PROJECT MANAGEMENT

THIRD EDITION

PROJECT MANAGEMENT
A Managerial Approach

JACK R. MEREDITH
SAMUEL J. MANTEL, JR.
University of Cincinnati

John Wiley & Sons, Inc.
New York • Chichester • Brisbane • Toronto • Singapore

Cover Photos: Alaskan Pipeline, G. Martin/Superstock
Inset Photo, The Rivera Collection/Superstock

Acquisitions Editor	Beth L. Golub
Marketing Manager	Debra Riegert
Senior Production Editor	John Rousselle
Senior Freelance Production Editor	Lois Lombardo
Designer	Laura Nicholls
Manufacturing Manager	Susan Stetzer
Photo Researcher	Lisa Passmore
Freelance Illustration Coordinator	Jaime Perea

This book was set in 10/12 Novarese Book by TCSystems and printed
and bound by R.R. Donnelley (Crawfordsville). The cover was printed
by Lehigh.

Library of Congress Cataloging in Publication Data:
Meredith, Jack R.
    Project management : a managerial approach / Jack R. Meredith,
Samuel J. Mantel, Jr.—3rd ed.

        p.   cm.—(Wiley series in production/operations management)
    Includes bibliographical references and indexes.
    ISBN 0-471-01626-8
    1. Industrial project management.   I. Mantel, Samuel J.
II. Title.   III. Series.

    HD69.P75M47   1995
    658.4'04—dc20   94-33876
                                                              CIP

Printed in the United States of America
10 9 8 7 6 5

Preface

▶ **APPROACH**

The use of projects and project management continues to grow in our society and its organizations. We are able to achieve goals through project organization that could be achieved only with the greatest of difficulty if organized in traditional ways. Though project management has existed since before the days of the great pyramids, it has enjoyed a surge of popularity beginning in the 1960s. A project put U.S. astronaut Neil Armstrong on the moon. A project called Desert Storm freed the nation of Kuwait. An annual project brings us Girl Scout cookies every spring. The use of project management to accomplish the many and diverse aims of society's varied organizations continues to grow.

Businesses regularly use project management to accomplish unique outcomes with limited resources under critical time constraints. In the service sector of the economy, the use of project management to achieve an organization's goals is even more common. Advertising campaigns, voter registration drives, political campaigns, a family's annual summer vacation, and even seminars on the subject of project management are organized as projects. Yet there have been relatively few books devoted to this way of managing, and there have been even fewer textbooks for teaching project management.

Of the books that are available, most fall into three categories. In the first category are "cookbooks" that describe in detail how to respond to a governmental Request for Proposal, how to set up the project office, what paper forms to use for which purposes, and where they should be filed. These books identify the details of *how* to carry out projects, but do not address the larger questions of *why* they are required and how they all fit together. We have not found this set of books particularly helpful in teaching managers, engineers, and others about the science, and art, of project management. They tend to ignore the managerial, organizational, and behavioral aspects of project management, which are both the strengths and the weaknesses of the project management concept.

In the second category are books that deal with very specific aspects of projects. Most common in this category are the math/network books describing PERT, CPM, or allied network techniques, which are extremely useful tools for project scheduling. But these books deal with projects, for the most part, as if good project management depended primarily on scheduling. We believe that this is misleading because scheduling is only one of several serious problems that the project manager must solve. Other such books cover cost estimating, team building, and similar special subjects. These works can be quite valuable for experienced project managers who need advanced education on specific areas of knowledge, but they do not deal with the subjects needed to understand the whole job of managing projects.

In the third category are the handbooks—collections of articles written mainly by academics and consultants on selected topics of interest to project managers. Handbooks do not, nor do they pretend to, offer broad coverage of the things project managers need to know. Like the second category previously described, once the project manager has been educated on the basics of project management these handbooks often represent valuable collections of relevant readings.

What is needed is a book that addresses project management from a *management* perspective rather than a cookbook, special area treatise, or collection of loosely associated articles. Such a book should address the basic nature of managing all types of projects—public, business, engineering, information systems, and so on—as well as the specific techniques and insights required to carry out this unique way of getting things done. It should deal with the problems of selecting projects, initiating them, and operating and controlling them. It should discuss the demands made on the project manager and the nature of the manager's interaction with the rest of the parent organization. The book should even cover the issues associated with terminating a project and with conducting a project that involves the use of people and organizations from different cultures.

This managerial perspective is the view we have taken here. The book is primarily intended for use as a college textbook for teaching project management at the advanced undergraduate or master's level. The book is also intended for current and prospective project managers who wish to share our insights and ideas about the field. We have drawn freely on our personal experiences working with project managers and on the experience of friends and colleagues who have spent much of their working lives serving as project managers in what they like to call the "real world."

As well as being a text that is equally appropriate for classes on the management of service, product, or engineering projects, we have found that information systems (IS) students in our classes find the material particularly helpful for managing their IS projects. Thus, we have expanded the coverage of material concerning information systems—particularly the systems development cycle and our thoughts on how IS projects differ from and are similar to regular business projects.

▶ ORGANIZATION AND CONTENT

Given this managerial perspective, we have arranged the book to use the *project life cycle* as the primary organizational guideline. We have found it to be a comfortable framework for the reader. Following an introductory chapter that comments on the role and importance of projects in our society and discusses project management as a potential career for aspiring managers, the book covers the major events and issues arising during the management of projects in the order in which they usually occur in the life of a project. *Part I, Project Initiation* describes how projects are selected for implementation. It also covers the role of the project manager and the various ways that projects can be organized. This is followed by a description of the project planning process and some tools used in project planning. Part I concludes with a topic of major importance to the project manager: negotiation.

Project budgeting, scheduling, resource allocation, monitoring/information systems, and controlling are then discussed in *Part II, Project Implementation*. Finally, *Part*

III, *Project Termination* concludes the discussion with a description of project auditing and termination. The final chapter is devoted to project management in an interdependent global economy. This material is placed at the end of the book because we feel it is necessary to understand project management before one can fully appreciate the problems raised by managing projects in a multicultural environment. The chapter concludes by noting three fundamental problems that must be solved if project management is to progress beyond its current state of sophistication.

We have relegated the discussion of two important aspects of projects that usually occur very early in the project life cycle—creativity/idea generation and technological forecasting—to two end-of-text appendixes. Although few project managers engage in either of these tasks (typically being appointed to project leadership after these activities have taken place), we believe that a knowledge of these subjects will make the project manager more effective.

Any way chosen to organize knowledge carries with it an implication of neatness and order that rarely occurs in reality. We are quite aware that projects almost never proceed in an orderly linear way through the stages and events we describe. The need to deal with change is the one constant task for the project manager. We have tried to reflect this in repeated references to the organizational, interpersonal, economic, and technical glitches that create crises in the life cycle of every project, and thus in the life of every project manager.

Finally, although we use a life cycle approach to organization, the chapters include material concerning the eight major areas of the Project Management Body of Knowledge (PMBOK) as defined by the Project Management Institute. Anyone wishing to prepare thoroughly in some of these areas may have to go beyond the information covered in this text.

- Human Resource Management (Chapters 4, 6, 11, and Appendix A)
- Communications Management (Chapters 3, 6, 10, and 11)
- Scope Management (Chapters 5 and 13)
- Quality Management (Chapters 11, 12, and 13)
- Scheduling/Time Management (Chapters 8, 9, and 10)
- Cost/Resource Management (Chapters 7, 9, 11, and Appendix B)
- Risk Management (Chapters 2, 12, and 13)
- Contract/Procurement Management (Chapter 2)

▶ PEDAGOGY

The primary use of this book is as a textbook, and we have included numerous pedagogical aids to foster this purpose. As in earlier editions, *short summaries* appear at the end of the text of each chapter, followed by *glossaries* defining key terms and concepts introduced in the chapter. End-of-chapter materials also include a *continuing assignment* for student project teams as well as *questions* and *problems* reviewing the materials covered in the chapter. There are also sets of conceptual *discussion questions* intended to broaden the students' perspectives and to force them to think beyond the chapter materials to its implications. The number and coverage of these questions and problems has been significantly extended over earlier editions.

As in the past, we have presented *incidents for discussion*; that is, "caselettes" oriented primarily toward the specific subjects covered in the chapter, but sometimes allowing use of materials and concepts covered in earlier chapters. In this edition, one or more major business *cases* have been added at the end of each chapter, in addition to *readings* drawn from important journal articles. We have extended chapter *bibliographies* with citations from articles and books published since our previous edition, but we have not deleted older citations in order to assist serious students who are interested in the background and history of project management and related subject areas. (Clearly, none of our chapter bibliographies pretends to complete coverage of any area. They are, however, considerably more extensive than those included in any other basic textbook of our acquaintance.)

We have made some assumptions about both student and professional readers in writing this text. First, we assume that all readers have taken an elementary course in management or have had equivalent experience. The reader with a background in management theory or practice will note that many of the principles of good project management are also principles of good general administrative management. Project management and administrative management are not entirely distinct. Further, we assume that readers are familiar with the fundamental principles of accounting, behavioral science, finance, and statistics as a typical manager would be. Because the assumption concerning statistics is not always met, we have added Appendix E on probability and statistics as an initial tutorial or as a refresher for rusty knowledge.

▶ WHAT'S NEW

In this third edition of the book we have updated and revised a number of topics as suggested by the reviewers, added some new material on total quality management, international and multicultural issues, ethics, behavioral and people aspects, teamwork and team building, and paid additional attention to information systems and service projects. These changes and additions are scattered throughout the entire text, sometimes amounting to a few words and sometimes to whole sections of a chapter. There is a new way of calculating the tracking signal (Chapter 7) that allows one to mix data from dissimilar forecasts, thereby speeding the process of getting an estimate of forecast bias. Similarly, we show a way of using optimistic and pessimistic PERT time estimates made at levels of precision much lower than the usual 99+ percent. Both of these changes were made in response to requests from practicing project managers.

Chapter 14 has been completely rewritten to discuss international and multicultural issues as well as noting some major unsolved problems that impact on project management's potential growth.

Particularly noticeable since the last edition has been the growth of microcomputer capabilities and project management software packages. Thus we have added considerable material in this area, including many examples of the use of Microsoft Project® and TimeLine® in Chapter 10. We chose these two application programs because they are probably the most widely used of the highly rated PC packages. Software exercises suitable for use with most of the PC-based project management programs are included in the material at the end of Chapter 10.

Initially, we had planned to spread Microsoft Project® and TimeLine® printouts throughout the book, particularly in those chapters describing a topic for which we could obtain a standard, preprogrammed printout. We found, however, that this was more confusing than helpful—when trying to understand a work breakdown structure, it is not helpful to be forced to learn computerese simultaneously. It seemed to us (and our students) easier to learn most of the basics of project management and *then* see how they are integrated in a project management software package with its various printouts and reports.

In addition to the new questions, problems, and cases noted in the pedagogy section, we have added a number of boxed real-life applications and real-life examples to the chapters in this edition. We have, however, kept some of the readings and cases from the previous edition that have become project management "classics." These are noted as such when they appear in the text.

▶ SUPPLEMENTS

The *Instructor's Resource Guide* has also been significantly expanded to provide additional assistance to the project management instructor. In addition to the answers/solutions to the problems, questions, and cases, this edition includes transparency masters, teaching tips, a test bank, and other such pedagogically helpful material.

▶ ACKNOWLEDGMENTS

We owe a debt of gratitude to all those who have helped us with this book. First, we thank the managers and students who helped us solidify our ideas about proper methods for managing projects and proper ways of teaching the subject. Second, we thank the project teams and leaders in all of our project management classes. We are especially grateful to Joseph Wert, whose youthful legwork preserved ours, and to Margaret Sutton, whose thoughtful skill with software and eye for inconsistency saved us countless hours of fumbling.

Special thanks are due those who have significantly influenced our thinking about project management or supplied materials to help us write this book: Desmond Cook, Ohio State University, Jeffrey Camm, James Evans, Martin Levy, John McKinney, and William Meyers, all of the University of Cincinnati, Jeffrey Pinto, Pennsylvania State University at Erie, Robert Riley, consultant, Gerhard Rosegger, Case Western Reserve University, and the Staff of the Project Management Institute.

We owe a massive debt of gratitude to the reviewers for previous editions: Nicholas Aquilano, University of Arizona, Edward Davis, University of Virginia, Herbert Spirer, University of Connecticut, Jerome Weist, University of Utah, Burton Dean, San Jose State University, and Samuel Taylor, University of Wyoming.

For this edition, we thank these reviewers: Robert J. Berger, University of Maryland, Howard Chamberlin, Texas A&M University, Jane E. Humble, Arizona State University, Richard H. Irving, York University, David L. Overbye, Keller Graduate School of Management, David J. Robb, University of Calgary, and James Willmann, University of Bridgeport.

Our appreciation of your counsel and encouragement is boundless and sincere. As always, responsibility for errors and omissions lies solely with us.

Jack R. Meredith
Samuel J. Mantel, Jr.

Contents

Projects in Contemporary Organizations

The past several decades have been marked by a rapid growth in the use of project management as a means by which organizations achieve their objectives. Project management provides an organization with powerful tools that improve its ability to plan, implement, and control its activities as well as the ways in which it utilizes its people and resources.

It is popular to ask, "Why can't they run government the way I run my business?" In the case of project management, however, business and other organizations learned from government, not the other way around. A lion's share of the credit for the development of the techniques and practices of project management belongs to the military, which faced a series of major tasks that simply were not achievable by traditional organizations operating in traditional ways. The United States Navy's Polaris program, NASA's Apollo space program, and more recently, the space shuttle and the strategic defense initiative ("star wars") programs are instances of the application of these specially developed management approaches to extraordinarily complex projects. Following such examples, nonmilitary government sectors, private industry, public service agencies, and volunteer organizations have all used project management to increase their effectiveness.

Project management has emerged because the characteristics of our late twentieth-century society demand the development of new methods of management. Of the many forces involved, three are paramount: (1) the exponential expansion of human knowledge; (2) the growing demand for a broad range of complex, sophisticated, customized goods and services; and (3) the evolution of worldwide competitive markets for the production and consumption of goods and services. All three forces combine to mandate the use of teams to solve problems that used to be solvable by individuals.

First, the expansion of knowledge allows an increasing number of academic disciplines to be used in solving problems associated with the development, production, and distribution of goods and services. Second, satisfying the continuing demand for more complex and customized products and services depends on our ability to make product design an integrated and inherent part of our production and distribution systems. Third, worldwide markets force us to include cultural and environmental differences in our managerial decisions about what, where, when, and how to produce and distribute output. The requisite knowledge does not reside in any one individual, no matter how well-educated or knowledgeable. Thus, under these conditions, teams are used for making decisions and taking action. This calls for a high level of coordination and cooperation between groups of people not particularly used to such interaction. Largely geared to the mass production of simpler goods, traditional organizational structures and management systems are simply not adequate to the task. Project management is.

The organizational response to the forces noted above cannot take the form of an instantaneous transformation from the old to the new. To be successful, the transition must be systematic, but it tends to be slow and tortuous for most enterprises. Accomplishing organizational change is a natural application of project management, and many firms have set up projects to implement their goals for strategic and tactical change.

Another important societal force is the intense competition among institutions, both profit and not-for-profit, fostered by our economic system. This puts extreme pressure on organizations to make their complex, customized outputs available as quickly as possible. "Time-to-market" is critical. Responses must come faster, decisions must be made sooner, and results must occur more quickly. Imagine the communications problems alone. Information and knowledge are growing explosively, but the allowable time to locate and use the appropriate knowledge is decreasing.

In addition, these forces operate in a society that assumes that technology can do anything. The fact is, this assumption is reasonably true, within the bounds of nature's fundamental laws. The problem lies not in this assumption so much as in a concomitant assumption that allows society to ignore both the economic and noneconomic costs associated with technological progress until some dramatic event forces our attention on the costs (e.g., the Chernobyl nuclear accident or the Exxon Valdez oil spill). At times, our faith in technology is disturbed by difficulties and threats arising from its careless implementation, as in the case of industrial waste, but on the whole we seem remarkably tolerant of technological change. For a case in point, consider California farm workers who waited more than 20 years to challenge a University of California research program devoted to the development of labor-saving farm machinery [37]. The acceptance of technological advancement is so strong it took more than two decades to muster the legal attack.

Finally, the projects we undertake are large and getting larger. The modern machine tool company, for example, advances from a numerically controlled milling machine to a *machining center* to a *flexible manufacturing system*. As each new capability extends our grasp, it serves as the base for new demands that force us to extend our reach even farther. Projects increase in size and complexity because the more we can do, the more we try to do. The path from earth orbit to lunar landing to interplanetary flight is clear—indeed, inevitable.

The projects that command the most public attention tend to be large, complex, multidisciplinary endeavors. Often, such endeavors are both similar to and different from previous projects with which we may be more or less familiar. Similarities with the past provide a base from which to start, but the differences imbue every project with considerable risk. The complexities and multidisciplinary aspects of projects require that the many parts be put together so that the prime objectives—performance, time (or schedule), and cost—are met.

While multimillion dollar, five-year projects capture public attention, the overwhelming majority of all projects are comparatively small—though nonetheless important to doer and user alike. They involve such outcomes, or *deliverables*, as a new basketball floor for a professional basketball team, a new insurance policy to protect against a specific casualty loss, a new casing for a four-wheel minivan transmission, a new industrial floor cleanser, the installation of a new method for peer-review of patient care in a hospital, even the development of new software to help manage projects. The list could be extended almost without limit. These undertakings have much in common with their larger counterparts. They are complex, multidisciplinary, and have the same general objectives—performance, time, and cost.

There is a tendency to think of a project solely in terms of its outcome—that is, its performance. But the time at which the outcome is available is itself a part of the outcome, as is the cost entailed in achieving the outcome. The completion of a building on time and on budget is quite a different outcome from the completion of the same physical structure a year late or 20 percent over budget, or both.

The prime objectives of project management are shown in Figure 1-1, with the three specified project objectives on each of the axes. This illustration implies that there is some "function" (not shown in the figure) that relates them, one to another. And so there is. Although the functions vary from project to project, and from time

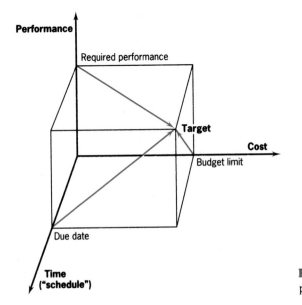

Figure 1-1: Performance, cost, time project targets.

to time for a given project, we will be constantly referring to these relationships, or *trade-offs*, throughout the rest of this book. The primary task of the project manager is to manage these trade-offs.

It is in this context that the project manager is expected to integrate all aspects of the project, ensure that the proper knowledge and resources are available when and where needed, and above all, ensure that the expected results are produced in a timely, cost-effective manner. For these reasons, we often refer to the project manager as a *supermanager*.

The complexity of the problems faced by the project manager taken together with the rapid growth in the number of project-oriented organizations has contributed to the professionalization of the project manager. The Project Management Institute (PMI) was established in 1969 and now has almost 10,000 members. Its mission is to foster the growth of project management as well as "building professionalism" in the field. The *Project Management Journal* and PM *Network* magazine were founded by the PMI as a means of communicating ideas about project management as well as solutions for commonly encountered problems. Another PMI objective is to codify the areas of learning required for competent project management. This project management body of knowledge, PMBOK, is meant to serve as the fundamental basis for education for project managers. The profession has flourished, with the result that many colleges and universities offer training in project management and some offer specialized degree programs in the area.

As we note in the coming chapters, the project manager's job is not without problems. There is the ever-present frustration of being responsible for outcomes while lacking full authority to command the requisite resources or personnel. There are the constant problems of dealing with the parties involved in any project—senior management, client, project team, and public, all of whom speak different languages and have different objectives. There are the ceaseless organizational and technical fires to be fought. There are vendors who cannot seem to keep "lightning-strike-me-dead" promises about delivery dates. This list of troubles only scratches the surface.

Difficult as the job may be, most project managers take a considerable amount of pleasure and job satisfaction from their occupation. The challenges are many and the risks significant, but so are the rewards of success. Project managers rarely lack organizational visibility, enjoy considerable variety in their day-to-day duties, and often have the prestige associated with work on the enterprise's high-priority objectives. The profession, however, is not one for the timid. Risk and conflict avoiders do not make happy project managers. Those who can stomach the risks and who enjoy practicing the arts of conflict resolution, however, can take substantial monetary and psychic rewards from their work.

This book identifies the specific tasks facing these supermanagers. We investigate the nature of the projects for which the project manager is responsible, the skills that must be used to manage projects, and the means by which the manager can bring the project to a successful conclusion in terms of the three primary criteria: performance, time, and cost. Before delving into the details of this analysis, however, we clarify the nature of *a project* and determine how it differs from the other activities that are conducted in organizations. We also note a few of the major advantages, disadvantages, strengths, and limitations of project management. At the end of the chapter we describe the approach followed in the remainder of this book.

Project Management in Practice
The Undersea England—France Chunnel

The idea of an undersea tunnel linking England and France was first seriously considered during Napoleon's reign, and even tried in 1880. It was tried again in 1975 but abandoned again. Now, the world's largest privately funded construction project is completing the dream. Funded by the largest banking syndicate ever put together, a consortium of 10 major British and French construction firms is building a trio of tunnels inside a mammoth cavern about 65 feet in diameter and 58 miles long under the ocean between England and France. Two of the tunnels will carry passenger and freight trains at speeds of 100 miles an hour, spanning the distance in about 35 minutes. The third tunnel is for service purposes and has its own transportation system also.

When the venture was first formed in 1986, the staff numbered six. At peak productivity, it rose to about 14,500 with daily expenditures of over 5.5 million dollars. The project, however, is much bigger than just the tunnels. In addition, there are two huge terminals at either end of the lines to handle the massive amounts of freight and passengers passing through the tunnels every day. Also, there are two massive crossover chambers located undersea to allow trains to change tracks for maintenance purposes. These chambers are the largest undersea caverns in the world and measure 527 feet long by 60 feet wide and 35 feet high. And then there are the support systems for the tunnels—drainage, cooling, ventilation, electrical, trackwork, rolling stock, fire control, electronics: 1,000 microcomputers, 160 megawatts peak power at 225,000 volts, 120 ton concrete tunnel doors, 140 tons of water an hour for fire control, 38 locomotives and 525 wagons to form trains half a mile long, and so on. Even building the concrete segments for the tunnels was the equal, in output terms, of any precast concrete works in the world.

Perhaps even more complex are the cultural differences between the British and French construction companies, as well as the two sets of political authorities. In order for

Source: J. K. Lemley, "The Channel Tunnel," PM *Network*, July 1992.

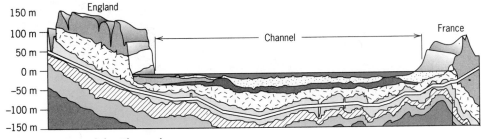

A cross-section of the Chunnel.

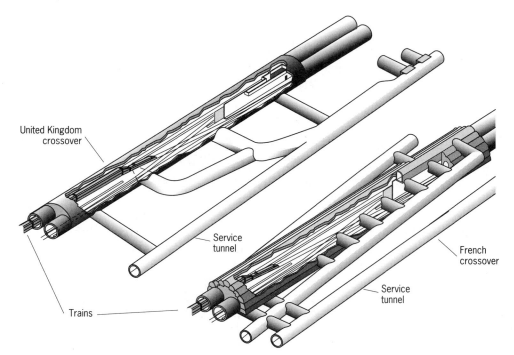

United Kingdom crossover

Service tunnel

French crossover

Service tunnel

Trains

Tunnel crossovers with trains switching tracks.

Breakthrough: The tunnel boring machine emerges on the French end.

this to be a privately funded project, the sponsors insisted on each government's agreement that the sponsors would be granted a concession for the right to operate the facility and benefit from their investment. In February 1986, the French and British governments signed what was known as the Treaty of Canterbury, which authorized a 55-year concession and provided guarantees against political cancellation in the future. With that authorization, work began in earnest. In December 1990 the service tunnel was completed and by June 1991, both running tunnels were completed, all several weeks ahead of schedule due to the wise use of project management throughout the complex phases of this massive, international project.

▶ 1.1   THE DEFINITION OF A "PROJECT"

There is a rich variety of projects to be found in our society. Although some may argue that the construction of the Tower of Babel or the Egyptian pyramids were some of the first "projects," it is probable that cavemen formed a project to gather the raw material for mammoth stew. It is certainly true that the construction of Boulder Dam and Edison's invention of the light bulb were projects by any sensible definition. Modern project management, however, is usually said to have begun with the Manhattan Project, which developed the atomic bomb. In its early days, project management was used mainly for very large, complex research and development (R & D) projects like the development of the ICBM and similar military weapon systems. Massive construction programs were also organized as projects—the construction of dams, ships, refineries, and freeways, among others.

As the techniques of project management were developed, mostly by the military, the use of project organization began to spread. Private construction firms found that project organization was helpful on smaller projects, such as the building of a warehouse or an apartment complex. The automotive companies used project organization to develop new automobile models. Both General Electric and Pratt & Whitney used it to develop new jet aircraft engines for the airlines as well as the Air Force. Project management has even been used to develop new models of shoes and ships (though possibly not sealing wax). More recently, the use of project management by international organizations, and especially organizations producing services rather than products, has grown rapidly. Advertising campaigns, global mergers, and capital acquisitions are often handled as projects, and the methods have spread to the nonprofit sector. Teas, weddings, Scout-o-ramas, fund drives, election campaigns, parties, and recitals have all made use of project management. Most striking has been the widespread adoption of project management techniques for the development of computer software.

In discussions of project management, it is sometimes useful to make a distinction between such terms as *project*, *program*, *task*, and *work packages*. The military, the source of most of these terms, generally uses the term *program* to refer to an exceptionally large, long-range objective that is broken down into a set of projects. These projects are further divided into *tasks*, which are, in turn, split into *work packages* that are themselves composed of *work units*. But exceptions to this hierarchical nomenclature abound. The Manhattan Project was a huge "program," but a "task force" was created to investigate the many potential futures of a large steel company.

In the broadest sense, a project is a specific, finite task to be accomplished. Whether large- or small-scale or whether long- or short-run is not particularly relevant. What is relevant is that the project be seen as a unit. There are, however, some attributes that characterize projects.

Purpose

A project is usually a one-time activity with a well-defined set of desired end results. It can be divided into subtasks that must be accomplished in order to achieve the project goals. The project is complex enough that the subtasks require careful coordination and control in terms of timing, precedence, cost, and performance. The project itself must often be coordinated with other projects being carried out by the same parent organization.

Life Cycle

Like organic entities, projects have life cycles. From a slow beginning they progress to a buildup of size, then peak, begin a decline, and finally must be terminated. (Also like other organic entities, they often resist termination.) Some projects end by being phased into the normal, ongoing operations of the parent organization. The life cycle is further discussed in Section 1.3 where an important exception to the usual description of the growth curve is mentioned.

Interdependencies

Projects often interact with other projects being carried out simultaneously by their parent organization; but projects *always* interact with the parent's standard, ongoing operations. Although the functional departments of an organization (marketing, finance, manufacturing, and the like) interact with one another in regular, patterned ways, the patterns of interaction between projects and these departments tend to be changing. Marketing may be involved at the beginning and end of a project, but not in the middle. Manufacturing may have major involvement throughout. Finance is often involved at the beginning and accounting (the controller) at the end, as well as at periodic reporting times. The project manager must keep all these interactions clear and maintain the appropriate interrelationships with all external groups.

Uniqueness

Every project has some elements that are unique. No two construction or R & D projects are precisely alike. Though it is clear that construction projects are usually more routine than research and development projects, some degree of customization is a characteristic of projects. In addition to the presence of risk, as noted earlier, this characteristic means that projects, by their nature, cannot be completely reduced to routine. The project manager's importance is emphasized because, as a devotee of *management by exception*, the manager will find there are a great many exceptions to manage by.

Conflict

More than most managers, the project manager lives in a world characterized by conflict. Projects compete with functional departments for resources and personnel. More serious, with the growing proliferation of projects, is the project versus project conflict for resources within multiproject organizations. The members of the project team are in almost constant conflict for the project's resources and for leadership roles in solving project problems.

The four parties-at-interest or "stake-holders" in any project (client, parent organization, project team, and the public) even define success and failure in different ways (see also Chapters 12 and 13). The client wants changes, and the parent organization wants profits, which may be reduced if those changes are made. Individuals working on projects are often responsible to two bosses at the same time, bosses with different priorities and objectives. Project management is no place for the timid.

▶ 1.2   WHY PROJECT MANAGEMENT?

The basic purpose for initiating a project is to accomplish some goals. The reason for organizing the task as a project is to focus the responsibility and authority for the attainment of the goals on an individual or small group.

In spite of the fact that the project manager often lacks authority at a level consistent with his or her responsibility, the manager is expected to coordinate and integrate all activities needed to reach the project's goals. In particular, the project form of organization allows the manager to be responsive to the client and to the environment, to identify and correct problems at an early date, to make timely decisions about trade-offs between conflicting project goals, and to ensure that managers of the separate tasks that comprise the project do not optimize the performance of their individual tasks at the expense of the total project—that is, that they do not *suboptimize.*

Actual experience [13] with project management indicates that the majority of organizations using it experience better control and better customer relations. A significant proportion of users also report shorter development times, lower costs, higher quality and reliability, and higher profit margins. Other reported advantages include a sharper orientation toward results, better interdepartmental coordination, and higher worker morale.

On the negative side, most organizations report that project management results in greater organizational complexity. Many also report that project organization increases the likelihood that organizational policy will be violated—not a surprising outcome, considering the degree of autonomy required for the project manager. A few firms reported higher costs, more management difficulties, and low personnel utilization.

As we will see in Chapter 4, the disadvantages of project management stem from exactly the same sources as do its advantages. The disadvantages seem to be the price one pays for the advantages. On the whole, the balance weighs in favor of project organization if the work to be done is appropriate for a project.

The tremendous diversity of uses to which project management can be put has had an interesting, and generally unfortunate, side-effect. While we assert that all projects are to some extent unique, there is an almost universal tendency for those working on some specific types of projects to argue, "Software (or construction, or R & D, or marketing, or machine maintenance, or. . .) projects are different and you can't expect us to schedule (or budget, or organize, or manage, or. . .) in the same way that other kinds of projects do." Disagreement with such pleas for special treatment is central to the philosophy of this book. The fundamental similarities between all sorts of projects, be they long or short, product- or service-oriented, parts of all-encompassing programs or stand-alone, are far more pervasive than are their differences.

There are real limitations on project management. For example, the mere creation of a project may be an admission that the parent organization and its managers cannot accomplish the desired outcomes through the functional organization. Further, conflict seems to be a necessary side-effect. As we noted, the project manager often lacks authority that is consistent with the assigned level of responsibility. Therefore, the project manager must depend on the goodwill of managers in the parent organization for some of the necessary resources. Of course, if the goodwill is not forthcoming, the project manager may ask senior officials in the parent organization for their assistance, but to use such power often reflects poorly on the skills of the project manager and, while it may get cooperation in the instance at hand, it may backfire in the long run.

We return to the subject of the advantages, disadvantages, and limitations of the project form of organization later. For the moment, it is sufficient to point out that project management is difficult even when everything goes well. When things go badly, project managers have been known to turn gray and take to hard drink. The trouble is that project organization is the only feasible way to accomplish certain goals. It is literally not possible to design and build a major weapon system, for example, in a *timely and economically acceptable manner*, except by project organization. The stronger the emphasis on achievement of results in an organization, the more likely it will be to adopt some form of project management. The stake or risks in using project management may be high, but no more so than in any other form of management. And for projects, it is less so. Tough as it may be, it is all we have—and it works!

All in all, the life of a project manager is exciting, rewarding, at times frustrating, and tends to be at the center of things in most organizations. Project management is now being recognized as a "career path" in a growing number of firms, particularly those conducting projects with lives extending more than a year or two. In such organizations, project managers may have to function for several years, and it is important to provide promotion potential for them. It is also common for large firms to put their more promising young managers through a "tour of duty" during which they manage one or more projects (or parts of projects). This serves as a good test of the aspiring manager's ability to coordinate and manage complex tasks and to achieve results in a politically challenging environment where negotiation skills are required.

Project Management in Practice
The Endicott, Alaska Oil Project

The first of the Prudhoe Bay, Alaska, oil production facilities was successfully completed nine months ahead of schedule and $600 million under budget through the use of special project management techniques. Endicott field contains approximately 350 million barrels of recoverable oil. The billion-dollar-plus production facility was developed and is operated by Standard Alaska Production Company on behalf of a consortium of oil companies.

Source: P. F. Flones, "Endicott Oil Field," *Project Management Journal*, December 1987.

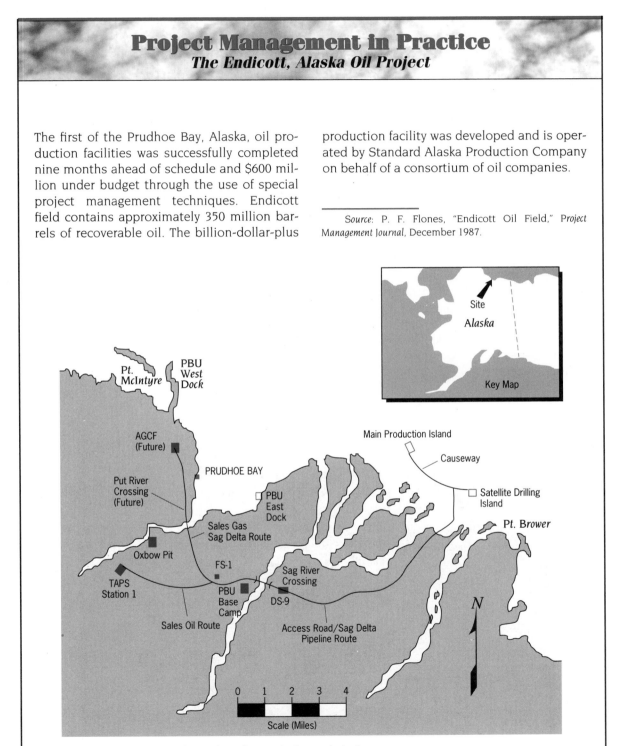

Endicott oil field map—located on the north shore of Alaska.

The Endicott field in Prudhoe Bay is located offshore where the ocean is frozen to depths of six feet for eight months of the year when the temperature ranges from -20 to -50 degrees Fahrenheit. To build facilities in this remote and extremely harsh environment, the project team conceived the idea of constructing the oil processing facilities inside large, barge-transportable, heated modules resembling large buildings. These modules were built in Louisiana and then transported via barges through the Panama Canal along the west coast of the United States to north Alaska. The shipping was scheduled to arrive at the north coast of Alaska in late July, just as the ice in the Arctic Ocean is breaking up, leaving them just enough time—4–6 weeks—to reach Endicott, be off-loaded, and return prior to the September refreeze.

The great diversity of design and construction abilities needed—roads, camps, power generation, communication, warehouses, pipelines, oil–gas separation facilities—required developing a unique contracting philosophy. The result was to split the work into discrete work packages that best matched the skills of various engineering and construction companies, avoiding unnecessary coordination and interface problems whenever possible. The project proceeded in two stages: first, a construction camp that would house 600 people was built. Then the processing facilities and support systems were constructed. Since the design of the processing facilities required 1.8 million engineering hours taking two and a half years, the processing facilities had to be constructed concurrently with their design in order to complete the project in time. The facility required the construction of two manufactured gravel islands connected by a three-mile long causeway, all requiring mining, hauling, and placing of 6.3 million yards of gravel. These islands provide a stable surface for the drilling, production, and construction facilities. The larger, 45-acre island will support the drilling

Main Production Island at Endicott Oil Field.

of up to 70 wells and the smaller, 10.5-acre island will support 50 wells. The processing facilities and support systems are also located on the larger island.

In October 1987, Endicott field began producing oil at the rate of 100,000 barrels a day. The project was completed significantly ahead of schedule and under budget, largely due to the creative approach taken by the project team toward contracting and the unique construction method developed for this project.

▶ 1.3 THE PROJECT LIFE CYCLE

Most projects go through similar stages on the path from origin to completion. We define these stages, shown in Figure 1-2, as the project's *life cycle*. The project is born (its start-up phase) and a manager is selected, the project team and initial resources are assembled, and the work program is organized. Then work gets under way and momentum quickly builds. Progress is made. This continues until the end is in sight. But completing the final tasks seems to take an inordinate amount of time, partly because there are often a number of parts that must come together and partly because team members "drag their feet" for various reasons and avoid the final steps.

The pattern of slow–rapid–slow progress toward the project goal is common. Anyone who has watched the construction of a home or building has observed this phenomenon. For the most part, it is a result of the changing levels of resources used during the successive stages of the life cycle. Figure 1-3 shows project effort, usually in terms of person-hours or resources expended per unit of time (or number

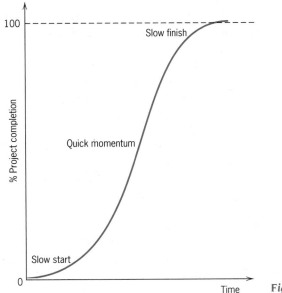

Figure 1-2: The project life cycle.

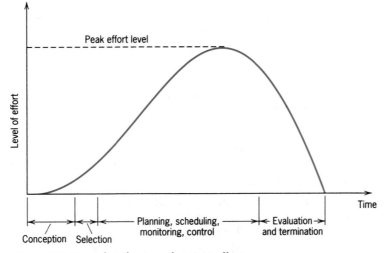

Figure 1-3: Time distribution of project effort.

of people working on the project) plotted against time, where time is broken up into the several phases of project life. Minimal effort is required at the beginning, when the project concept is being developed and is being subjected to project selection processes. (Later, we will argue that increasing effort in the early stages of the life cycle will improve the chance of project success.)

If this hurdle is passed, activity increases as planning is done, and the real work of the project gets underway. This rises to a peak and then begins to taper off as the project nears completion, finally ceasing when evaluation is complete and the project is terminated. While this rise and fall of effort always occurs, there is no particular pattern that seems to typify all projects, nor any reason for the slowdown at the end of the project to resemble the buildup at its beginning. Some projects end without being dragged out, as is shown in Figure 1-3. Others, however, may be like T. S. Eliot's world and end "not with a bang but a whimper," gradually slowing down until one is almost surprised to discover that project activity has ceased. In some cases, the effort may never fall to zero because the project team, or at least a cadre group, may be maintained for the next appropriate project that comes along. The new project will then rise, phoenix-like, from the ashes of the old.

The ever-present goals of meeting performance, time and cost are the major considerations throughout the project's life cycle. It was generally thought that performance took precedence early in the project's life cycle. This is the time when planners focus on finding the specific methods required to meet the project's performance goals. We refer to these methods as the project's *technology* because they require the application of a science or art.

When the major "how" problems are solved, project workers sometimes become preoccupied with improving performance, often beyond the levels required by the original specifications. This search for better performance delays the schedule and pushes up the costs.

At the same time that the technology of the project is defined, the project schedule is designed and project costs are estimated. Just as it was thought that performance took precedence over schedule and cost early in the life cycle, cost was thought to be of prime importance during the periods of high activity, and then schedule became paramount during the final stages, when the client is demanding delivery. This conventional wisdom turns out to be untrue. Recent research indicates that performance and schedule are more important than cost during *all* stages. The reality of time–cost–performance trade-offs will be discussed in greater detail in Chapter 3. In Chapter 7 we also note that not all projects have a life cycle that looks like Figure 1-2, a fact that is not only contrary to well-established conventional wisdom, but also has far-reaching implications about how resources should be allocated to projects having different types of life cycles.

It would be a great source of comfort if one could predict with certainty, at the start of a project, how the performance, time, and cost goals would be met. In a few cases, routine construction projects, for instance, we can generate reasonably accurate predictions, but often we cannot. There may be considerable uncertainty about our ability to meet project goals. The crosshatched portion of Figure 1-4 illustrates that uncertainty.

Figure 1-4 shows the uncertainty as seen at the beginning of the project. Figure 1-5 shows how the uncertainty decreases as the project moves toward completion. From project start time, t_0, the band of uncertainty grows until it is quite wide by the estimated end of the project. As the project actually develops, the degree of uncertainty about the final outcome is reduced. (See the estimate made at t_1, for example.) A later forecast, made at t_2, reduces the uncertainty still more. It is common to make new forecasts about project performance, time, and cost either at fixed intervals in the life of the project or when specific technological milestones are reached. In any event, the more progress made on the project, the less uncertainty there is about the final goal achievement.

Note that the focus in Figures 1-4 and 1-5 is on the uncertainty associated with project cost—precisely, the uncertainty of project cost at specific points in time.

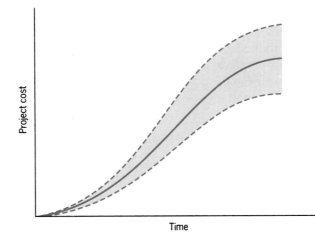

Figure 1-4: Estimate of project cost: estimate made at project start.

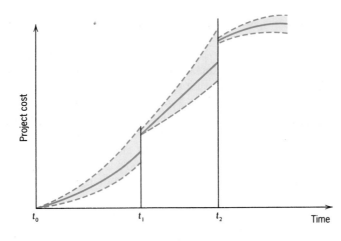

Figure 1-5: Estimates of project cost: estimates made at times t_0, t_1, and t_2.

Without significantly altering the shapes of the curves, we could exchange titles on the axes. The figures would then show the uncertainty associated with estimates of the project schedule, given specific levels of expenditure. The relationship between time and cost (and performance) is emphasized throughout this book. Dealing with the uncertainty surrounding this relationship is a major responsibility of the project manager.

Project Management in Practice
Project Management Style and the Challenger Disaster

The Space Shuttle Program was initiated by NASA in the early 1970s as a follow-on to the highly successful Apollo Manned Lunar Landings. At the time of its proposal, the Shuttle was expected to cost $10–13 billion to develop. However, the U.S. Congress reduced the development funding to $5.2 billion since this was meant to be a highly cost-effective program, using almost entirely well-established technologies, off-the-shelf items, and a reusable space vehicle. Fearing a cancellation of the Space Shuttle Program if they pointed out the developmental problems they faced, NASA acquiesed to the inadequate $5.2 billion budget.

This philosophical perspective of a cost-effective project became a major problem for NASA who was used to conducting highly ex-

pensive experimental projects, with extensive testing and safety procedures, and then completing them with great success and public acclaim. In the Shuttle program, they faced exactly the *opposite* situation. There was very little money for new development, testing, or safety; the objectives of placing astronauts in orbit were not particularly challenging; yet, the shuttle development problems and risks were in fact massive:

–The huge liquid-fueled shuttle engines had to be reused up to 50 times and were to be fired in the proximity of a gigantic external tank of propellants.

Source: A. Shenhar, "Project Management Style and the Space Shuttle Program (Part 2)," *Project Management Journal*, March 1992.

The space shuttle at launch.

–NASA had never used solid-fuel engines for launching manned flights.

–The atmospheric reentry of a large, winged space vehicle had never before been accomplished.

–The space vehicle, at 75 tons, would be the heaviest glider ever built.

–The space vehicle was expected to descend through both hypersonic and supersonic speeds to make a pinpoint landing 5000 miles from the point of reentry.

–A reusable thermal protection material had to be developed for reenty.

–The first flight test would require a live crew.

–There was to be no crew escape system!

Thus, the management style required of NASA was that appropriate to a routine, mass-production program of 24 launches a year while the reality was that this was a highly experimental program with overwhelming technical difficulties. As a result, portions of the program fell three years behind schedule and had cost overruns of 60 percent, even before the Challenger disaster. As the program moved into the operational flight stage, problems stemming from the inadequate development process surfaced in many areas, culminating in the Challenger explosion 73 seconds after launch on January 28, 1986.

▶ 1.4 THE STRUCTURE OF THIS TEXT

This book, a project in itself, has been organized to follow the life cycle of all projects. It begins with the creative idea that launches most projects and ends with termination of the project (followed by a short discussion of projects conducted in a multifunctional environment). This approach is consistent with our belief that it is helpful to understand the entire process of project management in order to understand and manage its parts. In addition, although this book is intended primarily for the student who wants to study project management, we feel it may also be of value to the prospective or acting project manager, and to senior managers who initiate projects and select, work with, or manage project managers. Therefore, our interests go beyond the issues of primary concern to the beginning student in this field.

Most projects will not be of the size and complexity addressed in many of our discussions. Though our point was not to confine our remarks only to large engineering-oriented projects, these are typically the most complex and place the greatest demands on project management. Smaller, simpler projects may therefore not require the depth of tools and techniques we will present, but the student or manager should be aware that such tools exist.

Project management actually begins with the initial concept for the project. We feel that this aspect of project management is so important, yet so universally ignored in books on project management, that we have included two appendices covering this area. In Appendix A we discuss the concepts of creativity and idea generation, and in Appendix B we describe the techniques of technological forecasting. We realize that these topics may be of more direct interest to the senior manager than the project manager. Though a project manager may prefer to skip this material, since what is past is past, we believe that history holds lessons for the future and wise project managers will wish to know the reasons for, and the history behind, the initiation of their project.

Following this introductory chapter, the material in Part I focuses on *project initiation* beginning with selection of the project. Chapter 2 describes the problems of evaluating and selecting projects, including descriptions of the major models used to select projects for funding in government as well as in industry. For those desiring additional depth, special models for evaluating R & D projects are included. In addition, this chapter also covers some of the technical details of proposals. The next step is selecting the project manager. Chapter 3, "The Project Manager," concerns the project manager's roles and responsibilities and some personal characteristics the project manager should possess. Next, Chapter 4 concentrates on establishing the project organization. Different organizational forms are described, together with their respective advantages and disadvantages. The staffing of the project team is also discussed. Chapter 5 deals with project planning where tools found to be useful in organizing and staffing the various project tasks are presented. Concluding this part of the book, Chapter 6 covers a subject of critical importance to the project manager that is almost universally ignored in project management texts, the art of negotiating for resources.

In Part II we consider *project implementation*. This section of the text treats the essentials of ongoing project management. Because of its importance, budgeting is addressed first in Chapter 7. Scheduling, a crucial aspect of project planning, is then described in Chapter 8, along with the most common scheduling models such as PERT, CPM, and precedence diagramming. Resource allocation is covered in Chapter 9. For single projects, the resource allocation problem concerns resource *leveling* to minimize the cost of the resources; but for multiple projects, the issue is how to allocate limited resources among several projects in order to achieve the objectives of each.

Chapter 10 discusses the information requirements of a project and the need for monitoring critical activities. Included in this chapter is a description of some common Project Management Information Systems (PMIS). In general, it is not possible to manage adequately any but the smallest of projects without the use of a computerized PMIS. There are many such systems available and several are briefly discussed, but in this book all examples using PMIS software will use either *Microsoft Project*® or Symantec's *TimeLine*®, two of the most popular systems for personal computers. Concluding the implementation phase, Chapter 11 describes the control process in project management. The chapter discusses standards for comparison and tools to aid the manager in maintaining control.

The final section of the book, Part III, concerns *project termination*. Chapter 12 deals with methods for both ongoing and terminal evaluations of a project, as well as identifying factors associated with project success and failure. Chapter 13 describes the different forms of project termination, such as outright shutdown, integration into the regular organization, or extension into a new project. Each of these forms presents unique problems for the project manager to solve. Finally, the future of project management is briefly discussed in Chapter 14, along with international issues.

With this introduction, let us begin our study, a project in itself, and, we hope, an interesting and pleasant one.

▶ SUMMARY

This chapter introduced the subject of project management and discussed its importance in our society. It defined what we mean by a "project," discussed the need for project management, and described the project life cycle. The final section explained the structure of this text and gave an overview of the material to be described in coming chapters.

The following specific points were made in the chapter.

- The Project Management Institute (PMI) was founded in 1969 to foster the growth and professionalism of project management.

- Project management is now being recognized as a valuable "career path" in many organizations, as well as a way to gain valuable experience with the organization.

- Project management, initiated by the military, provides managers with powerful planning and control tools.

- The three primary forces behind project management are (1) the growing demand for complex, customized goods and services, (2) the exponential expansion of human knowledge, and (3) the global production–consumption environment.

- The three prime objectives of project management are to meet specified performance within cost and on schedule.

- Our terminology follows in this order: program, project, task, work package, work unit.

- Projects are characterized by a singleness of purpose, a definite life cycle, complex interdependencies, some or all unique elements, and an environment of conflict.

- Project management, though not problem-free, is the best way to accomplish certain goals.

- Projects often start slowly, build up speed while using considerable resources, and then slow down as completion nears.

- This text is organized along the project life cycle concept, starting with *project initiation* in Chapters 2 to 6, where selection of the project and project manager occurs and project organization and planning begin. *Project implementation*, Chapters 7 to 11, is concerned with budgeting, scheduling, resource allocation, and activity monitoring and control. *Project termination*, concerning final evaluation and completion, is covered in Chapters 12 and 13. Chapter 14 concludes the text with a discussion of the future of project management and its global aspects.

We thus begin our discussion, in Chapter 2, with the topic of selecting the project. We might note, however, that this is not really where project management starts; the important preliminary work is creativity (Appendix A) and technological forecasting (Appendix B).

▶ GLOSSARY

Deliverables—The desired outcomes or results of a project.

Interdependencies—Relations between organizational functions where one function or task is dependent on others.

Life Cycle—A standard concept of a product or project wherein it goes through a start-up phase, a building phase, a maturing phase, and a termination phase.

Parties-at-Interest—Individuals or groups with a special interest in a project, usually the project team, client, senior management, and specific public interest groups.

Program—Often not distinguished from a project, but frequently meant to encompass a group of similar projects.

Project Management—The means, techniques, and concepts used to run a project and achieve its objectives.

Risk—The chance that outcomes will not turn out as planned.

Stakeholder—see "Parties-at-interest."

Suboptimize—Doing the best within a function or area but at a cost to the larger whole.

Supermanager—A person who successfully meets the requirements of a project and achieves the desired goals.

Task—One of the work elements in a project.

Technology—The means for accomplishing difficult tasks.

Trade-off—Taking less on one measure, such as performance, in order to do better on another, such as schedule or cost.

Uncertainty—Having only partial information about the situation or outcomes.

Work Package—A subelement of a task that needs to be accomplished in order to achieve the objectives of the task.

▶ MATERIAL REVIEW QUESTIONS

1. Name and briefly describe the societal forces that have contributed to the need for project management.

2. Why is the project manager often called a supermanager?

3. Describe the life cycle of a project in terms of the degree of project completion; in terms of required effort.

4. Describe the limitations of project management.

5. List the five main characteristics of a project and briefly describe the important features of each.

6. Name and briefly describe the three primary goals of a project.

7. Discuss the advantages and disadvantages of project management.

8. How do projects, programs, tasks, and work packages differ?

9. How would *you* define a project?

10. What are some of the interdependencies related to a project?

11. What are some sources of conflict the project manager must deal with?

▶ CLASS DISCUSSION QUESTIONS

1. Give several examples of projects found in our society, avoiding those discussed in the chapter.

2. Describe some situations in which project management would probably *not* be effective.

3. How does the rate-of-project-progress chart (Fig. 1-2) help a manager make decisions?

4. Expound on the adage, "Projects proceed smoothly until 90 percent complete, and then remain at 90 percent forever."

5. Discuss the duties and responsibilities of the project manager. How critical is the project manager to the success of the project?

6. Would you like to be a project manager? Why, or why not?

7. Discuss why there are tradeoffs among the three prime objectives of project management.

8. Why is the life cycle curve often "S" shaped?

9. How might project management be used when doing a major schoolwork assignment?

10. Did the change in management style required by the Space Shuttle Program bring about any ethical dilemmas?

▶ INCIDENTS FOR DISCUSSION

T.T.S Candle Company

Sue Miller, president of T.T.S. Candle Company, has just completed a two-day seminar on project management and is anxious to use the new techniques on a recurring problem faced by her company. About 60 percent of T.T.S.'s gross revenues result from the pre-Christmas sale of the firm's major product, XMAS-PAK. XMAS-PAK consists of twelve candles, all of one color and size. There are six different colors available in three different lengths. XMAS-PAK was introduced eight years ago, and sales have been increasing by approximately 20 percent per year.

Because of the seasonal nature of the product, all orders unfilled on December 16 are lost. Ms. Miller estimated that XMAS-PAK sales would have been about 10 percent higher last year were it not for lost orders. It was a frustrating problem because the loss was not due to a shortage of capacity. Sales forecasts were not very accurate, and her manufacturing managers had strict instructions to minimize investment in finished goods inventories. Miller was sure that project management could somehow help solve the problem without appreciably increasing inventories.

On her return from the seminar, she assigned Sam Joseph, marketing manager, and Kenneth Knight, vice-president of manufacturing, as project managers for this problem. She reviewed the problem with them and gave them eight years of historical sales data, broken down by line item and geographical region.

These were the data that she herself had used during her initial investigation. The project objective was to reduce lost sales to 0.5 percent within five years.

Question: Discuss Ms. Miller's approach to the problem and list the pros and cons.

Maladroit Machine Tool Company

The plant manager of the Maladroit Machine Tool Company must replace several of his milling machines that have become obsolete. He is about to take delivery of six machines at a total cost of $4 million. These machines must be installed and fully tested in time to be used on a new production line scheduled to begin operation in six months. Because this project is important, the plant manager would like to devote as much time as possible to the job, but he is currently handling several other projects. He thinks he has three basic choices: (1) He can handle the project informally out of his office; (2) he can assign the project to a member of his staff; or (3) the company that manufactures the machines is willing to handle the installation project for a fee close to what the installation would cost Maladroit.

Questions: Which of the three choices do you recommend, and why? If the project was one small machine at a total cost of $4,000, would your answer be different? Discuss the relative importance of the capital investment required versus the role of the investment in machinery.

▶ INDIVIDUAL EXERCISE

Select a recent major project you were extensively involved in, such as the selection of a college, the preparation of a resumé, an auto repair, home remodeling, planning a family trip with three small children, or landscaping. Review the tasks and the time it took to complete them. Construct a rate-of-progress chart and a distribution-of-effort chart similar to those in Figures 1-2 and 1-3. Also recall the initial estimates of either cost or performance and time to completion, and the variability of these estimates, to construct a chart similar to Figure 1-4. Plot the final actual values on the chart and describe the reason for the variance.

How accurate are these charts, in general? Do they picture adequately the concepts they are meant to describe? Archibald [2] portrays the target cost and time (Fig. 1-4) as an ellipse, rather than a band, that continually shrinks as the project nears completion. Is this a better portrayal? How would performance variability then be handled?

▶ PROJECT TEAM CONTINUING EXERCISE

Every chapter in this text will include assignments for project class teams to complete. The teams will be organized by your class instructor and will work on either individual projects or one large class project. The final project report or term paper will be assigned and discussed by your instructor, too.

For now, your task is to form into a team and, if so charged by the instructor, consider potential team projects. Be sure you clearly understand the performance requirements, completion due date, and resources available to conduct the project. Also, attempt to identify the project interdependencies and potential sources of conflict. The interdependencies will dictate how frequently you will have to communicate or have meetings and how much work can be done independently. Identifying the potential sources of conflict will help you avoid problems later on.

The purpose of this activity is to demonstrate in real terms the project management activities that we describe throughout this book. We hope that the tools, techniques, and concepts we discuss and illustrate will be helpful to you and your project team as you undertake and work to complete your project. Good luck!

▶ BIBLIOGRAPHY

1. ADAMS, J. R., S. E. BARNDT, AND M. D. MARTIN. *Managing by Project Management*. Dayton, OH: Universal Technology, 1979.

2. ARCHIBALD, R. D. *Managing High Technology Programs and Projects*. New York: Wiley, 1976.

3. AVOTS, I. "Why Does Project Management Fail?" *California Management Review*, Fall 1969.

4. AWANI, A. O. *Project Management Techniques*. Princeton, NJ: Petrocelli, 1983.

5. BAUMGARTNER, J. *Project Management*. Homewood, IL: Irwin, 1963.

6. BENNINGSON, L. "The Strategy of Running Temporary Projects." *Innovation*, September 1971.

7. BOBROWSKI, P. M. "A Basic Philosophy of Project Management." *Journal of Systems Management*, May–June 1974.

8. CLELAND, D. I. "Why Project Management." *Business Horizons*, Winter 1974.

9. CLELAND, D. I. *Project Management Handbook: Proceedings of the Third International Symposium*. New York: Van Nostrand Reinhold, 1988.

10. CLELAND, D. I. *Project Management Techniques Handbook—Advanced*. Centerville, VA: Management Control Institute, 1990.

11. CLELAND, D. I., AND W. R. KING. *Systems Analysis and Project Management*, 3rd ed. New York: McGraw-Hill, 1983.

12. CLELAND, D. I., AND W. R. KING, eds. *Project Management Handbook*. New York: Van Nostrand Reinhold, 1983.

13. DAVIS, E. W. "CPM Use in Top 400 Construction Firms." *Journal of the Construction Division*, American Society of Civil Engineers, 1974.

14. DAVIS, E. W. *Project Management: Techniques, Applications, and Managerial Issues*, 2nd ed. Norcross, GA: AIIE Monograph, 1983.

15. DEAN, B. V. *Project Management: Methods and Studies*. New York: Elsevier, 1985.

16. GOODMAN, L. *Project Planning and Management: An Integrated System for Improving Productivity*. New York: Van Nostrand Reinhold, 1987.

17. GRAHAM, R. J. *Project Management: Combining Technical and Behavioral Approaches for Effective Implementation*. New York: Van Nostrand Reinhold, 1985.

18. GROD, M. C., et al. *Project Management in Progress*. New York: Elsevier, 1986.

19. HARRISON, F. L. *Advanced Project Management*, 2nd ed. Halstead Press, New York, 1985.

20. HOCKNEY, J. W., AND K. K. HUMPHREYS. *Control and Management of Capital Projects*, 2nd ed. New York: McGraw-Hill, 1991.

21. HODGETTS, R. M. *An Interindustry Analysis of Certain Aspects of Project Management*, Ph.D. dissertation. Norman, OK: University of Oklahoma, 1968.

22. JACOBS, R. A. "Project Management—A New Style for Success." S.A.M. *Advanced Management Journal*, Autumn 1976.

23. KERZNER, H. *Project Management*. New York: Litton Educational Publishing, 1979.

24. KERZNER, H. *Project Management for Executives*. New York: Van Nostrand Reinhold, 1982.

25. KERZNER, H. *Project Management: A Systems Approach to Planning, Scheduling, and Controlling*, 3rd ed. New York: Van Nostrand Reinhold, 1989.

26. KERZNER, H., AND H. THAMHAIN. *Project Management for Small and Medium Sized Businesses*. New York: Van Nostrand Reinhold, 1983.

27. LOCK, D. *Project Management*, 4th ed. Hants, England: Gower Publications, 1988.

28. LOCK, D., ed. *Project Management Handbook*. Hants, England: Gower Publications, 1987.

29. MARTIN, C. C. *Project Management: How to Make It Work*. New York: AMACOM, 1976.

30. MARTINO, R. L. *Project Management*. Dayton, OH: MDI Publications, Management Development Institute, 1968.

31. ROMAN, D. D. *Managing Projects: A Systems Approach*. New York: Elsevier, 1986.

32. ROSENAU, M. D., JR. *Successful Project Management*, 2nd ed. New York: Van Nostrand Reinhold, 1991.

33. SILVERMAN, M. *Project Management: A Short Course for Professionals*, 2nd ed. New York: Wiley, 1988.

34. SPIRER, H. F. "The Basic Principles of Project Management." *Operations Management Review*, Fall 1982.

35. STEWART, J. M. "Making Project Management Work." *Business Horizons*, Fall 1965.

36. STUCKENBRUCK, L. C., ed. *The Implementation of Project Management: The Professional's Handbook*. Reading, MA: Addison-Wesley, 1981.

37. SUN, M. "Weighing the Social Costs of Innovation." *Science*, March 30, 1984.

38. TAYLOR, W. J., AND T. F. WATLING. *Successful Project Management*. London: Business Books, 1970.

39. TOELLNER, J. D. "Project Management: A Formula for Success." *Computerworld*, December 1978.

CASE

PEERLESS LASER PROCESSORS
Jack R. Meredith, Marianne M. Hill, and James M. Comer

Owner and President Ted Montague was sitting at his desk on the second floor of the small Groveport, Ohio plant that housed Peerless Saw Company and its new subsidiary, Peerless Laser Processors, Inc. As he scanned over the eight-page contract to purchase their third laser system, a 1200 watt computerized carbon dioxide (CO_2) laser cutter, he couldn't help but reflect back to a similar situation he faced three years ago in this same office. Conditions were significantly different then. It was amazing, Ted reflected, how fast things had changed in the saw blade market, especially for Peerless, which had jumped from an underdog to the technology leader. Market data and financial statements describing the firm and its market environment are given in Exhibits 1 and 2.

History of Peerless Saw Company

Peerless Saw Company was formed in 1931, during the Great Depression, in Columbus, Ohio, to provide bandsaw blades to Ford Motor Company. It survived the Depression and by 1971, with its non-unionized labor force, it was known for its quality bandsaw and circular saw blades.

But conditions inside the firm warranted less optimism. The original machines and processes were now very old and breaking down frequently, extending

Sources for the *Readings* and *Cases* are given in the *Sourcenotes* at the end of the text.

Sales		$5,028,067	
Costs:			
	Materials	1,860,385	
	Labor	905,052	
	Variable overhead	1,106,175	
	G&A	553,087	
Contribution to profit			603,368

Exhibit 1: Peerless Financial Data, 1983

order backlogs to 20 weeks. However, the owners were nearing retirement and didn't want to invest in new machinery, much less add capacity for the growing order backlog which had been building for years.

By 1974 the situation had reached the crisis point. The OPEC oil embargo provided the last straw, creating havoc in the saw blade market as in many other markets at the time as firms rushed to stockpile scare resources and critical materials, creating artificial shortages for everyone. At that point Ted Montague had appeared and, with the help of external funding, bought the firm from the original owners. Ted's previous business experience was in food processing and he had some concern about taking charge of a metal products company. But Ted found the 40 employees, 13 in the offices and 27 (divided among two shifts) on the shop floor, to be very helpful, particularly since they now had an owner who was interested in building the business back up.

Peerless survived the embargo, and the 1974 recession as well, so that by early 1976 Ted felt comfortable with his knowledge of the business. At that point he had a feel for what he believed were the more serious problems of the business and hired both a manufacturing manager and a manufacturing engineer, Con Wittkopp, to help him solve the problems.

The most shopworn machines at Peerless were the over 30-year-old grinding machines and vertical milling machines. Committed to staying in business, Ted arranged for capital financing to design and build a new facility and replace some of the aging equip-

Year	Sales (M)	Market Share (%)
1983	$5.028	29
1982	3.081	27
1981	2.545	25
1980	2.773	25

Exhibit 2: Sales and Market Data, 1983

ment. In 1977 the firm moved into new quarters in Groveport, not far from Columbus, with 7000 additional square feet of floor space. He also ordered seven new grinders from Germany and five new vertical mills. In order to determine what bottlenecks and inefficiencies existed on the shop floor, Ted also devised and installed a cost tracking system.

Laser Cutting Technology

By 1978, the competition had grown quite strong. In addition to the growing number of direct domestic competitors, foreign firms were mounting a devastating attack on the more common saw blade models, offering equivalent quality off the shelf for lower prices. Furthermore, many users were now tipping their own blades, or even cutting them themselves, further reducing the salable market. Sales were down while costs continued to increase and the remaining equipment continued to age and fail. Ted and Con looked into new technologies for saw blade cutting. They felt that Computer Numerical Control (CNC) machining couldn't be adapted to their needs, and laser cutting had high setup times, was underpowered, and exhibited a poor cut texture. (Ted remarked that "It looked as though an alligator had chewed on it.")

By early 1981, advances in laser cutting technology had received a considerable amount of publicity so Ted and Con signed up to attend a seminar on the subject sponsored by Coherent, one of the leaders in industrial laser technology. Unfortunately, at the last minute they were unable to attend the seminar and had to cancel their reservations.

Ted was under pressure from all sides to replace their worn out punch presses. No longer able to delay, he had contracts made up to purchase three state-of-the-art, quick-change, Minster punch presses. As he sat at his desk on the second floor of the Groveport building, scanning the Minster, Inc. contracts one last time before signing, Con came in with a small piece of sheet steel that had thin, smooth cuts through it.

It seems that a salesperson had been given Ted and Con's names from the seminar registration list and decided to pay them a call. He brought a small piece of metal with him that had been cut with a laser and showed it to Con. This was what Con brought into Ted's office. Impressed with the sample, Ted put the contracts aside and talked to the salesperson. Following their talk, Ted made arrangements to fly out to Coherent's headquarters in Palo Alto, California for a demonstration.

In July 1981, Ted and Con made the trip to Palo Alto and were impressed with the significant improvements made in laser cutting technology since 1978. Setups were faster, the power was higher, and the cuts were much cleaner. Following this trip, they arranged to attend the Hanover Fair in Germany in September to see the latest European technology. There they were guaranteed that the newer, higher powered lasers could even cut one-quarter inch steel sheets.

In November, Ted and Con returned to Palo Alto, making their own tests with the equipment. Satisfied, Ted signed a contract for a 700-watt laser cutter*, one of the largest then available, at a price close to $400,000 although the cutter couldn't be delivered until September 1982.

In addition to the risk of the laser technology, another serious problem now faced Ted and Con—obtaining adequate software for the laser cutter. Ted and Con wanted a package that would allow off-line programming of the machine. Furthermore, they wanted it to be menu-driven, operable by their current high school educated workers (rather than by engineers, as most lasers required), and to have pattern search capability.

Coherent, Inc. was simply not in the off-line software business. Since Ted and Con did not want to learn to write their own software for the cutter, Coherent suggested a seminar for them to attend where they might find the contact they needed. Con attended the session but was shocked at the "horror stories" the other attendees were telling. Nevertheless, someone suggested he contact Battelle Laboratories in Columbus for help. Fearing their high class price tag but with no other alternative, Ted and Con made arrangements to talk with the Battelle people.

The meeting, in March 1982, gave Ted and Con tremendous hope. Ted laid out the specifications for the software and, surprisingly, it appeared that what they wanted could possibly be done. The price would be expensive however—around $100,000—and would require seven months to complete. The timing was perfect. Ted arranged for a September completion, to coincide with the delivery of the laser cutter. In the next seven months Con worked closely with Battelle, constantly redesigning and respecifying the software

to improve its capabilities and avoid unsolvable problems and snags.

Finally, in September 1982, a two-inch high printout of Fortran code, programmed into a DEC PDP-ll computer, was delivered and matched via an RS-232 interface with the recently delivered laser cutter. But when the system was turned on, nothing happened. As Ted remarked: "Disaster City!" The software problem was solved within a day but the laser cutter had to be completely rebuilt on site. For almost 100 days the bugs had to be worked out of the system. "It was just awful."

The months of debugging finally resulted in a working system by December 1982. Meanwhile, Ted and the machine operator, Steve, spent four hours every Friday morning in training at Battelle to learn to use the system. Con and another operator did the same on Friday afternoons. Con and Ted later remarked that the "hardest" part of the training was learning to find the keys on the keyboard.

Initially, Ted and Con thought they might have enough business to keep the laser busy during one shift per day. As it turned out, running the system was considerably more operator dependent than they had expected for a computerized system. Though anyone in the shop could learn to use the system, the operator had to learn how to work *with* the system, finessing and overriding it (skipping routines, "tricking" it into doing certain routines) when necessary to get a job done. Ted described this as "a painful learning curve." Thus, only an experienced operator could get the volume of work through the system that was "theoretically" possible. Nevertheless, once thoroughly familiar with the system, one operator could easily handle two cutters at the same time, and probably even three.

Within the next 17 months, Peerless put 4000 saw patterns on the system and started running the cutter for two full shifts. Due to increased demand they added another laser cutter, using the same computer system, and by November 1983 were running both cutters throughout two full shifts.

Marketplace and Competitive Effects

As of 1984, Peerless saw a number of improvements in their operations, and some significant changes in their market as well. In 1979 they had a 14-week delivery lead time. Part of the reason for this was that 25 percent of their orders had to be renegotiated with the customer because the old tooling couldn't handle the job. This slowed down the work tremendously. With

---

*The contract included extensive ancillary equipment and hardware.

the laser cutter this has been reduced to just three weeks, heat treating being the bottleneck (two full weeks).

Though they weren't making any blades that *could not* be made in 1979, their product mix changed considerably. In 1979 they made primarily 8-, 10-, 12-, and 14-inch saw blades. With the new capabilities of the laser cutter they were now making a much wider variety of blades, and more complex blades as well. As a matter of fact, they were producing the more difficult blades now, and at less cost. For example, with the laser cutter, it took one-seventh the amount of time to cut a blade as it did previously, and one-eighth the number of machine operators. The resulting average cost saving was 5 to 10 percent per blade, reaching a maximum of 45 percent savings (on labor, material, and variable overhead) on some individual blades. Although cost savings allowed Peerless to cut prices on their blades, more significantly, they had an improved product, faster lead times, and more production capability.

Production capability was of particular importance. Peerless found that the ability to do things for customers that simply couldn't be done before changed the way customers ordered their blades. Because of their new capability, they were now seeing fewer repeat orders (although the batch size remained about the same) and considerably more "creativity" on the part of their customers. Orders now came to them as "The same pattern as last time except. . ." Customers were using Peerless' new capability to incrementally improve their saw blades, trying to increase capacity, or productivity, or quality by even one or two percent, based on their previous experimentation. Peerless had discovered, almost by accident, a significant competitive advantage.

Ted was intrigued with the *way* the laser cutter had revived Peerless. He stated that, based on payback or return on investment (ROI) criteria, he could not have justified the investment in the laser cutter beforehand. But more significantly, if he were to go through the figures now, after the tremendous success of the laser cutter, he *still* would not be able to justify the cutter on payback or ROI grounds. The point was, the new technology had changed the market Peerless was selling to, although the customers remained largely the same. The laser cutter in fact "created" its own market, one that simply could not exist prior to this technology. It filled a need that even the customers did not know existed.

Despite the increased speed of the laser cutter, it was not necessary to lay anyone off, though some employees' jobs changed significantly. The laser system was purposely packaged so that the existing employees could work with it and contribute to its success, even though they may have only had high school educations.

Ted continued to push the concept of a small, quality, technologically advanced business staying ahead of the same foreign competition that was wrecking havoc on the major corporations in America.

Ted summarized the benefits the new technology brought as:

- Decreased product cost
- Increased product quality
- Ability to use a sophisticated technology
- Ability to do what couldn't be done before, more responsive to the market
- An inspiration to visiting customers
- A positive image for the firm
- Adds "pizzazz" and "mystique" to the firm
- Allows entry into new fields

Peerless in 1984

In September 1984 Ted created a new division, Peerless Laser Processors, Inc. to handle general laser cutting of other types of parts besides saw blades. By then, Peerless had logged 10,000 hours on the laser cutters and had placed 6000 patterns on the system, adding new ones at the rate of 300 a month. Due to continuing customer requests that had never originally been considered, or even dreamed of, the software has been under constant revision and improvement by Battelle. Ted noted that, even though the need for revisions is expected to continue, it would neither pay to hire a software programmer, nor would the job be interesting enough to keep one for long.

Ted and Con felt that generic computer assisted design/computer aided manufacturing (CAD/CAM) systems available today would not help their situation. The unneeded capabilities tend to slow down the system, and in their new business the main competitive factor, given other constants such as quality, is: "How fast can you do the job?"

Peerless also hired two additional sales representatives, with one now in the field and two in the office at all times. They also hired an engineer to develop new applications on a full-time basis for Peerless Laser Processing. As Con noted, "The problem is recognizing new applications while still doing your own work." They discovered, for example, that they could now make their own shuttles for their double disk grinders instead of purchasing them.

Peerless now has five U.S. competitors in the laser cutting business. Of course, Germany and Japan, among others, are still major competitors using the older technology. For the future, Ted sees the lasers becoming more powerful and having better control. He sees applications growing exponentially, and lasers doing welding and general fabrication of parts as well. He sees other technologies becoming competitive also, such as water jet and electrodischarge machining (EDM).

For Peerless, Ted's immediate goal is to attain a two-week lead time for sawblades and even better customer service, possibly including an inventory function in their service offerings. For the long run, Ted's goal is to become a "showcase" operation, offering the best in technology and quality in the world. As Ted put it:

A company is like a tree. It only succeeds if it continues to grow and you've got to grow wherever there's an opportunity. There are a maximum number of sawblades needed in the world, but no cap on what else the technology can do. We're only limited by our own imagination and creativeness and desire to make technology do things. That's our only restriction. What it fundamentally comes down to is: Is a railroad a railroad or a transportation company? Are we a sawblade company or are we a company that fabricates metals into what anyone wants?

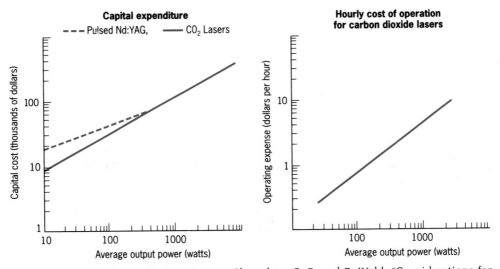

Exhibit 3: Laser characteristics. Source: Charschan, S. S. and R. Webb "Considerations for Lasers in Manufacturing," Laser Materials Processing (edited by M. Bass), North-Holland, 1983.

▶ QUESTIONS

1. How did the laser cutter "save" Peerless Saw Company when it could not be justified on payback or ROI grounds? Does this mean that the economics of automation are not important, or at least were not for Peerless?

2. Compare the decision Ted faces now—the 1200-watt laser purchase—with the decision he faced in 1981 when he was considering the three punch presses. Structure the investment decision for each of these cases. (Assume a computer cost in the neighborhood of $20,000 and software costs of $80,000. Training costs are included in this charge.) Consider costs, benefits, and risks. How has the decision environment changed? Is Ted more or less comfortable with this decision? How is this decision easier? How is it harder?

3. What do you think the potential problems might be in purchasing the 1200-watt laser? What about the potential benefits? Will this laser have the same impact on the business as the first laser? What are the strategic variables involved in these decisions?

4. Estimate costs and revenues for this new system to perform a payback analysis. Use the variable cost data in Exhibit 3; assume the laser cuts at the rate of 40 inches per minute, that a typical blade of 14 inches sells for $25 (33% discount for volumes near 100 units), and the same computer and software will be used as currently. Material load time for a 10-blade sheet of steel is one minute. Use a 3 inch arbor hole size and assume that a cut tooth doubles the cut distance. How would you address the quantification of the intan-gible benefits the new system might provide? Is the new system justified on an economic basis? How might this system be more or less justifiable on an economic basis than the first laser system?

5. What are the organizational/behavioral considerations involved in this purchase? Are they the same as the first laser? How might this system be more or less justifiable on a non-economic basis than the first laser system?

6. Ted is thinking about offering 25 of his largest customers the opportunity to tie into his system directly from their offices. What benefits would this offer to the customers and Peerless? What problems might it pose?

7. Advise Ted on the purchase of the new laser system.

▶ This adaptation is from a well-known classic in the complexities of managing projects. Initially, it describes the details of organizing a project and its unique characteristics in terms of scope, unfamiliarity, complexity, and stake. This is followed by a description of the special sources of trouble to which projects often give rise. Next, the actions required of executives, particularly top management, are described as guidelines. Finally, the author gives some advice concerning the management of human beings in a project setting.

Classic Reading

MAKING PROJECT MANAGEMENT WORK
John M. Stewart

Late last year, with a good deal of local fanfare, a leading food producer opened a new plant in a small midwestern town. For the community it was a festive day. For top management, however, the celebration was somewhat dampened by the fact that the plant had missed its original target date by six months and had overrun estimated costs by a cool $5 million.

A new high-speed, four-color press installed by a leading eastern printing concern has enabled a major consumer magazine to sharply increase its color pages and offer advertisers unprecedented schedule convenience. The printer will not be making money on the press for years, however. Developing and installing it took twice as long and cost nearly three times as much as management had expected.

Fiascos such as these are as old as business itself—as old, indeed, as organized human effort. The unfortunate Egyptian overseer who was obliged, 5000 years ago, to report to King Cheops that construction work on the Great Pyramid at Giza had fallen a year behind schedule had much in common with the vice-president who recoils in dismay as he and the chief executive discover that their new plant will be months late in delivering the production on which a major

---

Sources for the *Readings* and *Cases* are given in the *Sourcenotes* at the end of the text. "Classic" readings are articles that have been recognized over the years as being particularly well-written and offering timeless and invaluable advice.

customer's contract depends. The common thread: poor management of a large, complex, one-time "project" undertaking.

But unlike the Egyptian overseer, today's manager has available a set of new and powerful management tools with the demonstrated capacity to avert time and cost overruns on massive, complex projects. These tools can be successfully applied to a host of important, nonroutine undertakings where conventional planning and control techniques fail—undertakings ranging from a new product introduction or the launching of a national advertising campaign to the installation of an EDP system or a merger of two major corporations (Figure 1).

Project Management Organization

Commercial project management is usually a compromise between two basic forms of organization—pure project management and the more standard functional alignment. In the aerospace and construction companies (Figure 2), complete responsibility for the task, as well as all the resources needed for its accomplishment, is usually assigned to one project manager. Very large projects resemble a regular division, relatively independent of any other division or staff group. Outside the aerospace and construction industries, however, the project manager is usually not assigned complete responsibility for resources. Instead, the manager shares them with the rest of the organization, perhaps having only a handful of workers on temporary assignment from the regular functional organization. The functional managers, however, retain their direct line authority, monitor their staffs' contributions to the project, and continue to make all major personnel decisions.

The companies that have grasped the significance of project management concepts and learned to apply them enjoy an extraordinary advantage. They are bringing new products to market faster than their competitors, completing major expansions on schedule, and meeting crucial commitments more reliably than ever before.

Project management, however, is far from being a cure-all for the embarrassments, expenses, and delays that plague even the best-managed companies. First, project management requires temporary shifts of responsibilities and reporting relationships that may disturb the smooth functioning of the regular organization. Second, it requires unusually disciplined executive effort.

Basic to successful project management is the ability to recognize where it is needed and where it is not. When, in short, is a project a project? Executives must have methods to identify those undertakings that cannot be successfully managed by the regular functional organization working with routine planning and control methods. Although there are no simple rules of thumb, management can determine whether a given undertaking possesses this critical mass by applying four yardsticks: scope, unfamiliarity, complexity, and stake.

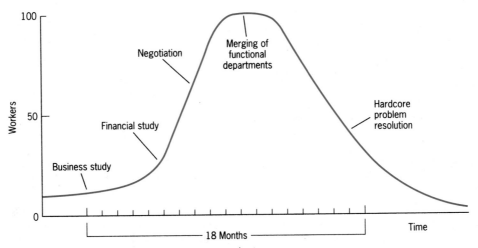

Figure 1: Labor commitment to a merger project.

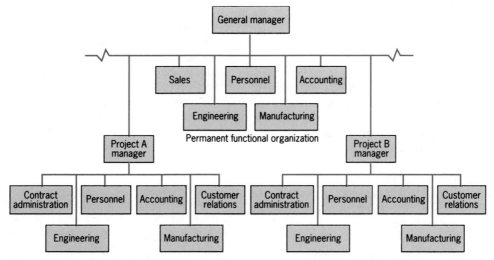

Figure 2: Typical project organization in the aerospace and construction industries.

Scope Project management can be profitably applied, as a rule, to a one-time undertaking that is (1) definable in terms of a single, specific end result, and (2) bigger than the organization has previously undertaken successfully. A project must, by definition, end at an objective point in time: the date the new plant achieves full production, the date the parent company takes over operating management of the new acquisition, or the date the new product goes on sale in supermarkets across the nation, to name a few.

The question of size is less easily pinned down. But where substantially more people, more dollars, more organizational units, and more time will be involved than on any other infrequent undertaking in the organization's experience, the test result is clearly positive. Such an undertaking, even though its component parts may be familiar, can easily overwhelm a divisional or corporate management. Project management forces a logical approach to the project, speeds decision making, and cuts management's job to a reasonable level. For example, a large service company, with years of experience in renovating district offices, established a project organization to renovate its 400 district offices over a two-year period. Even though each task was relatively simple, the total undertaking would have swamped the administrative organization had it been managed routinely.

In terms of the number of people and the organizational effort it involves, a project could typically be charted over time as a wave-like curve, rising gradually to a crest and dropping off abruptly with the accomplishment of the end result (see Figure 1).

Unfamiliarity An undertaking is not a project, in our sense of the term, unless it is a unique, or infrequent, effort by the existing management group. Lack of familiarity or lack of precedent usually leads to disagreement or uncertainty as to how the undertaking should be managed. Thus, though a single engineering change to one part of a product would not qualify for project management by this criterion, the complete redesign of a product line that had been basically unchanged for a decade would in most cases call for project management treatment. Individual managers could accomplish the first change easily, drawing on their own past experience, but each would have to feel his or her way by trial and error through the second.

Complexity Frequently the decisive criterion of a project is the degree of interdependence among tasks. If a given task depends on the completion of other assignments in other functional areas, and if it will, in turn, affect the cost or timing of subsequent tasks, project management is probably called for. Consider the introduction of a hypothetical new product. Sales promotion plans cannot be completed until introduction dates are known; introduction dates depend on product availability; and availability depends on tooling, which depends in turn on the outcome of a disagreement between engineering and product planning over performance specifications. If no one person can produce a properly detailed plan on which all those concerned can agree, if estimates repeatedly fail to withstand scrutiny, or if plans submitted by different departments prove difficult to reconcile or coordinate, the critical mass of a project has probably been reached.

Stake   A final criterion that may tip the scales in favor of project management is the company's stake in the outcome of the undertaking. Would failure to complete the job on schedule or within the budget entail serious penalties for the company? If so, the case for project management is strong.

The corporate stake in the outcome of a project is commonly financial; that is, the failure of a $50,000 engineering project might jeopardize $12 million in annual sales. But it may also involve costs of a different kind. As more than one World's Fair exhibitor can attest, failure to meet a well-publicized project schedule can sometimes do real harm to a company's reputation. In such cases, the powerful controls of project management offer a much firmer prospect of meeting the time, cost, and quality objectives of the major one-time undertaking.

The specific advantages of project management for ventures that meet the criteria just discussed are easily summarized. Project management provides the concentrated management attention that a complex and unfamiliar undertaking is likely to demand. It greatly improves, at very small cost, the chances of on-time, on-budget completion. And it permits the rest of the organization to proceed normally with routine business while the project is underway. But these benefits are available only if top management clearly understands the unique features of project management, the problems it entails, and the steps required to make it work.

The Nature of Project Management

With respect to organization, project management calls for the appointment of one person, the project manager, who has responsibility for the detailed planning, coordination, and ultimate outcome of the project. Usually appointed from the middle management ranks, the project manager is supplied with a team, often numbering no more than half a dozen people for a $10 million project. Team members, drawn from the various functional departments involved in the project, report directly to the project manager.

Within the limits of the project, the project manager's responsibility and authority are interfunctional, like that of top management for the company as a whole. Despite this similarity, however, this function cannot safely be superimposed on a top executive's normal workload. Every company I know that has tried giving operating responsibility for the management of a complex project to a division manager is soon swamped in a tidal wave of detail. Most projects call for more and faster decisions than does routine work, and clear precedents are usually lacking. Few projects are ever successfully managed on a part-time basis.

The essence of project management is that it cuts across, and in a sense conflicts with, the normal organization structure. Throughout the project, personnel at various levels in many functions of the business contribute to it. Because a project usually requires decisions and actions from a number of functional areas at once, the main flow of information and the main interdependencies in a project are not vertical but lateral. Up-and-down information flow is relatively light in a well-run project; indeed, any attempt to consistently send needed information from one functional area up to a common authority and down to another area through conventional channels is apt to cripple the project and wreck the time schedule. Projects are characterized by exceptionally strong lateral working relationships, requiring closely related activity and decisions by many individuals in different functional departments.

Necessarily though, a project possesses a vertical as well as a horizontal dimension, since those who are involved in it at various stages must often go to their superiors for guidance. Moreover, frequent project changes underline the necessity of keeping senior executives informed of the project's current status.

Special Sources of Trouble

Understandably, project managers face some unusual problems in trying to direct and harmonize the diverse forces at work in the project situation. Their main difficulties, observation suggests, arise from three sources: organizational uncertainties, unusual decision pressures, and vulnerability to top-management mistakes.

Organizational Uncertainties   Many newly appointed project managers find that their working relationships with functional department heads have not been clearly defined by management. Who assigns work to the financial analyst? Who decides when to order critical material before the product design is firm? Who determines the quantity and priority of spares? All these decisions vitally concern the project manager who must often forge guidelines for dealing with them. Unless done so skillfully, the questions are apt to be resolved in the interest of individual departments, at the expense of the project as a whole. In addition, the project manager must juggle the internal schedules of each department with the project schedule, avoid political problems that could create bottlenecks, expedite one department to compensate for another's failure to meet its schedule, and hold the project within a predetermined cost.

Unusual Decision Pressures   The severe penalties of delay often compel the project manager to base decisions on relatively little data, analyzed in haste. On a large project where a day's delay may cost $10,000 in salaries alone, one can hardly hold everything up for a week to perform an analysis that could save the company $5000. Decisions must be made fast, even if it means an intuitive decision that might lead to charges of rashness and irresponsibility from functional executives. Decisions to sacrifice time for cost, cost for quality, or quality for time, are common in most projects, and the project manager must be able to make them without panicking.

Vulnerability to Top-Management Mistakes   Though senior executives can seldom give the project manager as much guidance and support as a line manager enjoys, they can easily jeopardize the project's success by lack of awareness, ill-advised intervention, or personal whim. The damage that a senior executive's ignorance of a project situation can create is well illustrated by the following example. A project manager, battling to meet a schedule that had been rendered nearly impossible by the general manager's initial delay in approving the proposal, found functional cooperation more and more difficult to obtain. The functional heads, he discovered, had become convinced—rightly, as it turned out—that he lacked the general manager's full confidence. Unknown to the project manager, two department heads whom he had pressured to expedite their departments had complained to the general manager, who had readily sympathized. The project manager, meanwhile, had been too busy getting the job done to protect himself with top management. As a result, project performance was seriously hampered.

Executive Action Required

Because of the great diversity of projects, useful specific rules for project management are virtually impossible to formulate. From the experience of a number of industries, however, it is possible to distill some general guidelines.

Guideline 1: Define the Objective   Performing unfamiliar activities at a rapid pace, those involved in the project can easily get off track, with the result that many steps of the project may have to be retraced. To minimize this risk, management must clarify the objective of the project well in advance by (1) defining management's intent in undertaking the project, (2) outlining the scope of the project, that is, identifying the departments, companies, functions, and staffs involved, and the approximate degree of their involvement, and (3) describing the end results of the project and its permanent effects, if any, on the company or division.

Top managers who have spent hours discussing a proposed project can easily overlook the fact that middle managers charged with its execution lack their perspective on the project. An explicit description of how a new plant will operate when it is in full production, how a sales reorganization will actually change customer relationships, or how major staff activities will be coordinated after a merger, gives middle managers a much clearer view of what the project will involve and what is expected of them.

Guideline 2: Establish a Project Organization   For a functionally organized company, successful project management means establishing, for the duration of the project, a workable compromise between two quite different organizational concepts. The basic ingredients of such a compromise are (1) appointment of one experienced manager to run the project full-time, (2) organization of the project management function in terms of responsibilities, (3) assignment of a limited number of staff to the project team, and (4) maintenance of a balance of power between the functional heads and the project manager. In taking these steps, some generally accepted management rules may have to be broken, and some organizational friction will almost inevitably occur. But the results in terms of successful project completion should far outweigh these drawbacks and difficulties.

Though the project manager's previous experience is apt to have been confined to a single functional area of the business, he or she must be able to function on the project as a kind of general manager in miniature. It is important to assign an individual whose administrative abilities and skill in personal relations have been convincingly demonstrated under fire.

Experience indicates that it is desirable for senior management to delegate to the project manager some of its responsibilities for planning the project, for resolving arguments among functional departments, for providing problem-solving assistance to functional heads, and for monitoring progress. A general manager, however, should not delegate certain responsibilities, such as monitoring milestone accomplishments, resolving project-related disputes between senior managers, or evaluating the project performance of functional department managers. For the duration of the project, the project manager should also hold some responsibilities normally borne by functional department heads. These include responsibility for reviewing progress against schedule; organizing for, formulating, and approving a project plan; monitoring project cost performance; and, in place of the department heads normally involved, trading off time and cost. Functional department heads, however, should retain responsibility for the quality of their subordinates' technical performance, as well as for matters affecting their careers.

Functional department heads may view the project manager as a potential competitor. By limiting the number of staff on the project team, the problem is alleviated and the project manager's involvement in intrafunctional matters is reduced. Moreover, people transferred out of their own functional departments are apt to lose their inside sources of information and find it increasingly difficult to get things done rapidly and informally.

Because the project manager is concerned with change, while the department head must efficiently manage routine procedures, the two are often in active conflict. Though they should be encouraged to resolve these disputes without constant appeals to higher authority, their common superior must occasionally act as mediator. Otherwise, resentments and frustrations will impair the project's progress and leave a long-lasting legacy of bitterness. Short-term conflicts can often be resolved in favor of the project manager and long-term conflicts in favor of the functional managers. This compromise helps to reduce

friction, to get the job accomplished, and to prepare for the eventual phasing out of the project.

Guideline 3: Install Project Controls Though they use the same raw data as routine reports, special project controls over time, cost, and quality are very different in their accuracy, timing, and use. They are normally superimposed upon the existing report structure for the duration of the project and then discontinued. The crucial relationship between project time control and cost control is shown graphically in Figure 3.

The project in question had to be completed in twenty months instead of the twenty and a half months scheduled by a preliminary network calculation. The project manager, who was under strict initial manpower limitations, calculated the cost of the two weeks' acceleration at various stages of the project. Confronted by the evidence of the costs it could save, top management approved the project manager's request for early acceleration. The project was completed two working days before its 20-month deadline, at a cost only $6000 over the original estimate. Without controls that clearly relate time to cost, companies too often crash the project in its final stages, at enormous and entirely unnecessary cost.

Time Control Almost invariably, some form of network scheduling provides the best time control of a project. A means of graphically planning a complex undertaking so that it can be scheduled for analysis and control, network scheduling begins with the construction of a diagram that reflects the interdependencies and time requirements of the individual tasks that go to make up a project. It calls for work plans prepared in advance of the project in painstaking detail, scheduling each element of the plan, and using controls to ensure that commitments are met.

At the outset, each department manager involved in the project should draw up a list of all the tasks required of his department to accomplish the project. Then the project manager should discuss each of these lists in detail with the respective departmental supervisors in order to establish the sequence in the project in relation to other departments. Next, each manager and supervisor should list the information he or she will need from other departments, indicating which data, if any, are habitually late. This listing gives the project manager not only a clue to the thoroughness of planning in the other departments but also a

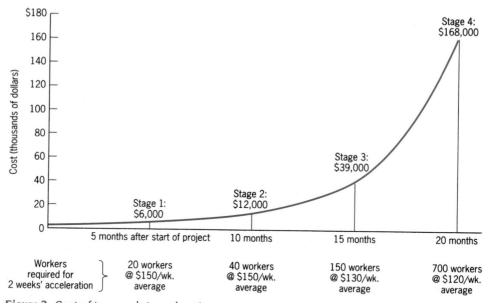

Figure 3: Cost of two weeks' acceleration at various project stages.

means of uncovering and forestalling most of the in-consistencies, missed activities, or inadequate planning that would otherwise occur.

Next, having planned its own role in the project, each department should be asked to commit itself to an estimate of the time required for each of its project activities, assuming the required information is supplied on time. After this, the complete network is constructed, adjusted where necessary with the agreement of the department heads concerned, and reviewed for logic.

Once the overall schedule is established, weekly or fortnightly review meetings should be held to check progress against schedule. Control must be rigorous, especially at the start, when the tone of the entire project is invariably set. Thus, the very first few missed commitments call for immediate corrective action.

Cost Control Project cost control techniques, though not yet formalized to the same degree as time controls, are no harder to install if these steps are followed: (1) break the comprehensive cost summary into work packages, (2) devise commitment reports for "technical" decision makers, (3) act on early, approximate report data, and (4) concentrate talent on major problems and opportunities.

Managing a fast-moving $15 million project can be difficult for even the most experienced top manager. For a first-line supervisor the job of running a

$500,000 project can be equally difficult. Neither manager can make sound decisions unless cost dimensions of the job are broken down into pieces of comprehensible size. Figure 4, which gives an example of such a breakdown, shows how major costs can be logically reduced to understandable and controllable work packages (usually worth $15,000 to $25,000 apiece on a major project), each of which can reasonably be assigned to a first-line manager.

Almost without exception, experience shows, 20 percent of the project effort accounts for at least 80 percent of the cost to which the company is committed. With the aid of a detailed cost breakdown and current information on cost commitment, the project manager is able, even after the project is underway, to take people off less important activities in order to concentrate more effort where it will do the most good in reducing costs. One company cut its product introduction costs by over $1 million in this way between the dates when the first print was released and the first machine assembled.

Quality Control Experience with a wide variety of projects—new-product introductions, mergers, plant constructions, introduction of organizational changes, to name a few—indicates that effective quality control of results is a crucial dimension of project success. Quality control comprises three elements: defining performance criteria, expressing the project

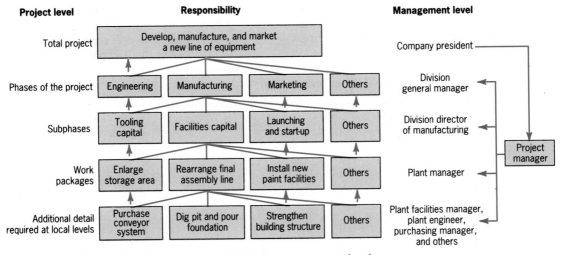

Project level — **Responsibility** — **Management level**

Figure 4: Breakdown of project cost responsibility by management level.

objection in terms of quality standards, and monitoring progress toward these standards.

The need to define performance criteria, though universally acknowledged, is generally ignored in practice. Such quality criteria can, however, be defined rather easily, that is, simply in terms of senior executives' expectations with respect to average sales per salesperson, market penetration of a product line, ratio of accounts to production workers, processing time for customer inquiries, and the like. If possible, these expectations should be expressed quantitatively. For example, the senior executive might expect the project to reduce emergency transportation costs from 15 percent to 5 percent of total shipping costs.

Since achievement of these quality goals is a gradual process, the project manager should review progress toward them with the general manager monthly or quarterly, depending on the length of the project. Sometimes there will be little noticeable change; in other cases major departures from expectations will be apparent. Here, as in the case of time and cost controls, the importance of prompt action to assure that the objectives will be met cannot be overemphasized.

Managing the Human Equation

The typical new project manager finds adjustment to this anomalous new role painful, confusing, and even demoralizing. Lacking real line authority, he or she must constantly lead, persuade, or coerce former peers through a trying period of change.

Too often, in these difficult early weeks, the project manager receives little support from senior management. Instead, he or she may be criticized for not moving faster and producing more visible results. Senior managers need to recognize that naming and needling the project manager is not enough. By giving support at the start, bringing a broad business perspective to bear on the overall project plan, and giving the project manager freedom in the details of the doing, senior executives can greatly enhance the prospects of success.

Another critical point comes at the conclusion of the project, when its results are turned over to the regular organization and the project manager and team must return to their permanent assignments. By virtue of the interfunctional experience gained under pressure, the project manager often matures in the course of a project, becoming a more valuable manager, but may have trouble slowing down to a normal organizational pace. The routine job is likely to seem less attractive in terms of scope, authority, and opportunity to contribute to the business. Even the best project manager, moreover, can hardly accomplish given project objectives without antagonizing some members of management, quite possibly the very executives who will decide his or her future. In one instance, a project manager who had brought a major project from the brink of chaos to unqualified success was let go at the end of the project because, in accomplishing the feat, he had been unable to avoid antagonizing one division manager. Such difficulties and dissatisfactions often lead a retired project manager to look for a better job at this time, in or out of the company.

To retain and profit by the superior management material developed on the fertile training ground of the project, senior executives need to be aware of these human problems. By recognizing the growth of project managers, helping them readjust to the slower pace of the normal organization, and finding ways to put their added experience and matured judgment to good use, the company can reap a significant side benefit from every successfully managed project.

PART

I

PROJECT INITIATION

This part of the text begins our formal analysis of project management. Chapter 2 takes the first step in project initiation: evaluating and selecting projects for implementation. That chapter also includes a short discussion of project proposals and their preparation. What is certainly a critically important task in the management of projects, the selection of a project manager, is treated in Chapter 3. The significance and nature of the project manager's role, responsibilities, and desirable personal characteristics are described in detail. Chapter 4 continues with a discussion of the advantages and disadvantages of several different forms of project organization. The nature and formation of the project staff are also briefly covered.

Chapter 5 opens the subject of project planning. Preparation of the fundamental planning document is covered, and some of the tools needed to organize and staff the numerous project tasks are described and illustrated through examples. Finally, Chapter 6 treats the most often used and least-discussed skill of an effective project manager, negotiation.

CHAPTER 2

Project Selection

Project selection is the process of evaluating individual projects or groups of projects, and then choosing to implement some set of them so that the objectives of the parent organization will be achieved. This same systematic process can be applied to any area of the organization's business in which choices must be made between competing alternatives. For example, a manufacturing firm can use evaluation/selection techniques to choose which machine to adopt in a part-fabrication process; a TV station can pick out which of several syndicated comedy shows to rerun in its 7:30 PM weekday time-slot; a trucking firm can use these methods to decide which of several tractors to purchase; a construction firm can select the best subset of a large group of potential projects on which to bid; a hospital can find the best mix of psychiatric, orthopedic, obstetric, pediatric, and other beds for a new wing; or a research lab can choose the set of R & D projects that holds the best promise of reaching a technological goal.

In this chapter we look at the procedures firms use to decide which creative idea to support, which new technology to develop, which repair to authorize. Each project will have different costs, benefits, and risks. Rarely are these known with certainty. In the face of such differences, the selection of one project out of a set is a difficult task. Choosing a number of different projects, a *portfolio*, is even more complex.

This chapter, like Appendixes A and B, may cover a subject not customarily covered in books on project management. Though the project manager often enters the picture at the stage of the project life cycle following selection, in many situations the project manager is the person who has worked and lobbied for the selection of this specific project, particularly if an RFP (Request For Proposal) was involved. Moreover, though project evaluation and selection is usually a task for senior management, this is an important part of the project life cycle because project success is judged by the degree to which the project meets its goals. Since project selection is based on a direct statement of those goals, the project manager needs to know them in order to perform effectively.

In this chapter we discuss several techniques that can be used to help decision makers select projects. Project selection is only one of many decisions associated with project management. To deal with all of these problems, we use *decision-aiding models*. We need such models because they abstract the relevant issues about a problem from the welter of detail in which the problem is embedded.

Realists cannot solve problems, only idealists can do that. Reality is far too complex to deal with in its entirety. The reality of this page, for instance, includes the weight of ink imprinted on it as well as the number of atoms in the period at the end of this sentence. Those aspects of reality are not relevant to a decision about the proper width of the left margin or the precise position of the page number. An "idealist" is needed to strip away almost all the reality from a problem, leaving only the aspects of the "real" situation with which he or she wishes to deal. This process of carving away the unwanted reality from the bones of a problem is called *modeling the problem*. The idealized version of the problem that results is called a *model*.

The model represents the problem's *structure*, its form. Every problem has a form, though often we may not understand a problem well enough to describe its structure. Several different types of models are available to make the job of modeling the problem easier. *Iconic* models are physical representations of systems. The category includes everything from teddy bears to the dowel rod and styrofoam model of an atom hanging from the ceiling of a high school chemistry lab. *Analogue* models are similar to reality in some respects and different in others. Traditionally, every student of elementary physics was exposed to the hydraulic analogy to explain electricity. This model emphasized the similarities between water pressure and voltage, between the flow of water and the flow of electrical current, between the reservoir and the capacitor. *Verbal* models use words to describe systems— George Orwell's novel *Animal Farm*, for example. *Diagrammatic* models may be used to explain the hierarchical command structure of an army battalion or a business firm, just as *graphic* models may be used to illustrate the equilibrium solution to problems of supply and demand. We will use all these models in this book, as well as *flow graph* and *network* models to help solve scheduling problems, *matrix* models to aid in project evaluation, and *symbolic* (mathematical) models for a number of purposes.

This wide variety of models allows the decision maker considerable choice. Most problems can be modeled in several different ways, and it is often not difficult to transform a problem from one model to another—the transformation from matrix to network to mathematical models, for instance, is usually straightforward. The decision maker usually has some leeway in selecting the model form.

Models may be quite simple to understand, or they may be extremely complex. In general, introducing more reality into a model tends to make the model more difficult to manipulate. If the input data for a model are not known precisely, we often use probabalistic information; that is, the model is said to be *stochastic* rather than *deterministic*. Again, in general, stochastic models are more difficult to manipulate. (Readers who are not familiar with the fundamentals of decision making might find a book such as *The New Science of Management Decisions* [57] or *Fundamentals of Management Science* [65] useful.) A few of the models we discuss employ mathematical programming techniques for solution. These procedures are rarely used, but they illustrate a logic that can be useful; and it is not necessary to understand mathematical programming to profit from the discussion.

This chapter relies heavily on the use of models for project evaluation and selection. First, we examine fundamental types of project selection models and the characteristics that make any model more or less acceptable. Next we consider the limitations, strengths, and weaknesses of project selection models, including some suggestions of factors to consider when making a decision about which, if any, of the selection models to use (see also the end of Section 2.3). We then discuss the problem of selecting projects when high levels of uncertainty about outcomes, costs, schedules, or technology are present. Finally, we comment on some special aspects of the information base required for project selection.

One might argue that we should discuss the *project proposal*, its contents and construction, before considering project selection models. It is, however, useful to understand how an idea will be evaluated before deciding on how best to present the idea. Further, we set aside the issue of where ideas come from and how they are introduced into the process that, sooner or later, results in a proposal. The subject is certainly of consequence, but project managers are rarely directly involved. As a result, consideration of idea generation is relegated to Appendix A. As noted, project proposals are discussed later in this chapter. We finish the chapter with a guess about the future of project selection models.

▶ 2.1 CRITERIA FOR PROJECT SELECTION MODELS

We live in the midst of what has been called the "knowledge explosion." We frequently hear such comments as "90 percent of all we know about physics has been discovered since Albert Einstein published his original work on special relativity"; and "80 percent of what we know about the human body has been discovered in the past 50 years." In addition, evidence is cited to show that knowledge is growing exponentially. Such statements emphasize the importance of the *management of change*. To survive, firms must develop strategies for assessing and reassessing the use of their resources. Every allocation of resources is an investment in the future. Because of the complex nature of most strategies, many of these investments are in projects.

To cite one of many possible examples, special visual effects accomplished through computer animation are common in the movies and television shows we watch daily. A few years ago they were unknown. When the capability was in its idea stage, computer companies as well as the firms producing movies and TV shows faced the decision whether or not to invest in the development of these techniques. Obviously valuable as the idea seems today, the choice was not quite so clear a decade ago when an entertainment company compared investment in computer animation to alternative investments in a new star, a new rock group, or a new theme park—or when the computer firm considered alternative investments in a new business software package, a higher resolution color monitor, or a faster processor.

The proper choice of investment projects is crucial to the long-run survival of every firm. Daily we witness the results of both good and bad investment choices. In our daily newspapers we read of Ashland Oil's decision to reformulate its automotive fuel in order to lower pollution at a cost of $0.03 to $0.05 per gallon—at the same time that British Petroleum decides to lower the volatility of its automotive fuel to lower pollution at a cost of $0.01 per gallon. We read of Chrysler's decision to make a major alteration in its passenger car line, of IBM's decision to make significant cuts in the prices of its personal computers, and of the United States congressional decision to withdraw funding from the Super Conducting Super Collider project. But can such important choices be made rationally? Once made, do they ever change, and if so, how? These questions reflect the need for effective selection models.

Within the limits of their capabilities, such models can be used to increase profits, to select investments for limited capital resources, or to improve the competitive position of the organization. They can be used for ongoing evaluation as well as initial selection, and thus are a key to the allocation and reallocation of the organization's scarce resources.

When a firm chooses a project selection model, the following criteria, based on Souder [60], are most important.

1. **Realism**   The model should reflect the reality of the manager's decision situation, including the multiple objectives of both the firm and its managers. Without a common measurement system, direct comparison of different projects is impossible. For example, Project A may strengthen a firm's market share by extending its facilities, and Project B might improve its competitive position by strengthening its technical staff. Other things being equal, which is better? The model should take into account the realities of the firm's limitations on facilities, capital, personnel, etc. The model should also include factors for risk—both the technical risks of performance, cost, and time and the market risk of customer rejection.

2. **Capability**   The model should be sophisticated enough to deal with multiple time periods, simulate various situations both internal and external to the project (e.g., strikes, interest rate changes, etc.), and *optimize* the decision. An optimizing model will make the comparisons that management deems important, consider major risks and constraints on the projects, and then select the best overall project or set of projects.

3. **Flexibility**   The model should give valid results within the range of conditions that the firm might experience. It should have the ability to be easily modified, or to be self-adjusting in response to changes in the firm's environment; for example, tax laws change, new technological advancements alter risk levels, and, above all, the organization's goals change.

4. **Ease of Use**   The model should be reasonably convenient, not take a long time to execute, and be easy to use and understand. It should not require special interpretation, data that are hard to acquire, excessive personnel, or unavailable equipment. The model's variables should also relate one to one with those real-world parameters the managers believe significant to the project. Finally, it should be easy to simulate the expected outcomes associated with investments in different project portfolios.

5. **Cost** Data-gathering and modeling costs should be low relative to the cost of the project and must surely be less than the potential benefits of the project. All costs should be considered, including the costs of data management and of running the model.

We would add a sixth criterion:

6. **Easy Computerization** It must be easy and convenient to gather and store the information in a computer data base, and to manipulate data in the model through use of a widely available, standard computer package such as Lotus 1-2-3®, Quattro Pro®, Excel®, and like programs.

▶ 2.2   THE NATURE OF PROJECT SELECTION MODELS

There are two basic types of project selection models, numeric and nonnumeric. Both are widely used. Many organizations use both at the same time, or they use models that are combinations of the two. Nonnumeric models, as the name implies, do not use numbers as inputs. Numeric models do, but the criteria being measured may be either objective or subjective. It is important to remember that the *qualities* of a project may be represented by numbers, and that *subjective* measures are not necessarily less useful or reliable than so-called *objective* measures. (We will discuss these matters in more detail in Section 2.5.)

Before examining specific kinds of models within the two basic types, let us consider just what we wish the model to do for us, never forgetting two critically important, but often overlooked, facts.

- Models do not make decisions; people do. The manager, not the model, bears responsibility for the decision. The manager may "delegate" the task of making the decision to a model, but the responsibility cannot be abdicated.
- All models, however sophisticated, are only partial representations of the reality they are meant to reflect. Reality is far too complex for us to capture more than a small fraction of it in any model. Therefore, no model can yield an optimal decision except within its own, possibly inadequate, framework.

We seek a model to assist us in making project selection decisions. This model should possess the characteristics discussed previously: ease of use, flexibility, low cost, and so on. Above all, it must evaluate potential projects by the degree to which they will meet the firm's objectives. (In general, we will not differentiate between such terms as *goals*, *objectives*, *aims*, etc.) To construct a selection/evaluation model, therefore, it is necessary to develop a list of the firm's objectives.

Such a list should be generated by the organization's top management. It is a direct expression of organizational philosophy and policy. The list should go beyond the typical clichés about "survival" and "maximizing profits," which are certainly real goals but are just as certainly not the only goals of the firm. Others might include maintenance of share of specific markets, development of an improved image with specific clients or competitors, expansion into a new line of business, decrease in sensitivity to business cycles, maintenance of employment for specific categories of workers, and maintenance of system loading at or above some percent of capacity, just to mention a few.

A model of some sort is implied by any conscious decision. The choice between two or more alternative courses of action requires reference to some objective(s), and the choice is thus made in accord with some, possibly subjective, "model."

In the past two or three decades, largely since the development of computers and the establishment of operations research as an academic subject area, the use of formal, numeric models to assist in decision making has expanded. A large majority of such models use financial measures of the "goodness" of a decision. Project selection decisions are no exception, being based primarily on the degree to which the financial goals of the organization are met [35]. As we will see later, this stress on financial goals, largely to the exclusion of other criteria, raises some serious problems for the firm, irrespective of whether the firm is for-profit or not-for-profit.

When the list of objectives has been developed, an additional refinement is recommended. The elements in the list should be weighted. Each item is added to the list because it represents a contribution to the success of the organization, but each item does not make an equal contribution. The weights reflect the different degree of contribution of each element in the set of goals.

Once the list of goals has been developed, one more task remains. A project is selected or rejected because it is predicted to have certain outcomes if implemented. These outcomes are expected to contribute to goal achievement. If the estimated level of goal achievement is sufficiently large, the project is selected. If not, it is rejected. The relationship between the project's expected results and the organization's goals must be understood. In general, the kinds of information required to evaluate a project can be listed under production, marketing, financial, personnel, administrative, and other such categories.

The following is a list of factors that contribute, positively or negatively, to these categories. In order to give focus to this list, we assume that the projects in question involve the possible substitution of a new production process for an existing one. The list is meant to be illustrative. It certainly is not exhaustive.

Production Factors
1. Time until ready to install
2. Length of disruption during installation
3. Degree of disruption during installation
4. Learning curve—time until operating as desired
5. Effects on waste and rejects
6. Energy requirements
7. Facility and other equipment requirements
8. Safety of process
9. Other applications of technology
10. Consistency with current technological know-how
11. Change in cost to produce a unit output

12. Change in time to produce a unit output
13. Change in raw material usage
14. Availability of raw materials
15. Required development time and cost
16. Impact on current suppliers
17. Change in quality of output
18. Change in quality control procedures

Marketing Factors

1. Size of potential market for output
2. Probable market share of output
3. Time until market share is acquired
4. Impact on current product line
5. Ability to control quality
6. Consumer acceptance
7. Impact on consumer safety
8. Estimated life of output
9. Shape of output life cycle curve
10. Spin-off project possibilities

Financial Factors

1. Profitability, net present value of the investment
2. Impact on cash flows
3. Payout period
4. Cash requirements
5. Time until break-even
6. Size of investment required
7. Impact on seasonal and cyclical fluctuations
8. Cost of getting system up to speed
9. Level of financial risk

Personnel Factors

1. Training requirements
2. Labor skill requirements
3. Availability of required labor skills
4. Level of resistance from current work force
5. Other worker reactions
6. Change in size of labor force
7. Change in sex, age, or racial distribution of labor force

8. Inter- and intra-group communication requirements
9. Support labor requirements
10. Impact on working conditions

Administrative and Miscellaneous Factors

1. Meet government safety standards
2. Meet government environmental standards
3. Impact on information system
4. Impact on computer usage
5. Need for consulting help, inside and outside
6. Reaction of stockholders and securities markets
7. Patent and trade secret protection
8. Impact on image with customers, suppliers, and competitors
9. Cost of maintaining skill in new technology
10. Vulnerability to single supplier
11. Degree to which we understand new technology
12. Elegance of new process
13. Degree to which new process differs from current process
14. Managerial capacity to direct and control new process

Some factors in this list have a one-time impact and some recur. Some are difficult to estimate and may be subject to considerable error. For these, it is helpful to identify a *range of uncertainty*. In addition, the factors may occur at different times. And some factors may have *thresholds*, critical values above or below which we might wish to reject the project.

Clearly, no single project decision need include all these factors. Moreover, not only is the list incomplete, but it contains redundant items. Perhaps more important, the factors are not at the same level of generality: *profitability* and *impact on organizational image* both affect the overall organization, but *impact on working conditions* is more oriented to the production system. Nor are all elements of equal importance. *Change in production cost* is usually considered more important than *impact on computer usage*. Later in this chapter we will deal with the problem of generating an acceptable list of factors and measuring their relative importance. At that time we will discuss the creation of a DSS (Decision Support System) for project evaluation and selection. The same subject will arise once more in Chapters 12 and 13 when we consider project auditing and termination.

Although the process of evaluating a potential project is time-consuming and difficult, its importance cannot be overstated. A major consulting firm has argued [37] that the primary cause for the failure of R & D projects is insufficient care in evaluating the proposal before the expenditure of funds. What is true of R & D projects also appears to be true for other kinds of projects. Careful analysis of a potential project is a *sine qua non* for profitability in the construction business. There are many horror stories [43] about firms that undertook projects for the installation of a computer information system without sufficient analysis of the time, cost, and disruption involved.

Later in this chapter we will consider the problem of conducting an evaluation under conditions of uncertainty about the outcomes associated with a project. Before dealing with this problem, however, it helps to examine several different evaluation/selection models and consider their strengths and weaknesses. Recall that the problem of choosing the project selection model itself will be discussed later in this chapter.

▶ 2.3   TYPES OF PROJECT SELECTION MODELS

Of the two basic types of selection models, numeric and nonnumeric, nonnumeric models are older and simpler and have only a few subtypes to consider. We examine them first.

Nonnumeric Models

The Sacred Cow   The project is suggested by a senior and powerful official in the organization. Often the project is initiated with a simple comment such as, "If you have the chance, why don't you look into . . . ," and there follows an undeveloped idea for a new product, for the development of a new market, for the installation of a new decision support system, for the adoption of Material Requirements Planning, or for some other project requiring an investment of the firm's resources. The immediate result of this bland statement is the creation of a "project" to investigate whatever the boss has suggested. The project is "sacred" in the sense that it will be maintained until successfully concluded, or until the boss, personally, recognizes the idea as a failure and terminates it.

The Operating Necessity   If a flood is threatening the plant, a project to build a protective dike does not require much formal evaluation. Republic Steel Corporation (now a part of LTV Corp.) has used this criterion (and the following criterion also) in evaluating potential projects. If the project is required in order to keep the system operating, the primary question becomes: Is the system worth saving at the estimated cost of the project? If the answer is yes, project costs will be examined to make sure they are kept as low as is consistent with project success, but the project will be funded.

The Competitive Necessity   Using this criterion, Republic Steel undertook a major plant rebuilding project in the late 1960s in its steel-bar-manufacturing facilities near Chicago. It had become apparent to Republic's management that the company's bar mill needed modernization if the firm was to maintain its competitive position in the Chicago market area. Although the planning process for the project was quite sophisticated, the decision to undertake the project was based on a desire to maintain the company's competitive position in that market.

In a similar manner, many business schools are restructuring their undergraduate and MBA programs to stay competitive with the more forward-looking schools.

In large part, this action is driven by declining numbers of tuiton-paying students and the stronger competition to attract them.

Investment in an *operating necessity* project takes precedence over a *competitive necessity* project, but both types of projects may bypass the more careful numeric analysis used for projects deemed to be less urgent or less important to the survival of the firm.

The Product Line Extension   A project to develop and distribute new products would be judged on the degree to which it fits the firm's existing product line, fills a gap, strengthens a weak link, or extends the line in a new, desirable direction. Sometimes careful calculations of profitability are not required. Decision makers can act on their beliefs about what will be the likely impact on the total system performance if the new product is added to the line.

Comparative Benefit Model   Assume that an organization has many projects to consider, perhaps several dozen. Senior management would like to select a subset of the projects that would most benefit the firm, but the projects do not seem to be easily comparable. For example, some projects concern potential new products, some concern changes in production methods, others concern computerization of certain records, and still others cover a variety of subjects not easily categorized (e.g., a proposal to set up a daycare center for employees with small children). The organization has no formal method of selecting projects, but members of the Selection Committee do think that some projects will benefit the firm more than others, even if they have no precise way to define or measure "benefit."

The concept of comparative benefits, if not a formal model, is widely adopted for selection decisions on all sorts of projects. Most United Way organizations use the concept to make decisions about which of several social programs to fund. The comparative benefit concept is also commonly used when making funding decisions on fundamental research projects. Organizations such as the National Science Foundation, the Office of Naval Research, and a great many other governmental, private, and university sponsors of research usually send project proposals to outside experts in the relevant areas who serve as "referees," a process known as *peer review*. The proposal is evaluated according to the referee's technical criteria, and a recommendation is submitted. Senior management of the funding organization then examines all projects with positive recommendations and attempts to construct a portfolio that best fits the organization's aims and its budget.

Of the several techniques for ordering projects, the *Q-Sort* [26] is one of the most straightforward. First, the projects are divided into three groups—*good, fair,* and *poor*—according to their relative merits. If any group has more than eight members, it is subdivided into two categories, such as *fair-plus* and *fair-minus*. When all categories have eight or fewer members, the projects within each category are ordered from best to worst. Again, the order is determined on the basis of relative merit. The rater may use specific criteria to rank each project, or may simply use general overall judgment. See Figure 2-1 for an example of a Q-Sort.

The process described may be carried out by one person who is responsible for evaluation and selection, or it may be performed by a committee charged with the responsibility. If a committee handles the task, the individual rankings can be devel-

Steps	Results at Each Step
1. For each participant in the exercise, assemble a deck of cards, with the name and description of one project on each card.	

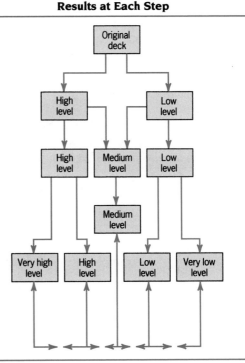

1. For each participant in the exercise, assemble a deck of cards, with the name and description of one project on each card.

2. Instruct each participant to divide the deck into two piles, one representing a high priority, the other a low-priority level. (The piles need not be equal.)

3. Instruct each participant to select cards from each pile to form a third pile representing the medium-priority level.

4. Instruct each participant to select cards from the high-level pile to yield another pile representing the very high level of priority; select cards from the low-level pile representing the very low level of priority.

5. Finally, instruct each participant to survey the selections and shift any cards that seem out of place until the classifications are satisfactory.

Figure 2-1: The Q-sort method. *Source:* [61]

oped anonymously, and the set of anonymous rankings can be examined by the committee itself for consensus. It is common for such rankings to differ somewhat from rater to rater, but they do not often vary strikingly because the individuals chosen for such committees rarely differ widely on what they feel to be appropriate for the parent organization. Projects can then be selected in the order of preference, though they are usually evaluated financially before final selection.

There are other, similar nonnumeric models for accepting or rejecting projects. Although it is easy to dismiss such models as unscientific, they should not be discounted casually. These models are clearly goal-oriented and directly reflect the primary concerns of the organization. The sacred cow model, in particular, has an added feature; sacred cow projects are visibly supported by "the powers that be." Full support by top management is certainly an important contributor to project success [43]. Without such support, the probability of project success is sharply lowered.

Numeric Models: Profit/Profitability

As noted earlier, a large majority of all firms using project evaluation and selection models use profit/profitability as the sole measure of acceptability. We will consider these models first, and then discuss models that go well beyond the profit test for acceptance.

Payback Period   The payback period for a project is the initial fixed investment in the project divided by the estimated annual cash inflows from the project. The ratio of these quantities is the number of years required for the project to repay its initial fixed investment. For example, assume a project costs $100,000 to implement and has annual cash inflows of $25,000. Then

$$\text{Payback period} = \$100,000/\$25,000 = 4 \text{ years}$$

This method assumes that the cash inflows will persist at least long enough to pay back the investment, and it ignores any cash inflows beyond the payback period. The method also serves as an inadequate proxy for risk. The faster the investment is recovered, the less the risk to which the firm is exposed.

Average Rate of Return   Often mistakenly taken to be the reciprocal of the payback period, the average rate of return is the ratio of the average annual profit (either before or after taxes) to the initial or average investment in the project. Because average annual profits are not equivalent to net cash inflows, the average rate of return does not equal the reciprocal of the payback period. Assume, in the example just given, that the average annual profits are $15,000:

$$\text{Average rate of return} = \$15,000/\$100,000 = 0.15$$

Neither of these evaluation methods is recommended for project selection, though payback period is widely used and does have a legitimate value for cash budgeting decisions. The major advantage of these models is their simplicity, but neither takes into account the time value of money. Unless interest rates are extremely low and the rate of inflation is nil, the failure to reduce future cash flows or profits to their present value will result in serious evaluation errors.

Discounted Cash Flow   Also referred to as the present value method, the discounted cash flow method determines the net present value of all cash flows by discounting them by the required rate of return (also known as the *hurdle rate, cutoff rate,* and similar terms) as follows,

$$\text{NPV (project)} = A_0 + \sum_{t=1}^{n} \frac{F_t}{(1 + k)^t}$$

where

    F_t = the net cash flow in period t,

    k = the required rate of return, and

    A_0 = initial cash investment (because this is an outflow, it will be negative).

To include the impact of inflation (or deflation) where p_t is the predicted rate of inflation during period t, we have

$$\text{NPV (project)} = A_0 + \sum_{t=1}^{n} \frac{F_t}{(1 + k + p_t)^t}$$

Early in the life of a project, net cash flow is likely to be negative, the major outflow being the initial investment in the project, A_0. If the project is successful, however, cash flows will become positive. The project is *acceptable* if the sum of the net present values of all estimated cash flows over the life of the project is positive. A simple example will suffice. Using our $100,000 investment with a net cash inflow of $25,000 per year for a period of eight years, a required rate of return of 15 percent, and an inflation rate of 3 percent per year, we have

$$\text{NPV (project)} = -\$100,000 + \sum_{t=1}^{8} \frac{\$25,000}{(1 + 0.15 + 0.03)^t}$$

$$= \$1939$$

Because the present value of the inflows is greater than the present value of the outflow—that is, the net present value is positive—the project is deemed acceptable.

PsychoCeramic Sciences, Inc.

PsychoCeramic Sciences, Inc. (PSI), a large producer of cracked pots and other cracked items, is considering the installation of a new manufacturing line that will, it is hoped, allow more precise quality control on the size, shape, and location of the cracks in its pots as well as in vases designed to hold artificial flowers.

The plant engineering department has submitted a project proposal that estimates the investment requirements as follows: an initial investment of $125,000 to be paid up-front to the Pocketa-Pocketa Machine Corporation, an additional investment of $100,000 to install the machines, and another $90,000 to add new material handling systems and integrate the new equipment into the overall production system. Delivery and installation is estimated to take one year, and integrating the entire system should require an additional year. Thereafter, the engineers predict that scheduled machine overhauls will require further expenditures of about $15,000 every second year, beginning in the fourth year. They will not, however, overhaul the machinery in the last year of its life.

The project schedule calls for the line to begin production in the third year, and to be up-to-speed by the end of that year. Projected manufacturing cost savings and added profits resulting from higher quality are estimated to be $50,000 in the first year of operation and are expected to peak at $120,000 in the second year of operation, and then to follow the gradually declining pattern shown in the table at the end of this box.

Project life is expected to be 10 years from project inception, at which time the proposed system will be obsolete and will have to be replaced. It is estimated that the machinery will have a salvage value of $35,000.

PSI has a 12 percent hurdle rate for capital investments and expects the rate of inflation to be about 3 percent over the life of the project. Assuming that the initial expenditure occurs at the beginning of the year and that all other receipts and expenditures occur as lump sums at the end of the year, we can prepare the Net Present Value analysis for the project shown in the table.

The Net Present Value of the project is positive and, thus, the project can be accepted. (The project would have been rejected if the hurdle rate were 14 percent.)

Just for the intellectual exercise, note that the total inflow for the project is $759,000, or

$75,900 per year *on average* for the 10 year project. The required investment is $315,000 (ignoring the biennial overhaul charges). Assuming 10 year, straight line depreciation or $31,500 per year, the payback period would be

$$PB = \frac{\$315,000}{\$75,900 + 31,500} = 2.9 \text{ years}$$

A project with this payback period would probably be considered quite desirable.

Year A	Inflow B	Outflow C	Net Flow D = (B − C)	Discount Factor $1/(1 + k + p)^t$	Net Present Value D(Disc. Fact.)
1996*	$ 0	$125,000	$−125,000	1.0000	$−125,000
1996	0	100,000	−100,000	0.8696	−86,960
1997	0	90, 000	− 90,000	0.7561	−68,049
1998	50,000	0	50,000	0.6575	32,875
1999	120,000	15,000	105,000	0.5718	60,039
2000	115,000	0	115,000	0.4972	57,178
2001	105,000	15,000	90,000	0.4323	38,907
2002	97,000	0	97,000	0.3759	36,462
2003	90,000	15,000	75,000	0.3269	24,518
2004	82,000	0	82,000	0.2843	23,313
2005	65,000	0	65,000	0.2472	16,068
2005	35,000		35,000	0.2472	8,652
Total	$759,000	$360,000	$ 399,000		$ 18,003

*$t = 0$ at the beginning of 1996.

Internal Rate of Return   If we have a set of expected cash inflows and cash outflows, the internal rate of return is the discount rate that equates the present values of the two sets of flows. If A_t is an expected cash outflow in the period t and R_t is the expected inflow for the period t, the internal rate of return is the value of k that satisfies the following equation (note that the A_0 will be positive in this formulation of the problem):

$$A_0 + A_1/(1 + k) + A_2/(1 + k)^2 + \ldots + A_n/(1 + k)^n = R_1/(1 + k) + R_2/(1 + k)^2$$
$$+ \ldots + R_n/(1 + k)^n \quad t = 1,2,3, \ldots ,n$$

The value of k is found by trial and error.

Profitability Index   Also known as the benefit–cost ratio, the profitability index is the net present value of all future expected cash flows divided by the initial cash investment. (Some firms do not discount the cash flows in making this calculation.) If this ratio is greater than 1.0, the project may be accepted.

Other Profitability Models   There are a great many variations of the models just described. These variations fall into three general categories: (1) those that subdivide net cash flow into the elements that comprise the net flow, (2) those that include specific terms to introduce risk (or uncertainty, which is treated as risk) into the evaluation, and (3) those that extend the analysis to consider effects that the project might have on other projects or activities in the organization. Two product line extension models, taken from Dean [16], will illustrate these methods.

Pacifico's Method   PI is the profitability index of acceptability where

$$PI = rdpc\ SP\ \sqrt{L}/C,$$

r = probability of research success,

d = probability of development success, given research success,

p = probability of process success, given development success, and

c = probability of commercial success, given process success.

The investment, C, is the estimated total cost of the R & D effort for the project. Risk is incorporated in the $rdpc$ term.

The cash flow is $SP\ \sqrt{L}$ where

S = estimated average annual sales volume in units of product,

P = estimated average annual profit per unit, and

L = estimated life of the product extension in years. (Note that although the profits are not formally discounted, they are "devalued" over time by multiplying them by $\sqrt{L}$ rather than by L.)

Dean's Profitability Method   Dean's model contains a term that subtracts the unit manufacturing cost and the unit selling and administrative costs from the unit price, multiplies the remainder by the expected number of units sold per year, and then subtracts tooling and development costs (a project risk factor is also included). All costs and revenues are time-indexed and discounted to the present. Dean modifies his model to deal with three distinct cases: (1) where the product extension has no significant impact on the existing system, (2) where the product extension may affect the profitability or the sales of existing products, or both, and (3) where the product extension is a replacement for an existing product.

Several comments are in order about all the profit–profitability numeric models. First, let us consider their advantages.

1. The undiscounted models are simple to use and understand.
2. All use readily available accounting data to determine the cash flows.
3. Model output is in terms familiar to business decision makers.
4. With a few exceptions, model output is on an "absolute" profit/profitability scale and allows "absolute" go/no-go decisions.
5. Some profit models account for project risk.
6. Dean's model includes the impact of the project on the rest of the organization.

The disadvantages of these models are the following.

1. These models ignore all nonmonetary factors except risk.
2. Models that do not include discounting ignore the timing of the cash flows and the time value of money.
3. Models that reduce cash flows to their present value are strongly biased toward the short run.
4. Payback-type models ignore cash flows beyond the payback period.

5. The IRR model can result in multiple solutions.

6. All are sensitive to errors in the input data for the early years of the project.

7. All discounting models are nonlinear, and the effects of changes (or errors) in the variables or parameters are generally not obvious to most decision makers.

8. Those models incorporating the risks of research and/or development and/or process (the commercial success risk factor is excluded from this comment) mislead the decision maker. It is not so much that the research–development–process success is risky as it is that the time and cost required to ensure project success is uncertain. The application of these risk terms applies mainly to R & D projects.

9. Some models, Dean's and Pacifico's, for example, are oriented only toward evaluation of projects that result in new products.

10. All these models depend for input on a determination of cash flows, but it is not clear exactly how the concept of cash flow is properly defined for the purpose of evaluating projects. (This problem is discussed later in this chapter.)

A complete discussion of profit/profitability models can be found in any standard work on financial management—see [1, 9, 67], for example. In general, the net present value models are preferred to the internal rate of return models.

In our experience the payback period model, occasionally using discounted cash flows, is one of the most commonly used models for evaluating projects and other investment opportunities. Managers generally feel that insistence on short payout periods tends to minimize the uncertainties associated with the passage of time. While this is certainly logical, we prefer evaluation methods that discount cash flows and deal with uncertainty more directly by considering specific risks. Using the payout period as a cash-budgeting tool aside, *its only virtue is simplicity*, a dubious virtue at best.

Project Management in Practice
Estimating Electronic System Costs for Future Projects

In the early 1980s, the U.S. Air Force found that it needed to be able to predict the flight test costs (one of eight cost predictions required for a full estimate) of electronic warfare systems such as radar warning receivers, electronic countermeasure radiating devices, and chaff dispensers. This task was an exceptionally difficult one due not only to the rapid technological advancements being made in the electronics field, but particularly because the estimates had to be made up to six years before the equipment would incur those costs; that is, even before the system was conceptualized or defined!

Source: J.R. Ward, "Project Management Cost Estimate: A Case Study in Electronic Warfare System Flight Test Costs," *Project Management Journal*, December 1984.

Cost estimating approaches based on estimating the costs of the system components could not be used because the components were often not even identified six years beforehand. Sometimes the only data available was the nature of the enemy system to be countered, or possibly, only the general type of equipment to be used. Thus, an approach was used based on independent variables with strong causal links to the dependent variable of interest: the flight test cost. Two general rules were employed to select variables to be included in a variety of statistical models available for test: (1) a logical, causal relationship must exist between the variable and the flight test cost, and (2) the variable must relate to an equipment characteristic that can be identified early in the equipment's conceptual phase. Based on these rules, the following variables were selected for testing:

weight, density, volume, input power, equipment type, whether new or modified equipment, and the phase of development for the flight tests.

Two statistical models offered good results (high correlations with actual flight test costs) but had problems unique to each of them. A linear regression model was unable to employ a number of key variables that would have offered good predictive ability. A principle components analysis model had two problems: (1) it used many cross-product variables whose causality was unclear, and (2) it only allowed a point estimate to be made without a confidence interval or trade-off figures.

Nevertheless, the study was considered highly successful, offering almost 90 percent explained variance for systems six years prior to actual use.

Numeric Models: Scoring

In an attempt to overcome some of the disadvantages of profitability models, particularly their focus on a single decision criterion, a number of evaluation/selection models that use multiple criteria to evaluate a project have been developed. Such models vary widely in their complexity and information requirements. The examples discussed illustrate some of the different types.

Unweighted 0–1 Factor Model A set of relevant factors is selected by management. These are usually listed in a preprinted form, and one or more raters score the project on each factor depending on whether or not it qualifies for that individual criterion. The raters are chosen by senior managers, for the most part from the rolls of senior management. The criteria for choice are a clear understanding of organizational goals and a good knowledge of the firm's potential project *portfolio*. Figure 2-2 shows an example of the rating sheet for an unweighted, 0–1 factor model.

The columns of Figure 2-2 are summed and those projects with a sufficient number of qualifying factors may be selected. The main advantage of such a model is that it uses several criteria in the decision process. The major disadvantages are that it assumes all criteria are of equal importance and it allows for no gradation of the degree to which a specific project meets the various criteria.

Unweighted Factor Scoring Model The second disadvantage of the 0–1 factor model can be dealt with by constructing a simple linear measure of the degree to which the project being evaluated meets each of the criteria contained in the list.

Project _____

Rater _____ Date _____

	Qualifies	Does Not Qualify
No increase in energy requirements	x	
Potential market size, dollars	x	
Potential market share, percent	x	
No new facility required	x	
No new technical expertise required		x
No decrease in quality of final product	x	
Ability to manage project with current personnel		x
No requirement for reorganization	x	
Impact on work force safety	x	
Impact on environmental standards	x	
Profitability		
Rate of return more than 15% after tax	x	
Estimated annual profits more than $250,000	x	
Time to break-even less than 3 years	x	
Need for external consultants		x
Consistency with current lines of business		x
Impact on company image		
With customers	x	
With our industry		x
Totals	12	5

Figure 2-2: Sample project evaluation form.

The x marks in Figure 2-2 would be replaced by numbers. Often a five-point scale is used, where 5 is very good, 4 is good, 3 is fair, 2 is poor, 1 is very poor. (Three-, seven-, and 10-point scales are also common.) The second column of Figure 2-2 would not be needed. The column of scores is summed, and those projects with a total score exceeding some critical value are selected. A variant of this selection process might select the highest-scoring projects (still assuming they are all above some critical score) until the estimated costs of the set of projects equaled the resource limit. The criticism that the criteria are all assumed to be of equal importance still holds.

The use of a discrete numeric scale to represent the degree to which a criterion is satisfied is widely accepted. To construct such measures for project evaluation, we proceed in the following manner. Select a criterion, say, "estimated annual profits in dollars." For this criterion, determine five ranges of performance so that a typical project, chosen at random, would have a roughly equal chance of being in any one of the five performance ranges. (Another way of describing this condition is: Take a large number of projects that were selected for support in the past, regardless of whether they were actually successful or not, and create five levels of predicted performance so that about one-fifth of the projects fall into each level.) This procedure will usually create unequal ranges, which may offend our sense of symmetry but need not concern us otherwise. It ensures that each criterion performance measure utilizes the full scale of possible values, a desirable characteristic for performance measures.

Consider the following two simple examples. Using the criterion just mentioned, "estimated annual profits in dollars," we might construct the following scale:

Score	Performance Level
5	Above $1,100,000
4	$750,001 to $1,100,000
3	$500,001 to $750,000
2	$200,000 to $500,000
1	Less than $200,000

As suggested, these ranges might have been chosen so that about 20 percent of the projects considered for funding would fall into each of the five ranges.

The criterion "no decrease in quality of the final product" would have to be restated to be scored on a five-point scale, perhaps as follows:

Score	Performance Level
	The quality of the final product is:
5	significantly and visibly improved
4	significantly improved, but not visible to buyer
3	not significantly changed
2	significantly lowered, but not visible to buyer
1	significantly and visibly lowered

This scale is an example of scoring cells that represent opinion rather than objective (even if "estimated") fact, as was the case in the profit scale.

Weighted Factor Scoring Model   When numeric weights reflecting the relative importance of each individual factor are added, we have a weighted factor scoring model. In general, it takes the form

$$S_i = \sum_{j=1}^{n} s_{ij}w_j \quad j = 1,2,3,\ldots,n$$

where

S_i = the total score of the *i*th project,

s_{ij} = the score of the *i*th project on the *j*th criterion, and

w_j = the weight of the *j*th criterion.

The weights, w_j, may be generated by any technique that is acceptable to the organization's policy makers. There are several techniques available to generate such numbers, but the most effective and most widely used is the Delphi technique. The Delphi technique was developed by Brown and Dalkey of the Rand Corporation during the 1950s and 1960s [15]. It is a technique for developing numeric values that are equivalent to subjective, verbal measures of relative value. (The method is also useful for developing technological forecasts. For a description of the technique see Appendix B and also reference [31] in the bibliography to that appendix.) The method of successive comparisons (or pairwise comparisons) may also be used for the same purpose. Originally described by Churchman, Ackoff, and Arnoff in their classic text on operations research [10], this technique asks the decision maker to make a series of choices between several different sets of alternatives. A set of numbers is then found that is consistent with the choices. These numbers can serve as weights in the scoring model. For an example of the use of this method, see [18]. Another popular and quite similar approach is the Analytic Hierarchy Process, developed by Saaty, see [54, 65] for details.

When numeric weights have been generated, it is helpful (but not necessary) to scale the weights so that

$$0 \le w_j \le 1 \qquad j = 1,2,3, \ldots, n$$

$$\sum_{j=1}^{n} w_j = 1$$

The weight of each criterion can be interpreted as the "percent of the total weight accorded to that particular criterion."

A special caveat is in order. It is quite possible with this type of model to include a large number of criteria. It is not particularly difficult to develop scoring scales and weights, and the ease of gathering and processing the required information makes it tempting to include marginally relevant criteria along with the obviously important items. Resist this temptation! After the important factors have been weighted, there usually is little residual weight to be distributed among the remaining elements. The result is that the evaluation is simply insensitive to major differences in the scores on trivial criteria. A good rule of thumb is to discard elements with weights less than 0.02 or 0.03. (If elements are discarded, and if you wish $\sum w_j = 1$, the weights must be rescaled to 1.0.) As with any linear model, the user should be aware that the elements in the model are assumed to be independent. This presents no particular problems for these scoring models because they are used to make estimates in a "steady state" system, and we are not concerned with transitions between states.

It is useful to note that if one uses a weighted scoring model to aid in project selection, the model can also serve as an aid to project *improvement*. For any given criterion, the difference between the criterion's score and the highest possible score on that criterion, multiplied by the weight of the criterion, is a measure of the potential improvement in the project score that would result were the project's performance on that criterion sufficiently improved. It may be that such improvement is not feasible, or is more costly than the improvement warrants. On the other hand, such an analysis of each project yields a valuable statement of the comparative benefits of project improvements. Viewing a project in this way is a type of *sensitivity analysis*. We examine the degree to which a project's score is sensitive to attempts to improve it—usually by adding resources. We will use sensitivity analysis several times in this book. It is a powerful managerial technique.

It is not particularly difficult to computerize a weighted scoring model by creating a template on Lotus 1-2-3 or one of the other standard computer spreadsheets. In Chapter 13, Section 13.3 we discuss an example of a computerized scoring model used for the project termination decision. The model is, in fact, a project selection model. The logic of using a "selection" model for the termination decision is straightforward: Given the time and resources required to take a project from its current state to completion, should we make the investment? A "Yes" answer to that question "selects" for funding the partially completed project from the set of all partially finished and not-yet-started projects.

Gettin' Wheels

Rather than using an example in which actual projects are selected for funding with a weighted factor scoring model (hereafter "scoring model") which would require tediously long descriptions of the projects, we can demonstrate the use of the model in a simple, common problem that many readers will have faced—the choice of an automobile for purchase. This problem is nicely suited to use of the scoring model because the purchaser is trying to satisfy multiple objectives in making the purchase and is typically faced with several different alternative cars from which to choose.

Our model must have the following elements:

1. A set of criteria on which to judge the value of any alternative;

2. A numeric estimate of the relative importance (i.e., the "weight") of each criterion in the set; and

3. Scales by which to measure or score the performance or contribution to value of each alternative on each criterion.

The criteria weights and measures of performance must be numeric in form, but this does not mean that they must be either "ob-

jective" or "quantitative." (If you find this confusing, look ahead in this chapter and read the subsection entitled "Comments on Measurement" in Section 2.5.) Criteria weights, obviously, are subjective by their nature, being an expression of what the decision maker thinks is important. The development of performance scales is more easily dealt with in the context of our example, and we will develop them shortly.

Assume that we have chosen the criteria and weights shown in Table A to be used in our evaluations.* The weights represent the relative importance of the criteria measured on a 10-point scale. The numbers in parentheses show the proportion of the total weight carried by each criterion. (They add to only .99 due to rounding.) Raw weights work just as well for decision making as their percentage counterparts, but the latter are usually preferred because they are a constant reminder to the decision maker of the impact of each of the criteria.

----

* The criteria and weights were picked arbitrarily for this example. Because this is typically an individual or family decision, techniques like Delphi or successive comparisons are not required.

Table A **Criteria and Weights for Automobile Purchase**

Criteria	Weight	(Value)
Appearance	4	(.10)
Braking	3	(.07)
Comfort	7	(.17)
Cost, operating	5	(.12)
Cost, original	10	(.24)
Handling	7	(.17)
Reliability	5	(.12)
Total	41	.99

Prior to consideration of performance standards and sources of information for the criteria we have chosen, we must ask, "Are there any characteristics that must be present (or absent) in a candidate automobile for it to be acceptable?" Assume, for this example, that to be acceptable, an alternative must not be green, must have air conditioning, must be able to carry at least four adults, must have at least 10 cubic feet of luggage space, and must be priced less than $33,000. If an alternative violates any of these conditions, it is immediately rejected.

For each criterion, we need some way of measuring the estimated performance of each alternative. In this case, we might adopt the measures shown in Table B. Our purpose is to transform a measure of the degree to which an alternative meets a criterion into a score, the s_{ij}, that is a general measure of the utility or value of the alternative with respect to that criterion. Note that this requires us to define the criterion precisely as well as to specify a source for the information.

Figure A shows the scores for each criterion transformed to a 5-point scale, which will suffice for our ratings.

Using the performance scores shown in Figure A, we can evaluate the cars we have identified as our alternatives: the Leviathan 8, the NuevoEcon, the Maxivan, the Sporticar 100, and the Ritzy 300. Each car is scored on each criterion according to the categories shown in Figure A. Then each score is multiplied by the criterion weight and the result is entered into the appropriate box in Figure B. Last, the results for each alternative are summed to represent the weighted score.

According to this set of measures, we prefer the Ritzy 300, but while it is a clear winner over the Leviathan 8 and the Maxivan, and scores about 8 percent better than the Sporticar, it rates only about 0.13 points or 4 percent above the NuevoEcon. Note that if we overrated the Ritzy by one point on Comfort or Handling, or if we underrated the NuevoEcon by one point on either of these criteria, the result would have been reversed. (We assume that the original cost data are accurate.) With the scores this close, we might want to evaluate these two cars by additional criteria (e.g., ease of carrying children, status,

Table B **Automobile Selection Criteria, Measures and Data Sources**

Criterion	Measure and Data Source
Appearance	Subjective judgment, personal
Braking	Distance in feet, 60–0 mph, automotive magazine[a]
Comfort	Subjective judgment, 30 min. road test
Cost, operating	Annual insurance cost plus fuel cost[b]
Cost, original	Dealer cost, auto-cost service[c]
Handling	Average speed through standard slalom, automotive magazine[a]
Reliability	Score on *Consumer Reports*, "Frequency-of-Repair" data (average of 2 previous years)

[a]Many automotive periodicals conduct standardized performance tests of new cars.

[b]Annual fuel cost is calculated as (17,500 mi/DOE ave. mpg) × $1.25/gal.

[c]There are several sources for dealer-cost data (e.g., AAA, which provides a stable data base on which to estimate the price of each alternative).

Criteria	1	2	3	4	5
Appearance	Ugh	Poor	Adequate	Good	WOW
Braking	>165	165–150	150–140	140–130	<130
Comfort	Bad	Poor	Adequate	Good	Excellent
Cost, operating*	>$2.5	$2.1–2.5	$1.9–2.1	$1.6–1.9	<$1.6
Cost, original*	>$26.5	$19–26.5	$14.5–19	$10–14.5	<$10
Handling	<45	45–49.5	49.5–55	55–59	>59
Reliability	Worst	Poor	Adequate	Good	Excellent

*Cost data in $1000s

Figure A: Performance measures and equivalent scores for selection of an automobile.

safety features like dual airbags or ABS, etc.) prior to making a firm decision.

All in all, if the decision maker has well delineated objectives, and can determine how specific kinds of performance contribute to those criteria, and finally, can measure those kinds of performance for each of the alternative courses of action, then the scoring model is a powerful and flexible tool. To the extent that criteria are not carefully defined, performance is not well linked to the criteria, and is carelessly or wrongly measured, the scoring model rests on a faulty foundation and is merely a convenient path to error.

Criteria and Weights

Alternatives	Appearance (0.10)	Braking (0.07)	Comfort (0.17)	Cost, operating (0.12)	Cost, original (0.24)	Handling (0.17)	Reliability (0.12)	$\Sigma s_{ij}w_i$
Leviathan 8	3×0.1 =0.30	1×0.07 =0.07	4×0.17 =0.68	2×0.12 =0.24	1×0.24 =0.24	2×0.17 =0.34	3×0.12 =0.36	2.23
NuevoEcon	3×0.1 =0.30	3×.07 =.21	2×0.17 =0.34	5×0.12 =0.60	4×0.24 =0.96	2×0.17 =0.34	4×0.12 =0.48	3.23
Maxivan	2×0.1 =0.20	1×0.07 =0.07	4×0.17 =0.68	4×0.12 =0.48	3×0.24 =0.72	1×0.17 =0.17	3×0.12 =0.36	2.68
Sporticar 100	5×0.1 =0.50	4×0.07 =0.28	3×0.17 =0.51	2×0.12 =0.24	2×0.24 =0.48	5×0.17 =0.85	2×0.12 =0.24	3.10
Ritzy 300	4×0.1 =0.40	5×0.07 =0.35	5×0.17 =0.85	2×0.12 =0.24	1×0.24 =0.24	4×0.17 =0.68	5×0.12 =0.60	3.36

Figure B: Scores for alternative cars on selection criteria.

Constrained Weighted Factor Scoring Model The temptation to include marginal criteria can be partially overcome by allowing additional criteria to enter the model as constraints rather than weighted factors. These constraints represent project characteristics that *must* be present or absent in order for the project to be acceptable. In our example concerning a product, we might have specified that we would not undertake any project that would significantly lower the quality of the final product (visible to the buyer or not).

We would amend the weighted scoring model to take the form:

$$S_i = \sum_{j=1}^{n} s_{ij} w_j \prod_{k=1}^{v} c_{ik}$$

where $c_{ik} = 1$ if the ith project satisfies the kth of v constraints, and 0 if it does not. Other elements in the model are as defined earlier.

Although this model is analytically tidy, in practice we would not bother to evaluate projects that are so unsuitable in some ways that we would not consider supporting them regardless of their expected performance against other criteria. For example, except under extraordinary circumstances, Procter & Gamble would not consider a project for adding a new consumer product or product line:

- that cannot be marketed nationally,
- that cannot be distributed through mass outlets (grocery stores, drugstores),
- that will not generate gross revenues in excess of $ ———— million,
- for which Procter & Gamble's potential market share is not at least 50 percent,
- that does not utilize Procter & Gamble's scientific expertise, manufacturing expertise, advertising expertise, or packaging and distribution expertise.

Again, a caveat is in order. Exercise care when adopting constraints. It may seem obvious that we should not consider any project if it has no reasonable assurance of long-run profitability. But such a constraint can force us to overlook a project that, though unprofitable itself, might have a strong, positive impact on the profitability of other projects in which we are interested.

Dean and Nishry's Model Beginning with the weighted factor scoring model, Dean and Nishry [16] cast the project selection decision in the form of an integer programming problem. In the problem

$$S_i = \sum_{j=1}^{n} w_j s_{ij}$$

$$\max x_i \left\{ \sum_{i=1}^{n} x_i S_i \right\}$$

such that

$$x_i = 0 \text{ or } 1$$

and

$$\sum_{i=1}^{n} x_i m_i \leq M$$

where m_i is the resource (labor, capital, etc.) requirement for the ith project, and M is the total amount of the resource available for use. The value of $x_i = 0$ or 1 depends on whether or not the ith project is selected.

In essence, the Dean and Nishry approach selects the highest-scoring project candidates from the scoring model, and selects them one after another until the available resources have been depleted. If there are several scarce resources, the selection problem can be recast and solved by dynamic programming methods. There are several other R & D project evaluation/selection models described in this excellent work [16]. Many are adaptable to a wide variety of project types.

Goal Programming with Multiple Objectives   Goal programming is a variation of the general linear programming method that can optimize an objective function with multiple objectives. In order to apply this method to project selection, we adopt a linear, 0–1 goal program.

First, establish a set of objectives such as "maximize equipment utilization," "minimize idle labor crews," "maximize profits," and "satisfy investment budget constraints." Alternative sets of projects are adopted or rejected based on their impact on goal achievement. A detailed discussion of goal programming is beyond the scope of this book. The interested reader should consult any modern text on management science, for example, [63, 65].

Because most real-world problems are too large for analytic solutions, heuristic solutions are necessary. Ignizio [30, pp. 202–206] has developed a heuristic approach that is easily applied to project selection.

As was the case with profitability models, scoring models have their own characteristic advantages and disadvantages. These are the advantages.

1. These models allow multiple criteria to be used for evaluation and decision, including profit/profitability models and both tangible and intangible criteria.

2. They are structurally simple and therefore easy to understand and use.

3. They are a direct reflection of managerial policy.

4. They are easily altered to accommodate changes in the environment or managerial policy.

5. Weighted scoring models allow for the fact that some criteria are more important than others.

6. These models allow easy sensitivity analysis. The trade-offs between the several criteria are readily observable.

The disadvantages are the following.

1. The output of a scoring model is strictly a relative measure. Project scores do not represent the value or "utility" associated with a project and thus do not directly indicate whether or not the project should be supported.

2. In general, scoring models are linear in form and the elements of such models are assumed to be independent.

3. The ease of use of these models is conducive to the inclusion of a large number of criteria, most of which have such small weights that they have little impact on the total project score.

4. Unweighted scoring models assume all criteria are of equal importance, which is almost certainly contrary to fact.

5. To the extent that profit/profitability is included as an element in the scoring model, this element has the advantages and disadvantages noted earlier for the profitability models themselves.

Selecting Projects within a Program

This project selection technique is a special type of weighted scoring model. Let us pose a more complex selection problem. Presume that one of a drug firm's three R & D laboratories has adopted a research program aimed at the development of a family of compounds for the treatment of a related set of diseases. An individual project is created for each compound in the family in order to test the compound's efficacy, to test for side effects, to find and install efficient methods for producing the compound in quantity, and to develop marketing strategies for each separate member of the drug family. Assume further that many aspects of the research work on any one compound both profits from and contributes to the work done on other members of the family. In such a case, how does one evaluate a project associated with any given member of the family? *One doesn't!*

To evaluate each project–drug family combination would require a separation of costs and revenues that would be quite impossible except when based on the most arbitrary allocations. Instead of inviting the political bloodletting that would inevitably accompany any such approach, let us attempt to evaluate the performance of *all* the projects as well as the laboratory that directed and carried out the entire program—and that may be conducting other programs at the same time.

B. V. Dean has developed an ingenious technique for accomplishing such an evaluation [17]. This tool not only helps identify the most desirable projects but can also be used as a planning tool to identify resource needs, especially for *large* projects. Consider Figure 2-3. R & D Laboratory A is conducting a set of interrelated projects in Program 1. Project i contributes to technology j, one of a set of desirable technologies that, in turn, makes a contribution to requirement k, one of a desired set of end requirements with some value V_k, the sum of all values being 1.0.

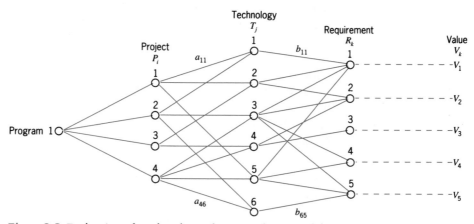

Figure 2-3: Evaluation of a related set of projects for R & D lab A.

Now consider the set of projects, P_i, and the technologies, T_j. We can form the transfer matrix

$$\mathbf{A} = |a_{ij}|$$

composed of ones and zeros as follows:

$$a_{ij} = \begin{cases} 1, & \text{if } P_i \text{ contributes to } T_j \\ 0, & \text{if } P_i \text{ does not contribute to } T_j \end{cases}$$

Similarly, we form the transfer matrix

$$\mathbf{B} = |b_{jk}|$$

composed of ones and zeros as follows:

$$b_{jk} = \begin{cases} 1, & \text{if } T_j \text{ contributes to } R_k \\ 0, & \text{if not} \end{cases}$$

Now find

$$\mathbf{C} = |c_{ik}|$$

where

$$\mathbf{C} = \mathbf{AB}$$

The resultant matrix will link P_i directly to R_k, thus indicating which projects contribute to which requirements.*

Now consider the value set V_k. "Normalize" V_k so that

$$\sum_k V_k = 1$$

Each normalized V_k will represent the *relative* value of R_k in the set $\{R_k\}$. The values can be written as a column matrix

$$\mathbf{V} = |V_k|$$

Note that a project, P_i, that contributes to a requirement, R_k, in c_{ik} ways will have a value

$$c_{ik} V_k$$

and that the *total* value of P_i is thus

$$e_i = \sum_k c_{ik} V_k$$

The column matrix $\mathbf{E} = |e_i|$ is the set of values for all projects in the laboratory, and the sum of all project values,

$$\mathbf{E}^* = \sum_i e_i = \mathbf{JE}$$

where $\mathbf{J}$ is a row matrix consisting of ones.

$$\begin{aligned} \mathbf{E}^* &= \mathbf{JE} \\ &= \mathbf{JCV} \\ &= \mathbf{JABV} \end{aligned}$$

---

*This step requires the arithmetic process of matrix multiplication. The process is not difficult. An explanation of the methods together with a short example is presented in Appendix D. The method is further illustrated in Case II of this chapter.

Example An R & D program consists of two projects, four technologies, and three requirements. Project 1 contributes to technologies 1 and 4 only but project 2 contributes to technologies 2, 3, and 4. Technology 1 contributes to requirement 2 only and technology 4 contributes to requirement 1 only. Technologies 2 and 3 contribute to requirements 1 and 3 and requirements 1 and 2, respectively. Requirements 1, 2, and 3 have relative values of 0.2, 0.5, and 0.3, respectively. What is the overall value of the program and which project is most important?

$$A = \begin{bmatrix} 1001 \\ 0111 \end{bmatrix} \quad B = \begin{bmatrix} 010 \\ 101 \\ 110 \\ 100 \end{bmatrix} \quad V = \begin{bmatrix} 0.2 \\ 0.5 \\ 0.3 \end{bmatrix}$$

The contribution of each project to each requirement is

$$C = AB = \begin{bmatrix} 110 \\ 311 \end{bmatrix}$$

The value of each project is

$$E = CV = \begin{bmatrix} .7 \\ 1.4 \end{bmatrix}$$

The value of the program is

$$E^* = JE = 2.1$$

Thus, project 2 is twice as important (valuable) as project 1.

If, in the preparation of matrix **A**, it seems desirable to differentiate between the different degrees by which a project contributes to a technology or a technology to a requirement, this is easily accomplished. Instead of a one-zero measure of contribution, one might use the following:

$$a = \begin{cases} 2, \text{ if } P_i \text{ makes a "major" contribution to } T_j \\ 1, \text{ if } P_i \text{ makes a "minor" contribution to } T_j \\ 0, \text{ if } P_i \text{ makes none} \end{cases}$$

Matrix **B** could also accommodate a more sensitive measure of the contributions of a technology to a requirement if the evaluator wishes.

Dean's method has wide applicability for evaluation of programs composed of multiple interdependent projects. Scores can be compared for several programs. When program life is extended over several time periods and generates outputs in these successive time periods, program performance can be compared between periods.

Choosing a Project Selection Model

Selecting the type of model to aid the evaluation/selection process depends on the philosophy and wishes of management. Liberatore and Titus [35] conducted a survey of 40 high-level staff persons from 29 *Fortune 500* firms. Eighty percent of their respondents report the use of one or more financial models for R & D project decision making. Although their sample is small and nonrandom, their findings are quite consistent with the present authors' experience. None of the respondent firms used mathematical programming techniques for project selection or resource allocation.

We strongly favor weighted scoring models for three fundamental reasons. First, they allow the multiple objectives of all organizations to be reflected in the important decision about which projects will be supported and which will be rejected. Second, scoring models are easily adapted to changes in managerial philosophy or changes in the environment. Third, they do not suffer from the bias toward the short run that is inherent in profitability models that discount future cash flows. This is not a prejudice against discounting and most certainly does not argue against the inclusion of profits/profitability as an important factor in selection, but rather *it is an argument against the exclusion of nonfinancial factors* that may require a longer-run view of the costs and benefits of a project. For a powerful statement of this point, see [25].

It is also interesting to note that Liberatore and Titus found that firms with a significant amount of contract research funded from outside the organization used scoring models for project screening much more frequently than firms with negligible levels of outside funding. It was also found that firms with significant levels of outside funding were much less likely to use a payback period [35, p. 969].

The structure of a weighted scoring model is quite straightforward. Its virtues are many. Nonetheless, the actual use of scoring models is not as easy as it might seem. Decision makers are forced to make difficult choices and they are not always comfortable doing so. They are forced to reduce often vague feelings to quite specific words or numbers. The Delphi method mentioned above and described in Appendix B is helpful, and is a satisfying process for decision makers. Even so, multiattribute, multiperson decision making is not simple. (For an interesting discussion of this process, see [31] as well as reference [31] in Appendix B.)

▶ 2.4 ANALYSIS UNDER HIGH UNCERTAINTY

At times an organization may wish to evaluate a project about which there is little information. Research and development projects sometimes fall into this general class. But even in the comparative mysteries of research and development activities, the level of uncertainty about the outcomes of R & D is not beyond analysis. As we noted when discussing Dean's profitability model, there is actually not much uncertainty about whether a product, process, or service can be developed, but there can be considerable uncertainty about *when* it will be developed and at *what* cost.

As they are with R & D projects, time and cost are also often uncertain in other types of projects. When the organization undertakes projects in which it has little or no recent experience—for example, the installation of a new computer, investment in an unfamiliar business, engaging in international trade, and a myriad of other projects common enough to organizations in general but uncommon to any single organization—there are three distinct areas of uncertainty. First, there is uncertainty about the timing of the project and the cash flows it is expected to generate.

Second, though not as common as generally believed, there may be uncertainty about the direct outcomes of the project—that is, what it will accomplish. Third, there is uncertainty about the side effects of the project, its unforeseen consequences.

Typically, we try to reduce such uncertainty by the preparation of *pro forma* documents. *Pro forma* profit and loss statements and break-even charts are examples of such documents. The results, however, are not very satisfactory unless the amount of uncertainty is reflected in the data that go into the documents. When relationships between inputs and outputs in the projects are complex, Monte Carlo simulation [34, 65] can handle such uncertainty by exposing the many possible consequences of embarking on a project. *Risk analysis* is a method based on such a procedure. With the great availability of microcomputers and user-friendly software, these procedures are becoming very common.

Risk Analysis

The term risk analysis is generally credited to David Hertz in his classic *Harvard Business Review* article, "Risk Analysis in Capital Investment" [27]. The principal contribution of this procedure is to focus the decision maker's attention on understanding the nature and extent of the uncertainty associated with some variables used in a decision-making process. Although the method can be used with almost any kind of variable and decision problem, risk analysis is usually understood to use financial measures in determining the desirability of an investment project.

Hertz [28] differentiates risk analysis from both traditional financial analysis and more general decision analysis with the diagrams in Figure 2-4. Figure 2-4a illustrates traditional financial analysis, Figure 2-4b risk analysis. The primary difference is that risk analysis incorporates uncertainty in the decision input data. Instead of point estimates of the variables, probability distributions are determined or subjectively estimated for each of the "uncertain" variables. With such inputs, the probability distribution for the rate of return (or NPV) is then usually found by simulation. The decision maker not only has probabilistic information about the rate of return and future cash flows but also gains knowledge about the *variability* of such estimates as measured by the standard deviation of the financial returns. Both the expectation and its variability are important decision criteria in the evaluation of the project. For an example, see the Reading at the end of this chapter.

When most managers refer to risk analysis, they are usually speaking of what Hertz and Thomas call "decision analysis." As Figure 2-4c shows, for decision analysis the manager's "utility function" for money must be determined. If the decision maker is seeking a decision that achieves several different objectives simultaneously, this method (utilizing a weighted factor scoring model, for example, rather than simulation) would be appropriate.

This approach is useful for a wide range of project-related decisions. For example, simulation risk analysis was used to select the best method of moving a computer to a new facility [64]. The major task elements and their required sequences were identified. Cost and time distributions were then programmed for analysis and a computer run of 2000 trials was made, simulating various failures and variations in cost and time for each of three methods of moving the computer. A cost–probability distribution was constructed (see Figure 2-5) to help identify the lowest-cost alternative and also the alternative with the lowest risk of a high cost, alternatives that are often not the same. As seen in the illustration, alternative 3 has the lowest expected cost (of 9) but also has the highest likelihood for a cost of 20 or more.

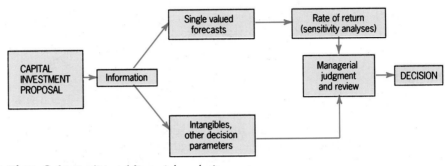

Figure 2-4a: Traditional financial analysis.

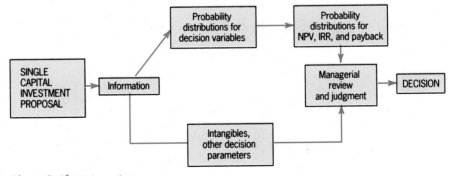

Figure 2-4b: Risk analysis.

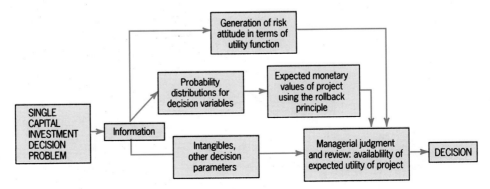

Figure 2-4c: Decision analysis. *Source:* [28]

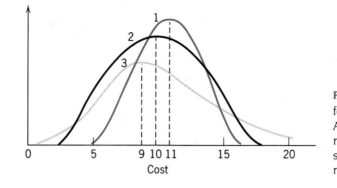

Figure 2-5: Probability density for three alternatives. Note: Alternative 3 has the lowest mean, but alternative 1 has a smaller variance and thus less risk.

A public utility faced with deciding between several R & D projects [21] used four separate cost-related distributions in a risk analysis simulation (Figure 2-6). (Total wage costs required two separate distributions, as shown in the figure.) The distributions were then combined to generate the distribution of a cost overrun for each potential project. In addition, sensitivity analysis was conducted to determine the effect of court rulings and specific task failures on project costs. High-risk projects were identified in this way, and tasks that posed high risk could then be moni-

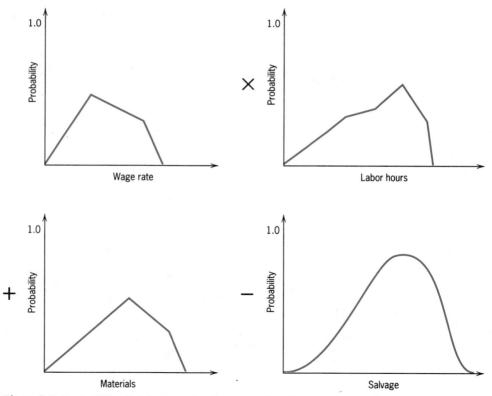

Figure 2-6: Probability distributions for elements of project cost for a utility.

tored with tight managerial controls. Following the cost analysis, project schedules were analyzed in the same way. Finally, time and cost analyses were combined to determine interactions and overall project effects.

General Simulation Analysis

Simulation combined with sensitivity analysis is also useful for evaluating R & D projects while they are still in the conceptual stage. Using the net present value approach, for example, we would support an R & D project if the net present value of the cash flows (including the initial cash investment) is positive and represents the best available alternative use of the funds. When these flows are estimated for purposes of the analyses, it is well to avoid the *full-cost* philosophy that is usually adopted. The full-cost approach to estimating cash flows forces the inclusion of arbitrarily determined overheads in the calculation—overheads which, by definition, are not affected by the change in product or process and thus are not relevant to the decision. The only relevant costs are those that will be changed by the implementation of the new process or product.

The determination of such costs is not simple. If the concept being considered involves a new process, it is necessary to go to the detailed *route sheet*, or *operations sequence sheet*, describing the operation in which the new process would be used. Proceeding systematically through the operating sequence step by step, one asks whether the present time and cost required for this step are likely to be altered if the new process concept is installed. If and only if the answer is yes, three estimates (optimistic, most likely, and pessimistic) are made of the size of the expected change. These individual estimated changes in the production cost and time, together with upstream or downstream time and cost changes that might also result (e.g., a production method change on a part might also alter the cost of inspecting the final product), are used to generate the required cash flow information—presuming that the time savings have been properly costed. This estimation process will be explained in detail in Chapter 8.

The analysis gives a picture of the proposed change in terms of the costs and times that will be affected. The uncertainty associated with each individual element of the process is included. Simulation runs will then indicate the likelihood of achieving various levels of savings. Note also that investigation of the simulation model will expose the major sources of uncertainty in the final cost distributions. If the project itself is near the margin of acceptability, the uncertainty may be reduced by doing some preliminary research aimed at reducing uncertainty in the areas of project cost estimation where it was highest. This preliminary research can be subjected to a cost–benefit analysis when the benefit is reduced uncertainty. For an example of such an approach see [41].

▶ 2.5 COMMENTS ON THE INFORMATION BASE FOR SELECTION

Our bias in favor of weighted scoring models is quite clear, but irrespective of which model is chosen for project selection, an annual or computerized data base must be created and maintained to furnish input data for the model. Directions for the actual construction of the data base go beyond the scope of this book, but some comments about the task are in order.

The use of either scoring models or profit/profitability models assume that the decision-making procedure takes place in a reasonably rational organizational environment. Such is not always the case. In some organizations, project selection seems to be the result of a political process, and sometimes involving questionable ethics, complete with winners and losers. In others, the organization is so rigid in its approach to decision making that it attempts to reduce all decisions to an algorithmic proceeding in which predetermined programs make choices so that humans have minimal involvement—and responsibility. In an interesting paper, Huber examines the impact that the organizational environment has on the design of decision support systems [29].

The remainder of this section deals with three special problems affecting the data used in project selection models.

Comments on Accounting Data

Whether managers are familiar with accounting systems or not, they can find it useful to reflect on the methods and assumptions used in the preparation of accounting data. Among the most crucial are the following.

1. Accountants live in a linear world. With few exceptions, cost and revenue data are assumed to vary linearly with associated changes in inputs and outputs.

2. The accounting system often provides cost–revenue information that is derived from standard cost analyses and equally standardized assumptions regarding revenues. These standards may or may not be accurate representations of the cost–revenue structure of the physical system they purport to represent.

3. As noted in the previous section, the data furnished by the accounting system may or may not include overhead costs. In most cases, the decision maker is concerned solely with cost–revenue elements that will be changed as a result of the project under consideration. Incremental analysis is called for, and great care must be exercised when using *pro forma* data in decision problems. Remember that the assignment of overhead cost is always arbitrary. The accounting system is the richest source of information in the organization, and it should be used—but with great care and understanding.

Comment on Measurements

It is common for those who oppose a project, for whatever reason, to complain that information supporting the project is "subjective." This epithet appears to mean that the data are biased and therefore untrustworthy.

To use the scoring methods discussed, we need to *represent* though not necessarily *collect* expected project performance for each criterion in numeric form. If a performance characteristic cannot be measured directly as a number, it may be useful to characterize performance verbally and then, through a word/number equivalency scale, use the numeric equivalents of verbal characterizations as model inputs.

Subjective versus Objective   The distinction between subjective and objective is generally misunderstood. All too often the word *objective* is held to be synonymous with *fact* and *subjective* is taken to be a synonym for *opinion*—where fact = true and opinion = false. The distinction in measurement theory is quite different, referring to the location of the standard for measurement. A measurement taken by reference to an external standard is said to be "objective." Reference to a standard that is internal to the system is said to be "subjective." A yardstick, incorrectly divided into 100 divisions and labeled "meter," would be an objective but inaccurate measure. The eye of an experienced judge is a subjective measure that may be quite accurate.

Quantitative versus Qualitative   The distinction between quantitative and qualitative is also misunderstood. It is not the same as numeric and nonnumeric. Both quantity and quality may be measured numerically. The number of words on this page is a quantity. The color of a red rose is a quality, but it is also a wavelength that can be measured numerically, in terms of microns. The true distinction is that one may apply the law of addition to quantities but not to qualities [66]. Water, for example, has a volumetric measure and a density measure. The former is quantitative and the latter qualitative. Two one-gallon containers of water poured into one container give us two gallons, but the density of the water, before and after joining the two gallons, is still 1.0.

Reliable versus Unreliable   A data source is said to be reliable if repetitions of a measurement produce results that vary from one another by less than a prespecified amount. The distinction is important when we consider the use of statistical data in our selection models.

Valid versus Invalid   Validity measures the extent to which a piece of information means what we believe it to mean. A measure may be reliable but not valid. Consider our mismarked yardstick 36 inches long but pretending to be a meter. It performs consistently, so it is reliable. It does not, however, match up well with other meter rules, so it would not be judged valid.

To be satisfactory when used in the previous project selection models, the measures may be either subjective or objective, quantitative or qualitative, but they must be numeric, reliable, and valid. Avoiding information merely because it is subjective or qualitative is an error and weakens our decisions. On the other hand, including information of questionable reliability or validity in selection models, even though it may be numeric, is dangerous. It is doubly dangerous if decision makers in the organization are comfortable dealing with the selection model but are unaware of the doubtful character of some input data. A condition a colleague has referred to as GIGO—garbage in, *gospel* out—may prevail.

Comment on Technological Shock

If the parent organization is not experienced in the type of project being considered for selection, performance measures such as time to installation, time to achieve

80 percent efficiency, cost to install, and the like are often underestimated. It is interesting to observe that an almost certain, immediate result of installing a new, cost–saving technology is that costs rise. Sometimes we blame the cost increases on resistance to change, but a more sensible explanation is that when we alter a system, we disturb it and it reacts in ways we did not predict. A steelmaker recalling the installation of the then new technology for manufacturing tinplate by electrolysis remarked: "We discovered and installed the world's first electrolytic method for making scrap. It took a year before we had that line running the way it was designed."

Of course, if the organization is experienced, underestimation is not likely to be a serious problem. The Reliance Electric Company undertook several "18-month" plant construction projects that they predicted, accurately, would require 36 months to build from decision to the point when the plant was capable of operating at or above three-fourths capacity. (Note the potential for ethical problems here.)

To the extent possible, past knowledge of system actions and reactions should be built into estimates of future project performance.

2.6   PROJECT PROPOSALS

Now that project selection methods have been discussed, it is appropriate to consider what documentation is needed to evaluate a project that is being considered. The set of documents submitted for evaluation is called the project proposal, whether it is brief (a page or two) or extensive, and regardless of the formality with which it is presented.

Several issues face firms preparing proposals, particularly firms in the aerospace, construction, defense, and consulting industries.

1.   Which projects should be bid on?
2.   How should the proposal-preparation process be organized and staffed?
3.   How much should be spent on preparing proposals for bids?
4.   How should the bid prices be set? What is the bidding strategy? Is it ethical?

Generally, these decisions are made on the basis of their overall expected values, perhaps as reflected in a scoring model.

In-house proposals submitted by a firm's personnel to that firm's top management do not usually require the extensive treatment given to proposals submitted to outside clients or such agencies as the Department of Defense. For the Department of Defense, a proposal must be precisely structured, meeting the requirements contained in the official RFP (Request for Proposal) or, more specifically, in the TPR (Technical Proposal Requirements) that is part of the RFP. The construction and preparation of a proposal to be submitted to the government or other outside funder is beyond the scope of this book. However, the subject has been well treated by Roman [52] and the interested reader is referred to his work as well as [24 and 53].

All proposals should begin with a short summary statement (an "Executive Summary") covering the fundamental nature of the proposal *in nontechnical language,* as well as the general benefits that are expected to accrue to its implementation. All proposals should be accompanied by a "cover letter." Roman [52, pp. 67–68] emphasizes that the cover letter is a key marketing document and is worthy of careful attention. In addition to the Executive Summary and the cover letter, every proposal should deal with four distinct issues: (1) the nature of the technical problem and how it is to be approached; (2) the plan for implementing the project once it has been accepted; (3) the plan for logistic support and administration of the project; and (4) a description of the group proposing to do the work, plus its past experience in similar work.

The precise way in which the contents of a proposal are organized usually follows the directions found in the TPR or RFP, the stated requirements of a specific potential funder, the traditional form used by the organization issuing the proposal, or, occasionally, the whim of the writer. As is the case with most products, the highest probability of acceptance will occur when the proposal meets the expectations of the "buyer," as to form and contents.

At times there is a tendency to feel that so-called "nontechnical" projects (by which is usually meant projects that are not concerned with the physical sciences or a physical product) are somehow exempt from the need to describe how the problem will be approached and how the project will be implemented—including such details as milestones, schedules, and budgets. To deal with nontechnical projects so casually is folly and casts considerable doubt on the proposer's ability to deliver on promises. (It is all too common for projects concerned with the development of art, music, drama, and computer software, among other "nontechnical" areas, to be quite vague as to what will be delivered, when, and at what cost.) On the other hand, when the proposal is aimed at another division or department of the same parent organization, the technical requirements of the proposal may be greatly relaxed, but the technical approach and implementation plan are still required—even if their form is quite informal.

The Technical Approach

The proposal begins with a general description of the problem to be attacked or project to be undertaken. If the problem is complex, the major subsystems of the problem or project are noted, together with the organization's approach to each. The presentation is in sufficient detail that a knowledgeable reader can understand what the proposer intends to do. The general method of resolving critical problems is outlined. If there are several subsystems, the proposed methods for interfacing them are covered.

In addition, any special client requirements are listed along with proposed ways of meeting them. All test and inspection procedures to assure performance, quality, reliability, and compliance with specifications are noted.

The Implementation Plan

The implementation plan for the project contains estimates of the time required, the cost, and the materials used. Each major subsystem of the project is listed along with estimates of its cost. These costs are aggregated for the whole project, and totals are shown for each cost category. Hours of work and quantities of material used are shown (along with the wage rates and unit material costs). A list of all equipment costs is added, as is a list of all overhead and administrative costs.

Depending on the wishes of the parent organization and the needs of the project, time charts, PERT/CPM, or Gantt charts are given for each subsystem and for the system as a whole. Personnel, equipment, and resource usages are estimated on a period-by-period basis in order to ensure that resource constraints are not violated. Major milestones are indicated on the time charts. Contingency plans are specifically noted. For any facility that might be critical, load charts are prepared to make sure that the facility will be available when needed.

The Plan for Logistic Support and Administration

The proposal includes a description of the ability of the proposer to supply the routine facilities, equipment, and skills needed now and then during any project. Having the means to furnish artist's renderings, special signs, meeting rooms, stenographic assistance, reproduction of oversized documents, computer graphics, word processing, conference telephone calls, and many other occasionally required capabilities provides a "touch of class." Indeed, their unavailability can be irritating. Attention to detail in all aspects of project planning increases the probability of success for the project—and impresses the potential funder.

It is important that the proposal contain a section explaining how the project will be administered. Of particular interest will be an explanation of how control over subcontractors will be administered, including an explanation of how proper subcontractor performance is to be insured and evaluated. The nature and timing of all progress reports, budgetary reports, audits, and evaluations are covered, together with a description of the final documentation to be prepared for users. Termination procedures are described, clearly indicating the disposition of project personnel, materials, and equipment at project end.

A critical issue, often overlooked, that should be addressed in the administrative section of the proposal is a reasonably detailed description of how change orders will be handled and how their costs will be estimated. Change orders are a significant source of friction (and lawsuits) between the organization doing the project and the client. The client rarely understands the chaos that can be created in a project by the introduction of a seemingly simple change. To make matters worse, the group proposing the project seems to have a penchant for misleading the potential client about the ease with which "minor" changes can be adopted during the process of implementing the project. Control of change orders is covered in Chapter 11.

Past Experience

All proposals are strengthened by including a section that describes the past experience of the proposing group. It contains a list of key project personnel together with their titles and qualifications. For outside clients, a full résumé for each principal should be attached to the proposal. When preparing this and the other sections of a proposal, the proposing group should remember that the basic purpose of the document is to convince a potential funder that the group and the project are worthy of support. The proposal should be written accordingly.

Project Management in Practice
The Military Mobile Communication System—A Procurement Innovation

In 1981, the U.S. military was using a hodge-podge of communication equipment that largely didn't intercommunicate. Different services used different vendors, each with their own protocol, and equipment for voice communication was completely different from that for data, facsimile, or e-mail. James Ambrose, then Undersecretary of the Army, thus initiated a $4.2 billion project to completely revamp the entire Army communications system, the largest communications program ever placed by the Army. His conception of the need included six unique acquisition guidelines that led to an extremely successful project:

1. The contractor is responsible for all aspects of systems acquisition, production, integration, fielding, training, logistics, and maintenance.

2. The contractor will satisfy 19 required design and functional features and as many of 82 desired features as possible.

3. The contractor will provide only fully developed, working equipment; there is to be virtually no engineering development.

4. Delivery of the system will start after 22 months and be completed 60 months after basic operations.

5. The contractor will buy every piece of equipment needed for each system, even if that equipment is already in use.

Source: A. A. Dettbarn, et al. "Excellence in Cost, Schedule and Quality Performance," PM N*etwork*, January 1992.

Depending on the new communications system during the Gulf War.

6. The contract is firm fixed price with the contractor accepting all cost risks.

In 1985, GTE won the bidding with a proposal $3 billion lower than the next competitor's. GTE has developed and refined their program management capabilities over a period of 35 years. A project team was assembled consisting of 32 subcontractors and 700 vendors to supply over 8000 mobile radios, 1400 telephone switching centers, and 25,000 telephones. This system can send and receive calls, electronic mail, data, and facsimiles to mobile units without interruption over an area of 37,500 square kilometers, even while the connective elements of the system are on the move. The system interconnects with the existing U.S. Army communications equipment as well as that of the other military services, NATO, and commercial satellite and landline telephone networks around the world. The system was tested in late 1985 for 10 slushy days during winter in eastern France. Mobile units crossed fields and roads, reconnecting between coverage areas, while switching centers jumped from location to location, just as would a regular Army corps during combat.

The final system met the requirement of 19 necessary features and 69 of the 82 desired features. The project also met the strict delivery deadlines and realized $21.7 million in cost savings as well. In 1991, the system was very successfully employed in the Persian Gulf for Operation Desert Shield/Storm. During the war period, the system operated for two straight weeks with only 45 minutes of downtime. It also was able to be set up and taken down in just the 30 minutes specified (completed in five minutes in one instance). It truly achieved the goal of "Effective communications from the foxhole to the theater commander to the President." This outstanding performance has been honored in four separate U.S. Army awards, including the DOD Value Engineering Contractor of the Year Award.

▶ 2.7   THE PAST AND FUTURE OF PROJECT EVALUATION/SELECTION MODELS

In 1964, Baker and Pound [6] surveyed the state of the art of evaluating and selecting R & D projects. Although their investigation focused solely on R & D projects, their findings, and the subsequent findings of Baker and Freeland [4, 5] lead to some tentative conclusions about the past, present, and future use of project selection methods.

The use of formal, numeric procedures for the evaluation and selection of projects is a recent phenomenon, largely post-World War II. At first, payback period (and the related "average annual rate of return") was widely used. It is still used by those who feel that the uncertainties surrounding project selection are so great that a higher level of sophistication is unwarranted.

The use of formal models slowly increased during the 1950s and 1960s, and a large majority of the models employed were strictly profit/profitability models. As we have noted, the emphasis on profitability models tended to shorten the time horizon of project investment decisions. This effect and the results of several studies on the use of project selection models are reported in Mansfield [39, App. A]; also see [40, pp. 15–16].

A similar effect on non-R & D projects is easily observed by noting the sharp decline of investment in long-term projects. The increasing interest rates seen during the 1970s forced cutoff ("hurdle") rates of return higher, which cut back investment in projects for which the time gap between investment and return was more than a very few years. For example, neither new steelmaking capacity nor copper-refining capacity was expanded nearly as rapidly as long-run growth in the demand for steel and copper seemed to justify during this period. Producers tended to blame the lack of investment on foreign competition, but given the aging capacity in the United States, it may well be that the level of foreign competition is as much a result of the lack of growth (that is, our failure to invest in newer technology) as it is a cause. Again, the reader is referred to Hayes and Abernathy [25].

A decade later, Baker [4] and Souder [60] reassessed R & D project selection. In this decade there was considerable growth in the use of formal models, again with great emphasis on profitability models. But Baker reported significant growth in the literature on models that use multiple criteria for decision making. He observed a trend away from decision models *per se*, and toward the use of decision information systems. Among other reasons for this change, he notes [4] that "the decision problem is characterized by multiple criteria, many of which are not easily quantified, and the typical approaches to quantifying subjective preferences are far from satisfactory." He also notes the development of interactive decision systems that allow users to examine the effects of different mixes of possible projects.

More than two decades have passed since Baker's 1974 study. Considerable progress has been made in the development of processes for measuring preferences that yield suitable input data for sophisticated scoring models, models which serve, in turn, as data for goal programming and other resource allocation models. Because it is easy to enter all the parts (data base, decision model, and list of potential projects) in a computer, it is feasible to simulate many solutions to the project selection problem. The decision maker can easily change the criteria being used, as well as the criteria weights. Decision makers can even investigate the sensitivity of their decisions to changes in the estimates of subjective input data, thus directly examining the potential impact of errors in their opinions. In spite of all these capabilities, Liberatore and Titus [35] have found that mathematical programming models are not used for project selection or resource allocation, at least in the firms they interviewed. They did find, however, that scoring models were used for selection—particularly when the firm dealt with outside funding agencies.

We believe that use of these techniques will be extended in the future. As we become more familiar with the construction and use of decision support and expert systems (see [65]), the simulation of project selection decisions will grow in popularity. It seems to us that two concurrent events will support this trend. First is the rapid growth in the ownership and use of microcomputers by organizational executives. The operation of a computer is no longer seen as restricted to computer specialists. Second is the growing realization that profitability alone is not a sufficient test for the quality of an investment.

Almost everyone who has studied project selection in recent years has noted the need for selection processes using multiple criteria. The writings of Michael

Porter [47, 48] and others have emphasized the role of innovation in the maintenance or improvement of a competitive position. Indeed, it is now clear that the firm's portfolio of projects is a key element in its competitive strategy. Suresh and Meredith [62] have added a "strategic approach" to the problem of selecting process technologies for implementation. In sum, the methodology and technology for multiple-criteria project selection not only exist but are widely available. Perhaps more important, we are beginning to understand the necessity for using them.

▶ SUMMARY

This chapter initiated our discussion of the project management process by describing procedures for evaluating and selecting projects. We first outlined some criteria for project selection models and then discussed the general nature of these models. From this basic overview, the chapter then described the types of models in use and their advantages and disadvantages. Considering the degree of uncertainty associated with many projects, a section was devoted to selection models concerned with risk and uncertainty. Concluding the discussion, some general comments were made about data requirements and the use of these models. Finally, two sections discussed the documentation of the evaluation/selection process via project proposals and the general trend of selection models in the past and for the probable future.

The following specific points were made in the chapter.

- Primary model selection criteria are realism, capability, flexibility, ease of use, and cost.

- Preparatory steps in using a model include identifying the firm's objectives, weighting them relative to each other, and determining the probable impacts of the project on the firm's competitive abilities.

- Project selection models can generally be classified as either numeric or nonnumeric; numeric models are further subdivided into profitability and scoring categories.

- Nonnumeric models include the sacred cow, the operating necessity, the competitive necessity, and comparative benefit.

- Profitability models include such standard forms as payback period, rate of return, discounted cash flow, and profitability index.

- Scoring models, the authors' preference, include the unweighted 0–1 factor model, the unweighted factor scoring model, the weighted factor scoring model, the constrained weighted factor scoring model, Dean and Nishry's model, and goal programming with multiple objectives.

- For handling uncertainty, *pro forma* documents, risk analysis, and simulation with sensitivity analyses are all helpful.

- Special care should be taken with the data used in project selection models. Of concern are data taken from an accounting data base, how data are measured and conceived, and the effect of technological shock.

- Project proposals generally consist of a number of sections: the technical approach, the implementation plan, the plan for logistic support and administration, and past experience.

- The history of project selection models has shown an increase in the use of formal models, particularly profitability models. We feel the future will extend the use of multiple criteria and simulation models, especially with the wide use of the microcomputer.

In the next chapter we consider the selection of the appropriate manager for a project and what characteristics are most helpful for such a position. We also address the issue of the project manager's special role, and the demands and responsibilities of this critical position.

GLOSSARY

Decision Support System—A computer package and data base to aid managers in making decisions. It may include simulation programs, mathematical programming routines, and decision rules.

Delphi—A formalized method of group decision making that facilitates drawing on the knowledge of experts in the group (described in Appendix B of this book).

Deterministic—Predetermined, with no possibility of an alternate outcome. Compare with stochastic.

Expert System—A computer package that captures the knowledge of recognized experts in an area and can make inferences about a problem based on decision rules and data input to the package.

Matrix—A table of numbers or other items with each row and column having a particular definition.

Model—A way of looking at reality, usually for the purpose of abstracting and simplifying it to make it understandable in a particular context.

Network—A group of items connected by some common mechanism.

Portfolio—A group or set of projects with varying characteristics.

Pro Forma—Projected or anticipated, usually applied to financial data such as balance sheets and income statements.

Programming—An algorithmic methodology for solving a particular type of complex problem, usually conducted on a computer.

Sensitivity Analysis—Investigation of the effect on the outcome of changing some parameters in the procedure or model.

Simulation—A technique for emulating a process, usually conducted a considerable number of times to understand the process better and measure its outcomes under different policies.

Stochastic—Probabilistic, or not deterministic.

MATERIAL REVIEW QUESTIONS

1. What are the four parts of a technical proposal?
2. By what criteria do you think managers judge selection models? What criteria *should* they use?
3. Contrast the competitive necessity model with the operating necessity model. What are the advantages and disadvantages of each?
4. What is a sacred cow? Give some examples.
5. Give an example of a Q-Sort process for project selection.
6. What are some of the limitations of project selection models?
7. What is the distinction between a qualitative and a quantitative measure?
8. How does the discounted cash flow method answer some of the criticisms of the payback period and average rate of return methods?
9. What are some advantages and disadvantages of the profit/profitability numeric models?
10. How is sensitivity analysis used in project selection?
11. How does Dean's program evaluation method work?
12. What ethical issues can arise when proposing an 18 month project that you know will require 36 months to complete?

CLASS DISCUSSION QUESTIONS

1. Explain why goal programming is classified as a scoring model. What is the real difference between profitability and scoring models? Describe a model that could fit both categories.
2. Can risk analysis be used for nonproject business decision making? Explain how.
3. Discuss how the following project selection models are used in real-world applications.

(a) Capital investment with discounted cash flow.
(b) Goal programming models.
(c) Simulation models.

4. Why do you think managers underutilize project selection models?

5. Would uncertainty models be classified as profitability models, scoring models, or some other type of model?

6. Contrast validity with reliability. What aspects, if any, are the same?

7. Contrast subjective and objective measures. Give examples of the proper use of each type of measure when evaluating competing projects.

8. Can a measure be reliable, yet invalid? Explain.

9. What are some possible extensions of project evaluation models for the future?

10. Are there certain types of projects that are better suited for nonnumeric selection methods as opposed to numeric ones?

11. Identify some of the ethical issues that can arise in a bid response to an RFP.

PROBLEMS

1. Two projects are proposed to a company. Project A will cost $250,000 to implement and will have annual cash flows of $75,000. Project B will cost $150,000 to implement and will have annual cash flows of $52,000. The company is very concerned about their cash flow. Using the payback period, which project is better, from a cash flow standpoint?

2. What is the average rate of return for a project that costs $200,000 to implement and has an average annual profit of $30,000?

3. A three-year project has net cash flows of $20,000; $25,000; and $30,000 in the next three years. It will cost $75,000 to implement the project. If the required rate of return is 0.2, what is the NPV?

4. What would happen to the NPV of the above project if the inflation rate was expected to be 7 percent in each of the next three years?

5. Given: An information systems program to develop a set of financial accounts systems consists of two projects, three packages, and three required deliverables, as shown (a contribution of 2 is twice that of 1).

$$A = \begin{bmatrix} 1 & 0 & 2 \\ 2 & 1 & 0 \end{bmatrix}$$

$$B = \begin{bmatrix} 0 & 2 & 1 \\ 0 & 1 & 2 \\ 1 & 2 & 0 \end{bmatrix}$$

$$V = \begin{bmatrix} 0.3 \\ 0.6 \\ 0.1 \end{bmatrix}$$

(a) Interpret the matrices A, B, and V.
(b) Calculate C and interpret it.
(c) Calculate E and interpret it.
(d) Calculate E* and interpret it.

6. Given the following military weapons program:

$$A = \begin{bmatrix} 0 & 0 & 1 & 1 & 0 \\ 1 & 0 & 1 & 0 & 1 \\ 0 & & 0 & 1 & 0 \\ 1 & 0 & 1 & 1 & 0 \\ 0 & 1 & 1 & 0 & 0 \\ 0 & 0 & 0 & 0 & 0 \end{bmatrix}$$

$$B = \begin{bmatrix} 1 & 0 \\ 0 & 1 \\ 0 & 1 \\ 0 & 1 \\ 1 & 0 \end{bmatrix} \quad V = \begin{bmatrix} 0.6 \\ 0.4 \end{bmatrix}$$

Calculate C, E, and E* and interpret the meaning of all the matrices.

7. Use a weighted score model to choose between three locations (A, B, C) for setting up a factory. The relative weights for each criterion are shown in the following table. A score of 1 represents unfavorable, 2 satisfactory, and 3 favorable.

		Location		
Category	Weight	A	B	C
Labor costs	20	1	2	3
Labor productivity	20	2	3	1
Labor supply	10	2	1	3
Union relations	10	3	3	2
Material supply	10	2	1	1
Transport costs	25	1	2	3
Infrastructure	10	2	2	2

8. Given:

$$A = \begin{bmatrix} 1 \\ 0 \\ 0 \\ 1 \\ 1 \end{bmatrix}$$

$$B = \begin{bmatrix} 0 & 0 & 1 & 1 & 1 & 0 & 0 \end{bmatrix}$$

$$V = \begin{bmatrix} 0.1 \\ 0.2 \\ 0.1 \\ 0.1 \\ 0.2 \\ 0.1 \\ 0.2 \end{bmatrix}$$

Describe the situation. Calculate **C**, **E**, and **E***.

9. Compare the value of the programs in Problems 5, 6, and 8.

10. Recompute the program value in Problem 6 if the unit values in **B** were each replaced with 2. Now how does the answer to Problem 6 compare to those of Problems 5 and 8?

11. A major consumer products company is determining the value of its program which includes two projects, A and B. There are three technologies that are affected: 1, 2, and 3. Project A has a major contribution to technology 1, no contribution to technology 2, and a major contribution to technology 3. Project B has no contribution to technology 1 and a minor contribution to technologies 2 and 3. There are two requirements, a and b, that are affected by these three technologies. Requirement a has a relative value of 0.6 and requirement b of 0.4. Technology 1 makes a contribution to requirement a but not to b. Technology 2 makes no contribution to requirement a but does to requirement b. Technology 3 makes a contribution to both requirements a and b. What is the overall value of this company's program?

12. Nina is trying to decide in which of four shopping centers to locate her new boutique. Some cater to a higher class of clientele than others, some are in an indoor mall, some have a much greater volume than others, and, of course, rent varies considerably. Because of the nature of her store, she has decided that the class of clientele is the most important consideration. Following this, however, she *must* pay attention to her expenses and rent is a major item, probably 90 percent as important as clientele. An indoor, temperature-controlled mall is a big help, however, for stores such as hers where 70 percent of sales are from passersby slowly strolling and window shopping. Thus, she rates this as about 95 percent as important as rent. Last, a higher volume of shoppers means more potential sales; she thus rates this factor as 80 percent as important as rent.

As an aid in visualizing her location alternatives, she has constructed the following table. A "good" is scored as 3, "fair" as 2, and "poor" as 1. Use a weighted score model to help Nina come to a decision.

	Location			
	1	2	3	4
Class of clientele	Fair	Good	Poor	Good
Rent	Good	Fair	Poor	Good
Indoor mall	Good	Poor	Good	Poor
Volume	Good	Fair	Good	Poor

▶ INCIDENTS FOR DISCUSSION

Multiplex Company

Multiplex Company is in its third year of using a rather complex and comprehensive strategic planning process. Billi Chase, CEO of Multiplex, is very pleased with the output of the planning process. Plans are logical, organized, and pertinent to the firm's business environment. However, implementation of the plans leaves something to be desired. Billi is convinced that her managers do a poor job of estimating the amount of resources and time required to complete the strategic projects associated with the plan.

This fiscal year, eleven new strategic projects were identified. There were six major types of projects: new products, modifications of existing products, research and development, new applications studies, manufacturing process improvements, and reorganization of the sales department. Each project is sponsored by one of the functional department managers, who is required to prepare a simple cost–benefit analysis and a Gantt chart (see Chapter 8, Section 8.3) showing the aggregate time required to finish a project. This sponsor usually, but not always, winds up being assigned as the project manager.

Tomorrow is the final day of the current year's strategic planning session. Ms. Chase plans to make a strong pitch to her managers to prioritize the strategic projects to ensure that those most important to the company get done. In the past it seemed as though all the projects lagged behind when resource problems arose. In the future she wants a consensus from the managers about which projects will go on the back burner and which are to proceed on schedule when problems are encountered.

Question: Ms. Chase is not sure how to go about ranking the projects. Will the managers be able to achieve consensus? Should they use the cost–benefit analysis done by the project sponsor? Perhaps the planning group could use their collective experience to rank the projects subjectively. What method would you recommend to Ms. Chase? Support your recommendation.

L & M Power

In the next two years a large municipal gas and electric company must begin construction on a new electric generating plant to accommodate the increased demand for electricity and to replace one of the existing plants that is fast becoming obsolete. The vice-president in charge of the new project believes there are two options. One is a new coal-fired steam plant and the other is a new nuclear plant. The vice-president has developed a project selection model and will use it in presenting the project to the president. For the models she has gathered the following information:

	Initial Cost	Generating Cost/KW	Exp. Life	Salv. Value
Steam plant	$10,000,000	$0.004	20 yr	10%
Nuclear plant	25,000,000	$0.002	15 yr	5%

Since the vice-president's background is in finance, she believes the best model to use is a financial one, net present value analysis.

Questions: Would you use this model? Why or why not? Base your answer on the five criteria developed by Souder and evaluate this model in terms of the criteria.

Billboard Publications

Billboard's top management, located in New York, has recently authorized a large number of data processing projects. However, when under pressure, they ask Bruce Johnson, manager of data processing, to reassign programmers to the latest "squeaky wheel." This situation was causing such turmoil that it was becoming impossible to manage the various projects, and staff morale was deteriorating rapidly.

Johnson's immediate project manager in Cincinnati agreed with him that this situation needed to be resolved, so a project evaluation and selection meeting was arranged. The meeting was held off-site to get away from the immediate pressures of business. It was attended by vice-presidents and department managers who had outstanding requests for data processing services or personnel assigned to such projects. In preparation for the meeting, Johnson gathered a portfolio of all project requests for data processing services with their labor and equipment requirements.

The meeting was held all day Monday and Tuesday. After the two long days and many discussions, all the projects had been evaluated and ranked. However, no one was truly pleased; there were not enough resources to go around, and no one received what he or she really wanted. But they had been heard and all agreed that, given the demands and the resources available, they would abide by the decisions of the group.

Johnson was exhausted after the meetings, but he returned to the office Wednesday and went right to work implementing the plans agreed to the day before. He held meetings with the project managers, programmers, and project personnel from user departments, explaining the "new" priorities. Much patience and persuasion was required, as some projects were placed on hold, staffing reduced on some and increased on others, and entirely new projects formed. The big selling point was that the working environment should be much more stable and professional because these assignments represented the consensus of management on projects to be pursued for the next several months.

Thursday morning, Johnson was looking forward to a calm, peaceful day in which to tackle the pile on his desk and contribute his individual expertise to some of the projects to which he was personally assigned. Before Johnson had made much progress, a call came from Bill Evans, vice-president of finance in New York, the functional manager to whom Johnson reported. Several managers had complained to Evans about the ranking of their pet projects and he had agreed to call Johnson and "discuss" how they could be "fit in." Johnson reminded Evans of the priorities that they had begun to implement only yesterday, and of the two-day meeting earlier that week that Evans had attended and chaired. All to no avail.

Johnson was now not only faced with reassigning personnel to deal with Evans's latest "squeaky wheels," but knew that it would most likely have to be done again tomorrow and then again on Monday. He asked himself, "Had anything really been accomplished?"

Questions: What project evaluation and selection methods do you think were used during the meeting? What should Johnson do? Do you think that hiring more personnel would help?

▶ INDIVIDUAL EXERCISE

Consider the purchase of a house. Develop a profitability model to compare alternative houses. Include depreciation, expenses, repairs, insurance, initial costs, and so on.

Next, devise a scoring model to evaluate the alternative purchases. How should you weight the various factors, and how do you decide?

Last, how would a risk analysis be used to make a decision? What factors would require distributions, and how might these be obtained? Which data are subjective and which objective? Which are qualitative and which are quantitative?

▶ PROJECT TEAM CONTINUING EXERCISE

For this topic, the project team is to develop a project proposal, as described in the chapter. *Pro forma* documents (e.g., a projected income statement) should be included, as well as a justification of the project. The team should endeavor to apply as many of the project selection methods as may be applicable, including both numeric and nonnumeric models. Both profitability and scoring models should certainly be included. How might goal programming or simulation models be useful here?

▶ **BIBLIOGRAPHY**

1. ALLEN, D. E. *Finance: A Theoretical Introduction.* New York: St. Martins Press, 1983.

2. ARCHIBALD, R. D. *Managing High Technology Programs and Projects.* New York: Wiley, 1976.

3. ATKINSON, A. C., and A. H. BOBIS. "A Mathematical Basis for the Selection of Research Projects." *IEEE Transactions on Engineering Management,* Jan. 1969.

4. BAKER, N. R. "R & D Project Selection Models: An Assessment." *IEEE Transactions on Engineering Management,* Nov. 1974.

5. BAKER, N. R., and J. FREELAND. "Recent Advances in R & D Benefit Measurement and Project Selection Models." *Management Science* June 1975.

6. BAKER, N. R., and W. H. POUND. "R & D Project Selection: Where We Stand." *IEEE Transactions on Engineering Management,* Dec. 1964.

7. BEALE, P., and M. FREEMAN. "Successful Project Execution: A Model," *Project Management Journal,* Dec. 1991.

8. BECKER, R. H. "Project Selection for Research, Product Development and Process Development." *Research Management,* Sept. 1980.

9. BLOCK, S., and G. HIRT. *Foundations of Financial Management.* 5th ed. Homewood, IL: Irwin, 1988.

10. CHURCHMAN, C. W., R. L. ACKOFF, and E. L. ARNOFF. *Introduction to Operations Research.* New York: Wiley, 1957.

11. CLARK, P. "A Profitability Project Selection Method." *Research Management,* Nov. 1977.

12. CLAYTON, R. "A Convergent Approach to R & D Planning and Project Selection." *Research Management,* Sept. 1971.

13. CLIFTON, D. S., JR., and D. E. FYFFE. *Project Feasibility Analysis: A Guide to Profitable Ventures.* New York: Wiley, 1977.

14. COCHRAN, M., E. B. PYLE, III, L. C. GREENE, H. A. CLYMER, and A. D. BENDER. "Investment Model for R & D Project Evaluation and Selection." *IEEE Transactions on Engineering Management,* Aug. 1971.

15. DALKEY, N. C. *The Delphi Method: An Experimental Study of Group Opinion* (RM-5888-PR). Santa Monica, CA: The Rand Corporation, June 1969.

16. DEAN, B. V. *Evaluating, Selecting, and Controlling R & D Projects.* New York: American Management Association 1968.

17. DEAN, B. V. "A Research Laboratory Performance Model." In *Quantitative Decision Aiding Techniques for Research and Development,* M. J. Cetron, H. Davidson, and A. H. Rubenstein, eds. New York: Gordon and Breach, 1972.

18. DEAN, B. V., and S. J. MANTEL, JR. "A Model for Evaluating Costs of Implementing Community Projects," *Analysis for Planning Programming Budgeting,* M. Alfandary-Alexander, ed. Potomac, MD: Washington Operations Research Council, 1968.

19. ENRICK, N. L. "Value Analysis for Priority Setting and Resource Allocation." *Industrial Management,* Sept.–Oct. 1980.

20. European Industrial Research Management Association. "Top–Down and Bottom–Up Approaches to Project Selection." *Research Management,* March 1978.

21. GARCIA, A., and W. COWDREY. "Information Systems: A Long Way from Wall-Carvings to CRTs." *Industrial Engineering,* April 1978.

22. GEE, R. E. "A Survey of Current Project Selection Practices." *Research Management,* Sept. 1971.

23. GOLABI, K., G. W. KIRKWOOD, and A. SICHERMAN. "Selecting a Portfolio of Solar Energy Projects Using Multi-Attribute Preference Theory." *Management Science,* Feb. 1981.

24. HAJEK, V. G. *Management of Engineering Projects,* 3rd ed. New York: McGraw-Hill, 1984.

25. HAYES, R., and W. J. ABERNATHY, "Managing Our Way to Economic Decline." *Harvard Business Review,* July–Aug. 1980.

26. HELIN, A. F., and W. E. SOUDER. "Experimental Test of a Q-Sort Procedure for Prioritizing R & D Projects." *IEEE Transactions on Engineering Management,* Nov. 1974.

27. HERTZ, D. B. "Risk Analysis in Capital Investment." *Harvard Business Review,* Sept.–Oct. 1979.

28. HERTZ, D. B., and H. THOMAS, *Risk Analysis and Its Applications.* New York: Wiley, 1983.

29. HUBER, G. P. "The Nature of Organizational Decision Making and the Design of Decision Support Systems," MIS *Quarterly*, June 1981.

30. IGNIZIO, J. P. *Goal Programming and Extensions*. Lexington, MA: Lexington Books, 1976.

31. IRVING, R. H., and D. W. CONRATH, "The Social Context of Multiperson, Multiattribute Decision-making," IEEE *Transactions on Systems, Man, and Cybernetics*, May–June 1988.

32. JOHNSTON, R. D. "Project Selection and Evaluating." *Long Range Planning*, Sept. 1972.

33. KHORRAMSHAHGOL, R., H. AZANI, and Y. GOUSTY. "An Integrated Approach to Project Evaluation and Selection," IEEE *Transactions on Engineering Management*, Nov. 1988.

34. LAW, A. M., and W. KELTON. *Simulation Modeling and Analysis*, 2nd ed. New York: McGraw-Hill, 1990.

35. LIBERATORE, M. J., and G. J. TITUS. "The Practice of Management Science in R & D Project Management." *Management Science*, Aug. 1983.

36. MAHER, P. M., and A. H. RUBENSTEIN. "Factors Affecting Adoption of a Quantitative Method for R & D Project Selection." *Management Science*, Oct. 1974.

37. *Management of New Products*. New York: BOOZ, Allen, and Hamilton, Inc., 1966.

38. MANN, G. A. "VERT: A Risk Analysis Tool for Program Management." *Defense Management*, May–June 1979.

39. MANSFIELD, E. *Industrial Research and Technological Innovation*. New York: Norton, 1968.

40. MANSFIELD, E., J. RAPOPORT, J. SCHNEE, S. WAGNER, and M. HAMBURGER. *Research and Innovation in the Modern Corporation*. New York: Norton, 1971.

41. MANTEL, S. J., JR., J. R. EVANS, and V. A. TIPNIS. "Decision Analysis for New Process Technology," in B. V. Dean, ed., *Project Management: Methods and Studies*. Amsterdam: North-Holland, 1985.

42. MASON, B. M., W. E. SOUDER, and E. P. WINKOFSKY. "R & D Budgeting and Project Selection: A Review of Practices and Models" ISMS, 1980.

43. MEREDITH, J. "The Implementation of Computer Based Systems." *Journal of Operations Management*, Oct. 1981.

44. MERRIFIELD, D. B. "How to Select Successful R & D Projects." *Management Review*, Dec. 1978.

45. MOORE, J. R., JR., and N. R. BAKER. "Computational Analysis of Scoring Models for R & D Project Selection." *Management Science*, Dec. 1969.

46. PAOLINI, A., JR., and M. A. GLASER. "Project Selection Methods That Pick Winners." *Research Management*, May 1977.

47. PORTER, M. E. *Competitive Strategy*. New York: Free Press, 1980.

48. PORTER, M. E. *Competitive Advantage*. New York: Free Press, 1985.

49. RAMSEY, J. E. "Selecting R & D Projects for Development." *Long Range Planning*, Feb. 1981.

50. REYNARD, E. L. "A Method for Relating Research Spending to Net Profit." *Research Management*, Dec. 1979.

51. ROBINSON, B., and C. LAKHANI. "Dynamic Models for New Product Planning." *Management Science*, June 1975.

52. ROMAN, D. D. *Managing Projects: A Systems Approach*. New York: Elsevier, 1986.

53. ROSENAU, M. D., JR. *Successful Project Management*, 2nd ed. New York: Van Nostrand Reinhold, 1991.

54. SAATY, T. S. *Decision for Leaders: The Analytic Hierarchy Process*. Pittsburgh, PA: University of Pittsburgh, 1990.

55. SCHMIDT, R. L. "A Model for R & D Project Selection with Combined Benefit, Outcome and Resource Interactions," IEEE *Transactions on Engineering Management*, Nov. 1993.

56. SCHWARTZ, S. L., and I. VERTINSKY. "Multi-Attribute Investment Decisions: A Study of R & D Project Selection." *Management Science*, Nov. 1977.

57. SIMON, H. *The New Science of Management Decisions*, rev. ed. Englewood Cliffs, NJ: Prentice Hall, 1977.

58. SOUDER, W. E. "Comparative Analysis of R & D Investment Models." AIIE *Transactions*, April 1972.

59. SOUDER, W. E. "Analytical Effectiveness of Mathematical Models for R & D Project Selection." *Management Science*, April 1973.

60. SOUDER, W. E. "Utility and Perceived Acceptability of R & D Project Selection Models." *Management Science*, Aug. 1973.

61. SOUDER, W. E. "Project Evaluation and Selection," in D. I. Cleland, and W. R. King, eds., *Project Management Handbook*. New York: Van Nostrand Reinhold, 1983.

62. SURESH, N. C., and J. R. MEREDITH. "Justifying Multimachine Systems: An Integrated Strategic Approach." *Journal of Manufacturing Systems*, Nov. 1985.

63. THOMPSON, G. E. *Management Science: An Introduction to Modern Quantitative Analysis and Decision Making.* Huntington, NY: Krieger, 1982.

64. TOWNSEND, H. W. R., and G. E. WHITEHOUSE. "We Used Risk Analysis to Move Our Computer." *Industrial Engineering*, May 1977.

65. TURBAN, E., and J. R. MEREDITH, *Fundamentals of Management Science*, 6th ed. Homewood, IL: Irwin, 1994.

66. VAN GIGCH, J. P. *Applied General Systems Theory*, 2nd ed. New York: Harper & Row, 1978.

67. VAN HORNE, J. C. *Fundamentals of Financial Management.* Englewood Cliffs, NJ: Prentice Hall, 1971.

68. WHALEY, W. M., and R. A. WILLIAMS. "A Profits-Oriented Approach to Project Selection." *Research Management*, Sept. 1971.

69. WILLIAMS, D. J. "A Study of a Decision Model for R & D Project Selection." *Operational Research Quarterly*, Sept. 1969.

70. ZALOON, V. A. "Project Selection Methods," *Journal of Systems Management*, Aug. 1973.

CASE I

WESTFIELD, INC.: PACKAGING ALTERNATIVES*

William McRay, project manager for the Consumer Packaging Group at Westfield, Inc. had just begun work on the 1988 Strategic Plan for the frozen concentrate juice business segment. These juices were currently packed in Westfield's traditional line of containers. However, this traditional line was being threatened by a host of alternative packaging technologies. Westfield had already experienced the painful effects of substitution when its largest segment of traditional container users switched to a new-material container in 1986. Bill wanted to do whatever was necessary to anticipate and minimize the negative effects of this substitution trend as it related to the frozen concentrate juice segment.

Westfield had recently licensed a new container technology called Formatek. The company's exclusive rights to this revolutionary process could provide Westfield with an answer to the substitution threat and a sustainable competitive advantage. But the technology was expensive, and there was no guarantee that the powerful customers within the frozen concentrate juice market would adopt the new containers. On the other hand, failure to innovate on Westfield's part could cause a reversal of fortunes for this container manufacturer that had been able to maintain a 13 percent compound annual growth rate over the last three years.

Company

Founded in 1903 in Georgia, Westfield began as a manufacturer of disposable paper cones for the growing textile industry. In its first year of operations, it generated sales of $17,000 and profits of $2000. The company projected sales of $739.6 million and net income of $42.4 million for the end of the current fiscal year, 1987, and employed more than 10,000 persons throughout the U.S. (see Exhibits 1 and 2 for recent financial data).

While Westfield had previously been considered strictly a paper company, acquisitions and internal developments transformed the firm into a packaging company. In fact, paper cones, once the company's mainstay, by 1987 represented only 5 percent of the business. Westfield was the leading manufacturer of paper tubes for the paper industry, the third largest manufacturer of traditional containers, and one of the country's largest users of waste paper.

When evaluating new projects, Westfield used an IRR analysis and required a 15 percent after-tax return on investment. Pricing for all new products was expected to cover the following costs: variable manufac-

---

*Copyright ©1987 by the Darden Graduate Business School Foundation, Charlottesville, Va.

	1987E	1986	1985	1984	1983
Net Sales	$739.6	$629.6	$568.3	$457.8	$453.3
Cost & Expenses					
Cost of Products Sold	585.3	500.8	456.5	368.2	349.8
Sell., Gen., & Admin.	71.4	60.7	53.9	46.8	42.2
Interest Expense	7.4	3.7	4.3	3.9	3.1
Profit Before Tax	75.5	64.4	53.6	38.9	58.2
Taxes on Income	35.6	30.0	23.9	16.5	26.6
Profit After Tax	39.9	34.4	29.7	22.4	31.6
Equity Earnings of Affiliates	2.5	1.6	1.9	2.3	1.3
Income from Continuing Operations	42.4	36.0	31.6	24.7	32.9
Discontinued Operations			(3.1)	(0.4)	(0.2)
Net Income	$42.4	$36.0	$28.5	$24.3	$32.7

Note: E 5 Estimated

Exhibit 1: Westfield, Inc.: Packaging Alternatives— Income Statement (dollars in millions)

turing costs; plant fixed costs; marketing, technical, and administrative costs (MTA); changes in working capital; and recovery of the initial capital outlay. Westfield used a straight-line depreciation period of eight years and allocated MTA as 5 percent of net sales. While MTA for most other companies was a fixed cost, it was considered variable by Westfield because of the company's exceptional growth rates. Accounts receivable and inventory averaged 25 days of sales and 50 days of sales, respectively.

Traditional Container Industry

The majority of the company's containers were made from a single type of material, one that was relatively easy and inexpensive to manufacture but that still met customers' needs. The containers were available in a wide range of sizes (circumferences measured in increments of $\frac{1}{16}$ of an inch) and with a choice of closure, either rigid or flexible.

These containers were an outgrowth of tube manufacturing in the late 1800s when such tubes were used for gun powder, oatmeal, and salt. Container use

	1987E	1986	1985	1984	1983
Cash and Equivalent	$16.2	$15.1	$8.2	$7.7	$20.6
Accounts Receivable	75.3	60.1	58.3	41.6	39.3
Inventories	75.0	61.5	54.0	50.2	38.8
Prepaid Expenses	3.0	6.5	4.9	2.5	1.1
Current Assets	169.5	143.2	125.4	102.0	99.8
Prop., Plant, & Equip.	209.1	171.0	169.7	171.7	154.5
Investment in Affiliate	12.3	12.6	11.7	11.6	12.1
Goodwill	30.6	16.6	15.5	16.7	12.1
Other Assets	4.2	3.5	3.4	3.2	2.7
TOTAL ASSETS	$425.7	$346.9	$325.7	$305.2	$281.2
Accounts Payable	$65.7	$47.0	$43.9	$35.4	$35.7
Short-Term Debt	8.1	9.3	10.5	26.2	8.2
Taxes	6.5	10.2	3.9	1.0	10.2
Current Liabilities	80.3	66.5	58.3	62.6	54.1
Long-Term Debt	62.4	26.8	35.8	29.5	25.3
Deferred Taxes	31.7	32.3	30.6	28.1	23.0
Stockholders' Equity	251.3	221.3	201.0	185.0	178.8
TOTAL LIABS. & EQUITY	$425.7	$346.9	$325.7	305.2	$281.2

Note: E = Estimated

Exhibit 2: Westfield, Inc.: Packaging Alternatives— Balance Sheet (dollars in millions)

grew steadily through the early 1950s, and advances in technology spurred additional applications including use for cleansers, caulk, frozen fruit juices, and refrigerated dough. During the 1950s, three significant manufacturing advances laid the groundwork for future growth of traditional containers:

- the development of higher speed winding and cut-off equipment;

- improved lining materials such as aluminum foil for greater product protection; and
- specially designed metal ends for improved seaming techniques.

Use of the traditional container for frozen concentrate juices, or FCJ (FCJ refers to all types of frozen concentrate juices), in 6- and 12-ounce sizes increased significantly during the 1960s. During this same period, the motor oil container gradually became the largest product segment within this industry.

While a limited number of major new markets were on the horizon, technical innovations and imaginative new applications offered good opportunities to convert several of these major segments. Such innovations included aseptic packaging, hot-filled cans, improved liner technology, and new advancements in end-seaming technologies. Potential applications for the future included coffees, peanuts and other snack foods, meat products, and institutional foods.

Competition

Traditional-container manufacturers had steadily been nibbling away at the metal can and glass markets by offering definite cost advantages. Still, the threat of substitutes remained very high. Since no proprietary technology was used in manufacturing, traditional containers were commodities. Companies competed on quality, service, and packaging innovation. Prices were already low—less than one-half cent per can so there was little room for price wars. Packaging innovation was either developed internally or at the insistence of a customer. Providing a new innovative package that solved a problem, offered a cost advantage, or differentiated the customer's product gave the manufacturer a competitive advantage. Companies were committed to research and development, and most were testing the potential of new technologies for their container lines.

Customer

Packaging provided a key marketing tool for customers. Customers tried to differentiate their products from competitors' products with eye-catching, attractive, informative labels or with a new, unique container. The outside package was usually the first thing the end user saw of the product, and many believed that packaging influenced buying behavior. Even though the container represented but a small portion of the total cost of the product, it needed to be appealing, functional, easy-to-fill, and long-lasting.

Westfield's product line satisfied these requirements. These traditional holders were strong, lightweight alternatives to metal and glass containers that could take advantage of high-speed filling equipment with minimal changeover costs. Additionally, the manufacturing process for these containers eliminated the side seam, giving the customer an unimpaired 360-degree billboard for graphics. Graphic quality was sharp and eye-catching for easy identification. Finally, the containers satisfied end users' demand for convenient resealable packaging.

Customers were large and extremely powerful, and few exhibited loyalty to a particular container manufacturer. Price was the key attribute in the decision-making process, followed by quality of both the service provided and the product, as well as the previous experience with a particular manufacturer. Customers often looked to container manufacturers that were innovators.

A revolutionary new container material on the market was receiving much attention. Until very recently, for example, motor oil had been packaged in the traditional containers supplied by Westfield and its competitors. But in late 1986, motor oil packaging was converted to this new container material. The switch was not cost driven; but rather the new material, molded with a spout, made pouring the oil easier and neater. Westfield feared further conversions from traditional containers to these new ones in other key market segments such as frozen concentrate juices.

Consumer Packaging Group

In 1986, the container unit was renamed the "Consumer Packaging Group" to emphasize, primarily internally, Westfield's desire to think beyond traditional containers to additional product lines that it might market to some of its existing customers. The Consumer Packaging Group had 16 plants strategically located near customers in order to be responsive to their needs and to save shipping costs. (See Exhibit 3 for a map of the plant locations.)

When the motor oil container market—the largest user of all segments—switched from the traditional material to the new material, the Consumer Packaging Group's sales declined because some of its customers switched to container manufacturers capable of producing the new material. Westfield reacted

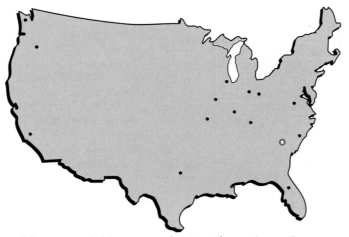

Exhibit 3: **Westfield, Inc.: Packaging Alternatives—Consumer Packaging Group Plant Locations**

by moving into production of these new containers. But because the conversion to the new material was capital intensive and because the company wanted to iron out any production problems before attempting large volume production, Westfield agreed to produce these new containers for only one of its major oil packer accounts. But the seriousness of the substitution threat hit home when the loss of sales was so extensive that one of the production lines for traditional motor oil containers was cut below a full shift.

Situation

Realizing that the decline of traditional containers to the motor oil market was likely the precursor to similar declines in other markets, Westfield sought to be proactive in its conversion of other key segments to the new containers. Bill McRay focused his attention on the frozen concentrate juices (FCJ) segment because it represented 19 percent of the division's sales and currently used only traditional containers. Westfield's reaction to this situation would likely influence the direction, and perhaps even the fate, of the firm.

Adding to the threat of substitution were the following factors: commodity product, basic technology, low price, low switching costs for customers, little brand loyalty, high bargaining leverage of customers. Mitigating the threat was the capital intensiveness of the industry.

The size of the FCJ market was an estimated 2.4 billion units, representing approximately $105 million

in sales (see Exhibit 4 for a list of the major FCJ customers). Wesfield had a 23 percent unit market share of the 2.4 billion unit market. Sales had been flat over recent years because of a consumer trend to drink chilled ready-to-serve juices, packed in cartons, instead of FCJ. Annual market growth was projected to be 3 percent for the next few years.

The net price of the traditional FCJ container was $52.35 with variable manufacturing costs of $43.79 (figures per thousand). In investigating alternative

Major Customers	Total Usage (in millions)	
	Units	Total Cost*
Coca-Cola Company	700	$37.0
Ventura Coastal Company	96	8.0
McCain's	60	4.3
Welch Foods	96	5.3
Seneca Foods	80	4.5

Others

Procter & Gamble
Treesweet
Bodiness

*Note that unit costs vary per customer because of differences in such factors as volume, length of time as customer, degree of customization required, special delivery arrangements, etc. The $52.34 price quoted in the case is an average across all customers.

Exhibit 4: **Westfield Inc.: Packaging Alternatives— Major FCJ Customers**

technologies, Westfield ran across a new material and manufacturing process, Formatek, that could offer substantial cost savings as its variable manufacturing costs were only $38.40 per thousand.

The Alternative

In July 1985, Westfield first uncovered this new process, Formatek, which was developed by an Australian company. Formatek introduced control in the high-speed manufacture of containers that had never before been achievable with other container materials. Uniformity of wall and base thickness, for example, was key to the manufacturing process, and Formatek's performance was excellent along those lines.

The fixed capital investment in this process (for one line) would be $2,099,000, and the annual volume output (operating 7 days a week, 3 shifts) would be 81 million units. These units would replace an equal number of traditional containers. In line with company practices, any currently operating equipment that would be replaced by the Formatek investment would be shipped to Westfield's overseas operations instead of being sold or disposed of. The terminal (book) value for the old equipment would be approximately $500,000 at the time of the installation of the new machine, and the Consumer Packaging Group would receive credit for the book value. The Formatek technology was not expected to become obsolete before 1995.

The plant's fixed costs for the Formatek machine would be $330,000, and the variable manufacturing costs would be $38.40 per thousand. Inflation was expected to average 5 percent a year over the life of the new licensed technology. (See Exhibit 5 for a summary of the costs and other assumptions for Formatek.)

An off-set printing technique was assumed in calculating the costs, but Bill wondered if the quality of the graphics would be an issue because multicolored inks were applied directly to the container and heat dried, so the quality depended on the surface and the inks. Slower printing speeds reduced blurred labels. The detail of off-set printing was not equivalent to that of paper labels used on traditional containers, but temperature extremes in filling and transporting FCJ limited labeling alternatives.

Formatek would give Westfield a proprietary technological competitive advantage and provide its customers with a container that Westfield's competitors could not offer. Westfield licensed this technology in early 1986 (agreeing to pay a royalty fee of 2.5 percent of sales) and had begun testing potential applications

Westfield's ROI Target (after tax)	15%
Annual Volume Estimated for 1988[a] (000s of units)	81,000
Royalty Deduction (% of sales)	2.5%
Miscellaneous Deduction (% of sales)	1.0%
Variable Mfg. Costs (per 000)	$38.40
Plant Fixed Costs ($000)	$330
Depreciation Life (straight line) years	8
Marketing, Technical, & Administrative Expenses (% of sales)	5%
Fixed Capital ($000)	$2099
Accounts Receivable (days of sales outstanding)	25
Inventories (days of sales outstanding)	50
Expected Inflation for Sales and Fixed Costs	5%
Expected Inflation for Variable Costs	5%
Tax Rate	34%

Note: All costs were estimates of those expected with the Formatek project.

[a]The 81 million units would replace an equal number of traditional containers.

Exhibit 5: Westfield, Inc.: Packaging Alternative—Summary of Formatek Machine Data.

in its pilot plant. Westfield's exclusive rights to the new technology would expire within two years if the technology were not put into operation before then.

In Bill's mind, the evaluation of the Formatek project had to be done on a stand-alone basis. Economically, the process for traditional containers was too entrenched to make an apples-to-apples comparison: the machines were fully depreciated; the workers had come quite a way down the learning curve; and the traditional containers were so profitable that Westfield would be extremely hard-pressed to find any new technology that could beat the traditional containers' margins. Even more importantly, though, the project had important *strategic* implications for the firm. Bill was far less interested in the incremental pennies per container that could be won or lost here than he was with the continuing viability of Westfield as a container manufacturer. For these reasons, the project needed to be evaluated as a stand-alone alternative.

To be consistent within this stand-alone analysis, Bill wanted to consider all the key factors—terminal value of old equipment; variable manufacturing costs; plant fixed costs; marketing, technical, and administrative costs (MTA); changes in working capital; and recovery of the initial capital outlay—as though this line were starting from scratch. Specifically, 25 days of accounts receivable and the 50 days of inventory would need to be built up the first year, and changes would be reflected in years thereafter. Bill also wanted to separate inflation for sales and fixed costs in his spreadsheet from inflation for variable costs to facilitate his sensitivity analysis.

Bill identified the following questions as key to his evaluation of the Formatek project:

- What would the IRR be over the life of the project if the new containers were introduced at the prevailing price of the traditional containers?

- What would the IRR be if the Formatek equipment was stretched two years past its estimated eight year life?

- What prices would Westfield have to charge to achieve the 15 percent hurdle rate required of

all of Westfield's capital expenditures under both the eight-year and 10-year scenarios?

- What are the key value drivers in the analysis? Could small changes in several drivers lead to big changes in the IRR? For example, what would happen if variable costs rose only 4.5 percent per year (because of learning curve improvements), the royalty fee could be negotiated down to 2.25 percent and/or the price could be raised to $52.84?

- Assume future technology improvements allow 2 percent annual increases in output. What would be the effect?

- What strategic factors should be considered?

Bill knew he had to move quickly if Westfield was to enter 1988 with Formatek capacity on line.

CASE II

PLANNING AND BUDGETING A SOCIAL SERVICE SYSTEM
Samuel J. Mantel, Jr.

The rapid increase of governmental interest in accountability from its agencies and from organizations using governmental funds has put considerable pressure on such agencies and organizations to develop and execute programs which meet the governmental requirements for accountability. As a response to these pressures, human services organizations have moved toward the adoption of such practices as Management by Objectives. Underlying these managerial methods is the assumption that organizational planning processes have been carried out proficiently and that the organization has structured itself to be efficient as well as effective.

The application of General Systems Theory as a planning aid for human services organizations has been most helpful [1], but specific planning techniques are needed in order to implement the basic planning strategies developed through systems analysis. This paper demonstrates one such technique.

A program entitled Employment Opportunities in Social Services (EOSS) was created in Ohio using Title

IV-A federal funds administered by the Ohio State Department of Welfare. The purpose was to provide human services job opportunities and salaries for current consumers of Aid for Families with Dependent Children or General Relief benefits. In this way, the program was aimed at allowing county welfare departments to increase their delivery of social services while, at the same time, providing earned income for unemployed welfare clients. Specifically, welfare consumers were to be employed in the following areas:

Chore Services

Day Care Services

Homemaker Services

Nursing Home Aide Services

Transportation Services

Other Services (as recommended by the county welfare departments and approved by the State Welfare Department)

The basic organizational structure required to administer the EOSS program was largely dictated by the organizational structure already existing in the various county welfare departments. Mechanisms also existed to search current welfare client lists in order to find likely candidates for the program. County welfare departments, however, had no organizational mechanism to screen candidates for their potential skills, nor was there a system developed for training and placing acceptable job candidates.

As a part of a week-long seminar in Planning for Human Service Organizations which was held at the School of Applied Social Sciences, Case Western Reserve University, a group of approximately fifteen social work agency executives undertook to design a structure to locate, screen, train, and place job candidates. An outcome of this exercise was the following flow chart denoting the basic tasks to be performed by the EOSS unit (Figure 1).

Given this structure, the seminar considered how to staff the operation and how to estimate its budget requirements. Several issues were raised by the staffing question. First, in addition to administering the program, several different human service skills had to be performed. Individual and group counseling was required at several stages of the process. Teaching skills were required for the various training programs, and job finding and placement skills were needed. It was noted that the number of people required to perform each of these tasks was directly dependent on the number of clients flowing through the system.

The problem was further complicated by the fact that the number of clients trained in any given substantive skill area should be constrained by the number of job openings available for the substantive skill. The agency executives agreed that it was all too common for job training programs to be oriented toward *a priori* goals that have little or no relation to actual job demand. This resulted in unmet expectations, frustrations, and disenchantment with the entire process.

For purposes of developing a specific solution to this general planning problem, the group decided to make some assumptions about the number of individuals that would be processed by the system in a given time period.* Clients would be processed in batches.

*The actual numbers used in this exercise were generated by the agency executives in the seminar. They were not chosen to be particularly realistic, but rather to clothe the planning problem with specific parameters and to allow numeric solutions to be generated.

Given an intake batch size of approximately 100 clients, it was estimated that about half would be trained in chore, day care, and homemaker services. The remainder would be split about equally between transportation and nursing home aide services. Because all training classes would feature demonstration and practice rather than theory, a class size of approximately 25 was seen as desirable. Based on this assumption, it was felt that the following levels of labor would be required:

Intake workers: $2\frac{1}{2}$

Skill screening: $\frac{1}{2}$

Teachers: 4

Job finding: 2

Placement counseling: 1

Follow-up counseling: $\frac{1}{2}$

Administration: $\frac{1}{2}$

Total personnel required: 11 people (full time equivalents)

Assuming about 25 applicants for these 11 staff positions, the problem of selecting the "best" 11 was seen by the agency executives to be nontrivial. The educational background of the applicants, experience levels, demonstrated human service job skills, and administrative ability would all be important. The group sought a general method for solving this problem that could be easily applied whether the size of the problem was large or small—and would be equally helpful when the specification of the system was less obvious than it was in this particular case.

We start, then, from a set of goals, define a set of tasks consistent with the goals, define the skills required to accomplish the tasks, and then select a set of individuals who possess the proper skills. This problem has the same form as a classic problem in the management of research and development activities. Given that the desired end results of R & D are known, i.e., that we know the mission, what science inputs are required to achieve the mission? Science and mission are related through technologies; and if we construct an incidence matrix that relates "mission" to "technology" and another which relates "technology" to "science," then multiply the two matrices, we derive a matrix which shows which sciences contribute to specific missions. [2] Dean uses a similar logic in evaluating research laboratory performance. [3]

Here, we can use this technique to relate goals to tasks, tasks to skills, and skills to individuals. The out-

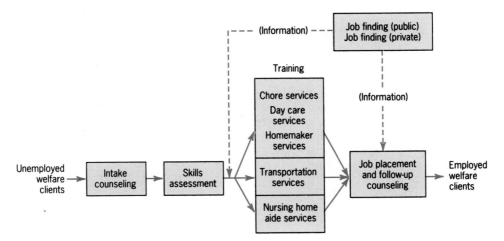

Figure 1: Flow chart for skill training and job placement program.

put of this model will be that set of individuals which can contribute to the goals of the program. Further, we can include information relating to the "degree of contribution" of a skill to a task, for example, or information which estimates the degree to which an individual possesses a given skill. To include such information will allow us to find those individuals who will "best" staff our program.

The problem of relating goals to specific tasks was, in this case, trivial; and an incidence matrix was not constructed for this step. The task of "job placement" was judged to make a direct contribution to each of the EOSS goals, which had been vaguely defined in any case. All other tasks directly supported job placement.

To develop the relationship between the tasks which must be performed by the EOSS project and the

social work skills required to perform these tasks, consider the set of tasks, T_i, and the set of skills, S_j. We can find the incidence matrix

$$\mathbf{A} = [a_{ij}]$$

which is a zero-one matrix defined as follows:

$$a_{ij} = \begin{cases} 1, \text{ if task } T_i \text{ requires skill } S_j \\ 0, \text{ if task } T_i \text{ does not require skill } S_j \end{cases}$$

The human service skills related to the tasks as defined by the seminar group are: (1) vocational counseling (individual), (2) vocational counseling (group), (3) placement counseling, (4) teaching, and (5) administration. The group constructed the following array, the elements of which form matrix **A**.

Matrix A

Tasks T_i	Vocational Counseling (individual)	Vocational Counseling (group)	Teaching	Job Placement Counseling	Administrative
Intake	1	1	0	0	0
Skill Screening	1	1	0	0	0
Job Training	0	0	1	0	0
Job Finding	0	0	0	1	0
Placement	0	0	0	1	0
Follow-up	0	0	0	1	0
Administration	0	0	0	0	1

In order to test the procedure of matching individual employees with the required social work skills, the agency executives presented 25 "simulated" applicants for the jobs. The simulated applicants were actual individuals known to the seminar members—typically, a member of his/her agency or a close associate. Academic training, job experiences, amount of experience in each type of job, and administrative experience were noted for each individual. The following scoring system was suggested and adopted:

Training

Specifically trained in skill	1
Not trained for skill	0

Job experience

Performed in skill area, less than 2 years	1
Performed in skill area, 2–5 years	2
Performed in skill area, more than 5 years	3
No experience in skill area	0

Each individual was scored on training and experience. These scores were summed and entered into an array where relevant.

The elements of this array form matrix **B**.

$$\mathbf{B} = (b_{jk})$$

where

$$b_{jk} = \begin{cases} n, \text{ if the individual } I_k \text{ is trained and/or has} \\ \quad \text{experience in skill } S_j \ (n = 1, 2, 3, 4). \\ 0, \text{ if the individual } I_k \text{ is not trained in and} \\ \quad \text{has no experience in skill } S_j. \end{cases}$$

Note that the number of non-zero elements in a column indicates the number of ways in which that individual can contribute to the skill requirements of the system. The sum of the numbers in a column is a measure of the value of that individual's contribution to the set of skills.

We can now calculate the contribution of an individual to the tasks which form the EOSS training/placement system. Suppose individual I_k has skill S_j which contributes to task T_j. This can be calculated as

$$\sum_j a_{ij} b_{jk} = m$$

If the relationship between **I** and **S**, or **S** and **T** does not exist, then

$$\sum_j a_{ij} b_{jk} = 0$$

If

$$c_{ik} = \sum_j a_{ij} b_{jk}$$

and we let **C** be the matrix of c_{ik}, we note that **C** can be found by matrix multiplication of matrices **A** and **B**, so that

$$\mathbf{C} = \mathbf{AB}$$

Using the numbers in the above arrays:

$$\mathbf{C} = \begin{bmatrix} 1 & 1 & 0 & 0 & 0 \\ 1 & 1 & 0 & 0 & 0 \\ 0 & 0 & 1 & 0 & 0 \\ 0 & 0 & 0 & 1 & 0 \\ 0 & 0 & 0 & 1 & 0 \\ 0 & 0 & 0 & 1 & 0 \\ 0 & 0 & 0 & 0 & 1 \end{bmatrix} \begin{bmatrix} 3 & 1 & 1 & 2 & 1 & 4 & \text{—} \\ 1 & 1 & 0 & 3 & 0 & 3 & \text{—} \\ 0 & 0 & 3 & 0 & 0 & 1 & \text{—} \\ 1 & 4 & 1 & 1 & 4 & 1 & \text{—} \\ 0 & 2 & 0 & 1 & 0 & 2 & \text{—} \end{bmatrix}$$

$$= \begin{bmatrix} 4 & 2 & 1 & 5 & 0 & 7 & \text{—} \\ 4 & 2 & 1 & 5 & 0 & 7 & \text{—} \\ 0 & 0 & 3 & 0 & 0 & 1 & \text{—} \\ 1 & 4 & 1 & 1 & 4 & 1 & \text{—} \\ 1 & 4 & 1 & 1 & 4 & 1 & \text{—} \\ 1 & 4 & 1 & 1 & 4 & 1 & \text{—} \\ 0 & 2 & 0 & 1 & 0 & 2 & \text{—} \end{bmatrix}$$

Matrix B

	Applicant I_k							
Skill S_j	1	2	3	4	5	6	—	25
Vocational Counselor (individual)	3	1	1	2	1	4	—	
Vocational Counselor (group)	1	1	0	3	0	3	—	
Teacher	0	0	3	0	0	1	—	
Placement Counselor	1	4	1	1	4	1	—	
Administrator	0	2	0	1	0	2	—	

As earlier, the number of non-zero elements in a column indicates the number of tasks to which an individual can contribute. The sum of the numbers in the column is a measure of the value of that individual's contribution to the system of tasks.

We still face the problem of selecting 11 FTE individuals from the 25 applicants. There are several decision rules that might be used; for example, we could choose the 11 highest column scores, constrained by the fact that at least 4 must have a non-zero entry in the "teaching" row, at least 2 1/2 (3) must have a non-zero entry in the "intake" row, and so forth. The agency executives adopted a slightly different method for selecting among applicants.

Referring to matrix **A**, they noted that each of the tasks to be performed had specific social work skills directly associated with it. For example, intake work required vocational counseling skills, job training required teaching skills, and so forth. Further, the tasks themselves formed clusters, with intake and skill assessment being a cluster; job finding, placement, and follow-up counseling being a cluster. Teaching and administration stood alone. After discussion, they decided that the job placement cluster was the most critical group of tasks, teaching the second most critical, intake the third most critical, and administration the least critical for the successful functioning of the EOSS program.

Taking the most critical skill set first, they found the contribution of each individual applicant, V_k, to the tasks of job finding, job placement counseling, and follow-up counseling, taken as a group.

$$V_k = \sum_i c_{ik}, \qquad i = 4, 5, 6$$

Since 3 1/2 FTE were required, they selected the four highest scores for this subset, settling ties by selecting those with the highest total column score. In the example above, applicants #2 and #5 score highest with 12 points; and applicant #2 has the highest total contribution with 18 points. Fortunately, one of the individuals (of the 25 analyzed) had experience in administration, so she was counted to fill the $\frac{1}{2}$ FTE administrative requirement.

They then proceeded to select four teachers and three intake worker/skill screeners in the same way. The program was now staffed. Since a large part of the budget for such a program is composed of personnel costs, the salary requirements for the selected applicants (plus the cost of a full-time secretary) amounted to approximately 85 percent of the total budget required to operate an EOSS program of the size they postulated.

The entire process, then, is quite straightforward.

1. From the goals (objectives) of a program, derive the set of tasks required to accomplish the goals.

2. Prepare an incidence matrix which indicates the direct relationship of goals and tasks. This may be a zero–one matrix, or the entries may reflect the importance of the relationships.

3. Find the set of work skills required to accomplish the tasks defined above and array these relationships in matrix form. The entries in the matrix may be zero–one or may reflect the importance of the relationships, as above.

4. Assess all potential workers for the skills determined in Step 3, and array these assessments in another matrix. Again, zero–one entries may be used or a score may be entered to reflect the strength of the relationship.

5. Sequentially multiply the matrices to find the contribution of each potential worker to the goals of the program.

6. Adopting any acceptable decision rule, select workers to staff the program.

7. Calculate the sum of worker salary requirements to determine the personnel budget for the program.

In conclusion, this model provides a method of evaluating the potential contributions of a set of individuals, each of whom possesses various unique combinations of skills, to the tasks to be performed by an organization. If these tasks are, in turn, related to the goals (or objectives) of an organization, the method will measure the contribution of individuals to those goals. Input data may include measures of the strength or criticality of the relationship between goals and tasks, tasks and skills, and skills and applicants. Stochastic variables may also be included. The larger the number of goals, tasks, skills, and applicants, the more powerful and time-saving the method becomes.

▶ REFERENCS

1. Holland, Thomas P., "Systems Theory and Its Application to Human Services Organizations," Human Services Design Laboratory, School of

Applied Social Sciences, Case Western Reserve University, Cleveland, Ohio, 1974.

2. Cetron, Marvin J., "QUEST Status Report." IEEE *Transactions on Engineering Management*, Vol. EM-14, No. 1, March 1967.

3. Dean, Burton V., "A Research Laboratory Performance Model," IEEE *Transactions on Engineering Management*, Vol. EM-14, No. 1, March 1967.

▶ **QUESTIONS**

1. How realistic is this matrix approach to the task?
2. Evaluate candidate #7 whose rating $b_{j7} = |1, 3, 2, 3, 3|$. How does the candidate contribute to V?
3. How might this model be extended? What other issues could be addressed?
4.. How might linear programming be used in this situation? Could it address the same task? Which would be better?

▶ The problem of justifying the adoption of advanced technologies is much the same as the project selection problem. The difference in perspective is primarily that there is some pre-existing hurdle that must be met in the justification problem and any number, or none, of the technologies may meet it. The aim of project selection, however, is to rank the projects along some set of criteria. This paper describes the justification/selection models in detail and gives examples.

READING

JUSTIFICATION TECHNIQUES FOR ADVANCED MANUFACTURING TECHNOLOGIES

Jack R. Meredith and Nallan C. Suresh

Introduction

It is now well recognized (see, for example, Kaplan 1984, Meredith 1985b, or Rosenthal 1984) that the major roadblocks to automating our factories are not engineering shortcomings in the equipment or manufacturing processes but rather managerial attitudes and policies. Foremost among such roadblocks is "the justification problem," as identified by Curtin (1984), Meredith *et al.* (1986), Michael and Millen (1984), and others.

The basic problem is that many of the advantages of these new manufacturing technologies lie not in the area of cost reduction but rather in more nebulous, "strategic" areas such as shorter lead times, simpler scheduling, and more consistent quality. Yet, since these manufacturing systems are largely equipment based, and manufacturing equipment has his-

torically been justified on the basis of cost reduction or capacity expansion (for example, see Grud 1984, McDonald and Hastings 1983, Meyer 1982, Muir 1984), these systems are typically expected to be justified on these same measures. In some cases that we identify later, this expectation is reasonable but in others it is not.

Our aim here is to identify those situations where economic justification policies are suitable and those where other justification procedures are more appropriate, according to a conceptual scheme developed (Meredith and Hill 1985) by matching the range of justification procedures observed with the intended use of the technology. In the process, we describe some new justification approaches that have been used by firms and give examples to illustrate their utility and methodology. First, however, we describe the automation technologies to which we are referring.

Advanced Manufacturing Technologies

As described in Meredith and Hill (1985), new manufacturing technologies can be considered to span a continuum (see Figure 1) in terms of level of integration from stand-alone equipment to full computer-integrated manufacturing (CIM). Robots and numerically controlled (NC) machine tools are often in the stand-alone category, although they can obviously be computer integrated into other systems and equipment also, such as material handling systems of manufacturing cells. The purpose of such equipment acquisitions is often to replace worn out or obsolete existing equipment.

When the stand-alone systems are linked together into cells, such as in group technology (GT) lines or flexible manufacturing systems (FMS), or more loosely, such as computer-aided design (CAD) with computer-aided process planning (CAPP), then an intermediate level of integration is achieved that exhibits a synergy between the independent systems. Other examples of such linked islands are automated storage/retrieval systems (AS/RS) with automated guided vehicle systems (AGVS) and manufacturing resource planning (MRP II) where the individual computer information systems are linked together.

When the design, planning, materials handling, manufacturing, and support systems (e.g., order entry, cost accounting, purchasing) are all linked together through computer control the factory is considered to be fully integrated, commonly known as CIM.

Two characteristics of all these advanced manufacturing technologies make their justification process more complex than such equipment has required in the past. First, these technologies are much more flexible, in most cases reprogrammable, than equipment has ever been before. As Gold (1982) points out, this flexibility maintains the value of the equipment over the long run, rather than letting its value depreciate. Fotsch (1983) reinforces this argument with the observation that companies are buying such equipment now because they believe they won't be spending for more equipment later. But the advantages of this flexibility are not easily captured in simple economic justification procedures.

The second characteristic of these new technologies that requires special consideration in the justification process was referred to earlier, their synergy when linked together. Users consistently report qualitative benefits from such linked systems, such as faster response to customer requests, that are deemed far more important than the normal cost savings. As Meredith (1985a) has shown, when such synergy is properly accounted for in the economic justification formulae, a significant increase in the calculated return on investment can be demonstrated.

Such outstanding benefits are not attained without risk however, and the risk involved in the acquisition of these enormously expensive systems is substantial. The risk is not only financial, but organizational as well since the entire company infrastructure (see Meredith 1986) must often be changed to obtain the benefits these systems offer. Consistent quality of input materials, new costing and payroll systems, and altered managerial structures are only a few of the many changes in the core fabric of the firm that are commonly required. The result is that the risks, as well as the benefits, are also inadequately considered in the economic justification procedures.

Three Justification Categories

Corresponding to the three categories of new manufacturing technologies in Figure 1, three separate approaches to the justification issue seem to exist. For stand-alone systems where the purpose is the straightforward replacement of old equipment, even if some economic benefits not usually considered (such as inventory or space reductions) are obtained, the standard economic justification approaches can be used with an allowance for the additional economic benefits or costs.

When synergy, flexibility, risk, and non-economic benefits are expected, as with the linked systems, more analytical procedures are needed. In some cases, subjective estimates of probability distribu-

Stand-alone	Linked	Integrated
Robots NC	GT FMS AS/RS CAD/CAPP MRP II	CIM

Figure 1: Advanced manufacturing technology continuum.

tions, or at least point estimates, are obtainable and can be included in the analysis.

Last, with systems approaching full integration, clear competitive advantages and major increments toward the firm's business objectives are usually being obtained. Here, strategic approaches are needed that take these benefits into consideration, although tactical and economic benefits may be accruing as well.

Each of these three justification categories spans a number of approaches, as illustrated in Figure 2. In the remainder of this paper we will describe these approaches and discuss their pros and cons.

Economic Justification Approaches

There exist a number of formulae and approaches that firms use for the economic justification of equipment. Examples include break-even analysis, MAPI (Machinery and Allied Products Institute) method, incremental rate of return, accounting rate of return, net present value, ROI (return on investment), and payback (or payout). All of these methods are well documented in the literature (e.g., Tombari 1978). Fotsch (1983) has determined, however, that the payback and ROI methods are used by the overwhelming majority (91%) of firms.

The advantages of the economic approaches are their simplicity, clarity, apparent "bottom-line" impact, and ease of data collection. But their disadvantages include their inability to capture non-economic

and strategic benefits. The primary disadvantage, however, is their use of a single value for decision making—a complex decision simply cannot be reduced to a single number and still contain the essential information needed for the decision. To do so gives the impression that the problem itself is simple, but gaining the complex benefits of advanced manufacturing technologies is reported by Gold (1982), Rosenthal (1984) and others, to involve serious repercussions throughout the organization.

Analytic Justification Approaches

The analytic techniques described in this section are again largely quantitative but more complex than the economic approaches. Also, they tend to capture more information and frequently consider uncertainty and multiple measures and effects. Their advantage is that they are more realistic, taking more factors and subjective judgments into account, and hence better reflect reality as understood by knowledgable managers. Their disadvantages are that more data are required and the analysis is considerably more complex and time-consuming, though the use of a computer can minimize this difficulty. (Comments about the data requirements for all the justification methods are made in a later section.) Nevertheless, the complexity of these methods is a deterrent to their use, both because of execution as well as understanding.

Three major approaches are typical of this category and we describe each in turn.

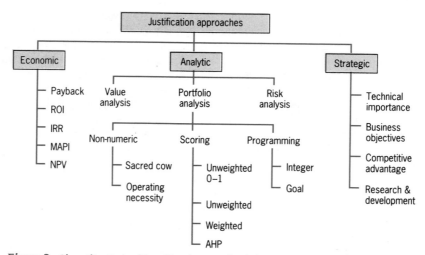

***Figure* 2:** Classification of justification methodologies.

Value Analysis This justification approach, described by Keen (1981), is used by some managers when assessing technical innovations. It consists of a two-stage process as depicted in Figure 3. In the pilot stage the project is treated as an investment in research and development (R & D) rather than as a capital investment (described in the strategic justification section). Here, *value* to the firm is considered first and then expected cost is determined to see if it is acceptable. In the second "build" stage, assuming the pilot stage was successful, the expected *cost* is considered first and then the expected benefits are evaluated for acceptability. These two stages are further described and illustrated below.

(1) Pilot Stage The decision to proceed with the pilot is based on an assessment of the expected, but not necessarily quantified, benefits. The pilot involves a small scale system, complete in itself but limited in its functional capability, to assess only a few of the expected benfits. The cost of the pilot is kept very low, for example, less than $20,000, to keep it in the R & D realm. When the pilot stage is finished the benefits are evaluated to verify their utility to the firm.

One example of this would be the development of a part classification and coding system with only a few digits (and thus limited ability) to determine the reduction in design, drafting, and process planning time. The reduction in lead time to delivery of new products, or decreased response time to customer inquiries might prove highly significant. Or perhaps the reduced hassle in design engineering, or smoother flows between design and process engineering, might be more valuable than expected.

Another example would be the use of a simple robot for limited production tasks such as spraying or material handling. The improvement in morale, or decrease in accidents, or reduction of pollution in the plant could be more important than had been surmized. Or perhaps less imporant.

And another example would be the installation of a simple manufacturing resource planning (MRP II) system, say on a microcomputer, that could coordinate production operations but had limited capabilities in terms of generating purchase orders and so on. Reduced scrap, better planning, smoother product flows, and so on might prove to be extremely valuable to the firm.

(2) Build Stage If the pilot stage was successful, that is, if the expected benefits were realized, then the full system development is considered next. At this stage the costs for the full system are evaluated very carefully and the expected value of the benefits obtained are compared with the cost to determine if they are justified. Clearly, various levels of costs can be

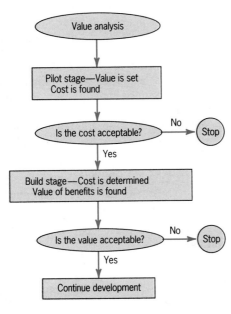

Figure 3: The value analysis process.

evaluated to determine value thresholds of the extended benefits, or "bells and whistles" as they are sometimes called.

To continue the examples above, the coding system would consider additional digits to further detail the parts and allow additional benefits in design, engineering, drafting, process planning, and possibly manufacturing also. More capable and expensive robots would be considered for more complex production tasks. And a larger MRP II system, perhaps for the mainframe, would be considered with significantly expanded capabilities for supporting other functions and departments.

Note that the pilot stage defined above was "broad" rather than "deep" and not the typical incremental approach used in engineering. That is, its *functional capability* was limited but not its *breadth of application*. The other way of handling a pilot stage, which can also be useful, is to reverse the process. For example, conduct the classification and coding for only a limited number of the firm's products, say, all turned parts. But the full set of digits would be used for these parts. And in the third example situation above, the firm would implement only one portion of the MRP II system, for example, the routings package. But it would be used on the mainframe and for all products made in the shop.

Either of these methods can help the firm approach factory automation with more understanding and less risk. The essence of value analysis is to separate the cost and the value derived to let managers intuitively ascertain if the value of the benefits obtained is worth their cost. It also provides an incremental approach to the automation process that lets managers control the cost and thus not let the risk to the firm get out of hand.

Portfolio Analysis   The scenario for portfolio analysis consists of a number of projects competing for limited capital funding. The task is to choose the best set of projects for implementation. The selection is made by creating a portfolio of projects that either maximizes value to the firm subject to capital investment or risk limitations, or minimizes risk or capital subject to attainment of a certain level of value. The value can be based on any number of factors such as return on investment, reduction in scrap, improvement in quality, and so on.

Three general types of portfolio models exist: non-numeric models, scoring models, and programming models. All three are discussed and illustrated in Meredith and Mantel (1985).

Risk Analysis   The usual approach of risk analysis (see, for example, Hertz 1964 or Turban and Meredith 1985) is to simulate the projects under consideration to determine the variables of interest—benefits, costs, yields, capacity, and so on—and describe the outcomes statistically or graphically. Cumulative distribution functions are determined for each variable of interest showing the likelihood of achieving a certain profit, capacity, return on investment, and so on. Various automation projects can thus be simulated beforehand and the results compared. Using the concepts of stochastic dominance as described by Whitmore and Findlay (1978), inferior policies or projects can be eliminated and only the most promising implemented (e.g., see Suresh and Meredith 1985). We illustrate the approach with a simple machine tool investment example below.

There are two potential investment alternatives to replace an existing manufacturing system that is old and overworked. The capital costs, hourly operating costs, and annual maintenance costs are given in Table 1. There are four products (A, B, C, and D) and several minor parts (P) currently being made on this equipment. The typical operation times required for each of the products and parts are given in Table 2 and the anticipated sales volume and price over the next eight years are listed in Tables 3 and 4, respectively. The sales volume estimates have an accuracy of plus or minus 250 units and the price accuracies are as shown.

Given the uncertainties in sales volumes and prices, a simulation risk analysis to determine factors such as net present value (NPV) and machine utilization of each of the alternatives is warranted. In the simulation model (written in SIMSCRIPT II.5), the sales volume is taken as a uniform random variate between the 250 unit accuracy limits. Prices are determined in the same manner. Following this, machine operating hours, equipment utilization, and then the

Table 1   Equipment Cost Elements

	Present Equipment	Alternatives 1	2
Capital cost	(salvage value, 5000)	40,000	32,500
Hourly operating cost	1.5	0.2	0.75
Annual maintenance cost	1000	1400	1250

Table 2   Operation Times

Product	Present Equipment	Alternative 1	Alternative 2
A	0.055	0.010	0.020
B	0.055	0.008	0.015
C	0.055	0.009	0.025
D	0.175	0.050	0.070
P	0.050	0.005	0.009

cash flows over the eight-year horizon are computed and the NPV found.

A number of factors may be analysed in the equipment selection decision process such as sales volume, revenue, idle time, and so on. Here we present, as examples, only two. In Figure 4 the cumulative probability distribution functions of the NPVs of the two alternatives are graphed and in Figure 5 the same is done for the equipment utilization.

As can be seen in Figure 4, the NPV distribution for alternative 1 falls to the left of that for alternative 2. Also, there is a considerable area of overlap between the two distributions, from 10,200 to 12,400. It is clear from the figure that alternative 2 is preferred. That is, the cumulative probability of achieving less than any particular NPV is always greater for alternative 1 than alternative 2. Thus, alternative 2 dominates alternative 1 by "first order stochastic dominance" (Whitmore and Findlay 1978).

However, equipment selection should not be viewed as a single criterion decision and other factors should also be considered. For example, Figure 5 shows that the distribution of machine utilization is also less for alternative 1 than alternative 2, thereby offering extra capacity with alternative 2 for possible future market growth. Clearly, other such factors may also be considered critical in any particular technology decision and their distributions should also be factored into the analysis.

Table 3   Anticipated Annual Sales Volumes

Product	Year								
	1	2	3	4	5	6	7	8
A	1500	1600	1700	1750	1750	1750	1600	1500
B	1600	1000	1200	1200	1200	1300	1200	1200
C	1100	1000	1000	1000	1000	1000	900	800
D	800	800	800	800	700	700	600	600
P	1500	1400	1400	1300	1200	1200	1100	1000

Table 4   Anticipated Annual Sales Price/(Accuracies)

Product	Year			
	1	2	3	4
A	191(2)	191(3)	190(3)	190(3.5)
B	195(2)	194(2)	194(2)	190(4)
C	194(2)	194(2)	194(2)	194(2)
D	191(2)	191(3)	190(3)	190(3.5)
P	192.5(1)	192.5(1)	191(1)	190(3)

Product	Year			
	5	6	7	8
A	188(3)	188(3)	186(3)	185(4)
B	190(4)	198(4)	198(4)	196(5)
C	194(2)	194(2)	194(2)	194(2)
D	188(3)	188(3)	186(3)	185(4)
P	190(2)	189(2)	189(2)	188(2)

Strategic Justification Approaches

The strategic approaches tend to be less technical than the two previous categories, though they are frequently used in combination with them. The advantage of the strategic approaches is their direct tie to the goals of the firm. A disadvantage is the possibility of overlooking the economic and tactical impacts of the projects, myopically focusing entirely on the strategic impacts. Economic justification calculations will commonly be made in combination with strategic considerations, but analytic evaluations are rarely included (usually due to their time and trouble). However, if a strategic approach is used, the economic and analytic implications should also be checked, simply for a clear understanding of all the impacts of the project.

Four main approaches are commonly used at this level.

Technical Importance   From a strategic viewpoint, a desired end cannot be attained unless this project is undertaken first. That is, justification under the concept of technical importance implies that the project is a prerequisite for an important follow-on activity. Its return may be negligible, or even disadvantageous, but later, more desirable work cannot be attempted without implementing this activity first. It is common for activities such as these to be grouped with the desired follow-on project in a "package" that is approved en masse by the approval board.

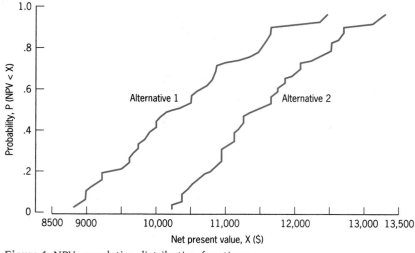

Figure 4: NPV cumulative distribution functions.

Many examples of such activities exist among advanced manufacturing technologies. Firms planning to use cellular manufacturing usually find it necessary to conduct a part–family classification and coding analysis first, though the analysis itself may appear to have no value to them. And it is commonly stated that inventory and bill of material records must be 95 percent accurate before implementing material requirements planning (MRP) systems. And finally, it is often stated as a truism, though it is not necessarily true at all, that a firm must quickly start somewhere in the factory automation process in order to get onto the automation learning curve before the competition gets so far ahead of the firm it can never catch up.

Business Objectives Justification of a project because it directly achieves the firm's business objectives is a clearly strategic approach. "Key indicators" or surrogate measures of this achievement are often used to verify the attainment of these objectives, and to measure when the firm is losing control in these areas and needs to intensify its efforts.

Examples in automation abound. For instance, just by employing the most sophisticated computerized production processes, firms give the impression to customers, vendors, visitors, and the media that they are progressive, advanced, and an up-and-coming organization. (Of course, this may not be true at all.) As another example, automation may allow the consistent attainment of uniform product quality, a top business objective in many firms these days. Or

again, automation may drastically reduce lead times and allow significantly better customer service, perhaps a strategic business objective of a company that is fighting foreign price competition.

Competitive Advantage In the competitive advantage justification approach an opportunity may exist for the firm to gain a significant advantage over its competitors by implementing this project. The advantage may not have been one of the strategic business objectives of the firm but it is too important for the company to pass up. The opportunity may have arisen from a unique set of circumstances or may be an outgrowth of a slight competitive advantage the firm already holds.

This situation occurs frequently in all areas of technology. A firm may hold a crucial patent that allows it to build on an existing base for a significant advantage over its competition. Also, many cases of automation in today's factories are raising opportunities for competitive advantages due to totally unexpected benefits such as reduced space requirements, better processing quality, higher performance capability, shorter design times, and so on.

A subcategory of this approach is "the competitive necessity." Here, the project is mandatory if the firm wishes to remain competitive in a particular market. This is the message so frequently spoken regarding all forms of automation these days and captured in the cliche "automate, emigrate, or evaporate."

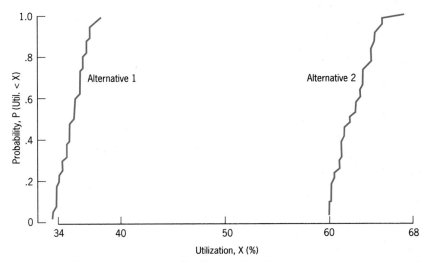

Figure 5: Utilization cumulative distribution functions.

Research and Development Treating a project as an R & D investment admits that it may fail but it holds sufficient strategic promise to justify the investment. The point is that one of many such projects will eventually come through and provide returns to the firm to reimburse all the failures. Without risk, nothing is gained.

A clear example of the R & D approach is the first stage of the value analysis approach described earlier, the pilot project. Another example is setting up one group technology line, or one manufacturing cell, to see how well it works, its costs, its problems, and its benefits. Firms often try to use this approach for promising automation ideas, but because of the risk, minimize the resources provided to the pilot project, whereupon it fails and the second stage of full implementation is abandoned. Companies must be careful not to pre-ordain failure by withholding needed resources at the pilot stage.

Comment on Data Requirements

With all these justification techniques, data acquisition can be a major problem since the technologies are so new. One solution is the pilot stage approach to data collection, as described in the section on value analysis. Another solution is to use the data reported in the literature (e.g., Rosenthal 1984, Meyer 1982), though caution must be advised. For example,

some articles are relatively unspecific about not only the conditions under which benefits have been attained but even the technology employed that gave the benefits, calling every technology "CIM." In many of the justification approaches, such as risk analysis, goal programming, portfolio analysis, and economic analysis, management's own subjective estimates are required concerning importance ratings, limitations on resources, goals, and probable effects of the automation on existing operations.

Although it may be true that the justification of these new technologies is difficult only because of the lack of data, as was originally also the case with office automation, numerical control, and even computers, we believe that there is a larger issue here because of the extensive interrelationships required for these technologies. When successfully used for strategic purposes, they may well alter the entire infrastructure of the organization, and even the organizational structure itself. Such extensive impacts have rarely been experienced with past technologies, thus the difficulty in assessing their benefits and justifying their use.

Conclusion

Historically, economic justification techniques have been used to gain approval for capital equipment expenditures. However, this approach cannot cope with the nature of the benefits offered, such as flexibility and synergy, and the risks inherent in today's advanced manufacturing technologies. Faced with this inadequacy, some firms have developed new justification approaches, the range of which has largely been identified here. The approaches were categorized as

1. economic—appropriate primarily for stand-alone replacement equipment with strictly economic benefits.

2. analytic—appropriate for systems with both economic and non-economic benefits and risks, particularly if the probability distributions can be subjectively estimated, and

3. strategic—appropriate for systems that contribute directly to the firm's business objectives.

When higher level (more stategic) approaches are employed, the lower level methods should also be used to reveal the full impacts of the decision. For example, a large machine tool manufacturer justified an FMS investment with a strategic level approach (business objectives) but nevertheless also conducted a risk and economic analysis of the investment to better understand its expected results. Obviously, stand-alone investments for economic reasons that have limited local impact need not be augmented with higher level justification analyses, since there are not expected to be any higher level impacts.

By recognizing the nature and purpose of the manufacturing systems they are contemplating and then using appropriate justification techniques, we hope that firms may be better able to justify the new manufacturing systems available to them today. By doing so, they may then be able to avoid the pitfall of failing to "economically justify" new manufacturing systems that might well determine whether they will become a competitive force in the market or disappear from it.

References

CURTIN, F. T., 1984, "The Executive Dilemma: How to Justify Investment in New Industrial Automation Systems." CIMCOM *Conference Proceedings*, Society of Manufacturing Engineers, Dearborn, Michigan.

FOTSCH, R. J., 1983, "Machine Tool Justification Policies: Their Effect on Productivity and Profitability." *Journal of Manufacturing Systems*, **3,** No. 2.

GOLD, B., 1982, "CAM Sets New Rules for Production." *Harvard Business Review*, November–December.

GRUD, J. M., 1984, "Can Manufacturing Systems Change be Justified?," *Production and Inventory Management*, 2nd Quarter.

HERTZ, D. B., 1964, "Risk Analysis in Capital Investment." *Harvard Business Review*, January–February.

KAPLAN, R. S., 1984, "Yesterday's Accounting Undermines Production." *Harvard Business Review*, July–August.

KEEN, P. G. W., 1981, ""Value Analysis: Justifying Decision Support Systems." MIS *Quarterly*, March.

McDONALD, J., and HASTINGS, W. F., 1983, "Selecting and Justifying CAD/CAM." *Assembly Engineering*, April.

MEREDITH, J. R., 1985a, "The Economics of Computer Integrated Manufacturing." In Nazemetz, J. W., Hammer, Jr., W. E., and Sadowski, R. P., *Computer Integrated Manufacturing Systems: Selected Readings*, Institute of Industrial Engineers, Norcross, Georgia.

MEREDITH, J. R., 1985b, *Results of the Manufacturing Management Council Study on Justification Procedures*, Society of Manufacturing Engineers, Dearborn, Michigan.

MEREDITH, J. R., 1986, "Include an Infrastructure in Your Automation Strategy." *Industrial Engineering*, May.

MEREDITH, J. R., and HILL, M. M., 1985, "Justifying Advanced Manufacturing Systems," *Working Paper*, University of Cincinnati.

MEREDITH, J. R., HYER. N. L., GERWIN, D., ROSENTHAL, S. R., and WEMMERLOV, U., 1986 "Research Needs in Managing Factory Automation." *Journal of Operations Management*, Feb.

MEREDITH, J. R., and MANTEL, S. J., 1985, *Project Management: A Managerial Approach*, Wiley, New York.

MEYER, R. J., 1982, "A Cookbook Approach to Robotic and Automation Justification," *Proceedings*, *Robots IV Conference*, Society of Manufacturing Engineers, Dearborn, Michigan.

MICHAEL, G. J., and MILLEN, R. A., 1984, "Economic Justification of Modern Computer-based Factory Automation Equipment: A Status Report," *Proceedings of the ORSA/TIMS First Special Interest Conference on FMS*, August.

MUIR, W. T., 1984, "An Alternative for Evaluating CIM Investments—A Case Study," CIMCOM *Conference Proceedings*, Society of Manufacturing Engineers, Dearborn, Michigan.

ROSENTHAL, S., 1984, "A Survey of Factory Automation in the U.S." *Operations Management Review*, Winter.

SURESH, N. C., and MEREDITH, J. R., 1985, "Justifying Multi-Machine Systems: An Integrated Strategic Approach." *Journal of Manufacturing Systems*, **5,** No. 2.

TOMBARI, H. A., 1978, "To Buy or Not to Buy? Weighing Capital Investments." *Production Engineering*, March.

TURBAN, E., and MEREDITH, J. R., 1985, *Fundamentals of Management Science*, 3rd edition. Business Publications, Inc., Plano, Texas.

WHITMORE, G. A., and FINDLAY, M. C., 1978, *Stochastic Dominance: An Approach to Decision Making Under Risk* D.C. Heath. Lexington, Massachussetts.

The Project Manager

In the last chapter we described how projects are evaluated and selected for development. Before more progress can be made, a project manager (PM) must usually be appointed. This person will take responsibility for planning, implementing, and completing the project, beginning with the job of getting things started. Actually, the way to get things started is to hold a meeting, but we will delay discussion of the initial project meeting until Chapter 5 because it is the first step in the process of planning the project.

The PM can be chosen and installed as soon as the project is selected for funding or at any earlier point that seems desirable to senior management. If the PM is appointed prior to project selection or if the PM originated the project, several of the usual start-up tasks are simplified. On occasion, a PM is chosen late in the project life cycle, usually to replace another PM who is leaving the project for other work. For example, a large agricultural products firm regularly uses a senior scientist as PM until the project's technical problems are solved and the product has been tested. Then it replaces the scientist with a middle manager from the marketing side of the firm as marketing becomes the focal point of the project. (The transition is difficult and, according to firm spokespeople, the results are sometimes unsatisfactory.)

Usually, a senior manager briefs the PM on the project so that the PM can understand where it fits in the general scheme of things in the parent organization, and its priority relative to other projects in the system and to the routine work of the organization. The PM's first set of tasks is typically to prepare a preliminary budget and schedule, to help select people to serve on the project team, to get to know the client, to make sure that the proper facilities are available, to ensure that any supplies required early in the project life are available when needed, and to take care of the routine details necessary to get the project moving.

As people are added to the project, plans and schedules are refined. The details of managing the project through its entire life cycle are spelled out, even to the point of planning for project termination when the work is finally completed.

Mechanisms are developed to facilitate communication between the PM and top management, the functional areas, and the client. As plans develop still further, the PM holds meetings and briefings to ensure that all those who will affect or be affected by the project are prepared in advance for the demands they will have to meet as the project is implemented.

In this chapter we discuss the unique nature of project management and some of the ways project management differs from *functional* management. Our emphasis is on the role and responsibilities of the PM. We concentrate on the demands placed on the PM, particularly on those unique to project management. For example, there is considerable difference between the demands placed on the following two information system project managers. One is responsible for converting a library's card catalog to a computerized system, including CD-ROMs. The other is responsible for the organization, planning, and implementation of the federal government's information superhighway. Based on our discussions of the nature of the PM's job, we complete the chapter by considering how to identify the skills and characteristics required of this supermanager.

It is best to describe the PM's job relative to some assumptions about the nature of projects and the organization within which the project must function. We assume that the parent firm is functionally organized and is conducting several projects simultaneously with its ongoing, routine operations. We also assume a fairly large firm, a project that has some technical components, with an output to be delivered to an "arms-length" customer. Clearly, not all, and possibly even not *most*, projects operate under these circumstances, but these are the most demanding and we address the most difficult problems a PM might have to face. Smaller, simpler projects may not require the tools we will present here, but the PM for these projects should be aware that such tools exist. The term *technical components* as we apply it includes more than hardware. Any firm with a well-defined methodology of carrying out its mission has a technical component, as we use the phrase. For example, a systems analysis and functional requirements are among the technical components in most information systems projects, as is the due diligence document in a security offering.

In this chapter two conditions receive special attention. Both have a profound effect on the outcome of the project, and neither is under the complete control of the PM—though the PM can greatly influence both by dealing with the conditions early in the project life. The first of these concerns the degree to which the project has the support of top management. If that support is strong and reasonably unqualified, the project has a much better chance of success.

The second condition concerns the general orientation of the project team members. If they are highly oriented toward their individual, functional disciplines, as opposed to the project itself, project success is threatened. If, on the other hand, they tend to be oriented toward the project (that is, problem-oriented rather than discipline-oriented), the likelihood of success is much greater. The PM cannot actually control these conditions, but there is often much that can be done to influence them.

▶ 3.1 SOME COMMENTS ON PROJECT MANAGEMENT AND THE PROJECT MANAGER

The Functional Manager versus the Project Manager

The best way to explain the unique role of the PM is to contrast it with that of a *functional* manager in charge of one of a firm's functional departments such as marketing, engineering, or finance (see Figure 3-1). Such department heads are usually specialists in the areas they manage. Being specialists, they are analytically oriented and they know something of the details of each operation for which they are responsible. When a technically difficult task is required of their departments, they know how to analyze and attack it. As functional managers, they are administratively responsible for deciding how something will be done, who will do it, and what resources will be devoted to accomplish the task.

A PM, by contrast, is usually a generalist with a wide background of experience and knowledge. A PM must oversee many functional areas, each with its own specialists (see Figure 3-2). Therefore, what is required is an ability to put many pieces of a task together to form a coherent whole—that is, the project manager must be more skilled at synthesis, whereas the functional manager must be more skilled at analysis. The functional manager uses the *analytic approach* and the PM uses the *systems approach*.

The phrase "systems approach" requires a short digression describing briefly what is meant by those words. A system can be defined as a set of interrelated components that accepts inputs and produces outputs in a purposeful manner. This simple statement is a bit more complicated than it appears. First, the word "purposeful" restricts our attention to systems that involve humans in some way. Machines are not purposeful, people are. Second, the notion of "inputs" and "outputs" implies some boundary across which the system's inputs arrive and outputs depart. This boundary differentiates the system from its "environment." Third, the nature of the interrelationships between the components defines the "structure" of the system.

The analytic method focuses on breaking the components of a system into smaller and smaller elements. We are not saying that this is the wrong thing to do, it is merely inadequate for understanding a complex system. Regardless of the dissector's skill or the degree to which, say, a frog is dissected, the dissection allows only a partial understanding of the total animal "frog." The systems approach maintains the policy that to understand a component, we must understand the system of which the component is a part. And to understand the system, we must understand the environment (or larger system) of which it is a part. At the beginning of his excellent book on the systems approach [44], John van Gigch quotes Blaise Pascal: "I

Figure 3-1: Functional management organization chart: marketing department of an insurance company.

Figure 3-2: Project management organization showing typical responsibilities of a project manager.

find as impossible to know the parts without knowing the whole, as to know the whole without specifically knowing the parts."

Adoption of the systems approach is crucial for the project manager. One cannot understand and, thus, cannot manage a project without understanding the organizational program of which the project is a part, and the organization in which the program exists, as well as the environment of the organization. Consider, if you will, the problem of managing a project devoted to the development of software that will create and maintain a database, and to undertake this task without knowing anything about the decision support system in which the database will be used, or the operating system of the computers that will contain the DSS, or the purposes for which the information in the database will be used, and so forth. The literature on the systems approach is extensive, but Sir Stafford Beer's works (see, for example [5], as well as [7, 8, 46 47]) which are classics in the field.

Back to our comparison between the PM and the functional manager. It reveals another crucial difference between the two. The functional manager is a direct, technical supervisor. The PM is a facilitator. Knowing the technology, the functional manager has the basic technical knowledge required to oversee and advise subordinates on the best ways to handle their work and solve problems met in the normal course of that work. The PM may have detailed technical knowledge in one or two specific areas, but he or she rarely has knowledge in depth beyond these few areas. The PM, therefore, cannot apply knowledge directly, but instead must facilitate cooperation between those who have the various kinds of specialized knowledge and those who need it. This distinction between facilitator and specialist is a key element in the decision to use generalists as PMs rather than specialists.

Three major questions face the PM in this task of synthesis: What needs to be done, when must it be done (if the project is not to be late), and how are the resources required to do the job to be obtained. In spite of the fact that the PM is responsible for the project, and depending on how the project is organized, the functional managers may make some of the fundamental and critical project decisions. For example, they may select the people who will actually do the work required to carry out the project. They may also develop the technological design detailing how the project will be accomplished. And they frequently influence the precise deployment of the project's resources. Once again, depending on how the project is organized, the functional managers may bear little or no direct responsibility for the results. As we will see later (and in Chapter 4, "Project Organization"), this separation of powers between functional and project managers, which may aid in the successful completion of the project, is also a source of considerable "discomfort" for both.

Note here that the PM is responsible for organizing, staffing, budgeting, directing, planning, and controlling the project. In other words, the PM "manages" it, but the functional managers may affect the choice of technology to be used by the project and the specific individuals who will do the work. (It is not uncommon, however, for the PM to negotiate with functional managers about the assignment of special individuals to carry out certain project work.) Arguments about the logic or illogic of such an arrangement will fall on deaf ears. The PM cannot allow the functional manager to usurp control of the project. If this happens, work on the project is likely to become secondary to the work of the functional group and the project will suffer. But the functional manager cannot allow the PM to take over authority for technical decisions in the functional area or to control the assignment of functional area personnel.

At times, a senior manager (the PM's immediate superior) will, in effect, take over the PM's job by exercising extremely close supervision over every action the PM takes, or will actually tell the PM precisely what to do. All of the powers normally delegated to the PM are withdrawn and the PM's boss runs the project. This condition is known as *micromanagement*. It stamps out any creativity or initiative from the PM or project workers, frustrates almost everyone connected with the project, and generally ensures mediocre performance, if not failure. The senior rationalizes the need for control with such statements as: "After all, the project is *my* responsibility," *or* "You must understand how important this project is to the firm," *or* "Superboss expects me to keep my eye on everything that goes on around here." Such nonsense sounds logical until subjected to analysis. The first comment denies the virtue of delegation. The second assumes that everyone except the speaker is stupid. The third is a paean to "self-importance." To be frank, we do not know how to cure or prevent micromanagement. It is practiced by individuals who have so little trust in their co-workers that they must control everything. Micromanagers are rarely likable enough for anyone to try to help them. Our considered advice to PMs who are micromanaged is to request a transfer.

At the other end of the spectrum, the relationship between the PM, the functional managers, the project team, and the PM's superior may be characterized as "collegial," and the organization may be populated by talented people. In such organizations conflict is minimized, cooperation is the norm, no one is terribly concerned with who gets the credit, and the likelihood of success is high. We will have more to say later in this chapter and in other chapters about building and maintaining teams. Effective teams tend to operate in a collegial mode. It is worth noting, however, that collegiality without talent leads to failure—even if the project team smiles a lot while failing.

Project Responsibilities

The PM's responsibilities are broad and fall primarily into three separate areas: responsibility to the parent organization, responsibility to the project, and responsibility to the members of the project team. Responsibilities to the firm itself include proper conservation of resources, timely and accurate project communications, and the careful, competent management of the project. Many formal aspects of the communications role will be covered in Chapter 9 when the Project Management Information System is discussed, but one matter must be emphasized here. It is very important to keep senior management of the parent organization fully informed about the project's status, cost, timing, and prospects. Senior managers should be warned about likely future problems. The PM should note the chances of running over budget or being late, as well as methods available to reduce the likelihood of these dread events. Reports must be accurate and timely if the PM is to maintain credibility, protect the parent firm from high risk, and allow senior management to intercede where needed. ***Above all, the PM must never, never, never allow senior management to be surprised!***

The PM's responsibility to the project is met by ensuring that the integrity of the project is preserved in spite of the conflicting demands made by the many parties who have legitimate interests in the project. The manager must deal with the engineering department when it resists a change advised by marketing, which is responding to a suggestion that emanated from the client. In the meantime, contract administration (or our attorney) says the client has no right to request changes without the submission of a formal Request for Change order. Manufacturing says that the argument is irrelevant because marketing's suggestion cannot be incorporated into the project without a complete redesign.

The PM is in the middle of this turmoil. The PM must sort out understanding from misunderstanding, soothe ruffled feathers, balance petty rivalries, and cater to the demands of the client. One must, of course, remember that none of these strenuous activities relieves the PM of the responsibility of keeping the project on time, within budget, and up to specifications.

In Chapter 4 it will become evident that it is very common for the PM to have no direct subordinates in spite of the fact that several, perhaps many, people "work for him/her" on the project. These people form what we have been referring to as the "project team." In spite of the strange circumstance where people are said to work for someone who is not their boss, the PM's relationship to the team may be considerably closer than one might expect, particularly when individuals are assigned to spend much or all of their time working on the project.

The project manager's responsibilities to members of the project team are dictated by the finite nature of the project itself and the specialized nature of the team. Because the project is, by definition, a temporary entity and must come to an end, the PM must be concerned with the future of the people who serve on the team. If the PM does not get involved in helping project workers with the transition back to their functional homes or to new projects, then as the project nears completion, project workers will pay more and more attention to protecting their own future careers and less to completing the project on time. These matters are discussed in more detail in Chapter 13, "Project Termination."

When some members of project teams are highly educated researchers, it has frequently been suggested that such specialists require a "special type" of managing. Often referred to as "tweed coat management," the implication is that Ph.D.s, scientific researchers, and academically oriented experts need careful shepherding. Articles describing the management of research seem to assume that the higher the level of formal education, the lower the level of "street smarts." To the best of our knowledge, there is no evidence supporting this odd assumption. Like most people, scientists seem to respond positively to a caring, supportive managerial style.

PM Career Paths

A large number of firms may have many different types and sizes of projects in progress simultaneously. Of these, it is typical to find that most are not large enough or sufficiently complex to require a full-time manager. Quite a few project managers are in charge of several projects simultaneously. For example, it is not unusual to find that when a medium or large firm undertakes a program to computerize written records, several hundred projects result. In order to ensure consistency and easy intergroup transfer of data, the program is commonly managed by the division or department housing the computer software group rather than being spread out in the units developing or using particular records. The entire process is apt to take several years.

At the same time that the computerization program is going on, the firm may be planning and building a new factory (three years), undertaking several dozen R & D projects (one to seven years), improving the landscape surrounding its factory in Mussent Point (two months), considering the acquisition of another firm (six months), upgrading the equipment in its thiotimolene plant (two years), buying art works produced by artists in each city in which the firm operates for display in corporate offices (one year), planning the annual stockholders' meeting (three months), and doing a large number of other things, many of which are organized as projects.

Who manages these projects? Where does the company find people competent to manage such a wide variety of projects? In Chapter 1, we referred to the professionalization and rapid growth of project management, to PMBOK (the project management body of knowledge), as well as to the development of college and university-level courses and degree programs available in the field. Although the percentage of PMs who are academically trained is increasing, most of the current group of project managers have no college-level training in the field. By far, the largest group got their training in one or more of three ways: on-the-job, project management seminars and workshops lasting from one-half day to two weeks, or active participation in the programs of the local chapters attached to the Project Management Institute.

The great number of fairly small, short-term projects being carried out, when managed by an experienced PM, serve a purpose beyond the output of the projects themselves. They provide an excellent training ground for new project managers who frequently begin their preparation with involvement in some major aspect of a small project. A number of firms, Procter & Gamble for one, often take management trainees and give them some project-management responsibility; for instance, the guidance of a new cosmetic through test procedures to ensure that it is not toxic to users. Such experience serves to teach trainees many things, not the least of which are the importance of an organized plan for reaching an objective, of "follow-through," of negotiation with one's co-workers, and of sensitivity to the political realities of organizational life. The skills and experiences gained from managing a project, even a small one, are a scaled-down version of what it is like to run a full-sized organization. Thus, projects provide an excellent growth environment for future executives and for developing managerial skills.

One final note on this subject. If we have made the process of project management seem orderly and rational, we apologize. If any single descriptor could be used to characterize project management, the adjective would be "messy." In an excellent article that should be read by anyone interested in understanding the reality of management, Kotter has shown that general managers are less organized, less formal, and less structured than college students are led to believe [26]. The same is undoubtedly true of project managers. This fundamental lack of organization and structure makes it all the more important that PMs implement good planning and organizational skills where possible, or the chaos becomes unmanageable.

The career path of a PM often starts with participation in small projects, and later in larger projects, until the person is given command over small and then larger projects. For example, the path could be tooling manager for small Project U, project engineer for larger Project V, manufacturing manager for large Project W, deputy project manager for large Project X, project manager for small Project Y, and project manager for large Project Z. If energy, luck, skill, and ambition remain, the PM may progress to corporate plant operations manager, vice-president of manufacturing, president, and chairman of the board.

The actual establishment of multiple career paths to the top of organizations is more talked about than acted on. Wishful thinking aside, with a very few notable exceptions,* we know of no *specific* career paths that can take project managers to CEO positions. In a great many firms, however, experience as a PM is seen as a mandatory or desirable step on the way up the corporate ladder. The logic of such a view is obvious. The capability of a PM to meet the demands of senior management positions is clearly evidenced by the PM's ability to achieve the project's goals without the need for *de jure* authority while operating in an environment typified by uncertainty, if not chaos.

---

* For example, Eli Lilly and Co., the pharmaceutical firm, finds that projects involving new drugs often last 8–12 years. No PM would be willing to manage a project that long without the opportunity for promotion. Lilly, therefore, has established a career path for their PMs that potentially leads to the top of the firm. They already had career paths progressing through "administration" or "R & D" to the top and have clearly demonstrated the reality of both paths.

Project Management in Practice
The Wreckmaster at a New York Subway Accident

At 12:16 A.M., Wednesday August 28, 1991, a 10-car subway train on the Lexington Line beneath New York City jumped the track and crashed in the subway tunnel. Damage was massive—five cars were derailed, one was cut in half, another bent in two, possibly 150 persons injured, four dead. The train ripped out 22 steel-girder support columns used to hold up the tunnel ceiling, as well as the street above which immediately sunk a half inch. Two tracks and a third rail had been ripped out and two signal sets, two switches, and an air compressor room destroyed.

When such an emergency occurs, the New York City Transit Authority (NYCTA) immediately appoints a project manager, called a "Wreckmaster," to oversee the handling of the disaster, coordinate rescue and repair activi-

---

Source: S. Nacco, "PM in Crisis Management at NYCTA: Recovering from a Major Subway Accident," PM Network, February 1992.

Subway accident damage.

ties, and make sure that operations are returned to a safe condition as soon as possible. In this case, the goal was to have the subway back to normal operation by Tuesday morning rush hour, September 3 after the three-day holiday weekend. Such disasters are handled in eight phases:

Phase 1: Respond to injury—Get people out of danger, provide needed medical care, remove bodies and ensure that no victims remain in the debris.

Phase 2: Secure the area—Simultaneously with phase 1, eliminate other threats to life or property by disconnecting power, providing emergency lighting and ventilation, stopping other trains from entering the area, keeping nonrelevant pedestrian and vehicular traffic out.

Phase 3: Initiate command facilities—Concurrent with phases 1 and 2, set up and activate command and coordination structure for all emergency activities.

Phase 4: Remove debris—Collect and remove the elements and debris of the accident which would hinder rescue, clean-up, or repair.

Phase 5: Remove damaged equipment—Use cranes, cutting torches, and other equipment to remove the large, major equipment.

Phase 6: Facility repair—Repair the facilities as quickly as possible for continuing and normal use.

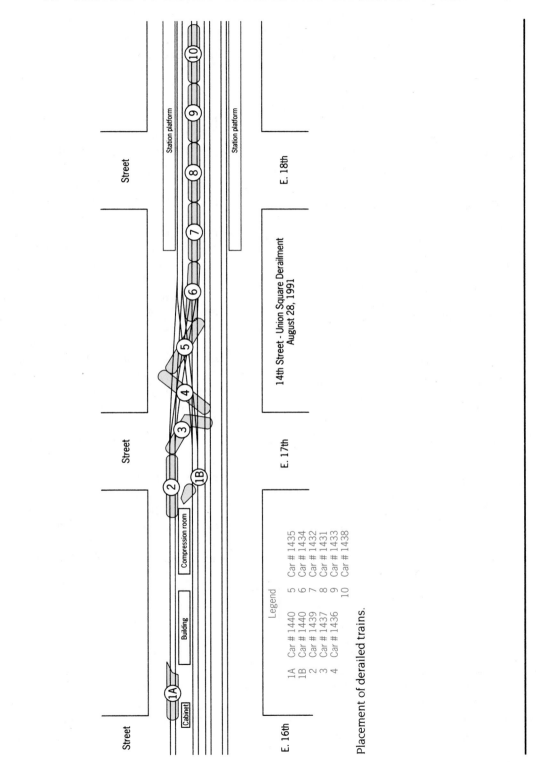

Placement of derailed trains.

Phase 7: Test—Make certain that all facilities are fully operational and safe by testing under the watchful eye of engineering, operations, and safety.

Phase 8: Clean-up—Clean the premises to the best possible state to permit normal operations.

The crash was heard at NYCTA's Union Square District 4 and about 40 transit police officers ran to assist passengers at the smoke-filled scene. Soon, officers from District 2, the Fire Department, and the Office of Emergency Management joined them. The Fire Department brought fans to help clear the smoke and steel cable to rope the wreckage to the support pillars so they could reach people still in the train cars without the roof caving in on them. Buses were dispatched to transport people to hospitals and the Red Cross provided food and drink for the injured. Some rescuers fainted from heat exhaustion as the temperature climbed over 110 degrees in the tunnel and two dozen police and fire workers were treated for injuries and smoke inhalation. Transit police officer Emanuel Bowser was riding the train when it crashed but helped people get off for more than four hours after the crash even though he had a broken arm and fingers himself.

After learning about the crash, NYCTA appointed Larry Gamache, general superintendent of track operations, as Wreckmaster. Larry set up team captains to coordinate activities throughout each phase of the disaster operations. A command center was established at a nearby subway station to direct and coordinate the operations. Gamache formulated a mental flow chart of how work needed to proceed. Each task had to be analyzed to determine what tasks had to precede it and what tasks could be conducted concurrently with it. Gamache also initiated regular meetings for all involved parties. This kept everyone informed of what progress had been made and provided them with estimates of future progress so activities could be coordinated and sequenced.

The plan was to remove the wreckage as quickly as possible from one track to allow worktrains to reach the disaster site, bringing needed materials to the site and removing debris. Since work had to continue throughout the Labor Day weekend on 12-hour shifts, facilities for the workers—food, drink, toilets—also had to be provided. Diesel trains pulled out the five cars that didn't derail but getting out the other five was a special problem. A new Hoersh hydraulic jacking system was brought in from another district that could lift a 44-ton car, move it sideways, and set it back down on the tracks. Using these jacks reduced by half the labor required to rerail the cars, thereby significantly expediting the recovery. As work progressed through the long weekend, it became apparent that the disaster recovery plan would meet its Tuesday morning completion goal and, in fact, trains began running again by late evening on Monday.

Lawrence Gamache, Wreckmaster

Larry Gamache started at NYCTA 24 years ago as a trackworker and progressed through many managerial positions on his way to general superintendent, track operations. His experience over those years clearly qualified him for the responsibility of this assignment, particularly his involvement as field supervisor of several earlier derailments. He was also highly involved in a three-year subway reconstruction project that required extensive coordination and negotiation with other city agencies, communities, and political leaders, all the while battling inclement weather and difficult conditions—yet, the project was completed ahead of time and well under budget. This experience, too, was valuable in coordinating the activities of the many groups involved in the disaster recovery.

Lawrence Gamache, Wreckmaster.

▶ 3.2   SPECIAL DEMANDS ON THE PROJECT MANAGER

A number of demands are unique to the management of projects, and the success of the PM depends to a large extent on how capably they are handled. These special demands can be categorized under the seven following headings.

Acquiring Adequate Resources

It was noted earlier that the resources initially budgeted for a project are frequently insufficient to the task. In part, this is due to the natural optimism of the project proposers about how much can be accomplished with relatively few resources; but it is also caused by the great uncertainty associated with a project. Many details of resource purchase and usage are deferred until the project manager knows specifically what resources will be required and when. For instance, there is no point in purchasing a centrifuge now if in nine months we will know exactly what type of centrifuge will be most useful.

The good PM knows there are resource trade-offs that need to be taken into consideration. A skilled machinist can make do with unsophisticated machinery to construct needed parts, but a beginning machinist cannot. Subcontracting can make up for an inadequate number of computer programmers, but subcontractors will have to be carefully instructed in the needs of the contractor, which is costly and may cause delays. Crises occur that require special resources not usually provided to the project manager. All these problems produce glitches in the otherwise smooth progress of the project. To deal with these glitches, the PM must scramble, elicit aid, work late, wheedle, threaten, or do whatever seems necessary to keep the project on schedule. On occasion, the additional required resources simply alter the project's cost–benefit ratio to the point that the project is no longer cost-effective. Obviously, the PM attempts to avoid these situations, but some of what happens is beyond the PM's control. This issue will be dealt with in detail in Chapter 13.

The problems of time and budget are aggravated in the presence of a phenomenon that has been long suspected but only recently demonstrated [11, 12]. The individual who has the responsibility for performing a task sometimes overestimates the time and cost required to do it. That individual's immediate supervisor often discounts the worker's pessimism but, in so doing, may underestimate the time and cost. Moving up the management hierarchy, each successive level frequently lowers the time and cost estimates again, becoming more optimistic about the ability of those working for them to do with less—or, perhaps, more forgetful about what things were like when they worked at such jobs. The authors have informally observed—and listened to complaints about—such doings in a variety of organizations. We suspect they reflect the superior's natural tendency to provide challenging work for subordinates and the desire to have it completed efficiently. The mere recognition of this phenomenon does not prevent it. Complaints to upper-level managers are usually met with a hearty laugh, a pat on the back, and a verbal comment such as, "I know you can do it. You're my best project manager, and you can. . . ."

Another issue may complicate the problem of resource acquisition for the PM. Project and functional managers alike perceive the availability of resources to be strictly limited and thus a strict "win–lose" proposition. Under these conditions, the "winners" may be those managers who have solid political connections with top management. Often, there are times in the life of any project when success or survival may depend on the PM's "friendship" with a champion high in the parent organization.

Acquiring and Motivating Personnel

A major problem for the PM is the fact that most of the people needed for a project must be "borrowed." With few exceptions, they are borrowed from the functional departments. The PM must negotiate with the functional department managers for the desired personnel, and then, if successful, negotiate with the people themselves to convince them to take on these challenging temporary project assignments.

Most functional managers cooperate when the PM comes seeking good people for the project, but the cooperative spirit has its limits. The PM will be asking for the services of the two types of people most needed and prized by the functional manager: first, individuals with scarce but necessary skills and, second, top producers. Both the PM and functional manager are fully aware that the PM does not want a "has-been," a "never-was," or a "never-will-be." Perceptions about the capabilities of individuals may differ, but the PM is usually trying to borrow precisely those people the functional manager would most like to keep.

A second issue may reduce the willingness of the functional manager to cooperate with the PM's quest for quality people. At times, the functional manager may perceive the project as more glamorous than his or her function and hence a potent source of managerial glory. The functional manager may thus be a bit jealous or suspicious of the PM, a person who may have little interest in the routine work of the functional area even if it is the bread and butter of the organization.

On its surface, the task of motivating good people to join the project does not appear to be difficult, because the kind of people who are most desired as members of a project team are those naturally attracted by the challenge and variety inherent in project work. Indeed, it would not be difficult except for the fact that the functional manager is trying to keep the same people that the PM is trying to attract. The subordinate who is being seduced to leave the steady life of the functional area for the glamour of a project can be gently reminded that the functional manager retains control of personnel evaluation, salary, and promotion for those people lent out to projects. (A few exceptions to these general rules will be discussed in Chapter 4.) There may even be comments about how easy it is to lose favor or be forgotten when one is "out of sight."

Unless the PM can hire outsiders with proven ability, it is not easy to gather competent people; but having gathered them, they must be motivated to work. Because the functional manager controls pay and promotion, the PM cannot promise much beyond the challenge of the work itself. Fortunately, as Herzberg has argued [21], that is often sufficient [also see 38]. Many of the project personnel are professionals and experts in their respective specialties. Given this, and the voluntary nature of their commitment to the project, there is the assumption that they must be managed "delicately."

It has long been assumed that in order to ensure creativity, professionals require minimal supervision, maximum freedom, and little control. As a matter of fact, William Souder has shown [44] that the output of R & D laboratories is actually not correlated with the level of freedom in the lab. This finding is significant. The most likely explanation is that individual scientists have unique requirements for freedom and control. Some want considerable direction in their work, whereas others find that a lack of freedom inhibits creativity. Those who need freedom thus tend to work in organizations where they are allowed considerable latitude, and those who desire direction gravitate to organizations that provide it.

Motivation problems are often less severe for routine, repeated projects such as those in construction, or for projects carried out as the sole activity of an organization (even if it is part of a larger organization). In such cases, the PM probably has considerable *de facto* influence over salary and promotion. Frequently, the cadre of these projects see themselves as engaged in similar projects for the long term. If the project is perceived as temporary, risky, and important, about all the PM can offer people is the chance to work on a challenging, high-visibility assignment, to be "needed," and to operate in a supportive climate. For most, this is sufficient incentive to join the project.

A story has it that when asked "How do you motivate astronauts?" a representative of NASA responded, "We don't motivate them, but, boy, are we careful about whom we select." The issue of motivating people to join and work creatively for a project is closely related to the kind of people who are invited to join. The most effective team members have some common characteristics. A list of the most important of these follows, but only the first is typically considered during the usual selection process.

1. **High-quality technical skills** Team members must be able to solve most of the technical problems of a project without recourse to outside assistance. Although the major technical problems faced by a project are generally solved by the functional departments, the exact way in which such solutions are ap-

plied invariably requires some adaptation. In addition, a great many minor technical difficulties occur, always at inconvenient times, and need to be handled rapidly. In such cases, project schedules will suffer if these difficulties must be referred back to the functional departments where they will have to stand in line for a solution along with (or behind) the department's own problems.

2. **Political sensitivity**   It is obvious that the PM requires political skills of a high order. Although it is less obvious, senior project members also need to be politically skilled and sensitive to organizational politics. As we have noted several times, project success is dependent on support from senior management in the parent organization. This support depends on the preservation of a delicate balance of power between projects and functional units, and between the projects themselves. The balance can be upset by individuals who are politically inept.

3. **Strong problem orientation**   Research conducted by Juri Pill [36] has shown that the chances for successful completion of a multidisciplinary project are greatly increased if project team members are *problem-oriented* rather than *discipline-oriented*. Pill indicates that problem-oriented people tend to learn and adopt whatever problem-solving techniques appear helpful, but discipline-oriented individuals tend to view the problem through the eyes of their discipline, ignoring aspects of the problem that do not lie in the narrow confines of their educational expertise. This is, of course, consistent with our insistence earlier in this chapter that the PM should adopt a systems approach to project management.

4. **Strong goal orientation**   Projects do not provide a comfortable work environment for individuals whose focus is on activity rather than on results. Work flow is rarely even, and for the professionals a 60-hour week is common, as are periods when there seems to be little to do. "Clock watchers" will not be successful team members.

5. **High self-esteem**   As we noted above, a prime law for projects (and one that applies equally well to the entire organization) is *never surprise the boss*. Projects can rapidly get into deep trouble if team members hide their failures, or even a significant risk of failure, from the PM. Individuals on the team should have sufficient self-esteem that they are not threatened by acknowledgement of their own errors, or by pointing out possible problems caused by the work of others. Egos must be strong enough that all can freely share credit and blame. We trust that the PM is aware that "shooting the messenger who brings bad news" will immediately stop the flow of any negative information from below—though negative surprises from above will probably be more frequent.

Dealing with Obstacles

One characteristic of any project is its uniqueness, and this characteristic means that the PM will have to face and overcome a series of crises. From the beginning of the project to its termination, crises appear without warning. The better the planning, the fewer the crises, but no amount of planning can take account of the myriad of changes that can and do occur in the project's environment. The successful PM is a fire fighter by avocation.

At the inception of the project, the "fires" tend to be associated with resources. The technical plans to accomplish the project have been translated into a budget and schedule and forwarded up the managerial hierarchy or sent to the client for approval. In an earlier section we noted that some of the budget and schedule is pared away at each successive step up the hierarchy. Each time this happens, the budget and schedule cuts must be translated into changes in the technical plans. Test procedures may be shortened, suppliers' lead times may be cut. The required cost and schedule adjustments are made, a nip here and a tuck there. To the people affected, these may well be crises.

The PM learns by experience; the wise PM learns from the experiences of others. Every project on which the PM has worked, whether as the project manager or not, is a source of learning. The war stories and horror tales of other PMs are vicarious experiences to be integrated with direct personal experience into a body of lore that will provide early-warning signals of trouble on the way. The lore will also serve as a bank of pretested remedies for trouble already at hand.

To be useful, experience must be generalized and organized. Managing a project is much like managing a business. Business firms often develop special routines for dealing with various types of fires. Expediters, order entry clerks, purchasing agents, dispatchers, shippers, and similar individuals keep the physical work of the system moving along from order to shipment. Human resource departments help put out "people fires" just as engineering helps deal with "mechanical fires." Fire fighting, to be optimally effective, should be organized so that fires are detected and recognized as early as possible. This allows the fires to be assigned to project team members who specialize in dealing with specific types of fires. Although this procedure does not eliminate crises, it does reduce the pain of dealing with them.

As the project nears completion, obstacles tend to be clustered around two issues: first, last-minute schedule and technical changes, and second, a series of problems that have as their source the uncertainty surrounding what happens to members of the project team when the project is completed. These two types of problems are very different from one another, as well as from the problems that faced the PM earlier in the life cycle of the project. The way to deal with last-minute schedule and technical changes is "the best you can." Beyond knowing that such changes will occur and will be disruptive to the project, there is little the PM can do except be prepared to "scramble."

Coping with the uncertainty surrounding what happens at the end of a project is a different matter. The issue will be covered at greater length in Chapter 13, but it deserves mention here because it is certainly an obstacle that the PM must overcome. The key to solving such problems is communication. The PM must make open communications between the PM and team members first priority. The notion of "open communications" requires that emotions, feelings, worries, and anxieties be communicated, as well as factual messages.

Making Project Goal Trade-offs

The PM must make trade-offs between the project goals of cost, time, and performance. The PM must also make trade-offs between project progress and process—that is, between the technical and managerial functions. The first set of trade-offs is required by the need to preserve some balance between the project time, cost, and performance goals. Conventional wisdom had it that the precise nature of the trade-offs varied depending on the stage of the project life cycle. At the beginning of the life cycle, when the project is being planned, performance was felt to be the most important of the goals, with cost and schedule sacrificed to the technical requirements of the project. Following the design phase, the project builds momentum, grows, and operates at peak levels. Because it accumulates costs at the maximum rate during this period, cost was felt to take precedence over performance and schedule. Finally, as the project nears completion, schedule becomes the high-priority goal, and cost (and perhaps performance) suffers. Research [25] has shown that these assumptions, sensible as they seem, are not true.

During the design or formation stage of the project life cycle, there is no significant difference in the importance project managers place on the three goals. It appears that the logic of this finding is based on the assumption that the project must be designed in such a way that it meets all the goals set by the client. If compromises must be made, each of the objectives is vulnerable. At times, however, a higher level of technical performance may be possible that, in the client's eyes, merits some softening of the cost or schedule goals. For example, a computer software project required that an information system be able to answer queries within 3 seconds 95 percent of the time. The firm designed such a system by ensuring that it would respond within 1.5 seconds 50 percent of the time. By meeting this additional standard, more stringent than that imposed by the client, it was able to meet the specified standard.

Schedule is the dominant goal during the buildup stage, being significantly more important than performance, which is in turn significantly more important than cost. Kloppenborg conjectures [25, p. 127] that this is so because scheduling commitments are made during the buildup stage. Scheduling and performance are approximately tied for primacy during the main stage of the life cycle when both are significantly more important than cost, though the importance of cost increases somewhat between the buildup and main stages. During the final stage, phaseout, performance is significantly more important than schedule, which is significantly more important than cost. Table 3-1 shows the relative importance of each objective for each stage of the project life cycle.

The second set of trade-offs concern sacrificing smoothness of running the project team for technical progress. Near the end of the project it may be necessary to insist that various team members work on aspects of the project for which they are not well trained or which they do not enjoy, such as copying or collating the final report. The PM can get a fairly good reading on team morale by paying attention to the response to such requests. This is, of course, another reason why the PM should select team members who have a strong problem orientation. Discipline-oriented people want to stick to the tasks for which they have been prepared and to which they have been assigned. Problem-oriented people have little hesitation in helping to do whatever is necessary to bring the project in on time, to "spec," and within budget.

The PM also has responsibility for other types of trade-offs, ones rarely discussed in the literature of project management. If the PM directs more than one

Table 3-1 Relative Importance of Project Objectives During Different Stages of the Project Life Cycle

Life Cycle Stage	Cost	Schedule	Performance
Formation	1	1	1
Buildup	3	1	2
Main	3	1	1
Phaseout	3	2	1

Note: 1 = most important.

(*Source:* [25, p. 78])

project, he or she must make trade-offs between the several projects. As noted earlier, it is critical to avoid the appearance of favoritism in such cases. Thus, we strongly recommend that when a project manager is directing two or more projects, care should be taken to ensure that the life cycles of the projects are sufficiently different that the projects will not demand the same constrained resources at the same time, thereby avoiding forced choices between projects.

In addition to the trade-offs between the goals of a project, and in addition to trade-offs between projects, the PM will also be involved in making choices that require balancing the goals of the project with the goals of the firm. Such choices are common. Indeed, the necessity for such choices is inherent in the nature of project management. The PM's enthusiasm about a project—a prime requirement for successful project management—can easily lead him or her to overstate the benefits of a project, to understate the probable costs of project completion, to ignore technical difficulties in achieving the required level of performance, and to make trade-off decisions that are clearly biased in favor of the project and antithetical to the goals of the parent organization. Similarly, this enthusiasm can lead the PM to take risks not justified by the likely outcomes.

Finally, the PM must make trade-off decisions between the project, the firm, and his or her own career goals. Depending on the PM's attitudes toward risk, career considerations might lead the PM to take inappropriate risks or avoid appropriate ones.

Failure and the Risk and Fear of Failure

In Chapter 13, we will consider some research on characteristics that seem to be associated with project success or failure, but sometimes it is difficult to distinguish between project failure, partial failure, and success. Indeed, what appears to be a failure at one point in the life of a project may look like success at another. If we divide all projects into two general categories according to the degree to which the project is understood, we find some interesting differences in the nature and timing of perceived difficulties in carrying out a project. These perceptions have a considerable effect on the PM.

Assume that Type 1 projects are generally well-understood, routine construction projects. Type 2 projects are at the opposite pole; they are not well understood, and there may be considerable uncertainty about specifically what must be done. When they are begun, Type 1 projects appear simple. As they progress, however, the natural flow of events will introduce problems. Mother Nature seems habitually hostile. The later in the life cycle of the project these problems appear, the more difficult it is to keep the project on its time and cost schedule. Contingency allowances for the time and cost to overcome such problems are often built into the budgets and schedules for Type 1 projects, but unless the project has considerable slack in both budget and schedule, an unlikely condition, little can be done about the problems that occur late in the project life cycle. As everyone from engineers to interior decorators knows, change orders are always received *after* the final design is set in concrete. And yet, Type 1 projects rarely fail because they are late or over budget, though they commonly are both. They fail because they are not organized to handle unexpected crises and deviations from plan and/or do not have the appropriate technical expertise to do so [37].

Type 2 projects exhibit a different set of problems. There are many difficulties early in the life of the project, most of which are so-called planning problems. By and large, these problems result from a failure to define the mission carefully and, at times, from a failure to get the client's acceptance on the project mission. Failure to define the mission leads to subsequent problems (e.g., failure to develop a proper schedule/plan, failure to have the proper personnel available to handle the technical problems that will arise, as well as failure to handle the crises that occur somewhat later in the project's life cycle) [37]. These failures often appear to result from the inability to solve the project's technical problems. In fact, they result from a failure to define project requirements and specifications well enough to deal with the technical glitches that always occur. (See Chapter 12 for a further discussion of this subject.)

Perhaps more serious are the psychic consequences of such technical snags. The occurrence and solution of technical problems tend to cause waves of pessimism and optimism to sweep over the project staff. There is little doubt that these swings of mood have a destructive effect on performance. The PM must cope with these alternating periods of elation and despair, and the task is not simple. Performance will be strongest when project team members are "turned on," but not so much that they blandly assume that "everything will turn out all right in the end," no matter what. Despair is even worse because the project is permeated with an attitude that says, "Why try when we are destined to fail?"

Maintaining a balanced, positive outlook among team members is a delicate job. Setting budgets and schedules with sufficient slack to allow for Murphy's law, but not sufficient to arouse suspicion in cost and time-conscious senior management, is also a delicate job. But who said the PM's job would be easy?

Breadth of Communication

As is the case with any manager, most of the PM's time is spent communicating with the many groups interested in the project [30]. Running a project requires constant selling, reselling, and explaining the project to outsiders, top management, functional departments, clients, and a number of other such parties-at-interest to the project, as well as to members of the project team itself. The PM is the project's liaison with the outside world, but the manager must also be available for problem solving in the lab, for crises in the field, for threatening or cajoling subcontractors, and for reducing interpersonal conflict between project team members. And all these demands may occur within the span of one day—a typical day, cynics would say.

To some extent, every manager must deal with these special demands; but for a PM such demands are far more frequent and critical. As if this were not enough, there are also certain fundamental issues that the manager must understand and deal with so that the demands noted can be handled successfully. First, the PM must know *why* the project exists; that is, the PM must fully understand the project's intent. The PM must have a clear definition of how *success* or *failure* is to be determined. When making trade-offs, it is easy to get off the track and strive to meet goals that were really never intended by top management.

Second, any PM with extensive experience has managed projects that failed. As is true in every area of business we know, competent managers are rarely ruined by a single failure, but repeated failure is usually interpreted as a sign of incompetence. On occasion a PM is asked to take over an ongoing project that appears to be heading for failure. Whether or not the PM will be able to decline such a doubtful honor depends on a great many things unique to each situation, such as the PM's relationship with the program manager, the degree of organizational desperation about the project, the PM's seniority and track record in dealing with projects like the one in question, and other matters, not excluding the PM's ability to be engaged elsewhere when the "opportunity" arises. Managing successful projects is difficult enough that the PM is, in general, well advised not to volunteer for undertakings with a high probability of failure.

Third, it is critical to have the support of top management. If support is weak, the future of the project is clouded with uncertainty. If the support is not broadly based in top management, some areas in the firm may not be willing to help the project manager when help is needed. Suppose, for example, that the marketing vice-president is not fully in support of the basic project concept. Even after all the engineering and manufacturing work has been completed, sales may not go all out to push the product. In such a case, only the chief executive officer (CEO) can force the issue, and it is very risky for a PM to seek the CEO's assistance to override a lukewarm vice-president. If the VP acquiesces and the product fails (and what are the chances for success in such a case?), the project manager looks like a fool. If the CEO does not force the issue, then the VP has won and the project manager may be out of a job. As noted earlier, political sensitivity and acumen are mandatory attributes for the project manager. The job description for a PM should include the "construction and maintenance of alliances with the leaders of functional areas."

Fourth, the PM should build and maintain a solid information network. It is critical to know what is happening both inside the project and outside it. The PM must be aware of customer complaints and department head criticism, who is favorably inclined toward the project, when vendors are planning to change prices, or if a strike is looming in a supplier industry. Inadequate information can blind the PM to an incipient crisis just as excessive information can desensitize the PM to early warnings of trouble.

Finally, the PM must be flexible in as many ways, with as many people, and about as many activities as possible throughout the entire life of the project. The

PM's primary mode of operation is to trade off resources and criteria accomplishment against one another. Every decision the PM makes limits the scope of future decisions, but failure to decide can stop the project in its tracks. Even here, we have a trade-off. In the end, regardless of the pressures, the PM needs the support of the noninvolved middle and upper-middle management.

Negotiation

In order to meet the demands of the job of project manager—acquiring adequate resources, acquiring and motivating personnel, dealing with obstacles, making project goal trade-offs, handling failure and the fear of failure, and maintaining the appropriate patterns of communication—the project manager must be a highly skilled negotiator. There is almost no aspect of the PM's job that does not depend directly on this skill. We have noted the need for negotiation at several points in the previous pages, and we will note the need again and again in the pages that follow. The subject is so important that Chapter 6 is devoted to a discussion of the matter.

▶ 3.3 SELECTING THE PROJECT MANAGER

Selection of the project manager is one of the two or three most important decisions concerning the project. In this section, we note a few of the many skills the PM should possess in order to have a reasonable chance of success.

The following is a list of some of the most popular attributes, skills, and qualities that have been sought when selecting project managers:

- A strong technical background.
- A hard-nosed manager.
- A mature individual.
- Someone who is currently available.
- Someone on good terms with senior executives.
- A person who can keep the project team happy.
- One who has worked in several different departments.
- A person who can walk on (or part) the waters.

These reasons for choosing a PM are not so much wrong as they are "not right." They miss the key criterion. Above all, the best PM is the one who can get the job done! As any senior manager knows, hard workers are easy to find. What is rare is the individual whose focus is on the completion of a difficult job. Of all the characteristics desirable in a PM, this *drive to complete the task* is the most important.

If we consider the earlier sections of this chapter, we can conclude that there are four major categories of skills that are required of the PM and serve as the key criteria for selection, given that the candidate has a powerful bias toward task completion. Moreover, it is not sufficient for the PM simply to possess these skills; they must also be perceived by others. The fact and the perception are equally important.

Credibility

The PM needs two kinds of credibility. First is *technical credibility*. The PM must be perceived by the client, senior executives, the functional departments, and the project team as possessing sufficient technical knowledge to direct the project. (We remind the reader that "technical credibility" includes technical knowledge in such arcane fields as accounting, law, psychology, anthropology, religion, history, playwriting, Greek, and a host of other non-hard sciences.) The PM does not have to have a high level of expertise, know more than any individual team members (or all of them), or be able to stand toe-to-toe and intellectually slug it out with experts in the various functional areas. Quite simply, the PM has to have a reasonable understanding of the base technologies on which the project rests, must be able to explain project technology to senior management, and must be able to interpret the technical needs and wants of the client (and senior management) to the project team.

Second, the PM must be *administratively credible*. The PM has several key administrative responsibilities that must be performed with apparently effortless skill. One of these responsibilities is to the client and senior management—to keep the project on schedule and within cost and to make sure that project reports are accurate and timely. This can place the PM in an ethically awkward situation sometimes. Another responsibility is to the project team—to make sure that material, equipment, and labor are available when needed. Still another responsibility is to represent the interests of all parties to the project (team, management, functional departments, and client) to one another. The PM is truly the "person in the middle." Finally, the PM is responsible for making the tough trade-off decisions for the project, and must be perceived as a person who has the mature judgment and courage to do so consistently.

Sensitivity

The preceding pages contain many references to the PM's need for political sensitivity. There is no point in belaboring the issue further. In addition to a good, working set of political antennae, the PM needs to sense interpersonal conflict on the project team or between team members and outsiders. Successful PMs are not conflict avoiders. Quite the opposite, they sense conflict very early and confront it before it escalates into interdepartmental and intradepartmental warfare.

The PM must keep project team members "cool." This is not easy. As with any group of humans, rivalries, jealousies, friendships, and hostilities are sure to exist. The PM must persuade people to cooperate irrespective of personal feelings, to set aside personal likes and dislikes, and to focus on achieving project goals.

Finally, the PM needs a sensitive set of technical sensors. It is common, unfortunately, for otherwise competent and honest team members to try to hide their failures. Individuals who cannot work under stress would be well advised to avoid project organizations. In the pressure-cooker life of the project, failure is particularly threatening. Remember that we staffed the team with people who are task-oriented. Team members with this orientation may not be able to tolerate their own failures (though they are rarely as intolerant of failure in others), and will hide failure rather than admit to it. The PM must be able to sense when things are being "swept under the rug" and are not progressing properly.

Leadership

Leadership has been defined [45] as "interpersonal influence, exercised in situations and directed through the communication process, toward the attainment of a specified goal or goals." But how is interpersonal influence generated? To all the skills and attributes we have mentioned, add enthusiasm, optimism, energy, tenacity, courage, and personal maturity. It is difficult to explain leadership. We tend to recognize it after the fact, rather than before. We define it anecdotally by saying that this person or that one acted like a leader. The PM must capitalize on people's strengths, cover their weaknesses, know when to take over and when to "give the team its head," know when to punish and when to reward, know when to communicate and when to remain silent. Above all, the PM must know how to get others to share commitment to the project. In a word, the PM must be a leader. (Note: [43] is an excellent article on leadership for the project manager.)

Another aspect of leadership that is important in a project manager is a strong sense of ethics. There is a considerable amount of attention to this topic in the news media these days (e.g., see [19]), both good and bad. For instance, Tylenol's decision to terminate their highly successful capsule line in the wake of the poisonings was as much an ethical decision as a marketing one. The insider trading scandals—Ivan Boesky, Michael Milken—it now appears, involved ethical issues also. Nixon [32] has identified some ethical missteps that are relatively common in business:

- "wired" bids and contracts (the winner has been predetermined)
- "buy-in" (bidding low with the intent of cutting corners or forcing subsequent contract changes)
- kickbacks
- "covering" for team members (group cohesiveness)
- taking "shortcuts" (to meet deadlines or budgets)
- using marginal (substandard) materials
- compromising on safety
- violating standards
- consultant (e.g., auditors) loyalties (to employer or to client or to public)

A project manager, particularly in the public sector, may easily become embroiled in the ethics concerning such issues as pollution, public safety, industrial plant locations, the use of public lands, and so on. There has even been a code of ethics proposed [23] for project managers at one of the annual PMI symposia, reproduced in Table 3-2. The extent of this subject is far beyond what we can cover here but, fortunately, there are a number of excellent books on the topic [4, 6, 34].

Ability to Handle Stress

Throughout this chapter and elsewhere in this book we have noted that the life of the project manager is rarely serene. While we know of no scientific research on the issue, casual observation leads us to believe that the basic environment surrounding projects is not fundamentally different from the environment existing in the par-

Table 3-2   Code of Ethics for Project Managers

PREAMBLE: Project Managers, in the pursuit of their profession, affect the quality of life for all people in our society. Therefore, it is vital that Project Managers conduct their work in an ethical manner to earn and maintain the confidence of team members, colleagues, employees, clients and the public.

ARTICLE I: Project Managers shall maintain high standards of personal and professional conduct.

   a. Accept responsibility for their actions.
   b. Undertake projects and accept responsibility only if qualified by training or experience, or after full disclosure to their employers or clients of pertinent qualifications.
   c. Maintain their professional skills at the state-of-the-art and recognize the importance of continued personal development and education.
   d. Advance the integrity and prestige of the profession by practicing in a dignified manner.
   e. Support this code and encourage colleagues and co-workers to act in accordance with this code.
   f. Support the professional society by actively participating and encouraging colleagues and co-workers to participate.
   g. Obey the laws of the country in which work is being performed.

ARTICLE II: Project Managers shall, in their work:

   a. Provide the necessary project leadership to promote maximum productivity while striving to minimize costs.
   b. Apply state-of-the-art project management tools and techniques to ensure schedules are met and the project is appropriately planned and coordinated.
   c. Treat fairly all project team members, colleagues and co-workers, regardless of race, religion, sex, age or national origin.
   d. Protect project team members from physical and mental harm.
   e. Provide suitable working conditions and opportunities for project team members.
   f. Seek, accept and offer honest criticism of work, and properly credit the contribution of others.
   g. Assist project team members, colleagues and co-workers in their professional development.

ARTICLE III: Project Managers shall, in their relations with employers and clients:

   a. Act as faithful agents or trustees for their employers or clients in professional or business matters.
   b. Keep information on the business affairs or technical processes of an employer or client in confidence while employed, and later, until such information is properly released.
   c. Inform their employers, clients, professional societies or public agencies of which they are members or to which they may make any presentations, of any circumstances that could lead to a conflict of interest.
   d. Neither give nor accept, directly or indirectly, any gift, payment or service of more than nominal value to or from those having business relationships with their employers or clients.
   e. Be honest and realistic in reporting project cost, schedule and performance.

ARTICLE IV: Project Managers shall, in fulfilling their responsibilities to the community:

   a. Protect the safety, health and welfare of the public and speak out against abuses in those areas affecting the public interest.
   b. Seek to extend public knowledge and appreciation of the project management profession and its achievements.

Source: [23]

ent organization within which the projects are being conducted. Life in some organizations is quite hectic and projects in those firms and agencies tend to be equally hectic.

There are a great many factors in life that cause stress and project managers are as subject to them as other humans. There do, however, appear to be four major causes of stress often associated with the management of projects. First, some PMs never develop a reasonably consistent set of procedures and techniques with which to manage their work. Second, many simply have "too much on their plates." Third, some have a high need to achieve that is consistently frustrated. Fourth, the parent organization is in the throes of major change.

This book is primarily devoted to helping the PM deal with the first cause of stress. As for the second cause, we would remind the PM to include him/herself as a "resource" when planning a project. Almost all project management software packages will signal the planner when a project plan calls for a resource to be used beyond its capacity (see Chapters 9 and 10). Such signals, at least, provide PMs with some evidence with which to discuss the work load with the appropriate senior manager.

Concerning the third cause of stress, Slevin [42] points out that stress results when the demands made on an individual are greater than the person's ability to cope with them, particularly when the person has a high need for achievement. It is axiomatic that senior managers give the toughest projects to their best project managers. It is the toughest projects that are most apt to be beset with unsolvable problems. The cure for such stress is obvious, except to the senior managers who continue the practice.

Finally, in this era of restructuring and downsizing, stress from worry about one's future is a common condition in modern organizations. Dealing with and reducing these stresses as well as the stress resulting from everyday life is beyond the scope of this book as well as the expertise of its authors. Fortunately, any bookstore will have entire sections devoted to the subject of stress and its relief. We refer the reader to such works.

Project Management in Practice
Selecting Project Managers at GTE Telecom, Inc.

The normal approach to selecting project managers for telecommunications projects is to select someone trained in engineering, since this person will undoubtedly have the appropriate technical background. However, GTE Telecom has found that this is an improper utilization of their resources and instead now uses managers trained in project management, free to draw upon engineering resources as needed. This allows their project managers to handle more than one project at a time and their engineers to work on multiple projects concurrently also. The project manager uses the skills concerning project

Source: V. L. Kendrick, "The Role of Project Managers in Telecommunication," *Project Management Journal*, Sept. 1990.

management—organization, scheduling, reporting, personnel selection and assignment—and the engineer uses the technical skills appropriate to the project as needed and only when needed.

This policy was formulated following three experiences with telecommunications projects, as described below. The first project was to implement a statewide multipoint data network in Indiana. An engineer was appointed to manage the project and was superior in developing the technical design and specifications for installation. However, throughout the rest of the project, the engineer continually had to seek help from another project manager for equipment ordering, dealing with purchasing, subcontractor negotiations, and coordination with operations. This was a misuse of the engineer's time, as well as a severe interruption of a project manager working on another project.

The second project involved the construction of a fiber optic route to extend a statewide fiber network to a new city. A project manager was assigned to this project and drew upon engineering, purchasing, contracts, operations, finance, and training, while still performing his project management functions

of schedule maintenance, monitoring subcontractors, and controlling expenditures. The project required four months to complete and on the final walkthrough, engineers were called in to check for any discrepancies from specs. But the project manager identified an over-billing error due to a construction over-estimate and received a $35,000 credit on the cost of the project.

The third project required the construction of a point-to-point fiber optic facility within a metropolitan area to provide connectivity to a statewide backbone network. An off-site project manager was assigned as team leader for this project with a full-time, on-site engineer as the local contact. The engineer spent full time monitoring the technical work and was able to identify problems early and inform the project manager, who then intervened to avoid the problems, in one case renegotiating with a subcontractor for additional resources to avoid a schedule delay. Thus, the engineer only needed to concern himself with technical aspects of the project and the project manager handled all negotiations and non-technical functions, such as progress reports, contract negotiation, departmental coordination, and vendor interfacing.

▶ SUMMARY

This chapter addressed the subject of the PM, a *super-manager*. The PM's role in the organization and responsibilities to both the organization and the project team were discussed first. Common PM career paths were also described. Next, the unique demands typically placed on project managers were detailed. Finally, the task of selecting the PM was addressed.

The following specific points were made in the chapter.

Two factors crucial to the success of the project are its support by top management and the existence of a problem orientation, rather than discipline orientation, within the team members.

Compared to a functional manager, a PM is a generalist rather than a specialist, a synthesizer rather than an analyst, and a facilitator rather than a supervisor.

The PM has responsibilities to the parent organization, the project itself, and the project team.

The unique demands on a PM concern seven areas:

- Acquiring adequate physical resources
- Acquiring and motivating personnel
- Dealing with obstacles
- Making goal trade-offs

- Maintaining a balanced outlook in the team
- Communicating with all parties
- Negotiating

The most common characteristics of effective project team members are

- High-quality technical skills
- Political sensitivity
- Strong problem orientation
- High self-esteem

To handle the variety of project demands effectively, the PM must understand the basic goals of the project, have the support of top management, build and maintain a solid information network, and remain flexible about as many project aspects as possible.

The best person to select as PM is the one who will get the job done.

Valuable skills for the PM are technical and administrative credibility, political sensitivity, and an ability to get others to commit to the project, a skill otherwise known as leadership.

In the next chapter we move to the first task of the PM, organizing the project. We deal there not only with various organizational forms, such as functional, project, and matrix, but also with the organization of the *project office*. This task includes setting up the project team and managing the human element of the project.

▶ GLOSSARY

Analytic Approach—Breaking problems into their constituent parts to understand the parts better and thereby solve the problem.

Benefit-Cost—A ratio to evaluate a proposed course of action.

Champion—A person who spearheads an idea or action and "sells" it throughout the organization.

Contingency Plan—An alternative for action if the expected result fails to materialize.

Discipline—An area of expertise.

Facilitator—A person who helps people overcome problems, either with technical issues or with other people.

Functional—One of the standard organization disciplines such as finance, marketing, accounting or operations.

Systems Approach—A wide-ranging, synthesizing method for addressing problems that considers multiple and interacting relationships. Commonly contrasted with the analytic approach.

Technological—Having to do with the methods and techniques for doing something.

Trade-Off—Allowing one aspect to get worse in return for another aspect getting better.

Tweed Coat Management—The concept that highly educated people such as engineers require a special type of management.

▶ MATERIAL REVIEW QUESTIONS

1. How does the project act as a stepping-stone for the project manager's career?
2. What are the main responsibilities of the project manager to his or her firm?
3. Name the categories of skills that should be considered in the selection of a project manager.
4. Why must the project manager be a generalist rather than a specialist?
5. Discuss the PM's responsibilities toward the project team members.
6. What are the major differences between functional managers and project managers?
7. What are some of the essential characteristics of effective project team members?
8. What is the most important characteristic of a project manager?
9. What project goals are most important during the project life cycle stages?
10. Why must project management team members have good technical skills?
11. Why does the project manager need to be a good negotiator?

▶ CLASS DISCUSSION QUESTIONS

1. Elaborate on " . . . it is not sufficient for the PM simply to possess these skills; they must also be perceived by others."

2. Can you think of several ways to assure "breadth of communication" in a project? Do you think "socialization" off the job helps or hinders?

3. Contrast the prime law for projects, "Never surprise the boss," with the corporate adage "Bad news never travels up."

4. "The successful PM is a fire fighter by avocation." How much do you think fire fighting is a result of the PM's style? Can some project managers anticipate problems better than others? Do some PMs create their own fires, perhaps out of a love for fire fighting?

5. Discuss why the project manager must be an overachiever.

6. How does a project manager, in some cases, work like a politician?

7. What are some of the conflicts that are bound to occur between parties that have legitimate interests in the project?

8. Project managers must be generalists rather than specialists. Yet, team members need to have more specialized, technical skills. Can a generalist manage a team of specialists effectively?

9. Why do you think cost drops in importance as an objective right after the formation stage?

10. Why is it more difficult to keep the project on its time and cost schedules the later the project gets in its life cycle?

11. Suppose you have a talented scientist temporarily working for you on a client contract who is due to be transferred back to her regular job. Although you could do without her efforts at this point of the contract, you happen to know that she will be laid off for lack of work at her regular job and her personal financial stituation is dire. You feel it is important that her talent be kept on the company payroll, although keeping her on the contract will increase expenses unnecessarily. Is the transfer decision a business decision or an ethical one? Why? If the decision were yours to make, what would you decide?

▶ INCIDENTS FOR DISCUSSION

Smithson Company

Eric Smithson is the CEO of the Smithson Company, a privately owned, medium-size manufacturing company. The company is 20 years old and, until recently, had experienced rapid growth. Mr. Smithson believes that the company's recent problems are closely related to the depressed U.S. economy.

Jane Smatters was hired as the director of corporate planning at Smithson six months ago. After reviewing the performance and financial statements of Smithson for the last few years, Ms. Smatters has come to the conclusion that the economic conditions are not the real problem, but rather exacerbate the real problems. She believes that Smithson Company products are becoming obsolete and that the company has done a bad job of reacting to market threats and opportunities. She also believes that the strong functional organization impedes the kinds of action required to remedy the situation. Accordingly, she has recommended that Mr. Smithson create a new position, manager of special operations, to promote and use project management techniques. The new manager would handle several critical projects in the role of project manager.

Mr. Smithson is cool to the idea. He believes that his functional departments are managed by capable professional people. Why can't these high-level managers work together more efficiently? Perhaps a good approach would be for him (Smithson) to give the group some direction (what to do, when to do it, who should do it) and then put the functional manager most closely related to the problems in charge of the group. He assumes that the little push from him (Smithson) as just described would be enough to "get the project rolling."

Questions: After this explanation Ms. Smatters is more convinced than ever that a separate, nonfunctional project manager is required. Is she right? If you were Smatters, how would you sell Mr. Smithson on the idea? If a new position is created, what other changes should be made?

Ohio Hospital

A 500-bed hospital in Ohio is in the planning and design stage of adding a new ambulatory service building and is scheduled to begin construction in two months. The engineering department is normally responsible for assigning a project manager for all projects within the hospital. Currently, the engineering department has no one with experience in the construction of an entire building. As a result, the president is considering using the architectural firm that is currently designing the building to do the project management as well. The engineering division head believes his senior project engineer can handle the job for three reasons: she has a good technical background, she pays meticulous attention to detail, and she is currently available.

Questions: If you were the president, what would your choice be? Why? What additional information would you try to obtain before making a decision? Would someone with experience in building construction be an even better choice?

▶ INDIVIDUAL EXERCISE

Assume that your class is faced with the task of producing an answer manual for this book within the next month. Assume that all pedagogical material has to have answers—all the questions, the exercises, the incidents, the problems, the cases. List the characteristics you would look for in choosing a classmate to lead this project. Then compare your list with the advice given in this chapter. What are the differences? Why do they exist? Would your list of characteristics differ if this project constituted 15 percent of your grade as compared to 85 percent? How would the list vary if you were the instructor and were attempting to choose a PM?

▶ PROJECT TEAM CONTINUING EXERCISE

The project team now needs to select its project manager. It should detail the various factors important in the selection of a PM and evaluate each member on each of the factors. A weighted scoring model might be appropriate here, with the heaviest weight on ability to get the job done. It is also important that the PM have the support of top management (the instructor) and be a talented facilitator rather than a knowledgeable supervisor.

Following selection of the PM, the team should proceed to evaluate the team members in terms of their effectiveness on the project. Pay particular attention to having a problem orientation rather than a discipline (e.g., marketing, finance) orientation.

▶ BIBLIOGRAPHY

1. ARCHIBALD, R. D. *Managing High Technology Programs and Projects.* New York: Wiley, 1976.

2. ATKINS, W. "Selecting a Project Manager." *Journal of Systems Management,* Oct. 1980.

3. AVOTS, I. "Making Project Management Work: The Right Tools for the Wrong Project Manager." S.A.M. *Advanced Management Journal,* Autumn 1975.

4. BARRY, V. *Moral Issues in Business.* Belmont, CA: Wadsworth, 1979.

5. BEER, S. *Diagnosing The System for Organizations.* New York: Wiley, 1985.

6. BLANCHARD, K., and N. V. PEALE. *The Power of Ethical Management.* New York: Morrow, 1988.

7. BOULDING, K. E. "General Systems Theory—The Skeleton of Science." *Management Science,* Vol. 2, No. 3, April 1956.

8. CHURCHMAN, C. W., *The Systems Approach,* rev.ed. New York: Delta, 1979.

9. FRIEND, F. L. "Be a More Effective Program Manager." *Journal of Systems Management*, Feb. 1976.

10. GADDIS, P. O. "The Project Manager." *Harvard Business Review*, May–June 1959.

11. GAGNON, R. J. *An Exploratory Analysis of the Relevant Cost Structure of Internal and External Engineering Consulting*, Ph.D. dissertation. Cincinnati: University of Cincinnati, 1982.

12. GAGNON, R. J., and S. J. MANTEL, JR. "Strategies and Performance Improvement for Computer-Assisted Design." *IEEE Transactions on Engineering Management*, Nov. 1987.

13. GEMMILL, G. R., and H. J. THAMHAIN. "The Power Styles of Project Managers: Some Efficiency Correlates." 20th Annual JEMC, *Managing for Improved Engineering Effectiveness*, Oct. 1972.

14. GEMMILL, G. R., and H. J. THAMHAIN. "Project Performance as a Function of the Leadership Styles of Project Managers: Results of a Field Study." *Convention Digest*. Philadelphia: 4th Annual Meeting of the Project Management Institute, Oct. 1972

15. GEMMILL, G. R., and H. J. THAMHAIN. "The Effectiveness of Different Power Styles of Project Managers in Gaining Project Support." *IEEE Transactions on Engineering Management*, May 1973.

16. GEMMILL, G. R., and H. J. THAMHAIN. "Influence Styles of Project Managers: Some Project Performance Correlates." *Academy of Management Journal*, June 1974.

17. GEMMILL, G. R., and D. L. WILEMON. "The Product Manager as an Influence Agent," *Journal of Marketing*, Jan. 1976.

18. GOODMAN, R. A. "Ambiguous Authority Definitions in Project Management." *Academy of Management Journal*, Dec. 1967.

19. HAGER, B. "What's Behind Business' Sudden Fervor for Ethics." *Business Week*, Sept. 22, 1991.

20. HAMBURGER, D. H. "The Project Manager: Risk Taker and Contingency Planner." *Project Management Journal.*, June and Dec. 1990.

21. HERZBERG, F. H. "One More Time: How Do You Motivate Employees?" *Harvard Business Review*, Jan.–Feb. 1968.

22. HODGETTS, R. M., "Leadership Techniques in the Project Organization." *Academy of Management Journal*, June 1968.

23. IRELAND, L. R., W. J. PIKE, and J. L. SCHROCK. "Ethics for Project Managers". *Proceedings of the 1982 PMI Seminar/Symposium on Project Management*, Toronto, Ont., Canada.

24. KIERCHNER, E. "The Project Manager." *Space Aeronautics*, Feb. 1965.

25. KLOPPENBORG, T. J., and S. J. MANTEL, JR. "Trade offs on Projects: They May Not Be What You Think." *Project Management Journal*, March 1990.

26. KOTTER, J. P. "What Effective General Managers Really Do." *Harvard Business Review*, Nov.–Dec. 1982.

27. LAWRENCE, P. R., and J. W. LORSCH. "New Management Job: The Integrator." *Harvard Business Review*, Nov.–Dec. 1967.

28. MAIELI, V. "Management by Hindsight: Diary of a Project Manager." *Management Review*, June 1971.

29. MELCHNER, A. J., and T. A. KAYSER. "Leadership Without Formal Authority: The Project Department." *California Management Review*, Winter 1970.

30. MINTZBERG, H. *The Nature of Managerial Work*. New York: Harper & Row, 1973.

31. MORTON, D. H. "The Project Manager, Catalyst to Constant Change: A Behavioral Analysis." *Project Management Quarterly*, March 1975.

32. NIXON, M. A. "Legal Lights: Business Ethics." *Project Management Journal*, Sept. 1987.

33. O'BRIEN, J. B. "The Project Manager: Not Just a Firefighter." S.A.M. *Advanced Management Journal*, Jan. 1974.

34. PASTIN, M. *The Hard Problems of Management*. San Francisco: Jossey-Bass, 1986.

35. PATTERSON, N. "Selecting Project Managers: An Integrated List of Predictors." *Project Management Journal*, June, 1991.

36. PILL, J. *Technical Management and Control of Large Scale Urban Studies: A Comparative Analysis of Two Cases*, Ph.D. dissertation. Cleveland: Case Western Reserve University, 1971.

37. PINTO, J. K., and S. J. MANTEL, JR. "The Causes of Project Failure." *IEEE Transactions on Engineering Management*, Nov. 1990.

38. PINTO, J. K., and D. P. SLEVIN "The Project Champion: Key to Implementation Success." *Project Management Journal*, Dec. 1989.

39. ROCHE, W. J., and N. L. MACKINNON. "Motivating People with Meaningful Work." *Harvard Business Review*, May–June 1970.

40. ROSENAU, M. D., JR. *Successful Project Management.* Belmont, CA: Lifetime Learning Publications, 1981.

41. RUBIN, I. M., and W. SEILIG. "Experience as a Factor in the Selection and Performance of Project Managers," *IEEE Transactions on Engineering Management,* Sept. 1967.

42. SLEVIN, D. P. *The Whole Manager.* New York: AMACOM, 1989.

43. SLEVIN, D. P., and J. K. PINTO "Project Leadership: Understanding and Consciously Choosing Your Style." *Project Management Journal,* Mar. 1991.

44. SOUDER, W. E. "Autonomy, Gratification, and R & D Output: A Small-Sample Field Study." *Management Science,* April 1974.

45. TANNENBAUM, R., and F. MASSARICK. "Leadership: A Frame of Reference." *Management Science,* Oct. 1957.

46. VAN GIGCH, J. P. *Applied General Systems Theory.* 2nd ed., New York: Harper & Row, 1978.

47. WEINBERG, G. M. *An Introduction to General Systems Thinking.* New York: Wiley, 1975.

48. WILEMON, D. L., and J. P. CICERO. "The Project Manager; Anomalies and Ambiguities." *Academy of Management Journal,* Sept. 1970.

CASE

GEARTRAIN INTERNATIONAL: MEDINA, OHIO
Jack R. Meredith

Dave Bergmann hurried back to his office following an extended CIM (computer integrated manufacturing) Task Force meeting where some important issues about the FMS (flexible manufacturing system) scheduling system had come up and needed to be addressed. He was expecting a phone call from division headquarters in Troy, Ohio about the status of the FMS Retrofit Proposal.

Coming down the narrow hall, he squeezed past Ruthie Winters, the plant manager's secretary, who was carrying a new plant for Mr. Daley's office. "A new philodendron for the boss's office?" he asked Ruthie. "Oh, hi Dave," said Ruthie. "Yes, the Boston fern was looking poorly so I'll take it home to nurse it and replace it with this in the meantime."

"Looks nice," said Dave. As he turned into his office he asked his secretary, John Shepherd, whether the call had come in yet. "Not yet, but Joan Kart dropped by and Don Morello called—the message is on your desk. Joan said she'd stop by later."

Don Morello was manager of industrial engineering for Dave and, according to his note, was having second thoughts about the overhead allocation procedure for the FMS. Joan Kart, also in IE, was senior project engineer for the FMS Retrofit. Dave himself had started out in the industrial engineering department here at Medina in 1971, 14 long years ago, before vol-

unteering in 1981 for the position of manufacturing engineering manager for their plant in Italy. Upon returning to the States this July, four years later, he was appointed manager of manufacturing engineering at Medina, a position that had recently been vacated.

As Dave sat down at his desk, thoughts about the retrofit filled his head. While waiting for the phone call from headquarters to come through, Dave took out a pencil to make some notes concerning the project.

History of the Medina Plant

The Medina plant, built in 1951, was originally known as the Axle Division of Troy Gear & Axle Company. The building was 379,000 square feet and the site included 61 acres. Original products were transfer cases and axles for military trucks. As the Korean Conflict grew, production in Medina grew until a peak of 2000 employees was reached in 1953. With the cessation of Korean hostilities, the plant then reduced in size.

Also in 1953, Troy Gear & Axle merged with Standard Gear Company and took the name Troy Geartrain Company. In 1955 the Medina plant was enlarged to 750,000 square feet with a $3 million addition in order to consolidate axle manufacturing processes from other plants and enter the civilian truck axle market.

In 1958, the firm changed its name to the Geartrain Corporation and the Medina plant became the Transmission and Axle Division. In 1972, the company name was changed once again, to Geartrain International, and Medina was extensively reorganized. Assembly operations were transferred to a new plant set up specifically for the work in Zanesville, Ohio, and a $14 million expansion and modernization program was instituted in Medina. A flexible manufacturing system (FMS) was purchased and installed for low-volume parts and later a transfer line was installed for high-volume parts. The FMS machining time ranged from 40 to 160 minutes compared to the one minute cycle time for the transfer machine. However, the setup time on the FMS was less than 30 minutes whereas the transfer line required two days to change over to a new part. Other modernization efforts were also undertaken resulting in infrared controlled heat treat furnaces, numerically controlled (NC) machining, and so on.

Operations at Medina

As of 1985, the Medina plant is operating with 1400 employees, of whom 210 are salaried. The hourly workers are represented by two unions: United Auto Workers (UAW) and International Brotherhood of Electrical Workers (IBEW). Given the age of the plant and its location, the average hourly worker at Medina already has 24 years of seniority, and many of the youngest employees have 12 years.

With its 750,000 square feet of space, the Medina plant is one of the largest domestic facilities in Geartrain. The equipment at Medina includes 1100 various kinds of machine tools, 60 of which are NC,

and a chip conveyor almost half a mile long. Most of the operations are arranged in "cellular" form to expedite throughput and reduce lead time. There are over 25,000 detail drawings covering their product lines and 40,000 drawings for individual tooling layout and details. There are also over 10,000 tooling numbers supported in the facility. In 1982, the Zanesville facility was closed and its axle assembly operations moved back into Medina, making Medina a fully integrated manufacturing and assembly facility.

With the spin-off of plants over the years to handle various segments of the high-volume axle business, Medina's main product lines now fall in the area of low to medium volume drive axles and service components, including transfer cases. Current product mix is 45 percent military and 55 percent commercial, all produced to order.

Though it has no sales representatives and all design work is done at headquarters in Troy, Ohio, Medina is organized as a profit center and deals directly with customers when working on their orders. A worldwide competitor, Medina's sales currently run slightly over a quarter of a billion dollars a year. Their primary domestic competitor is Eaton and, offshore, the Japanese. Customer pressures have been toward improving quality while the product itself is becoming a commodity, thereby giving rise to cost pressure. Their capital budget of $5 million is a reflection of the recent recession, having been $13 million in 1982. A typical product's costs would break out about 66 percent for materials, 5 percent for labor, and 29 percent for burden.

In terms of responsibility, the plant is organized as shown in Figure 1. In the most recent reorganization, "Manufacturing" was combined with "Materials"

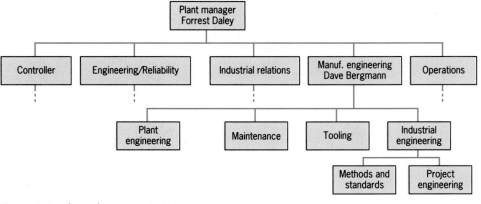

Figure 1: Medina plant organization.

into "Operations." Dave's area of responsibility, manufacturing engineering, consists of four subareas: plant engineering, maintenance, tooling, and industrial engineering. Industrial engineering (IE) consists primarily of two areas: methods and standards, the classical IE function, and project engineering, such as the FMS Retrofit.

Computer Integrated Manufacturing at Medina

When Dave took over as Manufacturing Engineering Manager he pulled the plant's various computer integrated manufacturing (CIM) projects together under one coordinating committee, the CIM Task Force. The aim of CIM at Medina is to improve quality, customer credibility, and productivity through advanced technology. The CIM committee includes representatives from manufacturing, industrial engineering (which also represents manufacturing engineering), materials, product engineering, data processing, and systems engineering (located in Troy, Ohio).

The task force's approach to integrating all the CIM projects is conceptually represented in Figure 2. At the top of the figure are the various areas of automation responsibility: manufacturing, engineering, and so on. Below these areas are the initial non-CIM methods for achieving each area's tasks (manual routings, etc.). Below these are the interim steps to becoming automated: material requirements planning (MRP I), and so forth. At the third level are the first islands of automation for achieving CIM: NC, computer aided design (CAD), computer aided process planning (CAPP), and manufacturing resource planning (MRP II). The next step, indicated by the question mark, will be to figure out how to pull all these areas together so they can communicate and provide Medina with a truly computer integrated manufacturing process.

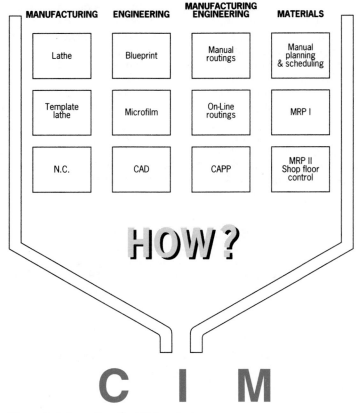

Figure 2: Integrating the CIM projects.

Medina's progress in each of these areas is continuing. The 60 NC machines largely fill their needs for now but CAD is still being implemented. The program began in April of 1984 with the approval to purchase the IBM CADAM® system for Troy headquarters and four "pilot" plants, Medina being one of the four. Five interactive work stations were provided at Medina, walls were torn down between departments, personnel were given four weeks of training, and a split shift was instituted to better utilize the work stations. In January 1985 drawings were successfully transmitted from Troy to Medina, and the CADAM UNI-APT® postprocessor created an NC part program from picture and word input. To date, about 1000 of Medina's tool drawings have been put on the system and the engineers are delighted with the result, stating that it clearly has improved their productivity by 300 percent.

Medina is also working on other areas of CIM, such as group technology and manufacturing resource planning. Currently, their MRP module is being run in batch mode over phone lines to Houston where centralized computing is located. Although there are no terminals in the factory as yet, shop floor control and capacity requirements planning modules are in the planning stages. The transfer machine and FMS are clearly major pieces of the CIM effort.

Medina's FMS

The original impetus for Medina's FMS was the condemnation of one of the Troy plants and the resulting need to produce low volume parts efficiently. Another problem was the lack of space at Medina due to increased business in higher volume lines. The solution was the transfer of assembly to Zanesville and the construction of an FMS in the newly available space.

The FMS layout is depicted in Figure 3. As can be seen, the FMS is composed of eight machining centers fed by an AGVS (automated guided vehicle system). Originally the system had six machining centers, a wash station, and a coordinate measuring machine. The coordinate measuring machine, which could never be properly interfaced with the system, and the wash station were removed in 1975 and two additional machining centers were put in their place for added capacity. (The coordinate measuring machine was sup-

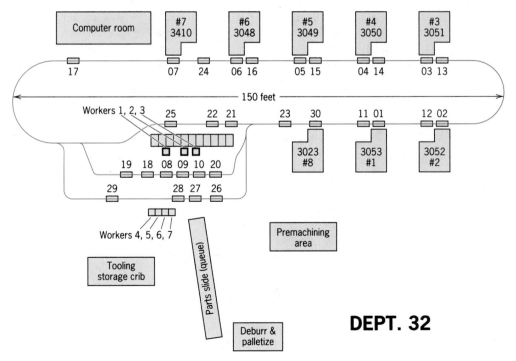

Figure 3: FMS layout.

plied by a third party and was not only inferior, but incompatible with the rest of the system.)

The AGVS includes 16 identical carts, 53 basically identical pallets, about 100 fixtures of either vertical or horizontal design, and about 150 subplates of various designs. Each cart carries a pallet with the work on it to a machine and transfers the pallet onto the machine's shuttle. (The shuttle rotates 180 degrees and can hold two pallets at a time—one that is being worked on and the other being loaded or unloaded.) Only one part, or job, is loaded on a pallet at a time. The load/unload workers build up the pallets by attaching a horizontal or vertical fixture to the pallet, depending on the job to be machined, and then bolting the most appropriate subplate onto the fixture. The part to be machined is then firmly bolted to the subplate. This is shown in Figure 4.

Through a tow–release mechanism, the AGVs follow a track of rails that run about 400 feet and include 30 zones for machine centers, load/unload stations, and accumulator (buffer) spaces. Only one cart is allowed in a zone at a time; if more than one are in a zone the computer shuts the system down. As a designated cart reaches its assigned zone, a limit switch embedded in the floor is thrown by the cart to tell the computer that the cart is in position. On occasion the carts get hung up in their position or in their load transfers to the shuttles and need a nudge from the machine operator to get them going again.

The entire system is controlled through two computers that transmit information back and forth between themselves. One computer serves as master and DNC (direct numerical control) computer for the machine tools and the other operates as a slave for the FMS system. The master handles the machine tool part program data, passes it to the machining centers, and interfaces with the machine operators.

The slave handles data files (part, route, tool, pallet), status files (machines, pallets, carts, etc.), and the AGVS. It checks and updates the files as activities are completed and the carts are moved from zone to zone. It interfaces with the AGVS through a digital multiplexor bay activated by relays, solenoids, and limit switches. It also interfaces with the load/unload crew at their stations.

Adjacent to the FMS is a dedicated tool crib. Medina maintains a total of over 10,000 different tooling numbers throughout the plant, though not all of them are used on the FMS. Here, tools are preset and staged for the next production run. The tools are delivered to the machine and manually loaded onto each machine's tool chain, which can store 59 tools at a time.

The FMS is currently programmed to machine 65 different parts in batch sizes ranging from 1 to 300. Cycle times on these parts range from 40 minutes for simple operations to 160 minutes for the most complex. Inspection is accomplished by programmed delays in the system for gauging purposes, which commonly take about five minutes each.

The FMS is currently operated by a four-person crew (two operators and two load/unload people) in the day shift and three in the evening and graveyard shifts (only one operator). Their time, and other over-

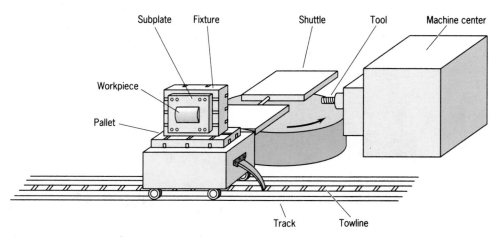

Figure 4: AGV cart and system at machine center.

head costs such as maintenance and setup, are allocated through standards for machining time. Although current plant burden rates are 250 percent variable and 300 percent fixed, the FMS is charged at 290 percent variable and 406 percent fixed due its minimal direct labor content.

The FMS Retrofit Proposal

One of the increasingly important advantages of the FMS to Medina has been its ability to replace worn out lines that made replacement parts for obsolete products. The FMS has also been particularly good for low volume startups on new products, especially prototypes.

However, the Medina FMS was one of the very early FMS installations and some aspects of the system tended to become bottlenecks or problems as the system throughput increased. About four years previously, Medina began to experience trouble with some of the electronic components. Fortunately, they had excellent electrical maintenance people who could solve the problems. But with age, some accuracy

problems also began to crop up. These became even more serious with the increased stress on quality by Medina's customers.

A list of the increasing maintenance problems as detailed by plant maintenance is given in Table 1. In essence, severe availability and compatibility problems are being experienced with replacement parts, primarily for two reasons. First, with the passage of time there are fewer suppliers and compatible replacement parts available. As noted in the table, some of the manufacturers of the FMS parts are not even in business anymore. And, of course, it is less worthwhile to keep old replacement parts for any piece of equipment, particularly one-of-a-kind equipment.

Secondly, as the FMS parts age, more and more components start wearing out and requiring replacement. Also, new or slightly different replacement parts place a heavier load on the existing parts until the new parts have "worn in," thus leading to even more failures of existing marginal parts.

Plant maintenance's comments about the system are typified by the following: "The printer is operating only by the grace of God. At present, it ejects three

---

Table 1. FMS Evaluation by Plant Maintenance

Category I: FMS Serviceability

1. FMS Computers: Serious incompatibility problems with new computer boards because of this being a prototype system. The computers are no longer serviced by the manufacturer and expensive third-party service is thus required.
2. 5MB Disk Drives: Obsolete; no longer serviced by manufacturer.
3. Digital Multiplexor Bay: Obsolete; no part availability; no longer serviced by manufacturer.
4. Hard Disk (for NC programs): Obsolete; no longer serviced by manufacturer.
5. Line Printer: Obsolete; manufacturer gone bankrupt.
6. Software: Obsolete; a prototype system no longer supported; written in an obsolete version of Fortran proprietary to OEM.
7. Relay Cabinets (10): Obsolete; parts totally unavailable; if one part fails an entire cabinet-full must be rebuilt.
8. Machine Centers: 14-years-old; wear in slides, ways, and ballscrews; cannot hold tolerances adequately to continue making two critical components on the FMS.
9. Track Relays (200): Becoming unreliable; replacements totally unavailable.

Category II: FMS Malfunctions

1. FMS down three times in the last six weeks.
2. CRT down six weeks last year.
3. Electronic malfunctions five times a week (on average), each taking about four hours to repair.
4. Mechanical malfunctions (table hang-ups, center of rotation problems, and shuttle failures, most commonly) require 25 hours a week in total to repair.

pages of blank paper between each printed sheet. We have not been able to repair this and replacing the printer is impractical due to FMS software compatibility." In conclusion, they note that upward compatibility of the FMS system was not maintained by the manufacturer and thus, individual elements cannot be continually replaced because they must electrically match the old components perfectly.

The retrofit proposal includes reworking all the machines and the software to bring them up-to-date. For example, plans are to rework the three-axis machines into state-of-the-art four-axis centers with a machine tool rapid travel speed increase from the current 150 inches-per-minute to 400. Further, the dual computer system would be upgraded to a single computer, such as a DEC VAX®, with system software and machine control drives designed by one of Medina's sister firms.

Dave and his team figure that the project will probably take almost two years to complete and cost about $3.5 million. (The original installation took over two years to get all the bugs out.) The project is divided into a hardware and a software/control system stage. The hardware stage, Phase I, runs 20 months and consists primarily of remanufacturing the eight machining centers and refurbishing the material handling system. The machines would be sent out two at a time for remanufacturing with a turnaround of approximately 20 weeks. This would allow the FMS to continue operating at Medina with a reduced operating capacity from the six remaining machines.

Phase II, the control system stage, consists of installing hardware and software and will run about 55 weeks, most of it concurrent with Phase I. The project would start in mid-1986 and finish in mid-1988 but over 90 percent of the expense would occur in 1987.

The proposal identified the approximate cost savings the retrofit would bring. Based on the current $12 million worth of parts put through the FMS, annual savings would accrue in four areas:

1.	Labor (@ 75% efficiency):	$20,000
2.	Maintenance:	
	Indirect repair labor	30,000
	Outside support	15,000
	Parts	50,000
3.	Scrap and rework (35% reduction):	10,000
4.	Reduced part subcontracting:	100,000

If the proposal is *not* funded, then additional outsourcing will be required at an annual expense of $200,000, plus a one-time, up-front tooling expense of $75,000.

However, there are some non-cost elements of the retrofit project that Forrest Daley also pointed out in the proposal. Perhaps chief among these was Medina's "plant mission" as Geartrain's supplier of low to mid-volume strategic parts such as product variations, prototypes, service parts, and general "cats and dogs." Strategic parts were defined in the proposal as "key proprietary components integral to our differential carrier and drive axle assemblies requiring close, in-house control of quality." Outsourcing these strategic parts would result in Geartrain losing control over both the proprietary manufacturing process and the required quality of the key parts.

As the proposal concluded: "This program is critical in supporting Medina's continuing role within the Corporation as a low-cost, highly flexible supplier of quality components. We must take some action if Medina is to continue over the long term manufacturing components on this line that will meet our world-class quality criterion."

Conclusion

The problem facing Dave was the amount of work that needed to be done in so many areas of technology. Although the *plant* was not particularly busy at the present time, no one seemed to realize that this is exactly when the staff are the busiest. The workloads are always countercyclic due to a number of reasons. First, when production volumes are down, there are more runs of smaller batches which thus require more tooling, more setup, and more of everything that is of a staff nature.

Second, when production, and thus profit, is lower, there is more need for cost improvement and other such "staff" types of programs (value analysis, zero defects, and so on). For example, with the reduced workload in the plant they now were instituting an SQC (statistical quality control) program. The FMS project was being undertaken at this time because throughput demand was lower than previously. For example, it was now running at only 92 percent utilization of two-shift capacity (one shift = 1800 labor hours/year).

Yet, because profits are down, Dave can't ask for additional people to help him accomplish the work.

Firms are more in a layoff mode of operation at such times, not a hiring mode. To hire staff while laying off line workers would certainly anger the employees.

But Dave was concerned about other CIM issues as well. For instance, due to the extreme seniority of the employees, the plant would be losing a number of skilled, knowledgeable employees in the next few years. How would he get the needed production information to new workers? CIM could be a big help with this problem by capturing the knowledge base of the employees in the computer system: drawings, specifications, tooling lists, setup instructions, feeds and speeds, gauges and checks, standards, volumes, materials, lot sizes, routings, suppliers, maintenance requirements, and so on.

Dave's major concern in this whole area related back to tying all the CIM elements together—determining a coherent "manufacturing strategy," or "technology strategy," in this process. In a way, he felt that this should be articulated, or at least coordinated,

from headquarters at Troy. But perhaps they felt too far removed from the daily operations in their various plants to elaborate such a strategy. Perhaps they were waiting for Mr. Daley and other plant managers to tell *them* how to implement these technologies. Would Forrest Daley then expect Dave to lay out the strategy or at least sketch in the outline of some potential such strategies?

It seemed to Dave that the FMS retrofit project should play a major role in this strategy, somehow. Although the cost savings from the retrofit were not impressive—neither an ROI nor a payback calculation was even included in the proposal—the project seemed to offer valuable intangible benefits that superseded the issue of costs. Even if the future of the plant depended on the project, could costs really be ignored? As Dave leaned back to consider the implications of all this, his secretary knocked on his door: "Your call from Troy, Mr. Bergmann."

▶ QUESTIONS FOR DISCUSSION

1. What are the payback and ROI of the retrofit proposal?

2. How important is Medina's "plant mission" to Geartrain?

3. Assume Geartrain does not have the liquid funds to invest in the FMS retrofit project. If you were their vice-president of finance, would you recommend borrowing at 17 percent interest to fund this project? What if you were the president?

4. What should Medina's strategy be and where does the FMS fit into it? Where does CIM fit into the strategy?

5. Is Dave also a project manager? What are the projects?

6. What should Dave do?

▶ The following article integrates two views about the requirements for good project managers. One view concerns the personal and managerial characteristics of PMs and their ability to lead a team, regardless of the project. The other view considers the critical problems in the project in question and the PM's talents relative to these problems.

A survey is first described and then the critical problems that projects face are identified from the survey responses. Next, the skills required of project managers, as indicated by the survey respondents, are detailed. Last, the skills are related back to the critical project problems for an integrated view of the requirements for a successful project manager.

READING

WHAT IT TAKES TO BE A GOOD PROJECT MANAGER
Barry Z. Posner

Selecting a good project manager is not a simple task. Being an effective project manager is an ongoing challenge. The complex nature and multifaceted range of activities involved in managing projects precludes easily identifying managerial talent and continually stretches the capabilities of talented project managers. Two seemingly contradictory viewpoints have been advanced about what is required to be a good project manager.

One perspective prescribes a set of *personal characteristics* necessary to manage a project [1]. Such personal attributes include aggressiveness, confidence, poise, decisiveness, resolution, entrepreneurship, toughness, integrity, versatility, multidisciplinary, and quick thinking.

However, Daniel Roman [2] maintains that it would take an extraordinary individual to have all of these critical personal characteristics. A more practical solution, he suggests, would be to determine the *critical problems* faced by project managers and to select a person who can handle such difficulties. The shortcoming with this second perspective, argue those like Michael Badaway [3], is that the primary problems of project managers are really not technical ones. The reason managers fail at managing projects, he contends, is because they lack critical organization and management skills.

Scholars like Roman and Badaway—as well as practitioners—may actually be raising different issues. On the one hand, good project managers understand the critical problems which face them and are prepared to deal with them. On the other hand, managing projects well requires a set of particular attributes and skills. But, are these two viewpoints really at odds with one another? In this study they were discovered to be two sides of the *same* coin!

Study of Project Manager Problems and Skills

Questionnaires were completed by project managers during a nationwide series of project management seminars. Project managers attending these seminars came from a variety of technology-oriented organizations. Responses to the survey instrument were both voluntary and confidential.

Information about the respondents and the nature of their projects was collected. The typical project manager was a 37-year-old male, had nine people reporting to him, and was responsible for a small to moderate size project within a matrix organization structure. More specifically, there were 189 men and 98 women in the sample (N = 287) and their ages ranged from 22 to 60 years of age (X = 37.4, S.D. = 8.3). Fifty-six percent indicated that they were the formal manager of the project. The size of their immediate project group ranged from 2 to over 100 people (median = 8.9). Fifty-nine percent reported that they worked primarily on small projects (involving few people or functions, with a short time horizon) as compared to large projects (involving many people or functions, with a long time horizon). More than 63 percent indicated they were working within a matrix organization structure. No information was collected about the specific nature (e.g., new product development, R & D, MIS) of their projects.

Two open-ended questions were asked (their order was randomized). The first asked about the skills necessary to be a successful project manager. The second question investigated the most likely problems encountered in managing projects. Responses to these questions were content analyzed. Content analysis is a systematic approach to data analysis, resulting in both qualitative assessments and quantitative information. Each respondent comment was first coded and then recoded several times as patterns of responses became apparent. The two questions were:

1. What factors or variables are *most* likely to cause you problems in managing a project?

2. What *personal* characteristics, traits, or skills make for "above average" project managers? What specific behaviors, techniques, or strategies do "above average" project managers use (or use better than their peers)?

Problems in Managing Projects

There were nearly 900 statements about what factors or variables created "problems" in managing a project. Most of these statements could be clustered into eight categories as shown in Table 1.

Inadequate resources was the issue most frequently mentioned as causing problems in managing a project. "No matter what the type or scope of your project," wrote one engineering manager, "if insufficient resources are allocated to the project, you have to be a magician to be successful." Not having the necessary budget or personnel for the project was a frequent complaint. However, the specific resource of *time*—and generally the lack thereof—was mentioned just about as often as the general inadequate resource lament. Typically, the problem of time was expressed as "having to meet unrealistic deadlines."

That resources are inadequate is caused by many factors, not the least of which being that resources are generally limited and costly. Before this hue is dismissed by veteran project managers as just so much bellyaching—"after all, there are never enough resources to go around"—it is important to examine the cause(s) of this problem. Respondents pointed out that resource allocation problems were usually created by senior management's failure to be clear about project objectives, which in turn, resulted in poor planning efforts. These two problems—lack of clear goals and effective planning—were specifically mentioned by more than 60 percent of the respondents. It is painfully obvious that vague goals and insufficient planning lead to mistakes in allocating the resources needed by project managers.

The three most significant problems reported by first-line research, development, and engineering su-

Table 1 Project Management Problems

1. Resources inadequate (69)
2. Meeting ("unrealistic") deadlines (67)
3. Unclear goals/direction (63)
4. Team members uncommitted (59)
5. Insufficient planning (56)
6. Breakdowns in communications (54)
7. Changes in goals and resources (42)
8. Conflicts between departments or functions (35)

Note: Numbers in parentheses represent percentage of project managers whose response was included in this cluster.

pervisors in Lauren Hitchcock's {4} study parallels those identified by project managers. He found "insufficient definition of policy from top downward, how to define the goal of a problem, and budgeting and manpower assignments" to be the major problems confronting supervisors. It remains true that senior management needs to articulate clearly where the project should be going, why, and what it expects from project personnel.

When project goals are not clear, it is difficult (if not impossible) to plan the project efficiently. The lack of planning contributes directly to unrealistic resource allocations and schedules. People assigned to the project are unlikely, therefore, to commit energetically to the endeavor. The lack of commitment (and poor motivation) among project personnel was reported as emerging more from the problems already mentioned than from issues associated with the project's technology or organizational structure (e.g., matrix form).

The communication breakdowns (problems which occur during the life of a project) were often referred to as "inevitable." These breakdowns occur as a result of the ambiguity surrounding the project, but also result from difficulties in coordinating and integrating diverse perspectives and personalities. The project manager's challenge is to handle communication breakdowns as they arise rather than being able to predict (and control) communication problems before they happen.

How the problems confronting project managers were interrelated is exemplified by how frequently problems of communication and dealing with conflicts were linked by respondents. The linkage between these two issues was demonstrated in statements like: "My problem is being able to effectively communicate with people when we disagree over priorities." "Conflicts between departments end up as major communication hassles." Conflicts between departments were also linked to earlier problems of poor goal-setting and planning.

Managing changes (e.g., in goals, specifications, resources, etc.) contributed substantially to project management headaches. This was often mentioned as "Murphy's Law," highlighting the context or environment in which project management occurs. Planning cannot accurately account for future possibilities (or better yet, unknowns). Interestingly, less than one in ten project managers mentioned directly a "technological" factor or variable as significantly causing them problems in managing a project.

Project Manager Skills

The second issue investigated was what project manager skills—traits, characteristics, attributes, behaviors, techniques—make a difference in successfully managing projects. Most respondents easily generated four to five items which they believed made the difference between average and superior project performance. The result was nearly 1400 statements. These statements were summarized into six skill areas as shown in Table 2. Several factors within each are highlighted.

Eighty-four percent of the respondents mentioned "being a good communicator" as an essential project manager skill. Being persuasive or being able to sell one's ideas was frequently mentioned as a characteristic of a good communicator within the project management context. Many people also cited the importance of receiving information, or good listening skills. As one systems engineer exclaimed: "The good project managers manage not by the seat of their pants but by the soles of their feet!"

Organizational skills represented a second major set of competencies. Characteristics included in this category were planning and goal-setting abilities, along with the ability to be analytical. The ability to prioritize, captured in the phrases "stays on track" and "keeps the project goals in perspective," was also identified as significant.

While successful project managers were viewed as good problem solvers, what really differentiated them from their so-so counterparts was their problem *finding* ability. Because of their exceptional communication skills, goal clarity and planning, effective project managers were aware of issues *before* they became problems. Problem finding gave them greater degrees of freedom, enabling them to avoid being seriously sidetracked by problems caused by unforeseen events.

The important team building skills involved developing empathetic relationships with other members of the project team. Being sensitive to the needs of others, motivating people, and building a strong sense of team spirit were identified as essential for effectively managing a project. "The best project managers use a lot of *'we'* statements in describing the project," wrote one computer programmer. Being clear about the project's objectives and subsequently breaking down the project into its component parts (e.g., schedules) helped project participants to understand their interdependencies and the need for teamwork.

Several different attributes and behaviors were catalogued under leadership skills. These included setting a good example, seeing the big picture, being enthusiastic, having a positive outlook, taking initiative, and trusting people. Having a vision is closely related to goal clarity (which was included as an organizational skill). The leadership component of this competency was best expressed by one financial analyst as "the ability to see the forest through the trees."

Since, as is often lamented, the only constant in managing a project is change, successful project managers require coping or stress-management skills. Respondents indicated that both flexibility and creativity were involved in effectively dealing (or coping) with change, as were patience and persistence. What project managers experience are generally high levels of stress. How well they handle stress ("grace under pressure") significantly affects their eventual success or failure.

The final cluster of skills was labeled technological. Successful project managers were seen as having relevant experience or knowledge about the technology required by the project. Seldom, however, were effective project managers seen as technological "experts." Indeed, expertise was often felt to be detrimental because it decreased flexibility and the willing-

Table 2   **Project Management Skills**

1. Communication Skills (84)
   • Listening
   • Persuading
	4. Leadership Skills (68)
	   • Sets example
	   • Energetic
	   • Vision (big picture)
	   • Delegates
	   • Positive

2. Organizational Skills (75)
   • Planning
   • Goal-setting
   • Analyzing
	5. Coping Skills (59)
	   • Flexibility
	   • Creativity
	   • Patience
	   • Persistence

3. Team Building Skills (72)
   • Empathy
   • Motivation
   • Esprit de corps
	6. Technological Skills (46)
	   • Experience
	   • Project knowledge

Note: Numbers in parentheses represent the percentage of project managers whose response was included in this cluster.

ness to consider alternative perspectives. Project managers do need to be sufficiently well versed in the technology to be able to ask the right questions because, as one senior military officer pointed out, "you've got to be able to know when people are blowing smoke at you."

Skills and Problems: Fundamentally Interconnected

It has been argued in the literature that project managers require certain skills in order to be effective. It has also been argued that project managers need to be able to handle certain problems in order to be effective. The results of this study suggest that these two perspectives are not contradictory but are fundamentally compatible. When the set of required skills is considered side-by-side with the set of critical problems project managers face, the complementary nature of these two perspectives is evident. This is illustrated in Table 3.

Without arguing which comes first, it is clear that either (a) project managers require certain skills in order to deal effectively with the factors most likely to create problems for them in managing the project, or (b) because certain problems are most likely to confront project managers, they require particular skills in order to handle them.

While this one-on-one matching in Table 3 obviously oversimplifies the dynamic nature of project management, it does have an inherent logical appeal. Since communication breakdowns are likely to create project management problems, effective project managers need to cultivate their communications (persuading and listening) skills. Project managers with good organizational skills are likely to be more effective at planning and subsequently allocating resources. Unless project managers are able to build strong project teams they are likely to be plagued by problems caused by poorly committed team members and interdepartmental conflict. Project goals are likely to be more easily understood when the project manager's leadership is consistent. Interpersonal conflicts will likely diminish when project managers set clear standards of performance and demonstrate their trust in, and respect for, others. The inevitable changes which accompany any project will be less problematic when not only coped with calmly, but also when handled with flexibility and creativity. Finally, problems

Table 3 Skills↔Problems: Interconnected in Project Management

Communication	Breakdowns in communications
Organizational	Insufficient planning
	Resources inadequate
Team Building	Team members uncommitted
	Weak inter-unit integration
Leadership	Unclear goals/direction
	Interpersonal conflicts
Coping	Handling changes
Technological	Meeting ("unrealistic") deadlines

created when deadlines and schedules are unrealistic may be minimized through a project manager's problem finding ability and experience in getting things back on track.

What was found underscores the claim that the primary problems of project managers are not technical, but human. Improving project managers' technological capabilities will be helpful only to the extent that this improves their ability to communicate, be organized, build teams, provide leadership, and deal comfortably with change. The challenge for *technical* managers, or for those moving from technical into managerial positions, is to recognize the need for, and to develop where necessary, their interpersonal skills.

References

1. Archibald, R. D. *Managing High-Technology Programs and Projects.* New York: John Wiley & Sons, 1976; Kernzer, H. *Project Management for Executives.* New York: Van Nostrand Reinhold, 1982; Stuckenbruck, L., "Ten Attributes of the Proficient Project Manager." *Proceedings of the Project Management Institute,* Montreal, 1976, 40–47; and Thamhain, H. and Wilemon, D., "Skill Requirements of Engineering Project Managers." *Twenty-Sixth IEEE Joint Engineering Management Conference,* 1978.

2. Roman, D. D. *Managing Projects: A Systems Perspective.* New York: Elsevier Science Publishing, 1985.

3. Badaway, M. *Developing Managerial Skills in Scientists and Engineers.* New York: Van Nostrand Reinhold, 1982.

4. Hitchcock, L. "Problems of First-Line Supervisors." *Research Management* Vol. 10 (6), 1967, 385–397.

CHAPTER

4

Project Organization

A firm, if successful, usually tends to grow, adding resources and people, developing an organizational structure. Commonly, the focus of the structure is specialization of the human elements of the group. As long as its organizational structure is sufficient to the tasks imposed on it, the structure tends to persist. When the structure begins to inhibit the work of the firm, pressures arise to reorganize along some other line. The underlying principle will still be specialization, but the specific nature of the specialization will be changed [see 24].

Any elementary management textbook covers the common bases of specialization [see 60, for example]. In addition to the ever-popular functional division, firms organize by product line, by geographic location, by production process, by type of customer, by subsidiary organization, by time, and by the elements of vertical or horizontal integration. Indeed, large firms frequently organize by several of these methods at different levels. For example, a firm may organize by major subsidiaries at the top level; the subsidiaries organize by product groups; and the product groups organize into customer divisions. These, in turn, may be split into functional departments that are further broken down into production process sections, which are set up as three-shift operating units.

When projects are initiated, two issues immediately arise. First, a decision must be made about how to tie the project to the parent firm. Second, a decision must be made about how to organize the project itself.

In the previous chapter we discussed the selection of the project manager (PM) and described the difficulties and responsibilities inherent in the PM's role. This chapter focuses on the interface between the project and its parent organization (i.e., how the project is organized as a part of its host). In the latter part of this chapter, we begin a discussion of how the project itself is organized, a discussion that will be continued in the next chapter.

First we look at the three major organizational forms commonly used to house projects and see just how each of them fits into the parent organization. We examine the advantages and disadvantages of each form, and discuss some of the critical factors that might lead us to choose one form over the others. We then consider some combinations of the fundamental forms and briefly examine the implications of using combination structures. Finally, we discuss some of the details of organizing the project team, describing the various roles of the project staff. We also describe some of the behavioral problems that face any project team.

To our knowledge, it is rare for a PM to have much influence over the interface between the organization and the project, choice of interface usually being made by senior management. The PM's work, however, is strongly affected by the project's structure, and the PM should understand its workings. Experienced PMs do seem to mold the project's organization to fit their notions of what is best. One project team member of our acquaintance remarked at length about how different life was on two projects (both matrix organized) run by different PMs. A study of the subtle impacts of the PM on project structure are beyond the scope of this book and deserve more attention from researchers in the behavioral sciences. (For an excellent review of relevant research, see [52].)

Project Management in Practice
Reorganizing for Project Management at AT&T

| 1889 | 1900 | 1939 | 1964 | 1969 | 1984 |

In 1988, as a result of the deregulation of the phone industry, AT&T announced that it was going to split itself into 19 separate Strategic Business Units. One of these, Business Communications Systems (BCS), is primarily focused on the customer PBX market. Following divestiture, the executives at BCS realized that the old ways of doing business would not be competitive in the new, open market they now faced and decided to reengineer their whole process of providing PBXs to the market. They decided that organizing by project management would give them better control over their business and bring a competitive advantage to BCS. Thus, they set the goal of becoming the leader in project management in the industry.

AT&T had previously used project managers in many of its activities but in a significantly different way. For instance, it was more a project coordination responsibility that could be successfully completed

Source: D. Ono, "Implementing Project Management in AT&T's Business Communications System," PM *Network*, October 1990.

through achieving the activities on a task list. However, the position was of low status and seen as only a temporary activity serving to carry someone on to a better functional position. Thus, the reward for doing a good job was to move into a functional position and get out of project management.

BCS realized it would have to change the whole nature of the project management role, and the entire structure of the organization as well, if it were to be successful in this strategy. They needed to develop professional project managers, plus a support system to maintain their abilities and careers in project management. The managerial mentality of two or three years on a project and then moving on to a functional job had to be changed to an attitude of professional pride in project management and staying in the field for the remainder of their careers. Equally important, the organizational mentality of admiring heroic rescues of projects in trouble had to be replaced with admiration for doing a competent job from the beginning and time after time. The challenge was to survive during the years it would take to evolve into a professional project management organization.

The reorganization for project management was a major project in itself, including the areas of candidate selection, education and training, compensation, career development, organizational restructuring, and methods development. In terms of organizational structure, a National Project Management (NPM) organization was created at the corporate level reporting to the service operating vice-president. Reporting to the director of NPM were three project directors spread across the United States, a systems support organization, and a methods and support staff. Program managers, project managers, and their subordinates reported to the project directors. This structure provided an integrated, self-contained project management group.

The project management career path now consists of:

- *Trainee*: a six-month position to learn about project management.
- *Cost Analysis/Schedule Engineer*: a 6–18 month team position reporting to a project manager.
- *Site Manager*: a 6–12 month position responsible for a large site and reporting to a program manager.
- *Small Project Manager*: sole responsibility for a $1M to $3M revenue project.
- *Project Manager*: responsible for $3M to $25M projects.
- *Program Manager*: responsible for multiyear projects and programs over $25M.

Candidates for the project manager career track are selected from BCS's Leadership Continuity Plan, a program to identify the people with the most potential to progress to middle and senior management levels of responsibility, as well as from career people within the organization. Particular skills sought are interpersonal leadership skills; oral and written communication skills; a presidential, big-picture perspective; political sensitivity; delegating, problem-solver orientation; optimistic, can-do attitude; planner mentality; *kaizen* (continuous improvement) spirit; and administrative, in-charge credibility.

BCS's Project Management organization now includes a staff in Denver and groups of project managers in Los Angeles, San Francisco, Atlanta, Chicago, Washington D.C., and New York City. These groups now manage over $500 million in projects, ranging in size from $1M to $92M. The project management approach is deemed the most capable in the field, setting the pace for AT&T's competitors.

▶ 4.1   THE PROJECT AS PART OF THE FUNCTIONAL ORGANIZATION

As one alternative for giving the project a "home," we can make it a part of one of the functional divisions of the firm. Figure 4-1 is the organizational chart for the University of Cincinnati, a functionally organized institution. If U.C. undertook the development of a Master of Science program in Project Management (or perhaps an MPM), the project would probably be placed under the *general supervision* of the senior vice president and provost, under the *specific supervision* of the dean of the College of Business Administration (and/or College of Engineering), and would be *managed* by a senior faculty member with a specialty in operations management—such as either of the authors of this book. (It might also be placed under the general supervision of the V.P. and dean for Graduate Studies and Research.) A project involving the construction of a new parking garage would fall under the V.P. for Business Affairs, as would a project to construct a local area network for all computers on the university campus. For functionally organized projects, the project is assigned to the functional unit that has the most interest in ensuring its success or can be most helpful in implementing it. As we noted in the case of the proposed MPM, more than one choice of parent may exist.

There are advantages and disadvantages of using functional elements of the parent organization as the administrative home for a project—assuming that one has chosen an appropriate function.

The major advantages are:

1. There is maximum flexibility in the use of staff. If the proper functional division has been chosen as the project's home, the division will be the primary administrative base for individuals with technical expertise in the fields relevant to the project. Experts can be temporarily assigned to the project, make the required contributions, and immediately be reassigned to their normal work.

2. Individual experts can be utilized by many different projects. With the broad base of technical personnel available in the functional divisions, people can be switched back and forth between the different projects with relative ease.

3. Specialists in the division can be grouped to share knowledge and experience. Therefore, the project team has access to whatever technical knowledge resides in the functional group. This depth of knowledge is a potential source of creative, synergistic solutions to technical problems.

4. The functional division also serves as a base of technological continuity when individuals choose to leave the project, and even the parent firm. Perhaps just as important as technological continuity is the procedural, administrative, and overall policy continuity that results when the project is maintained in a specific functional division of the parent firm.

5. Finally, and not the least important, the functional division contains the normal path of advancement for individuals whose expertise is in the functional area. The project may be a source of glory for those who participate in its successful completion, but the functional field is their professional home and the focus of their professional growth and advancement.

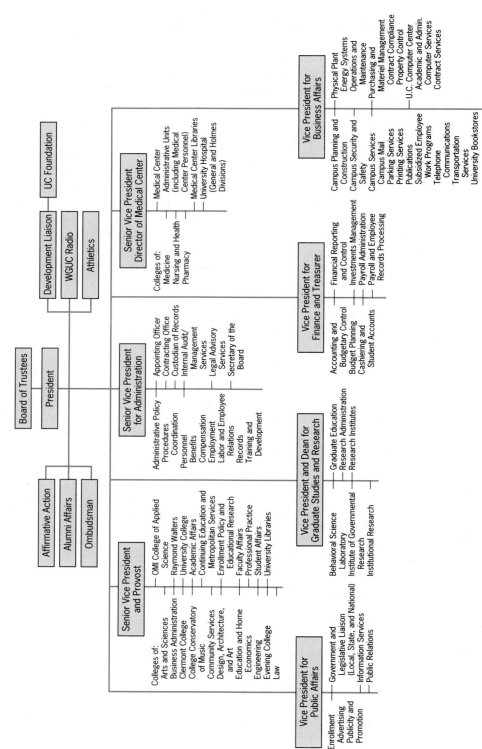

Figure 4-1: University of Cincinnati organization chart.

Just as there are advantages to housing the project in a functional area, there are also disadvantages:

1. A primary disadvantage of this arrangement is that the client is not the focus of activity and concern. The functional unit has its own work to do, which usually takes precedence over the work of the project, and hence over the interests of the client.

2. The functional division tends to be oriented toward the activities particular to its function. It is not usually problem-oriented in the sense that a project must be to be successful.

3. Occasionally in functionally organized projects, no individual is given full responsibility for the project. This failure to pinpoint responsibility usually means that the PM is made accountable for some parts of the project, but another person is made accountable for one or more other parts. Little imagination is required to forecast the lack of coordination and chaos that results.

4. The same reasons that lead to lack of coordinated effort tend to make response to client needs slow and arduous. There are often several layers of management between the project and the client.

5. There is a tendency to suboptimize the project. Project issues that are directly within the interest area of the functional home may be dealt with carefully, but those outside normal interest areas may be given short shrift, if not totally ignored.

6. The motivation of people assigned to the project tends to be weak. The project is not in the mainstream of activity and interest, and some project team members may view service on the project as a professional detour.

7. Such an organizational arrangement does not facilitate a holistic approach to the project. Complex technical projects such as the development of a jet transport aircraft or an emergency room in a hospital simply cannot be well designed unless they are designed as a totality. No matter how good the intentions, no functional division can avoid focusing on its unique areas of interest. Cross-divisional communication and sharing of knowledge is slow and difficult at best.

▶ 4.2 PURE PROJECT ORGANIZATION

At the other end of the organizational spectrum is pure project organization. The project is separated from the rest of the parent system. It becomes a self-contained unit with its own technical staff, its own administration, tied to the parent firm by the tenuous strands of periodic progress reports and oversight. Some parent organizations prescribe administrative, financial, personnel, and control procedures in detail. Others allow the project almost total freedom within the limits of final accountability. There are examples of almost every possible intermediate position. Figure 4-2 illustrates this pure project organization.

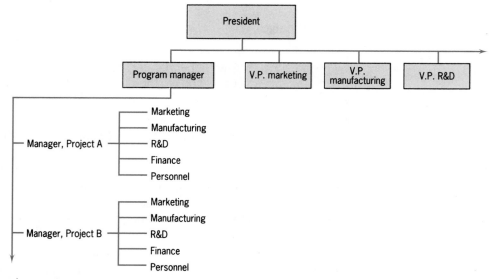

Figure 4-2: Pure project organization.

As with the functional organization, the pure project has its unique advantages and disadvantages. The former are:

1. The project manager has full line authority over the project. Though the PM must report to a senior executive in the parent organization, there is a complete work force devoted to the project. The PM is like the CEO of a firm that is dedicated to carrying out the project.

2. All members of the project work force are directly responsible to the PM. There are no functional division heads whose permission must be sought or whose advice must be heeded before making technological decisions. The PM is truly the project director.

3. When the project is removed from the functional division, the lines of communication are shortened. The entire functional structure is bypassed, and the PM communicates directly with senior corporate management. The shortened communication lines result in faster communications with fewer failures.

4. When there are several successive projects of a similar kind, the pure project organization can maintain a more or less permanent cadre of experts who develop considerable skill in specific technologies. Indeed, the existence of such skill pools can attract customers to the parent firm. Lockheed's famous "Skonk Works" was such a team of experts who took great pride in their ability to solve difficult engineering problems. The group's name, taken from the *Li'l Abner* comic strip, reflects the group's pride, irreverent attitude, and strong sense of identity.

5. The project team that has a strong and separate identity of its own tends to develop a high level of commitment from its members. Motivation is high and acts to foster the task orientation discussed in Chapter 3.

6. Because authority is centralized, the ability to make swift decisions is greatly enhanced. The entire project organization can react more rapidly to the requirements of the client and the needs of senior management.

7. Unity of command exists. While it is easy to overestimate the value of this particular organizational principle, there is little doubt that the quality of life for subordinates is enhanced when each subordinate has one, and only one, boss.

8. Pure project organizations are structurally simple and flexible, which makes them relatively easy to understand and to implement.

9. The organizational structure tends to support a holistic approach to the project. A brief explanation of the systems approach was given in Chapter 3, and an example of the problems arising when the systems approach is not used appears in Section 4.3 of this chapter. The dangers of focusing on and optimizing the project's subsystems rather than the total project are often a major cause of technical failure in projects.

While the advantages of the pure project organization make a powerful argument favoring this structure, its disadvantages are also serious:

1. When the parent organization takes on several projects, it is common for each one to be fully staffed. This can lead to considerable duplication of effort in every area from clerical staff to the most sophisticated (and expensive) technological support units. If a project does not require a full-time personnel manager, for example, it must have one nonetheless because personnel managers come in integers, not fractions, and staff are not shared across projects.

2. In fact, the need to ensure access to technological knowledge and skills results in an attempt by the PM to stockpile equipment and technical assistance in order to be certain that it will be available when needed. Thus, people with critical technical skills may be hired by the project when they are available rather than when they are needed. Similarly, they tend to be maintained on the project longer than needed, "just in case."

3. Removing the project from technical control by a functional department has its advantages, but it also has a serious disadvantage if the project is characterized as "high technology." Though individuals engaged with projects develop considerable depth in the technology of the project, they tend to fall behind in other areas of their technical expertise. The functional division is a repository of technical lore, but it is not readily accessible to members of the pure project team.

4. Pure project groups seem to foster inconsistency in the way in which policies and procedures are carried out. In the relatively sheltered environment of the project, administrative corner-cutting is common and easily justified as a response to the client or to technical exigency. "They don't understand our problems" becomes an easy excuse for ignoring dicta from headquarters.

5. In pure project organizations, the project takes on a life of its own. Team members form strong attachments to the project and to each other. A disease known as *projectitis* develops. A strong we–they divisiveness grows, distorting the relationships between project team members and their counterparts in the parent

organization. Friendly rivalry may become bitter competition, and political infighting between projects is common.

6. Another symptom of projectitis is the worry about "life after the project ends." Typically, there is considerable uncertainty about what will happen when the project is completed. Will team members be laid off? Will they be assigned to low-prestige work? Will their technical skills be too rusty to be successfully integrated into other projects? Will our team (that old gang of mine) be broken up?

▶ 4.3   THE MATRIX ORGANIZATION

In an attempt to couple some of the advantages of the pure project organization with some of the desirable features of the functional organization, and to avoid some of the disadvantages of each, the matrix organization was developed. In effect, the functional and the pure project organizations represent extremes. The matrix organization is a combination of the two. It is a pure project organization overlaid on the functional divisions of the parent firm.

Being a combination of pure project and functional organization structures, a matrix organization can take on a wide variety of specific forms, depending on which of the two extremes (functional or pure project) it most resembles. Because it is simpler to explain, let us first consider a strong matrix, one that is similar to a pure project. Rather than being a stand-alone organization, like the pure project, the matrix project is not separated from the parent organization. Consider Figure 4-3. The project manager of Project 1, PM_1, reports to a program manager who also exercises supervision over other projects.

Project 1 has assigned to it three people from the manufacturing division, one and one-half people from marketing, one-half of a person each from finance and

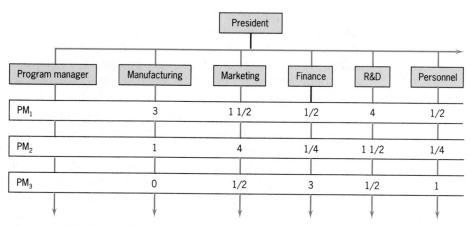

Figure 4-3: Matrix organization.

personnel, four individuals from R & D, and perhaps others not shown. These individuals come from their respective functional divisions and are assigned to the project full-time or part-time, depending on the project's needs. It should be emphasized that *the PM controls when and what these people will do, while the functional managers control who will be assigned to the project and what technology will be used.*

With heavy representation from manufacturing and R&D, Project 1 might involve the design and installation of a new type of manufacturing process. Project 2 could involve a new product or, possibly, a marketing research problem. Project 3 might concern the installation of a new, computerized, financial control system. All the while, the functional divisions continue on with their routine activities.

There is no single executive to whom PMs generally report. If a project is merely one of several in a specific program, the PM typically reports to a program manager, if there is one. It is not uncommon, however, for the PM to report to the manager of the functional area that has a particular interest in the program, or an interest in the project if it is not part of a program. If several projects on mathematics are being conducted for the Office of Naval Research (ONR), for instance, it would be normal for the PMs to report to the ONR section head for Mathematical Sciences. It is also common for PMs to report directly to the chief executive officer, the chief operating officer, or an executive vice-president in smaller firms with only a few projects.

At the other end of the spectrum of matrix organization is the weak matrix, one more like the functional organization. A project might, for example, have only one full-time person, the PM. Rather than having an individual functional worker actually assigned to the project, the functional departments lend *capacity* to the project. The PM might require engineering assistance, special software, product testing, or any other service that would be provided by the relevant functional unit. For example, the PM of a project set up to create a new database for personnel might request that the basic design be done by the systems analysis group in the administrative division. The personnel job would then be added to the normal workload of the systems group. The priority given to the design might be assigned by senior management or might be the result of negotiations between the PM and the head of the systems group. In some cases, the systems group's charges for the job might also be subject to negotiation.

Between these extremes, there are many different mixtures of project and functional responsibilities. When a functional group's work is frequently required by projects, it is common to operate the group as a functional unit rather than to transfer its people to the project. For instance, a toxicology unit in a cosmetic business, a quality assurance group in a multiproduct manufacturing firm, or a computer graphics group in a publishing firm might all be functionally organized and take on project work much like outside contractors. While the PM's control over the work is diminished by this arrangement, the project does have immediate access to any expertise in the group, and the group can maintain its technological integrity.

The impetus for the matrix organization was the fact that firms operating in high-technology areas had to integrate several functional specialties to work on a set of projects and wished to *time-share* expertise between individual projects in the set. Further, the technical needs of the projects often required a *systems* approach [11]. In earlier times, when a high-technology project was undertaken by a firm, it would start its journey through the firm in the R & D department. Concepts and ideas would be worked out and the result passed on to the engineering department, which would sometimes rework the whole thing. This result would then be forwarded to manufacturing, where it might be reworked once more in order to ensure that the output was manufacturable by the firm's current machinery. All of this required a great deal of time, and the emergent project might have scant resemblance to the original specifications.

In the meantime, another firm would be doing much the same thing on another project for the customer. These two projects might later have to be joined together, or to a third, and the combination was then expected to meet its intended function. For example, the first project might be a jet aircraft engine, the second a weapon system, and the third an airframe. The composite result rarely performed as originally conceived because the parts were not designed as a unified system. Military aircraft buffs may recall several World War II aircraft that used the Allison in-line engine (designed by Rolls Royce). The P-39 (Airacobra) was a mediocre combat aircraft. The P-38 (Lightning) was a fairly good plane. The P-51 (Mustang) was an outstanding combat machine. In all three cases, the engine, armament, and airframe were designed separately. In one case this approach to design worked well; in one it did not. A systems approach to design would require that engine, airframe, and weapon system be designed as a unit. The attempt is to optimize the composite system rather than the parts. This improves the chance of developing a P-51 and decreases the likelihood of making a P-39. Indeed, given the complexity of the systems going into a combat aircraft today, it is doubtful if a plane *could* be designed using the old methods.

The systems approach was adopted as an alternative to the traditional method described above. This did not mean that the same firm had to manufacture everything, but it did mean that one organization had to take responsibility for the integrity of project design—to make sure that the parts were compatible and that the combination would function as expected. This required that R & D, engineering, manufacturing, etc., work closely together, and that all these work closely with the client, all the while coordinating efforts with other firms that were supplying subsystems for the project.

Housing the project in a functional organization was simply too constraining. Setting it up as a pure project was workable but expensive because of the need to duplicate expensive technical talent when more than one project was involved. The matrix organization, which allows the PM to draw temporarily on the technological expertise and assistance of all relevant functions, was a way out of the dilemma. The effectiveness of the systems approach is well-demonstrated by the success of the Chrysler Corporation in designing and bringing to market their LH sedans (as well as by their new, small car, the Neon, and their sports car, the Viper). The LH design was the product of a process called "concurrent" or "simultaneous" engineering or design that involves marketing, engineering, manufacturing, design, quality assurance, and other departments working together from the outset. This process not only produced designs that have been widely rated as "outstanding," it also short-ened the design-to-street process by about 18 months. Quite apart from the value of a fine design, the economic value of the time saved is immense. The value de-rives from two sources: less design labor and overhead as well as earlier sales and return on the investment. For a more complete description of the use of design teams at Chrysler, see [49].

The matrix approach has its own unique advantages and disadvantages. Its strong points are:

1. The project is the point of emphasis. One individual, the PM, takes responsibil-ity for managing the project, for bringing it in on time, within cost, and to speci-fication. The matrix organization shares this virtue with the pure project organi-zation.

2. Because the project organization is overlaid on the functional divisions, tem-porarily drawing labor and talent from them, the project has reasonable access to the entire reservoir of technology in all functional divisions. When there are several projects, the talents of the functional divisions are available to all pro-jects, thus sharply reducing the duplication required by the pure project struc-ture.

3. There is less anxiety about what happens when the project is completed than is typical of the pure project organization. Even though team members tend to develop a strong attachment for the project, they also feel close to their func-tional "home."

4. Response to client needs is as rapid as in the pure project case, and the matrix organization is just as flexible. Similarly, the matrix organization responds flexi-bly and rapidly to the demands made by those inside the parent organization. A project nested within an operating firm must adapt to the needs of the parent firm or the project will not survive.

5. With matrix management, the project will have—or have access to—represen-tatives from the administrative units of the parent firm. As a result, consistency with the policies, practices, and procedures of the parent firm tends to be pre-served. If nothing else, this consistency with parent firm procedures tends to foster project credibility in the administration of the parent organization, a con-dition that is commonly undervalued.

6. Where there are several projects simultaneously under way, matrix organization allows a better companywide balance of resources to achieve the several differ-ent time/cost/performance targets of the individual projects. This holistic ap-proach to the total organization's needs allows projects to be staffed and scheduled in order to optimize total system performance rather than to achieve the goals of one project at the expense of others.

7. While pure project and functional organizations represent extremes of the orga-nizational spectrum, matrix organizations cover a wide range in between. We

have differentiated between strong and weak matrices in terms of whether the functional units supplied individuals or capacity to projects. Obviously, some functional units might furnish people and others only supply capacity. There is, therefore, a great deal of flexibility in precisely how the project is organized—all within the basic matrix structure—so that it can be adopted to a wide variety of projects and is always subject to the needs, abilities, and desires of the parent organization.

The advantages accruing to the matrix structure are potent. Unfortunately, the disadvantages are also serious:

1. In the case of functionally organized projects, there is no doubt that the functional division is the focus of decision-making power. In the pure project case, it is clear that the PM is the power center of the project. With matrix organizations, the power is more balanced. Often, the balance is fairly delicate. When doubt exists about who is in charge, the work of the project suffers. If the project is successful and highly visible, doubt about who is in charge can foster political infighting for the credit and glory. If the project is a failure, political infighting will be even more brutal to avoid blame.

2. While the ability to balance time, cost, and performance between several projects is an advantage of matrix organization, that ability has its dark side. The set of projects must be carefully monitored *as a set*, a tough job. Further, the movement of resources from project to project in order to satisfy the several schedules may foster political infighting among the several PMs, all of whom tend to be more interested in ensuring success for their individual projects than in helping the total system optimize organizationwide goals.

3. For strong matrices, problems associated with shutting down a project are almost as severe as those in pure project organizations. The projects, having individual identities, resist death. Even in matrix organizations, projectitis is still a serious disease.

4. In matrix-organized projects, the PM controls administrative decisions and the functional heads control technological decisions. The distinction is simple enough when writing about project management, but for the operating PM the division of authority and responsibility inherent in matrix management is complex. The ability of the PM to negotiate anything from resources to technical assistance to delivery dates is a key contributor to project success. Success is doubtful for a PM without strong negotiating skills.

5. Matrix management violates the management principle of unity of command. Project workers have at least two bosses, their functional heads and the PM. There is no way around the split loyalties and confusion that results. Anyone who has worked under such an arrangement understands the difficulties. Those who have not done so cannot appreciate the discomforts it causes. To paraphrase Plato's comment on democracy, matrix management "is a charming form of management, full of variety and disorder."

Project Management in Practice
Chrysler's Platform Team for New Auto Development

In a bold move, Chrysler has permanently changed the way it will develop cars in the future. Instead of the slow, functional, sequential approach, platform teams representing all functions are directly involved in the design of a new automobile up front. In authorizing the LH-body project, top management's goal was to meet all design objectives—performance, weight, fuel economy, quality, cost—up front and cut a year off the typical five-year new car development process.

The advantages of being able to design a car quickly are: (1) you can get the jump on competition and incorporate new technolgies before they find out what your design is; (2) the revenues occur sooner thereby providing higher profits on the investment; and (3) by starting closer to the target release date, the design will be more in line with what customers are demanding. Although Chrysler had used teams before to develop special vehicles (e.g., minivans, trucks), the team approach had never been institutionalized for regular new car development.

The platform team approach breaks down the barriers between the functions and empowers lower-level personnel with decision-making authority. Better communication between functions reduces the overall time to design the car. To speed up the process further, the engineers design the car through computer-based finite element analysis, in-cluding structural analysis and testing. Another difference in the team approach is the requirement to meet all design objectives before release, instead of leaving the more difficult ones to be ironed out in future model redesigns a few years later. In the LH project, the car passed all requirements in its first, real 35 mph crash test.

The LH project team was highly successful in meeting its goals, and finished the project in $3\frac{1}{2}$ years, six months ahead of schedule. And more recently, Chrysler's new Neon small sedan and mid-sized Cirrus and Stratus, are the hit of the 1994 Detroit auto show. According to media reports, the Neon offers a sporty engine, dual air bags, and a roomy interior for under $9000, a definite challenge to the $1000 more expensive Saturn and $2000 more expensive Civic and Tercel. And the Cirrus and Stratus, with their sophisticated engines, sleek good looks, thoughtful interiors, and 4- or 6-cylinder multivalve engines, are roomier and sportier than their Camry and Accord competitors but are priced $2000 to $3000 less. For now, it looks like the platform team concept has produced some more winners for Chrysler.

Sources: W. Raynal "Teaming with Enthusiasm," *Autoweek*, May 4, 1992; O. Suris, "Competitors Blinded by Chrysler's Neon," *The Wall Street Journal*, January 10, 1994.

▶ 4.4 MIXED ORGANIZATIONAL SYSTEMS

As noted in the introduction to this chapter, divisionalization is a means of dividing a large and monolithic organization into smaller, more flexible units. This enables the parent organization to capture some of the advantages of small, specialized organizational units while retaining some of the advantages that come with larger size.

Organizing projects by product involves establishing each product-project as a relatively autonomous, integrated element within the organization as a whole. Such primary functions as engineering and finance are then dedicated to the interests of the product itself. Software projects are a common type of project organized by "product." Software projects often occur in clusters—several different projects that are parts of the same overall information system or application software. Pursuing such projects as a group tends to ensure that they will be compatible, one with another, and even increases the likelihood that they will be completed as a group.

Consider a firm making lawn furniture. The firm might be divisionalized into products constructed of plastic or aluminum. Each product line would have its own specialized staff. Assume now two newly designed styles of furniture, one plastic and the other aluminum, each of which becomes a project within its respective product division. (Should a new product be a combination of plastic and aluminum, the pure project form of organization will tend to forestall interdivisional battles for turf.)

Similarly, organization by territory is especially attractive to national organizations whose activities are physically or geographically spread, and where the products have some geographical uniqueness, such as ladies' garments. Project organization across customer divisions is typically found when the projects reflect a paramount interest in the needs of different types of customers. Here customer preferences are more substantial than either territorial or product activities. The differences between consumer and manufacturer, or civilian and military, are examples of such substantial differences.

A special kind of project organization often found in manufacturing firms develops when projects are housed in process divisions. Such a project might concern new manufacturing methods, and the machining division might serve as the base for a project investigating new methods of removing metal. The same project might be housed in the machining division but include several people from the R & D lab, and be organized as a combination of functional and matrix forms.

Pure functional and pure project organizations may coexist in a firm. This results in the *mixed* form shown in Figure 4-4. This form is rarely observed with the purity we have depicted here, yet it is not uncommon. What is done, instead, is to spin off the large, successful long-run projects as subsidiaries or independent operations. Many firms nurture smaller projects that are not yet stable under the wing of an existing division, then wean them to pure projects with their own identity, and finally allow the formation of a *venture team*—or, for a larger project, *venture firm*—within the parent company. For example, Texas Instruments has done this with the Speak and Spell toy that was developed by one of its employees.

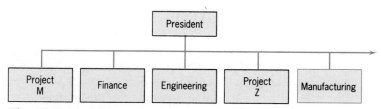

Figure 4-4: "Mixed" organization.

The hybridization of the mixed form leads to flexibility. It enables the firm to meet special problems by appropriate adaptation of its organizational structure. There are, however, distinct dangers involved in hybridization. Dissimilar groupings within the same accountability center tend to encourage overlap, duplication, and friction because of incompatibility of interests.

Figure 4-5 illustrates another common solution to the problem of project organizational form. The firm sets up what appears to be a standard form of functional organization, but it adds a staff office to administer all projects. This frees the functional groups of administrative problems while it uses their technical talents. In a large specialty chemical firm, this organizational form worked so well that the staff office became the nucleus of a full-scale division of the firm. The division's sole purpose is to administer projects.

In many ways this organizational form is not distinguishable from matrix management, but it is typically used for small, short-run projects where the formation of a full-fledged matrix system is not justified. This mixed form shares several advantages and disadvantages of the matrix structure, but the project life is usually so short that the disease of projectitis is rarely contracted. If the number or size of the projects being staffed in this way grows, a shift to a formal matrix organization naturally evolves.

Though the ways of interfacing project and parent organization are many and varied, most firms adopt the matrix form as the basic method of housing projects. To this base, occasional pure, functional, and hybrid projects are added if these possess special advantages in special cases. The managerial difficulties posed by matrix projects are more than offset by their relatively low cost and by their ability to get access to broad technical support. (Dinsmore recommends "flat, flexible structures," that are, as far as we can tell, not distinguishable from matrix structures in any significant way. He strongly emphasizes "lean and mean" for projects as well as a corporate way of life [16].)

▶ 4.5 CHOOSING AN ORGANIZATIONAL FORM

Even experienced practitioners find it difficult to explain how one should proceed when choosing the organizational interface between project and firm. The choice is determined by the situation, but even so is partly intuitive. There are few accepted

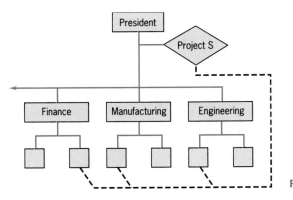

Figure 4-5: Staff organization.

principles of design, and no step-by-step procedures that give detailed instructions for determining what kind of structure is needed and how it can be built. All we can do is consider the nature of the potential project, the characteristics of the various organizational options, the advantages and disadvantages of each, the cultural preferences of the parent organization, and make the best compromise we can.

In general, the functional form is apt to be the organizational form of choice for projects where the major focus must be on the in-depth application of a technology rather than, for example, on minimizing cost, meeting a specific schedule, or achieving speedy response to change. Also, the functional form is preferred for projects that will require large capital investments in equipment or buildings of a type normally used by the function.

If the firm engages in a large number of similar projects (e.g., construction projects), the pure project form of organization is preferred. The same form would generally be used for one-time, highly specific, unique tasks that require careful control and are not appropriate for a single functional area—the development of a new product line, for instance.

When the project requires the integration of inputs from several functional areas and involves reasonably sophisticated technology, but does not require all the technical specialists to work for the project on a full-time basis, the matrix organization is the only satisfactory solution. This is particularly true when several such projects must share technical experts. But matrix organizations are complex and present a difficult challenge for the PM.

In choosing the structure for a project, the first problem is to determine the kind of work that must be accomplished. To do this requires an initial, tentative project plan. First, identify the primary deliverable(s) of the project. Next, list the major tasks associated with each deliverable. For each task, determine the functional unit that will probably be responsible for carrying out the task. These are the elements that must be involved in order to carry out the project. The problem is how best to bring them together—or, how best to integrate their work. Additional matters to be considered are the individuals (or small groups) who will do the work, their personalities, the technology to be employed, the client(s) to be served, the political relationships of the functional units involved, and the culture of the parent organization. Environmental factors inside and outside the parent organization must also be taken into account. By understanding the various structures, their advantages and disadvantages, a firm can select the organizational structure that seems to offer the most effective and efficient choice. Another view of the problem of selecting the appropriate interface between the project and its parent organization is found in [28].

Since it is our objective in this chapter to provide criteria for the selection of a project organization, we shall illustrate the process with two examples. In each case, we use the following procedure.

1. Define the project with a statement of the objective(s) that identifies the major outcomes desired.

2. Determine the key tasks associated with each objective and locate the units in the parent organization that serve as functional "homes" for these types of tasks.

3. Arrange the key tasks by sequence and decompose them into work packages.

4. Determine which project subsystems are required to carry out the work packages and which subsystems will work particularly closely with which others.

5. List any special characteristics or assumptions associated with the project—for example, level of technology needed, probable length and size of the project, any potential problems with the individuals who may be assigned to the work, possible political problems between different functions involved, and anything else that seems relevant, including the parent firm's previous experiences with different ways of organizing projects.

6. In light of the above, and with full cognizance of the pros and cons associated with each structural form, choose a structure.

Trinatronic, Inc.

Project objective: To design, build, and market a multitasking portable personal computer containing 8-, 16-, and 32-bit processors, 16 Mbytes RAM, at least 250 Mbytes of hard memory, at least 60MHz processing speed, weigh no more than 4 pounds, have an active matrix color display, have a battery life of 6 hours under normal operating conditions, and retail at $3000 or less.

Key Tasks	Organizational Units
A. Write specifications.	Mktg. Div. and R & D
B. Design hardware, do initial tests.	R & D
C. Engineer hardware for production.	Eng. Dept., Mfg. Div.
D. Set up production line.	Eng. Dept., Mfg. Div.
E. Manufacture small run, conduct quality and reliability tests.	Mfg. Div. and Q.A. Dept., Exec. V.P. staff
F. Write (or adopt) operating systems.	Software Prod. Div.
G. Test operating systems.	Q. A. Dept., Exec. V.P. staff
H. Write (or adopt) applications software.	Software Prod. Div.
I. Test applications software.	Q. A. Dept., Exec. V.P. staff
J. Prepare full documentation, repair and user manuals.	Tech. Writing Section (Eng. Div.) and Tech. Writing Section (Software Prod. Div.)
K. Set up service system with manuals and spare parts	Service Dept., Mktg. Div.
L. Prepare marketing program.	Mktg. Div.
M. Prepare marketing demonstrations.	Mktg. Div.

Without attempting to generate a specific sequence for these tasks, we note that they seem to belong to four categories of work.

1. Design, build, and test hardware.
2. Design, write, and test software.
3. Set up production and service/repair systems with spares and manuals.
4. Design marketing effort, with demonstrations, brochures, and manuals.

Based on this analysis, it would appear that the project will need the following elements:

- Groups to design the hardware and software.
- Groups to test the hardware and software.
- A group to engineer the production system for the hardware.
- A group to design the marketing program.
- A group to prepare all appropriate documents and manuals.
- And, lest we forget, a group to administer all the above groups.

These subsystems represent at least three major divisions and perhaps a half-dozen departments in the parent organization. The groups designing the hardware and the multiple operating systems will have to work closely together. The test groups may work quite independently of the hardware and software designers, but results seem to improve when they cooperate. We can prepare a simple responsibility chart for the tasks (Figure 4-6).

Trinatronics has people capable of carrying out the project. The design of the hardware and operating systems is possible in the current state of the art, but to design such systems at a cost that will allow a retail price of $3000 or less will require an advance in the state of the art. The project is estimated to take between 18 and 24 months, and to be the most expensive project yet undertaken by Trinatronics.

Based on the sketchy information above, it seems clear that a functional project organization would not be appropriate. Too much interaction between major divisions is required to make a single function into a comfortable organizational home for everyone. Either a pure project or matrix structure is feasible, and given the choice, it seems sensible to choose the simpler pure project organization if the cost of additional personnel is not too high. Note that if the project had required only part-time participation by the highly qualified scientific professionals, the matrix organization might have been preferable. Also, a matrix structure would probably have been chosen if this project were only one of several such projects drawing on a common staff base.

Tasks	Executive V.P. Staff		Marketing Division		Manufactur-ing Division		Engineering Division		Software Division		Research & Development Division
		Q.A. Dept.		Serv. Dept.		Eng. Dept.		Tech. Writ.		Tech. Writ.	
A			x								x
B											x
C						x					
D						x					
E		x			x						
F									x		
G		x									
H									x		
I		x									
J								x		x	
K			x								
L			x								
M			x								

Figure 4-6: Trinatronics, Inc. product task/organization responsibility chart.

Urban Hospital

Project objective: To develop and implement a computerized scheduling system for the hospital's operating rooms.

Key Tasks	Organizational Unit
A. Find and prioritize objectives of the system.	Syst. Anal. and Dept. of Surgery
B. Build preliminary model.	Syst. Anal.
C. Program and test preliminary model.	Syst. Anal.
D. Use model in parallel with current scheduling system.	Syst. Anal.
E. Compare results and present to Department of Surgery.	Syst. Anal. and Dept. of Surgery
F. If necessary, amend model and repeat tasks D and E.	Syst. Anal. and Dept. of Surgery
G. Install model, including full documentation.	Syst. Anal.
H. Train Department of Surgery clerks in operation of model.	Syst. Anal. and Dept. of Surgery

The order in which tasks should be performed is as shown above because all the work must be done sequentially. There are three major jobs.

1. Build the model based on input from the users.
2. Test model on an "as if" basis and amend if necessary.
3. Install model and train operators.

Only two units will be required for the project, a systems analysis group (housed in the Department of Administration) and a user group. Analysts and users will have to work together throughout the project. These groups each represent a different part of the parent organization.

Consideration was given to the use of an outside consultant to analyze the system and develop the model. The internal systems analysts are heavily involved in replacing an outside vendor's accounting software system with one of their own devising. They expect to be fully occupied for another six to eight months. On the other hand, some members of the Department of Surgery are worried that the hospital's own analysts will not be sensitive to the special needs of the department; they would be even less likely to tolerate and trust outsiders. Indeed, several of the sur-

geons are doubtful about the entire project. They are not sure that it makes any sense to set priorities on the objectives for scheduling the operating rooms because "quality of patient care is our only priority."

While the analysis group is currently engaged in a major project, it is estimated that they will be able to release an analyst to the OR scheduling project within three months. The project does not appear particularly difficult, and they feel it should not require more than two or three months to complete, given that the surgeons will consider cooperating in the analysis.

In this case, it seems best to house the project in the Department of Surgery. The project is small and involves only two departments. It is easy to move the analytic skill to the Department of Surgery, and there is nothing here that requires a separate project or matrix organization with the concomitant need for separate administration. Further, housing the project in Surgery would give that department a sense of control, which might act to allay their fears. It would, of course, be feasible to organize this endeavor as a staff project under the CEO of the hospital or the chief of the medical staff, but the psychological and political advantages of housing it in the Department of Surgery warrant the use of the functional organization.

▶ 4.6   THE PROJECT TEAM

In this section we consider the makeup of the project team, bearing in mind that different projects have vastly different staff needs. (For an interesting discussion of why teams are useful, see [17].) Then we take up some problems associated with staffing the team. Last, we deal with a few of the behavioral issues in managing this team.

Before discussing these issues, there is a seemingly unimportant item that needs mention because it is far more critical than it might seem. It is useful to have a *project office*, even for small projects—say, those having only a half-dozen people or so. The project office, sometimes called the *war room*, serves as a control center, chart room, conference room for visiting senior management and the project client, center for technical discussions, coffee shop, crisis center, and, in general, the focus of all project activity. It need not be sumptuous, but the PM's open cubicle will not suffice. (If space is tight, projects can share an office.) The war room represents the project "physically" and aids in instilling an *esprit de corps* in team members. If at all possible, the regular project team members should have their offices located near the project office. Certainly, the project manager's office should be nearby.

Now we continue with our discussion of the project team. To be concrete, let us use the example of an engineering project to determine how to form a project team. Assume that the size of our hypothetical project is neither particularly large nor small. In addition to the PM, the following key team members might be needed, plus an appropriate number of scientists, engineers, technicians, clerks, and the like.

- **Project Engineer**   The project engineer is in charge of product design and development and is responsible for functional analysis, specifications, drawings, cost estimates, quality/reliability, engineering changes, and documentation.

- **Manufacturing Engineer**   This engineer's task is the efficient production of the product or process the project engineer has designed, including responsibility for manufacturing engineering, design and production of tooling/jigs/fixtures, production scheduling, and other production tasks.

- **Field Manager**   This person is responsible for the installation, testing and support of the product/process once it is delivered to the customer.

- **Contract Administrator**   The administrator is in charge of all official paperwork, keeping track of customer changes, billings, questions, complaints, legal aspects, costs, and other matters related to the contract authorizing the project. Not uncommonly, the contract administrator also serves as project historian and archivist.

- **Project Controller**   The controller keeps daily account of budgets, cost variances, labor charges, project supplies, capital equipment status, etc. The controller also makes regular reports and keeps in close touch with both the PM and the company controller. If the administrator does not serve as historian, the controller can do so.

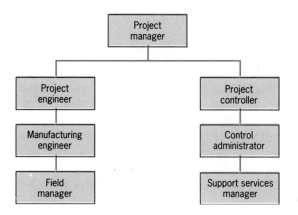

Figure 4-7: Typical organization for engineering projects.

- **Support Services Manager** This person is in charge of product support, subcontractors, data processing, and general management support functions.

Of these top project people, it is most important that the project engineer and the project controller report directly to the PM (see Figure 4-7). This facilitates control over two of the main goals of the project: technical performance and budget. (The project manager is usually in personal control of the schedule.) For a large project, all six project officials could work out of the project office and report directly to the PM.

To staff the project, the PM works from a forecast of personnel needs over the life cycle of the project. This is done with the aid of some special charts. First, a *work breakdown structure* is prepared to determine the exact nature of the tasks required to complete the project. (This chart is described in detail and illustrated in Chapter 5.) The skill requirements for these tasks are assessed and like skills are aggregated to determine work force needs. From this base, the functional departments are contacted to locate individuals who can meet these needs.

On occasion, certain tasks may be subcontracted. This option may be adopted because the appropriately skilled personnel are unavailable or cannot be located, or even because some special equipment required for the project is not available in-house. If the proper people (and equipment) are found within the organization, however, the PM usually must obtain their services from their home departments. Many firms insist on using "local" resources when they are available, in order to maintain better control over resource usage and quality. Typically, the PM will have to negotiate with both the department head and the employee, trying to "sell" the employee on the challenge and excitement of working on the project and trying to convince the department head that lending the employee to the project is in the department head's best interest.

There are some people who are more critical to the project's success than others and should report directly to the PM or to the PM's deputy (often the project engineer):

- Senior project team members who will be having a long-term relationship with the project.
- Those with whom the PM will require continuous or close communication.
- Those with rare skills necessary to project success.

Remember that the PM must depend on reason when trying to convince a department head to lend these valuable people to the project. The department head, who sees the project as a more or less glamorous source of prestige in which the department cannot share, has little natural motivation to be cooperative. Once again, it is obvious that success depends on the political skill of the PM as much as on the technical skill of the team.

Thus far, we have tacitly assumed a fairly strong matrix organization for the project in our example. In recent years, the use of weaker matrices has become more and more frequent. In many firms, when project managers are asked for the number of people who report directly to them, the answer "None!" is not uncommon. Most common of all, it seems to us, is the matrix organization with a project manager, one or two key skilled contributors who may be full-time members of the project, and a wide variety of services or capacity supplied to the project by functional groups in the parent organization. Such structures are often found in software projects that are part of larger programs being carried out by a parent firm. One or two programmers may be assigned to the project, but the work involved in integrating and testing the software, etc., is supplied to the project in the form of deliverables rather than people assigned to the project to carry out their work.

Although the project manager has to bargain for fewer individuals than in the case of stronger matrices, the PM's negotiating skills are just as critical. It is typical for the success of weak-matrix projects to be dependent on the skills of the few technical specialists who are assigned directly to the project. The ability of the PM to negotiate for skilled technicians as well as for the *timely* delivery of services from functional departments is a key determinant of success.

▶ 4.7 HUMAN FACTORS AND THE PROJECT TEAM

With the reminder of the need for the PM to possess a high level of political sensitivity, we can discuss some other factors in managing project teams, all the while remembering that the principles and practices of good, general management also apply to the management of projects. We discuss them from the viewpoint of the PM as an individual who must cope with the personal as well as the technical victories and frustrations of life on a project.

Meeting schedule and cost goals without compromising performance appears to be a technical problem for the PM. Actually, it is only partly technical because it is also a human problem—more accurately, a technical problem with a human dimension. Project professionals tend to be perfectionists. It is difficult enough to meet project goals under normal conditions, but when, out of pride of workmanship, the professionals want to keep improving (and thus changing) the product, the task becomes almost impossible. Changes cause delays. Throughout the project, the manager must continue to stress the importance of meeting due dates. It also helps if the PM establishes, at the beginning of the project, a *technical change procedure* to ensure control over the incidence and frequency of change. (It would not, however, be wise for the PM to assume that everyone will automatically follow such a procedure.) More on this subject in Chapters 5 and 11.

Another problem is motivating project team members to accomplish the work of the project. As we noted in Chapter 3 and in the discussion of matrix organizations in this chapter, the PM often has little control over the economic rewards and promotions of the people working on the project. This is certainly true when the matrix is weak. This does not, however, mean that the PM cannot motivate members of the project team. Frederick Herzberg, who studied what motivates technical employees such as engineers, scientists, and professionals on a project team, contends that recognition, achievement, the work itself, responsibility, advancement, and the chance to learn new skills are motivators [27]. It is the PM's responsibility to make sure that project work is structured in such a way as to emphasize these motivational factors. We have also found that the judicious use of "thank you" notes from the PM to those functional managers who have supplied the project with capable and committed individuals and/or effective and efficient capacity is a potent motivator—copies to the relevant individuals, of course.

The use of participative management is also a way of motivating people. This is not a new theory. It originated in the work of Argyris, Likert, McGregor and others in the 1950s and 1960s. The concept suggests that the individual worker (or team) should play a significant role in deciding what means should be employed in meeting desired ends, and in finding better ways of accomplishing things. Management By Objectives (MBO) was an early mechanism designed to develop participative management. Suggested by Drucker in 1954 [18], and advocated by others (e.g., [44]), MBO allowed the worker to take responsibility for the design and performance of a task under controlled conditions. More recently, such programs as Employee Involvement (EI) and Total Quality Management (TQM) have been developed that do not suffer from some of the problems associated with MBO. (There is a large body of literature on EI and TQM. Readers who are not familiar with these techniques might see [14 and 20 (especially Chapters 5, 10, and 11)] for excellent descriptions of both EI and TQM together with the associated behavioral theory and a discussion of implementing EI and TQM teams.)

The adoption of such methods *empowers* the team (as well as its individual members) to take responsibility and to be accountable for delivering project objectives. Some advantages of empowerment for project teams are:

1. It harnesses the ability of the team members to manipulate tasks so that project objectives are met. The team is encouraged to find better ways to do things.
2. Professionals do not like being micromanaged. Participative management does not tell them how to work but, given a goal, allows them to design their own methods.
3. The team members know they are responsible and accountable for achieving the project deliverables.
4. There is a good chance that synergistic solutions will result from team interaction.
5. Team members get timely feedback on their performance.
6. The PM is provided a tool for evaluating the team's performance.

All of the above items serve to increase motivation among members of the project team.

In Chapter 5, we cover the process of planning projects in detail, and we emphasize the use of an *action plan*, a concept borrowed directly from MBO. It is a detailed planning and scheduling technique directed toward achievement of the objectives of the project. The PM works with members of the project team and a comprehensive set of written plans is generated by this process. The resulting document is not only a plan, but also a control mechanism. Because the system of developing the plan is participative and makes team members accountable for their specific parts of the overall plan, it motivates them, and also clearly denotes the degree to which team members are mutually dependent. The importance of this latter outcome of the planning process is not well-recognized in the literature on team building.

There are a number of excellent works on team building, for example, see [19, 21, 32, 48, 51, and 57]. They cover a wide range of issues that affect team building and team operation. Such works, however, rarely mention a precondition that greatly eases the process of team formation, *mutual dependence required and recognized*, though this concept is, perhaps, implied by Katzenbach and Smith's emphasis on the fact that teams (rather than "working groups") "hold themselves mutually accountable" for reaching the team's performance goals [32, p. 112].

Bringing people together, even when they belong to the same organization and contribute their efforts to the same objectives, does not necessarily mean that they will behave like a team. Organizing the team's work in such a way that team members are mutually dependent and recognize it, will produce a strong impetus for the group to form a team. Project success will be associated with teamwork, and project failure will surely result if the group does not work as a team.* If many or most of the team members are also problem-oriented (see also Chapter 3, Section 3.2), the likelihood of the group forming an effective team is further increased.

Another major element posing a behavioral problem for the PM is interpersonal conflict. In 1975, Thamhain and Wilemon published the definitive work on the sources and nature of conflict in projects [56]. We have found their insights just as relevant today as they were in 1975. Table 4-1, based on [57], relates the most likely sources of conflict to specific stages of the project life cycle. The table also suggests some solutions. When the project is first organized, priorities, procedures, and schedules all have roughly equal potential as sources of conflict. During the buildup phase, priorities become significantly more important than any other conflict factor; procedures are almost entirely established by this time. In the main program phase, priorities are finally established and schedules are the most important cause of trouble within the project, followed by technical disagreements. Getting adequate support for the project is also a point of concern. At project finish, meeting the schedule is the critical issue, but interpersonal tensions that were easily ignored early in the project can suddenly erupt into conflict during the last hectic weeks of the life cycle. Worry about reassignment exacerbates the situation. Both Tables 4-1 and 4-2 show conflict as a function of stage in the project life cycle as well as by source of the conflict, but Table 4-2 also shows the *frequency* of conflict by source and stage of the life cycle. Figure 4-8 illustrates these tables.

Conflict can be handled in several ways, but one thing seems sure: Conflict avoiders do not make successful project managers. On occasion, compromise appears to be helpful, but most often, gently confronting the conflict is the method of choice. Much has been written about conflict resolution and there is no need to summarize that literature here beyond noting that the key to conflict resolution rests on the manager's ability to transform a win–lose situation into win–win. The Likerts have written [39] an interesting work on the nature and management of conflict, and Hill and White report [28] on how one particular project manager handled a difficult conflict:

---

* Though team formation is not even mentioned, a reading of A. S. Carlisle's article, "MacGregor" [6] is instructive. The article is a classic on the power of delegation and was clearly the inspiration for Blanchard and Johnson's *The One Minute Manager*. The Carlisle paper reports on a plant manager who delegates most operating decisions to his subordinates and insists that they help in solving one another's problems. As a result, they form a team that would be the envy of any project manager.

Table 4-1 Major Sources of Conflict During Various Stages of the Project Life Cycle

Life Cycle Phase	Major Conflict Source and Recommendations for Minimizing Dysfunctional Consequences	
	Conflict Source	**Recommendations**
Project formation	Priorities	Clearly defined plans. Joint decision making and/or consultation with affected parties. Stress importance of project to organization goals.
	Procedures	Develop detailed administrative operating procedures to be followed in conduct of project.
		Secure approval from key administrators.
		Develop statement of understanding or charter.
	Schedules	Develop schedule commitments in advance of actual project commencement.
		Forecast other departmental priorities and possible impact on project.
ʝup phase	Priorities	Provide effective feedback to support areas on forecasted project plans and needs via status review sessions.
	Schedules	Schedule work breakdown packages (project subunits) in cooperation with functional groups.
	Procedures	Contingency planning on key administrative issues.
ʝ program	Schedules	Continually monitor work in progress.
		Communicate results to affected parties.
		Forecast problems and consider alternatives.
		Identify potential trouble spots needing closer surveillance.
	Technical	Early resolution of technical problems.
		Communication of schedule and budget restraints to technical personnel.
		Emphasize adequate, early technical testing.
		Facilitate early agreement on final designs.
	Labor	Forecast and communicate staffing requirements early.
		Establish staffing requirements and priorities with functional and staff groups.
Phaseout	Schedules	Close schedule monitoring in project life cycle.
		Consider reallocation of available staff to critical project areas prone to schedule slippages.
		Attain prompt resolution of technical issues which may affect schedules.
	Personality and labor	Develop plans for reallocation of people upon project completion.
		Maintain harmonious working relationships with project team and support groups. Try to loosen up high-stress environment.

Source: [56]

The project manager did not flinch in the face of negative interpersonal feelings when listening to differences between people. "You have to learn to listen, keep your mouth shut, and let the guy get it off his chest."

- The project manager encouraged openness and emotional expression.

Table 4-2   Number of Conflicts During a Sample Project

Phase of Project				Sources of Conflict
Start	**Early**	**Main**	**Late**	
27	35	24	16	Project priorities
26	27	15	9	Admin. procedures
18	26	31	11	Technical trade-offs
21	25	25	17	Staffing
20	13	15	11	Support cost estimates
25	29	36	30	Schedules
16	19	15	17	Personalities

Source: [56]

- The manager set a role model for reacting to personality clashes. It was observed that a peer would often intercede and act out a third party conciliation role much like the manager.
- The manager seemed to exhibit the attitude that conflict could be harnessed for productive ends.
- Although managers usually confronted conflicts, they also avoided face-to-face meetings when the outside pressure was too high.

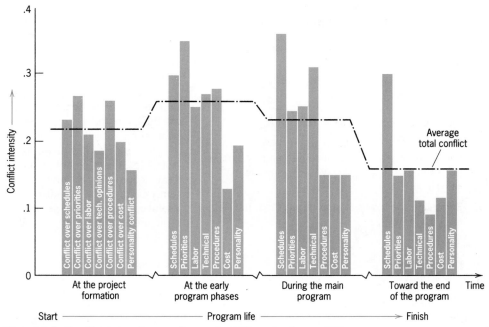

Figure 4-8: Conflict intensity over the project life cycle. *Source:* [56].

▶ SUMMARY

This chapter described the various organizational structures that can be used for projects, and detailed their advantages. An appropriate procedure for choosing the best form was described and two examples were given. The chapter then moved into a discussion of the project team itself, describing the organization of the project office staff and the human issues, such as motivation and conflict, the project manager will face. Specific points made in the chapter were these:

If the project is to be included in a functional organization, it should be placed in that unit with the greatest interest in its success or the unit that can provide the most help. Though there are advantages in this mode of organizing, the disadvantages are greater.

The project form of organizing has its advantages and disadvantages. Though the disadvantages are not as severe as with the functional form, they are nevertheless significant.

The matrix organization combines the functional and project forms in an attempt to reap the advantages of each. While this approach has been fairly successful, it also has its own unique disadvantages.

There are many variants of the pure forms of organization, and special hybrids are commonly used to handle special projects. The best form for a particular case requires consideration of the characteristics of the project compared with the various advantages and disadvantages of each form.

A useful procedure for selecting an organizational form for a project is:

1. Identify the specific outcomes desired.
2. Determine the key tasks to attain these outcomes and identify the units within the parent organization where these tasks would normally be assigned.
3. Sequence the key tasks and group them into logical work steps.

4. Determine which project subsystems will be assigned which steps and which subsystems must closely cooperate.
5. Identify any special firm or project characteristics, constraints, or problems that may affect how the project should be organized.
6. Consider all the above relative to the pros and cons of each organizational form as a final decision is made.

Every project should have a project office, even if it must be shared with another project.

Larger, more complex projects may include, in addition to the PM, a project engineer, manufacturing engineer, field manager, contract administrator, project controller, and support service manager.

Those on the project team who should report directly to the PM are the project engineer and project controller. So also should:

1. Senior team members who will have a long-term relationship with the project.
2. Those with whom the PM will be continuously or closely communicating.
3. Those with rare skills needed for project success.

Perfectionism, motivation, and conflict are often the major behavioral problems facing the PM. Management by Objectives (MBO) can be a useful tool for addressing the first two, while gentle confrontation usually works best for the latter.

Sources of project conflict are often priorities and policies at first, schedule and technical problems during the main phase, and schedule and personal issues near termination.

In the next chapter we move from organizational issues to project planning tasks. We address the topics of coordination, interface management, and systems engineering. We also present some extremely useful concepts and tools such as the work breakdown structure and linear responsibility chart.

▶ GLOSSARY

Action Plan—A detailed plan of what needs to be done and when (see Chapter 5 for more discussion and some examples).

Concurrent/Simultaneous Engineering—Originally, the use of a design team that included both design and manufacturing engineers, new expanded to include staff from quality control, purchasing, and other relevant areas.

Functional Management—The standard departments of the organization that represent individual disciplines such as engineering, marketing, purchasing, and so on.

Holistic—The whole viewed at one time rather than each piece individually.

Management by Objectives (MBO)—A management approach popular during the 1960s that encouraged managers to give their subordinates more freedom in determining how to achieve task objectives.

Matrix Organization—A method of organizing that maintains both functional supervisors as well as project supervisors. A strong matrix operates closer to a pure project organization while a weak matrix operates more like a functional organization.

Mixed Organization—This approach includes both functions (disciplines) and projects in its hierarchy.

Parent Organization—The firm or organization within which the project is being conducted.

Program Manager—This person is typically responsible for a number of related projects, each with its own project manager.

Projectitis—A social phenomenon, inappropriately intense loyalty to the project.

Subcontract—Subletting tasks out to smaller contractors.

Suboptimization—The optimization of a subelement of a system, perhaps to the detriment of the overall system.

War Room—A project office where the latest detail on project progress is available.

Work Breakdown Structure—A basic project document that describes all the work that must be done to complete the project and forms the basis for costing, scheduling, and work responsibility (see Chapter 5).

▶ MATERIAL REVIEW QUESTIONS

1. What is a program manager? How does this job differ from that of a project manager?

2. Identify the advantages and disadvantages of the matrix form of organization.

3. Name the four basic types of project organization and list at least one characteristic, advantage, and disadvantage of each.

4. Give some major guidelines for choosing an organizational form for a project.

5. Why is the project office so important?

6. Identify three ways of dealing with a conflict associated with projects. Does dealing with conflict always need to be a zero-sum game?

7. What are some advantages and disadvantages of housing a project in a functional form?

8. What are the project engineer's duties?

9. What are the major sources of conflict throughout the life cycle?

▶ CLASS DISCUSSION QUESTIONS

1. Discuss some of the differences between managing professionals and managing other workers or team members.

2. Human and political factors loom large in the success of projects. Given the general lack of coverage of this subject in engineering and science education, how might a PM gain the ability to deal with these issues?

3. A disadvantage of the pure project organization has to do with the tendency of project professionals to fall behind in areas of technical expertise

not used on the project. Name several ways that a project manager might avoid this problem.

4. Discuss the effects of the various organizational forms on coordination and interaction, both within the project team and between the team and the rest of the firm.

5. Can you think of any advantages other than those listed in the text associated with using MBO? Disadvantages?

6. How would you organize a project to develop a complex new product such as a new color fax-

copy machine? How would you organize if the product was simpler, such as a new disk drive?

7. How should the following projects be organized?

   (a) A bank's investment banking department
   (b) A firm's basic research laboratory
   (c) An international construction firm's project
   (d) A city's bus transportation project
   (e) A state's health service organization
   (f) A management consulting firm's project

8. What do you think may be the purpose of a work breakdown structure? How might it aid the PM in organizing the project?

9. Why do you think the average total conflict increases during the "early program phase" (Figure 4-8)?

10. What should the role of the project manager be in conflict management?

11. Is it ethical to employ participative management *solely* as a way to motivate employees?

▶ INCIDENTS FOR DISCUSSION

Shaw's Strategy

Rick Shaw has been tapped to be a project manager for the third time this year. Although he enjoys the challenges and opportunity for personal development afforded to him as a project manager, he dreads the interpersonal problems associated with the position. Sometimes he feels like a glorified baby-sitter handing out assignments, checking on progress, and making sure everyone is doing his or her fair share. Recently Rick read an article that recommended using MBO as an aid to the project manager in supervising and controlling team members. Rick thought this was a useful idea and decided to try it on his next project.

The project in question involved making a decision on whether to close one of the company's regional distribution centers. Rick had once been the manager of the distribution services department, so he felt very comfortable about his ability to lead the team and resolve this problem. He defined the objective of the project and detailed all the major tasks involved, as well as most of the subtasks. By the time the first meeting of the project team took place Rick felt more secure about the control and direction of the project than he had at the beginning of any of his previous projects. He had specifically defined objectives and tasks for each team member and had assigned completion dates for each task. He had even made up individual "contracts" for each team member to sign as an indication of their commitment to completion of the assigned tasks per schedule dates. The meeting went very smoothly, with almost no comments from team members. Everyone picked up a copy of his or her "contract" and went off to work on

the project. Rick was ecstatic about the success of this new approach.

Question: Do you think he will feel the same way six weeks from now? Compare his approach with the MBO process as well as his previous approach.

Better-Built

Better-Built Tape Recorder Company of Cleveland, Ohio, is planning to manufacture a new line of mini-tape recorders to compete with the small pocket recorders made by competitors. The company currently manufactures about 10,000 regular-size recorders per year and hopes to be manufacturing 5000 of the smaller version beginning in two years. The new recorder will require a 25 percent enlargement of the existing facility. The president of the company feels she must set up a project team to handle the engineering, manufacturing, financing, and support services. After considering several project managers she decided on the person she believes will get the job done and instructed her to select a project team.

Questions: Based on the above, what key people should the project manager try to enlist? What would their duties be?

Hydrobuck

Hydrobuck is a medium-sized producer of gasoline-powered outboard motors. In the past it has successfully manufactured and marketed motors in the 3- to 40-horsepower range. Executives at Hydrobuck are now interested in larger motors and would eventually like to produce motors in the 50- to 150-horsepower range.

The internal workings of the large motors are quite similar to those of the smaller motors. However, large, high-performance outboard motors require *power trim*. Power trim is simply a hydraulic system that serves to tilt the outboard motor up or down on the boat transom. Hydrobuck cannot successfully market the larger outboard motors without designing a power trim system to complement the motor.

The company is financially secure and is the leading producer of small outboard motors. Management has decided that the following objectives need to be met within the next two years:

1. Design a quality power trim system.

2. Design and build the equipment to produce such a system efficiently.

3. Develop the operations needed to install the system on the outboard motor.

The technology, facilities, and marketing skills necessary to produce and sell the large motors already exist within the company.

Questions: What alternative types of project organization would suit the development of the power trim system? Which would be best? Discuss your reasons for selecting this type of organization.

▶ INDIVIDUAL EXERCISE

Assume that you have been placed in charge of a project to educate the clerical staff on the advantages a microcomputer might offer them in their work. Assume that the organization is a large one and one you are familiar with, such as your own firm or school. Follow the procedure for selecting an organizational project form described in the chapter.

What special characteristics, constraints, or problems did you identify that a different project, or organization, might not have had? Were there any that seemed independent of the project? of the organization? What project structure pros and cons did you find to be relevant in this exercise? Would they probably be relevant for any project or organization? Was the procedure effective? In your estimation, were there any unnecessary steps? Were there any missing steps?

▶ PROJECT TEAM CONTINUING EXERCISE

In this exercise, you will have to determine how to organize the project team. A very important consideration will be the degree of independence versus interdependence the organizational structure provides. An initial work breakdown structure will be needed to determine the tasks to be completed. Then, tasks will have to be assigned to project personnel. Determine,

based on the size of the project and the personnel available, whether single individuals can be assigned individualized tasks (such as project controller) or if tasks must be grouped. Finally, try to anticipate where specific conflicts may arise over the course of the project and how you might handle them at that time.

▶ BIBLIOGRAPHY

1. ARCHIBALD, R. D. *Managing High Technology Programs and Projects.* New York: Wiley, 1976.

2. ARGYRIS, C. "Today's Problems with Tomorrow's Organizations." *Journal of Management Studies*, Feb. 1967.

3. BARNES, L. B. *Project Management and the Use of Authority: A Study of Structure, Role, and Influence*

Relationships in Public and Private Organizations, Ph.D. dissertation. Los Angeles: University of Southern California, 1971.

4. BARON, R. A., and J. GREENBERG. *Behavior in Organizations: Understanding and Managing the Human Side of Work.* Needham Heights, MA: Allyn & Bacon, Inc. 1989.

5. BOWDITCH, J. L., and A. F. BUONO. A *Primer on Organizational Behavior*, 2nd ed. New York: Wiley, 1990.

6. CARLISLE, A. S. "MacGregor," *Organizational Dynamics*. New York: AMACOM, Summer 1976.

7. CHAMBERS, G. J. "The Individual in a Matrix Organization," *Project Management Journal*, Dec. 1989.

8. CICERO, J. P., and D. L. WILEMON. "Project Authority: A Multidimensional View." *IEEE Transactions on Engineering Management*, May 1970.

9. CLELAND, D. I. *Matrix Management Systems Handbook*. New York: Van Nostrand Reinhold, 1983.

10. CLELAND, D. I. "The Age of Project Management," *Project Management Journal*, Mar. 1991.

11. CLELAND, D. I., and W. R. KING. *Systems Analysis and Project Management*, 3rd ed. New York: McGraw-Hill, 1983.

12. CROWSTON, W. B. "Models for Project Management." *Sloan Management Review*, Spring 1971.

13. DAVIS, S. M., and P. R. LAWRENCE. *Matrix*. Reading, MA: Addison-Wesley, 1977.

14. DEAN, J. W., JR. and J. R. EVANS, *Total Quality: Management, Organization, and Strategy*. St. Paul, MN: West, 1994.

15. DELBECQ, A. L., and A. C. FILEY. *Program and Project Management in a Matrix Organization: A Case Study*. Bureau of Business Research and Service, Madison: University of Wisconsin, 1974.

16. DINSMORE, P. C. "Flat, Flexible Structures: The Organizational Answer to Changing Times," in P. C. Dinsmore, ed., *The AMA Handbook of Project Management*. New York: AMACOM, 1993.

17. DINSMORE, P. C. "A Conceptual Team-Building Model: Achieving Teamwork Through Improved Communication and Interpersonal Skills," in P. C. Dinsmore, ed., *The AMA Handbook of Project Management*. New York: AMACOM, 1993.

18. DRUCKER, P. *The Practice of Management*. New York: HarperCollins, 1986.

19. DYER, W. G. *Team Building: Issues and Alternatives*, 2nd ed. Reading, MA: Addison-Wesley, 1987.

20. EVANS, J. R., and W. M. LINDSAY. *The Management and Control of Quality*, 2nd ed. St. Paul, MN: West, 1993.

21. FORD, R. C., and F. S. MCLAUGHLIN. "Successful Project Teams: A Study of MIS Managers," *IEEE Transactions on Engineering Management*, Nov. 1992.

22. FORRESTER, J. W. "A New Corporate Design." *Industrial Management Review*, Fall 1965.

23. GALBRAITH, J. R. "Matrix Organization Designs—How to Combine Functional and Project Forms." *Business Horizons*, Feb. 1971.

24. GREINER, L. E. "Evolution and Revolution as Organizations Grow." *Harvard Business Review*, July–Aug. 1972.

25 GUNZ, H. P., and A. PEARSON. "How to Manage Control Conflicts in Project Based Organizations." *Research Management*, March 1979.

26. HAMMER, M., and J. CHAMPY. *Reengineering The Corporation: A Manifesto for Business Revolution*. New York: Harper Business, 1993.

27. HERZBERG, F. H. "One More Time: How Do You Motivate Employees?" *Harvard Business Review*, Jan.–Feb. 1968.

28. HILL, R., and B. J. WHITE. *Matrix Organization and Project Management*, Michigan Business Paper #64. Ann Arbor: University of Michigan, 1979.

29. HOBBS, B. and P. MÉNARD, "Organizational Choices for Project Management," in P. C. Dinsmore, ed., *The AMA Handbook of Project Management*. New York: AMACOM, 1993.

30. ISGAR, T. *The Ten Minute Team: How Team Leaders Can Build High Performing Teams*. Longmont, CO: Seluera Press, 1989.

31. JANGER, A. R. "Anatomy of the Project Organization." *Business Management Record*, Nov. 1963.

32. KATZENBACH, J. R., and D. K. SMITH. "The Discipline of Teams," *Harvard Business Review*, March–April 1993.

33. KERZNER, H., and D. I. CLELAND. *Project/Matrix Management Policy and Strategy: Case and Situations*. New York: Van Nostrand Reinhold, 1984.

34. KETCHAM, L., and E. TRIST. *All Teams Are Not Created Equal: How Employee Empowerment Really Works*. Beverly Hills, CA.: Sage,1992.

35. KILLIAN, W. P. "Project Management—Future Organizational Concepts." *Marquette Business Review*, Feb. 1971.

36. KNIGHT, K. *Matrix Management*. New York: PBI-Petrocelli, 1977.

37. LARSON, E. W., and D. H. GOBELI. "Significance of Project Management Structure on Development Success," *IEEE Transactions on Engineering Management*, May 1989.

38. LAU, J. B., and A. B. SHANI. *Behavior in Organizations*, 5th ed. Homewood, IL: Irwin, 1991.

39. LIKERT, R., and J. G. LIKERT. *New Ways of Managing Conflict*. New York: McGraw-Hill, 1976.

40. MAINERO, L. A., and C. L. TROMLEY. *Developing Managerial Skills in Organizational Behavior*. Englewood Cliffs, NJ: Prentice Hall, 1989.

41. MARQUIS, D. G., and D. M. STRAIGHT, JR. "Organizational Factors in Project Performance," *School of Management Working Paper*. Cambridge: Massachusetts Institute of Technology, 1965.

42. McCOLLUM, J. K., and J. D. SHERMAN. "The Effects of Matrix Organization Size and Number of Project Assignments on Performance." *IEEE Transactions on Engineering Management*, Feb. 1991.

43. MIDDLETON, C. J. "How to Set Up a Project Organization." *Harvard Business Review*, March–April 1967.

44. ODIORNE, G. S. *Managing by Objectives: A System of Management Leadership*. New York: Pitman, 1965.

45. OUCHI, W. *Theory Z: How American Business Can Meet the Japanese Challenge*. Reading, MA: Addison-Wesley, 1981.

46. PADGHAM, H. E. "Choosing the Right Project Management Organization." *Project Management Journal*, Jun. 1989.

47. PEART, A. T. *Design of Project Management Systems and Records*. Cahners Books, 1971.

48. PINTO, M. B., and J. K. PINTO. "Determinants of Cross-Functional Cooperation in the Project Implementation Process." *Project Management Journal*, June 1991.

49. RAYNAL, W. "Teaming With Enthusiasm." *Auto Week*, May 4, 1992.

50. ROGERS, R. A. "Guidelines for Project Management Teams." *Industrial Engineering*, Dec. 1974.

51. ROSSY, G. L., and R. D. ARCHIBALD. "Building Commitment in Project Teams." *Project Management Journal*, June 1992.

52. SHAW, M. E. *Group Dynamics*, 3rd ed. New York: McGraw-Hill, 1981.

53. SHULL, F. A. *Matrix Structure and Project Authority for Optimizing Organizational Capacity*, Business Science Monograph No. 1, Business Research Bureau. Edwardsville, IL: Southern Illinois University, 1965.

54. SMYSLER, C. H. *A Comparison of the Needs of Program and Functional Management*, Masters thesis, School of Engineering. Dayton, OH: U.S. Air Force Institute of Technology, 1965.

55. SNOW, H. *The Power of Teambuilding Using Ropes Techniques*. San Diego, CA: Pfeffer 1992.

56. THAMHAIN, H. J., and D. L. WILEMON. "Conflict Management in Project Life Cycles." *Sloan Management Review*, Summer 1975.

57. TODRYK, L. "The Project Manager as Team Builder: Creating An Effective Team." *Project Management Journal*, Dec. 1990.

58. TSAI, M. C-P. *Contingent Conditions for the Creation of Temporary Management Organizations*, Masters thesis, School of Management. Cambridge: Massachusetts Institute of Technology, 1976.

59. WHITE, B. J. "Alternative Forms of Project Organization: Design and Evaluation." *Matrix Organization and Project Management*. Ann Arbor: Michigan Business Papers, 1979.

60. WREN, D. A., and D. VOICH, JR. *Management: Process, Structure and Behavior*. New York: Wiley, 1984.

61. WRIGHT, N. H. "Matrix Management, A Primer for the Administrative Manager." *Management Review*, May 1979.

CASE

OILWELL CABLE COMPANY, INC.
Jack R. Meredith

As Norm St. Laurent, operations manager for Oilwell Cable Company, pulled his Bronco 4x4 onto Kansas' Interstate 70, he heard on the CB about the traffic jam ahead of him due to icy road conditions. Although the traffic was moving some, Norm decided to get off at the eastern offramp for Lawrence, rather than the more direct western offramp, to save time. While waiting for the offramp to come up, Norm's mind drifted back to his discussion with Bill Russell, the general manager, on the previous day. Norm had been contemplating adding microprocessors to their rubber mixing equipment in order to save manual adjustments on these machines. This would improve throughput and reduce costs simultaneously, though without displacing any employees. Based on the data Norm had seen, it appeared that the microprocessors could cut the production time by one percent and reduce scrap from the current rate of one percent down to one-half of one percent.

However, it seemed that this might be an issue that should first be submitted to the production team in charge of rubber mixing for their thoughts on the idea. Once before, an even simpler change had been made without their knowledge and it wound up causing considerable trouble.

As the traffic wound around two cars in the ditch by the highway, Norm reflected on how difficult it was to make changes at this plant with their team management process, though there were advantages too. It probably stemmed from the way the company was originally set up.

History of Oilwell Cable Company (OCC)

Originally known as the Chord Cable Company and located in New Jersey, the firm had been experiencing severe management difficulties. When acquired by new management in 1983, they renamed it Oilwell Cable Company and relocated in Lawrence, Kansas so as to be closer to their primary customers in northeastern Oklahoma. Their product line consisted primarily of flat and round wire and cables for submersible pumps in oil wells.

The manager chosen to head up the new enterprise, Gino Strappoli, gave considerable thought to the organization of the firm. Gino envisioned a company where everyone took some responsibility for their own management and the success of the business. Gino preferred this approach not only for personal reasons but because cable manufacturing is a continuous process rather than a job shop-type of activity. The dedicated allegiance of the relatively few employees in a process firm is crucial to staying competitive. In such industries, direct labor commonly constitutes only 5 percent of the cost of the product, with indirect labor being another 5 percent. By contrast, in a job shop the wages paid for labor are a major determinant to being cost-competitive, often running 30 percent of product cost, thus introducing a potential conflict between labor and management. Gino reasoned that if he could obtain the employees' commitment to improving productivity, reducing scrap, being innovative with new technologies, and staying competitive in general, he would have a very viable firm.

With the approval of the new owners, Gino initiated his plan. Of the original labor force, only a few moved to Kansas, including Gino and the firm's controller, Bill Safford. All new equipment was purchased for the firm and a local labor force was selectively recruited. As the firm was organized, the team management process was developed. Eleven teams were formed, six of which constituted the production area. The remainder included the management team, the resource team (support functions such as computing services, accounting, etc.), the technical team (including the lab employees, R&D, and so on), the administrative team (office and clerical), and the maintenance team.

These teams basically set their own work schedules, vacation schedules, and job functions. They addressed common problems in their work area and interfaced with other teams when needed to solve problems or improve processes. With Gino's enthusiastic encouragement, the team approach grew and took on more responsibility such as handling grievances and reprimanding team members when needed.

In January 1985 the firm became profitable and later that year came fully on-stream. Gino soon thereafter left for another position and the operations manager, Bill Russell, was selected to succeed him. At this point, Norm was brought in to replace Bill as operations manager. Norm had years of experience in manufacturing and was a degreed mechanical engineer. (See Exhibit 1 for the organization structure.)

As Norm recalled, from 1985 to 1989 the firm rapidly increased productivity, improving profits significantly in the process and increasing in size to 140 employees. In so doing, they became the low cost leader in the industry and gained a majority of the market share. This resulted in a virtual fourfold increase in sales since the days of Chord Cable Co. They were now approaching almost $25 million in annual sales.

In 1989, however, the recession hit the oilwell industry. Added to this was the slowdown in energy consumption, effective conservation, and the oil glut. For almost a year, the company bided time and idle

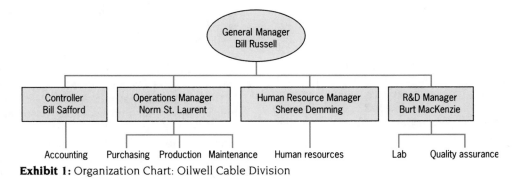

Exhibit 1: Organization Chart: Oilwell Cable Division

employees were paid for minimal production. Management felt a commitment to the employees to avoid a cutback, more so than in a normally organized firm. But finally, in 1990, top management told the teams that they would have to choose a method for handling this problem. Alternatives were shortened workweeks, layoffs, and other such measures. The teams chose layoffs. Next, management drew up a list of names of "recommended" layoff personnel representing a vertical slice through the organization—a top management employee, some professional and technical people, and a number of production employees. These lists were given to the teams who then decided what names to change and what names should remain.

Management largely went along with the teams' recommendations and the layoffs, about 20 in number, took place.

With a slimmer work force, the division increased their productivity even more significantly (see Exhibit 2), allowing them to cut their product prices from between 10 to 20 percent. As the country climbed out of the stagnant economy in 1991, the division was excellently poised to capitalize on the increased economic activity, although oil itself was still largely in the doldrums. Increased demand in mid-1991 forced the division to use overtime, and then temporary help. They didn't want to get back in the same work-force predicament they were in earlier.

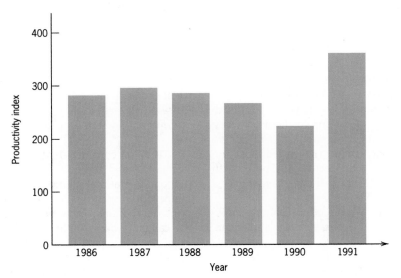

Exhibit 2: Productivity History

The Team Management Process

The 1990 layoff was a traumatic situation for the teams and the team process. Following that episode, the employees were unsure whether the team management process might require too much responsibility on their part. They had faced reprimanding employees in the past, and had even asked one employee to leave who tried to deceive them. In general, they were very receptive to employees' individual problems and had helped their colleagues through tough times on many occasions, but now they were unsure.

Team size varied from a low of three to a high of 17. The advantages to the firm of the team process seemed significant, in the minds of the team members and area managers. One member of the maintenance team noted that the team process gave much more responsibility to the employee and allowed the firm to obtain the maximum talent from each person. The firm, in response, spends $1000 per person per year on upgrading the skills of the employees in such areas as team effectiveness training, technical skill acquisition, communication skills, and general skill building. Bill Russell sees the major benefit of the team process as its production flexibility. Employees are also very receptive to change. Since the 1990 layoff, the employees have become much more sensitive to outside threats to their jobs. This spurred quality and productivity gains of over 30 percent in 1991.

The primary benefit of the team process to the employees is having a say in their own work schedule. A typical secondary benefit was the elimination of penalties for making an error. The employees feel that this is an excellent place to work; absenteeism is only 0.7 percent and only two people have voluntarily left since 1988.

Overall, the employees seemed to feel that this process worked well but wasn't utopia. "It doesn't give away the store," one employee commented. A disadvantage of the process, according to the employees, was the time and energy it required on their part to make decisions. As an example, they noted that it required three full days for the teams to come up with the revised layoff lists. Normally the teams met once a week for an hour and a half.

But when the teams made a decision, the implementation of the decision was virtually immediate, which was a big advantage over most managerially made decisions. Although this process required more time on the part of the employees, the total amount of time from idea to full implementation was probably less than that in a traditional organization, and was clearly more successful. When asked if he would ever be willing to work in a regular work environment again, one team member voiced the opinion that this process, while very good, really wasn't that much different from a good, open, traditional organization.

Teams realized that not every decision was put through them. They felt this was appropriate, however. They also recognized the difficulty facing management when trying to decide whether something should come through the teams or if it was unnecessary to consult them. Though the teams met on company time, they were not eager to spend more time on team meetings. Especially after the layoff crisis, the teams realized that self management was a two-way street and frequently hoped that upper management would make the tough decisions for them.

In summary, the teams felt that the process was based on trust, in both directions, and was working pretty well.

The Cable Production Process

As Norm pulled his truck into the OCC parking lot, he noticed there were quite a few empty spaces. This 1992 winter had been more severe than most people had expected, based on the November and December weather. The snow was almost over Norm's boots as he slogged his way to the buildings. Upstairs in his small, jumbled office, Norm pulled out the microprocessor file from his desk drawer and sat down to review the production process.

Their primary raw materials, which made up about 60 percent of the products' cost, included copper rods, lead, polypropylene, nylon, and rubber. Inspection consisted of submerging the cable in water and charging it with 30,000 volts. To date, none of their products had ever been returned. However, just in case they were ever queried about a cable they had produced, they kept samples of all their cables for five years back.

The firm considered itself very vulnerable to new technology and hence kept an active R & D lab in continuous operation. Simple advances in process technology or insulation and jacketing materials could wipe out their market overnight so they didn't want to be caught napping. Other methods of oil extraction were also a constant threat. Since they competed in a world market, they were highly exposed to foreign competition, and the location of their competitors was often a major factor in sales.

▶ QUESTIONS

1. If Norm chooses to go ahead with the micro-processor conversion on the machinery, what are the potential conflicts that might arise? What are the advantages of such a move?

2. If Norm decides to put the decision to the appropriate production team, what are the potential problems? What would be the advantages?

3. Can the firm always consult the teams before acting? What is the role of expediency in this process? Where should the line be drawn in what goes to the groups and what doesn't?

4. How much impact might microprocessors have on production costs? Assume that variable overhead represents the same percentage of costs as fixed overhead. Find the net present value if the microprocessors cost $25,000 and their installation runs another $5000.

5. Compare Norm's recollection of the division's productivity gains between 1985 and 1989 to Exhibit 2. Explain the inconsistency.

6. What would you recommend that Norm do?

▶ This article reports on a survey of the use and effectiveness of matrix management. It identifies three different kinds of matrix organizations and describes the advantages and disadvantages of matrix management in general, and of each of the three kinds in particular.

After a description of the study situation, the results are reported in terms of the usage of each of the three types of matrix and their effectiveness in those situations. Though usage was rather evenly distributed across the types, effectiveness was higher for the project matrix and below average for the functional matrix.

READING

MATRIX MANAGEMENT: CONTRADICTIONS AND INSIGHTS*
Erik W. Larson

Matrix management has been championed by many as the best way to manage the development of new products and services [1]. Born out of the aerospace race, matrix management is a "mixed" organizational form in which normal hierarchy is "overlayed" by some form of lateral authority, influence, or communication. In a matrix, there are usually two chains of command, one along functional lines and the other along project lines. Perham published, during the early 1970s, a list of matrix users which included such prestigious companies as American Cyanamid, Avco, Carborundum, Caterpillar Tractor, General Telephone and Electronics, Hughes Aircraft, ITT, 3M, Monsanto Chemical, TRW, and Texas Instruments [2].

While matrix enjoyed widespread popularity in the seventies, discord has begun to surface in the eighties. For example, Texas Instruments reportedly dumped its matrix system, citing it as one of the principle reasons for economic decline [3]. Medtronic, one of the leading producers of cardiac pacemakers, scrapped its formal matrix system after two years of frustration [4]. Similarly, Xerox recently abandoned matrix, claiming that it had created a stranglehold on product development [5]. Probably the most damning criticism can be found in the popular *In Search of Excellence*, in which Peters and Waterman assert that the tendency toward hopelessly complicated and ultimately unworkable structures "reaches its ultimate expression in the formal matrix organization structure [which] regularly degenerates into anarchy and rapidly becomes bureaucratic and noncreative." [6]

Is matrix management an unworkable system that eventually stifles the development of new products and services? Or is matrix management an effective mechanism for managing development projects in organizations? Hard evidence on the efficacy of matrix is virtually nonexistent. For the most part the literature consists of anecdotal success or failure stories. We believe that the issue has been obscured further by failing to recognize that there are different types of matrix. We further contend that the mixed reviews of matrix pertain more to different types of matrix rather than to matrix management in general.

While matrix has been applied to a number of different contexts (i.e., financial services, hospitals, construction), our focus is on its application to product development. To pursue this issue, we sampled over 500 managers, experienced in the development of new products and services, and collected data regarding both the usage and effectiveness of different matrix structures in their company. Before reporting the results, three different forms of matrix structures will be described and their relative advantages and disadvantages discussed.

Three Matrix Structures

Galbraith has distinguished different forms of matrix on a continuum which ranges from the functional organization to the pure project organization [7]. The functional organization is the traditional hierarchical structure in which the organization is usually broken down into different functional areas, such as engineering, research, accounting, and administration. When applied to a product development effort, the project is divided into segments and assigned to relevant functional groups with the heads of the functional groups responsible for their segments of the project. Coordination is provided by functional and upper levels of management.

At the other end of the spectrum is the project organization, in which all the resources necessary to complete a project are separated from the regular functional structure and set up as a self-contained team headed by a project manager. The project manager has direct authority over all the personnel on the project.

Matrix organizations lie between these two extremes by integrating the functional structure with a horizontal project structure. Instead of dividing a project into separate parts or creating an autonomous team, project participants report simultaneously to both project and functional managers. The open violation of the principle of unity of command is the trademark of a matrix management.

Companies apply this matrix arrangement in a variety of different ways. Some organizations set up temporary matrix systems to deal with specific projects while matrix may be a permanent fixture in other organizations. In addition, specialists may work full-time on one project or contribute to a variety of projects. One useful way to examine different forms of matrix management is in terms of the relative influence of project and functional managers; three different forms of matrix can be identified.

A *Functional Matrix* occurs when the project manager's role is limited to coordinating the efforts of the functional groups involved. Functional managers are responsible for the design and completion of technical requirements within their discipline. The project manager basically acts as a staff assistant with indirect authority to expedite and monitor the project. Conversely, *Project Matrix* refers to a situation in which the project manager has direct authority to make decisions about personnel and work flow activities. Functional managers' involvement is limited to providing services and advisory support. Finally, a *Balanced Matrix* is one in which the project manager is responsible for defining what needs to be accomplished while the functional managers are concerned with how it will be accomplished. More specifically, the project manager establishes the overall plan for completing the project, integrates the contributions of the different disciplines, sets schedules, and monitors progress. The functional managers are responsible for assigning personnel and executing their segment of the project according to the standards and schedules set by the project manager. The merger of "how and what" requires both parties to share responsibility and authority over work flow operations. Table 1 summarizes these descriptions, as well as the functional and project organization from reference [8].

Matrix is essentially a compromise between the traditional functional organization and a pure project organization. It is more flexible than a functional organization but not as flexible as a project team. At the same time, it is more efficient than a project team, but incurs administrative cost which is unnecessary in a

Table 1 Project Management Structures

Functional Organization:	The project is divided into segments and assigned to relevant functional areas and/or groups within functional areas. The project is coordinated by functional and upper levels of management.
Functional Matrix:	A person is formally designated to oversee the project across different functional areas. This person has limited authority over functional people involved and serves primarily to plan and coordinate the project. The functional managers retain primary responsibility for their specific segments of the project.
Balanced Matrix:	A person is assigned to oversee the project and interacts on an equal basis with functional managers. This person and the functional managers jointly direct work flow segments and approve technical and operational decisions.
Project Matrix:	A manager is assigned to oversee the project and is responsible for the completion of the project. Functional managers' involvement is limited to assigning personnel as needed and providing advisory expertise.
Project Team:	A manager is put in charge of a project team composed of a core group of personnel from several functional areas and/or groups, assigned on a full-time basis. The functional managers have no formal involvement.

functional organization. Table 2A summarizes the major advantages and disadvantages reported in the literature.

Many of the problems associated with matrix are in contradiction with its strengths. Critics have described matrix as being costly, cumbersome, and overburdening to manage, while proponents praise its efficiency and flexibility. Everyone agrees that matrix is a delicate system to manage, but few have discussed the relative efficacy of different types of matrix. With this in mind, the three types of matrix structures will be compared according to the advantages and disadvantages associated with matrix. Table 2B summarizes the tentative conclusions of this discussion.

Advantages:

- **Efficient Use of Resources** All three forms of matrix allow specialists as well as equipment to be shared across multiple projects.

- **Project Integration** Granting the project manager more control over work activities should increase project integration, but at the same time quality may suffer since input from functional areas is less concentrated.

- **Flexibility** The multidisciplinary involvement inherent in all three kinds of matrix should enhance flexibility and adaptive reactions. This should be especially true for the Balanced Matrix in which consensus through give-and-take are necessary to win joint approval. The Functional Matrix and Project Matrix are likely to be less flexible since authority is more clearly defined, making decisions less negotiable.

- **Information Flow** Vertical information flow should be enhanced under all forms of matrix, since one of the roles of the project manager is to be a central communication link with top management. Lateral communication, however, should be strongest in a Balanced Matrix. This is probably due more to necessity than design. Shared decision making places a premium on close communication through which agreements are eventually shaped. Conversely, lateral communication may suffer a bit under a project using Functional Matrix since the project manager and functional managers are not as dependent upon each other as in a Balanced Matrix.

- **Discipline Retention** A key advantage that matrix has over the pure project team approach is that it allows participants to sustain their link with their functional area while working on multidisciplinary projects. This not only provides a home port for specialists to return to once work on the project is completed but also helps participants to remain technically sharp in their discipline. Still, the ability of participants to maintain ties with their specialty area is likely to decline as their involvement becomes more and more under the jurisdiction of the project manager.

Table 2A   Advantages and Disadvantages of a Matrix Organization

Advantages

+ Efficient use of resources—Individual specialists as well as equipment can be shared across projects.
+ Project integration—There is a clear and workable mechanism for coordinating work across functional lines.
+ Improved information flow—Communication is enhanced both laterally and vertically.
+ Flexibility—Frequent contact between members from different departments expedites decision making and adaptive responses.
+ Discipline retention—Functional experts and specialists are kept together even though projects come and go.
+ Improved motivation and commitment—Involvement of members in decision making enhances commitment and motivation.

Disadvantages

- Power struggles—Conflict occurs since boundaries of authority and responsibility deliberately overlap.
- Heightened conflict—Competition over scarce resources occurs especially when personnel are being shared across projects.
- Slow reaction time—Heavy emphasis on consultation and shared decision making retards timely decision making.
- Difficulty in monitoring and controlling—Multidiscipline involvement heightens information demands and makes it difficult to evaluate responsibility.
- Excessive overhead—Double management by creating project managers.
- Experienced stress—Dual reporting relations contributes to ambiguity and role conflict.

Table 2B   Comparative Advantages and Disadvantages of Three Types of Matrix Structures

Advantages	Functional Matrix	Balanced Matrix	Project Matrix
+ Resource efficiency	High	High	High
+ Project integration	Weak	Moderate	Strong
+ Discipline retention	High	Moderate	Low
+ Flexibility	Moderate	High	Moderate
+ Improved information flow	Moderate	High	Moderate
+ Improved motivation and commitment	Uncertain	Uncertain	Uncertain

Disadvantages			
- Power struggles	Moderate	High	Moderate
- Heightened conflict	Low	Moderate	Moderate
- Reaction time	Moderate	Slow	Fast
- Difficulty in monitoring and controlling	Moderate	High	Low
- Excessive overhead	Moderate	High	High
- Experienced stress	Moderate	High	Moderate

- **Motivation and Commitment** Inherent in all types of matrix is a high degree of involvement in decision making, which should enhance personal commitment and motivation. Team spirit, however, is likely to be high under a Project Matrix since participant involvement is more project focused. Still, many specialists find interacting with different types of people and performing a wide range of activities frustrating. It is difficult to conclude which structure will elicit the highest levels of commitment and motivation.

Disadvantages:

- **Power Struggles** Matrix is predicated on tension between functional managers and project managers who are in competition for control over the same set of resources. Such conflict is viewed as a necessary mechanism for achieving an appropriate balance between complex technical issues and unique project requirements. While the intent is noble, the effect is sometimes analogous to opening Pandora's box. Legitimate conflict spills over to a more personal level, resulting from conflicting objectives and accountabilities, disputes about credit and blame, and attempts to redress infringements on professional domains. The Balanced Matrix is more susceptible to these kinds of problems since power and authority are more negotiable under this system. Power struggles should be reduced under functional and project matrices since the relative authority of each party is more clearly defined.

- **Heightened Conflict** Any situation in which equipment and people are being shared across projects lends itself to conflict and competition for scarce resources. A Functional Matrix, however, should alleviate some of these problems since specialists can directly appeal to their functional superiors to resolve conflicting demands on their time and energy.

- **Reaction Time** While shared decision making enhances the flexibility of the Balanced Matrix, the drawback is the time necessary to reach agreement. The Project Matrix should produce faster results since the project man-

ager is not necessarily bound to a consensus style of decision making, which is formalized in a Balanced Matrix. For the same reason, the Functional Matrix should be quicker than the Balanced Matrix, but not as fast as the Project Matrix since decision making has to be coordinated across functional lines.

- **Monitoring and Control** Matrix is susceptible to passing the buck, abdication of responsibility, and cost accounting nightmares. This is particularly true for Balanced Matrix in which responsibility is explicitly shared across functional and project lines. While in principle each functional area is responsible for its particular segment of the project under a Functional Matrix, contributions naturally overlap, making it difficult to determine accountability. The Project Matrix centralizes control over the project, permitting more efficient cost-control and evaluation systems.

- **Excessive Overhead** All three forms of matrix increase administrative overhead by instituting the role of project manager. Administrative costs, in the form of salaries, are likely to be higher for the Balanced and Project forms of matrix due to the greater roles of the project manager.

- **Experienced Stress** The very nature of development projects tends to make it a very stressful experience for participants. Matrix management appears to exacerbate this problem. Multiple reporting relationships and divided commitment across projects heighten role conflict and ambiguity. Stress is likely to be a more serious problem where ambiguity is the greatest: the Balanced Matrix. Both the Functional Matrix and the Project Matrix are likely to reduce ambiguity and associated stress, since lines of authority and responsibility are more clearly defined.

Overall, these comparisons indicate that the advantages and disadvantages associated with matrix are not necessarily true for all three forms of matrix and that each type of matrix has its own unique set of strengths and weaknesses. The comparisons also suggest that the Project Matrix is superior in many ways to the other two forms of matrix. The Project Matrix is likely to enhance project integration, decrease reaction time, diminish power struggles, and improve the control and monitoring of project activities and costs. On the down side, technical quality may suffer since functional areas have less control over their contributions.

The Functional Matrix is likely to improve technical quality as well as provide a better system for managing conflict across projects. The Achilles' heel is that functional control is maintained at the likely expense of poor project integration. The Balanced Matrix represents a compromise between the two extreme approaches and as such shares to a lesser degree several of the advantages of the two other approaches. At the same time, it is the most delicate system to manage and is more likely to succumb to many of the problems associated with matrix.

The questions that need to be addressed are: What has been the experience of actual companies with these different matrix structures? Which form of matrix is the most widely used? More to the point, does practice support theory? Do practitioners support our conclusion that the Project Matrix is the most effective form of matrix for developing new products and services?

The Study This study is part of a research program sponsored by the Project Management Institute (PMI). PMI is the professional association for practitioners of project management and has over 5000 members worldwide. Data were collected by means of a mailed questionnaire which was sent to randomly selected PMI members in both Canada and the United States. Repeated mailings yielded a 64 percent response rate. This study is based on the 510 respondents who reported that they were primarily involved in development projects directed at creating new products, services, and/or processes.

Over 30 percent of the sample were either project managers or directors of project management programs within their firm. Sixteen percent were members of top management (i.e., president, vice-president, or division manager), while 26 percent were managers in functional areas such as marketing, operations, and accounting. Eighty percent share the common experience of having been a project manager at some time during their career.

The sample represents a wide variety of industries. For example, 40 percent were involved in developing pharmaceutical products, 10 percent were in aerospace, and 10 percent were involved in developing computer and data processing products. Among the other industries represented in lesser numbers are telecommunications, medical instruments, glass products, petrochemical products, software development, and housewares goods.

As we report our findings, we are keenly aware that individual perceptions do not provide the best basis for drawing inferences about effectiveness. Still, the breadth of the study provides a useful referent point for assessing the current status of matrix in North America.

Matrix: Usage In order to ascertain experience with matrix, respondents were asked two questions: Has your organization ever used matrix management to develop new products or services? If so, what is the likelihood matrix will be used again? If they responded that it would not be used again, then they were asked to state the reasons why. Figure 1 represents the results for these two questions.

Over three-quarters of respondents reported that their company has used matrix. Of those who responded yes, 89 percent felt that matrix would probably or definitely continue to be used. Only 1 percent reported that matrix would definitely not be used again. Among the reasons given for dropping matrix were breakdowns in coordination between functional and project managers, a shift toward using project teams to complete projects, and the size of their organization was too small to take advantage of a matrix system. Still, the overwhelming opinion was that matrix is the dominant mode for managing development projects in the organizations sampled and will continue to be so.

These results address matrix in general. The usage of the three types of matrix was measured by having respondents indicate the number of current projects ("many," "few," or "none") in their organization that utilized each structure (see Figure 2). Respondents based their responses on a capsule description of each structure (as presented in Table 1).

All three forms of matrix were widely used. Project Matrix was the most popular, with over 78 percent of the respondents reporting that this form of matrix was being used to manage development projects in their company. Seventy-four percent reported that their firm used the Functional Matrix while 68 percent reported using the Balanced Matrix.

Since size affects economies of scale, availability of resources, and integration requirements, usage rates for the different structures were compared to the size of the firm. The only significant variation occurred in companies with less than 100 employees. Over 84

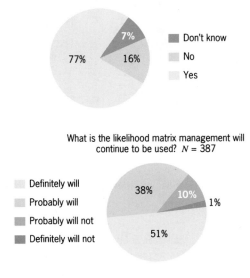

Has your company ever used
"matrix management" for development projects?

7%
77%   16%

■ Don't know
■ No
■ Yes

What is the likelihood matrix management will
continue to be used? $N = 387$

■ Definitely will
■ Probably will
■ Probably will not
■ Definitely will not

38%   10%   1%

51%

Figure 1: Questionnaire responses.

percent of respondents working in small firms reported using a Project Matrix while the usage levels were lower for both the Balanced Matrix (62 percent) and Functional Matrix (56 percent). No differences were revealed in the usage patterns of large and medium-sized firms.

Matrix: *Effectiveness* Respondents were asked to rate the effectiveness of each of the matrix structures they had experienced. Controlling cost, meeting schedule, and achieving technical performance parameters were among the factors considered in evaluating the different structures. The average rating for

each form of matrix is reported in Figure 3. The results indicate a strong preference for the Project Matrix, which was rated above effective. The Balanced Matrix was considered effective, while the Functional Matrix was rated below effective.

The ratings for the total sample are somewhat clouded by the fact that not all the respondents had direct experience with each of the three matrix structures. A more valid reference point can be obtained from the 123 respondents who had direct experience with all three structures. Their ratings are also reported in Figure 3, and here the pattern is further rein-

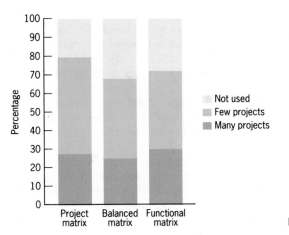

Percentage

100
90
80
70
60
50
40
30
20
10
0

Project matrix   Balanced matrix   Functional matrix

■ Not used
■ Few projects
■ Many projects

Figure 2: Usage of different matrix structures.

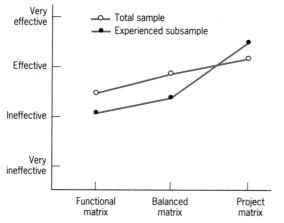

Figure 3: Rated effectiveness of different matrix structures.

forced. The Project Matrix received the highest rating while the Functional Matrix was rated as ineffective. The Balanced Matrix received only a marginal rating.

Potential variations in the above results were examined for the size of the firm. One of the reasons mentioned for dropping matrix was that the organization was too small to sustain a matrix structure. However, when effectiveness ratings were examined according to size of the firm, size had little impact on the ratings. For example, both respondents in firms of less than 100 employees and respondents in firms of greater than 1000 employees rated Project Matrix as the most effective.

The results indicate a strong preference for a Project Matrix in which the project manager has primary responsibility and control over development activities. These results may have been tempered by self-interest since a significant portion of the sample was project managers. To examine this potential bias, the ratings of project managers were compared with those of top management and managers in other functional areas. These results revealed only minor differences in the ratings of the three groups. Top management, project managers, and even functional managers were in agreement that the Project Matrix is the most effective form of matrix. The Functional Matrix was considered the least effective, even by the functional managers.

Discussion and Conclusions   While matrix might be viewed as being cumbersome, chaotic, and anarchical by critics, it is still widely used by North American businesses. Over three-fourths of the respondents re-

ported that their organization has tried matrix and will continue to use it. These results contradict the notion that the popularity of matrix is waning, suggesting instead that matrix is the dominant mode for completing development projects. The support is strong, but not without reservations. The following comment from one respondent is typical of the feelings toward matrix management: "Matrix management works, but it sure seems difficult at times. All matrix managers must keep up their health and take stress tabs."

More specifically, all three forms of matrix were popular, with the Project Matrix having a slightly higher usage rate than either the Balanced Matrix or the Functional Matrix. Size of the firm affected usage patterns only with regard to small firms which were found to have a much stronger preference for the Project Matrix. The effectiveness data confirmed our prediction concerning the relative efficacy of the different matrix structures. The Project Matrix was consistently rated superior to the other two forms of matrix. The Balanced Matrix received a marginal rating, while the Functional Matrix was considered ineffective. These effectiveness ratings were not affected by the size of the firm.

The results of this study reveal an interesting contradiction. If the Project Matrix form is considered the most effective, why are the other two forms used nearly as often?

One explanation for this contradiction can be found in the work of Davis and Lawrence [9]. They argue that matrix systems tend to evolve over time, beginning first with a Functional Matrix, followed by a shift toward a Balanced Matrix, and ultimately maturing into a Project Matrix. The comparable usage patterns among the matrix structures suggest that the organizations sampled may be at different stages of matrix development.

A related factor is resistance to change. Matrix management, especially the Project Matrix form, represents a radical departure from the conventional functional approach to organizing. Such change is likely to evoke strong resistance. This is especially true among functional managers, who perceive their authority being usurped by the project manager. Since authority typically resides along functional lines before the introduction of matrix, it would seem only natural that vested interests play a role in choosing a weaker form of matrix. Several project managers commented that their company's reliance on a Functional Matrix was politically motivated and that their functional counterparts strongly opposed

expanding the role of project managers over projects.

This condition also underscores once again the need to recognize that not all matrix structures are the same. Our position is that much of the recent criticism leveled at matrix is more relevant to the balanced and functional forms of matrix. Conversely, much of the support for matrix probably comes from those using the Project Matrix form. While more rigorous studies are needed to substantiate this claim, the responses from practitioners in this study support this argument. The final lesson to be learned is a relatively simple one: managers who are concerned with the development of new products and services should consider moving to a Project Matrix if they haven't already done so, especially if they see the disadvantages of a Functional Matrix and a Balanced Matrix occurring in their firms.

References

1. See, for example, Leonard Sayles, "Matrix Management: The Structure with a Future," *Organizational Dynamics* (Autumn 1976), pp. 2–17; W. C. Goggin, "How the Multi-Dimensional Structure Works at Dow-Corning," *Harvard Business Review* (January/February 1974), pp. 54–65; Jay Galbraith, ed., *Matrix Organizations: Organization Design for High Technology* (Cambridge, MA: MIT Press, 1971).

2. H. Perham, "Matrix Management: A Tough Game to Play," *Dun's Review* (August 1970), pp. 31–34.

3. *Business Week*, "An About Face in TI's Culture," July 5, 1982, p. 77.

4. David H. Gobeli and W. R. Rudelius, "Managing Innovation: Lessons from the Cardiac Pacing Industry," *Sloan Management Review* (Summer 1985), pp. 29–43.

5. *Business Week*, "How Xerox Speeds Up the Birth of New Products," March 19, 1984, pp. 58–59.

6. Tom Peters and Robert Waterman, *In Search of Excellence* (New York: HarperCollins, 1982), p. 49.

7. Jay Galbraith, "Matrix Organization Designs—How to Combine Functional and Project Forms," *Business Horizons* (February 1971), pp. 29–40.

8. For those readers interested in a more comprehensive description of matrix, we recommend: Stanley Davis and Paul Lawrence, *Matrix* (Reading, MA: Addison-Wesley Publishing Co., 1977); D. R. Kingdon, *Matrix Organization* (London: Tavistock. 1973); Lynn Stuckenbruck, "The Matrix Organization," *Project Management Quarterly* (1979), pp. 21–33.

9. Stanley Davis and Paul Lawrence, *op. cit.*

5

Project Planning

In the previous chapter we discussed the problem of structuring the interface between the project and its parent organization. We then introduced several issues bearing on the formation and management of the project team. It is now time to consider how to plan the work of the project and to examine how the project plan impacts on the structure of the project team as well as on its relationship to its parent.

There is an extensive literature on project planning. Some of it is concerned with the strategic aspects of planning, being focused on the choice of projects that are consistent with the organization's goals (e.g., [3, 9, 13, 19, 25, and 42]). Another group of works is aimed at the process of planning individual projects, given that they have been chosen as strategically acceptable (e.g., [1, 6, 12, 13, 19, 21, 27, 30, 32, 35, and 44]). Laufer [23], in particular, offers an interesting discussion on the theory of planning that includes some practical implications. Most fields have their own accepted set of project planning processes, though they are all similar, as we shall soon see. For example, in the field of Information Systems they refer to the standard "systems development cycle" for software projects, consisting of four or six or seven "phases", depending on which author is being consulted (e.g., see [36]). It is even standard to use the example of building a house to communicate the activities involved in each phase, as illustrated below:

- **Definition Phase** Here the problem is defined in a Requirements Document. A house would need heating, plumbing, lighting, space, storage, etc.
- **Analysis Phase** This phase produces the Functional Specifications ("deliverables") for the house such as the location of vents for central heating and air conditioning or outlets for phone service.

- **Design Phase**   Here a system is proposed to solve the problem. The system is divided into functional components and the components are interconnected. These would include the rooms, ventilation, wiring.

- **Programming Phase**   This is the actual work that is conducted to bring the system into being. It is the building of the house.

- **System Test Phase**   This phase brings the pieces together and tests them as a whole. In the house, we test the plumbing, the electricity, the roof, and so on.

- **Acceptance Phase**   The customer now tests the completed system for acceptance and payment. Minor problems are fixed at the time; major problems require negotiation (see Chapter 6). The house buyer may ask for repairs to cracked plaster, or an outlet. A major problem would be if the buyer had specified two fireplaces and the contractor had only built one.

- **Operation Phase**   This includes installation and use. The house buyer moves in and lives in the house. If problems develop or are found upon use, the contractor fixes them during the warranty period. This does not include maintenance, or upgrades and extensions.

Prentis [35] breaks the general planning process into seven steps, while Roman [38] describes it as a set of six planning sequences. First comes preliminary coordination where the various parties involved in the project get together and make preliminary decisions about what will be achieved (project objectives) and by whom. These preliminary plans serve as the basis for the second step: a detailed description of the various tasks that must be undertaken and accomplished in order to achieve the objectives of the project. In addition, the very act of engaging in the preliminary planning process increases member commitment to the project.

These work plans are used for the third and fourth sequences, deriving the project budget and schedule. Both the budget and the schedule directly reflect the detail (or lack of it) in the project work plan, the detailed description of project tasks. The fifth planning sequence is a precise description of all project status reports, when they are to be produced, what they must contain, and to whom they will be sent. Finally, plans must be developed that deal with project termination, explaining in advance how the project pieces will be redistributed once its purpose has been completed.

This chapter deals only with the first two of Roman's six planning sequences, or the first three of Prentis', but we develop planning techniques that link the first two stages to each of the other sequences, which are covered in later chapters. Project budgets are discussed in Chapter 7, schedules in Chapter 8, status reports in Chapter 10, and project termination in Chapter 13.

Before we begin, we assume in this chapter that the purpose of planning is to facilitate later accomplishment. The world is full of plans that never become deeds. The planning techniques covered here are intended to smooth the path from idea to accomplishment. It is a complicated process to manage a project, and plans act as a map of this process. The map must have sufficient detail to determine what must be done next but be simple enough that workers are not lost in a welter of minutiae.

In the pages that follow we discuss a somewhat formal method for the development of a project plan. Almost all project planning techniques lead to plans that contain the same basic elements. They differ only in the ways they approach the process of planning. We have adopted an approach that we think makes the planning process straightforward and fairly systematic, but it is never as systematic and straightforward as planning theorists would like you to believe. At its best, planning is tortuous. It is an iterative process yielding better plans from not-so-good plans, and the iterative process of improvement seems to take place in fits and starts. The process may be described formally, but it does not occur formally. Bits and pieces of plans are developed by individuals, by informal group meetings, or by formalized

Project Management in Practice
Planning Anchorage's Bid for the Winter Olympics

Hosting the Olympic Games is always a massive project, but even the preparation of the bid proposal is a major project itself, involving the conceptualization and selling of the Olympics project. Just before the 1984 Winter Olympics in Sarajevo, a group of managers of the Alyeska Ski Resort, while meeting for lunch, wondered aloud, "Why couldn't we host a Winter Olympics in Anchorage?" Anchorage was already studying the construction of Olympic-caliber sports facilities and being an Olympic training site. Why not the Olympics themselves? As public discussion of the idea grew, a steering committee was formed to investigate the issue. Some members went to observe the Winter Games, some visited former winter sites, and some visited the U.S. Olympic Headquarters. Assessing their information, the steering committee decided that it was feasible for Anchorage to make a bid by 1989 to host the 1996 Winter Olympic Games, so in late 1984 the Anchorage Organizing Committee (AOC) was incorporated as a nonprofit organization.

The project was planned to be slow and deliberate, gaining the inside track over time. However, in March 1985, the United States Olympic Committee (USOC) asked the AOC and four other interested cities to bid in June for the 1992 winter games. The winning USOC bid would be forwarded to the International Olympic Committee (IOC) for the final selection decision in September. With only 90 days to prepare their bid, the AOC, as well as the citizens of Anchorage, were galvanized into action. A number of committees were formed and a fund-raiser was hired. The bid was completed in 30 days but the preparation of the presentation took another 45 days. The project garnered wide public support and volunteers. On June 15, the USOC selected Anchorage's bid to forward to the International Committee! In October 1986, the AOC made its bid

Source: Mystrom, R., D. Baumeister, and R. Nerland. "Anchorage Organizing Committee for the 1994 Olympics," Project Management Journal, June 1988.

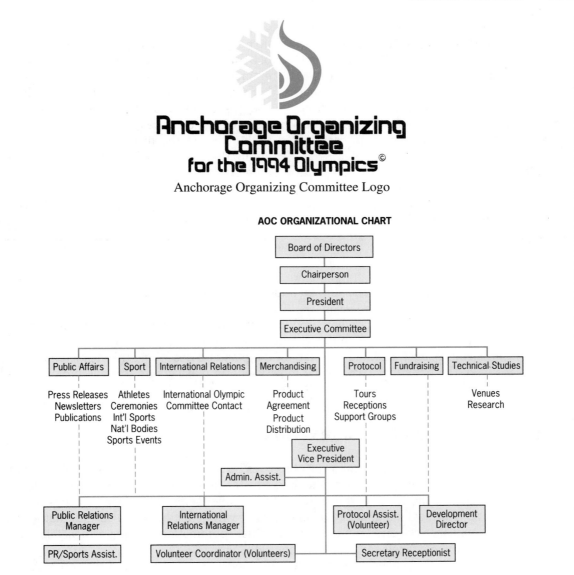

Anchorage Organizing Committee Logo

AOC ORGANIZATIONAL CHART

presentation to the International Committee. More than 200 Anchorage residents traveled at their own expense to Lausanne, Switzerland for the presentation, but the selection went to Albertville, France. The Anchorage presentation had been impressive, however, and established the serious Olympic credentials of the city. Thus, when the IOC announced a month later that future winter games would be staggered from the summer games, beginning with the winter games in 1994 (rather than 1996), the USOC, with little debate, reselected Anchorage as its bid.

Again, the AOC began the preparations to make a serious bid for the next winter games. Cost of the bid effort was estimated to be $2.8 million, one of the least expensive bids ever (Paris' bid cost $22 million) due to the massive community volunteer effort and support. Two-thirds of all Alaskans (158,000) made a $5 contribution from their 1986 "dividend" checks to support the bid effort, and the 1987 contributions are expected to double that. In addition, corporate and private donations are expected to bring in $1 million and merchandise marketing should earn another $600,000.

The committee formalized its organization (see chart) and did an extensive economic analysis. One study on the long-term impact concluded that the Alaskan economy would receive between $150 and $750 million in net value from the games. The financial plan was to stage the games without any government funding. Television revenues would bring in two-thirds of the cost; sponsorships and ticket sales would provide most of the rest. The biggest expense would be the cost of facilities while the major operating expense during the games would be the cost of communications.

(*Note:* Anchorage was not selected by the IOC for the 1994 Winter Olympics.)

planning teams [32], and then improved by other individuals, groups, or teams, and improved again, and again.

If the appropriate end product is kept firmly in mind, this untidy process yields a project *master plan*. In this chapter and several following chapters, we discuss the end product, defining the parts of the plan and describing the characteristics each of the parts must have to be most useful in making sure that the project is completed and achieves its objectives.

5.1 INITIAL PROJECT COORDINATION

It is crucial that the project's objectives be clearly tied to the overall mission of the firm. Senior management should define the firm's intent in undertaking the project, outline the scope of the project, and describe the project's desired results. Without a clear beginning, project planning can easily go astray. It is also vital that a senior manager call and be present at an initial coordinating meeting as a visible symbol of top management's commitment to the project.

At the meeting, the project is discussed in sufficient detail that potential contributors develop a general understanding of what is needed. If the project is one of many similar projects, the meeting will be quite short and routine, a sort of "touching base" with other interested units. If the project is unique in most of its aspects, extensive discussion may be required.

Whatever the process, the outcome must be that: (1) technical objectives are established (though perhaps not "cast in concrete"), (2) basic areas of performance responsibility are accepted by the participants, and (3) some tentative schedules and budgets are spelled out. Each individual/unit accepting responsibility for a portion of the project should agree to deliver, by the next project meeting, a preliminary but detailed plan about how that responsibility will be accomplished. Such plans should contain descriptions of the required tasks, budgets, and schedules.

These plans are then reviewed by the group and combined into a composite *project plan*. The composite plan, still not completely firm, is approved by each participating group, by the project manager, and then by senior organizational management. Each subsequent approval hardens the plan somewhat, and when senior management has endorsed it, any further changes must be made by processing a formal *change order*. However, if the project is not large or complex, informal written memoranda can substitute for the change order. The main point is that no *significant* changes in the project are made, without written notice, following top management's approval. The definition of "significant" depends on the specific situation and the people involved.

The PM generally takes responsibility for gathering the necessary approvals and assuring that any changes incorporated into the plan at higher levels are communicated to, and approved by, the units that have already signed off on the plan. Nothing is as sure to enrage functional unit managers as to find that they have been committed by someone else to alterations in their carefully considered plans without being informed. Violation of this procedure is considered a betrayal of trust. Several incidents of this kind occurred in a firm during a project to design a line of children's clothing. The anger at this *change without communication* was so great that two chief designers resigned and took jobs with a competitor.

Because senior managers are almost certain to exercise their prerogative to change the plan, the PM should always return to the contributing units for consideration and reapproval of the plan as modified. The final, approved result of this procedure is the project plan, also known as the *master plan*, or the *baseline plan*.

Project Management in Practice
Integrating Company Policy with Company Strategy

A major insurance company decided, as a matter of corporate strategy, that they should embark on a campaign of new product development. Further, they wished to make some other significant changes in their operation, for example, computerization of all forms and records. In order to accomplish these objectives, the Research and Development group, working with senior executives, developed a methodology that formalized the developmental process from the examination of a new idea, through its definition, design, production, and implementation stages. The following flow chart was developed that spelled out the entire process and denoted a series of "check points" at which progress could be measured and controlled. Company management felt that this methodology for new product project development would help make sure that corporate strategy could be embodied in projects—as well as ensure that projects were consistent with and advanced corporate strategy.

Source: Mantel, S. J., Jr. Consulting Project.

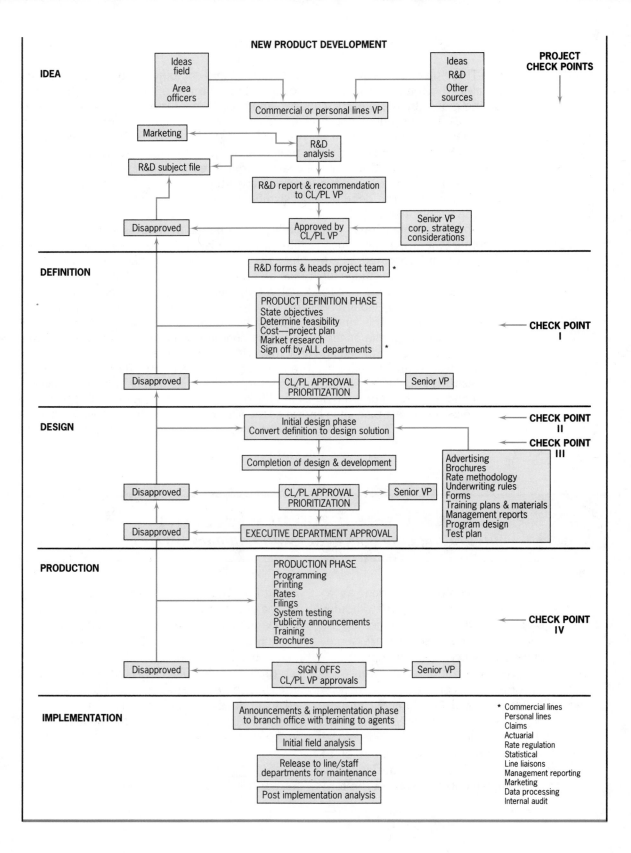

NEW PRODUCT DEVELOPMENT

PROJECT CHECK POINTS

IDEA

Ideas field / Area officers

Ideas R&D / Other sources

Commercial or personal lines VP

Marketing

R&D analysis

R&D subject file

R&D report & recommendation to CL/PL VP

Disapproved

Approved by CL/PL VP

Senior VP corp. strategy considerations

DEFINITION

R&D forms & heads project team *

PRODUCT DEFINITION PHASE
State objectives
Determine feasibility
Cost—project plan
Market research
Sign off by ALL departments *

CHECK POINT I

Disapproved

CL/PL APPROVAL PRIORITIZATION

Senior VP

DESIGN

Initial design phase
Convert definition to design solution

CHECK POINT II

CHECK POINT III

Completion of design & development

Advertising
Brochures
Rate methodology
Underwriting rules
Forms
Training plans & materials
Management reports
Program design
Test plan

Disapproved

CL/PL APPROVAL PRIORITIZATION

Senior VP

Disapproved

EXECUTIVE DEPARTMENT APPROVAL

PRODUCTION

PRODUCTION PHASE
Programming
Printing
Rates
Filings
System testing
Publicity announcements
Training
Brochures

CHECK POINT IV

Disapproved

SIGN OFFS
CL/PL VP approvals

Senior VP

IMPLEMENTATION

Announcements & implementation phase to branch office with training to agents

Initial field analysis

Release to line/staff departments for maintenance

Post implementation analysis

* Commercial lines
Personal lines
Claims
Actuarial
Rate regulation
Statistical
Line liaisons
Management reporting
Marketing
Data processing
Internal audit

Outside Clients

When the project is to deliver a product/service (often referred to as the project's *deliverables*) to an outside client, the fundamental planning process is unchanged except for the fact that the specifications cannot be altered without the *client's* permission. A common "planning" problem in these cases is that marketing has promised deliverables that engineering may not know how to produce on a schedule that manufacturing may be unable to meet. This sort of problem usually results when the various functional areas are not involved in the planning process at the time the original proposal is made to the potential client.

Two objections to such early participation by engineering and manufacturing are likely to be raised by marketing. First, the sales arm of the organization is trained to sell and is expected to be fully conversant with all technical aspects of the firm's products/services. Further, salespeople are expected to be knowledgeable about design and manufacturing lead times and schedules. On the other hand, it is widely assumed by marketing (with some justice on occasion) that manufacturing and design engineers do not understand sales techniques, will be argumentative and/or pessimistic about client needs in the presence of the client, and are generally not "housebroken" when customers are nearby. Second, it is expensive to involve so much technical talent so early in the sales process—typically, prior to issuing a proposal. It can easily cost a firm more than $10,000 to send five technical specialists on a trip to consider a potential client's needs. The willingness to accept higher sales costs puts even more emphasis on the selection process.

The rejoinder to such objections is simple. It is usually cheaper, faster, and easier to do things right the first time than to redo them. When the product/service is a complex system that must be installed in a larger, more complex system, it is appropriate to treat the sale like a project. The sale *is* a project and deserves the same kind of planning. A great many firms that consistently operate in an atmosphere typified by design and manufacturing crises have created their own panics. (Software producers and computer system salespeople take note!) In fairness, it is appropriate to urge that anyone meeting customers face to face should receive some training in the tactics of selling.

Project Plan Elements

Given the project plan, approvals really amount to a series of authorizations. The PM is authorized to direct activities, spend monies (usually within preset limits) request resources and personnel, and start the project on its way. Senior management's approval not only signals its willingness to fund and support the project, but also notifies subunits in the organization that they may commit resources to the project.

The process of developing the project plan varies from organization to organization, but any project plan must contain the following elements:

- **Overview** This is a short summary of the objectives and scope of the project. It is directed to top management and contains a statement of the goals of the project, a brief explanation of their relationship to the firm's objectives, a description of the managerial structure that will be used for the project, and a list of the major milestones in the project schedule.

- **Objectives** This contains a more detailed statement of the general goals noted in the overview section. The statement should include profit and competitive aims as well as technical goals.

- **General Approach** This section describes both the managerial and the technical approaches to the work. The technical discussion describes the relationship of the project to available technologies. For example, it might note that this project is an extension of work done by the company for an earlier project. The subsection on the managerial approach takes note of any deviation from routine procedure—for instance, the use of subcontractors for some parts of the work.

- **Contractual Aspects** This critical section of the plan includes a complete list and description of all reporting requirements, customer-supplied resources, liaison arrangements, advisory committees, project review and cancellation procedures, proprietary requirements, any specific management agreements (e.g., use of subcontractors), as well as the technical deliverables and their specifications, delivery schedules, and a specific procedure for changing any of the above. (Project change orders will be discussed in Chapter 11.) Completeness is a necessity in this section. If in doubt about whether an item should be included or not, the wise planner will include it.

- **Schedules** This section outlines the various schedules and lists all milestone events. The estimated time for each task should be obtained from those who will do the work. The project master schedule is constructed from these inputs. The responsible person or department head should sign off on the final, agreed-on schedule.

- **Resources** There are two primary aspects to this section. The first is the budget. Both capital and expense requirements are detailed by task, which makes this a *project budget* (discussed further in Chapter 7). One-time costs are separated from recurring project costs. Second, cost monitoring and control procedures should be described. In addition to the usual routine elements, the monitoring and control procedures must be designed to cover special resource requirements for the project, such as special machines, test equipment, laboratory usage or construction, logistics, field facilities, and special materials.

- **Personnel** This section lists the expected personnel requirements of the project. Special skills, types of training needed, possible recruiting problems, legal or policy restrictions on work force composition, and any other special requirements, such as security clearances, should be noted here. (This reference to "security" includes the need to protect trade secrets and research targets from competitors as well as the need to protect the national security.) It is helpful to time-phase personnel needs to the project schedule. This makes clear when the various types of contributors are needed and in what numbers. These projections are an important element of the budget, so the personnel, schedule, and resources sections can be cross-checked with one another to ensure consistency.

- **Evaluation Methods**   Every project should be evaluated against standards and by methods established at the project's inception. This section contains a brief description of the procedure to be followed in monitoring, collecting, storing, and evaluating the history of the project.

- **Potential Problems**   Sometimes it is difficult to convince planners to make a serious attempt to anticipate potential difficulties. One or more such possible disasters such as subcontractor default, technical failure, strikes, bad weather, sudden required breakthroughs, critical sequences of tasks, tight deadlines, resource limitations, complex coordination requirements, insufficient authority in some areas, and new, complex, or unfamiliar tasks are certain to occur. The only uncertainties are which ones will occur and when. In fact, the timing of these disasters is not random. There are times, conditions, and events in the life of every project when progress depends on subcontractors, or the weather, or coordination, or resource availability, and plans to deal with unfavorable contingencies should be developed early in the project's life cycle. Some PMs disdain this section of the plan on the grounds that crises cannot be predicted. Further, they claim to be very effective firefighters. It is quite possible that when one finds such a PM, one has discovered an arsonist. No amount of current planning can solve the current crisis, but preplanning may avert some.

These are the elements that constitute the project plan and are the basis for a more detailed planning of the budgets, schedules, work plan, and general management of the project. Once this basic plan is fully developed and approved, it is disseminated to all interested parties. For an example of a project plan, see the case at the end of this chapter.

5.2   SYSTEMS INTEGRATION

Systems integration (sometimes called *systems engineering*) plays a crucial role in the performance aspect of the project. We are using this phrase to include any technical specialist in the science or art of the project who is capable of performing the role of integrating the technical disciplines to achieve the customer's objectives, and/or integrating the project into the customer's system. As such, systems integration is concerned with three major objectives.

1. **Performance**   Performance is what a system does. It includes system design, reliability, quality, maintainability, and repairability. Obviously, these are not separate, independent elements of the system, but are highly interrelated qualities. Any of these system performance characteristics is subject to overdesign as well as underdesign but must fall within the design parameters established by the client. If the client approves, we may give the client more than the specifications require simply because we have already designed to some capability, and giving the client an overdesigned system is faster and less expensive than

delivering precisely to specification. At times, the esthetic qualities of a system may be specified, typically through a requirement that the appearance of the system must be acceptable to the client.

2. ***Effectiveness*** The objective is to design the individual components of a system to achieve the desired performance in an optimal manner. This is accomplished through the following guidelines:

- Require no component performance specifications unless necessary to meet one or more systems requirements.
- Every component requirement should be traceable to one or more systems requirements.
- Design components to optimize system performance, not the performance of a subsystem.

It is not unusual for clients to violate any or all of these seemingly logical dicta. Tolerances specified to far closer limits than any possible system requirement, superfluous "bells and whistles," and "off the shelf" components that do not work well with the rest of the system are so common they seem to be taken for granted by both client and vendor. The causes of these strange occurrences are probably associated with some combination of inherent distrust between buyer and seller, the desire to overspecify in order "to be sure," and the feeling that "this part will do just as well." As we will see in Chapter 6, these attitudes can be softened and replaced with others that are more helpful to the process of systems integration.

3. ***Cost*** Systems integration considers cost to be a design parameter, and costs can be accumulated in several areas. Added design cost may lead to decreased component cost, leaving performance and effectiveness otherwise unchanged. Added design cost may yield decreased production costs, and production cost may be traded off against unit cost for materials. *Value engineering* (or *value analysis*) examines all these cost tradeoffs and is an important aspect of systems integration [31]. It can be used in any project where the relevant cost tradeoffs can be estimated. It is simply the consistent and thorough use of cost/effectiveness analysis. For an application of value engineering techniques applied to disease control projects, see [13].

Systems integration plays a major role in the success or failure of any project. If a risky approach is taken by systems integration, it may delay the project. If the approach is too conservative, we forego opportunities for enhanced project capabilities or advantageous project economics. A good design will take all these tradeoffs into account in the initial stages of the technical approach. A good design will also avoid locking the project into a rigid solution with little flexibility or adaptability in case problems occur later on or changes in the environment demand changes in project performance or effectiveness.

The details of systems integration are beyond the scope of this book. The interested reader is referred to [4, 7]. In any case, the ability to do systems integration or engineering depends on at least a minimal level of technical knowledge about most parts of the project. It is one of the reasons project managers are expected to have some understanding of the technology of the projects they head.

▶ **5.3   SORTING OUT THE PROJECT**

In this and the following sections of this chapter, and in Chapters 7 and 8 on budgeting and scheduling, we move into a consideration of the details of the project. We need to know exactly what is to be done, by whom, and when. All activities required to complete the project must be precisely delineated and coordinated. The necessary resources must be available when and where they are needed, and in the correct amounts. Some activities must be done sequentially, but some may be done simultaneously. If a large project is to come in on time and within cost, a great many things must happen when and how they are supposed to happen. In this section, we propose a conceptually simple method to assist in sorting out and planning all this detail.

To accomplish any specified project, several major activities must be completed. First, list them in the general order in which they would normally occur. A reasonable number of major activities might be anywhere between two and 20. Break each of these major activities into two to 20 subtasks. There is nothing sacred about these limits. Two is the minimum possible breakdown and 20 is about the largest number of interrelated items that can be comfortably sorted and scheduled at a given level of task aggregation. Second, preparing a network from this information, as we will in Chapter 8, is much more difficult if the number of activities is significantly greater than 20.

It is important to be sure that all items in the list are at roughly the same level of task generality. In writing a book, for example, the various chapters tend to be at the same level of generality, but individual chapters are divided into finer detail. Indeed, subdivisions of a chapter may be divided into finer detail still. It is difficult to overstate the significance of this simple dictum. It is central to the preparation of most of the planning documents that will be described in this chapter and those that follow.

Sometimes a problem arises because some managers tend to think of outcomes (events) when planning and others think of specific tasks (activities). Many mix the two. The problem is to develop a list of both activities and outcomes that represents an exhaustive, nonredundant set of results to be accomplished (outcomes) and the work to be done (activities) in order to complete the project.

The procedure proposed here is a *hierarchical* planning system. First, the goals must be specified. This will aid the planner in identifying the set of required activities for the goals to be met, the *project action plan*. Each activity has an outcome (event) associated with it, and these activities and events can be decomposed into subactivities and subevents, which may, in turn, be subdivided again. The *project plan* is the set of these action plans. The advantage of the project plan is that it contains all planning information in one document.

Assume, for example, that we have a project whose purpose is to acquire and install a large machining center in an existing plant. In the hierarchy of work to be accomplished for the installation part of the project, we might find such tasks as "Develop a plan for preparation of the floor site" and "Develop a plan to maintain plant output during the installation and test period." These tasks are two of a larger set of jobs to be done. The task " . . . preparation of the floor site" is subdivided into its elemental parts, including such items as "Get specifics on machine center mounting points," "Check construction specifications on plant floor," and "Present final plan for floor preparation for approval." A form that may help to organize this information is shown in Figure 5-1. (Additional information about each element of the project will be added to the form later when budgeting and scheduling are discussed.) Figure 5-2 shows an action plan for a college "Career Day." (Clearly, Figure 5-2 is not complete. For example, the list of activities does not show such items as "setting and decorating the tables." In the interest of simplicity and in order to avoid doubling the length—and cost—of this book, the examples shown in this and following chapters are meant to be indicative, not exhaustive.)

A short digression is in order before continuing this discussion on action plans. The actual form the action plan takes is not sacrosanct. As we will show in this and the coming chapters, not even all elements of the action plan shown in Figure 5-1 are necessary in all cases. In some cases, for example, the amounts of specific resources required may not be relevant. In others, "due dates" may be substituted for activity durations. The appearance of action plans differs in different organizations, and may even differ between departments or divisions of the same organization (though standardization of format is usual, and probably desirable in any given firm). In some plans, numbers are used to identify activities; in others, letters. In still others, combinations of letters and numbers are used. In this chapter, we will illustrate several different forms of action plans drawn from "real life." Our purpose is not to confuse the reader, but to focus the reader's attention on the *content* of the plan, not its *form*.

A tree diagram can be used to represent a hierarchical plan as in Figure 5-3. Professor Andrew Vazsonyi has called this type of diagram a *Gozinto chart* after the famous Italian mathematician, Prof. Zepartzat Gozinto, of Vazsonyi's invention. (Readers familiar with the Bill of Materials in a Materials Requirements Planning—MRP—system will recognize the parallel to nested hierarchical planning.)

ACTION PLAN

Deliverables ____________________

Measure(s) of accomplishment ____________________

Key constraints and assumptions ____________________

TASKS	ESTIMATED RESOURCES	IMMEDIATE PREDECESSOR TASKS	ESTIMATED TIME DURATION(S)	ASSIGNED TO

Figure 5-1: A form to assist hierarchical planning.

ACTION PLAN

Steps	Responsibility	Time (weeks)	Prec.	Resources
Objective: Career Day				
I. Contact Organizations				
a. Print forms	Secretary	6	–	Print shop
b. Contact organizations	Program manager	15	1.a	Word processing
c. Collect display information	Office manager	4	1.b	
d. Gather college particulars	Secretary	4	1.b	
e. Print programs	Secretary	6	1.d	Print shop
f. Print participants' certificates	Graduate Assistant	8	–	Print shop
2. Banquet and Refreshments				
a. Select guest speaker	Program manager	14	–	
b. Organize food	Program manager	3	1.b	Caterer
c. Organize liquor	Director	10	1.b	Dept. of Liquor Control
d. Organize refreshments	Graduate Assistant	7	1.b	Purchasing
3. Publicity and Promotion				
a. Send invitations	Graduate Assistant	2	–	Word processing
b. Organize gift certificates	Graduate Assistant	5.5	–	
c. Arrange banner	Graduate Assistant	5	1.d	Print shop
d. Contact faculty	Program manager	1.5	1.d	Word processing
e. Advertise in college paper	Secretary	5	1.d	Newspaper
f. Class announcements	Graduate Assistant	1	3.d	Registrar's office
g. Organize posters	Secretary	4.5	1.d	Print shop
4. Facilities				
a. Arrange facility for event	Program manager	2.5	1.c	
b. Transport materials	Office manager	.5	4.a	Movers

Figure 5-2: Partial action plan for college "Career Day."

If the project does not involve capital equipment and special materials, estimates may not be necessary. Some projects require a long chain of tasks that are mostly sequential—for example, the real estate syndication of an apartment complex or the development and licensing of a new drug. Other projects require the coordination of many concurrent tasks that finally come together—for example, the design and manufacture of an aircraft engine or the construction of a house. Still others have the characteristics of both. An example of a plan to acquire a subsidiary is illustrated in Figures 5-4a and 5-4b. A verbal "action plan" was written in the form of a memorandum, Figure 5-4a, and was followed by the more common, tabular plan shown in Figure 5-4b. Only one page of a five-page plan is shown. The individu-

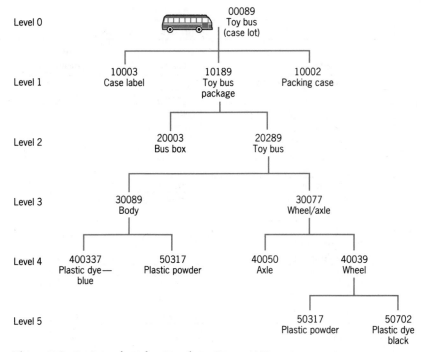

Figure 5-3: Gozinto chart for a toy bus. *Source:* [15]

als and groups mentioned developed similar plans at a greater level of detail. (Names have been changed at the request of the firm.)

The importance of careful planning can scarcely be overemphasized. Pinto and Slevin [33, 34] developed a list of ten factors that should be associated with success in implementation projects. The factors were split into strategic and tactical clusters. Of interest here are the strategic factors:

1. **Project mission.** It is important to spell out clearly defined and agreed-upon goals in the beginning of the project.

2. **Top management support.** It is necessary for top managers to get behind the project at the outset and make clear to all personnel involved that they support successful completion.

3. **Project schedule or plan.** A detailed plan of the required steps in the implementation process needs to be developed, including all resource requirements (money, raw materials, staff, and so forth).

Extensive empirical testing showed these factors to be required for implementation project success. (Tactical factors are also necessary for success, but they are not a consideration here.)

At this point, it might be helpful to sum up this section with a description of how the planning process actually works in many organizations. Assume that you, the PM, have been given responsibility for developing the computer software re-

---

MEMO

To allow Ajax to operate like a department of Instat by April 1, 1996, we must do the following by the dates indicated.

September 24

Ajax Management to be advised of coming under Instat operation. The Instat sales department will begin selling Ajax Consumer Division production effective Jan. 1, 1996. There will be two sales groups: (1) Instat, (2) Ajax Builder Group.

October 15

Instat Regional Managers advised—Instat sales department to assume sales responsibility for Ajax products to distribution channels, Jan. 1, 1986.

October 15

Ajax regional managers advised of sales changes effective Jan. 1, 1996.

October 15

Instat Management, Bob Carl, Van Baker, and Val Walters visit Ajax management and plant. Discuss how operations will merge into Instat.

October 22

Ajax regional managers advised Ajax sales personnel and agents of change effective Jan. 1, 1996.

October 24

Brent Sharp and Ken Roadway visit Instat to coordinate changeover.

October 29

Instat regional managers begin interviewing Ajax sales personnel for possible positions in Instat's sales organization.

November 5

Instat regional managers of Ajax for sales training session.

November 26

Walters visits Ajax to obtain more information.

November 30

Data Processing (Morrie Reddish) and Mfg. Engineering (Sam Newfield): Request DP tapes from Bob Cawley, Ajax, for conversion of Ajax to Instat eng. records: master inventory file, structure file, bill of materials file, where-used file, cross-reference Instat to Ajax part numbers, etc.

Allow maximum two weeks until December 14, 1995, for tapes to be at Instat.

December 3

ADMINISTRATIVE (Val Walters): Offer Norwood warehouse for sublease.

December 3

SALES (Abbott and Crutchfield): Week of sales meeting . . . instruction of salespeople in Ajax line . . . including procedure in writing Ajax orders on separate forms from Instat orders . . . temporarily, adding weight and shipping information, and procedure below:

Crutchfield to write procedure regarding transmission of orders to Instat, credit check, and transmission of order information to shipping point, whether Norwood, San Francisco, or, later, Instat Cincinnati.

Figure 5-4a: Action plan for merger of Ajax Hardware into Instat Corp. (page 1 of 5)

quired to transmit a medical X ray from one location to another over a telephone line. There are several problems that must be solved to accomplish this task. First, the X ray image must be translated into computer language. Second, the computerized image must be transmitted and received. Third, the image must be displayed (or printed) in a way that makes it intelligible to the person who must interpret it. You have a team of four programmers and a couple of assistant programmers as-

ACTION PLAN

Objective: Merger of Ajax Hardware into Instat Corp. by April 1, 1996			
Steps	**Due Date**	**Responsibility**	**Precedent**
1. Ajax management advised of changes	September 24	Bob Carl, Van Baker	–
2. Begin preparing Instat sales dept. to sell Ajax Consumer Division products effective 1/1/96	September 24	Bob Carl	1
3. Prepare to create two sales groups; (1) Instat, (2) Ajax Builder Group effective 1/1/96	September 24	Bob Carl	1
4. Advise Instat regional managers of sales division changes	October 15	Bob Carl	2,3
5. Advise Ajax regional managers of sales division changes	October 15	Van Baker	2,3
6. Visit Ajax management and plan to discuss merger of operations	October 15	Bob Carl, Van Baker, Val Walters	4,5
7. Advise Ajax sales personnel and agents	October 22	Van Baker	6
8. Visit Instat to coordinate changeover	October 24	Brent Sharp, Ken Roadway	6
9. Interview Ajax sales personnel for possible positions	October 29	Instat regional managers	7
10. Sales training sessions for Ajax products	November 5	Instat regional managers	9
11. Visit Ajax again	November 26	Val Walters	8,10
12. Request DP tapes from Bob Cawley for conversion	November 30	Morrie Reddish, Sam Newman	6
13. Offer Norwood warehouse for sublease	December 3	Val Walters	11
14. Write order procedures	December 3	Doug Crutchfield	10
15. Sales meeting (instruction—product line and procedures)	December 3	Fred Abbott, Doug Crutchfield	14
16. DP tapes due for master inventory file, bill of materials, structure file	December 14	Bob Cawley	12
. . .			
. . .			
. . .			

Figure 5-4b: Tabular action plan for Ajax-Instat merger based on Figure 5-4a.

signed to you. You also have a specialist in radiology assigned part-time as a medical advisor.

Your first action is to meet with the programmers and medical advisor in order to arrive at the technical requirements for the project. From these requirements, the project mission statement and detailed specifications will be derived. (Note that the original statement of your "responsibility" is too vague to act as an acceptable mission statement.) The basic actions needed to achieve the technical requirements for the project are then developed by the team. For example, one technical requirement would be to develop a method of measuring the density of the image at every point on the X ray and to represent this measurement as a numerical input for the computer. This is the first level of the project's action plan.

Responsibility for accomplishing the first level tasks is delegated to the project team members who are asked to develop their own action plans for each of the first level tasks. These are the second level action plans. The individual tasks listed in the second level plans are then divided further into third level action plans detailing how each second level task will be accomplished. The process continues until the lowest level tasks are perceived as "units" or "packages" of work.

Early in this section, we advised the planner to keep all items in an action plan at the same level of "generality" or detail. One reason for this is now evident. The tasks at any level of the action plan are usually monitored and controlled by the level just above. If senior managers attempt to monitor and control the highly detailed work packages several levels down, we have a classic case of micromanagement. Another reason for keeping all items in an action plan at the same level of detail is that planners have an unfortunate tendency to plan in great detail all activities they understand well, and to be dreadfully vague in planning activities they do not understand well. The result is that the detailed parts of the plan are apt to be carried out and the vague parts of the plan are apt to be given short shrift.

In practice, this process is iterative. Members of the project team who are assigned responsibility for working out a second, third, or lower-level action plan generate a tentative list of tasks, resource requirements, task durations, predecessors, etc., and bring it to the delegator for discussion, amendment, and approval. This may require several amendments and take several meetings before agreement is reached. The result is that delegator and delegatee both have the same idea about what is to be done, when, and at what cost. Not uncommonly, the individuals and groups that make commitments during the process of developing the action plan actually *sign-off* on their commitments. The whole process involves negotiation and will be further developed in the chapters to follow. Of course, like any managers, delegators can micromanage their delegatees, but micromanagement cannot be mistaken for negotiation—especially by the delegatee.

Project Management in Practice
Planning for Public Project Management: Milwaukee's Sewerage Renovation/Expansion

In 1977, by judicial and regulatory order, Milwaukee was ordered to renovate and expand their inadequate and outdated sewerage system. To do so would cost over $2 billion, involve 27 separate municipalities, and take approximately 20 years, all without disrupting existing sewerage services. To date, it has involved 306 construction and procurement

Source: H. F. Padgham, "The Milwaukee Water Pollution Abatement Program: Its Stakeholder Management," PM Network, April 1991.

Reconstructed treatment plant on the Milwaukee project.

contracts ranging from $100,000 to $200 million, 121 firms, and 1500 construction personnel. The project includes 20 miles of deep tunnels, ranging from 17 to 32 feet in diameter and 270 to 325 feet underground, and 62 miles of near-surface tunnels and sewers.

To manage this project, a Program Management Office (PMO) was established and given a set of seven physical objectives, seven community objectives, and five funding objectives. Overall, the PMO is responsible for six major functions: evaluation and planning, design management, cost/schedule management, construction, support service, and startup. Rather than PMO hiring all the workers needed for this project as city employees and bearing the costs of hiring, unemployment insurance, etc., an engineering consulting firm experienced in managing large municipal projects was engaged to "schedule, coordinate, and technically manage the various project elements of this program."

In addition to hiring construction and engineering contractors, a number of legal and public relations firms were also engaged to handle the many public conflicts that would invariably occur. One of these developed that seriously threatened the project when USA *Today* published a story that linked the Milwaukee Sewage Processing Plant with an illness contracted by three football players. The public relations firm engaged a number of medical authorities to study the data and offer opinions. They did, and discounted the possibility of any connection, a position affirmed by the national Environmental Protection Agency. The danger blew over.

Another critical point requiring political and public relations expertise concerned which of two major approaches were to be taken to the renovation: the separation of sewer and storm drains/tunnels (favored by excavators and pavers, plus newer communities who already had separate systems) versus the construction of deep underground storage facilities to allow the treatment plants time to process the polluted storm water (a much cheaper solution). Critical support from

Milwaukee community leadership organizations and public officials eventually led to selecting the second approach.

A more difficult problem, still not resolved, is how to pay for the project. Most of the suburbs preferred that the capital (investment) costs be paid through user charges based on the volume of wastewater entering the system. The city and other suburbs preferred that the capital costs be paid through property taxes, and operating costs be paid through user charges. The issue has been in and out of many courts, the state legislature, the state utility regulators, and the Public Service Commission.

In addition to the community leadership organizations, public agencies, and various engineering firms and contractors involved in the project, other stakeholders that need to be considered in the project's decisions include the EPA, the Wisconsin Department of Natural Resources, the U.S. Army Corps of Engineers, the operating staff of the Milwaukee Metropolitan Sewerage District (who will assume operating control of the new system when completed), local and state politicians, the governmental councils of the 27 municipalities, and the citizens and media of Milwaukee and its municipalities. As a tribute to the Milwaukee community, the contracting engineering firm designed a Milwaukee Riverwalk and solicited endorsements and funding for it. Today it is a reality.

▶ 5.4   THE WORK BREAKDOWN STRUCTURE AND LINEAR RESPONSIBILITY CHARTS

As was the case with project action plans and contrary to popular notion, the Work Breakdown Structure (WBS) is not one thing. It can take a wide variety of forms, which, in turn, serve a wide variety of purposes. It often pictures a project subdivided into hierarchical units of tasks, subtasks, work packages, etc., as a type of Gozinto chart or tree constructed directly from the project's action plans. Many of the project management software packages actually create WBSs automatically, given that the action plans have been input. These WBSs are usually in the form of outlines with the first level tasks at the left, and successive levels appropriately indented.

Another popular type of WBS shows the organizational elements associated with specific categories of tasks. Figure 5-5 is such a WBS. The project is to build a robot. The control group of the Electronics Department of the organization has responsibility for developing control systems for the robot. Five different control functions are shown, each of which is presumably broken down into more detailed tasks. In this case, the account numbers for each task are shown so that proper charges can be assigned to each piece of work done for the project.

Some writers recommend using the WBS as the fundamental tool for planning [16, for instance]. We find nothing logically wrong with this approach, but it seems overly structured when compared to the way that firms noted for high-quality planning actually proceed. If this approach is used, the PM is well advised to adopt the general philosophy of building the WBS that was used when building the action plan (see Section 5.3). Other writers pay scant attention to the WBS, giving the subject little more than a mention [4 and 26, among others]. We do not find this a fatal error as long as the planning activity is otherwise carried out to an appropriate level of detail.

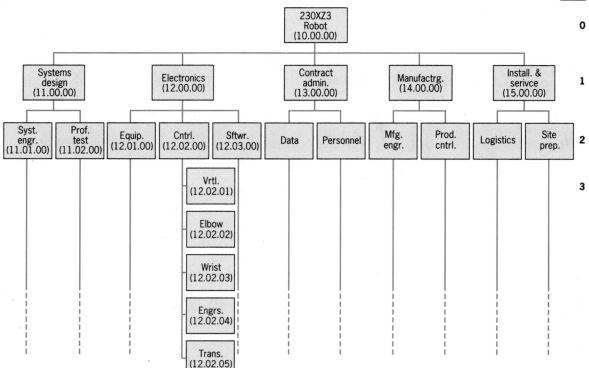

Figure 5-5: Work breakdown structure (account numbers shown).

In general, the WBS is an important document and can be tailored for use in a number of different ways. It may illustrate how each piece of the project contributes to the whole in terms of performance, responsibility, budget, and schedule. It may, if the PM wishes, list the vendors or subcontractors associated with specific tasks. It may be used to document that all parties have signed-off on their various commitments to the project. It may note detailed specifications for any work package, establish account numbers, specify hardware/software to be used, and identify resource needs. It may serve as the basis for making cost estimates (see Chapter 7) or estimates of task duration (see Chapter 8). Its uses are limited only by the needs of the project and the imagination of the PM. No one version of the WBS will suit all needs, so the WBS is not *a* document, but any given WBS is simply one of many possible documents.

The following general steps explain the procedure for designing and using the WBS. For small or moderate-size projects, and depending on the use for which the WBS is designed, some of the following steps might be skipped, combined, extended, and handled less formally than our explanation indicates, particularly if the project is of a type familiar to the organization.

1. Using information from the action plan, list the task breakdown in successively finer levels of detail. Continue until all meaningful tasks or work packages have

been identified and each task can be individually planned, budgeted, scheduled, monitored, and controlled.

2. For each such work package, identify the data relevant to the WBS (e.g., vendors, durations, equipment, materials, special specifications, etc.). List the personnel and organizations responsible for each task. It is helpful to construct a *linear responsibility chart* (sometimes called a *responsibility matrix*) to show who is responsible for what. This chart also shows critical interfaces between units that may require special managerial coordination. With it, the PM can keep track of who must approve what and who must report to whom. Such a chart is illustrated in Figure 5-6. If the project is not too complex, the responsibility chart can be simplified (see Figure 5-7). Figure 5-8 shows one page of a verbal responsibility chart developed by a firm to reorganize its distribution system. In this case, the chart takes the form of a 30-page document covering 116 major activities.

3. All work package information should be reviewed with the individuals or organizations who have responsibility for doing or supporting the work in order to verify the WBS' accuracy. Resource requirements, schedules, and subtask relationships can now be aggregated to form the next higher level of the WBS, continuing on to each succeeding level of the hierarchy. At the uppermost level, we have a summary of the project, its budget, and schedule.

4. For the purpose of pricing a proposal, or determining profit and loss, the total project budget should consist of four elements: direct budgets from each task

Responsibility						
WBS		**Project Office**				**Field Oper.**
Subproject	Task	Project Manager	Contract Admin.	Project Eng.	Industrial Eng.	Field Manager
Determine Need	A1	○		●	▲	
	A2	■	○	▲	●	
Solicit Quotations	B1	○	■	▲		●
Write Approp. Request	C1	■	▲	○	●	
	C2		●	○	▲	
	C3	●	■	▲		■
"	"					
"	"					
"	"					

Legend:
▲ Responsible
● Support
■ Notification
○ Approval

Figure 5-6: Linear responsibility chart.

	Vice-president	General manager	Project manager	Manager engineering	Manager software	Manager manufacturing	Manager marketing	Subprogram manager manufacturing	Subprogram manager software	Subprogram manager hardware	Subprogram manager services
Establish project plan	6	2	1	3	3	3	3	4	4	4	4
Define WBS		5	1	3	3	3	3	3	3	3	3
Establish hardware specs		2	3	1	4	4	4				
Establish software specs		2	3	4	1		4				
Establish interface specs		2	3	1	4	4	4				
Establish manufacturing specs		2	3	4	4	1	4				
Define documentation		2	1	4	4	4	4				
Establish market plan	5	3	5	4	4	4	1				
Prepare labor estimate		3	1	1	1			4	4	4	4
Prepare equipment cost estimate		3	1	1	1			4	4	4	4
Prepare material costs		3	1	1	1			4	4	4	4
Make program assignments		3	1	1	1			4	4	4	4
Establish time schedules		5	3	1	1	1	3	4	4	4	4

1 Actual responsibility   4 May be consulted
2 General supervision   5 Must be notified
3 Must be consulted   6 Final approval

Figure 5-7: Simplified linear responsibility chart.

as just described; an indirect cost budget for the project, which includes general and administrative overhead costs (G & A), marketing costs, potential penalty charges, and other expenses not attributable to particular tasks; a project "contingency" reserve for unexpected emergencies; and any residual, which includes the profit derived from the project, which may, on occasion, be intentionally negative. In Chapter 7 we argue that the budget used for pricing or calculation of profit should not be the same budget that the PM uses to control the project.

5. Similarly, schedule information and milestone (significant) events can be aggregated into a *project master schedule*. The master schedule integrates the many different schedules relevant to the various parts of the project. It is comprehensive and may include contractual commitments, key interfaces and sequencing, milestone events, and progress reports. In addition, a time contingency reserve for unforeseeable delays might be included. A graphic example of a master schedule is shown in Figure 5-9.

Activities	Initiate Action	Responsible Individuals Work with	Clear Action with
Distribution System and its Administration			
1. Recommend distribution system to be used.	Mktg Officers	ILI & IHI LOB MCs M-A Cttee VP &Agcy Dir	Sr VP Mktg
	Mktg Officers	Group LOB MC M-A Cttee VP & Agcy Dir	Sr VP Mktg
	Mktg Officers	IA LOB MC M-A Cttee VP & Agcy Dir	Sr VP Mktg
Compensation			
2. Determine provisions of sales compensation programs (e.g., commissions, subsidies, fringes).	Compensation Task Force	Mktg, S&S & Eqty Prod Offrs	President
	Compensation Task Force	Mktg, S&S & Eqty Prod Offrs	
	Compensation Task Force	Mktg, S&S & Eqty Prod Offrs	President
3. Ensure cost-effectiveness testing of sales compensation programs.	Compensation Task Force	Mktg, S&S & Eqty Prod Offrs	President
Territory			
4. Establish territorial strategy for our primary distribution system.	VP & Agcy Dir	Dir MP&R M-A Cttee	Sr VP Mktg
5. Determine territories for agency locations and establish priorities for starting new agencies.	VP & Agcy Dir	Dir MP&R M-A Cttee	Sr VP Mktg
6. Determine agencies in which advanced sales personnel are to operate.	Dir Ret Pln Sls Dir Adv Sls	VP S&S	Sr VP Mktg

Legend: IA, ILI, IHI: Product lines
LOB: Line of business
MC: Management committee
M-A Cttee: Marketing administration committee
S&S: Sales and service
MP&R: Marketing planning and research

Figure 5-8: Verbal responsibility chart.

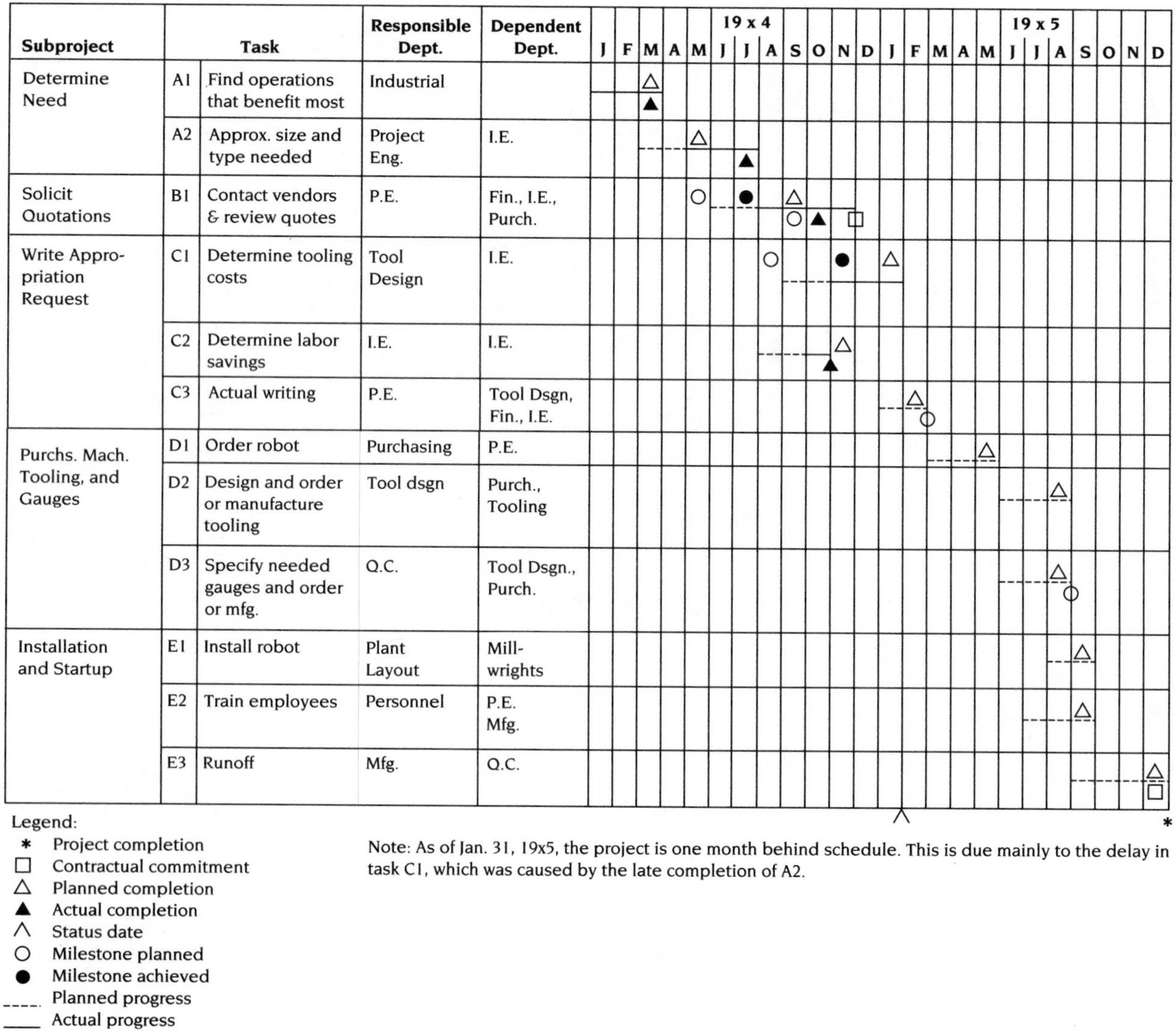

Subproject		Task	Responsible Dept.	Dependent Dept.	19 x 4 J F M A M J J A S O N D	19 x 5 J F M A M J J A S O N D
Determine Need	A1	Find operations that benefit most	Industrial		△ ▲	
	A2	Approx. size and type needed	Project Eng.	I.E.	△ ▲	
Solicit Quotations	B1	Contact vendors & review quotes	P.E.	Fin., I.E., Purch.	○ ● △ ○▲ ▢	
Write Appropriation Request	C1	Determine tooling costs	Tool Design	I.E.	○ ● △	
	C2	Determine labor savings	I.E.	I.E.	△ ▲	
	C3	Actual writing	P.E.	Tool Dsgn, Fin., I.E.	△ ○	
Purchs. Mach. Tooling, and Gauges	D1	Order robot	Purchasing	P.E.		△
	D2	Design and order or manufacture tooling	Tool dsgn	Purch., Tooling		△
	D3	Specify needed gauges and order or mfg.	Q.C.	Tool Dsgn., Purch.		△ ○
Installation and Startup	E1	Install robot	Plant Layout	Mill-wrights		△
	E2	Train employees	Personnel	P.E. Mfg.		△
	E3	Runoff	Mfg.	Q.C.		△ ▢

Legend:
* Project completion
▢ Contractual commitment
△ Planned completion
▲ Actual completion
∧ Status date
○ Milestone planned
● Milestone achieved
____ Planned progress
____ Actual progress

Note: As of Jan. 31, 19x5, the project is one month behind schedule. This is due mainly to the delay in task C1, which was caused by the late completion of A2.

Figure 5-9: Project master schedule.

Listed items 1 to 5 focus on the WBS as a planning tool. It may also be used as an aid in monitoring and controlling projects. Again, it is important to remember that no single WBS contains all of the elements described and any given WBS should be designed with specific uses in mind.

6. As the project is carried out, step by step, the PM can continually examine actual resource use, by work element, work package, task, and so on up to the full project level. By comparing actual against planned resource usage at a given time, the PM can identify problems, harden the estimates of final cost, and make sure that relevant corrective actions have been designed and are ready to implement if needed. It is necessary to examine resource usage in relation to results achieved because, while the project may be over budget, the results may be farther along than expected. Similarly, the expenses may be exactly as planned, or even lower, but actual progress may be much less than planned. Control charts showing these *earned values* are described in more detail in Chapter 10.

7. Finally, the project schedule may be subjected to the same comparisons as the project budget. Actual progress is compared to scheduled progress by work element, package, task, and complete project, to identify problems and take corrective action. Additional resources may be brought to those tasks behind schedule to expedite them. These added funds may come out of the budget reserve or from other tasks that are ahead of schedule. This topic is discussed further in Chapter 9.

▶ 5.5 INTERFACE MANAGEMENT

The most difficult aspect of implementing the project plan is the coordination of the various elements of the project so that they meet their joint goals of performance, schedule, and budget. The PM must control the process and timing of this coordination as a part of the everyday task of managing the project. The term *interface* is used to denote both the process and fact of this coordination. The linear responsibility chart discussed above is clearly a useful aid to the PM in performing this managerial task because it displays the multiple ways the project's people must interact and what the rights, duties, and responsibilities of each will be.

A more formal and detailed approach to this problem has been developed [6] by Benningson. This analytic approach is called TREND (Transformed Relationships Evolved from Network Data) and was designed to illustrate important relationships between work groups, to alert the project manager to potential problems associated with interfaces, and to aid in the design of effective ways to avoid or deal with the potential interface problems.

Three key concepts are added in Benningson's approach: interdependence, uncertainty, and prestige. The project master schedule, the WBS, and task networks can be used to provide some of the information required to delineate the nature of these concepts, to understand their potential impacts on the interface between individuals and groups, and to denote task and group interdependencies. Figure 5-10 is an organizational chart that has been modified according to TREND procedures.

Interdependencies are shown by lines, with the primary direction of the interdependence indicated by the arrows.

The uncertainty facing each task group or individual and the relative prestige levels of each of the task groups/individuals need to be established. Uncertainty levels are assumed to correlate with such factors as the length of the project time horizon, the level of reliance on formal authority, and the degree of task orientation of the work. If estimates are available, the spread between the optimistic and pessimistic time estimates reflects the level of uncertainty of the schedule. See the shaded boxes in Figure 5-10.

Prestige is inferred from organization charts or from known anecdotal information. See the right-hand scale in Figure 5-10. Although using position on the organization chart as a surrogate for organizational prestige is questionable, no better overall measure seems to be available. The analyst would be well advised to check this assumption for each particular case when employing this model. All three elements—prestige, uncertainty, and interdependence—can be depicted on an organization chart to illustrate potential coordination problems.

Dependence is shown by an arrow from the preceding task group/person to the following, dependent task group/person. Uncertainty is denoted by shading those groups/persons with high task uncertainty and not shading those with low uncertainty. Prestige is read directly off the chart by noting the level of the group/person in the organizational structure. See [6] for a detailed example.

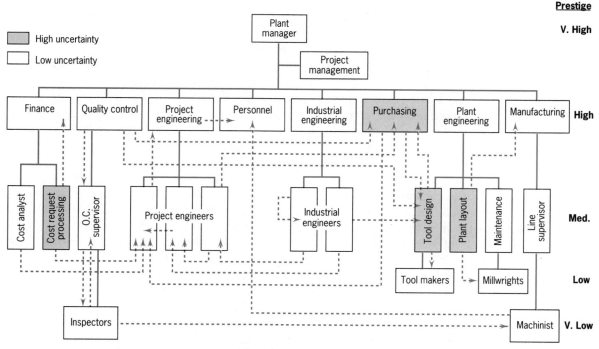

Figure 5-10: TREND organizational overlay.

A complete description of the project interfaces can be shown by mapping all dependencies in the project together with the average uncertainty faced by each group/person. Similarly, the different phases of the project life cycle can be displayed using TREND, and can be examined to see what problems might arise within particular time periods. For instance, the work of a particular group might consist mostly of work having low uncertainty, but at project startup, for example, the group may be assigned to some high uncertainty tasks. The PM would give this group special attention during startup in order to react quickly to problems that arose during that period, but could afford to relax attention to this specific group during other phases of the project's life cycle. This pattern of high uncertainty followed by low uncertainty is common. Design of the foundation for a large building may have high uncertainty until test borings are completed, and low uncertainty thereafter. The same is true for most R & D projects, there being high uncertainty until an approach is proven, and then low uncertainty.

Problems also tend to occur when a high-prestige group is dependent on a low-prestige group, when a high-uncertainty task follows another high-uncertainty task, when complex multiple uncertainties exist, and so on. The various combinations of uncertainty and group prestige differentials have various potentials for problems and can best be controlled by managerial strategies formulated specifically to deal with unique situations. Table 5-1 describes some potential interface problems in Figure 5-10 together with possible managerial solutions.

Table 5-1 Analysis of TREND Overlay

Effect	Coordination Required
1. Industrial Engs. and Project Engs.—self-dependencies.	Monitor internal coordination.
2. Quality Control Mgr./Q.C. Supervisor—same functional areas, same low uncertainty, low status depends on high status.	Depend on planning, regular coordination.
3. Q.C. Mgr./Tool Design—different functional areas, mixed uncertainty, low status depends on high status.	Set up interfunctional system for coordination. Monitor regularly.
4. Personnel Mgr./Machinist—different functional area, low uncertainty, high status depends on low status.	Interface as coordinator and translator.
5. Project Engineer/Purchasing Mgr.—different functional area, mixed uncertainty, reciprocal dependence, different status.	Set up regular review meetings for coordination. Project manager chairs meetings.
6. Tool designers/Purchasing Mgr.—different functional area, same high uncertainty, different status, reciprocal dependence.	Set up regular review meetings. Plant eng. mgr. and purch. mgr. to rotate chairing meeting. Perhaps include the project engineers in the meeting.
7. Project Eng. Mgr./Project Engineers—same functional area, high status depends on low, same low uncertainty.	Depend on regular authority and information structure. Stay informed. Encourage frequent discussion.

TREND is hardly a complete system for interface management and its full-scale, formal use is rarely justified, but the conceptual approach is valuable. Experienced PMs are aware of many of the problems TREND exposes, but the technique provides an excellent framework for the inexperienced and a check for "old hands." For an excellent discussion of the behavioral problems in interface management as well as the entire project implementation process, see [29].

▶ SUMMARY

In this chapter we initiated planning for the project in terms of identifying and addressing the tasks required for project completion. We emphasized the importance of initial coordination of all parties involved and the smooth interpretation of the various systems required to achieve the project objectives. Last, we described some tools such as the Work Breakdown Structure (WBS), the linear responsibility chart, the action plan, TREND, and the Gozinto chart to aid in the planning process.

Specific points made in the chapter were these:

- The preliminary work plans are important because they serve as the basis for personnel selection, budgeting, scheduling, and control.

- Top management should be represented in the initial coordinating meeting where technical objectives are established, participant responsibility is accepted, and preliminary budgets and schedules are defined.

- The approval and change processes are complex and should be handled by the project manager.

- Common elements of the project plan are the overview, statement of objectives, general approach, contractual requirements, schedules, budget, cost control procedures, evaluation procedures, and potential problems.

- Systems integration concerns the smooth coordination of project systems in terms of cost, performance, and effectiveness.

- The hierarchical approach to project planning is most appropriate and can be aided by a tree diagram of project subsets, called a Gozinto chart, and a Work Breakdown Structure (WBS). The WBS relates the details of each subtask to its task and provides the final basis for the project budget, schedule, personnel, and control.

- A linear responsibility chart is often helpful to illustrate the relationship of personnel to project tasks and to identify where coordination is necessary.

- A tool particularly helpful in identifying potential interface and coordination problems is the TREND organization chart overlay, based on differences in status or prestige level, task dependence, and uncertainty.

Based on the now-established project plan and WBS, we can consider the task of negotiating for the resources to implement the project. This topic completes Part I of the text.

▶ GLOSSARY

Baseline Plan—The nominal plan to which deviations will be compared.

Bill of Materials—The set of physical elements required to build a product.

Control Chart—A graph showing how a statistic is changing over time compared to its average and extreme values.

Deliverables—The physical items to be delivered from a project. This typically includes reports and plans as well as physical objects.

Earned Value—A measure of project progress, frequently related to tasks accomplished and milestones achieved.

Effectiveness—Achieving the objectives set beforehand; to be distinguished from efficiency, which is measured by the output realized for the input used.

Engineering Change Orders—Product improvements that engineering has designed after the initial product design was released.

Gozinto Chart—A pictorial representation of a product that shows how the elements required to build a product fit together.

Hierarchical Planning—A planning approach that breaks the planning task down into the activities that must be done at each managerial level. Typically, the upper level sets the objectives for the next lower level.

Interface Management—Managing the problems that tend to occur between departments and disciplines, rather than within individual departments.

Material Requirements Planning (MRP)—A planning and material ordering approach based on the known or forecast final demand requirements, lead times for each fabricated or purchased item, and existing inventories of all items.

Systems Engineering—The engineering tasks involved in the complete system concerning the project and the integration of all the subsystems into the overall system.

Value Engineering—An approach that examines each element of a product or system to determine if there is a better or cheaper way of achieving the same function.

Work Statement—A description of a task that defines all the work required to accomplish it, including inputs and desired outputs.

▶ MATERIAL REVIEW QUESTIONS

1. List the six component planning sequences of project planning.

2. Any successful project plan must contain nine key elements. List these items and briefly describe the composition of each.

3. What are the basic guidelines for systems design which assure that individual components of the system are designed in an optimal manner?

4. What are the general steps for managing each work package within a specific project?

5. How may the three key concepts in the TREND approach be depicted on an organizational chart, and how are potential problems recognized and possibly averted using this method?

6. What is shown on a linear responsibility chart? How is it useful to a PM?

7. What should be accomplished at the initial coordination meeting?

8. Why is it important for the functional areas to be involved in the project from the time of the original proposal?

9. What are the three major objectives of systems integration?

10. What are the basic steps to design and use the Work Breakdown Structure?

11. What is the objective of interface management?

▶ CLASS DISCUSSION QUESTIONS

1. What percentage of the total project effort do you think should be devoted to planning? Why?

2. Why do you suppose that the coordination of the various elements of the project is considered the most difficult aspect of project implementation?

3. What kinds of problem areas might be included in the project plan?

4. What is the role of systems integration in project management? What are the three major objectives of systems integration?

5. In what ways may the WBS be used as a key document to monitor and control a project?

6. Describe the process of subdivision of activities and events that composes the tree diagram

known as the Work Breakdown Structure or Gozinto chart. Why is the input of responsible managers and workers so important an aspect of this process?

7. Why is project planning so important?

8. What are the pros and cons concerning the early participation of the various functional areas in the project plan?

9. What tradeoffs might exist among the three objectives of system integration?

10. Task 5-C is the critical, pacing task of a rush project. Fred always nitpicks anything that comes his way, slowing it down, driving up its costs, and irritating everyone concerned. Normally, Fred would be listed as "Notify" for task 5-C on the responsibility matrix but the PM is considering "forgetting" to make that notation on the chart. In this unethical, political, or just smart management?

▶ INCIDENTS FOR DISCUSSION

Ringold's Pool and Patio Supply

John Ringold, Jr., just graduated from a local university with a degree in industrial management and joined his father's company as executive vice-president of operations. Dad wants to break John in slowly and has decided to see how he can do on a project that John Sr. has never had time to investigate. Twenty percent of the company's sales are derived from the sale of above-ground swimming pool kits. Ringold's does not install the pools. John Sr. has asked John Jr. to determine whether or not they should get into that business. John Jr. has decided that the easiest way to impress Dad and get the project done is personally to estimate the cost to the company of setting up a pool and then call some competitors and see how much they charge. That will show whether or not it is profitable.

John Jr. remembered a method called the work breakdown structure (WBS) that he thought might serve as a useful tool to estimate costs. Also, the use of such a tool could be passed along to the site supervisor to help evaluate the performance of work crews. John Jr.'s WBS is shown in Table 5-2. The total cost John Jr. calculated was $185.00, based on 12.33 labor-hours at $15.00/labor-hour. John Jr. found that, on average, Ringold's competitors charged $229.00 to install a similar pool. John Jr. thought he had a winner. He called his father and made an appointment to present his findings the next morning. Since he had never assembled a pool himself, he decided to increase the budget by 10 percent, "just in case."

Questions: Is John Jr.'s WBS projection reasonable? What aspects of the decision will John Sr. consider?

HAC Computer Company

The board members of HAC Computer Company approved the building of a new facility approximately six months ago. The facility is to be constructed in South Carolina and will be used to manufacture a new line of microcomputers. The company is currently manufacturing only minicomputers and workstations but because of the tremendous market for the micro, they plan to enter this field also. The company has already selected the project manager and the project team. The project manager is ready to get the project under way and has begun work on the project master plan. The three aspects of the master plan that she is most concerned about are schedules, resources, and personnel. Since she is so concerned about scheduling, she decided to get a head start and do the project scheduling estimates for the milestone events herself. For the resource planning she developed some capital

Table 5-2   Pool Installation WBS

Work Tasks		Labor-hours (estimated)
Prepare ground surface		2.67
Clear	1	
Rake	1/3	
Level	1	
Sand bottom	1/3	
Lay out pool frame		2.50
Bottom ring	1	
Side panels	1/2	
Top ring	1	
Add plastic liner		0.50
Assemble pool		1.66
Build wooden support		3.00
Lay out	1	
Assemble	2	
Fill and test		2.00
Total		12.33

requirements for the various parts of the project that would be continuing throughout the project, and for personnel she developed a preliminary forecast of what skills she felt might be needed, and when, over the life of the project.

Questions: If you were the project manager, would you handle these three aspects of the master plan the same or differently? Explain. What elements of resource planning and personnel planning should be included?

INDIVIDUAL EXERCISE

Recall a recent or current project in a formal group, such as a church committee or social group, of which you are a member. Construct a detailed Gozinto chart and Work Breakdown Structure for the project. Then lay out a linear responsibility chart for the project along the lines of Figure 5-7. Next, design a general organization chart that includes all the parties identified on the linear responsibility chart.

PROJECT TEAM CONTINUING EXERCISE

For this exercise, initial project planning must be conducted. To construct the overall project plan, start with the action plan and construct the work breakdown structure, a Gozinto chart, and determine a linear responsibility chart. Include the instructor in your plans as a representative of top management. From this set of information, build a preliminary project budget and determine a master schedule with major milestones. Finally, use the TREND procedure to build an organizational overlay, identify potential problem areas, and suggest possible remedies. Are there any missing information sets or aids that could be helpful for your specific project?

BIBLIOGRAPHY

1. AGARWAL, J. C. "Project Planning at Kennecott." *Research Management*. May 1974.
2. ANDERSON, J., and R. NARASIMHAN. "Assessing Project Implementation Risk: A Methodical Approach." *Management Science*, June 1979.
3. ARCHIBALD, R. D. "Projects: Vehicles for Strategic Growth." *Project Management Journal*, Sept. 1988.
4. BADIRU, A. B. *Project Management in Manufacturing and High Technology Operations*. New York: Wiley, 1988.
5. BAUMGARTNER, J. S. *Project Management*. Homewood, IL: Irwin, 1963.
6. BENNINGSON, L. A. "TREND: A Project Management Tool." *Proceedings of the Project Management Conference*, Philadelphia, Oct. 1972.
7. BLANCHARD, B. S., and W. FABRYCKY. *Systems Engineering and Analysis*, 2nd ed. Englewood Cliffs, NJ.: Prentice Hall, 1990.
8. BLANNING, R. W. "How Managers Decide to Use Planning Models." *Long Range Planning*, April 1980.
9. CLELAND, D. I., and R. K. KIMBALL. "The Strategic Context of Projects." *Project Management Journal*, Aug. 1987.
10. DAVIS, E. W. *Project Management: Techniques, Applications, and Managerial Issues*, 2nd ed. Norcross, GA.: Institute of Industrial Engineers, 1983.
11. FRIEND, F. L. "Be A More Effective Program Manager." *Journal of Systems Management*, Feb. 1976.
12. GOODMAN, L. J., and R. N. LOVE, eds. *Project Planning Management*. New York: Pergamon Press Inc., 1980.
13. GROSS, R. N. "Cost–Benefit Analysis and Social Planning." M. Alfandary-Alexander, ed., *Analysis of Planning Programming Budgeting*. Potomac, MD.: Washington Operations Research Council, 1968.
14. GUNDERMAN, J. R., and F. R. McMURRY. "Making Project Management Effective." *Journal of Systems Management*, Feb. 1975.
15. HARRIS, R. D., and R. F. GONZALEZ. *The Operations Manager*. St. Paul: West, 1981.

16. HUBBARD, D. G. "Work Structuring," in P. C. Dinsmore, ed., *The AMA Handbook of Project Management*. New York: AMACOM, 1993.

17. HUGHES, E. R. "Planning: The Essence of Control." *Managerial Planning*, June 1978.

18. JOHNSON, J. R. "Advanced Project Control." *Journal of Systems Management*, May 1977.

19. KAHERLAS, H. "A Look at Major Planning Methods: Development, Implementation, Strengths and Limitations." *Long Range Planning*, Aug. 1978.

20. KERZNER, H. *Project Management: A Systems Approach to Planning, Scheduling, and Controlling*, 3rd ed. New York: Van Nostrand Reinhold, 1984.

21. KNUTSON, J., and M. SCOTT. "Developing a Project Plan." *Journal of Systems Management*, Oct. 1978.

22. KONDINELL, D. A. "Planning Development Projects: Lessons from Developing Countries." *Long Range Planning*, June 1979.

23. LAUFER, A. "Project Planning: Timing Issues and Path of Progress." *Project Management Journal*, June 1991.

24. LAVOLD, G. D. "Developing and Using the Work Breakdown Structure," in Cleland, D. I., and W. R. King, *Project Management Handbook*. New York: Van Nostrand Reinhold, 1983.

25. LIBERATORE, M. J. "A Decision Support System Linking Research and Development Project Selection with Business Strategy." *Project Management Journal*, Nov. 1988.

26. LOVE, S. F. *Achieving Problem Free Project Management*. New York: Wiley, 1989.

27. MARTIN, J. "Planning: The Gap between Theory and Practice." *Long Range Planning*, Dec. 1979.

28. MARTYN, A. S. "Some Problems in Managing Complex Development Projects." *Long Range Planning*, April 1975.

29. MORRIS, W. T. *Implementation Strategies for Industrial Engineers*. Columbus, OH: Grid, 1979.

30. NUTT, P. C. "Hybrid Planning Methods." *Academy of Management Review*, July 1982.

31. PALEY, A. I. "Value Engineering and Project Management: Achieving Cost Optimization," in P. C. Dinsmore, ed., *The AMA Handbook of Project Management*. New York: AMACOM, 1993.

32. PELLS, D. L. "Project Management Plans: An Approach to Comprehensive Planning for Complex Projects," in P. C. Dinsmore, ed., *The AMA Handbook of Project Management*. New York: AMACOM 1993.

33. PINTO, J. K., and D. P. SLEVIN. "Critical Factors in Successful Project Implementation." *IEEE Transactions on Engineering Management*, Feb. 1987.

34. PINTO, J. K., and D. P. SLEVIN. "Project Success: Definitions and Measurement Techniques." *Project Management Journal*, Feb. 1988.

35. PRENTIS, E. L. "Master Project Planning: Scope, Time and Cost." *Project Management Journal*, Mar. 1989.

36. RAKOS, J. J. *Software Project Management*. Englewood Cliffs, NJ: Prentice Hall, 1990.

37. ROLEFSON, J. F. "Project Management—Six Critical Steps." *Journal of Systems Management*, April 1975.

38. ROMAN, D. *R & D Management*. New York: Appleton-Century-Crofts, 1968.

39. SCHULTZ, R. L., D. P. SLEVIN, and J. K. PINTO. "Strategy and Tactics in a Process Model of Project Implementation." *Interfaces*, May–June 1987.

40. SJOQUIST, P. *Program Management Handbook*. Bloomington, MN: Control Data Corporation (now Ceridian Corp.), undated.

41. STEWART, J. M. "Guides to Effective Project Management." *Management Review*, Jan. 1966.

42. WEBSTER, J. L., W. E. REIF, and J. S. BRACKER. "The Manager's Guide to Strategic Planning Tools and Techniques." *Planning Review*, Nov./Dec. 1989, reprinted in *Engineering Management Review*, Dec. 1990.

43. WEDLEY, W. C., and A. E. J. FERRIE. "Perceptual Differences and Effects of Managerial Participation on Project Implementation." *Operations Research*, March 1978.

44. WESTNEY, R. E., "Paradigms for Planning Productive Projects," in P. C. Dinsmore, ed., *The AMA Handbook of Project Management*. New York: AMACOM, 1993.

45. WHEELWRIGHT, S. C., and R. L. BLANK. "Involving Operating Managers in Planning Process Evaluation." *Sloan Management Review*, Summer 1979.

CASE

A PROJECT MANAGEMENT AND CONTROL SYSTEM FOR CAPITAL PROJECTS

Herbert F. Spirer and A. G. Hulvey

Introduction

Heublein, Inc., develops, manufactures, and markets consumer food and beverage products domestically and internationally. The business of Heublein, Inc., their sales revenue, and some of their better known products are shown in Figure 1. Highlights of Figure 1 include:

The four major businesses ("Groups") use different manufacturing plants, equipment, and processes to produce their products. In the Spirits Group large, continuous-process bottling plants are the rule; in the Food Service and Franchising Group, small fast food restaurants are the "manufacturing plants."

The amount of spending for capital projects and support varies greatly among the Groups, as would be expected from the differences in the magnitude of sales revenues.

The engineering departments of the Groups have responsibility for operational planning and control of capital projects, a common feature of the Groups. However, the differences among the Groups are reflected in differences in the sizes of the engineering departments and their support services. Similarly, financial tracking support varies from full external support to self-maintained records.

Prior to the implementation of the Project Management and Control System (PM&C) described in this paper, the capital project process was chiefly concerned with the financial justification of the projects, as shown in Figure 2. Highlights include:

A focus on cost–benefit analysis.

Minimal emphasis on execution of the projects; no mechanism to assure that non-financial results were achieved.

In the late 1970s the following factors focused attention on the execution weaknesses of the process:

Some major projects went over budget.

The need for optimal utilization of capital funds intensified since depreciation legislation was not keeping pace with the inflationary rise in costs.

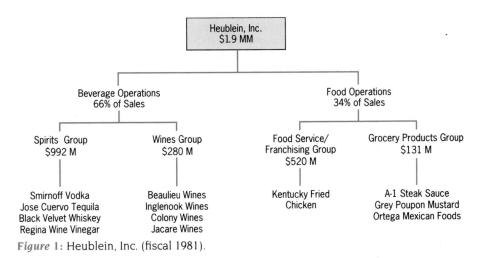

Figure 1: Heublein, Inc. (fiscal 1981).

Group recognizes
need or opportunity

|

Group prepares a Capital Appropriation Request—
primarily cost/benefit analysis

|

Group management reviews,
approves/disapproves

|

Corporate Finance Department reviews,
approves/disapproves

|

Corporate Facilities and Manufacturing Planning
reviews, approves/disapproves

|

Corporate Management reviews,
approves/disapproves

|

Group implements project

|

Group reports status monthly to Corporate

|

If significant cost variance occurs, Group prepares
Capital Appropriation Revision and process repeated
from step 3

|

Project completed

Figure 2: Capital project progress prior to PM&C

Responding to these factors, Heublein's corporate management called for a program to improve execution of capital projects by implementing PM&C. Responsibility for this program was placed with the Corporate Facilities and Manufacturing Department, which, in addition to reviewing all Capital Appropriation Requests, provided technical consulting services to the corporation.

Feasibility Study

Lacking specialized expertise in project management, the Director of Facilities and Manufacturing Planning decided to use a consultant in the field. Interviewing of three consultants was undertaken to select one who had the requisite knowledge, compatibility with the style and goals of the firm, and the ability to communicate to all levels and types of managers. The latter requirement was important because of the diversity of the engineering department structures and

personnel involved. The first author was selected as the consultant.

With the consultant selected, an internal program manager for PM&C was selected. The deferral of this choice until after selection of the consultant was deliberate, to allow for development of interest and enthusiasm among candidates for this position and so that both the selected individual and the selection committee would have a clear picture of the nature of the program. A program manager was chosen from the corporate staff (the second author).

Having the key staff in place, ground rules were established as follows:

> The PM&C program would be developed internally to tailor it to the specific needs of the Groups. A "canned" or packaged system would limit this flexibility, which was deemed essential in this application of project management principles.

> The directors of the engineering departments of each of the Groups were to be directly involved in both the design and implementation of the PM&C system in total and for their particular Group. This would assure the commitment to its success that derives from ownership and guarantees that those who know the needs best determine the nature of the system.

> To meet the above two ground rules, a thorough fundamental education in the basic principles of project management would be given to all involved in the system design.

The emphasis was to be project *planning* as opposed to project *control*. The purpose of PM&C was to achieve better performance on projects, not catch mistakes after they have occurred. Success was the goal, rather than accountability or identification of responsibility for failure.

Program Design

The option of defining a uniform PM&C system, to be imposed on all engineering departments by corporate mandate was rejected. The diversity of projects put the weight in favor of individual systems, provided planning and control was such that success of the projects was facilitated. The advantage to corporate staff of uniform planning and reporting was given second place to accommodation of the unique needs of each Group and the wholehearted commitment of each engineering manager to the effective use of the adopted system. Thus, a phased implementation of PM&C within Heublein was planned in advance. These phases were:

Phase 1. Educational overview for engineering department managers. A three-day seminar with two top-level educational objectives: (1) comprehension by participants of a maximal set of project management principles and (2) explanation of the corporate objectives and recommended approach for any PM&C system. Despite some expressed initial concern, the response to this session was positive. It was correctly perceived as the first step in a sincere attempt by corporate management to develop a jointly defined PM&C system that would be useful to the managers of projects, rather than to satisfy a corporate reporting need.

Phase II. PM&C system design. A "gestation period" of three weeks was deliberately introduced between Phases I and II to allow for absorption, discussion, and review of the project management principles and objectives by the engineering department managers. At the end of this period a session was called for the explicit purpose of defining the system. The session was chaired by the consultant, a deliberate choice to achieve the "lightning rod" effect whereby any negative concern was directed to an outsider. Also, the consultant—as an outsider—could criticize and comment in ways that should not be done by the engineering department managers who will have long-term working relationships among each other. It was agreed in advance that a consensus would be sought to the greatest possible extent, avoiding any votes on how to handle particular issues which leaves the "nay" votes feeling that their interests have been overridden by the majority. If consensus could not be achieved, then the issue would be sidestepped to be deferred for later consideration; if sufficiently important then a joint solution could be developed outside the session without the pressure of a fixed closing time. The dynamics of this design session included the development of consensus statements which were displayed on overhead transparencies to be worked into shape. As soon as this was acceptable to the Group as a whole, one of two attending stenographers would record the agreement, leave the room and return later with a typed version for group consideration. The use of two group stenographers assured that one was always in attendance. The enthusiasm expressed by the

engineering department managers for this meeting was high.

Phase III. Project plan development. The output of Phase II (the set of consensus conclusions) represented both guidelines and specific conclusions concerning the nature of a PM&C system. Recognizing that the PM&C program will be viewed as a model project and that it should be used as such, serving as an example of what is desired, the program manager prepared a project plan for the PM&C program. The remainder of this paper is primarily concerned with the discussion of this plan, both as an example of how to introduce a PM&C system and how to make a project plan. The plan discussed in this paper and illustrated in Figures 3 to 11 is the type of plan that is now required before any capital project may be submitted to the approval process at Heublein.

Phase IV. Implementation. With the plan developed in Phase III approved, it was possible to move ahead with implementation. Implementation was in accordance with the plan discussed in the balance of this paper. Evaluation of the results was considered a part of this implementation.

Project Plan

A feature of the guidelines developed by the engineering managers in Phase II was that a "menu" of component parts of a project plan was to be established in the corporate PM&C system, and that elements of this menu were to be chosen to fit the situational or corporate tracking requirements. The menu is:

1. Introduction
2. Project Objectives
3. Project/Program Structure
4. Project/Program Costs
5. Network
6. Schedule
7. Resource Allocation
8. Organization and Accountability
9. Control System
10. Milestones or Project Subdivisions

In major or critical projects, the minimal set of choices from the menu is specified by corporate staff (the definition of a "major" or "critical" project is a part of the PM&C procedure). For "routine" projects, the choice from the menu is left to the project manager.

In the PM&C plan, items 6 and 7, Schedule and Resource Allocation, were combined into one section for reasons which will be described as part of the detailed discussions of the individual sections which follow.

Introduction

In this PM&C system, the Introducton is an executive summary, with emphasis on the justification of the project. This can be seen from the PM&C Program Introduction shown in Figure 3. It is to the advantage of everyone concerned with a project to be fully aware of the reasons for its existence. It is as important to the technicians as it is to the engineers or the corporate financial department. When the project staff clearly comprehends the reason for the project's existence it is much easier to enlist and maintain their support and wholehearted efforts. In the Heublein PM&C system, it is expected that the introduction section of a project plan will include answers to these questions: What type of project is involved? What is the cost–benefit relationship? What are the contingency plans? Why is it being done this way (that is, why were alternatives rejected)? Figure 3 not only illustrates this approach, but is the executive summary for the Heublein PM&C system.

Objectives

Both anecdotal and research inputs have established the importance of clearly stated objectives: von Clauswitz' "Principles of the Objective: A clearly defined, attainable goal" (*On War*, the Modern library, 1943), holds for projects in business. Goals for a project at Heublein must be stated in terms of *deliverable items*. To so state a project objective forces the definition of a clear, comprehensible, measurable and tangible objective. Often, deliverable items resulting from a project are documents. In constructing a residence, is the deliverable item "the house" or is it "the certificate of occupancy"? In the planning stages of a project (which can occur during the project as well as at the beginning), asking this question is as important as getting the answer. Also, defining the project in terms of the deliverables tends to reduce the number of items which are forgotten. Thus, the Heublein PM&C concept of objectives can be seen to be similar to a "statement of work" and is not meant to encompass specifications (detailed descriptions of the attributes of a deliverable item) which can be included as appendices to the objectives of the project.

Figure 4 shows the objectives stated for the Heublein PM&C program. It illustrates one of the principles set for objective statement: that they be hierarchically structured, starting with general statements

---

External and internal factors make it urgent to ensure most efficient use of capital funds. Implementation of a project management and control ("PM&C") system has been chosen as one way to improve the use of capital funds. In March 1979, the Corporate Management Committee defined this need.

Subsequently, Corporate Facilities and Manufacturing Planning performed a feasibility study on this subject. A major conclusion of the study was to develop the system internally rather than use a "canned" system. An internally developed system can be tailored to the individual Groups, giving flexibility which is felt to be essential to success. Another conclusion of the study was to involve Group engineering managers in the design and implementation of the system for better understanding and acceptance.

This is the detailed plan for the design and implementation of a corporate-wide PM&C System. The short term target of the system is major capital projects; the long term target is other types of projects, such as new product development and R&D projects. The schedule and cost are:

Completion Date: June 1980.
Cost: $200,000, of which $60,000 is out of pocket.

Figure 3: Introduction to PM&C program project plan.

General Objectives

1. Enable better communication between Group and Corporate management with regard to the progress of major projects.
2. Enable Group management to more closely monitor the progress of major projects.
3. Provide the capability for Group personnel to better manage and control major projects.

Specific Objectives[a]

1. Reporting and Control System
   - For communication of project activity within Group and between Group and Corporate.
   - Initially for high-cost capital projects, then for "critical," then all others.
2. Procedures Manual
   - Document procedures and policies.
   - Preliminary manual available by October 20, 1979, for use in general educational seminars.
3. Computer Support Systems
   - Survey with recommendations to establish need for and value of computer support.
4. General Educational Package
   - Provide basic project planning and control skills to personnel directly involved in project management, to be conducted by academic authority in field.
   - Technical seminars in construction, engineering, contract administration, and financial aspects of project management.

[a]Defined at the July 1979 PM&C Workshop, attended by representatives of Operating Groups.

Figure 4: Objectives of PM&C program.

and moving to increasingly more detailed particular statements. When both particular and general objectives are defined, it is imperative that there be a logical connection; the particular must be in support of the general. Ambiguity and confusion at this point is not unusual and where they exist, they are a source of considerable conflict among client, project management, and staff.

A project (the PM&C Program) satisfying the broadly expressed needs of the Introduction (Figure 3) is more precisely defined in Figure 4. Here we see first that the primary thrust of this system is *General Objectives* item number 3, to provide Group personnel with the ability to do their jobs better. We believe it is important that these general objectives, which were set in a Corporate Management Committee meeting, are not concerned with assigning blame or setting the stage for tighter corporate control, but are in fact positive goals which not only answer desires of Corporate and Group management, but also resolve issues often raised by the operational level personnel.

The specific objectives follow the general objectives in Figure 4, which is largely in accord with our

own standards for expression of specific objectives in terms of deliverables. It is now apparent that this could have been carried further; but the success of the program supports the view that these objectives were good enough for their purpose.

Project Structure

Having a definition of deliverables, the project manager needs explicit structuring of the project to:

Relate the specific objectives to the general.

Define the elements which comprise the deliverables.

Define the activities which yield the elements and deliverables as their output.

Show the hierarchical relationship among objectives, elements, and activities.

The WBS is the tool used to meet these needs. While the WBS may be represented in either indentured (textual) or tree (graphical) formats, the graphic tree format has the advantage of easy comprehension

---

Work Breakdown Structure

HEUBLEIN PM&C PROGRAM

1000 Program Plan

2000 PM&C System

  2100 Design-Phase Reports
    2101 Analyze Project Scope
    2102 Define Performance Reports
    2103 Define Project Planning
    2104 Define Revision Procedure
    2105 Define Approval/Signoff Procedure
    2106 Define Opening/Closing Procedure
    2107 Define Authority/Responsibility Procedure
    2108 Define Record-keeping Requirements
    2109 Define Estimating Requirements
    2110 Define Reporting and Control System
    2111 Determine Accounting Support Capabilities
    2112 Define Estimating Procedures
    2113 Define Record-keeping Procedures
    2114 Prepare Organization Impact Analysis (Include Ongoing training)
    2115 Define Policy Requirements
    2116 Define Public Relations Policy
    2117 Define Legal Policies—Environmental, OSHA, EEO, Government Agencies, Land Use
    2118 Define Personal Liability Policy
    2119 Define Financial Policy—Capital Expense, Cash Flow
    2120 Define Purchasing Policy—Contracts vs PO, Contractor Qualification, $ Approvals
    2121 Define Record Retention Policy
    2122 Define Computer Support Systems Requirements
  2200 Procedures Manual
    2201 Preliminary Manual
    2202 Final Manual
  2300 Reporting and Control System
  2400 Computer Support Survey
    2401 PERT/CPM
    2402 Scheduling
    2403 Accounting

3000 General Training

  3100 Project Planning and Control Seminar
    3101 Objective Setting
    3102 WBS
    3103 Networks
    3104 Scheduling
    3105 Cost Estimating
    3106 Record Keeping
    3107 Control
  3200 Technical Seminars
    3201 Construction Engineering
    3202 Contract Administration
    3203 Financial Aspects
  3300 Ongoing Training

Figure 5: Project structure.

at all levels. The tree version of the WBS also has the considerable advantage that entries may be made in the nodes ("boxes") to indicate charge account numbers, accountable staff, etc.

Figure 5 is the WBS for the PM&C Program, showing the nature of the WBS in general and the structure of the PM&C Program project in particular. At this point we can identify the component elements and the activities necessary to achieve them. A hierarchical numbering system was applied to the elements of the WBS, which is always a convenience. The 22 Design Phase Reports (2100 series in Figure 5) speak for themselves, but it is important to note that this WBS is the original WBS: All of these reports, analyses, and determinations were defined prior to starting the program and there were no requirements for additional items. In this area, there was no change of scope problem because the cooperation of all involved functions was obtained at the start of the program. The breadth of the definition task for this company, which does not contract or subcontract to public agencies (with their own special requirements), gives some idea of the considerations that must be taken into account when setting up a PM&C System. The rest of the WBS is self-explanatory and it is hoped that it can serve as a starting point for others wishing to implement similar programs.

Project Costs

The WBS provides a listing of the tasks to be performed to achieve the project objectives; with only the WBS in hand it is possible to assemble a *preliminary* project estimate. The estimates based only on the WBS are preliminary because they reflect not only uncertainty (which varies considerably among types of projects), but because the allocation of resources to meet schedule difficulties cannot be determined until both the network and the schedule and resource evaluations have been completed. However, at this time the project planner can begin to hierarchically assemble costs for use at any level. First the lowest level activities of work (sometimes called "work packages") can be assigned values. These estimates can be aggregated in accordance with the WBS tree structure to give higher level totals. At the root of the tree there is only one element—the project—and the total preliminary estimated cost is available.

Figure 6 shows the costs as summarized for the PM&C program plan. This example is supplied to give the reader an idea of the nature of the costs to be ex-

pected in carrying out such a PM&C program in this type of situation. Since a project-oriented cost accounting system does not exist, out-of-pocket costs are the only incremental charges. Any organization wishing to cost a similar PM&C program will have to do so within the framework of the organizational approach to costing indirect labor. As a guide to such costs, it should be noted that in the Heublein PM&C Program, over 80 percent of the costs—both out-of-pocket and indirect—were in connection with the General Training (WBS code 3000).

Seminars were limited to two and two-and-a-half days to assure that the attendees perceived the educational process as efficient, tight, and not unduly interfering with their work; it was felt that it was much better to have them leaving with a feeling that they would have liked more rather than the opposite. Knowing the number of attendees, it is possible to determine the labor-days devoted to travel and seminar attendance; consultant/lecturer's fees can be obtained (expect preparation costs) and the incidentals (travel expenses, subsistence, printing, etc.) are easily estimated.

Network

The PM&C system at Heublein requires networks only for major projects, but encourages their use for all projects. The project manager is allowed the choice of whatever type of network (activity-on-node or event-on-node) he or she prefers to use. For this reason, all educational activities provided instruction in both types of network.

Figure 7 shows a segment of the network for the PM&C Plan. All the usual principles of network cre-

Labor costs	
Development & Design	$ 40,000
Attendees' time in sessions	60,000
Startup time of PM&C in Group	40,000
Basic Educational Package	
Consultants' fees	20,000
Attendees' travel & expenses	30,000
Miscellaneous	10,000
Total Program Cost	$200,000

Out-of-pocket costs: $60,000

Figure 6: Program costs.

Act'y Short Descr.	Time (weeks)	Immediate Predecessors
4000 prepare final rpt	2	2000, 2122, 3200
2000 monitor system	6	2000: hold group workshops
2000 hold group w'shps	2	2000: obtain approval
2000 prepare final proc	2	2000: monitor system
2000 prepare final proc manual, revise syst	2	2116–2121: approvals
2000 monitor system	8	2000: hold group workshops
2000 prepares for impl'n	2	3100: hold PM&C seminar
2122 get approval	2	2122: define com'r supp needs
2122 def comp supp needs	4	3100: hold PM&C sem
3200 hold tech seminars	4	3200: prepare seminars
3200 prepare seminars	8	3200: obtain approvals
3200 obtain approvals	2	3200: def tech sem needs
3200 def tech sem needs	2	3100: hold PM&C sem
3100 hold PM&C seminar	3	3100: integrate proc man in sem 2201: revise prel proc man
3100 int. proc man in sem	1	2201: prel. proc manual
2201 revise prel proc man	.6	2201–2300: get approval
2201–2300 get approval	1	2214: org impact analysis
2214 org impact analysis	.4	2201: prel. proc manual
2201 prepare prel. pm	1	2213: def recd kpng proc
2213 def recd kpng proc	1	2111: det acctg supp
2111 det acctg supp	2	2103, 2108, 2109
2112 def est proc	2	2103, 2108, 2109
2300 revise rep cont sys	6	2110: get approval
2110 get approval	1	2110: define rep/contr sys
2110 def rep/con sys	1	2101: analyze scopes 1000: revise prog plan 2104–7: def proc's 2103, 2108, 2109
2116–21 get approval	2	2116–21: define policies
2116–21 define pol'y's	8	2115: def pol'y req'ts
2115 def pol'y req'ts	3	1000: prep. program plan
2101 analyze scopes	1	1000: ditto
1000 rev prog plan	.4	1000: get appr plan
1000 get appr plan	2	1000: prep. program plan
2104-7 4-revision 5-appr/signoff 6-open/close 7-auth/resp'y	1.8	2102: def perf repts
2102 def perf repts	1	1000: prep. program plan
2103, 2108, 2109 3-proj planning 8-recd-kpng 9-estimating	2	2102: def perf repts
3100 prepare PM&C sem	4	3100: get appr content
3100 get appr content	1	1000: prep. program plan

Note: Because of space limitations, the network is given in the form of a precedence table. An activity-on-node diagram may be directly constructed from this table. Numerical designations refer to the WBS on Figure 5.

Figure 7: Network of PM&C program.

ation and analysis (for critical path, for example) may be applied by the project manager to the extent that it facilitates planning, implementation, and control. Considerable emphasis was placed on network creation and analysis techniques in the educational phases of the PM&C Program because the network is the basis of the scheduling methods presented, is potentially of great value and is one of the hardest concepts to communicate.

In the Heublein PM&C system, *managerial* networks are desired—networks which the individual project managers will use in their own management process and which the staff of the project can use to self-direct where appropriate. For this reason, the view toward the network is that no one network should exceed 50 nodes. The top-level network represents the highest level of aggregation. Each activity on that network may well represent someone else's next lower level network consisting of not more than 50 nodes; any activity on that second-level network may represent someone else's third-level network consisting of not more than 50 nodes; and so on. Networks with hundreds of nodes are to be avoided because of the difficulty of reading them and also because of the negative attitudes toward formal network planning methods generated by experiences with huge (over 5000 nodes, for example) networks in the past. This is not to say that there are not thousands of activities possible in a Heublein project, but that at the working managerial level, each manager or project staff person responsible for a networked activity is expected to work from a single network of a scope that can be easily comprehended. It is not an easy task to aggregate skillfully to reduce network size, but the exercise of this discipline has value in planning and execution in its own right.

The network shown reflects the interdependencies of activities for Heublein's PM&C Program; they are dependent on the design of the Program and the needs of the organization. Each organization must determine them for themselves. But what is important is that institution of a PM&C Program be planned this way. There is a great temptation in such programs to put all activities on one path and not to take advantage of parallel activities and/or not to see just what is the critical path and to focus efforts along it. Even where there is no special urgency in completion, it is important that all parts of the program work smoothly. If the PM&C Program team cannot assure that all necessary materials are on hand when the seminar attendees arrive to be instructed in methods of assuring timely completion of projects, the PM&C system will be viewed with great cynicism.

Schedule and Resource Allocation

The network defines the mandatory interdependency relationships among the tasks on a project; the schedule is the realization of the *intent* of the project manager, as it shows when the manager has determined that tasks are to be done. The schedule is constrained in a way that the network is not, for the schedule must reflect calendar limitations (vacations, holidays, plant and vendor shutdowns, etc.) and also the limitations on resources. It is with the schedule that the project manager can develop the resource loadings and it is the schedule which ultimately is determined by both calendar and resource constraints.

Organization and Accountability

Who is responsible for what? Without clear, unambiguous responses to this question there can be no assurance that the task will be done. In general, committees do not finish projects and there should be one organizational unit responsible for each element in the work breakdown structure and one person in that organizational unit who holds final responsibility. Thus responsibility implies a single name to be mapped to the task or element of the WBS, and it is good practice to place the name of the responsible entity or person in the appropriate node on the WBS.

However, accountability may have multiple levels below the top level of complete responsibility. Some individuals or functions may have approval power, veto power without approval power, others may be needed for information or advice, etc. Often, such multilevel accountability crosses functional and/or geographical boundaries and hence communication becomes of great importance.

A tool which has proved of considerable value to Heublein where multilevel accountability and geographical dispersion of project staff is common is the "accountability matrix." An accountability matrix for a part of the PM&C Program project is shown in Figure 8.

The accountability matrix reflects considerable thought about the *strategy* of the program. In fact, one of its great advantages is that it forces the originator (usually the project manager) to think through the process of implementation. Some individuals must be involved because their input is essential. For example, all engineering managers were essential inputs to establish the exact nature of their needs. On the other hand, some individuals or departments are formally involved to enlist their support, even though a satisfactory program could be defined without them.

Activity	PM&C Mgr	Consultant	Mgrs. of Eng. FS/F GPG Wines Spirits	Dir F&MP
Program Plan	I	P		A
Design-Phase Reports	I	P	P P P P	
Procedures Manual	I			A
Reporting & Control System	I	P	P P P P	
Computer Support Survey	I	P		P
Project Planning & Control Seminar	A	I		P
Technical Seminars	I		P P P P	A

Legend: I: Initiate/Responsibility
         A: Approve
         P: Provide input

Figure 8: Accountability matrix for PM&C program.

Control System

The basic loop of feedback for control is shown in Figure 9. This rationale underlies all approaches to controlling projects. Given that a plan (or budget) exists, we then must know what is performance (or actual); a comparison of the two may give a variance. If a variance exists, then the cause of the variance must be sought. Note that any variance is a call for review; as experienced project managers are well aware, underspending or early completions may be as unsatisfactory as overspending and late completions.

The PM&C program did not involve large purchases, or for that matter, many purchases. Nor were large numbers of people working on different tasks to

be kept track of and coordinated. These reasons of scale made it possible to control the PM&C Program through the use of Gantt conventions, using schedule bars to show plan and filling them in to show performance. Progress was tracked on a periodic basis, once a week.

Figure 10 shows the timing of the periodic reviews for control purpose and defines the nature of the reports used.

Milestones and Schedule Subdivisions

Milestones and Schedule Subdivisions are a part of the control system. Of the set of events which can be defined (in the Event-on-Node network, or implicitly

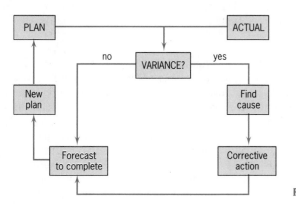

Figure 9: The basic feedback loop of control.

1. Periodic status checking will be performed monthly.
2. Labor costs will be collected manually and estimated where necessary from discussion with Group engineering management.
3. Out-of-pocket costs will be collected through commitments and/or invoice payment records.
4. Monthly status reports will be issued by the PM&C Program project manager including:
    a. Cost to date summaries.
    b. Cost variances.
    c. Schedule performance relative to schedule in Gantt format.
    d. Changes in scope or other modifications to plan.
5. Informal control will be exercised through milestone anticipation by the PM&C Program project manager.

Figure 10: Control system.

in the Activity-on-Node network), milestones form a limited subset of events, in practice rarely exceeding 20 at any given level. The milestones are predetermined times (or performance states) at which the feedback loop of control described above (Figure 9) should be exercised. Other subdivisions of the project are possible, milestones simply being a subdivision by events. Periodic time subdivisions may be made, or division into phases, one of the most common. Figure 11 shows the milestones for the PM&C Program.

Summary

The Heublein PM&C Program met the conditions for a successful project in the sense that it was completed on time and within the budgeted funds. As is so often the case, the existence of a formal plan and continuing reference to it made it possible to deal with changes of scope. Initial reaction to the educational package was so favorable that the population of attendees was increased by Group executives and en-

gineering managers; by reference to the original plan it was possible to predict cost increases in advance. Thus, there was no overrun in any sense.

To deliver on time and within budget, but to deliver a product which does not serve the client's needs is also unsatisfactory. Did this PM&C Program achieve the "General Objectives" of Figure 5? We all know the difficulties of quantifying and measuring such objectives within the real-world environment, where the concept of a proper research design is not allowable: We rarely deliberately experiment with organizations. This is a similar problem to that faced in medical research; if we have a methodology that can save or make millions of dollars, can we deny it to any group, even if we are not absolutely certain of its value?

Thus, as is so often the case in managerial systems and educational programs, we are forced to rely on the perceptions of the clients. In this PM&C Program, the clients are Corporate Management, Group Management, and most importantly, the Managers of Engineering and their staffs. In the short

Date	Description
09/05/79	Program plan approved by both Corporate & Groups
09/26/79	Reporting and control system approved by Corporate and Groups
10/05/79	Organizational impact analysis report issued
11/07/79	Basic project planning and control seminars completed
01/07/80	Reporting and control system implemented
03/24/80	Final procedures manual approved
05/19/80	Technical Seminars completed
	Computer support systems survey completed
06/30/80	Final impact assessment report issued

Figure 11: Milestones.

run, the latter two operational clients are primary. In addition to informal feedback from them, formal feedback was obtained in the form of Impact Statements (item number 4000 in the WBS of Figure 5). The Impact Statements concerned the impact of the PM&C Program on the concerned organization ("How many labor-hours are expected to be devoted to the PM&C System?) and response to the PM&C Program ("Has this been of value to you in doing your job better?").

Clearly, the response of perceived value from the operating personnel was positive, or this paper would not have been written. Can we put any measure on it? We sought no formal instruments for measurement, relying instead on subjective, free form, and anecdotal responses. Can we measure the improvement which we believe to be taking place in the implementation of capital and other projects? It may be years before the

impact (positive or negative) can be evaluated, and even then there may be such confounding with internal and external variables that no unequivocal, quantified response can be defined.

At this point we base our belief in the value of the PM&C Program on the continuing flow—starting with Impact Statements—of positive perceptions. The following is an example of such a response, occurring one year after the exposure of the respondent:

. . . find attached an R&D Project Tracking Diagram developed as a direct result of the [PM&C] seminar . . . last year. [In the seminar we called it] a Network Analysis Diagram. The Product Development Group has been using this exclusively to track projects. Its value has been immeasurable. Since its inception, fifteen new products have gone through the sequence. . . .

▶ QUESTIONS

1. Which of the project planning aids (WBS, etc.) described in the chapter was used in the case?

2. For each of the aids used in the case, describe how they were constructed and if there were any modifications in form.

3. How were each of the aids applied in the case?

4. Would a TREND organizational overlay have been useful in this situation? What potential problems might it have shown?

5. What was the purpose of the PM&C project? Was it successful?

6. What was wrong with the previous focus on cost–benefit? Does the PM&C system still include a cost–benefit analysis?

7. Why did lagging depreciation legislation increase the importance of using capital funds optimally?

▶ This article investigates the dual importance of strategy and tactics in project management. It uses a project life cycle framework to illustrate its points and postulates ten critical project success factors, some strategic and some tactical. Four types of major errors are described and illustrated with four example firms. Then the ten critical success factors are derived for each of the firms to show their interplay.

READING

BALANCING STRATEGY AND TACTICS IN PROJECT IMPLEMENTATION

Dennis P. Slevin
Jeffrey K. Pinto

Successful project implementation is complex and difficult. Project managers must pay attention simultaneously to a wide variety of human, financial, and technical factors—and they are often made responsible for project outcome without being given sufficient authority, money, or manpower.

Project-based work tends to be very different from other organizational activities. Projects usually have a specific goal or goals, a defined beginning and end, and a limited budget. Often developed by a team of individuals with special expertise, projects usually consist of a series of complex tasks requiring high levels of coordination.

Perhaps not surprisingly, the project manager's job is characterized by role overload, frenetic activity, and superficiality. He or she needs tools that will help to identify critical issues and to prioritize them over the life of the project.

Project management tools must acknowledge that the manager is of necessity a generalist as well as a specialist: he or she must know how to *plan* effectively and *act* efficiently. Unfortunately, the "dreamers" who are effective strategists often lack the operational skills to realize their plans. Likewise, project managers who are uncomfortable with planning prefer to address concrete, well-defined problems. Balancing the interplay between planning and action—strategy and tactics—may be a project manager's most important job.

Despite the fact that many project managers are uneasy with either the strategic or the tactical side of their work, project management research to date has generally failed to address this important issue. This article provides some conceptual tools designed to do so. It proposes ten project management "critical success factors," defines their relationship to one another, and describes how they fit into a strategic–tactical framework. In addition, it pinpoints errors likely to occur if strategy is well managed but tactics are not, and vice versa. Finally, it offers some pragmatic advice about strategic and tactical project management.

The Project Life Cycle

The concept of a *project life cycle* provides a useful framework for looking at project dynamics over time. The idea is familiar to most managers; it is used to conceptualize work stages and the budgetary and organizational resource requirements of each stage [1]. As Figure 1 shows, this frame of reference divides projects into four distinct phases of activity.

- **Conceptualization.** The initial project stage. Top managers determine that a project is necessary. Preliminary goals and alternative project approaches are specified, as are the possible ways to accomplish these goals.

- **Planning.** The establishment of formal plans to accomplish the project's goals. Activities include scheduling, budgeting, and allocation of other specific tasks and resources.

- **Execution.** The actual "work" of the project. Materials and resources are procured, the project is produced, and performance capabilities are verified.

- **Termination.** Final activities that must be performed once the project is completed. These include releasing resources, transferring the project to clients, and, if necessary, reassigning project team members to other duties.

As Figure 1 shows, the project life cycle is useful for project managers because it helps to define the level of effort needed to perform the tasks associated

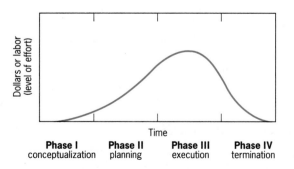

Source: Adams and Barndt: "Behavioral implications of the Project Life Cycle." In *Project Management Handbook*, ed. Cleland and King. Copyright © 1983 by Van Nostrand Reinhold Co. Inc. Reprinted by permission of the publisher.

Figure 1: Stages in the project life cycle.

with each stage. During the early stages, requirements are minimal. They increase rapidly during late planning and execution and diminish during termination. Project life cycles are also helpful because they provide a method for tracking the status of a project in terms of its stages of development.

Project Critical Success Factors

In recent years the authors and other researchers have focused on identifying those factors most critical to project success and have generated both theoretical models and lists of "success" factors [2]. Through a recent study, we have developed and refined a set of critical success factors that we believe will make conceptual sense to managers, and that is general enough to be supported across a wide range of project types [3]. As we shall see, these factors fit into a broader framework that models the dynamic project implementation process. They have also led to the development of a Project Implementation Profile (PIP) that can be used to monitor and update the factors' status throughout a project's life. First, though, we should define the factors [4].

- **Project Mission.** Initial clarity of goals and general direction.

- **Top Management Support.** Willingness of top management to provide the necessary resources and authority or power for project success.

- **Project Schedule/Plans.** Detailed specification of the individual action steps required for project implementation.

- **Client Consultation.** Communication and consultation with, and active listening to, all affected parties.

- **Personnel.** Recruitment, selection, and training of the necessary personnel for the project team.

- **Technical Tasks.** Availability of the required technology and expertise to accomplish the specific technical action steps.

- **Client Acceptance.** The act of "selling" the final project to its intended users.

- **Monitoring and Feedback.** Timely provision of comprehensive control information at each stage in the implementation process.

- **Communication.** Provision of an appropriate network and necessary data to all key actors in the project implementation.

- **Trouble Shooting.** Ability to handle unexpected crises and deviations from plan.

A 50-item instrument has been developed to measure a project's score on each of the 10 factors in comparison to the over 400 projects studied here. The Project Implementation Profile provides a quantitative way of quickly profiling a project on these ten key factors.

As Figure 2 shows, we have developed a framework of project implementation based on the ten factors. This framework is intended to demonstrate that these ten factors are not only all critical to project success, but that there is also a relationship *among* the factors. In other words, these factors must be examined in relation to each other as well as to their individual impact on successful implementation. Conceptually, the factors are sequenced logically rather than randomly. For example, it is important to set goals or define the mission and benefits of the program before seeking top management support. Similarly, unless consultation with clients occurs early in the process, chances of subsequent client acceptance will be lowered. In actual practice considerable overlap can occur among the various factors, and their sequencing is not absolute. The arrows in the model represent information flows and sequences, not causal or correctional relationships.

As Figure 2 shows, in addition to the seven factors that can be laid out on a sequential critical path, three additional factors are hypothesized to play a more overriding role in the project implementation. These factors, monitoring and feedback, communication, and trouble shooting, must all necessarily be present at each point in the implementation process. Further, a good argument could be made that these three factors are essentially different facets of the same general concern (i.e., project communication). Communication is vital for project control, for problem solving, and for maintaining beneficial contacts with both clients and the rest of the organization.

Strategy and Tactics

As one moves through the ten-factor model, it becomes clear that the factors' general characteristics change. The first three (mission, top management support, and schedule) are related to the early, "plan-

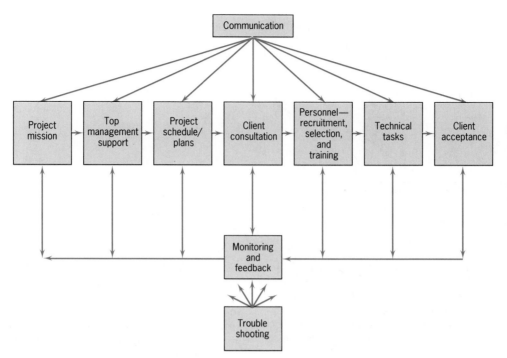

Figure 2: Ten key factors of the Project Implementation Profile.

ning" phase of project implementation. The other seven are concerned with the actual implementation or "action" of the project. These planning and action elements can usefully be considered *strategic*—the process of establishing overall goals and of planning how to achieve those goals—and *tactical*—using human, technical, and financial resources to achieve strategic ends. Briefly, the critical success factors of project implementation fit into a strategic/tactical breakout in the following way:

- **Strategic:** mission, top management support, project schedule/plans.
- **Tactical:** client consultation, personnel, technical tasks, client acceptance, monitoring and feedback, communication, trouble shooting.

Strategy and Tactics over Time While both strategy and tactics are essential for successful project implementation, their importance shifts as the project moves through its life cycle. Strategic issues are most important at the beginning, tactical issues gain in importance toward the end. There should, of course, be

continuous interaction and testing between the two—strategy often changes in a dynamic corporation, so regular monitoring is essential. Nevertheless, a successful project manager must be able to make the transition between strategic and tactical considerations as the project moves forward.

As Figure 3 shows, a recent study of more than 400 projects charted the shifting balance between strategic and tactical issues over the project's life cycle [5]. The "importance" value was measured by regression beta weights showing the relationships among strategy, tactics, and project success over the life cycle stages. During the two early stages, conceptualization and planning, strategy is significantly more important to project success than tactics. As the project moves toward the final stage, they achieve almost equal importance. Throughout the project, initial strategies and goals continue to "drive" or shape tactics.

These changes have important implications. A project manager who is a brilliant strategist but an ineffective tactician has a strong potential for committing certain types of errors as the project moves for-

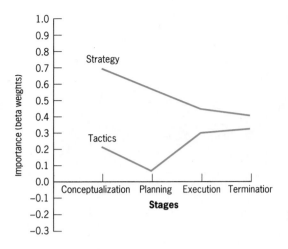

Figure 3: Changes in strategy and tactics across the Project Life Cycle (n = 418).

ward. These errors may occur after substantial resources have been expended. In contrast, the project manager who is excellent at tactical execution but weak in strategic thinking has a potential for committing different kinds of errors. These will more likely occur early in the process, but may remain undiscovered because of the manager's effective execution.

Strategic and Tactical Performance Figure 4 shows the four possible combinations of strategic and tactical performance and the kinds of problems likely to occur in each scenario. The values "high" and "low" represent strategic and tactical *quality*, i.e., effectiveness of operations performed.

A *Type* I error occurs when an action that should have been taken was not. Consider a situation in which strategic actions are adequate and suggest development and implementation of a project. A Type I error has occurred if tactical activities are inadequate, little action is subsequently taken, and the project is not developed.

A *Type* II error happens if an action is taken when it should not have been. In practical terms, a Type II error is likely to occur if the project strategy is ineffective or inaccurate, but goals and schedules are implemented during the tactical stage of the project anyway.

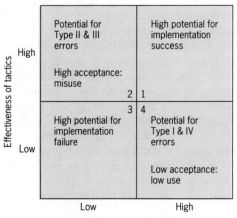

Type I error: Not taking an action when one should be taken.
Type II error: Taking an action when none should be taken.
Type III error: Taking the wrong action (solving the wrong problem).
Type IV error: Addressing the right problem, but solution is not used.

Figure 4: Strategy/tactics effectiveness matrix. *Source*: Schultz, Slevin and Pinto (1987).

A *Type* III error can be defined as solving the wrong problem, or "effectively" taking the wrong action. In this scenario, a problem is identified, or a project is desired, but because of a badly performed strategic sequence, the wrong problem is isolated, so the implemented project has little value—it does not address the intended target. Such situations often involve large expenditures of human and budgetary resources (tactics) for which there is inadequate initial planning and problem recognition (strategy).

A *Type* IV is the final kind of error common to project implementation: the action taken does solve the right problem, but the solution is not used. That is, if project management correctly identifies a problem, proposes an effective solution, and implements that solution using appropriate tactics—but the project is not used by the client for whom it was intended—then a Type IV error has occurred.

As Figure 4 suggests, each of these errors is most likely to occur given a particular set of circumstances.

- **Cell 1: *High Strategy/High Tactics.*** Cell 1 is the setting for projects rated effective in carrying out both strategy and tactics. Not surprisingly, most projects in this situation are successful.

- **Cell 3: *Low Strategy/Low Tactics.*** The reciprocal of the first is the third cell, where both strategic and tactical functions are inadequately performed. Projects in this cell have a high likelihood of failure.

- **Cell 4: *High Strategy/Low Tactics.*** The results of projects in the first two cells are intuitively obvious. Perhaps a more intriguing question concerns the likely outcomes for projects found in the "off diagonal" of Figure 4, namely, High Strategy/Low Tactics and Low Strategy/High Tactics. In Cell 4, the project strategy is effectively developed but subsequent tactics are ineffective. We would expect projects in this cell to have a strong tendency toward "errors of inaction" such as low acceptance and low use by organization members or clients for whom the project was intended. Once a suitable strategy has been determined, little is done in the way of tactical follow-up to operationalize the goals of the project or to "sell" the project to its prospective clients.

- **Cell 2: *Low Strategy/High Tactics.*** The final cell reverses the preceding one. Here, project strategy is poorly conceived or planning is inadequate, but tactical implementation is well managed. Projects in this cell often suffer from "errors of action." Because of poor strategy, a project may be pushed into implementation even though its purpose has not been clearly defined. In fact, the project may not even be needed. However, tactical follow-up is so good that the inadequate or unnecessary project is implemented. The managerial attitude is to "go ahead and do it"; not enough time is spent early in the project's life assessing whether the project is needed and developing the strategy.

Case Study Illustrations

In the section that follows, we discuss four instances in which strategic and tactical effectiveness were measured by project participants using the Project Implementation Profile. We caution that the results were reported in three instances by only one observer—the project manager—so they are obviously not meant as evidence in support of an argument, but rather as an illustration of distinct project-outcome types. In each case, a ten-factor profile is provided, using the actual scores from the PIP based on input from the project managers.

High Strategy/High Tactics: The New Alloy Development   One department of a large organization was responsible for coordinating the development and production of new stainless steel alloys for the automotive exhaust market. This task meant overseeing the efforts of the metallurgy, research, and operations departments. The project grew out of exhaust component manufacturers' demands for more formable alloys. Because this product line represented a potentially significant portion of the company's market, the project was given high priority.

As Figure 5(a) demonstrates, the scores for this project as assessed by the project team member were uniformly high across the ten critical success factors. Because of the importance of the project, its high priority was communicated to all personnel, and this led to a strong sense of project mission and top management support. The strategy was clear and was conveyed to all concerned parties, including the project

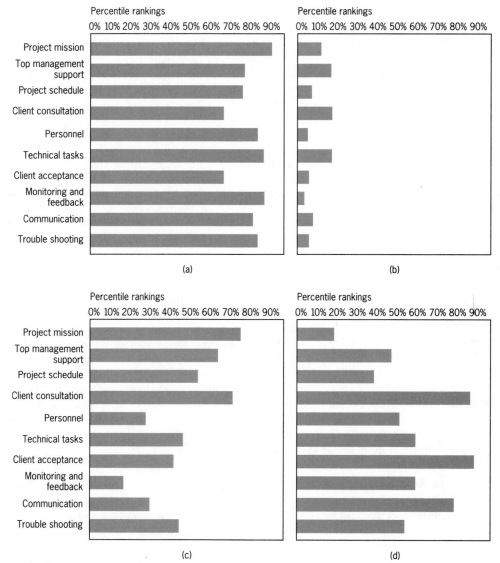

Figure 5: (a) High strategy/high tactics project, (b) Low strategy/low tactics project, (c) High strategy/low tactics project, (d) Low strategy/high tactics project.

team, which was actively involved in early planning meetings. Because the project team would include personnel from research, metallurgy, operations, production, and commercial departments, great care was taken in its selection and coordination. Use throughout the project team of action plans and daily exception reports was reflected in high scores on Technical Tasks and Trouble Shooting.

In the new alloy development project, a strong, well-conceived strategy was combined with highly competent tactical follow-up. The seeds of project success were planted during the conceptual and planning stages and were allowed to grow to their potential through rigorous project execution. Success in this project can be measured in terms of technical excellence and client use, as well as project team satisfaction and commercial profitability. In a recent follow-up interview, a member of a major competitor admitted that the project was so successful that the company still has a virtual lock on the automotive exhaust market.

Low Strategy/Low Tactics: The Automated Office
A small, privately owned company was attempting to move from a nonautomated paper system to a fully integrated, automated office that would include purchasing, material control, sales order, and accounting systems. The owner's son, who had no previous experience with computers, was hired as MIS director. His duties consisted of selecting hardware and software, directing installation, and learning enough about the company to protect the family's interests. Figure 5(b) shows a breakdown of the ten critical success factors as viewed by a project team member.

Several problems emerged immediately. Inadequate "buy-in" on the part of organization members, perceived nepotism, and lack of interaction with other top managers in purchasing decisions were seen as problems while the project was still in its strategy phase. A total lack of a formal schedule or implementation plan emphasized other strategic inadequacies destined to lead to tactical problems as well.

Tactically, the project was handled no better. Other departments that were expected to use the system were not consulted about their specific needs; the system was simply forced upon them. Little effort was made to develop project control and trouble-shooting mechanisms, perhaps as a direct result of inadequate scheduling.

Project results were easy to predict. As the team member indicated and Figure 5(b) reinforces, the project was over budget, behind schedule, and coolly received—all in all, an expensive failure. The owner's son left the company, the manager of the computer department was demoted, the mainframe computers were found to be wholly inadequate and were sold, and upper management forfeited a considerable amount of employee goodwill.

High Strategy/Low Tactics: The New Bank Loan Setup   The purpose of this project was to restructure the loan procedures used at a major bank. The project was intended to eliminate duplicate work done by branches and the servicing department and to streamline loan processes. These goals were developed and strongly supported by upper management, which had clearly conveyed them to all concerned parties. The

project was kicked off with a great deal of fanfare; there was a high expectation of speedy and successful completion. Trouble started when the project was turned over to a small team that had not been privy to the initial planning, goal setting, and scheduling meetings. In fact, the project team leader was handed the project after only three months with the company.

Project tactics were inadequate from the beginning. The team was set up without any formal feedback channels and with few communication links with either the rest of the organization or top management. The project was staffed on an ad hoc basis, often with nonessential personnel from other departments. This staffing method resulted in a diverse team with conflicting loyalties. The project leader was never able to pull the team together.

As the project leader put it, "Although this project hasn't totally failed, it is in deep trouble." Figure 5(c) illustrates the breakdowns for the project as reported by two team members. Almost from the start of its tactical phase, the project suffered from the team's inability to operationalize the initial goals. This failure caused frustration both within the project team and throughout the rest of the organization. The frustration resulted from having a clear idea of the initial goals without having prescribed the means to achieve them. As of this writing, the project continues to stagger along, with cost overruns and constantly revised schedules. Whether or not it achieves its final performance goals, this project will be remembered with little affection by the rest of the organization.

Low Strategy/High Tactics: The New Appliance Development   A large manufacturing company initiated the development of a new kitchen appliance to satisfy what upper management felt would be a consumer need in the near future. The project was perceived as the pet idea of a divisional president and was rushed along without adequate market research or technical input from the R&D department. A project team was formed to develop the product and rush it to the marketplace.

Figure 5(d) shows the breakdowns of the ten critical success factors for this project. Organizational and project team commitment was low. Other members of upper management felt the project was being pushed along too fast and refused to get behind it. Initial planning and scheduling developed by the divisional president and his staff were totally unrealistic.

What happened next was interesting. It was turned over to an experienced, capable manager who succeeded in taking the project, which had gotten off to such a shaky start, and successfully implementing it. He reopened channels of communication within the organization, bringing R&D and marketing on board. He met his revised schedule and budget, using trouble-shooting and control mechanisms. Finally, he succeeded in getting the project to the market in a reasonable time frame.

In spite of the project manager's effective tactics, the product did not do well in the market. As it turned out, there was little need for it at the time, and second-generation technology would make it obsolete within a year. This project was highly frustrating to project team members, who felt, quite correctly, that they had done everything possible to achieve success. Through no fault of their own, this project was doomed by the poor strategic planning. All the tactical competence in the world could not offset the fact that the project was poorly conceived and indifferently supported, resulting in an "error of action" [6].

Implications for Managers

These cases, and the strategy/tactics effectiveness matrix, suggest practical implications for managers wishing to better control project implementation.

Use a multiple-factor model. Project management is a complex task requiring attention to many variables. The more specific a manager can be regarding the definition and monitoring of those variables, the greater the likelihood of successful project outcome. It is important to use a multiple-factor model to do this, first to understand the variety of factors affecting project success, then to be aware of their relative importance across project implementation stages [7]. This article offers such a model: ten critical success factors that fit into a process framework of project implementation; within the framework, different factors become more critical to project success at different points in the project life cycle.

Additionally, both the project team and clients need to perform regular assessments to determine the "health" of the project. The time for accurate feedback is when the project is beginning to develop difficulties that can be corrected, not down the road when the troubles have become insurmountable. Getting the project team as well as the clients to perform status checks has the benefit of giving insights from a variety of viewpoints, not just that of the project manager. Further, it reinforces the goals the clients have in mind, as well as their perceptions of whether the project satisfies their expectations.

Think strategically early in the project life cycle. It is important to consider strategic factors early in the project life cycle, during conceptualization and planning. As a practical suggestion, organizations implementing a project should bring the manager and his or her team on board early. Many managers make the mistake of not involving team members in early planning and conceptual meetings, perhaps assuming that the team members should only concern themselves with their specific jobs. In fact, it is very important that at an early stage both the manager *and* the team members "buy in" to the goals of the project and the means to achieve those goals. The more team members are aware of the goals, the greater the likelihood of their taking an active part in monitoring and trouble shooting.

Think more tactically as the project moves forward in time. As Figure 4 shows in the later project stages, strategy and tactics are of almost equal importance to project implementation success. Consequently, it is important that the project manager shift the team's emphasis from "What do we do?" to "How do we want to do it?" The specific critical success factors associated with project tactics tend to reemphasize the importance of focusing on the "how" instead of the "what." Factors such as personnel, communication, and monitoring are concerned with better managing specific action steps in the project implementation process. While we argue that it is important to bring the project team on board during the initial strategy phase, it is equally important to manage their shift into a tactical, action mode in which their specific project duties are performed to help move the project toward completion.

Consciously plan for and communicate the transition from strategy to tactics. Project monitoring will include an open, thorough assessment of progress at several stages of implementation. The assessment must acknowledge that the transition from a strategic to a tactical focus introduces an additional set of critical success factors.

Project managers should regularly communicate with team members about the shifting status or focus of the project. Communication reemphasizes the importance of a joint effort, and it reinforces the status of the project relative to its life cycle. The team is kept aware of the degree of strategic versus tactical activity necessary to move the project to the next life-cycle stage. Finally, communication helps the manager to track the various activities performed by the project team, making it easier to verify that strategic vision is not lost in the later phases of tactical operationalization.

***Make strategy and tactics work for you and your
project team***.   Neither strong strategy nor strong tactics by themselves will ensure project success. When strategy is strong and tactics are weak, there is a potential for creating projects that never get off the ground. Cost and schedule overruns, along with general frustration, are often the side effects of projects that encounter "errors of inaction." On the other hand, a project that starts off with a weak or poorly conceived strategy and receives strong subsequent tactical operationalization is likely to be successfully implemented, but to address the wrong problem. New York advertising agencies can tell horror stories of advertising campaigns that were poorly conceived but still implemented, sometimes costing millions of dollars, and that were ultimately judged disastrous and scrubbed.

In addition to having project strategy and tactics working together, it is important to remember (again following Figure 3) that strategy should be used to "drive" tactics. Strategy and tactics are not independent of each other. At no point do strategic factors become unimportant to project success; instead, they must be continually assessed and reassessed over the life of the project in light of new project developments and changes in the external environment.

References

The authors wish to acknowledge the comments of Robert W. Zmud and an anonymous reviewer on a draft of this article.

1. The four-stage project life cycle is based on work by J. Adams and S. Barndt, "Behavorial Implications of the Project Life Cycle," in *Project Management Handbook*, eds., D. I. Cleland and W. R. King (New York: Van Nostrand Reinhold, 1983), pp. 222–244.

2. For an alternative methodology for the development of critical success factors for the implementation of organizational systems, see the work of M. Shank, A. Boynton, and R. W. Zmud, "Critical Success Factor Analysis as a Methodology for MIS Planning." MIS *Quarterly*, June 1985, pp. 121–129. See further, A. Boynton and R. W. Zmud, "An Assessment of Critical Success Factors," *Sloan Management Review*, Summer 1984, pp. 17–27.

3. D. P. Slevin and J. K. Pinto, "The Project Implementation Profile: New Tool for Project Managers," *Project Management Journal*, 17 (1986): 57–70.

4. J. K. Pinto and D. P. Slevin, "Critical Factors in Successful Project Implementation," IEEE *Transactions on Engineering Management*, EM-34, Feb. 1987, pp. 22–27.

5. J. K. Pinto, "Project Implementation: A Determination of Its Critical Success Factors, Moderators, and Their Relative Importance across Stages in the Project Life Cycle" (Pittsburgh, PA: University of Pittsburgh, unpublished doctoral dissertation, 1986).

6. Pinto (1986).

7. For a copy of the full 100-item Project Implementation Profile, see Slevin and Pinto (1986).

8. R. L. Schultz, D. P. Slevin, and J. K. Pinto, "Strategy and Tactics in a Process Model of Project Implementation," *Interfaces*, May–June 1987, pp. 34–46.

6

Negotiation and Conflict Resolution

As we noted in Chapter 5, the process of planning a project usually requires inputs from many people. Even when the project is relatively small and simple, planning involves the interaction of almost every functional and staff operation in the organization. It is virtually impossible for these interactions to take place without conflict, and when a conflict arises, it is helpful if there are acceptable methods to reduce or resolve it.

Conflict has been defined as "the process which begins when one party perceives that the other has frustrated, or is about to frustrate, some concern of his" [29, p. 891]. While conflict can arise over issues of belief or feelings or behavior, our concern in this chapter is focused for the most part on goal conflicts that occur when an individual or group pursues goals different from those of other individuals or groups [25, Ch. 12]. A party to the conflict will be satisfied when the level of frustration has been lowered to the point where no action, present or future, against the other party is contemplated. When all parties to the conflict are satisfied to this point, the conflict is said to be resolved.

There are, of course, many ways to resolve conflict. Brute force is a time-honored method, as is the absolute rule of the monarch, but the rule of law is the method of choice for modern societies—in spite of occasional lapses. Conflict resolution is the ultimate purpose of law.

Organizations establish elaborate and complex sets of rules and regulations to settle disputes between the organization itself and the individuals and groups with whom it interacts. Contracts between a firm and its suppliers, its trade unions, and its customers are written to govern the settlement of potential conflicts. But the various parties-at-interest do not always agree about the meaning of a law or a provision in a contract. No agreement, however detailed, can cover all the circumstances that might arise in the extensive relationships between the buyer and the seller of complicated industrial equipment, between the user and the supplier of engineering consulting services, between the producer and user of computer programs—the list of potential conflicts is endless. Our overcrowded courts are witness to the extent and variety of conflict. More than 500,000 lawyers in the United States [30] are employed in helping conflicting parties to adjudicate or settle their differences.

In this chapter we examine the nature of negotiation as a means of reducing or resolving the kinds of conflict that typically occur within projects. But *before we begin the discussion, it must be made quite clear that this chapter is not a primer on how to negotiate;* a course in negotiation is beyond the scope of this book and beyond our expertise (for such information, the reader is referred to the bibliography). Rather, this chapter focuses on the roles and applications of negotiation in the *management* of projects. Note also that we have excluded negotiations between the organization and outside vendors. In our experience, this type of negotiation is conducted sometimes by the project manager, sometimes by the project engineer, but most often by members of the organization's purchasing department. In any case, negotiations between buyer and seller are admirably covered by [14 and 25].

Of course, conflict may produce positive outcomes for the organization. Debate over the proper technical approach to a problem often generates a collaborative solution that is superior to any solution orginally proposed. Conflict often educates individuals and groups about the goals/objectives of other individuals and groups in the organization, thereby satisfying a precondition for valuable win–win negotiations (see Section 6.3). Indeed, the act of engaging in win–win negotiations serves as an example of the positive outcomes that can result from such an approach to conflict resolution.

In Chapter 3 we noted that negotiation was a critical skill required of the project manager. In this chapter we describe typical areas of project management where this skill is mandatory. In addition, we will cover some of the appropriate and inappropriate approaches to negotiation, as well as a few of the characteristics of successful negotiation suggested by experts in the field or indicated by our experience. We will also note some ethical issues regarding negotiation. There are probably more opportunities for ethical missteps in handling conflicts and negotiations than in any other aspect of project management. Unlike other chapters, we will use comparatively few illustrative examples. Successful negotiation tends to be idiosyncratic to the actual situation, and most brief examples do little to help transform theory into practice. We have, however, included a vignette at the end of the chapter. This vignette was adapted from "real life"; the names were changed to protect innocent and guilty alike.

No project manager should attempt to practice his/her trade without explicit training in negotiation. We are appalled that the subject is rarely mentioned in books on project management, excepting [14] on buyer–seller negotiations.

Project Management in Practice
Using Project Management to Avoid Conflicts During the AT&T/NCR Merger

The $7.4 billion AT&T/NCR merger was the largest corporate takeover of 1991, and probably the most risky. Many in the financial community were predicting doom because of the inherent conflicts that would arise between the two huge firms. In particular, the computer systems of the two firms were scheduled to be integrated at the time of the official merger, in 90 days. Sensing the short lead time and tremendous complexity of this effort, involving 12 independent divisions spread around the world, 55,000 employees, 450 projects, and 3000 activities, NCR engaged a private consulting firm with experience in managing projects involving substantial intangibles with inherent potential for conflicts.

The consulting firm set about defining a work breakdown structure (WBS) and master schedule for the integration process. The final WBS involved 12 level-two aggregate processes that were then taken down to the fifth level, resulting in 450 discrete work projects that could be definitively scheduled. Reports were generated for each project showing every interorganizational activity that might represent a potential conflict; in this way a number of conflicts were identified early and avoided. In one case, for example, it was found that marketing was planning on releasing a product before production had finished it.

Activity slippage charts were also generated and color-coded according to the following criteria: high risk (red)—slipped 14 days or more, or no schedule, or adversely impacted another division; medium risk (yellow)—slipped 6–13 days, or incomplete schedule, or adversely impacted by another division; and low risk (green)—less than 5 days late, complete schedule, or no interdivisional conflicts.

To further identify where conflicts might occur, a functional risk assessment chart was prepared, again using red, yellow, and green signals for potential conflicts, that matrixed functional areas of the firm against each other. This "stoplight" chart provided a higher-level display of overall risk for top management to stay focused on throughout the merger.

In this fashion, the systems were successfully integrated without disrupting ongoing operations and conflicts were avoided. Using project management to guide the systems merger "enabled us to eliminate surprises that could have derailed the effort." By a year after the merger, AT&T/NCR's revenue and operating income have been strong and getting stronger, and there have been no disruptions or other problems between the firms, or their customers.

Source: E. Hofstadter "The Science of the Deal: Project Management Meets Wall Street," PM *Network*, Nov. 1992.

▶ 6.1 THE NATURE OF NEGOTIATION

The favored technique for resolving conflict is *negotiation*. What is negotiation? Wall [33, Preface] defines negotiation as "the process through which two or more parties seek an acceptable rate of exchange for items they own or control." Dissatisfied with this definition, he spends part of a chapter extending and discussing the concept [33, Chapter 1], without a great deal of improvement. Cohen [9, p. 15] says that "Negotiation is a field of knowledge and endeavor that focuses on gaining the favor of people from whom we want things." Other authors define negotiation differently, but do not appreciably extend Cohen's definition. Even if no single definition neatly fits all the activities we label "negotiation," we do recognize that such terms as "mediate," "conciliate," " make peace," "bring to agreement," "settle differences," "moderate," "arbitrate," "adjust differences," "compromise," "bargain," "dicker," and "haggle," [27, pp. 504–505, 534, 545] are synonyms for " negotiate" in some instances.

Most of the conflicts that involve the organization and outsiders have to do with property rights and contractual obligations. In these cases, the parties to negotiation see themselves as opponents. Conflicts arising inside the organization may also appear to involve property rights and obligations, but they typically differ from conflicts with outsiders in one important way: As far as the firm is concerned, they are conflicts between allies, not opponents. Wall [33, pp. 149–50] makes this point neatly:

> Organizations, like groups, consist of interdependent parts that have their own values, interests, perceptions, and goals. Each unit seeks to fulfill its particular goal . . . and the effectiveness of the organization depends on the success of each unit's fulfillment of its specialized task. Just as important as the fulfillment of the separate tasks is the integration of the unit activities such that each unit's activities aid or at least do not conflict with those of the others.

One of the ways in which organizations facilitate this integration is to establish "*lateral relations* [which] allow decisions to be made horizontally across lines of authority" [33, p. 150]. Because each unit will have its own goals, integrating the activities of two or more units is certain to produce the conflicts that Wall says should not take place. The conflicts may, however, be resolved by negotiating a solution, if one exists, that produces gains (or minimizes losses) for all parties. Raiffa [25, p. 139] defines a Pareto optimal solution to the two-party conflict and discusses the nature of the bargaining process required to reach optimality, a difficult and time-consuming process. While it is not likely that the conflicting parties will know and understand the complex tradeoffs in a real world, project management, many-persons/many-issues conflict [see 25, Chapters 17–23], the general objective is to find a solution such that no party can be made better off without making another party worse off by the same amount or more—i.e., a Pareto optimal solution.

Approaching intraproject conflicts with a desire to win a victory over other parties is inappropriate. The proper outcome of this type of negotiation should be to optimize the outcome in terms of overall organizational goals. Although it is not always obvious how to do this, negotiation is clearly the correct approach.

During the negotiation process, an ethical situation often arises that is worth mentioning. Consider the situation where a firm requests an outside contractor to develop a software package to achieve some function. When the firm asks for a specific objective to be accomplished, it frequently does not know if that is a major job or a trivial task because it lacks technical competence in that area. Thus, the contractor has the opportunity to misrepresent the task to its customer, either inflating the cost for a trivial task or minimizing the impact of a significant task in order to acquire the contract and then boosting the cost later. The ethics of the situation require that each party in the negotiation be honest with the other, even in situations where it is clear there will not be further work between the two.

▶ 6.2 PARTNERING, CHARTERING, AND CHANGE

Projects provide ample opportunity for the project manager (PM) to utilize her/his skills at negotiation. There are, however, three situations commonly arising during projects that call for the highest level of negotiating skill the PM can muster: the use of subcontractors, the development of the project's mission statement, and the management of changes ordered in the project's deliverables and/or priorities after the project is underway. The former probably accounts for more litigation than all other aspects of the project combined. The latter two are, in the authors' experience, by far the most common and most troublesome issues project managers report facing.

Partnering

Generally, relations between the organization carrying out a project and a subcontractor working on the project are best characterized as adversarial. The parent organization's objectives are to get the deliverable at the lowest possible cost, as soon as possible. The subcontractor's objectives are to produce the deliverable at the highest possible profit with the least effort. These conflicting interests tend to lead both parties to work in an atmosphere of mutual suspicion and antagonism. Indeed, it is almost axiomatic that the two parties will have significantly different ideas about the exact nature of the deliverable, itself. The concept of "partnering" has been developed to replace this atmosphere with one of cooperation and mutual helpfulness.

In their excellent article on the subject, Cowan, Gray, and Larson define partnering as follows:

> *Project partnering is a method of transforming contractual relationships into a cohesive, cooperative project team with a single set of goals and established procedures for resolving disputes in a timely and effective manner.* [8, p. 5, italics in original]

They present a multistep process for building partnered projects. First, the parent firm must make a commitment to partnering, select subcontractors who will also make such a commitment, engage in joint team-building exercises, and develop a "charter" for the project. (See next subsection for a description of such a charter.) Second, both parties must implement the partnering process with a four-part agreement on: (1) "joint evaluation" of the project's progress, (2) a method for resolving any problems or disagreements, (3) acceptance of a goal for continuous improvement (also known as TQM) for the joint project, and (4) continuous support for the process of partnering from senior management of both parties. Finally, the parties commit to a joint review of "project execution" when the project is completed.

Clearly, each step in this process must be accompanied by negotiation, and just as clearly, the negotiations must be nonadversarial. The entire concept is firmly rooted in the assumption of mutual trust between the partners and this assumption, too, requires nonadversarial negotiation. Finally, the article focuses on partnering when the partners are members of different organizations. We think the issue is no less relevant when the partners are from different divisions or departments of the same parent organization. Identical assumptions hold, identical steps must be taken, and interparty agreements must be reached for partnering to succeed. (Also see [3].)

Chartering

A project charter is simply a written agreement between the PM, senior management, and the functional managers who are committing resources and/or people to the project [20]. Like planning documents, WBSs, and responsibility charts, the charter may take many different forms. Typically, it details the expected project deliverables, often including the project's schedule and budget. It attests to the fact that senior management, functional managers, and the PM are "on the same page," agreeing about what is to be done, when, and at what cost. Note that if there is such an agreement, there is also an implication that none of the parties will change the agreement unilaterally, or, at least, without prior consultation with the other parties.

Most projects do not have charters, which is one reason for observing that most projects are not completed on specification, on time, and on budget. Also note the additional fact that project managers are among the most frustrated people in American industry.

In the previous chapter, we described an iterative process for developing project action plans wherein individuals responsible for a task or subtask provided an action plan for completing it. We noted that it is not uncommon for the individuals or groups who make commitments during the process of developing the projects's action plan to sign-off on their commitments. This signed-off set of action plans might constitute a project charter, particularly if senior management has signed-off on the overall mission statement, *and if it is recognized as a charter by all parties to the plan.*

A somewhat less specific charter appears in [8], in which the various members of the partnering team sign a commitment to

- Meet design intent
- Complete contract without need for litigation
- Finish project on schedule:
  - Timely resolution of issues
  - Manage joint schedule
- Keep cost growth to less than 2 percent . . . etc. [8 Figure 2, p. 8]

Of course, even this charter assumes some agreement on the "design intent," the schedule, and costs.

Change

No matter how carefully a project is planned, it is almost certain to be changed before completion. There are three basic causes for change in projects. Some changes result because planners erred in their initial assessment about how to achieve a given end or erred in their choice of the proper goal for the project. Technological uncertainty is the fundamental causal factor for either error. The foundation for a building must be changed because a preliminary geological study did not reveal a weakness in the structure of the ground on which the building will stand. An R & D project must be altered because metallurgical test results indicate another approach should be adopted. The project team becomes aware of a recent innovation that allows a faster, cheaper solution to the conformation of a new computer.

Other changes result because the client/user or project team learns more about the nature of the project deliverable or about the setting in which it is to be used. An increase in user or team knowledge or sophistication is the primary factor leading to change. A computer program must be extended or rewritten because the user thinks of new uses for the software. Physicians request that intensive care units in a hospital be equipped with laminar air-flow control in order to accommodate patients highly subject to infection who might otherwise not be admissible in an ICU. The fledgling audio-addict upgrades the specifications for a system to include very high frequencies so that his/her dog can enjoy the music, too.

A third source of change is the mandate. A new law is passed. A government regulatory unit articulates a new policy. A trade association sets a new standard. The parent organization of the user applies a new criterion for its purchases. In other words, the rules of conduct for the project are altered. A state approved pollution control system must be adopted for each chemical refinery project. The state government requires all new insurance policies to conform to a revised law specifying that certain information must be given to potential purchasers. At times, mandates affect only priorities. The mandate in question might move a very important customer to the "head of the line" for some scarce resource or service.

In Chapter 11, we discuss some procedures for controlling the *process* of changing projects, but whatever the nature of the change, specifications of the deliverables must be altered, and the schedule and budget must be recalculated. Obviously, negotiation will be required to develop new agreements between the parties-at-interest to the project. These negotiations are difficult because most of the stakeholders will have a strong interest in maintaining the *status quo*. If the proposed change benefits the client and increases the cost of the project, the producer will try to sequester some of the user's potential benefit in the form of added charges to offset the added cost. The client will, of course, resist. All parties must, once again, seek a Pareto optimal solution—always a difficult task.

Change by mandate raises an additional problem. Not only are the project's deliverables, budget, and schedule usually changed, the *priorities* of other projects are typically changed, too. Suddenly, a PM loses access to key resources, because they are urgently required elsewhere. Key contributors to a project miss meetings or are unable to keep promised task-delivery dates. All too often, the PM's response to this state of affairs is anger and/or discouragement. Neither is appropriate.

After discussing priorities with both PMs and senior managers, it has become clear to us that most firms actually have only three levels of priority (no matter how ornate the procedure for setting project priorities might seem to be). First, there are the high-priority projects, that is the set of projects currently being supported. Second, there are the lower-priority projects, the projects "we would like to do when we have the time and money." Third, occasionally, there are urgent projects, mandates, that must be done immediately. "Customer `A's' project must be finished by the end of the month." "The state's mandate must be met by June 30th." Everything else is delayed to ensure that mandates are met. As noted above, we will have more to say on this subject in Chapter 11.

While project charters and partnerships would certainly help the PM deal with conflicts that naturally arise during a project, neither charters nor partnering are widely utilized at this time. It is understandably difficult to convince senior managers to make the firm commitments implied in a project charter in the face of a highly uncertain future. Functional managers are loath to make firm commitments for precisely the same reason. So, too, the client, aware of her/his own ignorance about the degree to which the project output will meet his/her needs, is cautious about commitment—even when a procedure for negotiating change exists.

Partnering is a recently developed concept, and in our litigious society any system for conflict resolution that asks parties to forego lawsuits is viewed with considerable suspicion. Indeed, we find that a great many organizations preach "team building," "TQM," and "employee involvement," but comparatively few practice what they preach. For each participative manager you find, we can show you a dozen micromanagers. For each team player ready to share responsibility, we can show you a dozen "blame placers." The era of project charters and partnering is approaching, but it is not yet here.

▶ 6.3   CONFLICT AND THE PROJECT LIFE CYCLE

In this section, following a brief discussion of the project life cycle, we will categorize the types of conflicts that frequently occur in the project environment, and then amplify the nature of these conflicts. Finally, we will link the project life cycle with the fundamental conflict categories and discover that certain patterns of conflict are associated with the different periods in the life of a project. With this knowledge, the PM can do a faster and more accurate job of diagnosing the nature of the conflicts he/she is facing, thereby reducing the likelihood of escalating the conflict by dealing with it ineffectually.

More on the Project Life Cylcle

Various authors define the stages of the project life cycle (see Figures 1-2 and 1-3 in Chapter 1) in different ways. Two of the most commonly cited definitions are those of Thamhain and Wilemon [29] and Adams and Barndt [1]. The former use a four-stage model with project formation, buildup, main program, and phaseout identified as the stages of the life cycle. Adams and Barndt also break the project life cycle into four stages: conceptualization, planning, execution, and termination.

For our purposes, these two views of the cycle are not significantly different. During the first stage, senior management tentatively, sometimes unofficially, approves preliminary planning for a project. Often, this management recognition is preceded by some strictly unofficial "bootleg" work to test the feasibility of an idea. Initial planning is undertaken, basic objectives are often adopted, and the project may be "scoped out." The second stage is typified by detailed planning, budgeting, scheduling, and the aggregation of resources. In the third stage, the lion's share of the actual work on the project is accomplished. During the final stage of the life cycle, work is completed and products are turned over to the client or user. This stage also includes disposition of the project's assets and personnel. It may even include preparation for the initial stage of another related project to follow.

Categories of Conflict

All stages of the project life cycle appear to be typified by conflict. In Chapter 4, we discussed some of the human factors that require the PM to be skilled at reducing interpersonal tensions. In that chapter we also introduced the work of Thamhain and Wilemon [29, 30] on conflict in the project. These conflicts center on such matters as schedules, priorities, staff and labor requirements, technical factors, administrative procedures, cost estimates, and, of course, personality conflicts. Thamhain and Wilemon collected data on the frequency and magnitude of conflicts of each type during each stage of the project life cycle. Multiplying frequency by a measure of conflict magnitude and adjusting for the proportion of PMs who reported each specific type of conflict, they derived an estimate of the "intensity" of the conflicts (see Tables 4-1 and 4-2). Figure 4-8 illustrates these conflicts and is repeated here as Figure 6-1 for the reader's convenience.

On examination of the data, it appears that the conflicts fall into three fundamentally different categories:

1. Groups working on the project may have different goals and expectations.
2. There is considerable uncertainty about who has the authority to make decisions.
3. There are interpersonal conflicts between people who are parties-at-interest in the project.

Some conflicts reflect the fact that the day-to-day work on projects is usually carried out by many different units of the organization, units that often differ in their objectives and technical judgments. The result is that these units have different expectations about the project, its costs and rewards, its relative importance, and its timing. Conflicts about schedules, intra-and interproject priorities, cost estimates, and staff time tend to fall into this category. At base, they arise because the project manager and the functional managers have very different goals. The PM's concern is the project. The primary interest of the functional manager is the daily operation of his/her function.

Other conflicts reflect the fact that both technical and administrative procedures are important aspects of project management. Uncertainty about who has the authority to make decisions on resource allocation, on administrative procedures,

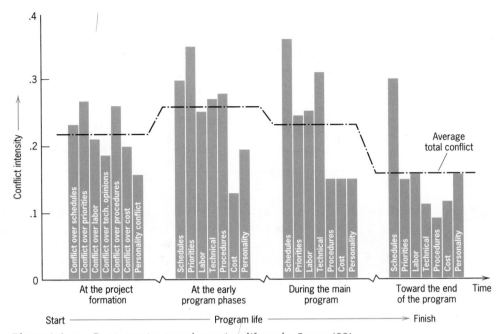

Figure 6-1: Conflict intensity over the project life cycle. *Source:* [29]

on communication, on technological choices, and on all the other matters affecting the project produces conflict between the PM and the other parties. It is simple enough (and correct) to state that in a matrix organization, the functional manager controls who works on the project and makes technical decisions, while the project manager controls the schedule and flow of work. In practice, in the commonly hectic environment of the project, amid the day's countless little crises faced by project and functional manager alike, the distinction is rarely clear.

Finally, some conflicts reflect the fact that human beings are an integral part of all projects. In an environment that depends upon the cooperation of many persons, it seems inevitable that some personalities will clash. Also, in conflicts between the project and the client, or between senior management and the project, it is the project manager who personifies the project and thus is generally a party to the conflict.

We can categorize these conflicts as conflict over differing goals, over uncertainty about the locus of authority, and between personalities. For the entire array of conflict types and parties-at-interest, see Table 6-1.

The three types of conflict seem to involve the parties-at-interest to the project in identifiable ways. The different goals and objectives of the project manager, senior management, and functional managers are a major and constant source of conflict. For example, senior management (at times, arbitrarily) is apt to fix all three parameters of the project—time, cost, and performance—and then to assume that the PM will be able to achieve all the preset targets. As we will see in Chapter 7 on budgeting, underestimation of cost and time is a natural consequence of this prac-

Table 6–1   Project Conflicts by Category and Parties-at-Interest

Parties-at-Interest	Categories of Conflict		
	Goals	Authority	Interpersonal
Project team	Schedules Priorities	Technical	Personality
Client	Schedules Priorities	Technical	
Functional and senior management	Schedules Priorities Labor cost	Technical Administrative	Personality

tice, and it leads directly to conflict between the PM, as a representative of the project team, and senior management. A second consequence is that the PM tries to pass the stringent cost and time estimates along to functional managers whose units are expected to perform certain work on the project. More conflict arises when the functional managers complain that they cannot meet the time and cost restrictions. All this tends to build failure into the job of managing a project, another source of conflict between the PM and senior management.

Functional managers also may not see eye-to-eye with the PM on such issues as the project's priority or the desirability of assigning a specifically named individual to work on the project, or even the applicability of a given technical approach to the project. In addition, the client's priorities and schedule, whether an inside or outside client, may differ radically from those of senior management and the project team. Finally, the project team has its own ideas about the appropriateness of the schedule or level of project staffing. The Thamhain and Wilemon data show that these goal-type conflicts occur in all stages of the project's life cycle, though they are particulary serious in the early stages (see Figure 6-1). Regardless of the timing, in many cases it is not certain just whose priorities are ruling.

There are, of course, a number of methods for settling conflicts about priorities between projects, as well as intraproject conflicts. Often, the project selection model used to approve projects for funding will generate a set of projects ranked by some measure of value. It is also common for senior management to determine interproject priorities. The relative importance of the various tasks in an individual project is set by the project manager, who allocates scarce resources depending on the requirements of schedule, task difficulty, resource availability, and similar considerations. The existence of these methods for resolving priority conflicts is all too often irrelevant, because there is a powerful tendency for both project and functional managers to optimize their individual interests, with little regard for the total organization.

In matrix organizations, the center of authority is particularly unclear. Locus-of-authority conflicts are endemic to matrix-organized projects. The project team and the client tend to focus on the technical procedures, debating the proper approach to the project, or perhaps how to solve individual problems that can occur at any stage. Senior management has other fish to fry. Not only do they insist that the project manager adopt and maintain a set of administrative procedures that conform to organizational and legal standards, but they also are quite concerned with who reports to whom and whose permission is required to take what action. The astute reader will note that such concerns are not entirely appropriate for matrix-organized projects. Our discussions with senior managers lead us to the not-surprising conclusion that it is common for senior management to want the efficiency and other advantages of matrix management but simultaneously to attempt to maintain the managerial comforts of traditional hierarchical structures—a sure source of conflict.

The conflict-resolution potential of partnering and project charters should be quite clear. Neither technique will stop conflicts from arising, but they will sharply lower the intensity of the conflicts as well as provide a framework for resolving conflict. They will even allow an environment in which the PM and functional managers can take positions that support the total organization rather than suboptimizing the project or the function.

Project managers will often find themselves arguing for scheduling or resource priorities from functional managers who outrank them by several levels. Neither the functional nor the project managers are quite sure about who has what authority. (The reader will recall that the pure project form of organization has a tendency to breed deviant administrative behaviors, and that matrix organization is characterized by superior–subordinate confusion.) A constant complaint of project managers is "I have to take the responsibility, but I have no authority at all."

People problems arise, for the most part, within the project team, though functional managers may clash with PMs—the former accusing the latter of being "pushy," and the latter accusing the former of "foot dragging." In our experience, most personality clashes on the project team result from differences in technical approach or philosophy of problem solving, and in the methods used to implement the project results. Of course, it is quite possible that a personality conflict *causes* a technical conflict. It is also possible that any type of conflict will appear, at first blush, to be a personality clash.

Next we put these conflicts into the chronological perspective of the project life cycle.

Project Formation

In the initial stage of the project life cycle, most of the conflict centers around the inherent confusion of setting up a project in the environment of matrix management. Almost nothing about the project or its governance has been decided. Even the project's technical objectives, not clearly defined or established, are apt to be understood only in the most general sense. Moving from this state of semi-chaos to the relatively ordered world of the buildup stage is difficult. To make this transition, four fundamental issues must be handled, although not necessarily in the order presented here.

First, the technical objectives of the project must be specified to a degree that will allow the detailed planning of the buildup stage to be accomplished. Second, commitment of resources to the project must be forthcoming from senior management and from functional managers. Third, the priority of the project, relative to the priorities of the parent organization's other projects, must be set and communicated. (Our comments about priorities at the end of Section 6.2 notwithstanding, we feel the project's priority must be set as early as possible in the life of the project. While it will probably not save the project from delay in the event of a mandate, it stands as an important political signal to functional managers about which projects take precedence in case of resource conflicts.) Fourth, the organizational structure of the project must be established to an extent sufficient for the WBS and a linear responsibility chart, or its equivalent, to be prepared during the next stage of the life cycle.

These conditions are not sufficient, but they are most certainly necessary if the conflicts typical of the formation stage are to be resolved—at least at a reasonable level—and not simply carried forward to the buildup stage in an exacerbated state.

The project manager who practices conflict avoidance in this stage is inviting disaster in the next. The four fundamental issues above underlie such critical but down-to-earth matters as these: Which of the functional areas will be needed to accomplish project tasks? What will be the required level of involvement of each of the functional areas? How will conflicts over resources/facility usage between this and other projects be settled? What about those resource/facility conflicts between the project and the routine work of the functions? Who has the authority to decide the technical, scheduling, personnel, and cost questions that will arise? Most important, how will changes in the parent organization's priorities be communicated to everyone involved?

Note that three of the four fundamental issues—delimiting the technical objectives, getting management commitment, and setting the project's relative priority—must be resolved irrespective of what organizational form is selected for the project. It should also be noted that the organizational structure selected will have a major impact on the ways in which the conflicts are handled. The stronger the matrix, having the pure project as its limit, the more authoritative the role played by the PM. The weaker the matrix, having functional organization as its limit, the more authority is embedded in the functional managers. Lack of clarity about the relative power/influence/authority of the PM and the functional managers is a major component of all conflicts involving technical decisions, resource allocation, and scheduling.

Project Buildup

Thamhain and Wilemon note that conflict occurring in the buildup stage "over project priorities, schedules, and administrative procedures . . . appears as an extension from the previous program phase" [29, pp. 39]. This is the period during which the project moves (or should move) from a general concept to a highly detailed set of plans. If the project's organizational format is a strong matrix, the PM seeks a commitment of *people* from the functional departments. If the project if organized as a weak matrix, the PM seeks a commitment of *work* from the functional departments. In either case, the PM seeks commitment from functional managers who are under pressure to deliver support to other projects as well as, and in addition to, the routine, everyday demands made on their departments.

As the project's plans become detailed, conflicts over technical issues build—again, conflicts between the PM and the functional areas tend to predominate. Usually, the functional departments can claim more technical expertise than the

PM, who is a "generalist." On occasion, however, the PM is also a specialist. In such situations, discussions between the functional manager and the project manager about the best technical approach often result in conflict. The total level of conflict is at its highest in this transition period.

Main Program

Schedules are still a major source of conflict in the main program phase of the project life cycle, though the proximate cause of schedule-related conflict is usually different than in the earlier stages. Project plans have been developed and approved by everyone involved (although, perhaps, grudgingly), and the actual work is under way. Let us make an assumption that is certain to be correct; let us assume that some activity runs into difficulty and is late in being completed. Every task that is dependent on this late activity will also be delayed. Some of these subsequent activities will, if sufficiently late and if the late work is not made up, delay the entire project.

In order to prevent this consequence, the PM must try to get the schedule back on track. But catching up is considerably more difficult than falling behind. Catching up requires extra resources that the functional groups who are doing the "catching up" will demand, but which the PM may not have.

The more complex the project, the more difficult it is to trace and estimate the impact of all the delays, and the more resources that must be consumed to get things back on schedule. Throughout this book we have referred to the PM's job of managing time/cost/performance trade-offs. Maintaining the project schedule is precisely an exercise in managing trade-offs, but adding to the project's cost or scaling down the project's technical capabilities in order to save time are trade-offs the PM will not take if there is any viable alternative. The PM's ability to make trade-offs is often constrained by contract, company policy, and ethical considerations. In reality, trade-off decisions are extremely difficult.

Like schedule conflicts, technical conflicts are frequent and serious during the main program stage. Also like schedule conflicts, the source of technical conflict is somewhat different than in earlier stages. Just as a computer and a printer must be correctly linked together in order to perform properly, so must the many parts of a project. These linkages are known as *interfaces*. The number of interfaces increases rapidly as the project gets larger, which is to say that the system gets more complex. The need to manage these interfaces and to correct incompatibilities is the key to the technical conflicts in the main program phase.

Project Phaseout

As in the main program stage, schedule is the major source of conflict during project phaseout. If schedule slippage has occurred in the main program stage (and it most certainly will have), the consequences will surely be felt in this final stage. During phaseout, projects with firm deadlines develop an environment best described as hectic. The PM, project team, and functional groups often band together to do what is necessary to complete the project on time and to specification. Cost overruns, if not outrageously high, are tolerated—though they may not be forgiven and they will certainly be remembered.

Technical problems are comparatively rare during phaseout because most have been solved or bypassed earlier. Similarly, working interfaces have been developed and put in place. If the project involves implementing a technology in an outside client's system, technical conflicts will probably arise, but they are usually less intense.

Thamhain and Wilemon [30, p. 41] note that personality conflicts are the second-ranked source of conflict during phaseout. They ascribe these conflicts to interpersonal stress caused by the pressure to complete the project, and to individuals' natural anxiety about leaving the project either to be assigned to another, or be returned to a functional unit. In addition, we have observed conflict, sometimes quite bitter, focused on the distribution of the project's capital equipment and supplies when the project is completed. Conflict also arises between projects phasing out and those just starting, particularly if the latter need resources or personnel with scarce talents being used by the former.

The upshot is simple. As we noted in the first section of Chapter 1, conflict is an inherent characteristic of projects, and the project manager is constantly beset by conflict. The ability to reduce and resolve conflict in ways that support achievement of the project's goals is a prime requisite for success as a PM. The primary tool to accomplish conflict resolution and reduction is negotiation, and the method of handling conflict established in the project formation stage will set the pattern for the entire project. Therefore, the style of negotiation adopted by the PM is critical.

Much has been written on conflict resolution. Burke's classic paper [5] on the confrontation–problem solving method of resolving conflicts is offered as a "Reading" at the end of this chapter. The similarities between the confrontation–problem solving technique for conflict resolution and win–win negotiation covered in the following section are quite striking. Dyer [11] also writes of resolving conflicts, focusing on conflict between members of a team, and [2] is a general work on the subject.

Project Management in Practice
A Consensus Feasibility Study for Montreal's Archipel Dam

In 1979, Quebec conducted a short interdepartmental evaluation to assess the need for a feasibility study evaluating the costs and benefits of constructing a dam for watershed development within the St. Lawrence river basin in the Montreal metropolitan area. The evaluation concluded that a feasibility study that considered the hydroelectric power generated, the flood control possible, and the shoreline restoration for recreation for the 3 million local area residents was justified. It was recommended that a central authority act as project manager for the study and that arbitration procedures be instituted for the interests of all affected parties.

Thus, a new body called "Secretariat Archipel" was created to directly supervise the feasibility study. Secretariat Archipel,

Source: R. Desbiens, R. Houde, and P. Normandeau. "Archipel Feasibility Study: A Questionable Consensus Approach," *Project Management Journal*, March 1989.

however, rejected the recommendations of the prior evaluation and chose to use a more democratic "consensus" approach between all involved agencies rather than a central authority approach. Doing so avoided the need for arbitration procedures as well. In addition, a matrix structure was put in place to guarantee a veto right to each of the ten governmental departments involved in the process. It was believed that this consensus approach would lead to a solution acceptable to all, while protecting the jurisdictional responsibilities of all departments.

Although this approach apparently avoided difficult conflicts, and the concomitant need to arbitrate them, a post-study evaluation of the process concluded that it was neither effective nor efficient. By discarding the recommendation for a central authority body, a leadership gap arose in the decision framework and veto rights were abused by many of the participants. The leadership gap led, for example, to no one identifying incompatible objectives, rules for making decisions, or common priorities.

In terms of effectiveness, the recommendations of the study are questionable: that the dam be postponed until the year 2015 while only $35 million—less than the cost of the feasibility study—be spent on recreational facilities. Considering efficiency, it was found that many of the expensive support studies authorized by the Secretariat did not add significantly to the feasibility process. Also, the study appeared to take one to two years longer than necessary, with a correspondingly higher cost.

The evaluation proposed three probable causes of the lack of decisiveness in this study process:

1. Fear of litigation between the governmental departments and municipalities,

2. Difficulty comparing positive and negative impacts due to a lack of decision rules, and

3. Long delays and unavoidable sacrifices through a failure of the consensus process.

In retrospect, the consensus approach appeared to have been selected to protect the fields of jurisdiction of each governmental department rather than for defining the best project for the community. Since many of the goals were incompatible to start with, a consensual decision process with veto override would simply have to reject any recommendation—no matter how appropriate for the community—that was incompatible with another goal or disliked by any of the ten departments involved in the study. Although consensus is a highly desirable goal for public studies, leadership cannot be abandoned in the process. Attempting to avoid conflict through mandated consensus simply defeats the purpose of any study in the first place, except a study to determine what everyone commonly agrees upon.

▶ 6.4 SOME REQUIREMENTS AND PRINCIPLES OF NEGOTIATION

The word "negotiation" evokes many images: Bill Clinton and Congress, the "Uruguay Round" of the GATT talks, a player's agent and the owner of an NFL team, the buyer and seller of an apartment complex, attorneys for husband and wife in a divorce settlement, union and management working out a collective bargaining agreement, tourist and peddler haggling over a rug in an Ankara market. But as we noted in the introduction to this chapter, none of these images is strictly appropriate for the project manager who must resolve the sorts of conflicts we have considered in the previous section.

The key to understanding the nature of negotiation as it applies to project management is the realization that few of the conflicts arising in projects have to do with *whether* or not a task will be undertaken or a deliverable produced; rather, they have to do with *how* results will be achieved, by *whom*, *when*, and at *what cost*. The implication is clear: *The work of the project will be done.* If conflicts between any of the parties to the project escalate to the point where negotiations break down and work comes to a halt, everyone loses. *One requirement for the conflict reduction/resolution methods used by the PM is that they must allow the conflict to be settled without irreparable harm to the project's objectives.*

A closer consideration of the attorneys negotiating the divorce settlement makes clear a second requirement for the PM negotiating conflicts between parties-at-interest to the project. While the husband and wife (or the rug peddler and tourist) may employ unethical tactics during the negotiation process and, if not found out, profit from them at the expense of the other party, it is much less likely for the attorneys representing the husband and wife to do so—particularly if they practice law in the same community. The lawyers know they will have to negotiate on other matters in the future. Any behavior that breeds mistrust will make future negotiations extremely difficult, perhaps impossible. The rug peddler assumes no further contact with the tourist, so conscience is the sole governor of his or her ethics. A *second requirement for the conflict resolution/reduction methods used by the* PM *is that they allow (and foster) honesty between the negotiators.*

The conflicting parties-at-interest to a project are not enemies or competitors, but rather allies—members of an alliance with strong common interests. It *is a requirement of all conflicting parties to seek solutions to the conflict that not only satisfy their own individual needs, but also satisfy the needs of other parties to the conflict, as well as the needs of the parent organization.* In the language of negotiation, this is called a "win–win" solution. Negotiating to a win–win solution is the key to conflict resolution in project management.

Fisher and Ury [13] have developed a negotiation technique that tends to maintain these three requirements. They call it "principled negotiation." The method is straightforward; it is defined by four points [13, p. 11].

1. **Separate the people from the problem.**   The conflicting parties are often highly emotional. They perceive things differently and feel strongly about the differences. Emotions and objective fact get confused to the point where it is not clear which is which. Conflicting parties tend to attack one another rather than the problem. To minimize the likelihood that the conflict will become strictly interpersonal, the substantive problem should be carefully defined. Then everyone can work on it rather than each other.

2. **Focus on interests, not positions.**   Positional bargaining occurs when the PM says to a functional manager: "I need this subassembly by November 15." The functional manager responds: "My group can't possibly start on it this year. We might be able to deliver it by February 1." These are the opening lines in a dialogue that sounds suspiciously like the haggling of the tourist and the rug peddler. A simple "Let's talk about the schedule for this subassembly" would be sufficient to open the discussion. Otherwise each party develops a high level of ego involvement in his/her position and the negotiation never focuses on the

real interests and concerns of the conflicting parties—the central issues of the conflict. The exchange deteriorates into a series of positional compromises that do not satisfy either party and leave both feeling that they have lost something important.

In positional negotiation, the "positions" are statements of immediate wants and assume that the environment is static. Consider these positional statements: "I won't pay more than $250,000 for that property." Or, as above, "We might be able to deliver it by February 1." The first position assumes that the bidder's estimates of future property values are accurate, and the second assumes that the group's current workload (or a shortage of required materials) will not change. When negotiation focuses on interests, the negotiator must determine the underlying concern of the other party. The real concerns or interests of the individuals stating the positions quoted above might be to earn a certain return on the investment in a property, or to not commit to delivery of work if delivery on the due date cannot be guaranteed. Knowledge of the other party's interests allows a negotiator to suggest solutions that satisfy one party's interests without agreeing with the other's position.

3. ***Before trying to reach agreement, invent options for mutual gain.*** The parties-in-conflict usually enter negotiations knowing the outcome they would like. As a result, they are blind to other outcomes and are not particulary creative. Nonetheless, as soon as the substantive problems are spelled out, some effort should be devoted to finding a wide variety of possible solutions—or elements thereof—that advance the mutual interests of the conflicting parties. Success at finding options that produce mutual gain positively reinforces win–win negotiations. Cohen [9] reports on a conflict between a couple in which "he" wanted to go to the mountains and "she" wanted to go to the shore. A creative win–win solution sent them both to Lake Tahoe.

4. ***Insist on using objective criteria.*** Rather than bargaining on positions, attention should be given to finding standards (e.g., market value, expert opinion, law, company policy) that can be used to determine the quality of an outcome. Doing this tends to make the negotiation less a contest of wills or exercise in stubbornness. If a functional manager wants to use an expensive process to test a part, it is acceptable for the PM to ask if such a process is required to ensure that the parts meet specified quality standards.

Fisher and Ury [13] have had some success with their approach, "principled negotiation," in the Harvard (Graduate School of Business) Negotiation Project. Use of their methods increases the chance of finding win–win solutions.

There are many books on negotiation, some of which are listed in the bibliography of this chapter. Most of these works are oriented toward negotiation between opponents, not an appropriate mindset for the project manager, but all of them contain useful, tactical advice for the project manager. Wall's book [33] is an excellent academic treatment of the subject. Fisher and Ury [13] is a clear presentation of principled negotiation, and contains much that is relevant to the PM. In addition, Herb Cohen's *You Can Negotiate Anything* [9] is an outstanding guide to win–win negotiation.

Among the tactical issues covered by most books on negotiation are things the project manager, as a beginning negotiator, needs to know. For example, what should a negotiator who wishes to develop a win–win solution do if the other party to the conflict adopts a win–lose approach? What do you do if the other party tries to put you under psychological pressure by seating you so that a bright light shines in your eyes? What do you do if the other party refuses to negotiate in order to put you under extreme time pressure to accept whatever solution he/she offers? How do you settle what you perceive to be purely technical disputes? How should you handle threats? What should be your course of action if a functional manager, with whom you are trying to reach agreement about the timing and technology of a task, goes over your head and attempts to enlist the aid of your boss to get you to accept a solution you feel is less than satisfactory? How can you deal with a person you suspect dislikes you?

In addition, the reader will find books on body language and communication in the bibliography. These works explain the nonverbal aspects of communication. At times, nonverbal messages are at variance with verbal messages, providing proof of that old adage, "actions speak louder than words." When negotiating, the PM must be sensitive to *all* the messages being communicated, not merely those in verbal form.

Almost every writer on negotiation emphasizes the importance of understanding the interests of the person with whom you are negotiating. As we noted above, the positions taken by negotiators are not truly understandable without first understanding the interests and concerns that prompt those positions. The statement that a test requested for May 15 cannot be run until June 2 may simply mean that the necessary test supplies will not be delivered until the latter date. If the PM can get the supplies from another source in time for the May 15 deadline, the test can be run on schedule. But the ability to do this depends on knowing *why* the test was to be delayed. If the negotiation remains a debate on positions, the PM will never find out that the test could have been run on time. *The key to finding a negotiator's interests and concerns is to ask "Why?" when he/she states a position.* The following vignette demonstrates the maintenance of a nonpositional negotiating style. This vignette is based on an actual event and was described to the authors by an "actor" in the case.

▶ 6.5   NEGOTIATION IN ACTION—THE QUAD SENSOR PROJECT

Dave Dogers, an experienced project manager, was assigned the project of designing and setting up a production system for an industrial instrument. The instrument would undoubtedly be quite delicate, so the design and fabrication methods for the shipping container were included in the project. Production of containers capable of meeting the specifications in this case were outside the experience of the firm, but one engineer in the container group had worked with this type of package in a previous job. This engineer, Jeff Gamm, was widely recognized as the top design engineer in the container group.

During the initial meetings on the project, which was organized as a weak matrix, Dogers asked Tab Baturi, manager of the Container Group, to assign Gamm to the project because of his unique background. Baturi said he thought they could work it out, and estimated that the design, fabrication of prototypes, and testing would require about four weeks. The package design could not start until several shape parameters of the instrument had been set and allowable shock loadings for the internal mechanisms had been determined. The R&D group responsible for instrument design thought it would require about nine months of work before they could complete specifications for the container. In addition to the actual design, construction, and test work, Gamm would have to meet periodically with the instrument design team to keep track of the project and to consult on design options from the container viewpoint. It was estimated that the entire project would require about 18 months.

Seven months into the project, at a meeting with Dave Dogers, the senior instrument design engineer, Richard Money casually remarked: "Say, Dave, I thought Jeff Gamm was going to do the package for the Quad Sensor."

"He is, why?" Dogers replied.

"Well," said the engineer, "Gamm hasn't been coming to the design team meetings. He did come a couple of times at the start of the project, but then young McCutcheon showed up saying that he would substitute for Gamm and would keep him informed. I don't know if that will work. That package is going to be pretty tricky to make."

Dogers was somewhat worried by the news the engineer had given him. He went to Gamm's office, as if by chance, and asked, "How are things coming along?"

"I'm up to my neck, Dave," Gamm responded. "We've had half a dozen major changes ordered from Baker's office (V.P. Marketing) and Tab has given me the three toughest ones. I'm behind, getting behinder, and Baker is yelling for the new container designs. I can't possibly do the Quad Sensor package unless I get some help—quick. It's an interesting problem and I'd like to tackle it, but I just can't. I asked Tab to put McCutcheon on it. He hasn't much experience, but he seems bright."

"I see," said Dogers. "Well, the Quad Sensor package may be a bit much for a new man. Do you mind if I talk to Tab? Maybe I can get you out from under some of the pressure."

"Be my guest!" said Gamm.

The next day Dogers met with Tab Baturi to discuss the problem. Baturi seemed depressed. "I don't know what we're supposed to do. No sooner do I get a package design set and tested than I get a call changing things. On the Evans order, we even had production schedules set, had ordered the material, and had all the setups figured out. I'm amazed they didn't wait till we had completed the run to tell us to change everything."

Baturi continued with several more examples of changed priorities and assignments. He complained that he had lost two designers and was falling further and further behind. He concluded: "Dave, I know I said you could use Gamm for the Quad Sensor job, but I simply can't cut him loose. He's my most productive person, and if anyone can get us out from under this mess, he can. I know McCutcheon is just out of school, but he's bright. He's the only person I can spare, and I can only spare him because I haven't got the time to train him on how we operate around here—if you can call this 'operating.'"

The two men talked briefly about the poor communications and the inability of senior management to make up its collective mind. Then Dogers suggested, "Look,

Tab, Quad Sensor is no more screwed up than usual for this stage of the project. How about this? I can let you borrow Charlotte Setter for three or four weeks. She's an excellent designer and she's working on a low-priority job that's not critical at the moment. Say, I'll bet I can talk Anderson into letting you borrow Levy, too, maybe half time for a month. Anderson owes me a favor."

"Great, Dave, that will help a lot, and I appreciate the aid. I know you understand my problem and you know that I understand yours." Baturi paused and then added, "You realize that this won't take much pressure off Jeff Gamm. If you can get him the designing help he needs he can get more done, but I can't release him for the amount of time you've got allocated for the Quad Sensor."

They sat quietly for a while, then Dogers said, "Hey, I've got an idea. Container design is the hard problem. The production setup and test design isn't all that tough. Let me have Gamm for the container design. I'll use McCutcheon for the rest of the project and get him trained for you. I can get Carol Mattson to show him how to set up the shock tests and he can get the word on the production setup from my senior engineer, Dick Money.

Baturi thought a moment. "Yeah, that ought to work," he said. "But Gamm will have to meet with your people to get back up to speed on the project. I think he will clean up Baker's biggest job by Wednesday. Could he meet with your people on Thursday?"

"Sure, I can arrange that," Dogers said.

Baturi continued. "This will mean putting two people on the package design. McCutcheon will have to work with Gamm if he is to learn anything. Can your budget stand it?"

"I'm not sure," Dogers said, "I don't really have any slack in that account, but . . ."

"Never mind," interrupted Baturi, "I can bury the added charge somewhere. I think I'll add it to Baker's charges. He deserves it. After all, he caused our problem."

▶ SUMMARY

This chapter addressed the need for negotiation as a tool to resolve project conflicts. We first discussed the nature of negotiation and its purpose in the organization. We then described various categories of conflict and related them to the project life cycle. We followed this by identifying a number of requirements and principles of negotiation. Finally, we presented a short vignette illustrating an actual negotiation situation.

Specific points made in the chapter were these:

- Negotiation within the firm should be directed at obtaining the best outcome for the organization, not winning.

- There are three major categories of conflict: goal-oriented, authority-based, and interpersonal.

- There are also three primary sources of conflict. They are the project team itself, the client, and functional and senior management.

- Critical issues to handle in the project formation stages are delimiting technical objectives, getting management commitment, setting the project's relative priority, and selecting the project organizational structure.

- The total level of conflict is highest during the project buildup stage.

- Scheduling and technical conflicts are most frequent and serious in the project buildup and main program stages, and scheduling conflicts in particular during the phaseout stage.

- Project negotiation requirements are that conflicts must be settled without permanent damage, the methodology must foster honesty, and the solution must satisfy both individuals' and the organization's needs.
- One promising approach to meeting the requirements of project negotiation is called principled negotiation.

This chapter concludes the subject of project initiation. In the next part of the text we address project implementation, starting with the subject of budgeting. We look at various budgeting methods. The chapter also addresses the issue of cost estimation and its difficulty.

▶ GLOSSARY

Interfaces—The boundaries between departments or functions.

Lateral Relations—Communications across lines of equivalent authority.

Pareto Optimal Solution—A solution such that no party can be made better off without making another party worse off by the same amount or more.

Positional Negotiation—Stating immediate wants on the assumption that the environment is static.

Principled Negotiation—A process of negotiation that aims to achieve a win–win result.

Parties-at-Interest—Those who have a vested interest in the outcome of the negotiations.

Win–Win—When both parties are better off in the outcome.

▶ MATERIAL REVIEW QUESTIONS

1. Construct a definition of negotiation that generally encompasses all the meanings discussed in the chapter.
2. Review and justify the placement of the seven types of conflicts into the nine cells of Table 6-1.
3. Discuss each of the four fundamental issues for potential conflict during the project formation stage.
4. Identify the types of likely conflicts during the project buildup, main program, and phaseout stages.

5. What are the three main requirements of project negotiation?
6. Describe the four points of principled negotiation.
7. What is the objective of negotiation?
8. What are the three categories of conflict?
9. What is "principled negotiation"?
10. What are some reasons for conflict during project phaseout?

▶ CLASS DISCUSSION QUESTIONS

1. Summarize the vignette in the chapter in terms of the negotiation skill used. Comment on the appropriateness and ethical aspects related to "burying" the cost.
2. What will be the likely result of a win–win style manager negotiating with a win–lose style manager? What if they are both win–lose styled?
3. Reallocate the placement of the seven types of conflicts into the nine cells of Table 6-1 according to your own logic.

4. Describe the effect of practicing "conflict avoidance" in the project formation stage in terms of the resulting problems during the buildup stage.
5. How does the type of project organization affect each of the types of conflicts that occur over the project life cycle?
6. Project managers are primarily concerned with project interfaces. At what rate do these interfaces increase with increasing project size?

7. The critical term in the concept of principled negotiation is "position." Elaborate on the multiple meanings of this term relative to negotiation. Can you think of a better term?

8. Give an example of a Pareto optimal solution in a conflict.

9. Why are scheduling conflicts so serious in the phaseout stage?

10. Given that many conflicts are the result of different parties having different interests, is it possible to achieve a win–win situation?

11. Contractors always try to make a task sound more difficult than it is so they can charge more. When, if ever, does this become unethical?

12. The chairman of Cadbury Schweppes PLC, G.A.H. Cadbury, suggests [7] the following test for an ethical action: Would you be embarrassed to have it described in the newspaper? Is this a sufficient test for ethics? Can you think of any others?

▶ INCIDENTS FOR DISCUSSION

Pritchard Soap Co.

Samantha ("Sam") Calderon is manager of a project that will completely alter the method of adding perfume to Pritchard Soap's "Queen Elizabeth" gift soap line. The new process will greatly extend the number of available scents and should result in a significant increase in sales. The project had been proceeding reasonably well, but fell several weeks behind when the perfume supplier, the Stephen Marcus Parfumissary, was unable to meet its delivery deadline because of a wildcat strike.

Under normal circumstances this would not have caused problems, but the project had been subject to a particularly long evaluation study and now was in danger of not being ready for the Christmas season. The major scheduling problem concerned Pritchard's toxicity lab. Mike Lee, lab manager, had been most cooperative in scheduling the Queen Elizabeth perfumes for toxicity testing. He had gone out of his way to rearrange his own schedule to accommodate Calderon's project. Because of the strike at Marcus, however, Calderon cannot have the perfumes ready for test as scheduled, and the new test date Lee has given Sam will not allow her to make the new line available by Christmas. Calderon suspects that the project might not have been approved if senior management had known that they would miss this year's Christmas season.

Questions: What are Sam's alternatives? What should she do?

Sutton Electronics

Harold Frank was still basking in the glory of his promotion to project manager for Sutton Electronics Corporation, manufacturer of fire alarm systems for motels, offices, and other large-scale installations. Frank's first project involved the development of an alarm system based on sophisticated circuitry that would detect and identify a large number of dangerous gases as well as smoke and very high temperatures. The device was the brainchild of Ira Magoo, vice-president of research and the technical wizard responsible for many of Sutton's most successful products

It was unusual for so young and relatively inexperienced an employee as Frank to be given control of such a potentially important project, but he had shown skill in handling several complex, though routine, jobs. In addition, he had the necessary scientific background to allow him to understand the nature of Magoo's proposed gas detection system.

Four weeks into the project, Frank was getting quite worried. He had tried to set up an organizational and basic planning meeting several times. No matter when he scheduled the meeting, the manager of the marketing department, Jaki Benken, was unable to attend. Finally, Frank agreed that marketing could be represented by young Bill Powell, a Benken protégé who had just graduated from college and joined Sutton Electronics. Frank was doubtful that Powell could contribute much to the project.

Frank's worry increased when Powell missed the first planning meeting completely and did not appear at the second meeting until it was almost over. Powell seemed apologetic and indicated that departmental crises had kept him away from both meetings. The project was now seven weeks old and Frank was almost five weeks late with the master plan. He was thinking about asking Ira Magoo what to do.

Questions: Do you think that Frank should involve Magoo at this point? If so, what outcome would you expect? If not, what should he do?

▶ INDIVIDUAL EXERCISE

Review two recent incidents where you had a conflict with another person, one a success and one a failure. Describe the incidents in terms of the types of conflicts discussed in the chapter and the approaches to negotiation that were used. Were the requirements of project negotiation followed? Would the points of principled negotiation have helped?

▶ PROJECT TEAM CONTINUING EXERCISE

As your project progresses, record the negotiation process that group members encounter throughout the term of the project. Consider both negotiations between members of the team as well as negotiations with outsiders, such as for resources, information, or even time. Make note if the principles of good negotiation were used and how the outcome evolved. Was it a "win–win" process or not? At what point in the project life cycle did each issue arise?

▶ BIBLIOGRAPHY

1. ADAMS, J. R., and S. E. BARNDT. "Behavorial Implications of the Project Life Cycle." In D. I. Cleland and W. R. King, eds., *Project Management Handbook*. New York: Van Nostrand Reinhold, 1983.

2. AFZALUR, R. M., *Managing Conflict in Organizations*. Westport, CT: Praeger, 1992.

3. BAKER, S. T., "Partnering: Contracting for The Future." *Cost Engineering*, April 1990.

4. BROCKS, E., and G. S. ODIORNE. *Managing by Negotiation*. Melbourne, FL: Krieger 1990.

5. BURKE, R. J. "Methods of Resolving Interpersonal Conflict." *Personnel Administration*, July–August, 1969.

6. BURTON, J. *Conflict Resolution and Prevention*. New York: St. Martins, 1990.

7. Cadbury, G. A. H. "Ethical Managers Make Their Own Rules." *Harvard Business Review*, Sept.–Oct. 1987.

8. COWEN, C., C. GRAY, and E. LARSON. "Project Partnering." *Project Management Journal*, December 1992.

9. COHEN, H. *You Can Negotiate Anything*. Secaucus, N.J.: Lyle Stuart Inc., 1980.

10. DOLAN, J. P. *Negotiate Like the Pros*. San Jose, CA: Putnam, 1992.

11. DYER, W. G., *Team Building*, 2nd ed. Reading, MA: Addison-Wesley, 1987.

12. FAST, J. *Body Language*. New York: Pocket Books, 1971.

13. FISHER, R., and W. URY, *Getting to Yes*. Harmondsworth, Middlesex, G.B.: Penguin Books, 1983.

14. HAJEK, V. G. *Management of Engineering Projects*, 3rd. ed. New York: McGraw Hill, 1984.

15. HELPERN, A. *Negotiating Skills*. Holmes Beach, FL: W. W. Gaunt, 1992.

16. ILICH, J. *The Art and Skill of Successful Negotiation.* Englewood Cliffs, N.J.: Prentice Hall, 1983.

17. ILICH, J. *Power Negotiating.* Reading, MA: Addison-Wesley, 1980.

18. JANDT, F. E. *Win–Win Negotiating.* New York: Wiley, 1987.

19. KUHN, R. L. *Deal Maker.* New York: Wiley, 1988.

20. LOVE, S. F. *Achieving Problem Free Project Management.* New York: Wiley, 1989.

21. NIERENBERG, G. I. *Fundamentals of Negotiating.* New York: HarperCollins, 1987.

22. NIERENBERG, G. I., and H. H. CALERO. *How to Read a Person Like a Book.* New York: Pocket Books, 1971.

23. NIERENBERG, G. I., and H. H. CALERO, *Meta-talk.* New York: Pocket Books, 1975.

24. Obrodovitch, M. M, and S. E. Stephenou. *Project Management: Risks and Productivity* (see Chapter 11, "Ethics"). Bend, OR: Daniel Spencer Pub., 1990.

25. RAIFFA, H. *The Art and Science of Negotiation.* Cambridge: Belknap/Harvard Press, 1982.

26. RECK, R., and B. G. LONG. *The Win–Win Negotiator:* *How to Negotiate Favorable Agreements that Last.* Portage, MI: Spartan, 1987.

27. *Roget's International Thesaurus.* New York: Thomas Y. Crowell, 1946.

28. STEER, R. M. *Introduction to Organizational Behavior,* 3rd ed. Glenview, IL: Scott, Foresman, 1988.

29. THAMHAIN, H. J., and D. L. WILEMON. "Conflict Management in Project Life Cycles." *Sloan Management Review*, Summer 1975.

30. THAMHAIN, H. J., and D. L. WILEMON. "Diagnosing Conflict Determinants in Project Management." *IEEE Transactions on Engineering Management*, February 1975.

31. THOMAS, K. W. "Conflict and Conflict Management." In M.D. Dunnette, ed., *Handbook of Industrial and Organizational Psychology.* New York: Rand McNally, 1976.

32. U.S. Bureau of the Census. *Statistical Abstract of the United States:* 1987. Washington, DC: US Government Printing Office, 1986.

33. WALL, J. A., JR. *Negotiation: Theory and Practice.* GLENVIEW, IL: Scott, Foresman, 1985.

CASE

CINCINNATI MILACRON INC.: ROBOT WELDING
James M. Comer and Marianne M. Hill

Cincinnati Milacron Inc. is engaged in the design, manufacture, and sale of process equipment and systems for industry, along with the supplies and accessories sold for use in those systems. Formed as Cincinnati Screw and Tap Company in 1884, the company originally sold screws, taps, and dies. The portion of the company devoted to milling machines was purchased in 1889 and named the Cincinnati Milling Machine Co.

In 1970 the Cincinnati Milling Machine Co. was renamed Cincinnati Milacron. By 1983 the company had eleven plants in the United States and eight overseas, employing some 10,000 people and having annual sales in excess of $500 million. Industry sources in 1983 ranked Cincinnati Milacron first in dollar sales of robotics in the United States, although these sales represented less than 10 percent of total company sales.

The company has three divisions: Machine Tools, Plastics Processing Machinery, and Industrial Specialty Products. The Machine Tool Division (see Figure 1) has a number of departments including Metal Fabrication. The welding shop and the foundry are two parts of the Metal Fabrication Division.

The Welding Shop Project

In the late 1960s, Cincinnati Milacron had workable robotic technology. One of the first interests of management was the application of this new technology in

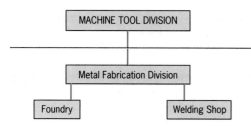

Figure 1: Partial organization design.

other corporate divisions. One division that seemed to have a natural fit was in the Metal Fabrication Division because it had many repetitive jobs and the opportunity for significant cost savings.

In the early 1970s the division ignored the robotic technology. They showed no inclination to seek out and use the robots in their operations despite their apparent advantages. The president of Cincinnati Milacron, along with upper management, as an incentive, offered to provide robots without cost or overhead charges to the divisions. Despite this offer, no strong interest was evidenced in their adoption and use.

In the period 1977–79 an executive committee reviewed the entire company's manufacturing processes. One of their decisions was to move ahead and apply the company's existing expertise in robot welding to the firm's own operations in the Metal Fabrication Division. They told the weld shop that a welding robot would be installed because: (1) other divisions of the company developed and marketed robots including robots for welding and they needed a readily available customer demonstration site—thus an on-site application could be used as a marketing and selling tool; (2) customer-specific technological problems could be investigated in-house rather than going outside; (3) there were some welding applications in Milacron's manufacturing process that would be improved by the use of robotic welding techniques. For example, Cincinnati Milacron welded box-type enclosures such as hydraulic tanks and electrical cabinets which were particularly appropriate for robotic applications.

Project Development and Implementation

The project was initiated in September 1980 when the feasibility study on the first welding robot indicated the potential for a good return on the investment. The first group that worked on the project consisted of a manager, an engineer who was familiar with welding,

and a welder from another division brought in as a technician. None of them were experienced with robot welding.

The year 1981 was spent in the welding shop developing techniques and methods for the robot cell. The project initially experienced resistance by some people in the weld shop. In January 1982 the project was physically moved into the production area where its capabilities were demonstrated to the foundry management and welders alike. By June 1982 this resistance had disappeared with the demonstration of the robot welding hydraulic tanks. The quality, consistency, and speed of the robot dispelled any reluctance to adopt it. A second robot welder was requested by welding shop management and installation was completed by January 1983. The third, devoted solely to heavy welding, was put into operation in July 1983.

Robot Applications

Initial Situation

Prior to 1980 the welding shop consisted of well-trained and closely supervised people hand welding both light (16 gauge to $\frac{1}{4}$") and thick (up to 3") metals. Spot and arc welding were used on the light metals with arc welding exclusively applied to heavier plate metal. Typical welding problems were "warping" (the heat induced from the welding causing the light metals to bend) and "seam tracking" (keeping the weld straight) in the heavy welding. In the manual welding operation when the welder received a job, he or she would put the parts to be welded on a welding table or the floor, move them around to achieve the desired angle, and then hold them down with hand clamps or by foot while performing the necessary welding.

Robot Installation and Work Force

In 1982 when the initial robot welder was installed in the shop, management chose not to use an experienced welder to operate the robot. In fact, a person was selected and trained to operate it who had had no previous welding experience. The reason was quite simply that management knew that experienced welders would find it difficult, if not impossible, to ignore their own training and years of experience and operate the machine accordingly. Training of a new person to the necessary proficiency to operate the robot required about six months, although the robot could be operated adequately with one month's training. On the other hand, training of a manual welder to perform simple seam welding required about five to six weeks. Training a welder to interpret engineering drawings and competently assemble a variety of pieces required about one year. The existing work force of manual welders were promised during negotiations that only new work would be given to the robots.

Applications of Robot Welding

The company found that the installation of the robot had a number of effects both on the operation of the welding shop as well as in operations upstream and downstream from it. In the welding of tanks, ladders, and cabinets these effects could be readily seen.

Customers of the company used or sold tanks to hold such products as liquids. Previously these tanks were welded by hand on both the inside and the outside of the tanks and, when completed, these welds usually had to be sanded smooth. There were some problems with weld quality on these tanks so this operation was chosen as the first application for robot welding. When the robot first started welding these tanks, it was programmed to weld both the inside and outside just as the manual welder had done. Very quickly, however, management found that the robot

was so accurate and steady that only one side had to be welded. This reduced welding cost and production time while increasing the quality of the finished product. The quality was so reliable that pressure and leak testing were no longer necessary. An additional unexpected benefit was that the robot weld was so smooth that it required little or no finishing.

A second instance where the robot proved its value was in the welding of robot ladders (see Figure 2). The human welder was instructed to weld in a pattern such as A,E,C,D,B,F, so that heat wouldn't build up in one area causing warpage and ladders which had to be scrapped because they were "out of square." At first, under direct supervision and instruction, the welder would weld the ladder in the proper sequence. An experienced welder typically could do about two to three ladders a day. Without direct supervision, however, welders too often succumbed to the temptation to weld the ladder in the quickest manner such as A,D,E,B,C,F. The result was that the ladder scrappage rate commonly ran as much as 33 percent of production.

Given the problems in the ladder welding, the robot welder was assigned to weld ladders. The robot, however, did exactly as it was programmed to do time after time with no variation. It was able to weld five ladders a day perfectly and with no scrappage.

In welding box-type enclosures such as electrical cabinets there is considerable accuracy necessary in the cutting and bending process prior to welding. A sheet of metal is cut in the shape illustrated in Figure 3 and the four peninsulas are then bent upward to form a box. The corners must then be welded and finished to have a solid product. When the company relied on hand welding the welder would take the pieces of metal, put them in a convenient spot (usually on

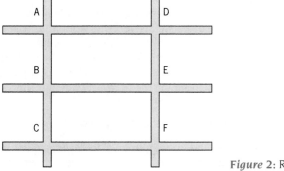

Figure 2: Robot ladder.

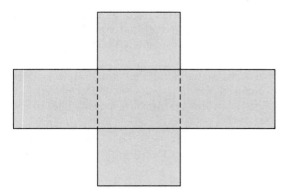

Figure 3: Sheet metal cut for box.

the floor!), and twist them around to the proper angle by hand or hoist as was needed to complete the job. If the worker saw an improper cut or bend he or she would "adjust" for the difference by twisting or bending the metal by force. The welder could also compensate for imperfections by adjusting the welding process.

A robot is not able to identify imperfections in the metal sheets and make on-the-spot adjustments. Thus the installation of the robot to weld cabinets dictated that a number of changes be made both upstream of the welding operation as well as in the operation itself. First, the company had to design, acquire, and install a complete set of relatively elaborate fixturing to hold the metal parts at precisely the right position and angle every time. Second, when two pieces of metal did not match properly, the robot couldn't compensate by bending or twisting the metal until it matched as did a human operator. Thus the company had to buy new shears to cut parts more accurately and a new press brake to bend the metal more precisely.

In all three operations, the robot's speed and accuracy had direct impacts on middle management's planning requirements. For example, management had to be much more accurate in acquiring raw materials as well as maintaining in-process inventory to avoid machine downtime. In addition, materials handling equipment and procedures had to be more closely monitored to ensure compatibility with robot operation.

Evaluation

The company conducted a number of post audits of the impact of the robot welding process on shop operation. They were uniformly favorable in that the robot quality was not only higher than the human operator but was also more consistent. From a marketing and sales perspective, however, only three or four general customer tours visited the robot-welding operation. Reportedly no customers or prospective customers requested or were given direct experience with the robot welding process.

As of June 1983 the welding robots were being used solely on new business with none of the existing welders replaced by the technology. Management's objective was to have some 80 percent of Cincinnati Milacron's welding operations performed by robot in the future.

In general, management was extremely pleased with the installation and operation of the robot welding process. Problems arose with the initial installation but these were viewed as minor compared to the improvement in the welding operation.

▶ QUESTIONS

1. Was this a project situation involving partnering between the executive committee and the project group, chartering of the welding robot project, or change? If so, which one(s)?

2. Why did the Metal Fabrication Division management not seek out the robotic technology even though it offered significant cost advantages and was a "free good"?

3. Was there anything unusual about the justification for introducing robot technology in this case? Why? Was there any implicit reason for the introduction?

4. Does an in-house demonstration site seem to be the best way to market a product/process? What do you expect might have gone wrong? What other alternatives are there? What are the implications of choosing another alternative?

5. At what stage of the project life cycle did the major conflicts arise? Were the sources of the conflicts one of the higher-intensity categories depicted in Figure 6-1? Which one(s)?

6. Burke (see [5] or the *Classic Reading* for this chapter) categorizes the methods for resolving conflict into five categories: withdrawing, smoothing, compromising, forcing, and confrontation-problem solving. Which one(s) was used in this situation?

7. What assumption(s) did the firm make when they promised that only "new work" would go to the robot? What are the firm's responsibilities to the welders?

8. Would the four points of "principled negotiation" have helped in this situation? If so, which ones and why?

9. Why did management choose to use a development team that was relatively inexperienced with robotics?

▶ This classic article describes a number of methods for negotiating and handling conflicts. The author identifies effective and ineffective methods ranging from withdrawal to forcing. Each method is then illustrated with a number of examples. Finally, the most effective method, confrontation-problem solving, is described in terms of its many characteristics.

Classic Reading

METHODS OF RESOLVING INTERPERSONAL CONFLICT
Ronald J. Burke

The management of conflict in creative and useful ways, rather than its containment or abolition, has been proposed by many writers. Various strategies for dealing with conflict at different levels and for managing disagreements have also been proposed. Most of these methods have not been experimentally evaluated. Given the central and inevitable role of conflict in human affairs, a high priority of importance is to be placed on learning the most effective way to resolve it.

Purpose of This Study

In a previous investigation, Burke (1969a) collected questionnaire data from 74 managers, in which they described the way they and their superiors dealt with conflict between them. It was possible to relate five different methods of conflict resolution originally proposed by Blake and Mouton (1964)—Withdrawing, Smoothing, Compromising, Forcing, and Confrontation or Problem Solving—to two major areas of the superior–subordinate relationship. These were (1) constructive use of differences and disagreements, and (2) several aspects of the superior–subordinate relationship in planning job targets and evaluating accomplishments.

In general, the results showed that Withdrawing and Forcing behaviors were consistently negatively related to these two areas. Compromising was not related to these two areas. Use of Smoothing was inconsistently related, sometimes positive and sometimes negative. Only Confrontation-Problem Solving was always related positively to both. That is, use of Confrontation was associated with constructive use of differences and high scores on various measures of the superior–subordinate relationship.

This study has the dual purpose of attempting to specify more precisely the characteristics of the Confrontation-Problem Solving method of conflict resolution, and replicating the earlier study (Burke, 1969a) using different methodology.

Method

Subjects: The respondents were managers from various organizations who were enrolled in a university course emphasizing behavioral science concepts relevant to the functions of management. Their organizational experience ranged from one year to over 30 years.

Procedure: Each respondent was asked to describe a time when he felt particularly GOOD (or BAD) about the way in which an interpersonal conflict was resolved. The specific instructions stated:

"Think of a time when you felt especially GOOD (or BAD) about the way an interpersonal conflict or disagreement (e.g., boss–subordinate, peer-peer, etc.) in which you were involved was resolved. It may have been on your present job, or any other job, or away from the work situation.

"Now describe it in enough detail so a reader would understand the way the conflict or differences were handled."

This statement appeared at the top of a blank sheet of paper.

Approximately half the respondents were first to describe the instance when they felt particularly good, followed by the instance when they felt particularly bad. The remaining respondents described the instances in the reverse order. No apparent effects were observed from the change in order, so the data from both groups will be considered together in this report.

Results

Fifty-three descriptions of effective resolution of conflict (felt especially GOOD) and 53 descriptions of ineffective resolutions of conflict (felt especially BAD) were obtained. These were provided by 57 different individuals. Some individuals provided only one example. The response rate was about 70 percent of the total available population.

The written descriptions were then coded into one of the five methods of conflict resolution proposed by Blake and Mouton (1964). (1) *Withdrawing*— easier to refrain than to retreat from an argument; silence is golden. "See no evil, hear no evil, speak no evil." (2) *Smoothing*—play down the differences and emphasize common interests; issues that might cause divisions or hurt feelings are not discussed. (3)

Compromising—splitting the difference, bargaining, search for an intermediate position. Better half a loaf than none at all; no one loses but no one wins. (4) *Forcing*—a win–lose situation; participants are antagonists, competitors, not collaborators. Fixed positions, polarization. Creates a victor and a vanquished. (5) *Confrontation-Problem Solving*—open exchange of information about the conflict or problem as each sees it, and a working through of their differences to reach a solution that is optimal to both. Both can win.

Table 1 presents the method of conflict resolution associated with effective resolution (left half of Table 1) and ineffective resolution (right half of Table 1). Considering the left half of the table, Confrontation-Problem Solving was the most common method for effective resolution (58.5%), followed by Forcing (24.5%), and Compromise (11.3%). The prominence of Confrontation as an effective method is consistent with the earlier study (Burke, 1969a) but the value for Forcing was higher than expected. When these 13 cases are considered as a group, 11 of them are similar in that the party providing the written description benefited as a result of the Forcing. That is, Forcing was perceived as an effective method of resolving conflict by the victor, but not by the vanquished.

Moving to the right half of Table 1, Forcing was the most commonly used method for ineffective resolution, followed in second place by Withdrawal with only 9.4 percent. The vast majority of individuals pro-

Table 1   Methods Associated with Effective and Ineffective Conflict Resolution

	Effective Resolution (N = 53)		Ineffective Resolution (N = 53)	
	N	%	N	%
Withdrawal	0	0.0*	5	9.4*
Smoothing	0	0.0	1	1.9
Compromise	6	11.3	3	5.7
Forcing	13	24.5*	42	79.2*
Confrontation- problem solving	31	58.5*	0	0.0*

Other (still unresolved;
  unable to determine
  how resolved; irrelevant
  to assignment; etc.)
	3	5.7	2	3.8

*Percentage difference between groups is significant at the .05 level of confidence.

viding written descriptions of Forcing methods were victims or "losers" as a result of Forcing behavior.

In summary, the major differences in methods of conflict resolution found to distinguish effective versus ineffective examples were: (1) significantly greater use of Confrontation in the effective examples (58.5% vs. 0.0%); (2) significantly less use of Forcing in the effective examples (24.5% vs. 79.2%); and (3) significantly less use of Withdrawing in the effective examples (0.0% vs. 9.4%).

When Forcing was seen to be effective, the authors of the examples were "winners" of a win–lose conflict; when Forcing was seen to be ineffective, the authors of the examples were "losers" of a win–lose conflict. Whether the resolution of conflict via Forcing would actually be perceived to be effective by members of the organization outside the conflict (i.e., objectively seen as effective), as it was perceived to be effective by the "winners," remains to be determined by future research.

Effective Conflict Resolution

A few of the examples of effective conflict resolution are provided to highlight specific features of Confrontation. These were taken verbatim from the written descriptions.

1. *This example highlights the presentation of a problem of mutual interest—meeting deadlines more often at the earliest opportunity (when the problem is observed). Superior is open-minded and asking for help.*

"I once was given the responsibility for managing a small group of technicians engaged in turning out critical path schedules. I spent some time trying to get organized and involved with the group, but I sensed a hostile atmosphere, accompanied by offhand sarcastic remarks. At the end of the day very little work had been accomplished.

"The next day when I came in, I called the group together and told them that we were falling behind, and asked them to help me find a solution. After the initial distrust had been dissipated, the group produced some good ideas on work reallocation, office arrangement, priorities and techniques. I told the group that all of their agreed-upon suggestions would be implemented at once, and their reply was that the backlog would be cleared in three days and would not build up again.

"Within three days the backlog was gone, the group worked together better, and for the six months I

was in charge, schedules were always ready before they were required."

2. *This example highlights emphasis on facts in determining the best resolution of conflict. Both had strong convictions but one willingly moved to the other's position when facts indicated that this position was best.*

"The project engineer and I disagreed about the method of estimating the cost of alternative schemes in a highway interchange. Neither of us could agree on the other's method. Eventually I was able to satisfy him using algebra. We were both happy with the result."

3. *Like Example 2, this one highlights an emphasis on facts and the conviction that by digging and digging, the truth will be discovered. Although the superior had a vested interest in the "old" system (a product of his thinking), the discussion was never personalized. That is, it did not involve "me" versus "you," but rather a comparison of two systems, two concepts or two ideas.*

"About a year ago I developed a new system for processing the accounting of the inventory of obsolete material on hand in our plant. It was my estimation that it would prove to be an easier system to operate and control and would also involve a considerable monetary saving for the company.

"When I approached my boss with the system, he immediately turned it down as he had developed the present system and was sure it was the best possible system. As I was sure my new system was superior to the present one, I then convinced him to join me in analyzing a comparison of the two systems, pointing out the strengths and weaknesses of the two. After a period of evaluation involving many differences of opinion, we were able to resolve that my system had definite merit and should be brought into operation."

4. *This example highlights the fact that through problem solving both parties can benefit. Instead of compromising, the issues are disussed until a solution completely satisfactory to both is found. Often this is superior to the ones initially favored by the separate parties.*

"In the—Board of Education, there were eight inspectors of Public Schools and four superintendents. Last February the inspectors were given the assignment of developing an in-service plan for the training of teachers for the school year 1968–69. The inspectors gave the assignment to a group of three of their number who were to bring a report to the next inspectors' meeting. I was not a member of the in-service committee but in conversations with the committee members I discovered that they contemplated having an in-service program for two teachers from each school (there are about 85 schools) once a month for the entire year in mathematics. I felt that this would be a very thin coverage of our 2000 or so teachers.

"Consequently I worked on a plan whereby utilizing two Thursday mornings a month and the specialized teaching help available in—, every teacher would have the opportunity to become involved in an in-service training session in a subject of his or her choice once during the year. At the inspectors' meeting the sub-committee presented its report and after some procedural wrangling I was permitted to present my plan. The two were diametrically opposed and it looked as if my plan would be voted down except the chairman suggested that both plans be presented to the superintendents.

"At the meeting of the superintendents, the sub-committee made its report and I presented my plan. As the meeting progressed there was some give and take and instead of one or the other being discarded both plans were adopted. For this school year mathematics is stressed for the first eight Thursday mornings (their plan in a rather concentrated form); then for the next eight months on the second and fourth Thursday my plan is used. We came out of this meeting with a combination of the two plans which was better than either one individually."

Ineffective Conflict Resolution

Examples 5, 6, and 7 illustrate Forcing methods of conflict resolution. A win–lose situation is set up, and usually the superior wins. The individual with the greater power triumphs (a personalized disagreement) rather than the one whose position is supported by the most factual evidence.

5. "In a previous job, I worked for a major management consulting group as a consultant. One assignment, lasting four months, was to use a simulation technique to evaluate the most preferable investment decision using defined quantitative criteria. At the end of the job two alternatives were shown to be marginally better than the other. However, later sensitivity tests also showed that the analytical technique could not rate one to be substantially better than the other.

"Therefore, I wrote a 'technically honest' report stating that our analysis could not provide the one best alternative. My manager, feeling that we were hired to recommend a 'one best' alternative, wanted to cover up the limitations of our methodology.

"We disagreed and I was overruled. The manager wrote a 'technically dishonest' version of the report and the revised report was sent to the client indicating the 'one best' alternative."

6. "Recently in my firm, management had sprung a secrecy agreement contract upon all of the technical people. No word of introduction or explanation was given. It was simply handed out and we were asked to sign it. Most of us found objection in several clauses in the agreement. However, management officials stated that the agreement would probably not stand up in a court of law. They further stated that it was something that was sent from corporate in the U.S. and was not their idea. The employees continued to show reluctance.*

"The vice-president called on everyone individually and stated that there would be no room for advancement for anyone who did not sign the contract. As a result everyone signed."

7. "I was assigned a project by my boss to determine the optimum way, using predetermined times, to lay out an assembly line. It would have to provide optimum efficiency with the following variables: (a) different hourly production rates (e.g., 100/hr. Mon., 200/hr. Tues.) which would mean different numbers of operators on the line; (b) different models of the product (electric motors). The group was on group incentive.

"After much research and discussion, the system was installed utilizing the floating system of assembly (operators could move from station to station in order to keep out of the bottleneck operation). This system was working out well. However, at this time I was informed by my boss that he and the foreman of the area decided that they wished to use the 'paced' system of assembly. This would mean the conveyor belt would be run at set speeds and that the stripes would be printed on the belt indicating that one device would have to be placed on each mark and operators would not float.

"I was dead against this since I had considered it and rejected it in favor of the implemented method. I was, however, given the order to use their proposed system *or else*. There was *no* opportunity for discussion or justification of the method."

8. *This example is a classic description of Withdrawal as a mode of conflict resolution. Clearly the problem is not resolved.*

"On the successful completion of a project which involved considerable time and effort, I was praised and thanked for a job well done by my immediate supervisor and his supervisor, the vice-president in charge of manufacturing. They promised me that on my next salary review I would receive a substantial increase.

"The next salary review came up and my immediate supervisor submitted an amount that he and I felt was a good increase. The amount I received was one-third of this figure. I felt insulted, cheated, and hurt that the company considered I was worth this 'token' amount.

"I had a personal interview with the vice-president where I argued that I felt I should receive more. He agreed in sort of an offhanded way—he felt the whole salary schedule should be reviewed and that my area of responsibility should be increased. He said the company wants people to 'prove themselves' before they give them increases; and he suggested a salary review. I felt I had just done this in my last project—I felt I was being put off, but agreed to the salary review.

"One month passed and nothing happened. I became frustrated—I purposely slowed down the amount of work I turned out.

"Another month passed and still no action. I became disillusioned with the company and resolved at this point to look for another position. Several months later with still no action, I resigned and accepted another position."

Inability to Resolve Conflict

These descriptions of ineffective resolution of conflict indicate that an impressive number of respondents included termination or change of employment of one member in the situation (19 of 53, 26%). These cases tended to be of two types.

The first is represented by Example 8. Here an employee decides to quit because he felt the problem was not resolved in a satisfactory manner. Forcing is likely to be associated with instances of voluntary termination.

The second centered around an inability to resolve the conflict. Then the "problem employee" (a visible symptom of the conflict) was dismissed.

9. *The following example illustrates this:*

"This concerned a young girl about 18 years old who was a typist in our office. This girl lacked a little maturity, but was not really all that bad. She was tuned to all the latest fashions in both dress and manners.

"I felt and still feel that this girl was a potentially good employee. But it was decided that she should be let go. The argument used was that she was not a good worker and lacked the proper attitude for office work. Rather than spend a little time and effort to understand the girl and perhaps develop her into a good employee, the easy way was taken and the girl was fired."

There were two other clear cases of "effective" conflict resolution resulting in voluntary employee terminations. In both instances a Forcing mode was employed and the "loser" resigned from the organization soon after. Our finding is that these were given as examples of effective conflict resolution by the "winner." In another effective example of Forcing, the "loser" was dismissed.

Conclusions

The results of this investigation are consistent with an earlier study (Burke, 1969a), and the data of Lawrence and Lorsch (1967a, 1967b) in showing the value of Confrontation–Problem Solving as a method of conflict resolution. About 60 percent of the examples of effective conflict resolution involved use of the method, while no examples of ineffective conflict resolution did. The poorest method of conflict resolution was Forcing. This method accounted for 80 percent of the examples of ineffective conflict resolution and only 24 percent of the examples of effective conflict resolution. The latter conclusion is somewhat at odds with Lawrence and Lorsch's findings that Forcing was an effective backup method to Confrontation, from an organizational effectiveness standpoint. In fact, the earlier study (Burke, 1969a) found that the use of these methods tended to be negatively correlated. Managers high in use of one of them tended to be low in use of the other.

Characteristics of Problem Solving

Let us now consider more specific features of Confrontation, the most effective method of resolving interpersonal conflict. Insights from the present investigation and the writings of others (e.g., Blake, Shepard and Mouton, 1964; Maier, 1963; Maier and Hoffman, 1965) becomes relevant. The following then are characteristics of Confrontation as a method of managing conflict:

(1) Both people have a vested interest in the outcome. (Examples 1, 2, 3, and 4).

(2) There is a belief on the part of the people involved that they have the potential to resolve the con-

flict and to achieve a better solution through collaboration.

(3) There is a recognition that the conflict or the problem is mainly in the relationship between the individuals and not in each person separately. If the conflict is in the relationship, it must be defined by those who have the relationship. In addition, if solutions are to be developed, the solutions have to be generated by those who share the responsibility for assuring that the solution will work and for making the relationship last.

(4) The goal is to solve the problem, not to accommodate different points of view. This process identifies the causes of reservation, doubt, and misunderstanding between the people confronted with conflict and disagreement. Alternative ways of approaching conflict resolution are explored and tested (Examples 2 and 3).

(5) The people involved are problem-minded instead of solution-minded; "fluid" instead of "fixed" positions. Both parties jointly search out the issues that separate them. Through joint effort, the problems that demand solutions are identified, and later solved.

(6) There is a realization that both aspects of a controversy have potential strengths and potential weaknesses. Rarely is one position completely right and the other completely wrong. (Example 4).

(7) There is an effort to understand the conflict or problem from the other person's point of view, and from the standpoint of the "real" or legitimate needs that must be recognized and met before problem solving can occur. Full acceptance of the other is essential.

(8) The importance of looking at the conflict objectively rather than in a personalized sort of way is recognized. (Example 3).

(9) An examination of one's own attitudes (hostilities, antagonisms) is needed before interpersonal contact on a less effective basis has a chance to occur.

(10) An understanding of the less effective methods of conflict resolution (e.g., win–lose, bargaining, etc.) is essential.

(11) One needs to present "face-saving" situations. Allow people to "give" so that a change in one's viewpoint does not suggest weakness or capitulation.

(12) There is need to minimize effects of status differences, defensiveness, and other barriers which prevent people from working together effectively.

(13) It is important to be aware of the limitations of arguing or presenting evidence in favor of your own position while downgrading the opponent's position.

This behavior often stimulates the opponent to find even greater support for his position (increased polarization). In addition, it leads to selective listening for weaknesses in the opponent's position rather than listening to understand his/her position.

Attitude, Skill, and Creativity

Two related themes run through these characteristics, one dealing with attitudes, and the other with skills (interpersonal, problem solving) of the individuals involved. As the research of Maier and his associates has shown, differences and disagreements need not lead to dissatisfaction and unpleasant experiences but rather can lead to innovation and creativity. One of the critical variables was found to be the leader's attitudes toward disagreement. The person with different ideas, especially if he or she is a subordinate, can be seen as a problem employee and troublemaker or as an innovator, depending on the leader's attitude. There are some people that go through life attempting to sell their ideas, to get others to do things they do not want to do. They set up a series of win–lose situations, and attempt to emerge victorious. Many of these people are able to accomplish their ends. There are others who are more concerned with the quality and effectiveness of their operations, and who, with creative solutions to problems, are genuinely open-minded and able and willing to learn from others (and to teach others), in a collaborative relationship.

The interpersonal skills are related to the development of a "helping relationship" and include among other things, mutual trust and respect, candid communication, and awareness of the needs of others. The problem solving skills center around locating and stating the problem, seeking alternatives, exploring and testing alternatives, and selecting the best alternative. Knowledge and insight gained through experience with the benefits of problem solving and the dysfunctional effects of other strategies would be valuable in developing interpersonal skills.

Further Research Needed

Two additional areas need immediate research consideration. The first needs to explore the notions of conflict resolution from the organizational as well as the individual viewpoint. Lawrence and Lorsch report that Forcing was an effective back-up mode to Confrontation from the organization's standpoint, because at least things were being done. Our data in two separate investigations indicate that this mode of conflict resolution is very unsatisfactory from the standpoint of the one forced, the "loser," and may also have dysfunctional consequences.

The second research area concerns the application of these principles of effective conflict resolution (Confrontation–Problem Solving, with their more specific attitudinal and skill components) in an attempt to arrive at more constructive use of disagreement. Preliminary results from an experiment simulating conflict situations using role playing suggest that knowledge of these principles and some limited practice in their use increases one's ability to use differences constructively in obtaining a quality solution, and decreases the tendency to engage in "limited war" (Burke, 1969b).

References

BLAKE, R. R., and J. S., MOUTON. *The Managerial Grid*, Houston: Gulf Publishing Company, 1964.

BLAKE, R. R., H. A. SHEPARD, and J. S MOUTON. *Managing Intergroup Conflict in Industry*, Houston: Gulf Publishing Company, 1964.

BOULDING, K. "A pure theory of conflict applied to organization." In R. I. Kahn and E. Boulding (eds.), *Power and Conflict in Organizations*. New York: Basic Books, Inc., 1964, pp. 136–145.

BURKE, R. J. "Methods of managing superior–subordinate conflict: Their effectiveness and consequences." Unpublished manuscript, 1969a.

BURKE, R. J. "Effects of limited training on conflict resolution effectiveness." Unpublished manuscript, 1969b.

KATA, D. "Approaches to managing conflict." In R. L. Kahn and E. Boulding (eds.), *Power and Conflict in Organizations*. New York: Basic Books, Inc., 1964, pp. 105–114.

LAWRENCE, P. R., and J. W. LORSCH. "Differentiation and intergration in complex organizations." *Administrative Science Quarterly*, 1967a, 12, 1–47.

LAWRENCE, P. R., and J. W LORSCH. *Organization and Environment*, Boston: Division of Research, Harvard Business School, Harvard University, 1967b.

MAIER, N. R. F. *Problem-Solving Discussions and Conferences*. New York: McGraw-Hill, 1963.

MAIER, N. R. F., and L. R. HOFFMAN. "Acceptance and quality of solutions as related to leaders' attitudes toward disagreement in group problem-solving." *Journal of Applied Behavioral Science*, 1965, 1, pp. 373–386.

McGREGOR, D. *The Professional Manager*. New York: McGraw-Hill, 1967.

SHEPARD, H. A. "Responses to situations of competition and conflict." In R. L. Kahn and E. Boulding (eds.), *Power and Conflict in Organizations*. New York: Basic Books, Inc., 1964, pp. 127–135.

II

PROJECT IMPLEMENTATION

At this point in the book we turn to a detailed description of project implementation. Chapter 7 initiates our discussion with a description of budgeting as a logical extension of the planning techniques from Chapter 5. Project scheduling, considered by some to be the meat of project management, and certainly the most written-about area of the field, is addressed in Chapter 8. Such well-known techniques as PERT and Gantt charts are described with illustrations. Chapter 9 then covers the topic of resource allocation, both within a single project and among multiple projects.

Chapter 10 is devoted to the linkage between planning and control: monitoring and information systems. This chapter includes a brief description of some of the commonly used computerized Project Management Information Systems (PMIS).

Chapter 11 concludes this part of the text with a full description and discussion of the control processes for project management. Standards for comparison, common control techniques, and the basic role of control are covered here.

C H A P T E R

7

Budgeting and Cost Estimation

In Chapter 5 we reviewed the planning process, gave some guidelines for designing the project plan, and then discussed the art of negotiation to achieve that plan in Chapter 6. We are now ready to begin implementation. First priority is, of course, obtaining resources with which to do the work. Senior management approval of the project budget does exactly that. A budget is a plan for allocating resources. Thus, the act of budgeting is the allocation of scarce resources to the various endeavors of an organization. The outcomes of the allocation process often do not satisfy managers of the organization who must live and work under budget constraints. It is, however, precisely the pattern of constraints in a budget that embodies organizational policy. The degree to which the different activities of an organization are fully supported by an allocation of resources is one measure of the importance placed on the outcome of the activity. Most of the senior managers we know try hard to be evenhanded in the budgetary process, funding each planned activity at the "right" level—neither overfunding, which produces waste and encourages slack management, nor underfunding, which inhibits accomplishment and frustrates the committed.

The budget is not simply one facet of a plan, nor is it merely an expression of organizational policy; it is also a control mechanism. The budget serves as a standard for comparison, a baseline from which to measure the difference between the actual and planned uses of resources. As the manager directs the deployment of resources to accomplish some desired objective, resource usage should be monitored carefully. This allows deviations from planned usage to be checked against the progress of the project, and exception reports can be generated if resource expenditures are not consistent with accomplishments. Indeed, the pattern of deviations (variances) can be examined to see if it is possible, or reasonable, to forecast significant departures from budget. With sufficient warning, it is sometimes possible to implement corrective actions. In any event, such forecasting helps to decrease the number of undesirable surprises for senior management.

Budgets play an important role in the entire process of management. It is clear that budgeting procedures must associate resource use with the achievement of organizational goals or the planning/control process becomes useless. If budgets are not tied to achievement, management may ignore situations where funds are being spent far in advance of accomplishment but are within budget when viewed by time period. Similarly, management may misinterpret the true state of affairs when the budget is overspent for a given time period but outlays are appropriate for the level of task completion. Data must be collected and reported in a timely manner, or the value of the budget in identifying and reporting current problems or anticipating upcoming problems will be lost. The reporting process must be carefully designed and controlled. It is of no value if the data are sent to the wrong person or the reports take an inordinately long time to be processed through the system. For example, one manager of a large computer company complained that, based on third-quarter reports, he was instructed to act so as to alter the fourth-quarter results. However, he did not receive the instructions until the first quarter of the following year.

In Chapter 5 we described a planning process that integrated the planning done at different levels of the project. At the top level is the overall project plan, which is then divided and divided again and, perhaps, still again into a "nest" of plans. Project plans were shown to be the verbal equivalents of the WBS. If we cost the WBS, step by step, we develop a project budget. If we cost project plans, we achieve exactly the same end. Viewed in this way, *the budget is simply the project plan in another form.*

Let us now consider some of the various budgeting methods used in organizations. These are described in general first, then with respect to projects. We also address some problems of cost estimation, with attention to the details and pitfalls. We consider some of the special demands and concerns with budgeting for projects. Finally, we present a method for improving one's skills at budget estimation, or estimation and forecasting of any kind. Printouts of project budgets from PM software packages will be shown in Chapter 10 where we cover project management information systems.

Project Management in Practice
Financing the Flight of the Voyager

On the morning of December 23, 1986, Dick Rutan and Jeana Yeager landed their strange-looking canard aircraft at Edwards Air Force Base in California, culminating an historic 9-day, 25,000 mile nonstop circumnavigation of the globe without refueling. The plane is as stunning as the flight itself: an enormous flexible wing with a span of over 110 feet whose tips can move 30 feet up or down and has a

Source: D. E. Swanton, "The Voyager Aircraft Odyssey," *Project Management Journal*, April 1988.

surface area equivalent to that of a Boeing 727 airliner, a structural weight of only 2250 pounds but with a capacity for over 7000 pounds of fuel, a pusher and a puller engine, but the puller engine is turned off in flight, and numerous other such unexpected characteristics.

The flight itself was just as unusual. The noise level in the cockpit was too deafening for the two pilots to tolerate for nine days so a sine wave generator was installed to cancel the engine noise and piped into their earphones. A special oxygen supply was added to allow the plane to climb to the necessary 20,000 feet to fly over Africa. And the plane had a tendency to "porpoise" early in the flight and had to be continuously fought by the pilots for the first three days.

Yet, during the entire first two years of the project most of the time was not spent working on the plane, nor even on the flight plans—80 percent of the time was spent trying to raise funds! Volunteer project participants struggled from week to week for funding. With such a revolutionary concept and goal, the team thought it would be easy to secure corporate funding to back their efforts. With only one exception, no one, including Lee Iacocca and Ross Perot, was willing to help them—the exception was a Japanese firm, whose offer was politely declined. As flight tests began, however, media coverage increased and the public awareness brought donations as well as some corporate sponsors for the plane's components. The primary reason the plane could be built at a minimal cost was the focus on simplicity and essentials. Eliminating the nonessential items saved time and money, and possibly weight, and may have been the real reason the project was able to be completed successfully!

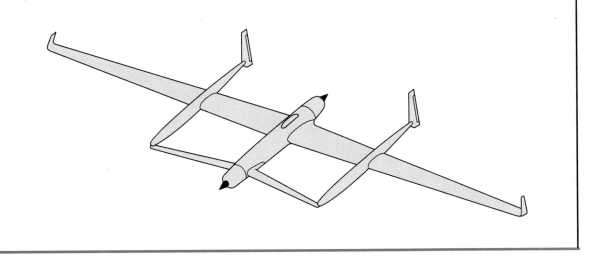

▶ 7.1 ESTIMATING PROJECT BUDGETS

In order to develop a budget, we must forecast what resources the project will require, the required quantity of each, when they will be needed, and how much they will cost—including the effects of potential price inflation. Uncertainty is involved in any forecast, though some forecasts have less uncertainty than others. An experienced cost estimator can forecast the number of bricks that will be used to construct a brick wall of known dimensions within 1 to 2 percent. (The estimator knows almost exactly how many bricks are needed to build the wall and must simply add a small allowance for some faulty (broken or discolored) bricks and a few more being broken during the construction process.) On the other hand, the errors are apt to be much larger for an estimate of the number of programmer hours or lines of code that will be required to produce a specific piece of software (see Section 7.2). While the field of software science makes such estimations quite possible, the level of uncertainty is considerably higher and the typical error size is much larger.

In many fields, cost estimation methods are well codified. The office walls of organizational purchasing departments are lined with catalogues detailing what materials, services, and machines are available, from whom, and at what prices. Also on the book shelves are volumes devoted to the techniques of estimating the quantities of materials and labor required to accomplish specific jobs. Every business has its own rules of thumb for cost estimation. These usually distill the collective experience gained by many estimators over many years. An experienced producer of books, for example, can leaf through a manuscript and, after asking a few questions about the number and type of illustrations and the quality of paper to be used, can make a fairly accurate estimate of what it will cost to produce a book.

At times, the job of cost estimation for entire complex projects may be relatively simple because experience has shown that some formula gives a good *first approximation* of the project's cost. For example, the Goodyear Aircraft Company makes an initial estimate of the cost of building a blimp by multiplying the estimated weight of the blimp by a specific dollar factor. (The weight is estimated in pounds, presumably prior to the blimp's inflation with helium.) The cost of buildings is commonly estimated as dollars per square foot times the square feet of floor area. Obviously these approximations must be adjusted for any special characteristics associated with each individual project, but this adjustment is far easier than making an estimate from scratch.

We will have more to say about gathering data shortly. Before doing so, however, and before discussing budget construction and presentation, it is helpful to understand that developing project budgets is much more difficult than developing budgets for more permanent organizational activities. The influence of history is strong in the budget of an ongoing activity and many entries may ultimately become just "last year's figure plus X percent," where X is any number the budgeter feels "can be lived with," and is probably acceptable to the person or group who approves the budgets. No single item in the budget for an ongoing activity is apt to be crucial, because over the course of years the budget has gained sufficient slack that internal adjustments will probably take care of minor shortages in the key accounts.

But the project budgeter cannot depend on tradition. At project inception, there are no past budgets to use as a base. At times, the budgeter may have budgets and audit reports for similar projects to serve as guides, but these are rough guides at best. Tradition, however, has another impact on budgeting, this time a helpful one. In the special case of R & D projects, it has been found [12] that project budgets are stable over time when measured as a percent of the total allocation to R & D from the parent firm, though within the project the budget may be reallocated among activities. There is no reason to believe that the situation is different for other kinds of projects, and we have some evidence that shows stability similar to R & D projects.

For multiyear projects, another problem is raised. The plans and schedules for such projects are set at the beginning of project life, but over the years, the forecast resource usage may be altered by the availability of alternate or new materials, machinery, or personnel—available at different costs than were estimated. The longer the project life, the less the PM can trust that traditional methods and costs will be relevant. As if that were not enough, the degree of executive oversight and review is usually much higher for projects than for ongoing operations, so the budgeter must expect to defend any and all budget entries.

Tradition has still another impact on project budgeting. Every organization has its idiosyncrasies. One firm charges the project's R & D budget with the cost of training sales representatives on the technical aspects of a new product. Another adopts special property accounting practices for contracts with the government. Unless the PM understands the organizational accounting system, there is no way to exercise budgetary control over the project. The methods for project budgeting described below are intended to avoid these problems as much as possible, but complete avoidance is out of the question. Further, it is not politically feasible for the PM to plead a special case with the accountants, who have their own problems. The PM simply must be familiar with the organization's accounting system!

One aspect of cost estimation and budgeting that is not often discussed has to do with the *actual* use of resources as opposed to the accounting department's assumptions about how and when the resources will be used. For instance, presume that you have estimated that $5000 of a given resource will be used in accomplishing a task that is estimated to require five weeks. The actual use of the resource may be none in the first week, $3000 worth in the second week, none in the third week, $1500 in the fourth week, and the remaining $500 in the last week. Unless this pattern of expenditure is detailed in the plan, the accounting department, which takes a linear view of the world, will spread the expenditure equally over the five-week period. This may not affect the project's budget, but it most certainly affects the project's cash flow. The PM must be aware of both the resource requirements and the specific time pattern of resource usage. The subject will be mentioned again in Chapter 9.

Another aspect of preparing budgets is especially important for project budgeting. Every expenditure (or receipt) must be identified with a specific project task (and with its associated milestone, as we will see in the next chapter). Referring back to Figure 5-5, we see that each element in the WBS has a unique account number to which charges are accrued as work is done. These identifiers are needed for the PM to exercise budgetary control.

With these things in mind, the issue of how to gather input data for the budget becomes a matter of some concern. There are two fundamentally different strategies for data gathering, top–down and bottom–up.

Top–Down Budgeting

This strategy is based on collecting the judgments and experiences of top and middle managers, and available past data concerning similar activities. These managers estimate overall project cost as well as the costs of the major subprojects that comprise it. These cost estimates are then given to lower-level managers, who are expected to continue the breakdown into budget estimates for the specific tasks and work packages that comprise the subprojects. This process continues to the lowest level.

The process parallels the hierarchical planning process described in the last chapter. The budget, like the project, is broken down into successively finer detail, starting from the top, or most aggregated level following the WBS. It is presumed that lower-level managers will argue for more funds if the budget allocation they have been granted is, in their judgment, insufficient for the tasks assigned. However, this presumption is often incorrect. Instead of reasoned debate, argument sometimes ensues, or simply sullen silence. When senior managers insist on maintaining their budgetary positions—based on "considerable past experience"—junior managers feel forced to accept what they perceive to be insufficient allocations to achieve the objectives to which they must commit.

Discussions between the authors and a large number of managers support the contention that lower-level managers often treat the entire budgeting process as if it were a zero-sum game, a game in which any individual's gain is another individual's loss. Competition among junior managers is often quite intense.

The advantage of this top–down process is that aggregate budgets can often be developed quite accurately, though a few individual elements may be significantly in error. Not only are budgets stable as a percent of total allocation, the statistical distribution of the budgets is also stable, making for high predictability [12]. Another advantage of the top–down process is that small yet costly tasks need not be individually identified, nor need it be feared that some small but important aspect has been overlooked. The experience and judgment of the executive is presumed automatically to factor all such elements into the overall estimate.

Bottom–Up Budgeting

In this method, elemental tasks, their schedules, and their individual budgets are constructed, again following the WBS. The people doing the work are consulted regarding times and budgets for the tasks to ensure the best level of accuracy. Initially, estimates are made in terms of resources, such as labor hours and materials. These are later converted to dollar equivalents. Standard analytic tools such as learning curve analysis (discussed in the next section) and work sampling are employed where appropriate to improve the estimates. Differences of opinion are resolved by the usual discussions between senior and junior managers. If necessary, the project manager and the functional manager(s) may enter the discussion in order to ensure the accuracy of the estimates. The resulting task budgets are aggregated to give the total direct costs of the project. The PM adds such indirect costs as general and administrative (G & A), a project reserve for contingencies, and a profit figure to arrive at the final project budget.

Bottom–up budgets should be, and usually are, more accurate in the detailed tasks, but it is critical that all elements be included. It is far more difficult to develop a complete list of tasks when constructing that list from the bottom up than from the top down. Just as the top–down method may lead to budgetary game playing, the bottom–up process has its unique managerial budget games. For example, individuals overstate their resource needs because they suspect that higher management will probably cut all budgets by some percentage. Their suspicion is, of course, quite justified, as Gagnon [15, 16] and others have shown. Managers who are particularly persuasive sometimes win, but those who are consistently honest and have high credibility win more often.

The advantages of the bottom–up process are those generally associated with participative management. Individuals closer to the work are apt to have a more accurate idea of resource requirements than their superiors or others not personally involved. In addition, the direct involvement of low-level managers in budget preparation increases the likelihood that they will accept the result with a minimum of grumbling. Involvement also is a good managerial training technique, giving junior managers valuable experience in budget preparation as well as the knowledge of the operations required to generate a budget.

While top–down budgeting is common, true bottom–up budgets are rare. Senior managers see the bottom–up process as risky. They tend not to be particularly trusting of ambitious subordinates who may overstate resource requirements in an attempt to ensure success and build empires. Besides, as senior managers note with some justification, the budget is the most important tool for control of the organization. They are understandably reluctant to hand over that control to subordinates whose experience and motives are questionable. This attitude is carried to an extreme in one large corporation that conducts several dozen projects simultaneously, each of which may last five to eight years and cost in excess of $1 million. Project managers do not participate in the budgeting process in this company, nor do they have access to project budgets during their tenure as PMs. (In the past few years, the firm has decided to give PMs access to project budgets but they are still not allowed to participate in the budgetary process.)

An Iterative Budgeting Process—Negotiation-in-Action

In Chapter 5, we recommended an iterative planning process with subordinates* developing action plans for the tasks for which they were responsible. Superiors review these plans, perhaps suggesting amendments. (See also the latter part of Section 5.3.) The strength of this planning technique is that primary responsibility for the design of a task is delegated to the individual accountable for its completion, and thus it utilizes participative management (or "employee involvement"). If done correctly, estimated resource usage and schedules are a normal part of the planning process at all planning levels. Therefore, the individual concocting an action plan at the highest level would estimate resource requirements and durations for each of the steps in the highest level action plan. Let us refer to these as r_i and t_i, the resource and task time requirements for the ith task respectively. Similarly, the

---

*We use the terms "superior" and "subordinate" here for the sole purpose of identifying individuals working on different relative levels of a project's set of action plans. We recognize that in a matrix organization it is not uncommon for PMs ("superiors") to delegate work to individuals ("subordinates") who do not report to the PM and who may be senior to the PM on the parent firm's organizational chart.

subordinate estimates the resource and time requirements for each step of the lower-level action plan. Let us denote the *aggregate* resource and time requirements for the lower level action plan as r_i' and t_i', respectively.

In a perfect world, r_i would equal r_i'. (As regards t_i and t_i', our argument holds for duration estimates as well as resource estimates.) We do not, however, live in a perfect world. As a matter of fact, the probable relationship between the original estimates made at the different levels is $r_i \ll r_i'$. This is true for several reasons, three of which are practically universal. First, as Gagnon has found [15], the farther one moves up the organizational chart away from immediate responsibility for doing the work, the easier, faster, and cheaper the job looks to the superior than to the one who has to do it. This is because the superior either does not know the details of the task, or has conveniently forgotten the details, as well as how long the job takes and how many problems can arise. Second, wishful thinking leads the superior to underestimate cost (and time), because the superior has a stake in representing the project to senior management as a profitable venture. Third, the subordinate is led to build-in some level of protection against failure by adding an allowance for "Murphy's Law" onto a budget that already has a healthy contingency allowance.

Assuming that the superior and subordinate are reasonably honest with one another (any other assumption leads to a failure in win–win negotiations), the two parties meet and review the subordinate's action plan. Usually, the initial step toward reducing the difference in cost estimates is made by the superior who is "educated" by the subordinate in the realities of the job. The result is that r_i rises. The next step is typically made by the subordinate. Encouraged by the boss's positive response to reason, the subordinate surrenders some of protection provided for by the budgetary "slop," and r_i' falls. The subordinate's cost estimate is still greater than the superior's, but the difference is considerably decreased.

The pair now turn their attention to the technology of the task at hand. They carefully inspect the subordinate's work plan, trying to find a more efficient way to accomplish the desired end; that is, they practice total quality management (TQM) and/or value engineering. It may be that a major change can be made that allows a lower resource commitment than either originally imagined. It may be that little or no further improvement is possible. Let us assume that moderate improvement is made, but that r_i' is still somewhat greater than r_i, although both have been altered by the negotiations thus far. What should the superior do, accept the subordinate's estimate or insist that the subordinate make do with r_i? In order to answer this question, we must digress and reconsider the concept of the project life cycle.

In Chapter 1, we presented the usual view of the project life cycle in Figure 1-2, shown here as Figure 7-1 for convenience. It is important to note that this figure shows "Percent project completion" as a function of "Time." The life-cycle function is essentially unchanged if, for the horizontal axis, we use "Resources" instead. In effect, the life cycle shows what an economist might call "return on input"; that is, the amount of project completion resulting from inputs of time and/or resources.

While this view of the life cycle reflects reality on many projects, it is seriously misleading for others. To understand the difference, let us consider the baking of a cake. Once the ingredients are mixed, we are instructed to bake the cake in a 350° (F) oven for 35 minutes. At what point in the baking process do we have "cake"?

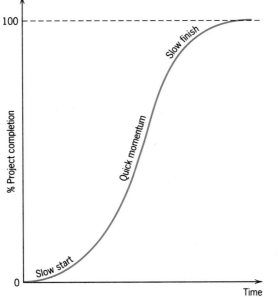

Figure 7-1: The project life cycle
(Figure 1-2 reproduced).

Experienced bakers know that the mixture changes from "goop" (a technical term well-known to bakers and cooks) to "cake" quite rapidly in the last few minutes of the baking process. The life cycle of this process looks like the curve shown in Figure 7-2. A number of actual projects have a similar life cycle; for example, some projects devoted to the development of computer software, or some projects in chemistry and chemical engineering. In general, this life cycle may exist for projects in which the output is composed or constructed of several subunits (or subroutines) that have little use in and of themselves, but are quite useful when put together. It would also be typical for projects where a chemical-type reaction occurs that rapidly transforms the project from useless to useful. For example, the preparation of the manuscript for the current edition of this book is such a project. A great deal of information must be collected, a great deal of rewriting must be done, new materials

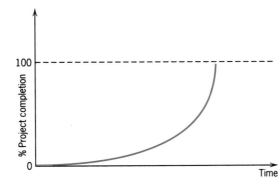

Figure 7-2: Another possible project life cycle.

have to be gathered, but there is no visible result until everything is assembled at the last minute.

Figure 7-1 shows that, as the project nears completion, continued inputs of time or resources result in successively smaller increments of completion—diminishing marginal returns. Figure 7-2 shows the opposite. As these projects near completion, successive inputs of time or resources result in successively larger increments of completion—increasing marginal returns. In order to decide whether to adopt the subordinate's resource estimate, r_i', or the superior's, r_i, we need to know which picture of the life cycle is representative of the task under consideration. Note that we are treating the subordinate's action plan as if it were a project, which is perfectly all right because it has the characteristics of a project that were described in Chapter 1. Also note that we do not need to know the shape of the life cycle with any precision, merely if its last stage is concave or convex to the horizontal axis.

Remember that the superior's and subordinate's resource estimates are not very far apart as a result of the negotiations preceding this decision. If the latter part of the life-cycle curve is concave (as in Figure 7-1), showing diminishing marginal returns, we opt for the superior's estimate because of the small impact on completion that results from withholding a small amount of resources. The superior might say to the subordinate, "Jeremy, what can you get me for r_i? We will have to live with that." If, on the other hand, the life cycle curve is convex, showing increasing marginal returns, the subordinate's estimate should be chosen because of the potentially drastic effect a resource shortage would have on project completion. In this event, the superior might say, "OK, Brandon, we have got to be sure of this job. We'll go with your numbers." If the disagreement had concerned schedule (duration) instead of resources, the negotiation process and underlying logic would be unaltered.

This is a time-consuming process. At the same time the PM is negotiating with the several subordinates responsible for the pieces of the PM's action plan, each of the subordinates are negotiating with their subordinates, and so on. This multilevel process is messy and not particularly efficient, but it allows a free-flow of ideas up and down the system at all levels.

It is worth noting that ethics is just as important in negotiations within an organization as in negotiations between an organization and an outside party. In this case, the superior and subordinate have the responsibility to be honest with each other. For one thing, they must continue to work together in the future under the conditions of mutual trust. Second, it is ethically necessary to be honest in such negotiations.

Comments on the Budget Request Process

The budget process often begins with an invitation from top management for each division to submit a *budget request* for the coming year. Division heads pass the invitation along to departments, sections, and subsections, each of which presumably collects requests from below, aggregates them, and passes the result back up the organizational ladder.

This sounds like bottom–up budgeting, but there is an important difference between this procedure and a true bottom–up system. Along with the formal invitation for submission of a budget request, in the iterative system another message is passed down—a much less formal message that carries the following kinds of information: the percent by which the wage bill of the organization will be allowed to be increased, organizational policy on adding to the work force, the general attitude toward capital expenditures, knowledge about which projects and activities are considered to be high priority and which are not, and a number of other matters that, in effect, prescribe a set of limits on lower-level managers. As the budget requests are passed back up the organization, they are carefully inspected for conformity to guidelines. If they do not conform, they are "adjusted," often with little or no consultation with the originating units.

The less autocratic the organization (and the less pressured it is by current financial exigencies), the greater the probability that this process will allow dialogue and some compromise between managerial levels. Even the most *participative* firms, however, will not long tolerate lower-level managers who are not sensitive to messages relating to budget limitations. It makes little difference whether budget policy is passed down the system by means of formal, written policy statements or as a haphazard set of oral comments informally transmitted by some senior managers and practically neglected by others; the PM's budget request is expected to conform to policy. Ignorance of the policy is no excuse. Repeated failure to conform will be rewarded with a ticket to corporate Siberia. It is the budget originator's responsibility to find out about budget policy. Again we see the importance of political sensitivity. The PM's channels of communication must be sensitive enough to receive policy signals even in the event that a noncommunicative superior blocks those signals.

Activity Budgeting vs. Program Budgeting

Thus far we have discussed one facet of an organization's philosophy of budgeting. Another facet has to do with the degree to which a budget is activity-oriented or program-oriented, a distinction we have mentioned before. The traditional organizational budget is activity-oriented. Individual expenses are classified and assigned to basic budget *lines* such as phone, materials, personnel–clerical, utilities, direct labor, etc. These expense lines are gathered into more inclusive categories, and are reported by organizational unit—for example, by section, department, and division. In other words, the budget can be overlaid on the organizational chart. Table 7-1 shows one page of a typical, activity-oriented monthly budget report for a real estate project.

With the advent of project organization, it became necessary to organize the budget in ways that conformed more closely to the actual pattern of fiscal responsibility. Under traditional budgeting methods, the budget for a project could be split up among many different organizational units, which diffused control so widely that it was frequently nonexistent. It was often almost impossible to determine the actual size of major expenditure categories in a project's budget. In light of this problem, ways were sought to alter the budgeting process so that budgets could be associated directly with the projects that used them. This need gave rise to *program budgeting*. Table 7-2 shows a program-oriented project budget divided by task and expected time of expenditure. In an interesting paper, Brimson [6] critiques both systems separately, and then combines them.

Table 7-1   Typical Monthly Budget for a Real Estate Project (Page 1 of 6)

	Current			
	Actual	**Budget**	**Variance**	**Pct.**
Corporate—Income Statement				
Revenue				
8430 Management fees				
8491 Prtnsp reimb—property mgmt	7,410.00	6,222.00	1,188.00	119.0
8492 Prtnsp reimb—owner acquisition	.00	3,750.00	3,750.00−	.0
8493 Prtnsp reimb—rehab	.00	.00	.00	.0
8494 Other income	.00	.00	.00	.0
8495 Reimbursements—other	.00	.00	.00	.0
Total revenue	7,410.00	9,972.00	2,562.00−	74.3
Operating expenses				
Payroll & P/R benefits				
8511 Salaries	29,425.75	34,583.00	5,157.25	85.0
8512 Payroll taxes	1,789.88	3,458.00	1,668.12	51.7
8513 Group ins & med reimb	1,407.45	1,040.00	387.45−	135.3
8515 Workmens compensation	43.04	43.00	.04−	100.0
8516 Staff apartments	.00	.00	.00	.0
8517 Bonus	.00	.00	.00	.0
Total payroll & P/R benefits	32,668.12	39,124.00	6,457.88	83.5
Travel & entertainment expenses				
8512 Travel	456.65	300.00	156.65−	152.2
8522 Promotion, entertainment & gift	69.52	500.00	430.48	13.9
8523 Auto	1,295.90	1,729.00	433.10	75.0
Total travel & entertainment exp	1,822.07	2,529.00	706.93	72.1
Professional fees				
8531 Legal fees	419.00	50.00	369.00−	838.0
8532 Accounting fees	289.00	.00	289.00−	.0
8534 Temporary help	234.58	200.00	34.58−	117.2
8535 Commissions & consulting	4,398.50	2,532.00	1,866.50−	173.7
8536 Data processing services	61.46	125.00	63.54	49.1
Total professional fees	5,402.54	2,907.00	2,495.54−	185.8
Facility expense				
8541 Rent & parking	8,860.60	8,816.00	44.60−	100.5
8542 Telephone	1,306.26	800.00	506.26−	163.2
8543 Office supplies & expense	664.62	700.00	35.38	94.9
8544 Photocopy	.00	.00	.00	.0
8545 Postage	302.45	200.00	102.45−	151.2
8546 Repairs & maintenance	440.00	350.00	90.00−	125.7
8547 Insurance	67.50	.00	67.50−	.0

Table 7-2   Project Budget by Task and Month

Task	I	J	Estimate	Monthly Budget (£)							
				1	2	3	4	5	6	7	8
A	1	2	7000	5600	1400						
B	2	3	9000		3857	5143					
C	2	4	10000		3750	5000	1250				
D	2	5	6000		3600	2400					
E	3	7	12000				4800	4800	2400		
F	4	7	3000				3000				
G	5	6	9000			2571	5143	1286			
H	6	7	5000					3750	1250		
I	7	8	8000						2667	5333	
J	8	9	6000								6000
			75000	5600	12607	15114	14192	9836	6317	5333	6000

Source: [17]

Program budgeting is the generic name given to a budgeting system that aggregates income and expenditures across programs (projects). In most cases, aggregation by program is in addition to, not instead of, aggregation by organizational unit. The project has its own budget. In the case of pure project organizations, the budgets of all projects are aggregated to the highest organizational level. When functional organization is used for projects, the functional department's budget will be arranged in whatever manner is standard for the organization, but the income/expense associated with each project will be shown. The physical arrangement of such budget reports varies widely, but usually takes the form of a spreadsheet with the standard budget categories listed down the left-hand side of the sheet and category totals disaggregated into "regular operations" and charges to the various projects. Project charges will be split out and spread across the page, with special columns devoted to each project. For example, the columns shown in Table 7-1 would be repeated for each project.

Two special forms of program budgeting have received considerable notoriety in the past. One is planning-programming-budgeting systems (PPBS) and the other is zero-base budgeting (ZBB). While neither PPBS nor ZBB is now widely used, both have influenced managerial thinking. We know of no organizations that currently use ZBB and only a few that have permanently adopted PPBS, mainly social service agencies. But we do know of several corporations that occasionally require PPBS-type cost–benefit analyses. We even know a few senior managers who considered preparing zero-base budgets, but none have actually done so yet. Again, because these concepts have influenced managerial thinking in ways that are important to PMs, they are briefly discussed here.

Planning-Programming-Budgeting System (PPBS)

PPBS was developed in the late 1960s through then Secretary of Defense Robert McNamara's efforts to deal rationally with the budget of the Department of Defense. PPBS is basically a program budgeting (and planning) system oriented to identifying, planning, and controlling projects that will maximize achievement of the organization's long-run goals. The system focuses on funding those projects that will bring the greatest progress toward organizational goals for the least cost. The PPBS budgeting process entails four major steps:

1. The identification of goals and objectives for each major area of activity. This is the "planning" portion of PPBS.

2. Analysis of the programs proposed to attain organizational objectives; multi-year programs are considered as well as short-term programs. This step requires a good description of the nature of each project so that its intent and the character of its proposed contribution to the organization are understood. This is the "programming" part of PPBS.

3. Estimation of total costs for each project, including indirect costs. Time phasing of costs is detailed for multiyear projects.

4. Final analysis of the alternative projects and sets of projects in terms of expected costs, expected benefits, and expected project lives. Cost–benefit analyses are performed for each program so that the programs can be compared with one another in preparation for selecting a set of projects (i.e., a "portfolio," for funding).

PPBS was mandated by the Department of Defense for contractors, and at the time was deemed useful and effective. With the advent of cost/schedule control systems criteria (see Chapter 10) in the late 1960s, PPBS has fallen from grace and now enjoys only limited use by a few state and local government agencies and some social service organizations. Its precepts, however, have been embodied in the budgeting procedures of many organizations.

Zero-Base Budgeting (ZBB)

ZBB came into favor in the 1970s as a reaction to the automatic budget increases given year after year to government agencies. As a form of program budgeting, the goal of ZBB was to link the level of funding directly to the achievements associated with specific programs. As opposed to making incremental changes in programs and their accompanying budget allocations, the philosophy of ZBB is that the fundamental desirability of every program should be reviewed and justified each year before the program receives any funding at all. The objective is to cut waste by culling out projects that have outlived their utility and are continuing simply because of the inertia of policymakers.

The ZBB procedure is to describe each project/program, evaluate each one, and rank them in terms of cost–benefit or some other appropriate measure. Funds can then be allocated in accordance with this ranking.

As PPBS is associated with Robert McNamara, ZBB is associated with President Jimmy Carter. He employed ZBB as governor of Georgia and promised (threatened) to do so as president. Like PPBS, ZBB has had no great success. Whereas PPBS involved difficult implementation problems, particularly in the area of measuring costs and benefits (see [30], among many other critiques), ZBB raises a different problem. The primary effect of ZBB is to challenge the existence of every budgetary unit every budget period. Any project that cannot justify continued funding is sentenced to administrative death. The threat of ZBB is so great that organizations subjected to this budget process tend to devote more and more of their energies to defending their existence.

ZBB has a great deal of opposition and little support from the people who must supply the data for the analyses. Few governments have sufficient political clout to adopt and operate a true ZBB system, but some executives employ the logic of ZBB to challenge the continuation of projects they see as inefficient or ineffective. We feel this use of ZBB has considerable merit. For most cases, we feel that use of ZBB is rarely a cost-effective means of project budget control, but the concept is useful for helping to make decisions about whether or not to terminate projects. In Chapter 13 we illustrate an approach to the termination decision based on ZBB. Please note, however, that ZBB is not applied to projects that are clearly successful or are obvious failures, but to projects that cannot be identified as belonging to either group.

Project Management in Practice
Completing the Limerick Nuclear Facility under Budget

On January 8, 1990, the Limerick nuclear power generating facility in Pennsylvania began commercial operation, thereby setting a construction record for nuclear facilities. In an era when it is common to hear of nuclear plants that massively overrun their budgets and completion schedules, Limerick was completed eight months ahead of its 49-month schedule and came in $400 million under its $3.2 billion budget. Limerick has truly set a standard for the industry.

It was no accident that Limerick was completed ahead of schedule and under budget. When construction started in February 1986, a project goal was to complete the project eight months ahead of the planned completion, which would help keep the costs under the budget limit as well. To achieve this early target, a series of innovative approaches were taken. Two of the major ones were to accelerate ramp-up staffing and to use an ex-

tensive, fully-supported second shift. The momentum of the speedy start-up set the fast pace for the remainder of the project. The second shift earned a very favorable premium, as well as having a full complement of managers and engineers to work with the manual workers. In this fashion, the second shift productivity was equal to, if not higher than, the first shift's.

Other decisions and actions further helped either the cost or the schedule. For example, it was decided that overtime would not be worked since a second shift was being used. And as a condition of the project approval, a project labor agreement with the local unions (rather than the national) had to be developed that would eliminate strikes,

Source: T. P. Gotzis, "Limerick Generating Station Unit 2," PM *Network*, January 1991.

Limerick Nuclear Facility contractor logos and lost-time clock.

lockouts, and delays and provide for peaceful resolution of disputes. Also, an incentive fee contract with the building contractor was signed whereby the contractor would share equally in cost/schedule overruns or underruns, with limits set.

With such attention to the goal of an early and underbudget completion, the team, numbering almost 3000 workers by June 1987, worked diligently and with high morale, meeting the goal in January 1990.

▶ 7.2   IMPROVING THE PROCESS OF COST ESTIMATION

The cooperation of several people is required to prepare cost estimates for a project. If the firm is in a business that regularly requires bids to be submitted to its customers, it will have "professional" cost estimators on its staff. In these cases, it is the job of the PM to generate a description of the work to be done on the project in sufficient detail that the estimator can know what cost data must be collected. Frequently, the project will be too complex for the PM to generate such a description without considerable help from experts in the functional areas.

Even with the finest of experts working to estimate resource usage, the one thing that is certain is that things will not go precisely as planned. There are two fundamentally different ways to deal with the chance events that occur on every project. The simpler and far more common way is to make an allowance for contingencies—usually 5 or 10 percent of the estimated cost. Just why these numbers are chosen in preference to $6\frac{7}{8}$ or $9\frac{1}{4}$, for instance, we do not know. We strongly prefer another method in which the forecaster selects "most likely, optimistic, and pessimistic" estimates. This method is described in detail in Chapter 8 when we cover the issue of estimating the duration of elements in the action plan. The method described in Chapter 8 is applicable, unchanged, to the estimation of resource requirements.

Turning now to the problem of estimating direct costs,* project managers often find it helpful to collect direct cost estimates on a form that not only lists the level of resource needs, but also indicates *when* each resource will be needed, and notes if it is available (or will be available at the appropriate time). Figure 7-3 shows such a form. It also has a column for identifying the person to contact in order to get specific resources. This table can be used for collating the resource requirements for each task element in a project, or for aggregating the information from a series of tasks onto a single form.

Note that Figure 7-3 contains no information on overhead costs. The matter of what overhead costs are to be added and in what amounts is unique to the firm, beyond the PM's control, and generally a source of annoyance and frustration to one and all. The allocation of overhead is arbitrary by its nature, and when the addition of overhead cost causes an otherwise attractive project to fail to meet the organization's economic objectives, the project's supporters are apt to complain bitterly about the "unfairness" of overhead cost allocation.

---

*Our emphasis on estimating direct costs and on focusing on resources that are "direct costed" in the action plan is based on our feeling that the PM should be concerned with only those items over which he/she has some control—which certainly excludes overheads. The PM, however, may wish to add some nonchargable items to the resource column of the action plan simply to "reserve" that item for use at a specific time.

Project Name _____

Date _____

Task Number _____

RESOURCES NEEDED

Resources	Person to Contact	How Many/ Much Needed	When Needed	Check (✓) If Available
People: Managers, Supervisors				
Professional & Technical				
Nontechnical				
Money				
Materials: Facilities				
Equipment				
Tools				
Power				
Space				
Special Services: Research & Test				
Typing/clerical				
Reproduction				
Others				

Figure 7-3: Form for gathering data on project resource needs.

At times, firms fund projects that show a significant incremental profit over direct costs but are not profitable when fully costed. Such decisions can be justified for a number of reasons, such as:

- To develop knowledge of a technology
- To get the organization's "foot in the door"
- To obtain the parts or service portion of the work
- To be in a good position for a follow-on contract
- To improve a competitive position
- To broaden a product line or a line of business.

All of these are adequate reasons to fund projects that, in the short term, may lose money but provide the organization with the impetus for future growth and profitability. It is up to senior management to decide if such reasons are worth it.

Learning Curves

If the project being costed is one of many similar projects, the estimation of each cost element is fairly routine. If the project involves work in which the firm has little experience, cost estimation is more difficult, particularly for direct labor costs. For example, consider a project that requires 25 units of a complex electronic device to be assembled. The firm is experienced in building electronic equipment but has never before made this specific device, which differs significantly from the items it routinely assembles.

Experience might indicate that if the firm were to build many such devices, it would use about seventy hours of direct labor per unit. If labor is paid a wage of $12 per hour, and if benefits equal 28 percent of the wage rate, the estimated labor cost for the 25 units is

$$(1.28)(\$12/\text{hr.})(25 \text{ units})(70 \text{ hours/unit}) = \$26,880$$

In fact, this would be an underestimate of the actual labor cost because more time per unit output is used early in the production process. Studies have shown that human performance usually improves when a task is repeated. In general, performance improves by a fixed percent each time production doubles. More specifically, *each time the output doubles, the worker hours per unit decrease to a fixed percentage of their previous value.* That percentage is called the *learning rate*. If an individual requires 10 minutes to accomplish a certain task the first time it is attempted and only 8 minutes the second time, that person is said to have an 80 percent learning rate. If output is doubled again from two to four, we would expect the fourth item to be produced in

$$8(.8) = 6.4 \text{ minutes}$$

Similarly, the eighth unit of output should require

$$6.4(.8) = 5.12 \text{ minutes}$$

and so on. The time required to produce a unit of output follows a well-known formula:

$$T_n = T_1 n^r$$

where

T_n = the time required for the nth unit of output,
T_1 = the time required for the initial unit of output,
n = the number of units to be produced, and
r = log decimal learning rate/log 2.

The total time required for all units of a production run of size N is

$$\text{total time} = T_1 \sum_{n=1}^{N} n^r$$

Tables are widely available with both unit and total values for the learning curves, and have been calculated for many different improvement ratios (learning rates—e.g., see [26]).

In the example of the electronic device just given, assume that after producing the twentieth unit, there is no significant further improvement (i.e., assembly time has reached a steady state at 70 hours). Further assume that previous study established that the usual learning rate for assemblers in this plant is about 85 percent. We can estimate the time required for the first unit by letting $T_n = 70$ hours by the unit $n = 20$. Then

$$r = \log .85/\log 2$$
$$= -.1626/.693$$
$$= -.235$$

and

$$70 = T_1(20)^r$$
$$T_1 = 141.3 \text{ hours}$$

Now we know the time for the initial unit. Using a table that shows the total time multipler (see [26, p. 347–348] for example), we can find the appropriate total time multiplier for this example—the multiplier for 20 units given a learning rate of 85 percent. With this multiplier, 12.40, we can calculate the total time required to build all 20 units. It is

$$(12.40)(141.3 \text{ hrs.}) = 1752.12 \text{ hours}$$

The last 5 units are produced in the steady-state time of seventy hours each. Thus the total assembly time is

$$1752.12 + 5(70 \text{ hrs.}) = 2102.12 \text{ hours}$$

We can now refigure the direct labor cost.

$$2102.12(\$12)(1.28) = \$32,288.56$$

Our first estimate, which ignored learning effects, understated the cost by

$$\$32,288.56 - \$26,880 = \$5,408.56$$

or about 17 percent. Figure 7-4 illustrates this source of the error.

The conclusion is simple. For any task where labor is a significant cost factor and the production run is reasonably short, the PM should take the learning curve into account when estimating costs. The implications of this conclusion should not be overlooked. We do not often think of projects as "production," but they are. Research [16] has shown that the learning curve effect is important to decisions about the role of engineering consultants on computer-assisted design (CAD) projects. The failure to consider performance improvement is a significant cause of project cost underestimation.

Other Factors

The number of things that can produce errors in cost estimates is almost without limit, but some problems occur with particularly high frequency. Changes in resource prices is one of these. The most commonly used solution to this problem is to increase all cost estimates by some fixed percentage. A more useful approach is to identify each input that accounts for a significant portion of project cost and estimate the direction and rate of price change for each.

The determination of which inputs account for a "significant" portion of project cost is not difficult, though it may be somewhat arbitrary. Suppose, for example, that our initial, rough cost estimate (with no provision for future price changes) for

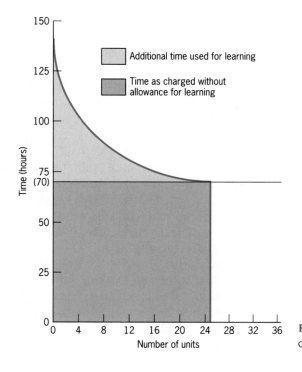

Figure **7-4:** Effect of ignoring learning curve.

a project is $1 million and is to be spent over a three-year period in approximately equal amounts per year. If we think personnel costs will comprise about 40 percent of that total, also spread equally over time, the wage/salary bill will be about $400,000. Split into three equal amounts, we have expenditures of $133,333 per year. If we estimate that wage/salary rates will increase by 6 percent per year, our expense for the second year rises to $141,333 (an increase of $8,000), and to $149,813 in the third year (an increase of $8,480). Failure to account for wage/salary inflation would result in an underestimate of project cost of about $16,500. This is an error of slightly more than 4 percent of the personnel cost and almost 2 percent of the total project budget.

Further improvements can be made by taking into account the fact that the prices of different inputs often change at very different rates. A quick examination of the Bureau of Labor Statistics (BLS) wage and price indices, which cover a very large number of specific commodities and wage rates, will reveal that even in periods of stable prices, the prices of some things rise while others fall and still others do not change appreciably. Thus, the PM may wish to use different *inflators* for each of several different classes of labor or types of commodities.

The proper level of breakdown in estimating the impact of price changes simply depends on the organization's willingness to tolerate error. Assume that management is willing to accept a 5 percent difference between actual and estimated cost for each major cost category. In the example above, expected increases in wage/salary costs will use more than four-fifths of that allowance. That leaves less than 1 percent (about $3,500) of allowable error, and the need to add one part-time clerk to the project for a single year would more than use the remaining allowance.

Other elements that need to be factored into the estimated project cost include an allowance for waste and spoilage. No sane builder would order "just enough" lumber to build a house. Also, personnel costs can be significantly increased by the loss and subsequent replacement of project professionals. Not only must new people go through a learning period—which, as we have seen, will have a negative effect on production—but professional starting salaries often rise faster than the general rate of annual salary increases. Thus, it may well cost more to replace a person who leaves the project with a newcomer who has approximately the same level of experience.

We have already mentioned the inclination PMs have toward understating the costs of a project in order to make it appear more profitable to senior managers, as well as the proclivity of lower-level project workers to overestimate costs in order to protect themselves. If the project is in its initial planning stage as a response to an RFP from an outside organization, over- and underestimation of cost can have a serious impact on the probability of winning the contract—or on the level of profit, if a win occurs. (A large proportion of such projects are bid on a "cost plus" basis.)

Serious ethical problems may arise during the process of estimating costs and submission of bids in response to a Request for Proposal (RFP). If the job is to be paid on a cost-plus basis, or even if it is a fixed-fee project, with fee increases allowed for special circumstances, some bidders may "low ball" a contract (submit underestimated costs). By doing this, they hope to win the bid, counting on the opportunity to increase costs or to plead special circumstances once the job is underway.

At times, clients have been known to give favored bidders a "last look" at supposedly sealed bids so that the favored bidder can submit a winning bid, often with an unwritten agreement to allow some cost escalation at a later date. There is considerable opportunity for unethical behavior during cost estimation and bidding. Further, estimation and bidding practices vary widely from industry to industry.

Finally, there is plain bad luck. Delays occur for reasons that cannot be predicted. Machinery with the reliability of a railroad spike suddenly breaks down. That which has never failed fails. Every project needs an "allowance for contingencies."

Some writers and instructors differentiate four bases for estimating costs: experience, quantitative (statistical) methods, constraints, and worksheets. They discuss the advantages and disadvantages of each and then, typically, decide that one or another gives the best results. We feel strongly that all four are useful and that no approach to cost estimation should be accepted as the best or rejected out of hand. The best estimators seem to employ an eclectic approach that uses, as one said, "anything that works." The wise PM takes into account as many known influences on the project budget as can be predicted. What cannot be predicted must then, by experience, simply be "allowed for." There are two other factors, particularly common to projects involving intangible outputs such as software programming, that need to be mentioned relating to cost-estimation and the schedule. These two factors have been identified in a classic and highly-readable work—*The Mythical Man-Month*—by Brooks [7].

First, most projects involve a tangible medium that tends not to be under our control—the wood splits, the paint smears—and thus we blame implementation problems of our "good" ideas on these physical elements. So, when we are working with a purely intellectual medium that has no physical elements, such as computer code, we are highly optimistic and foolishly assume that all will go well. However, when any project consisting of a series of components can only be successful if all of the components are successful, and each component has a small probability of failing, the chances of the overall project being successful are in fact very poor. Consider, for example, a software program consisting of 1000 lines of code, each of which is 99.9 percent reliable. The chance of the program itself working is only about 36 percent! Brooks' experience has led him to the following rule of thumb for software projects. As a fraction of the total time of the project, planning consumes about $\frac{1}{3}$, coding consumes $\frac{1}{6}$, component test consumes $\frac{1}{4}$, and system test consumes $\frac{1}{4}$. Thus, if a project estimate is made based on the expected coding time (the main element for which we can derive an estimate), this in reality will usually represent only about 17 percent of the entire project time rather than the 80 to 90 percent commonly assumed.

The second factor is what Brooks calls "the mythical man month" and relates to our tendency to assume that workers and time are interchangeable. Thus, when a schedule slips, the traditional response is to add labor which is like trying to douse a fire with gasoline. Our assumption that workers and time are interchangeable is correct only when a task can be partitioned such that there is no communication needed between the workers, such as in picking cotton by hand. Most projects, however, especially computer programming, are not set up that way and the more workers that are added require even more workers to train, as well as lines of communication to coordinate their efforts. Thus, three workers require three times as much pairwise intercommunication as two, and four require six times as much, etc. This result is captured in Brooks' law: *Adding manpower to a late software project makes it later.*

The Emanon Aircraft Corporation

Emanon Aircraft is a major manufacturer of aircraft parts, specializing in landing gear parts and assemblies. They are located in a highly industrialized midwestern state. The local area suffers from somewhat higher than average unemployment, partly because Emanon has experienced a downturn in business. In the past three years, they have lost out on a number of landing gear contracts, being underbid by competitors from other areas of the country. Senior management studied the problem, but has come to no conclusion about what can be done. They have hired a consulting team from a nearby university to study the situation and make a recommendation.

Business in the aircraft industry is not significantly different than in many other industries specializing in the building of complex machines. Aircraft builders are primarily assembly operations. They build planes from subassemblies and parts manufactured by themselves or by subcontractors who, in turn, specialize in specific subassemblies; for example, landing gear, avionics, passenger seats, heating and air conditioning, etc. When an order is received to build some number of a given type of plane, the builder (prime contractor) requests bids for the proper number of a certain part or subassembly from appropriate subcontractors. All relevant specifications for the part or subassembly are included in the RFP. The subcontractors who wish to participate in the project submit proposals that include a complete description of the proposed subassem-

bly together with price information, delivery dates, and any other pertinent conditions of sale.

The university consulting team studied three aspects of Emanon's landing gear operation: the manufacturing process, the cost structure, and the bidding behavior and profit structure on landing gear bids. They determined that the manufacturing process was reasonably efficient and not significantly different from Emanon's competitors. Second, they found that all competitors were using approximately the same level of mark-up when determining their cost-plus price. When examining the cost structure, however, they noted that in the past three years, the firm consistently ran negative cost variances in material accounts. That is, the amount of material actually used in the construction of landing gears was approximately 10 percent less than the plan indicated. The team was unsure of this finding because there were only a few winning contracts for landing gears during the past three years.

An investigation was conducted on the estimation and purchase of materials for this department. It exposed the following facts. Three and one-half years ago, Emanon was late making a delivery of landing gear parts. The firm paid a large penalty and was threatened with loss of further business with the prime contractor. The late delivery resulted when Emanon ordered an insufficient quantity of a special steel alloy used in landing gear struts, and was unable to purchase any on the open market. The steel company required a manufacturing lead time of more than 90 days, so Emanon's delivery was late.

As a result, the purchasing official who had responsibility for this contract was demoted. The new purchasing official handled the problem in a straightforward fashion by in-flating the material estimates by approximately 10 percent. The cost of material is about half of the total cost of landing gear production, which resulted in bids that were approximately 5 percent above the competition.

On Making Better Estimates

Cost overruns are so frequent for all types of projects that senior managers often develop a cynical attitude when examining a project budget. They assume it is significantly understated. A common explanation for this phenomenon is that the PM purposely underestimates the project budget in order to improve its benefit–cost ratio, thereby increasing the probability that the project will be funded. Once the project is underway, the reasoning goes, and a monetary and psychic investment has been made in the work, the firm will not let a "good" project die and will make up for budget shortages, albeit grudgingly. It is interesting to note that in recent years computer experts (both hard- and software specialists) have replaced engineers as the people who "cannot be believed" in the industrial world. The "fact" that they will seriously underestimate both the time and cost required to do anything is taken as gospel.

Nevertheless, we will assume that budget estimation errors are not the result of a conspiracy to mislead senior managers, but rather derive from honest errors on the part of the PM, the project cost estimators, or anyone else involved in the estimation process. As we have already noted, there are a number of reasons why "honest" underestimation errors occur. Furthermore, to senior managers the job even looks easier, faster, and less expensive than it appears to the person who must do the job. Nonexpert cost estimators tend to overlook details necessary to the completion of a set of tasks. Neophyte and expert project managers alike seem to assume that Murphy's Law has been repealed in the case of their personal project.

Ambrose Bierce, in *The Devil's Dictionary*, defined "experience" as "The wisdom that enables us to recognize as an undesirable old acquaintance the folly that we have already embraced." It is axiomatic that we should learn through experience. It is a truism that we do not. Nowhere is this more evident than in project management, and yet it is not difficult to improve one's estimation/forecasting skills.

Recall that there are two generic types of estimation error. First, there is *random error* in which overestimates and underestimates are equally likely. Second, there is *bias*, which is *systematic* error. For biased estimates, the chance of over- and underestimates are not equally likely. Using the ubiquitous Lotus 1-2-3®, we can construct a spreadsheet that captures the essence of a person's performance as an estimator. Two simple statistical measures are used: the mean absolute deviation (MAD), and

	A	B	C	D	E	F	G
1	This is a template for improving one's estimating skills						
2							
3	MAD = SUM (|A(t) − F(t)|)/n						
4	Tracking Signal = SUM (A(t) − F(t))/MAD		A Measure of Bias				
5							Tracking
6	Period	Estimate	Actual	A(t) − F(t)	|A(t) − F(t)|	MAD	Signal
7							
8	1	155	163	8	8		
9	2	242	240	−2	2	5.00	1.20
10	3	46	67	21	21	10.33	2.61
11	4	69	78	9	9	10.00	3.60
12	5	75	71	−4	4	8.80	3.64
13	6	344	423	79	79	20.50	5.41
14	7	56	49	−7	7	18.57	5.60
15	8	128	157	29	29	19.88	6.69
16							
17				133	159		
18							
19							

Figure 7-5: Lotus 1-2-3® template for improving cost estimation.

the tracking signal (TS). The printout* of such a Lotus 1-2-3® spreadsheet is shown in Figure 7-5. Appendix E and references [11 and 26] include information on probability, statistics, and forecasting.

Figure 7-5 assumes that for each period (Column A) someone has made an estimate of a variable (Column B), and that the actual value of that variable is, sooner or later, known (Column C). (It should be noted that Column A need not be time periods. This column simply counts the number of estimates made and links estimates with their respective actuals.) Column D calculates the difference between the actual value, A(t), and the estimate or forecast for that period, F(t). Column E contains the absolute value of that difference. We can now calculate a statistic known as the *mean absolute deviation* (MAD).

As the information in Row 3 of the spreadsheet shows:

$$MAD = \Sigma(|A(t)-F(t)|)/n$$

where n is the number of differences. The MAD is therefore the arithmetic average of the absolute values of the differences—the mean absolute deviation.

Students of statistics may note that the MAD has certain logical similarities to the standard deviation. Assuming that the forecast errors are normally distributed, the MAD is approximately 80 percent of a standard deviation (see [11] and else-

---

*The data for Figures 7-5 and 7-6 were prepared using a Lotus 1-2-3® spreadsheet, transferred to Excel®, and printed. Any of the common spreadsheet programs can easily handle all of the calculations shown in this chapter. Almost all will accept the formulas and calculations from any of the others.

where). Thus, if the MAD is a sizable fraction of the variable being estimated, the average error is large and the forecast or estimate is not very accurate.

Now, consider Column D. The sum of the entries in this column for any number of periods is the sum of the forecast errors, often referred to as the "running sum of the forecast errors" (RSFE). If the estimator's errors are truly random, their sum should approach zero; that is, the RSFE should be a small number because positive errors should be offset by negative errors. If either positive or negative errors are more numerous or consistently larger than the other, the estimation process is said to be biased and the errors are not random. In Figure 7-5, RSFE = 133, so the forecast is quite positively biased.

The tracking signal measures the estimator's bias. It is easily found:

$$TS = RSFE/MAD$$

Note that it calculates the number of MADs in the RSFE (see column G in Figure 7-5, and recall the similarity between MAD and standard deviation). If the RSFE is small, approaching zero, the TS will also approach zero. As the RSFE grows, the TS will grow, indicating bias. Division of the RSFE by the MAD creates a sort of "index number," the TS, that is independent of the size of the variables being considered. We cannot say just how much bias is acceptable in an estimator/forecaster. We feel that a TS $\geq$ 3 is too high unless the estimator is a rank beginner. Certainly, an experienced estimator should have a much lower TS. (It should be obvious that the TS may be either negative or positive. Our comment actually refers to the absolute value of the TS.)

Perhaps more important than worrying about an acceptable limit on the size of the tracking signal is the practice of keeping track of it and analyzing why the estimator's bias, if there is one, exists. Similarly, the estimator should consider how to reduce the MAD, the average estimation error. Such analysis is the embodiment of "learning by experience." The Lotus 1-2-3® template makes the analysis simple to conduct, and should result in descreasing the size of both the MAD and the TS. (For those familiar with Lotus 1-2-3®, the formulas used for Figure 7-5 are shown in Figure 7-6.)

Some estimators would like to speed up the process of improving their estimation skills by grouping forecasts of different resources to generate more data points when calculating their MADs and TSs. Use of the tracking signal requires that the input data, estimates (forecasts) and actuals, be collected and processed separately for each variable being estimated. Cost estimates and actuals for different resources, for instance, would be used to find the MAD and TS for each individual resource. The reason for this inconvenience is that resources come in different units and the traditional caution about adding apples and oranges applies. (Even if all resources are measured in dollars, we still have scale problems when we mix resource costs of very different sizes.) Fortunately, there is a way around the problem.

Instead of defining the estimation error as the *difference* between actual and forecast, we can define it as the *ratio* of actual to forecast. Therefore, the new error for the first forecast (Period 1) in Figure 7-5 is not 8 units, but rather is

$$A(t)/F(t) = 163/155 = 1.052$$

	A	B	C	D	E	F	G
1							
2							
3							Tracking
4	Period	Estimate	Actual	A(t) − F(t)	|A(t) − F(t)|	MAD	Signal
5							
6	1	155	163	=C6²B6	=ABS (C6²B6)		
7	2	242	240	=C7²B7	=ABS (C7²B7)	=(SUM($E$6:E7))/A7	=(SUM($D$6:D7))/F7
8	3	46	67	=C8²B8	=ABS (C8²B8)	=(SUM($E$6:E8))/A8	=(SUM($D$6:D8))/F8
9	4	69	78	=C9²B9	=ABS (C9²B9)	=(SUM($E$6:E9))/A9	=(SUM($D$6:D9))/F9
10	5	75	71	=C10²B10	=ABS (C10²B10)	=(SUM($E$6:E10))/A10	=(SUM($D$6:D10))/F10
11	6	344	423	=C11²B11	=ABS (C11²B11)	=(SUM($E$6:E11))/A11	=(SUM($D$6:D11))/F11
12	7	56	49	=C12²B12	=ABS (C12²B12)	=(SUM($E$6:E12))/A12	=(SUM($D$6:D12))/F12
13	8	128	157	=C13²B13	=ABS (C13²B13)	=(SUM($E$6:E13))/A13	=(SUM($D$6:D13))/F13
14							
15				=SUM (D6:D14)	=SUM (E6:E14)		
16							

Figure 7-6: Lotus 1-2-3® formulas for Figure 7-5.

or a 5.2 percent error. In order to produce measures similar in nature and concept to the MAD and TS, we will subtract 1 from the ratio. Thus, when the actual is *greater* than the forecast, the measure (i.e., the error ratio minus 1) will be positive, and if the actual is *less* than the forecast, the measure will be negative. Figure 7-7 shows the calculations of {A(t)/F(t) − 1} for the data used in Figure 7-5. Column E shows the absolute value of column D, and column F lists the MAR (mean absolute ratio). The tracking signal is calculated as usual by dividing the "running sum of the forecast ratios" (RSFR) by the MAR,

$$TS = RSFR/MAR$$

	A	B	C	D	E	F	G
1							
2							
3							Tracking
4	Period	Estimate	Actual	(A(t) / F(t))−1	|(A(t) / F(t))−1|	MAR	Signal
5	1	155	163	0.052	0.052		
6	2	242	240	−0.008	0.008	0.030	1.448
7	3	46	67	0.457	0.457	0.172	2.904
8	4	69	78	0.130	0.130	0.162	3.898
9	5	75	71	−0.053	0.053	0.140	4.120
10	6	344	423	0.230	0.230	0.155	5.205
11	7	56	49	−0.125	0.125	0.151	4.523
12	8	128	157	0.227	0.227	0.160	5.670
13							
14				0.908	1.281		
15							
16							

Figure 7-7: Estimation template using ratios.

	A	B	C	D	E	F	G
1							
2							
3							Tracking
4	Period	Estimate	Actual	(A(t) / F(t))−1	|A(t) / F(t)−1|	MAR	Signal
5							
6	1	155	163	=(C6/B6)−1	=ABS((C6/B6)−1)		
7	2	242	240	=(C7/B7)−1	=ABS((C7/B7)−1)	=(SUM($E$6:E7))/A7	=(SUM($D$6:D7))/F7
8	3	46	67	=C8/B8−1	=ABS((C8/B8)−1)	=(SUM($E$6:E8))/A8	=(SUM($D$6:D8))/F8
9	4	69	78	=C9/B9−1	=ABS((C9/B9)−1)	=(SUM($E$6:E9))/A9	=(SUM($D$6:D9))/F9
10	5	75	71	=C10/B10−1	=ABS((C10/B10)−1)	=(SUM($E$6:E10))/A10	=(SUM($D$6:D10))/F10
11	6	344	423	=C11/B11−1	=ABS((C11/B11)−1)	=(SUM($E$6:E11))/A11	=(SUM($D$6:D11))/F11
12	7	56	49	=C12/B12−1	=ABS((C12/B12)−1)	=(SUM($E$6:E12))/A12	=(SUM($D$6:D12))/F12
13	8	128	157	=C13/B13−1	=ABS((C13/B13)−1)	=(SUM($E$6:E13))/A13	=(SUM($D$6:D13))/F13
14							
15				=SUM (D6:D14)	=SUM(E6:E14)		
16							

Figure 7-8: Formulas for Figure 7-7.

Notice that this calculation does not suffer from unit or scale effects because the ratio of actual to forecast is a dimensionless number and we are finding the percent error rather than the "real" error.

One caution remains. While this technique will allow one to aggregate dissimilar data and, thereby, measure the degree of random error and bias faster than when using differences, care must be exercised to aggregate only data for which there is good reason to believe that the amount of bias and uncertainty is roughly the same for all resource estimations. The Lotus 1-2-3® formulas for Figure 7-7, again translated into Excel®, are shown in Figure 7-8.

A *final note:* At the beginning of this discussion, we made the assumption that estimation errors were "honest." That assumption is not necessary. If a manager suspects that costs are purposely being under- or overestimated, it is usually not difficult to collect appropriate data and calculate the tracking signal for an individual estimator—or even for an entire project team. If it is known that such information is being collected, one likely result is that the most purposeful bias will be sharply reduced.

▶ **SUMMARY**

This chapter initiated the subject of project implementation by focusing on the project budget, which authorizes the project manager to obtain the resources needed to begin work. Different methods of budgeting were described along with their impacts on project management. Then, a number of issues concerning cost estimation were discussed, particularly the effect of learning on the cost of repetitive tasks and how to use the concept of the learning curve. Finally, methods for improving cost estimation skills were described.

Specific points made in the chapter were these:

- The intent of a budget is to communicate organizational policy concerning the organization's goals and priorities.

- There are a number of common budgeting methods: top–down, bottom–up, the budget request, PPBS, ZBB.

- The intent of PPBS is to focus on cost–benefit

relative to the organization's goals for selecting projects to fund.

- The intent of ZBB is to avoid automatic percentage budgeting in each budget period by focusing on the total value of each project to the organization's goals.

- A form identifying the level of resource need, when it will be needed, who the contact is, and its availability is especially helpful in estimating costs.

- It is common for organizations to fund projects whose returns cover direct but not full-costs in order to achieve long-run strategic goals of the organization.

- If projects include repetitive tasks with significant human input, the learning phenomenon should be taken into consideration when preparing cost estimates.

- The learning curve is based on the observation that the amount of time required to produce one unit decreases a constant percentage every time the cumulative output doubles.

- A method for determining whether or not cost estimations are biased is described. The method can be used to improve any estimation/forecasting process.

- Other major factors, in addition to learning, that should be considered when making project cost estimates are inflation, differential changes in the cost factors, waste and spoilage, personnel replacement costs, and contingencies for unexpected difficulties.

In the next chapter we address the subject of task scheduling, a topic of major importance in project management. More research and investigation has probably been conducted on the subject of scheduling than any other element of project management.

▶ GLOSSARY

Bottom–Up Budgeting—A budgeting method that begins with those who will be doing the tasks estimating the resources needed. The advantage is more accurate estimates.

Learning Rate—The percentage of the previous worker hours per unit required for doubling the output.

Planning-Programming-Budgeting-System (PPBS)—A system developed in the 1960s for dealing rationally with budgeting through maximization of the chances for attaining the organization's long-run goals.

Program Budgeting—Aggregating income and expenditures by project or program, often in addition to aggregation by organizational unit or activity.

Top–Down Budgeting—A budgeting method that begins with top managers' estimates of the resources needed for a project. Its primary advantage is that the aggregate budget is typically quite accurate because no element has been left out. Individual elements, however, may be quite inaccurate.

Variances—The pattern of deviations in costs and usage used for exception reporting to management.

Zero-Based Budgeting—A budgeting method from the 1970s that was devised as an alternative to the incremental approach. Every program budget had to be totally justified every budget cycle.

▶ MATERIAL REVIEW QUESTIONS

1. What are the advantages of top–down budgeting? Of bottom–up budgeting? What is the most important task for top management to do in bottom–up budgeting?

2. In preparing a budget, what indirect costs should be considered?

3. What is the procedure for zero-base budgeting? Is it a good method to use in planning a state or national budget? Why, or why not?

4. List the four main steps involved in PPBS. Why has it become obsolete?

5. Describe the top–down budgeting process.

6. What is a variance?

7. Describe the learning curve phenomenon.

8. How might you determine if cost estimates are biased?

9. What is "program budgeting"?

10. What is the difference between activity- and task-oriented budgets?

▶ CLASS DISCUSSION QUESTIONS

1. Discuss ways in which to keep budget planning from becoming a game.

2. List some of the pitfalls in cost estimating. What steps can a manager take to correct cost overruns?

3. Why do consulting firms frequently subsidize some projects? Is this ethical?

4. What steps can be taken to make controlling costs easier? Can these steps also be used to control other project parameters, such as performance?

5. Which budgeting method is likely to be used with which type of organizational structure?

6. What are some potential problems with the top–down and bottom–up budgeting processes? What are some ways of dealing with these potential problems?

7. How is the budget planning process like a game?

8. Would any of the conflict resolution methods described in the previous chapter be useful in the budget planning process? Which ones?

9. Why hasn't ZBB caught on with project managers?

10. Why is learning curve analysis important to project management?

11. Why is it "ethically necessary to be honest" in negotiations between a superior and subordinate?

▶ INCIDENTS FOR DISCUSSION

Preferred Widget Company

Larry Cole has been appointed project manager of the Preferred Widget Company's new widget manufacturing process project. Widgets are extremely price-sensitive and Preferred has done a great deal of quantitative work so it can accurately forecast changes in sales volume relative to changes in pricing.

The company president, "J. R." Widget, has considerable faith in the firm's sensitivity model and insists that all projects that affect the manufacturing cost of widgets be run against the sensitivity model in order to generate data to calculate the return on investment. The net result is that project managers, like Larry, are under a great deal of pressure to submit realistic budgets so go/no–go project decisions can be made quickly. J. R. has canceled several projects that appeared marginal during their feasibility stages and recently fired a project manager for overestimating project costs on a new model widget. The project was killed very early in the design stage and six months later a competitor introduced a similar widget that proved to be highly successful.

Larry's dilemma is how to go about constructing a budget that accurately reflects the cost of the proposed new manufacturing process. Larry is an experienced executive and feels comfortable with his ability to come close to estimating the cost of the project. However, the recent firing of his colleague has made him a bit gun-shy. Only one stage out of the traditional four-stage widget manufacturing process is being changed, so he has detailed cost information about a good percentage of the process. Unfortunately, the tasks involved in the process stage being modified are unclear at this point. Larry also believes that the new modification will cause some minor changes in the other three stages, but these changes have not been clearly identified. The stage being addressed by the project represents almost 50 percent of the manufacturing cost.

Questions: Under these circumstances, would Larry be wise to pursue a top–down or a bottom–up budgeting approach? Why? What factors are most relevant here?

General Ship Company

General Ship Company has been building nuclear destroyers for the Navy for the last 20 years. It has recently completed the design of a new class of nuclear destroyer and will be preparing a detailed budget to be followed during construction of the first destroyer.

The total budget for this first destroyer is $90 million. The controller feels the initial project cost estimate prepared by the planning department was too low because the waste and spoilage allowance was underestimated. Thus, she is concerned that there may be a large cost overrun on the project and wants to work closely with the project manager to control the costs.

Question: How would you monitor the costs of this project?

▶ INDIVIDUAL EXERCISE

Use the work breakdown structure from the chapter exercise in Chapter 5 to design a project budget for that project. Organize it hierarchically by task, etc. How would a top–down budgeting process proceed for this project? Compare it to a bottom–up process.

Then consider the tasks within the WBS itself. Are any of the tasks repetitive, with a high labor content?

Might the learning curve apply here? If mechanical tasks requiring tools or machinery follow an 80 percent learning rate whereas simply memory/learning tasks follow a 60 percent learning rate, what rate would you estimate for these tasks?

▶ PROJECT TEAM CONTINUING EXERCISE

At this point, the team must establish the detailed project budget. Start with the work breakdown structure and then estimate, both from the bottom up and the top down, what the appropriate budget will be. Examine any discrepancies between the two budgets for errors, misunderstandings, or oversights. If any of

the tasks are repetitious, use the learning curve to predict their cost by unit. If the task is mechanical, use a 75–80 percent rate; if more mental, use a 65–70 percent rate. Finally, describe how a PPBS and ZBB approach might apply to your project.

▶ BIBLIOGRAPHY

1. AUSTIN, A. L. *Zero-Based Budgeting: Organizational Impact and Effects.* New York: AMACOM, 1977.
2. BACON, J. *Managing the Budget Function.* Washington, DC: National Industrial Conference Board, 1970.
3. BARTIZAL, J. R. *Budget Principles and Procedures.* Englewood Cliffs, NJ: Prentice Hall, 1940.
4. BLOCK, E. B. "Accomplishment/Cost: Better Project Control." *Harvard Business Review,* May 1971.
5. BRIGGS, G. R. *The Theory and Practice of Management Control.* New York: American Management Association, 1970.
6. BRIMSON, J. A. "Activity Product Cost." IEEE *Engineering Management Review,* Spring 1992.
7. BROOKS, F. P. *The Mythical Man-Month.* Reading, MA: Addison-Wesley, 1975.
8. BROWN, R., and J. D. SUVER. "Where Does Zero-Base Budgeting Work?" *Harvard Business Review,* Dec. 1977.
9. BUNGE, W. R. *Managerial Budgeting for Profit Improvement.* New York: McGraw-Hill, 1968.
10. BURKHEAD, J. *Budgeting and Planning.* General Learning Press, 1971.
11. CHASE, R. B., and N. J. AQUILANO. *Production and Operations Management,* 5th ed. Homewood, IL: Irwin, 1989.
12. DEAN, B. V., S. J. MANTEL, JR., and L. A. ROEPCKE.

"Research Project Cost Distributions and Budget Forecasting." IEEE *Transactions on Engineering Management*, Nov. 1969.

13. DEARDON, J. *Cost and Budget Analysis.* Englewood Cliffs, NJ: Prentice Hall, 1962.

14. EITEMAN, J. W. *Graphic Budgets.* Ann Arbor, MI: Masterco Press, 1949.

15. GAGNON, R. J. *An Exploratory Analysis of the Relevant Cost Structure of Internal and External Engineering Consulting*, Ph.D. dissertation. Cincinnati: University of Cincinnati, 1982.

16. GAGNON, R. J., and S. J. MANTEL, JR. "Strategies and Performance Improvement for Computer-Assisted Design." IEEE *Transactions on Engineering Management*, Nov. 1987.

17. HARRISON, F. L. *Advanced Project Management.* Hants, Eng: Gower, 1983.

18. HECKERT, J. B. *Business Budgeting and Control.* New York: Ronald, 1967.

19. HITCH, C. J. "Plans, Programs and Budgets in The Department of Defense." *Operations Research*, Jan.–Feb. 1963.

20. HITCH, C. J. "A Planning-Programming-Budgeting System." In F. E. Kast and J. E. Rosensweig, eds. *Science, Technology and Management.* New York: McGraw-Hill, 1963.

21. HOVER, L. D. *A Practical Guide to Budgeting and Management Control Systems: A Functional and Performance Evaluation Approach.* Lexington, MA: Lexington Books, 1979.

22. LIN, T. "Corporate Planning and Budgeting: An Integrated Approach." *Managerial Planning*, May 1979.

23. MACIARIELLO, J. A. "Making Program Management Work." *Journal of Systems Management*, July 1974.

24. MACLEAD, R. K. "Program Budgeting Works in Non-Profit Institutions." *Harvard Business Review*, Sept. 1971.

25. MCKEAN, R. N. "Remaining Difficulties in Program Budgeting." In Enke, S., ed., *Defense Management.* Englewood Cliffs, NJ: Prentice Hall, 1967.

26. MEREDITH, J. R. *The Management of Operations*, 4th ed. New York: Wiley, 1992.

27. NTUEN, M. "Applying Artificial Intelligence to Project Cost Estimates." *Cost Engineering*, No. 5, 1987.

28. PYHRR, PETER A. *Zero-Base Budgeting: A Practical Management Tool for Evaluating Expenses.* New York: Wiley, 1973.

29. STEDRY, ANDREW C. *Budget Control and Cost Behavior.* Englewood Cliffs, NJ: Prentice Hall, 1960.

30. STEINER, G. "Program Budgeting: Business Contribution to Government Management." *Business Horizons*, Spring 1965.

CASE

AUTOMOTIVE BUILDERS, INC.: THE STANHOPE PROJECT
Jack Meredith

It was a cold, gray October day as Jim Wickes pulled his car into ABI's parking lot in their corporate offices in suburban Detroit. The leaves, in yellows and browns, swirled around his feet as he walked into the wind toward the lobby.

"Good morning, Mr. Wickes," said his secretary as he came into the office. "That proposal on the Stanhope project just arrived a minute ago. It's on your desk."

"Good morning, Debbie. Thanks. I've been anxious to see it."

This was the day Jim had scheduled to review the 1986 supplemental capital request and he didn't want any interruptions as he scrutinized the details of the flexible manufacturing project planned for Stanhope, Iowa. The Stanhope proposal, compiled by Ann Williamson, project manager and the managerial "champion" on this effort, looked like just the type of project to fit ABI's new strategic plan, but there was a large element of risk in the project. Before recommending the project to Steve White, the executive vice president of ABI, Jim wanted to review all the details one more time.

History of ABI

ABI started operations as the Farm Equipment Company just after the First World War. Employing new technology to produce diesel engine parts for tractors, the firm grew with the growth of farming and became a multimillion dollar company by 1940.

During the Second World War, the firm switched over to producing tank and truck parts in volume for the military. At the war's end, the firm converted its equipment over to the production of automotive parts for the expanding automobile industry. To reflect this major change in their product line, the company was renamed Automotive Builders, Inc. (ABI), though they remained a major supplier to the farm equipment market.

A Major Capital Project

The farm equipment industry in the 1970s had been doing well but there were some disturbing trends. Japanese manufacturers had entered the industry and were beginning to take a significant share of the domestic market. More significantly, domestic labor costs were significantly higher than overseas and resulted in price disadvantages that couldn't be ignored any longer. And perhaps most important of all, quality differences between American and Japanese farm equipment, including tractors, were becoming quite noticeable.

To improve the quality and costs of their incoming materials, many of the domestic tractor manufacturers were beginning to single-source a number of their tractor components. This allowed them better control over both quality and cost, and made it easier to coordinate delivery schedules at the same time.

In this vein, one of the major tractor engine manufacturers, code-named "Big Red" within ABI, let its suppliers know that it was interested in negotiating a contract for possible 100 percent sourcing of 17 versions of special piston heads destined for a new line of high-efficiency tractor engines which were expected to replace the current conventional engines in both new and existing tractors. These were all six-cylinder diesel engines and thus would require six pistons each.

This put ABI in an interesting situation. If they failed to bid on this contract, they would be inviting competition into their very successful and profitable diesel engine parts business. Thus, to protect their existing successful business, and to pursue more such business, ABI seemed required to bid on this contract. Should ABI be successful in their bid, this would result in 100 percent sourcing in both the OEM market as well as the replacement market with its high margins. Furthermore, the high investment required to produce these special pistons at ABI's costs would virtually rule out future competition.

ABI had two plants producing diesel engine components for other manufacturers and believed they had a competitive edge in engineering of this type. These plants, however, could not accommodate the volume Big Red expected for the new engine. Big Red insisted at their negotiations that a 100 percent supplier be able to meet peak capacity at their assembly plant for this new line.

As Jim looked over the proposal, he decided to refer back to the memos which restated their business strategy and started them thinking about a new Iowa plant in the heart of the farm equipment industry for this project. In addition, Steve White had asked the following basic, yet rather difficult questions about the proposal at their last meeting and Jim wanted to be sure he had them clearly in mind as he reviewed the files.

- ABI is already achieving an excellent return on investment (ROI). Won't these investments simply tend to dilute it?
- Will the cost in new equipment be returned by an equivalent reduction in labor? Where's the payoff?
- What asset protection can we get? This proposal requires us to invest in new facilities before knowing whether we will get a long-term contract that will reimburse us for our investment.
- Does this proposal maximize ROI, sales potential, or total profit?

To address these questions adequately, Jim decided to recheck the expected after-tax profits, return on investment (internal rate of return), and the payback period for himself when he reached the financial portion of the proposals. These figures should give a clear indication of the "quality" of the investment. There were, however, other aspects of capital resource allocation to consider besides just the financial elements. One of these was certainly the new business strategy of the firm, as recently articulated by ABI's executive committee.

The Business Strategy

A number of elements of ABI's business strategy were directly relevant to this proposal. Jim took out a note pad to jot each of them down and assign them a priority.

1. To bid only on good margin products that have the potential for maintaining their margins over a long term.
2. To pursue only those new products whose design or production process is of a proprietary nature and that lie in those areas where our technical abilities enable us to maintain a long-term position.
3. To employ, if at all possible, the most advanced technology in new projects that is either within our experience or requires the next step up in experience.
4. To foster the "project champion" approach to innovation and creativity. The idea is to encourage entrepreneurship by approving projects that individual managers are committed to and have taken on as personal "causes" because of their belief that the idea, product, or process is in our best interest.
5. To maintain small plants of no more than 480 employees. These have been found to be the most efficient and enjoy the best labor relations.

With these in mind, Jim reopened the proposal and started reading at critical sections.

Demand Forecasts and Scenarios

For this proposal, three scenarios were analyzed in terms of future demand and financial impacts. The baseline "Scenario I" assumed that the new line would be successful. "Scenario II" assumed the Japanese would soon follow and compete successfully with Big Red in this line. "Scenario III" assumed that the new line was a failure. The sales volume forecasts under these three scenarios are shown in Table 1.

There was, however, not a lot of confidence in any of these forecasts. In the preceding few years Japan had become a formidable competitor, not only in

Table 1   Demand Forecasts (000s engines)*

Year	Baseline I	Scenario II	Scenario III
1987	69	69	69
1988	73	72	72
1989	90	81	77
1990	113	95	68
1991	125	87	62
1992	145	74	47

* Each engine requires six pistons.

price but also in more difficult areas of competition, such as quality and reliability. Furthermore, the economic situation in 1986 was taking a severe toll on American farmers and economic forecasts indicated there was no relief in sight. Thus, as stated in the proposal:

The U.S. farm market will be a difficult battleground for world farm equipment manufacturers and any forecast of a particular engine's potential in this market must be considered as particularly risky. How much risk do we want to take on? Every effort should be made to minimize our exposure on this investment and maximize our flexibility.

Manufacturing Plan

The proposal stressed two primary aspects of the manufacturing process. First, a learning curve was employed in calculating production during the 1000-unit ramp-up implementation period so as to not be overly optimistic. A learning rate of 80 percent was assumed. Second, an advanced technology process using a flexible manufacturing system based largely on turning centers was recommended since it came in at $1 million less than conventional equipment and met the strategy guidelines of using sophisticated technology when appropriate.

Since ABI had closely monitored Big Red's progress in the engine market, it had been anticipating the request for bids. In preparation for this, Jim had authorized a special manufacturing process study to determine more efficient and effective ways of producing piston heads. The study considered product design, process selection, quality considerations, productivity, and manufacturing system planning. Three piston manufacturing methods were considered in the study: batch manufacture via computer numerically controlled (CNC) equipment, a flexible manufacturing system (FMS), and a high volume, low-unit-cost transfer machine.

The resulting recommendation was to install a very carefully designed FMS if it appeared that the additional flexibility might be required in the future for other versions, or even other manufacturers. Though such a system would be expensive, the volume of production over the FMS' longer lifetime would offset that expense. Four preferred machine builders were contacted for equipment specifications and bids. It was ABI's plan to work closely with the selected vendor in designing and installing the equipment, thus building quality and reliability into both the product and the process and learning about the equipment at the same time.

To add further flexibility for the expensive machinery, all design features that would facilitate retool or changeover to other products were incorporated. For example, the machining centers would also be capable of machining other metals, such as aluminum or nodular iron, and would be fitted with variable feed and speed motors, feed-force monitors, pressure-controlled clamping of workpieces, and air-leveling pallets. Also, fully interchangeable chucks, spindles, pallets, tooling, and risers would be purchased to minimize the spares inventories.

Plant Operation and Organization

As stated in the proposal, many innovative practices were also to be employed at the new plant.

- Machine operators will be trained to do almost all of their own machine maintenance.
- All employees will conduct their own statistical process control and piston heads will be subject to 100 percent inspection.
- There will only be four skill classes in the plant. Every employee in each of those classes will be trained to do any work within that class.
- There will not be any time clocks in the plant.

The organizational structure for the 11 salaried workers in the new plant is shown in Figure 1 and the complete labor summary is illustrated in Figure 2, including the shift breakdown. As can be seen, the plant will be relatively small, with 65 employees in the ratio of 1:5 salaried to hourly. The eight month acquisition of the employees during the ramp-up is illustrated in

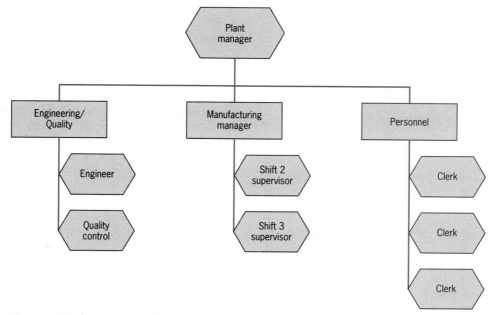

Figure 1: Stanhope organization.

Salaried Labor

plant manager	1
manufacturing managers (3 shifts)	3
quality control manager	1
engineering	2
personnel manager	1
clerical	3
	11

Hourly Labor

	Days	Afternoons	Nights
direct	14	14	10
inspection	1	1	1
maintenance	2	1	1
tooling	2	2	1
rec./shp./mtl.	2	1	1
total	21	19	14

Summary

salary	11
hourly	54
total	65

Figure 2: Stanhope labor summary.

Financial Considerations

Figure 3, with full employment occurring by March 1987.

Financial aspects of new proposals at ABI were considered from a number of perspectives, in part because of the interdependent nature of many proposals. The results of not investing in a proposal are normally compared with the results of investing and the differences noted. Variations on the investment assumptions are also tested, including errors in the forecast sales volumes, learning rates, productivities, selling prices, and cancellations of both current and future orders for existing and potential business.

For the Stanhope proposal, the site investment required is $3,012,000. The details of this investment are shown in Table 2. The total investment required amounts to $7,108,000 (plus required working capital of $1,380,000). The equipment is depreciated over an eight year life. ABI, under the revised tax laws, is in the 34 percent tax bracket. The price of the piston heads has been tentatively set at $25.45 apiece. ABI's expected costs are shown in Table 3.

Some Concerns

Jim had spoken with some of his colleagues about the FMS concept after the preliminary financial results

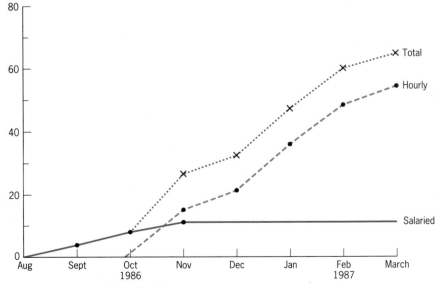

Figure 3: Stanhope labor buildup.

Table 2   Stanhope Site Capital Costs

Land and Site Preparation

land	$246,000
access roads/parking lot	124,000
landscaping	22,000

Building Costs

building (67,000 sq. ft.)	1,560,000
air conditioning	226,000
power	205,000
employee services	177,000
legal fees and permits	26,000

Auxiliary Equipment

ABI company sign	25,000
containers, racks, etc.	33,000
flume	148,000
coolant disposal	97,000
furnishings	51,000
fork lift trucks	72,000
total	3,012,000

had been tabulated. Their concerns were what now interested him.

For example, he remembered one manager asking: "Suppose Bid Red's sales only reach 70 percent of our projections in the 1989–90 time period, or say, perhaps as much as 150 percent; how would this affect the project? Does the FMS still apply or would you

Table 3   Piston Head Cost Summary

material	$8.47
labor	1.06
variable overhead	2.23
fixed overhead	2.44
freight	0.31
total factory cost	14.51
general & admin.	1.43
scrap	0.82
testing	0.39
total cost	17.15

consider some other form of manufacturing equipment, possibly conventional or CNC with potential aftermarket application in the former case or a transfer machine in the latter case?"

Another manager wrote his thoughts down as a memo to forward to Jim. He had two major concerns:

- The "Scenario II" analysis assumes the loss of substantial volume to competition. This seems rather unlikely.

- The after-tax margins seem unreasonably high. Can we get such margins on a sole-source contract?

Jim wondered what these changes in their assumptions would do to the ROI of the proposal and its overall profitability.

Conclusion

Jim had some concerns about the project also. He was wondering how realistic the demand forecasts were, given the weak economy and what the Japanese might do. If the demand didn't materialize, they might be very sorry they had invested in such an expensive piece of equipment as an FMS.

Strategically, it seemed like ABI had to make this investment to protect its profitable position in the diesel engine business but how far should arguments like that be carried? Were they letting their past investments color their judgment on new ones? He was also concerned about the memo questioning the high profit margins. They did seem high in the midst of a sluggish economy.

▶ QUESTIONS

1. What are the answers to Steve White's questions?
2. What other factors are relevant to this issue?
3. How do the changes in assumptions mentioned by the other managers affect the proposal?
4. What position should Jim take? Why?

▶ This article clearly describes the importance and impact of cost-related issues on a project. These issues can significantly alter the profitability and even success of a project. Costs are discussed from three viewpoints: that of the project manager, the accountant, and the controller. Not only are the amounts of expenditures and encumbrances important, but their timing is critical also. Perhaps most important is having a project cost system that accurately reports costs and variances in a way that can be useful for managerial decisions.

READING

THREE PERCEPTIONS OF PROJECT COST— COST IS MORE THAN A FOUR LETTER WORD
David H. Hamburger

Project cost seems to be a relatively simple expression, but "cost" is more than a four letter word. Different elements of the organization perceive cost differently, as the timing of project cost identification affects their particular organizational function. The project manager charged with on-time, on-cost, on-spec execution of a project views the "on cost" component of his responsibility as a requirement to stay within the allocated budget, while satisfying a given set of specified conditions (scope of work), within a required time frame (schedule). To most project managers this simply means a commitment to project funds in accordance with a prescribed plan (time based budget). Others in the organization are less concerned with the commitment of funds. The accounting department addresses expense recognition related to a project or an organizational profit and loss statement. The accountant's ultimate goal is reporting profitability, while positively influencing the firm's tax liability. The comptroller (finance department) is primarily concerned with the organization's cash flow. It is that person's responsibility to provide the funds for paying the bills, and putting the unused or available money to work for the company.

To be an effective project manager, one must understand each cost, and also realize that the timing of cost identification can affect both project and corporate financial performance. The project manager must be aware of the different cost perceptions and the manner in which they are reported. With this knowledge, the project manager can control more than the project's cost of goods sold (a function often viewed

as the project manager's sole financial responsibility). The project manager can also influence the timing of cost to improve cash flow and the cost of financing the work, in addition to affecting revenue and expense reporting in the P&L statement.

Three Perceptions of Cost

To understand the three perceptions of cost—commitments, expenses, and cash flow—consider the purchase of a major project component. Assume that a $120,000 compressor with delivery quoted at six months was purchased. Figure 1 depicts the order execution cycle. At time 0 an order is placed. Six months later the vendor makes two shipments, a large box containing the compressor and a small envelope containing an invoice. The received invoice is processed immediately, but payment is usually delayed to com-

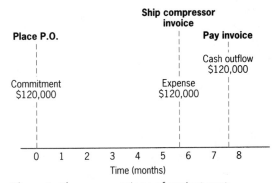

Figure 1: Three perceptions of project cost.

ply with corporate payment policy (30, 60, 90 or more days may pass before a check is actually mailed to the vendor). In this example, payment was made 60 days after receipt of the invoice or 8 months after the order for the compressor was given to the vendor.

Commitments—The Project Manager's Concern Placement of the purchase order represents a *commitment* to pay the vendor $120,000 following satisfactory delivery of the compressor. As far as the project manager is concerned, once this commitment is made to the vendor, the available funds in the project budget are reduced by that amount. When planning and reporting project costs the project manager deals with commitments. Unfortunately, many accounting systems are not structured to support project cost reporting needs and do not identify commitments. In fact, the value of a purchase order may not be recorded until an invoice is received. This plays havoc with the project manager's fiscal control process, as he cannot get a "handle" on the exact budget status at a particular time. In the absence of a suitable information system, a conscientious project manager will maintain personal (manual or computer) records to track his project's commitments.

Expenses—The Accountant's Concern Preparation of the project's financial report requires identification of the project's revenues (when applicable) and all project *expenses*. In most conventional accounting systems, expenses for financial reporting purposes are recognized upon receipt of an invoice for a purchased item (not when the payment is made—a common misconception). Thus, the compressor would be treated as an expense in the sixth month.

In a conventional accounting system, revenue is recorded when the project is completed. This can create serious problems in a long-term project in which expenses are accrued during each reporting period with no attendant revenue, and the revenue is reported in the final period with little or no associated expenses shown. The project runs at an apparent loss in each of the early periods and records an inordinately large profit at the time revenue is ultimately reported—the final reporting period. This can be seriously misleading in a long-term project which runs over a multi-year period.

To avoid such confusion, most long-term project P&L statements report revenue and expenses based on a "percentage of completion" formulation. The general intent is to "take down" an equitable percentage of the total project revenue (approximately equal to the proportion of the project work completed) during each accounting period, assigning an appropriate level of expense to arrive at an acceptable period gross margin. At the end of each accounting year and at the end of the project, adjustments are made to the recorded expenses to account for the differences between actual expenses incurred and the theoretical expenses recorded in the P&L statement. This can be a complex procedure. The misinformed or uninformed project manager can place the firm in an untenable position by erroneously misrepresenting the project's P&L status; and the rare unscrupulous project manager can use an arbitrary assessment of the project's percentage of completion to manipulate the firm's P&L statement.

There are several ways by which the project's percentage of completion can be assessed to avoid these risks. A typical method, which removes subjective judgments and the potential for manipulation by relying on strict accounting procedures is to be described. In this process a theoretical period expense is determined, which is divided by the total estimated project expense budget to compute the percentage of total budget expense for the period. This becomes the project's percentage of completion which is then used to determine the revenue to be "taken down" for the period. In this process, long delivery purchased items are not expensed on receipt of an invoice, but have the value of their purchase order prorated over the term of order execution. Figure 2 shows the $120,000 compressor in the example being expensed over the six-month delivery period at the rate of $20,000 per month.

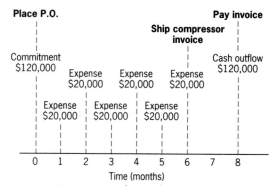

Figure 2: Percentage of completion expensing.

Cash Flow—The Comptroller's Concern   The comptroller and the finance department are responsible for managing the organization's funds, and also assuring the availability of the appropriate amount of cash for payment of the project's bills. Unused funds are put to work for the organization in interest-bearing accounts or in other ventures. The finance department's primary concern is in knowing when funds will be needed for invoice payment in order to minimize the time that these funds are not being used productively. Therefore, the comptroller really views project cost as a *cash outflow*. Placement of a purchase order merely identifies a future cash outflow to the comptroller, requiring no action on his part. Receipt of the invoice generates a little more interest, as the comptroller now knows that a finite amount of cash will be required for a particular payment at the end of a fixed period. Once a payment becomes due, the comptroller provides the funds, payment is made, and the actual cash outflow is recorded.

It should be noted that the compressor example is a simplistic representation of an actual procurement cycle, as vendor progress payments for portions of the work (i.e., engineering, material, and delivery) may be included in the purchase order. In this case, commitment timing will not change, but the timing of the expenses and cash outflow will be consistent with the agreed-upon terms of payment.

The example describes the procurement aspect of project cost, but other project cost types are treated similarly. In the case of project labor, little time elapses between actual work execution (a commitment), the recording of the labor hours on a time sheet (an expense), and the payment of wages (cash outflow). Therefore, the three perceptions of cost are treated as if they each occur simultaneously. Subcontracts are treated in a manner similar to equipment purchases. A commitment is recorded when the subcontract is placed and cash outflow occurs when the monthly invoice for the work is paid. Expenses are treated in a slightly different manner. Instead of prorating the subcontract sum over the performance period, the individual invoices for the actual work performed are used to determine the expense for the period covered by each invoice.

Thus the three different perceptions of cost can result in three different time-based cost curves for a given project budget. Figure 3 shows a typical relationship between commitments, expenses, and cash outflow. The commitment curve leads and the cash

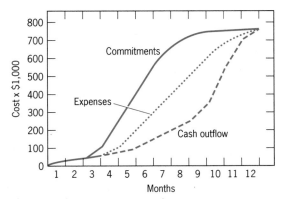

Figure 3: Three perceptions of cost.

outflow curve lags, with the expense curve falling in the middle. The actual shape and the degree of lag/lead between the curves are a function of several factors, including: the project's labor, material, and subcontract mix; the firm's invoice payment policy; the delivery period for major equipment items; subcontract performance period and the schedule of its work; and the effect of the project schedule on when and how labor will be expended in relation to equipment procurement.

The conscientious project manager must understand these different perceptions of cost and should be prepared to plan and report on any and all approaches required by management. The project manager should also be aware of the manner in which the accounting department collects and reports "costs." Since the project manager's primary concern is in the commitments, he or she should insist on an accounting system which is compatible with the project's reporting needs. Why must a project manager resort to a manual control system when the appropriate data can be made available through an adjustment in the accounting department's data processing system?

Putting Your Understanding of Cost to Work

Most project managers believe that their total contribution to the firm's profitability is restricted by the ability to limit and control project cost, but they can do much more. Once the different perceptions of cost have been recognized, the project manager's effectiveness is greatly enhanced. The manner in which the project manager plans and executes the project can improve company profitability through influence on financing expenses, cash flow, and the reporting of revenue and expenses. To be a completely effective project manager one must be totally versed in the cost accounting practices which affect the firm's project cost reporting.

Examination of the typical project profit & loss statement (see Table 1) shows how a project sold for profit is subjected to costs other than the project's costs (cost of goods sold). The project manager also influences other areas of cost as well, addressing all aspects of the P&L to influence project profitability positively.

Specific areas of cost with examples of what a project manager can do to influence cost of goods sold, interest expense, tax expense, and profit are given below:

Cost of Goods Sold (Project Cost)

- Evaluation of alternate design concepts and the use of "trade-off" studies during the development phase of a project can result in a lower project cost, without sacrificing the technical quality of the project's output. The application of value engineering principles during the initial design period will also reduce cost. A directed and controlled investment in the evaluation of alternative design concepts can result in significant savings of project cost.

- Excessive safety factors employed to ensure "on-spec" performance should be avoided. Too frequently the functional members of the project team will apply large safety factors in their effort to meet or exceed the technical specifications. The project team must realize that such excesses increase the project's cost. The functional staff should be prepared to justify an incremental investment which was made to gain additional performance insurance. Arbitrary and excessive conservatism must be avoided.

- Execution of the project work must be controlled. The functional groups should not be allowed to stretch out the project for the sake of improvement, refinement, or the investigation of the most remote potential risk. When a functional task has been completed to the project manager's satisfaction (meeting the task's objectives), cut off further spending to prevent accumulation of "miscellaneous" charges.

- The project manager is usually responsible for controlling the project's contingency budget. This budget represents money that one expects to expend during the term of the project for specific requirements not identified at the project onset. Therefore, these funds must be carefully monitored to prevent indiscriminate spending. A functional group's need for a portion of the contingency budget must be justified and disbursement of these funds should only be made after the functional group has exhibited an effort to avoid or limit its use. It is imperative that the contingency budget be held for its intended purpose. Unexpected problems will ultimately arise, at which time the funds will be needed. Use of this budget to finance a scope change is neither advantageous to the project manager nor to management. The contingency budget represents the project manager's authority in dealing with corrections to the project work. Management must be made aware of the true cost of a change so that financing the change will be based on its true value (cost–benefit relationship).

- In the procurement of equipment, material and subcontract services, the specified requirements should be identified and the lowest priced, qualified supplier found. Adequate time for price "shopping" should be built into the project schedule. The Mercury project proved to be safe and successful even though John Glenn, perched in the Mercury capsule

Table 1 Typical Project Profit & Loss Statement

Revenue (project sell price)	$1,000,000
(less) cost of goods sold (project cost)	($ 750,000)
Gross margin	$ 250,000
(less) selling, general & administrative expenses	($ 180,000)
Profit before interest and taxes	$ 70,000
(less) financial expense	($ 30,000)
Profit before taxes	$ 40,000
(less) taxes	($ 20,000)
Net profit	$ 20,000

atop the Atlas rocket prior to America's first earth orbiting flight, expressed his now famous concern that "all this hardware was built by the low bidder." The project manager should ensure that the initial project budget is commensurate with the project's required level of reliability. The project manager should not be put in the position of having to buy project reliability with unavailable funds.

- Procurement of material and services based on partially completed drawings and specifications should be avoided. The time necessary for preparing a complete documentation package before soliciting bids should be considered in the preparation of the project schedule. Should an order be awarded based .on incomplete data and the vendor then asked to alter the original scope of supply, the project will be controlled by the vendor. In executing a "fast track" project, the project manager should make certain that the budget contains an adequate contingency for the change orders which will follow release of a partially defined work scope.

- Changes should not be incorporated in the project scope without client and/or management approval and the allocation of the requisite funds. Making changes without approval will erode the existing budget and reduce project profitability; meeting the project manager's "on-cost" commitment will become extremely difficult, if not impossible.

- During periods of inflation, the project manager must effectively deal with the influence of the economy on the project budget. This is best accomplished during the planning or estimating stage of the work, and entails recognition of planning in an inflationary environment for its effect by estimating the potential cost of two distinct factors. First, a "price protection" contingency budget is needed to cover the cost increases that will occur between the time a vendor provides a firm quotation for a limited period and the actual date the order will be placed. (Vendor quotations used to prepare an estimate usually expire long before the material is actually purchased.) Second, components containing certain price volatile materials (e.g., gold, silver,

etc.) may not be quoted firm, but will be offered by the supplier as "price in effect at time of delivery." In this case an "escalation" contingency budget is needed to cover the added expense that will accrue between order placement and material delivery. Once the project manager has established these inflation related contingency budgets, the PM's role becomes one of ensuring controlled use.

Financial Expense

- The project's financial cost (interest expense) can be minimized by the project manager through the timing of order placement. Schedule slack time can be used to defer the placement of a purchase order so that the material is not available too early and the related cash outflow is not premature. There are several risks associated with this concept. Delaying an order too long could backfire if the desired material is unavailable when needed. Allowing a reasonable margin for error in the delivery cycle, saving some of the available slack time for potential delivery problems, will reduce this risk. Waiting too long to place a purchase order could result in a price increase which can more than offset the interest savings. It is possible to "lock-up" a vendor's price without committing to a required delivery date, but this has its limitations. If vendor drawings are a project requirement, an "engineering only" order can be placed to be followed by hardware release at the appropriate time. Deferred procurement which takes advantage of available slack time should be considered in the execution of all projects, especially during periods when the cost of money is excessively high.

- Vendors are frequently used to help "finance the project" by placing purchase orders which contain extended payment terms. Financially astute vendors will build the cost of financing the project into their sell price, but only to the extent of remaining competitive. A vendor's pricing structure should be checked to determine if progress payments would result in a reduced price and a net project benefit. A discount for prompt payment should be taken if the discount exceeds the interest savings that could result from deferring payment.

- Although frequently beyond the project manager's control, properly structured progress payment terms can serve to negate most or all project financial expenses. The intent is simple. A client's progress payment terms can be structured to provide scheduled cash inflows which offset the project's actual cash outflow. In other words, maintenance of a zero net cash position throughout the period of project execution will minimize the project's financial expense. In fact, a positive net cash position resulting from favorable payment terms can actually result in a project which creates interest income rather than one that incurs an interest expense. Invoices to the client should be processed quickly, to minimize the lost interest resulting from a delay in receiving payment.

- Similarly, the project manager can influence receipt of withheld funds (retention) and the project's final payment to improve the project's rate of cash inflow. A reduction in retention should be pursued as the project nears completion. Allowing a project's schedule to indiscriminately slip delays project acceptance, thereby delaying final payment. Incurring an additional expense to resolve a questionable problem should be considered whenever the expense will result in rapid project acceptance and a favorable interest expense reduction.

- On internally funded projects, where retention, progress payments, and other client related financial considerations are not a factor, management expects to achieve payback in the shortest reasonable time. In this case, project spending is a continuous cash outflow process which cannot be reversed until the project is completed and its anticipated financial benefits begin to accrue from the completed work. Unnecessary project delays, schedule slippages, and long-term investigations extend system startup and defer the start of payback. Early completion will result in an early start of the investment payback process. Therefore, management's payback goal should be considered when planning and controlling project work, and additional expenditures in the execution of the work should be considered if a shortened schedule will adequately hasten the start of payback.

Tax Expense and Profit.

- On occasion, management will demand project completion by a given date to ensure inclusion of the project's revenue and profit within a particular accounting period. This demand usually results from a need to fulfill a prior financial performance forecast. Delayed project completion by only a few days could shift the project's entire revenue and profit from one accounting period to the next. The volatile nature of this situation, large sums of revenue and profit shifting from one period to the next, results in erratic financial performance which negatively reflects on management's ability to plan and execute their efforts.

- To avoid the stigma of erratic financial performance, management has been known to suddenly redirect a carefully planned, cost-effective project team effort to a short-term, usually costly, crash exercise, directed toward a project completion date, artificially necessitated by a corporate financial reporting need. Unfortunately, a project schedule driven by influences external to the project's fundamental objectives usually results in additional cost and reduces profitability.

- In this particular case, the solution is simple if a percentage of completion accounting process can be applied. Partial revenue and margin take-down during each of the project's accounting periods, resulting from this procedure (rather than lump sum take down in a single period at the end of the project, as occurs using conventional accounting methods) will mitigate the undesirable wild swings in reported revenue and profit. Two specific benefits will result. First, management's revenue/profit forecast will be more accurate and less sensitive to project schedule changes. Each project's contribution to the overall forecast will be spread over several accounting periods and any individual performance change will cause the shift of a significantly smaller sum from one accounting period to the next. Second, a project nearing completion will have had 90–95 percent of its revenue/profit taken down in earlier periods which will lessen or completely eliminate management pressure to complete the work to satisfy a financial reporting demand. Inordinate, unnecessary spending to meet such unnatural demands can thereby be avoided.

- An Investment Tax Credit*, a net reduction in corporate taxes gained from a capital investment project (a fixed percentage of the project's installed cost), can be earned when the project actually provides its intended benefit to the owner. The project manager should consider this factor in scheduling the project work, recognizing that it is not necessary to complete the entire project to obtain this tax benefit as early as possible. Failure to substantiate beneficial use within a tax year can shift this savings into the next tax year. The project manager should consider this factor in establishing the project's objectives, diligently working toward attainment by scheduling the related tasks to meet the tax deadline. Consideration should also be given to expenditures (to the extent they do not offset the potential tax savings) to reach this milestone by the desired date.

- In managing the corporate P&L statement, the need to shift revenue, expenses, and profit from one tax period to the next often exists. By managing the project schedule (expediting or delaying major component procurements or shifting expensive activities) the project manager can support this requirement. Each individual project affords a limited benefit, but this can be maximized if the project manager is given adequate notice regarding the necessary scheduling adjustments.

- Revenue/profit accrual based on percentage of completion can create a financial problem if

---

* The proposed tax law revisions under consideration in Congress at the time this article was written include a provision which eliminates the Investment Tax Credit.

actual expenses greatly exceed the project budget. In this case the project's percentage of completion will accumulate more quickly than justified and the project will approach a theoretical 100 percent completion before all work is done. This will "front load" revenue/profit take down and will ultimately require a profit reversal at project completion. Some managers may find this desirable, since profits are being shifted into earlier periods, but most reputable firms do not wish to overstate profits in an early period which will have to be reversed at a later time. Therefore, the project manager should be aware of cost overruns and, when necessary, reforecast the project's "cost on completion" (increasing the projected cost and reducing the expected profit) to reduce the level of profit taken down in the early periods to a realistic level.

Conclusion

Cost is not a four letter word to be viewed with disdain by the project manager. It is a necessary element of the project management process which the project manager must comprehend despite the apparent mysteries of the accounting systems employed to report cost. The concept of cost is more than the expenses incurred in the execution of the project work: the manner in which cost is treated by the organization's functional elements can affect project performance, interest expenses and profitability. Therefore, the conscientious project manager must develop a complete understanding of project cost and the accounting systems used to record and report costs. The project manager should also recognize the effect of the timing of project cost, and the differences between commitments, expenses, and cash flow. The project manager should insist on the accounting system modifications needed to accommodate project cost reporting and control requirements. Once an appreciation for these concepts has been gained, the project manager can apply this knowledge towards positively influencing project and organizational profitability in all areas of cost through control of the project schedule and the execution of the project's work.

CHAPTER

8

Scheduling

The previous chapter initiated our discussion of project implementation. In this and the following three chapters, we continue with the implementation of the project plans we made in Chapter 5. In this chapter we examine some scheduling techniques that have been found to be useful in project management. We cover the Program Evaluation and Review Technique (PERT), the Critical Path Method (CPM), Gantt charts, and briefly discuss Precedence Diagramming, the Graphical Evaluation and Review Technique (GERT), and report-based methods.

In Chapter 9, we consider the special problems of scheduling when resource limitations force conflicts between concurrent projects, or even between two or more tasks in a single project. We also look at ways of expediting activities by adding resources. Following a discussion of the monitoring and information system function in Chapter 10, we discuss the overall topic of project control in Chapter 11.

8.1 BACKGROUND

A schedule is the conversion of a project action plan into an operating timetable. As such, it serves as a fundamental basis for monitoring and controlling project activity and, taken together with the plan and budget, is probably the major tool for the management of projects. In a project environment, the scheduling function is more important than it would be in an ongoing operation because projects lack the continuity of day-to-day operations and often present much more complex problems of coordination. Indeed, project scheduling is so important that a detailed schedule is sometimes a customer-specified requirement. In later chapters we discuss the fact that a properly designed, detailed schedule can also serve as a key input in establishing the monitoring and control systems for the project.

Not all project activities need to be scheduled at the same level of detail. In fact, there may be several schedules: the master schedule, the development and testing schedule, the assembly schedule, and so on. These schedules are typically based on the previously determined action plan and/or work breakdown structure (WBS), and it is good practice to create a schedule for each major task level in the WBS which will cover the work packages. It is rarely necessary however, to list all work packages. One can focus mainly on those that need to be monitored for maintaining adequate control over the project. Such packages are usually difficult, expensive, or have a relatively short time frame for their accomplishment.

When making a schedule, it is important that the dates and time allotments for the work packages be in precise agreement with those set forth in the project master schedule. It is also important that the work units that aggregate into work packages be in agreement with the times in the master schedule. These times are control points for the PM. It is the project manager's responsibility to insist on and maintain this consistency, but the actual scheduling of the task and work packages is usually done by those responsible for their accomplishment—after the PM has established and checked appropriate due dates for all tasks. This procedure ensures that the final project schedule reflects the interdependencies among all the tasks and departments involved in the project, and maintains consistency among them.

The basic approach of all scheduling techniques is to form an actual or implied network of activity and event relationships that graphically portrays the sequential relations between the tasks in a project. Tasks that must precede or follow other tasks are then clearly identified, in time as well as function. Such a network is a powerful tool for planning and controlling a project and has the following benefits:

- It is a consistent framework for planning, scheduling, monitoring, and controlling the project.
- It illustrates the interdependence of all tasks, work packages, and work units.
- It denotes the times when specific individuals must be available for work on a given task.
- It aids in ensuring that the proper communications take place between departments and functions.
- It determines an expected project completion date.
- It identifies so-called critical activities which, if delayed, will delay the project completion time.
- It also identifies activities with slack that can be delayed for specified periods without penalty, or from which resources may be temporarily borrowed without harm.
- It determines the dates on which tasks may be started—or must be started if the project is to stay on schedule.
- It illustrates which tasks must be coordinated to avoid resource or timing conflicts.
- It also illustrates which tasks may be run, or must be run, in parallel to achieve the predetermined project completion date.

- It relieves some interpersonal conflict by clearly showing task dependencies.
- It may, depending on the network form used, allow an estimate of the probability of project completion by various dates, or the date corresponding to a particular *a priori* probability.

Project Management in Practice
Replacing the Atigun Section of the TransAlaska Pipeline

In June of 1977, the TransAlaska Pipeline was put into service as the successful conclusion of one of the most difficult projects in history. As part of the maintenance of the 48-inch diameter pipeline, instrumented "pigs" are run along the pipeline every year to detect both internal and external corrosion. In the fall of 1988, data from the pig run indicated that excessive external corrosion had occurred in an 8.5 mile section of the pipeline located in the Atigun River flood plain, 135 miles north of the Artic Circle (see map).

Thus, in the spring of 1989 a project team was formed to take total responsibility for replacing this portion of the buried pipeline with another buried pipe that had much better external corrosion protection, fusion bonded epoxy covered with 1.25 inches of concrete, an articulated concrete mat, and then five to fifteen feet of dirt. As part of the project objectives, the oil flow of two million barrels per day at pressures exceeding 800 psi was *not* to be interrupted, and there could be absolutely no oil spills!

Polar bears at construction site—Atigun Section of TransAlaska Pipeline.

Sidebooms lower new pipe into ditch at −50°F temperatures.

This meant that a bypass system had to be constructed while the pipe was being replaced, all in a very hostile work environment. The site is subject to flooding, rockslides, avalanches, mudslides, temperatures that reach − 60° F in the winter (tires break like glass and gasoline turns to jelly at that temperature), and as little as three hours of sunshine in which to work during the winter months. To minimize exposure to the spring-time avalanches, they worked in another area first and then used explosives to trigger potential avalanches and unstable snow deposits. Also, a full-time avalanche control and forecasting expert was present during con-

struction in the danger area. Blasting was also used to dig the ditch, ironically, to protect the existing pipeline which was only 30 feet away. Another ironic aspect of the project was the constant curiosity of the wildlife in the area: "What impressed me most was completing this project right there in the middle of all these animals, and seeing that we didn't affect them at all—that was gratifying."

The project began in September of 1989 and was completed in December 1991, a 27-month duration. Scheduling was a major facet of the project, not just due to the limited hours of sunshine, but also in obtaining facilities and materials for the project. For exam-

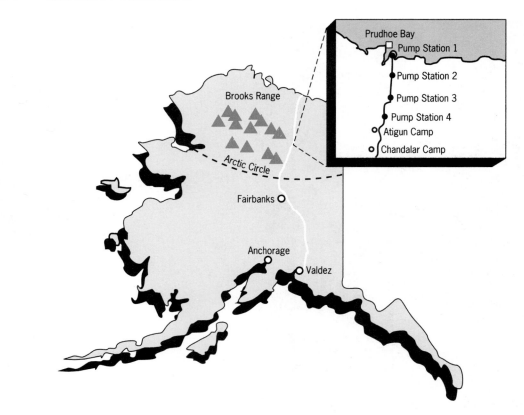

ple, some elements of the replacement pipeline had to be shipped to Saudia Arabia for corrosion treatment and then shipped back, all just prior to the Persian Gulf war. Yet, the project met or exceeded all expectations, without one oil spill. More surprisingly, the project was completed 34 percent under bud-get through careful analysis of the financial and physical risks and assignment to the most appropriate contractor.

Source: Project Team "Atigun Mainline Reroute Project," PM *Network*, Jan. 1993.

▶ 8.2   NETWORK TECHNIQUES: PERT AND CPM

With the exception of Gantt charts, to be discussed below, the most common approach to project scheduling is the use of network techniques such as PERT and CPM. The Program Evaluation and Review Technique was developed by the U.S. Navy in cooperation with Booz-Allen Hamilton and the Lockheed Corporation for the Polaris missile/submarine project in 1958. The Critical Path Method was developed by DuPont, Inc., during the same time period.

In application, PERT has primarily been used for R & D projects, the type of projects for which it was developed, though its use is more common on the "development" side of R & D than it is on the "research" side. CPM was designed for construction projects and has been generally embraced by the construction industry. (There are many exceptions to these generalities. The Eli Lilly Company, for example, uses CPM for its research projects.)

The two methods are quite similar and are often combined for educational presentation. Throughout most of this chapter we will not distinguish between them except where the differences are of direct interest to us. We will write "PERT/CPM" whenever the distinction is not important. Originally, however, PERT was strictly oriented to the time element of projects and used probabilistic activity time estimates to aid in determining the probability that a project could be completed by some given date. CPM, on the other hand, used deterministic activity time estimates and was designed to control both the time and cost aspects of a project, in particular, time/cost trade-offs. In CPM, activities can be "crashed" (expedited) at extra cost to speed up the completion time. Both techniques identified a project *critical path* whose activities could not be delayed, and also indicated *slack* activities that could be somewhat delayed without lengthening the project completion time.

We might note in passing that the *critical* activities in real-world projects typically constitute less than 10 percent of the total activities. In our examples and simplified problems in this chapter, the critical activities constitute a much greater proportion of the total because we use smaller networks to illustrate the techniques.

Before explaining the mechanics of these methods, we must note that their value in use is not totally accepted by everyone. Research on the use of PERT/CPM [11, 24, 25] conducted in the 1960s and early 1970s found that there was no significant difference in the technological performance on projects where PERT/CPM was used and where it was not. This research found, however, that there was a significantly lower probability of cost and schedule overruns when PERT/CPM was used. In our experience, the use of network scheduling techniques has increased markedly in recent years, particularly with the proliferation of project management software packages that are inexpensive and reasonably friendly to PMs who are familiar with the fundamental concepts of PERT/CPM, and who are also sensible enough to avoid trying to construct complex networks by hand.

Recent research [9] finds that a greater use of "project management techniques" (PERT/CPM among a number of others) occurs on R & D type projects, on projects with greater levels of complexity, and on projects with resource limitations, than on other types of projects or those with lower levels of complexity and fewer resource limitations. Unfortunately, this otherwise excellent research did not investigate whether or not the use of project management software influenced the number of project management techniques used. The use of project management software for scheduling projects will be discussed and illustrated in Chapter 10.

Terminology

Let us now define some terms used in our discussion of networks.

Activity   A specific task or set of tasks that are required by the project, use up resources, and take time to complete.

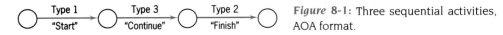

Figure 8-1: Three sequential activities, AOA format.

Event   The result of completing one or more activities. An identifiable end state occurring at a particular time.

Network   The combination of all activities (usually drawn as *arcs*) and events (usually drawn as *nodes* at the beginning and end of each arc) define the project and the activity precedence relationships. Networks are usually drawn starting on the left and proceeding to the right. Arrowheads placed on the arcs are used to indicate the direction of flow—that is, to show the proper precedences. Before an event can be *realized*—that is, achieved—all activities that immediately precede it must be completed. These are called its *predecessors*. Thus, an event represents an instant in time when each and every predecessor activity has been finished. Events themselves have no time duration and use no resources. They are merely points on the network, conditions of the system that can be recognized.

Path   The series of connected activities (or intermediate events) between any two events in a network.

Critical   Activities, events, or paths which, if delayed, will delay the completion of the project. A project's *critical path* is understood to mean that sequence of critical activities (and critical events) that connect the project's start event to its finish event.

To transform a project plan into a network, one must know what activities comprise the project and, for each activity, what its predecessors (and/or successors) are. An activity can be in any of these conditions: (1) it may have a successor(s) but no predecessor(s), (2) it may have a predecessor(s) but no successor(s), and (3) it may have both predecessor(s) and successor(s). The first of these is an activity that starts a network. The second ends a network. The third is in the middle. Figure 8-1 shows each of the three types of activities. Arrows are labeled with the appropriate type numbers. More than one arrow can start a network, end a network, or be in the middle. Any number of arrows can end at a node or depart from a node, as in Figure 8-2.

The interconnections depend on the technological relationships described in the action plan. For example, when one paints a room, filling small holes and cracks in the wall and masking windows and woodwork are predecessors to painting the walls. Similarly, removing curtains and blinds, as well as pictures and picture hooks

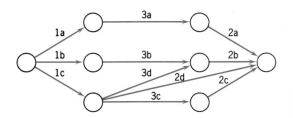

Figure 8-2: Activity network, AOA format.

from the wall are predecessors to spackling and masking. It is the nature of the work to be done that determines predecessor–successor relationships.

In the examples above, arrows represent activities while nodes stand for events. This is an AOA (activity-on-arrow) network. Another format for drawing networks is AON (activity-on-node). In this case, activities are represented by nodes and arrows to show the precedence relationships. In AON notation, when there are multiple activities with no predecessors, it is usual to show them all emanating from a single node called "start." Similarly, when multiple activities have no successors, it is usual to show them connected to a node called "end," as in Figure 8-3.

The choice between AOA and AON representation is largely a matter of personal preference. Our impression is that users of PERT favor AOA and users of CPM favor AON, but both approaches appear in the educational literature. Both are also used in commercially available computer packages, though AON is typically used in the most popular PC-based software. AOA networks are slightly harder to draw, but they identify events (milestones) clearly. AON networks do not require the use of *dummy* activities (defined below) and are easier to draw. Throughout most of this chapter we adopt the AOA format of PERT. In Section 8.4, we use the AON representation that is standard with that method. In this way, the reader can become familiar with both types of networks. This chapter is intended as an introduction to project scheduling at a level sufficient for the PM who wishes to use most commercial computerized project scheduling packages. For a deeper understanding of PERT/CPM, we refer the reader to [4, 12, 15, 17, 19, 37, 40, 55].

Recall the planning documents we developed in Chapter 5. In particular, the action plan contains the information we need. It is a list of all activities that must be undertaken in order to complete a specified task, the time each activity is expected to take, any nonroutine resources that will be used by the activity, and the predecessor activities for each activity. For example, we might have an action plan like that shown in Figure 8-4.

Constructing the Network

Let us start by assuming the node numbered 1 denotes the event called "START." Activities **a** and **b** have no predecessors, so we assume their source is at START (node 1) and their destination at nodes we will number 2 and 3, respectively (Figure 8-5). As explained above, the arrowheads show the direction of flow.

Activity **c** follows **a**, activity **d** follows **b**, and activity **e** also follows **b**. Let's add these to our network in Figure 8-6. Note that we number the event nodes sequentially from left to right as we construct the network. No great damage occurs if we do not use this convention, but it is convenient.

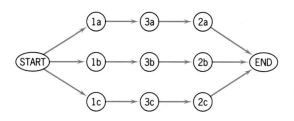

Figure 8-3: Activity network, AON format.

ACTION PLAN

Objective: To complete. . . . .

. . . .

Measures of Performance. . . . .

. . . .

Constraints. . . . .

Tasks	Precedence	Time	Cost	Who Does
a	—	5 days	—	—
b	—	4 days	—	—
c	a	6 days	—	—
d	b	2 days	—	—
e	b	5 days	—	—
f	c,d	8 days	—	—

Figure 8-4: Sample action plan.

Now note that activity **f** must follow both **c** and **d,** but *any given activity must have its source in one, and only one node.* Therefore, it is clear that **c** and **d,** both of which must precede **f,** must conclude in the same node from which **f** originates. We can now redraw the network, collapsing nodes 4 and 5 (and renumbering them) as in Figure 8-7.

The action plan does not indicate any further activity is required to complete the task, so we have reached the end of this particular plan. Once again, we can redraw the network to show that the final activities (those with no successors) end in a single node, Figure 8-8.

This process of drawing and redrawing the network may seem a bit awkward, and is. If the list of activities associated with a project is long, with complicated in-

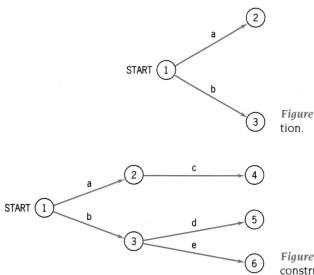

Figure 8-5: Sample of network construction.

Figure 8-6: Sample of network construction.

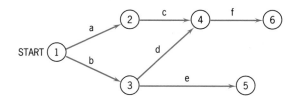

Figure 8-7: Sample of network construction.

terrelationships, this way of constructing the network would be too time-consuming to be practical. In Chapter 10 we will describe some computer software that can automatically generate the network.

Construction of a network may not be straightforward in some cases. For instance, there may be a need for a dummy activity to aid in indicating a particular precedence, via a dashed arc. A dummy activity has no duration and uses no resources. Its sole purpose is to indicate a technological relationship.

Figure 8-9 illustrates the proper way to use a dummy activity *if two* activities occur between the same *two* events. Figure 8-9 also shows why dummy activities may be needed for AOA networks. An activity is identified by its starting and ending nodes as well as its "name." For example, activities **a** and **b** both start from node 1 and end at node 2. Many computer programs that are widely used for finding the critical path and time for networks require the nodes to identify which activity is which. In our example, **a** and **b** would appear to be the same, both starting at node 1 and ending at node 2.

Figure 8-10 illustrates how to use a dummy activity when activities **a, b,** and **c** must precede activity **d,** but only **a** and **b** must precede activity **e.** Last, Figure 8-11 illustrates the use of dummy activities in a more complex setting.

Let us now consider a small project with ten activities in order to illustrate the network technique. Table 8-1 lists the activities, their most likely completion times, and the activities that must precede them. The table also includes optimistic and pessimistic estimates of completion time for each activity in the list. Actual activity

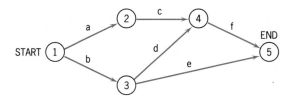

Figure 8-8: Sample of network construction.

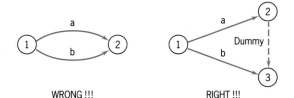

Figure 8-9: Networking concurrent activities.

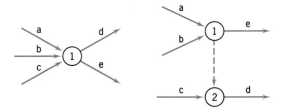

Figure 8-10: Activity **c** not required for **e.**

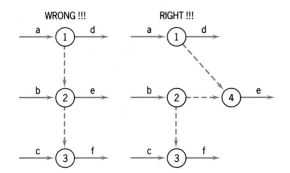

Figure 8-11: **a** precedes **d**; **a** and **b** precede **e**; **b** and **c** precede **f** (**a** does not precede **f**).

time is expected rarely to be less than the optimistic time or more than the pessimistic time. (More on this matter shortly.)

As described earlier, we start the network by finding those activities that have no predecessors. In the table activities **a, b,** and **c** meet the test. Therefore, they can all be drawn emerging from our starting node.

Next, we look for activities that only require **a, b,** or **c,** or some combination of **a, b,** and **c,** to precede them. Activity **d** requires that **a** be completed, and **e, f,** and **g** all require that **b** and **c** be completed. Note that a dummy will be necessary unless we begin the network from separate nodes for **b** and **c.** Last, **h** requires only that **c** be completed. To this point, the network might look like Figure 8-12.

Table 8-1 Project Activity Times and Precedences

Activity	Optimistic Time	Most Likely Time	Pessimistic Time	Immediate Predecessor Activities
a	10	22	22	—
b	20	20	20	—
c	4	10	16	—
d	2	14	32	a
e	8	8	20	b,c
f	8	14	20	b,c
g	4	4	4	b,c
h	2	12	16	c
i	6	16	38	g,h
j	2	8	14	d,e

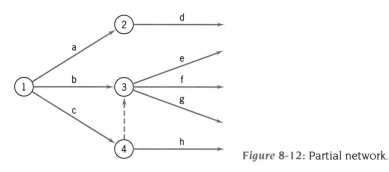

Figure **8-12:** Partial network.

The last two activities, **i** and **j**, are drawn in the same manner. Activity **i** requires that both **g** and **h** be completed, so **g** and **h** are directed to a single node (node 5). Similarly, activity **j** requires the completion of both **d** and **e,** which are directed to node 6. Since no activities require that **f, i,** or **j** precede them, these activities are directed to the project completion node, 7. The complete project network is shown in Figure 8-13.

Calculating Activity Times

The next step is to calculate expected activity completion times from the data in Table 8-1. These expected completion times are found by using the three time estimates (optimistic, pessimistic, and most likely) in the table.

Once again, a short digression is helpful. Precisely what is meant by "optimistic," "pessimistic," and "most likely"? Assume that all possible times for some specific activity might be represented by a statistical distribution (e.g., the asymmetrical distribution in Figure 8-14). The "most likely" time, m, for the activity is the mode of this distribution. In theory, the "optimistic" and "pessimistic" times are selected in the following way. The PM, or whoever is attempting to estimate a and b, is asked to select a such that the actual time required by the activity will be a or greater about 99 percent of the time. Similarly, b is estimated such that about 99 percent of the time the activity will have a duration of b or less. (We know of no project managers or workers who are comfortable making estimates at this level of precision, but we will delay dealing with this problem for the moment.)

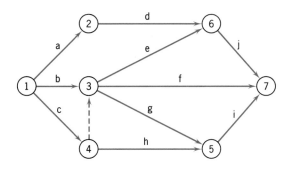

Figure **8-13:** The complete network from Table 8-1.

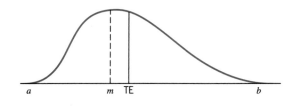

Figure 8-14: Distribution of all possible activity times for an activity.

The expected time, TE, is found by

$$TE = (a + 4m + b)/6$$

where

    a = optimistic time estimate,

    b = pessimistic time estimate, and

    m = most likely time estimate, the mode.

Note in Table 8-1 that some activity durations are known with certainty, which is to say that a, b, and m are the same (see activity **b**, for instance). Note further that the most likely time may be the same as the optimistic time ($a = m$) as in activity **e,** or that the most likely time may be identical to the pessimistic time ($m = b$) as in activity **a.** The range about m may be symmetric where

$$m - a = b - m$$

as in activity **c,** or may be quite asymmetric, as in activities **h** and **j.**

The above formula for calculating expected times is usually said to be based on the beta statistical distribution.* This distribution is used rather than the more common normal distribution because it is highly flexible in form and can take into account such extremes as where $a = m$ or $b = m$.

TE is an estimate of the mean of the distribution. It is a weighted average of a, m, and b with weights of 1-4-1, respectively. Again, we emphasize that *this same method can be applied to finding the expected level of resource usage given the appropriate estimates of the modal resource level as well as optimistic and pessimistic estimates.*

Recently, Sasieni noted [48] that writers (including himself) have been using the formula used here to estimate TE. He pointed out that it could not be derived from the formula for the beta distribution without several assumptions that were not necessarily reasonable, and he wondered about the original source of the formula. Fortunately, for two generations of writers on the subject, Littlefield and Randolph [27] cited a U.S. Navy paper that derives the approximations used here and states the not unreasonable assumptions on which they are based. Gallagher [16] makes a second derivation of the formula using a slightly different set of assumptions.

---

*We remind readers who wish a short refresher on elementary statistics and probability that one is available in Appendix E at the end of this book.

Table 8-2   Expected Activity Times (TE), Variances (σ^2), and Standard Deviations (σ)

Activity	Expected Time, TE	Variance, σ^2	Standard Deviation, σ
a	20	4	2
b	20	0	0
c	10	4	2
d	15	25	5
e	10	4	2
f	14	4	2
g	4	0	0
h	11	5.4	2.32
i	18	28.4	5.33
j	8	4	2

The results of the expected value calculations are shown in Table 8-2 and are included on Figure 8-15 as well. Also included in the table and on the network are measures of the *uncertainty* for the duration of each activity, the *variance*, $\sigma,^2$ that is given by

$$\sigma^2 = ((b - a)/6)^2$$

and the *standard deviation*, σ, which is given by

$$\sigma = \sqrt{\sigma^2}$$

This calculation of σ is based on the assumption that the standard deviation of a beta distribution is approximately one-sixth of its range, $(b - a)/6$.

Critical Path and Time

Consider the hypothetical project shown in Figure 8-15. Assume, for convenience, that the time units involved are days. How long will it take to complete the project?

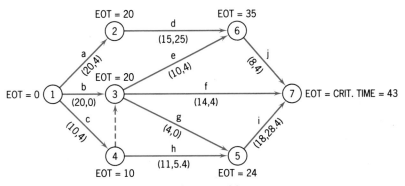

Figure 8-15: The complete network from Table 8-2.

(For the moment we will treat the expected times as if they were certain.) If we start the project on day zero, we can begin simultaneously working on activities **a, b,** and **c,** each of which have no predecessor activities. We will reach event 2 in 20 days, event 3 in 20 days, and event 4 in ten days. We have shown these times just above or below their respective nodes. They are labelled EOT (earliest occurrence time) because they represent the earliest times that the event can occur. Activity **d,** for example, cannot begin before event 2 has occurred, which means that all activities that precede event 2 must be completed. In this case, of course, activity **a** is the only predecessor of event 2.

Note that event 3 not only requires the completion of activity **b,** but also requires the completion of activity **c,** as shown by the dummy activity. (Refer to Figure 8-9 for a refresher.) The dummy requires neither time nor resources, so it does not affect the network time in any way. Event 3 does not occur until all paths leading to it have been completed. Therefore, the EOT for event 3 is equal to the time required by the *longest* path leading to it. The path from event 1 to event 3 requires the completion of activity **b** (20 days) *and* the completion of activities **c** and **dummy** (ten + zero days). Because the two paths may be followed simultaneously, we can reach event 3 in 20 days. Therefore, the earliest starting time (EST) for any activity emanating from event 3 is 20 days.

Proceeding similarly, we see that event 6 has two predecessor activities, **d** and **e.** Activity **d** cannot start until day 20, (EST = 20) and it requires 15 days to complete. Thus, its contribution to event 6 will require a total of 35 days from the start of the project. Activity **e** may also start after 20 days, the EOT for event 3, but it requires only ten days, a total of 30 days from the project start. Because event 6 requires the completion of both activities **d** and **e,** the EOT for event 6 is 35 days, the *longest* of the paths to it. Event 5 has an EOT of 24 days, the longest of the two paths leading to it, and event 7, the completion event of the network, has a time of 43 days. The EOTs are shown in Figure 8-15.

There are eight activity paths leading to event 7. They are

a-d-j=20 + 15 + 8=43 days   **c-dummy-e-j**=10 + 0 + 10 + 8=28 days
b-e-j=20 + 10 + 8=38 days   **c-dummy-f** =10 + 0 + 14   =24 days
b-f=20 + 14   =34 days   **c-dummy-g-i**=10 + 0 + 4 + 18=32 days
b-g-i=20 + 4 + 18=42 days
c-h-i=10 + 11 + 18=39 days

The longest of these paths is **a-d-j** using 43 days, which means that 43 days is the *shortest* time in which the entire network can be completed. This is called the *critical* time of the network, and **a-d-j** is the critical path, usually shown as a heavy line.

In a simple network such as our example, it is easy to find and evaluate every path between start and finish. Many real networks are considerably more complex, and finding all paths can be taxing. Using the method illustrated above, there is no need to worry about the problem. Every node is characterized by the fact that one or more activities lead to it. Each of these activities has an expected duration and originates in an earlier node. As we proceed to calculate the EOT of each node, beginning at the start, *we are actually finding the critical path and time to each of the nodes in the net-*

work. Note that event 5 has an EOT (critical time) of 24 days, and its critical path is **b-g** rather than **c-h** which requires 21 days, or **c-dummy-g** which takes 14 days.

The number of activities directly entering an event tells us the number of paths we must evaluate to find the EOT for that event. Here, *path* is defined as originating at immediate predecessor events, not at the network origin. With event 5, that number is two, so we find the EOT and activity times for the two immediate predecessors. For event 7, we have three evaluations to do, the EOT of event 6 plus the duration of activity **j** (43 days), the EOT of event 3 plus the duration of **f** (34 days), and the EOT of event 5 plus the duration of **i** (42 days). There is, therefore, no need to find, list, and evaluate all possible start-to-finish paths in the network.

Although we will assume throughout this chapter that we always employ the "as-soon-as-possible" approach to scheduling tasks ("early start"), there are situations where other approaches are sometimes used. One example is the simultaneous start, where all resources are launched at the beginning. Another is the simultaneous finish, where a facility can be moved to its next location once all the tasks are finished. Of course, delay early on in a project runs the risk of delaying the overall project if some other activities inadvertently become delayed. One important reason for using an "as-late-as-possible" approach is that it delays the use of resources as much as possible, thereby optimizing the cash flow of the project, but again at some risk of delay.

Slack

Thus far in this discussion we have focused mostly on the events in the network. We found the EOTs for the project milestones. It is now helpful to focus on the activities by finding their earliest starting times (EST) and latest possible starting times (LST). As noted in the previous section, the EST for an activity is equal to the EOT for the event from which the activity emanates. Activity **i** cannot start until event 5 has occurred. Event 5 has an EOT of 24 days, and so activity **i** has an EST of 24 days. An important question for the PM is this: What is the latest time (LST) activity **i** could start without making the entire project late?

Refer again to Figure 8-15. The project has a critical time of 43 days. Activity **i** requires 18 days to be accomplished. Therefore, **i** must be started no later than day 25 (43 − 18 = 25) if the project is to be complete on day 43. The LST for activity **i** is day 25. Because **i** cannot begin until event 5 has occurred, the latest occurrence time (LOT) for event 5 is also day 25. The difference between the LST and the EST for an activity is called its *slack* or *float.* In the case of activity **i,** it *must* be started no later than day 25, but *could* be started as early as day 24, so it has one day of slack. It should be immediately obvious that all activities on the critical path have zero slack. They cannot be delayed without making the project late.

For another example, consider activity **f.** Its EST is day 20, which is equal to the EOT for event 3 from which it emanates. The LST for activity **f** is 43 − 14 = 29. If **f** is started later than day 29, it will delay the entire project. Activity **f** has slack of LST − EST = 29 − 20 = 9 days.

To find the slack for any activity or the LOT for any event, we make a backward pass (right to left) through the network just as we made a forward pass (left to right) to find the critical path and time and the EOTs for all events (which are also the

ESTs for successor activities). There is one simple convention we must adopt: *When there are two or more noncritical activities on a path, it is conventional to calculate the slack for each activity as if it were the only activity in the path.* Thus, when finding the slack for activity **i,** for example, we assume that none of **i**'s predecessors are delayed, and that event 5 occurred on its EOT of day 24. Of course, if some activity, **x,** had six days of slack (given a specific EOT for the immediate preceding event), and if an earlier activity was late, causing the event to be delayed say two days, then activity **x** would have only four days of slack, having lost two days to the earlier delay.

It is simple to calculate slack for activities that are immediate predecessors of the final node. As we move to earlier activities, it is just a bit more complicated. Consider activity **g.** Remembering our assumption that the other activities in the same path use none of the available slack, we see that activity **i** must follow **g,** and that **g** emanates from event 3. Starting with the network's critical time of 43 days, we subtract 18 days for activity **i** and four more days for **g** ($43 - 18 - 4 = 21$). Thus **g** can begin no later than day 21 without delaying the network. The EST for **g** (EOT for event 3) is day 20, so **g** has one day of slack.

To find the LOT for event 3, we must investigate each path that emanates from it. We have already investigated two paths, one with activity **g** and one with activity **f.** Recall that **f** could start as late as day 29. For **f** not to delay the network, event 3 would have to be complete not later than day 29. But activity **g** must start no later than day 21, so event 3 must be complete by day 21 or the **g-i** path will cause a delay. Now consider activity **e,** the only remaining activity starting from event 3. Activity **e** must be completed by day 35 or event 6 will be late and the network will be delayed. (Note that we do not have to work backward from the end of the network to find the slack for any activity that ends at a node on the critical path. All events and activities on the critical path have zero slack, so any activity ending on this path must arrive at event 6 not later than day 35.) The LST for **e** is $35 - 10 = 25$. Its EST is day 20, so activity **e** has five days of slack.

We now can see that the LOT for event 3 is day 21, the most restrictive (earliest) time required, so that no activity emanating from it will cause the network to be late. Table 8-3 shows the LST, EST, and slack for all activities, and the LOT, EOT, and slack for all events.

On occasion, the PM may negotiate an acceptable completion date for a project which allows for some slack in the entire network. If, in our example, an acceptable date was 50 working days after the project start, then the network would have a total of $50 - 43 = 7$ days of slack. This is the latest occurrence time minus the earliest occurrence time for the ending node, 7, of the network.

Uncertainty of Project Completion Time

When discussing project completion dates with senior management, the PM should try to determine the probability that a project will be completed by the suggested deadline—or find the completion time associated with a predetermined level of risk. With the information in Table 8-2, this is not difficult.

If we assume that the activities are statistically independent of each other, then the variance of a set of activities is equal to the sum of the variances of the individual activities comprising the set. Those who have taken a course in statistics will recall that the variance of a population is a measure of the population's dispersion

Table 8-3 Times and Slacks for Network
in Figure 8-15

Event	LOT	EOT	Slack
1	0	0	0
2	20	20	0
3	21	20	1
4	14	10	4
5	25	24	1
6	35	35	0
7	43	43	0
Activity	**LST**	**EST**	**Slack**
a	0	0	0
b	1	0	1
c	4	0	4
d	20	20	0
e	25	20	5
f	29	20	9
g	21	20	1
h	14	10	4
i	25	24	1
j	35	35	0

and is equal to the square of the population's standard deviation. The variances in which we are interested are the variances of the activities on the critical path.

The critical path of our example includes activities **a, d,** and **j**. From Table 8-2 we find that the variances of these activities are 4, 25, and 4, respectively; and the variance for the critical path is the sum of these numbers, 33 days. Assume, as above, that the PM has promised to complete the project in 50 days. What are the chances of meeting that deadline? We find the answer by calculating Z, where

$$Z = (D - \mu)/\sqrt{\sigma_\mu^2}$$

and

D = the desired project completion time

μ = the critical time of the project, the sum of the TEs for activities on the critical path

σ_μ^2 = the variance of the critical path, the sum of the variances of activities on the critical path

Z = the number of standard deviations of a normal distribution (the *standard normal deviate*)

Z, as calculated above, can be used to find the probability of completing the project on time.

Using the numbers in our example, D = 50, μ = 43, and σ_μ^2 = 33 (the square root of σ_μ^2 is 5.745), we have

$$Z = (50 - 43)/5.745$$
$$= 1.22 \text{ standard deviations}$$

Table 8-4   Cumulative (Single Tail) Probabilities of the Normal Probability Distribution (Areas under the Normal Curve from $-\infty$ to Z)

z	00	.01	.02	.03	.04	.05	.06	.07	.08	.09
.0	.5000	.5040	.5080	.5120	.5160	.5199	.5239	.5279	.5319	.5359
.1	.5398	.5438	.5478	.5517	.5557	.5596	.5636	.5675	.5714	.5753
.2	.5793	.5832	.5871	.5910	.5948	.5987	.6026	.6064	.6103	.6141
.3	.6179	.6217	.6255	.6293	.6331	.6368	.6406	.6443	.6480	.6517
.4	.6554	.6591	.6628	.6664	.6700	.6736	.6772	.6808	.6844	.6879
.5	.6915	.6950	.6985	.7019	.7054	.7088	.7123	.7157	.7190	.7224
.6	.7257	.7291	.7324	.7357	.7389	.7422	.7454	.7486	.7517	.7549
.7	.7580	.7611	.7642	.7673	.7704	.7734	.7764	.7794	.7823	.7852
.8	.7881	.7910	.7939	.7967	.7995	.8023	.8051	.8078	.8106	.8133
.9	.8159	.8186	.8212	.8238	.8264	.8289	.8315	.8340	.8365	.8389
1.0	.8413	.8438	.8461	.8485	.8508	.8531	.8554	.8577	.8599	.8621
1.1	.8643	.8665	.8686	.8708	.8729	.8749	.8770	.8790	.8810	.8880
1.2	.8849	.8869	.8888	.8907	.8925	.8944	.8962	.8980	.8997	.9015
1.3	.9032	.9049	.9066	.9082	.9099	.9115	.9131	.9147	.9162	.9177
1.4	.9192	.9207	.9222	.9236	.9251	.9265	.9279	.9292	.9306	.9319
1.5	.9332	.9345	.9357	.9370	.9382	.9394	.9406	.9418	.9429	.9441
1.6	.9452	.9463	.9474	.9484	.9495	.9505	.9515	.9525	.9535	.9545
1.7	.9554	.9564	.9573	.9582	.9591	.9599	.9608	.9616	.9625	.9633
1.8	.9641	.9649	.9656	.9664	.9671	.9678	.9686	.9693	.9699	.9706
1.9	.9713	.9719	.9726	.9732	.9738	.9744	.9750	.9756	.9761	.9767
2.0	.9772	.9778	.9783	.9788	.9793	.9798	.9803	.9808	.9812	.9817
2.1	.9821	.9826	.9830	.9834	.9838	.9842	.9846	.9850	.9854	.9857
2.2	.9861	.9864	.9868	.9871	.9875	.9878	.9881	.9884	.9887	.9890
2.3	.9893	.9896	.9898	.9901	.9904	.9906	.9909	.9911	.9913	.9916
2.4	.9918	.9920	.9932	.9925	.9927	.9929	.9931	.9932	.9934	.9936
2.5	.9938	.9940	.9941	.9943	.9945	.9946	.9948	.9949	.9951	.9952
2.6	.9953	.9955	.9956	.9957	.9959	.9960	.9961	.9962	.9963	.9964
2.7	.9965	.9966	.9967	.9968	.9969	.9970	.9971	.9972	.9973	.9974
2.8	.9974	.9975	.9976	.9977	.9977	.9978	.9979	.9979	.9980	.9981
2.9	.9981	.9982	.9982	.9983	.9984	.9984	.9985	.9985	.9986	.9986
3.0	.9987	.9987	.9987	.9988	.9988	.9989	.9989	.9989	.9990	.9990
3.1	.9990	.9991	.9991	.9991	.9992	.9992	.9992	.9992	.9993	.9993
3.2	.9993	.9993	.9994	.9994	.9994	.9994	.9994	.9995	.9995	.9995
3.3	.9995	.9995	.9995	.9996	.9996	.9996	.9996	.9996	.9996	.9997
3.4	.9997	.9997	.9997	.9997	.9997	.9997	.9997	.9997	.9997	.9998

We turn now to Table 8-4, which shows the probabilities associated with various levels of Z. (Table 8-4 also appears as Appendix C. It is shown here for the reader's convenience.) We go down the left column until we find Z = 1.2, and then across to column .02 to find Z = 1.22. The probability value of Z = 1.22 shown in the table is .8888, which is the likelihood that we will complete the critical path of our sample project within 50 days of the time it is started. Figure 8-16 shows the resulting probability distribution of the project completion times.*

---

*Our use of the normal distribution is allowed by the Central Limit Theorem which attests to the fact that the sum of independent activity times is normally distributed if the number of activities is large.

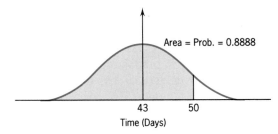

Figure 8-16: Probability distribution of project completion times.

We can work the problem backward, too. What deadline is consistent with a .95 probability of on-time completion? First, we go to Table 8-4 and look through the table until we find .95. The Z value associated with .95 is 1.645. (The values in the table are not strictly linear, so our interpolation is only approximate.) We know that μ is 43 days, and that $\sqrt{\sigma_\mu^2}$ is 5.745. Solving the equation for D, we have

$$D = \mu + 5.745(1.645)$$
$$= 43 + 9.45$$
$$= 52.45 \text{ days}$$

Thus, there is a 95 percent chance of finishing the project by 52.45 days.

Note that as D approaches μ, Z gets smaller, approaching zero. Table 8-4 shows that for Z = 0, the chance of on-time completion is 50–50. The managerial implications are all too clear. If the PM wants a reasonable chance of meeting a project deadline, there must be some slack in the project schedule. When preparing a project budget, it is quite proper to include some allowance for contingencies. The same principle holds for preparing a project schedule. The allowance for contingencies in a schedule is network slack, and the wise PM will insist on some.

Finally, to illustrate an interesting point, let's examine a noncritical path, activities **b-g-i**. The variance of this path (from Figure 8-15) is $0 + 0 + 28.4 = 28.4$, which is slightly less than the variance of the critical path. The path time is 42 days. The numerator of the fraction $(D - \mu)/\sqrt{\sigma_\mu^2}$ is larger, and in this case the denominator is smaller. Therefore, Z will be larger, and the probability of this path delaying project completion is less than for the critical path. But consider the noncritical path **c-h-i** with a time of $10 + 11 + 18 = 39$ days, and a total variance of 37.8. (Remember, we are trying to find the probability that this noncritical path with its higher variance but shorter completion time will make us late, given that the critical path is 43 days.)

$$Z = (50 - 39)/6.15$$
$$Z = 1.79$$

The result is that we have a 96 percent chance for this noncritical path to allow the project to be on time.

If the desired time for the network equaled the critical time, 43 days, we have seen that the critical path has a 50–50 chance of being late. What are the chances that the noncritical path **c-h-i,** will make the project late? D is now 43 days, so we have

$$Z = \frac{(43 - 39)}{6.15}$$
$$= .65$$

$Z = .65$ is associated with a probability of .74 of being on time, or $1 - .74 = .26$ of being late.

Assuming that these two paths (**a-d-j** and **c-h-i**) are independent, the probability that *both* paths will be completed on time is the product of the individual probabilities, $(.50)(.74) = .37$, which is considerably less than the 50–50 we thought the chances were. (If the paths are not independent, the calculations become more complicated.) Therefore, it is a good idea to consider noncritical paths that have activities with large variances and/or path times that are close to critical in duration (i.e., those with little slack).

Simulation is an obvious way to check the nature and impacts of interactions between probabilistic paths in a network. While this used to be difficult and time consuming, software has now been developed which simplifies matters greatly. Two excellent software packages have been developed which link to widely available spreadsheets: Crystal Ball® which runs as a part of Excell®, and At Risk® which runs as a part of Lotus 1-2-3®. Both allow easy simulation of network interactions.

Toward Realistic Time Estimates

The calculations of expected network times, and the uncertainty associated with those time estimates performed in the preceding sections are based, as we noted, on estimating optimistic and pessimistic times at the .99 level. That is, *a* is estimated such that the actual time required for an activity will be *a* or higher 99 percent of the time and will be *b* or lower 99 percent of the time. We then noted, parenthetically, that no project managers of our acquaintance are comfortable making estimates at that level of precision.

Fortunately, in practice it is not necessary to make estimates at the one-in-a-hundred level. Unless the underlying distribution is very asymmetric, no great error is introduced in finding TE if the pessimistic and optimistic estimates are made at the 95 percent, or even at the 90 percent levels; that is to say, only once in 20 times (or ten times for the 90 percent level) will the actual activity time be greater than or less than the pessimistic or optimistic estimates, respectively. The formula for calculating the variance of an activity, however, must be modified.

Recall that the calculation of variance is based on the assumption that the standard deviation of a beta distribution is approximately one-sixth of its range. Another way of putting this assumption is that *a* and *b* are estimated at the -3σ and $+3\sigma$ limits respectively—roughly at the 99+ percent levels. Let the 95 percent estimates be represented by a' and b' and the 90 percent estimates by a'' and b''. If we use a 95 or 90 percent estimation level, we are actually moving both *a* and *b* in from the distribution's tails so that the range will no longer represent $\pm 3\sigma$. See Figure 8-17.

It is simple to correct the calculation of variance for this error. Consider the 95 percent estimates. Referring to Table 8-4 we can find the Z associated with .95 of the area under the curve from a' to ∞. For .95, Z is approximately -1.65. (Of course, this applies to the normal distribution rather than to the beta distribution, but this huristic appears to work quite well in practice.) Similarly, $Z = 1.65$ for the area under the curve from $-\infty$ to b'.

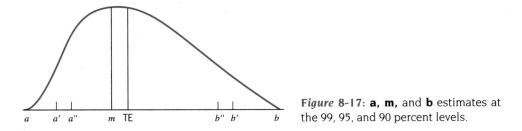

Figure 8-17: **a, m,** and **b** estimates at the 99, 95, and 90 percent levels.

The range between b' and a' represents $2(1.65)\sigma = 3.3\sigma$, rather than the 6σ used in the traditional estimation of the variance. Therefore when estimating a' and b' at the 95 percent level, we should change the variance calculation formula to read

$$\sigma^2 = ((b' - a')/3.3)^2$$

For estimations at the 90 percent level (a'' and b'' in Figure 8-17), Z is approximately 1.3 and the variance calculation becomes

$$\sigma^2 = ((b'' - a'')/2.6)^2$$

In order to verify that this modification of the traditional estimator for the variance of a beta distribution gave good estimates of the true variance, we ran a series of trials using Statistical Analysis Systems (SAS) PROC IML for beta distributions of different shapes and estimated a and b at the 95 and 90 percent levels. We then compared these estimates of a and b with the true variance of the distribution and found the differences to be quite small, consistently under five percent.

An alternate method for approximating the mean and variance of a beta distribution when a and b are estimated at the 95 percent level is given in the last section of Appendix E. For the full exposition of the method, see reference 5 of Appendix E.

Another Lotus 1-2-3® File

Just as we did in Chapter 7 on budgeting, we can construct a Lotus 1-2-3® template to do the calculations for finding the expected times, variances, and standard deviations associated with a series of three-time estimates for PERT/CPM networks. Figure 8-18 shows the file itself and Figure 8-19 shows the formulas used. Remember that the formula for calculation of variance must be modified according to the previous section unless a and b are estimated at the 99 + percent levels.

Most of the widely used project management software will not accept three-time estimates or do the necessary calculations to use such estimates, but a large majority of such software packages will routinely exchange information with Lotus 1-2-3,® Excel,® and similar spreadsheet software. It is therefore quite simple to enter the three-time estimates into a Lotus 1-2-3® file and enter the expected activity times, TEs, into a project management scheduling package where they can be used as if they were deterministic times in finding a project's critical path and time. Calculations of the probability of completing a project on or before some elapsed time can easily be done by hand.

	A	B	C	D	E	F	G
1	This is a template for three-time PERT schedule estimates						
2							
3	a = optimistic time estimate						
4	b = pessimistic time estimate						
5	m = typical (modal) time estimate						
6							
7	Activity	a	m	b	TE	Variance	Std. Dev.
8							
9	a	5	6	8	6.17	0.250	0.500
10	b	4	7	8	6.67	0.444	0.667
11	c	6	8	12	8.33	1.000	1.000
12	d	7	7	7	7.00	0.000	0.000
13	e	6	7	8	7.00	0.111	0.333
14	f	4	5	12	6.00	1.778	1.333
15	g	4	6	9	6.17	0.694	0.833
16							

Figure 8-18: A spreadsheet template for PERT schedules.

▶ 8.3 GANTT CHARTS

One of the oldest and still one of the most useful methods of presenting schedule information is the Gantt chart, developed around 1917 by Henry L. Gantt, a pioneer in the field of scientific management. The Gantt chart shows planned and actual progress for a number of tasks displayed against a horizontal time scale. It is a particularly effective and easy-to-read method of indicating the actual current status for each of a set of tasks compared to the planned progress for each item of the set. As a result, the Gantt chart can be helpful in expediting, sequencing, and reallocating resources among tasks, as well as in the valuable but mundane job of keeping track of how things are going. In addition, the charts usually contain a number of special symbols to designate or highlight items of special concern to the situation being charted.

	A	B	C	D	E	F	G
1							
2							
3	Activity	a	m	b	TE	Variance*	Std. Dev.
4							
5	a	5	6	8	=(B5+(4*C5)+D5)/6	=(((D5−B5)/6)^2)	=F5^0.5
6	b	4	7	8	=(B6+(4*C6)+D6)/6	=(((D6-B6)/6)^2)	=F6^0.5
7	c	6	8	12	=(B7+(4*C7)+D7)/6	=(((D7-B7)/6)^2)	=F7^0.5
8	d	7	7	7	=(B8+(4*C8)+D8)/6	=(((D8-B8)/6)^2)	=F8^0.5
9	e	6	7	8	=(B9+(4*C9)+D9)/6	=(((D9-B9)/6)^2)	=F9^0.5
10	f	4	5	12	=(B10+(4*C10)+D10)/6	=(((D10-B10)/6)^2)	=F10^0.5
11	g	4	6	9	=(B11+(4*C11)+D11/6	=(((D11-B11)/6)^2)	=F11^0.5
12							

*Adjust variance formula for level of precision (99+, 95, or 90).

Figure 8-19: Template formulas for PERT spreadsheet.

There are several advantages to the use of Gantt charts. First, even though they may contain a great deal of information, they are easily understood. While they do require frequent updating (as does any scheduling/control device), they are easy to maintain *as long as task requirements are not changed or major alterations of the schedule are not made.* Gantt charts provide a clear picture of the current state of a project.

Another significant advantage of Gantt charts is that they are easy to construct. While they may be constructed without first drawing a PERT diagram, there is a close relationship between the PERT/CPM network and the Gantt chart. We use the example in the previous section to illustrate this relationship and, at the same time, demonstrate how to construct such a chart.

First, the PERT/CPM network of Figure 8-15 is redrawn so that the lengths of each arc are in proportion to the respective task times. In essence, we redraw the network along a horizontal time scale. This modified network is shown in Figure 8-20. The heavy line, **a-d-j** is the critical path, and the horizontal dashed line segments indicate slack times. The vertical dashed line segments are dummy activities (as between events 3 and 4), or merely connectors (as elsewhere in the drawing). Note that to transform the network in this manner requires that we "explode" single nodes into multiple nodes when multiple activities emanate from the single node. In this modified network, each activity must originate from an individual node, although several activities still can have a common destination node.

The nodes of Figure 8-15 are placed at their EOTs (the early start times for ensuing activities), and the slack is shown *after* the activity duration. (We have used an arrowhead to separate the activity duration from its slack.) To draw the modified diagram only requires that the nodes be placed at their EOTs listed on the PERT/CPM network and the activity durations drawn out from them as solid lines. Precedence is shown by connecting the duration lines with dashed line segments, showing each specific connection to the appropriate nodes.

The Gantt chart can be drawn directly from the modified PERT/CPM diagram. A list is made of all activities required to complete the project. Activities are usually listed in alphanumeric order—which is most often the order in which they were

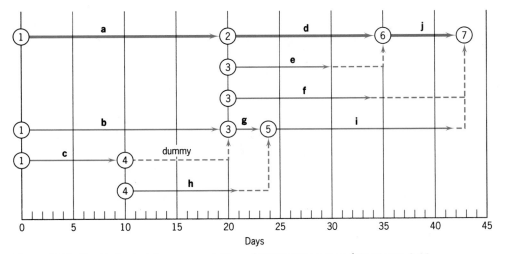

Figure 8-20: Gantt chart style representation of PERT/CPM network in Figure 8-15.

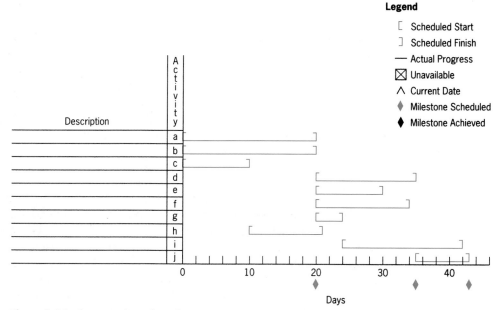

Figure 8-21: Gantt project chart from Figure 8-15.

listed in the action plan or whatever source document was originally used. As Figure 8-21 shows, activity times are superimposed on a linear calendar, much as in Figure 8-20. Precedence relationships are preserved by not allowing the activity line or bar for a successor activity to begin until its predecessors are complete. Scheduled activity times are drawn as light lines or hollow bars. A heavy line or a filled-in bar indicates actual progress. Color is sometimes used for easy visibility. The PM's ability to customize Gantt charts is limited only by the PM's imagination and the software being used.

Figure 8-21 transforms the modified PERT/CPM network into a Gantt chart. Note that three milestones are shown as diamonds below the baseline. These are the events that occur along the critical path. While there is no particular rule mandating the use of critical path events as project milestones, it is common for them to be chosen in this way. (If there are many critical events, some may be ignored and only the particularly noteworthy critical events are selected as milestones.) We can also see that while all precedence relationships must be preserved, it is not possible to distinguish easily their technical relationships simply by observing the chart itself. For example, activities **a** and **b** both have a duration of 20 days. Activities **d, e, f,** and **g** begin on the twentieth day. Using the Gantt chart, however, it is not possible to determine which, **a** or **b,** is predecessor to which of **d, e, f,** or **g.** If a single activity is completed at some time, it is reasonable to assume that other activities starting at that point are dependent on the first one; but if two or more activities end at the same time, the relationships between them and subsequent activities are unclear. Gantt charts, therefore, are generally inadequate for showing technological dependencies.*

*Actually, precedence relationships can be shown on Gantt charts, but the charts become cluttered and very difficult to read.

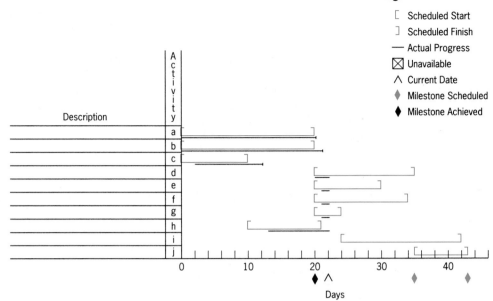

Figure 8-22: Gantt chart showing progress of project on Day 22.

Figure 8-22 pictures the project as it might appear on its twenty-second day. Actual progress is shown as a heavy line added just below the scheduled progress line. Activity **a** started and finished on time, while **b** started on time but was completed one day late. Activity **c** was begun two days late and finished three days late, which delayed the start of **h**. (In this case, the predecessor relationship of **c** to **h** is clear.) Activity **d** is under way and was started on time. Activities **e, f,** and **g** were all started one day late. Even with some activities starting late, nothing has happened to delay the actual critical path. While it is not clear from the Gantt chart, the network (Figure 8-15) shows that the delay in **b** means that the **b-g-i** path has gone critical.

This example illustrates both the strength and weakness of the Gantt chart. Its major strength is that it is easy to read. All popular project management software will prepare Gantt charts, and most have some options available for customization. Gantt charts are often mounted on the wall of the project office and updated frequently. Anyone interested in the project can see the state of progress easily, even if the interested party knows little about the actual nature of the work being done. The weakness of the Gantt chart is simply that one needs the PERT/CPM network (or the WBS) to interpret what appears on the Gantt chart beyond a cursory level—or to plan how to compensate for lateness.

Another advantage is the ease of construction of the chart. In our example, we converted the PERT/CPM network in Figure 8-15 to a Gantt chart by modifying the network as in Figure 8-20. In practice, this intermediate stage is not necessary, and one can easily go from network to chart in a single step. On balance, ease of construction and ease of use have made the Gantt chart the most popular method for displaying a project schedule [25]. Nonetheless, a PERT/CPM network is still needed for the PM to exercise control over the schedule.

In many ways, the Gantt chart is similar to the project master schedule described in Chapter 5. Both are types of bar charts and are used similarly. The major difference is that the Gantt chart is intended to monitor the detailed progress of work, whereas the master schedule contains only major tasks and is oriented toward overall project management rather than precise control of the detailed aspects of the project.

While PERT/CPM and Gantt charts are both scheduling techniques, they are not merely different ways of achieving the same ends; they are complementary rather than competitive. The budget can be directly related to the Gantt chart, as shown in Figure 8-23.

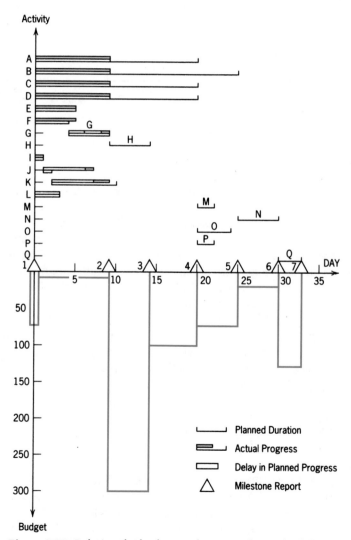

Figure 8-23: Relating the budget to the Gantt chart schedule.

Project Management in Practice
Hosting the Annual Project Management Institute Symposium

Planning and implementing a national conference for a society that will draw about 1000 attendees is a major project. The tasks involved in hosting such an event are considerable and involve selecting a program committee, choosing a theme, contacting exhibitors, making local arrangements, planning the program, and on and on.

Pittsburgh was selected as host city/chapter for the 1992 Project Management Institute's annual September seminar/symposium. The objectives for the event were three: (1) to deliver a high-quality, value-added program that would be useful and last for years to come, (2) to offer a social and guest program that would reflect well on the host city, and (3) to meet strict financial criteria. The first task after selecting the city and hotel facilities was to put together the project team and chairperson. This included managers in charge of each of the tracks, the social program, the local arrangements, and all the other details as shown in the organization

Source: PMI Staff, "Catch the Spirit. . .at Pittsburgh," PM *Network*, May 1992.

Pittsburgh—host city for the PMI Annual Symposium.

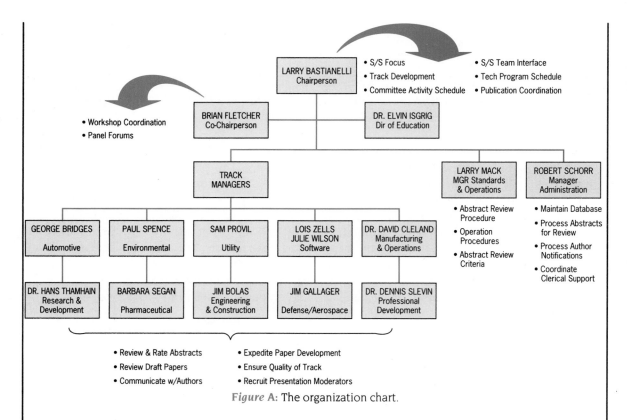

Figure A: The organization chart.

WORK BREAKDOWN STRUCTURE AND TASKS

S/S Project Management
Recruit Project Team
Establish Organizational
  Procedures
Establish CAO Support Levels
  and Budget
Issue Reports to VP-Tech and
  Board of Directors
Develop S/S Goals and
  Objectives
Assemble and Issue Post-S/S
  Report

Technical Program
Develop S/S Theme
Strategize Tracks and SIGs
Recruit Technical Program Team
Develop Selection Process
  Procedures
Interface with Education
  Committee on Workshops
Plan and Issue Call for
  Papers/Panel Discussions

Recruit Invited Papers/Panel
  Discussions
Recruit Moderators
Develop and Issue Master
  Schedule for Presentations
Select Printer
Plan and Issue Abstract Books
  and Proceedings
Organize Awards for Speakers'
  Breakfasts
Identify Audio/Visual
  Requirements
Develop and Issue Post-S/S
  Technical Report

Social Guest Program
Establish Objectives
Identify Available Activities
Analyze Cost-Benefit
Identify Recommendations
Complete Contracts
Recruit Staff

Speakers
Identify Candidates and Related
  Benefits and Costs
Make Recommendations and
  Obtain Approval
Complete Contracts
Maintain Periodic Contact
Host Speakers

Publicity/Promotion
Theme Establishment and
  Approval
Logo Development and
  Approval
Video Production
Promotional Materials
  Identification and Approval
Advertising: PMI, Public and
  Trade Media Releases
Regional Newsletter Articles

Finance
Initiate Code of Accounts

Figure B: The work breakdown structure.

360

Develop Procedures of Financial Operation

Develop Independent Auditing Procedure

Initiate Separate Banking Account

Develop Cash Flow Estimates/ Projections

Develop and Issue Standard Reports

Interact with CAO on Account Reconciliation

Develop and Issue Post-S/S Financial Report

Corporate Sponsorship

Establish Participation Philosophy

Target Prime Corporations

Solicit Participation Recognition

Facilities Vendor/CAO Support

Contract with Host and Backup Hotels

Staff Recruiting

(Details to be Identified and Scheduled with PMI Executive Director and Events Manager)

Figure B: (continued)

ACTIVITY DESCRIPTION — timeline 1988 | 1989 | 1990 | 1991 | 1992 | 1993 (months)

S/S PROJECT MANAGEMENT
- RECRUIT PROJECT TEAM
- ESTABLISH ORGANIZATIONAL PROCEDURES
- ESTABLISH C.A.D. SUPPORT LEVELS AND BUDGET
- ISSUE REPORTS TO V.P. TECH & BOARD OF DIRECTORS
- DEVELOP S/S GOALS & OBJECTIVES
- 1992 SEMINAR/SYMPOSIUM
- ASSEMBLE & ISSUE POST S/S REPORT

TECHNICAL PROGRAM
- DEVELOP S/S THEME
- RECRUIT TECHNICAL PROGRAM
- STRATEGIZE TRACKS & SPECIAL INTEREST GROUPS
- DEVELOP SELECTION PROCESS PROCEDURES
- INTERFACE W/EDUCATION COMMITTEE ON WORKSHOPS
- PLAN & ISSUE CALL FOR PAPERS/PANEL DISCUSSIONS
- RECRUIT "INVITED" PAPERS/PANEL DISCUSSIONS
- SELECT PRINTER
- RECRUIT MODERATORS
- PLAN & ISSUE ABSTRACT BOOKS & PROCEEDINGS
- DEVELOP & ISSUE MASTER SCHEDULE OF PRESENTATIONS
- ORGANIZE AWARDS FOR SPEAKER'S BREAKFAST
- IDENTIFY AUDIO/VISUAL REQUIREMENTS
- DEVELOP & ISSUE POST S/S TECHNICAL REPORT

FINANCE
- DEVELOP CASH FLOW ESTIMATES/PROJECTIONS
- DEVELOP PROCEDURES OF FINANCIAL OPERATION
- INITIATE CODE OF ACCOUNTS
- INITIATE SEPARATE BANKING ACCOUNT
- DEVELOP INDEPENDENT AUDITING PROCEDURE
- DEVELOP & ISSUE STANDARD REPORTS
- INTERACT WITH PMI CAD ON ACCOUNT RECONCILIATION
- DEVELOP & ISSUE POST S/S FINANCIAL REPORT

CORPORATE SPONSORSHIP
- ESTABLISH PARTICIPATION PHILOSOPHY
- TARGET PRIME CORPORATION PHILOSOPHY
- SOLICITING PARTICIPATION
- RECOGNITION

FACILITIES/VENDOR/C.A.D. SUPPORT
- CONTRACT WITH HOST AND BACKUP HOTELS
- ESTABLISH OBJECTIVES
- IDENTIFY AVAILABLE ACTIVITIES
- STAFF RECRUITING
- IDENT & SCHED DETAILS W/EX DIR & EVENTS MGR.
- RECRUIT STAFF

FACILITIES/VENDOR/C.A.D. SUPPORT
- ANALYZE COST-BENEFIT: IDENTIFY RECOMMENDATIONS
- COMPLETE CONTRACTS

SOCIAL/GUEST PROGRAM
- IDENTIFY CANDIDATES & RELATED BENEFITS & COSTS
- MAKE RECOMMENDATIONS AND OBTAIN APPROVAL
- COMPLETE CONTRACTS
- MAINTAIN PERIODIC CONTACT
- HOST SPEAKERS

SPEAKERS
- THEME ESTABLISHMENT AND APPROVAL
- LOGO DEVELOPMENT AND APPROVAL
- ADVERTISING PMI PUBLIC & TRADE MEDIA RELEASES
- VIDEO PRODUCTION
- PROMOTIONAL MATERIALS IDENTIFICATION & APPROVAL
- REGIONAL NEWSLETTER ARTICLES

Planning Unit: month	PITTSBURGH '92 PROJECT TEAM
	1992 SEMINAR/SYMPOSIUM PROJECT PLAN

FALL '92 REPORT TO PMI

Date	Revisions	Checked	Approved

Primavera Systems, Inc.
Project Start: 1SEPT88
Project Finish: 31MAR93

Data Date: 1FEB92
Plot Date: 20MAR92

Figure C: Gantt chart.

structure in Figure A. The project team was organized using a functional approach. Pittsburgh PMI Chapter officers had most of the primary responsibilities, with members from nine other chapters assisting in other duties.

Next was the development of the work breakdown structure, shown in Figure B, and the Gantt chart of activity schedules, shown in Figure C. As seen in the Gantt chart, scheduling all the work for a major conference such as this is an overwhelming effort. In the WBS, the major task was the development of the technical program. For PMI '92, the technical program offered 22 workshops composed of 70 technical papers, special panel discussions, and case studies. The technical tracks included engineering and construction, pharmaceuticals, utilities, software, automotive,

R&D, defense, education, and manufacturing. The workshops included sessions on preparing for the PMI certification examinations, learning about Taguchi concepts of statistical quality control, and future practice in project management. All of these also required careful scheduling.

The vendor program included exhibits by dozens of vendors and a large number of showcase sessions for in-depth demonstrations of their wares. The social program included a golf tournament, numerous social activities to meet with colleagues, tours of Pittsburgh's attractions, and a wide variety of entertainment opportunities.

All in all, a conference such as PMI's is as difficult a project as many firms face in their competitive markets.

▶ 8.4 EXTENSIONS AND APPLICATIONS

There have been a large number of extensions to the basic ideas of PERT and CPM. These extensions are often oriented toward handling rather specific problem situations through additional program flexibility, computerizing some of the specific problems, fine-tuning some of the concepts for special environments, and combining various management approaches with the PERT/CPM concepts—for example, the TREND approach discussed in Chapter 5.

Another interesting extension deals with the case when it is very difficult to estimate activity times because no one has experience with the activity, or because the activity is ill-defined. In this case, the concepts of fuzzy-set theory are applied [34]. There are also opportunities for using simulation on stochastic PERT networks in order to make estimates of project finish time, as well as to examine the likelihood that noncritical paths have sufficient variance to become critical [51].

In this section we discuss some of these extensions and look at the utility of network scheduling models in general. However, we delay our coverage of extensions aimed primarily at resource allocation and formal applications of CPM until Chapter 9.

Precedence Diagramming

One shortcoming of the PERT/CPM network method is that it does not allow for leads and lags between two activities without greatly increasing the number of subactivities to account for this. In construction projects, in particular, it is extremely common for the following restrictions to occur.

- Activity B must not start before activity A has been in progress for at least two days (Figure 8-24a).

- Activity A must be complete at least three days before activity B can be finished (Figure 8-24*b*).

- Activity B cannot begin before four days after the completion of A (Figure 8-24*c*).

- Activity B cannot be completed before eight days from the start of A (Figure 8-24*d*).

Precedence diagramming is an AON network method that allows for these leads and lags within the network. Node designations are illustrated in Figure 8-24*e*. Because of the increased flexibility regarding required lead and lag times, it must be

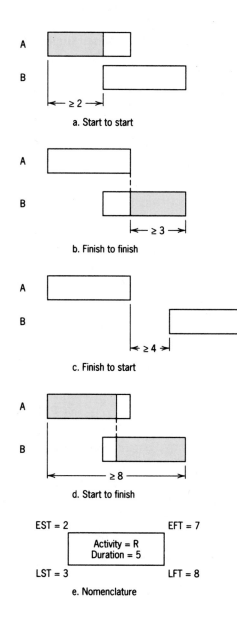

a. Start to start

b. Finish to finish

c. Finish to start

d. Start to finish

e. Nomenclature

Figure 8-24: Precedence diagramming conventions.

known whether each activity can be *split* or not. Splitting allows easier satisfaction of the lead and lag restrictions. If splitting is not allowed, the project may be significantly delayed.

Some anomalies tend to occur in precedence diagramming that are not encountered in PERT/CPM. For example, because of the lead and lag requirements, activities may appear to have slack when they really do not. Also, the critical path of the network will frequently go backward through an activity, with the result that increasing the activity time may actually decrease the project completion time. Such an activity is called *reverse critical*. This happens when the critical path enters the completion of an activity through a finish constraint (Figure 8-24*b* or *d*), continues backward through the activity, and leaves through a start constraint (Figure 8-24*a* or *d*).

Network node times are calculated in a manner similar to PERT/CPM times. Because of the lead and lag restrictions, it is often helpful to lay out a Gantt chart to see what is actually happening.

Precedence diagramming seems to be gaining in popularity. The richer set of precedence relationships it allows is pertinent for a variety of projects, particularly construction projects. For more details on this technique, see [1, 12 (Chapters 6 and 17), and 37]. Most current project management software will allow leads, lags, delays, and other constraints in the context of their standard AON network and Gantt chart programs.

GERT

The Graphical Evaluation and Review Technique (GERT) is a network model developed to deal with more complex modeling situations than can be handled by PERT/CPM. GERT combines signal flowgraph theory, probabilistic networks, PERT/CPM, and decision trees all in a single framework. Its components consist of *logical nodes* (defined below) and directed arcs (or branches) with *two* parameters; the probability that a given arc is taken (or "realized") and the distribution function describing the time required by the activity. Evaluation of a GERT network yields the probability of each node being realized and the elapsed time between all nodes.

At this point, it may be useful to compare GERT and PERT/CPM in order to focus on what is different about GERT.

GERT	**PERT/CPM**
Branching from a node is probabilistic.	Branching from a node is deterministic.
Various possible probability distributions for time estimates.	Only the beta distribution for time estimates.
Flexibility in node realization.	No flexibility in node realization.
Looping back to earlier events is acceptable.	Looping back is not allowed.
Difficult to use as a control tool.	Easy to use for control.
Arcs may represent time, cost, reliability, etc.	Arcs represent time only.

While there are computer programs that optimize PERT/CPM problems, GERT and its various enhancements are computer simulations. Most of the programs (and the enhancements) are the result of work conducted by Pritsker [44]. His modeling package called Q-GERT simulates queues, or waiting lines, in the network. (There are other extensions of PERT that have some features similar to GERT and Q-GERT—VERT, for example—but GERT seems to be the most widely used extension.)

The steps employed in using GERT are these:

1. Convert the qualitative description of the project action plan into a network, just as in the use of PERT/CPM.

2. Collect the necessary data to describe the arcs of the network, focusing not only on the specific activity being modeled, but also on such characteristics of the activity as the likelihood it will be realized, the chance it might fail, any alternative activities that exist, and the like.

3. Determine the *equivalent function* of the network.

4. Convert the equivalent function of the network into the following two performance measures:

The probability that specific nodes are realized.

The "moment generating function" of the arc times.

5. Analyze the results and make inferences about the system.

It is not appropriate to deal here with the complex solution techniques employed for GERT networks. They make use of topology equations, equivalent functions, moment generating functions, and extensive calculation. The interested reader is urged to consult the papers of Pritsker and others [1, 44, 50] for formal descriptions of the methods involved in formulating and solving GERT networks. Instead, we will describe how to construct a GERT network of a simple situation.

The list of common GERT symbols, together with a few examples, is given in Figure 8-25. This figure describes the left, or input side of the nodes first, and then the right-hand output side next. All combinations of input and output symbols are feasible, as shown in the examples.

Now let us describe a manufacturing project situation developed by Pritsker and portray it through the GERT approach. This situation concerns the initiation of a new production process developed by manufacturing engineering for an electronic component. The resulting GERT model could just as well describe an R & D project, a government project, or a Girl Scout project.

Sample Problem, Modeled with GERT

A part is manufactured on a production line in four hours. Following manufacture, parts are inspected. There is a 25 percent failure rate, and failed parts must be reworked. Inspection time is a stochastic variable, exponentially distributed, with a mean of 1 hour. Rework takes 3 hours, and 30 percent of the reworked parts fail the next inspection and must be scrapped. Parts that pass their original inspection or

Symbol	Name	Explanation
		INPUT
K	Exclusive—or	Any branch leading into the node causes the node to be realized, but only one branch can occur.
<	Inclusive—or	Any branch causes the node to be realized and at the time of the earliest branch.
(	And	The node is realized only after ALL branches have occurred.
		OUTPUT
)	Deterministic	All branches out must occur if the node is realized.
>	Probabilistic	Only one of the branches may occur if the node is realized.
		EXAMPLES
D⟨		Beginning node with branches that must occur.
 a b ◁		Ending node that occurs whenever **a** or **b** occurs.
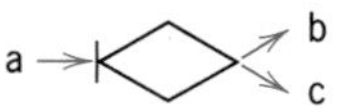 a →K⟩ b c		Intermediate node that occurs if **a** occurs with either **b** or **c** following.
 a b c ⟩ d e		Intermediate node that occurs when all **a, b,** and **c** occur with either **d** or **e** following.

Figure 8-25: GERT symbols.

pass inspection after rework are sent to finishing, a process that requires 10 hours 60 percent of the time and 14 hours otherwise. A final inspection rejects 5 percent of the finished parts, which are then scrapped.

We can now model this situation as a GERT network so that it can be solved for the expected percentage of good parts and the expected time required to produce a good part. This GERT network is illustrated in Figure 8-26.

Activity **a** represents the output of the four-hour manufacturing process. The outputs enter an inspection from which 75 percent are passed, **c,** and 25 percent

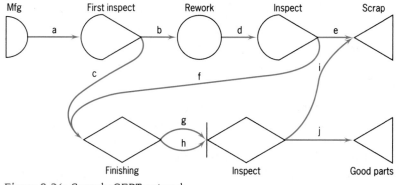

Figure 8-26: Sample GERT network.

fail, **b.** The latter go to rework, with flow **d** emerging. Another inspection takes place—**e** (30 percent of 25 percent = 7.5%) flows to scrap, while the successfully reworked parts (70 percent of 25 percent = 17.5 percent), represented by **f,** go with the other good parts, **c,** to the finishing process. Sixty percent of this input requires 10 hours of work, **g,** and the remainder (40 percent) needs 14 hours, **h.** The final inspection process discards 5 percent of the output, **i** which goes to scrap, and the remainder (which is 87.875 percent of the original input) is sent to "good parts," **j.**

The time for an "average" part to proceed through the network can be found in much the same way as we calculated the output. The result of the entire analysis is therefore considerably richer than the simpler PERT/CPM. It should, however, be obvious that the input information requirements for GERT are more extensive and the computational requirements are far more extensive than for PERT/CPM, particularly for large networks. As always, the PM should adopt the simplest scheduling technique consistent with the needs of the project.

Other Methods

Two straightforward methods for project scheduling that do not use networks or Gantt charts are employed by some agencies of the U.S. government. The Goddard Space Flight Center develops its project schedules in three phases. Phase I is advanced schedule planning, where the basic project schedule is developed directly from the work breakdown structure. Phase I lists all major elements of the project. This is used for presenting the proposed project to NASA and to the Congress and its many committees.

Phase II consists of the preparation of the operational schedule. This is the equivalent of the project master schedule. Phase III is schedule administration. In this last phase, the project is monitored and the master schedule is updated through the use of biweekly reports. Any necessary corrections and alterations to the project master schedule are made as a result of this process.

The Department of General Services uses a project scheduling system that provides planning, scheduling, and control in three distinct but closely related stages. Activity scheduling is the initial stage. At this point the planner attempts to develop optimum timing for the start and completion of all tasks associated with the project. Labor-hour and progress scheduling is carried out in the second stage. This identifies the labor (and other resources) required to initiate project activities on time and to sustain the necessary rate of progress to keep the project on schedule. Progress reporting takes place in the final stage. In this third stage, the project is monitored and a more or less constant stream of reports are filed so that appropriate action can be taken to keep the project on schedule. The information reported to senior management shows the project status relative to activity milestones and actual progress relative to planned progress. The value of the progress achieved as well as the estimated value of progress remaining is used to calculate (forecast) the labor-hours required to complete the remaining work on schedule.

Note that these methods parallel the basic concept of the project action plan with its specific steps to be taken, its estimate of resource requirements, times, and precedences, and most important, with each step in the higher-level plans broken down into lower-level action plans.

A Mild Caveat

Many researchers, most recently Richard Schonberger [49], have exposed some interesting anomalies in PERT/CPM networks which show that deterministic times are optimistically biased. In essence, the effect comes about when one or more paths in the network have times that are close to the critical path time. If the noncritical path is delayed and becomes critical, it may extend the average completion time for the network, as we noted earlier. Schonberger develops a simple example to illustrate this finding. His critique extends to the three-time estimate method, which allows for activity time variance on a path-by-path analysis, but does not consider delays caused by path interaction. (Remember that the ability to calculate path variance as the sum of the variances of individual activities is based on the assumption of independence between activities—and paths.)

Several possible conclusions may be drawn from Schonberger's insight:

- Projects will probably be late—relative to the deterministic critical path.
- Network simulation is probably not worth the added expense.
- Deterministic time estimates should be used in place of the three time estimates.
- The network developed from these deterministic time estimates should be subjectively reevaluated for any path interaction factors that would tend to make the project late.
- Critical or near-critical activities should be intensively managed, the usual practice of project managers.

While it is helpful to be aware of these issues, we are not entirely in agreement with Schonberger's conclusions. The costs of simulation techniques are decreasing rapidly, and there are several inexpensive simulation computer programs readily available. GERT is an example of a simulation-based technique that is quite valuable *if the required information base and computational power are readily available*. GERT and other computer programs come in sufficient variety to have a great many applications in project management.

A stronger area of disagreement is our belief that three time estimates are far more informative to the PM than deterministic time estimates. The degree of activity variability is a clear indicator of the need for adaptive planning. In any case, for most project managers, the use of deterministic times does not mean that they estimate the variance of each and every activity to be zero, but rather that they assume that optimistic and pessimistic times are symmetrically distributed around the most likely times and cancel out. The distinction between a deterministic time and an average time is easily ignored by the unsophisticated. Further, this error is compounded because it leads to the false assumption that the expected time approach is the same as the deterministic approach. Clearly, the critical times would be the same in either case, which leads the unwary to the error.

As we illustrated earlier with Lotus 1-2-3®, readily available and inexpensive computer software makes the additional computational cost of three time estimates a trivial matter. Perhaps more serious is the advice to increase the calculated network time by subjective evaluation of the effects of path interaction. This will extend the network time by some arbitrary amount, usually in the form of network slack, a time-consuming but nonresource-consuming "activity" added to the end of the project, which automatically adds duration to the critical path. (In Chapter 9 we will define a similar activity as a "pseudo-activity".)

This practice makes the operation of *Parkinson's Law* a clear and present danger. The work done on project elements is almost certain to "expand to fill the additional time," as Schonberger himself and many others have observed. We favor a different way of handling the problem. If three time estimates are used, and if various completion dates with their associated probabilities are calculated, and, finally, if the PM and senior management can agree on a mutually acceptable completion date for the project, the PM can be held accountable for on-time delivery. If an additional allowance is needed for path interdependence, some mutually acceptable network slack can be added. It should not, however, make the PM any less accountable for project performance.

Using These Tools

We have heard differing opinions on the value of each of the tools we have described, including many of the computerized project management information systems (PMISs). We have been told, "No one uses PERT/CPM/Precedence Diagramming," "No one uses three-time PERT," and "No one uses___computer package." But we have first-hand knowledge of PERT users, of CPM users, of precedence diagram users. We know PMs who collect and use three time PERT. For example, refer to the boxed Apartment Complex example (Figure 8-27).

Figure 8-27 is a portion of a 48-step action plan for the syndication of an apartment complex. Note that several of the steps are obvious composites of multistep action plans designed for a lower level (e.g., see 1-4). Figure 8-28 is an AON network of Figure 8-27. The firm also has a Gantt chart version of the network that is used for tracking each project. Figure 8-27 also contains three time estimates of the "calendar" time used for each step (in days) and of the "resource" time used for each step (in hours). The time estimate 2(10) is read, "2 days, 10 labor-hours." The duplicate data are useful for scheduling work loads.

We are reluctant to give advice about which tools to use. If the PM indulges in a bit of experimentation with the major systems, their relative advantages and disadvantages *in a given application* will become evident. We have noted Bubshait and Selen's work [9] on the use of project management techniques, and Digman and Green [14] have developed an interesting and useful framework for evaluating the various planning and control techniques. The PM should opt for the simplest method sufficient to the needs of the project and its parent firm. If a computerized PMIS is used, the problem is avoided. Most require inputs of specific form and produce their own unique outputs. Again, a thorough demonstration of the PMIS should be a prerequisite to purchase or lease. In the end, these tools are intended to help the PM manage the project. The PM should select those that seem most useful—and most comfortable. The PMISs will be discussed in more detail in Chapter 10.

Task	a (days,hours)	m	b	TE (days)	σ^2 (days)	TE (hr)	σ^2 (hr)
1. Product package received by Secy. in Real Estate (R.E.) Dept.	n/a	(.3)	(.4)				
2. Secy. checks for duplicates, and forwards all packages in Atlanta region (but not addressed to R.E. staff member) to Atl. via fast mail. Atl. office sends copy of submittal log to L.A. office on weekly basis.	n/a	(.2)	(.3)				
3. Secy, date stamps, logs, checks for duplication, makes new file, checks for contact source, adds to card file all new packages. Sends criteria letter to new source. Send duplication letter. Forwards package to Admin. Asst. (AA).	(.7)	(.7)	(.9)				
4. AA reviews package, completes Property Summary Form, forwards to L.A. Reg. Acquisit. Director (RAD) officer or to R.E. staff member to whom package is addressed.	(.5)	(.5)	(.7)				
Total 1-4	1(1.7)	1(1.7)	3(2.3)	1.3	0.11	1.8	0.01
5. Person to whom package forwarded determines action. (May refer to other or retain for further review.) "Passes" sent to Secy. for files. "Possibles" retained by RAD for further review.	1(.5)	1(.5)	1(1)	1.0		.58	0.01
6. RAD gets add'l data as needed, gets demographics and comparables. Rough numbers run. Looks for the "opportunities." If viable, continue.	4(3)	5(3)	3(2.3)	5.5	0.69	3.83	0.69
• • •	• • •	• • •	• • •		• • •		
45. Prop. Mgt./Fin. prepares for closing and take-over. At closing, prorations of taxes, rents, service contracts.	3(4)	5(8)	10(24)	5.5	1.36	10.0	11.11
46. PM final inspect. On-site at close.	1(4)	1(8)	2(12)	1.2	0.03	8.0	1.78
47. Legal closes.	2(8)	2(14)	4(25)	2.3	0.11	14.83	8.03
48. Legal issues Post Closing Memorandum.	2(5)	5(8)	10(10)	5.3	1.78	7.83	0.69

Figure 8-27: Action plan for syndication of an apartment complex.

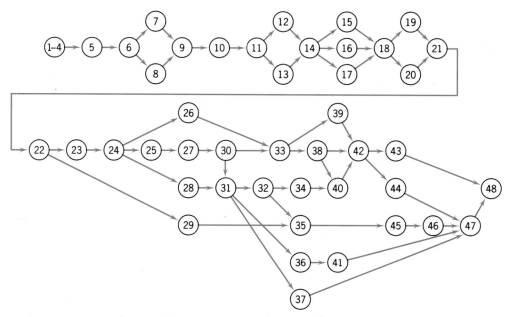

Figure 8-28: Apartment complex network.

▶ SUMMARY

In this chapter the scheduling aspect of project implementation was addressed. Following a description of the benefits of using a network for planning and controlling a project, the PERT/CPM approach was described. Next, Gantt charts were described and their relation to the PERT/CPM diagram was illustrated. Finally, precedence diagramming, GERT, and a few other extensions were discussed.

Specific points covered in the chapter were these:

- Scheduling is particularly important to projects because of complex coordination problems.

- The network approach to scheduling offers a number of specific advantages of special value for projects.

- Critical project tasks typically constitute fewer than 10 percent of all the project tasks.

- Although research indicates technological performance is not significantly affected by the use of PERT/CPM, there did seem to be a significantly lower probability of cost and schedule overruns.

- Network techniques can adopt either an activity-on-node or activity-on-arc framework without significantly altering the analysis.

- Networks are usually constructed from left to right, indicating activity precedence and event times as the network is constructed. Through use of the network, critical activities and events are identified, early and late activity start times are found, available slacks for each activity are determined, and probabilities of project completion by various times are calculated.

- Gantt charts, a monitoring technique, are closely related to network diagrams, but are more easily understood and provide a clearer picture of the current state of the project. However, while offering some advantages, they also have some drawbacks, such as not clearly indicating task precedence and dependencies.

- GERT is one of the more common extensions of PERT/CPM and allows:
  Probabilistic branching from nodes,
  Various probability distributions for the activity times,
  Looping in the network,

Representation of project elements other than time, such as cost or reliability.

In the next chapter we investigate the scheduling problem further when multiple projects require a set of common resources to be shared. Again, a number of techniques are useful for resource allocation and activity expediting under such circumstances.

▶ GLOSSARY

Activity—A specific project task that requires resources and time to complete.

Activity-On-Arc (Node)—The two ways of illustrating a network: placing the activities on the arcs or on the nodes.

Arc—The line connecting two nodes.

Crash—In CPM, an activity can be conducted at a normal pace or at an expedited pace, known as *crashed*, at a greater cost.

Critical—An activity or event that, if delayed, will delay project completion.

Event—An end state for one or more activities that occurs at a specific point in time.

Gantt Chart—A manner of illustrating multiple, time-based activities on a horizontal time scale.

Milestone—A clearly identifiable point in a project or set of activities that commonly denotes a reporting requirement or completion of a large or important set of activities.

Network—A combination of interrelated activities and events depicted with arcs and nodes.

Node—An intersection of two or more lines or arrows, commonly used for depicting an event or activity.

Path—A sequence of lines and nodes in a network.

Project Management Information System (PMIS)—The systems, activities, and data that allow information flow in a project, frequently computerized but not always.

Trade-off—The amount of one factor that must be sacrificed in order to achieve more or less of another factor.

▶ MATERIAL REVIEW QUESTIONS

1. Define *activity*, *event*, and *path* as used in network construction. What is a dummy activity?

2. What characteristic of the critical path times makes them critical?

3. What two factors are compared by Gantt charting? How does the Gantt chart differ in purpose from the project master schedule?

4. How is the GERT technique different from the PERT technique?

5. When is each scheduling technique appropriate to use?

6. What is the difference between activity-on-node and activity-on-arrow diagrams?

7. What does it mean to "crash" an event?

8. Briefly summarize how a network is drawn.

9. Define "late start time" and "early start time."

10. How is the critical path determined?

11. What is "slack"?

▶ CLASS DISCUSSION QUESTIONS

1. How do you think the network technique could be used to estimate costs for manufacturing?

2. What are some benefits of the network approach to project planning? What are some drawbacks?

3. What is your position on the conclusions in the Caveat section?

4. Why is PERT of significant value to the project manager?

5. How is uncertainty in project scheduling dealt with?

6. Are there any drawbacks to using GERT?

7. How are activity times estimated?

8. Should the critical path activities be managed differently from noncritical path activities? Explain.

▶ PROBLEMS

1. Given the following information, draw the PERT/CPM diagram:

Activity	Immediate Predecessor
1	—
2	—
3	1,4
4	2
5	2
6	3,5

2. Given the diagram below, find:
   (a) The critical path.
   (b) How long it will take to complete the project.

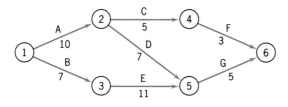

3. Given the following activities and precedences, draw a PERT/CPM diagram:

Activity	Immediate Predecessor
A	—
B	—
C	A
D	A,B
E	A,B
F	C
G	D,F
H	E,G

4. Given the following network:
   (a) What is the critical path?

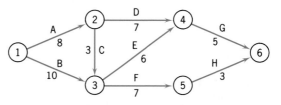

   (b) How long will it take to complete this project?
   (c) Can activity **B** be delayed without delaying the completion of the project? If so, how many days?

5. Given the estimated activity times below and the network in 4 above:

Activity	a	m	b
A	6	7	14
B	8	10	12
C	2	3	4
D	6	7	8
E	5	5.5	9
F	5	7	9
G	4	6	8
H	2.5	3	3.5

What is the probability that the project will be completed within:
   (a) 21 days?
   (b) 22 days?
   (c) 25 days?

6.

Activity*	a	m	b
AB	3	6	9

---

*The nomenclature AB means the activity *between* events A and B.

Activity*	a	m	b
AC	1	4	7
CB	0	3	6
CD	3	3	3
CE	2	2	8
BD	0	0	6
BE	2	5	8
DF	4	4	10
DE	1	1	1
EF	1	4	7

Find:

(a) the critical path;
(b) all event slacks;
(c) critical path to event D;
(d) probability of completion in 14 days;
(e) the effect if CD slips to 6 days; to 7 days; to 8 days.

7.

Activity*	TE
AB	1
AC	2
AD	3
DC	4
CB	3
DE	8
CF	2

Activity*	TE
BF	4
IJ	2
CE	6
EF	5
FG	10
FH	11
EH	1
GH	9
EJ	3
GI	8
HJ	6

(a) Draw the PERT diagram.
(b) Find the critical path.
(c) Find the completion time.

8. The Denver Iron & Steel Company is expanding its operations to include a new drive-in weigh station. The weigh station will be a heated/air-conditioned building with a large floor and small office. The large room will have the scales, a 15–foot counter, and several display cases for its equipment.

Before erection of the building, the project manager evaluated the project using PERT/CPM analysis. The activities with their corresponding times were recorded in Table A:

Table A

Times

#	Activity	Optimistic	Most Likely	Pessimistic	Preceding Tasks
1	Lay foundation	8	10	13	—
2	Dig hole for scale	5	6	8	—
3	Insert scale bases	13	15	21	2
4	Erect frame	10	12	14	1,3
5	Complete building	11	20	30	4
6	Insert scales	4	5	8	5
7	Insert display cases	2	3	4	5
8	Put in office equipment	4	6	10	7
9	Finishing touches	2	3	4	8,6

*See nomenclature note in Problem 6.

Using PERT/CPM analysis, find the critical path, the slack times, and the expected completion time.

9. The Dock B Shipbuilding Company received a contract from the government to build the prototype of a new U.S. Navy destroyer. The destroyer is to be nuclear-powered, include advanced weapon systems, and have a small crew. The Dock B Shipbuilding Company has assigned to the task a project manager who, in turn, has delegated minor subprojects to subordinate managers.

The project was evaluated using PERT/CPM analysis. Due to the extensive length of the project, many activities were combined: The following is the result.

Activity*	Time (months)
AB	3
BC	6
BD	2
BF	5
BE	4
CD	9
DG	20
FG	6
EH	11
EI	19
GJ	1
HK	3
IL	9
LM	12
KN	7
JO	4
MN	15
NP	13
OP	10

Find the critical path and expected completion date.

10. The following PERT chart was prepared at the beginning of a small construction project.

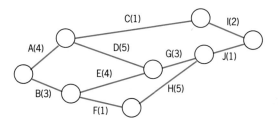

The duration, in days, follows the letter of each activity. What is the critical path? Which activities should be monitored most closely?

At the end of the first week of construction, it was noted that activity **A** was completed in 2.5 days, but activity **B** required 4.5 days. What impact does this have on the project? Are the same activities critical?

11. Given the following project, find the probability of completion by 17 weeks. By 24 weeks. By what date is management 90 percent sure completion will occur?

Times (weeks)

Activity	Optimistic	Most Likely	Pessimistic
1–2	5	11	11
1–3	10	10	10
1–4	2	5	8
2–6	1	7	13
3–6	4	4	10
3–7	4	7	10
3–5	2	2	2
4–5	0	6	6
5–7	2	8	14
6–7	1	4	7

---

*See nomenclature note in Problem 6.

If the firm can complete the project within 18 weeks it will receive a bonus of $10,000. But if the project delays beyond 22 weeks it must pay a penalty of $5000. If the firm can choose whether or not to bid on this project, what should its decision be if the project is only a breakeven one normally?

12. Given a project with the following information:

Activity	Standard Deviation	Critical?	Duration
a	2	yes	2
b	1		3
c	0	yes	4
d	3		2
e	1	yes	1
f	2		6
g	2	yes	4
h	0	yes	2

Find:

(a) The probability of completing this project in 12 weeks (or less).
(b) The probability of completing this project in 13 weeks (or less).
(c) The probability of completing this project in 16 weeks (or less).
(d) The number of weeks required to assure a 92.5 percent chance of completion.

13. Given a PERT network:

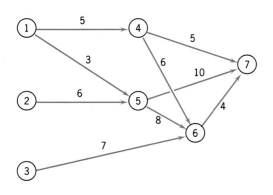

Note that three activities can start immediately. Find:

(a) The critical path.
(b) The earliest time to complete the project.
(c) The slack on activities **4-6**, **5-6**, and **4-7**.
(d) Draw the network on a Gantt chart.

14. The events of the project below are designated as 1, 2, and so on.

(a) Draw the PERT network and the Gantt chart.
(b) Find the critical path.
(c) Find the slacks on all the events and activities.

Activity	Prec. Evt.	Suc. Evt.	TE (weeks)	Prec. Activ.
a	1	2	3	none
b	1	3	6	none
c	1	4	8	none
d	2	5	7	a
e	3	5	5	b
f	4	5	10	c
g	4	6	4	c
h	5	7	5	d,e,f
i	6	7	6	g

15. Given the following PERT network (times are in weeks):

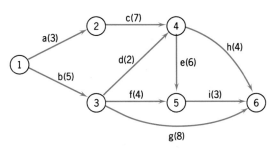

Determine:
(a) The EOT and LOT for each event.
(b) The slacks on all events and activities.
(c) The critical activities and path.

16. Given the schedule in Table B for a liability work package done as part of an accounting audit in a corporation, find:
(a) The critical path.
(b) The slack time on "process confirmations."
(c) The slack time on "test pension plan."
(d) The slack time on "verify debt restriction compliance."

Table B

Activity	Duration (days)	Preceding Activities
a. Obtain schedule of liabilities	3	none
b. Mail confirmation	15	a
c. Test pension plan	5	a
d. Vouch selected liabilities	60	a
e. Test accruals and amortization	6	d
f. Process confirmations	40	b
g. Reconcile interest expense to debt	10	c,e
h. Verify debt restriction compliance	7	f
i. Investigate debit balances	6	g
j. Review subsequent payments	12	h,i

17. In the project network shown in the figure below, the number alongside each activity designates the activity duration (TE) in weeks.

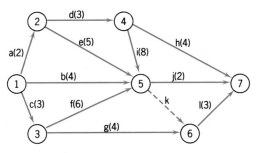

Determine:
(a) The EOT and LOT for each event.
(b) The earliest time that the project can be completed.

(c) The slack on all events and activities.
(d) The critical events and activities.
(e) The critical path.

18. Given the following information regarding a project:

Activity	TE (weeks)	Preceding Activities
a	3	none
b	1	none
c	3	a
d	4	a
e	4	b
f	5	b
g	2	c,e
h	3	f

(a) Draw the PERT network and the Gantt chart.
(b) What is the critical path?
(c) What will the scheduled (earliest completion) time for the entire project be?
(d) What is the critical path to event 4 (end of activities **c** and **e**)? What is the earliest time that this event can be reached?
(e) What is the effect on the project if activity **e** takes an extra week? Two extra weeks? Three extra weeks?

19. Construct a network for the project below and find its critical path.

Activity	TE (weeks)	Preceding Activities
a	3	none
b	5	a
c	3	a
d	1	c
e	3	b
f	4	b,d
g	2	c
h	3	g,f
i	1	e,h

20. Construct a network for the project:

Activity	TE (weeks)	Preceding Activities
a	3	none
b	5	none
c	14	a
d	5	a
e	4	b
f	7	b
g	8	d,e
h	5	g,f

(a) Draw the PERT network and the Gantt chart.
(b) Find the critical path.
(c) Assume activity **a** took five weeks. Replan the project.
(d) From where would you suggest transferring resources, and to what activities so that the original target date may be maintained?

21. Resolve part (d) of Problem 6 assuming the values of a and b are given at the 95 percent level. Repeat, assuming the values are given at the 90 percent level.

▶ INCIDENTS FOR DISCUSSION

Yankee Chair Company

The Yankee Chair Company was anxious to get a new model rocking chair onto the market. Past efforts to introduce new models had resulted in frustrating failures. Jim Ricks, president of Yankee Chair, was determined that it would not happen again with the newest model. He had no confidence in his current management team, so he hired Jan Dymore, a local consultant, to organize and manage this project. He assigned a Yankee Chair manager, Tom Gort, to work with Dymore to start developing some talent for project management within the company. Dymore decided to set up a PERT network and guided Gort through the process of listing activities, assigning precedence, and estimating completion times. She also explained the critical path concept to Gort, who by this time had a reasonable grasp of the project direction. At the first review session with Mr. Ricks, the PERT approach was accepted enthusiastically, but toward the end of the review Dymore made some critical remarks about the product design and was subsequently released from the project.

Ricks then asked Gort if he could carry on the PERT approach by himself. Gort jumped at the chance, but later in his office he began to question whether or not he really could use the PERT network effectively. Dymore had made a guess at what the critical path would be and how long the project would take, but she had also told Gort that several other calculations had to be made in order to calculate the exact time estimates for each activity and the variances of those activity times. Gort really did not understand the mathematics involved and certainly did not want to look bad in Ricks' eyes, so he decided to take Dymore's guess at the critical path and get the best possible estimates of those activity times. By concentrating his attention on the critical path activities and ignoring the variance issues, he figured he could bring the project in on time.

Questions: Will Gort's approach work? How much more of a gamble is Gort taking than any project manager normally takes? What should Gort watch out for?

Cincinnati Equipment Company

Cincinnati Equipment Company, which specializes in the manufacture of modern construction equipment, will be building a facility to house a new foundry. The company has selected a project manager and team to follow the project through to completion. The project team is very interested in selecting an appropriate scheduling technique for the project. The project man-ager has thus set the following guidelines for the selection process: simple; able to show durations of events, the flow of work, and the relative sequence of events; able to indicate planning and actual flow, which items may proceed at the same time, and how far they are from completion. The assistant project manager favors the Gantt chart, the finance representative likes PERT, and the construction supervisor prefers CPM.

Question: If you were the project manager, which method would you use, and why?

▶ PROJECT TEAM CONTINUING EXERCISE

The task for the project team is to formulate the schedule for the project from the work breakdown structure. Use optimistic, most likely, and pessimistic times for each activity; construct the PERT diagram; and conduct a full analysis of the data, including likelihoods of delay by certain amounts of time and 80, 90, and 99 percent likelihood of completion times. Identify the project's critical path, the critical path to each event, the slacks for each activity, and the earli-est and latest occurrence times. Show the schedule as an AON and an AOA network, as well as a Gantt chart with milestones. Graph the budget from Chapter 7 on the Gantt chart to illustrate cash flow needs. Comment on the applicability of one of the other network approaches such as GERT or precedence diagramming to your project. As the project progresses, update the charts at each milestone.

▶ BIBLIOGRAPHY

1. AL-HAMMED, A. and S. ASSAF. "A Survey of Cost Reduction Techniques Used by Construction Firms in Saudi Arabia." *American Association of Cost Engineers Transactions,* 1988.

2. ARCHIBALD, R. D., and R. L. VILLORIA. *Network Based Management Systems (PERT/CPM).* New York: Wiley, 1967.

3. AYERS, R. H., R. M. WALSH, and R. G. STAPLES. "Project Management by the Critical Path Method." *Research Management,* July 1970.

4. BAKER, B. N., and R. L. ERIS. *An Introduction to PERT-CPM.* Homewood, IL: Irwin, 1964.

5. BENNINGSON, L. A. TREND—*New Management Information from Networks.* Sandoz Co. Reprint, 1974.

6. BERKWITT, G. W. "Management Rediscovers CPM." *Dun's Review,* May 1971.

7. BLYSTONE, E. E., and R. G. ODUM. "A Case Study of CPM in a Manufacturing Situation." *Journal of Industrial Engineering,* Nov.–Dec. 1964.

8. BRENNAN, J. *Applications of Critical Path Techniques.* New York: Elsevier, 1968.

9. BUBSHAIT, K. A., and W. J. SELEN. "Project Characteristics That Influence The Implementation of Project Management Techniques: A Survey. "*Project Management Journal,* June 1992.

10. CLARK, C. G., D. G. MALCOM, J. H. ROSENBLOOM, and W. FAZAR. "Applications of a Technique for Research and Development Program Management." *Operations Research,* Sept.–Oct. 1959.

11. DAVIS, E. W. "Networks: Resource Allocation." *Industrial Engineering,* April 1974.

12. DEAN, B. V. *Project Management: Methods and Studies.* New York: Elsevier, 1985.

13. DECOSTER, D. T. "PERT/Cost—The Challenge." *Management Services,* May–June 1964

14. DIGMAN, L. A., and G. I. GREEN. "A Framework of Evaluating Network Planning and Control Techniques." *Research Management,* Jan. 1981.

15. EVARTS, H. E. *Introduction to PERT.* Boston: Allyn and Bacon, 1964.

16. GALLAGHER, C. "A Note on Pert Assumptions." *Management Science,* October 1987.

17. GIDO, J. *An Introduction to Project Planning*, 2nd ed. Industrial Press, 1986.

18. GOLFARB, N., and W. K. KAISER. *Gantt Charts and Statistical Quality Control*. New York: Hofstra University Press, 1964.

19. HOROWITZ, J. *Critical Path Scheduling: Management Control Through CPM and PERT*. Melbourne, FL: Krieger, 1980.

20. JENETT, E. "Experience with and Evaluation of Critical Path Methods." *Chemical Engineering*, Feb. 1969.

21 KARNS, L. A., and L. A. SWANSON. "The Effect of Activity Time Variance on Critical Path Scheduling." *Project Management Quarterly*, Dec. 1973.

22. KELLY, J. E., and M. R. WALKER. "Critical Path Planning and Scheduling." *Proceedings, Eastern Joint Computer Conference*, 1959.

23. KERZNER, H. *Project Management: A Systems Approach to Planning, Scheduling, and Controlling*, 2nd ed. New York: Van Nostrand Reinhold, 1989.

24. KIRKPATRICK, C. A., and R. C. LEVINE. *Planning and Control with PERT/CPM*. New York: McGraw-Hill, 1966.

25. LEVY, F. K., G. L. THOMPSON, and J. D. WEIST. "The ABC's of the Critical Path Method." *Harvard Business Review*, Sept–Oct. 1963.

26. LIBERATORE, M. J., and G. J. TITUS. "The Practice of Management Science in R & D Project Management." *Management Science*, Aug. 1983.

27. LITTLEFIELD, T. K., JR., and P. H. RANDOLPH. "An Answer to Sasieni's Question on PERT Times." *Management Science*, Oct. 1987.

28. LOCKYER, K. G. *An Introduction to Critical Path Analysis*. Woodstock, NY: Beckman, 1969.

29. LOWE, C. W. *Critical Path Analysis by Bar Chart*. London: Business Books, 1966.

30. MACCRIMMON, K. R., and C. R. RYAVEC. "An Analytical Study of PERT Assumptions." *Operations Research*, Jan–Feb. 1964.

31. MALLON, J. C. "Verifying Cost and Schedule During Design." *Project Management Journal*, Mar. 1992.

32. MARQUIS, D. G. "A Project Team Plus PERT= Success. Or Does It?" *Innovation*, 1969.

33. MARTINO, R. L. *Project Management and Control*, Vol. I. New York: American Management Association, 1964.

34. MCCAHON, C. S. "Using PERT as an Approximation of Fuzzy Project–Network Analysis." *IEEE Transactions on Engineering Management*, May 1993.

35. MEYER, W. C., J. B. RITTER, and L. R. SHAFFER. *The Critical Path Method*. New York: McGraw-Hill, 1965.

36. MILLS, N. L. "The Development of a University Sports Complex: A Project Management Application." *Computers and Industrial Engineering*, 17:149–153, 1989.

37. MODER, J. J., C. R. PHILLIPS, and E. W. DAVIS. *Project Management with CPM, PERT, and Precedence Diagramming*, 3rd ed. New York: Van Nostrand Reinhold, 1983.

38. MORRIS, L. N. *Critical Path, Construction and Analysis*. Oxford, G.B: Pergamon Press, 1967.

39. MUTH, J. F., and G. L. THOMPSON. *Industrial Scheduling*. Englewood Cliffs, NJ: Prentice Hall, 1963.

40. NAIK, B. *Project Management: Scheduling and Monitoring by PERT/CPM*. Advent Books, 1984.

41. ORCZYK, J. J., and L. CHANG. "Parametric Regression Model for Project Scheduling." *Project Management Journal*, Dec. 1991.

42. PAZER, H. H., and L. A. SWANSON. *PERTsim, Text and Simulation*. International Textbook, 1969.

43. POWERS, J. R. "A Structured Approach to Schedule Development and Use." *Project Management Journal*, Nov. 1988.

44. PRITSKER, A. A. B. "GERT Networks." *The Production Engineer*, Oct. 1968.

45. RAITHE, A. W., ed. *Gantt on Management*. New York: American Management Association, 1961.

46. SAITOW, A. R. "CSPC: Reporting Project Progress to the Top." *Harvard Business Review*, Jan–Feb. 1969.

47. SANTELL, M. P., J. R. JUNG, and J. C. WARNER. "Optimization in Project Coordination Scheduling through Application of Taguchi Methods." *Project Management Journal*, Sept. 1992.

48. SASIENI, M. W. "A Note on PERT Times." *Management Science*, Dec. 1986.

49. SCHONBERGER, R. J. "Why Projects Are Always Late: A Rationale Based on Manual Simulation of a PERT/CPM Network." *Interfaces*, Oct. 1981.

50. SILVERBERG, E. C. "Predicting Project Completion." *Research-Technology Management*, May–June 1991.

51. TOELLE, R. A., and J. WITHERSPOON. "From 'Managing the Critical Path' to 'Managing Critical Activities.'" *Project Management Journal*, December 1990.

52. TURBAN, E. "The Line of Balance—A Management by Exception Tool." *Journal of Industrial Engineering,* Sept. 1968.

53. VAZSONYI, A. "L'Histoire de Grandeur et la Decadence de la Methode PERT." *Management Science,* April 1979.

54. WEIST, J. D. "A Heuristic Model for Scheduling Large Projects with Limited Resources." *Management Science,* Feb. 1967.

55. WEIST, J. D., and F. K. LEVY. *A Management Guide to PERT/CPM,* 2nd ed. Englewood Cliffs, NJ: Prentice Hall, 1977.

56. WOODGATE, H. S. *Planning by Network.* Woodstock, NY: Beckman 1977.

CASE

THE SHARON CONSTRUCTION CORPORATION
E. Turban and Jack R. Meredith

The Sharon Construction Corporation has been awarded a contract for the construction of a 20,000-seat stadium. The construction must start by February 15 and be completed within one year. A penalty clause of $15,000 per week of delay beyond February 15 of next year is written into the contract.

Jim Brown, the president of the company, called a planning meeting. In the meeting he expressed great satisfaction at obtaining the contract and revealed that the company could net as much as $300,000 on the project. He was confident that the project could be completed on time with an allowance made for the usual delays anticipated in such a large project.

Bonnie Green, the director of personnel, agreed that in a normal year only slight delays might develop due to a shortage of labor. However, she reminded the president that for such a large project, the company would have to use unionized employees and that the construction industry labor agreements were to expire on November 30. Past experience indicated a fifty–fifty chance of a strike.

Jim Brown agreed that a strike might cause a problem. Unfortunately, there was no way to change the contract. He inquired about the prospective length of a strike. Bonnie figured that such a strike would last either eight weeks (70 percent chance) or possibly 12 weeks (30 percent chance).

Jim was not too pleased with these prospects. However, before he had a chance to discuss contingency plans he was interrupted by Jack White, the vice-president for engineering. Jack commented that an extremely cold December had been predicted. This factor had not been taken into consideration during earlier estimates since previous forecasts called for milder weather. Concrete pouring in a cold December would require in one out of every three cases (depending on the temperature) special heating that cost $500 per week.

This additional information did not please Jim at all. The chances for delay were mounting. And an overhead expense of $500 per week would be incurred in case of any delay.

The technical details of the project are given in the appendix to this case.

The management team was asked to consider alternatives for coping with the situation. At the end of the week five proposals were submitted.

1. Expedite the pouring of seat gallery supports. This would cost $20,000 and cut the duration of the activity to six weeks.

2. The same as proposal 1, but in addition, put a double shift on the filling of the field. A cost of $10,000 would result in a five-week time reduction.

3. The roof is very important since it precedes several activities. The use of three shifts and some overtime could cut six weeks off the roofing at an additional cost of only $9000.

4. Do nothing special until December 1. Then, if December is indeed cold, defer the pouring of the seat gallery supports until the cold wave breaks, schedule permitting, and heat whenever necessary. If a strike occurs, wait until it is over (no other choice) and then expedite *all* remaining activities. In that case, the duration of any activity

could be cut but to no less than one third of its normal duration. The additional cost per activity for any week which is cut would be $3000.

5. Do not take any special action; that is, hope and pray that no strike and no cold December occur (no cost).

Appendix: Technical Details of the Stadium

The stadium is an indoor structure with a seating capacity of 20,000. The project begins with clearing the site, an activity that lasts eight weeks. Once the site is clear, the work can start simultaneously on the structure itself and on the field.

The work in the field involves subsurface drainage which lasts eight weeks, followed by filling for the playing field and track. Only with the completion of the filling (14 weeks) can the installation of the artifi-cial playing turf take place, an activity that consumes 12 weeks.

The work on the structure itself starts with excavation followed by the pouring of concrete footings. Each of these activities takes four weeks. Next comes the pouring of supports for seat galleries (12 weeks), followed by erecting pre-cast galleries (13 weeks). The seats can then be poured (4 weeks) and are ready for painting. However, the painting (3 weeks) cannot begin until the dressing rooms are completed (4 weeks). The dressing rooms can be completed only after the roof is erected (8 weeks). The roof must be erected on a steel structure which takes 4 weeks to install. This activity can start only after the concrete footings are poured.

Once the roof is erected, work can start simultaneously on the lights (5 weeks) and on the scoreboard and other facilities (4 weeks). Assume there are 28 days in February and that February 15 falls on a Monday.

▶ QUESTIONS

1. Analyze the five proposals and make recommendations based on expected costs.

2. What other basis might be used to make a decision besides expected costs? What then might the decision be?

3. What other factors might enter into the decision such as behavioral, organizational, and political?

4. What decision would you make as the president?

▶ This article addresses the issue of what to do if the project schedule exceeds the required due date. The author recommends two major approaches: compressing activities along the critical path(s) and building contingencies into the schedule. Compression methods include ways to reduce task durations as well as techniques to alter precedence relationships. In the area of contingency building, we would add that every PERT schedule has only a certain probability of completion by any required due date, whether the expected completion time is before or after the required due date, and thus the addition of contingencies is simply an attempt to improve that probability.

READING

"ON TIME" PROJECT COMPLETION— MANAGING THE CRITICAL PATH
David H. Hamburger

Completing a project "on time" (meeting a specified end date), is often attempted or achieved at the expense of the project's specification and/or budget. Stringent deadlines are frequently established by a client, project sponsor or management for sound business reasons with little or no regard for the reality of attainment; and the project manager is then charged with making someone's unrealistic wish come true. The Space Shuttle disaster is a tragic reminder of what can happen—lives were lost, the project delayed for several years and NASA's image damaged, possibly beyond repair.

So what is a project manager to do? If an unrealistic end date is accepted and a schedule is developed by arbitrarily making the necessary project tasks "fit" the predetermined time constraint, the plan is likely to be ineffective. The project will either be late, or if completed within the allotted time, specified performance and/or quality are not likely to be achieved. If the time and specification requirements are met, they will probably be achieved at a premium cost. The concept of making a schedule fit a predefined time frame, without knowledge of where the problems specifically occur, offers little or no chance for project success.

To maximize the probability of success, the project planner must first establish a realistic expected completion date—defined by the project's Critical Path—with no regard for an arbitrary end date; and then selectively compress this required sequence of tasks by judicious resource management and prudent risk taking. To ensure "on time" project completion, the plan must also accommodate the uncertainties of task execution. This is achieved by compressing the Critical Path to meet an earlier end date than specified—effectively establishing a schedule contingency. In this way, the "shotgun" approach of forcing the tasks to fit a given time constraint is avoided; and additional expenditures are incurred, or risks taken, only where they will do the most good. Should this process fail to provide a realistic plan for meeting the specified end date, management or the client must be advised.

The Natural Inclination

Once a required project completion date has been defined, the natural inclination is to schedule the work from back to front, fitting the tasks within the time limit. At one time or another each of us has used this technique as a "logical" procedure for developing a schedule that "works" (fitting the constraint). In so doing we may have established irrational precedence relationships or allocated arbitrary, unrealistic task durations to make the tasks fit.

Using faulty precedence relationships will result in a schedule which makes little or no sense. Work execution will not be controllable, as actual task performance cannot be made to follow an illogical sequence. The true Critical Path may not be properly identified and the project manager's attention will be drawn to less critical issues, inhibiting control of the critical tasks and timely project completion. Arbitrary division of the available time between the required tasks is also dangerous. Apportioning time at the discretion of the planner, without considering the needs of the individuals responsible for execution, will probably result in one of two undesirable outcomes. If the task is completed within the allocated time, the quality of the effort will likely suffer; meeting a schedule does not guarantee acceptable results. If the functional staff does its job properly, they are likely to exceed the understated time allocation and the desired project end date will slip.

The Proper Approach

Instead of planning from back to front—arbitrarily selecting precedence relationships and task durations—to make the project schedule fit the defined time constraint, disregard the required completion date and lay out a network schedule based on the responsible functional managers' needs. A workable schedule, acceptable to the functional staff, will result; but it will not satisfy the project sponsor or management, as the required completion date will probably be missed. However, this ideal schedule *will* have compression potential for meeting a reasonable completion target.

This length of the ideal network schedule's Critical Path defines the minimum expected project completion time and the difference between the required and expected completion times represents the minimum amount of schedule compression needed to ensure success. Since the Critical Path contains the specific activities which cause the project to take longer than desired, schedule compression should be selectively applied to those activities, and only to the extent that a reduction in project duration results. Excessive compression will shift the Critical Path to a secondary path. Once this happens, redirect compression accordingly.

Consider the following in compressing the Critical Path:

- Selectively reduce task durations or alter precedence relationships.
- Evaluate the incremental cost and performance risk of each potential compression step, then maximize the schedule benefit for the least cost, at the lowest possible risk.
- Where possible, compress the earlier tasks. As a general rule, the early project tasks are easier and less costly to compress than the later

ones. The professionals responsible for the project's initial effort can be easily motivated, once they are convinced that a realistic urgency exists. Later tasks either have greater labor requirements or employ trades or skills which command premium pay for overtime.

• Favor early compression over late compression to save the reduction potential of the final tasks for later use, as unexpected execution problems are likely to cause a schedule slip. In addition, the potential savings available in the early tasks will be lost, if not taken before the tasks are completed.

• Do not be deceived into believing that early compression may not be necessary because time may somehow be gained during project execution. Lucky breaks just don't happen. If one does occur, it will likely result from a planned effort and not from a stroke of good fortune.

Compressing the Critical Path

Every potential opportunity should be considered in the schedule revision process to get the maximum benefit at minimum incremental cost, while incurring minimum additional risk. Evaluate each task to determine its potential for duration reduction and consider altering each precedence relationship; then select the most promising, cost effective, combination.

Reducing Task Duration The most common and most frequently misunderstood task reduction technique uses additional resources to shorten the required period of performance. In some cases staff increases result in a proportional activity duration reduction at no additional cost; but this is not always the case, as many functions do not fit the linear model, and those situations which do are only effective over a limited range. (For example; a brick wall requiring ten days for a single bricklayer to erect can probably be erected in five days by two bricklayers, but it is extremely unlikely that ten bricklayers can accomplish the task in a day.)

Unfortunately, adding resources does not always work [1]. Situations exist in which increasing staff size actually results in a longer performance period. Programmers are aware of this fact, as the efficiency of a programming staff can actually be reduced by adding resources, unless staff communications are

also enhanced. When adding resources to reduce performance time, consider the availability and quality of the extra personnel. With an effective network schedule as the basis for compression, the required personnel may be found assigned to less critical tasks and reassignment is possible.

Overtime is also used to reduce activity duration. This can be effective if the overtime is limited to short intervals. Employee burnout, personnel inefficiencies, and lost time during the workweek for personal activities normally accomplished during overtime hours are serious factors which reduce overtime's long term efficacy. Using selective overtime for specific task duration reductions will be far more effective than a long term program of schedule overtime, or the panic crash that frequently occurs near the end of a project, when it is finally realized that the "fitted" schedule is not working.

The cost of overtime is also a factor which will vary with the type of resource and the accounting system employed to account for premium labor expenses. Many salaried employees are not paid overtime, in which case no additional cost will be incurred if they work the extra hours. Other employees are paid a premium which must be considered. The premium (half time to double time) represents compression cost. Some organizations treat overtime premium as an overhead expense which is included in the average hourly rate applied to all labor. In this case no additional expense results when overtime is actually used.

Shortcuts also support schedule compression, but undue risk or the creation of a downstream problem must be avoided. For example, piping design time may be reduced by eliminating the requirement for piping details, if field installation in accordance with a piping schematic is opted. However, the added installation expense and the increased risk of errors and rework must be considered in making this shortcut decision. Typical shortcuts include:

• Selecting an alternate technology, method or production process.

• Selecting material or components based on delivery rather than specification or cost.

• Reducing the level of detail included in a design.

• Reducing equipment or product test time.

• Sole source equipment, material, or services procurement.

- Restricting a bidder's proposal preparation time.
- Waiving contractual approval, review or inspection requirements.

The "Make or Buy" decision can be used to select the option offering best delivery. However, consideration must also be given the decision's effect on product performance and quality, disclosure of proprietary information, potential creation of a competitor, other inhouse work, and the organization's image or reputation, in addition to assessing schedule reduction cost.

Altering Defined Precedence Relationships Not all project activity precedence relationships are fixed and some sequences may be changed to shorten a Critical Path. Using this technique requires an understanding of precedence relationships, the extent to which they can be altered and the cost and/or risk associated with making such changes. Precedence relationships fall into three categories:

- Natural Precedences
- Environmental Precedences
- Preferential Precedences

Natural precedence relationships represent unalterable constraints of nature which control the sequence of work execution. Since they are dictated by the nature of the work involved, nothing can be done to change them. The project manager must either find a creative alternative process or accept their inevitability. The foundation construction sequence—Excavate, Set Forms, Place Rebar, Pour Concrete—results from the natural precedence relationships of these tasks. No other sequence will work, nor can two tasks be performed in parallel. Imagine the futility of an attempt to place rebar after the concrete has been poured, or the mess that would result if the two tasks were performed concurrently.

The unalterable characteristic of a natural precedence relationship precludes effective schedule modification. Any attempt to change one will prove to be fruitless. Fortunately, the other precedence types can be altered—either at incremental cost or by incurring added risk—to obtain a desired schedule compression. Therefore, the project manager intent on shortening a schedule should concentrate on modifying the originally established Environmental and Preferential Precedence relationships.

Environmental precedence relationships represent constraints unique to a particular working environment or organization. If only one crane were available at a high rise building construction site and two independent tasks requiring a crane had to be performed (e.g., siding installation and placing mechnical equipment on the roof), the tasks would have to be done in series. The sequence may not be inportant because of task independence, but the resource constraint would necessitate series execution. If a second crane were available, the two independent tasks could be executed in parallel. Therefore, altering the environment by acquiring additional resources (renting a crane) can reduce project duration if the action allows parallel execution of two serial Critical Path tasks. Environmental constraints can be altered by:

- reassigning personnel and/or other resources to parallel independent tasks which are scheduled in series because of a resource constraint (no additional cost),
- using temporary personnel (at a premium expense and a potential risk of less efficient performance), or
- renting or purchasing additional equipment to meet a specific need.

Preferential precedence relationships represent the planner's work sequence choice, which generally reflects the safest, most conservative approach to task execution. However, conservatism can be sacrificed and an alternate, higher risk, work sequence selected to shorten a schedule.

In the example shown in Figure 1a; material required for fabrication of a newly designed component is normally purchased after design drawings have been checked. However, material procurement can be started before checking to reduce project duration. As seen in Figure 1b, the schedule can be shortened by the length of the checking period. The risk of purchasing the wrong material is assumed to gain schedule compression.

If checking discloses a material selection error, the time gained will probably be lost and an additional cost may be incurred. The extent of the loss will depend on disposition of the material in question, the point in time the error is identified, and the speed of problem rectification. An effective risk decision requires knowledge of the potential risk, the desired benefit (reward), the probabilities of success and failure, and the remedy to be implemented should the risk become reality. Given this information the project

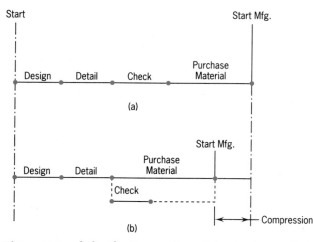

Figure 1(a) and (b): Altering a preferential precedence relationship.

manager can judge whether the potential benefit is worth the risk.

Altering a preference to improve a schedule is a common planning practice, as functions which are best performed serially are occasionally performed in parallel or overlapped. The risk associated with many of these choices is frequently low. Preparation of detail drawings is often started before a design has been completed, or a test may be run before test procedure release. In other cases, greater risk may be assumed to obtain the desired compression. Making a commitment to a vendor or subcontractor, before drawings and specifications have been completed, can have severe financial consequences if extensive changes become necessary. Yet, this is frequently done on "fast track" projects where completion time is critical.

Although altering Preferential Precedence relationships is a common practice, project managers rarely recognize the extent of the risk being assumed to gain a time reduction. To be effective, make each decision with an awareness of the added risk involved and have a contingency or recovery plan ready for implementation, should the assumed risk become a reality during execution.

Building in Contingency

The uncertainty of an activity duration estimate must also be considered in the scheduling process. After all, a schedule is only a plan or model of what is to transpire during project execution, and the quality of the model is only as good as the available information and the experience of the people who prepare the plan. Time estimates are by no means perfect; tasks are not always well defined or fully understood and things can go wrong during execution, thus creating a degree of uncertainty in every project. The extent of the uncertainty is a function of the nature of the tasks. The more developmental the project—the greater the uncertainty and the greater the degree of uncertainty—the less likely "on time" completion becomes. As a result, a contingency that compensates for project uncertainty is needed to improve the chances of "on time" completion.

An important lesson regarding the potential for "on time" completion and the need for a schedule contingency can be learned from PERT. Probabilistic PERT theory concludes that project expected completion time is the sum of a series of independent random variables—the expected completion times for all Critical Path tasks—and the sum of these times is normally distributed. Each expected or mean task duration is computed from three estimates—an optimistic time, a pessimistic time, and a most likely time. The expected and required project completion dates are compared (see Figure 2) and the probability of "on time" completion is assessed. Specific probability judgments are not important to this discussion, but the fact that the chance of "on time" completion improves as the favorable difference between expected and required completion dates increases (Figure 2c) is significant. If project completion is expected *after* the required date (Figure 2a), the probability of "on time" completion, defined by the shaded area under the normal probability distribution curve, will be low, the later completion is expected, the lower the chance of

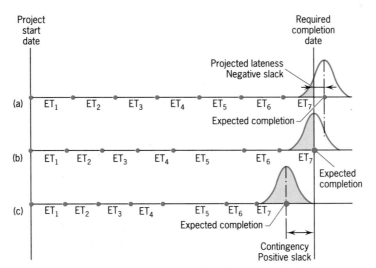

Figure 2(a)-(e): Critical path probability of success distribution.

success. When project completion is expected earlier than the specified date, a higher chance of success results. When the expected and required completion dates are the same (Figure 2b), the probability of "on time" or earlier completion, to the surprise of many people, will only be fifty percent.

The fallacy of forcing a schedule to fit a defined completion requirement is further emphasized by the probabilistic PERT relationships. Even if the fitting process were absolutely perfect—each precedence relationship properly defined, the assigned task durations equal to the functional managers' desires and the expected completion date matching the required completion date—the probability of "on time," or earlier, completion would only be fifty percent. In fact this probability assessment is apt to be optimistic, as the most likely time estimate, used to make most schedules, is usually lower than the expected time which reflects performance uncertainty. This results from the probability distribution curve's inherent skewness (the pessimistic estimate delay being more severe than the optimistic estimate savings). Since the length of the Critical Path is likely to be longer than estimated, it must be concluded that a "perfectly fitted" schedule's chance of success will be *less than* fifty percent, and this probability will diminish further as the degree of project uncertainty increases.

A limited chance of success will also be true of a schedule that is properly developed by compressing the Critical Path to the point at which the expected and required completion dates match. To improve the chances of "on time" completion, schedule compres-

sion should not stop when the specified target has been met, but should be applied further to provide positive slack (schedule contingency) along the Critical Path. As seen in Figure 2, the greater the slack or contingency, the greater the chance of completing the project on time. The degree of contingency will vary with the nature of the project. As a project's uncertainty increases, more contingency becomes necessary to ensure meeting a specified end date. The experienced project manager will consider every opportunity for increasing the contingency to improve the chance for meeting, and possibly beating, the required completion date.

Obtaining the compression needed to either better, or at least meet, the required completion date is not always possible. When this occurs, the project manager must advise the client, project sponsor, and/or management of the unattainability of their completion requirement. The network schedule defining the initial expected completion date and the minimum compression needed to meet the required date, and the improvements resulting from the steps taken to meet the specified target, should serve as justification for schedule relief, increased funding, or additional resources.

If the client or management reject the evidence developed through this systematic approach and "want the date met anyway," the project manager can still benefit from the planning effort. The project manager can accept the requirement as a challenge, offering a "best shot." If the end date is met, it will result from the project manager's efforts and if the effectively compressed plan proves to be correct and the end date is missed, the project manager cannot be rightfully faulted for failing to support a mandated requirement. Of course, it is best to have an agreement on the schedule, as successful project completion, and not placement of blame, is the common goal.

Managing the Contingency

Once a contingency has been established, the project manager must ensure that the available time is not misused by the functional staff executing the work, or that the client or management does not take advantage of the potential time savings to "improve" the required completion date. Contingency should be viewed as an element of the project's duration, representing time that will ultimately be spent during the period of performance, but neither the specific tasks requiring the extra time nor the cause are known to the project manager when the contingency is established. The project manager should support contingency use only when needed to solve a particular problem, as unused contingency will result in early project completion. Therefore, contingency should be treated as a reserve, controlled by the project manager, for use by the functional staff when needed to deal with specific execution issues.

Do not hide a contingency in the schedule by spreading the spare time among the project tasks and do not permit estimate "padding." If a task duration is overstated to include a contingency, the extra time will most likely be lost during execution, as Parkinson's law will prevail. The work will expand to fit the available time and the buried contingency will ultimately erode.

Identify any extra time as a contingency and keep it separated from the specified tasks, incorporated as a distinct block of time at the end of the schedule. If the project manager is concerned about the risk of highlighting the extra time (e.g., relaxation by the functional staff executing the work, or a client or management move to shorten the schedule at the expense of the contingency), then the contingency should be disguised. This can be achieved by either creating a fictitious task at the end of the project containing the total contingency or by inflating the duration of the *final* project task or tasks, the immediate predecessors of completion. In either case, the functional staff, client, project sponsor or management will not easily abuse the contingency and any slippage experienced during the project will eat into the time allocated to these final tasks. If an adequate contingency has been established, this erosion will merely reduce the available time for these tasks to their original duration estimates. Disguising the contingency is not encouraged, as an open and honest working relationship between functional and project personnel is important to a successful project; and the client, sponsor, and management must be aware of true project status, if their complete support is expected. However, disguising the contingecy is an approach available to the project manager who has previously experienced schedule abuse and ultimate contingency erosion.

Summary

Completing a project "on time" (meeting a specified end date) is not a responsibility to be taken lightly. "Wishing" will not make it so, nor will preparing an unsubstantiated plan that gives the appearance of feasibility. One cannot force fit a schedule into a predefined time constraint and then casually assume that the work will be done on time. If the plan is not based on sound information and logical work flow patterns, as delineated by the functional entities responsible for executing the work, then the plan will offer little chance for success. The key to successful schedule performance lies in first developing a realistic schedule, acceptable to the functional organization, and then using this schedule as the basis for controlling the work as it is performed.

Reference

1. Brooks, Fredrick P. Jr. 1975. *The Mythical Man Month*. Boston: Addison-Wesley.

Resource Allocation

In the previous chapter we looked at a special type of resource allocation problem, that of allocating time among project tasks, better known as *scheduling*. Now we consider the allocation of physical resources as well. Also, we are concerned with using resources in both individual and in multiple, simultaneous projects. The subject relates directly to the topic of scheduling because altering schedules can alter the need for resources and—just as important—alter the timing of resource needs. At any given time, the firm may have a fixed level of various resources available for its projects. The fixed resources might include labor-hours of various types of special professional or technical services, machine-hours of various types of machinery or instrumentation, hours of computing time, and similar scarce resources needed for accomplishing project tasks. For example, if the need for some resource varies between 70 and 120 percent of resource capacity, then that resource will be under utilized (and wasted if no alternative use exists) at one point in the project and in insufficient supply at another. If the project schedule can be adjusted to smooth the use of the resource, it may be possible to avoid project delay and, at the same time, not saddle the project with the high cost of excess resources "just to make sure."

This chapter addresses situations that involve resource problems. We discuss the trade-offs involved, the difference between allocation to one project and allocation between multiple projects, the relationship between resource loading and leveling, and some of the approaches employed to solve allocation problems, including the Critical Path Method (CPM) and several other well-known techniques. Although CPM is not actually a resource allocation method, we include it here because we view time as a resource, and trade-offs between time and other resources are a major problem in resource management. Finally, we note the major impact that current project management software has had on the PM's ability—and willingness—to deal with resource loading and leveling.

▶ 9.1 CRITICAL PATH METHOD

In Chapter 8 we mentioned that CPM is similar to PERT. In the original versions of CPM and PERT there was one important difference: CPM included a way of relating the project schedule to the level of physical resources allocated to the project. This allowed the PM to trade time for cost, or vice versa. In CPM, two activity times and two costs are specified, if appropriate, for each activity. The first time/cost combination is called *normal* and the second set is referred to as *crash*. Normal times are "normal" in the same sense as the *m* time estimate of the three times used in PERT. Crash times result from an attempt to expedite the activity by the application of additional resources—for example, overtime, special equipment, additional staff or material, and the like.

It is standard practice with PERT/CPM to estimate activity times under the assumption of resource loadings that are normal. To discuss a time requirement for any task without some assumption about the level of resources devoted to the task makes no real sense. At the same time, it does not make sense to insist on a full list of each and every resource that will be spent on each of the hundreds of activities that may comprise a PERT/CPM network. Clearly, there must have been some prior decision about what resources would be devoted to each task, but much of the decision making is, in practice, relegated to the common methods of standard practice and rules of thumb. The allocation problem requires more careful consideration if it is decided to speed up the accomplishment of tasks and/or the total project. We need to know what additional resources it will take to shorten completion times for the various activities making up the project.

While standard practice and rules of thumb are sufficient for estimating the resource needs for normal progress, careful planning is critical when attempting to expedite (crash) a project. Crash plans that appear feasible when considered activity by activity may incorporate impossible assumptions about resource availability. For example, we may need to crash some activities on the Wild Horse Dam Project. To do so, we have all the labor and materials required, but we will need a tractor-driven crawler crane on the project site not later than the eighth of next month. Unfortunately, our crane will be in Decatur, Illinois, on that date. No local contractor has a suitable crane for hire. Can we hire one in Decatur or Springfield and bring ours here?

And so it goes. When we expedite a project, we tend to create problems; and the solution to one problem often creates several more problems that require solutions.

Difficulties notwithstanding, the wise PM adopts the Scout's motto: "Be prepared." If deterministic time estimates are used, and if project deadlines are firm, there is a high likelihood that it will be necessary to crash the last few activities of most projects. Use of the three probabilistic time estimates of PERT may reduce the chance that crashing will be needed because they include uncertainties that are sometimes forgotten or ignored when making deterministic time estimates. Even so, many things make crashing a way of life on some projects—things such as last-minute changes in client specifications, without permission to extend the project deadline by an appropriate increment. An example of one of the problems that commonly result from the use of deterministic time estimates can be seen in the boxed example that follows.

Architectural Associates, Inc.

Architectural Associates, Inc. (AAI) specializes in large, industrial, retail, and public projects, including shopping malls, manufacturing complexes, convention centers, and the like. The firm is considered to be one of the region's most effective and creative design studios. Their design facility is located in a large, midwestern city and is housed on the second floor of an old building, originally used for light manufacturing. The offices are at one end of the floor, and about two-thirds of the floor space is occupied by the design staff and technicians. The entire space devoted to design is a single, open area and workstations are laid out in such a way as to encourage communication between individuals working on a common project.

A senior executive of AAI noticed that, for the past year or two, the chance of bringing design projects in on time and on budget had decreased to the point where the only uncertainty was how late and how much over budget a project would be. Architectural projects, like computer programming and a few other creative processes, seem to be typified by the need to crash projects at the last minute, but even with the usual crash, AAI was still late and, consequently, over budget.

An examination of the workplace disclosed a large, green felt, display board mounted on the wall where it was visible to the entire design staff. The board listed the names of individual designers and technicians vertically, and design contract numbers across the horizontal axis. The times allocated for work on each project by appropriate staff members were shown at the intersections of the rows and columns. The time estimates were made by senior managers, themselves architects, based on their experience. The individuals with direct responsibility for design work generally felt that the time estimates were reasonable.

The work process was studied and the following problem was revealed. If the design of the electrical systems involved in a plan was estimated to take five days, for example, the individual(s) responsible for the work planned it in such a way that it used the five days allowed. If a problem occurred on the first day, the worker(s) simply stayed late or speeded up work the next day in order to get back on schedule. Problems on the second day, and even on the third and fourth days were handled in the same way, by crashing the work. Problems occurring on the fifth day, however, could not be handled so easily and this part of the project would be late. Because most of the different systems (the mechanicals, landscape, etc.) were designed simultaneously and staffed to require about the same number of days (rather than being sequential), and because problems were very likely to arise late in the design process of at least one of the systems, the overall design project, which required all tasks to be completed on time, was almost invariably late.

In an attempt to solve the problem, a simple check-mark to show job assignments was substituted for time allocations on the green board. Additionally, senior management made normal, optimistic, and pessimistic time estimates for each task and calculated "TE," also used to help estimate project cost. These estimates were not given to the design staff who were simply told to do the work involved as efficiently and effectively as they could. The result was that the range of task times increased slightly, but the average time required for the various tasks fell somewhat since they were now designed for efficiency rather than X days. Roughly the same number of tasks were accomplished in less than the expected time as tasks that took more than the expected time.

Consider the data in Table 9-1. First, we compute a cost/time *slope* for each activity that can be expedited (crashed). Slope is defined as follows:

$$\text{slope} = \frac{\text{crash cost} - \text{normal cost}}{\text{crash time} - \text{normal time}}$$

that is, the cost per day of crashing a project. The slope is negative, indicating that as the time required for a project or task is decreased, the cost is increased. Note that activity **c** cannot be expedited. Table 9-2 shows the time/cost slopes for our example.

A clear implication of this calculation is that activities can be crashed in increments of one day (or one period). Often, this is not true. A given activity may have only two or three technically feasible durations. The "dollars per day" slope of such activities is relevant only if the whole crash increment is useful. For example, if an activity can be carried out in either eight days or four days, with no feasible intermediate times, and if an uncrashable parallel path goes critical when the first activity is reduced from eight down to six days, then the last two days (to four days) of time reduction are useless. (Of course, there are times when the PM may expedite activities that have little or no impact on the network's critical time, such as when the resources used must be made available to another project.)

One must remember that crashing a project results in a change of the technology with which something is done. In the language of economics, it is a change in the "production function." At times, crashing may involve a relatively simple decision to increase groups of resources already being used. If the project, for instance, is to dig a ditch of a certain length and depth, we might add units of labor-shovel to shorten the time required. On the other hand, we might replace labor-shovel units with a Ditch Witch. Discontinuities in outcomes usually result. Different amounts of labor-shovel input may result in a job that takes anywhere from one to three days. Use of the Ditch Witch may require three hours. There may be no sensible combination of resources that would complete the job in, say, six hours. In some cases, technology cannot be changed, and task duration is fixed. A 30-day toxicity test for a new drug requires 30 days—no more, no less.

Not only do changes in technology tend to produce discontinuities in outcomes, they also tend to produce discontinuities in cost. As the technology is changed to speed a project, the cost curve relating input costs to time is apt to jump as we move from less to more sophisticated production systems. Not only is the curve displaced, it almost certainly will not be parallel to the earlier curve, but will change at a different rate. (For an extended treatment of this subject, see [37] (chapter 13)).

Table 9-1   An Example of CPM

Activity	Precedence	Duration, Periods (normal, crash)	Cost (normal, crash)
a	—	3,2	$ 40,80
b	a	2,1	20,80
c	a	2,2	20,20
d	a	4,1	30,120
e	b	3,1	10,80

Table 9-2 Activity Slopes—
Cost per Period for Crashing

Activity	Slope ($/period)
a	$40/-1 = -40$
b	$60/-1 = -60$
c	—
d	$90/-3 = -30$
e	$70/-2 = -35$

To use CPM, we develop a table or graph of the cost of a project as a function of the project's various possible completion dates. This can be obtained by either of two approaches.

The first approach is to start with the normal schedule for all project activities, and then to crash selected activities, one at a time, to decrease project duration at the minimum additional cost. This approach is illustrated in Figure 9-1. The normal schedule is shown in network 9-1a. (Note the required dummy activity. We use the AOA representation to illustrate that this procedure can be used with PERT as well as with CPM.)

The critical path of network 9-1 is **a–b–e.** To reduce the total network duration, we must reduce the time required by one of the activities along this critical path. Inspecting Table 9-2 to see which critical activity can be reduced at the least cost, we find it is **e,** at a cost of $35 per day. If we crash **e** by one day, we have a seven-day project duration at a cost of $155, as shown in Figure 9-1b.

Crashing **e** by a day has created a second critical path, **a–d–dummy.** To reduce project duration further, we might cut one day off this new critical path in addition to another day from activity **e.** (Remember that the path **a–b–e** is also critical.) Activity **d** has the most favorable cost-per-day rate among the critical activities. This adds $30 to the $35 required to reduce **e,** for a total cost increment of $65. We will still have two critical paths. Another alternative, however, is to crash an activity common to both critical paths, activity **a.** Reducing **a** by one day at a cost of $40 is less expensive than crashing both **e** and **d,** so this is preferred (see Figure 9-1c). Because **a** cannot be further reduced, we now cut **e** and **d** to lower total project duration to five days, which raises the project cost to $260 (see Figure 9-1d).

Activity **e** has now been crashed to its maximum (as has **a**), so additional cuts will have to be made on **b** to reduce the **a–b–e** critical path. Cutting one day from **b** (which is expensive) and **d** results in the final network that now has a time of four days and a cost of $350, more than 200 percent of the cost for normal time. The project duration cannot be reduced further, since both critical paths have been crashed to their limits.

The second approach to CPM is to start with an all-crash schedule, compute its cost, and "relax" activities one at a time. Of course, the activities relaxed first should be those that do not extend the completion date of the project—that is, those not on the critical path. In our example, this is possible. The all-crash cost is $380, and the project duration is four days. Activity **d,** however, could be extended by one day at a cost saving of $30 without altering the project's completion date. This can be

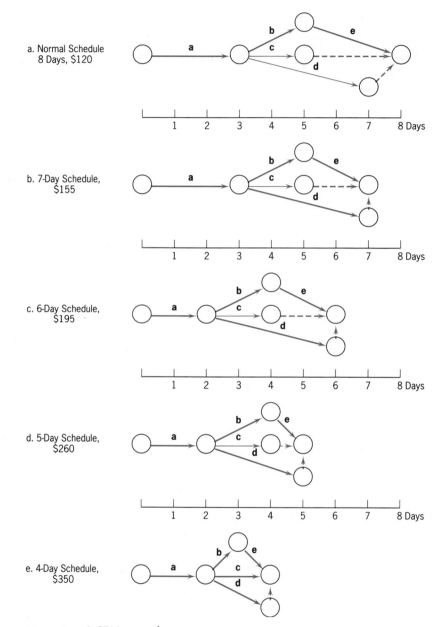

a. Normal Schedule
8 Days, $120

b. 7-Day Schedule,
$155

c. 6-Day Schedule,
$195

d. 5-Day Schedule,
$260

e. 4-Day Schedule,
$350

Figure 9-1: A CPM example.

seen in Figure 9-1e, where activity **d** is shown taking two days. Continuing in this
manner would eventually result in the all-normal schedule of eight days and a cost
of $120, as shown in Figure 9-1a.

   The time/cost relationships of crashing are shown in Figure 9-2. Starting at the
right (all-normal), note that the curve of cost per unit of duration gets steeper and

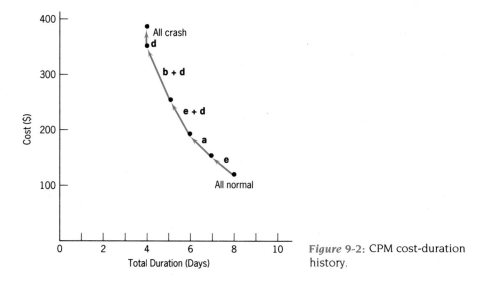

Figure 9-2: CPM cost-duration history.

steeper the more the project duration is reduced. It becomes increasingly costly to squeeze additional time out of the project. Economists will recognize that attempts to expedite a project are subject to decreasing marginal returns.

Charts such as the one shown in Figure 9-2 are useful to the PM in exercising control over project duration and cost. They are particularly helpful in dealing with senior managers who may argue for early project completion dates with little understanding of the costs involved. Similarly, such data are of great benefit when clients plead for early delivery. If the client is willing to pay the cost of crashing, or if the firm is willing to subsidize the client, the PM can afford to listen with a sympathetic ear. (While we advise the PM to ignore overhead cost over which he/she has no control, it should be noted that indirect costs are often altered when a project is crashed.)

Some organizations have more than one level of crashing. Table 9-3 illustrates such a case. In this example, the firm has two distinct levels of expediting a project, rush and blitz. The differences in the precedence relationships between tasks are noted in the table, as are differences in resource commitments. The last two rows of the table show the expected changes in cost and time if the project is expedited.

Finally, if a project has a penalty clause that makes the organization liable for late delivery, the cost/duration trade-off curve contains the information the PM needs to know in order to determine whether crashing the project or paying the penalty is the more economic course of action.

▶ 9.2 THE RESOURCE ALLOCATION PROBLEM

A shortcoming of the scheduling procedures covered In the previous chapter is that they do not address the issues of resource utilization and availability. They focus on time rather than physical resources. Also, in the discussion that follows it will not

Table 9-3 Official Pace of a Project

Title	Normal	Rush	Blitz
Approved Project Definition	Full	Some abbreviations from normal pace.	Only as necessary for major management decisions, purchasing and design engineering.
Study of Alternates	Reasonable	Quick study of major profitable items.	Only those not affecting schedule.
Engineering Design	Begins near end of Approved Project Definition.	Begins when Approved Project Definition 50–75% complete.	Concurrently with such Approved Project Definition as is done.
Issue Engineering to Field	Allow adequate time for field to plan and purchase field items. Usually 1/2–2 months lead time between issue and field erection.	Little or no lead time between issue and field erection.	No lead time between issue and field erection.
Purchasing	Begins in latter stages of Approved Project Definition.	Done concurrently with Approved Project Definition. Rush purchase of all long delivery items. Many purchases on "advise price" basis.	Done concurrently with such Approved Project Definition as is done. Rush buy anything that will do job. Overorder and duplicate order to guarantee schedule.
Premium Payments	Negligible	Some to break specific bottlenecks.	As necessary to forestall any possible delays.
Field Crew Strength	Minimum practical or optimum cost.	Large crew with some spot overtime.	Large crew; overtime and/or extra shifts.
Probable Cost Difference Compared with Normal Pace, as a Result of:			
*Design and Development	Base	5–10% more	15% and up, more
*Engineering and Construction costs	Base	3–5% more	10% and up, more
Probable Time	Base	Up to 10% less	Up to 50% less

be sufficient to refer to resource usage simply as "costs." Instead, we must refer to individual types of labor, specific facilities, kinds of materials, individual pieces of equipment, and other discrete inputs that are relevant to an individual project but are limited in availability. Last, we must not forget that time itself is always a critical resource in project management, one that is unique because it can neither be inventoried nor renewed.

The relationship between progress, time, and resource availability/usage is the major focus of this chapter. Schedules should be evaluated not merely in terms of meeting project milestones, but also in terms of the timing and use of scarce resources. A fundamental measure of the PM's success in project management is the skill with which the trade-offs among performance, time, and cost are managed. It is a continuous process of cost–benefit analysis: "I can shorten this project by a day at a cost of $400. Should I do it?" "If I buy 300 more hours of engineering time, I may be able to improve performance by 2 or 3 percent. Should I do it?"

Occasionally it is possible that some additional (useful) resources can be added at little or no cost to a project during a crisis period. At other times, some resources in abundant supply may be traded for scarce ones (á la M.A.S.H.'s "Radar"). Most of the time, however, these trades entail additional costs to the organization, so a primary responsibility for the PM is to make do with what is available.

The extreme points of the relationship between time use and resource use are these:

- **Time Limited:** The project must be finished by a certain time, using as few resources as possible. But it is time, not resource usage, that is critical.
- **Resource Limited:** The project must be finished as soon as possible, but without exceeding some specific level of resource usage or some general resource constraint.

The points between these two extremes represent time/resource-use trade-offs. As in Figure 9-2, they specify the times achievable at various resource levels. Equivalently, they specify the resources associated with various completion times. Clearly, the range of time or resource variability is limited.

Occasionally, both time and resources may be limited, but in this case, the specifications cannot also be fixed. If all three variables—time, cost, specifications—are fixed, the system is "overdetermined." The PM has lost all flexibility to perform the trade-offs that are so necessary to the successful completion of projects. Of course, it is possible that all three variables might be fixed at levels that allowed the PM plenty of maneuvering room, but this is most unlikely. Far more likely, our project manager acquaintances tell us, is the case in which senior management assigns budgets, schedules, and specifications without regard for the uncertainties of reality. It is the PM's responsibility, possibly with help from the project's champion, to warn senior management of the impropriety of such restrictions in spite of the chance that a senior manager might respond with "I'll get someone who can. . .!"

On occasion, it may be that one or more tasks in a project are *system-constrained*. A system-constrained task requires a fixed amount of time and known quantities of resources. Some industrial processes—heat treating, for instance—are system-constrained. The material must "cook" for a specified time to achieve the desired effect. More or less "cooking" will not help. When dealing with a system-constrained task or project, no trade-offs are possible. The only matter of interest in these cases is to make sure that the required resources are available when needed.

In the following sections we discuss approaches for understanding and using these relationships in various project situations.

▶ 9.3   RESOURCE LOADING

Resource loading describes the amounts of individual resources an existing schedule requires during specific time periods. Therefore, it is irrelevant whether we are considering a single work unit or several projects; the loads (requirements) of each resource type are simply listed as a function of time period. Resource loading gives a general understanding of the demands a project will make on a firm's resources. It is an excellent guide for early, rough project planning. Obviously, it is also a first step in attempting to reduce excessive demands on certain resources, regardless of the specific technique used to reduce the demands. Again, we caution the PM to recognize that the use of resources on a project is often nonlinear. Much of the project management software does not always recognize this fact [20].

The PERT/CPM network technique is well suited for the job of generating time-phased resource requirements. A Gantt chart could be adapted, but the PERT/CPM diagram, particularly if modified to illustrate slacks, will be helpful in the analysis used for resource leveling. Let us illustrate with the PERT/CPM network used as an example in the previous chapter. The network (Table 8-2) reappears as Figure 9-3, and resource usage is illustrated for two hypothetical resources, A and B, on the arcs. The expected activity time is shown above the arc and resource usage is shown in parentheses just below the arc, with the use of A shown first and B second—e.g., (5,3) would mean that five units of A and three units of B would be used on the activity represented by the arc. Figure 9-4 shows the "calendarized" PERT/CPM diagram, similar to the familiar Gantt chart. Resource demands can now be summed by time period across all activities.

The loading diagram for resource A is illustrated in Figure 9-5a, and that for resource B in Figure 9-5b. The loads are erratic and vary substantially over the duration of the project. Resource A, used in tasks **a, b,** and **c,** has a high initial demand that drops through the middle of the project and then climbs again. Resource B, on the other hand, has low initial use but increases as the project develops. The PM must be aware of the ebbs and flows of usage for each input resource throughout

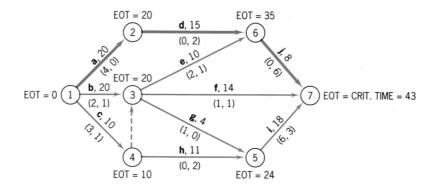

Figure 9-3: The complete network from Figure 8-15.

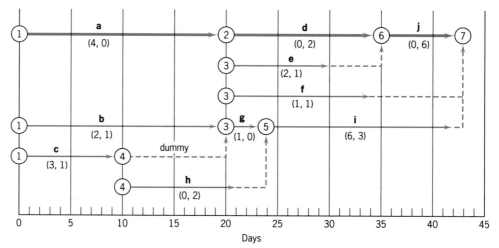

Figure 9-4: Modified PERT/CPM diagram showing resource usage (from Figure 9-3).

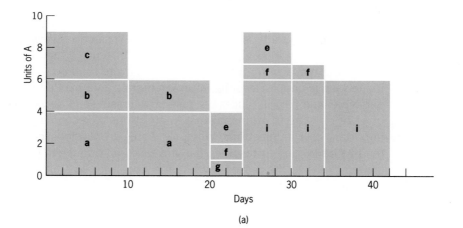

(a)

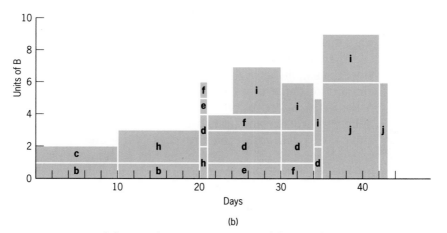

(b)

Figure 9-5a: Load diagram for resource A. *b*: Load diagram for resource B.

the life of the project. It is the PM's responsibility to assure that the required resources, in the required amounts, are available when and where they are needed. In the next three sections, we will discuss how to meet this responsibility.

▶ 9.4 RESOURCE LEVELING

In the example above, we noted that the project began with the heavy use of resource A, used smaller amounts during the middle of the project, and then continued with rising usage during the project's latter stages. Usage of B started low and rose throughout the project's life. Large fluctuations in the required loads for various resources are a normal occurrence—and are undesirable from the PM's point of view. Resource leveling aims to minimize the period-by-period variations in resource loading *by shifting tasks within their slack allowances.* The purpose is to create a smoother distribution of resource usage.

There are several advantages to smoother resource usage. First, much less hands-on management is required if the use of a given resource is nearly constant over its period of use. The PM can arrange to have the resource available when needed, can have the supplier furnish constant amounts, and can arrange for a backup supplier if advisable. Moreover, the PM can do this with little error. Second, if resource usage is level, the PM may be able to use a "just-in-time" inventory policy without much worry that the quantity delivered will be wrong. If the resource being leveled is people, leveling improves morale and results in fewer problems in the personnel and payroll offices because of increasing and decreasing labor levels.

Not only are there managerial implications to resource leveling, there are also important cost implications. When resources are leveled, the associated costs also tend to be leveled. If resource use increases as time goes by, and if resources are shifted closer to the present by leveling, costs will be shifted in the same way. The opposite is true, of course, if resource usage is shifted to the future. Perhaps most important from a cost perspective is leveling employment throughout a project or task. For most organizations, the costs of hiring and layoff are quite significant. It is often less expensive to level labor requirements in order to avoid hiring and layoff, even if it means some extra wages will be paid. In any case, the PM must be aware of the cash flows associated with the project and of the means of shifting them in ways that are useful to the parent firm.

The basic procedure for resource leveling is straightforward. For example, consider the simple network shown in Figure 9-6a. The activity time is shown above the arc, and resource usage (one resource, workers) is in parentheses below the arc. Activities **a, b,** and **c** follow event 1, and all must precede event 4. Activity **a** requires two workers and takes two days, **b** requires two workers and takes three days, and **c** needs four workers and five days. (We addressed the problem of trade-offs between labor and activity time in the first section of this chapter.) If all these tasks are begun on their early start dates, the resource loading diagram appears as shown in Figure 9-6b, steps of decreasing labor demand varying from eight workers to four workers. If, however, task **b** is delayed for two days, the full length of its slack in this particular case, the resource loading diagram is smoothed, as shown in Figure 9-6c.

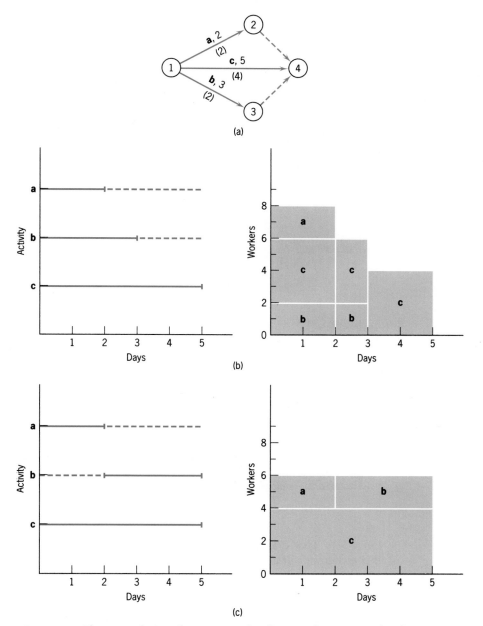

Figure 9-6a: The network. *b:* Before resource leveling. *c:* After resource leveling.

The same result would have occurred if **b** were started as early as possible and task **a** were delayed until day 3.

Resource leveling is a procedure that can be used for almost all projects, whether or not resources are constrained. If the network is not too large and there are only a few resources, the leveling process can be done manually. For larger networks and multiple resources, resource leveling becomes extremely complex, far be-

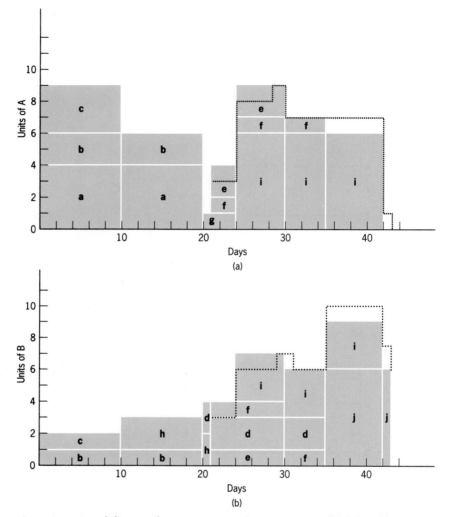

Figure 9-7a: Load diagram for resource A with activities **e** and **f** delayed by one day each.
b: Load diagram for resource B with activities **e** and **f** delayed by one day each.

yond the power of manual solutions. Fortunately, a number of computer programs can handle most leveling problems efficiently (discussed in Chapter 10).

Reconsider the load diagrams of Figures 9-5a and b. Assume it is desired to smooth the loading of resource B, which is particularly jagged. Both activities **e** and **f** can be delayed (**e** has five days of slack and **f** has nine). If we delay both for one day, we remove the peak on day 20 without increasing any of the other peaks (see Figure 9-7b). If we do this, however, it also alters the use of resource A and deepens the "valley" on day 20 (see Figure 9-7a). If we further delay **f** another seven days in order to level the use of A toward the end of the project, we would deepen the valley between days 20 and 24, and the resultant use of A would be as shown by the dotted lines on Figure 9-7a. Activity **f** would begin on day 29 (and would become critical). The effect on the usage of B is easy to see (Figure 9-7b). The change would lower usage by one unit beginning on day 21 (remember that we have already delayed **f** one day), and increase usage by one unit beginning on day 35, continuing to the end of the project. This action increases peak use of B from nine to ten units.

It is important to emphasize that if the network under consideration is more complex and the number of resources to be leveled is realistically large, a manual leveling process is out of the question. Computer-aided leveling is not only mandatory, it is also helpful because it allows the PM to experiment with various patterns of resource usage through simulation.

In the next section we raise the most general problem of minimizing resource usage while still achieving various completion dates—or the inverse problem, minimizing completion times while operating with specified limits on resources.

Project Management in Practice
A Resource Leveling Information System for Scheduling at Sacramento Municipal Utility District

The Sacramento Municipal Utility District had been using color-coded magnetic scheduling boards for over 20 years to keep track of line construction, meter, and service job status for its 426,000 customers and to make daily crew assignments. But with explosive population growth and increased systems maintenance requirements, the system was overloaded, resulting in a backlog of over 3000 line construction jobs. Thus, a new, computerized forecasting, planning, scheduling, and monitoring system was needed. Management dictated three requirements: (1) Keep it simple, (2) Allow for future expansion, and (3) Assure compatibility with existing information systems.

The project proceeded in phases:

Definition—managerial interviews and analysis of needs

Design and approval of action plan—work scope, resource requirements, schedule

Information gathering—interviews with working personnel

Analysis and documentation—constructing CPM schedules, process flowcharts, data dictionaries

System specification—specifications and programming

Data loading and testing—issuing status reports and meeting to resolve problems

Documentation and training—provide for later in-house modification ability.

Schedule construction is now a two-step process (see figure). First, CPM schedules are loaded into the system for each construction project. Second, the program reschedules the jobs based on priorities and worker availability, always maintaining customer-required dates. Any conflicts are worked out by a central planning/scheduling group with line management and the customer.

To gain scheduler acceptance, a one-month trial period was undertaken to get feedback about the system. Indeed, comments from the schedulers led to a change in the manner of scheduling on the computer, as well as some significant customization of the report-writing capabilities of the system. However, with these changes the system was well accepted by the users.

Source: C. J. Pospisil, "A PC-Based Scheduling System for a Transmission and Distribution Construction Department," *Project Management Journal*, Sept. 1990.

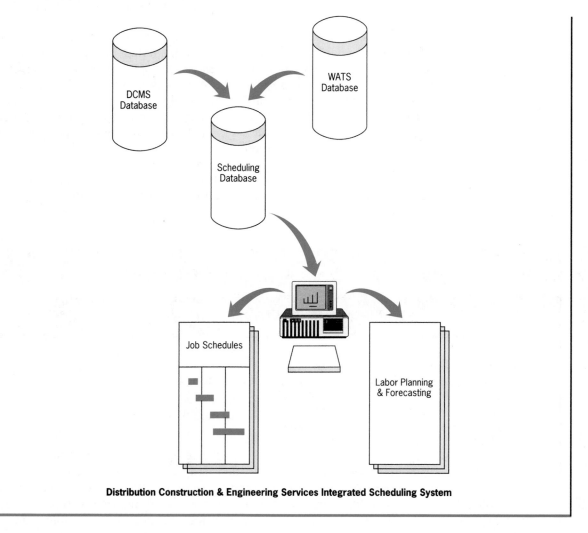

Distribution Construction & Engineering Services Integrated Scheduling System

▶ 9.5 CONSTRAINED RESOURCE SCHEDULING

There are two fundamental approaches to constrained allocation problems: heuristics and optimization models. Heuristic approaches employ rules of thumb that have been found to work reasonably well in similar situations. They seek better solutions. Optimization approaches seek the best solutions but are far more limited in their ability to handle complex situations and large problems. We will discuss each separately.

Most of the readily available PC software designed for project management will level resources and handle resource conflicts, but usually with a limited number of heuristic approaches. In leveling resources, TimeLine® gives priority to activities with earlier start dates while SuperProject® uses the least slack rule, and Primavera® will use any of several rules. In an interesting experiment, Johnson tested ten widely available project management packages for PCs against optimal solutions to a set of resource leveling problems [25]. In this particular test, Timeline® scored best with an average error of 5 percent. Figure 9-8a shows a Timeline® generated report on a resource conflict, while Figure 9-8b shows a resource-leveled solution to the conflict. (The example was extracted from a project presented in Chapter 10.)

Heuristic Methods

Heuristic approaches to constrained resource scheduling problems are in wide, general use for a number of reasons. First, they are the only feasible methods of attacking the large, nonlinear, complex problems that tend to occur in the real world of project management. Second, while the schedules heuristics generate may not be

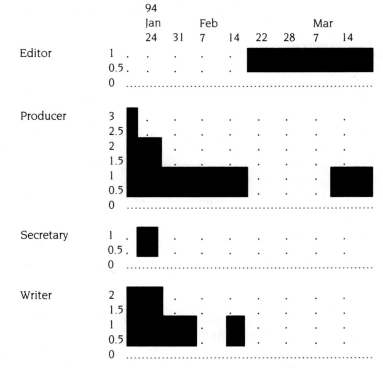

Schedule Name : Producing a Video Tape
Responsible   : Project Manager
As-of Date   : 19-Jan-94   8:00am
End Date   : 17-Mar-94   5:00pm

Select filter: Resource

Figure 9-8a: Resource conflict, two resources used beyond capacity.

Schedule Name : Producing a Video Tape
Responsible   : Project Manager
As-of Date   : 19-Jan-94 8:00a
End Date   : 29-Mar-94 5:00pm

Select filter: Resource

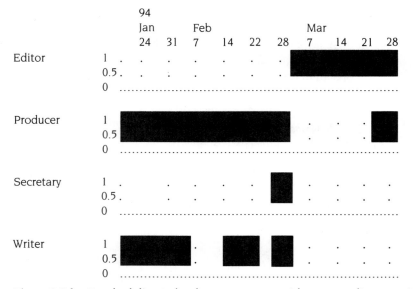

Figure 9-8 b: Rescheduling to level resource usage without exceeding capacity.

optimal, they are usually quite good—certainly good enough for most purposes. Commercially available computer programs handle large problems and have had considerable use in industry. Further, modern simulation techniques allow the PM to develop many different schedules quickly and to determine which, if any, are significantly better than current practice. If a reasonable number of simulation runs fails to produce significant improvement, the PM can feel fairly confident that the existing solution is a good one.

Most heuristic solution methods start with the PERT/CPM schedule and analyze resource usage period by period, resource by resource. In a period when the available supply of a resource is exceeded, the heuristic examines the tasks in that period and allocates the scarce resource to them sequentially, according to some priority rule. The major difference among the heuristics is in the priority rules they use. *Remember that the technological necessities always take precedence.* Some of the most common priority rules are these:

As Soon as Possible   The default rule for scheduling. This provides the general solution for critical path and time.

As Late as Possible   All activities are scheduled as late as possible without delaying the project. The usual purpose of this heuristic is to defer cash outflows as long as possible.

Shortest Task First   Tasks are ordered in terms of duration, with the shortest first. In general, this rule will maximize the number of tasks that can be completed by a system during some time period.

Most Resources First   Activities are ordered by use of a specific resource, with the largest user heading the list. The assumption behind this rule is that more important tasks usually place a higher demand on scarce resources.

Minimum Slack First   This heuristic orders activities by the amount of slack, least slack going first. (It is common, when using this rule, to break ties by using the shortest-task-first rule.)

Most Critical Followers   Tasks are arranged by number of critical activities following them. The ones with the greatest number of critical followers go first.

Most Successors   This is the same as the previous rule, except that *all* followers, not merely critical ones, are counted.

There are many such priority rules employed in scheduling heuristics. Most of them are simple adaptations and variations of the heuristics used for the traditional "job shop scheduling" problem of production/operations management, a problem that has much in common with multiproject scheduling and resource allocation. Also, most heuristics use a combination of rules—a primary rule, with a secondary rule used to break ties.

Several researchers [19, 28, 29] have conducted tests of the more commonly used schedule priority rules. Although their findings vary somewhat because of slightly different assumptions, the minimum slack rule was found to be best or near-best quite often and rarely caused poor performance. It usually resulted in the minimum amount of project schedule slippage, the best utilization of facilities, and the minimum total system occupancy time.

As the scheduling heuristic operates, one of two events will result. The routine runs out of activities (for the current period) before it runs out of the resources, or it runs out of resources before all activities have been scheduled. (While it is theoretically possible for the supply of resources to be precisely equal to the demand for such resources, even the most careful planning rarely produces such a tidy result.) If the former occurs, the excess resources are left idle, assigned elsewhere in the organization as needed during the current period, or applied to future tasks required by the project—always within the constraints imposed by the proper precedence relationships. If one or more resources are exhausted, however, activities requiring those resources are slowed or delayed until the next period when resources can be reallocated.

If the minimum slack rule is used, resources would be devoted to critical or nearly critical activities, delaying those with greater slack. Delay of an activity uses some of its slack, so the activity will have a better chance of receiving resources in the next allocation. Repeated delays move the activity higher and higher on the priority list. We consider later what to do in the potentially catastrophic event that we run out of resources before all critical activities have been scheduled.

The heuristic procedure just described is probably the most common. There are, however, other heuristic procedures that work in a similar manner. One works in reverse and schedules jobs from the end of the project instead of from its beginning. Activities that just precede the project finish are scheduled to be completed just barely within their latest finish times. Then, the next-to-last tasks are considered, and so on. The purpose of this approach is to leave as much flexibility as possible for activities that will be difficult to schedule in the middle and early portions of the project. This logic seems to rest on the idea that flexibility early in the project gives the best chance of completing early and middle activities on time and within budget, thereby improving the chances of being on time and budget with the ending activities.

Other heuristics use the *branch and bound* approach. They generate a wide variety of solutions, discard those that are not feasible and others that are feasible but poor solutions. This is done by a *tree search* that prunes infeasible solutions and poor solutions when other feasible solutions dominate them. In this way, the heuristic narrows the region in which good, feasible solutions may be found. If the "tree" is not too large, this approach can locate optimal solutions, but more computer search time will be required. See [55] for further details.

These heuristics are usually embedded in a computer simulation package that describes what will happen to the project(s) if certain schedules or priority rules are followed. A number of different priority rules can be tried in the simulation in order to derive a set of possible solutions. Simulation is a powerful tool and can also handle unusual project situations. Consider, for example, the following problem in *resource contouring*.

Given the network and resource demand shown in Figure 9-9, find the best schedule using a constant crew size. Each day of delay beyond 15 days incurs a penalty of $1000. Workers cost $100 per day, and machines cost $50 per day. Workers are interchangeable, as are machines. Task completion times vary directly with the number of workers, and partial work days are acceptable. The critical time for the project is 15 days, given the resource usage shown in Figure 9-9. (There are other jobs in the system waiting to be done.)

Figure 9-9 lists the total worker-days and machines per day normally required by each activity (below the activity arc). Because activity times are proportional to worker demands, path **b–c–e–i** is most demanding and this path uses 149 worker-days.

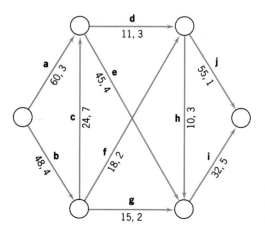

Figure 9-9: Network for resource load simulation. *Note:* The numbers on the arcs represent, respectively, worker-days, machines per day.

The fact that completion times vary with the number of workers means that activity **a** could be completed in 6 days with ten workers or in 10 days with six workers. Applying some logic and trying to avoid the penalty, which is far in excess of the cost of additional resources, we can add up the total worker-days required on all activities, obtaining 319. Dividing this by the 15 days needed to complete the project results in a requirement of slightly more than 21 workers–say, 22. How should they be allocated to the activities? Figure 9-10 shows one way, arbitrarily determined. Workers are shown above the "days" axis and machines below. We have 22 workers at $100 per day for 15 days ($33,000) and 128.5 machine days at $50 per day ($6425). The total cost of this particular solution is $39,425.

The "critical path" illustrated in Figure 9-10 is **a–g–i,** which takes 15 days. However, inspecting Figure 9-9, activity **g** does not follow activity **a** so how can this be a true "critical path"? The reason is: when resources are shared among activities, the resources for one activity may not be available because an earlier activity (though not necessarily a predecessor) is still using them. Thus, in theory, **g** (and **f** too) could have started at day 4 when **b** was completed but there were no workers available.

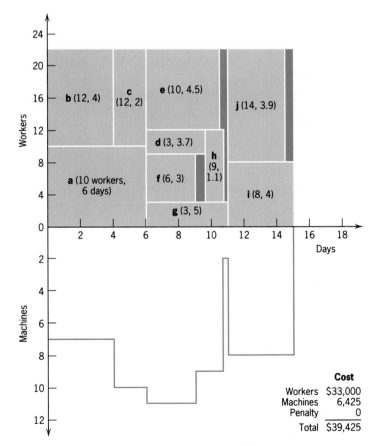

Figure 9-10: Load chart for a simulation problem.

The availability of workers is indicated by the shaded regions in Figure 9-10. Thus, if we use the 6 idle workers shown between activities **f** and **h** (for 0.7 days, thereby releasing 4.2 worker-days) to reduce the length of activity **g,** we could reduce it by 4.2/3 (workers) = 1.4 days, finishing now at 9.6 days. However, path **b–c–d–h** would then become critical at 10.8 days, resulting in only 0.2 days of overall project reduction. Using the 4.2 worker-days to reduce not only activity **g** but also activities **d** and **e,** would allow us to complete all of activities **e, h,** and **g** at day 10.32, thereby reducing the project time by 0.68 days. The idle labor following activity **j** could be used similarly to reduce activity **i.**

After all reallocations, it is important to recalculate the demand for machines since this will also change. Note that we have assumed that machine use depends only on time and is independent of the number of workers: if this is not the case, then a different set of calculations are required to determine the machine requirements. Finally, there may be limitations on the total number of workers or machines that are available at any one time and this can affect the solution. For example, how would the solution change if only 20 workers were available?

The purpose of reassignments is not to decrease labor cost in the project. This is fixed by the base technology implied by the worker/machine usage data. The reassignments do, however, shorten the project duration and make the resources available for other work sooner than expected. If the tradeoffs are among resources, for instance, trading more labor for fewer machines or more machines for less material input, the problem is handled in the same way. Always, however, the technology itself constrains what is possible. The Chinese build roads in the mountains by using labor. In the United States machines are used. Both nations exercise an option because either labor-intensive or machine-intensive technology is feasible. The ancient Israelites, however, could not substitute labor for straw in making bricks: No straw, no bricks.

On small networks with simple interrelationships among the resources, it is not difficult to perform these resource trade-offs by hand. But for networks of a realistic size, a computer is clearly required. If the problem is programmed for computer solution, many different solutions and their associated costs can be calculated. But, as with heuristics, simulation does not guarantee an optimal, or even feasible, solution. It can only test those solutions fed into it.

Another heuristic procedure for leveling resource loads is based on the concept of minimizing the sum of the squares of the resource requirements in each period. That is, the smooth use of a resource over a set of periods will give a smaller sum of squares than the erratic use of the resource that averages out to the same amount as the smooth use. This approach, called *Burgess's method*, was applied by Woodworth and Willie |61| to a multiproject situation involving a number of resources. The method was applied to each resource sequentially, starting with the most critical resource first.

Next, we briefly discuss some optimizing approaches to the constrained resource scheduling problem.

Optimizing Methods

The methods to find an optimal solution to the constrained resource scheduling problem fall into two categories: mathematical programming (linear programming for the most part) and enumeration. In the 1960s, the power of LP improved from being able to handle three resources and 15 activities to four resources and 55 activities. But even with this capacity, LP is usually not feasible for reasonably large projects where there may be a dozen resources and thousands of activities. (See [18] and [41] for more detail.)

In the late 1960s and early 1970s, limited enumeration techniques were applied to the constrained resource problem with more success. Tree search and branch and bound methods [50] were devised to handle up to five resources and perhaps 200 activities. Advances in LP techniques now allow LP to be used on large constrained resource scheduling problems.

More recent approaches have combined programming and enumeration methods. Patterson and Huber [42], for example, employ an integer programming approach combined with a minimum bounding procedure to reduce the computation time for minimizing project duration. Similarly, Talbot [52] uses integer programming and implicit enumeration to formulate and solve problems where the completion time is a function of the resources allocated to the project.

One problem with even the newer combination of approaches is that the characteristics of problems that can be usefully addressed with these methods is still largely unknown. Why various methods will work on one problem and not on a similar problem is still being researched.

Project Management in Practice
Benefits of Resource Constraining at Pennsylvania Electric

Pennsylvania Electric Company, headquartered in Johnstown, PA, operates generating facilities with a capacity of 6950 megawatts to serve 547,000 customers over an area of 17,600 square miles. The Generation Division Planning Group is responsible for planning all maintenance and capital projects. In the early 1980s, the group used a manual method of planning with hand-drawn charts. The planning process has now been computerized, which is faster, allows "what-if" analyses, and controls more than just the previously monitored critical path. In bringing the planning process in-house, the group also saved $100,000 a year in service fees from an outside engineering firm who was planning their construction activities.

A special feature of the computerized system is its resource constraining module which establishes labor requirements across all jobs. In the pilot program to test the new software, $300,000 was saved when it was discovered that a job could be done with 40 percent fewer mechanics than normally used and still complete the job on time. In another application, it was found that a turbine disassembly and inspection could be added to the task list without delaying the project or exceeding the project budget.

After worker-hours are input to the program by activity, actual progress is monitored (see figure) and schedule and cost deviations are highlighted for management attention. This allows management to make adjustments to recover the schedule, slow the project down, or acquire more funds to get the

Source: A. J. Cantanese, "At Penelec, Project Management is a Way of Life," *Project Management Journal*, December 1990.

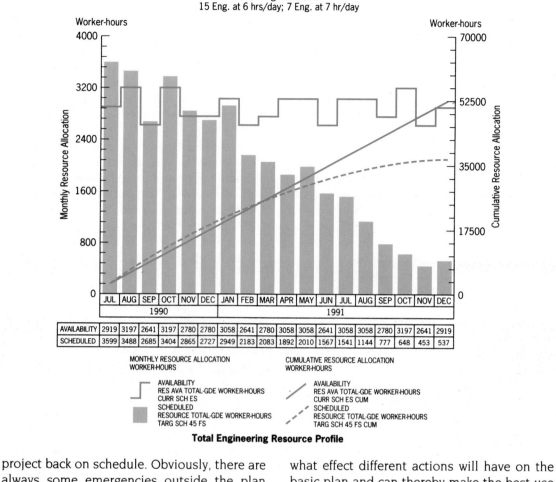

Total Engineers-GDE
15 Eng. at 6 hrs/day; 7 Eng. at 7 hr/day

	JUL	AUG	SEP	OCT	NOV	DEC	JAN	FEB	MAR	APR	MAY	JUN	JUL	AUG	SEP	OCT	NOV	DEC
AVAILABILITY	2919	3197	2641	3197	2780	2780	3058	2641	2780	3058	3058	2641	3058	3058	2780	3197	2641	2919
SCHEDULED	3599	3488	2685	3404	2865	2727	2949	2183	2083	1892	2010	1567	1541	1144	777	648	453	537

MONTHLY RESOURCE ALLOCATION
WORKER-HOURS

    AVAILABILITY
    RES AVA TOTAL-GDE WORKER-HOURS
    CURR SCH ES
    SCHEDULED
    RESOURCE TOTAL-GDE WORKER-HOURS
    TARG SCH 45 FS

CUMULATIVE RESOURCE ALLOCATION
WORKER-HOURS

    AVAILABILITY
    RES AVA TOTAL-GDE WORKER-HOURS
    CURR SCH ES CUM
    SCHEDULED
    RESOURCE TOTAL-GDE WORKER-HOURS
    TARG SCH 45 FS CUM

Total Engineering Resource Profile

project back on schedule. Obviously, there are always some emergencies outside the plan that must be handled on an exception basis. But with this software, management knows what effect different actions will have on the basic plan and can thereby make the best use of available resources to handle the emergency with minimal impact on the plan.

▶ 9.6   MULTIPROJECT SCHEDULING AND RESOURCE ALLOCATION

Scheduling and allocating resources to multiple projects is much more complicated than for the single-project case. The most common approach is to treat the several projects as if they were each elements of a single large project. (A more detailed explanation is given below when we consider a specific multiproject scheduling heuristic.) Another way of attacking the problem is to consider all projects as completely independent; see [28, 29], for example. As [28] shows, these two approaches lead to different scheduling and allocation outcomes. For either approach, the conceptual basis for scheduling and allocating resources is essentially the same.

There are several projects, each with its own set of activities, due dates, and resource requirements. In addition, the penalties for not meeting time, cost, and performance goals for the several projects may differ. Usually, the multiproject problem involves determining how to allocate resources to, and set a completion time for, a new project that is added to an existing set of ongoing projects. This requires the development of an efficient, dynamic multiproject scheduling system.

To describe such a system properly, standards are needed by which to measure scheduling effectiveness. Three important parameters affected by project scheduling are: (1) schedule slippage, (2) resource utilization, and (3) in-process inventory. The organization (or the PM) must select the criterion most appropriate for its situation.

Schedule slippage, often considered the most important of the criteria, is the time past a project's due date or delivery date when the project is completed. Slippage may well result in penalty costs that reduce profits. Further, slippage of one project may have a ripple effect, causing other projects to slip. Indeed, expediting a project in order to prevent slippage may, and usually does, disturb the overall organization to the point where slippage due to resource shortages may then be caused in other projects. The loss of goodwill when a project slips and deliveries are late is important to all producers. As is the case with many firms, Grumman Aircraft, purchased by the Northrup Corporation in 1994, jealously guards its reputation for on-time delivery. During a project to install a new machine control system on a production line, Grumman insisted that the project be designed to minimize disturbance to operations in the affected plant and avoid late shipments. This increased the cost of the project, but the firm maintained delivery schedules.

A second measure of effectiveness, *resource utilization*, is of particular concern to industrial firms because of the high cost of making resources available. A resource allocation system that smooths out the peaks and valleys of resource usage is ideal, but it is extremely difficult to attain while maintaining scheduled performance because all the projects in a multiproject organization are competing for the same scarce resources. In particular, it is expensive to change the size of the human resource pool on which the firm draws.

While it is relatively easy to measure the costs of excess resource usage required by less than optimal scheduling in an industrial firm, the costs of uncoordinated multiproject scheduling can be high in service-producing firms, too. In the real estate syndication firm used as an example of an AON network in Chapter 8 (see Figure 8-28), the scarce resource is executive judgment time. If two deals arrived at the same time, one would have to wait. This is undesirable because other potential buyers are seeking properties, and the process must move along without delay.

The third standard of effectiveness, the amount of *in-process inventory*, concerns the amount of work waiting to be processed because there is a shortage of some resource(s). Most industrial organizations have a large investment in in-process inventory, which may indicate a lack of efficiency and often represents a major source of expense for the firm. The remedy involves a trade-off between the cost of in-process inventory and the cost of the resources, usually capital equipment, needed to reduce the in-process inventory levels. It is almost axiomatic that the most time-consuming operation in any production system involving much machining of metals is an operation called "wait." If evidence is required, simply observe parts sitting on the plant floor or on pallets waiting for a machine, or for jigs, fixtures, and tools.

All these criteria cannot be optimized at the same time. As usual, trade-offs are involved. A firm must decide which criterion is most applicable in any given situation, and then use that criterion to evaluate its various scheduling and resource allocation options.

At times, the demands of the marketplace and the design of a production/distribution system may require long production runs and sizable levels of in-process inventory. This happens often when production is organized as a continuous system, but sales are organized as projects, each customized to a client order. Items may be produced continuously but held in a semifinished state and customized in batches.

A mattress manufacturing company organized to produce part of its output by the usual continuous process; but the rest of its production was sold in large batches to a few customers. Each large order was thought of as a project and was organized as one. The customization process began after the metal frames and springs were assembled. This required extensive in-process inventories of semifinished mattresses.

As noted earlier, experiments by Fendley [19] revealed that the minimum-slack-first rule is the best overall priority rule, generally resulting in minimum project slippage, minimum resource idle time, and minimum system occupancy time (i.e., minimum in-process inventory) for the cases he studied. But the most commonly used priority rule is first come, first served—which has little to be said for it except that it fits the client's idea of what is "fair." In any case, individual firms may find a different rule more effective in their particular circumstances and should evaluate alternative rules by their own performance measures and system objectives.

Fendley found that when a new project is added to a multiproject system, the amount of slippage is related to the average resource load factor. The load factor is the average resource *requirement* during a set time period divided by resource *availability* for that time period. When the new project is added, the load factor for a resource increases and slippage rises. Analysis of resource loads is an important element in determining the amount of slippage to expect when adding projects.

Given these observations, let us examine some examples of the various types of multiproject scheduling and resource allocation techniques. We begin with a short description of one optimization method, briefly cover several heuristics, and then discuss one heuristic in greater detail.

Mathematical Programming

Mathematical programming [16, 18, 41, 55] can be used to obtain optimal solutions to certain types of multiproject scheduling problems. These procedures determine when an activity should be scheduled, given resource constraints. In the following discussion, it is important to remember that each of the techniques can be applied to the activities in a single project, or to the projects in a partially or wholly interdependent set of projects. Most models are based on integer programming that formulates the problem using 0–1 variables to indicate (depending on task early start times, due dates, sequencing relationships, etc.) whether or not an activity is scheduled in specific periods. The three most common objectives are these:

1. Minimum total throughput time (time in the shop) for all projects

2. Minimum total completion time for all projects

3. Minimum total lateness or lateness penalty for all projects.

Constraint equations ensure that every schedule meets any or all of the following constraints, given that the set of constraints allow a feasible solution.

1. Limited resources

2. Precedence relationships among activities

3. Activity-splitting possibilities

4. Project and activity due dates

5. Substitution of resources to assign to specified activities

6. Concurrent and nonconcurrent activity performance requirements

In spite of its ability to generate optimal solutions, mathematical programming has some serious drawbacks when used for resource allocation and multiproject scheduling. As noted earlier, except for the case of small problems, this approach has proved to be extremely difficult and computationally expensive.

Heuristic Techniques

Because of the difficulties with the analytical formulation of realistic problems, major efforts in attacking the resource-constrained multiproject scheduling problem have focused on heuristics. We touched earlier on some of the common general criteria used for scheduling heuristics. Let us now return to that subject.

There are scores of different heuristic-based procedures in existence. A great many of the procedures have been published (see [18] and [40], for example), and descriptions of some are generally available in commercial computer programs.

The most commonly applied rules were discussed in Section 9.5. The logical basis for these rules predates PERT/CPM. They represent rather simple extensions of well-known approaches to job-shop scheduling. Some additional heuristics for resource allocation have been developed that draw directly on PERT/CPM. All these are commercially available for computers, and most are available from several different software vendors in slightly different versions.

Resource Scheduling Method   In calculating activity priority, give precedence to that activity with the minimum value of d_{ij} where

d_{ij} = increase in project duration resulting when activity **j** follows activity **i**.

= Max $[0; (EFT_i - LST_j)]$

where

EFT_i = early finish time of activity **i**

LST_j = latest start time of activity **j**

The comparison is made on a pairwise basis among all activities in the *conflict set*.

Minimum Late Finish Time   This rule assigns priorities to activities on the basis of activity finish times as determined by PERT/CPM. The earliest late finishers are scheduled first.

Greatest Resource Demand   This method assigns priorities on the basis of total resource requirements, with higher priorities given for greater demands on resources. Project or task priority is calculated as:

$$\text{Priority} = d_j \sum_{i=1}^{m} r_{ij}$$

where

d_j = duration of activity **j**

r_{ij} = per period requirement of resource **i** by activity **j**

m = number of resource types

Resource requirements must be stated in common terms, usually dollars. This heuristic is based on an attempt to give priority to potential resource bottleneck activities.

Greatest Resource Utilization   This rule gives priority to that combination of activities that results in maximum resource utilization (or minimum idle resources) during each scheduling period. The rule is implemented by solving a 0–1 integer programming problem, as described earlier. This rule was found to be approximately as effective as the minimum slack rule for multiple project scheduling, where the criterion used was project slippage. Variations of this rule are found in commercial computer programs such as RAMPS (see [35]).

Most Possible Jobs   Here, priority is given to the set of activities that results in the greatest number of activities being scheduled in any period. This rule also requires the solution of a 0–1 integer program. It differs from the greatest-resource-utilization heuristic in that the determination of the greatest number of possible jobs is made purely with regard to resource feasibility (and not with regard to any measure of resource utilization).

Heuristic procedures for resource-constrained multiproject scheduling represent the only practical means for finding workable solutions to the large, complex multiproject problems normally found in the real world. Let us examine a multiproject heuristic in somewhat more detail.

A Multiproject Scheduling Heuristic

To attack this problem, recall the hierarchical approach to project planning we adopted in Chapter 5. A project plan is a nested set of plans, composed of a set of generalized tasks, each of which is decomposed into a more detailed set of work packages that are, in turn, decomposed further. The decomposition is continued until the work packages are simple enough to be considered "elemental." A PERT/CPM diagram of a project might be drawn for any level of task aggregation. A single activity (arrow) at a high level of aggregation would represent an entire network of activities at a lower level (see Figure 9-11). Another level in the planning hierarchy is shown as a Gantt chart in Figure 9-12.

If an entire network is decomposed into subnetworks, we have the equivalent of the multiproject problem where each of the projects (subnetworks) is linked to predecessor and successor projects (other subnetworks). In this case, the

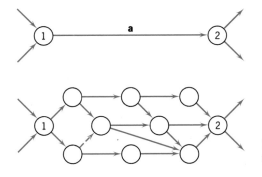

Figure 9-11: Task **a** decomposed into a network of subtasks.

predecessor/successor relationships depend on the technology of the parent project. In the true multiproject case, these relationships may still depend on technological relationships—for example, a real estate development project being dependent on the outcome of a land procurement project. The relationships may, however, be determined more or less arbitrarily, as when projects are sequenced on a first-come, first-served basis, or by any other priority-setting rule, or undertaken simultaneously in the hope that some synergistic side effects might occur. Or the relationship among the projects may simply be that they share a common pool of resources.

With this conceptual model, assume we have a set of projects. Each individual

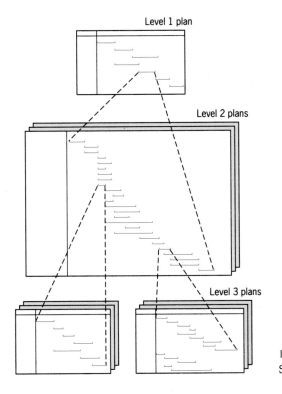

Figure 9-12: Hierarchy of Gantt charts.
Source: [23]

project is represented by a network of tasks. We can form a single network of these projects by connecting them with dummy activities (no resources, no duration) and/or pseudoactivities (no resources, some duration). Both dummy activities and pseudoactivities represent dependency relationships, but these dependencies, as noted above, may be technological or quite arbitrary.*

As usual, and excepting dummy and pseudoactivities, each task in each network requires time and resources. The amount of time required may or may not vary with the level of resources applied to it. The total amount of resources and/or amounts of individual resources are limited in successive scheduling periods. Our problem is to find a schedule that best satisfies the sequence and resource constraints and minimizes the overall duration of the entire network. The resulting schedule should indicate when to start any activity and at what level of resources it should be maintained while it is active.

Before undertaking the allocation of resources, it is proper to consider the quantity of resources available for allocation. (For the moment, we consider "resources" as an undifferentiated pool of assets that can be used for any purpose.) At the beginning of any period (hour, day, week, month, etc.) we have available any resources in inventory, R_I, which is to say, left over as excess from the previous allocation process. Changes in the inventory can be made from within the system of projects or by importing or exporting inventory from the outside. Excluding activities that have been completed in previous periods, every activity planned by the project is in one of four states; ongoing, stopping, waiting and technologically able to start, or waiting and technological unable to start.

Figure 9-13 illustrates these conditions. We label ongoing activities as "resource users." Those stopping are "resource contributors." Those waiting and able to start are "resource demanders." Those waiting and unable to start can be ignored for the present. The amount of resources available for allocation is, therefore, the amount in inventory plus the amount contributed, $R_I + R_C$. If the amount demanded is less than this sum, there will be a positive inventory to start the next period. If not, some demanders will go unfunded.

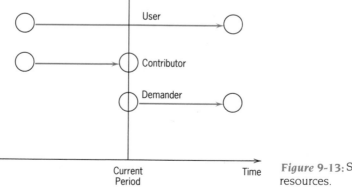

Figure 9-13: Sources and uses of resources.

*This exposition is based on Weist's work [59], and on Corwin's application of Weist's papers to resource allocation among multiple R & D projects [11].

Weist's heuristic (SPAR-1, Scheduling Program for Allocation of Resources) allocates resources to activities in order of their early start times. In the first period, we would list all available tasks and order them by their slack, from least to most. (Calculation of slack is based on the assumption that activities will be supported at *normal* resource levels.) Activities are selected for support and scheduling one by one, in order. As activities at the top of the list are supported, the relevant resource stocks are debited. Tasks are scheduled sequentially until the list of available jobs is completed, or until the stock of one or more resources is depleted. If we deplete resources before completing the task list, remaining tasks are delayed until the next period. Postponed activities lose slack and rise toward the top of the priority list.

The information requirements for this heuristic are straightforward. Each period, we need a period-by-period updating of the list of currently active tasks continued from the previous period, including the resource usage level for each active task, the current scheduled (or expected) completion date, and the current activity slack. We need to know the currently available stocks of each type of resource, less the amounts of each in use. We also need a list of all available tasks together with their slacks and normal resource requirements. As activities are completed, their resources are "credited" to the resource pool for future use.

Thus, resources are devoted to activities until the supply of available resources or activities is exhausted. If we use up the resources before all critical activities are scheduled, we can adopt one of two subheuristics. First, we may be able to borrow resources from currently active, but noncritical, tasks. Second, we may "deschedule" a currently active, noncritical task. The former presumably slows the progress of the work, and the latter stops it. In both cases, some resources will be released for use on critical tasks. Obviously, if a critical task is slowed, descheduled, or not supported, the duration of the associated project will be extended.

The decision about which of these courses of action to take, borrowing or descheduling, can be made by adopting the same logic used in Chapter 7 when we discussed the budget negotiations between subordinate and superior. The decision to borrow or deschedule depends on our estimate of the impact either action would have on the task under consideration, given its current state of completion. Figure 9-14 shows two different versions of the project or task life cycle discussed in Chapter 7. If the task is a Type 1, borrowing would minimize the damage to the task unless it is quite near completion and we are willing to accept the outcome in its current state, in which case we can deschedule. If the task is Type 2, borrowing is

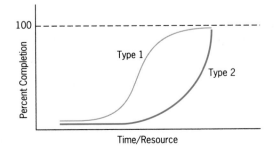

Figure 9-14: Project or task life cycles.

apt to have a catastrophic effect on the task and we should either deschedule it (and start it again later) or reject it as a source of resources.

If the size of the resource pool is more than sufficient for the list of active and available tasks, the extra resources may be used to crash critical activities in order to put some slack in the critical path as insurance against project delays caused by last-minute crises. In fact, it is often possible to borrow resources from tasks with plenty of slack in order to crash critical items that are frequent causes of project delay.

As a result of this scheduling process, each task from the previous period, along with any tasks newly available for support, will be:

1. Continued as is, or newly funded at a normal level
2. Continued or funded at a higher level of resources as a result of criticality
3. Continued or funded at a lower-than-normal level as a result of borrowing
4. Delayed because of a resource shortage.

If there is more than one scarce resource, a separate activity can be created for each type of scarce resource. These "created" activities must be constrained to start in the same period as the parent activity, and to have the same level of resource assig nment (normal, crash, or minimal.) Figure 9-15 shows a flow diagram for SPAR-1.

As we have noted, many commercially available software packages have the ability to schedule constrained resources and deal with resource conflicts [21, 25, 57]. The *Project Management Journal* published by the Project Management Institute is an excellent source of reviews on project management software. These reviews typically include a discussion of the package's capabilities. Many will allow the user to solve the problem either automatically, using the program's heuristics, or by hand in which case the user can adopt any method desired. If a set of projects is linked together by dummy activities so that it can be treated like a single project, the software will report resource usage conflicts; that is, cases in which the scheduled utilization of a resource is greater than the supply of that resource.

In one sense this chapter's emphasis on resource shortages is misleading. The common case of shortage applies not to resources in general, but to one or two highly specific resources. For example, an insurance firm specializing in casualty insurance has a typical kind of scarce resource, a "Walt." Walter A. is a specialist in certain types of casualty losses in the firm's commerical lines business. He is the only such specialist in the firm, and his personal knowledge is required when designing new policies in the field. His knowledge is based on years of experience and an excellent, analytical mind. It is common for projects involving the modification or creation of policies in the commercial lines area to have problems associated with the fact that the firm has one, and only one Walt. Walt-capacity cannot be hired, trained, or subcontracted within an appropriate time frame. The firm's ability to extend its Walt-capacity is not sufficient to satisfy its Walt-demand. Left with no alternative, some projects must be delayed so that others can proceed.

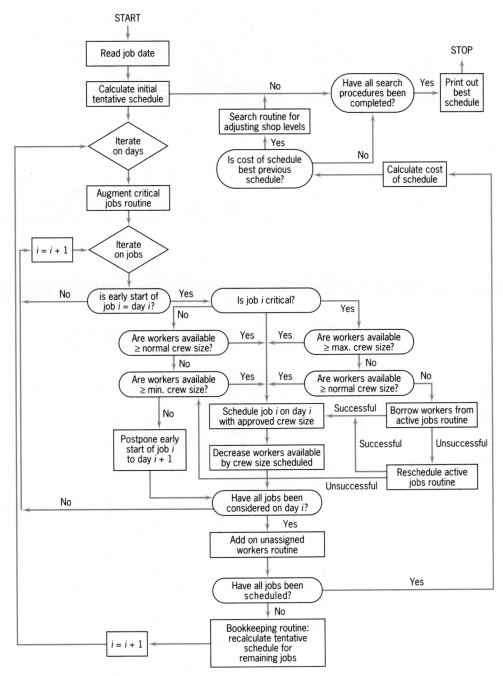

Figure 9-15: Flow diagram for SPAR-1. *Source:* [59]

Project Management in Practice
Tying Projects to Resources and Constraints at the Minnesota Department of Transportation

The Minnesota Department of Transportation is responsible for facility construction and maintenance for highways, bridges, airports, waterways, railroads, and even bicycle paths. At any given time, there will be approximately 1100 projects—typically, highway improvements—in active development, with a turnover of about 300 per year. These projects will range from $50,000 paint jobs to multimillion dollar freeway interchanges. The computerized Project Management and Scheduling System (PMSS) used to manage these projects is based on a work breakdown structure detailing about 100 activities involving 75 functional groups, 40 of which are in-house groups and the rest being consultants.

The PMSS encompasses three major areas: scheduling, funding, and human resource planning. It allows planning, coordination, and control of the work progress and resource requirements for multiple projects over a multiyear time span, since projects may continue

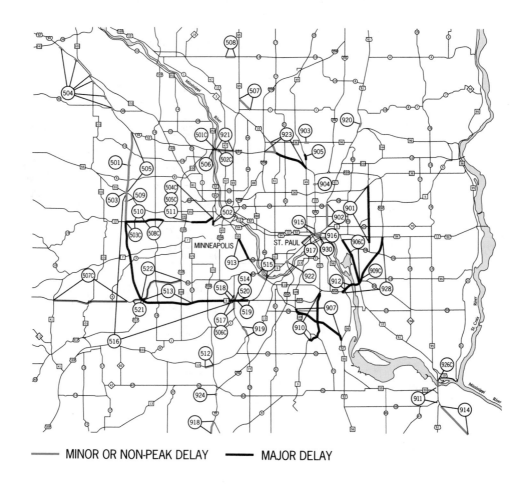

—— MINOR OR NON-PEAK DELAY   —— MAJOR DELAY

for up to four years in some cases. This integration offers the capability to relate work plans to funding availability as well as human resource availability. Conversely, resource use can be planned according to the construction project schedule. Other constraints can also be included in the system and its reports, such as avoiding projects that might overly congest a high-traffic area (see figure) or properly sequencing subprojects such as grading, surfacing, and finishing.

The PMSS system gives management a "big picture" perspective of what is happening in terms of workflow over time and geography. It has also enhanced the department's ability to answer questions about activities, funding, labor, and equipment, and to present reports in a variety of configurations to satisfy the needs of many different parties.

Source: R. Pearson, "Project Management in the Minnesota Department of Transportation," PM *Network*, November 1988.

▶ SUMMARY

In this chapter we looked at the problem of allocating physical resources, both among the multiple activities of a project and among multiple projects. The continuous problem to the PM is finding the best trade-offs among resources, particularly time. We considered resource loading, allocation, and leveling, and presented methods and concepts to aid in all these tasks.

Specific points made in the chapter were these:

- The critical path method (CPM) is a network constructed in the same manner as PERT but considers the possibility of adding resources to tasks (called crashing) to shorten their duration, thereby expediting the project.

- The resource allocation problem is concerned with determining the best trade-offs between available resources, including time, throughout the duration of a project.

- Resource loading is the process of calculating the total load from project tasks on each resource for each time period of the project's duration.

- Resource leveling is concerned with evening out the demand for various resources required in a project by shifting tasks within their slack allowances. The aid of a computer is mandatory for realistic projects.

- There are two basic approaches to addressing the constrained resources allocation problem:

    Heuristic methods are realistic approaches that may identify feasible solutions to the problem. They essentially use simple priority rules, such as shortest task first, to determine which task should receive resources and which task must wait.

    Optimizing methods, such as linear programming, find the best allocation of resources to tasks but are limited in the size of problems they can efficiently solve.

- For multiproject scheduling, three important measures of effectiveness are schedule slippage, resource utilization, and level of in-process inventory.

- When a new project is added to a multiproject system, the amount of slippage is directly related to the average resource load.

- Mathematical programming models for multiproject scheduling aim either to minimize total throughput time for all projects, minimize the completion time for all projects, or minimize the total lateness (or lateness penalty) for all projects. These models are limited to small problems. There are a number of heuristic methods, such as the resource scheduling method, available for the multiproject scheduling problem.

In the next chapter we move to the ongoing implementation of the project and consider the project information systems used for monitoring progress, costs, performance, and so on. The chapter also describes some available computer packages for this function.

▶ GLOSSARY

Cost/Time Slope—The ratio of the increased cost for expediting to the decreased amount of time for the activity.

Followers—The tasks that logically follow a particular task in time.

Heuristic—A formal process for solving a problem, like a rule of thumb, that results in an acceptable solution.

Mathematical Programming—A general term for certain mathematical approaches to solving constrained optimization problems, including linear programming, integer programming, and so on.

Predecessors—The tasks that logically precede a particular task in time.

Priority Rules—Formal methods, such as ratios, that rank items to determine which one should be next.

Resource Leveling—Approaches to even out the peaks and valleys of resource requirements so that a fixed amount of resources can be employed over time.

Resource Loading—The amount of resources of each kind that are to be devoted to a specific activity in a certain time period.

Successors—See followers.

Tree Search—The evaluation of a number of alternatives that logically branch from each other like a tree with limbs.

▶ MATERIAL REVIEW QUESTIONS

1. Identify several resources that may need to be considered when scheduling projects.

2. What is resource loading? How does it differ from resource leveling?

3. What is an activity slope and what does it indicate?

4. Name four priority rules. What priority rule is best overall? How would a firm decide which priority rule to use?

5. Name three efficiency criteria that might be considered when choosing a multiproject scheduling system.

6. What is the average resource load factor? How is it used to determine project completion times?

7. What are two methods for addressing the constrained resources allocation problem?

8. What are three measures of effectiveness for multiproject scheduling?

9. What is a "system constrained" task?

10. How does the resource scheduling method heuristic work?

▶ CLASS DISCUSSION QUESTIONS

1. Why are large fluctuations in the demands for particular resources undesirable? What are the costs of resource leveling? How would a PM determine the "best" amount of leveling?

2. When might a firm choose to crash a project? What factors must be considered in making this decision?

3. Why is the impact of scheduling and resource allocation more significant in multiproject organizations?

4. How much should a manager know about a scheduling or resource allocation computer program to be able to use the output intelligently?

5. With the significantly increased power of today's computers, do you think the mathematical programming optimization approaches will become more popular?

6. What are some of the limitations of CPM?

7. Why is leveling of resources needed?

8. What are some implications of resource allocation when an organization is involved in several projects at once?

9. What are some of the indirect costs of crashing?

10. How might CPM be used for strategic planning purposes?

▶ PROBLEMS

1. Given the following network, determine the first activity to be crashed by the following priority rules:
 (a) Shortest task first
 (b) Minimum slack first
 (c) Most critical followers
 (d) Most successors.

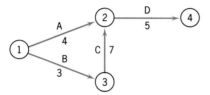

2. Using the network above and the additional information below, find:

 (a) The crash cost per day
 (b) Which activities should be crashed to meet a project deadline of 13 days at minimum cost.

Activity	Crash Time	Normal Cost	Crashed Cost (total)	Normal Time (days)
A	3	$300	$500	4
B	1	250	325	3
C	4	400	550	7
D	3	150	250	5

3. Consider the following network:

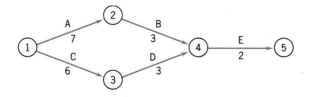

(a) Construct a schedule showing
 ESTs for all activities
 LSTs for all activities
 EOTs for all events
 LOTs for all events
 Slacks for all activities and events
 Critical path
(b) Given the following:

Activity	Crash Time	Normal Cost	Crashed Cost (total)	Normal Time (days)
A	4	$500	$ 800	7
B	2	200	350	3
C	4	500	900	6
D	1	200	500	3
E	1	300	550	2
			$3100	

 1. Find the crash cost per day.
 2. Which activities should be crashed to meet a project deadline of 10 days with a minimum cost?
 3. Fine the new cost.

4. Given the following:

Activity	Immediate Predecessor	Activity Time (months)
A	——	4
B	——	6
C	A	2
D	B	6
E	C,B	3
F	C,B	3
G	D,E	5

 (a) Draw the network.
 (b) Find the ESTs, LSTs, EOTs, LOTs, and Slacks.

(c) Find the critical path.

(d) If the project has a 1 1/2 year deadline, should we consider crashing some activities? Explain.

5. Given the following network with resource demands, construct a modified PERT chart with resources and a resource load diagram. Suggest how to level the load if you can split operations. The project is due at day 36.

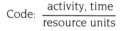

Code: $\dfrac{\text{activity, time}}{\text{resource units}}$

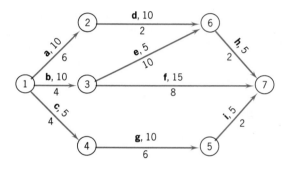

6. Reconsider Problem 14 in Chapter 8 under the constraint that the problem *must* be completed in 16 weeks. This time, however, activities **c, f, h,** and **i** may be crashed as follows.

Activity	Crash Time (weeks)	Additional Cost per Week
c	7	$40
f	6	20
h	2	10
i	3	30

Find the best schedule and its cost.

7. The following data were obtained from a study of the times required to overhaul a chemical plant:

Activity	Crash Schedule Time	Crash Schedule Cost	Normal Schedule Time	Normal Schedule Cost
1–2	3	$6	5	$4
1–3	1	5	5	3
2–4	5	7	10	4
3–4	2	6	7	4
2–6	2	5	6	3
4–6	5	9	11	6
4–5	4	6	6	3
6–7	1	4	5	2
5–7	1	5	4	2

Note: Costs are given in thousands of dollars, time in weeks.

(a) Find the all-normal schedule and cost.

(b) Find the all-crash schedule and cost.

(c) Find the total cost required to expedite all activities from all-normal (case a) to all-crash (case b).

(d) Find the *least-cost* plan for the all-crash time schedule. Start from the all-crash problem (b).

8. Given the data in Problem 7, determine the first activities to be crashed by the following priority rules:

(a) Shortest task first.

(b) Most resources first (use normal cost as the basis).

(c) Minimum slack first.

(d) Most critical followers.

(e) Most successors.

9. Consider Problem 10 in Chapter 8 again. Suppose the duration of both activities **A** and **D** can be reduced to one day, at a cost of $15 per day of reduction. Also, activities **E, G,** and **H** can be reduced in duration by one day at a cost of $25 per day of reduction. What is the least cost approach to crash the project two days? What is the shortest "crashed" duration, the new critical path, and the cost of crashing?

10. Given a network with normal times and crash times (in parentheses), find the optimal time–cost plan. Assume indirect costs are $100 per day. The data are:

Activity	Time Reduction Direct Cost per Day
1–2	$30 first, $50 second
2–3	$80 each
3–4	$25 first, $60 second
2–4	$30 first, $70 second, $90 third

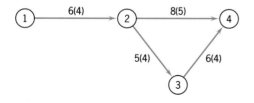

11. The network shown in the table has a fixed cost of $90 per day, but money can be saved by shortening the project duration. Find the least cost schedule.

Activity	Normal Time	Crash Time	Cost Increase (1st, 2nd, 3rd day)
1–2	7	4	$30, 50, 70
2–3	9	6	40, 45, 65
1–3	12	10	60, 60
2–4	11	9	35, 60
3–4	3	3	—

▶ INCIDENTS FOR DISCUSSION

Bryce Power Tool Company

George Ertle is the director of engineering for the Bryce Power Tool Company. A decision was made recently to modernize Bryce's entire tool line. The president of Bryce has indicated that he expects the modernization program to result in a significant improvement in design technology. Ertle is concerned with the possibility that his department will not have adequate resources to support the modernization program. Ertle believes he has enough staff to handle the aggregate engineering requirements, but he is not too sure he will be able to supply engineering personnel at the times and quantities requested by the company's project manager.

To complicate matters further, the tool modernization program will be under the control of four different project managers. Each major market segment has been recognized as a separate business unit with the authority to modernize the key tools for that segment based on a schedule that makes sense for it.

Ertle knows a little bit about resource allocation techniques. He remembers that one of the most effective allocation techniques is to work first on the activity with the minimum slack, so he has instructed his staff to approach any tasks they are assigned as members of a project team on that basis.

Questions: Is this technique a reasonable way to schedule the engineering resources of Bryce? Why or why not? What complication is added by making this four separate projects?

Critical Care Hospital

Critical Care Hospital will be purchasing a CATSCAN (computerized axial tomography scanner) in the next six months. The CATSCAN equipment will be installed in the radiology department and will require a significant renovation for the area. The scanner will arrive in about five months, but the construction project cannot be started until the unit is set in place. This will result in a project length of approximately 12 months. The hospital estimates the equipment will generate an income of $25,000 per month and is therefore in a hurry to complete the project. The project manager feels she may be able to cut the time on some aspects of the project, but at an increased cost. She has decided, in an effort to make the best decision, to use a resource allocation version of CPM.

Questions: What information must the project manager gather to use this method properly? How should she use this version of CPM to reduce the project time?

▶ PROJECT TEAM CONTINUING EXERCISE

The project team now is to address the problem of identifying and allocating resources for the project. First, determine what the resource loads are for each activity and what the resource availabilities are. Also determine whether activities can be speeded up by the allocation of additional resources; that is, the cost/time trade-offs. Conduct a CPM analysis to see where crashing may be desirable to meet an expedited completion and derive the cost-duration history graph. (If some activities have already been completed, conduct the analysis in retrospect.)

Next, plot the multiple resource needs for the project on a Gantt chart and evaluate their loadings. Use various heuristics and priority rules to level the loads and evaluate the time–resource trade-offs. Are there "natural" points of high efficiency or resource usage? What heuristics and priority rules seem to work best? Might any of the programming or optimizing methods seem applicable for your project? Might the SPAR heuristic be useful for your project? Why or why not?

BIBLIOGRAPHY

1. ANDERSON, D. R., D. J. SWEENEY, and T. A. WILLIAMS. *An Introduction to Management Science*, 6th ed. Minneapolis, MN: West Publishing, 1991.

2. ARROW, K. J., and L. HURWICZ. *Studies In Resource Allocation Processes.* Cambridge, GB: Cambridge University Press, 1977.

3. BALAS, E. "Project Scheduling with Resource Constraints." *Applications of Mathematical Programming Techniques*, Pittsburgh: Carnegie-Mellon Univ., 1970.

4. BENSON, L. A., and R. F. SEWALL, "Dynamic Crashing Keeps Projects Moving." *Computer Decisions*, Feb. 1972.

5. BERMAN, E. B. "Resource Allocation in a PERT Network Under Continuous Activity Time–Cost Functions." *Management Science*, July 1964.

6. BILDSON, R. A., and J. R. GILLESPIE. "Critical Path Planning PERT Integration." *Operations Research*, Nov.–Dec. 1962.

7. BUFFA, E. S., and J. G. MILLER. *Production-Inventory Systems: Planning and Control*, 3rd ed. Homewood, IL: Irwin, 1979.

8. CARRUTHERS, J. A., and A. BATTERSBY. "Advances in Critical Path Methods." *Operational Research Quarterly*, Dec. 1966.

9. CHARNES, A., and W. W. COOPER. "A Network Interpretation and a Direct Subdual Algorithm for Critical Path Scheduling." *Journal of Industrial Engineering*, July–Aug. 1962.

10. CLARK, E. "The Optimum Allocation of Resources among the Activities of a Network." *Journal of Industrial Engineering*, Jan.–Feb. 1961.

11. CORWIN, B. D. "Multiple R and D Project Scheduling with Limited Resources." *Technical Memorandum No. 122*, Dept. of Operations Research, Cleveland: Case Western Reserve University, 1968.

12. CROFT, F. M. "Putting a Price Tag on PERT Activities." *Journal of Industrial Engineering*, July 1966.

13. CROWSTON, W., and G. L. THOMPSON. "Decision CPM: A Method for Simultaneous Planning, Scheduling, and Control of Projects." *Operations Research*, May–June 1967.

14. DAVIES, E. M. "An Experimental Investigation of Resource Allocation in Multiactivity Projects." *Operational Research Quarterly*, Dec. 1973.

15. DAVIS, E. W. "Networks: Resource Allocation." *Industrial Engineering*, April 1974.

16. DAVIS, E. W. *Project Management: Techniques, Applications, and Managerial Issues*, 2nd ed. Norcross, GA: Institute of Industrial Engineers, 1983.

17. DAVIS, E. W., and G. E. HEIDORN. "An Algorithm for Optimal Project Scheduling Under Multiple Resource Constraints." *Management Science*, Aug. 1971.

18. DAVIS, E. W., and J. H. PATTERSON. "A Comparison of Heuristic and Optimum Solutions in Resource-Constrained Project Scheduling." *Management Science*, April 1975.

19. FENDLEY, L. G. "Towards the Development of a Complete Multiproject Scheduling System." *Journal of Industrial Engineering*, Oct. 1968.

20. GILYUTIN, I. "Using Project Management in a Nonlinear Environment." *Project Management Journal*, Dec. 1993.

21. GLAUBER, L. W. "Project Planning With Scitor's PS5000." *Project Management Journal*, June 1985.

22. GORENSTEIN, S. "An Algorithm for Project (Job) Sequencing with Resource Constraints." *Operations Research*, July–Aug. 1972.

23. HARRISON, F. L. *Advanced Project Management.* Hants, GB Gower, 1983.

24. HASTINGS, N. A. J. "On Resource Allocation in Networks." *Operational Research Quarterly,* June 1972.

25. JOHNSON, R. V. "Resource Constrained Scheduling Capabilities of Commercial Project Management Software." *Project Management Journal,* Dec. 1992.

26. KELLEY, J. "Critical Path Planning and Scheduling: Mathematical Basis." *Operations Research,* May–June 1961.

27. KRONE, W. T. B., and H. V. PHILLIPS. "SCRAPP, a Reporting and Allocation System for a Multi-Project Situation." *Applications of Critical Path Techniques.* London: English University Press, 1968.

28. KURTULUS, I., and E. W. DAVIS. "Multi-Project Scheduling: Categorization of Heuristic Rules Performance." *Management Science,* Feb. 1982.

29. KURTULUS, I., and S. C. NARULA. "Multi-Project Scheduling: Analysis of Project Performance." *IEEE Transactions on Engineering Management,* March 1985.

30. LAMBERSON, L. R., and R. R. HOCKING. "Optimum Time Compression in Project Scheduling." *Management Science,* June 1970.

31. MARCHBANKS, J. L. "Daily Automatic Rescheduling Technique." *Journal of Industrial Engineering,* March 1966.

32. MILLS, N. L. "The Development of a University Sports Complex: A Project Management Application." *Computers and Industrial Engineering,* 1989.

33. MODER, J. J., C. R. PHILLIPS, and E. W. DAVIS. *Project Management With CPM, PERT and Precedence Diagramming,* 3rd ed. New York: Van Nostrand Reinhold, 1983.

34. MOODIE, C. L., and D. E. MANDEVILLE. "Project Resource Balancing by Assembly Lines Balancing Techniques." *Journal of Industrial Engineering,* July 1965.

35. MOSHMAN, J., J. R. JOHNSON, and M. LARSEN. "RAMPS—A Technique for Resource Allocation and Multiproject Scheduling." *Proceedings,* Spring Joint Computer Conference, 1963.

36. NAVARRE, C., and J. SCHAAN. "Design of Project Management Systems from Top Management's Perspective," *Project Management Journal,* Jun. 1990.

37. NICHOLAS, J. M. *Managing Business & Engineering Projects.* Englewood Cliffs, NJ: Prentice Hall, 1990.

38. PARNCUTT, G. "Concepts of Resource Allocation and Cost Control and Their Utility in Project Management." *Project Management Quarterly,* 1974.

39. PARRIS, T. P. E. "Practical Manpower Allocation of a Project Mix Via Zero-Float CPM Networks." *Project Management Institute Proceedings,* 1972.

40. PASCOE, T. L. "An Experimental Comparison of Heuristic Methods for Allocating Resources." Ph.D. Dissertation, Department of Engineering, Cambridge, GB: Cambridge University Press, 1965.

41. PATTERSON, J. H. "Alternate Methods of Project Scheduling with Limited Resources." *Naval Research Logistics Quarterly,* Dec. 1973.

42. PATTERSON, J. H., and W. D. HUBER. "A Horizon-Varying, Zero-One Approach to Project Scheduling." *Management Science,* Feb. 1974.

43. PRITSKER, A. A. B., L. J. WALTERS, and P. M. WOLFE. "Multi-Project Scheduling with Limited Resources: A Zero-One Programming Approach." *Management Science,* Sept. 1969.

44. ROBINSON, D. R. "A Dynamic Programming Solution to Cost-Time Trade-off for CPM." *Management Science,* Oct. 1975.

45. SAKAREV, I., and M. DEMIROV. *Solving Multi-Project Planning by Network Analysis.* Amsterdam: North-Holland, 1969.

46. SCHRAGE, L. "Solving Resource-Constrained Network Problems by Implicit Enumeration—Non-Preemptive Case." *Operations Research,* 1970.

47. SHIH, W. "A New Application of Incremental Analysis in Resource Allocations." *Operational Research Quarterly,* Dec. 1974.

48. SHIH, W. "A Branch and Bound Procedure for a Class of Discrete Resource Allocation Problems with Several Constraints." *Operational Research Quarterly,* June 1977.

49. STINSON, J. P. "A Branch and Bound Algorithm for a General Class of Resource Constrained Scheduling Problems." *AIIE Conference Proceedings,* Las Vegas, 1975.

50. STINSON, J. P., E. W. DAVIS, and B. KHUMAWALA. "Multiple Resource-Constrained Scheduling Using Branch and Bound." *AIIE Transactions,* Sept. 1978.

51. SUNAGE, T. "A Method of the Optimal Scheduling for a Project with Resource Restrictions." *Journal of the Operations Research Society of Japan*, March 1970.

52. TALBOT, F. B. "Project Scheduling with Resource-Duration Interactions: The Nonpreemptive Case." Working paper No. 200, Graduate School of Business Administration, Ann Arbor, MI: University of Michigan, Jan. 1980.

53. TALBOT, F. B., and J. H. PATTERSON. "Optimal Methods for Scheduling Under Resource Constraints." *Project Management Quarterly*, Dec. 1979.

54. TONGE, F. M. *A Heuristic Program for Assembly Line Balancing.* Englewood Cliffs, NJ: Prentice Hall, 1961.

55. TURBAN, E., and J. R. MEREDITH. *Fundamentals of Management Science*, 6th ed. Homewood, IL: Irwin, 1994.

56. WALTON, H. "Administration Aspects of Network Analysis." *Applications of Critical Path Techniques.* London: English Universities Press, 1968.

57. WEAVER, J. "Mainframe ARTEMIS: More Than a Project Management Tool." *Project Management Journal*, April 1988.

58. WHITEHOUSE, G. E., and J. R. BROWN. "GENRES: An Extension of Brook's Algorithm for Project Scheduling with Resource Constraints." *Computers and Industrial Engineering*, No. 3, 1979.

59. WEIST, J. D. "A Heuristic Model for Scheduling Large Projects with Limited Resources." *Management Science*, Feb. 1967.

60. WEIST, J. D. "Heuristic Programs for Decision Making." *Harvard Business Review*, Sept.–Oct. 1965.

61. WOODWORTH, B. M., and C. T. WILLIE. "A Heuristic Algorithm for Resource Levelling in Multi-Project, Multi-Resource Scheduling." *Decision Sciences*, 1975.

CASE

D. U. SINGER HOSPITAL PRODUCTS CORP.
Herbert F. Spirer

D. U. Singer Hospital Products Corp. has done sufficient new product development at the research and development level to estimate a high likelihood of technical success for a product of assured commercial success: A long-term antiseptic. Management has instructed Singer's Antiseptic Division to make a market entry at the earliest possible time; they have requested a complete plan up to the startup of production. Marketing and other plans following startup of production are to be prepared separately after this plan has been completed.

Project responsibility is assigned to the division's Research and Development Group; Mike Richards, the project scientist who developed the product, is assigned responsibility for project management. Assistance will be required from other parts of the company: Packaging Task Force, R & D Group; Corporate Engineering; Corporate Purchasing; Hospital Products Manufacturing Group; Packaged Products Manufacturing Group.

Mike was concerned about the scope of the project. He knew from his own experience that a final formula had yet to be developed, although such development was really a "routine" function. The remaining questions had to do with color, odor, and consistency additives rather than any performance-related modification. Fortunately, the major regulatory issues had been resolved and he believed that submission of regulatory documentation would be followed by rapid approval as they already had a letter of approval contingent on final documentation.

But there were also issues in packaging that had to be resolved; development of the packaging design was one of his primary concerns at this time. Ultimately, there will have to be manufacturing procedures in accordance with corporate policies and standards: capital equipment selection and procurement, installation of this equipment and startup.

Mike was concerned about defining the project unambiguously. To that end, he obtained an interview with S. L. Mander, the group vice-president.

When he asked Mander where his responsibility should end, the executive turned the question back to him. Mike had been prepared for this and said that he would like to regard his part of the project as done when the production process could be turned over to manufacturing. They agreed that according to Singer practice, this would be when the manufacturing operation could produce a 95 percent yield of product (fully packaged) at a level of 80 percent of the full production goal of 10 million liters per year.

"But I want you to remember," said Mander, "that you must meet all current FDA, EPA, and OSHA regulations and you must be in compliance with our internal specification—the one I've got is dated September and is RD78/965. And you know that manufacturing now—quite rightly, I feel—insists on full written manufacturing procedures."

After this discussion, Mike felt that he had enough information about this aspect to start to pin down what had to be done to achieve these results. His first step in this effort was to meet with P. H. Docent, the director of research.

"You are naive if you think that you can just start right in finalizing the formula," said Docent. "You must first develop a product rationale (a).* This is a formally defined process according to company policy. Marketing expects inputs at this stage, manufacturing expects their voice to be heard, and you will have to have approvals from every unit of the company that is involved; all of this is reviewed by the Executive Committee. You should have no trouble if you do your homework, but expect to spend a good eight weeks to get this done."

"That certainly stretches things out," said Mike. "I expected to take 12 weeks to develop the ingredient formula (b) and you know that I can't start to establish product specifications (c) until the formula is complete. That's another three weeks."

"Yes, but while you are working on the product specifications you can get going on the regulatory documentation (d). Full internal specifications are not required for that work, but you can't start those documents until the formula is complete."

"Yes, and I find it hard to believe that we can push through both preparation of documents *and* get-

---

*Tasks which must be accounted for in a network plan are identified by lower-case alphabetic symbols in parentheses. Refer to Exhibit 1.

ting approval in three weeks, but Environmental swears it can be done."

"Oh, it can be done in this case because of the preparatory work. Of course, I won't say that this estimate of three weeks is as certain as our other time estimates. All we need is a change of staff at the Agency and we are in trouble. But once you have both the specifications and the approval, you can immediately start on developing the processing system (g)."

"Yes, and how I wish we could get a lead on that, but the designers say that there is too much uncertainty and they won't move until they have both specifications and regulatory documentation and approval. They are offering pretty fast response; six weeks from start to finish for the processing system."

"They are a good crew, Mike. And of course, you know that you don't have to delay on starting the packaging segment of this project. You can start developing the packaging concept (e) just as soon as the product rationale has been developed. If my experience is any judge, it will take a full eight weeks; you'll have to work to keep the process from running forever."

"But as soon as that is finished we can start on the design of the package and its materials (f) which usually takes about six weeks. Once that is done we can start on the packaging system (h) which shouldn't take longer than eight weeks," concluded Mike. At this point he realized that although Docent would have general knowledge, he needed to talk directly to the Director of Manufacturing.

"The first step, which follows the completion of the development of processing and packaging systems," said the Director of Manufacturing, "is to do a complete study of the facilities requirements (i). You won't be able to get that done in less than four weeks. And that must precede the preparation of the capital equipment list (j) which should take about three-quarters as long. Of course, as soon as both the process system and packaging system are completed, you could start on preparing the written manufacturing procedures (q)."

"But," said Mike, "Can I really finish the procedures before I have installed and constructed the facilities (p)?"

"No, quite right. What you can do is get the first phase done, but the last three of the ten weeks it will take to do that will have to wait for the installation and construction."

"Then this means that I really have two phases for the writing, that which can be completed without the

Activity	Packaging Task Force	R & D Group	Corp. Eng.	H-P Manuf.	Pack. Prod. Manuf.	Maint.	Purchasing	Material & Other Direct Charges
a—prod. rationale	1	12	1	1	2	0	0	$ 0
b—dev. formula	0	16	4	2	0	0	0	500
c—prod. spec.	1	6	3	1	1	0	1	0
d—reg. document	0	12	4	2	0	0	0	0
e—dev. pkg. conc.	12	8	4	2	8	0	2	4000
f—design pkg.	12	2	3	0	3	0	3	2000
g—dev. proc. sys.	0	18	12	12	0	0	0	0
h—dev. pkg. sys.	24	8	8	0	8	0	2	0
i—study fac. req.	0	4	16	2	2	0	0	0
j—cap. equip. list	0	1	3	0	0	0	1	0
k—procure proc. eqpt.	0	1	1	1	0	0	7	40,000
l—procure pkg. eqpt.	1	0	1	0	1	0	9	160,000
m—procure facil.	0	0	1	1	1	1	6	30,000
n—install proc. eqpt.	0	2	4	8	0	4	1	4000
o—install pkg. eqpt.	2	0	4	0	8	4	1	8000
p—install fac.	0	0	5	5	5	10	1	6000
q,q'—written procedures	5	5	5	10	15	10	0	5000
r—pilot test	3	6	6	6	6	6	0	0

Exhibit 1: Labor Requirements (Worker-weeks)

installation and construction (q), and that which has to wait for those inputs (q′).″

″True. Now you realize that the last thing you have to do is to run the equipment in a pilot test (r) which will show that you have reached a satisfactory level?″

″Yes. Since that must include debugging, I've estimated a six-week period as adequate.″ The director of manufacturing assented. Mike continued, ″What I'm not sure of is whether we can run all the installation tasks in parallel.″

″You can let the purchase orders and carry out the procurement of process equipment (k), packaging equipment (l), and facilities (m) as soon as the capital equipment list is complete. The installation of each of these types of equipment and facilities can start as soon as the goods are on hand (n,o,p).″

″What do you estimate for the times to do these tasks?″ asked Mike. The director of manufacturing estimated 18, 8, and 4 weeks for the purchasing phases for each of the subsystems in that order and four weeks for each of the installations. ″Then I can regard my job as done with the delivery of the procedures and when I show my 95 percent yield,″ said Mike, and the director of manufacturing agreed, but reminded Mike that none of the purchasing cycles could start until the capital equipment list had been prepared and approved (j) which he saw as a three-week task.

The executive committee of D. U. Singer Hospital Products Corporation set a starting date for the project of December 10 and asked Mike to project a completion date with his submission of the plan. The committee's request implied that whatever date Mike came up with was acceptable, but Mike knew that he would be expected to show how to shorten the time to complete the project. However, his task in making the schedule was clear; he had to establish the resource requirements and deal with calendar constraints as best as he could.

To this end, Mike had to get an estimate of resources which he decided to do by making a list of the

activities and asking each group involved what was their level of employee input. The results of this survey are shown in Exhibit 1.

For the purposes of overall planning, the accounting department told Mike that he could estimate a cost of $600 per week per employee. This would enable him to provide a cash flow forecast along with his plan, which the chief accountant said would be expected, something that Mike had not realized.

Mike knew that it was customary at D. U. Singer to provide the following as parts of a plan to be submitted to the executive committee:

1. Statement of Objectives.
2. Work Breakdown Structure.
3. A network, either activity-on-node (CPM) or event-on-node (PERT).
4. A determination of the critical path or paths and the duration along the critical path.
5. An Early-Start Schedule, in which every activity would be started at its Early Start, regardless of resource constraints.
6. A period labor requirements graph for:
   a. Each group.
   b. Project as a whole.
7. Cumulative labor requirements plot for:
   a. Each group.
   b. Project as a whole.
8. A schedule based on the best leveling of labor requirements that could be achieved without lengthening project duration by more than 15 percent in calendar days.
9. A cash flow requirements graph for the project when leveled, assuming that commitments for materials and other direct charges are made at the start of the activity but that arrivals of purchased goods are uniformly distributed through the first two-thirds of the activity.

▶ QUESTIONS

1. Construct the nine elements of the plan identified above.
2. Analyze the plan for potential problems.
3. Analyze the plan for opportunities.
4. Should the executive committee approve the plan? Why or why not?
5. What alternatives might the executive committee suggest for analysis?

▶ This article compares a number of different PM software packages and describes their differences, particularly as regards resource leveling. The packages are then compared in terms of their ability to optimally schedule 110 projects that have over-scheduled resources.

READING

RESOURCE CONSTRAINED SCHEDULING CAPABILITIES OF COMMERCIAL PROJECT MANAGEMENT SOFTWARE

Roger V. Johnson

Introduction

Several commercial microcomputer project management software packages are tested for their ability to optimally schedule 110 projects in which early finish schedules have over-scheduled resources. Each examined package has the ability to remove the over-scheduled positions with resource leveling. It was found that no package consistently finds a schedule in which the project completion time is minimized. The best package obtains schedules for the 110 projects that average 5.03 percent longer than the optimal schedule of each; the weakest package obtains schedules that average 25.6 percent longer than optimal.

Commercial project management packages level resources that are over-scheduled to their earliest start schedule differently, seldom attaining the same or the shortest possible schedule. This article compares the schedules of 110 projects[1] generated by 13 versions of seven commercial software packages: SuperProject Expert 1.0 and SuperProject 2.0, Timeline 2.0 and 4.0, Primavera 4.00, 4.1 and 5.0, Microsoft Project for Windows 1.0 and 3.0, Harvard Total Project Manager II and Harvard Project Manager 3.0, Pertmaster Advanced[2], and Hornet[2]; with two academic procedures: Talbot's [8] optimizer, and Patterson's [4] heuristic.

All packages that use PERT or the Critical Path Method compute the same early and late start and finish times from the same project data—unless *resource leveling* is required to remove over-scheduled conditions. Then, it is often very difficult to find the optimal (shortest feasible) schedule, and no commercial package examined consistently does so. Why? When two tasks require the same resource, it is not always obvious which should be scheduled first. Consider the five-task project depicted in Figure 1.

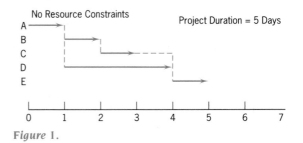

Figure 1.

In the absence of resource constraints, this project can be completed in five days, and the critical path is A-D-E. The total slack of Tasks A, D, and E is 0, and is 1 for Tasks B and C. (Total slack is the time which a task might be delayed beyond its early start without causing the project to be late. Wiest and Levy [9] provide a clear description of this and other critical path basics.) But suppose the only available unit of Resource R is required by Tasks B and D, which are scheduled to be performed simultaneously in the earliest start schedule. To find the shortest schedule, it is necessary to try B earlier, and also try D earlier. Only then is it clear to schedule B earlier than D to complete the project in six days. Both schedules are provided in Figure 2.

An appealing way to resolve a two-task resource conflict is to schedule the task with less total slack earlier. This is what some commercial packages do, and it is very often the correct choice. But not always, as demonstrated in Figure 2, in which Task B should be performed first to shorten the project's duration, even though it has more slack than D.

The difficulty of determining the optimal schedule lies in the vast number of combinations of tasks and schedules. To be sure of obtaining an optimal schedule, it is necessary to enumerate each option at every conflict. If 20 two-task resource conflicts exist, there are 1,048,576 schedules to enumerate. To do

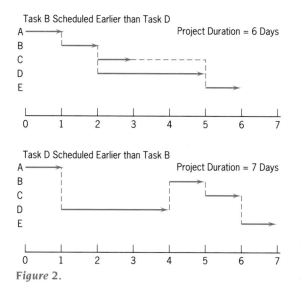

Figure 2.

this, it is necessary to identify each conflict and keep track of those enumerated. Davis and Heidorn [1], Demeulemeester and Herroelen [2], Stinson, Davis and Khumawala [7], and Talbot and Patterson [8] show how this can be done. Each have clever ways of shortening the enumeration process, such as to

- Keep track of task completion times of partial solutions and then either identify and eliminate dominated partial solutions; or to

- Compute time bounds for unscheduled tasks and eliminate all solutions containing the partial solution if the project necessarily exceeds the completion time of another solution already identified.

Each of the four optimizing approaches provides the optimal resource-constrained schedule to small or moderately sized projects. All four require excessive computer time for large projects (Demeulemeester's requires the least), and the Davis and Stinson procedures require large amounts of computer memory for large projects. Patterson [5] describes and evaluates the earlier three approaches in detail.

Large Number of Heuristics

Heuristic schedules are built by applying the selected heuristic (rule), such as "least total slack," to each task assignment decision. A rule can be implemented in several ways:

- Using dynamic or static allocation (depending on whether task properties are recalculated after each task assignment);

- Using forward or backward allocation (depending on whether the project sequence is built from the start or end of the project);

- Using serial or parallel allocation (depending on whether the tasks are sequenced strictly in order of the heuristic priority, or whether the schedule is built in chronological order with conflicts decided by the selected rule); and

- Allowing tasks to be split or not.

So there are 2^4, or 16, ways to implement a single rule if no ties occur. Ties often do occur: such as when two or more tasks have the same total slack. To break a tie, another rule such as "shortest imminent task" or "earliest late finish" can be used. If a tie still ensues, a third rule can be used. The use of four tie-breaking rules increases the number of distinct implementations by a factor of 4! to 384.

Packages Evaluated and Data Preparation

Each of the procedures identified in the opening paragraph were used to schedule the 110 projects assembled by Patterson.

Converting Data to the Format of Commercial Packages The transfer of data between packages was accomplished by using five custom FORTRAN programs in conjunction with the data conversion programs supplied with two of the packages and with the import and export facilities provided by the packages.

Resource Leveling Default Options Used If a package offers resource leveling options, the default settings were used in the experiments. The assumptions made internally by each package are the same: tasks cannot be split, over-scheduled positions are not used, etc. Thus, each package schedules identical projects under the same conditions.

SuperProject. The automatic leveling feature is used by selecting "yes" to Resource Leveling, and "no" to Level by Priority. This invokes leveling by float (i.e., by least slack) (pages 4-37 and 13-13, Super-Project Expert 1.0 User Manual). Version 1.0 appears to use a static, backward, and parallel implementation. Super-Project 2.0 incorporates improvements.

Timeline. Releas.es 2.0 and 4.0 generate identical schedules. Version 4.0 is much faster. A task with

Table 1. Completion Times of 110 Resource Constrained Projects When Scheduled by Twelve Logic Systems

Problem #	# of Tasks	Resource Units* #1	#2	#3	Talbot (Optimal)	Patterson's Heuristic	SuperProject Expert 1.0	SuperProject 2.0	Timeline 2.0/4.0	Harvard TPM II/3.0	Primavera (1)	Primavera (2)	MS Project for Windows 1.0	MS Project for Windows 3.0	PertMaster Advanced	Hornet
1	14	2	1	2	19	21	19	20	19	19	19	19	22	22	19	19
2	7	5	5	3	7	7	7	7	8	8	9	8	7	7	10	8
3	13	6	7	6	20	20	23	23	22	23	23	23	24	23	31	22
4	22	15	20	20	6	6	6	6	6	6	6	6	6	6	6	6
5	22	13	15	15	7	7	7	7	7	7	7	7	7	7	7	7
6	22	13	13	13	8	8	8	8	8	8	8	8	8	8	8	8
7	9	5			8	10	8	8	8	11	11	8	9	10	8	8
8	9	4			11	11	11	11	13	11	14	11	13	13	11	11
9	18	8			19	19	21	19	21	19	25	31	29	21	31	24
10	8	4	3		14	14	14	14	14	14	14	14	14	14	14	14
11	8	3	3		18	18	18	18	18	18	18	18	18	18	18	18
12	23	11	5	8	13	13	13	13	13	14	13	14	20	13	14	13
13	22	10	10	10	20	20	26	21	27	25	23	27	32	27	24	27
- Table abbreviated -																
100	27	10	10	10	33	39	37	36	37	41	40	42	47	37	42	38
101	51	10	12	10	75	79	80	77	79	81	80	90	87	79	86	77
102	51	10	12	12	83	83	85	83	83	85	83	97	110	83	96	85
103	51	14	14	12	56	56	58	56	58	58	58	58	64	56	58	58
104	51	12	12	10	79	80	79	80	79	80	79	79	87	80	79	79
105	51	10	10	10	77	77	77	77	77	77	77	86	92	77	86	77
106	51	10	10	10	60	63	62	62	63	61	64	63	80	63	63	66
107	51	10	12	10	78	78	78	78	78	78	78	79	107	78	79	78
108	51	10	10	10	61	63	64	63	65	65	63	71	94	63	65	64
109	51	12	12	10	60	63	64	62	63	65	63	62	78	64	72	63
110	51	10	12	10	50	52	53	51	51	65	52	69	57	52	69	53
Total					3836	4061	4113	4064	4029	4219	4184	4382	4818	4074	4377	4048
Mean percent over optimal					0	5.87	7.22	5.94	5.03	9.98	9.07	14.23	25.60	6.20	14.10	5.53
Optimal schedules					110	30	28	31	35	21	18	19	10	31	18	33

* All problems required one, two, or three resources. Available units of each resource are shown.

1. This schedule was generated without using Primavera's "Schedule before level?" option.

2. This schedule was generated using Primavera's "Schedule before level?" option.

an earlier start date takes precedence over one with a later start date. Ties are broken in favor of the task with the longer duration (page 6-12, Timeline User Manual 4.0). The implementation appears to be static, forward, and parallel.

Primavera. Primavera offers several ways of resource leveling. The default setting selects the "least slack" schedule. The option "Should this project be scheduled prior to leveling?" proved important, so results for both the "no" and "yes" option are reported. The "Smooth resource during leveling?" option is not selected. Scheduling before leveling appears to generate a static schedule.

Harvard Project Manager. The resource leveling option is selected. Its scheduling approach is not apparent, and the manual does not state which rule is used.

Microsoft Project for Windows 1.0 and 3.0. The resource leveling option is used. The early start date is used to sequence tasks. Ties are broken by favoring the task with the least slack. Second-order ties are broken in favor of the task with the shortest duration. Remaining ties are broken favoring the task with the largest task ID. Version 1.0 contains a logic error which has been corrected in Version 3.0, which accounts for the different results.

This package should not be confused with the DOS-based Microsoft Project, which has the ability to level resources only within the total slack of the schedule. For most of the 110 projects, an over-scheduled position remained, so Microsoft Project is not included in the study.

Patterson's Heuristic. Patterson [4] constructed a regression equation for each of the eight one-pass heuristics. "Patterson's heuristic" schedules a particular project with the rule predicted by his regression equations to provide the shortest schedule for a particular project. The equations do not always select the best heuristic.

Computations Results

In Table 1 the optimal project durations provided by Talbot's optimizer are listed with those of other procedures.

Timeline is the most successful of the tested commercial packages. It obtains the optimal (shortest

Table 2.   Project 13 Data

Task Number	Duration	Required Followers	Required Units for Resource		
			1	**2**	**3**
1	0	2, 3, 4, 17, 18	0	0	0
2	2	5, 6	2	3	6
3	4	7, 8, 9	1	5	0
4	3	10, 11	4	2	3
5	2	13	2	1	5
6	3	12	4	3	1
7	1	12	3	2	7
8	2	14, 20	6	0	3
9	4	15, 16	5	3	6
10	3		3	8	3
11	1	13, 15, 16	2	4	0
12	1	19	1	2	1
13	5	19	6	1	5
14	2		7	5	2
15	3		4	4	3
16	3	21	0	5	7
17	0	19	2	2	3
18	0	21	4	1	5
19	4	22	1	3	0
20	3	22	4	2	2
21	2	22	2	1	2
22	0		0	0	0
Resource availability:		Resource number:	1	2	3
		Available Units:	10	10	10

possible) schedule duration for 35 of the 110 projects, and is an average of 5.03 percent over the optimal duration. The least successful package, Microsoft Project for Windows Version 1.0, finds the optimal schedule for 10 of the 110 projects, and is an average of 25.60 percent over the shortest duration. (Version 3.0 is much improved.)

A useful feature of Primavera is its choice of leveling options: several can be used and the best schedule selected. When the better of the two schedules generated by the Primavera options used in this study is selected, the project duration is an average of 7.45 percent over the optimal duration.

An Analysis of Problem 13

Problem 13 is examined in more detail because the schedules created by the various packages are so different. The data of this project is provided in Table 2, followed in Figure 3 by its schedule when resource requirements are ignored. The schedules obtained by the various packages are provided in Table 3.

Table 3 shows that all procedures create the same schedule for the first three days, except for

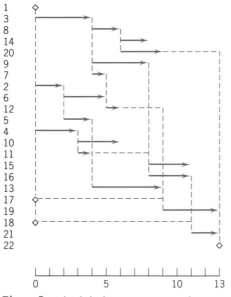

Figure 3: Schedule for Project 13 without resource leveling.

Timeline's placement of Tasks 17 and 18, which are milestone activities of negligible duration. On the fourth day, there is a shortage of the second resource, calling for a decision. Tasks 3 and 5, which started on Days 1 and 3, respectively, use six of the ten available units of this resource on Day 4. Task 6 requires three units and Task 11 requires four units of the second resource. Table 3 reveals that some packages schedule Task 6 here, while others schedule Task 11.

Conclusion

Commercial packages usually do not create optimal schedules when resource leveling is necessary. The problem is that no single heuristic scheduler is consistently best, and optimizers sometimes take excessive time. Yet using a sub-optimal schedule is inconsistent with the new ethic of competing on time as espoused, for example, by Stalk [6]. The impact of unnecessarily slow projects on a business is often underestimated: particularly losses from getting to market later and subsequently losing market share. The more easily estimated lateness costs of over-budget labor and equipment, and late penalties are only some of the consequences. This suggests commercial software vendors should provide optimal scheduling as an option.

The author's solution to the problem of obtaining optimal resource-levelled schedules is a FORTRAN program that takes a commercial package's exported data, computes an optimal schedule using an optimizing algorithm, then provides the optimal schedule in a form that the commercial package can import—thus providing an optimal schedule within a commercial package.

Endnotes

1   I am grateful to Professor James H. Patterson of Indiana University for providing the data set and project durations using Talbot's and Patterson's procedures.

2   I am also grateful to Professor Dr. W. Herroelen and E. Demeulemeester of the Katholieke Universiteit Leuven for providing an English translation of portions of their student Michel Moreau's thesis [3], the source of Pertmaster Advanced and Hornet results.

Table 3. Project 13 Schedules Generated by Ten Logic Systems

Task start and finish times generated by:

Task #	Duration	Talbot (Optimum)	Patterson's Heuristic	Primavera (1)	Primavera (2)	Timeline 2.0/4.0	Harvard TPM II/3.0	SuperProject Expert 1.0	SuperProject 2.0	MS Project for Windows 1.0	MS Project for Windows 3.0
1	0	1-1	1-1	1-1	1-1	1-1	1-1	1-1	1-1	1-1	1-1
2	2	1-2	1-2	1-2	1-2	1-2	1-2	1-2	1-2	1-2	1-2
3	4	1-4	1-4	1-4	1-4	1-4	1-4	1-4	1-4	1-4	1-4
4	3	1-3	1-3	1-3	1-3	1-3	1-3	1-3	1-3	1-3	1-3
5	2	3-4	3-4	3-4	3-4	3-4	3-4	3-4	3-4	3-4	3-4
6	3	4-6	4-6	4-6	5-7	5-7	5-7	5-7	5-7	5-7	9-11
7	1	15-15	15-15	5-5	17-17	14-14	17-17	14-14	5-5	17-17	14-14
8	2	14-15	14-15	6-7	14-15	14-15	14-15	14-15	15-16	17-18	14-15
9	4	5-8	5-8	8-11	5-8	10-13	5-8	5-8	6-9	8-11	5-8
10	3	12-14	12-14	12-14	21-23	20-22	23-25	15-17	10-12	22-24	20-22
11	1	7-7	7-7	5-5	4-4	4-4	4-4	4-4	4-4	4-4	4-4
12	1	16-16	16-16	7-7	18-18	15-15	18-18	15-15	8-8	18-18	15-15
13	5	9-13	9-13	12-16	9-13	5-9	9-13	9-13	10-14	12-16	9-13
14	2	19-20	19-20	17-18	19-20	26-27	21-22	21-22	20-21	31-32	26-27
15	3	9-11	9-11	19-21	9-11	23-25	9-11	18-20	13-15	25-27	23-25
16	3	16-18	16-18	17-19	14-16	16-18	14-16	22-24	16-18	19-21	16-18
17	0	1-1	1-1	1-1	1-1	8-8	1-1	1-1	1-1	1-1	1-1
18	0	1-1	1-1	1-1	1-1	8-8	1-1	1-1	1-1	1-1	1-1
19	4	17-20	17-20	20-23	24-27	16-19	19-22	18-21	16-19	25-28	16-19
20	3	16-18	16-18	8-10	16-18	16-18	18-20	18-20	17-19	28-30	23-25
21	2	19-20	19-20	20-21	18-19	19-20	17-18	25-26	19-20	28-29	26-27
22	0	20-20	20-20	23-23	27-27	21-21	25-25	26-26	20-20	30-30	27-27
Project		1-20	1-20	1-23	1-27	1-27	1-25	1-26	1-21	1-32	1-27

1. This schedule generated with "no" reply to Primavera's question "Schedule before level?"

2. This schedule generated with "yes" reply to Primavera's question "Schedule before level?"

References

1. DAVIS, EDWARD W., and G. E., HEIDORN. 1971. "Optimal Project Scheduling Under Multiple Resource Constraints." *Management Science*, 17, 12 (August), B803-B816.

2. DEMEULEMEESTER, ERIC, and WILLY, HERROELEN. 1992. "A Branch-and-Bound Procedure for the Multiple Resource-Constrained Project Scheduling Problem." Forthcoming *Management Science*.

3. MOREAU, MICHEL. 1990. "Het evalueren van project-plannings software met betrekking tot behandeling van hulpmiddelenbeperkingen." Masters thesis. Belgium: Katholieke Universiteit Leuven.

4. PATTERSON, JAMES H. 1976. "Project Scheduling: The Effects of Problem Structure on Heuristic Performance." *Naval Research Logistics Quarterly*, 23, 1 (March), 95-123.

5. PATTERSON, JAMES H. 1984. "A Comparison of Exact Approaches for Solving the Multiple Constrained Resource, Project Scheduling Problem." *Management Science*, 30, 7 (July), 854–867.

6. STALK, GEORGE. 1988. "Time—The Next Source of Competitive Advantage." *Harvard Business Review*, (July-August), 41–51.

7. STINSON, JOEL P., EDWARD W. DAVIS, and BASHEER M. KHUMAWALA. 1978. "Multiple Resource Constrained Scheduling Using Branch and Bound." AIIE *Transactions*, 10, 3 (September), 252–259.

8. TALBOT, F. BRIAN, and JAMES H. PATTERSON. 1978. "An Efficient Integer Programming Algorithm with Network Cuts for Solving Resource Constrained Scheduling Problems." *Management Science*, 24, 11 (July), 1163–1174.

9. WEIST, JEROME D., and FERDINAND K. LEVY. 1977. A *Management Guide to* PERT/CPM. Englewood Cliffs, NJ: Prentice Hall.

10

Monitoring and Information Systems

In this chapter, perhaps more than in any other, it would be helpful if we could consider everything at once. How is it possible to discuss monitoring without specifying what is to be controlled? On the other hand, how is it possible to specify a control system without understanding what aspects of a project are subject to measurement and how the measurement is to be accomplished? As a matter of fact, one could just as easily argue that evaluation, the primary subject of Chapter 12, should precede both monitoring and control. The placement of these chapters is arbitrary, and readers may feel free to read them in any order they wish. Irrespective of the order in which one considers these subjects, however, their interdependence is clear.

Our fundamental approach to evaluation and control of projects is that these activities are, at base, the opposite sides of project selection and planning. The logic of selection dictates the components to be evaluated, and the details of planning expose the elements to be controlled. The ability to measure is prerequisite to either.

Monitoring is collecting, recording, and reporting information concerning any and all aspects of project performance that the project manager or others in the organization wish to know. In our discussion it is important to remember that monitoring, as an activity, should be kept distinct from controlling (which uses the data supplied by monitoring to bring actual performance into approximate congruence with planned performance), as well as from evaluation (through which judgments are made about the quality and effectiveness of project performance).

First we expand on the nature of this link between planning and control, including a brief discussion of the various aspects of project performance that need to be monitored. We also examine some of the problems associated with monitoring a project. Finally, we report on several computer software packages that can greatly increase the speed and effectiveness of project monitoring.

This book is addressed to practicing PMs as well as students of project management. Students resist the idea that PMs do not have immediate access to accurate information on every aspect of the project. But PMs know it is not always easy to find out what's going on when working on a project. Records are frequently out of date, incomplete, in error, or "somewhere else" when needed. A hospital executive of our acquaintance carried out a project that was designed to generate a major improvement in profitability by altering the patient mix. The hospital's accounting system could not report on the results of the project until six months later.

Throughout the chapter, our primary concern is to ensure that all parties interested in the project have available, *on a timely basis*, the information needed to exercise effective control over the project. The other uses for monitoring (e.g., auditing, learning from past mistakes, or keeping senior management informed), important as they are, must be considered secondary to the control function when constructing the monitoring system. The key issue, then, is to create an information system that gives project managers the information they need to make informed, timely decisions that will keep project performance as close as possible to the project plan.

One final note. In this chapter we frequently refer to a "project monitor," a "project controller," or even to the "group" responsible for monitoring. These individuals and groups do in fact exist on most large projects. On a small project, it is likely that the person in charge of monitoring is the same person as the project controller—and the same person as the PM. That is, when we refer to the project monitor and controller, we are referring to roles needed in project management, not necessarily to different individuals.

Project Management in Practice
Using Project Management Software to Schedule the 1988 Olympic Winter Games in Calgary

The XV Olympiad in Calgary involved nearly 2000 athletes from 57 countries in 129 competitive events, attracted over 1,500,000 spectators, was covered by over 5000 journalists, and was run by a staff of 600 professionals complemented by 10,000 volunteers. For those 600 responsible for organizing, planning, scheduling, coordinating, and handling the information requirements for the 16-day extravaganza, the task was overwhelming. The top managers of the organizing committee thus turned to a Computer Based Project Planning and Scheduling (CBPPS) system for scheduling and managing the 30,000 tasks organized into 50 projects, the first time this

had ever been done. (Although tried in the 1984 Los Angeles Games, the attempt was dropped when the scheduled completion was found to be late 1986.)

The goal for the Calgary Games was to provide the best games ever, but within the budget. The philosophy employed was to let each project manager plan his/her own project but meet firm completion dates and budget limits. This made a lot of additional work for the upper managers since each project's

Source: R. G. Holland, "The XV Olympic Winter Games: A Case Study in Project Management," PM *Network*, November 1989.

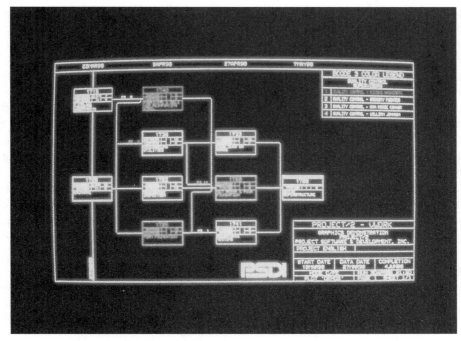

Computerized system used to schedule Olympic games.

Skier checking time clock before run at the Olympics.

reports and needs were different from every other project's. However, two major features of the project helped make this a success: (1) Knowing that the Games would happen on the scheduled date regardless of whether they were ready or not, and (2) Being such a high-visibility, challenging project that demands exceptional focus on the task.

To schedule the entire Winter Games, the 129-event, 16-day Olympics was broken down into 15-minute periods, except for short-track speed skating which was segmented into 1-minute intervals. There was a printout for every day by venue, minute by minute, and a complete set of drawings of every site, building, and room. Meticulous scheduling was necessary to ensure that the 2500 or so competitors, members of royalty, and government officials were at the right place at the right time. Support staff, including medical and security personnel, were also carefully scheduled for each event as crowds shifted from competition to competition. Transportation—600 buses—also had to be scheduled, oftentimes on short notice. The biggest concern was the weather, and sure enough, the Chinook winds forced the rescheduling of over 20 events, some of them twice!

Yet, the 1988 Calgary Games were the best yet, and organized better than ever before. Moreover, as compared to the budget overruns of many other cities, this Olympiad was completed under budget!

▶ 10.1 THE PLANNING–MONITORING–CONTROLLING CYCLE

Throughout this book we have stressed the need to plan, check on progress, compare progress to the plan, and take corrective action if progress does not match the plan. The key things to be planned, monitored, and controlled are time (schedule), cost (budget), and performance (specifications). These, after all, encompass the fundamental objectives of the project.

There is no doubt that some organizations do not spend sufficient time and effort on planning and controlling projects. It is far easier to focus on doing, especially because it appears to be more effective to "stop all the talk and get on with the work." We could cite firm after firm that incurred great expense (and major losses) because the planning process was inadequate for the tasks undertaken.

- A major construction project ran over budget by 63 percent and over schedule by 48 percent because the PM decided that, since "he had managed similar projects several times before, he knew what to do without going into all that detail that no one looks at anyway."

- A large industrial equipment supplier "took a bath" on a project designed to develop a new area of business because they applied the same planning and control procedures to the new area that they had used (successfully) on previous, smaller, less complex jobs.

- A computer store won a competitive bid to supply a computer, five terminals, and associated software to the Kansas City office of a national firm. Admittedly insufficient planning made the installation significantly late. Performance of the software was not close to specified levels. This botched job prevented the firm from being invited to bid on more than 20 similar installations planned by the client.

The planning (budgeting and scheduling) methods we propose "put the hassles up front." They require a significantly greater investment of time and energy early in the life of the project, but they significantly reduce the extent and cost of poor performance and time/cost overruns. Note that this is no guarantee of a trouble-free project, merely an improvement in the risk of failure.

It is useful to perceive the control process as a *closed loop* system, with revised plans and schedules (if warranted) following corrective actions. We delay a detailed discussion on control until the next chapter, but the planning—monitoring—controlling cycle is continuously in process until the project is completed. The information flows for such a cycle are illustrated in Figure 10-1. Note the direction of the flows, information flowing from the bottom toward the top and authority flowing from the top down.

It is also useful to construct this process as an internal part of the organizational structure of the project, not something external to and imposed on it or, worse, in conflict with it. Finally, experience tells us that it is also desirable, though not mandatory, that the planning–monitoring–controlling cycle be the normal way of life in the parent organization. What is good for the project is equally good for the parent firm. In any case, unless the PM has a smoothly operating monitoring/control system, it will be difficult to manage the project effectively.

Designing the Monitoring System

The first step in setting up any monitoring system is to identify the key factors to be controlled. Clearly, the PM wants to monitor performance, cost, and time but must

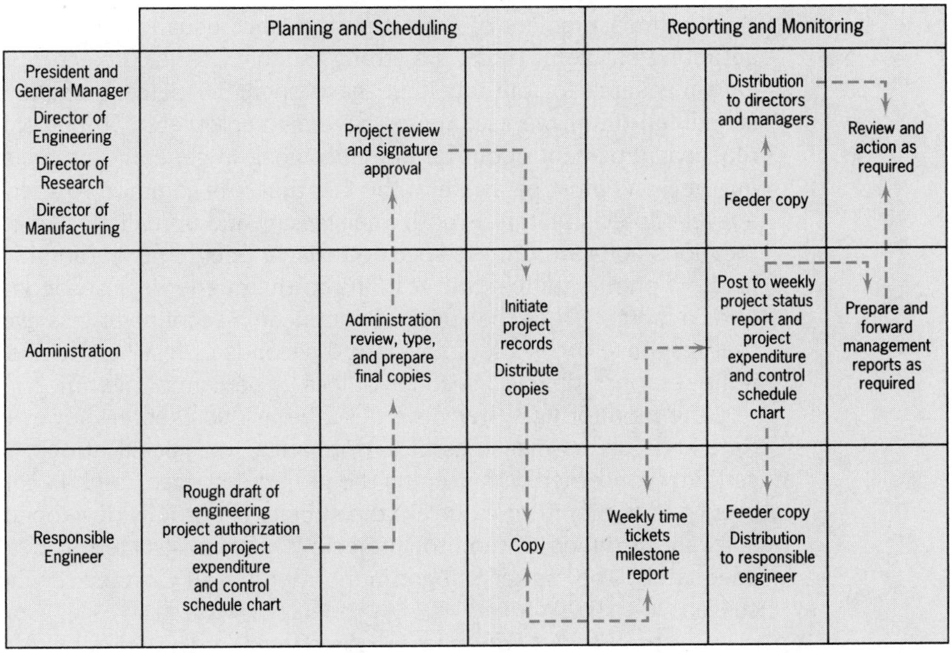

Figure 10-1: Project authorization and expenditure control system information flow.
Source: [12]

define precisely which specific characteristics of performance, cost, and time should be controlled and then establish exact boundaries within which control should be maintained. There may also be other factors of importance worth noting, at least at milestones or review points in the life of the project. For example, the number of labor hours used, the number or extent of engineering changes, the level of customer satisfaction, and similar items may be worthy of note on individual projects.

But the best source of items to be monitored is the project action plan–actually, the set of action plans that describe what is being done, when, and the planned level of resource usage for each task, work package, and work unit in the project. The monitoring system is a direct connection between planning and control. If it does not collect and report information on some significant element of the plan, control can be faulty or missing. The action plan furnishes the key items that must be measured and reported to the control system, but it is not sufficient. For example, the PM might want to know about changes in the client's attitudes toward the project. Information on the morale of the project team might be useful in preparing for organizational or personnel changes on the project. These two latter items may be quite important, but are not reflected in the project's action plans.

Unfortunately, it is common to focus monitoring activities on data that are easily gathered—rather than important—or to concentrate on "objective" measures that are easily defended at the expense of softer, more subjective data that may be more valuable for control. Above all, monitoring should concentrate primarily on measuring various facets of output rather than intensity of activity. It is crucial to remember that effective PMs are not primarily interested in how hard their project teams work. They are interested in achieving results.

The measurement of project performance usually poses the most difficult data gathering problem. There is a strong tendency to let project inputs serve as surrogate measures for output. If we have spent 50 percent of the budget (or of the scheduled time), we assume we have also completed 50 percent of the project or reached 50 percent of our performance goal. In general, this assumption is in error. Further, one must be aware of the fact that it is common to specify performance to a level of precision that is both unnecessary and unrealistic. For example, a communications software project specified that a telephone "information" system had to locate a phone number and respond to the querier in 5 seconds or less. Is 5.1 seconds a failure? Does the specification mean 5 seconds or less every time, or merely that response times should average 5 seconds or less? Is the specification satisfied if the response time is 5 seconds or less 90 percent of the time?

The monitoring systems we describe in this chapter, however, focus mainly on time and cost as measures of performance, not specifications. While we are most certainly concerned with keeping the project "on spec," and do consider some of the problems of monitoring output, the subject is not fully developed here because the software designed to monitor projects is not constructed to deal with the subject adequately. The matter will get more attention in Chapter 12 when auditing is discussed.

Given all this, performance criteria, standards, and data collection procedures must be established for each of the factors to be measured. The criteria and data collection procedures are usually set up for the life of the project. The standards themselves, however, may not be constant over the project's life. They may change as a result of altered capabilities within the parent organization or a technological breakthrough made by the project team; but, perhaps more often than not, standards and criteria change because of factors that are not under the control of the PM.

For example, they may be changed by the client. One client who had ordered a special piece of audio equipment altered performance specifications significantly when electronic parts became available that could filter out random noises.

Standards may also be changed by the community as a response to some shift in public policy—witness the changes in the performance standards imposed on nuclear power installations or automotive exhaust systems. Shifts in the prime rate of interest or in unemployment levels often alter the standards that the PM must use for making project related decisions. The monitoring process is based on the criteria and standards because they dictate, or at least constrain, the set of relevant measures.

Next, the information to be collected must be identified. This may consist of accounting data, operating data, engineering test data, customer reactions, specification changes, and the like. The fundamental problem is to determine precisely which of all the available data should be collected. It is worth repeating that the typical determinant for collecting data too often seems to be simply the ease with which they can be gathered. Of course the nature of the required data is dictated by the project plan, as well as by the goals of the parent organization, the needs of the client, and by the fact that it is desirable to improve the process of managing projects.

Perhaps the most common error made when monitoring data is to gather information that is clearly related to project performance but has little or no probability of changing significantly from one collection period to the next. Prior to its breakup, the American Telephone and Telegraph Company used to collect monthly statistics on a very large number of indicators of operating efficiency. The extent of the collection was such that it filled a telephone-book-sized volume known as "Ma Bell's Green Book." For a great many of the indicators, the likelihood of a significant change from one month to the next was extremely small. When asked about the matter, one official remarked that the mere collection of the data kept the operating companies "on their toes." We feel that there are other, more positive and less expensive ways of motivating project personnel. Certainly, "collect everything" is inappropriate as a monitoring policy.

Therefore, the first task is to examine the project plans in order to extract performance, time, and cost goals. These goals should relate in some fashion to each of the different levels of detail; that is, some should relate to the project, some to its tasks, some to the work packages, and so on. Data must be identified that measure achievement against these goals, and mechanisms designed that gather and store such data.

Similarly, the process of developing and managing projects should be considered and steps taken to ensure that information relevant to the diagnosis and treatment of the project's organizational infirmities and procedural problems are gathered and collected. A reading of the fascinating book *The Soul of a New Machine* [24] reveals the crucial roles organizational factors, interpersonal relationships, and managerial style play in determining project success.

How to Collect Data

Given that we know *what type* of data we want to collect, the next question is *how* to collect this information. At this point in the construction of a monitoring system, it is necessary to define precisely what pieces of information should be gathered and *when*. In most cases, the PM has options. Questions arise. Should cost data be gathered before or after some specific event? Is it always mandatory to collect time and cost information at exactly the same point in the process? What do we do if a specific item is difficult to collect because the data source (human) fears reporting any information that might contribute to a negative performance evaluation? What do we do about the fact that some use of time is reported as "hours charged" to our project, and we are quite aware that our project has been charged for work done on another project (but for the same customer) that is over budget? Are special forms needed for data collection? Should we set up quality control procedures to ensure the integrity of data transference from its source to the project information system? Such questions merely indicate the broad range of knotty issues that must be handled.

A large proportion of all data collected take one of the following forms, each of which is suitable for some types of measures.

1. **Frequency counts**   A simple tally of the occurrence of an event. This type of measure is often used for "complaints," "number of times a project report is late," "days without an accident," "bugs in a computer program," and similar items. The data are usually easy to collect and are often reported as events per unit time or events as a percent of a standard number.

2. **Raw numbers**   Dates, dollars, hours, physical amounts of resources used, and specifications are usually reported in this way. These numbers are reported in a wide variety of ways, but often as direct comparisons with an expected or standard number. Also, "variances" are commonly reported either as the difference between actual and standard or as the ratio of actual to standard. Differences or ratios can also be plotted as a time series to show changes in system performance.

3. **Subjective numeric ratings**   These numbers are subjective estimates, usually of a quality, made by knowledgeable individuals or groups. They can be reported in most of the same ways that objective raw numbers are, but care should be taken to make sure that the numbers are not manipulated in ways only suitable for quantitative measures. (See Chapter 2 for comments on measurements.) Ordinal rankings of performance are included in this category.

4. **Indicators**   When the PM cannot measure some aspect of system performance directly, it may be possible to find an indirect measure or indicator. The speed with which change orders are processed and changes are incorporated into the project is often a good measure of team efficiency. Response to change may also be an indicator of the quality of communications on the project team.

When using indicators to measure performance, the PM must make sure that the link between the indicator and the desired performance measure is as direct as possible.

5. ***Verbal measures***   Measures for such performance characteristics as "quality of team member cooperation," "morale of team members," or "quality of interaction with the client" frequently take the form of verbal characterizations. As long as the set of characterizations is limited and the meanings of the individual terms consistently understood by all, these data serve their purposes reasonably well.

Drug Counseling Program

A social service agency applied for and received funding for a special project to counsel male drug addicts between 18 and 24 years of age, and to secure full-time employment for each client (or part-time employment for clients who were still in school). To qualify for the program, the addicts must have been arrested for a crime, but not be classed as "repeat offenders." Further, the addict must be living with at least one member of his family who is a parent or guardian. Among other conditions placed on the grant, the agency was asked to develop a measure of effectiveness for the counseling program that was acceptable to the funding agency.

The primary measure of effectiveness adopted by most drug programs was "rate of recidivism." A recidivistic incident is defined as any rearrest for a drug-related crime, or any behavior that resulted in the individual reentering the social service system after completing the program and being discharged.

While a "rearrest" is most surely recidivistic, there were several cases in which former clients contacted the agency and asked to be readmitted to the program. These voluntary readmissions resulted when a former client either began to use drugs again or was fearful that he would begin again. It seemed to the agency professionals that voluntary readmissions were successes, not failures.

A new measure of effectiveness was developed to replace "rate of recidivism." It was composed of scores on three different measures, combined with equal weighting.

1. Number of successive weeks of "clean urines."

2. Number of successive months of satisfactory employment (or schooling) experience.

3. Number of successive months of satisfactory behavior at home.

Scores on the second and third measures were based on interviews with employers, teachers, and parent(s).

After data collection has been completed, reports on project progress should be generated. These include project status reports, time/cost reports, and variance reports, among others. Causes and effects should be identified and trends noted. Plans, charts, and tables should be updated on a timely basis. Where known, "com-

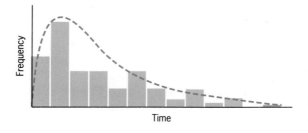

Figure 10-2: Number of bugs found during test of Datamix program.

parables" should be reported, as should statistical distributions of previous data if available. Both help the PM (and others) to interpret the data being monitored. Figures 10-2 and 10-3 illustrate the use of such data. Figure 10-2 shows the results of a count of "bugs" found during a series of tests run on a new piece of computer software. (Bugs found were fixed prior to subsequent tests.) Figure 10-3 shows the percent of the time a computer program retrieved data within a specified time limit. Each point represents a series of trials.

The PM can fit a statistical function to the data shown in Figure 10-2 and make a rough estimate of the number of tests that will have to be run to find some predetermined number of additional bugs in the program. By fitting a curve (formally or "by eyeball") to the data in Figure 10-3, the PM can estimate the cost and time (the number of additional trials and adjustments) required to get system performance up to the specified level.

The nature of *timeliness* will be amplified below, but it is important that the PM make sure that the PERT/CPM and Gantt charts in the project war room (office) are frequently updated. Monitoring can serve to maintain high morale on the project team as well as to alert team members to problems that will have to be solved.

The purpose of the monitoring system is to gather and report data. The purpose of the control system is to act on the data. To aid the *project controller*, it is helpful for the *monitor* to carry out some data analysis. Significant differences from plan should be highlighted or "flagged" so that they cannot be overlooked by the controller. The methods of statistical quality control are very useful for determining what size variances are "significant" and sometimes even help in determining the probable cause(s) of variances. Where causation is known, it should be noted. Where it is not

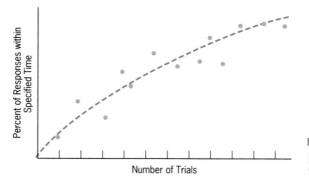

Figure 10-3: Percent of specified performance met during repeated trials.

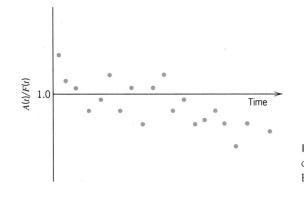

Figure 10-4: Ratio of actual material cost to estimated material cost, Emanon Aircraft Company.

known, an investigation may be in order. The decisions about when an investigation should be conducted, by whom, and by what methods are the prerogative of the project controller, although the actual investigation may be conducted by the group responsible for monitoring.

The Emanon Aircraft Company example presented in Chapter 7 is a case in point. While the study team collected and analyzed a great deal of cost information during the process of finding the problem, the method used for the analysis was actually quite simple. The team compared forecast or estimated cost, F(t), with actual cost, A(t), for each batch of output from the manufacturing system. This analysis was done for each cost center. The ratio of actual cost to estimated cost was calculated and plotted as a time series, as in Figure 10-4.* Note that $A(t)/F(t) < 1$ when the cost forecast for a cost center is greater than actual. In this case, the cost involved was "material cost." Though careful statistical analysis was not necessary in this specific case, the application of standard quality control techniques has wide application to project management (see any book on statistical quality control, [13] for example). Time series analysis can often give the PM an early warning of problems.

At base, this provides a *management by exception* reporting system for the PM. But management by exception has its flaws as well as its strengths. It is essentially an "after-the-fact" approach to control. Variances occur, are investigated, and only then is action taken. The astute PM is far more interested in preventing problems than curing them. Therefore, the monitoring system should develop data streams that indicate variances yet to come. Obviously, such indicators are apt to be statistical in nature, hinting at the likelihood of a future problem rather than predicting it with certainty. An example would be a trend in the data showing a system heading out of control. Interested readers are referred to the "2-5-7 Rule" (see [36], quality chapters). The PM may waste time and effort trying to deal with trouble that will not actually occur. This may be frustrating, but the costs of dealing with some nonproblems is usually minor when compared to the costs of dealing with real problems too late.

---

*Actual data were not used in constructing Figure 10-4, but the figure reflects the consultants' findings.

In creating the monitoring system, some care should be devoted to the issues of honesty and bias. The former is dealt with by setting in place an internal audit. The audit serves the purpose of ensuring that the information gathered is honest. No audit, however, can prevent bias. All data are biased by those who report them, advertently or inadvertently. The controller must understand this fact of life. The first issue is to determine whether or not the possibility of bias in the data matters significantly. If not, nothing need be done. Bias finding and correcting activities are worthwhile only if data with less or no bias are required.

The issue of creating an atmosphere that fosters honesty on a project is widely ignored, but it is of major importance. A set of instructions to the PM on how to do this is not beyond the scope of this book, but if such instructions exist, we do not know of them. We do, however, have some advice to offer. The PM can tolerate almost any kind of behavior except dishonesty. Projects are vulnerable to dishonesty, far more vulnerable than the ongoing operations of the parent organization. Standard operations are characterized by considerable knowledge about expected system performance. When the monitoring system reports information that deviates from expectations, it is visible, noteworthy, and tends to get attention. In the case of many projects, expectations are not so well known. Deviations are not recognized for what they are. The PM is often dependent on team members to call attention to problems. To get this cooperation, the PM must make sure that the bearer of bad news is not punished; nor is the admitter-to-error executed. On the other hand, the hider-of-mistakes may be shot with impunity—and then sent to Siberia.

There is some tendency for project monitoring systems to include an analysis directed at the assignment of blame. This practice has doubtful value. While the managerial dictum "rewards and punishments should be closely associated with performance" has the ring of good common sense, it is actually not good advice. Instead of motivating people to better performance, the practice is more apt to result in lower expectations. If achievement of goals is directly measured and directly rewarded, tremendous pressure will be put on people to understate goals and to generate plans that can be met or exceeded with minimal risk and effort.

▶ 10.2 INFORMATION NEEDS AND THE REPORTING PROCESS

Everyone concerned with the project should be appropriately tied into the project reporting system. The monitoring system ought to be constructed so that it addresses every level of management, but reports need not be of the same depth or at the same frequency for each level. Lower-level personnel have a need for detailed information about individual tasks and the factors affecting such tasks. Report frequency is usually high. For the senior management levels, overview reports describe progress in more aggregated terms with less individual task detail. Reports are issued less often. In both cases, the structure of the reports should reflect the WBS, with each managerial level receiving reports that allow the exercise of control at the relevant level. At times it may be necessary to move information between organizations, as illustrated in Figure 10-5, as well as between managerial levels.

The relationship of project reports to the project action plan or WBS is the key to the determination of both report content and frequency. Reports must contain

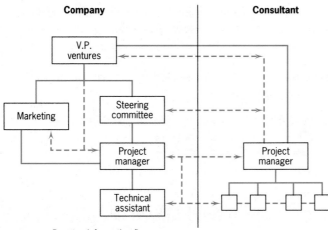

Figure 10-5: Reporting and information flows between organizations working on a common project.

data relevant to the control of specific tasks that are being carried out according to a specific schedule. The frequency of reporting should be great enough to allow control to be exerted during or before the period in which the task is scheduled for completion. For example, efficacy tests of drugs do not produce rapid results in most cases. Thus, there is no reason for weekly (and perhaps not even monthly) reports on such tests. When test results begin to occur, more frequent reports and updates may be required.

In addition to the criterion that reports should be available in time to be used for project control, the timing of reports should generally correspond to the timing of project milestones. This means that project reports may not be issued periodically—excepting progress reports for senior management. There seems to be no logical reason, except for tradition, to issue weekly, monthly, quarterly, etc., reports. Few projects require attention so neatly consistent with the calendar. This must not be taken as advice to issue reports "every once in a while." Reports should be scheduled in the project plan. They should be issued on time. The report schedule, however, need not call for *periodic* reports.

Identification of project milestones depends on who is interested. For senior management, there may be only a few milestones, even in large projects. For the PM there may be many critical points in the project schedule at which major decisions must be made, large changes in the resource base must be initiated, or key technical results achieved. The milestones relevant to lower levels relate to finer detail and occur with higher frequency.

The nature of the monitoring reports should be consistent with the logic of the planning, budgeting, and scheduling systems. The primary purpose is, of course, to ensure achievement of the project plan through control. There is little reason to burden operating members of the project team with extensive reports on matters that are not subject to control—at least not by them. For example, overhead costs or the in-house rental cost of the project war room are simply not appropriate considerations for a team member who is supervising a research experiment in polymer chemistry or designing the advertising campaign for a new brand of coffee. The scheduling and resource usage columns of the project action plan will serve as the key to the design of project reports.

There are many benefits of detailed reports delivered to the proper people on a timely basis. Among them are:

- Mutual understanding of the goals of the project
- Awareness of the progress of parallel activities and of the problems associated with coordination among activities
- More realistic planning for the needs of all groups and individuals working on the project
- Understanding the relationships of individual tasks to one another and to the overall project
- Early warning signals of potential problems and delays in the project
- Minimizing the confusion associated with change by reducing delays in communicating the change
- Faster management action in response to unacceptable or inappropriate work
- Higher visibility to top management, including attention directed to the immediate needs of the project
- Keeping the client and other interested outside parties up to date on project status, particularly regarding project costs, milestones, and deliverables.

Report Types

For the purposes of project management, we can consider three distinct types of reports: routine, exception, and special analysis. The routine reports are those issued on a regular basis; but, as we noted above, *regular* does not necessarily refer to the calendar. For senior management, the reports will usually be periodic, but for the PM and lower-level project personnel, milestones may be used to trigger routine reports. At times, it may be useful to issue routine reports on resource usage periodically, occasionally on a weekly or even daily basis.

Exception reports are useful in two cases. First, they are directly oriented to project management decision making and should be distributed to the team members who will have prime responsibility for decisions or who have a clear "need to know." Second, they may be issued when a decision is made on an exception basis and it is desirable to inform other managers as well as to document the decision—in other words, as part of a sensible procedure for protecting oneself. (PMs should be aware that overuse of exception reporting will be perceived by top management as sheeplike, overly cautious behavior.)

Special analysis reports are used to disseminate the results of special studies conducted as part of the project or as a response to special problems that arise during the project. Usually they cover matters that may be of interest to other PMs, or make use of analytic methods that might be helpful on other projects. Studies on the use of substitute materials, evaluation of alternative manufacturing processes, availability of external consultants, capabilities of new software, and descriptions of new governmental regulations are all typical of the kinds of subjects covered in special analysis reports. Distribution of these reports is usually made to anyone who might be interested.

Meetings

Thus far, we have implicitly assumed that "reports" were written and disseminated by hard-copy or E-mail. More and more often, however, all three types of reports are delivered in face-to-face meetings, and in telephone conference-calls. For a large majority of managers, meetings are as welcome as bad checks or unmentionable diseases. The main complaints are that they are interminably long, come to no conclusions, and waste everyone's time.

There is no doubt, though, that meetings of project teams are necessary and helpful. Indeed, there is no particular reason why meetings should be run in such a way as to cause attendees to hate them with such passion. A few simple rules can remove most of the onus associated with project meetings.

- Use meetings for making group decisions or getting input for important problems. Avoid "show-and-tell" meetings, sometimes called "status and review meetings." If the latter type of meeting has been used to keep project team members informed about what others are doing on the project, insist that such information be communicated personally or electronically by the relevant individuals to the relevant individuals. Only when there is a clear need, such as informing senior management of the project's status, and it is difficult for team members to "get together" on their own, are status and review meetings appropriate.

- Have preset starting and stopping times as well as a written agenda. Stick with both, and above all, do not penalize those who show up on time by making them wait for those who are tardy.

- Make sure that you (and others) do their homework prior to the meeting. Be prepared!

- If you chair the meeting, take your own minutes. Reality (and the minutes become reality as soon as the meeting is over) is too important to be left to the most junior person present. Distribute the minutes as soon as possible after the meeting, not later than the next work day.

- Avoid attributing remarks or viewpoints to individuals in the minutes. Attribution makes people quite wary about what they say in meetings and damps creativity as well as controversy. Also, do not report votes on controversial matters. It is, for example, inappropriate to report in the minutes that the project team voted to send a "Get Well" card to the boss; 4 yea and 3 nay.

- Avoid overly formal rules of procedure. A project meeting is not a parliament and is not the place for Robert's Rules of Order, though courtesy is always in order.

- If a serious problem or crisis arises, call a meeting for the purpose of dealing with that issue *only*. The stopping time for such meetings may be "When the problem has been solved."

Some types of meetings should never be held at all. A large, diversified manufacturing firm holds monthly "status and review" meetings in each of its divisions at which the managers of all projects report to a Project Review Committee (PRC). The divisional PRCs are made up of senior managers. At least one, and we are told more than one, of the PRCs apparently models its meetings on "Hell Week" at a nearby university fraternity. Hazing and humiliating the project managers who must report to the committee is standard practice. The results are to be expected. Projects are managed defensively. Creativity is avoided. Project managers spend time printing and distributing résumés. The best PMs do not stay long.

Common Reporting Problems

There are three common difficulties in the design of project reports. First, there is usually too much detail, both in the reports themselves and in the input being solicited from workers. Unnecessary detail usually results in the reports not being read. Also, it prevents project team members from finding the information they need. Furthermore, the demand for unnecessary, highly detailed input information often results in careless preparation of the data, thereby casting doubt on the validity of reports based on such data. Finally, the preparation and inclusion of unnecessary detail is costly, at the very least.

A second major problem is the poor interface between the project information system and the parent firm's information system. Data are rarely comparable, and interaction between the PM and the organization's accountants is often strained. In our experience, the PM may try to force a connection. It rarely works well. The parent organization's information system must serve as the definitional prototype for the project's information system. In effect, this means that the parent's accounting, engineering, marketing, finance, personnel, and production information systems should be used as the base on which the project's information system is built. Obviously, different types of reports must be constructed for managing the project, but they can be built by using standard data for the most part. The PM can feel free to add new kinds of data to the information base but cannot insist that costs, resource usage, and the like be reported in the project differently from how they are reported in the parent organization.

The third problem concerns a poor correspondence between the planning and the monitoring systems. If the monitoring system is not tracking information directly related to the project's plans, control is meaningless. This often happens when the firm's existing information system is used for monitoring without modifications specifically designed for project management. For example, an existing cost tracking system oriented to shop operations would be inappropriate for a project with major activities in the area of research and development. But as we noted just above, the option of running the project from a different database is generally not viable. The PM's problem is to fit standard information into a reporting and tracking system that is appropriate for the project.

The real message carried by project reports is in the comparison of actual activity to plan and of actual output to desired output. Variances are reported by the monitoring system, and responsibility for action rests with the controller. Because the project plan is described in terms of performance, time, and cost, variances are reported for those same variables. Project variance reports usually follow the same format used by the accounting department, but at times they may be presented differently.

The Earned Value Chart

Thus far, our examples have covered monitoring for parts of projects. The monitoring of performance for the entire project is also crucial because performance is the *raison d'être* of the project. *Individual* task performance must be monitored carefully because the timing and coordination between individual tasks is important. But *overall* project performance is the crux of the matter and must not be overlooked. One way of measuring overall performance is by using an aggregate performance measure called *earned value*. A history of earned value from its origin in PERT/Cost to its culmination in C/SCSC (Cost/Schedule Control System Criteria) together with its techniques, advantages, and disadvantages is reported in a series in PMN*etwork* starting with [16].

A serious difficulty with comparing actual expenditures against budgeted or *baseline* expenditures for any given time period is that the comparison fails to take into account the amount of work accomplished relative to the cost incurred. The earned value of work performed (*value completed*) for those tasks in progress is found by multiplying the estimated percent completion for each task by the planned cost for that task. The result is the amount that should have been spent on the task thus far. This can then be compared with the actual amount spent.

Estimating the "percent completion" of each task (or work package) is nontrivial. If the task is to write a piece of software, percent completion can be estimated as the number of lines of code written divided by the total number of lines to be written—given that the latter has been estimated. But what if the task is to test the software? We have run a known number of tests, but how many remain to be run? There are several conventions used to aid in estimating percent completion. The most popular seems to be the 50–50 estimate. Fifty percent completion is assumed when the task is begun, and the remaining 50 percent when the work is complete. Other conventions include the 0–100 percent rule which allows no credit for work until the task is complete, or assignment of credit according to the amount of a critical input that has been used.

A graph such as that shown in Figure 10-6 can be constructed and provides a basis for evaluating cost and performance to date. If the total value of the work accomplished is in balance with the planned (baseline) cost (i.e., minimal scheduling variance), then top management has no particular need for a detailed analysis of individual tasks. Thus the concept of earned value combines cost reporting and aggregate performance reporting into one comprehensive chart.

We can identify three variances on the earned value chart. The *time variance* is the difference in the time scheduled for the work that has been performed (STWP) and the actual time used to perform it (ATWP). The *cost or spending variance* is the differ-

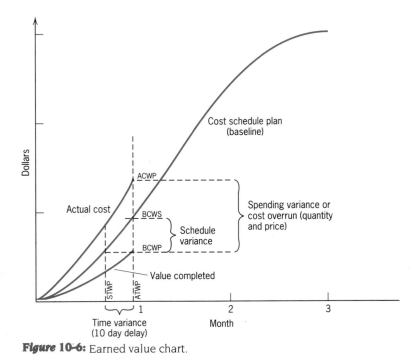

Figure 10-6: Earned value chart.

ence between the amount of money we budgeted for the work that has been performed (BCWP) to date and the actual cost of that work (ACWP). The *schedule variance* is the difference between the budgeted cost of the work performed (BCWP) to date and the cost of the work we scheduled to be performed to date (BCWS).* In compact form,

$$STWP - ATWP = \text{time variance (TV, delay is negative)}$$
$$BCWP - ACWP = \text{cost variance (CV, overrun is negative)}$$
$$BCWP - BCWS = \text{schedule variance (SV, behind is negative)}$$

Typically, the variances are defined in such a way that they will be negative when the project is behind schedule and/or over cost, though this practice is not universal either in the literature or in practice. The variances are also often stated as ratios rather than differences so that the TV ratio = STWP/ATWP, the CV ratio = BCWP/ACWP, and the SV ratio = BCWP/BCWS, malperformance being indicated by a ratio less than one. Use of ratios is particularly helpful when an organization wishes to compare the performance of several projects—or project managers. As we just noted, however, the accuracy and usefulness of these performance mea-

---

*A fourth variance can be found. It is the difference between the cost the project budget says should have been expended to date (BCWS) and the actual cost incurred to date by the project (ACWP). BCWS − ACWP is what we call the *resource flow variance*. (Note that the resource flow variance is not a "cash flow" variance.)

sures are dependent on the degree to which estimates of percent completion reflect reality.

Cost and schedule variances are most commonly used. A short example illustrates this. Assume that operations on a work package has been scheduled to cost $1500 to complete the package. It was originally scheduled to have been finished today. As of now, however, we have actually expended $1350, and we estimate that we have completed two-thirds of the work. What are the cost and schedule variances?

$$\text{cost variance} = \text{BCWP} - \text{ACWP}$$
$$= \$1500(2/3) - 1350$$
$$= -\$350$$

$$\text{schedule variance} = \text{BCWP} - \text{BCWS}$$
$$= \$1500(2/3) - 1500$$
$$= -\$500$$

In other words, we are spending at a higher level than our budget plan indicates, and given what we have spent, we are not as far along as we should be (i.e., we have not completed as much work as we should have).

If the earned value chart shows a cost overrun or performance underrun, the PM must figure out what to do to get the system back on target. Options include such things as borrowing resources from activities performing better than expected, or holding a meeting of project team members to see if anyone can suggest solutions to the problems, or perhaps notifying the client that the project may be late or over budget.

Cost/Schedule Control System Criteria (C/SCSC)

C/SCSC was developed by the U.S. Department of Defense in the late 1960s and is generally required for defense projects. Fundamentally, it is an extension of earned value analysis. C/SCSC, as its name implies, spelled out a number of standards of organization, accounting, budgeting, etc., that firms must meet if they are to be considered acceptable for government contracts. For an excellent extended discussion of C/SCSC together with the process for accomplishing it, see [26].

As usual, if remedial action is contemplated, it is important to make the analysis at the lowest feasible level of the action plan or WBS. The need to keep project performance, cost, and schedule related when monitoring projects has been emphasized in this chapter. This emphasis will be reinforced in Chapter 11. For purposes of control, it is just as important to emphasize the need to relate the realities of time, cost, and performance with the project's master plan. C/SCSC takes just such an approach, but there is a major caveat that must be heeded: *The set of project action plans (the project master plan) must be kept up to date.* These plans contain descriptions of each task together with estimates of the time and resources required by each. The plans are therefore the primary source of the STWPs, BCWSs, and BCWPs and the framework within which the ATWPs and ACWPs are collected.

Differences between work scheduled and work planned can develop from several different causes; for example, official change orders in the work elements required to accomplish a task, informal alterations in the methods used to accom-

Name	BCWS	BCWP	ACWP	Sch. Variance	Cost Variance	BAC	FAC	Variance	QTR 1, 1994 Jan Feb Mar	QTR 2, 1994 Apr May Jun
Contact Organizations	$3,797.30	$3,980.00	$3,920.00	$182.70	($60.00)	$3,980.00	$3,920.00	($60.00)		
Print forms	$645.00	$645.00	$645.00	$0.00	$0.00	$645.00	$645.00	$0.00		
Contact organizations	$840.00	$840.00	$728.00	$0.00	($112.00)	$840.00	$728.00	($112.00)		
Collect display information	$660.00	$660.00	$660.00	$0.00	$0.00	$660.00	$660.00	$0.00		
Gather college particulars	$520.00	$520.00	$520.00	$0.00	$0.00	$520.00	$520.00	$0.00		
Print programs	$687.30	$870.00	$922.00	$182.70	$52.00	$870.00	$922.00	$52.00		
Print participants' certificate	$445.00	$445.00	$445.00	$0.00	$0.00	$445.00	$445.00	$0.00		
Banquet and Refreshments	$1,220.00	$1,220.00	$1,200.00	$0.00	($20.00)	$1,220.00	$1,200.00	($20.00)		
Select guest speaker	$500.00	$500.00	$500.00	$0.00	$0.00	$500.00	$500.00	$0.00		
Organize food	$325.00	$325.00	$325.00	$0.00	$0.00	$325.00	$325.00	$0.00		
Organize liquor	$100.00	$100.00	$100.00	$0.00	$0.00	$100.00	$100.00	$0.00		
Organize refreshments	$295.00	$295.00	$275.00	$0.00	($20.00)	$295.00	$275.00	($20.00)		
Publicity and Promotion	$2,732.55	$2,297.75	$2,039.00	($434.80)	($258.75)	$3,010.00	$2,870.00	($140.00)		
Send invitations	$700.00	$700.00	$560.00	$0.00	($140.00)	$700.00	$560.00	($140.00)		
Organize gift certificates	$330.00	$330.00	$330.00	$0.00	$0.00	$330.00	$330.00	$0.00		
Arrange banner	$570.00	$570.00	$570.00	$0.00	$0.00	$570.00	$570.00	$0.00		
Contact faculty	$280.00	$280.00	$280.00	$0.00	$0.00	$280.00	$280.00	$0.00		
Advertise in college paper	$165.00	$82.50	$65.00	($82.50)	($17.50)	$165.00	$165.00	$0.00		
Class announcements	$99.00	$0.00	$0.00	($99.00)	$0.00	$220.00	$220.00	$0.00		
Organize posters	$588.55	$335.25	$234.00	($253.30)	($101.25)	$745.00	$745.00	$0.00		
Facilities	$200.00	$0.00	$0.00	($200.00)	$0.00.	$200.00	$200.00	$0.00		
Arrange facility for event	$52.00	$0.00	$0.00	($52.00)	$0.00	$52.00	$52.00	$0.00		
Transport materials	$148.00	$0.00	$0.00	($148.00)	$0.00	$148.00	$148.00	$0.00		

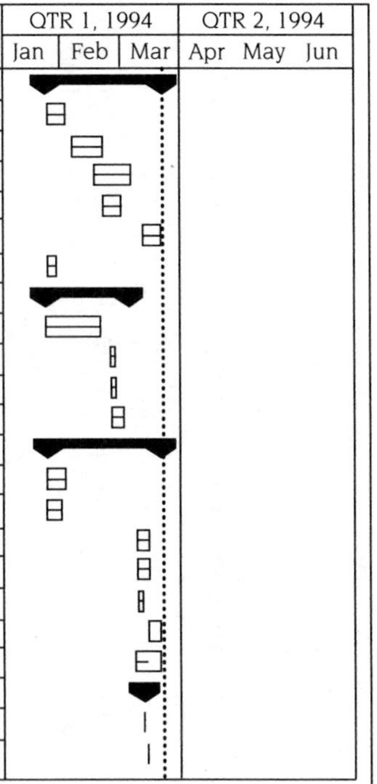

Project: Career Day
Date: 1/24/94

Critical   Progress   Summary
Noncritical   Milestone   Rolled up

Figure 10-7: Microsoft Project for Windows®, budget sheet for career day project (cf. Chapter 5).

plish specific tasks, or official or unofficial changes in the tasks to be accomplished. Similarly, cost variances can result from any of the above as well as from changes in input factor prices, changes in the accounting methods used by the project, or changes in the mix of input factors needed to accomplish a given task. If the plan is not altered to reflect such changes, comparisons between plan and actual are not meaningful.

Figure 10-7 shows a budget for the Career Day project described in Chapter 5, Section 5.3. This budget was generated as a standard report from Microsoft Project®. (A similar report is available through Time Line®, and most other PC project management packages.) Note that the project is reported on at the work package level. The first two tasks, *Contact Organizations* and *Banquet and Refreshments* have been completed, and the third task, *Publicity and Promotion* is currently underway. The first four work packages under *Publicity and Promotion* have been completed, but the fifth and seventh are only partially finished. The sixth has not been started, nor has the fourth task, *Facilities*, been started. A compressed Gantt chart is shown on the right side.

The three columns of data on the right, BAC, FAC, and Variance, are "Budget at Completion," "Forecast at Completion" and the Variance or difference between BAC and FAC. For all activities that have been completed, BAC = BCWP and FAC = ACWP. The work packages that have not been completed, however, tell a different story. *Advertise in college paper* is 50 percent complete, and *Organize posters* is 45 percent complete. (The percent complete data are from another report.) *Class announcements* has not yet been started. Note that for *Advertise in the college paper*, the BCWP is 50 percent of the BCWS, which is to say that \$82.50 is 50 percent of the BAC and FAC. Similarly for *Organize posters*, with \$335.25 being 45 percent of BAC and FAC (\$335.25/.45 = \$745.00). When the two work packages are completed, however, and if there is still a cost variance, then BAC and FAC will no longer be equal. For a completed work package, the cost variance (BCWP − ACWP) = BAC − FAC.

Project Management in Practice
Applying the BCWP Concept at the U.S. Environmental Protection Agency

Over a period of eight years, the R&D laboratory of the EPA developed, implemented, and revised a project management system (PMS) that attempted to incorporate the budgeted cost of work performed (BCWP) concept. In the mid-1970s, a project team was formed to help R&D manage a subcontracted set of environmental control projects totaling \$40–60 million. The technical staff of 45 engineers and scientists thus had over a million dollars worth of projects to oversee, per person. The PMS project objectives were identified as:

– To provide contractor progress reports to the laboratory director.

Source: C. B. Oldham, C. T. Ripberger, and J. E. Cook "Project Management in a Federal Research and Development Laboratory: An Application of the Elusive Budgeted Cost of Work Performed," *Project Management Journal*, Sept. 1986.

- To provide project officers information on cost and schedule to better manage their contracts.
- To relieve project officers of the burden of preparing monthly progress reports.
- To facilitate data input and updating of the integrated information system by standardizing reports and formats.
- To collect pertinent data for identifying schedule slippages.

The concept of the PMS was to have each contractor disaggregate project costs by the lowest level of detail in the work breakdown structure. Then, the schedule of tasks to be completed would give the budgeted cost of work scheduled (BCWS) and actual schedule and cost progress, shown as the BCWP and ACWP, respectively, which could be compared monthly against the BCWS to identify cost and schedule variances. A number of performance indexes, such as cost (BCWP/ACWP), schedule (BCWP/BCWS), percent spent, and percent complete, were to be calculated and reported monthly as well to give project man-

agers and administrators a quick way to identify projects needing attention.

In implementation, however, the project team found that the data collection forms were not being properly or uniformly filled out. Upon investigation, it was realized that the project officers considered PMS as a top management monitoring system rather than as a tool to help them better manage their projects. Thus, they did not even check the forms from the contractor, and the contractors, in turn, simply gave them to their accountants, who were not in touch with the progress of each project, to fill out. Three flaws in the system were then identified: (1) feedback from the supervisor of the R&D project officers was missing since the reports bypassed this level of management; (2) as noted above, the project officers considered this a system for top management; and (3) the project officers had no involvement in designing the system and thus no interest in using it, seeing it as a reporting system being forced upon them. Yet, the project officers believed that the basic concept in PMS was a good one

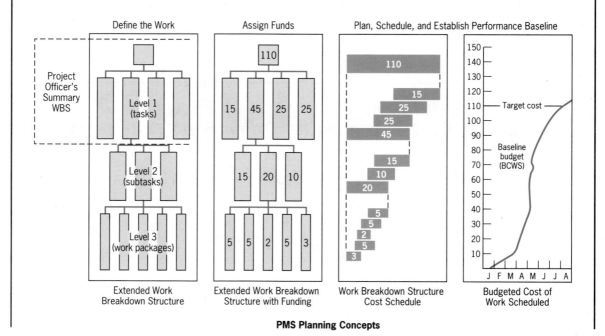

PMS Planning Concepts

and necessary for sound oversight of their projects.

In the next phase, top management of the R&D laboratory changed and the system was discontinued for three years. After seven years since the original PMS project began, the system was reintroduced as a set of tools for project officers to use and adapt as they found useful. The evaluation of project officers was changed to a system whereby they would be evaluated by their supervisors based on results achieved instead of the use of project management tools. Training in the use of PMS was provided and the system is now receiving much wider acceptance.

Milestone Reporting

We referred earlier to milestone reports. A typical example of such a report is shown in Figure 10-8a, b, and c. In this illustration, a sample network with milestones is shown, followed by a routine milestone report form. A model top management project status report is illustrated in the next chapter. When filled out, these reports show project status at a specific time. They serve to keep all parties up to date on

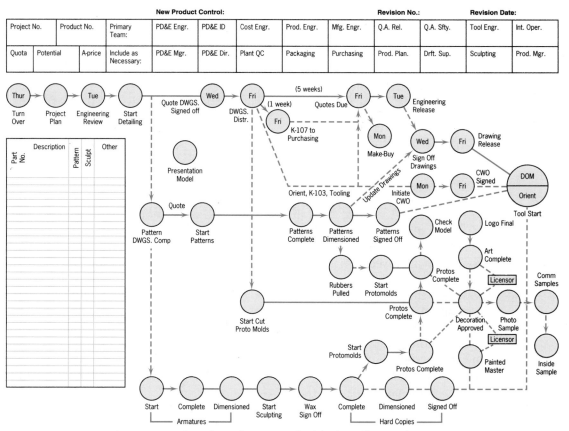

Figure 10-8a: Sample project network with sign-off control.

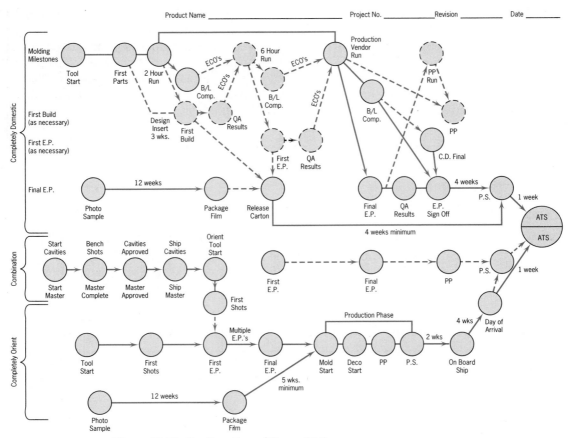

Figure 10-8*b*: Continuation of Figure 10-8*a*.

what has been accomplished. If accomplishments are inadequate or late, these reports serve as starting points for remedial planning.

Figures 10-8a and b show the network for a new product development project for a manufacturer. A steady flow of new products is an essential feature of this firm's business, and each new product is organized as a project as soon as its basic concept is approved by a project selection group. If we examine Figures 10-8a and b closely, we see that the sign-off control boxes at the top of the page correspond with sequences of events in the network. For example, look at the bottom line of the network in Figure 10-8a. The design of this product requires a sculpture that is formed on an armature. The armature must be constructed, and the sculpture of the product completed and signed off. Note that the sculpture is used as a form for making models that are, in turn, used to make the prototype product. The completion of the sculpture is signed off in the next-to-last box in the lower line of boxes at the top of the page.

A careful examination of Figure 10-8b reveals that it is a continuation of the previous page. Figure 10-8a is primarily concerned with product design and Figure 10-8b with production. The expected times for various activities are noted on the

NAME					PROJECT PLAN	ENGR. REVIEW	DESIGN REVIEW	QUOTE QUES.	PAT SCULP COMPL	PAT SCULP COMPL	QUOTES DUE	MAKE BUY
PROJECT NO.	PRODUCT NO.	MFG SOURCE	TURNOVER	ORIGINAL								
				CURRENT								
A=PRICE	QUOTA	POTENTIAL		ACTUAL								

ENGR. RELEASE	PROJECT REVIEW	RELEASE DWGS.	TOOL START	PHOTO SAMPLES	INSIDE SAMPLES	PKG. FILM	INSTR. LAYOUT	INSTR. FILM. ART	FINAL PARTS	FIRST EP	FINAL EP	EP SIGN-OFF	ORIENT PS	OBS	PROD. PILOT	PT SIGN-OFF	PROD. START	ATS

NAME					PROJECT PLAN	ENGR. REVIEW	DESIGN REVIEW	QUOTE QUES.	PAT SCULP COMPL	PAT SCULP COMPL	QUOTES DUE	MAKE BUY
PROJECT NO.	PRODUCT NO.	MFG SOURCE	TURNOVER	ORIGINAL								
				CURRENT								
A=PRICE	QUOTA	POTENTIAL		ACTUAL								

ENGR. RELEASE	PROJECT REVIEW	RELEASE DWGS.	TOOL START	PHOTO SAMPLES	INSIDE SAMPLES	PKG. FILM	INSTR. LAYOUT	INSTR. FILM. ART	FINAL PARTS	FIRST EP	FINAL EP	EP SIGN-OFF	ORIENT PS	OBS	PROD. PILOT	PT SIGN-OFF	PROD. START	ATS

Figure 10-8c: Milestone monitoring chart for Figures 10-8a and b.

network, along with the various operations that must be performed. Figure 10-8c is a summary milestone report that covers several concurrent projects—four, in the case of this page. Each project has a series of steps that must be completed. Each has an original schedule that may be amended for use as a current schedule. Steps are completed in actual times. This form helps program managers coordinate several projects by trying to schedule the various steps to minimize the degree to which the projects interfere with one another by being scheduled for the same facilities at the same time.

The next section of this chapter, which discusses computerized project management information systems, contains several other examples of project reports.

▶ 10.3 COMPUTERIZED PMIS (PROJECT MANAGEMENT INFORMATION SYSTEMS)

The project examples used in Chapters 8 and 9 were small, so that the concepts could be demonstrated. But real projects are often extremely large, with many hundreds or thousands of tasks and hundreds of thousands of work packages. Diagramming, scheduling, and tracking all these tasks is clearly a job for the computer, and computerized PMISs were one of the earlier business applications for computers (e.g., see [44]). Initially, the focus was on simple scheduling packages, but this quickly extended to include costs, earned values, variances, management reports, and so on.

The earlier packages were typically written in FORTRAN and ran on large, expensive mainframe computers; thus, only the larger firms had access to them. Still, the use of these packages for managing projects on a day-to-day basis was not particularly successful, except perhaps in construction and contracting firms. This was because of the inability of project managers to update plans in real time, mainframe computers typically being run in a batch rather than online mode. With the development and proliferation of microcomputers, and the corresponding availability of a wide variety of project management software, project managers are showing a renewed interest in PMIS.

These new microcomputer-based PMIS are considerably more sophisticated than earlier systems and use the microcomputer's graphics, color, and other features more extensively. The systems are available for small, medium, and even large firms. They also offer much more support capability. The current trend in PMIS is integration of software, including spreadsheets, databases, word processing, communications, graphics, and other such capabilities. In this section, we briefly describe a few of the larger, more complex software packages and then we proceed to a discussion of packages for small- and medium-sized projects. Finally, we illustrate two of the more popular micropackages.

This area is developing so rapidly that any information given must be considered dated by the time it reaches print. The reader interested in current capabilities would be wise to refer to recent annual or monthly software reviews, such as [27, 30, and 59], and those in PM *Network* (e.g., May and Aug., 1994). Finally, it is worth noting that these systems can be misused or inappropriately applied—as can any tools. The most common error of this type is managing the PMIS rather than the project itself. This and other such errors are described by Thamhain [52] and listed below.

- **Computer paralysis.** Excessive computer involvement with computer activity replacing project management; loss of touch with the project and its realities.
- **PMIS verification.** PMIS reports may mask real project problems, be massaged to look good, or simply verify that real problems exist, yet are not acted upon.
- **Information overload.** Too many reports, too detailed, or the distribution of reports, charts, tables, data, and general information from the PMIS to too many people overwhelms managers and effectively hides problems.

- **Project isolation.** The PMIS reports replace useful and frequent communication between the project manager and top management, or even between the PM and the project team.
- **Computer dependence.** PM or top management wait for the computer reports/results to react to problems rather than being proactive and avoiding problems in the first place.
- **PMIS *misdirection*.** Due to the unequal coverage of the PMIS, certain project subareas are overmanaged and other areas receive inadequate attention; symptoms of problems are monitored and managed (budget overruns, schedule slippages), rather than the problems themselves.

Large PMIS Capabilities

Current PMISs that run on mainframes and minis are intended for large, complex, engineering-based projects such as major defense or aerospace contracts. In these situations, the firm is a prime contractor or major subcontractor and is facing years of work involving thousands of tasks, perhaps millions of labor-hours, and multiple interfaces with many subcontractors. The entire project must be well coordinated and tightly controlled if performance requirements are to be achieved and schedules met.

The first step in such projects is to *scope out* the work in a major work phase diagram. Such a chart is illustrated in Figure 10-9. The scope document is usually a RFP (Request for Proposal) or the firm's proposal in response to an RFP. From this, phase I of project definition is initiated. This includes constructing a summary WBS for the project, laying out the major project milestones, and getting an estimate of the general order of magnitude of the project in terms of total labor-hours required.

The next phase (II) is the definition of the work package in more detail. This involves determining exactly what must be done (the WBS), when, who will do it, and how much it will cost. Following this, baseline input data requirements are specified in phase III. This includes such items as estimates of activity durations, budgets, labor requirements, constraints, and the other items listed in Figure 10-9.

Phase IV is ongoing monitoring where input data on project status are collected through system modules for schedules, costs, cash flows, and so forth. The final phase (V) is the definition of output management reports for the control function. This consists of defining the data analyses that must be conducted and report formatting and generation. Example outputs would be exception, earned value, cost status, schedule status, variance, and other such reports described earlier and in the following chapter.

The chores that must be handled when managing a large project are not significantly different in concept from those involved in small projects. The difference in size, however, increases the complexity of the job by orders of magnitude. PMISs for mainframe and minicomputers retail for somewhere between $2000 and $500,000. Most run on IBM and DEC hardware and software, but sometimes on Hewlett Packard, Data General, and others. Two of the most widely used are Artemis® and Project/2®. There is also TRAK® which, in spite of its claim to be "a fully integrated on-line Project Management system," is mainly an excellent, integrated, project database, data management, and reporting device.

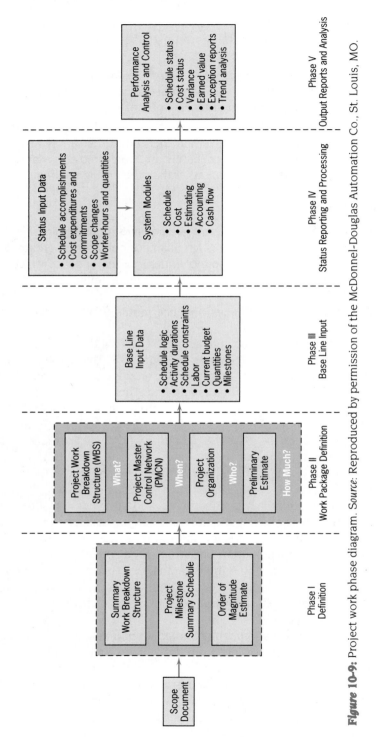

Figure 10-9: Project work phase diagram. *Source:* Reproduced by permission of the McDonnel-Douglas Automation Co., St. Louis, MO.

Rather than discussing the various things that these large systems can do, we simply advise the user who needs a large system to investigate several of them carefully. When such investigations do take place, they usually involve several individuals from the computer department. While we have no prejudice against including software/hardware specialists in the search for a good product, it is even more important to include people who have considerable experience in project management, and who understand what the software can and will be asked to do.

It is clear that large, defense-type, engineering projects require the use of a mainframe or minicomputer to handle the mass of data. Also, customer requirements for complex reports are easily handled by these packages. Note, however, that the lion's share of projects are not so large—even though they do require the same rigorous and extensive planning, scheduling, costing, monitoring, and control capabilities. PMISs for these projects can fit on a microcomputer.

Small PMIS Capabilities

An explosive growth in PMISs has occurred in the area of small- to medium-sized PMISs intended for microcomputers. There are now over 500 packages on the market and the number continues to grow. These packages come in a wide variety of capabilities and prices. Several packages cost less than $50 and a few cost several thousand dollars, with one or two above $25,000. Our interest here is in reasonably priced ($500–$2000 list-priced) software that is capable of applying reasonably sophisticated project management techniques (e.g., resource leveling, C/SCSC-type budget reports, project tracking, and updating) to projects of reasonable size (>5000 activities per project) with multiproject capability, and with a reasonable set of reporting options (such as Gantt and PERT/CPM charts, WBS or action plans, resource reports, cost reports, etc.). We assume the ability to import and export data and reports to the standard word processing and spreadsheet packages. We also assume reasonably good graphic capabilities.

Based on these criteria, and based on a number of software ratings made by magazines devoted to PC users [15 among many others], software rating firms [37, for example], and individuals (consultants and academics) writing for project management journals or books [for instance, 14, 21, 28, 30, and 42], we have selected two packages to illustrate a few types of output that are typical of the genre: Microsoft Project for Windows® 3.0 and Time Line® 5.0. Both list for just under $700, and both are widely available at prices less than $450, sometimes considerably less. Both are widely used, probably being the two most popular pieces of project management software. Both can be used on a LAN—as can most of the popular project management software.

Our approach here will be to describe PMIS's needs briefly and generically. We then illustrate some typical outputs available with our chosen packages. It is worth noting that many of the articles rating project management software are written by software authorities rather than project managers, and the judgments expressed in such articles may not be particularly relevant for experienced PMs. Likewise, Avots [2] maintains that package reviews and comparative evaluations in computer trade journals are not a dependable basis for comparing PMISs. Our discussion of user needs is based largely on two surveys [49, 58] conducted on PMs.

- **Friendliness.**   For the novice user, this included clear and logical manuals, help screens, tutorials, a menu-driven structure, easy editing, and so on. For the advanced user, this meant well-documented and easy-to-program commands.
- **Schedules.**   Gantt charts were mandatory, as well as automatic recalculation with updates of times, costs, and resources. Plots of earliest start, scheduled start, slack/float, latest finish, planned finish, and actual finish times were desired.
- **Calendars.**   Either a job shop and/or calendar dates are necessary, plus the ability to indicate working days, non-working days, and holidays.
- **Budgets.**   The ability to include a budget for planning, monitoring, and control was deemed necessary. Especially desirable was the ability to interface this with a spreadsheet program.
- **Reports.**   Individualizing of report formats was considered most desirable. Again, having the ability to interface the reports with a word processing package was highly desired.

While half the respondents mentioned the desirability of the following additional features, in our opinion these features would also be considered mandatory today.

- **Graphics.**   The ability to see the schedule and interactions was especially important.
- **PERT/CPM Network.**   The depiction of the network was deemed desirable by those familiar with this mode of project presentation.
- **Charts.**   Charts for responsibility and histograms for resources were deemed particularly useful.
- **Migration.**   The ability to migrate other software systems such as databases, spreadsheets, word processing, other project management packages, the organization's mainframe programs, graphics programs, and engineering and manufacturing software to and from the PMIS was considered valuable. Furthermore, general telecommunications and the ability to upload and download were deemed useful as well.
- **Integration/complexity.**   Akin to user friendliness, an *appropriate* level of one-key-does-it-all integration and package complexity was considered important. Extensive integration makes errors difficult to correct, and overcomplexity, while adding capability, makes the PMIS less easy to use.

A number of respondents also mentioned the desirability of the PMIS supporting appropriate output devices (color printers, plotters, high-speed printers), having windowing capability, allowing three-time PERT estimates, and including precedence relationships and activity-on-arrow diagrams. There is one item missing from the survey list of desired and mandatory features that we consider critically important, the *ability to update all data based on actuals*. Unless the software allows updating both schedule and resources, it is only useful for planning and cannot be used to monitor and control projects. With the exception of three-time PERT and AOA networks, many current PC project management computer packages will support all these capabilities.

It is important to remember that no one package will meet all needs. Numerous trade-offs exist not only between price and capability but also between functional capability, ease of use, complexity, and speed. In general, there are five areas of PMIS internal capabilities, separate from the ability to migrate data and communicate externally, that should be considered. These are project planning, resource management, tracking/monitoring, report generation, and decision aiding. We discuss each below.

Project planning.   In this initial area, consideration should be given to the number of activities per project, the use of various calendars and time units, data recording and organization, time estimation, graphics generation, Gantt chart and PERT/CPM chart capabilities, early and late starts, and the ability to handle subnetworks (i.e., nested networks). Of particular interest in this category is the ability to reschedule/update automatically.

Resource management.   The issues here are similar and include the number of resource types, the number of resources per project, sharing of resources, resource leveling, scheduling by resource load, resource updating, resource usage conflicts, multiproject resource analysis, resource planning and analysis, cost estimating, and financial modeling and analysis.

Tracking/monitoring.   This area includes critical path analysis, subnetwork analysis, early warning systems, baseline and actual schedule updating and display, resource updating and display, and similar items.

Report generation.   This topic includes project status summaries, computer-assisted report generation, sophisticated data evaluation, resource lists and histograms, schedule lists, task detail, updating of report periods, resource detail, resource assignments, and current Gantt and PERT/CPM diagrams.

Decision aiding.   This area includes a number of capabilities, some involving external software packages. Generally, what-if analysis, expert system capability, multiproject tracking with cross analysis and other such types of capabilities are useful.

The potential purchaser of a PMIS would be wise to consider the intended use of the package, the background and needs of all the potential users, and the organizational setting where the package is to be employed, including the needs and orientation of those who will be receiving the reports and graphics. In terms of need, for example, is it really necessary to monitor costs or update schedules or resource usage? Are we dealing with large projects, or ones with large numbers of critical resources? How complex are the activity interrelationships? All these questions need to be addressed before selecting a final package.

A general PMIS selection process based on Levine's excellent work |30| is as follows:

1. Establish a comprehensive set of selection criteria, considering the questions and five areas of capabilities detailed above.

2. Set priorities for the criteria, separating "must have" items from "nice to have" items and "not needed" items.

3. Conduct a preliminary evaluation of the software packages relative to the criteria using vendor-supplied data, product reviews, and software surveys.

4.   Narrow the candidate packages to three and obtain demos of each, evaluating the vendors at the same time in terms of interest, software maintenance, and support.

5.   Evaluate each package with a standard project typical of your current and projected future needs. Make note of any weaknesses or strengths that are particularly relevant to your situation.

6.   Negotiate on price, particularly if you are making a volume purchase or contemplating a site license. Include descriptions of vendor support, training, and product maintenance in the contract.

Figures 10-10 through 10-18 illustrate some typical outputs available from Microsoft Project for Windows® 3.0 (MPW) and Time Line® 5.0 (TL). These packages, along with a great many others, are competent products, not difficult for computer-literate PMs to learn. Each has its strengths and idiosyncrasies. MPW, for example, has excellent graphics. TL is an excellent resource leveler.

Figure 10-10 shows the MPW version of a small software evaluation project plan. Note that the display shows WBS identification numbers at two levels of the action plan. Included are scheduled start and finish dates together with a Gantt chart. Figure 10-11 is the MPW project calendar for December. There is room on the calendar to note project meetings and other dates of importance. Figure 10-12 shows the same project in a TL draft version. The WBS code is more detailed and the resources are shown along with task and work package durations. The Gantt chart is also displayed. Figure 10-13 is TL's PERT/CPM network for the project. Note that three levels of work are shown with the appropriate WBS numbers and are surrounded on the network with dotted lines. In both MPW and TL versions, summary activities (tasks) are also shown on the Gantt charts.

In another project devoted to the production of a video tape, Figure 10-14 shows the TL network, with the critical path highlighted. Figure 10-15 shows a TL Gantt chart, customized to show the action plan, start dates, resource needs, and finish dates with slack. Again, the critical path is highlighted. Figures 10-16 and 10-17 show the same project with MPW outputs. The critical path is shown on the Gantt chart and on the network. The network was customized to show scheduled starts and finishes, and durations. Both software packages give the PM considerable latitude to customize output, as do almost all current software packages in this and higher priced categories. For example, Figure 10-18 shows a TL Gantt chart that includes both baseline data and predicted "actuals" for the construction of a house. The project, in this example, was updated on September 28 at which point the "Foundation/Lot" task was late. The predicted impact on the rest of the project is shown. Also note that "percent achieved" is shown using the 0/100 percent convention. Finally, note that "Concrete" and "Grading" were scheduled to start on September 29, but actually were completed when the update was performed on the 28th. Figure 10-7, appearing earlier in this chapter, shows one version of an MPW budget display. Figures 9-8*a* and *b* show typical TL resource-usage histograms.

As we have noted several times, there are many project management software packages from which to choose. When decision time comes, the user must read current product review materials. Fortunately, these are plentiful. Finally, the user must

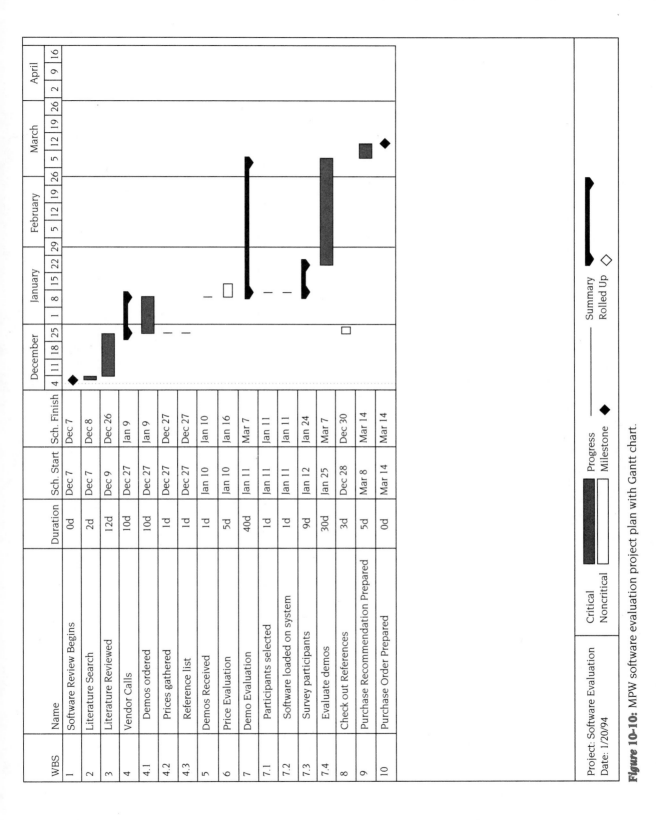

WBS	Name	Duration	Sch. Start	Sch. Finish
1	Software Review Begins	0d	Dec 7	Dec 7
2	Literature Search	2d	Dec 7	Dec 8
3	Literature Reviewed	12d	Dec 9	Dec 26
4	Vendor Calls	10d	Dec 27	Jan 9
4.1	Demos ordered	10d	Dec 27	Jan 9
4.2	Prices gathered	1d	Dec 27	Dec 27
4.3	Reference list	1d	Dec 27	Dec 27
5	Demos Received	1d	Jan 10	Jan 10
6	Price Evaluation	5d	Jan 10	Jan 16
7	Demo Evaluation	40d	Jan 11	Mar 7
7.1	Participants selected	1d	Jan 11	Jan 11
7.2	Software loaded on system	1d	Jan 11	Jan 11
7.3	Survey participants	9d	Jan 12	Jan 24
7.4	Evaluate demos	30d	Jan 25	Mar 7
8	Check out References	3d	Dec 28	Dec 30
9	Purchase Recommendation Prepared	5d	Mar 8	Mar 14
10	Purchase Order Prepared	0d	Mar 14	Mar 14

Project: Software Evaluation
Date: 1/20/94

Critical
Noncritical

Progress
Milestone

Summary
Rolled Up

Figure 10-10: MPW software evaluation project plan with Gantt chart.

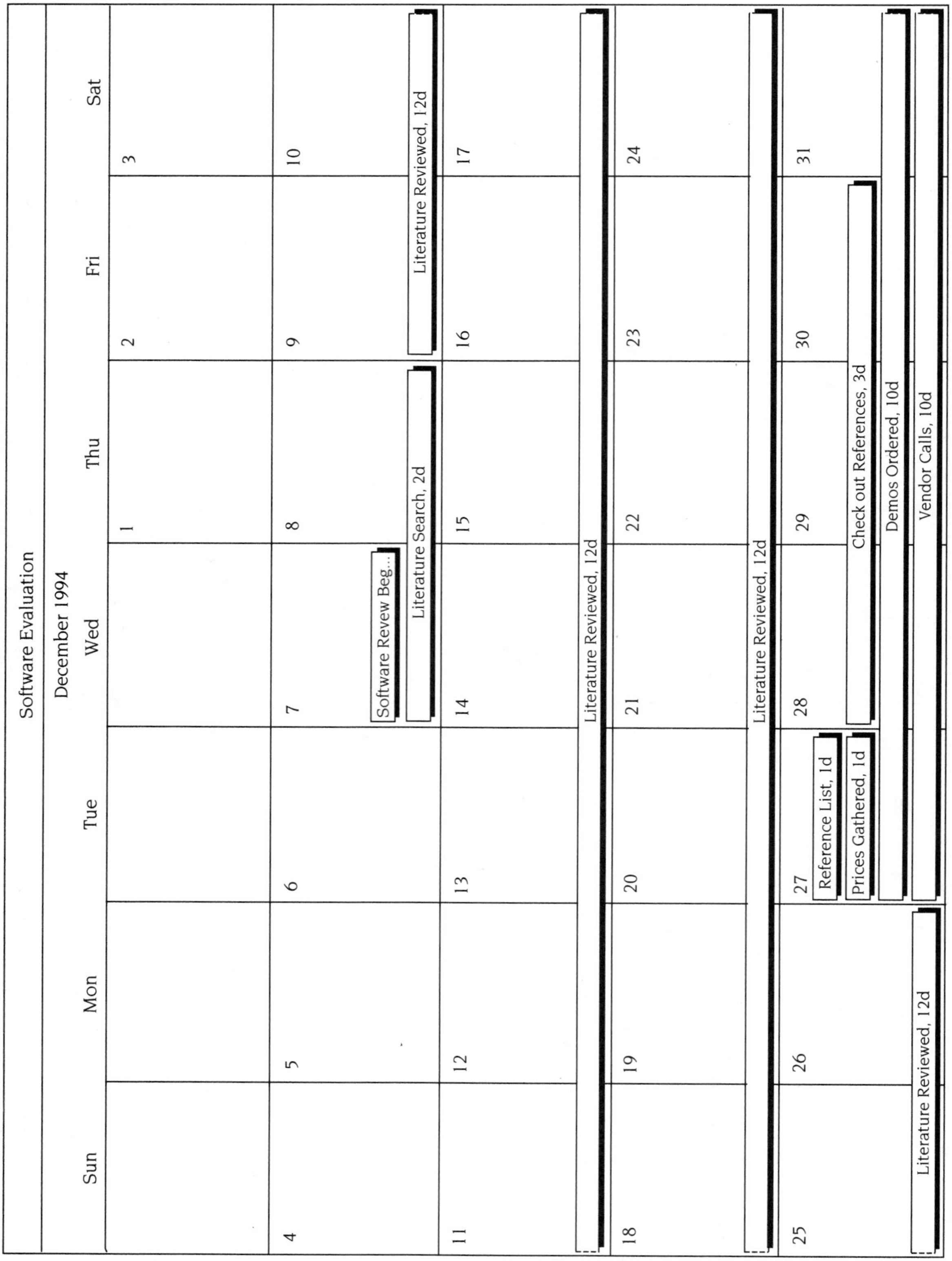

Software Evaluation

December 1994

Sun	Mon	Tue	Wed	Thu	Fri	Sat
				1	2	3
4	5	6	7 Software Revew Beg… Literature Search, 2d	8	9	10 Literature Reviewed, 12d
11	12	13	14	15	16	17
18	19	20	21 Literature Reviewed, 12d	22	23	24
25 Literature Reviewed, 12d	26 Literature Reviewed, 12d	27 Reference List, 1d / Prices Gathered, 1d	28 Literature Reviewed, 12d	29 Check out References, 3d / Demos Ordered, 10d / Vendor Calls, 10d	30	31

Figure 10-11: MPW December calendar for software evaluation project.

Schedule Name : Software Evaluation

As-of Date   : 20-Jan-94 8:00a
End Date   : 26-Apr-94 5:00pm

WBS Code	Task Name	Duratn (Days)	Resources
001	Software Review Begins	0	
002	Literature Search	2	Secretary
003	Price Evaluation	5	Bus Office
004	Literature Review	12	System Mgr
005	Vendor Calls	10	Secretary, System Mgr
005.01	Demos Ordered	10	
005.02	Prices Gathered	1	
005.03	Reference List	1	
006	Demos Received	0	
007	Demo Evaluation	39	System Mgr, Secretary, Tech Spec
007.01	Participants Selected	1	System Mgr
007.02	Software Loaded on System	1	Tech Spec, System Mgr
007.03	Survey Participants	9	
007.03.01	Survey Design	3	System Mgr, Info Spec
007.03.02	Survey Prepared	4	Secretary
007.03.03	Survey Distributed	2	Secretary
007.04	Evaluate Demos	30	
008	Check Out References	3	System Mgr, Secretary
009	Purchase Recommendation	5	System Mgr
010	Purchase Order Prepared	0	Bus Office

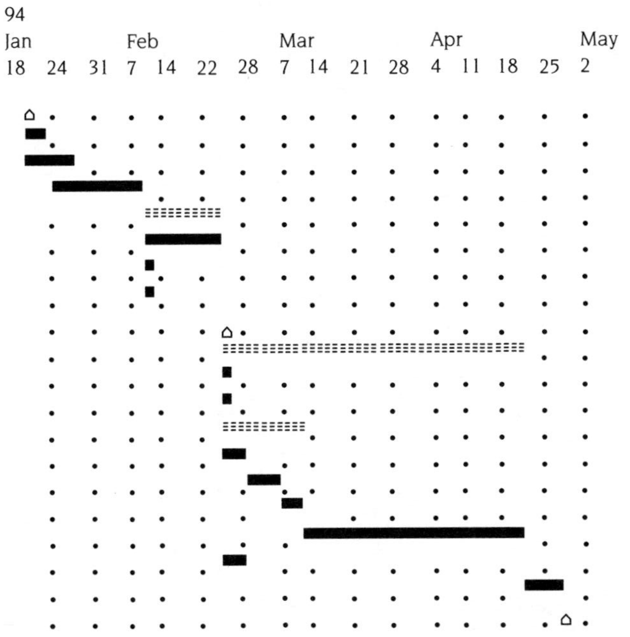

Legend:
- ▐ Detail Task   ░░░ Summary Task   ∘∘∘∘∘ Baseline
- (Progress)   (Progress)   ▲▲▲ Conflict
- ..-- (Slack)   ===-- (Slack)   ▪ Resource delay   ◁ Milestone
- Progress shows Proportional % Achieved on Actual
- Scale: 8 hours per character

TIME LINE Gantt Chart Report, Strip 1

Figure 10-12: TL draft mode of software evaluation plan with Gantt chart.

Software Evaluation

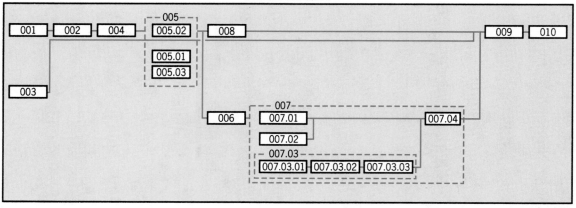

Figure 10-13: TL PERT network for software evaluation project with WBS identification numbers.

always be aware that no piece of software will do all things. At times, the user must be inventive and "force" the software to accomplish the desired ends. When suffering from the frustrations that inevitably accompany learning any new software, the user must also remember that managing any but the smallest of projects is nearly impossible without the computer's help. The information contained in a PMIS is interesting, but its real value comes when it is used to plan and control the project, helping it to reach its goals.

Producing a Video Tape

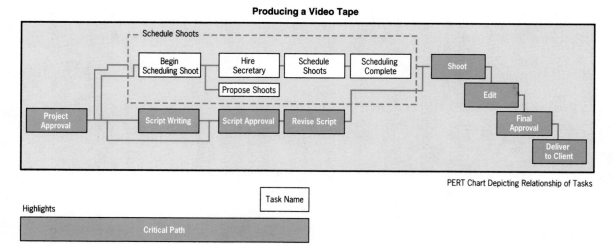

PERT Chart Depicting Relationship of Tasks

Figure 10-14: TL video project network (critical path highlighted).

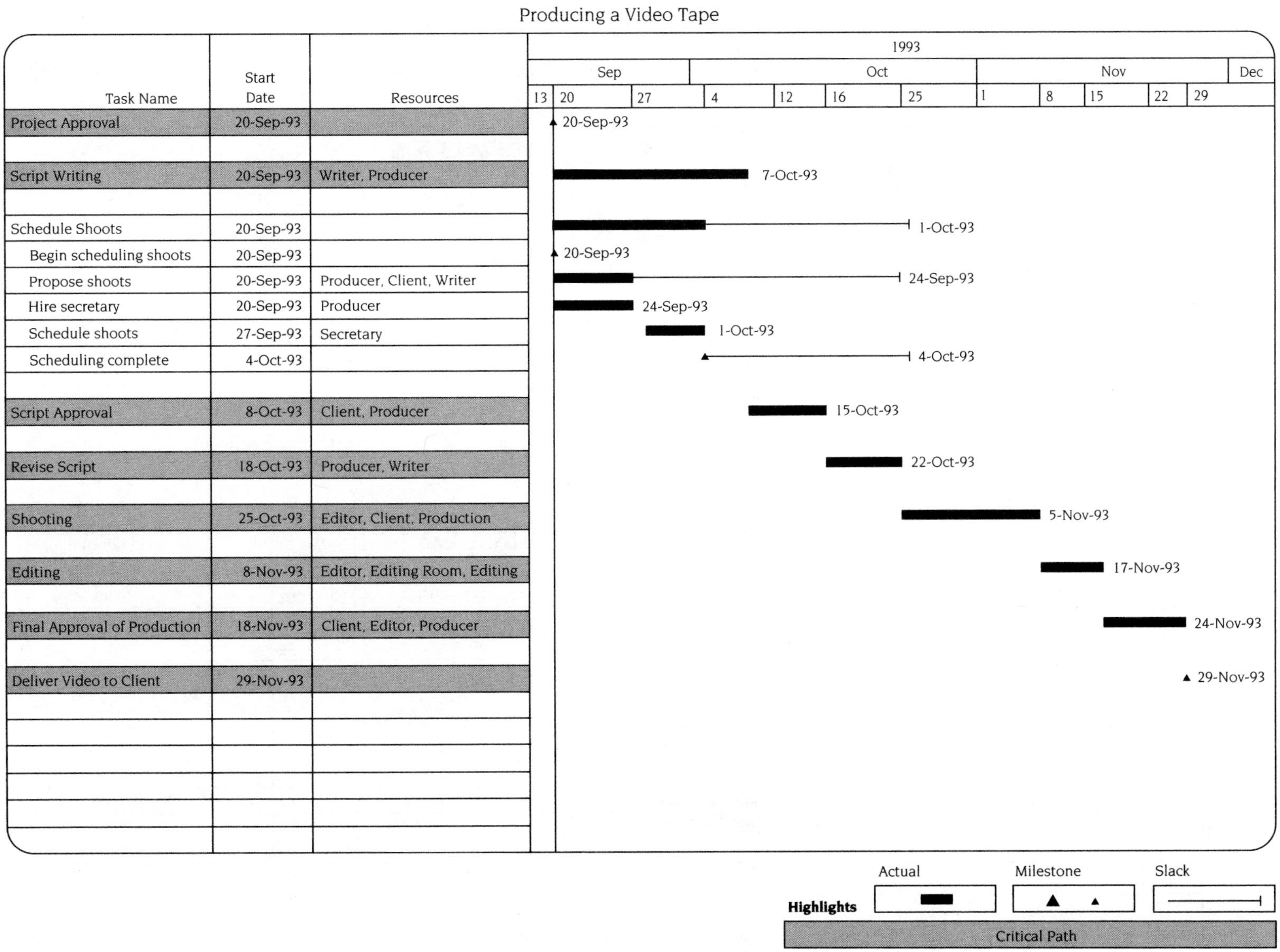
Producing a Video Tape
Task Name
Start Date
Resources
1993
Sep
Oct
Nov
Dec
13
20
27
4
12
16
25
1
8
15
22
29
Project Approval
20-Sep-93
20-Sep-93
Script Writing
20-Sep-93
Writer, Producer
7-Oct-93
Schedule Shoots
20-Sep-93
1-Oct-93
Begin scheduling shoots
20-Sep-93
20-Sep-93
Propose shoots
20-Sep-93
Producer, Client, Writer
24-Sep-93
Hire secretary
20-Sep-93
Producer
24-Sep-93
Schedule shoots
27-Sep-93
Secretary
1-Oct-93
Scheduling complete
4-Oct-93
4-Oct-93
Script Approval
8-Oct-93
Client, Producer
15-Oct-93
Revise Script
18-Oct-93
Producer, Writer
22-Oct-93
Shooting
25-Oct-93
Editor, Client, Production
5-Nov-93
Editing
8-Nov-93
Editor, Editing Room, Editing
17-Nov-93
Final Approval of Production
18-Nov-93
Client, Editor, Producer
24-Nov-93
Deliver Video to Client
29-Nov-93
29-Nov-93
Highlights
Actual
Milestone
Slack
Critical Path

Figure **10-15:** TL Gantt chart for video project (critical path highlighted).

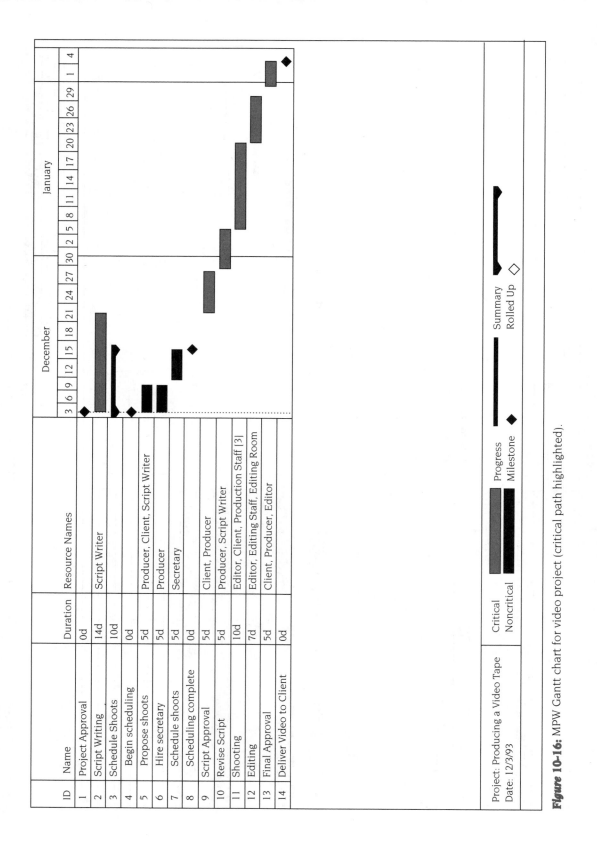

The following table represents the data shown in the Gantt chart:

ID	Name	Duration	Resource Names
1	Project Approval	0d	
2	Script Writing	14d	Script Writer
3	Schedule Shoots	10d	
4	Begin scheduling	0d	
5	Propose shoots	5d	Producer, Client, Script Writer
6	Hire secretary	5d	Producer
7	Schedule shoots	5d	Secretary
8	Scheduling complete	0d	
9	Script Approval	5d	Client, Producer
10	Revise Script	5d	Producer, Script Writer
11	Shooting	10d	Editor, Client, Production Staff [3]
12	Editing	7d	Editor, Editing Staff, Editing Room
13	Final Approval	5d	Client, Producer, Editor
14	Deliver Video to Client	0d	

Project: Producing a Video Tape
Date: 12/3/93

Critical
Noncritical

Progress
Milestone

Summary
Rolled Up

Figure 10-16: MPW Gantt chart for video project (critical path highlighted).

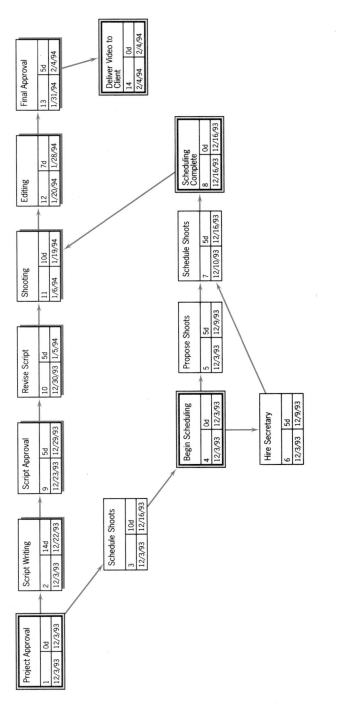

Project: Producing a Video Tape
Date: 12/3/93

Figure 10-17: MPW network for video project (critical path shown).

Building a House

Task Name	Start Date	Duratn (Days)	Pct Achvd
Begin Construction of House	15-Sep	0	100
Foundation/Lot	15-Sep	11	100
Survey	15-Sep	2	100
Layout	17-Sep	2	100
Excavation	21-Sep	3	100
Footers	23-Sep	2	100
Blockwork	27-Sep	2	100
Concrete	29-Sep	0.5	100
Final grading	29-Sep	0.5	100
Framing	30-Sep	4	0
Subfloors/walls	30-Sep	4	0
Roof trusses and decking	30-Sep	4	0
Electrical	6-Oct	3	0
Plumbing	12-Oct	3	0
Insulation	15-Oct	2	0
HVAC	15-Oct	2	0
Drywall	19-Oct	5	0
Painting	26-Oct	7	0
Finish Carpentry	4-Nov	2	0
Interior Doors	4-Nov	2	0
Trim/Baseboards	4-Nov	2	0
Cabinets/Shelves	4-Nov	2	0
Floors	8-Nov	4	0
Roofing	19-Oct	1	0
Exterior Trim	20-Oct	6	0
Siding	20-Oct	2	0
Soffits/gutters	20-Oct	2	0
Doors/windows	22-Oct	4	0
Landscaping	28-Oct	3	0
House Completed	15-Nov	0	0

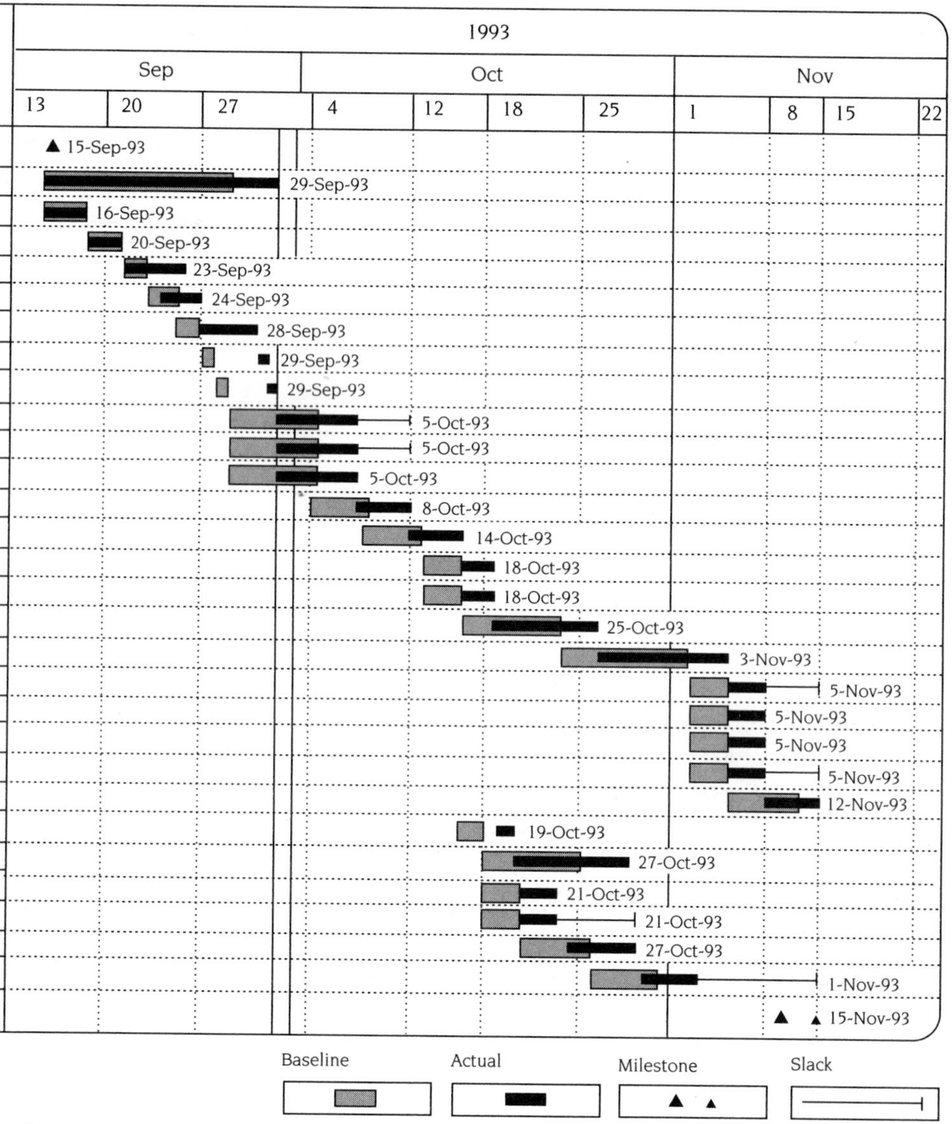

Updated 9/28/93

Figure 10-18: TL updated Gantt chart for house project (baseline and predicated actuals shown).

Project Management in Practice
Developing an Integrated Project Management System at Lederle Laboratories

The Medical Development Section (MDS) of Lederle Laboratories is responsible for conducting clinical drug studies, monitoring adverse drug reactions and complaints, preparing clinical supplements and submissions, producing brochures and publications for professional and promotional use, and developing exhibits for booth displays at scientific meetings. In the 1970s, MDS was using a set of four independent systems to conduct their work:

- *Clinical Study Administrative Information*: Includes investigator data, a study description, study design and protocol variables, personnel resources, and milestone planning and completion dates.

- *Study Grants Financial Information*: Includes study identification, total grant cost, payments to date, estimated payments, and monies returned.

- *Task Management System*: Provides information on progress toward utilization of clinical data and includes task identifiers, task manager, objectives, and estimated and actual dates.

- *Automated Project Management System*: Provides project analysis capability to plan and control projects.

These four systems were developed independently and did not intercommunicate. The result was duplicate data entry, data inconsistency, incomplete reports, and user confusion, all of which resulted in a lack of confidence in MDS and its work. Thus, MDS designed a single-entry Medical Development Information Management System (MDIMS) that would integrate the information supplied to MDS and return results to administrative databases for ultimate reporting. The user requirements were identified as:

- Eliminate duplicate data entry.
- Eliminate contradictory data.
- Develop data standards.
- Standardize data collection procedures.
- Consolidate schedule estimates.
- Enhance existing databases.
- Integrate all independent systems.
- Create unified turnaround and output reports.
- Extend automated project planning to all project teams.

An MDIMS project team was created and accomplished the above requirements within the first year. The last requirement was solved by creating generic work packages for each project, including any activities and constraints usually associated with it. In this way, a project manager can quickly create a project plan by simply fetching the generic work packages needed and assembling them into a larger plan.

As MDIMS was put into service, users identified weaknesses in the system and asked for the following additional features, which are being added:

Source: F. P. Funk, "The Development of an Integrated Project Management System in the Medical Development Section of Lederle Laboratories," *Project Management Journal*, September 1989.

1. Standardize project names to facilitate communication among users and administrators.

2. Redesign the turnaround reports to facilitate user updates as well as administrative data changes.

3. Add two new financial reports that combine project and study cost information.

4. Delete half of the work packages and focus on milestones instead to better manage projects.

5. Add the capability for users to view their own grant reports.

6. Add query capability to the system.

7. Provide uniform training to all system users.

SUMMARY

In this chapter we reviewed the monitoring function, relating it to project planning and control, and described its role in the project implementation process. The requirements for monitoring were discussed, in addition to data needs and reporting considerations. Last, some techniques for monitoring progress were illustrated and some computerized PMISs were described.

Specific points made in the chapter were these:

- It is important that the planning–monitoring–controlling cycle be a closed loop cycle based on the same structure as the parent system.

- The first task in designing the monitoring system is to identify the key factors in the project action plan to be monitored and to devise standards for them. The factors should concern results, rather than activities.

- The data collected are usually either frequency counts, numbers, subjective numeric ratings, indicators, or verbal measures.

- Project reports are of three types: routine, exception, and special analysis.

- Project reports should include an amount of detail appropriate to the target level of management with a frequency appropriate to the need for control (i.e., probably not weekly or other such regular basis). More commonly, reports occur near milestone dates.

- Three common project reporting problems are too much detail, poor correspondence to the parent firm's reporting system, and a poor correspondence between the planning and monitoring systems.

- The earned value chart depicts scheduled progress, actual cost, and actual progress (earned value) to allow the determination of spending, schedule, and time variances.

- There currently exist a number of computerized PMISs that are available for PMs, the greatest growth occurring in microcomputer PMISs.

- Project managers' preferred PMIS features were friendliness, schedules, calendars, budgets, and reports, with graphics, networks, charts, migration, and integration also frequently being mentioned.

- The five areas of internal PMIS capabilities are project planning, resource management, tracking/monitoring, report generation, and decision making.

In the next chapter we move into the final phase of project implementation, project control. We discuss the different types of control and describe some techniques useful to the PM in controlling the project.

GLOSSARY

Computer Paralysis—Excessive fascination or activity with the computer rather than the project itself such that the project suffers.

Earned Value—An approach for monitoring project progress that relies on the budgeted cost of activities completed to ascribe value.

Friendliness—When applied to computer use, this term refers to how easy it is to learn and/or use a computer or software package.

Hard Copy—Printed information output, as opposed to screen output.

Information Overload—Having an excess of information so that the information desired is difficult to locate.

Migration—The ability to move files and data between software packages.

Monitor—To keep watch in order to take action when progress fails to match plans.

Schedule Variance—The budgeted cost of work completed less the budgeted cost of work scheduled at this time.

Software—The instructions for running a computer.

Spending Variance—The budgeted cost of work completed less the actual cost at this time.

Spreadsheet—A matrix of data used with a computer. As the data in particular cells are changed, the results of other cells change also to keep in accordance.

Time Variance—The scheduled time for the work completed less the actual time.

Variance—A deviation from plan or expectation.

Windowing—A computer software feature that allows different functions to be conducted in a separate section of the screen, called a window.

 MATERIAL REVIEW QUESTIONS

1. Define *monitoring*. Are there any additional activities that should be part of the monitoring function?

2. Identify the key factors that need to be considered when setting up a monitoring system.

3. List some factors that would be difficult to monitor.

4. Describe routine reports and some problems with them.

5. What are the primary difficulties experienced in the design of project reports?

6. Describe the three variances of an earned value chart and explain their significance.

7. Can you identify other symptoms of computer misuse besides those in section 10.3?

8. Compare the PMIS features desired by PMs with the capabilities of microcomputer PMISs. Which are available; which are not?

9. What types of measures do data come in?

10. What is "earned value"?

 CLASS DISCUSSION QUESTIONS

1. Discuss the benefits of timely, appropriate, detailed information. How can a value be assigned to those characteristics?

2. What are the advantages for a PM of having a computerized system over a manual one? The disadvantages?

3. A project is usually a one-time activity with a well-defined purpose. What is the justification of setting up a PMIS for such a project?

4. A more intensive, and extensive, monitoring system is needed in project management than in a functional organization. Why?

5. The earned value chart is an attempt to put the three-dimensional concept of Figure 1-1 (see

Chapter 1) into a two-dimensional format. Is it successful? What is missing?

6. Will all future PMISs eventually be microcomputer based?

7. How might a variance be traced back to its source?

8. How would a Project Management Information System differ from an ordinary Management Information System?

9. Why would project managers resist using a computerized PMIS?

10. What type of general purpose software might project managers find useful?

11. How should a PMIS be chosen?

12. Discuss the uses of a PMIS in the different stages of the project life cycle.

13. Is it unethical, in an attempt to avoid a "shoot-the-messenger" response, to simply not mention bad news? To hide a mistake?

▶ PROBLEMS

1. Find the schedule variance for a project that has an actual cost at month 22 of $540,000, a scheduled cost of $523,000, and an earned value of $535,000.

2. A project at month 5 had an actual cost of $34,000, a planned cost of $42,000, and a value completed of $39,000. Find the spending and schedule cost variances.

3. A project at day 70 exhibits an actual cost of $78,000, a scheduled cost of $84,000, and a value completed of $81,000. What are the spending and schedule cost variances? Estimate the time variance.

4. A project has an actual cost in month 17 of $350,000; a planned cost of $475,000; and a value completed of $300,000. Find the spending and schedule cost variances.

5. A project has an actual cost in month 10 of $23,000; a scheduled cost of $17,000; and a value completed of $20,000. Find the schedule variance.

▶ INCIDENTS FOR DISCUSSION

Jackson Excavating Company

Donald Suturana joined Jackson Excavating Company six months ago. He is an experienced management information systems executive who has been given the task of improving the responsiveness of Jackson's data processing group to the end user. After several months of investigation, Suturana felt certain he understood the current situation clearly enough to proceed. First, approximately 90 percent of all end user requests came to data processing (DP) in the form of a project, with the DP output either the final product of the project, or, more commonly, one step of a project. Accordingly, Don felt he should initially direct his efforts toward integrating DP's approach to projects with the company's formal project management system.

It has been Don's experience that most problems associated with DP projects revolve around poor project definition and inadequate participation by the end user during the system design phase. Typically, the end user does not become heavily involved in the project until the new system is ready to install. At that point, a great deal of work is required to adapt the system to meet end-user requirements. Don decided to institute a procedure that put end-user cooperation and participation on the front end of the project. The idea was to define the objective and design of the system so thoroughly that implementation would become almost mechanical in nature rather than an introduction to the end user of "his or her new system."

Don also recognized that something had to be done to control the programming quality of DP's output. A more effective front-end approach to DP projects would subject DP managers to more intense pressure to produce results within user's needs, including time constraints. Don was concerned that the quality of the DP output would deteriorate under those conditions, especially given the lack of technical expertise on the part of end users and outside project managers. To solve this problem, Don recommended the creation of a DP quality assurance (QA) manager who would approve the initial steps of the projects and review each additional step. The QA manager would have the authority to declare any step or portion of the output inadequate and to send it back to be reworked.

Questions: Is this a good control system for DP? Why or why not? Does it also represent a good control point for company projects using DP to accomplish one portion of the project objective? What would your answer be if you were a non-DP project manager?

Guillotine Company

The Guillotine Razor Blade Company recently decided to update its plant by replacing eight metal-cutting machines with computerized machines. Management feels that one of the existing machines should be replaced every two months for the duration of the project rather than attempting to replace all the machines at once. The project manager has been setting up the project for the last couple of weeks and is now trying to develop an effective way to monitor the project to ensure it proceeds according to plan. The monitoring system she has developed is based on certain key factors in the project progress. Also, she has developed performance criteria to keep herself abreast of project performance. She believes that by basing the system on these two elements, she can effectively monitor the project.

Question: If you were the project manager, would you be satisfied with this system? Describe any additions or changes you would make.

The U.S. Army Corps of Engineers

The U.S. Army Corps of Engineers has contracted with a medium-size excavation firm to construct a small series of three earthen dams as part of a flood control project in North Carolina. For economic reasons, dams #1 and #2 have to be constructed at the same time and dam #3 can only be built after #1 and #2 are completed. There is also a very important scheduled completion date that has to be met (relating to next year's flood season). The project is being handled by Bill Johnson, who has been with the company for about a year.

This is a new job for Mr. Johnson in that he had never before headed more than one project at a time. About three months into the building of dams #1 and #2, he began to notice an information problem. He had supervisors from dams #1 and #2 reporting to him, but he never knew how far along they were in relation to each other. Since dam #3 cannot be built until both dams are fully complete, he cannot tell if it will be started on time and therefore completed on time. Realizing the situation was becoming serious, he began to wonder about how he could coordinate the projects. How could he tell where the projects were in relation to each other? How far were they *jointly* behind? Bill's major problem was his inability to monitor and record the dual projects effectively.

Question: What would you recommend to Bill?

▶ PROJECT TEAM CONTINUING EXERCISE

At this point, the project team should determine how progress will be monitored and reported. This includes the PMIS as well as the description of the regular (e.g., milestone) and exception reports that will be generated. The team and top management must decide here what will be measured and reported. One of the reports should be the earned value chart, so the cost of planned work must be determined as well as the time schedule for the project. All actual variances should be computed and reported separately throughout the project, as well as shown on the chart.

The team should determine and describe the PMIS features that will be important for the project. For example, is file migration or resource leveling important for the project? Follow the PMIS selection process described in the chapter and recommend one of the available packages. Then employ such a package in the project, using its features and reporting on a regular basis.

▶ BIBLIOGRAPHY

1. ANTHONY, R. N. *Planning and Control Systems: A Framework for Analysis.* Division of Research, Graduate School of Business Administration, Boston: Harvard University, 1965.

2. AVOTS, I. "How Useful Are the Mass Market Project Management Systems?" *Project Management Journal*, Aug. 1987.

3. BARNES, N. M. L. "Cost Modelling—An Integrated Approach to Planning and Cost Control." *American Association of Chemical Engineers Transactions*, March 1977.

4. BERGER, W. C. "What A Chief Executive Should Know about Major Project Management." *Price Waterhouse Review*, Summer–Autumn 1972.

5. BOBROWSKI, P. M. "Project Management Control Problems: An Information Systems Focus." *Project Management Journal.*, June 1989.

6. BRACKETT, S. W., and A. M. ISBELL. "PMIS—An Integrated Approach for the Management and Distribution of Project Information." *Project Management Journal*, September 1989.

7. BRANDON, D. H., and M. GRAY. *Project Control Standards*. Brandon/Systems Press, 1970.

8. CASPE, M. S. "Monitoring People to Perform on Design and Construction Projects." *Project Management Quarterly*, Dec. 1979.

9. CASPE, M. S. "Developing A Management Support System for Performing Design and/or Construction Management." *Project Management Quarterly*, Sept. 1981.

10. CLARKE, W. "The Requisites for a Project Management System." *Project Management Institute Proceedings*, 1979.

11. CLELAND, D. I., and W. R. KING. *Systems Analysis and Project Management*, 3rd ed. New York: McGraw-Hill, 1983.

12. DEAN, B. V. *Evaluating, Selecting, and Controlling R & D Projects*. New York: American Management Association Research Study 89, 1968.

13. EVANS, J. R., and W. M. LINDSAY. *The Management and Control of Quality*, 2nd ed. Minneapolis: West, 1993.

14. FARID, F., and KANGARI, R. "A Knowledge-Based System for Selecting Project Management Microsoftware Packages." *Project Management Journal*, Sept. 1991.

15. FERSKO-WEISS, H. "Project Management Software Gets A Grip on Usability." PC *Magazine*, July 1992.

16. FLEMING, Q. W. and J. M. KOPPELMAN "The 'Earned Value' Concept: Back to The Basics." PM *Network*, January 1994.

17. FORD, R. C., and F. S. McLAUGHLIN. "Ten Questions and Answers on Managing MIS Projects." *Project Management Journal*, Sept. 1992.

18. HODGE, B., and R. HODGSON. *Management and the Computer in Information and Control Systems*. New York: McGraw-Hill, 1969.

19. HOWARD, D. C. "Cost/Schedule Control Systems." *Management Accounting*, Oct. 1976.

20. JOHNSON, J. R. "Advanced Project Control." *Journal of Systems Management*, May 1977.

21. JOHNSON, R. V. "Resource Constrained Scheduling Capabilities of Commercial Project Management Software." *Project Management Journal*, Dec. 1992.

22. KELLY, J. F. *Computerized Management Information Systems*. New York: Macmillan, 1970.

23. KHATIAN, G. A. "Computer Project Management—Proposal, Design, and Programming Phases." *Journal of Systems Management*, Aug. 1976.

24. KIDDER, T. *The Soul of a New Machine*. Boston: Little, Brown, 1981.

25. KOEMTZOPOULOS, G. A. "Matrix Based Cost Control Systems for the Construction Industry." *Project Management Institute Proceedings*, 1979.

26. LAMBERT, L. R. "Cost/Schedule Control System Criteria (C/SCSC): An Integrated Project Management Approach Using Earned Value Techniques." In P. C. Dinsmore, ed., *The AMA Handbook of Project Management*. New York: AMACOM, 1993.

27. LEE, T. "Project Management for the Rest of Us." *Datamation*, Jan. 1, 1993.

28. LEVINE, H. A. "The Usability Factor: A Follow-Up." PM *Network*, Jan. 1994.

29. LEVINE, H. A. *Project Management Using Microcomputers*. Berkeley, CA: Osborne/McGraw-Hill, 1986.

30. LEVINE, H. A. "PM Software Forum." *Project Management Journal*, 1987 on (all issues). See "Hints for Software Selection," June and December 1987.

31. LIBRATORE, M. J. "A Decision Support System Linking Research and Development." *Project Management Journal*, Nov. 1988.

32. MANDAKOVIC, T., and L. A. SMITH. "Defining Project Management Software." *Proceedings*, Decision Sciences Institute, November 1986.

33. MARCHBANKS, J. L. "Daily Automatic Rescheduling Technique." *Journal of Industrial Engineering*, March 1976.

34. MATTHEWS, M. D. "A Conceptual Framework for Project Management Software." *Project Management Journal*, Aug. 1987.

35. McFARLAN, W. "Portfolio Approach to Information Systems." *Journal of Systems Management*, Jan. 1982.

36. MEREDITH, J. R. *The Management of Operations*, 4th ed. New York: Wiley, 1993.

37. National Software Testing Laboratories, Inc. "Ratings Report." *Software Digest*, Oct. 1991.

38. PALLA, R. W. "Introduction to Microcomputer Software Tools for Project Information Management." *Project Management Journal*, Aug. 1987.

39. PEART, A. T. *Design of Project Management Systems and Records*. London: Gower Press, 1971.

40. POSPISIL, C. J. "A PC-Based Scheduling System for a Transmission and Distribution Construction

Department." *Project Management Journal*, Sept. 1990.

41. PRINCE, T. *Information Systems for Management Planning and Control*. Homewood, IL: Irwin, 1970.

42. RAKOS, J. J. *Software Project Management*. Englewood Cliffs, NJ: Prentice Hall, 1990.

43. RANDALL, P. *Lotus Guide to One-Two-Three: Release 2.2*. New York: Lotus Books,1990.

44. SAITOW, A. R. "CSPC: Reporting Project Progress to the Top." *Harvard Business Review*, Jan.–Feb. 1969.

45. SANDERS, J. "Effective Estimating Process Outlined." *Computer World*, April 7, 14, and 21, 1980.

46. SEATON, S. J. "Field Product Performance Reports." *Journal of Systems Management*, Oct. 1978.

47. SETHI, N. K. "Project Management." *Industrial Management*, Jan.–Feb. 1980.

48. SHULL, F., and R. J. JUDD. "Matrix Organizations and Control Systems." *Management International Review*, June 1971.

49. SMITH, L. A., and S. GUPTA. "Project Management Software in P&IM." *P&IM Review and APICS News*, June 1985.

50. SMITH, M. G. "PCS: A Project Control System," Doctoral dissertation. Cambridge, MA: Massachusetts Institute of Technology,1973.

51. SPINNER, M. *Elements of Project Management: Plan, Schedule, and Control*. Englewood Cliffs, NJ: Prentice Hall, 1981.

52. THAMHAIN, H. J. "The New Product Management Software and Its Impact on Management Style." *Project Management Journal*, Aug. 1987.

53. TURBAN, E. "The Line of Balance—a Management by Exception Tool." *Journal of Industrial Engineering*, Sept. 1968.

54. VAN GIGCH, J. P. *Applied General Systems Theory*, 2nd ed. New York: Harper & Row, 1978.

55. VOICH, M. S. *Information Systems for Operations and Management*. Cincinnati: South Western, 1975.

56. WEBSTER, F. M., JR. *Survey of Project Management Software Packages*. Drexel Hill, PA: Project Management Institute, 1987.

57. WETZEL, J. J. "Project Control at the Managerial Level in the Automotive Engineering Industry," Masters dissertation, Sloan School of Management. Cambridge, MA: Massachusetts Institute of Technology, 1973.

58. WITTE, O. R. "Software for Project Management." *Architecture*, April 1987.

59. YAHDAV, D. "Project Spotlight: Project Management Gets Easier." *Computerworld*, Oct. 19, 1992.

CASE

RIVERVIEW CHILDRENS HOSPITAL*

On Thursday, February 15, 1990, Louis Bernard, the Assistant Executive Director of Finance at Riverview Children's Hospital in Toronto, reviewed the latest financial statements from the new computerized financial system. His fears of a slower than expected implementation were confirmed. The fiscal year-end of March 30 was fast approaching and the new system was not ready for the external auditors who would begin their audit in mid-April. Even though the implementation was already eight months late, Louis was tempted to delay the system implementation until after the audit.

Riverview Hospital Background

Founded in 1899 as a "Home for Incurable Children," Riverview Children's Hospital had developed over the years into a modern 87-bed children's facility providing long-term care and rehabilitation for infants, children, and young adults. Riverview patients were chronically ill, physically handicapped children who were

---

*Copyright 1991, The University of Western Ontario. This case was prepared by Bradley J. Dixon of the Western Business School. Reprinted with permission Western Business School.

educable. The most common afflictions were: cerebral palsy, spina bifida, and muscular dystrophy. Officially classified as a chronic care hospital, it had become one of the most respected pediatrics facilities in Canada. Riverview currently enjoyed a three-year accreditation status, the highest award granted by the Canadian Council on Hospital accreditation. (See attached Mission Statement—Exhibit 1.)

Since his arrival in 1987, Mark Thompson, the executive director, had guided Riverview toward enhancing its leadership role in providing services to its target population. Recently, Riverview had expanded into providing long-term acute care for eight ventilator-dependent children. This program re-

Exhibit 1: A Statement of Mission

PHILOSOPHY

Riverview Children's Hospital is committed to providing high quality inpatient and outpatient services for physically disabled children and young adults through ongoing programs of rehabilitation, health care, education, and research. This care involves the family or guardian, and is provided in an environment serving the whole person to promote optimum individual growth, development and integration into the community.

STRUCTURE AND ROLE

Riverview Children's Hospital, an 87-bed chronic care facility, shall operate within the requirements of the Ontario Public Hospitals Act and strive to:

- Assess and meet each patient's physical, mental, spiritual, social, recreational, and educational needs.

- Promote an atmosphere of caring support to patients, their families, staff, and volunteers.

- Liaise with other health services to fulfill its role in providing a continuum of care to the community.

- Encourage research and scholarly works to enhance the quality of life for the disabled.

- Provide education and training for health care personnel and the public.

- Exclude service for the management of those conditions which primarily require ongoing critical and/or diagnostic services of an acute care hospital.

quired special approval from the Ministry of Health to fund the additional staffing and specialized equipment requirements. Additionally, many other programs had been expanded or enhanced since Mark Thompson's arrival at Riverview to replace the previous executive director who was removed by the board of trustees.

More than 95 percent of the operating budget of $10 million came from the Ontario Ministry of Health. The 1989 fiscal operating deficit of $200,000 was funded by the Riverview Foundation which had grown into a sizable ($20 million in assets) foundation that supported disabled children through grants to Riverview and other institutions.

Riverview, like all public hospitals, was run by a board of trustees. The board had always consisted of a large majority of women, as women had started Riverview when they were driven from the board of a major children's hospital more than 90 years ago. The board took an active role in the administration of the hospital and met regularly with the hospital executive management group.

The board had several committees that also met regularly to set policy and review management decisions: the Executive Committee, the Joint Planning Committee, and the Finance and Audit Committee. The Finance and Audit Committee met every month and comprised nine board members, three of whom were Chartered Accountants.

In April 1987, Riverview had been given the responsibility for managing the eventual closing down of another chronic care children's hospital 20 kilometers north of Riverview in Thornhill, Ontario. The Thornhill Heights Hospital had been privately owned and the physical condition was deemed too inadequate by the Ministry of Health to warrant continued operation. The Ministry purchased the facility and gave the management team at Riverview the responsibility for managing the Thornhill Heights facility until it was closed. The phase out period was estimated to be at least 5 to 7 years.

Louis Bernard

Louis obtained an undergraduate degree in Business Administration in 1982, joined a major accounting firm, and received his Chartered Accountant designation in 1985. At the accounting firm, Louis had the opportunity to learn about health care accounting as an external auditor of hospitals and medical supply companies. Through his accounting firm's consultancy practice, he was given the opportunity to become the interim finance director at Riverview in April 1987. The opening at Riverview had arisen from the recent dismissal, by the hospital board, of the previous assistant executive director of finance who had held the position for less than nine months. In August 1987, Louis was offered the position of assistant executive director (AED) of finance.

The assistant executive director of finance was responsible for all facets of the finance function at Riverview: Treasury, Accounting, Auditing, and Office Management (see Exhibit 2). When Thornhill Heights was acquired in April 1987, a part-time AED of finance was hired. In the fall of 1987, the part-time contract was not renewed and Louis was given the finance responsibility for both facilities. Louis spent between one and two days per week at Thornhill.

Exhibit 2: Assistant Executive Director of Finance Job Responsibilities

The assistant executive director of Finance is responsible for all facets of the finance function at Riverview and Thornhill: Treasury, Accounting, Auditing, and Office Management.

Treasury responsibilities include:
  Negotiate revenue from the Ministry of Health.
  Manage the cash and investments of the Riverview Hospital and Foundation.
  Prepare capital assets budgeting.
  Advise the Board of the financial implications of decisions.
  Oversee all donations, bequests, and estate matters.

The Accounting and Audit responsibilities include:
  Submit financial statements to Board of Trustees.
  Produce quarterly reports to the Ministry of Health.
  Ensure the accounting system is current and accurate.
  Establish policies and procedures to prevent errors and fraud.

The Office Management Responsibilities include:
  Ensure smooth functioning of all financial procedures.
  Respond to questions and requests from the departments.
  Manage the telephone system and photocopiers.
  Supervise office staff.

Finance and Computer Departments

As the assistant executive director of finance, Louis Bernard was responsible for all aspects of financial management at Riverview and Thornhill. At Riverview, his staff consisted of seven people organized into two departments, Accounting and Materials Management (see Exhibit 3). Three Thornhill staff reported to Louis, the accounting clerk, the payroll clerk, and the receptionist. Job responsibilities, educational background, employment history, and Louis' comments on the staff are detailed in Exhibit 4.

The computer and communications department was formed in January 1989 at the same time that a computer room was being constructed to house the new computer hardware. Wilma Lo was promoted to computer coordinator reporting to Mark Thompson, who was overseeing the new system implementation. Previously, Wilma was the word processing coordinator and reported to Louis Bernard. The computer vendor's technical staff were favourably impressed with Wilma Lo's enthusiasm and felt that she could manage the computer operations. As the computer coordinator, Wilma was responsible for the operations and the technical management of the new computer system in addition to her current word processing support and telephone system management responsibilities. Wilma felt overextended by her new responsibilities.

I feel I am so busy all the time, there is so much going on. I never have the time to do anything right. There is so much to learn about the new computer, I have never worked with such a large system before. Working with the new computer is enjoyable, there wasn't much challenge in my job of providing support for all the word-processing users. Now the word-processor users always phone, often at awkward times, and expect me to come running to solve their problems. Mark tells me to not worry about them too much, but I used to be a word-processing clerk, they are my friends.

Wilma Lo also maintained the telephone system and reported to Louis Bernard, who had overall responsibility for the telephone system. The telephone system was not a big part of Wilma's job, but Louis felt that her priorities were not always logical.

Whenever I asked Wilma to make a minor change to the telephone system, it would be done immediately, even if I specifically men-

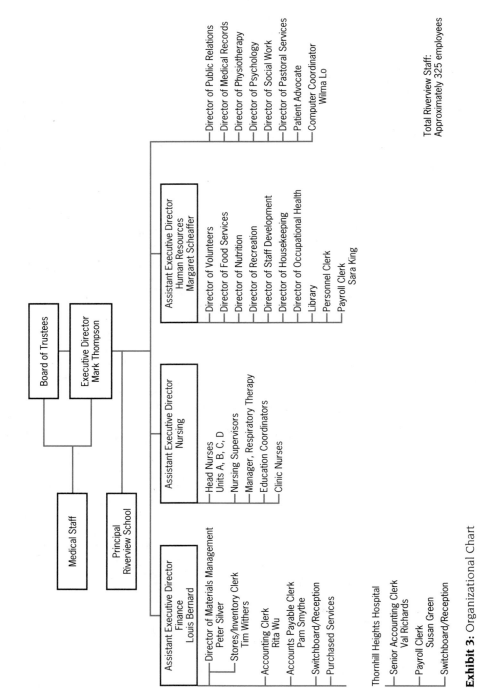

Exhibit 3: Organizational Chart

Exhibit 4: Biographical Details of Employees and Louis Bernard's Comments on Employees

Louis Bernard's comments on the performance of selected employees are shown in *Italics*.

RIVERVIEW CHILDREN'S HOSPITAL

Sarah King—Payroll Clerk
  5 years at Riverview
  High School Education
  Previous experience in Payroll Department in industry
  Poor management skills. Not detail-oriented.
  Weak comprehension skills, learned by copying procedures.
  Good worker, but progressively poor attendance record.
  Increasingly becoming flustered and missing details.
  Part-time assistant was necessary because of work load.

Rita Wu—Senior Accounting Clerk
  6 years at Riverview
  High School Education
  Runs the current microcomputer accounting system
  Relatively independent, did not need much direction.
  Learned the new system well.
  Responsible for General Ledger and Management Reports.

Pam Smythe—Accounts Payable Clerk
  6 years at Riverview
  High School Education
  Recently received Hospital Accounting Course Certificate.
  Not too confident—tends to hesitate.
  Procrastinates—somewhat insecure about the system.

Peter Silver—Materials Management Supervisor
  15 years at Riverview
  College in Portugal
  Community college—High marks—Transcript posted on wall.
  Not a delegator - runs the department very tightly.
  Workaholic, tries to do everything.
  Never used computer before but learns quick.

Tim Withers—Stores Inventory Clerk
  10 years at Riverview
  Educated in Ireland
  Very laid back—likes to visit with the sales representatives.
  Prompt—arrives and leaves on time.
  Recent heart attack.

Wilma Lo—Coordinator of Computer and Communication Department
  7 years at Riverview
  Diploma in computers from DeVry Institute
  Formerly supported the secretaries with their word processors
  Chosen (based on recommendations from ICS personnel) to head computer department.
  Very busy worker, but poorly organized.
  Writes copious notes, but takes time for her to comprehend.
  Management skills are lacking—does not prioritize well.

THORNHILL HEIGHTS HOSPITAL

Val Richards—Senior Accounting Clerk
  19 years at Thornhill
  Bookkeeping training
  High School Education
  Knows everyone, friendly.
  No computer experience.

Susan Green—Payroll Clerk
  5 years at Thornhill
  High School Education
  Was junior clerk in payroll department at large employer
  Intelligent, learns quickly.

tioned that this could wait. I thought her service was great, until my staff complained about Wilma's service. I realized she was doing everything I asked because I was the assistant executive director and her former supervisor.

The computer department at Riverview should logically have reported to the AED Finance, but Louis had no time or desire to manage it at that stage. In Canada, hospital computer departments usually report to the AED Finance, except the largest (500 plus beds) hospitals, where a chief information officer would manage the computer department. Louis felt that Wilma Lo, the computer department coordinator, was in over her head, and Mark Thompson was having to spend more time than he would like managing her and the computer problems. Louis remarked that he would need an accounting supervisor to look after the office and the day-to-day accounting issues before he could even consider managing the computer department.

Louis was concerned that the organizational structure of the administration departments did not make sense. Louis felt that the payroll department should not report to the same manager as the personnel department. More than 70 percent of a hospital's costs are salary expense. Proper audit and control practices dictate that the person who enters the hours worked into the system should work in the accounting department.

However, I am not sure I would want Sarah King, the payroll clerk, reporting to me anyway. I have had numerous incidents with her and I do not have much confidence in her abilities. Once I even pushed to have her fired, but the AED of Human Resources, Margaret Scheaffer, protects her staff and supported Sarah.

Purchasing the New System

Louis had become involved in the process of purchasing a new computer system soon after his arrival in 1987. Even though he did not have any experience installing computer systems, Louis was interested in introducing a hospital financial system into Riverview.

A computer evaluation committee had been formed to decide which computer system to purchase. The committee consisted of Mark Thompson, the three assistant executive directors, the director of Medical Records, and Wilma Lo.

There were six reasons for purchasing a system to replace the existing microcomputer-based accounting system and to automate other areas of the hospital. First, the existing system was inadequate and could not provide the department managers with anything beyond basic reports outlining the departmental expenses. Because the system had not been designed for hospitals it could not produce the necessary statistical and budgeting reports that the department managers needed in an increasingly cost-conscious health care environment. Good management reports are important to enable managers to control costs.

Second, the Canadian Hospital Association had just finished the Management Information Systems (MIS) guidelines. These guidelines covered how management information should be recorded, managed, and disseminated in hospitals. While the guidelines were just recommendations, it would only be a matter of time until adherence to MIS guidelines would become a prerequisite of receiving Hospital Accreditation.

Third, the payroll deposits and earnings statements had been processed by an off-site computer service bureau which cost $1300 per month. To update payroll and personnel information involved filling out forms that were couriered to the service bureau where they were entered into the computer. The entire process was slow, error prone, and cumbersome.

Fourth, the existing microcomputer system, purchased in 1982, was running out of capacity and increasingly breaking down. The computer would have to be replaced or upgraded soon.

Fifth, the executive director realized that proper financial systems were an important factor that the Ontario Ministry of Health would consider before allowing Riverview to expand programs. The Ministry of Health encouraged all hospitals to install financial systems that would support the management of a hospital, in addition to simply maintaining the accounting ledgers. Louis felt that Riverview's installation of a new system had been a consideration in the recent approval of the new program for ventilator-dependent children.

Finally, the management of patient information was entirely manual. The patient record, a binder that contained a record of all treatments, diagnoses, and progress reports for a patient, was located in a central records room. Computerized patient care information would enhance productivity, reduce errors, and move Riverview into the 1990s by providing greater analysis of treatment outcomes, faster access to medical histories by medical staff, and automatic output of the mandatory statistical reports for various governments.

In late autumn 1987 a consultancy firm specializing in hospital systems had been retained to prepare a needs analysis report of Riverview's systems requirements. After much discussion with the computer committee, the report was the basis of a Request For Proposal (RFP) which was sent to several computer system vendors in May 1988. The 195-page RFP was analyzed by the vendors who responded with elaborate proposals, addressing each question in the RFP. The proposals were reviewed by the committee with assistance from the consultants. A short list of three vendors was selected in June 1988. After numerous visits to other sites and further analysis of the proposals submitted by the vendors, a system was selected in August. A contract for purchasing the hardware, software and implementation services for $499,000 was finally signed in November 1988 with a major computer hardware vendor, Integrated Computer Systems (ICS).

ICS proudly advertised that they were the only single source health care systems vendor in Canada. ICS was responsible in the contract for managing the training, hardware installation, software implementation, and hardware support for Riverview. Louis was impressed that the training and implementation costs were lower than other vendors' proposals. The hardware to be installed at Riverview was an ICS-A1 mainframe computer with 25 terminals connected to the computer.

The software comprised two parts: the first part was the patient-care system which automated the patient information flow and computerized the Medical Records department. The patient-care software was developed by ICS in their Winnipeg office and the software trainers were ICS employees. The second part was the financial system which automated the Materials Management, Payroll and Accounting departments. The financial system consisted of many interrelated subsystems, or modules (see Exhibit 5), that had to be implemented in a coordinated fashion. There were few connections between the financial and patient-care systems; each system could be implemented independently of the other. The financial soft-

---

Exhibit 5: Financial System Modules

GENERAL LEDGER AND BUDGETING

The purpose of this application is to maintain and report the financial data arising from the operation of the hospital and its various departmental units. This system assists in cost control through more timely financial reports, prepared with less clerical effort.

The system provides an on-line auditing capability that allows the users and auditors to easily track the movements of data to and from the general ledger accounts.

The general ledger system accepts input transactions automatically from other applications, such as accounts payable, accounts receivable, payroll, purchasing, and inventory control. Users can also input transactions manually, and inquire about the status of any general ledger account. The system allows use of the new chart of accounts described in the MIS Guidelines for Canadian Hospitals. A user-defined chart of accounts is also allowed.

The system generates financial reports as specified by the user. It can provide comparative reporting by period, by departmental unit or any other desired basis. The system also provides consolidated financial statements for the hospital.

The system monitors actual expenditures against the budget for the hospital and all departments. It generates monthly budget variance reports for each department and cost centre.

ACCOUNTS PAYABLE

The purpose of this application is to assure the proper receipt of goods, to support the orderly payment of supplier accounts, and to assure authorization of payments. This system allows the hospital staff to have current information on volume of purchases and minimizes the time required to find the status of a supplier order. It also helps the hospital staff to avoid missing supplier discount dates.

The system regularly prints a list of invoices or accounts which should be paid. The user can make modifications to this pre-payment register. When a user is satisfied, the system prints the required cheques.

The user can, at any time, request the printing of a single cheque, which is charged against a specified general ledger account (e.g., an expense account). The user can also write cheques manually and enter the details, which the system uses to keep all account balances up to date. The system keeps track of outstanding cheques and performs a reconciliation with the monthly bank statements.

The system generates purchase analysis reports by department, product type, and supplier. It can also produce other useful reports such as product price histories and supplier delivery performance. On-line inquiry to all accounts payable information is available.

PAYROLL

The purpose of this application is to maintain time and attendance data for all hospital personnel and calculate the payroll. This system minimizes the clerical effort required to produce the payroll and other labour statistics. The system can generate a report of payroll costs and full-time equivalents used by department, cost centre and job description. It can produce consolidated reports for the hospital. It can also produce reports which monitor vacation days, sick leave, overtime hours, etc. by employee.

Time and attendance data for all full-time and permanent part-time staff are entered from time

Exhibit 5: (*continued*)

sheets. The system can handle multiple pay cycles. Some employees are paid on a weekly basis; others can be paid biweekly, semi-monthly, etc. The hospital is a multi-union environment. The system is flexible, allowing changes to union contracts and pay scales to be made with a minimum amount of effort.

In most cases, employees are paid through an automatic funds transfer to their bank accounts. The system can also issue cheques for those employees not on automatic deposit.

The system automatically prints record of employment forms for terminated employees. The system retains certain information on terminated employees for retroactive and reference purposes.

The system has the capability to calculate vacation pay, sick pay, bonuses, etc.

PURCHASING

The purpose of this application is to oversee the acquisition of commodities, parts, supplies and any other material goods required by the hospital. The system captures requisition data from multiple departments, assists in the preparation of purchase orders and monitors the receipt of goods received.

The normal flow of operation within the purchasing application is:

(1) A purchase requisition is created within a hospital department. This requisition is sent to the purchasing department for approval and creation of a purchase order.

(2) The purchasing department will review the requisition. They will, when necessary, select the appropriate vendor. They may negotiate prices and discounts. They will ensure that delivery is for the required date. Once they approve the requisition, they will enter it into the computer.

(3) The computer will generate the purchase order. A copy of this purchase order will be sent to the supplier. The system also automatically produces stock purchase orders based on inventory reorder points and economic order quantities.

(4) The supplier will deliver the goods.

(5) The receiving department will count the items received. Their receipt will update the inventory control and open purchase order records.

INVENTORY CONTROL

The purpose of this application is to control the issue and stocking levels of most hospital stock items, including medical and surgical supplies, sterile supplies for nursing units, reusable linen items, dietary material and utensils, pharmaceutical supplies, and paper supplies. The system attempts to prevent stockouts, while minimizing inventory carrying costs.

The inventory control system maintains a file of all stock items, including newly purchased, reusable, and manufactured items. The system records all requisitions and issues. Details of supplier orders and receipt of goods are automatically received from the purchasing system. It assists in physical inventory taking, and upon authorized clearance makes any necessary adjustments to the file.

The system calculates order points and quantities for all items. It regularly generates a report of all items near their order level.

The system prints product item catalogues for departments to use when requisitioning items from stores or non-stores.

The system allows for multiple stores locations. It maintains cart profiles for the multiple supply carts found throughout the hospital. It also provides information for charging supplies usage to the various cost centres.

The system allows on-line inquiry for inventory item status and purchase order status.

---

ware was sold by ICS but written by Dovetail Software, a London, Ontario-based software firm, under contract to provide hospital financial software exclusively to ICS. The Dovetail financial software was one of the most advanced hospital financial systems in Canada. The software's many features, coupled with the fiscal control from the disciplined procedures the software required, made Dovetail software popular with larger, 400-plus bed, hospitals.

Implementing the System

A schedule for implementing the financial modules was agreed upon in the contract between the computer vendor and Riverview's computer committee (see Exhibit 6). The computer hardware was installed in the computer room during January and February, 1989. A project manager was appointed in March 1989 and the 10-week implementation schedule was initiated. As executive director, Mark Thompson would

Exhibit 6: Implementation Schedule—Financial Modules

TASK #						WEEKS				
	1	2	3	4	5	6	7	8	9	10
1a. Initiate Team Formation	X									
1b. Identify Dovetail Modifications										
Define Modifications for:										
(a) Accounts Payable	X									
(b) General Ledger	X									
(c) Financial Reports	X									
2. Analysis of Modifications Requested										
(a) Develop Specifications		X								
(b) Provide Cost Estimates			X							
(c) Provide Implementation Estimates			X							
3. Acceptance of Modifications										
(a) Priorities				X						
(b) Approval				X						
(c) Signoff/Acceptance				X						
4. Revise Implementation Plan										
Revise Due to Modifications					X					
5. Consultation for User Training										
(a) Core Trainers Assigned	X									
(b) Develop Training Plan	X									
6. Customization & Programming										
(a) Programming Commences					X	X	X			
(b) Testing						X	X	X		
(c) Incorporate in System							X	X	X	
(d) Documentation Changes Made						X	X			
7. User Training										
Implement Training Plan						X	X	X	X	
8. Determine Conversion Methodology										
Manual vs. Tape-to-Disk		X								
Internal vs. Contracted		X								
9. Prepare Conversion Data										
(a) Define Conversion Data			X							
(b) Review & Cost Conversion Specs.			X							
10. Perform Conversion										
(a) Write Conversion Programs				X						
(b) Test Validity of Programs				X	X					
11. Test Accounts Payable										
(a) Test for Integrity of Data						X				
(b) Test Scripts						X				
12. A/P Acceptance										
Evaluate and Accept A/P							X			
13. Test General Ledger										
Test for Integrity of Data						X				
Test Scripts						X				
14. G/L Acceptance										
Evaluate and Accept G/L							X			
15. Test Financial Reporting										
Test for Integrity of Data							X			
Test Scripts							X			

Exhibit 6: (*continued*)

TASK #		1	2	3	4	5	6	7	8	9	10
						WEEKS					
16.	Financial Reporting Acceptance										
	Evaluate & Accept Financial Reporting								X		
17.	Test Payroll										
	Test Integrity of Data								X		
	Test Scripts								X		
18.	Payroll Acceptance										
	Evaluate & Accept Payroll									X	
19.	Live Implementation										
	(*a*) Provide Conversion Coverage										X
	(*b*) Prepare for Operations										X
	(*c*) Implement Plan (See 4)										X
20.	System Shakedown										
	Allow Time Post-Implementation to										
	Resolve any Problems								X	X	
21.	Post-Implementation Review										
	(*a*) A/P										
	(*b*) G/L										
	(*c*) F/R										
	(*d*) Payroll/Personnel										

oversee the entire project and liaise with ICS. Louis would direct the financial system portion and the director of Medical Records would manage the patient-care system portion. The expected date for the financial system to be fully operational or 'live' was early July. The patient accounting system would be implemented after the financial system. The entire implementation was expected to take 6 to 7 months.

The implementation budget, to cover project management and miscellaneous technical support expenses to get the system 'live,' was $64,000. This amount was included in the negotiated contract price and was estimated to cover a 6 to 8 month implementation. Riverview relied on ICS to employ the appropriate project management candidate. ICS, in turn, subcontracted Sharon Picalle from a computer consultancy firm in March 1989: Sharon had worked extensively with ICS computers and had project management experience in the banking industry. This was her first project working with patient-care and hospital financial software. Sharon reported to both Venkat Halambi, the support manager at ICS, and Mark Thompson at Riverview. Venkat actually employed Sharon but any major decisions that Sharon referred to him were made after consultations with the ICS marketing account manager for Riverview.

After a few days on the job, Sharon realized that Wilma Lo, the computer coordinator, was not understanding the computer system and would require extra training and technical support. Sharon asked Venkat to provide an ICS technical support person to spend extra time with Wilma Lo to help her understand the system and enable her to solve the minor technical problems that invariably arose. The technical support person was billed to the project at $480 per day for time spent solving problems where ICS had determined they were not at fault or responsible. Fortunately for Riverview, there was not another system installed at the same time. The technical support person was available to spend the extra time Wilma needed to learn the system.

Training for the first financial module (General Ledger) started in April. The users complained to Sharon that the training was too rushed and after talking to the Dovetail trainers Sharon realized that the days allocated for training in the contract had been cut roughly in half. Sharon learned from ICS's marketing department that the training days had been reduced because Riverview, at 87 beds, was less than half the size of all the hospitals that had purchased the system to date. Sharon reviewed the training days' shortfall with Mark Thompson and Louis. Louis felt that the training he attended for the General Ledger module did not seem rushed. He wondered if days recommended by Dovetail were actually needed. Louis felt that Sharon should be able to help the staff with implementing the system. Sharon, Mark, and Louis agreed to keep to the original training plan rather than incur costs of $650 per day for a Dovetail trainer for the extra 30 days that were cut.

In May it became apparent to Sharon that the frequency of computer problems was not decreasing. Wilma Lo was still having trouble with the computer system, although the technical support person was spending 2 to 3 days per week at Riverview assisting Wilma. The computer was constantly going down, inconveniencing the users. Louis was not surprised when Sharon mentioned to him that she was postponing the second training sessions until the end of May to correct the hardware problems. The system "live" date was delayed by one month to July.

Many difficulties were created for Sharon by Riverview staff's lack of familiarity with computers. Although Sharon was spending extra time working with the staff, the users still complained that there was not enough time to learn the system. Sharon found that she had to be increasingly assertive and persistent to ensure that users completed any assigned project tasks. Payroll was the most complicated of all the financial systems and it became apparent to Margaret and Louis that the payroll clerk, Sarah King, would not be able to handle going live until sometime in the fall. Louis was disappointed that Riverview would not be able to realize the monthly savings from implementing Payroll earlier.

During June several of Louis's staff mentioned that they felt increasingly uncomfortable working with Sharon. Louis saw Sharon only a couple of times per week, and always asked how things were going. Sharon was positive about the system, the staff, and the prospects for going live with everything but payroll in August. Louis increasingly wondered why Sharon was spending so much time to manage this project. Louis knew that the $64,000 budget was based on a part-time project manager.

Shortly after completion of the training sessions in June, Tim Withers, the stores inventory clerk, suffered a major heart attack. Tim would be off work recovering until October. Peter Silver, the director of Material Management, was taking holidays in September. Louis realized that the Material Management module implementation would be delayed until November. Summer holidays interfered with the implementation plans of the other financial modules as well. Louis agreed with Sharon that the live dates for the other financial modules would have to be pushed back to October.

Louis' concerns about the amount of time Sharon was spending were realized in early July when he received an invoice from ICS for $59,000 for the implementation costs to date. The invoice did not provide a breakdown of the hours spent and Louis requested, through Mark Thompson, that a breakdown be provided. Eventually, the hour totals revealed that over 400 hours, or 50 days, of billable technical support were charged between March and June. Louis and Mark met with Sharon and representatives from ICS and expressed their concern with the amount of the bill. Sharon felt confident that the implementation would not be delayed further.

Louis noticed that Sharon's style was becoming more controlling, demanding, and aggressive. Sharon annoyed Margaret, the AED of Human Resources, by her manner during meetings to discuss the payroll implementation. Louis learned that Wilma felt she was being treated "like a child" by Sharon. The situation reached a crisis in late August when ICS submitted an invoice for $20,000, which included an additional $15,000 charge over the remaining budget to cover extra implementation costs. Louis refused to pay the $15,000. Louis, Margaret, and Mark Thompson met to discuss the project and Sharon's role. They felt Sharon's handling of the project was inadequate and Mark Thompson told ICS not to renew Sharon's contract, effective September 1.

The New Project Manager

At the end of August, Louis approached John Deans, the Dovetail trainer for the accounts payable and general ledger modules, about assuming the project management responsibilities. Louis and John had developed a good relationship from working together on the general ledger module over the past several months. Dovetail prepared a proposal that outlined the implementation dates, the project management days, and the extra training required (see Exhibit 7).

The Riverview board was very concerned about cost overruns. Louis was concerned how the board would react to a request for an additional $32,000 to cover project management costs. After discussions with Mark, Louis rearranged the computer budget by

Exhibit 7: Proposal for Project Management and Training

This proposal is for the balance of the training required, the implementation assistance, and the project management required to implement the system successfully to meet the target dates.

Based on our daily rate of $525.00, the cost would be $32,025 excluding travel and lodging costs. We estimate our travel and lodging expenses to be approximately $150 per day. We look forward to discussing the details with you to ensure that we mutually understand the project requirements.

TRAINING REQUIREMENTS

Training required to implement Dovetail is outlined by module below:

Material Management: 6–9 Days

Refresher training at both Thornhill and Riverview is highly recommended due to the delays between the original training and the implementation date. Recommended training is 2–3 days per site.

Implementation support is recommended when system goes live. This support is usually requested by hospitals and has proven extremely valuable to eliminate implementation problems and minimize future system issues. Suggested support is 2–3 days when system is going live.

Management Information: 2–3 Days

Outstanding training in management information will cover payroll and other complex reporting. This training would be scheduled over the next few months as data become available on the system.

General Ledger and Accounts Payable: 1–2 Days

Implementation support and review are recommended for these modules. This time would be scheduled concurrently with the implementation date.

Payroll and Personnel Training: 19 Days

There are five outstanding tasks before the payroll system can go live. The major items and their associated training days include:

Test with subset of 25 employees	5 Days (Riverview Only)
	4 Days (Thornhill Only)
Department head training	1 Day
Parallel payroll	5 Days
Miscellaneous payroll functions	3 Days
Review outstanding issues	1 Day

Operations Training: 5 Days

Consideration should be given to scheduling 5 days of operations training, 2–3 days when the system goes live and the remainder after several months of operation.

PROJECT MANAGEMENT

Schedule

In order to project the number of days required for project management, a summary schedule was developed based on conversations with hospital personnel coupled with past experience at other hospitals.

Key Milestone Dates

G/L, A/P Implementation:	1-Oct-89
Material Management Live:	1-Nov-89
Conversion of Payroll Data:	?-Nov-89
Payroll/Personnel	1-Dec-89

Projected Days Required

The days required for project management are listed below. These days are based on the above schedule and our previous experience with implementing Dovetail. These days are our best estimate and are, therefore, subject to mutually agreed revisions as the project progresses.

September	5 Days
October	9 Days
November	5 Days
December	3 Days
January	1 Day
TOTAL:	23 Days

Project Management Approach

Dovetail is committed to working with our customers toward the common goal of a smooth implementation of the Dovetail system. We believe that communication among all people involved in the implementation is vital. We will strive to keep communication open and as up to date as possible.

Successful projects are implemented in an environment of cooperation, communication, and team work. We believe that Dovetail's project management skill will be a positive addition to this implementation.

deferring a software purchase for a year. Louis was able to find enough funds to pay for the extra project management costs without requesting additional funds from the board. John Deans was appointed project manager in mid-September.

John realized how concerned Riverview was with their expenses. Riverview had a strict policy regarding overtime, and employees mentioned that several years back people had been asked to take unpaid leave in order to meet the budget. John submitted status reports every week detailing the days spent to date and was careful not to spend any unnecessary time at Riverview.

During October, John's visits focused on getting the general ledger and payroll system live. The payroll system live date of December 1 was delayed until January 1, 1990, because of problems in obtaining the specialized forms and making custom modifications to the software. Delaying the implementation of payroll past January 1 would cause more complications from converting tax and benefit deductions that were based on a calendar year.

The implementation of the general ledger went smoothly and by the middle of November the closing balances from the old system were transferred to the new system, reconciled, and financial reports were prepared in time to be included in the 1990 budget packages for distribution to department managers by the end of November. The managers would review their results and prepare a budget which was to be submitted to finance by mid-January. Then the entire finance department faced 4 or 5 very busy weeks to consolidate the data, review and prepare preliminary *pro forma* statements for budget meetings, then revise the statements and prepare final reports, meanwhile performing the required daily duties.

Each time John visited the hospital he would check with the accounting and materials management staff to inquire about how the implementation was going and was always told that everything was going as planned. John's schedule of training and consulting at three other hospitals prevented him from travelling to Riverview during most of November and early December.

After an absence of 5 weeks, John arrived at Riverview on December 18. Louis told John that it appeared that everything was progressing as planned and the Accounting and Material Management staffs were not having any major problems. Louis acknowl-

edged, however, that he was not confident that everything was going as well as his staff let on. Louis remarked that he had been too busy to spend time down in Materials Management to learn what was really happening. John spent the morning investigating the status of the system and generating computer reports. After analyzing the computer output John realized things were not going as planned and arranged a meeting with Louis.

Louis, there are three concerns that I have with the system. First, the accounts payable invoices for November are not entered into the new system. Pam assured me, the last time we talked, that she was right on schedule. She has not spent any overtime doing this. Second, the Materials Management department is not looking at their daily computer reports, and I believe the inventory balances are not accurate; they blame the delays in entering Purchase Orders into the system. This leads me to believe that they are not managing their inventory or their module well. Third, the payroll will not be able to go live January 1, because the programmer who was writing the software to convert the files from the service centre to the new computer is very sick with pneumonia and nobody else will be able to finish the job in time.

Louis and John discussed the problems and arrived at an action plan to correct the problem. Louis agreed to encourage Pam Smythe, the accounts payable clerk, to spend time entering November's invoices into the system and to speak with Peter, the Materials Management manager, about his module. John mentioned that he would arrange for the Dovetail Materials Management trainer to come and review the system with the Materials Management staff as soon as possible.

In January, John worked with Pam to enter the November invoices into the system. Louis talked with Pam and realized that his earlier requests for working overtime went largely ignored because the staff thought they would not get paid for overtime. Louis assured them that they would get paid overtime.

Entering the invoices was complicated by the elapsed time since the goods had arrived and the many errors in purchase orders. Invoices could only be entered against a purchase order previously entered into the system, and then only when the order was marked by the receiver as having been received. When the system was notified that the goods had been received, a liability was created for the value of the goods as per the purchase order. The invoice was entered into the system, and if it matched the liability exactly, a cheque was produced. In the conversion, all the purchase orders, receipts, and invoices were entered for one month as a parallel to ensure that the old and the new systems were matched and this also provided an accounting "trail" for the auditors to follow.

The Decision

By Monday, February 12, all the November invoices were entered and matched to the purchase orders. The system was ready for the first month end to be run overnight. The month end failed because Material Management had not run their month end first. After investigating further, John found that the Materials Management manager did not know how to run a month end and thought that accounting was responsible for starting the run.

After both the Inventory and Accounts Payable month ends had been run on Tuesday evening, Louis requested the computer to generate the first set of financial statements Wednesday morning. The financial statements were worse than Louis imagined. First, the accounts payable liabilities for November were $1.4 million, not even close to the current system's liability of $50,000. Additionally, the inventory value was shown as over $1 million dollars when it should have been about $70,000. Finally, three months of inventory issues had been entered into November's expenses.

After a long discussion with John, Louis realized he could either parallel the system for four months from November to February or start fresh after the audit and the year end stock count sometime in April.

Louis spent most of Wednesday and Thursday working with the statements trying to understand the magnitude of the errors. His main concern was inventory, where there were some obvious mistakes, like photocopier paper inventoried at about $1 per sheet. With 200 items in inventory, correcting errors would require at least a half hour per item just to investigate the problems. Some of the discrepancies arose from mistakes on purchase orders or the corresponding goods receipts. With about 800–900 purchase orders generated over the past four months, it could take a couple of weeks of analysis to sort out the purchase order problems. If all the accounts payable invoices were entered, the program to match invoices to purchase orders would help Materials Management to find a lot of the problems. To date, only November invoices had been entered into the system; it could take Pam Smythe 40 to 50 hours to enter a month's invoices.

Louis felt that his odds were "50–50" of being able to balance the statements to the old system in time. Louis did not feel confident that even with all invoices, purchase orders, and receipts entered and checked that all the errors could be found before the audit started in April. Louis wondered how the work would get done. Should he attempt to utilize temporary employees who would know nothing about the system, or spend the money and utilize the Dovetail trainers, at $650 per day, or should he rely on his staff to work enough overtime at an overtime rate of about $20 per hour?

Louis was concerned that delaying the implementation would prolong the frustration until next May or June. Louis knew the morale of the staff working with the new system was not good. The accounting staff had just finished working on the budget, a very busy time of the year. Wilma Lo was in especially bad shape; she was irritable, constantly blaming everyone else for each petty incident, and Louis noticed during one coffee break that she was shaking when she held her cup. The system was constantly going down; Louis believed that Wilma was too preoccupied to schedule preventive maintenance to catch problems in time. Pam Smythe was frustrated with all the obstacles in both the new and the old systems. Louis was also worried about how much longer Tim Withers would be able to handle the stress, given his heart condition.

Louis wondered if the current microcomputer system would be able to last much longer. During the last month, the microcomputer had been broken for six days and there were a number of corrupt files on the disk which was overloaded. To work around the problems, Pam Smythe was having to trick the system into producing accounts payable checks.

Louis knew that the audit would keep his accounting staff very busy during the month of April, and it would be a messy and difficult audit if based on the old system. Louis could not imagine which was worse, trying to implement the system during April while doing an audit or implementing the system now. If he continued to implement the new system, and the systems did not balance by March 30, his audit would become extremely complicated; the fees could double from the typical bill of $15,000. The auditors would not regard a botched implementation lightly. They could cast Louis in a most unfavourable light in the management report that was prepared by the auditors for the Finance and Audit committee.

Louis questioned why he had not known about the problems earlier, and wondered what changes were necessary to prevent this lack of communication from recurring?

The Finance and Audit committee would not be pleased with another delay in the system implementation. Implementing in April would push computer implementation expenses into another fiscal year, something Louis was sure the board would want to avoid.

Louis had to make a decision soon; the Finance and Audit Committee of the board of directors was to meet on Tuesday, February 20. They expected an update on the status of the system implementation.

This article describes four guideline pitfalls in implementing PMISs. These are related to C/SCSC and numerous real-world examples are given for each of the pitfalls. On the surface, each guideline appears to be quite logical but can easily lead the inexperienced astray.

READING

PROJECT MANAGEMENT CONTROL PROBLEMS: AN INFORMATION SYSTEMS FOCUS
Paul M. Bobrowski

Introduction

Managing a project is much like managing any other business effort. The key functions are planning, organizing, and controlling the effort for it to be successful. A successful project is a quality product, that meets the product's specifications, stays within its budget and is delivered on schedule. Over the last 30 years, the study of project management has become commonplace. Almost all college business majors and most engineering students are given an introduction to project management. The primary problem with much of the education on project management is the emphasis has historically been on the first two managerial functions, planning and organizing.

There are numerous examples of projects that have been well planned and organized initially, but when consistent control over all the elements is lacking throughout the project duration, the project failed. The ability to control projects is dependent on the ability of project management to obtain accurate, timely information and convert it into the required actions. This capability is usually described as an information and control system. To aid in the management of the program, this system should be in place as the project begins. Past experience with the aerospace/electronics industry suggests that even expecting such a system within a year of project start might be overly optimistic. Some efforts to provide this control capability have exceeded two years on projects that are only four years long. Delays this long seriously impair the process of evaluating the project status, forecasting potential problems, evaluating contingencies, and accurately estimating scheduled completion and cost at completion.

To better understand the control aspects of project management, more insight is needed into the management information systems that aid in controlling the project and, in particular, an awareness of the life cycle of these systems is required. Numerous authors and organizations have defined the information system life cycle and most fit within the following general phases defined by Ahituv and Newmann [2]: definition, construction, implementation, and operation. Project management often focuses on the life cycle of the program or project they are charged with managing. To be successful in the latter endeavor, they must not only be aware of the information system life cycle, but of some warning signs of potential danger that affect the information system and ultimately the project.

Even though management information systems that service projects are diverse and are dependent upon the company and the particular project, there are underlying concepts that are common to almost all project management information systems. The objective here is to identify four of these concepts that are accepted in the information system literature, and illustrate by use of examples how some project management information systems have failed to provide the proper control information.

Key concepts that have not received the appropriate attention in the development of project management information systems are:

1. the proper definition of the system user,
2. the determination of what top management support is,
3. the shortcomings of a bottom–up design approach, and
4. the reasonable expectations for a computerized information system.

To assist in the development of these ideas, examples have been selected from defense-related projects (aerospace/electronics). Selecting this category of projects has several advantages. First, the government requires selected contractors to implement information and control systems that meet a set of standards for validation. Second, there exists almost twenty years of information and control systems design, implementation, and validation experience in this segment. Third, the set of general guidelines and standards used by the government has remained largely unchanged over the past 20 years. Lastly, the experiences and knowledge gained by implementing control systems in this sector are applicable to systems development efforts in most industries and environments.

Prior to developing these information system concepts within the project management environment, the next section provides a brief history and description of the general guidelines and standards used by the government.

Cost/Schedule Control Systems Criteria

Since the late 1960s, the Department of Defense (DOD) has required the implementation of the Cost/Schedule Control Systems Criteria (C/SCSC) on certain research and development and production contracts as specified in DOD Instruction 7000.2.

Initially, these requirements were applied to only the largest contractors who typically received the majority of contracts meeting the specified thresholds. The aircraft and missile development and production contracts of the early 1970s are representative examples. As the DOD moved into a greater number of high-technology electronic developments and inflation simultaneously increased the price of doing research and development, the number of firms winning contracts that met the C/SCSC thresholds increased. By the end of 1981, a total of 425 Army, Navy and Air Force efforts, [5] required the implementation of C/SCSC. In the years since, the trend has continued with large contracts being awarded to smaller government contractors who previously had not been required to meet the requirements of C/SCSC.

C/SCSC is not a government designed management information system that is being thrust on the management of defense firms who win major contracts. Rather, the focus of C/SCSC is on a set of sound management principles and standards that must be included in the contractor's management information and control system, in a manner and design consistent with the way the contractor manages his business. The Criteria are listed under the generic headings such as organization, planning and budgeting, accounting, scheduling, analysis and revisions. The purpose of the Criteria according to Abba [1] is twofold: (1) for contractors to use effective internal cost and schedule management control systems, and (2) for the government to be able to rely on timely auditable data produced by those systems for determining product-oriented contract status. The imposition of the Criteria then requires that a contractor's internal management information system meet these general management principles or standards by including them in their system description and demonstrating that the system performs as described.

A plan for a potential contractor to demonstrate how his system will comply with C/SCSC typically is part of the contractor's proposal. A typical contractor proposal calls for a documented and demonstrated system fulfilling the criteria within the first six months after contract award. Of course, this proposed quick road to a government validated information system can be attributed in a large part to "bidding hype." However, it seems reasonable to expect a validated government compliant information system within the first year after contract award. This affords time for system design, document preparation, and system demonstration (the first three phases of the information life cycle) as well as allowances for government delays and other miscellaneous problems. The evidence from the aerospace/electronics industry suggests that even a year has been overly optimistic.

Each contractor who has experienced a lengthy design and implementation process could provide an itemized list of what went wrong. However, a majority of these problems could be narrowed down to a few categories. The categories are most appropriately labeled by the following phrases that should serve as warning signs:

1. "Give customers what they want!"
2. "This effort has the full support of top management."
3. "All we need to do is tie the existing subsystems together."
4. "The system will prevent any problems."

Warning Sign #1: Give Customers What They Want

Consider the example of the large aerospace manufacturer whose program manager had the monthly cost/schedule performance report sent directly to the customer without so much as a review of what was being said to the customer. As the lower level members of the project team soon realized, the report primarily filled a contractual requirement and did not provide a means of surfacing and solving problems. Since the information system had practically no impact on the program manager's decision making, the quality of analysis degraded, recommendations became a routine, repeating what was said previously, and all effort to increase the timeliness of the report ceased. The system of tracking the cost and schedule performance had largely become a means to satisfy a contractual requirement.

The requirement of C/SCSC on a contract with the accompanying monthly contract performance reports is often viewed as the price for doing business with a government agency. This attitude is reflected in a system design that equates the customer as the sole system "user." With this definition, the stated objective of an internal management information system is ignored. The result is a proliferation of information and information sources that are often in conflict rather than in agreement with each other.

Even when the user group is expanded to include the program manager and the top functional managers, this still is a narrow view of the system users which can limit the effectiveness of the information system. In the general system design literature, Bostrom and Heinen [3] point out that an inadequate definition of the "user" often ignores secondary users on whom the success of the system often depends and whose jobs are most critically affected by the information system design. The typical design strategy has concentrated on the delivery of the end product, the monthly contract performance report, in a timely manner. Forgotten in this strategy is the expense of the time and effort required by the more widely defined user set which includes analysts, program control staff, accounting personnel, clerks, cost account managers, and data processing managers and staff. Ignoring all these users of the system in deference to the customer and the project's upper management results in an end product that may meet the letter of the contract, but the information system is an ineffective managerial tool for locating potential problems and communicating them.

Warning Sign #2: Full Support of Top Management

When a project management information and control system is required for a project to comply with the contract, all levels of the project management team are quick to assure that top management has given this requirement their full and uncompromising support. This complete and unqualified support appears in different forms and at different times for a new effort. First, this support, or something similar to it appears as a preface to the information system implementation plan put forth in the proposal. At contract award, when a more realistic schedule for project management information system implementation is defined, top management's support is still in evidence to assure the project manager as well as the customer that developing an information and control system is not suddenly of secondary importance. Top management's support continues to be used as a means of assuring anxious questioners when the system still is unable to produce accurate, auditable information on the contract performance. After witnessing the repeated use of top management's support for the effort, there is a certain amount of skepticism and it becomes apparent that more important than the repetitious assurances are top management's actions that demonstrate their commitment.

Top management commitment or lack of commitment can take many forms. The following three examples show how top management's words do not correspond with their actions.

In the first example, an electronics manufacturer possessed an organizational structure similar to the one shown in Figure 1. It was a fairly typical functional organization that used a matrix organizational structure to plan and execute the contracted electronics project. Despite the promise of full management support, the project office was responsible for the design and development of the information and control system. A staff of information system specialists was readily identifiable within the organization, but top management would not commit skilled resources to this effort. Without assistance, coordination, support or any other tangible connection to the corporate department in charge of overseeing information system development, several poor design decisions were made that made the system cumbersome, inflexible to change and resulted in a two year delay in producing accurate and auditable information to the detriment of the company as well as the customer.

The second example shows how top management's commitment is not reflected in its personnel policies. In this electronics firm, design responsibility was given to the project's business manager. The business manager was a key member involved in project planning, scheduling and budgeting, and subcontract management as well as other key areas in the daily management of the electronics development project. This business manager and his boss, the project manager, were without the resources necessary to have each job—business management and information system development and implementation—adequately accomplished. The result was that neither job was performed satisfactorily. In this case, knowledge about the process of planning, budgeting, and executing the electronics project plan was not sufficient to translate the design process into a timely, accurate information system.

In the final example, the commitment of top management is needed not only when a new system is designed from scratch, but is as equally important when an existing information and control system is being transferred and implemented from some other facility. In this case, the project manager, who was responsible for a $65 million, four and one half year, electronics development program, was satisfying the requirement for a project management information system by transferring a validated system from a sister division in a different geographic location. The program manager was given full responsibility for the implementation which turned out to be a sizable distraction from his primary task of managing the electronics development effort during the critical first year of

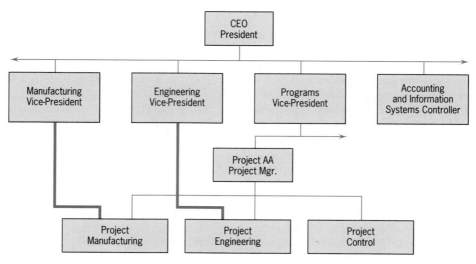

— Matrix responsibility

Figure 1: Organizational structure.

work. Top management was lax in assuming that this particular project, and its project manager, should assume sole responsibility for transferring and implementing a system which in the long term would benefit the entire facility.

These three examples and a more detailed case study by Schmitt and Kozar [6] are typical of the difference between what top management says and what is really done. A wary project manager is much better served by getting top management to act and commit resources through written direction and additional budget resources rather than to use top management's stated commitment as a shield.

Warning Sign #3: All We Need to Do Is Tie the Subsystems Together

Since the Criteria are not a system in themselves, the fundamentals that constitute the Criteria exist in various systems that the firm might already be using. A large manufacturer can be expected to have a material system, a tooling system, an order status system, production order release system, an engineering release and parts list system, a direct labor performance evaluation system, and an inventory system among its various planning and control information systems.

When a contractual requirement for a validated management information and control system is initially received, a typical response from such a firm is that its existing systems already do 90 percent of what is required and all that is needed are the mechanisms to transfer the information between the various subsystems. The perceived benefit is that minimal design costs will be incurred because the independent subsystems that capture, edit, reduce and formulate the information already exist. The relatively minor design investment is for the infrastructure needed to couple or combine these independent subsystems. Usually, this effort is seen as a series of input/output interfaces between the various subsystems.

Figure 2 is an example of one of these "pieced together subsystem" systems. The diagram represents how the information is gathered for the monthly contract performance report. The problem with these systems is that the parts do not always talk the same "language," and therefore the interface that enables the systems to talk together is often a labor intensive manual system. A simple example of a communication problem would be a material system trying to "talk" to an order release system. An order

release system tracks by means of an order number while the material system tracks the material by the stock order number. Even though the communication problem is identified, neither system is usually changed. Instead, some cumbersome translation mechanism is programmed to sit between the two pieces. When the fix cannot be mechanized, the system is usually hand manipulated to filter and correct the information. This leads to the problem of the firm becoming dependent on a very few people for the system to produce the accurate information required. Also, the system is not readily auditable without the total reliance on one of these experts. As an example, the system shown in Figure 2 has only three people capable of tracing the information from the report to the source, and this is for a division of a major aerospace contractor who has over 5000 employees at the facility.

The top managment, as well as the project manager, who expect accurate information in a short period of time because the source subsystems already exist, are underestimating the effort required to untangle the subsystems and arrange them into a unified design. Too often it is only after several years of operating this make-shift connected system—and living with the problems that arise from accuracy, redundancy, and traceability problems that the real cost of a bottom–up approach to information system design is realized.

Warning Sign #4: The System Will Prevent Any Problems

Once the computerized information gathering system is operational, this last warning sign surfaces. Management believes that the control mechanisms for the project have been fully automated. The emphasis of most computerized information systems is the collection of data, the editing of the data and finally the formulation of the data into meaningful accurate information. In the first example cited above, the electronics manufacturers dealt with a program manager who had the information collected, edited, and analyzed prior to sending it to the customer directly. Absent in that example was a key component for the system to be effective. Missing was an internal method or procedure that would present the analyzed information to the project's management on a periodic basis for changing the project or anticipating changes that would affect the project.

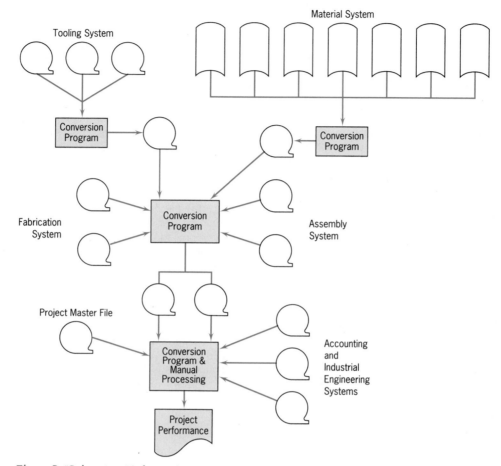

Figure 2: "Subsystem" information system.

In the C/SCSC environment, a computerized information system provides at the minimum, both the current and cumulative cost and schedule variances accumulated by major work efforts and products within the project. The manual portion of this control system arrangement provides, at a minimum, a means by which the appropriate individuals can address the reasons for these variances and supplement them with a detailed analysis. If this is the total output of the combined computerized information and manual control system, then the result is an expensive method for looking at what has happened. The problem with this type of system is that there is no way for the information to assist in improving the internal management of the project's future activities and tasks. Often the reason for this operational problem can be traced to the personnel required to plan and execute the project. Consider their background.

Projects such as the ones used here as examples are usually dominated by engineers, scientists, and other technical personnel. Historically these individuals have primarily addressed decision making from the technical perspective without seriously considering the impact on the ultimate cost and delivery date or completion date of the project. Since a majority of the project managers come from this technically oriented group, there is usually no mechanism or forum that allows the technical managers to integrate their scientific and/or engineering analysis with the cost and schedule analysis.

With this group of technically oriented people who represent a majority of the personnel associated with the project team, the task of evaluating the budgeted performance to the planned performance and the planned performance to the actual performance is sometimes seen as a waste of a scarce resource. Usually, it is felt that time of the technical personnel is more fruitfully spent on technical issues. This leads to the creation of a cadre of analysts who possess some technical expertise but whose responsibility initially is to perform the business-oriented tasks of evaluating where the project is, where it should be, and what is the future direction. Unfortunately, the analysts soon inherit the task of providing the technical analyses required once the cost and schedule variance thresholds are broached. Thus, the people responsible for the work, having a technical background, are no longer involved in the analysis. Therefore, the integration of the technical, cost, and schedule ramifications of a problem is no longer possible. Ultimately this results in separate systems—one to raise technical problems and another to review cost and schedule performance—with no means of reconciling the two.

Conclusions

Controlling the project has been primarily associated with the problem of having information available. The first three warning signs identified in this paper addressed this issue. The concepts of top management support, definition of the system user, and the subsystem design approach all address the problem of obtaining accurate information in a timely manner. These concepts focused on the information system during the first two phases of its life cycle, definition, and construction. Problems here were shown to be a serious detriment in controlling the project. A more subtle problem was identified with the last warning sign; providing timely, accurate information alone was not enough for a control system to succeed in improving control of the overall project. The information system needs to be coupled with ancillary systems and

procedures that enable the conversion of information into action.

These four warning signs do not portray all of the potential control system design and operation problems; however, they do point to an important underlying conclusion. Even though a project has a computerized information system in place, the issue of project control is still very much a people-oriented issue. When these four warning signs are overlaid on the system life cycle, all the control problems are people dependent whether they be top management, the system "users," system designers or the project management team.

Finally, an information system alone is not a control system. Manual procedures, management structures, and the integration of people provide the means of using the output of the information system to control a project that must act and react in a dynamic environment.

References

1. ABBA, WAYNE. "Cost/Schedule Control Systems Criteria." *Program Manager*, 9, 45–57, 1986.
2. AHITUV, N., and S. NEWMANN. *Principles of Information Systems for Management*, 2nd Ed. Dubuque, Iowa: WC Brown, 1986.
3. BOSTROM, ROBERT P., and J. STEPHEN, HEINEN. "MIS Problems and Failures: A Socio-Technical Perspective—Part I: The Causes." MIS *Quarterly*, September 1977, 17–32.
4. DOD Instruction 7000.2. "Performance Measurement for Selected Acquisitions." June 10, 1977.
5. GADEKEN, OWEN C., and THOMAS S. TISON. "The Cost of C/SCSC." *Program Manager*, 5, 13–18.
6. SCHMITT, JOHN W. and KENNETH A. KOZAR. "Management's Role in Information System Development Failures: A Case Study." MIS *Quarterly*, June 1978, 7–16.

11

Project Control

In the previous chapter we described the monitoring and information gathering process that would help the PM to control the project. *Control* is the last element in the implementation cycle of planning–monitoring–controlling. Information is collected about system performance, compared with the desired (or planned) level, and action taken if actual and desired performance differ enough that the *controller* (manager) wishes to decrease the difference. Note that reporting performance, comparing the differences between desired and actual performance levels, and accounting for why such differences exist are all parts of the control process. In essence, control is the *act* of reducing the difference between plan and reality.

As has been emphasized throughout this book, control is focused on three elements of a project—performance, cost, and time. The PM is constantly concerned with these three aspects of the project. Is the project delivering what it promised to deliver or more? Is it making delivery at or below the promised cost? Is it making delivery at or before the promised time? It is strangely easy to lose sight of these fundamental targets, especially in large projects with a wealth of detail and a great number of subprojects. Large projects develop their own momentum and tend to get out of hand, going their own way independent of the wishes of the PM and the intent of the proposal.

Think, for a moment, of a few of the things that can cause a project to require the control of performance, costs, or time.

Performance

Unexpected technical problems arise.

Insufficient resources are available when needed.

Insurmountable technical difficulties are present.

Quality or reliability problems occur.

Client requires changes in system specifications.

Interfunctional complications arise.

Technological breakthroughs affect the project.

Cost

Technical difficulties require more resources.

The scope of the work increases.

Initial bids or estimates were too low.

Reporting was poor or untimely.

Budgeting was inadequate.

Corrective control was not exercised in time.

Input price changes occurred.

Time

Technical difficulties took longer than planned to solve.

Initial time estimates were optimistic.

Task sequencing was incorrect.

Required inputs of material, personnel, or equipment were unavailable when needed.

Necessary preceding tasks were incomplete.

Customer-generated change orders required rework.

Governmental regulations were altered.

And these are only a few of the relatively "mechanistic" problems that can occur. Actually, there are no purely mechanistic problems on projects. All problems have a human element, too. For example, humans, by action or inaction, set in motion a chain of events that leads to a failure to budget adequately, creates a quality problem, leads the project down a technically difficult path, or fails to note a change in government regulations. If, by chance, some of these or other things happen (as a result of human action or not), humans are affected by them. Frustration, pleasure, determination, hopelessness, anger, and many other emotions arise during the course of a project. They affect the work of the individuals who feel them— for better or worse. It is over this welter of confusion, emotion, fallibility, and general cussedness that the PM tries to exert control.

All of these problems, always combinations of the human and mechanistic, call for intervention and control by the project manager. There are infinite "slips 'twixt cup and lip," especially in projects where the technology or the deliverables are new and unfamiliar, and PMs, like most managers, find control is a difficult function to perform. There are several reasons why this is so. One of the main reasons is that PMs, again like most managers, do not discover problems. Managers discover what Russell Ackoff once described as a "mess" [1]. A "mess" is a general condition of a system that, when viewed by a manager, leads to a statement that begins, "%#^@*&±#!" and goes downhill from there. It is the discovery of a mess that leads the PM to the conclusion that there is a problem(s) lurking somewhere around. In systems as complex as projects, the task of defining the problem(s) is formidable, and thus knowing what to control is not a simple task. Another reason control is difficult is because, in spite of an almost universal need to blame some person for any trouble, it is often almost impossible to know if a problem resulted from human error or from the random application of Murphy's Law.

PMs also find it tough to exercise control because the project team, even on large projects, is an "in-group." It is "we," while outsiders are "they." It is usually hard to criticize friends, to subject them to control. Further, many PMs see control as an *ad hoc* process. Each need to exercise control is seen as a unique event, rather than as one instance of an ongoing and recurring process.

Because control of projects is such a mixture of feeling and fact, of human and mechanism, of causation and random chance, we must approach the subject in an extremely orderly way. In this chapter we start by examining the general purposes of control. Then we consider the basic structure of the process of control. We do this by describing control theory in the form of a cybernetic control loop. While most projects offer little opportunity for the actual application of automatic feedback loops, this system provides us with a comprehensive but reasonably simple illustration of all the elements necessary to control any system. From this model, we then turn to the types of control that are most often applied to projects. The design of control systems is discussed as are the impacts that various types of controls tend to have on the humans being controlled. The specific requirement of "balance" in a control system is also covered, as are two special control problems: control of creative activities, and control of change.

▶ 11.1   THE FUNDAMENTAL PURPOSES OF CONTROL

The two fundamental objectives of control are:

1.   The regulation of results through the alteration of activities.
2.   The stewardship of organizational assets.

Most discussions of the control function are focused on regulation. The PM needs to be equally attentive to both regulation and conservation. Because the main body of this chapter (and much of the next) concerns the PM as regulator, let us emphasize the conservationist role here. The PM must guard the physical assets of the organization, its human resources, and its financial resources. The processes for conserving these three different kinds of assets are different.

Physical Asset Control

Physical asset control requires control of the *use* of physical assets. It is concerned with asset maintenance, whether preventive or corrective. At issue also is the timing of maintenance or replacement as well as the quality of maintenance. Some years ago, a New England brewery purchased the abandoned and obsolete brewing plant of a newly defunct competitor. It put a project manager in charge of this old facility with the instruction that the plant should be completely "worn out" over the next five-year period, but that it should be fully operational in the meantime. This presented an interesting problem: the controlled deterioration of a plant while at the same time maintaining as much of its productive capability as possible. Clearly, both objectives could not be achieved simultaneously, but the PM met the spirit of the project quite well.

If the project uses considerable amounts of physical equipment, the PM also has the problem of setting up maintenance schedules in such a way as to keep the equipment in operating condition while minimizing interference with ongoing work. It is critical to accomplish preventive maintenance prior to the start of that final section of the project life cycle known as the Last Minute Panic (LMP). (Admittedly, the timing of the LMP is not known, which makes the planning of pre-LMP preventive maintenance somewhat difficult.)

Physical inventory, whether equipment or material, must also be controlled. It must be received, inspected (or certified), and possibly stored prior to use. Records of all incoming shipments must be carefully validated so that payment to suppliers can be authorized. The same precautions applied to goods from external suppliers must also be applied to suppliers from inside the organization. Even such details as the project library, project coffee maker, project room furniture, and all the other minor bits and pieces must be counted, maintained, and conserved.

Human Resource Control

Stewardship of human resources requires controlling and maintaining the growth and development of people. Projects provide particularly fertile ground for cultivating people. Because projects are unique, differing one from another in many ways, it is possible for people working on projects to gain a wide range of experience in a reasonably short time.

Measurement of physical resource conservation is accomplished through the familiar audit procedures. The measurement of human resource conservation is far more difficult. Such devices as employee appraisals, personnel performance indices, and screening methods for appointment, promotion, and retention are not particularly satisfactory devices for ensuring that the conservation function is being properly handled. The accounting profession has worked for some years on the development of *human resource accounting*, and while the effort has produced some interesting ideas, human resource accounting is not well accepted by the accounting profession.

Financial Resource Control

Though accountants have not succeeded in developing acceptable methods for human resource accounting, their work on techniques for the conservation (and regulation) of financial resources has most certainly resulted in excellent tools for financial control. This is the best developed for the basic areas needing control.

It is difficult to separate the control mechanisms aimed at conservation of financial resources from those focused on regulating resource use. Most financial controls do both. Capital investment controls work to conserve the organization's assets by insisting that certain conditions be met before capital can be expended, and those same conditions usually regulate the use of capital to achieve the organization goal of a high return on investments.

The techniques of financial control, both conservation and regulation, are well known. They include current asset controls, and project budgets as well as capital investment controls. These controls are exercised through a series of analyses and audits conducted by the accounting/controller function for the most part. Representation of this function on the project team is mandatory. The structure of the techniques applied to projects does not differ appreciably from those applied to the general operation of the firm, but the context within which they are applied is quite different. One reason for the differences is that the project is accountable to an outsider—an external client, or another division of the parent firm, or both at the same time.

The importance of proper conformance to both organizational and client control standards in financial practice and recordkeeping cannot be overemphasized. The parent organization, through its agent, the project manager, is responsible for the conservation and proper *use of* resources owned by the client or owned by the parent and charged to the client. Clients will insist on, and the courts will require the practice of, *due diligence* in the exercise of such responsibility. While some clients may not be aware of this responsibility on the part of firms with whom they contract, the government is most certainly aware of it. In essence, due diligence requires that the organization proposing a project conduct a reasonable investigation, verification, and disclosure, in language that is understandable, of every material fact relevant to the firm's ability to conduct the project, and to omit nothing where such omission might ethically mislead the client. It is not possible to define, in some general way, precisely what might be required for any given project. The firm should, however, make sure that it has legal counsel competent to aid it in meeting this responsibility.

One final note on the conservationist role of the controller. The attitude or mind-set of the conservationist is often antithetical to the mind-set of the PM, whose attention is naturally on the use of resources rather than their conservation. The conservationist reminds one of the fabled librarian who is happiest when all the books are ordered neatly on the library shelves. The PM, often the manager and controller at one and the same time, is subject to this conflict and has no choice but to live with it. The warring attitudes must be merged and compromised as best they can.

Project Management in Practice
Formalizing the Program Control System at Battelle Laboratories

In the late 1970s, Battelle's Pacific Northwest Laboratory made the decision to develop the Research Project Management System, including a program control segment, for projects over $100,000. As a part of the management information and support function,

the program control specialists are charged with the development, implementation, and

Source: R. K. Johnson, "Program Control from the Bottom Up—Exploring the Working Side," *Project Management Journal*, March 1985.

maintenance of program control systems for Battelle-Northwest's research programs. These systems are not the usual monitoring systems used to provide information to top management for decision making but instead are meant for the lower-level project managers, contract administrators, personnel specialists, and others who have a direct impact on project success or failure.

The goal of the program control segment is to ensure a quality product, on schedule, within cost. In some Federal projects, such as with DOD or DOE, the implementation of a full cost/schedule control system criteria (C/SCSC) is required for control purposes, but for many other projects, particularly R&D projects, such control is not required. With a good system in place, chances of cost overruns and missed scheduled milestones are reduced, hence the need for a program control function such as Battelle's.

To date, the payoffs from incorporating this function in their project management system have been high. In the DOE's $178 million Fuels Refabrication and Development Program, Battelle's program control function is credited with achieving a high level of success and an overall performance rating of "excellent." Again, in the Seasonal Thermal Energy Program, another "excellent" performance rating was achieved. Paying attention to the control aspect of project management appears to be paying off.

▶ 11.2 THREE TYPES OF CONTROL PROCESSES

The process of controlling a project (or any system) is far more complex than simply waiting for something to go wrong and then, if possible, fixing it. We must decide at what points in the project we will try to exert control, what is to be controlled, how it will be measured, how much deviation from plan will be tolerated before we act, what kinds of interventions should be used, and how to spot and correct deviations before they occur, among a great many other things. In order to keep these and other such issues sorted out, it is helpful to begin a consideration of control with a brief exposition on the theory of control.

No matter what our purpose in controlling a project, there are three basic types of control mechanisms we can use: cybernetic control, go/no-go control, and postcontrol. In this section we will describe these three types and briefly discuss the information requirements of each. Remember that we describe cybernetic control systems in order to clarify the elements that must be present in any control system, as well as the information requirements of control systems.

Cybernetic Control

Cybernetic, or steering, control is by far the most common type of control system. (*Cyber* is the Greek word for "helmsman.") The key feature of cybernetic control is its automatic operation. Consider the diagrammatic model of a cybernetic control system shown in Figure 11-1.

As Figure 11-1 shows, a system is operating with inputs being subjected to a process that transforms them into outputs. It is this system that we wish to control. In order to do so, we must monitor the system output. This function is performed by a sensor that measures one or more aspects of the output, presumably those aspects one wishes to control. Measurements taken by the sensor are transmitted to

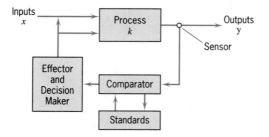

Figure 11-1: A cybernetic control system.

the comparator, which compares them with a set of predetermined standards. The difference between actual and standard is sent to the decision maker, which determines whether or not the difference is of sufficient size to deserve correction. If the difference is large enough to warrant action, a signal is sent to the effector, which acts on the process or on the inputs to produce outputs that conform more closely to the standard.

A cybernetic control system that acts to reduce deviations from standard is called a *negative feedback loop*. If the system output moves away from standard in one direction, the control mechanism acts to move it in the opposite direction. The speed or force with which the control operates is, in general, proportional to the size of the deviation from standard. (Mathematical descriptions of the action of negative feedback loops are widely available. See for example [48].) The precise way in which the deviation is corrected depends on the nature of the operating system and the design of the controller. Figure 11-2 illustrates three different response patterns. Response path A is direct and rapid, while path B is more gradual. Path C shows oscillations of decreasing amplitude. An aircraft suddenly deflected from a stable flight path would tend to recover by following pattern C.

Types of Cybernetic Control Systems Cybernetic controls come in three varieties, or *orders*, differing in the sophistication with which standards are set. Figure 11-1 shows a simple *first-order* control system, a goal-seeking device. The standard is set and there is no provision made for altering it except by intervention from the outside. The common thermostat is a time-worn example of a first-order controller. One sets the standard temperature and the heating and air-conditioning systems operate to maintain it.

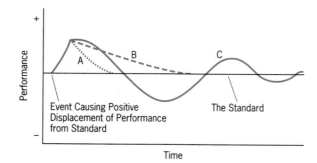

Figure 11-2: Typical paths for correction of deviation of performance from standard.

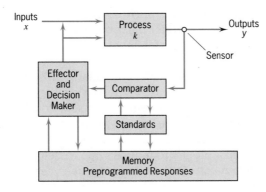

Figure 11-3: A second-order feedback system—preprogrammed goal changer.

Figure 11-3 shows a second-order control system. This device can alter the system standards according to some predetermined set of rules or program. The complexity of second-order systems can vary widely. The addition of a clock to the thermostat to allow it to maintain different standards during day and night makes the thermostat a second-order controller. An interactive computer program may alter its responses according to a complex set of preprogrammed rules, but it is still only a second-order system. Many industrial projects involve second-order controllers—for example, robot installations, flexible manufacturing systems, and automated record-keeping or inventory systems.

A *third-order* control system (Fig. 11-4) can change its goals without specific preprogramming. It can reflect on system performance and decide to act in ways that are not contained in its instructions. Third-order systems have reflective consciousness and, thus, must contain humans. Note that a second-order controller can be programmed to recognize patterns, and to react to patterns in specific ways. Such systems are said to "learn." Third-order systems can learn without explicit preprogramming, and therefore can alter their actions on the basis of thought or whim. An advantage of third-order controllers is that they can deal with the unforeseen and unexpected. A disadvantage is that, because they contain human elements, they may lack predictability and reliability. Third-order systems are of great interest to the PM, for reasons we now discuss.

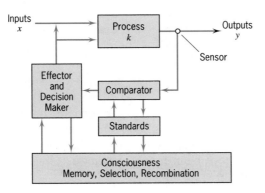

Figure 11-4: A third-order feedback system—reflective goal changer.

Information Requirements for Cybernetic Controllers In order to establish total control over a system, the controller must be able to take a counteraction for every action the system can take. This statement is a rough paraphrase of Ashby's Law of Requisite Variety [41]. This implies that the PM/controller is aware of the system's full capabilities. For complex systems, particularly those containing a human element, this is simply not possible. Thus, we need a strategy to aid the PM in developing a control system. One such strategy is to use a cost/benefit approach to control—to control those aspects of the system for which the expected benefits of control are greater than the expected costs. We are reminded of a firm that manufactured saw blades. It set up a project to reduce scrap losses for the high-cost steel from which the blades were made. At the end of the one-year project, the firm had completed the project—cost $9700, savings $4240. (Of course, if the savings were to be repeated for several years, the rate of return on the project would be acceptable. The president of the firm, however, thought that the savings would decline and disappear when the project ended.)

Relatively few elements of a project (as opposed to the elements of a system that operates more or less continuously) are subject to automatic control. An examination of the WBS or the details of an action plan will reveal which of the project's tasks are largely mechanistic and represent continuous types of systems. If such systems exist, and if they operate across a sufficient time period to justify the initial expense of creating an automatic control, then a cybernetic controller is useful.

Given the decisions about what to control, the information requirements of a cybernetic controller are easy to describe, if not to meet. First, the PM must define precisely what characteristics of an output (interim output or final output) are to be controlled. Second, standards must be set for each characteristic. Third, sensors must be built that will measure those characteristics at the desired level of precision. Fourth, measurements must be transformed into a signal that can be compared to a "standard" signal. Fifth, the difference between the two is sent to the decision maker, which detects it, if it is sufficiently large, and sixth, transmits a signal to the effector that causes the operating system to react in a way that will counteract the deviation from standard. If the control system is designed to allow the effector to take one or more of several actions, an additional piece of information is needed. There must be built-in criteria that instruct the effector on which action(s) to take.

Knowledge of cybernetic control is important because all control systems are merely variants, extensions, or nonautomatic modifications of such controls. Because most projects have relatively few mechanistic elements that can be subjected to classic cybernetic controls, this concept of control is best applied to tracking the system and automatically notifying the PM when things threaten to get out of control.

Go/No-go Controls

Go/no-go controls take the form of testing to see if some specific precondition has been met. This type of control can be used on almost every aspect of a project. For many facets of performance, it is sufficient to know that the predetermined specifications for project output have been met. The same is often true of the cost and time elements of the project plan.

It is, of course, necessary to exercise judgment in the use of go/no-go controls. Certain characteristics of output may be required to fall within precisely determined limits if the output is to be accepted by the client. Other characteristics may be less precisely defined. In regard to time and cost, there may be penalties associated with nonconformance with the approved plans. Penalty clauses that make late delivery costly for the producer are often included in the project contract. At times, early delivery can also carry a penalty (e.g., when a just-in-time supply system is involved). Cost overruns may be shared with the client or borne by the project. Some contracts arrange for the first $X of cost overrun to be shared by client and producer, with any further overrun being the producer's responsibility. The number and type of go/no-go controls on a project is limited only by the imagination and desire of the contracting parties.

The project plan, budget, and schedule are all control documents, so the PM has a predesigned control system complete with prespecified milestones as control checkpoints. Control can be exercised at any level of detail that is supported by detail in the plans, budgets, and schedules. The parts of a new jet engine, for instance, are individually checked for quality conformance. These are go/no-go controls. The part passes or it does not, and every part must pass its own go/no-go test before being used in an engine. Similarly, computer programs are tested for bugs. The program passes its tests or it does not.

While cybernetic controls are automatic and will check the operating systems continuously or as often as designed to do so, go/no-go controls operate only when and if the controller uses them. In many cases, go/no-go controls function periodically, at regular, preset intervals. The intervals are usually determined by clock, calendar, or the operating cycles of some machine system. Such periodicity makes it easy to administer a control system, but it often allows errors to be compounded before they are detected. Things begin to go awry just after a quarterly progress check, for instance, and by the time the next quarterly check is made, some items may be seriously out of control.

Project milestones do not occur at neat, periodic intervals; thus, *controls should be linked to the actual plans and to the occurrence of real events, not simply to the calendar.* This is not to say that periodic reports are inappropriate. All projects should be reviewed by senior management at reasonably frequent intervals. We will discuss such reports shortly, but the PM cannot control the project properly with a periodic reporting system.

The PM must keep abreast of all aspects of the project, directly or through deputies. Competent functional managers understand the importance of *follow-up*, and the project manager's work provides no exception. Control is best exerted while there is still time for corrective action. To this end, the PM should establish an *early warning system* so that potential problems can be exposed and dealt with before they metamorphose into full-fledged disasters. One way to construct such an early warning system is to set up a project forecast data sheet. On this sheet, outputs or progress are forecast by period. Actual output or progress is then checked against the forecast, period by period. Figure 11-5 illustrates such a data sheet.

For an early warning system to work, it must be clear that the messenger who brings bad news will not be shot, and that anyone caught sweeping problems and mistakes under the rug will be. As we have said before, the most important rule for

DATE

PROD OR PROG TITLE

CUSTOMER

DATE REC'D.	CONTRACT START DATE	SUBMISSION OR COMPLETE DATE	CUST. CONT. OR REQ. NO.	BUYER

CUST. - ENG. - DEPT.	T.E.P. NO.	REL. G & A PROJ. NO'S.	G & A CODE

CAPITAL EQUIPMENT	REL. ACCTG. CODE NO.	TOTAL G & A

DESCRIPTION OF PRODUCT OR PROGRAM

REASON FOR INTEREST:

EXPLOITATION PLAN SUMMARY - (ATTACH SHEETS FOR DETAIL AND PROGRESS):

FORECAST PERIOD	REC. G & A	TOTAL R & D	TOTAL PRODUCT	PLAN R & D	PLAN PRODUCT	PROB. FACT.	VAL. FACT.	FIG. OF MERIT	COMPETITIVE POSITION						
									1	2	3	4	5	6	7
1															
2															
3															
4															
1															
2															
3															
4															
1															
2															
3															
4															
1															
2															
3															
4															

TOTAL BEYOND DETAILED FORECAST PERIODS						PLAN APPROVAL	DATE	ASSIGNED TO	DATE
						PER.			
						SALES			
						ENG.			
							SUMMARY INDEX NO.		

(SEE REVERSE SIDE FOR DETAIL G & A CODE)

Figure 11-5: Project forecast data sheet.

any subordinate is the Prime Law of Life on a project: Never let the boss be surprised!

Controls have a tendency to terrorize the insecure and to induce high anxiety in everyone else. The result is avoidance, and avoidance is exactly what the PM cannot tolerate. Unless deviation from plan is discovered, it cannot be corrected. Therefore, a spirit of trust between superior and subordinate at all levels of the project is a prime requisite for the effective application of control.

Information Requirements for Go/No-Go Controls   Most of the input information needed to operate go/no-go project control has already been referenced directly or implied by the previous discussion. The project proposal, plans, specifications, schedules, and budgets (complete with approved change orders) contain all the information needed to apply go/no-go controls to the project. Milestones are the key events that serve as a focus for ongoing control activity. These milestones are the project's deliverables in the form of in-process output or final output. If the milestones occur on time, on budget, and at the planned level of quality, the PM can take comfort from the fact that things are proceeding properly. Perhaps just as important to the PM, senior management can be equally comfortable with the project—and with the project manager as well.

Except for a few important projects, senior management usually cannot keep up with the day-to-day or week-to-week progress of work; nor should they try. Senior management does, however, need a monthly or quarterly status review for all projects. The project status report contains a list of the important milestones for each project together with the status of each. If many of the projects are similar—such as construction projects or marketing projects, for example—the milestones will be of similar type, and one table can show the status of several projects in spite of the fact that each milestone may not be applicable to each and every project. The Elanco Products Company (the agricultural products division of Eli Lilly and Company, now DowElanco) uses such a report. A generalized version of Elanco's Project Status Report is shown in Figure 11-6. The Gantt chart (see Chapter 8) is also a convenient way to present senior managers with information on project status.

Either of these report forms can be altered to contain almost any additional information that might be requested. For example, the Gantt chart can be annotated with footnotes indicating such matters of interest as the resources required to get a late milestone back on schedule, or a statement of how an activity must be changed if it is to be approved by a regulatory agency. The information requirements for such extensions of standard reports must be set on an *ad hoc* basis. For the most part,

Task	Project		
	#1	#2	#3
Priorities set	C	C	C
PM selected	C	C	C
Key members briefed on RFP	C	C	C
Proposal sent	C	C	C
Proposal accepted as negotiated	C	C	C
Preliminary design developed	C	W/10	C
Design accepted	C	W/12	C
Software developed	C	NS/NR	N/A
Product test design	C	W/30	W/15
Manufacturing scheduled	C	NS/HR	W/8
Tools, jigs, fixtures designed	W/1	NS/HR	W/2
Tools, jigs, fixtures delivered	W/2	NS/HR	W/8
Production complete	NS/HR	NS/HR	NS/HR
Product test complete	NS/HR	NS/HR	NS/HR
Marketing sign-off on product	NS/HR	NS/HR	NS/HR

Figure 11-6: Sample project status report.

Notes:

N/A—Not applicable	W—Work in progress (number refers to month required)	NS—Not started
C—Completed		NR—Need resources
		HR—Have resources

such information will be readily available within the project, but occasionally, external sources must be utilized. If the PM ensures that the status reports given to senior management contain information that is current enough to be actionable (and always is as accurate as required for control), little else can be done to furnish the decision makers with the proper data for them to exercise control. The PM is well advised to insist that status reports make clear the implications of specific conditions where those implications might be overlooked—or not understood—by senior managers. If meetings between senior management and project managers are used to report project status and progress, it is critical to remember that the process employed in such meetings should not be punitive or intimidating. As we pointed out in Chapter 10, punitive meetings do far more damage than good.

Postcontrol

Postcontrols (also known as postperformance controls or postproject controls) are applied after the fact. One might draw parallels between postcontrol and "locking the barn after the horse has been stolen," but postcontrol is not a vain attempt to alter what has already occurred. Instead, it is a full recognition of George Santayana's observation that "Those who cannot remember the past are condemned to repeat it." Cybernetic and go/no-go controls are directed toward accomplishing the goals of an ongoing project. Postcontrol is directed toward improving the chances for future projects to meet their goals.

Postcontrol is applied through a relatively formal document that is usually constructed with four distinct sections.

The Project Objectives The postcontrol report will contain a description of the objectives of the project. Usually, this description is taken from the project proposal, and the entire proposal often appears as an appendix to the postcontrol report. As reported here, project objectives include the effects of all change orders issued and approved during the project.

Because actual project performance depends in part on uncontrollable events (strikes, weather, failure of trusted suppliers, sudden loss of key employees, and other acts of God), the key initial assumptions made during preparation of the project budget and schedule should be noted in this section. A certain amount of care must be taken in reporting these assumptions. They should not be written with a tone that makes them appear to be excuses for poor performance. While it is clearly the prerogative, if not the duty, of every PM to protect himself politically, he or she should do so in moderation to be effective.

Milestones, Checkpoints, and Budgets This section of the postcontrol document starts with a full report of project performance against the planned schedule and budget. This can be prepared by combining and editing the various project status reports made during the project's life. Significant deviations of actual schedule and budget from planned schedule and budget should be highlighted. Explanations of why these deviations occurred will be offered in the next section of the postcontrol report. Each deviation can be identified with a letter or number to index it to the explanations. Where the same explanation is associated with both a schedule and budget deviation, as will often be the case, the same identifier can be used.

The Final Report on Project Results When significant variations of actual from planned project performance are indicated, no distinction is made between favorable and unfavorable variations. Like the tongue that invariably goes to the sore tooth, project managers focus their attention on trouble. While this is quite natural, it leads to complete documentation on why some things went wrong and little or no documentation on why some things went particularly well. Both sides, the good and the bad, should be chronicled here.

Not only do most projects result in outputs that are more or less satisfactory, most projects operate with a process that is more or less satisfactory. The concern here is not on what the project did but rather on how it did it. Basically descriptive, this part of the final report should cover project organization, an explanation of the methods used to plan and direct the project, and a review of the communication networks, monitoring systems, and control methods, as well as a discussion of intraproject interactions between the various working groups.

Recommendations for Performance and Process Improvement The culmination of the postcontrol report is a set of recommendations covering the ways that future projects can be improved. Many of the explanations appearing in the previous section are related to one-time happenings—sickness, weather, strikes, or the appearance of a new technology—that themselves are not apt to affect future projects, although other, different one-time events may affect them. But some of the deviations from plan were caused by happenings that are very likely to recur. Examples of recurring problems might be a chronically late supplier, a generally noncooperative functional department, a habitually optimistic cost estimator, or a highly negative project team member. Provision for such things can be factored into future project plans, thereby adding to predictability and control.

Just as important, the process of organizing and conducting projects can be improved by recommending the continuation of managerial methods and organizational systems that appear to be effective, together with the alteration of practices and procedures that do not. In this way, the conduct of projects will become smoother, just as the likelihood of achieving good results, on time and on cost, is increased.

Postcontrol can have a considerable impact on the way projects are run. A large, market-driven company in consumer household products developed new products through projects that were organized in matrix form, but had a functional tie to the marketing division. PMs were almost always chosen from the marketing area. Members of the project team who represented R & D had argued that they should be given a leadership role, particularly early in the project's life. Marketing resisted this suggestion on the grounds that R & D people were not market-oriented, did not know what would sell, and were mainly interested in pursuing their own "academic" interests. After reading the perennial R & D request in a postcontrol report, the program manager of one product line decided to reorganize a project as requested by R & D. The result was not merely a successful project, but was the first in a series of related projects based on extensions of ideas generated by an R & D group not restricted to work on the specific product sought by marketing. Following this successful experiment, project organization was modified to include more input from R & D at an earlier stage of the project.

There is no need to repeat the information requirements for postcontrol here. It should be noted, however, that we have not discussed the postcontrol audit, a full review and audit of all aspects of the project. This is covered in Chapter 12.

▶ 11.3   COMMENTS ON THE DESIGN OF CONTROL SYSTEMS

Irrespective of the type of control used, there are some important questions to be answered when designing any control system: Who sets the standards? How realistic are the standards? How clear are they? Will they achieve the project's goals? What output, activities, behaviors should be monitored? Should we monitor people? What kinds of sensors should be used? Where should they be placed? How timely must the monitoring be? How rapidly must it be reported? How accurate must the sensors be? How great must a difference between standard and actual be before it becomes actionable? What corrective actions are available? Are they ethical? What are the most appropriate actions for each situation? What rewards and penalties can be used? Who should take what action?

If the control system is to be acceptable to those who will use it and those who will be controlled by it, the system must be designed so that it appears to be sensible. Standards must be achievable by the mechanical systems used. Control limits must be appropriate to the needs of the client—that is, not merely set to show "how good we are." Like punishment, rewards and penalties should "fit the crime."

In addition to being sensible, a good control system should also possess some other characteristics.

- The system should be flexible. Where possible, it should be able to react to and report unforeseen changes in system performance.

- The system should be cost effective. The cost of control should never exceed the value of control. As we noted above, control is not always less expensive than scrap.

- The control system must be truly useful. It must satisfy the real needs of the project, not the whims of the PM.

- The system must operate in an ethical manner.

- The system must operate in a timely manner. Problems must be reported while there is still time to do something about them, and before they become large enough to destroy the project.

- Sensors and monitors should be sufficiently accurate and precise to control the project within limits that are truly functional for the client and the parent organization.

- The system should be as simple to operate as possible.
- The control system should be easy to maintain. Further, the control system should signal the overall controller if it goes out of order.
- The system should be capable of being extended or otherwise altered.
- Control systems should be fully documented when installed and the documentation should include a complete training program in system operation.

No matter how designed, all control systems we have described use feedback as a control process. Let us now consider some more specific aspects of control. To a large extent, the PM is trying to anticipate problems or catch them just as they begin to occur. The PM wants to keep the project out of trouble because upper management often bases an incremental funding decision on a review of the project. This review typically follows some particular milestone and, if acceptable, leads to a follow-on authorization to proceed to the next review point. If all is not going well, other technological alternatives may be recommended; or if things are going badly, the project may be terminated. Thus, the PM must monitor and control the project quite closely.

The control of performance, cost, and time usually requires different input data. To control performance, the PM may need such specific documentation as engineering change notices, test results, quality checks, rework tickets, scrap rates, and maintenance activities. For cost control, the manager compares budgets to actual cash flows, purchase orders, labor hour charges, amount of overtime worked, absenteeism, accounting variance reports, accounting projections, income reports, cost exception reports, and the like. To control the schedule, the PM examines benchmark reports, periodic activity and status reports, exception reports, PERT/CPM networks, Gantt charts, the master project schedule, earned value graphs, and probably reviews the WBS and action plans.

Some of the most important analytic tools available for the project manager to use in controlling the project are variance analysis and trend projection, both of which have been discussed earlier in this book. The essence of these tools is shown in Figure 11-7. A budget, plan, or expected growth curve of time or cost for some

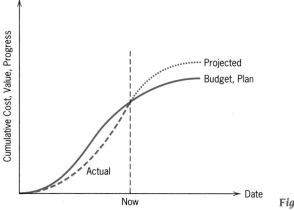

Figure 11-7: Trend projection.

task is plotted. Then actual values are plotted as a dashed line as the work is actually finished. At each point in time a new projection from the actual data is used to forecast what will occur in the future if the PM does not intervene. Based on this projection, the manager can decide if there is a problem, what action alternatives exist, what they will cost and require, and what they will achieve. Based on this analysis, the PM will decide what to do. Trend projection charts can even be used for combined performance/cost/time charts, as illustrated in Figure 11-8.

Earned value analysis was also described earlier. On occasion it may be worthwhile, particularly on large projects, for the PM to calculate a set of *critical ratios* for all project activities. The critical ratio is

(actual progress/scheduled progress) × (budgeted cost/actual cost)

The critical ratio is made up of two parts; the ratio of actual progress to scheduled progress, and the ratio of budgeted cost to actual cost. (In the language of C/SCSC, the budgeted cost is the BCWP and the actual cost is the ACWP.) *Cæteris paribus,* to

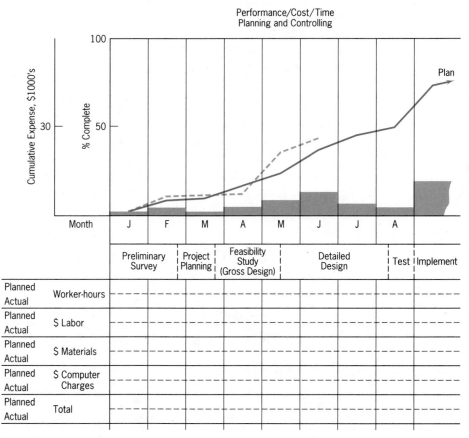

Figure 11-8: Integrated performance cost/time chart. *Source:* [31]

Table 11-1   (Actual Progress/Scheduled Progress) × (Budgeted Cost/Actual Cost)

Task Number	Actual Progress		Scheduled Progress		Budgeted Cost		Actual Cost		Critical Ratio
1	(2	/	3)	×	(6	/	4)	=	1.0
2	(2	/	3)	×	(6	/	6)	=	.67
3	(3	/	3)	×	(4	/	6)	=	.67
4	(3	/	2)	×	(6	/	6)	=	1.5
5	(3	/	3)	×	(6	/	4)	=	1.5

quote any economist who ever lived,[*] a ratio of actual to scheduled progress greater than one is "good." If the ratio is less than one, it is "bad." Similarly with the ratio of budgeted to actual cost—never forgetting *cæteris paribus*. Assuming moderately accurate measures for each element of each ratio (an assumption that rivals *cæteris paribus* for its *chutzpa*), the critical ratio is a good measure of the general health of the project. Note that the critical ratio is the product of the two separate ratios. This way of combining the two underlying ratios weights them equally, allowing a "bad" ratio for one part to be offset by an equally "good" ratio in the other. The PM may or may not agree that this results in a valid measure of project "health."

Consider Table 11-1. We can see that the first task is behind schedule but also below budget. If lateness is no problem for this activity, the PM need take no action. The second task is on budget but its physical progress is lagging. Even if there is slack in the activity, the budget will probably be overrun. The third task is on schedule but cost is running higher than budget, creating another probable cost overrun. The fourth task is on budget but ahead of schedule. A cost saving may result. Finally, the fifth task is on schedule and is running under budget, another probable cost saving.

Tasks 4 and 5 have critical ratios greater than 1 and might not concern some PMs, but the thoughtful manager wants to know why they are doing so well (and the PM may also want to check the information system to validate the unexpectedly favorable findings). The second and third activities need attention, and the first task may need attention also. The PM may set some critical-ratio control limits intuitively. The PM may also wish to set different control limits on different activities, controlling progress in the critical path more closely than on paths with high slack.

Charts can be used to monitor and control the project through the use of these ratios. Figure 11-9 shows an example. Note that the PM will ignore critical ratios in some ranges, and that the ranges are not necessarily symmetric around 1.0. Different types of tasks may have different control limits. Control charts can also be used to aid in controlling costs (Figure 11-10), work force levels, and other project parameters.

---

[*]For those who have never been blessed with a course in economics, this Latin phrase means "other things being equal." The phrase is the economist's equivalent of the physicist's frictionless plane. It does not and cannot exist in fact.

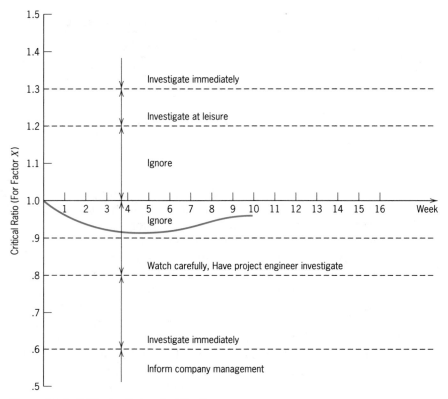

Figure 11-9: Critical ratio control limits.

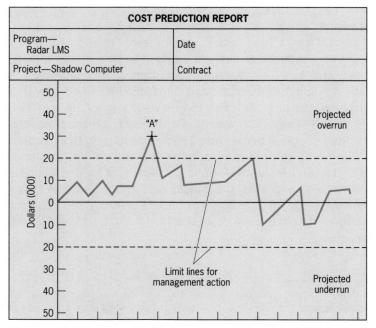

Figure 11-10: Cost control chart. *Source*: [17]

Auditing will be discussed in Chapter 12, but it needs a brief mention here. It is basically an investigation and count to identify and locate all elements of a project. The PM may find a particular activity perplexing or not understand why it is taking longer than it should or costing more than expected. An audit would provide the data to explain the unusual nature of the discrepancy. The PM may choose to do the audit or have the organization's accountant perform the work.

Project Management in Practice
Schedule and Cost Control for Australia's Immense New Parliament House

Over seven years in the making, Australia's new Parliament House at Canberra is actually a suite of buildings costing about $982 million! Meant to be an enduring symbol of the values and expectations of the Australian nation, and a source of pride for its citizens, the complex will consist of 5000 rooms, 40,000 items of furniture, 50,000 square meters of stonework, 7350 doors, and 170,000 square meters of drywall. To excavate the site, over

Source: T. R. Nixon, "Project Management at the New Parliament House, Canberra," *Project Management Journal,* Sept. 1987.

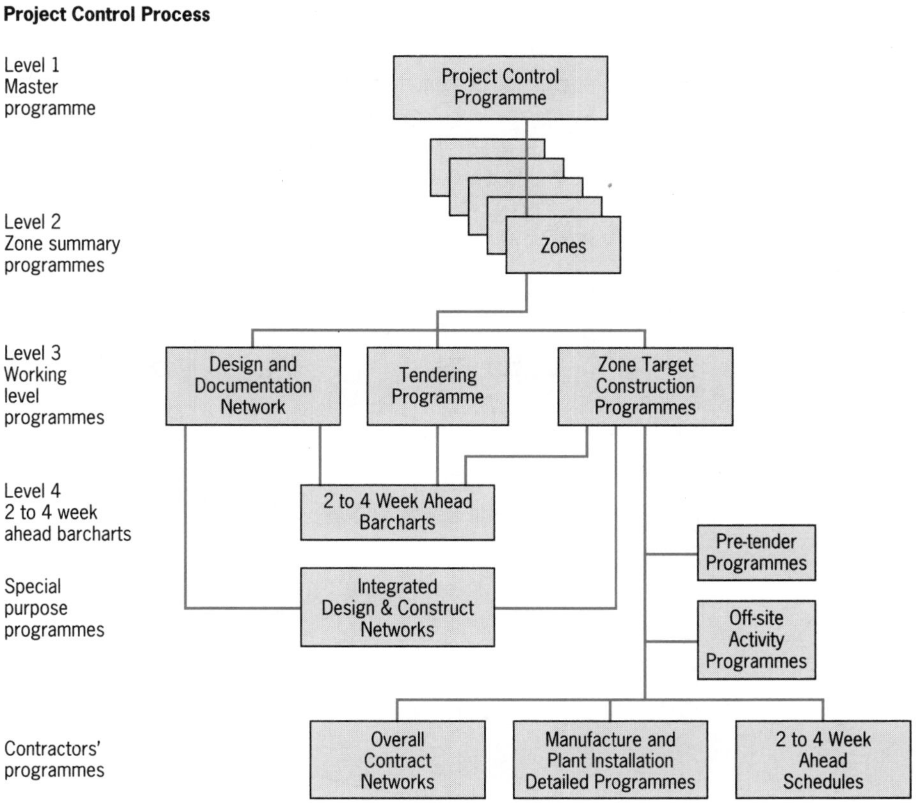

Project Control Process

Level 1
Master
programme — Project Control Programme

Level 2
Zone summary
programmes — Zones

Level 3
Working
level
programmes — Design and Documentation Network; Tendering Programme; Zone Target Construction Programmes

Level 4
2 to 4 week
ahead barcharts — 2 to 4 Week Ahead Barcharts; Pre-tender Programmes

Special
purpose
programmes — Integrated Design & Construct Networks; Off-site Activity Programmes

Contractors'
programmes — Overall Contract Networks; Manufacture and Plant Installation Detailed Programmes; 2 to 4 Week Ahead Schedules

one million cubic meters of rock was moved, and 170,000 cubic meters of concrete was poured to form the foundation. At its busiest point, the complex was costing $1.2 million per working day.

Given the immensity of the project, the information systems to control its design, construction, and furnishing were equally extensive. Procedures were devised for planning, cost control, tendering, contract commencement, drawing and samples, purchasing, stores control, contracts administration, accounts, general administration, and accident prevention. In the area of contracts alone, 540 separate contracts were awarded. And 20,000 drawings were prepared, with 750,000 prints issued. Thus, computerized systems were de-

veloped for the data associated with contracts and bids, drawings, information requests, site instructions, change proposals, shop drawings, asset registers, time reporting, cost reporting, budgetary control, contracts payments, consultants' fees, and reimbursables.

Time control is based on monitoring at four levels of detail giving progressively more programming detail on aspects of the project. Special purpose programs are included for specific problems or requirements. In addition to exception reports, progress review and coordination meetings help management focus attention on the areas of concern. The overall control system is illustrated in the previous figure.

Layout of Separate Buildings within the Parliament House

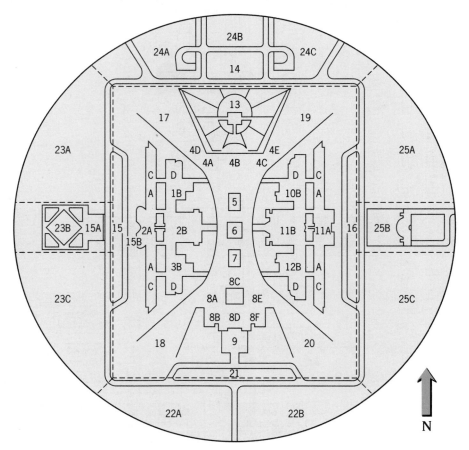

The old parliament house (foreground) and the complex of buildings that comprise the new parliament house (background) in Canberra, Australia.

Cost control is based on the philosophy that 80 percent of the cost is designed in and only 20 percent is due to construction variations. Thus, attention was focused on three points during the design process: early on, to identify allocations and deviations; halfway through to check costs again; and at the completion. Still, ongoing cost control is necessary and performance against budget is measured monthly. Forecasts are also revised every six months to check for any problems ahead.

With such attention to control, the citizens of Australia are looking forward to the completion of their new "house."

▶ 11.4   CONTROL AS A FUNCTION OF MANAGEMENT

With a few rare exceptions, control of projects is always exercised through people. Senior managers in the organization are governed by the CEO who is directed by such groups as the executive committee and/or board of directors/trustees. Senior managers, in turn, try to exercise governance of project managers, and project managers try to exert control over the project team and others representing functions that are involved with the project. The purpose is always the same—to bring the actual schedule, budget, and deliverables of the project into reasonably close congruence with the planned schedule, budget, and deliverables. In this and the following sections of this chapter, we discuss the design and use of control systems with some emphasis on the ways in which people respond to various types of control. A number of the points we cover in these sections are discussed at greater length in William Newman's excellent book, *Constructive Control* [33]. Its insights are as fresh today as they were two decades ago when the book was written.

Finally, it should be noted that much of the literature on total quality management (TQM), ISO 9000 standards, employee involvement (EI), and the functioning of teams is devoted to techniques for developing creativity and synergistic problem-solving through effective teamwork. What is almost never discussed is the implicit assumption that teams have a sense of direction, and are attempting to achieve some specified objectives. All of this implies control. Even the most chaotic brainstorming session (see Appendix A) is aimed at the solution of specific problems. Control is a necessary and inherent part of life in any organization. It is not helpful to think of control as coercive, though, at times, it may be. We prefer to think of control as the maintenance of ethical goal-directed behavior.

The PM is always subject to such eternal verities as the law of gravity, the laws of thermodynamics, and the brute fact that the exercise of managerial control will result in distorting the behavior of subordinates. The job of the PM/controller is to set controls that will encourage those behaviors/results that are deemed desirable and discourage those that are not. The unspoken assumption here is that control systems motivate individuals to behave in certain ways. While this may seem obvious, it is not the bland assertion it appears. The entire subject of motivation is a complex and rich field for research and there are several theories about the nature of motivation. Each has its supporters and critics. We adopt no particular theory here; we do, however, argue that the control mechanisms described in this chapter provide a context within which motivation takes place. Thus, while control does not provide a good explanation for the presence or absence of motivation, control does indicate the direction toward which the motivated person will move [28].

Though control does not ensure motivated behavior, individual reactions to the various types of control systems do affect levels of motivation. By and large, people respond to the goal-directedness of control systems in one of three general ways: (1) by active and positive participation and goal seeking, (2) by passive participation in order to avoid loss, and (3) by active but negative participation and resistance— usually not active resistance to the goal, but failure to undertake those activities that will result in goal achievement. Which of the three resemble a given individual's reaction to control depends on several variables, including such things as the specific control mechanism used, the nature of the goal being sought, the individual's self-image, assessment of the value of the goal, expectation of being able to achieve the goal, and basic tolerance for being controlled.

While human response to specific types of control is typified by its variety, some generalizations are possible.

Cybernetic Controls   Human response to steering controls tends to be positive. Steering controls are usually viewed as helpful rather than as a source of unwelcome pressure if the controllees perceive themselves as able to perform inside the prescribed limits. Contrary to the popular song, it is not the "impossible dream" that motivates goal-seeking behavior, but rather a moderately good chance of success.

Of course, response to steering control is dependent on the individual's acceptance of the goal as appropriate. Indeed, no control system is acceptable if the objective of control is not acceptable. Further, the source of control must be seen as legitimate for the control mechanism to be accepted.

While it appears to be true that humans respond positively to steering controls, they may not be so positive about the monitoring systems that drive the control mechanisms. Grant, *et al.* [16] have shown that computerized performance monitoring and control systems are viewed as mixed blessings and have both functional and dysfunctional effects. These monitoring systems, though not used for true cybernetic controls, are fairly common in software projects.

Go/No-go Controls Response to go/no-go controls tends to be neutral or negative. The reason appears to be related to the inherent nature of this type of control system. With go/no-go control systems, "barely good enough" results are just as acceptable as "perfect" results. The control system itself makes it difficult for the worker to take pride in high-quality work because the system does not recognize gradations of quality. In addition, it is all too common to be rather casual about setting the control limits for a go/no-go control; the limits should be very carefully set. The fact that this kind of control emphasizes "good enough" performance is no excuse for the nonchalant application of careless standards.

While go/no-go control is the most frequent type of control exercised on projects, the impact of such control on the project team seems, to us, to be less negative than Newman suggests [33, pp. 41–42]. Perhaps this is because *project team performance* is the primary focus of control rather than specific items of work performed by individuals. The quality of the project taken as a whole serves as the source of satisfaction to the group, not the quality of bits and pieces. It also appears clear that the quality of the project also serves as a source of satisfaction with the *process* of doing projects. The entire subject of human response to control in a project environment is a prime area for additional research.

Postcontrols Postcontrols are seen as much the same as a report card. They may serve as a basis for reward or punishment, but they are received too late to change current performance. Whether reaction to postcontrol is positive, neutral, or negative seems to depend on the "grade" received. In cases where a series of similar projects must be undertaken, postcontrols are regarded as helpful in planning for future work, but considerable care must be devoted to ensuring that controls are consistent with changing environmental conditions. To be effective, management must provide an incentive for project managers to study postcontrol reports, and to determine corrective procedures for problems exposed by the reports, as well as procedures that will replicate the techniques and systems that appear particularly helpful.

Because postcontrols are placed on the process of conducting a project, as well as on the usual time, cost, and performance standards, they may be applied to such areas as interproject communications, cooperation between the groups working on related task elements, the quality of project management, and the nature of interaction with the client. Application of control to such matters presents severe measurement problems. Often it is difficult to detect gross differences in the quality of intergroup communications, for example, or to relate these differences, if detected, to aspects of the project that can be controlled. To say that these matters are difficult to measure and control is not, of course, to obviate the need for control. The soft side of project performance is no less important in the longer run than the easier-to-measure hard side.

▶ 11.5 BALANCE IN A CONTROL SYSTEM

When developing a control system, it is important that the system be well *balanced*. Unfortunately, the concept of balance is fuzzy—difficult to explain, difficult to achieve, and difficult to recognize. Though precise definition is impossible, we can describe some general features of a balanced control system, and also indicate some of the things a controller can do to achieve good balance in a system.

- A balanced control system is built with cognizance of the fact that investment in control is subject to sharply diminishing returns. Costs increase exponentially as the degree of control increases.
- A balanced control system recognizes that as control increases past some point, innovative activity is more and more damped, and then finally shut off completely.
- A balanced control system is directed toward the correction of error rather than toward punishment. This requires a clear understanding of the fact that the past cannot be changed, no matter how loudly the manager yells.
- A balanced system exerts control only to the degree required to achieve its objectives. It rarely pays to spend dollars to find lost pennies, nor is it sensible to machine a part to the ten-thousandth if the client's requirements are to the tenth.
- A balanced system utilizes the lowest degree of hassle consistent with accomplishing its goals. The controller should avoid annoying those people whose cooperation is required to reach system objectives.

To sum up, a balanced control system is cost-effective, well geared for the end results sought, and not overdone. The causes of imbalance are legion. For example, the application of across-the-board controls is usually not a good idea. Treating everyone alike appeals to a naive sense of equity, but better results are usually achieved by treating everyone individually.

Across-the-board freezes on expenditures or on hiring tend to reward those who have already overspent or overhired and to penalize the frugal and efficient. The side effects of this are often quite odd. Several years ago, Procter & Gamble put a freeze on hiring into effect for an engineering development laboratory. Project managers who were shorthanded hired temporary labor, including highly skilled technicians, from Manpower and similar firms. P & G's accounting system allowed temporary labor to be charged to material accounts rather than to the salary account. The lesson to be learned is that results-oriented, creative project managers tend to see across-the-board controls as a challenge and a barrier to be circumvented.

Other common causes of imbalance are these:

1. Placing too much weight on easy-to-measure factors and too little weight on difficult-to-measure, soft factors (the so-called "intangibles").
2. Emphasizing short-run results at the expense of longer-run objectives.
3. Ignoring the changes in the structure of organizational goals that result from the passage of time or changes in the firm's circumstances. For example, high

quality and strict adherence to delivery schedules might be extremely important to a new firm. Later, perhaps, expense control might be more important.

4. Overcontrol by an aggressive executive often causes trouble. In an attempt to create a reputation for on-time delivery, one overly zealous PM put so much pressure on the project team that on-time shipments took precedence over proper test procedures. The result was serious malfunctions of the product and its subsequent recall.

5. Monitoring and controlling items may lead some people to ignore anything that is not measured. "If it isn't counted, it doesn't count," is the attitude. This factor was responsible for the failure of many attempts at management by objectives.

Achieving balance in a control system is rather easy to discuss but quite difficult to accomplish. Several principles must be simultaneously upheld. Perhaps most important is the need to tie controls directly to project objectives. Occasionally, firms establish tortuous, indirect linkages between control and objective, apparently on the theory that people should not be aware of or understand the controls under which they must operate. It is as if the firm were trying to unethically trap employees. Such control systems rarely work because they rest on two fallacious assumptions: (1) that people are generally perverse and will avoid trying to accomplish a known objective, and (2) that people are too stupid to see through the misdirection.

In addition to linking controls to objectives, controls should be closely and directly related to specific performance outcomes. Start by defining the desired results as precisely as possible. System actions that can cause deviation from the desired results are then examined and controls are designed for these actions, beginning with those that can be the source of serious deviation, particularly those that cause trouble with high frequency.

The PM should also examine all controls in terms of the probable reactions of individuals to the proposed controls. One asks, "How will the various members of the project team react to this control?" If negative reaction is likely, the control should be redesigned.

The problem of developing a good balance between long-run and short-run control objectives is delicate, not because the blending is inherently difficult, but because the PM is often preoccupied with urgent short-run problems rather than longer-run problems that can always be "temporarily" set aside no matter how important the results may be at some later date. Even the timing and sequences of monitoring and controlling can affect the likelihood of time and cost overruns [35].

A good rule for the controller is to place the control as close as possible to the work being controlled and to design the simplest possible mechanism to achieve control. Giving the worker direct control over quality has had impressive results in Japanese production processes as well as at the Lincoln Electric Company in the United States. Similar results were achieved by a major producer of housing units. Carpenters, masons, electricians, and other workers were given considerable discretion over specific production methods. Projects on which this approach was employed showed significantly improved quality when compared to projects built by standard methods.

The most important step in constructing a balanced control system must be taken far in advance of the time when control systems are usually designed. Every step of project planning must be undertaken with the understanding that *whatever work is planned will also have to be controlled*. As we have emphasized, planning and control are opposite sides of the same coin. No amount of planning can solve the current crisis, but planning combined with the design and installation of appropriate control mechanisms can go a long way toward crisis prevention.

An excellent example of integrating the planning and control functions is provided by Mead Data Central, a producer of large-scale database systems and a subsidiary of Mead Corporation. In its *Project Management Development Guide*, Mead describes six stages of the project life cycle as seen from its point of view. For each stage, the purpose is carefully explained and the deliverables for that stage are listed. For example, the list of deliverables for the feasibility stage contains these items: project description, project number, preliminary business case, project requirements document, and so forth. For each deliverable, the individual(s) and/or groups responsible are noted.

An extensive glossary of terms is included in the document so that inexperienced project workers can understand what is meant by such diverse terms as "escalation document," "functional audit," "milestone," "not-to-do list," "project cost tracking," and "release readiness statement." In addition, the *Development Guide* summarizes the tasks that must be performed by each of the functional areas or individuals during each stage of the life cycle. The work of the Idea Champion, the Market Managers, the Business Management Process Director, the Project Review Committee, and so on is well defined. The result is an effective integration of planning and control that is available to anyone working on the organization's projects.

A senior executive at a large industrial firm that carries out many projects each year sees control in a slightly different light. Noting that differences between plan and reality usually represent problems for project managers, he remarked: "If you are solving problems faster than they are arriving to be solved, you have the project under control. If not, you haven't."

▶ 11.6   CONTROL OF CREATIVE ACTIVITIES

Some brief attention should be paid to the special case of controlling research and development projects, design projects, and similar processes that depend intimately on the creativity of individuals and teams. First, the more creativity involved, the greater the degree of uncertainty surrounding outcomes. Second, too much control tends to inhibit creativity. But neither of these dicta can be taken without reservation. As noted in Appendix A, control is not necessarily the enemy of creativity [45]; nor, popular myth to the contrary, does creative activity imply complete uncertainty. While the exact outcomes of creative activity may be more or less uncertain, the process of getting the outcome is usually not uncertain.

In order to control creative projects, the PM must adopt one or some combination of three general approaches to the problem: (1) progress review, (2) personnel reassignment, and (3) control of input resources.

Progress Review

The progress review focuses on the process of reaching outcomes rather than on the outcomes *per se*. Because the outcomes are partially dependent on the process used to achieve them—uncertain though they may be—the process is subjected to control. For example, in research projects the researcher cannot be held responsible for the outcome of the research, but can most certainly be held responsible for adherence to the research proposal, the budget, and the schedule. The process is controllable even if the precise results are not.

Control should be instituted at each project milestone. If research results are not as expected or desired, milestones provide a convenient opportunity to assess the state of progress, the value of accomplishment to date, the probability of valuable results in the future, and the desirability of changes in the research design. Again, the object of control is to ensure that the research design is sound and is being carried out as planned or amended. The review process should be participative. Unilateral judgments from the superior are not apt to be accepted or effective. Care must be taken not to overstress method as opposed to result. Method is controllable, and should be controlled, but results are still what count.

Personnel Reassignment

This type of control operates in a very straightforward way. Individuals who are productive are kept. Those who are not are moved, to other jobs or to other organizations. Problems with this technique can arise because it is easy to create an elite group. While the favored few are highly motivated to further achievement, everyone else tends to be demotivated. It is also important not to apply control with too fine an edge. While it is not particularly difficult to identify those who fall in the top and bottom quartiles of productivity, it is usually quite hard to make clear distinctions between people in the middle quartiles.

Control of Input Resources

In this case, the focus is on efficiency. The ability to manipulate input resources carries with it considerable control over output. Obviously, efficiency is not synonymous with creativity, but the converse is equally untrue. Creativity is not synonomous with extravagant use of resources.

The results flowing from creative activity tend to arrive in batches. Considerable resource expenditure may occur with no visible results, but then, seemingly all of a sudden, many outcomes may be delivered. The milestones for application of resource control must therefore be chosen with great care. The controller who decides to withhold resources just before the fruition of a research project is apt to become an ex-controller.

Sound judgment argues for some blend of these three approaches when controlling creative projects. The first and third approaches concentrate on process because process is observable and can be affected. But process is not the matter of moment; results are. The second approach requires us to measure (or at least to recognize) output when it occurs. This is often quite difficult. Thus, the wise PM will use all three approaches: checking process and method, manipulating resources, and culling those who cannot or do not produce.

▶ 11.7 CONTROL OF CHANGE

In Chapter 6, we discussed the fact that the original plans for projects are almost certain to be changed before the projects are completed. The changes, we noted, result from three basic causes: uncertainty about the technology on which the work of the project or its output is based, an increase in the knowledge base or sophistication of the client/user, or a modification of the rules applying to the process of carrying out the project or to its output. When either the process or output of a project is changed, there is almost always a concomitant change in the budget and/or schedule.

Conversations in recent years with more than 500 project managers have convinced us that coping with changes and changing priorities is perceived as the most important single problem facing the PM—or if not the most important, certainly the most irritating. When a senior financial officer of a toy manufacturing firm makes an offhand, negative comment about the color of a toy, and triggers a "total redesign" of the toy, thereby invalidating an already approved design, schedule, and budget, the project manager and the design artist may consider murder. (It is probable that a knowledgeable jury would find their action justifiable.)

The most common changes, however, are due to the natural tendency of the client and project team members to try to improve the product or service. New demands and performance requirements become apparent to the client which were not realized at the time of project initiation. New technologies become available or better ideas occur to the team as work progresses. As noted earlier, the later these changes are made in the project, the more difficult and costly they are to complete. Without control, a continuing accumulation of little changes can have a major negative impact on the project's schedule and cost.

There is, however, no insurance against the risks associated with project changes. Total quality management and employee involvement will help if both the deliverable and the process by which it is to be produced are carefully studied by thoughtful teams that represent the interests of the major stakeholders in any project, the client, senior management, the project team, and the community. Also, a thorough knowledge of production processes will help avoid some manufacturability-related engineering changes [38]. Since prevention of change is not possible, the PM's best hope seems to lie in controlling the process by which change is introduced and accomplished.

This is accomplished with a formal *change control system* which, in some industries, is a part of their *configuration management system* responsible for integrating and coordinating changes throughout the systems development cycle. The purpose of the formal *change control system* is to:

- review all requested changes to the project (both content and procedures)
- identify all task impacts
- translate these impacts into project performance, cost, and schedule
- evaluate the benefits and costs of the requested changes
- identify alternative changes that might accomplish the same ends

- accept or reject the requested changes
- communicate the changes to all concerned parties
- ensure that the changes are implemented properly
- prepare monthly reports that summarize all changes to date and their project impacts.

The following simple guidelines, applied with reasonable rigor, can be used to establish an effective change control procedure.

1. All project contracts or agreements must include a description of how requests for a change in the project's plan, budget, schedule, and/or deliverables, will be introduced and processed.

2. Any change in a project will be in the form of a *change order* that will include a description of the agreed-upon change together with any changes in the plan, budget, schedule, and/or deliverables that result from the change.

3. Changes must be approved, in writing, by the client's agent as well as by an appropriate representative of senior management of the firm responsible for carrying out the project.

4. The project manager must be consulted on all desired changes prior to the preparation and approval of the change order. The project manager's approval, however, is not required.

5. Once the change order has been completed and approved, the project master plan should be amended to reflect the change, and the change order becomes a part of the master plan.

The process of controlling change is not complicated. If the project is large, Roman suggests a change control board [37, p. 274], a group representing all interested parties that processes all requests for change. For the typical small- or medium-sized project, however, the problem of handling change need not be complex. The main source of trouble is that too many project managers, in an attempt to avoid anything that smacks of bureaucracy, adopt an informal process of handling requests for change. Misunderstanding often arises from this informality, and the PM finds that the project becomes committed to deliver a changed output, but will have to swallow the additional cost involved, and will have to scramble to meet the old, unchanged schedule.

The problems associated with dealing with change orders informally are particularly severe in the case of software and information system projects. We resist the notion that computer-oriented projects are significantly different from other types of projects in this regard. (For a diametric view, see [36].) Nonetheless, the precise techniques of managing projects are not independent of the technology applied on the project. Service sector projects often require different planning and control methods than do construction projects or R & D projects.

The severity of the problem of dealing with change in software projects, it seems to us, is caused by two, interrelated factors. First, software and information systems experts too often fail to explain adequately to the client the real nature of the systems they develop. Second, clients too often fail to make an adequate effort to understand the systems that become the lifeblood for their organizations. All too often, the systems developer is preoccupied by the technical demands of the systems and ignorant of the user's needs. And all too often, the user views the systems developer as a practitioner of some arcane art that cannot be penetrated by normal minds.

Given this basic failure to communicate, the client has no real idea of what is involved in changing a software project in order to provide another useful feature not specified in the original project requirements. The software technician, eager to please the customer, agrees to provide the utility, but does not make clear to the client the level of effort and time that will be required. The project is late, over budget, and the customer is angry. This scenario is played out again and again with neither side profiting from the experience. The formal process for change suggested above tends to reduce the degree of misunderstanding—and disappointment.

Difficult as it may be, control is an important part of the PM's job on every project. Perhaps the most helpful advice we can give the PM is, in the language of the 1970s, to "hang loose." One effective project manager of our acquaintance tells his project team, "I will not accept crises after 4:30 PM. You are limited to one crisis per day. Crises are not cumulative. If you don't get yours in today, you do not get two tomorrow." All this is said, of course, with good humor. Team members understand that the PM is not serious, but his projects seem to progress with exceptional smoothness. Crises do occur from time to time, but everyone on the team works to prevent them by applying control in an effective and timely manner.

Project Management In Practice
Better Control of Product Development Projects at Johnson Controls

The Automotive Systems Group of Johnson Controls was having trouble controlling their product development programs with each project being managed differently, disagreements about who was responsible for what, projects failing because of rapid company growth, and new employees having trouble fitting into the culture. For a solution, they went to their most experienced and successful project managers and condensed their knowledge into four detailed procedures for managing projects. Because these procedures are now common to all projects, they can be used to train new employees, standardize practices, create a common language, tie together different company functions, create common experiences, act as implicit job descriptions, and create a positive overall project management culture.

The first procedure is project approval for authorizing the expenditure of funds and use of resources. The sales department must first provide a set of product/market information, including financial data, project scope, critical dates, and engineering resource requirements before management will approve the project. Thus, projects are now scrutinized much more closely before work is started and money spent—when more questions are asked and more people are involved, better decisions tend to be made.

The second procedure is the statement-of-work, identifying agreements and assump-

Source: W. D. Reith and D. B. Kandt, "Project Management at a Major Automotive Seating Supplier," *Project Management Journal,* September 1991.

tions for the project. Here, both the customer and top management must sign off before product design work begins, thereby reducing misunderstandings regarding not only product specifications, prices, and milestones but also intangible product requirements, explicit exclusions, and generic performance targets. Maintaining this documentation over the life of the project has helped avoid problems caused by late product changes from the customer, particularly for 3–5 year projects where the personnel rotate off the project. Customers have, however, been slow to agree to this level of documentation because it limits their ability to change timing, prices, and specifications late in the program when they are more knowledgable about their needs.

The third procedure is the work breakdown structure, consisting of nine critical lifecycle phases running from definition through production. Included in each of these nine

phases are four key elements: the tasks, the timing of each task, the responsible individuals, and the meeting dates for simultaneous engineering (a formalized procedure at Johnson Controls).

The fourth procedure is a set of management reviews, crucial to successful project completion. Both the content and timing of these reviews are specified in advance and progression to the next phase of a project cannot occur until senior management has approved the prespecified requirements, objectives, and quality criteria for that phase. The procedure also specifies questions that must be answered and work that must be reviewed by senior management.

Through the use of these procedures, which are updated and improved with each new project experience, the learning that occurs in the organization is captured and made useful for future projects.

▶ SUMMARY

As the final subject in the project implementation part of the text, this chapter described the project control process in the planning–monitoring–controlling cycle. The need for control was discussed and the three types available were described. Then the design of control systems was addressed, including management's role, achieving the proper balance, and attaining control of creative activity as well as handling changes.

Specific points made in this chapter were these:

- Control is directed to performance, cost, and time.
- The two fundamental purposes of control are to regulate results through altering activity and to conserve the organization's physical, human, and financial assets.
- The three main types of control processes are cybernetic (either first-, second-, or third-order), go/no-go, and postcontrol.
- The postcontrol report contains four sections:
  Project objectives

  Milestones and budgets
  Final project results
  Recommendations for improvement

- The trend projection curve, critical ratios, and the control chart are useful control tools.
- Control systems have a close relationship to motivation and should be well-balanced; that is, cost-effective, appropriate to the desired end results, and not overdone.
- Three approaches to the control of creativity are progress review, personnel reassignment, and control of inputs.
- The biggest single problem facing a PM is the control of change.

In the next chapter we initiate the project termination part of the text, beginning with evaluation and auditing. This topic is closely related to the postcontrol topics in this chapter.

▶ GLOSSARY

Champion—A person with organizational clout who takes on personal responsibility (though not usually day-to-day management) for the successful completion of a project for the organization.

Control—Assuring that reality meets expectations or plans. Usually involves the process of keeping actions within limits to assure that certain outcomes will in fact happen.

Control Chart—A chart of a measure of performance—commonly a quality characteristic—over time, showing how it changes compared to a desired mean and upper and lower limits.

Critical Ratio—A ratio of progress (actual/scheduled) times a cost ratio (budgeted/actual).

Cybernetic—An automatic control system containing a negative feedback loop.

Early Warning System—A monitoring system that forewarns the project manager if trouble arises.

Go/No-Go—Initially, a type of gauge that quickly tells an inspector if an object's dimension is within certain limits. In the case of project management, this can be any measure that allows a manager to decide whether to continue, change, or terminate an activity or a project.

▶ MATERIAL REVIEW QUESTIONS

1. What is the purpose of control? To what is it directed?

2. What are the three main types of control systems? What questions should a control system answer?

3. What tools are available to the project manager to use in controlling a project? Identify some characteristics of a good control system.

4. What is the mathematical expression for the critical ratio? What does it tell a manager?

5. Describe the relationship between motivation and control.

6. How is creativity controlled?

7. What are go/no-go gauges?

8. What is a champion?

9. Describe a cybernetic control system.

10. What should the postcontrol report include?

11. How should change be controlled?

▶ CLASS DISCUSSION QUESTIONS

1. How could MBO be used in project control?

2. How might the project manager integrate the various control tools into a project control system?

3. How could a negative feedback control system be implemented in project management to anticipate client problems?

4. Compare the trend projection curve and the earned value chart. Could they be combined to aid the PM's control?

5. What other project parameters might a control chart be used for? How would their limits be set?

6. Control systems are sometimes classified into two categories, preventive and feedback. How do the three types of systems described in the chapter relate to these two categories?

7. How do internal and external controls differ?

8. What are some difficulties encountered when attempting project control?

9. How might the information required for control systems be collected?

10. How might the information collected through the control system be used on subsequent projects?

11. How does the control of creative projects differ from the control of ordinary projects?

12. Where might ethical issues arise for a PM in the stewardship of the company's resources?

13. Why is the control of change such a difficult problem for a PM?

▶ PROBLEMS

1. Given the following information, calculate the critical ratios and indicate which activities are on target and which need to be investigated.

Activity	Actual Progress	Scheduled Progress	Budgeted Cost	Actual Cost
A	2 days	2 days	$40	$35
B	4 days	6 days	$30	$40
C	1 day	3 days	$50	$70
D	3 days	2 days	$25	$25

2. Calculate the critical ratios for the following activities and indicate which activities are probably on target and which need to be investigated.

Activity	Actual Progress	Scheduled Progress	Budgeted Cost	Actual Cost
A	4 days	4 days	$60	$40
B	3 days	2 days	$50	$50
C	2 days	3 days	$30	$20
D	1 day	1 day	$20	$30
E	2 days	4 days	$25	$25

3. Given the following information, which activities are on time, which are early, and which are behind schedule?

Activity	Budgeted Cost	Actual Cost	Critical Ratio
A	$60	$40	1.0
B	$25	$50	0.5
C	$45	$30	1.5
D	$20	$20	1.5
E	$50	$50	0.67

4. Design and plot a critical ratio for a project that had planned constant, linear progress from 0 to an earned value of 200 over a 100 day duration. In fact, progress for the first 20 days has been: 2, 3, 4, 6, 7, 9, 12, 14, 15, 17, 20, 21, 21, 22, 24, 26, 27, 29, 31, 33. What can you conclude about this project?

5. Design and plot a critical ratio for a project that has planned constant, linear spending from 0 to a total of 1000 over a 100 day duration. In fact, daily spending for the first 15 days has been: 11, 10, 9, 10, 11, 12, 11, 9, 8, 9, 10, 12, 14, 11, 7. What can you conclude about this project?

6. Empire State Building, Inc., has two project teams installing virtually identical buildings for a customer in two separate cities. Both projects have a planned daily cost of 100 and a planned daily earned value of 100. The first six days for each team have progressed as follows:

Day	Team A: Earned Value	Team B: Earned Value	A: Cost	B: Cost
1	90	90	95	95
2	92	88	98	94
3	94	95	101	102
4	98	101	106	109
5	104	89	116	99
6	112	105	126	118

Compare the two projects in terms of general progress and according to critical ratios.

7. World Trade Building, Ltd., is also constructing an identical building for the same customer as in Problem 6 and has the following earned values and costs for the first six days: EV: 90, 88, 95, 101, 89, 105; Cost: 92, 88, 93, 98, 85, 100. Compare this project to the two in Problem 6.

▶ INCIDENTS FOR DISCUSSION

Speciality Pak, Inc.

Speciality Pak, Inc., is a custom packing operation serving the chemical industry in seven states. S. P. has one operation in each state, and they vary in size from 50 to 240 employees. A disturbing trend has been developing for the last couple of years that S. P. management wishes to stop. The incidence of tardiness and absenteeism is on the increase. Both are extremely disruptive in a custom packing operation. S. P. is nonunion in all seven locations, and since management wants to keep this situation, it wants a careful, low-key approach to the problem. Roger Horn, assistant personnel manager, has been appointed project manager to recommend a solution. All seven operations managers have been assigned to work with him on this problem.

Roger has had no problem interfacing with the operations managers. They have very quickly agreed that three steps must be taken to solve the problem:

1. Institute a uniform daily attendance report that is summarized weekly and forwarded to the main office. (Current practice varies from location to location, but comments on attendance are normally included in monthly operations reports.)

2. Institute a uniform disciplinary policy, enforced in a uniform manner.

3. Initiate an intensive employee education program to emphasize the importance of good attendance.

The team has further decided that the three-point program should be tested before a final recommendation is presented. They have decided to test the program at one location for two months. Roger wishes to control and evaluate the test by having the daily attendance report transmitted to him directly at headquarters, from which he will make the final decision on whether to present the program in its current format or not.

Questions: Does this monitoring and control method appear adequate? What are the potential problems?

Night Tran Construction Company

Night Tran Construction Company specializes in building small power plants, mostly for utility companies. The company was awarded a contract approximately two years ago to build such a power plant. The contract stated a project duration of three years, after which a 1 percent penalty would be invoked for each additional month of construction. Project records indicate the utility plan is only 50 percent completed and is encountering continuing problems. The owner of Night Tran Company, concerned over the potential losses, investigated the project and found the following: There were an excessive number of engineering design changes; there was a high work rejection rate; and the project was generally understaffed. As a result, she directed the project manager to develop a better system of project control and present this method to the board members in one week.

Questions: If you were the project manager, what characteristics would you be looking for in the new control system? Will a new control system be adequate for the problem? Explain.

▶ PROJECT TEAM CONTINUING EXERCISE

For this assignment, design a project control system for your team project. Determine how you will control performance, cost, and time. Will you use go/no-go, postcontrol, or cybernetic controls, and if the latter, a first-, second-, or third-order system? Are these dynamic or static controls? What will you measure? What tools will you employ: control charts, critical ratios, trend projections? Will you attempt to control change? If so, how? Justify your control system in terms of cost effectiveness, appropriateness, and ability to motivate team members. Then apply the control system in retrospect to those activities already completed and analyze its success. Modify as appropriate and continue using it throughout the remainder of the project.

▶ BIBLIOGRAPHY

1. ACKOFF, R. L. "Beyond Problem Solving." *Decision Sciences*, April 1974.

2. ADAMS, J. R., S. E. BARNDT, and M. D. MARTIN. *Managing by Project Management.* Dayton, OH:. Universal Technology Corp.,1979.

3. AMRINE, H. T., J. A. RITCHEY, and O. S. HULLEY.

Manufacturing Organization and Management, 5th ed. Englewood Cliffs, NJ: Prentice Hall, 1987.

4. ARCHIBALD, R. D. *Managing High Technology Programs and Projects.* New York: Wiley, 1976.

5. BARNES, N. M. L. "Cost Modelling—An Integrated Approach to Planning and Cost Control."

American Association of Chemical Engineers Transactions, March 1977.

6. BENT, J. A. "Project Control Concepts." *Project Management Proceedings*, 1979.

7. BLOCK, E. B. "Accomplishment/Cost: Better Project Control." *Harvard Business Review*, May 1971.

8. BOBROWSKI, P. M. "Project Management Control Problems: An Information Systems Focus." *Project Management Journal*, June 1989.

9. BRAZ, E. F. "Project Management Oversight: A Control Tool of Owners of Engineering and Construction Projects." *Project Management Journal*, March 1989.

10. BUFFA, E. S. *Basic Production Management*, 2nd ed. New York: Wiley, 1975.

11. CAMMANN, C., and D. A. NADLER. "Fit Control Systems to Your Management Style." *Harvard Business Review*, Jan.–Feb. 1976.

12. CESTIN, A. A. "What Makes Large Projects Go Wrong." *Project Management Quarterly*, March 1980.

13. DAVIS, S. M., and P. LAWRENCE. *Matrix*. Reading, MA: Addison-Wesley, 1977.

14. ELLIOTT, D. P. "Paper and Cost Control." *Project Management Proceedings*, 1979.

15. FRAZIER, HAUGG, and THACKERY. "Developing A Project Management Package." *Journal of Systems Management*, Dec. 1976.

16. GRANT, R. A., C. A. HIGGINS, and R. H. IRVING. "Computerized Performance Monitors: Are They Costing You Customers?" *Sloan Management Review*, Spring 1988.

17. HAJEK, V. G. *Management of Engineering Projects*. New York: McGraw Hill, 1977.

18. HIGGINS, J. C., and R. FINN. "Managerial Attitudes Toward Computer Models for Planning and Control." *Long Range Planning*, Dec. 1976.

19. HOLLANDER, G. L. "Integrated Project Control, Part II: TCP/Schedule: A Model for Integrated Project Control." *Project Management Quarterly*, June 1973.

20. HOROVITZ, J. H. "Strategic Control: A New Task for Top Management." *Long Range Planning*, June 1979.

21. HOWARD, D. C. "Cost Schedule Control Systems." *Management Accounting*, Oct. 1976.

22. JOHNSON, J. R. "Advanced Project Control." *Journal of Systems Management*, May 1977.

23. KARAA, F. A., and B. ABDALLAH. "Coordination Mechanisms During the Construction Project Life Cycle." *Project Management Journal*, Sept. 1991.

24. KEANE, A. "Timing for Project Management Control." *Data Management*, 1979.

25. KERZNER, H. "Evaluation Techniques in Project Management." *Journal of Systems Management*, Feb. 1980.

26. LARSEN, S. D. "Control of Construction Projects: An Integrated Approach." *The Internal Auditor*, Sept. 1979.

27. LIKIERMAN, A. "Avoiding Cost Escalation on Major Projects." *Management Accounting*, Feb. 1980.

28. LIVINGSTON, J. L., and R. RONEN. "Motivation and Management Control Systems." *Decision Sciences*, April 1975.

29. MARTYN, A. S. "Some Problems in Managing Complex Development Projects." *Long Range Planning*, April 1975.

30. MORAVEC, M. "How Organizational Development Can Help and Hinder Project Managers." *Project Management Quarterly*, Sept. 1979.

31. MURDICK, R. G. *et al. Information Systems for Modern Management*, 3rd ed. Englewood Cliffs, NJ: Prentice Hall, 1984.

32. MYERS, G. "Forms Management; Part 5—How to Achieve Control." *Journal of Systems Management*, Feb. 1977.

33. NEWMAN, W. H. *Constructive Control*. Englewood Cliffs, NJ: Prentice Hall, 1975.

34. NEWNEM, A. "Planning Ahead with an Integrated Management Control System." *Project Management Proceedings*, 1979.

35. PARTOVI, F. Y., and J. BURTON. "Timing of Monitoring and Control of CPM Projects." *IEEE Transactions on Engineering Management*, Feb. 1993.

36. ROETZHEIM, W. H. "Managing Software Projects: Unique Problems and Requirements." in P. C. Dinsmore, ed., *The AMA Handbook of Project Management*. New York: AMACOM, 1993.

37. ROMAN, D. D. *Managing Projects: A Systems Approach*. New York: Elsevier, 1986.

38. SAEED, B. I., D. M. BOWEN, and V. S. SOHONI. "Avoiding Engineering Changes through Focused

Manufacturing Knowledge." IEEE *Transactions on Engineering Management*, Feb. 1993.

39. SAITOW, A. R. "CSPC: Reporting Project Progress to the Top." In E. W. Davis, ed., *Project Management: Techniques, Applications and Managerial Issues*. Norcross, GA: American Institute of Industrial Engineers, 1976.

40. SANDERS, J. "Effective Estimating Process Outlined." *Computer World*, April 7, 14, and 21, 1980.

41. SCHODERBEK, C. G., P. P. SCHODERBEK, and A. G. KEFALAS. *Management Systems*, 4th ed. Homewood, IL: Irwin, 1989.

42. SCHOOF, G. "What Is the Scope of Project Control?" *Project Management Proceedings*, 1979.

43. SETHI, N. K. "Project Management." *Industrial Management*, Jan–Feb. 1980.

44. SNOWDON, M. "Measuring Performance in Capital Project Management." *Long Range Planning*, Aug. 1980.

45. SOUDER, W. E. "Autonomy, Gratification, and R & D Outputs: A Small-Sample Field Study." *Management Science*, April 1974.

46. TIONG, R. L. K. "Effective Controls for Large Scale Construction Projects." *Project Management Journal*, Mar. 1990.

47. TOELLNER, J. D. "Project Management: A Formula for Success." *Computer World*, Dec. 1978.

48. VAN GIGCH, J. P. *Applied General Systems Theory*, 2nd ed. New York: Harper & Row, 1978.

49. WEBER, F. M. "Ways to Improve Performance on Projects." *Project Management Quarterly*, Sept. 1981.

50. YUNUS, N. B., D. L. BABCOCK, and C. BENJAMIN. "Development of a Knowledge-Based Schedule Planning System." *Project Management Journal*, Dec. 1990.

51. ZELDMAN, M. *Keeping Technical Projects on Target*. New York: American Management Association, 1978.

CASE

CORNING GLASS WORKS: THE Z-GLASS PROJECT*
Kim B. Clark

After several highly successful years, 1977 had been a difficult one at Corning Glass Work's Harrisburg plant. In July the yields and productivity of the Z-Glass process had begun a long decline, and the entire plant organization was working overtime trying to correct the problem. Morale was plummeting as yields continued to decline throughout the summer and fall. In December of 1977, a team of engineers from the corporate Manufacturing and Engineering (M&E) staff had been assigned to the plant; its charter was to focus on long-term process improvement while the line organization concentrated on day-to-day operations.

On the morning of March 24, 1978, Eric Davidson, leader of the M&E project team at Harrisburg, sat in his office and reflected on the group's first three months in the plant. The project had not gone well, and Davidson knew that his team members were discouraged. The technical problems they faced were difficult enough, but it seemed that the line organization had resisted almost everything the M&E team had

tried to do. In addition to conflicts over responsibility and authority, there were deep disagreements about the sources of the problems and how best to deal with them. Real cooperation was almost nonexistent, and the relationships between team and line personnel in some departments were tense. Davidson felt that a change in the direction of the project had to be made immediately.

---

* This case has become a classic in the project implementation literature for its lessons in human behavior as well as technical analysis of laboratory data. Though somewhat dated now, the lessons are still highly relevant. Copyright 1981 by the President and Fellows of Harvard College. Harvard Business School Case 681-091. This case was prepared by Kim B. Clark as a basis for class discussion rather than to illustrate either effective or ineffective handling of an administra-tive situation. Reprinted by permission of the Harvard Business School.

As he began to sift through the comments and memos from his team, he recalled what David Leibson, vice president of Manufacturing and Engineering, had said to him shortly after he accepted the Harrisburg assignment:

> Eric, this is the M&E group's first major turnaround project and the first real project of any kind in the Industrial Products division. I picked you for this job because you're the kind of guy who gets things done. This is a key one for our group, and I think a big one for the company. In situations like this, you either win big or you lose big. There's very little middle ground.

Corning Glass Works in the 1970s

During the late 1960s and early 1970s Corning Glass Works was a corporation in transition: long a leader in the development of glass and ceramic products for industrial and commercial uses, Corning had entered several consumer goods markets during the 1960s. Under the direction of Lee Waterman, president from 1962 to 1971, Corning developed a strong marketing emphasis to go along with several new consumer products.

Although the public's perception of Corning in the 1960s was no doubt dominated by its well-known Pyrex and Ovenware cooking products, and Pyroceram dinnerware, its most successful consumer-oriented product was actually TV tube casings. Utilizing an innovative glass-forming process, Corning entered the market for TV tube funnels and front plates in 1958 and soon developed a strong market position. Throughout the mid- to late 1960s, growth in TV at Corning was rapid, and the profits at the TV division constituted the backbone of the income statement.

During the heyday of TV, Corning's organization was decentralized. The operating divisions had considerable control over marketing and manufacturing decisions, and corporate staffs in these areas were relatively small. Only in research and development did corporate staff personnel play a major role in the direction of the company. The Technical Staffs Division was responsible for all research and development activities, as well as for manufacturing engineering. New products were regarded as the lifeblood of the corporation, and the director of new product development, Harvey Blackburn, had built a creative and energetic staff. It was Blackburn's group that developed the glass-forming process that made TV tube production

possible, and it was to this group that the corporation looked when growth in the TV division and other consumer products began to slow in the late 1960s.

Changes in TV and Corporate Reorganization

The critical year for the TV division at Corning was 1968. Up to that point, sales and profits had grown rapidly, and Corning had carved out a substantial share of the market. In 1968, however, RCA (a major Corning customer) opened a plant in Ohio to produce glass funnels and front plates. Several of the engineering and management personnel at the new RCA plant were former Corning employees. RCA's decision to integrate backward into glass production had a noticeable effect on the performance of the TV division. Although the business remained profitable, growth over the next three years was much less rapid, and Corning's market share declined.

Slower growth in TV in the 1969–72 period coincided with reduced profitability in other consumer products as costs for labor and basic materials escalated sharply. These developments resulted in weaker corporate financial performance and prompted a reevaluation of the basic direction of the company.

The outcome of these deliberations was a reemphasis of the technical competence of the company in new project development and a focus on process excellence and productivity. A major step in the new approach to operations and production was the establishment of the Manufacturing and Engineering Division (M&E) at the corporate level. This reorganization brought together staff specialists in processes, systems, and equipment under the direction of David Leibson, who was promoted from the job of director of manufacturing at the TV division and was named a corporate vice president.

Shortly after the M&E Division was formed, Thomas MacAvoy, who was the general manager of the Electronics Division and the former director of physical research on Corning's technical staff, was named president of the company. MacAvoy was the first Corning president in recent times with a technical background; he had a PhD in chemistry and a strong record in research and development. An internal staff memorandum summed up the issues facing Corning under MacAvoy:

> Our analysis of productivity growth at Corning from 1960 to 1970 shows that we per-

formed no better than the average for other glass products manufacturers (2–4 percent per year) and in the last two years have actually been below average. With prices on the increase, improved productivity growth is imperative. At the same time, we have to improve our ability to exploit new products. It appears that research output has, if anything, increased in the last few years (Z-Glass is a prime example), but we have to do a much better job of transferring products from the lab into production.

The Manufacturing and Engineering Division

Much of the responsibility for improved productivity and the transfer of technology (either product or process) from research to production fell to the new and untried M&E division. Because of the company's historical preference for a small, relatively inactive manufacturing staff, building the M&E group into a strong and effective organization was a considerable challenge. Looking back on the early days, David Leibson reflected on his approach.

I tried to do two things in the first year:

1. Attract people with very strong technical skills in the basic processes and disciplines in use at Corning; and
2. Establish a working relationship with the manufacturing people in the operating divisions. I think the thing that made the difference in that first year was the solid support we got from Tom MacAvoy. It was made clear to all of the division general managers that productivity growth and cost reduction were top priorities.

From 1972 to 1977 engineers from the M&E division were involved in numerous projects throughout Corning involving the installation of new equipment and process changes. A typical project might involve four to five M&E engineers working with a plant organization to install a new type of conveyor system, possibly one designed in the M&E division. The installation project might last three to four months, and the M&E team would normally serve as consultants thereafter.

In addition to equipment products and internal consulting, the M&E group became involved in the transfer of products from R&D to production. After laboratory development and prototype testing, new products were assigned to an M&E product team which took responsibility for the design of any new equipment required and for engineering and implementing the new process. Leibson felt that successful transfer required people who appreciated both the development process and the problems of production. In many respects M&E product teams served as mediators and translators; especially in the first few projects, their primary task was to establish credibility with R&D group and with the manufacturing people in the operating divisions.

By 1976, the M&E division had conducted projects and helped to transfer new products in most of Corning's divisions, although its role in industrial products was still quite limited. The manufacturing organization in that division had been relatively strong and independent, but Leibson felt that the reputation and expertise of his staff was increasing and that opportunities for collaboration were not far off. He also felt that M&E was ready to take on a completely new kind of responsibility: a turnaround project. From time to time parts of a production process, even whole plants, would experience a deterioration in performance. In some instances, these situations would last for several months and could have serious competitive consequences. It was Leibson's view that a concentrated application of engineering expertise could shorten the turnaround time significantly and could have a measurable impact on overall corporate productivity.

The Z-Glass Project

The opportunity for M&E involvement in a major turnaround effort and for collaboration with the Industrial Products division came in late 1977. Since June of that year, yields on the Z-Glass process at the division's Harrisburg plant had experienced a sharp decline (see Exhibit 1). Substantial effort on the part of the plant organization failed to change the downward drift in yields, and in October, Oliver Williams, director of manufacturing for industrial products, met with David Leibson to establish an M&E project at Harrisburg.

Williams, a chemical engineer with an MBA from NYU, had been named director of manufacturing in November of 1976, after 18 years of experience in various engineering and operations positions at Corning. He felt that the importance of the product (corporate expectations for Z-Glass were very high) and the seriousness of the problem warranted strong measures.

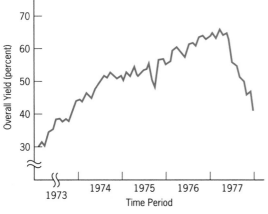

Exhibit 1: Overall Yield 1973–1977

The agreement he worked out with Leibson called for an M&E project team to work in the plant under the general supervision of a Review Board composed of Leibson, Williams, Martin Abramson, head of process engineering in the M&E division, and Bill Chenevert, head of M&E equipment development group. (See Exhibit 2 for an organization chart.) The team's charter was to increase yields, define and document the process and train the operating people (see Exhibit 3). A budget, the size of the team, specific goals, and timetable were to be developed in the first month of the team's operation.

While the plant manager and his staff had not been involved in the decision to bring in the M&E team, Williams and Leibson agreed that their involvement and support were essential. A decision was made to allocate all M&E charges to the Industrial Products division in order to relieve the plant of the extra overhead expense. Moreover, M&E specialists assigned to the project would be located in the plant on a full-time basis.

Since this was M&E's first turnaround project, Leibson was personally involved in the selection of the team leader and key project engineers. He had no trouble finding people willing to work on the project. It was clear to everyone in the M&E group that "turnarounds" were the next major activity for the group and that those working on the first team would be breaking a lot of new ground. Leibson chose Eric Davidson to lead the Harrisburg project. He was 32 years old, had a masters degree in mechanical engineering from Cornell, and six years of experience at Corning. Davidson had completed several projects in the M&E division, including one in France, and had also worked as an assistant plant manager. A close friend and colleague commented on Davidson's reputation:

> To say that Eric is on the fast track is a bit of an understatement. He has been given one challenging assignment after another and has been very successful. The word around M&E is that if you have a tough problem you want solved, just give it to Eric and get out of the way.

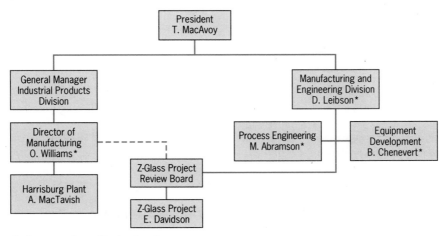

*Indicates members of Review Board.

Exhibit 2: Organization Chart

MEMORANDUM

To: E. Davidson E. D.   November 24, 1977
From: Harrisburg project team
Re: Team charter

    The charter of the project team is yield improvement as a top priority, definition and documentation of the process, and operator training. Enclosed is a copy of the proposed Process Definition and Documentation Program; it will serve as the framework for process diagnosis and control. Its main elements are as follows:

Priority

1. Define best known *operating setpoint* for each major variable.

2. Establish auditing system to track variables daily with built-in feedback loop.

3. Develop and implement *process troubleshooting* guides.

4. Write and implement *Operating Procedures*.

5. *Train* operating personnel in procedure usage.

6. *Audit* operating procedures on random frequency.

7. Write and implement *Machine Specification Procedures*.

Your comments on the program are encouraged.

Exhibit 3

    Working under Leibson's direction, Davidson spent the first two weeks of his assignment meeting with the plant management and selecting members of the M&E team. At the outset, he chose four specialists to work on the first phase of the project—data collection and problem definition:

    Richard Grebwell: 35 years old, an expert in statistical process analysis with 10 years of experience at Corning. While Grebwell was considered by some to be a bit eccentric, his characteristically brilliant use of statistical analysis was vital to the project.

    Jennifer Rigby: 28 years old, with a master's degree in industrial engineering from the University of Texas. She had worked in the Harrisburg plant for six months on her first assignment at Corning.

    Arthur Hopkins: 40 years old, a mechanical engineer with 12 years of Corning experience. Hopkins had worked with Davidson on the French project and was, in Davidson's words, a "wizard with equipment."

    Frank Arnoldus: 37 years old, a chemist with Corning for six years. He also had worked on the French project and had earned Davidson's admiration for his ability to solve processing problems.

    Davidson's plan for the first two to three weeks was to use the small group to identify problems and then expand the team as specific tasks and subprojects were established. His objectives were focused on the long term:

    I'm after increases in yields as soon as we can get them, but what I'm really shooting for is permanent improvements in the process. To do what we've go to do to define the process and document its operation. My whole approach is based on the idea of "receivership": whatever solutions we come up with have to be received, or accepted, by the plant organization. And I mean really accepted; they have to "own" the changes. That's why I will be taking a team approach—each project we do will have two co-leaders, one from M&E (the transferer) and one from the plant (the receiver).

    After a brief period to get acquainted and develop a plan, Davidson and his M&E team began working in the plant on December 10, 1977.

Z-Glass: Product and Process

Z-Glass was Corning's code name for a multilayered, compression-molded glass product which was exceptionally strong and impact-resistant for its weight. Its durability and hardness, combined with its low weight and competitive cost, made it an attractive substitute for ceramic and plastic products used in the construction and auto industries. Introduced in 1973, Z-Glass products were an immediate success. From 1973 to 1977 production capacity grew 35 to 40 percent per year and still had failed to keep up with demand (see Exhibit 4). Many people thought that the current array of products was only the beginning of Z-Glass applications.

To Corning's knowledge, no other company in the world had yet developed the capability to make a product like Z-Glass, and if one did, it was assumed that they would have to license the technology from Corning. In fact, much of this technology was still an artform in the sense that a number of the characteristics of most Z-Glass products were not completely explainable in terms of known glass technology: people knew what it could do and roughly why it could do it but were still utilizing trial-and-error methods to perfect existing products and develop new ones.

Z-Glass had been developed by Harvey Blackburn and his staff during the early 1970s. In every sense of the word, the product was Blackburn's "baby." He not only conceived of the idea, but typical of the way Corning operated before the M&E division was created, he and his staff solved numerous technical problems, built all the machinery and equipment needed for prototype production, and even worked in the plant during startup. Furthermore, Blackburn had championed the product in discussions with top management. Several times when the project was not going well, his reputation and skills of persuasion were

what kept funding going. When yields began to fall in 1977, engineers at Harrisburg had consulted Blackburn on an ad hoc basis; he still felt responsible for the product and was a walking encyclopedia of information on its nuances and subtleties.

The Process

The production of Z-Glass products consisted of three main steps: melting, molding, and finishing, which were closely linked and had to be carried out in a fixed time sequence. The process required precise control over the composition and thicknesses of the various glass layers, as well as careful timing and monitoring during the molding and finishing operations. Maintaining this precision in a high-volume environment required continuous, tight controls as well as a "feel" for the process.

Melting

The first step was the preparation of the different types of molten glass which composed the various layers. These mixtures were prepared in separate electrically heated vats, which were designed and built by Corning. Each vat had to be carefully monitored to ensure that the ingredients of the glass were in correct proportion, distributed evenly throughout the vat, and at the appropriate temperature.

The "base" layer was poured continuously onto a narrow (two–three foot) moving strip. The outer layers were poured on top of each other at precisely controlled intervals so that when the layered strip arrived at the molding stage each layer of the multilayered

	Z1*		Z4†		Z10		Z35		Z12		Total	
	Pieces	Amount	Pieces	Amount	Pieces	Amount	Pieces	Amount	Pieces	Amount	Pieces	Amount
1973	—	—	—	—	119	$2,220.1	495	$5,217.8	—	—	614	$ 7,431.9
1974	—	—	—	—	232	4,315.2	549	6,313.5	—	—	781	10,628.7
1975	384	$ 5,161.5	—	—	239	4,983.2	552	6,513.6	—	—	1,175	16,658.3
1976	784	11,514.2	45	$ 552.3	268	5,831.9	591	7,541.7	82	$1,213.2	1,770	26,653.3
1977	803	12,005.0	407	5,372.4	264	6,087.6	671	8,689.5	534	8,410.5	2,679	40,565.0
1978‡	171	2,565.1	35	493.5	145	1,957.5	250	2,975.2	61	988.3	662	8,979.6

*Introduced in early 1975.

†Introduced in late 1976.

‡Data for 1978 cover reporting periods 1–3 (i.e., first 12 weeks of 1978). Note that because of seasonal factors it is not possible to arrive at an accurate indication of annual output of a particular product by multiplying the 1978 (1–3) results by 13/3.

Exhibit 4: Harrisburg Plant Sales by Product Line 1973–1978 (000s)

glass sandwich was at the proper temperature and thickness for molding. Minor (and, at the beginning of process development, almost unmeasurable) deviations from the "recipe" could lead to major problems, which often could be solved only on an ad hoc basis utilizing the unprogrammable skill of the operators and technicians.

Some of these problems were clearly identifiable with the melting operations. For example, the existence of "blisters" (tiny bubbles in one or more of the glass layers), "stones" (unmelted bits of sand), and "streaks" (imperfectly melted or mixed ingredients) were observable visually and were obvious indicators of problems. Separation of the different layers, either after the molding or finishing operations, often could also be traced to improper execution during melting. But when the glass sandwich did not mold properly, there was usually some question as to which operation was at fault.

A process engineer explained the difficulty of melting control:

> The secret to avoiding problems at the melting state is maintaining its stability. Sometimes it's easy to tell when something has gone wrong there, but more often you don't find out until something goes wrong at a later stage. And usually it takes a long time to determine whether you've really solved the problem or are simply treating a symptom of a larger problem. It's tough to keep on top of what is going on in each of those melting vats because it's largely a chemical operation.

Despite the difficulty of maintaining control over the melting operation and of correcting it when problems developed, Corning had been able to achieve yields of as high as 95 percent at this stage of the process.

Molding

In contrast to melting, molding was basically a physical operation: rectangles of the soft glass sandwich were cut off the moving strip and moved onto a series of separated conveyor belts. Each slab was inserted between the jaws of a compression-molding device which contained a number of molds for the particular parts being produced. After the parts were stamped out, they continued down the conveyor line while the glass trim was discarded. Depending on the product

mix, several conveyors might pool their contents before the parts entered the finishing stage.

Despite the apparent simplicity of this process (problems could be detected quickly and usually corrected quickly), so many different kinds of problems arose and so many different variables could be manipulated that it was generally considered to be even more of a problem to control this stage than the melting stage. Typical problems included the basic dimensional specifications of the product, its edge configuration, and "buckling" and "flattening" after molding. The occurrence of these problems, together with machine downtime associated both with correcting problems and changing the product mix, made it difficult to achieve more than an 80 percent efficiency (good output to rated machine capacity) during this stage of the process.

Finishing

The finishing operation consisted of heat treating the molded objects, then applying one of a variety of possible coatings to them. Heat treating both stabilized the internal tensions generated by the molding operation and appeared to improve the lamination between the various layers of the glass sandwich as well. Since it required a precise sequence of temperatures and their duration, this operation took place while the objects passed through long ovens on their conveyor belts. It usually did not present a problem, but if cracks or layer separation occurred, the heat-treating operation was sometimes the cause.

The application of coatings, on the other hand, was more of a job-shop operation and could be done off-line. There were a number of possible kinds of coatings that could be applied, from either purely practical (improving the reflective, insulating, or electrical conducting properties of surface) to purely ornamental. Sometimes decals were also applied either in place of or in addition to a coating. The number of possible coatings was steadily increasing, and one process engineer characterized the process as "a continual bother: lots of short runs but a necessity to maintain high speeds." The target yield was 95 percent, but it was seldom attained.

The differing characteristics of the three stages made overall control and fine-tuning of the total process quite difficult. The backgrounds and skills of the "hot end" workers were very different from those at the "cold end," and completely different branches of engineering were involved. When problems arose, many of them were undetectable for some time and often only showed up during destructive testing of parts after they had proceeded completely through the process. Then it was often difficult to isolate which part of the process was at fault because there appeared to be a high degree of interrelation between them. And finally, once a problem and its cause were identified, it sometimes took a long period of trial-and-error fiddling until people could be convinced that it was indeed corrected.

The Harrisburg Plant

The decision to put Z-Glass into the Harrisburg plant had been based on its availability. Long devoted to the production of headlights and other auto products (the plant was built in 1958), the plant had experienced several years of excess capacity in the late 1960s. In 1972, headlight production was consolidated in the Farwell, Ohio, plant, and Harrisburg was set up for Z-Glass production. Several of the production foremen and manufacturing staff members were transferred to Farwell and replaced by individuals who had been involved in Z-Glass prototype production. (Exhibit 5 contains a profit and loss statement for the Harrisburg plant in 1975–76.)

The plant manager at Harrisburg was Andrew MacTavish, a 54-year-old native of Scotland. He came

	1976	1977
Sales*	$26,653.3	$40,565.0
Direct expenses		
Materials	9,947.2	16,214.2
Labor	3,714.3	6,194.7
Gross profit	12,991.8	18,156.1
Manufacturing overhead		
Fixed[†]	6,582.6	11,016.9
Variable[‡]	1,429.3	2,114.4
Plant administrative expenses	1,784.5	2,715.2
Plant profit	$ 3,195.4	$ 2,219.6

*Capacity utilization (on a nominal sales basis) was 92 percent in 1976 and 84 percent in 1977.

[†]Includes depreciation, insurance, taxes, maintenance, utilities, and supervision.

[‡]Includes fringe benefits, indirect labor and tools, and supplies.

Exhibit 5: Z-Glass Project, Harrisburg Plant Profit and Loss Statement, 1976–77 ($000)

to the United States shortly after World War II and began working at Corning as a helper on a shipping crew at the old main plant. Over the years, MacTavish had worked his way up through various supervisory positions to production superintendent and finally to plant manager. He was a large man with a ruddy complexion and a deep booming voice. Although his temper was notorious, most people who had worked with him felt that some of his notorious tirades were more than a little calculated. Whatever peoples' perceptions of his personality might be, there was no question as to who was in charge at Harrisburg.

In mid-1977 MacTavish had been at Harrisburg for six years. From the beginning he had developed a reputation as a champion of the "little people," as he called them. He wore what the workers wore and spent two to three hours each day on the factory floor talking with foremen, supervisors, and production workers. If he had a philosophy of plant operations, it was to keep management as close to the people as possible and to rely on the experience, judgment, and skill of his workers in solving problems.

The Harrisburg plant was organized along department lines, with a production superintendent responsible for three general foremen who managed the melting, forming, and finishing departments. Ron Lewis, production superintendent, had come to the plant in 1975 after eight years of Corning experience. He was quietly efficient and had developed a good rapport with the foremen and supervisors. Besides Lewis, three other managers reported to MacTavish: Al Midgely, director of maintenance and engineering; Arnie Haggstrom, director of production planning and inventory control; and Royce Ferguson, head of personnel.

By June of 1977 the management group at the Harrisburg plant had worked together for two years and had established what MacTavish thought was a solid organization. Speaking to a visitor in May of 1977 he commented:

> I've seen a lot of plant organizations in my time, but this one has worked better than any of them. When we sit down in staff meetings every morning, everyone is on top of their situation, and we've learned to get to the heart of our problems quickly. With the different personalities around here you'd think it would be a dogfight, but these people really work together.

Of all the managers on his staff, MacTavish worked most closely with Al Midgely. Midgely, 46 years old, had come to the plant with MacTavish, had a B.S. in mechanical engineering, and was regarded as a genius when it came to equipment ("He can build or fix anything," MacTavish claimed). He was devoted to MacTavish:

> Ten years ago, Andy MacTavish saved my life. I had some family problems after I lost my job at Bausch and Lomb, but Andy gave me a chance and helped me pick up the pieces. Everything I have I owe to him.

Several other people in the Harrisburg plant gratefully acknowledge MacTavish's willingness to help his people.

The M&E Project at Harrisburg

Davidson's first priority in the first two weeks of the project was to define the problem. Overall yields had declined, but there had been no analysis of available information to identify the major causes. It seemed clear to the M&E group that the plant organization had spent its time on firefighting during the past six months, and there had been little overall direction. Richard Grebwell concerned himself with analyzing the historical data collected by the production control

department. The rest of the team spent the first two weeks familiarizing themselves with the process, meeting with their counterparts in the plant organization, and meeting together to compare notes and develop hypotheses about what was going on.

One problem surfaced immediately: the relative inexperience of the department supervisors. As MacTavish explained to them, four of the six supervisors had been in the plant less than nine months. The people they replaced had been with the Z-Glass process since its prototype days. MacTavish felt that part of the explanation for the decline in yields was the departure of people who knew and understood the process extremely well. He expressed confidence in the new people and indicated that they were rapidly becoming quite knowledgeable.

Grebwell's preliminary statistical work (see Exhibit 6) pointed to the molding department as the primary source of defects, with finishing the second major source. The team identified four areas for immediate attention: overall downtime, trim settings, glass adhesion and layer separation. As Grebwell's work proceeded, other projects in other departments were identified, and additional staff members were added to the team. By the middle of January it was evident that the overall project would have to encom-

---

MEMORANDUM

To: M&E Project Team
From: R. Grebwell
Re: Yield report for December 1977

Below are data on yields in period 13 (provided by the production control department) along with notes based on preliminary observations. Rejects are based on 100 percent inspection. Note that selecting a reason for rejection is based on the concept of "principal cause"—if more than one defect is present, the inspector must designate one as the primary reason for rejection.

Harrisburg Plant
Yield Report Period 13, 1977

	Good Output as a Percent of Rated Capacity[a]					Downtime[b] as a Percent of Total Available Time
	Z1	Z4	Z10	Z35	Z12	
I. Melting:						
Glass	70.4	65.4	72.3	73.5	66.9	—
Equipment downtime	—	—	—	—	—	10.3

Exhibit 6

	Percent Rejected by Product, Reason, and Department[c]					Downtime[b] as a Percent of total Available Time
	Z1	**Z4**	**Z10**	**Z35**	**Z12**	
II. Molding and finishing:						
A. Molding						
Trim[d]	6.4	12.8	4.1	3.4	10.2	—
Structural	3.7	6.2	1.7	2.8	5.7	—
Adhesion	4.5	8.3	2.5	3.1	8.5	—
Downtime	—	—	—	—	—	15.2
B. Finishing						
Cracks	0.8	4.2	.03	1.2	3.6	—
Separation	2.6	3.8	1.5	2.2	4.4	—
Coatings	1.9	2.4	0.6	1.7	2.1	—
Downtime	—	—	—	—	—	12.6

	Good Output as a Percent of Rated Capacity					
	Z1	**Z4**	**Z10**	**Z35**	**Z12**	**Total**
III. Summary[e]:						
Melting	70.4	65.4	72.3	73.5	66.9	—
Molding	72.4	61.6	77.8	76.9	64.1	—
Finishing	82.8	78.3	85.3	82.9	78.6	—
Overall	42.2	31.5	48.0	46.9	33.7	40.7

[a]This is overall yield and includes the effects of glass defects as well as downtime.

[b]No data are available on equipment downtime by product; the overall figure is applied to each product.

[c]The data are presented by department. They indicate the percentage of *department* output rejected and the principal reason for rejection. Total overall process yield (good output as a percent of rated capacity) depends on both product defects and downtime.

[d]The reasons for rejection breakdown as follows:

Molding:

Trim: This is basically two things—dimensions and edge configuration. It looks to me like the biggest problem is with the edges. The most common cause of defects in the runs I have watched is that the settings drift out of line. Apparently this depends on where the settings are established, how they are adjusted, and the quality of the glass.

Structural: Pieces are rejected if they buckle or if the surface has indentations. This one is a real mystery—it could be a problem with the equipment (not right specs) or the operating procedures. Without some testing it's hard to tell. One possibility we need to check is whether the temperature of the incoming glass is a factor.

Adhesion: If compression ratios are too low or if the glass temperature is not "just right" or the glass has stones, then the glass adheres to the surface of the molds. The operators check the ratios, but the ideal range is marked on the gauges with little bits of tape, and I suspect the margin of error is pretty large.

Finishing:

Cracks: Pieces sometimes develop cracks after heat treating. The principal suspect is consistency of temperature and flame zone. It is very hard to tell whether this is due to poor initial settings or changes in flames once the process starts. Inconsistencies in the material may be another source of cracks.

Layer separation: Layer separation seems to be caused by same factors as cracks.

Castings: This is almost entirely a problem of operator error—handling damage, poor settings on the equipment, inattention to equipment going out of spec, and so forth.

[e]There are four steps to calculating overall yield:

1. For a given product in a given department, add up reject rates by reason and subtract from 1.

Exhibit 6 (*continued*)

2. Then multiply by (1 – percent downtime) to get department yield for that product (e.g., molding yield for Z12 = (1 – .244) (1 – .152) = .641).
3. Multiply department yields to get overall yield by product (e.g., yield for Z12 = .669 × .641 × .786 = .337).
4. To get overall yield, take a weighted average of product yields, with share in total output (on a total-pieces basis) as weights: in period 13 these weights were Z1 = .3, Z4 = .15, Z10 = .10, Z35 = .25, and Z12 = .2.

Exhibit 6 (*continued*)

pass activities throughout the plant. It was decided that the only way to measure performance equitably was to use overall yield improvement. A timetable for improved yields was established and approved by the Review Board in late January of 1978.

Davidson commented on the first six weeks of the project:

> Our initial reception in the plant was luke-warm. People were a little wary of us at first, but we did establish a pretty good relationship with Ron Lewis and some of the people in the production control group. I was confident that with time we could work together with MacTavish and people in other departments, but I wasn't as confident that the problems themselves could be solved. My objective was to obtain long-term improvements by defining and documenting the process, but when I arrived I found an inadequate data base and a process more complex than anyone had imagined.

Davidson also found resistance to the very idea of process documentation. The view of MacTavish and other people in the plant was aptly summarized by Harvey Blackburn, who appeared in Harrisburg off and on throughout the first three months of the M&E project. On one such visit he took Davidson into a conference room and had the following conversation:

Blackburn (after drawing on the blackboard): Do you know what this is? This is a corral and inside the corral is a bucking bronco. Now what do you suppose this is?

Davidson: It looks like a cowboy with a book in his hand.

Blackburn: That's right, sonny, it's a greenhorn cowboy trying to learn how to ride a bucking bronco by reading a book. And that's just what you are trying to do with all your talk about documentation. And you'll end right where the greenhorn is going to end up; flat on your face.

The Emergence of Conflict

Following the Review Board's acceptance of the proposed timetable, it was Davidson's intent to create subproject teams, with an M&E specialist and a plant representative as co-leaders. Despite Blackburn's lecture, Davidson pressed ahead with plans for process definition and documentation. A key element of the program was the development of instrumentation to collect information on the critical operating variables (glass temperature, machine speeds, timing, and so forth). Beginning in early January, Frank Arnoldus had spent three weeks quietly observing the process, asking questions of the operators, and working on the development of instruments. He had decided to debug and confirm the systems on one production line (there were five separate lines in the plant) before transferring the instruments to other lines.

The instrumentation project was scheduled to begin on February 1, with the installation of sensors to monitor glass temperature in the molding process. However, no plant representative for the project had been designated by that time, and Davidson postponed the installation. A series of meetings between Davidson and MacTavish then followed, but it was not until two days before the next Review Board meeting on February 23 that plant representatives for each subproject were chosen. Even then, things did not go smoothly. Frank Arnoldus described his experience:

> I didn't want to impose the instrumentation program on the people; I wanted them to understand that it was a tool to help them do their jobs better. But I had a terrible time getting Hank Gordel (the co-leader of the project team) to even talk to me. He claimed he was swamped with other things. The thing of it is, he *was* busy. The plant engineering group had several projects of their own going, and those people were working 15 hours a day. But I knew there was more to it than that when people stopped talking to me and even avoided me in elevators and the cafeteria.

The other subprojects suffered a similar fate. The only team to make any progress was the group working on materials control. Ron Lewis thought the program was a good one, and he supported it; he had appointed one of his better supervisors to be co-leader. In the other areas of the plant, however, little was ac-

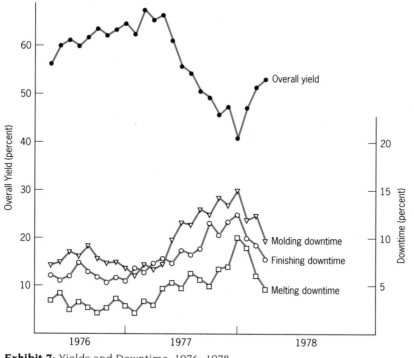

Exhibit 7: Yields and Downtime, 1976–1978

complished. Attempts to deal with people in the plant organization on an informal basis (lunch, drinks after work) were not successful, and Davidson's meetings with MacTavish and his requests for support were not fruitful. Indeed, it was MacTavish's view that the M&E team was part of the problem. His view was expressed forcefully in a meeting with Davidson in late March of 1978:

> I've said right from the beginning that this yield problem is basically a people problem. My experienced production people were promoted out from under me, and it has taken a few months for the new people to get up to speed. But this kind of thing is not going to happen again. I've been working on a supervisor backup training program that will give me some bench strength.
>
> I'm not saying we don't have problems. I know there are problems with the process, but the way to solve them is to get good people and give them some room. What this process needs now is some stability. Last year two new products were introduced, and this year I've got you

and your engineers out there with your experiments and your projects, fiddling around with my equipment and bothering my people.

> And then there's Blackburn. He blows in here with some crazy idea and goes right out there on the floor and gets the operators to let him try out his latest scheme. The best thing for this plant right now would be for all of you to just get out and let us get this place turned around.
>
> I am convinced we can do it. In fact, we've already been doing it. You've seen the data for the last 12 weeks.[*] Yields have been increasing steadily, and we're now above average for last year. While you people have been making plans and writing memos, we've been solving the problem.

Resolving the Crisis

Eric Davidson sat at his desk in the Harrisburg plant on March 24, 1978, and reviewed the events of the last

---

[*]Data from the preliminary yield report are presented in Exhibits 7 and 8.

Department	Product Lines					
	Z1	Z4	Z10	Z35	Z12	Total
Melting	74.6	69.3	76.6	77.9	70.9	—
Molding	79.7	71.3	83.5	83.8	72.4	—
Finishing	85.8	83.7	88.7	87.6	84.9	—
Overall	51.0	41.4	56.7	57.2	43.6	53.4

Exhibit 8: Harrisburg Plant Summary of Yields, Period 3, 1978

three months. He realized that he also had been guilty of excessive firefighting and had not taken the time to step back from the situation and plot out a course of action. The situation demanded careful thought.

He was genuinely puzzled by the recent improvement in yield performance; since the M&E team had done very little beyond data analysis, the improvement must have come from somewhere else. All his training and experience supported the concept of definition and documentation, but he had never encountered such a complex process. Perhaps MacTavish was right . . . but he just couldn't bring himself to believe that.

Several options came to mind as he thought of ways to resolve the crisis; none of them were appealing. He could go to Leibson and Williams and ask (demand?) that MacTavish be replaced with someone more supportive. He could continue to try to build alliances with supporters in the plant (there were a few such people) and get a foothold in the organization. Or he could develop a new approach to the problem (perhaps new people?) and attempt to win over MacTavish. Davidson knew that his handling of this situation could have important consequences for the M&E Division, for the company, and for the careers of several people, including his own.

QUESTIONS

1. Analyze the decline in yields to determine their cause.

2. Evaluate Davidson's approach to his assignment from Leibson's point of view.

3. Explain MacTavish's reaction to Davidson.

4. Analyze Davidson's position. What should he do now?

5. Is the M&E idea a viable concept? Is it needed?

This article reports on a study of hundreds of project managers and the challenges and barriers they perceived in successfully controlling projects. The potential problems leading to schedule slips and budget overruns are identified and compared to the directly observed reasons. Also, the general managers' reasons for the slips and overruns are compared to the project managers' reasons and significant differences are noted. Last, the criteria that seem to be important to control are listed and discussed.

The value of this article for managers is the insight it gives concerning what needs to be controlled to bring about successful projects. The major factors are defining a detailed project plan that includes all key project personnel, reaching agreement on the plan among the project team members and the customer, obtaining the commitment of management, defining measurable milestones, and detecting problems early.

READING

CRITERIA FOR CONTROLLING PROJECTS ACCORDING TO PLAN
Hans J. Thamhain
David L. Wilemon

Introduction

Few project managers would argue the need for controlling their projects according to established plans.

The challenge is to apply the available tools and techniques effectively. That is, to manage the effort by leading the multifunctional personnel toward the agreed-on objectives within the given time and resource constraints. Even the most experienced practitioners often find it difficult to control programs in spite of apparent detail in the plan, personnel involvement, and even commitment. As summarized in Table 1, effective program management is a function of properly defining the work, budgets, and schedules and then monitoring progress. Equally important, it is related to the ability to keep personnel involved and interested in the work, to obtain and refuel commitment from the team as well as from upper management, and to resolve some of the enormous complexities on the technical, human, and organizational side.

Responding to this interest, a field study was initiated to investigate the practices of project managers regarding their project control experiences. Specifically, the study investigates:

1. Type of project control problems experienced by project managers.
2. Project management practices and performance.
3. Criteria for effective project control.

Method of Investigation

Data were collected over a period of three years from a sample of over 400 project leaders in predominantly technical undertakings, such as electronics, petrochemical, construction, and pharmaceutical projects. The data were collected mostly by questionnaires from attendees of project management workshops and seminars, as well as during inplant consulting work conducted by the authors. Selectively, questionnaires were followed up by personal interviews. All data were checked for relevent sourcing to assure that the people who filled in the questionnaire had the minimum project leadership qualifications we established. These included: two years of experience in managing multidisciplinary projects, leading a minimum of three other project professionals, and being formally accountable for final results.

Sample Characteristics

The final qualifying sample included 304 project leaders from 183 technical projects. The leaders had an average of 5.2 years of project management experience. As shown by the sigma/standard deviation[1] the sample data are distributed widely:

Number of Project Leaders in Sample	304
Number of Projects in Sample	183
Number of Project Leaders per Project	1.66 ($\sigma = 1$)
Project Size (Average)	$850K ($\sigma = 310K$)
Project Duration (Average)	12 Months ($\sigma = 4$)
Multidisciplinary Nature (Average)	8 Team Members ($\sigma = 5$)
Project Management Experience/PM	5.2 Years ($\sigma = 2.5$)
Number of Previous Projects/PM	6 ($\sigma = 4.5$)

Data were collected in three specific modes: (1) Open-ended questions leading to a broad set of data, such as condensed in Table 2, and used for broad classifications and further, more detailed investigations; (2) Specific questions, requested to be answered on a tested five-point scale, such as shown in Figure 1. The scores enabled subsequent data ranking and correlation analysis; and (3) Interviews leading to a discussion of the previous findings and further qual-

Table 1 Challenges of Managing Projects According to Plan

Rank	Challenge	Frequency (Mentioned by % of PMs)
1	Coping with End-Date Driven Schedules	85%
2	Coping with Resource Limitations	83%
3	Communicating Effectively among Task Groups	80%
4	Gaining Commitment from Team Members	74%
5	Establishing Measurable Milestones	70%
6	Coping with Changes	60%
7	Working Out Project Plan Agreement with Team	57%
8	Gaining Commitment from Management	45%
9	Dealing with Conflict	42%
10	Managing Vendors and Subcontractors	38%
11	Other Challenges	35%

---

[1]The distribution of the sample data is skewed. The sigma/standard deviation listed in parentheses corresponds to the positive side only.

Rank by General Managers	Rank by Project Managers	Reason or Problem	Rarely 1 — Sometimes 2 — Often 3 — Most Likely 4 — Always 5	Agreement Between GM & PM
1	10	Insufficient Front-End Planning	PM ... GM	Disagree
2	3	Unrealistic Project Plan		Strongly Agree
3	8	Project Scope Underestimated		Disagree
4	1	Customer/Management Changes		Disagree
5	14	Insufficient Contingency Planning		Disagree
6	13	Inability to Track Progress	PM GM	Disagree
7	5	Inability to Detect Problems Early		Agree
8	9	Insufficient Number of Checkpoints		Agree
9	4	Staffing Problems		Disagree
10	2	Technical Complexities		Disagree
11	6	Priority Shifts		Disagree
12	10	No Commitment by Personnel to Plan		Agree
13	12	Uncooperative Support Groups		Agree
14	7	Sinking Team Spirit		Disagree
15	15	Unqualified Project Personnel		Agree

Figure 1: Directly observed reasons for schedule slips and budget overruns.

itative investigations into the practices and experiences of project managers and their superiors.

All associations were measured by utilizing Kendall's Tau rank-order correlation. The agreement between project managers and their superiors on the reason for project control problems was tested by using the nonparametric Kruskal-Wallis one-way analysis of variance by ranks, setting the null-hypothesis for agreement at various confidence levels depending on the strength of the agreement or disagreement as specified in the write-up.

Discussion of Results

The results of this study are being presented in four parts. First, the reasons for poor project control are analyzed as they relate to budget overruns and schedule slips. Second, the less tangible criteria for these control problems are discussed. This part shows that many of the reasons blamed for poor project performance, such as insufficient front-end planning and underestimating the complexities and scope, are really rooted in some less obvious organizational, managerial, and interpersonal problems. Third, the relationship between project performance and project management problems is discussed, and fourth, the criteria for effective project controls are summarized.

The Reasons for Poor Project Control Figure 1 summarizes an investigation into 15 problem areas regarding their effects on poor project performance. Specifically, project managers and their superiors (such as senior functional managers and general managers) indicate on a five-point scale their perception of how frequently certain problems are responsible for schedule slips and budget overruns. The data indicate that project leaders perceive these problem areas in a somewhat different order than their superiors.

While *project leaders* most frequently blame the following reasons as being responsible for poor project performance:

1. Customer and Management Changes
2. Technical Complexities
3. Unrealistic Project Plans

4. Staffing Problems

5. Inability to Detect Problems Early.

senior management ranks these reasons somewhat differently:

1. Insufficient Front-End Planning

2. Unrealistic Project Plans

3. Underestimated Project Scope

4. Customer and Management Changes

5. Insufficient Contingency Planning.

On balance, the data support the findings of subsequent interviews that project leaders are more concerned with external influences such as changes, complexities, staffing, and priorities while senior managers focus more on what should and can be done to avoid problems.

In fact, the differences between project leaders' and senior/superior management's perceptions were measured statistically by using a Kruskal-Wallis analysis of variance by ranks, based on the following test statistics:

Strong Agreement:	If acceptable at > 99% confidence
Agreement:	If acceptable at > 90% confidence
Weak Agreement:	If acceptable at > 80% confidence
Disagreement:	If rejected at 80% confidence

Project leaders disagree with their superiors on the ranking of importance for all but six reasons. What this means is that while both groups of management actually agree on the basic reasons behind schedule slips and budget overruns, they attach different weights. The practical implication of this finding is that senior management expects proper project planning, organizing, and tracking from project leaders. They further believe that the "external" criteria, such as customer changes and project complexities, impact project performance only if the project had not been defined properly and sound management practices were ignored. On the other side, management's view that some of the subtle problems, such as sinking team spirit, priority shifts, and staffing, are of lesser importance might point to a potential problem area. Management might be less sensitive to these struggles, get less involved, and provide less assistance in solving these problems.

Less Obvious and Less Visible Reasons for Poor Performance Managers at all levels have long lists of "real" reasons why the problems identified in Figure 1 occur. They point out, for instance, that while insufficient front-end planning eventually got the project into trouble, the real culprits are much less obvious and visible. These subtle reasons, summarized in Table 2, strike a common theme. They relate strongly to organizational, managerial, and human aspects. In fact, the most frequently mentioned reasons for poor project performance can be classified in five categories:

1. Problems with organizing project team

2. Weak project leadership

3. Communication problems

4. Conflict and confusion

5. Insufficient upper management involvement

Most of the problems in Table 2 relate to the manager's ability to foster a work environment conducive to multidisciplinary teamwork, rich in professionally stimulating and interesting activities, involvement, and mutual trust. The ability to foster such a high-performance project environment requires sophisticated skills in leadership, technical, interpersonal, and administrative areas. To be effective, project managers must consider all facets of the job. They must consider the task, the people, the tools, and the organization. The days of the manager who gets by with technical expertise or pure administrative skills alone, are gone. Today the project manager must relate socially as well as technically. He or she must understand the culture and value system of the organization. Research[2] and experience show that effective project management is directly related to the level of proficiency at which these skills are mastered. This is also reflected in the 30 potential problems of our study (see Table 2) and the rank-order correlations summarized in Table 3. As indicated by the correlation figure of $\tau = -.45$, the stronger managers felt about the

---

[2] For a detailed discussion of skill requirements of project managers and their impact on project performance see H. J. Thamhain & D. L. Wilemon, "Skill Requirements of Project Managers," *Convention Record*, IEEE Joint Engineering Management Conference, October 1978, and H. J. Thamhain, "Developing Engineering Management Skills" in *Management of R & D and Engineering*, North Holland Publishing Company, 1986.

Table 2 Potential Problems* (Subtle Reasons) Leading to Schedule Slips and Budget Overruns

01	Difficulty of Defining Work in Sufficient Detail
02	Little Involvement of Project Personnel During Planning
03	Problems with Organizing and Building Project Team
04	No Firm Agreement to Project Plan by Functional Management
05	No Clear Charter for Key Project Personnel
06	Insufficiently Defined Project Team Organization
07	No Clear Role/Responsibility Definition for P-Personnel
08	Rush into Project Kick-off
09	Project Perceived as Not Important or Exciting
10	No Contingency Provisions
11	Inability to Measure True Project Performance
12	Poor Communications with Upper Management
13	Poor Communications with Customer or Sponsor
14	Poor Understanding of Organizational Interfaces
15	Difficulty in Working across Functional Lines
16	No Ties between Project Performance and Reward System
17	Poor Project Leadership
18	Weak Assistance and Help from Upper Management
19	Project Leader Not Involved with Team
20	Ignorance of Early Warning Signals and Feedback
21	Poor Ability to Manage Conflict
22	Credibility Problems with Task Leaders
23	Difficulties in Assessing Risks
24	Insensitivity to Organizational Culture/Value System
25	Insufficient Formal Procedural Project Guidelines
26	Apathy or Indifference by Project Team or Management
27	No Mutual Trust among Team Members
28	Too Much Unresolved/Dysfunctional Conflict
29	Power Struggles
30	Too Much Reliance on Established Cost Accounting System

*The tabulated potential problems represent summaries of data compiled during interviews with project personnel and management.

Table 3 Correlation of Project Management Practices to Performance

Potential Problems vs. Actual	Correlation of (1) Potential Problems (Table 2) and (2) Directly Observed Reasons for Budget and Schedule Slips (Figure 1)	$\tau = -.45^*$
Potential Problems vs. Performance	Correlation of (1) Potential Problems Leading for Budget and Schedule Slips (Table 2) and (2) Project Performance (Top Management Judgment)	$\tau = -.55^*$
Actual Problems vs. Performance	Correlation of (1) Directly Observed Reasons for Budget and Schedule Slips (Figure 1) and (2) Project Performance	$\tau = -.40^*$

*99% Confidence Level (p = .01)

All Tau values are Kendall Tau Rank-Order Correlation

reasons in Figure 1, the stronger they also felt about the problems in Table 2 as reasons for poor project performance. This correlation is statistically signifi- cant at a confidence level of 99 percent and supports the conclusion that both sets of problem areas are re- lated and require similar skills for effective manage- ment.

Management Practice and Project Performance Managers appear very confident in citing actual and potential problems. These managers are sure in their own mind that these problems, summarized in Figure 1 and Table 2, are indeed related to poor project per- formance. However, no such conclusion could be drawn without additional data and the specific statis- tical test shown in Table 3. As indicated by the strongly negative correlations between project perfor- mance and (1) potential problems ($\tau = -.55$) and (2) actual problems ($\tau = -.40$), the presence of either problem will indeed result in lower performance. Specifically, the stronger and more frequently project managers experience these problems, the lower was the manager judged by superior managers regarding overall on-time and on-budget performance.

Furthermore, it is interesting to note that the more subtle potential problems correlate most strongly to poor performance ($\tau = -.55$). In fact, spe- cial insight has been gained by analyzing the associa- tion of each problem to project performance sepa- rately. Taken together, it shows that the following problems seem to be some of the most crucial *barriers* to high project performance:

- Team organization and staffing problems
- Work perceived as not important, challenging, having growth potential
- Little team and management involvement during planning
- Conflict, confusion, power struggle
- Lacking commitment by team and management
- Poor project definition
- Difficulty in understanding and working across organizational interfaces
- Weak project leadership
- Measurability problems
- Changes, contingencies, and priority problems
- Poor communications, management involvement and support

To be effective, project leaders must not only recognize the potential barriers to performance, but also know where in the life cycle of the project they most likely occur. The effective project leader takes preventive actions early in the project life cycle and fosters a work environment that is conducive to active participation, interesting work, good communications, management involvement, and low conflict.

Criteria for Effective Project Control

The results presented so far focused on the reasons for poor project performance. That is, what went wrong and why were analyzed. This section concentrates on the lessons learned from the study and extensive interviews investigating the forces driving high project performance. Accordingly, this section summarizes the criteria which seem to be important for controlling projects according to plan. The write-up follows a recommendations format and flows with the project through its life cycle wherever possible.

1. **Detailed Project Planning.** Develop a detailed project plan, involving all key personnel, defining the specific work to be performed, the timing, the resources, and the responsibilities.

2. **Break the Overall Program into Phases and Sub-**

systems. Use Work Breakdown Structure (WBS) as a planning tool.

3. **Results and Deliverables.** Define the program objectives and requirements in terms of specifications, schedule, resources and deliverable items for the total program and its subsystems.

4. **Measurable Milestones.** Define measurable milestones and checkpoints throughout the program. Measurability can be enhanced by defining specific results, deliverables, technical performance measures against schedule and budget.

5. **Commitment.** Obtain commitment from all key personnel regarding the problem plan, its measures and results. This commitment can be enhanced and maintained by involving the team members early in the project planning, including the definition of results, measurable milestones, schedules, and budgets. It is through this involvement that the team members gain a detailed understanding of the work to be performed, develop professional interests in the project and desires to succeed, and eventually make a firm commitment toward the specific task and the overall project objectives.

6. **Intra-Program Involvement.** Assure that the interfacing project teams, such as engineering and manufacturing, work together, not only during the task transfer, but during the total life of the project. Such interphase involvement is necessary to assure effective implementation of the developments and to simply assure "doability" and responsiveness to the realities of the various functions supporting the project. It is enhanced by clearly defining the results/deliverables for each interphase point, agreed upon by both parties. In addition, a simple sign-off procedure, which defines who has to sign off on what items, is useful in establishing clear checkpoints for completion and to enhance involvement and cooperation of the interphasing team members.

7. **Project Tracking.** Define and implement a proper project tracking system which captures and processes project performance data conveniently summarized for reviews and management actions.

8. **Measurability.** Assure accurate measurements of project performance data, especially technical progress against schedule and budget.

9. **Regular Reviews.** Project should be reviewed regularly, both on a work package (subsystem) level and total project level.

10. **Signing-On.** The process of "signing-on" project personnel during the initial phases of the project or each task seems to be very important to a proper understanding of the project objectives, the specific tasks, and personal commitment. The sign-on process that is so well described in Tracy Kidder's book, *The Soul of a New Machine*, is greatly facilitated by sitting down with each team member and discussing the specific assignments, overall project objectives, as well as professional interests and support needs.

11. **Interesting Work.** The project leader should try to accommodate the professional interests and desires of supporting personnel when negotiating their tasks. Project effectiveness depends on the manager's ability to provide professionally stimulating and interesting work. This leads to increased project involvement, better communications, lower conflict, and stronger commitment. This is an environment where people work toward established objectives in a self-enforcing mode requiring a minimum of managerial controls. Although the scope of a project may be fixed, the project manager usually has a degree of flexibility in allocating task assignments among various contributors.

12. **Communication.** Good communication is essential for effective project work. It is the responsibility of the task leaders and ultimately the project manager to provide the appropriate communication tools, techniques, and systems. These tools are not only the status meetings, reviews, schedules, and reporting systems, but also the objective statements, specifications, list of deliverables, the sign-off procedure and critical path analysis. It is up to the project leaders to orchestrate the various tools and systems, and to use them effectively.

13. **Leadership.** Assure proper program direction and leadership throughout the project life cycle. This includes project definition, team organization, task coordination, problem identification and a search for solutions.

14. **Minimize Threats.** Project managers must foster a work environment that is low on personal conflict, power struggles, surprises, and unrealistic demands. An atmosphere of mutual trust is necessary for project personnel to communicate problems and concerns candidly and at an early point in time.

15. **Design a Personnel Appraisal and Reward System.** This should be consistent with the responsibilities of the people.

16. **Assure Continuous Senior Management Involvement, Endorsement, and Support of the Project.** This will surround the project with a priority image, enhance its visibility, and refuel overall commitment to the project and its objectives.

17. **Personal Drive.** Project managers can influence the climate of the work environment by their own actions. Concern for project team members, ability to integrate personal goals and needs of project personnel with project goals, and ability to create personal enthusiasm for the project itself can foster a climate of high motivation, work involvement, open communication, and ultimately high project performance.

A Final Note

Managing engineering programs toward established performance, schedule, and cost targets requires more than just another plan. It requires the total commitment of the performing organization plus the involvement and help of the sponsor/customer community. Successful program managers stress the importance of carefully designing the project planning and control system as well as the structural and authority relationships. All are critical to the implementation of an effective project control system. Other organizational issues, such as management style, personnel appraisals and compensation, and intraproject communication, must be carefully considered to make the system self-forcing; that is, project personnel throughout the organization must feel that participation in the project is desirable regarding the fulfillment of their professional needs and wants. Furthermore, project personnel must be convinced that management involvement is helpful in their work. Personnel must be convinced that identifying the true project status and communicating potential problems early will provide them with more assistance to problem solving, more cross-functional support, and in the end will lead to project success and the desired recognition for their accomplishments.

In summary, effective control of engineering programs or projects involves the ability to:

- Work out a detailed project plan, involving all key personnel
- Reach agreement on the plan among the project team members and the customer/sponsor
- Obtain commitment from the project team members
- Obtain commitment from management
- Define measurable milestones
- Attract and hold quality people
- Establish a controlling authority for each work package
- Detect problems early

References

1. ADAMS, J. R., & S. E. BARNDT. "Behavioral Implications of the Project Life Cycle," Chapter 12 in D. D. Cleland and W. R. King, *Project Management Handbook*. New York: Van Nostrand Reinhold, 1983.
2. ARCHIBALD, Russel C. "Planning the Project." In *Managing High-Technology Programs and Projects*. New York: Wiley, 1976.
3. CASHER, J. D. "How to Control Project Risks and Effectively Reduce the Chance of Failure." *Management Review*, June, 1984.
4. DELANEY, W. A. "Management by Phases." *Advanced Management Journal*, Winter, 1984.
5. KING, W. R., & D. I. CLELAND. Life Cycle Management. Chapter 11 in D. D. Cleland and W. R. King, *Project Management Handbook*. New York: Van Nostrand Reinhold, 1983.
6. McDOUNOUGH, E. F., & R. M. KINNUNEN. "Management Control of a New Product Development Project." IEEE *Transactions on Engineering Management*, February 1984.
7. PESSEMIER, E. A. *Product Management*. New York: Wiley, 1982.
8. SPIRER, H. F. "Phasing Out the Project." Chapter 13 in D. D. Cleland and W. R. King, *Project Management Handbook*. New York: Van Nostrand Reinhold, 1983.
9. STUCKENBRUCK, L. C. "Interface Management." Chapter 20 in *Matrix Management Systems Handbook*. New York: Van Nostrand Reinhold, 1984.
10. THAMHAIN, H. J. *Engineering Program Management*. New York: Wiley, 1984.
11. THAMHAIN, H. J., & D. L. WILEMON. "Project Performance Measurement, The Keystone to Engineering Project Control." *Project Management Quarterly*, January 1982.
12. THAMHAIN, H. J., & D. L. WILEMON. "Conflict Management in Project Lifecycles." *Sloan Management Review*, Summer 1975.
13. TUMINELLO, J. A. "Case Study of Information/KnowHow Transfer." IEEE *Engineering Management Review*, June 1984.
14. URBAN, G. L., & J. R. HAUSER. *Design and Marketing of New Products*. Englewood Cliffs, NJ: Prentice-Hall, 1980.
15. U.S. Air Force. *Systems Management—System Program Office Manual*, AFSCM 375-3, Washington DC, 1964.

▶ III ◀

PROJECT TERMINATION, MULTICULTURAL PROJECTS, AND UNSOLVED PROBLEMS

The final part of the book addresses critical but often slighted aspects of project management: evaluation and termination. In Chapter 12 we look specifically at the role and importance of audits and evaluations. We also discuss some methods for conducting an ongoing or a terminal audit/evaluation.

Chapter 13 outlines the various methods for terminating a project and describes the pros and cons of each. Any method presents its own set of problems for the project manager, and these problems, together with some possible solutions, are covered. The Project Final Report is also described.

Chapter 14 discusses some of the managerial issues raised by multicultural projects. The chapter closes with short descriptions of three critical, unsolved problems in project management.

Project Auditing

In the previous chapter we discussed postcontrol. The purpose of postcontrol is not an attempt to change what has already happened. Quite the opposite, postcontrol tries to capture the essence of project successes and failures so that future projects can benefit from past experiences. To benefit from past experiences implies that one understands them, and understanding requires evaluation.

But project evaluation is not limited to after-the-fact analysis. While the project as a whole is evaluated when it has been completed, project evaluation should be conducted at a number of points during the life cycle.

A major vehicle for evaluation (but by no means the only one) is the *project audit*, a more or less formal inquiry into any aspect of the project. We associate the word *audit* with a detailed examination of financial matters, but a project audit is highly flexible and may focus on whatever matters senior management desires.

The term *evaluate* means to set the value of or appraise. Project evaluation appraises the progress and performance of a project compared to that project's planned progress and performance, or compared to the progress and performance of other, similar projects. The evaluation also supports any management decisions required for the project. Therefore, the evaluation must be conducted and presented in a manner and format that assures management that all pertinent data have been considered. The evaluation of a project must have credibility in the eyes of the management group for whom it is performed and also in the eyes of the project team on whom it is performed. Accordingly, the project evaluation must be just as carefully constructed and controlled as the project itself.

In this chapter, we describe the project audit/evaluation, its various forms and purposes, and some typical problems encountered in conducting an audit/evaluation. For an excellent general work on evaluation, see [16].

▶ 12.1   PURPOSES OF EVALUATION—GOALS OF THE SYSTEM

A primary purpose of evaluation is to aid in achieving the project's goals as a contribution to the parent organization's goals. To do this, all facets of the project are studied in order to identify and understand the project's strengths and weaknesses. It is the equivalent of an application of TQM to project management. The result is a set of recommendations that can help both ongoing and future projects to:

- Identify problems earlier
- Clarify performance, cost, and time relationships
- Improve project performance
- Locate opportunities for future technological advances
- Evaluate the quality of project management
- Reduce costs
- Speed the achievement of results
- Identify mistakes, remedy them, and avoid them in the future
- Provide information to the client
- Reconfirm the organization's interest in and commitment to the project

These purposes—and there are many others—relate quite directly to how well the project team is meeting the stated project objectives. (For brevity, we will refer to them as "direct goals.") They ignore, however, many costs and benefits to the project, to its team members, and to the parent organization that are not overtly established as objectives. Evaluation often makes recommendations that relate to these ancillary, unplanned but important contributions to the project and its parent. Some examples of recommendations concerning these "ancillary goals" include attempts to:

- Improve understanding of the ways in which projects may be of value to the organization
- Improve the processes for organizing and managing projects
- Provide a congenial environment in which project team members can work creatively together
- Identify organizational strengths and weaknesses in project-related personnel, management, and decision-making techniques and systems
- Identify risk factors in the firm's use of projects
- Improve the way projects contribute to the professional growth of project team members
- Identify project personnel who have high potential for managerial leadership

Identification of the direct goals of a project is *relatively* easy. It requires only a careful reading of the project proposal and a close examination of any documentation that indicates why the project was selected or undertaken. Refer again to Figure

11-5, a reproduction of a project management data form used by a firm in the aerospace industry. Immediately following the project description is a section headed "Reason for Interest." This is a statement of the project's direct goals. If no such document exists, and all too often it will not, a few interviews with the individuals in charge of making decisions about projects will help to expose the direct goals that the firm is seeking by supporting the project. On the other hand, identification of ancillary goals is a difficult and politically delicate task.

The adjective "ancillary" is not a sufficient descriptor, though it is the best single word we could find. Synonyms are "helpful," "subsidiary," "accessory," and the like, and we have all these things in mind. In addition, the ancillary goals are usually not overtly identified. For the most part, they are "hidden" by accident, not by purpose. Finding them requires deductive reasoning. Organizational decisions and behaviors imply goals, often very specific goals, that are simply not spelled out anywhere in the organizational manuals. For example, most executives desire to operate their organizations in such a way that people enjoy the work they do and working together, but only occasionally do firms publish such statements. Few firms would disavow this objective, they simply do not *overtly* subscribe to it. Even so, this particular objective affects the decisions made in almost every firm we know.

There are tough problems associated with finding the ancillary goals of a project. First, and probably the most important, is the obvious fact that one cannot measure performance against an unknown goal. Therefore, if a goal is not openly acknowledged, project team members need not fear that their performance can be weighed and found wanting. The result is that goals appearing in the project proposal must be recognized, but "unwritten" goals can often be ignored. Again, ancillary goals are rarely disclaimed; they are merely not mentioned.

Whether or not such anxiety is deserved is not relevant. Particularly in this era of corporate "restructuring," anxiety is present. It is heightened by the fear that an evaluation may not be conducted "fairly," with proper emphasis on what is being accomplished rather than stressing shortcomings. If the self-image of the project team is very strong, this barrier to finding ancillary goals of the project may be weak, but it is never absent.

A second problem arises during attempts to find the ancillary goals of a project. Individuals pursue their own individual ends while working for organizations. At times, however, people may be unwilling to admit to personal goals, which they may see as not entirely consistent with organizational objectives. For example, a person may seek to join a project in order to learn a new skill, one that increases that person's employment mobility. At times, the scientific direction taken by R & D projects is as much a function of the current interest areas of the scientists working on the project as it is the scientific needs of the project. While such purposes are not illegitimate or unethical, they are rarely admitted.

A third problem arises through lack of trust. Members of a project team are never quite comfortable in the presence of an auditor/evaluator. If the auditor/evaluator is an "outsider" — anyone who cannot be identified as a project team member—there is fear that "we won't be understood." While such fears are rarely specific, they are nonetheless real. If the auditor/evaluator is an "insider," fear focuses on the possibility that the insider has some hidden agenda, is seeking some personal advantage at the expense of the "rest of us." The motives of insider and outside alike are distrusted. As a result, project team members have little or no incentive to be forthcoming about their individual or project ancillary goals.

Finally, a fourth problem exists. Projects, like all organizations that serve human ends, are multipurposed. The diverse set of direct and ancillary, project and individual goals do not bear clear, organizationally-determined (or accepted) priorities. Various members of the project team may have quite different ideas about which purposes are most important, which come next in line, and which are least important. In the absence of direct questions about the matter, no one has to confront the issue of who is right and who is wrong. As long as the goals and priorities are not made explicit, project team members can agree on *what* things should be done without necessarily agreeing (or even discussing) *why* those things should be done. Thus, if some of the project's objectives are not openly debated, each member can tolerate the different emphases of fellow team members. No one is forced to pick and choose, or even to argue such matters with co-workers.

All in all, the task of finding the ancillary goals of a project is difficult. Most evaluations simply ignore them, but the PM is well-advised to take a keen interest in this area, and to request that evaluations include ancillary goals, the project's and the parent organization's, if not those of individuals. Even though one must usually be satisfied with rough, qualitative measures of ancillary-goal achievement, the information can be valuable. It may provide insight into such questions as: What sorts of things motivate people to join and work on projects? What sorts of rewards are most effective in eliciting maximum effort from project personnel? What are the major concerns of specific individuals working on the project?

In Chapter 4, we alluded to the importance of the project "war room" (office) as a meeting place for the project team, as a display area for the charts that show the project's progress, as a central repository for project files and reports, and as an office for the PM and other project administrators. The war room is also the "clubhouse" for the project team members and serves an important ancillary goal. It is to the project what the local pub was to "that old gang of mine." The camaraderie associated with a successful, well-run project provides great satisfaction to team members. The project office, therefore, fills an emotional need as well as meeting its more mundane, direct administrative goals.

Project Management in Practice
Evaluating the Results of a Sewerage Project in Barbados

In 1983, an evaluation of the results of a sewerage project in Bridgetown, Barbados, was conducted. The project was designed to receive 2.4 million gallons of sewage a day from about 38,000 users, process the sewage by contact stabilization, treat the sludge for farm use, and discharge the effluent into the sea 1000 feet offshore in 40 feet of water. The project took ten years and was completed in 1982.

On the plus side, the project has checked

Source: J. Khan "The Development Project Cycle and a Barbadian Project," *Project Management Journal*, June 1991.

the disposal of untreated sewage at sea, improved sanitation and public health of the target areas, reduced the marine and beach pollution, improved the clarity of water, and fostered the return of large fish to the area. It also provided Bridgetown with a sewage system, facilitated urban renewal, enhanced the quality of life for 38,000 users, boosted tourism, and generally improved the aesthetic conditions of the area.

However, a seabed evaluation indicated that the water quality and health of the ma-
rine community continued to deteriorate. An evaluation of the sewage plant found that process and flow control was frequently difficult to achieve. Either one year's arrest of pollution has not yet been enough to reverse the environmental decline or, perhaps, the chlorine being used to treat the sewage might be contributing to the deterioration. At this point, more training of the sewage plant personnel is being planned, as well as continuing evaluation of the seabed near the site of the outfall.

▶ 12.2   THE PROJECT AUDIT

The project audit is a thorough examination of the management of a project, its methodology and procedures, its records, its properties, its budgets and expenditures, and its degree of completion. It may deal with the project as a whole, or only with a part of the project. The formal report may be presented in various formats, but should, at a minimum, contain comments on the following points:

1. ***Current status of the project***   Does the work actually completed match the planned level of completion?

2. ***Future status***   Are significant schedule changes likely? If so, indicate the nature of the changes.

3. ***Status of crucial tasks***   What progress has been made on tasks that could decide the success or failure of the project?

4. ***Risk assessment***   What is the potential for project failure or monetary loss?

5. ***Information pertinent to other projects***   What lessons learned from the project being audited can be applied to other projects being undertaken by the organization? This point will be discussed later in this chapter, and again in Chapter 14.

6. ***Limitations of the audit***   What assumptions or limitations affect the data in the audit?

These six parts of the audit report will be discussed in more detail in the next section of this chapter.

Note that the project audit is not a financial audit. The audit processes are similar in that each represents a careful investigation of the subject of the audit, but the outputs of these processes are quite different. The principal distinction between the two is that the financial audit has a limited scope. It concentrates on the use and preservation of the organization's assets. The project audit is far broader in scope and may deal with the project as a whole or any component or set of components of the project. It may be concerned with any aspect of project management. Table 12–1 lists the primary differences between financial and project audits.

Table 12-1 Comparison of Financial Audits with Project Audits

	Financial Audits	Project Audits
Status	Confirms status of business in relation to accepted standard	Must create basis for, and confirm, status on each project
Predictions	Company's state of economic well-being	Future status of project
Measurement	Mostly in financial terms	Financial terms plus schedule, progress, resource usage, status of ancillary goals
Record-keeping system	Format dictated by legal regulations and professional standards	No standard system, uses any system desired by individual organization or dictated by contract
Existence of information system	Minimal records needed to start audit	No records exist, data bank must be designed and used to start audit
Recommendations	Usually few or none, often restricted to management of accounting system	Often required, and may cover any aspect of the project or its management
Qualifications	Customary to qualify statements if conditions dictate, but strong managerial pressure not to do so	Qualifications focus on shortcomings of audit process (e.g., lack of technical expertise, lack of funds or time)

While the project audit may be concerned with any aspect of project management, it is not a traditional management audit. Management audits are primarily aimed at ensuring that the organization's management systems are in place and operative. The project audit goes beyond this. Among other things, it is meant to ensure that the project is being *appropriately* managed. Some managerial systems apply fairly well to all projects; for example, the techniques of planning, scheduling, budgeting, and so forth. On the other hand, some management practices should differ with different types of projects. For an interesting discussion of the project management audit, see [21, the reading for this chapter].

In the previous chapter, we argued that software projects were not *significantly* different from other types of projects. We stand on that position, but we also note that they possess some unique characteristics worthy of recognition and response. For example, computer-based projects are ordinarily very labor intensive while many engineering projects, for instance, are highly capital intensive. A thoughtful manager will simply not adopt the same managerial approach to each. The need for and value of a participative style (TQM, EI, etc.) is well established in the case of labor-intensive projects where problems are often ill-structured. If the project is capital intensive and characterized by well-structured problems, the need for and value of a participative style is *relatively* diminished. (The reader must not read these statements as degrading the value of participative management. It is simply more valuable and relevant in some cases than others.)

To sum up, the management audit looks at managerial systems and their use. The project audit studies the financial, managerial, and technical aspects of the project as an integrated set—applied to a specific project in a specific organizational environment.

Depth of the Audit

There are several practical constraints that may limit the depth of the project auditor's investigation. Time and money are two of the most common (and obvious) limits on the depth of investigation and level of detail presented in the audit report. Of course, there are costs associated with the audit/evaluation process over and above the usual costs of the professional and clerical time used in conducting the audit. Accumulation, storage, and maintenance of auditable data is an important cost element. Remember that such storage may be critically important in meeting the test of "due diligence" noted in Chapter 11.

Also serious, but less quantifiable, are two often overlooked costs. First, no matter how skilled the evaluator, an audit/evaluation process is always distracting to those working on the project. No project is completely populated with individuals whose self-esteem (defined by Ambrose Bierce as "an erroneous appraisement" [2]) is so high that evaluation is greeted without anxiety. Worry about the outcome of the audit tends to produce an excessive level of self-protective activity, which, in turn, lowers the level of activity devoted to the project. Second, if the evaluation report is not written with a "constructive" tone, project morale will suffer.* Depending on the severity of the drop in morale, work on the project may receive a serious setback. The more difficult the technical problems of the project, the more project workers are apt to react strongly to negative criticism. Because the whole process is threatening to the auditees, the auditor should exercise care and discretion in writing the report.

It is logical to vary the depth of the investigation depending on circumstances and needs unique to each project. While an audit can be performed at any level the organization wishes, three distinct levels are easily recognized and widely used: the general audit, the detailed audit, and the technical audit. The general audit is normally most constrained by time and resources and is usually a brief review of the project, touching lightly on the six concerns noted earlier. A typical detailed audit is conducted when a follow-up to the general audit is required. This tends to occur when the general audit has disclosed an unacceptable level of risk or malperformance in some part(s) of the project. The depth of the detailed audit depends on the importance of the questionable issues and their relationship to the objectives of the project—the more serious, or potentially serious, the greater the depth. The evaluation of the then-revolutionary J. C. Penney guaranteed "lifetime" automotive battery required several thousand pages.

At times, the detailed audit cannot investigate problems at a satisfactory technical level because the auditor does not possess the technical knowledge needed. In such cases, a technical audit is required. Technical audits are normally carried out by a qualified technician under the direct guidance of the project auditor. In the

---

*The evaluator is well-advised to remember two fundamental principles: (1) Constructive criticism does not feel all that constructive to the criticizee; and (2) Fix first, then blame—if you have any energy left.

case of very advanced or secret technology, it may be difficult to find qualified technical auditors inside the organization. In such cases, it is not uncommon for the firm to use academic consultants who have signed the appropriate nondisclosure documents. Although not a hard and fast rule, the technical audit is usually the most detailed.

Timing of the Audit

Like audit depth, the timing of a project audit will depend on the circumstances of a particular project. Given that all projects of significant size or importance should be audited, the first audits are usually done early in the project's life. The sooner a problem is discovered, the easier it is to deal with. Early audits are often focused on the technical issues in order to make sure that key technical problems have been solved or are under competent attack. Ordinarily, audits done later in the life cycle of a project are of less immediate value to the project, but are of more value to the parent organization. As the project develops, technical issues are less likely to be matters of concern. Conformity to the schedule and budget becomes the primary interest. Management issues are major matters of interest for audits made late in the project's life (e.g., disposal of equipment or reallocation of project personnel).

Postproject audits are conducted with several basic objectives in mind. First, a postproject audit is often a legal necessity because the client specified such an audit in the contract. Second, the postproject audit is a major part of the Postproject Report, which is, in turn, the main source of managerial feedback to the parent firm. Third, the postproject audit is needed to account for all project property and expenditures.

Additional observations on the timing and value of audits are shown in Table 12-2.

▶ 12.3 CONSTRUCTION AND USE OF THE AUDIT REPORT

The type of project being audited and the uses for which the audit is intended dictate some specifics of the audit report format. Within any particular organization, however, it is useful to establish a general format to which all audit reports must conform. This makes it possible for project managers, auditors, and organizational management all to have the same understanding of, and expectations for, the audit report as a communication device. If the audit report is to serve as a communication device, there must also be a predetermined distribution list for such documents. When distribution is highly restricted, the report is almost certain to become the focus for interpersonal and intergroup conflict and tension.

While a few PMs insist on a complicated format for evaluation reports tailored to their individual projects, the simpler and more straightforward the format, the better. The information should be arranged so as to facilitate the comparison of predicted versus actual results. Significant deviations of actual from predicted results should be highlighted and explained in a set of footnotes or comments. This eases the reader's work and tends to keep questions focused on important issues rather than trivia. This arrangement also reduces the likelihood that senior man-

Table 12-2   Timing and Value of Project Audits/Evaluations

Project Stage	Value
Initiation	Significant value if audit takes place early—prior to 25 percent completion of initial planning stage
Feasibility study	Very useful, particularly the technical audit
Preliminary plan/schedule budget	Very useful, particularly for setting measurement standards to ensure conformance with standards
Master schedule	Less useful, plan frozen, flexibility of team limited
Evaluation of data by project team	Marginally useful, team defensive about findings
Implementation	More or less useful depending on importance of project methodology to successful implementation
Postproject	More or less useful depending on applicability of findings to future projects

agers will engage in "fishing expeditions," searching for something "wrong" in every piece of data and sentence of the report. Once again, we would remind PMs of the dictum "Never let the boss be surprised."

Negative comments about individuals or groups associated with the project should be avoided. Write the report in a clear, professional, unemotional style and restrict its content to information and issues that are relevant to the project. The following items cover the *minimum* information that should be contained in the audit report.

1. **Introduction**   This section contains a description of the project to provide a framework of understanding for the reader. Project objectives (direct goals) must be clearly delineated. If the objectives are complex, it may be useful to include explanatory parts of the project proposal as an addendum to the report.

2. **Current Status**   Status should be reported as of the time of the audit and, among other things, should include the following measures of performance:

   Cost: This section compares actual costs to budgeted costs. The time periods for which the comparisons are made should be clearly defined. As noted in Chapter 7, the report should focus on the *direct* charges made to the project. If it is also necessary to show project *total* costs, complete with all overheads, this cost data should be presented in an *additional* set of tables.

   Schedule: Performance in terms of planned events or milestones should be reported (see Figures 10-8c and 11-5 as examples). Completed portions of the project should be clearly identified, and the percent completion should be reported on all unfinished tasks for which estimates are possible.

   Progress: This section compares work completed with resources expended. Earned value charts (see Figure 10-6) may be used for this purpose if desired, but they usually lack the appropriate level of detail. The requirement here is for information that will help to pinpoint problems with specific tasks or sets of tasks. Based on this information, projections regarding the timing and amounts of remaining planned expenditures are made.

Quality: Whether or not this is a critical issue depends on the type of project being audited. Quality is a measure of the degree to which the output of a system conforms to prespecified characteristics. For some projects, the prespecified characteristics are so loosely stated that conformity is not much of an issue. At times, a project may produce outputs that far exceed original specifications. For instance, a project might require a subsystem that meets certain minimum standards. The firm may already have produced such a subsystem— one that meets standards well in excess of the current requirements. It may be efficient, with no less effectiveness, to use the previously designed system with its excess performance. If there is a detailed quality specification associated with the project, this section of the report may have to include a full review of the quality control procedures, along with full disclosure of the results of quality tests conducted to date.

3. **Future Project Status** This section contains the auditor's conclusions regarding progress together with recommendations for any changes in technical approach, schedule, or budget that should be made in the remaining tasks. Except in unusual circumstances, for example when results to date distinctly indicate the undersirability of some preplanned task, the auditor's report should consider only work that has already been completed or is well under way. No assumptions should be made about technical problems that are still under investigation at the time of the audit. Project audit/evaluation reports are not appropriate documents in which to rewrite the project proposal.

4. **Critical Management Issues** All issues that the auditor feels require close monitoring by senior management should be included in this section, along with a brief explanation of the relationships between these issues and the objectives of the project. A brief discussion of time/cost/performance tradeoffs will give senior management useful input information for decisions about the future of the project.

5. **Risk Analysis** This section should contain a review of major risks associated with the project and their projected impact on project time/cost/performance. If alternative decisions exist that may significantly alter future risks, they can be noted at this point in the report. Once again, we note that the audit report is not the proper place to second-guess those who wrote the project proposal. The Postproject Report, on the other hand, will often contain sections on the general subject of "If only we knew then what we know now."

6. **Caveats, Limitations, and Assumptions** This section of the report may be placed at the end or may be included as a part of the introduction. The auditor is responsible for the accuracy and timeliness of the report, but senior management still retains full responsibility for the interpretation of the report and for any action(s) based on the findings. For that reason, the auditor should specifically include a statement covering any limitations on the accuracy or validity of the report.

Responsibilities of the Project Auditor/Evaluator

First and foremost, the auditor should "tell the truth." This statement is not so simplistic as it might appear. It is a recognition of the fact that there are various levels of truth associated with any project. The auditor must approach the audit in an objective and ethical manner and assume responsibility for what is included and excluded from consideration in the report. Awareness of the biases of the several parties interested in the project—including the auditor's own biases—is essential, but extreme care is required if the auditor wishes to compensate for such biases. (A note that certain information *may* be biased is usually sufficient.) Areas of investigation outside the auditor's area of technical expertise should be acknowledged and assistance sought when necessary. The auditor/evaluator must maintain political and technical independence during the audit and treat all materials gathered as confidential until the audit is formally released.

Walker and Bracey [28] develop an even stronger case for the "independence" of the auditor. They argue that independence is essential for management's ability to assemble information that is both timely and accurate. They also list the following steps for carrying out an audit:

- Assemble a small team of experienced experts.
- Familiarize the team with the requirements of the project.
- Audit the project on site.
- After completion, debrief the project's management.
- Produce a written report according to a prespecified format.
- Distribute the report to the PM and project team for their response.
- Follow up to see if the recommendations have been implemented.

If senior management and the project team are to take the audit/evaluation seriously, all information must be presented in a credible manner. The accuracy of data should be carefully checked, as should all calculations. The determination of what information to include and exclude is one that cannot be taken lightly. Finally, the auditor should engage in a continuing evaluation of the auditing process in a search for ways to improve the effectiveness, efficiency, and value of the process.

Project Management in Practice
Auditing a Troubled Project at Atlantic States Chemical Laboratories

In early 1980, Atlantic States Chemical Laboratories (ASCL) received a contract from an entrepreneurial firm, Oretec, to conduct a unique type of chemical analysis on special alloys they had created in their own laboratories in the interest of identifying potentially successful commercial alloys. The contract emphasized quality of the effort and speed of continuing laboratory analyses. The contract duration would be open-ended with payment at the monthly rate of $100,000. The liaison officer from Oretec would have access to ASCL's laboratory work for observation.

As work progressed during mid- to late-1980, the liaison officer became more involved in the project, pressuring the team to alter their approach and skip the usual repeat-verification procedures in the interest of time. On two occasions, the ASCL team devised an analysis indicating that a commer-

Source: J. R. Meredith, consulting project.

cially successful product could be produced. The liaison officer was gratified with the effort and asked for suggestions on how to produce the product commercially. However, tests at Oretec indicated that these approaches would not work. As early-1981 passed, the pressure for more and faster analyses increased even more, with the liaison officer becoming more belligerent and difficult to please. In May of 1981, the president of ASCL received a letter from Oretec voicing a number of complaints and terminating the contract effective immediately. Puzzled by the unexpected displeasure of their client with no indication of trouble on the project from internal sources, the president requested a comprehensive but quick audit of the project.

The audit reported the following:

1. **Overview Points:**

   - The original approach to the project was sound but was altered by the client's liaison officer; nevertheless, significant findings were still made.

   - The analyses themselves were conducted properly.

   - There were several analytical successes during the project (each identified).

   - Commercialization was not ASCL's responsibility but the client's, even if ASCL suggested some possible processes.

   - There was excessive involvement of the liaison officer in the management of the project, including frequent changes of direction.

   - Ongoing project management decisions and changes were not documented by ASCL, nor communicated to the client.

2. **Analysis of Client's Criticism** (about half of the criticisms were valid, details described)

3. **Further Points of Note:**

   - The commercialization processes proposed by ASCL have, in fact, been successfully used in similar instances. The client's tests indicating their unacceptability are incorrect.

   - The reports provided by ASCL and criticized by the client as incomplete were redirected by the liaison officer to be prepared quickly and informally. The reports of project analysis success would not have been understandable to the client's management, only to technical personnel or the liaison officer.

   - Management gave insufficient guidance/support to the project leader in his relations with the client.

4. **Recommendation:** Establish a formal procedure for identifying high-risk projects at the contract stage and monitoring them carefully for deviations from plan. The factors contributing to making this a high-risk project were inadequate funding, insufficient time, low chance of success, an unsophisticated client, and excessive access to ongoing project activities by the client.

▶ 12.4   THE PROJECT AUDIT LIFE CYCLE

Thus far we have considered the project audit and project evaluation as if they were one and the same. In most ways they are. The audit contains an evaluation, and an evaluator must conduct some sort of audit. Let us now consider the audit as a formal document required by contract with the client. If the client is the federal government, the nature of the project audit is more or less precisely defined, as is the audit process.

Like the project itself, the audit has a *life cycle* composed of an orderly progression of well-defined events. There are six of these events.

1. **Project Audit Initiation**   This step involves starting the audit process, defining the purpose and scope of the audit, and gathering sufficient information to determine the proper audit methodology.

2. **Project Baseline Definition**   The purpose of this phase is to establish performance standards against which the project's performance and accomplishments can be evaluated. This phase of the cycle normally consists of identifying the performance areas to be evaluated, determining standards for each area, ascertaining management performance expectations for each area, and developing a program to measure and assemble the requisite information.

   Occasionally, no convenient standards exist. For example, a commodity pricing model was developed as part of a large marketing project. No baseline data existed that could serve to help evaluate the model. Because the commodity was sold by open bid, the firm used its standard bidding procedures. The results formed baseline data against which the pricing model could be tested on an "as if" basis. Table 12-3 shows the results of one such test. CCC is the firm and the contracts on which it bid *and won*, together with the associated revenues (mine net price × tonnage), are shown. Similar information is displayed for Model C, which was used on an "as if" basis so the Model C Revenue column shows those bids the model *would have won*, had it actually been used.

3. **Establishing an Audit Database**   Once the baseline standards are established, execution of the audit begins. The next step is to create a database for use by the audit team. Depending on the purpose and scope of the audit, the database might include information needed for assessment of project organization, management and control, past and current project status, schedule performance, cost performance, and output quality, as well as plans for the future of the project. The information may vary from a highly technical description of performance to a behaviorally based description of the interaction of project team members.

   Because the purpose and scope of audits vary widely from one project to another and for different times on any given project, the audit database is frequently quite extensive. The required database for project audits should be specified in the project master plan. If this is done, the necessary information will be available when needed. Nonetheless, it is important to avoid collecting "anything that might be useful," since this can place extraordinary information collection and storage requirements on the project.

4. **Preliminary Analysis of the Project**   After standards are set and data collected, judgments are made. Some auditors eschew judgment on the grounds that such a delicate but weighty responsibility must be reserved to senior management. But judgment often requires a fairly sophisticated understanding of the technical aspects of the project, and/or of statistics and probability, subjects that may elude some managers. In such an event, the auditor must analyze the

Table 12-3 Performance Against Baseline Data

		19xx Bid Performance for Model "C"—State of _____ Award				
Destination	Tonnage	CCC Bid	Model "C" Bid	Mine Net Price	CCC Revenue	Model "C" Revenue
DI-2	3800		X	$4.11		$15,618
DI-7	1600		X	3.92		6,272
D2-7	1300		X	4.11		5,343
D3-2	700	X		5.13		3,591
D3-3	500	X		5.22	$2610	
D3-4	600		X	5.72		3,432
D3-5	1200		X	5.12		6,144
D3-6	1000		X	5.83		5,830
D4-6	700		X	4.88		3,416
D4-8	600		X	5.34		3,204
D5-1	500	X		3.54	1770	
D6-1	1000	X	X	4.02–3.92	4020	3,920
D6-2	900	X		4.35	3915	
D6-5	200	X		3.75	750	
D6-6	800		X	3.17		2,536
D7-5	1600		X	5.12		8,192
D7-8	2600		X	5.29		13,754
D8-2	1600	X	X	4.83	7728	7,728
D8-3	2400		X	4.32		10,368
				Total revenue	$20,793	$99,348
				Total tonnage	4700	21,500
				Average mine net	$4.42	$4.62

data and then present the analysis to managers in ways that communicate the real meaning of the audit's findings. It is the auditor's duty to brief the PM on all findings and judgments *before* releasing the audit report. The purpose of the audit is to improve the project being audited as well as to improve the entire process of managing projects. It is not intended as a device to embarrass the PM.

5. **Audit Report Preparation** This part of the audit life cycle includes the preparation of the audit report, organized by whatever format has been selected for use. A set of recommendations, together with a plan for implementing them, is also a part of the audit report. If the recommendations go beyond normal practices of the organization, they will need support from the policy-making level of management. This support should be sought and verified *before* the recommendations are published. If support is not forthcoming, the recommendations should be modified until satisfactory. Figure 12-1 is one page of an extensive and detailed set of recommendations that resulted from an evaluation project conducted by a private social service agency.

6. **Project Audit Termination** As with the project itself, after the audit has accomplished its designated task, the audit process should be terminated. When the

Final Report, Agency Evaluation, Sub-Committee II
Physical Plant, Management of Office, Personnel Practices

Summary of Recommendations

Recommendations which require Board action.

1. The Board of _____ should continue its efforts to obtain additional funds for our salary item.
2. The cost of Blue Cross and Blue Shield insurance coverage on individual employees should be borne by _____.

Recommendations which can be put into effect by *Presidential Order* to committees, staff, or others.

3. The House Committee should activate, with first priority, the replacement of the heating/air conditioning system. Further, this committee should give assistance and support to the Secretary to the Executive Director in maintenance and repair procedures.
4. A professional library should be established even if part time workers must share space to accomplish this.
5. Our insurance needs should be re-evaluated.
6. All activities related to food at meetings should be delegated to someone other than the Secretary to the Executive Director.
7. Majority opinion—position of Administrative Assistant and Bookkeeper will need more time in the future.
   Minority opinion—positions of Administrative Assistant, Bookkeeper and Statistical Assistant should be combined.
8. The Personnel Practices Committee should review job descriptions of Bookkeeper and Statistical Assistant and establish salary ranges for those two positions and that of the Administrative Assistant.
9. Dialogue between the Executive Director, his secretary, and the Administrative Assistant should continue in an effort to streamline office procedures and expedite handling of paperwork.
10. The written description of the Personnel Practices Committee should include membership of a representative of the non-professional staff.
11. The Personnel Practices Committee should study, with a view toward action, the practice of part time vs. full time casework staff.

Figure 12-1: Sample recommendations for a social service agency.

final report and recommendations are released, there will be a review of the audit process. This is done in order to improve the methods for conducting the audit. When the review is finished, the audit is truly complete and the audit team should be formally disbanded.

▶ 12.5 SOME ESSENTIALS OF AN AUDIT/EVALUATION

For an audit/evaluation (hereinafter, simply a/e) to be conducted with skill and precision, for it to be credible and generally acceptable to senior management, to the project team, and to the client, several essential conditions must be met. The a/e team must be properly selected, all records and files must be accessible, and free contact with project members must be preserved.

The A/E Team

The choice of the a/e team is critical to the success of the entire process. It may seem unnecessary to note that team members should be selected because of their ability to contribute to the a/e procedure, but sometimes members are selected merely because they are available. The size of the team will generally be a function of the size and complexity of the project. For a small project, one person can often handle all the tasks of an a/e audit, but for a large project, the team may require representatives from several different constituencies. Typical of the areas that might furnish a/e team members are:

- The project itself
- The accounting/controller department
- Technical specialty areas
- The customer
- The marketing department
- Senior management
- Purchasing/asset management
- The personnel department
- The legal/contract administration department

The main role of the a/e team is to conduct a thorough and complete examination of the project or some prespecified aspect of the project. The team must determine which items should be brought to management's attention. It should report information and make recommendations in such a way as to maximize the utility of its work. The team is responsible for constructive observations and advice based on the training and experience of its members. Members must be aloof from personal involvement with conflicts among project team staff and from rivalries between projects. The a/e is a highly disciplined process and all team members must willingly and sincerely subject themselves to that discipline.

Access to Records

In order for the a/e team to be effective, it must have free access to all information relevant to the project. This may present some problems on government projects that may be classified for reasons of national security. In such cases, a subgroup of the a/e team may be formed from qualified ("cleared") individuals.

Most of the information needed for an a/e will come from the project team's records or from various departments such as accounting, personnel, and purchasing. Obviously, gathering the data is the responsibility of the a/e team, and this burden should not be passed on to the project management team, though the project team is responsible for collecting the usual data on the project and keeping project records up to date during the project's life.

In addition to the formal records of the project, some of the most valuable information comes from documents that predate the project—for example, correspondence with the customer that led to the RFP, minutes of the Project Selection Committee, and minutes of senior management committees that decided to pursue a specific area of technical interest. Clearly, project status reports, relevant technical memoranda, change orders, information about project organization and management methods, and financial and resource usage information are also important. The a/e team may have to extract much of this data from other documents because the required information is often not in the form needed. Data collection is a time-consuming task, but careful work is absolutely necessary for an effective, credible a/e.

As information is collected, it must be organized and filed in a systematic way. Systematic methods need to be developed for separating out useful information. Most important, stopping rules are needed to prevent data collection and processing from continuing far past the point of diminishing returns. Priorities must be set to ensure that important analyses are undertaken before those of lesser import. Also, safeguards are needed against duplication of efforts. The careful development of forms and procedures will help to standardize the process as much as possible.

Access to Project Personnel and Others

Contact between a/e team members and project team members, or between the a/e team and other members of the organization who have knowledge of the project, should be free. One exception is contact between the a/e team and the customer; *such contacts are not made without clearance from senior management.* This restriction would hold even when the customer is represented on the audit team, and should also hold for in-house clients.

In any case, there are several rules that should be followed when contacting project personnel. Care must be taken to avoid misunderstandings between a/e team members and project team members. Project personnel should always be made aware of the in-progress a/e. Critical comments should be avoided. Particularly serious is the practice of delivering on-the-sport, off-the-cuff opinions and remarks that may not be appropriate or represent the consensus opinion of the a/e team.

The a/e team will undoubtedly encounter political opposition during its work. If the project is a subject of political tension, attempts will most certainly be made by the opposing sides to co-opt the a/e team. As much as possible, they should avoid becoming involved. At times, information may be given to a/e team members in confidence. Discreet attempts should be made to confirm such information through nonconfidential sources. If it cannot be confirmed, it should not be used. The auditor/evaluator must protect the sources of confidential information and must not become a conduit for unverifiable criticism of the project.

▶ 12.6 MEASUREMENT

Measurement is an integral part of the a/e process. Many issues of what and how to measure have been discussed in earlier chapters, particularly in Chapter 2. Several aspects of a project that should be measured are obvious and, fortunately, rather easy to measure. For the most part, it is not difficult to know if and when a milestone has been completed. We can directly observe the fact that a building foundation has been poured, that all required materials for a corporate annual report have been collected and delivered to the printer, that all contracts have been let for the rehabilitation of an apartment complex, that the navigation instruments for a new fighter aircraft have been tested, or that all case workers have been trained in the new case management techniques. At times, of course, milestone completion may not be quite so evident. It may be difficult to tell when a chemical experiment is finished, and it is almost impossible to tell when a complex computer program is finally "bug free." Largely, however, milestone completion can be measured adequately.

Similarly, performance against planned budget and schedule usually poses no major measurement problems. We may be a bit uncertain whether or not a "nine-day" scheduled completion time should include weekend days, but most organizations adopt conventions to ease these minor counting problems. Measuring the actual expenditures against the planned budget is a bit trickier and depends on an in-depth understanding of the procedures used by the accounting department. It is common to imbue cost data with higher levels of reality and precision than is warranted. Still, while there may be some unique difficulties raised when we attempt to measure the time/cost/performance dimensions of a project, these problems are usually tractable.

When the objectives of a project have been stated in terms of profits, rates of return, or discounted cash flows, as in the financial selection models discussed in Chapter 2, measurement problems may be more obstinate. The problem does not often revolve around the accounting conventions used, though if those conventions have not been clearly established in advance there may be bitter arguments about what costs are appropriately assigned to the individual project being evaluated. A far more difficult task is the determination of what revenues should be assigned to the project.

Assume, for example, that a drug firm creates a project for the development of a new drug and simultaneously sets up a project to develop and implement a marketing strategy for the potential new drug and two existing allied drugs. Assume further that the entire program is successful and large amounts of revenue are generated. How much revenue should be assigned to the credit of the drug research project? How much to the marketing project? Within the marketing project, how much should go to each of the subprojects for the individual drugs? If the entire program is treated as one project, the problem is less serious; but R & D and marketing are in different functional areas of the parent organization and each may be evaluated on the basis of its contribution to the parent firm's profitability. The year-end bonuses of divisional managers are determined in part (often in large part) by the profitability of the units they manage. Figure 12-2 illustrates project baseline data established for a new product. This figure shows the use of multiple measures including price, unit sales, market share, development costs, capital expenditures, and other measures of performance.

There is no theoretically acceptable solution to such measurement problems, but there are politically acceptable solutions. All the cost/revenue allocation decisions must be made when the various projects are initiated. If this is done, the battles are fought "up front," and the equity of cost/revenue allocations ceases to be so

PROJECT EVALUATION DATA

PRODUCT_____ DATE _____

MARKET_____

DATE OF FIRST SALE: U.S. _____

O.U.S. _____

	1ST YEAR			2ND YEAR			3RD YEAR			4TH YEAR			5TH YEAR			TOTAL		
	MIN	B.E.*	MAX	MIN	B.E.	MAX	MIN	B.E.	MAX	MIN	B.E.	MAX	MIN	B.E.	MAX	MIN	B.E.	MAX
1. Total Market Size:																		
2. Expected Market Share:																		
3. Kg. or Units:																		
4. Est. Selling Price:																		
5. Gross Sales:																		
6. Est. COPS %:																		
7. Gross Margin %:																		
8. Est. Marketing Expense %:																		
9. Marketing Margin %:																		
10. Loss on Profit from other Products: List:																		
11. Est. Profit:																		
12. Development Expenses:																		
13. Capital Expenditures:																		

Figure 12-2: Baseline marketing data for a new product.

*Best Estimate

serious an issue. As long as allocations are made by a formula, major conflict is avoided—or, at least, mitigated.

If multi-objective scoring models rather than financial models are being used for project selection, measurement problems are somewhat exacerbated. There are more elements to measure, some of which are objective and measured with relative ease. But some elements are subjective and require reasonably standard measurement techniques if the measures are to be reliable. Interview and questionnaire methods for gathering data must be carefully constructed and carried out if the project scores are to be taken seriously. Criteria weights and scoring procedures should be decided at the start of the project.

A Note to The Auditor/Evaluator

A kindly critic and colleague uses what he calls the "rules of engagement" to explain to his students how to schedule interviews, conduct interviews, get copies, limit the scope of activities, and handle the many mundane tasks included in auditing/evaluating projects. While the phrases, "rules of engagement," seems a bit warlike to us, we do have some similar advice for the auditor/evaluator.

Above all else, the a/e needs "permission to enter the system." It is difficult precisely to describe what is meant by that phrase, but every experienced auditor or evaluator will know. Senior management can assign an individual to the job of heading an audit/evaluation team, but this does not automatically imply that project personnel will accept that person as a legitimate a/e. There will be several indicators if the a/e is not accepted. Phone calls from the a/e will be returned only at times when the a/e is not available. Requests for information will be politely accepted, but little or no information will be forthcoming—though copious, sincere apologies and semi-believable excuses will be. Interviews with project team members will be strangely contentless. Attempts to determine the project's ancillary goals will be unavailing, as will attempts to get team members to discuss intrateam conflict. Everyone will be quite pleasant, but somehow promises of cooperation do not turn into fact. Always, there are good excuses and wide-eyed innocence.

If the a/e is reasonably likable and maintains a calm, relaxed attitude, the project team generally begins to extend limited trust. The usual first step is to allow the a/e qualified access to information about the project. Missing information from the official project files is suddenly found. The a/e has then been given tentative permission to enter the system. If the a/e deals gently with this information, neither ignoring nor stressing the project's shortcomings while recognizing and appreciating the project's strengths, trust will be extended, and the permission to enter the system will no longer be tentative.

Trust-building is a slow and delicate process, easily thwarted. The a/e needs to understand the politics of the project team and the interpersonal relationships among its members, and must deal with this confidential knowledge respectfully. On this base is trust built and meaningful audit/evaluation constructed. There is an almost universal propensity for the a/e to mimic Sgt. Friday—"Just give me the facts, ma'am." It is not that simple, nor are any processes involving human beings that simple.

▶ SUMMARY

This chapter initiated our discussion of the final part of the text, project termination. A major concluding step in the termination process is the evaluation of the project process and results, otherwise known as an audit. Here we looked at the purposes of evaluation and what it should encompass: the audit process and measurement considerations, the demands placed on the auditor, and the construction and design of the final report.

Specific points made in the chapter were these:

- The purposes of the evaluation are both goal-directed, aiding the project in achieving its objectives, and also aimed at achieving unspecified, sometimes hidden, yet firmly held, ancillary objectives.

- The audit report should contain at least the current status of the project, the expected fu-

ture status, the status of crucial tasks, a risk assessment, information pertinent to other projects, and any caveats and limitations.
- Audit depth and timing are critical elements of the audit because, for example, it is much-more difficult to alter the project based on a late audit than an early audit.
- The difficult responsibility of the auditor is to be honest in fairly presenting the audit results. This may even require data interpretation on occasion.
- The audit life cycle includes audit initiation, project baseline definition, establishing a

database, preliminary project analysis, report preparation, and termination.
- Several essential conditions must be met for a credible audit: a credible a/e team, sufficient access to records, and sufficient access to personnel.
- Measurement, particularly of revenues, is a special problem.

In the next chapter we move into the final state of the project management process, termination. There we will look at when to terminate a project and the various ways the termination can be conducted.

GLOSSARY

Audit—A formal inquiry into some issue or aspect of a system.
Baseline—A standard for performance, commonly established early on for later comparisons.
Evaluate—To set a value for or appraise.

Risk Analysis—An evaluation of the likely outcomes of a policy and their probability of occurrence, usually conducted to compare two or more scenarios or policies.

MATERIAL REVIEW QUESTIONS

1. Give some examples of ancillary project objectives.
2. When should an audit be conducted during a project? Is there a "best" time?
3. What occurs in each stage of the audit life cycle?
4. What items should be included in the audit status report?
5. What access is required for an accurate audit?
6. Why is measurement a particular problem in auditing?
7. What is a "baseline"?
8. What is the purpose of a risk analysis?
9. What are the essential conditions of a credible audit?

CLASS DISCUSSION QUESTIONS

1. In a typical project, do you feel frequent brief evaluations or periodic major evaluations are better in establishing control? Why?
2. Do you think that project evaluations cost-justify themselves?
3. What steps can be taken to ease the perceived threat to team members of an external evaluation?
4. What feedback, if any, should the project team get from the evaluation?
5. During the project audit, a tremendous amount of time can be wasted if a systematic method of information handling is not adopted. Briefly explain how this systematic method may be developed.

6. "Evaluation of a project is another means of project control." Comment.

7. Why is it better to rely on several sources of information than just a few?

8. What could be some advantages and disadvantages of the following sources of information: (*a*) charts, (*b*) written reports, and (*c*) firsthand observation?

9. Why is it important to use outside auditors rather than inside auditors who would be more familiar with the company and the project?

10. What kinds of reports might be sent to customers?

11. What would you identify as the ethical responsibilities of an auditor?

▶ INDIVIDUAL EXERCISE

Refer back to one of the earlier projects used for a chapter exercise or the following Gerkin "Incident for Discussion." Design an audit for the project. What data would you need? To whom should you talk? What are the goals of the project? The ancillary goals? When should the audit be conducted in the project? What sections should the final report contain? Describe the audit process and its life cycle.

▶ INCIDENTS FOR DISCUSSION

Gerkin Manufacturing Co.

Tina Lasket was the project manager of a project with the objective of determining the feasibility of moving a significant portion of Gerkin's manufacturing capacity to another geographical location. Project completion was scheduled for 28 weeks. Tina had the project team motivated and at the end of the twentieth week the project was on schedule. The next week, during a casual lunch conversation, Tina discovered that the vice-president of manufacturing had serious doubts about the validity of the assumptions the team was using to qualify sources of supply for a critical raw material.

Tina tried to convince him that he was wrong during two follow-up meetings, with no success. In fact, the more they talked, the more convinced the vice-president became that Tina was wrong. The project was too far along to change any assumptions without causing significant delays. In addition, the vice-president was likely to inherit the responsibility for implementing any approved plans for a new plant. For those reasons, Tina felt it was essential to resolve the disagreement before the scheduled completion of the project. Tina requested a project auditor be as-

signed to audit the project, paying special attention to the methodology behind the sourcing assumptions.

Questions: Is this a good use of the audit technique? Will it be helpful here? Why or why not?

General Ship Building Company

General Ship Building has a contract with the Department of the Navy to build three new aircraft carriers over the next five years. During the construction of the first ship, the project manager formed an auditing team to audit the construction process for the three ships. After picking the audit team members, he requested that they develop a set of minimum requirements for the projects and use this as a baseline in the audit. While reviewing the contract documents, an auditing team member discovered a discrepancy between the contract minimum requirements and the Navy's minimum requirements. Based on his findings, he has told the project manager that he has decided to contact the local Navy contract office and inform them of the problem.

Questions: If you were the project manager, how would you handle this situation? How can a customer be assured of satisfactory contract completion?

▶ PROJECT TEAM CONTINUING EXERCISE

This assignment involves an audit and written report on the findings. The audit and project evaluation should be conducted around the midpoint of the project, preferably at some midterm milestone. The auditor should be an outside evaluator or the project controller or other reporter. The determination of factors for measurement should be specifically addressed in the report, particularly costs and revenues. It should include project goals, the status of all tasks, the project prognosis, a risk assessment, and any caveats and limitations.

▶ BIBLIOGRAPHY

1. BALACHANDRA, R., and J. A. RAELIN. "How to Decide When to Abandon A Project." *Research Management*, July 1980.

2. BIERCE, A. *The Devil's Dictionary*. New York: Dell Publishing, 1991.

3. BUELL, C. K. "When to Terminate a Research and Development Project." *Research Management*, July 1967.

4. CERULLO, M. J. "Determining Post-Implementation Audit Success." *Journal of Systems Management*, March 1979.

5. COOPER, M. J. "Evaluation System for Project Selection." *Research Management*, March 1979.

6. DEAN, B. V. "A Research Laboratory Performance Model." In M. J. Cetron, H. Davidson, and A. H. Rubenstein, eds. *Quantitative Decision Aiding Techniques for Research and Development*. New York: Gordon and Breach, 1972.

7. DeCOTIIS, T. A., and L. DYER. "Defining and Measuring Project Performance." *Research Management*, Jan. 1979.

8. DEVAUX, S. A. "When the DIPP Dips: A P&L Index for Project Decisions." *Project Management Journal*, Sept. 1992.

9. FREEMAN, M., and P. BEALE. "Measuring Project Success." *Project Management Journal*, March 1992.

10. HICKS, C. F., and L. L. SCHMIDT, JR. "Post-Auditing: The Capital Investment Decision." *Management Accounting*, Aug. 1971.

11. HILDENBRANT, S. "The Changing Role of Analysis in Effective Implementation of Operations Research and Management Science." *European Journal of Operational Research*, Dec.. 1980.

12. JACKSON, B. "Decision Methods for Evaluating R & D Projects." *Research Management*, June-Aug. 1983.

13. KELLY, J. F. *Computerized Management Information Systems*. New York: Macmillan, 1970.

14. KERZNER, H. "Evaluation Techniques in Project Management." *Journal of Systems Management*, Feb. 1980.

15. MEREDITH, J. "Program Evaluation Techniques in The Health Services." *American Journal of Public Health*, Nov. 1976.

16. MEYERS, W. R. *The Evaluation Enterprise*. San Francisco: Jossey-Bass, 1981.

17. NASH, C., and D. PEARCE. "Criteria for Evaluating Project Evaluation Techniques." *Journal of the American Institute of Planners*, March 1975.

18. NEWTON, J. K. "Computer Modeling for Project Evaluation." *Omega*, May 1981.

19. PHILLIPS, J. P. "MS Implementation: A Parable." *Interfaces*, Aug. 1979.

20. ROSENAU, M. D., JR. "Assessing Project Value." *Industrial Research Development*, May 1979.

21. RUSKIN, A. M., and W. E. ESTES. "The Project Management Audit: Its Role and Conduct." *Project Management Journal*, Aug. 1985.

22. SCHNELL, J. S., and R. S. NICOLOSI. "Capital Expenditure Feedback: Project Reappraisal." *The Engineering Economist*, Summer 1974.

23. SOUDER, W. E. "System for Using R & D Project Evaluation Methods." *Research Management*, Sept. 1978.

24. Stuckenbruck, L. C., and C. L. Myers. "Project Evaluation." A Special Summer Issue of the *Project Management Journal*, Aug. 1985.

25. Thierauf, R. J. *Management Auditing*. New York: AMACOM, 1980.

26. Thamhain, H. J., and D. L Wilemon. "Conflict Management in Project Life Cycles." *Sloan Management Review*, Spring 1975.

27. Turner, W. S., III. *Project Auditing Methodology*. Amsterdam: North Holland, 1980.

28. Walker, M. G., and R. Bracey. "Independent Auditing As Project Control." *Datamation*, March 1980.

CASE
DELTA ELECTRONICS, INC.*
Robert D. Landel

"Well, it's finally done. I hope." John Wilson sat back and looked at the recommendations he had made concerning the redesign of the order processing activities at Delta Electronics, Inc.

John worked in the planning department at Delta Electronics and had been put on special assignment two months ago to analyze the system of processing customer orders. The system was considered by many executives in the company to be overly complicated and inefficient and, therefore, unnecessarily expensive. Moreover, years of poor delivery performance had tarnished the company's record as a dependable supplier of replacement parts and new products. Only in the last 15 months had the company seen its customer service improve dramatically. In a few days John hoped to be able to present to top management his recommendations on streamlining the order entry system and consolidating order entry groups. It was early in 1982 and, with the recession that had gripped their industry, no one had to tell John how important cost savings projects were for Delta Electronics. Still, the five-year business plan he had been working on before this special assignment was important, too, and he was anxious to get back to it. He wondered how Mr. Andy Roders, the company's vice-president of finance (and his immediate superior), would respond to his recommendations. Would Roders signal his approval by scheduling a presentation of John's recommendations at next week's executive staff meeting or would Roders send him back to the drawing board?

Company Background

Delta Electronics, Inc., with world headquarters in Chicago, Illinois, employed approximately 3000 people in the design, development, manufacturing, and marketing of high technology instrumentation, controls, and computer systems for power generation and industrial automation in the process industries and the utility markets.

Through the years, Delta had pioneered a host of developments in control and systems technology which had earned it a worldwide reputation as a leading supplier of instrumentation and control systems. Delta strived to provide systems which allowed tighter process control, more efficient fuel consumption, and less maintenance. Delta instruments and controls offered an impressive degree of flexibility, reliability, and system compatibility to serve the varying needs of industry. Delta analog and digital controls were widely used and ranged from the simplest flowmeter to sophisticated, microprocessor-based control equipment. Its advanced systems for monitoring and control employed digital-based distributed information and control architecture, with colorgraphic display and a data communications loop.

In 1951, Delta Electronics started with ten employees. By 1981, they had grown into a company operating three manufacturing plants, a large replacement parts distribution center, and 43 sales and service offices across the United States, with subsidiaries in Canada, Australia, and Brazil. They also had licensees in several European and Asian countries which manufactured and sold Delta Electronics products. In 1981, Delta Electronics was bought out by a major international manufacturing firm and operated as a wholly owned subsidiary. Delta Electronics sales were approximately $250 million in 1981.

Delta's customer base included both government contracts and utilities, which generally required long lead times, and industrial firms (such as iron and steel, chemical, pulp, and paper) which were, in late 1981, characterized as "wanting quick order turnarounds." John Wilson's business planning studies had indicated a trend toward less capital spending by Delta's customers and more emphasis on the retrofitting of existing processes and control equipment.

Low Cost Producer Initiatives

In mid-1981, Bob Morris was promoted from the position of vice-president of engineering to president of Delta Electronics. As president, he confronted the undesirable situation that Delta Electronics was most likely the high cost producer in industrial and utilities markets where business volume activity was down by at least 15 percent for most competitors. Accordingly, Bob Morris and his executive staff met weekly during the summer months to formulate goals and programs which would transform Delta Electronics into the low cost producer position and industry leader in the instrumentation and controls business. The intermediate-term goals developed by the executive staff group over several weeks in August 1981 are shown in Exhibit 1. Bob Morris charged each functional executive with developing specific goal-oriented improvement initiatives and presenting them to the executive staff group. A selection of those adopted by the group in the fall of 1981 is shown in Exhibit 2.

Parts, Products, and Systems

As the product line grew in size and diversity, Delta Electronics separated its business into three categories: parts, products, and systems. Parts were the simplest components available. They were usually simply designed, easily describable items such as

Exhibit 1: DELTA ELECTRONICS, INC. Immediate-Term Executive Staff Goals

1. We must restructure our business to respond to a fundamental shift from electro-mechanical to digital/electronic designs.
2. The new structure must serve as the basis for even more rapid growth than experienced in the last two years.
3. We will not sacrifice responsiveness to our customers and, in fact, will strive to improve it further.
4. We will not generate additional overdue shipments and we will continue to work toward providing the most reliable delivery performance in the industry.
5. We will become *the* cost leader in the instrumentation business.
6. We will continue to search for the most qualified people for every position ensuring that high performers are rewarded and that low performers are replaced.
7. Our original 1982 Business Plan commitments must be achieved in spite of the industry-wide downturn in business.

Source: Executive staff group minutes, August 1981.

adapter tubing and connectors. Products were more specialized, more complex items, typically assembled by Delta Electronics from hundreds of purchased and manufactured parts. Examples of products were pressure gauges, gas analyzers, and universal drives. Finally, systems were the most complex items sold and were usually custom-designed for specific applications such as process control systems for nuclear and fossil power electrical utility stations. Systems were usually designed by an engineering project team based on customer performance and reliability requirements and then manufactured from purchased and fabricated products.

Parts, products, and systems were separated to help organize a diverse product line and because very different marketing strategies supported each. Parts were generally low-priced items and were used primarily as replacement components by customers, usually on Delta's products or systems. Parts often required immediate delivery to get critical equipment running again; therefore, customer service and quick

Exhibit 2: DELTA ELECTRONICS, INC. Executive Staff Group Initiatives

1. Engineering and marketing will develop internal documentation methods to significantly reduce both the elapsed time and costs to process bid proposals for systems business.

2. A salary headcount reduction program will be formulated, calling for each manager to identify and eliminate poor performers in order to achieve a 10 percent reduction in force. A forced order ranking procedure will be developed and implemented during the fall of 1981.

3. Early retirements will be introduced and voluntary layoff procedures will be designed.

4. Aggressive, competitive bidding will be encouraged among Delta's vendors, and larger purchase discount opportunities will be pursued.

5. Short work weeks will be used in order to prevent finished goods inventory build-up.

6. All summer picnics and the national sales meeting will be cancelled for the 1982 year.

7. Annual increases for salaried employees will be indefinitely postponed.

8. A hiring freeze will be instituted in all areas with new hires being available only by prior approval of the executive staff group.

9. Finance will examine the overall order entry process for possible acceleration where the goal is to reduce indirect salary costs and to provide greater responsiveness in delivery.

10. Monthly expenses will be reviewed at the executive staff meetings.

11. Engineering will accelerate the new product releases.

12. Engineering will accelerate the processing of dirty product orders and systems orders.

13. A cooperative and highly aggressive formal program of product cost reduction, directed toward making Delta the low cost leader will be defined, sponsored, and directed by manufacturing. This program will be in place by 10/1/81. Reviews of the ten most significant cost accomplishments will be held by manufacturing for the executive staff on a monthly basis.

14. An inventory reduction program of $10 million will be developed by manufacturing and marketing by 10/1/81.

15. Quality assurance will put in place an aggressive schedule with manufacturing cooperation to implement and follow up on machine and assembly capabilities studies.

16. Marketing will accelerate its development of innovative approaches to gain share of near-term *product* business to offset, as nearly as possible, the $11 million needed to cover the projected 1982 factory load short-fall due to the business downturn.

Source: Executive staff group minutes, Fall 1981.

delivery were much more important than price or any special features which may have differentiated Delta Electronics' parts from their competition's. There were usually enough physical differences between various manufacturers' replacement parts to make switching inconvenient for the price. Customer service pressures were often aggravated by the practice within Delta Electronics manufacturing of filling customer orders for products by scavenging from parts inventories. Replacement parts generally carried high margins. The replacement parts services offered by Delta Electronics are described in Exhibit 3.

On the other hand, products were more competitive than parts, but without the extreme requirements for rapid delivery. Since many products were essentially standard within the industry, competitors' products were often interchangeable; thus, the products market was more price sensitive and required Delta to sell at lower profit margins. Several of Delta's product categories were priced higher than competing lines because of the technical performance and reliability advantages or unique features of Delta's products.

The lowest margins were on systems orders, although they were permitted the longest delivery and commanded the highest price. Delta's marketing effort emphasized superior design performance and features and reasonable pricing in an extremely competitive market.

Exhibit 3: DELTA ELECTRONICS, INC. Replacement Parts Services

Delta replacement parts services are centralized at our Chicago headquarters, where customer service representatives are available to assist you. Our representatives work individually with you to provide the personal assistance that is part of the total Delta customer service package.

In order to meet your replacement parts needs quickly and efficiently, we offer the following customer services:

- Delta customer service representatives are assigned to individual customer accounts, providing personal attention and prompt response.

- Delta customer service representatives are capable of providing instant order status via on-line CRT's.

- Delta replacement parts service updates a parts price list throughout the year to ensure accuracy of price and delivery quotations.

- Delta customer service representatives provide order verification and accuracy through a sophisticated order entry system.

- Delta customer service representatives are aware of all substitution parts in order to expedite your parts requests.

EMERGENCY SERVICE: 24–HOUR SHIPPING

Over the years, Delta has learned to deal with many potential emergencies in all phases of our business. To respond to your demand for quick shipment of replacement parts, we make it possible to ship most parts within 24 hours of order receipt.

Emergency orders have top priority at each point in the Delta order cycle.

CENTRAL WAREHOUSING FOR FASTER SHIPMENT

In order to streamline the replacement parts order process, we have centralized the storage and shipment of high demand replacement parts at our warehouse facility in Easton, Illinois. In order to meet our customers' special stock requests, we also maintain a stock of obsolete product line parts. The Delta Replacement Parts Distribution Center uses a computerized information and retrieval system to keep you informed of parts availability and lead times. Through coordinated efforts with our Chicago headquarters and Easton warehouse, we are able to provide you with Delta "total customer service" for your spare parts needs.

Order Processing

Just as there was a difference in profit margins and level of competition between parts, products, and systems, so there were differences in the way orders were taken and handled at Delta Electronics. Customer order logging, data entry, and cleaning-up activities were performed by three separate order processing groups (see Exhibit 4). Parts order entry and products order entry were the responsibility of finance while systems order entry was in the marketing function's project management department.

The order entry process for *products* is shown in Exhibit 5. Ninety percent of all products orders were placed into the Delta Electronics order entry process by the regional salesforce personnel (10 percent were sent directly by the customer to the main office). The salesperson recorded a customer's order on a Field

Requisition Form and then mailed the form to the Chicago main office for "logging."

The logging step was the first entry of any order-related data into the company's computer system. A data entry clerk in the products order processing group, using information on the Field Requisition Form, entered the following data: customer name, customer identification number (obtained from customer lists in a separate reference book), customer purchase order number (if available), date the order was received, and other general shipping and invoicing information concerning the order. A preformatted CRT data screen guided the entry of data at this step. A Delta control number was assigned to each customer order so it could be tracked through the entire order entry process. The data entry clerk also wrote this same information on the top section of the Order Review Sheet (Exhibit 6). At the completion of this

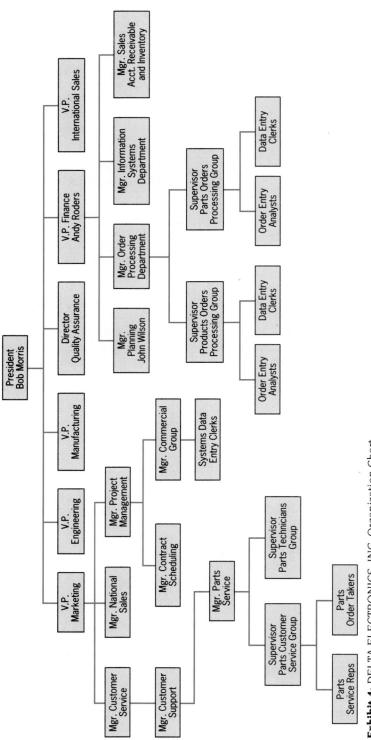

Exhibit 4: DELTA ELECTRONICS, INC. Organization Chart

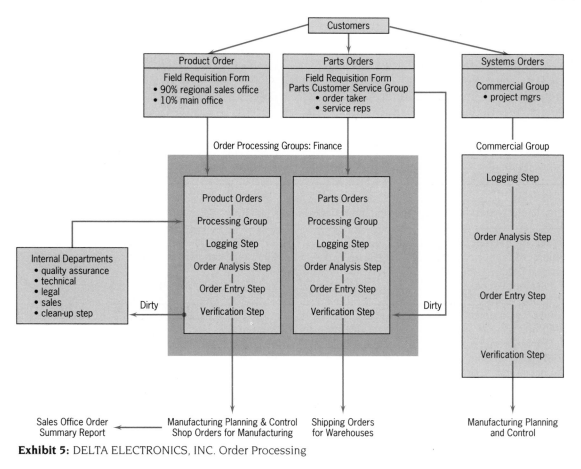

Exhibit 5: DELTA ELECTRONICS, INC. Order Processing

logging step, a computer-prepared postcard was printed and mailed to the customer. It acknowledged receipt of the customer's request for Delta Electronics equipment and it also informed the customer of the Delta control number that should be referred to on any future correspondence.

The order analysis step followed the logging of Field Requisition Forms. The supervisor of the products order processing group (see Exhibit 5) assigned an order entry analyst to fill out the remainder of the Order Review Sheet from the Field Requisition Form and actual customer purchase order, if one had been received. At this step, the order would be delayed if the appropriate credit information, international export requirements, or special shipping instructions

were missing from the Field Requisition Form or the customer order. Not until the relevant information was received could a completed Order Review Sheet be returned to a data entry clerk for entry into the order processing system.

During the order entry step, a data entry clerk entered the second section of data on the Order Review Sheet into the computer, following a preformatted CRT data screen. The computer was programmed to check all their data entries, whenever possible, against master computer data files to verify that all numbers were valid. In this verification step, any preformatted entry left blank or determined by the computer to be invalid caused the order to be classified as "dirty" and automatically printed out by the computer

Logging Step   Date _____

Purchase Order No. _____	Delta Control No. _____
Field Requisition Form Date _____	Contract No. _____
Customer Ident. No. _____	
Proposal No. _____	Date _____
Invoice To _____	Attention _____
Ship To _____	Attention _____
Acknowledgment To _____	Attention _____
Engineer _____	Contractor _____
Order Type _____	Log Operator _____

Order Analysis Step (with Customer Purchase Order)

Order Analyst _____	Partial Ship Code _____
Shipment Date _____	Customer Requisition Date _____
Invoice Data:	
Payment Terms ____ Method ____	No. Invoice Requisition ____
Billing Terms _____	
Invoice Comments _____	
Shipping Data:	
Delivery Terms _____	
Shipment Mode _____	Packaging _____
Special Instructions _____	

Data Entry Clerk _____   Technician _____

Exhibit 6: DELTA ELECTRONICS, INC. Order Review Sheet

system at a printer in the products order processing group. For instance, a dirty order would result from the absence of the product calibration specifications desired by the customer. This information needed to be obtained from the customer.

Depending on what information was missing or incorrect, a dirty order was returned either to the salesperson or to the appropriate main office department for "clean up." Except for the limited number of data entries verified by the computer master files, this was the first point in order processing in which the entire order was checked for accuracy and completeness. No individual or group who had worked with the order up to this point had a direct responsibility or an explicit goal for generating complete and accurate orders.

Product orders were complicated to clean up because of the technical specification details which were required to identify exactly the product desired by the customer. There were many different pressure gauges,

for example, depending on the desired range and sensitivity of the device, its accuracy, physical size, and durability. Each variation required a separate product identification code. Only about 50 percent of all product orders completed the first pass through order entry clean. Cleaning dirty product orders could be very time consuming because it frequently necessitated sending the complete order file back to the regional salesperson or through the main office for technical clarification or further detail, often involving additional customer contact. Personnel in the products orders processing group were assigned responsibility for getting an order cleaned up in the shortest possible time. There was almost no routine cause of dirty orders known to management of the group. No systematic analysis of probable causes had been conducted in the past two years.

Once the product order passed the verification step clean, a shop order was printed. Shop orders were accumulated by the manufacturing planning and control department, where staff professionals developed the manufacturing schedule. The regional sales office was then notified with a Sales Office Order Summary Report. It indicated the date that a customer order had been released to manufacturing.

The ordering process for parts and systems varied slightly from the ordering process for products. Whereas product orders were usually taken by salespersons with an occasional repeat customer calling in directly, all replacement parts orders were taken over the telephone or received through the mail without salesperson involvement. This was possible because parts were generally much easier to order since they had a specific catalog part number. Part orders were taken by service representatives in the marketing function's parts customer service group (see Exhibit 4). Employees in this group filled out Field Requisition Forms and sent them to be logged and entered into the computer by personnel in the parts orders processing group within the finance function. Data entry clerks and analysts performed processing tasks similar to those described in the products order entry process.

Parts orders were more likely to complete the first pass through entry clean because the catalogues of replacement parts provided complete parts data. Typically, about 15 percent of parts orders needed to be cleaned up. This was a relatively simple task since the most common missing pieces of information (part number or customer identification number) readily could be found in the parts catalog or customer listings. Dirty parts orders were not cleaned up by the data entry clerks but, instead, were sent back to the service representatives in the parts customer service group for necessary additions or corrections. Once the parts order was declared clean by the service representative, the data was entered in the computer, and then a shipping order was printed and sent to the appropriate warehouse.

Systems orders generated average sales of $600,000 per order, with some systems generating as much as $20 million for Delta Electronics. Primarily due to the intricate design specification and warranty provisions of systems contracts, the order processing activities for systems were necessarily more complex than those required for parts and products. When the company was interested in bidding on a system contract, a project manager and several engineers were assigned to a system team. If an order resulted from Delta Electronics' bid, the project manager took the order, usually in the form of a customer purchase order referencing Delta Electronics' written bid proposal. The purchase order was sent to the main office and was referred to the commercial group within the marketing function (see Exhibit 5). The commercial group reviewed the terms and conditions set forth in the customer's purchase order to verify that they were within standard Delta Electronics terms and conditions. Once approved by the manager of the commercial group, the order was logged by data entry clerks in that group and subsequently processed in that group in an activity sequence similar to a part or product order.

In most cases, systems orders needed considerable time-consuming analysis and cleaning up. Consequently, virtually 100 percent of all systems orders were rejected as "dirty" the first time through order entry and returned to the appropriate project manager for action.

The Order Processing Working Committee—1977 to 1981

In 1977 Delta Electronics' management faced stiffening competition, increasing customer delivery service problems, and rising payroll costs. The major response, made by the previous president at Delta Electronics and Andy Roders, was to form the order processing working committee. The committee, made up of 12 representatives from marketing, manufacturing, finance, and engineering and chaired by a manager in the management information systems department, was given the charter in late 1977 to:

1. Examine the existing system(s) and procedures being used for processing parts, products, and systems orders,

2. Define, analyze, and detail the real departmental needs for order processing within Delta Electronics, and

3. Design new, streamlined, and automated order processing system(s) and procedures to reduce fixed costs while maintaining and improving current customer service levels.

By early 1978, the committee had found that order processing at Delta Electronics required a large amount of paper handling for each order and a great deal of redundant work. Many of the processing delays were caused by errors in transferring data between order-entry documents. The original timetable proposed by the committee recommended that a new computer controlled order processing system be designed by July 1979 and fully implemented throughout the company by February 1981. The goal had to be attained, however, while at least maintaining, and preferably improving, Delta Electronics' customer service. Once the computer system was in place, its capabilities would be expanded to include manufacturing scheduling and MRP analysis.

As a working committee, issues were brought up, tasks assigned, and alternative solutions discussed and resolved by agreement of the committee. The work of the committee was broken into three phases.

Phase I was a feasibility study and included the following:

1. **Analysis of Current Systems.** A complete review of all existing systems was done. This included documenting the paperwork flows for parts, products, and systems orders. All forms were gathered and documented.

2. **Definition and Analysis of Information and Processing Requirements.** Each member of the committee submitted the information and processing requirements from his or her area of interest. These were analyzed and combined to form a set of data entry specifications.

3. **Design of New System.** A macro design of a new order processing system was formulated using the information and processing requirements and documentation of the current systems.

The full committee met frequently with various user subcommittees covering specific order processing problems. The major subcommittees and their activities were:

1. **Coding.** Reviewed the parts and products coding techniques being used at Delta, analyzed them, and recommended a new, more efficient means of coding.

2. **Order Numbering.** Reviewed the current customer order numbering techniques and offered solutions to the problems caused by the ineffective numbering system.

3. **Short Term Order Processing.** Developed and implemented a short term fix to reduce front-end order entry time for parts orders from 20–40 days to 8–20 days. This effort interrupted the working committee's work for six months (from February to August 1978).

4. **Design.** Developed the paperwork flow for the new order processing system.

The feasibility study was completed and issued January 29, 1979. Exhibit 7 presents the key needs and objectives the committee identified as impacting the order processing activities at Delta Electronics. Phase II involved the design and implementation of the new system while Phase III would be the evaluation of the system.

The committee decided to pursue an in-house design for their new order processing system after visiting several companies. Several outside vendors were also considered but discarded due to the need for extensive modifications and high cost.

Phase II design activities were focused into four modules. Each module was defined in such a way that it could be implemented independently of the others. The committee's goal was a continual stream of achievements that would maintain a high degree of enthusiasm by the users. The modules were to be prioritized, designed, and implemented in a sequence which tracked the major steps of the order processing flow.

The working committee's design timetable proved to be too optimistic. Work was hampered by labor union contract problems during the summer and fall of 1979, resulting in a seven-month delay of scheduled milestones. The general system design was completed in February 1980, seven months behind schedule. The order logging module was successfully implemented in April of 1980. The design and implementation of the data entry, shipping, and invoicing modules for parts and product orders was originally scheduled to be completed late 1981 or early 1982.

In the fall of 1980 an evaluation was done on the remainder of the project. A revised approach was taken by the committee which entailed implementing the data entry module for all orders (parts, products, and systems orders) but continuing to print the old paperwork at each step of the entire process. This would allow shipping and invoicing to function using the paperwork from the old system with only minor changes.

The data entry module was implemented in the fall of 1981. As of March 1982, the shipping and invoicing modules had not been implemented.

In reviewing the project history, the casewriter was told, "We only sell automation, we do not seem to use it in our internal processes." This seemed to be re-

Exhibit 7: DELTA ELECTRONICS, INC. Order Processing System Feasibility Study and Evaluation, January 29, 1979

NEED

The need for an order processing system is demonstrated by the following:

1. Long Order Processing Times: Front-end order processing durations for parts orders takes 20–40 days; for product orders up to 60 days. This time must be reduced to remain competitive in the marketplace.

2. Outdated System: The current system was implemented piecemeal over many years and does not meet the needs of today's organization. Maintenance accounts for 40–60 percent of the available software support thus leaving little time for any major development work.

3. Data: The system does not supply the data needed. Data must be gathered, organized, and stored for easy retrieval. Production of meaningful reports is currently near impossible on a company-wide basis. Similar reports must be cannibalized manually to produce one meaningful management report, thus producing excessive paperwork.

4. Lack of Backlog Control: Data needed to locate and classify an all-company backlog is extremely difficult to control, time consuming to generate and manage, and almost impossible to change.

5. Excessive Paperwork: The current system is bogged-down by voluminous amounts of paperwork which is extremely difficult to control, time consuming to generate and manage, and almost impossible to change.

KEY OBJECTIVES

The new system must respond to these critical needs:

1. Decrease order processing time for parts and product orders to three days.

2. Produce an order acknowledgment, preferably within three days, but no later than ten days from receipt of order on all orders that will not ship within ten days.

3. Generate an invoice within one working day of shipment.

4. Create one order entry system for the processing of all Delta Electronics business.

5. Measure order processing paperwork against a plan.

6. Provide a base of data or foundation for all future systems development.

7. Reduce paperwork.

Source: Paraphrased from Feasibility Study, 1/29/79, pages 2 and 3.

---

flected throughout the working committee's results. A computer system was designed and partially installed but the remainder of the order entry working environment was left intact. The casewriter was also told: "A committee member would say he needed feature XYZ and it was usually put into the system design without question. Too many special features and not enough fundamental aspects were installed. The head of MIS was a central computer fanatic. He wanted everything hardwired and under his department's control."

John Wilson's Special Assignment

In early 1982, Mr. J. W. Lindley, an outside consultant to Delta Electronics, was called in to review the cost reducing efforts under way in the marketing and man-

ufacturing areas. Among his findings was the apparent slow progress of the order processing working committee. As of March 1982, only two of the originally proposed four order processing modules had been even partially implemented. The two modules currently in place were designed to simplify the logging and data entry activities of the process. The changes that had been made had done little more than reduce the number of typewriters and increase the number of computer keyboards being used strictly as typewriters.

It disturbed Mr. Lindley to find that not only was implementation of the new order processing system well behind schedule, but no reduction in labor or decrease in paperwork had resulted. In fact, there was actually one more level of paperwork per order now than there had been when the project was begun (Order Review Sheet). The order processing working committee was still organized but had not been active for some time. They had spent a great deal of effort making sure a system was designed, but had not taken an aggressive role in pushing for implementation.

When Bob Morris, president of Delta Electronics, became aware of Mr. Lindley's findings, he immediately assigned John Wilson to "find out why projected net savings of $275,000 per year have not been realized." John began his work by learning all he could about the order processing working committee and the order processing activities at Delta. First, he read all published reports and committee meeting minutes from the past 4 1/2 years. Next, he interviewed committee members and employees involved with order processing. Finally, he observed work flow in the three order processing groups noting how people and equipment were allocated.

From John's observations and analyses he reached the following conclusions:

1. The schedule set by the order processing working committee for implementing a new order processng system was currently 13 months behind. The software that had been completed and implemented did little to streamline order processing. Implementation had dragged on so slowly that system users had lost interest, making it doubtful the rest of the system would ever be implemented successfully.

2. Start-up of the new computer-based order processing system had caused a great deal of frustration throughout the company. No individual appeared directly responsible for the final structure of the system or its software as it was installed. Operators in the user's group did not know exactly what the software programming could do, and user's manuals and operating procedures were promised but never supplied.

3. The new order processing system was basically a word processor. The entire system was still primarily handled with paper flows rather than through the electronic data systems capabilities of the computer. The extra form (Order Review Sheet) now in the order process was recently initiated by one of the order processing group supervisors. He felt that a printed copy was necessary at one more stage of the process to insure against the computer losing valuable information.

4. At least 12 departments and groups in Delta's main office and 60 individuals routinely interacted with the order processing computer system. This included people responsible for initial logging, data entry as well as the cleaning-up of parts, products, and systems orders.

5. Parts, products, and systems orders were processed by three entirely separate organizations even though the logging, order reviewing, and data entry aspects of the processing were very similar.

6. With the order processing groups working with the same customers, no one group seemed to feel responsible for maintaining an accurate list of current customers. The number of customer files had been growing rapidly since no group had purged inactive accounts. Computer response was noticeably slow when using these files.

Based on the conclusions shown above, John Wilson developed his recommendations for Andy Roders for immediate consideration.

John Wilson's Recommendations

Order Processing Activities Recommendations

A. Reorganize the order processing activities by combining the existing employees in the parts and products order processing groups, the parts service departmen t, and certain specialized technical functions into a *customer order service* (COS) *group*. The specific features of the COS group are listed below.

1. Parts, products, and systems orders are to be processed by a single organizational unit. Members of the project management commercial group who log and enter systems orders are to be pulled into the COS Group (see Exhibit 8). The functional reporting relationships would have to be determined.

2. Technicians who can be identified with cleaning up dirty orders on parts and products are to be pulled into the COS group.

3. Data entry job duties are to be redesigned so that all data are entered from and checked against source documents rather than the Order Review Sheet. The Order Review Sheet will be dropped.

4. Define the charter of the COS group to include:

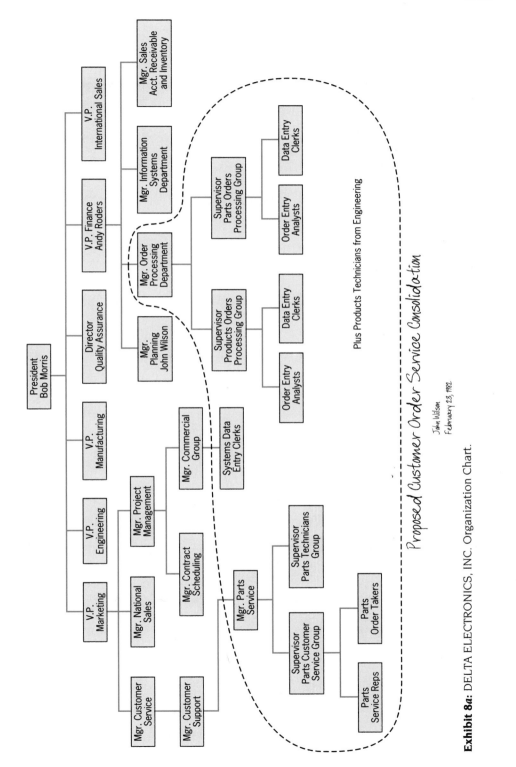

Plus Products Technicians from Engineering

John Wilson
February 23, 1982

Proposed Customer Order Service Consolidation

Exhibit 8a: DELTA ELECTRONICS, INC. Organization Chart.

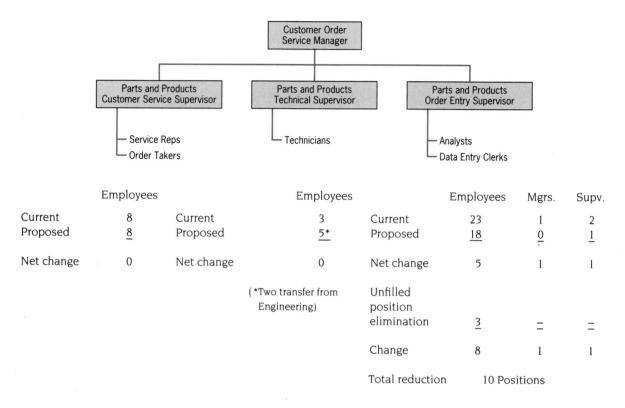

	Employees		Employees		Employees	Mgrs.	Supv.
Current	8	Current	3	Current	23	1	2
Proposed	8	Proposed	5*	Proposed	18	0	1
Net change	0	Net change	0	Net change	5	1	1
		(*Two transfer from Engineering)		Unfilled position elimination	3	=	=
				Change	8	1	1
				Total reduction		10 Positions	

Summary of 10 Position Reductions

1 supervisor from Parts and Products Order Processing Groups
1 manager from Mgr., Order Processing Dept.
5 clerks and analysts Parts and Products Order Processing Groups
3 data entry clerk currently unfilled

Exhibit 8*b*: DELTA ELECTRONICS, INC. Proposed Customer Order Service Organization.

- the parts and products businesses;
- acting as a single point of contact for inquiries from customers or salespeople on parts and products, domestic and international;
- receiving feedback and measuring error rates in data entry;
- an emphasis upon target goals to appraise the timely and accurate entry of customer purchase order data; and
- performance direction to ensure that orders are filled on-time a high percentage (95%) of the time.

B. MIS management should prepare a plan for expediting the installation of the billing and shipping modules for the order processing system. The plan should include:

1. Three alternative systems completion dates (rush date, normal conditions expected date, extended horizon date) and the scope, methodology, and resources associated with each date for management review.

2. Listings of equipment needed, location of copying machines, groups affected, and other environmental factors.

3. A summary of any proposed changes to administrative planning and control systems.

4. Proposal for organizaton of a new implemention group (disband the order processing working committee!).

Future Management Information System Plans Recommendations

Future MIS systems should be implemented under the following administrative conditions:

1. An individual should be responsible for making decisions about what is included in the proposed computer system (a project manager).

2. An executive should have overall responsibility for computer and administrative system changes.

3. An implementation plan for the computer work should include impact statements with respect to organizational and administrative changes.

4. Computer system introduction should be implemented on a "drop dead date" or all-system-go basis rather than a sequential gradual introduction.

5. Introduction of the computer system should be accompanied by user's manuals and operating procedures for the affected groups.

Mr. Roders' Assessment

Mr. Roders wrestled with the implications of John's recommendations. John had stated, "My COS Group design will allow three currently unfilled data entry positions to be eliminated. Furthermore, seven people currently employed by the parts and products order processing groups can be let go, since there are no other positions in the company for them to fill."

The data entry clerks and analysts and the parts and products technicians in the new customer order service group would be responsible for cleaning up part and product orders as well as the actual data entry for part, product, and system orders. They would still not be required to clean up systems orders, however, since this would often be much more complicated and time consuming. John's plan called for eliminating much of the existing paperwork in the ordering system. People who were unaware of the capabilities and dependability of the new computer-driven order processing system were sure to resist elimination of the Order Review Sheet paper back-up system.

The most recent monthly report data for Gene Vince, manager of the order processing department, showed the calendar day duration for the processing of parts and products orders. Mr. Roders wondered how this performance history ought to be factored into his analysis (see Exhibit 9).

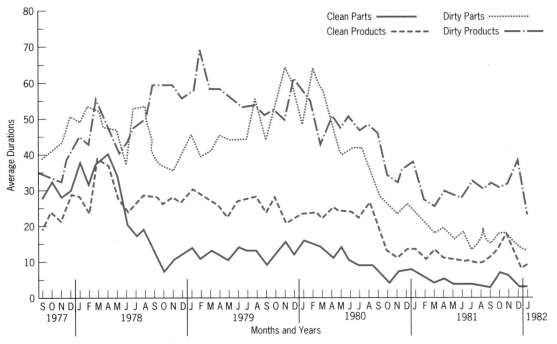

Exhibit 9: DELTA ELECTRONICS, INC: Order Processing Durations (In Calendar Days)

▶ QUESTIONS

The real questions Mr. Roders faced in accepting or rejecting all or part of John's plan were:

1. Can data entry, analysis, and clean-up jobs for parts, products, and, to some degree, systems really be combined into one group as John Wilson suggested?

2. Depending on which people are eliminated, the new organization will either have ex-analysts doing order entry or ex-data entry clerks doing analysis and clean-up. How will these people react to these changes?

3. With such a major departmental redesign, can John really be sure 10 is the right number of peo-

ple to eliminate? John Wilson had not conducted work activity time studies on any of the processing functions. How could you ever decide exactly how many? What happens if the volume of orders drops off or increases dramatically in the near future?

4. What criteria should be used in evaluating service effectiveness? How big an effect on customer service level, a very important issue at Delta Electronics, would this restructing have, during and after the change?

▶ This article provides a general overview of the audit purpose and process. It discusses why an audit is desirable, what it entails, when it should be conducted (both planned and unplanned), who should conduct it, and how it should be executed. Preparation, implementation, and reporting are also described in detail. Some hazards and cautions are given for final guidance.

The value of this article for managers is the guidance it provides for the effective use of the audit. For general managers, it describes the utility of the audit for overseeing projects and their implementation. For project managers, it helps them understand the need for an audit and how it can be helpful to them in achieving the project's objectives for the organization.

READING

THE PROJECT MANAGEMENT AUDIT: ITS ROLE AND CONDUCT

Arnold M. Ruskin
W. Eugene Estes

Introduction

Projects are managed by people, and most people are at least a little imperfect. These imperfections can cause them to manage projects poorly. Moreover, project managers are subject to conflicting pressures that can confuse or distort the way they see their projects. Various tools are therefore used to compensate for project managers' shortcomings. Among these tools are formalized planning and control techniques, contingency allowances, reporting procedures, supervisory relationships, design reviews, and so forth. Another useful tool that does not cost much is the project management audit.

A project management audit is concerned with much more than the project's financial records. Rather, it concerns all of the project elements, including objectives, plans, resources, schedules, budgets, accomplishments, and so forth. While project management audits have been mentioned in the literature, they are not widely understood, and it is worthwhile examining them in some detail.

Projects fail because mistakes occur in planning and execution and then are not corrected. The project manager may not understand their significance, may be lazy or too busy to correct them at the time, or may feel that it would be good politics to keep them quiet. Project management audits can nip these in the bud.

In addition, audits give other stakeholders, such as the organization's general management, readings on just how their projects stand and what immediate actions they might have to take to protect their interests.

This paper discusses the why, when, who, what and how of project management audits so that the reader can decide when and if a project should be audited and how to proceed.

Why

Why audit a project? What can an audit do that is not provided in the ordinary course of reporting project plans and progress?

Audits are generally performed because management and investors or clients need to know the true status of their projects. Otherwise, they may be unpleasantly surprised later, when the situation cannot be salvaged. They need to be assured that their resources are being used as planned. They need to know that the results will indeed meet their objectives, or failing that, what the shortfall will be and what corrective measures can be taken. And they need to know that the reports on the project are complete, objective, and accurate. Project management audits serve these needs.

To elaborate, many projects are complex in their goals, approaches, or relationships. These complexities cloud the project staff's vision of the true endpoints of their work so that they are commonly lost from view. An experienced auditor who has little or no connection with the project can probe it in ways that no one involved with the project is likely to do. Thus, he or she can determine whether management's and the investors' or client's interests are really being met.

Even without complexities, timely audits can reduce the chance of project failure. Projects fail for a number of reasons. Some projects should never have been started in the first place. Timely audits will discover such unfortunate circumstances and prompt their early termination as an alternative to a later failure, saving resources in the process. Other projects fail because mistakes are not corrected when they occur, even when one or several staff members are well aware of them. When mistakes are allowed to survive, time elapses and further steps may compound the errors. Situations that were repairable then become project failures.

Mistakes survive and are compounded because of indolence, lack of courage, or moral or intellectual dishonesty, together with a lack of thorough and im-

partial examination. Timely project management audits can force prompt recognition of mistakes for what they are and lead to their correction.

Also, highly competent project managers are often spread too thin. Audits help bring such situations to light and prompt corrective action before something bad happens.

What

A project management audit is a comprehensive, thorough fact-finding exercise. It unearths and examines the status of a project, including the quality and quantity of the work and whether it meets the client's needs; the resources expended and the resources required to complete the work; the suitability of the schedule for the work done and work to be done; organizational issues; and so forth. In making this examination, the audit delves into:

1. the detailed plans
2. monitoring and control procedures
3. risks and contingency allowances
4. staffing arrangements
5. internal interfaces
6. reporting arrangements
7. customer relations
8. subcontractor and vendor relations
9. relations with third parties
10. accounting, invoicing, and billing
11. other mundane but essential matters.

Since the aim of an audit is to establish the true status of the entire project and not become a witch hunt (which would make a lot of key personnel defensive), it is not particularly focused on exceptional items unless and until they appear. Cause and effect analyses are frequently included, but they are not essential. When they are included, their purpose is to identify how certain unfortunate effects can be prevented in the future. Again, witch hunts are not intended.

Unpleasant facts, however, are not shunned or left unexamined. On the contrary, the project management audit is structured, staffed, and conducted precisely to find and characterize any unpleasantness there might be with minimum defensiveness and acrimony. An audit serves a project uniquely in this regard.

A project management audit is superior, for example, to most supervisory relationships in dealing with unpleasantness. A project manager and his or her supervisor have a continuing relationship that complicates any current probe. While the best relationships are based on honesty, they also include loyalty, trust, and sensitivity to the other's feelings. When honesty and loyalty conflict, who can predict that honesty will dominate? When trust exists, who can predict that the search will be thorough? When one is sensitive to another's feelings, who can predict that problems will be described accurately? For these reasons, the independent audit has certain advantages over supervisory examinations.

A project management audit also has advantages over design reviews when it comes to ascertaining the status of the entire project. The purpose of design reviews is to assure that the customer's specifications are being met and will continue to be met. While this is indeed one aspect of an audit, it is only one aspect. A project management audit also examines whether the project's detailed objectives are correct; whether the project plan, resources, arrangements, and processes are appropriate and working; and whether there are any hidden agendas or other insidious factors that threaten the success of the project. These are largely internal matters to the organization that is doing the project, and many, if not most of them, are unlikely to be aired in a design review.

Audits also serve projects in a way that they cannot possibly serve themselves. They provide independent verification of project status. While a project manager who is skillful, conscientious, honest, and on top of the job may learn nothing new from audits, audits nevertheless reduce doubts in the minds of others about project status. They are like *Good Housekeeping* Seals of Approval, which enhance the credibility of the project managers who win them. This increase in credibility enhances their effectiveness in dealing with others, especially with their managements and customers.

When

Project management audits can be either planned or unplanned, and each has its place.

Planned Audits Complex projects should have planned audits and their timing might follow this schedule:

1. Review of the project plan in draft form.

2. A *first* audit soon after the project has been organized and is well underway.

3. A *second* audit when about 20 percent of the scheduled time or money has been spent, whichever comes first.

4. *Third* and *subsequent* audits at key turning or decision points as needed to verify that corrective actions identified in prior audits have been taken.

An example audit schedule might look like this:

Project Schedule Time: 50 weeks

Review of the project plan	week one
1st audit	week three
2nd audit	week ten
3rd audit	optional
Project completion	week fifty

Except in rare instances, the project management audit should not be a surprise event. By giving advance notice, the project manager and staff can prepare for the audit and make it productive. Advance notice helps everyone involved to be knowledgeable of the true project status and lessen procrastination in doing necessary but perhaps difficult tasks.

Unplanned Audits If members of general management perceive that a project is in trouble or heading for trouble or if they are uncertain of its status, then a project management audit is appropriate. In this case, they will get an accurate assessment of the project that will either allay their fears or give them the information they need to correct the situation intelligently.

A project management audit is also appropriate when there is a change in project managers. If project managers change unexpectedly after the project is well underway, then a special audit gives the incoming project manager a clear understanding of conditions at the time of takeover. Both the outgoing project manager and the incoming project manager should be present. This type of audit minimizes surprises and allows the incoming project manager to take timely corrective action.

Although rare, there is a third condition that calls for an unplanned audit, which is also unannounced in advance. When investors have good reason to suspect that some sort of skulduggery is at work and advance notice would precipitate a cover-up or interfere with taking corrective action, then a surprise audit is in order.

Who

The prerequisites for a project management auditor include all or nearly all of the following:

1. The auditor should not have been directly involved in the proposal effort, the project planning stage (except to review and critique the draft project plan), or the staffing decisions and actions for the project. He or she must not be involved in doing the work or in supervising it. The auditor needs to have an unfettered outlook.

2. The auditor should have much diverse experience. This experience should include a number of years in working on projects and in managing projects. The auditor needs to have first-hand experience with the real problems that all projects face and needs to be familiar with many of the typical pitfalls. Extensive technical experience in the technical areas that the project is involved with is not necessary as long as there is a general understanding of the field. The auditor also needs to be able to distinguish between the important and the trivial.

3. The auditor should have a reputation of being fair, objective, and thorough, and should not be considered naive. The auditor must be a good listener who is able to draw people out and should pay attention to detail rather than jumping to conclusions.

Once the project management auditor is selected, the person must be given sufficient authority to perform the audit in a thorough manner with a minimum of time expenditure. The auditor must have the authority to discuss the project with all internal personnel. Outside personnel should be contacted, however, only with the advice or consent from general management.

The auditor must have the authority to look at all records, documentation, correspondence and financial records and must be able to observe all actions in process on the project.

How

A project management audit is not a spontaneous affair, although the need for one might not be recognized until a precipitous event occurs. Whether the audit is planned ahead or decided upon urgently, it nevertheless must be prepared and performed carefully if it is to be successful.

Preparing for An Audit Preparing for a project management audit includes:

1. estimating the schedule and budget for the audit
2. selecting the auditor
3. establishing the auditor's reporting level
4. agreeing on the outline or format of the audit report
5. notifying the project manager of the audit
6. arranging the time and place of the audit
7. telling the project manager what to provide in advance of the audit.

The auditor should report at a level that is higher than every individual connected with the project. Such individuals include functional group heads and support service heads whose staffs contribute to the projects as well as any technical and marketing experts and others assigned to the project who may outrank the project manager. One aim of this condition is to ensure that the auditor is taken seriously. Another aim is to ensure that the person receiving the report cannot have rank pulled on him or her by an unhappy project team member if changes are made as a result of the audit.

The auditor and the person to whom the auditor will report need to agree in advance on the goal and scope of the audit and the outline of the audit report. There usually is no good opportunity to redo a portion of an audit if it should be necessary later to fill in some overlooked details. All the information must be gathered the first time. Thus, the auditor and the audit recipient need to have a common understanding at the outset regarding the audit's goal and scope and the report's outline.

Once the auditor has been charged with the duty, general management should notify the *de jure* project manager and the *de facto* project manager, if different, that there will be an audit and tell them the name of the auditor. The auditor can then arrange the place and time for the audit. Normally, the place should be where the work is being done. The auditor needs access to the work, the personnel who are working on the project, and their records. If the work is dispersed, the auditor may have to travel from one place to another.

The time of the audit also needs to be calendared. There is little point in the auditor showing up when the project manager and other key personnel are simply not available. Arranging an appointment, however, may not be a simple job. No time seems to be convenient to a project manager who is desperately trying to get or keep a project on track. The auditor may therefore have to simply announce when the audit will take place and insist that the project manager be there, prepared as described in the next paragraph. The auditor's level of reporting will be a major asset in enforcing this mandate.

The auditor should instruct the project manager regarding the materials to be provided in advance of the audit. Normally, these include the statement of work, the plan, drawings, bills of material, documentation, instructions, manuals, guidelines, codes and regulations, the contract, purchase orders, subcontracts, invoices, progress reports, and financial reports. These items should be provided to the auditor sufficiently in advance of the audit so that they can be reviewed before meeting the project personnel.

Performing An Audit   Performing a project management audit involves:

1. acquiring information
2. examining the information and comparing pieces of it with other pieces and with the auditor's experience to determine its relevance, completeness, and accuracy
3. drawing conclusions about the status of the project from the comparisons
4. presenting the results and discussing them with the individual(s) who commissioned the audit.

Information is acquired from two types of sources, from the materials listed in the previous discussion on preparing for the audit and from interviews.

The materials should provide:

1. a general description of the project, including its objectives;
2. the reasons for the objectives;
3. assumptions, either implicit or explicit, that affect the project or the way it is performed;
4. the project schedule;
5. the project budget;
6. the approach or method to be used;
7. the people and organization doing the project, including any subcontractors;
8. interfaces between the project and the customer and between the project and third parties;

9. the provision of equipment and material;
10. the plan for controlling quality;
11. the work authorization plan;
12. the schedule control plan;
13. the cost control plan;
14. reporting plans; and
15. assessments of risk and contingency plans and allowances.

As the auditor reviews the materials, relevant questions include:

1. Are the main objectives and subobjectives clear and correct? Are there any conflicts inherent among them? If so, how will the conflicts be resolved?
2. How will the project manager and the customer know when the objectives have been successfully met?
3. Why are various elements of the overall project plan present? Are they reasonable? Are they based on facts? If not, are they based on reasonable assumptions? Are the assumptions explicit or implicit? Are any important elements or details missing?
4. Does the project have enough of the right talent, information, equipment, moral and tangible support, etc.? Are the plans for deploying these resources satisfactory?
5. Are the project's monitoring and control provisions appropriate, sufficient, and timely?
6. Are the reporting plans appropriate?
7. Are difficulties and risks clearly identified and appropriately assessed? Are contingency plans and allowances adequate?

These questions should help the auditor determine if the foundation of the project is sound enough to enable a successful outcome. If not, the auditor needs to find out through interviews if the shortcomings have been rectified.

Whether or not the project's foundation is sound, the auditor should interview the project manager and other personnel who might have either a corroborating or contrasting viewpoint. If the foundation is sound, the purpose is to confirm that it is as good as it seems and that it is being followed. If the foundation is not sound, the purpose is to discover what supplementary steps are being taken and how well they are working.

The auditor can identify potential interviewees in several ways. The organization chart for the project should show the key personnel on the project, all of whom should be interviewed. Then each of them can be asked who else is acquainted with the various parts of the project that bear further examination. Personnel who interface with the project should also be considered, and they, or at least their functions, can be identified from the project plans. As in any sleuthing, the auditor should develop leads wherever possible; not all will be productive, but some may turn out to be crucial.

The interviews should be done individually. The auditor might begin by asking each interviewee to describe the project briefly as he or she understands it and to then comment on the parts of it that could be improved. As the auditor listens to the various discussion, it is important to be alert to distortions, ambiguities, gaps and omissions, and conflicting information or viewpoints. Attention should be paid not only to what interviewees say but also to what they might have said and did not.

Some points may have to be explored further if they pertain to significant aspects of the project. The auditor should have no qualms about asking "darn fool questions" to elicit information. And as interviewees make assertions or allegations, the auditor should ask for specific examples unless there is already incontrovertible evidence supporting the claims.

A key to the success of a project is its standing in the priority queue of all the work being done by each person involved. It is important, therefore, to discover how much time and attention each work element is getting from each party. If individual efforts are insufficient, too fragmented, or not timely, the project will suffer, perhaps disastrously, as needed work is done inadequately or too late. The auditor should look for such opportunities for the project to fail in order to correct them in time.

Also, the auditor should determine the extent to which limitations or constraints are handicapping the project. If there are such handicaps, the auditor should ask the personnel involved for their rationales. Often project difficulties can be relieved by removing unwarranted constraints.

It often pays for the auditor to be available for project personnel and other staff to talk with informally. They sometimes have something to say but are unlikely to be interviewed because no one else suggests them and they do not necessarily have a visible

position. It helps, therefore, for the auditor's presence to be well known, that there is some uncommitted time while on the scene, and that people know where the auditor is staying if he or she is from out-of-town.

Reporting Audit Findings Following the interviews, the auditor must prepare and present a report that summarizes all of the work, conclusions, and recommendations. The report should include:

1. a description of the project status,
2. what was seen and heard,
3. the auditor's own opinions,
4. a listing of other opinions found by the auditor, and
5. the auditor's recommendations for corrective action.

This report should normally be addressed to the person who commissioned the audit, and a copy of it should be provided to the project manager.

Hazards and Cautions

Project management auditing is not without its hazards. The auditor is likely to find errors of omission and commission, and the project team subjects know this. Consequently, they may be defensive or reluctant to cooperate. Worse yet, traps may be set. It pays the auditor, therefore, to work with a measure of caution and prudence, lest a hornet's nest be opened without being prepared.

The auditor's style has a major impact on the level of cooperation. If the auditor is belligerent or accusatory, defensive reactions will be engendered from everyone. If friendly and accessible, cooperation is likely, at least from those who would normally cooperate.

At the same time, the auditor should not accept half answers or otherwise be put off. If an interviewee demurs on a question, the auditor can ask why the respondent is reluctant to answer. Then the auditor can say that he or she understands the other person's reluctance but wants to proceed anyway because it will help make the whole project a healthy one. An auditor needs to be persuasive and persistent to get the information needed.

While rare, an auditor sometimes meets someone who is intimidating by virtue of knowledge, skill, force of personality, fame or some other awesome characteristic. When this happens, the auditor can be immobilized by a fear that the intimidator could destroy the auditor's credibility. An auditor should recognize the situation when it occurs and overcome it. Simply proceed with the audit, making sure that the facts are straight and can be substantiated.

Occasionally an auditor is engaged by one who is an underlying cause of any trouble there may be on the project. The person who is the cause may or may not welcome the insight the auditor will bring. The auditor needs to prepare this individual to accept the information. It helps if the auditor can tell the person first that there are some delicate matters that are perhaps unpleasant to hear but must nevertheless be voiced if the project is to be made healthy. The emphasis needs to be on improving the project, not on accusing the guilty party.

The person who is the underlying cause of trouble may have requested the audit in order to place blame elsewhere. The auditor now has a moral dilemma of the first order. While there is usually enough blame to find several who are responsible, it is possible that no real good can result unless the one who engaged the auditor also reforms. In this case, the auditor needs to advise this person as to what he or she needs to do in order to allow the project to succeed. Here also the emphasis needs to be on corrective actions all around and not on who has done what in the past.

Summary

A project management audit is an examination designed to determine the true status of work performed on a project and its conformance with the project statement of work, including schedule and budget constraints. It is an independent, structured assessment of the state of affairs conducted by a competent examiner. By inference or extrapolation, it provides insight into the work needed to meet project objectives and the adequacy of the schedule and budget to do so. In addition, it can illuminate mistakes that can cause project failure and thus can trigger timely corrective action.

The why, when, who, what, and how of project management audits are discussed. Project management audits are compared and contrasted with normal supervision of project management, with reviews conducted for the customer (whether internal or external), and with financial audits. Guidelines are presented for choosing a qualified auditor, and a structured format is offered for preparing, performing, and reporting an audit.

By following good methods and procedures, such as given here, many managers, clients, owners, and investors will find the project management audit a useful tool that can pay big dividends.

References

1. KIRSCHNER, D. "Construction Audit Services for Owners." *The CPA Journal*, Volume XLIX, No. 1, January 1979, pp. 19–25.

2. ROSS, F. E. "Technical Reviews and Audits: Keeping Track of Progress in Development Projects." *Management Review*, Volume 65, No. 8, August 1976 pp. 11–18.

3. WALKER, M. G., and BRACEY, R. "Independent Auditing as Project Control." *Datamation*, Volume 26, No. 3, March 1980, pp. 201–202.

Project Termination

As it must to all things, termination comes to every project. At times, project death is quick and clean, but more often it is a long process; and there are times when it is practically impossible to establish that death has occurred. The skill with which termination, or a condition we might call "near termination," is managed has a great deal to do with the quality of life after the project. The termination stage of the project rarely has much impact on technical success or failure, but it has a great deal to do with residual attitudes toward the project—the "taste left in the mouth" of the client, senior management, and the project team.

At this point, the joy of discovery is past. Problems have been solved, by-passed, lived with, and/or ignored. Implementation plans have been carried out. The client is delighted, angry, or reasonably satisfied. In construction-type projects where the project cadre remains intact, the termination issue is eased because the team moves on to another challenge. For nonrecurring projects, the issue is far more akin to the breakup of a family. While the members of the family may be on the best of terms, they must now separate, go their individual ways, divide or dispose of the family property, and make plans for individual survival. The change is stressful. For projects organized as weak matrices, there will be only a few individuals, perhaps only the project manager, who "belong" to the project. This may represent an even more stressful situation than the breakup of a large project family because there is less peer group support and few or no sympathetic colleagues with whom to share the anxieties associated with transfer to a new project or back to a functional group.

The process of termination is never easy, always complicated, and, as much as we might wish to avoid it, almost always inevitable. The problem is how to accomplish one of the several levels of what is meant by project termination with a minimum of trouble and administrative dislocation.

In this chapter we examine the variety of conditions that may be generally referred to as *project termination*. As indicated above, some projects are not actually terminated, but rather are severely slowed down. We then view some decision-aiding models that can assist an organization in making the termination decision. This requires us to return to the subject of evaluation and discuss indicators of success and failure in projects. We also discuss some procedures that decrease the pain of termination, and others that reduce the administrative problems that often arise after projects have been terminated. We look into the typical causes of termination, and finally note that the preparation of a project history is an integral part of the termination process.

▶ 13.1   THE VARIETIES OF PROJECT TERMINATION

For our purposes, a project can be said to be terminated when work on the substance of the project has ceased or slowed to the point that further progress on the project is no longer possible, when the project has been indefinitely delayed, when its resources have been deployed to other projects, or when project personnel (especially the PM) become *personae non gratae* with senior management and in the company lunchroom. There may seem to be a spark of life left, but resuscitation to a healthy state is most unlikely. On rare occasions, projects are reborn to a new, glorious existence. But such rebirth is not expected, and project team members who "hang on to the bitter end" have allowed optimism to overcome wisdom. The PM must understand that the ancient naval tradition that the captain should go down with the ship does not serve the best interests of the Navy, the crew, the ship, and most certainly not the captain.

On the other hand, the captain must not, ratlike, flee the "ship" at the first sign of trouble. In the next section of this chapter, we note many of the signs and signals that indicate that the project may be in real trouble. At this point, it is appropriate to consider the ways in which a project can be terminated. There are four fundamentally different ways to close out a project: extinction, addition, integration, and starvation.

Termination by Extinction

The project is stopped. It may end because it has been successful and achieved its goals: The new product has been developed and handed over to the client; the building has been completed and accepted by the purchaser; or the software has been installed and is running.

The project may also be stopped because it is unsuccessful or has been superseded: The new drug failed its efficacy tests; the yield of the chemical reaction was too low; there are better/faster/cheaper/prettier alternatives available; or it will cost too much and take too long to get the desired performance. Changes in the external environment can kill projects, too. The explosion of the Challenger stopped a number of space shuttle projects overnight. More recently, extraordinary cost escalation in the technology and materials associated with automotive racing caused the ruling bodies of both Formula 1 and Indy-car racing to stop (and even repeal) technological change in their respective venues.

A special case of termination by extinction is "termination by murder."* There are all sorts of murders. They range from political assassination to accidental projecticide. When senior executives vie for promotion, projects for which the loser is champion are apt to suffer. Corporate mergers often make certain projects redundant or irrelevant. NCR was forced to cancel several projects following its merger into AT&T. Two important characteristics of termination by murder, premeditated or not, are the suddenness of project demise and the lack of obvious signals that death is imminent.

When a decision is made to terminate a project by extinction, the most noticeable event is that all activity on the *substance* of the project ceases. A great deal of organizational activity, however, remains to be done. Arrangements must be made for the orderly release of project team members and their reassignment to other activities if they are to remain in the parent organization. The property, equipment, and materials belonging to the project must be disbursed according to the dictates of the project contract or in accord with the established procedures of the parent organization. Finally, the Project Final Report, also known as the *project history*, must be prepared. These subjects will be covered in greater detail later in this chapter.

Termination by Addition

Most projects are "in-house," that is, carried out by the project team for use in the parent organization. If a project is a major success, it may be terminated by institutionalizing it as a formal part of the parent organization. NCR Corporation (now merged with AT&T and recently renamed "AT&T Global Information Solutions"), for example, uses this method of transforming a project into a division of the firm and then, if real economic stability seems assured, into an independent subsidiary. Essentially the same process occurs when a university creates an academic department out of what originally was a few courses in an existing department. For example, most software engineering and/or information systems departments began by reorganizing an engineering or business school "sub-specialty" into a full-fledged department.

When the project is made a more or less full-fledged member of the parent, it lives its first years in a protected status—much as any child is protected by the adults in the family. As the years pass, however, the child is expected gradually to assume the economic responsibilities of full adulthood.

When project success results in termination by addition, the transition is strikingly different from termination by extinction. In both cases the project ceases to exist, but there the similarity stops. Project personnel, property, and equipment are often simply transferred from the dying project to the newly born division. The metamorphosis from project to department, to division, and even to subsidiary is accompanied by budgets and administrative practices that conform to standard procedure in the parent firm, by demands for contribution profits, by the probable decline of political protection from the project's corporate "champion," indeed by a greater exposure to all the usual stresses and strains of regular, routine, day-to-day operations.

---

*The authors thank Professor Samuel G. Taylor (University of Wyoming) for noting this special case of termination by extinction.

It is not uncommon, however, for some of the more adventurous members of the project team to request transfers to other projects or to seek the chance to start new projects. Project life is exciting, and some team members are uncomfortable with what they perceive to be the staid, regulated existence of the parent organization. The change from project to division brings with it a sharply diminished sense of freedom.

This transition poses a difficult time for the PM, who must see to it that the shift is made smoothly. In Part I of this book, and especially in Chapter 3, we referred repeatedly to the indispensable requirement of political sensitivity in the PM. The transition from project to division demands a superior level of political sensitivity for successful accomplishment. Projects lead a sheltered life, for all the risks they run. The regular operating divisions of a firm are subjected to the daily infighting that seems, in most firms, to be a normal result of competition between executives.

Project Management in Practice
Nucor's Approach to Termination by Addition

Nucor, one of the early steel "minimills," is a highly entrepreneural firm with a compound growth rate of 23 percent per year. In 1987, its sales were $851 million with an executive staff of only 19 monitoring the operations of 23 plants and 4600 employees. As part of its strategy, Nucor in 1983 decided to move into the flat rolled steel market, the largest market for steel products. They thus initiated the construction of a major plant in Crawfordsville, Indiana, which would comprise over 20 percent of their total assets.

As another part of its strategy, Nucor does its own construction management, with most of the construction team then transitioning into permanent positions in the newly constructed plant. In this case, four managers started the conceptual team for the new facility and then brought in 19 other people from outside the company to form the rest of the construction team, none of them ever having built a steel mill before. The manager on the conceptual team for the new plant was the lead person on the site determination team and became the general manager of the facility. The field shift superintendents on the construction project will have permanent managerial responsibility for the melt shop, the hot mill, and the cold mill. The engineers will become supervisors in the mill. Even the secretary/clerk will have a position in the new facility.

Nucor also relies heavily on the services and capabilities of its suppliers in the construction process, since they are such a small firm. But it also reflects Nucor's "lean and mean" philosophy. In this case, the only error the construction team made was underestimating the engineering time required from suppliers, the time coming in at about double the estimate. Even so, the engineering costs (and probably most other labor costs, too) apparently only ran about 20 percent of what it historically costs to build this type of steel facility!

Source: R. Kimball, "Nucor's Strategic Project," *Project Management Journal*, Sept. 1988.

Termination by Integration

This method of terminating a project is the most common way of dealing with successful projects, and the most complex. The property, equipment, material, personnel, and functions of the project are distributed among the existing elements of the parent organization. The output of the project becomes a standard part of the operating systems of the parent, or client.

In some cases, the problems of integration are relatively minor. The project team that installed a new machining center, instructed the client in its operation and maintenance, and then departed probably left only minor problems behind it, problems familiar to experienced operations managers. If the installation was an entire flexible manufacturing system, however, or a minicomputer complete with multiple terminals and many different pieces of software, then the complexities of integration are apt to be much more severe. In general, the problems of integration are inversely related to the level of experience that the parent organization (or client) has had with: (1) the technology being integrated and (2) the successful integration of other projects, regardless of technology.

Most of the problems of termination by addition are also present when the project is integrated. In the case of integration, the project may not be viewed as a competitive interloper, but the project personnel being moved into established units of the parent organization will be so viewed. Also, the project, which flourished so well in its protected existence as a project, may not be quite so healthy in the chill atmosphere of the "real world." The individuals who nurtured the project may have returned to their respective organizational divisions, and may have new responsibilities. They tend to lose their fervid interest in the "old" project.

Following is a list of a few of the more important aspects of the transition from project to integrated operation that must be considered when the project functions are distributed.

1. ***Personnel***   Where will the project team go? Will it remain a team? If the functions that the team performed are still needed, who will do them? If ex-team members are assigned to a new project, under what conditions or circumstances might they be temporarily available for help on the old project?

2. ***Manufacturing***   Is training complete? Are input materials and the required facilities available? Does the production system layout have to be replanned? Did the change create new bottlenecks or line-of-balance problems? Are new operating or control procedures needed? Is the new operation integrated into the firm's computer systems?

3. ***Accounting/Finance***   Have the project accounts been closed and audited? Do the new department budgets include the additional work needed by the project? Have the new accounts been created and account numbers been distributed? Has all project property and equipment been distributed according to the contract or established agreements?

4. ***Engineering***   Are all drawings complete and on file? Are operating manuals and change procedures understood? Have training programs been altered appropriately for new employees? Have maintenance schedules been adjusted for the change? Do we have a proper level of "spares" in stock?

5. **Information Systems/Software**   Has the new system been thoroughly tested? Is the software properly documented and are "comments" complete? Is the new system fully integrated with current systems? Have the potential users been properly trained to use the new system?

6. **Marketing**   Is the sales department aware of the change? Is marketing in agreement about lead times? Is marketing comfortable with the new line? Is the marketing strategy ready for implementation?

7. **Purchasing, Distribution, Legal, etc.**   Are all these and other functional areas aware of the change? Has each made sure that the transition from project to standard operation has been accomplished within standard organizational guidelines and that standard administrative procedures have been installed?

Termination by Starvation

There is a fourth type of project termination, although strictly speaking, it is not a "termination" at all. It is "slow starvation by budget decrement." Almost anyone who has been involved with projects over a sufficient period of time to have covered a business recession has had to cope with budget cuts. Budget cuts, or decrements, are not rare. Because they are common, they are sometimes used to mask a project termination.

There may be a number of reasons why senior management does not wish to terminate an unsuccessful or obsolete project. In some firms, for example, it is politically dangerous to admit that one has championed a failure, and terminating a project that has not accomplished its goals is an admission of failure. In such a case, the project budget might receive a deep cut—or a series of small cuts—large enough to prevent further progress on the project and to force the reassignment of many project team members. In effect, the project is terminated, but the project still exists as a legal entity complete with sufficient staff to maintain some sort of presence such as a secretary who issues a project "no-progress" report each year. In general, it is considered bad manners to inquire into such projects or to ask why they are still "on the books."

▶ 13.2   WHEN TO TERMINATE A PROJECT

The decision to terminate a project early, by whatever method, is difficult. As we emphasized in Chapter 4, projects tend to develop a life of their own—a life seemingly independent of whether or not the project is successful. In an early article [12] on the subject of terminating R & D projects, Buell suspected that the main reason so little information was available on the subject was that it was hard to spell out specific guidelines and standards for the decision. He expressed strong doubts about the ability to "wrap everything up in a neat set of quantitative mathematical expressions," and then went on to develop an extensive set of questions that, if answered, should lead management to a decision. While these questions were aimed at R & D projects, they have wide, general applicability. Paraphrased and slightly modified to broaden and extend them beyond R & D projects, they are:

* Is the project still consistent with organizational goals?

- Is it practical? Useful?
- Is management sufficiently enthusiastic about the project to support its implementation?
- Is the scope of the project consistent with the organization's financial strength?
- Is the project consistent with the notion of a "balanced" program in all areas of the organization's technical interests? In "age"? In cost?
- Does the project have the support of all the departments (e.g., finance, manufacturing, marketing, etc.) needed to implement it?
- Is organizational project support being spread too thin?
- Is support of this individual project sufficient for success?
- Does this project represent too great an advance over current technology? Too small an advance?
- Is the project team still innovative, or has it gone stale?
- Can the new knowledge be protected by patent, copyright, or trade secret?
- Could the project be farmed out without loss of quality?
- Is the current project team properly qualified to continue the project?
- Does the organization have the required skills to achieve full implementation or exploitation of the project?
- Has the subject area of the project already been "thoroughly plowed"?
- Has the project lost its key person or champion?
- Is the project team enthusiastic about success?
- Can the potential results be purchased or subcontracted more efficiently than developed in-house?
- Does it seem likely that the project will achieve the minimum goals set for it? Is it still profitable? timely?

We could add many other such questions to Buell's list. For instance:

- Has the project been obviated by technical advances or new products/services developed elsewhere?
- Is the output of the product still cost-effective?
- Is it time to integrate or add the project as a part of the regular, ongoing operation of the parent organization?
- Would we support the project if it were proposed today at the time and cost required to complete it?
- Are there better alternative uses for the funds, time, and personnel devoted to the project?
- Has a change in the environment altered the need for the project's output?

Such questions clearly overlap, and the list could easily be extended further. Dean [16] reports that the probabilities of technical and/or commerical failure are the two most important reasons for terminating projects (see Table 13–1), according to the

Table 13-1   Rank-Order of Important Factors Considered in Terminating R&D Projects (36 Companies)

Factors	No. of Companies Reporting the Factor as Being Important
Technical	
Low probability of achieving technical objectives or commercializing results	34
Technical or manufacturing problems cannot be solved with available R&D skills	11
Higher priority of other projects requiring R&D labor or funds	10
Economic	
Low profitability or return on investment	23
Too costly to develop as individual product	18
Market	
Low market potential	16
Change in competitive factors or market needs	10
Others	
Too long a time required to achieve commerical results	6
Negative effect on other projects or products	3
Patent problems	1

Source: [16]

executives he surveyed. Balachandra and Raelin [9, 38] performed a discriminant analysis on 23 factors involved in terminating projects, not as a decision model, but as a way of highlighting the various factors involved and their relevance to the termination problem, as related to projects in general.

Compared to the great level of research and thought that went into the project selection decision before the 1980s (see also Chapter 2), there was relatively little research published on the termination decision. But even this bit was more than the work devoted to defining project success. As interest in project termination increased in the mid-1980s, interest in understanding project success also rose. Baker, Green, Bean, *et al.* [7,8] looked at factors associated with R & D project success and failure. Pinto and Slevin [34, 35, 36] surveyed experienced PMs and found ten factors that the managers felt to be critical to successful project implementation (see Table 13–2). Many other researchers also attacked the problem of defining success [17, 29, for example].

A particularly important finding of Baker *et al.* is that the *factors associated with project success are different for different industries.* Baker's work was restricted to R & D projects, but the Pinto and Slevin study covered many different types of projects. They found that the success-related factors differed between fundamentally different types of projects—between R & D and construction projects, for example. At the very least, the factors and their relative importance are idiosyncratic to the industry, to the project type, and, we suggest, possibly to the firm.

Table 13-2 Critical Success Factors in Order of Importance

1. *Project Mission*—Initial clearly defined goals and general directions.
2. *Top-Management Support*—Willingness of top management to provide the necessary resources and authority/power for project success.
3. *Project Schedule/Plan*—A detailed specification of the individual action steps for project implementation.
4. *Client Consultation*—Communication, consultation, and active listening to all impacted parties.
5. *Personnel*—Recruitment, selection, and training of the necessary personnel for the project team.
6. *Technical Tasks*—Availability of the required technology and expertise to accomplish the specific technical action steps.
7. *Client Acceptance*—The act of "selling" the final project to its ultimate intended users.
8. *Monitoring and Feedback*—Timely provision of comprehensive control information at each stage in the implementation process.
9. *Communication*—The provision of an appropriate network and necessary data to all key actors in the project implementation.
10. *Trouble-shooting*—Ability to handle unexpected crises and deviations from plan.

Source: [34]

Out of this work came some models that could be used to predict project success or failure, based on certain project characteristics or practices. Pinto and Mantel [33], using Pinto's work cited above, reported on factors that were associated with project failure. The factors differed for the type of project involved (R & D vs. construction), for the project's position in the life cycle, as well as for the precise way in which "failure" was defined. Green, Welsh, and Dehler found that a poor fit with the firm's existing technological expertise and/or with its existing marketing area and channels was a good early predictor of project termination [19]. Kloppenborg and Plath [25] described precursors to success and failure for projects intended to implement expert systems, and Beale and Freeman [10] modeled project success, differentiating between factors exogenous and endogenous to the project and the project team.

In the face of this diversity of success factors, it is interesting to note that there are relatively few fundamental reasons why some projects fail to produce satisfactory answers to Buell's questions.

1. **A Project Organization Is Not Required** The use of the project form of organization was inappropriate for this particular task or in this particular environment. The parent organization must understand the conditions that require instituting a project.

2. **Insufficient Support from Senior Management** Projects invariably develop needs for resources that were not originally allocated. Arguments between functional departments over the command of such resources are very common. Without the direct support of a champion in senior management, the project is almost certain to lose the resource battle.

3. **Naming the Wrong Person as Project Manager**   This book is testimony to the importance of the PM. A common mistake is to appoint as PM an individual with excellent technical skills but weak managerial skills or training.

4. **Poor Planning**   This is a very common cause of project failure. In the rush to get the substance of the project under way, competent planning is neglected. In such cases, crisis management becomes a way of life, difficulties and errors are compounded, and the project slowly gets farther behind schedule and over budget.

These, and a few other reasons, are the base causes of most project failures. The specific causes of failure, for the most part, derive from these fundamental items. For example:

- No use was made of earlier project Final Reports that contained a number of recommendations for operating projects in the future.
- Time/cost estimates were not prepared by those who had responsibility for doing the work.
- Starting late, the PM jumped into the tasks without adequate planning.
- Project personnel were moved without adjusting the schedule, or were reassigned during slow periods and then were unavailable when needed.
- Project auditors/evaluators were reluctant to conduct careful, detailed meaningful evaluations.
- The project was allowed to continue in existence long after it had ceased to make cost-effective progress.
- Evaluations failed to determine why problems were arising during the early phases of the project life cycle.

All these causes of failure underline the need for careful evaluation at all stages of the project. But at the same time, it is most important for the reader to note that the lion's share of the attention given to the termination issue is focused on the failing project. It is equally or more important to terminate successful projects at the right time and by proper methods. One rarely mentioned problem affecting many organizations is the inability or unwillingness of successful project managers working on successful projects to "let their projects go." This is a particularly difficult problem for in-house projects. The PM (and team) simply will not release the project to the tender care of the client department. An outstanding technical specialist and manager conducting communications projects was released from employment simply because she insisted on maintaining semi-permanent control of projects that had essentially been completed, but which were not released to the users because they "needed further testing" or "fine-tuning."

Also, little consideration has been given to *how* the termination decision is made and *who* makes it. We feel that a broadly based committee of reasonably senior executives is probably best. The broad organizational base of the committee is needed to diffuse and withstand the political pressure that accompanies all terminations—successes and failures alike. To the extent possible, the criteria used by the termination committee should be written and explained in some detail. It is, however, important to write the criteria in such a way that the committee is not frozen into a mechanistic approach to a decision. There are times when hunches should be followed (or rejected) and blind faith should be respected (or ignored). It depends on whose hunches and faith are under consideration.

▶ 13.3 THE TERMINATION PROCESS

The termination process has two distinct parts. First is the decision whether or not to terminate. Second, if the decision is to terminate the project, the decision must be carried out.

The Decision Process

Decision-aiding models for the termination decision fall into two generic categories. First, there are models that base the decision on the degree to which the project qualifies against a set of factors generally held to be associated with successful (or failed) projects. Second, there are models that base the decision on the degree to which the project meets the goals and objectives set for it.

Most of the research on factors associated with success and failure can be used to "predict" project success. Pinto's work with Slevin and others [particularly 33 and 35] can be used in that way. Tadisina [46], working with a set of factors associated with project success found by Baker, *et al.* [7, 8], suggested a variety of termination-decision models that could be used if the success-related factors were monitored and used as input data in the models. Freeman and Beale [17] focused their decision model on the net present value of the project, which is determined by transforming a number of success-related factors (from the sponsor's and the project manager's points of view) into NPV equivalents. Riggs, *et al.* [39] determined a set of success-related factors pertaining to government (NASA) projects by polling experienced managers using the Delphi method. From this, they developed statistically-generated "success predictor models" for manned and unmanned space projects.

The use of models that measure project success or failure based on its achievement of present goals is subject to debate.

Balachandra and Raelin [9, 38] state that project selection models are not appropriate for the project termination decision. They argue that the data requirements for selection models are too large and costly. They also argue that the evaluation of factors in project selection models may change as projects are evaluated at different stages in their life cycles. They note that the probability of technical success of a project is usually estimated to be close to 1.0 early in the life cycle, but lower during later stages when the technical problems are known. This, they say, would bias decisions in favor of new projects and against ongoing ones.

We think [27] that the first argument is generally untrue of those selection models actually being used, which are typically of modest size. As we have remarked elsewhere in this book, the uncertainty associated with most projects is not concerned with whether or not the project objective is technically achievable, but rather with the time and cost required to achieve it.

Adopting the position that sunk costs are not relevant to current investment decisions, we hold that the primary criterion for project continuance or termination is *whether or not the organization is willing to invest the estimated time and cost required to complete the project, given the project's current status and current expected outcome.* We emphasize that this criterion can be applied to any project. Balachandra and Raelin were , of course, discussing only R & D projects.

Shafer and Mantel [42] have developed a project termination decision support system (DSS) based on the widely available Lotus 1–2–3® spreadsheet and using a constrained weighted factor scoring model (see Chapter 2). The capabilities of Lotus 1–2–3® (as well as Excel®, and several other spreadsheets), allow direct modeling of the scoring model, allow customized menus, and allow decision makers to adapt and enhance the model as they gain experience in the use of the DSS. The database requirements include data on the project, on the parent organization, and on the environment. The criteria on which projects are rated, the specifics of the scores, and the relative weights of the criteria are often developed by organizational executives using the Delphi method. (For a description of the use of the Delphi method to develop weights, see [28].) If it seems desirable, the weights may be determined through discriminant analysis, as in [9, 38, 46].

Just as decision criteria, constraints, weights, and environmental data are unique to each organization, so are the specifics of using this (or any) decision model. A detailed discussion of various potential decision rules that might be useful with such a model can be found in [42]. Figure 13–1 illustrates the structure of this model.

The Implementation Process

Once it has been decided to terminate a project, the process by which it will be terminated must be implemented. The actual termination can be planned and orderly, or a simple hatchet job. The former is apt to have significantly better results, and so we suggest that the termination process be planned, budgeted, and scheduled just as is done for any other phase of the project life cycle. Such a project is illustrated in Figure 13–2. Archibald [4] has prepared an extensive checklist of items covering the closeout of both the administrative and substantive parts of the project (see Figures 13–3a and b).

In some organizations, the processing of the project closeout is conducted under the direct supervision of the PM, but this often raises dilemmas. For many PMs, termination signals the end of their reign as project leader. If the PM has another project to lead, the issue may not be serious; but if there is no other project and if the PM faces a return to a staid life in a functional division, there may be a great temptation to stretch out the termination process.

An examination of Figures 13–2 and 13–3a and 13–3b shows that implementing termination is a complex process. Note that in Figure 13–3b such items as A-4, B-4, C-3, and G-2, among many others, are actually small projects. It is all too easy, at this final stage of the game, to give this mountain of paperwork a "lick and a promise"—easy, but foolish. Someone must handle all the bureaucratic tasks, and if the PM leaves many loose ends, he or she will rapidly get a reputation for being slipshod, a characterization not associated with career success.

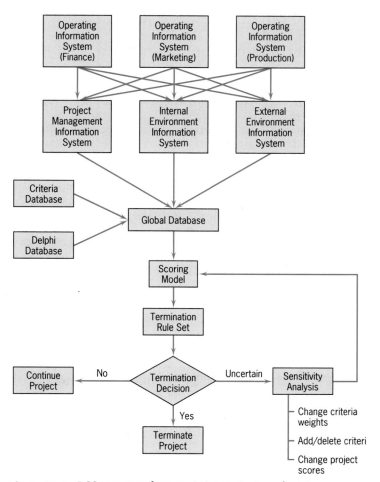

Figure 13-1: DSS structure for a project termination decision.

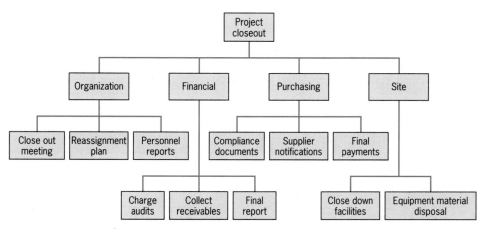

Figure 13-2: Design for project termination.

PROJECT TITLE _____   COMPLETION DATE _____

CONTRACT NO. _____   COST TYPE _____

CUSTOMER _____   PROJECT MGR. _____

The project close-out check lists are designed for use in the following manner:

Column I—Item No.: Each task listed is identified by a specific number and grouped into categories. Categories are based on functions, not on organizations or equipment.

Column II—Task Description: Task descriptions are brief tasks that could apply to more than one category but are listed only in the most appropriate category.

Column III—Required, Yes or No: Check whether the item listed applies to the project.

Column IV—Date Required: Insert the required date for accomplishment of the task.

Column V—Assigned Responsibility: Insert the name of the person responsible to see that the task is accomplished on schedule. This may be a member of the Project Office or an individual within a functional department.

Column VI—Priority (PR): A priority system established by the Project Manager may be used here, e.g., Priority #1 may be all tasks that must be accomplished before the contractual completion date, Priority #2 within 2 weeks after the completion date, etc.

Column VII— Notes, Reference: Refer in this column to any applicable Procedures, a government specification that may apply to that task, etc.

Figure 13-3a: Instructions for project termination checklist.

Item No.	Task Description	Required		Required Date	Assigned Responsibility	PR.	Notes Reference
		Yes	No				
A.	**Project Office (PO) and Project Team (PT) Organization**						
1.	Conduct project close-out meeting						
2.	Establish PO and PT release and reassignment plan						
3.	Carry out necessary personnel actions						
4.	Prepare personal performance evaluation on each PO and PT member						
B.	**Instructions and Procedures**						
	Issue Instructions for:						
1.	Termination of PO and PT						
2.	Close-out of all work orders and contracts						
3.	Termination of reporting procedures						
4.	Preparation of final report(s)						
5.	Completion and disposition of project file						
C.	**Financial**						
1.	Close out financial documents and records						
2.	Audit final charges and costs						

Figure 13-3b: Checklist for project termination. *Source:* [4]

Item No.	Task Description	Required Yes	Required No	Required Date	Assigned Responsibility	PR.	Notes Reference
3.	Prepare final project financial report(s)						
4.	Collect receivables						
D.	**Project Definition**						
1.	Document final approved project scope						
2.	Prepare final project breakdown structure and enter into project file						
E.	**Plans, Budgets, and Schedules**						
1.	Document actual delivery dates of all contractual deliverable end items						
2.	Document actual completion dates of all other contractual obligations						
3.	Prepare final project and task status reports						
F.	**Work Authorization and Control**						
1.	Close out all work orders and contracts						
G.	**Project Evaluation and Control**						
1.	Assure completion of all action assignments						
2.	Prepare final evaluation report(s)						
3.	Conduct final review meeting						
4.	Terminate financial, manpower, and progress reporting procedures						
H.	**Management and Customer Reporting**						
1.	Submit final report to customer						
2.	Submit final report to management						
I.	**Marketing and Contract Administration**						
1.	Compile all final contract documents with revision, waivers, and related correspondence						
2.	Verify and document compliance with all contractual terms						
3.	Compile required proof of shipment and customer acceptance documents						
4.	Officially notify customer of contract completion						
5.	Initiate and pursue any claims against customer						
6.	Prepare and conduct defense against claims by customer						
7.	Initiate public relations announcements re. contract completion						
8.	Prepare final contract status report						

Figure 13-3b: (continued)

Item No.	Task Description	Required		Required Date	Assigned Responsibility	PR.	Notes Reference
		Yes	No				
J.	**Extension-New Business**						
1.	Document possibilities for project or contract extensions, or other related new business						
2.	Obtain commitment for extension						
K.	**Project Records Control**						
1.	Complete project file and transmit to designated manager						
2.	Dispose of other project records as required by established procedures						
L.	**Purchasing and Subcontracting**						
	For each Purchase Order and Subcontract:						
1.	Document compliance and completion						
2.	Verify final payment and proper accounting to project						
3.	Notify vendor/contractor of final completion						
M.	**Engineering Documentation**						
1.	Compile and store all engineering documentation						
2.	Prepare final technical report						
N.	**Site Operations**						
1.	Close down site operations						
2.	Dispose of equipment and material						

Figure 13-3b: (continued)

The PM also has another option, to ignore the termination process entirely. The evaluation has already been conducted and praise or censure has been delivered. Rather than deal with termination, the PM may let the project administrator handle things. Project team members may well have similar feelings and reactions, and may seek new jobs or affiliations before the project actually ends, thereby dragging out some final tasks interminably.

Special *termination managers* are sometimes useful in completing the long and involved process of shutting down a project. In such cases, the PM is transferred to another project or reassigned to a functional "home." The termination manager does not have to deal with substantive project tasks and therefore may be a person familiar with the administrative requirements of termination and the environment within which the project will be operating (if it continues to live).

If technical knowledge is required during the termination process, a member of the project team may be upgraded and assigned responsibility for the termination. This "promotion" is often a motivator and will provide development experience for the team member.

The primary duties of the termination manager are encompassed in the following eight general tasks:

1. Ensure completion of the work, including tasks performed by subcontractors.

2. Notify the client of project completion and ensure that delivery (and installation) is accomplished. Acceptance of the project must be acknowledged by the client.

3. Ensure that documentation is complete, including a terminal evaluation of the project deliverables and preparation of the project's Final Report.

4. Clear for final billings and oversee preparation of the final invoices sent to the client.

5. Redistribute personnel, materials, equipment, and any other resources to the appropriate places.

6. Determine what records (manuals, reports, and other paperwork) to keep. Ensure that such documents are stored in the proper places and that responsibility for document retention is turned over to the parent organization's archivist.

7. Ascertain any product support requirements (e.g., spares, service, etc.), decide how such support will be delivered, and assign responsibility.

8. Oversee the closing of the project's books.

It is likely that tasks 1 to 3 will be handled by the regular PM immediately before the project termination process is started. If the termination manager must handle these tasks, technical support will almost certainly be needed. Of course, many of the tasks on this list will be quite simple if the project is not large, but even with small- or medium-sized projects, the PM should make sure all items are covered.

Item 5 on this list deserves some amplification. The PM can do a great deal to reduce the problems of termination by dealing with these issues well before the actual termination process begins. As we noted in Chapter 2, arrangements for the distribution and disposal of property and equipment belonging to the project should be included in the proposal and/or in the contract with the client. Obviously, this does not stop all arguments, but it does soften the conflicts. Dealing with project personnel is more difficult.

Most PMs delay the personnel reassignment/release issue as long as possible for three main reasons: a strong reluctance to face the interpersonal conflicts that might arise when new assignments and layoffs are announced; worry that people will lose interest and stop work on the project as soon as it becomes known that termination is being considered; or concern—particularly in the case of a pure project organization—that team members will try to avoid death by stretching out the work as far as possible.

As long as the PM has access to the functional managers' ears, any team member who "quits work" before the project is completed or stalls by stretching out tasks or creating task extensions would be subject to the usual sanctions of the workplace. The PM should make it quite clear that on-the-job-resignations and tenure-for-life are equally unacceptable.

The first problem results when project leadership is held by a managerially weak PM. The height of weakness is demonstrated when the PM posts a written list of reassignments and layoffs on the project's bulletin board late Friday afternoon and then leaves for a long weekend. A more useful course of action is to speak with project members individually or in small groups, let them know about plans for termination, and offer to consult with each in order to aid in the reassignment process or to assist in finding new work. (A preliminary announcement to the entire project team is in order because the interviews may cover several weeks or months.) It is almost impossible to keep termination plans a secret, and to confront the matter immediately tends to minimize rumors.

In a large project, of course, the PM will not be able to conduct personal interviews except with a few senior assistants. The project's personnel officer, or a representative from the parent firm's personnel department, can serve instead. This may seem like an unnecessary service to the team members, but a reputation of "taking care of one's people" is an invaluable aid to the PM when recruiting for the next project.

Termination by murder makes it very difficult to follow these suggestions about dealing with project personnel. The project's death often occurs with so little warning that the PM learns of the fact at the same time as the project team—or, as sometimes happens, learns about it from a member of the project team.

There is little the PM can do in such a case except to try to minimize the damage. The team should be assembled as rapidly as possible and informed, to the best of the PM's ability, about what has happened. At this point the PM should start the reassignment/release process.

Project Management in Practice
A Smooth Termination/Transition for Suncor's Ontario Refinery

Suncor of Ontario, Canada was committed to bringing a petroleum refinery on-line quickly and by a certain date due to contractual requirements. Normally, the start-up activities of a multi-million dollar project such as this are only studied in detail after construction is well underway. However, in this situation the lead time was short and the possibilities for schedule overruns were large due to labor problems in the area.

This difficulty was approached in a number of ways. For one thing, considerable effort was expended to attain and maintain good relations and communication with the tradespeople and laborers. But equally important

was the transition process devised for the facility. The nearly 200 logistical systems comprising the facility were analyzed separately in terms of handoff to operating personnel for start-up. These systems were then carefully documented in detail regarding all the requirements for handoff and start-up, and prioritized to achieve full compatability with the necessary start-up sequence. Computerized scheduling analyses were then executed to ensure that each system would be completed

Source: A. Rustin, "The Challenge of Project Management," Project Management Journal, Sept. 1985.

by its required date and in coordination with the construction schedule.

This early planning allowed the construction personnel to concentrate on the construction activities and plant operations to receive the plant in the manner and sequence that was necessary to enable a successful start-up. The end result was that all facilities were operating successfully very shortly after total construction completion.

13.4   THE FINAL REPORT—A PROJECT HISTORY

Good project management systems have a memory. The embodiment of this memory is the Project Final Report. The final report is not another evaluation; rather, it is the history of the project. It is a chronicle of the life and times of the project, a compendium of what went right and what went wrong, of who served the project in what capacity, of what was done to create the substance of the project, of how it was managed.

The elements that should be covered in the final report are listed below. When considering these elements it is also beneficial to consider where the source materials can be found. For the most part, the required information is contained in the project master plan, a document that includes the proposal, all action plans, budgets, schedules, change orders, and updates of the above. In addition to the master plan, all project audits and evaluations also contain required input data. Almost everything else required by the final report is reflective, based on the thoughts of the PM and others involved in the project. There is little problem in knowing where the needed documents should be kept—in the project's files. Making sure that they are, in fact, there and that they are, in fact, up-to-date is a serious concern, indeed.

The precise organization of the final report is not a matter of great concern; the content is. Some are organized chronologically, while others feature sections on the technical and administrative aspects of the project. Some are written in a narrative style and some contain copies of all project reports strung together with short commentaries. What matters is that several subjects should be addressed, one way or another, in the final report.

1. **Project Performance**   A key element of the report is a comparison of what the project achieved (the terminal evaluation) with what the project tried to achieve (the project proposal). This comparison may be quite extensive and should include explanations of all significant deviations of actual from plan. Because the report is not a formal evaluation, it can reflect the best judgment of the PM on why the triumphs and failures occurred. This comparison should be followed with a set of recommendations for future projects dealing with like or similar technical matters.

2. **Administrative Performance**   The substantive side of the project usually gets a great deal of attention, while the administrative side is often ignored until administrative problems occur. There is also a strong tendency on the part of almost everyone to treat the "pencil pushers" with grudging tolerance, at best. The administration of a project cannot solve technical problems, but it can enable good technology to be implemented (or prevent it). Administrative prac-

tices should be reviewed, and those that worked particularly well or poorly should be highlighted. It is important, when possible, to report the reasons why some specific practice was effective or ineffective. If poor administration is to be avoided and good practices adopted, it is necessary to understand why some things work well and others do not *in the environment of a particular organization*. This becomes the basis for the recommendations that accompany the discussion.

3. **Organizational Structure** Each of the organizational forms used for projects has its own, unique set of advantages and disadvantages. The final report should include comments on the ways the structure aided or impeded the progress of the project. If it appears that a modification to the accepted form of project organization—or a change to a different basic organizational form—might be helpful for project management, such a recommendation should be made. Obviously, recommendations should be accompanied by detailed explanations and rationales.

4. **Project and Administrative Teams** On occasion, individuals who are competent and likable as individuals do not perform well as members of a team when a high level of interpersonal communication and cooperation is required. A *confidential* section of the final report may be directed to a senior personnel officer of the parent organization, recommending that such individuals not be assigned to projects in the future. Similarly, the PM may recommend that individuals or groups who are particularly effective when operating as a team be kept together on future projects or when reassigned to the firm's regular operations.

5. **Techniques of Project Management** The outcome of the project is so dependent on the skill with which the forecasting, planning, budgeting, scheduling, resource allocation, and control are handled that attention must be given to checking on the way these tasks were accomplished. If the forecasts, budgets, and schedules were not reasonably accurate, recommendations for improved methods should be made. The techniques used for planning and control should also be subject to scrutiny.

For each element covered in the final report, recommendations for changing current practice should be made and defended. Insofar as is possible, the implications of each potential change should be noted. Commonly ignored, but equally important, are comments and recommendations about those aspects of the project that worked unusually well. Most projects, project teams, and PMs develop informal procedures that speed budget preparation, ease the tasks of scheduling, improve forecasts, and the like. The final report is an appropriate repository for such knowledge. Once reported, they can be tested and, if generally useful, can be added to the parent organization's list of approved project management methods.

The fundamental purpose of the final report is to improve future projects. It is ultimately focused on the project itself and on the process by which the project was conducted. Data on the project and its outcomes are available in the many interim reports, audits, and evaluations conducted during the project's life. But data on the process come largely from the PM's recollections. To ensure that significant issues are included, the PM should keep a diary. The PM's diary is not an official project document, but rather an informal collection of thoughts, reflections, and commentaries on project happenings. Such a diary tends to be a rich source of unconventional wisdom when written by a thoughtful PM. It may also be a great source of learning for a young, aspiring PM. Above all, it keeps ideas from "getting lost" amid the welter of activity on the project.

Occasionally, the project diary serves a purpose not originally intended. A PM working for a Minnesota highway construction company made a habit of keeping a project diary, mostly for his own interest and amusement. The firm was sued as the result of an accident on a road under construction. The plaintiff alleged that the highway shoulder was not complete nor was it marked "Under Construction" at the time of the accident. The PM's diary noted daily progress on the road, and it showed that the relevant piece of the road had been completed several days prior to the accident. The company successfully defended its position. All company PMs keep diaries now. A vice-president of the firm mentioned that they are the same type of diary his high-school-aged daughter uses.

▶ SUMMARY

At last, we come to the completion of our project—termination. In this chapter we looked at the ways in which projects can be terminated, how to decide if a project should be terminated, the termination process, and the preparation of the Project Final Report.

Specific points made in the chapter were these:

- A project can be terminated in one of four ways: by extinction, addition, integration, or starvation.

- Making a decision to terminate a project before its completion is difficult, but a number of factors can be of help in reaching a conclusion.

- Most projects fail because of one or more of the following reasons:

  Inappropriate use of the project form of organization
  Insufficient top-management support
  Naming the wrong project manager
  Poor planning

- Studies have shown that the factors associated with project success are different for different industries and the various types of projects.

- Success-related factors, or any factors management wishes, can be used in termination decision models.

- Special termination managers are often used, and needed, for closing out projects. This task, consisting of eight major duties, is a proj. ect in itself.

- The Project Final Report incorporates the process knowledge gained from the project. In addition to preservation of project records, the Final Report embodies the experience from which we learn. It should include:

  Project performance comments
  Administrative performance comments
  Organizational structure comments
  Personnel suggestions, possibly a confidential section

▶ GLOSSARY

Termination by Addition—Bringing the project into the organization as a separate, ongoing entity.

Budget Decrement—A reduction in the amount of funds for an activity.

Termination by Extinction—The end of all activity on a project without extending it in some form, such as by inclusion or integration.

Termination by Integration—Bringing the project activities into the organization and distributing them among existing functions.

Termination by Murder—Terminating a project suddenly and without warning, usually for a cause not related to the project's purpose.

Termination by Starvation—Cutting a project's budget sufficiently to stop progress without actually killing the project.

Termination Manager—An administrator responsible for wrapping-up the administrative details of a project.

MATERIAL REVIEW QUESTIONS

1. List and briefly describe the ways projects may be terminated.
2. What problems may occur if the project manager does not have a follow-on project when the current project nears termination?
3. What are the primary duties of a termination manager?
4. On termination of a project, what happens to the information gathered throughout the course of the project?

5. What is a budget decrement?
6. Identify the four reasons for project termination.
7. What does the Project Final Report include?
8. What factors are considered most important in the decision to terminate a project?
9. What issues should be considered when using the termination-by-integration method?

CLASS DISCUSSION QUESTIONS

1. Discuss the impact, both positive and negative, of termination on the project team members. How might the negative impact be lessened?
2. If the actual termination of a project becomes a project in itself, what are the characteristics of this project? How is it different from other projects?
3. Discuss some reasons why a Project Final Report, when completed, should be permanently retained by the firm.
4. What elements of the termination process may be responsible for making a project unsuccessful?

5. How is discriminant analysis used in project management?
6. What are some characteristics of a good termination manager?
7. How might one choose which termination method to use?
8. Why might a failing project not be terminated?
9. How can termination for reasons other than achievement of project goals be avoided?
10. What must the project manager do in planning, scheduling, monitoring, and closing out the project?

INDIVIDUAL EXERCISE

Using the same project used for the Chapter 12 exercise, plan a project termination by *each* of the four methods described in the chapter. How would a decision regarding early termination be made? What would the critical factors be? If the project were to become a failure, what would the most likely reason be? Does it fall within the categories given in this chapter?

▶ INCIDENTS FOR DISCUSSION

Industrial Mop and Supply Co.

IMSCO began manufacturing and distributing mops and brooms to industrial customers 43 years ago. Mr. Bretting, president of IMSCO, has been toying with the idea of using IMSCO's manufacturing and distribution expertise to begin making and selling consumer products. He has already decided that he cannot sell any of his current products to consumers. Also, if IMSCO is going to go to the trouble of developing consumer markets, Mr. Bretting feels very strongly that their first product should be something new and innovative that will help establish their reputation. He thinks that the expertise required to develop a new product exists within the company, but no one has any real experience in organizing or managing such a project. Fortunately, Mr. Bretting is familiar with a local consulting firm that has a good reputation and track record of leading companies through projects such as this, so he contacted them.

Three months into the project, Mr. Bretting contacted the program manager/consultant and mentioned that he was worried about the amount of risk involved in trying to introduce such an innovative consumer product with his current organization. He was worried that the project was oriented too strongly towards R&D and did not consider related business problems in enough depth. (This was a complete about-face from his feelings three months earlier, when he had approved the first plan submitted with no changes.)

Mr. Bretting suggested that the consultant modify the existing project to include the introduction of a "me-too" consumer product before IMSCO's new product was defined and tested. Mr. Bretting thought that some experience with a "me-too" product would provide IMSCO management with valuable experience and would improve later performance with the new product. He allowed the R&D portion of the project to continue concurrently, but the "me-too" phase would have top priority as far as resources were concerned. The consultant said she would think about it and contact him next week.

Questions: If you were the consultant, what would you recommend to Mr. Bretting? Would you continue the relationship?

Excel Electronics

Excel Electronics is nearing completion of a three-year project to develop and produce a new pocket computer. The computer is no larger than a cigarette pack but has all the power and features of a $5000 microcomputer. The assembly line and all the production facilities will be completed in six months and the first units will begin production in seven months. The plant manager believes it is time to begin winding the project down. He has three methods in mind for terminating the project: extinction, addition, and integration, but he is not sure which method would be best.

Question: Which of the three methods would you recommend, and why?

▶ PROJECT TEAM CONTINUING EXERCISE

This assignment marks the completion of the project team's activity. The team should prepare a Project Final Report detailing the method of project termination, the reasons for termination, and the tasks the termination manager will have to complete to terminate the project. Also include the process knowledge gained from the project concerning performance, administration, organization structure, and personnel.

Last, suggest a termination evaluation model that includes what your team considers to be the relevant project success and failure factors. Note the potential for interaction between project manager factors, organizational factors, and project factors, in particular.

▶ BIBLIOGRAPHY

1. ADAMS, J. R., S. E. BARNDT, and M. D. MARTIN. *Managing by Project Management.* Dayton, OH: Universal Technology Corp., 1979.

2. AMRINE, H. T. et al. *Manufacturing Organization and Management*, 5th ed. Englewood Cliffs, NJ: Prentice Hall, 1987.

3. ANDREWS, K. R. *The Concept of Corporate Strategy*, 3rd ed. Homewood, IL: Dow Jones-Irwin, 1986.

4. ARCHIBALD, R. D. *Managing High Technology Programs and Projects.* New York: Wiley, 1976.

5. AVOTS, I. "Making Project Management Work— The Right Tool for The Wrong Project Manager." *Advanced Management Journal*, Autumn 1975.

6. AVOTS, I. "Why Does Project Management Fail?" *California Management Review*, Fall, 1969.

7. BAKER, N. R., S. G. GREEN, and A. S. BEAN. *A Multivariate Analysis of Environmental Organizational and Process Variables in the Process of Organized Technological Innovation. Vol. II. Technical Summary.* Final Report on National Science Foundation Award No. ISI 7921581, College of Business Administration. Cincinnati: University of Cincinnati, Jan. 1984.

8. BAKER, N. R., S. G. GREEN, A. S. BEAN, W. BLANK, and S. K. TADISINA. "Sources of First Suggestion and Project Success/Failure in Industrial Research." *Proceedings*, Conference on the Management of Technological Innovation, Washington, D.C., 1983.

9. BALACHANDRA, R., and A. J. RAELIN. "How to Decide When to Abandon a Project." *Research Management*, July 1980.

10. BEALE, P., and M. FREEMAN. "Successful Project Execution: A Model." *Project Management Journal*, December 1991.

11. BENNINGSON, L. A. "The Strategy of Running Temporary Projects." *Innovation*, Sept. 1971.

12. BUELL, C. K. "When to Terminate a Research and Development Project." *Research Management*, July 1967.

13. CERULLO, M. J. "Determining Post-Implementation Audit Success." *Journal of Systems Management*, March 1979.

14. CLELAND, D. I., and W. R. KING. *Systems Analysis and Project Management*, 2nd. ed. New York: McGraw-Hill, 1975.

15. CONNOR, P. E. et al., eds. *Dimension in Modern Management.* Boston: Houghton Mifflin, 1974.

16. DEAN, B. V. *Evaluating, Selecting, & Controlling R & D Projects.* New York: American Management Association, 1968.

17. FREEMAN, M., and P. BEALE. "Measuring Project Success." *Project Management Journal*, March 1992.

18. GRAY, C. F. *Essentials of Project Management.* Princeton, NJ: Petrocelli Books, 1981.

19. GREEN, S. G., M. A. WELSH, and G. E. DEHLER. "Red Flags at Dawn or Predicting Project Terminations at Start Up." *Research-Technology Management*, May-June 1993.

20. HOCKNEY, J. W., and K. HUMPHREYS. *Control and Management of Capital Projects*, 2nd ed. New York: McGraw-Hill, 1991.

21. HOLZMANN, R. T. "To Stop or Not—The Big Research Decision." *Chemical Technology*, 1972.

22. KEMP, P. S. "Post-Completion Audits of Capital Investment Projects." *Management Accounting*, Aug. 1966.

23. KERZNER, H. *Project Management, A Systems Approach to Planning, Scheduling, and Controlling*, 2nd ed. New York: Van Nostrand Reinhold, 1989.

24. KERZNER, H. "Evaluation Techniques in Project Management." *Journal of Systems Management*, Feb. 1980.

25. KLOPPENBORG, T. J., and D. A. PLATH. "Effective Project Management Practices during Expert Systems Implementation." *Project Management Journal*, December 1991.

26. KOONTZ, H. *Appraising Managers as Managers.* New York: McGraw-Hill, 1971.

27. LEE, W., and S. J. MANTEL, JR. "An Expert System for Project Termination." *Proceedings*, First International Conference on Engineering Management, Arlington, VA, Sept. 1986.

28. MANTEL, S. J., JR., A. L. SERVICE, et al. "A Social Service Measurement Model." *Operations Research*, March-April 1975.

29. MIGHT, R., and FISCHER, W. A. "The Role of Structural Factors in Determining Project Management Success." *IEEE Transactions on Engineering Management*, Vol. 32, 1985.

30. MONTGOMERY, J. L. "Appraising Capital Expenditures." *Management Accounting*, Sept. 1965.

31. NORTHCRAFT, G. B., and NEALE, M. A. "Opportunity Costs and the Framing of Resource Allocation Decisions." *Organizational Behavior and Human Decision Processes*, 1986, pp. 348–356.

32. NORTHCRAFT, G. B., and WOLF, G. "Dollars, Sense, and Sunk Costs: A Life Cycle Model of Resource Allocation Decisions." *Academy of Management Review*, No. 2 1984.

33. PINTO, J. K., and S. J. MANTEL, JR. "The Causes of Project Failure." *IEEE Transactions on Engineering Management*, Nov. 1990.

34. PINTO, J. K., and D. P. SLEVIN. "Critical Factors in Successful Project Implementation." *IEEE Transactions on Engineering Management*, February 1987.

35. PINTO, J. K., and D. P. SLEVIN. "Project Success: Definitions and Measurement Techniques." *Project Management Journal*, February 1988.

36. PINTO, J. K., and D. P. SLEVEN. "Critical Success Factors Across The Project Life Cycle." *Project Management Journal*, June 1988.

37. "Project Management Tasks: Wrap Up." *Design News*, April 19, 1982.

38. RAELIN, J. A., and R. BALACHANDRA. "R&D Project Termination in High-Tech Industries." *IEEE Transactions on Engineering Management*, Feb. 1985.

39. RIGGS, J. L., M. GOODMAN, R. FINLEY, and T. MILLER. "A Decision Support System for Predicting Project Success." *Project Management Journal*, September 1992.

40. RINGSTROM, N. H. "Making Project Management Work." *Business Horizons*, Fall 1965.

41. ROSENAU, M. D. *Successful Project Management*, 2nd ed. New York: Van Nostrand Reinhold, 1991.

42. SHAFER, S. M., and S. J. MANTEL, JR. "A Decision Support System for the Project Termination Decision." *Project Management Journal*, June 1989.

43. SILVERMAN, M. *Project Management: A Short Course for Professionals*, 2nd ed. New York: Wiley, 1988.

44. STAW, B. M., and ROSS, J. "Knowing When to Pull the Plug." *Harvard Business Review*, March-April, 1987.

45. STUCKENBRUCK, L. C., ed. *The Implementation of Project Management: The Professionals Handbook*. Project Management Institute, Reading, MA: Addison-Wesley, 1981.

46. TADISINA, S. K. "Support System for the Termination Decision in R&D Management." *Project Management Journal*, Nov. 1986.

47. WOLFF, M. F. "Knowing When the Horse Is Dead." *Research Management*, Nov. 1981.

CASE I

CINCINNATI MILACRON INC.: CASTING CLEANING
Marianne M. Hill and James M. Comer

In early 1982 Malcolm Davis, manager of manufacturing process development of Cincinnati Milacron, Inc. faced a decision regarding the continuation of the robot-aided casting cleaning project. Although it had taken much longer than planned to tool and program the robot, it had successfully cleaned two types of castings during December 1981. There was some concern, however, about continuing the development of the cleaning applications for the remainder of the 30 castings in the foundry's medium castings line.

Industry and Company Background

Cincinnati Milacron Inc. is engaged in the design, manufacture, and sale of process equipment and systems for industry, along with the supplies and accessories sold for use in these systems. Incorporated as Cincinnati Screw and Tap Company in 1884, the company originally sold screws, taps, and dies. After discovering a market for milling machines, the portion of the company devoted to these machines was pur-

Table I Cincinnati Milacron, Inc.

	1974	1975	1976	1977	1978	1979	1980	1981
			in thousands, except per-share amounts					
Summary of Operations								
Sales	$424,760	$431,225	$420,396	$497,073	$592,563	$702,120	$816,402	$934,395
Earnings (loss) from continuing operations	6,390	8,356	7,572	18,357	31,219	52,577	52,441	60,787
Percent of sales	1.5%	1.9%	1.8%	3.7%	5.3%	7.5%	6.4%	6.5%
Percent of average shareholder's equity	4.3%	5.4%	4.8%	10.8%	16.2%	22.8%	18.4%	18.3%
Per common share	0.28	0.37	0.34	0.83	1.40	2.34	2.32	2.68
Net earnings (loss)	10,259	9,946	9,991	20,869	33,184	55,439	75,644	60,787
Percent of average shareholder's equity	6.9%	6.4%	6.3%	12.3%	17.2%	24.1%	26.6%	18.3%
Per common share	0.47	0.45	0.45	0.95	1.49	2.47	3.35	2.68
Financial Position at Year End								
Working capital	169,132	167,561	160,719	165,436	182,758	206,335	253,923	266,983
Property, plant and equipment—net	95,300	95,379	101,792	109,109	118,864	146,148	156,944	184,440
Total assets	421,560	376,891	393,824	426,422	482,049	570,562	626,696	715,779
Long-term debt and lease obligations	124,076	116,304	110,917	106,919	108,053	108,723	100,786	104,715
Total debt	188,449	149,249	141,635	136,012	136,908	139,340	127,343	126,993
Shareholder's equity	152,356	157,015	161,752	178,065	206,937	253,521	316,145	349,315
Per common share	6.77	6.99	7.20	7.86	9.01	11.03	13.75	15.17
Other Data								
Dividends paid to common shareholders	5,044	5,047	5,051	5,809	7,017	9,902	14,571	16,283
Per common share	0.2333	0.2333	0.2333	0.2667	0.3167	0.4416	0.6467	0.7200
Capital expenditures	26,752	12,029	18,793	22,683	24,922	36,288	43,752	49,655
Depreciation	7,365	7,948	8,886	9,352	10,008	11,748	14,542	17,326
Unfilled orders at year end	346,226	216,166	250,082	320,738	471,231	673,316	698,288	476,856
Employees (average)	14,915	13,369	12,445	13,011	13,379	13,743	13,750	13,602
U.S. plants					16	18	17	19
Overseas plants					14	13	11	11

Source: 1983 Annual Report

Table 2   Cincinnati Milacron, Inc. Annual Sales and Operating Earnings (in millions)

	1978	1979	1980	1981
Machine Tool Group				
Sales	$374	$449	$563	$640
Operating Earnings	47	68	89	97
Plastics Machinery Group				
Sales	144	155	129	137
Operating Earnings	19	23	12	14
*Industrial Specialty Products Group**				
Sales	75	99	125	158
Operating Earnings	5	13	12	13

*1980–81: robots, cutting fluids, grinding wheels, semiconductor material, printed circuit board material

1978–79 (called Industrial Products): specialty chemicals, cutting fluids, grinding wheels, semiconductor material, printed circuit board material. In these years, robots are included in "Machine Tools."

Source: 1982–1983 Annual Reports

chased in 1889 and named the Cincinnati Milling Machine Company. The "Cincinnati Milacron" name was adopted in 1970. In 1981 the firm had 19 plants in the United States and 11 overseas, employed over 13,000 people, and had annual sales approaching $1 billion. Financial data for the years 1974–1981 are found in Table 1.

The company has three major divisions: machine tools, plastics processing machinery, and industrial specialty products. In 1981, the machine tool group accounted for 68.5 percent of total sales and 78.1 percent of total operating earnings, and the plastics machinery group provided 14.6 percent of total sales and 11.6 percent of operating earnings. The third group, industrial specialty products, accounted for 16.9 percent of sales and 10.3 percent of operating earnings. The five product lines in this group include robots, cutting fluids, grinding wheels, semiconductor materials (silicon epitaxial wafers), and printed circuit board materials. Although industry sources rank Milacron first in dollar sales of robots in the United States, robot sales represent less than 10 percent of total company sales. Table 2 shows annual sales and operating earnings for the three product groups for the years 1978–1981.

A major component of the machine tool division is a large jobbing foundry, which has provided gray and ductile iron castings for Milacron's machine tools for over 70 years.* With recent capacity expansion and

modernization facilitating the marketing of castings to other firms, plans are currently underway to change the foundry to a cost center. There are three separate departments in the foundry served by two cupolas and an electric holding furnace producing approximately 2500 different types of castings in lot sizes from 1 to 600 in small, medium, or large sizes. The small castings range in size from 4 ounces to 200 pounds; the medium castings range from 200 to 2000 pounds and account for the largest percentage of iron poured; and, the large castings range from 2000 to 40,000 pounds.

In 1980, foundry shipments dropped significantly from 1979 levels. Even with this decline, iron foundries were the nation's fifth largest manufacturing industry in 1981 and the second largest metal producing industry (surpassed only by rolled steel). Table 3 gives gray and ductile iron shipment figures in the United States for the years 1969–1981.

Casting and Cleaning Process

Iron castings are made in the following manner. Typically, a pattern is first made which conforms to the external shape of the casting. In the sand molding process, this pattern is then used to form a cavity in

---

*A glossary of terms used in this case is found in the case appendix.

Table 3 Total U.S. Shipments (000 Net Tons) of Ductile Iron and Gray Iron Castings

| | Gray Iron | | Ductile Iron | |
	Total	For Sale	Total	For Sale
1969	14,649	9,206*	1,286	N.A.
1970	12,388	8,146*	1,607	N.A.
1971	11,865	7,909*	1,712	N.A.
1972	13,467	7,153	1,835	1,037
1973	14,801	7,688	2,246	1,320
1974	13,459	7,260	2,203	1,505
1975	10,622	5,235	1,824	1,202
1976	11,923	5,455	2,245	1,405
1977	12,371	5,477	2,736	1,808
1978	13,140	6,316	3,005	1,993
1979	12,512	6,084	2,890	1,865
1980	9,399	4,788	2,400	1,669
1981	9,610	5,063	2,191	1,524

* Includes ductile iron for sale

Source: Bureau of the Census

the sand which is shaped to the desired contours and dimensions of the casting. Sand is packed firmly around the pattern. After the pattern is removed, cores are set in place; the cores form the interior surface in the casting. The mold is then closed, and the casting is poured. After the iron has solidified, the casting is removed from the mold, the sand is broken away, and the casting is sandblasted. It is then sent to the casting cleaning area to remove all extraneous metal. After final cleaning, it is sent to the paint line. A flowchart of a typical foundry operation is included in Exhibit 1.

Casting cleaning is the most labor intensive operation in the foundry and one of the most difficult to staff. A casting is dumped on the floor in the cleaning area; the casting cleaners stand over it while cleaning and use crowbars and an overhead crane (which is shared among all the men) to move it and turn it over. The system of risers, runners, and gates that created a path for the molten iron to enter the mold cavity is removed. Fins and other protrusions are also trimmed with the use of chisels, grinders, etc. The casting cleaners originally worked under very difficult conditions. The position was viewed by workers primarily as an entré into a desirable organization, since one of the "incentives" of the job was the ability to transfer to another position.

Foundry Modernization

A comprehensive internal study of the foundry was instituted in 1973. The committee investigated forecasted needs, workflows, floor plans, and health and safety concerns in order to develop an effective foundry modernization plan. The plan called for the modernization to begin first in the core room, proceed to molding, and then to the cleaning process. It was to start with the small casting line and then move on to the medium and large lines. The project began in 1976 and the scheduled completion date for the plan was 1986.

An accident in 1980 caused by a cracked wheel on an old grinder prompted an adjustment to the plan. Four grinders with improved safety features immediately replaced the remaining older ones. Also in 1980, OSHA cited Milacron for unacceptable levels of noise and respirable dust in the cleaning areas.*

The modernization project in the cleaning areas specified the installation of "cleaning booths." The

---

*Noise levels are calculated as weighted daily averages of all exposure to noise, including that produced by the worker him- or herself and other workers within hearing range.

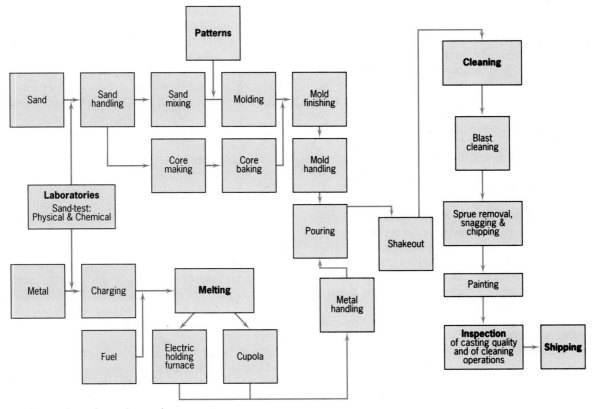

Exhibit 1: Flow Chart of Foundry Operations.

first booth was installed in the fall of 1980, and the twelfth was to be completed at the end of 1982, all in the small and medium castings lines. Three-sided booths for large castings are planned for 1986.

Castings enter a cleaning booth on a conveyor, and each booth has its own crane for lifting the casting onto a table. This table both rotates and elevates the casting so that the large grinders can be used. Previously, a 40–pound limit had been placed on castings that could be lifted by human operators. Castings weighing over 40 pounds were left on the floor and smaller grinders were used on them, which greatly increased the cleaning times.

In the booths, the air is circulated and cleaned. Although the air quality in the booths is such that helmet respirators are not needed, they are still worn for two reasons: they greatly reduce potential eye injury, and management wants consistency in the treatment of casting cleaners both in and out of the booths. The booths also provide isolation from noise associated with other cleaners. Although the booths and helmets did not constitute an engineering solution to the dust and noise problem, all OSHA regulations have been satisfied in these areas.

The booths result in a more orderly flow of work, improved material handling, and a decrease in tool repair. Tools are now conveniently located instead of being tossed around the cleaning area. There is also improved "housekeeping" in the booths. Management attributes this to the increased "pride of ownership" on the part of the casting cleaners. The turnover rate of cleaners has subsequently decreased dramatically.

The Introduction of Advanced Manufacturing Technologies

During 1977–79 an executive committee reporting directly to the president was established at Cincinnati Milacron to examine the trend in manufacturing throughout the entire firm. In general, the committee concluded that the company had to modernize and update the way in which they manufactured products in order to stay competitive with the foreign competition. More specifically, studies of the future trends in the work force had indicated that workers would become unavailable for undesirable jobs, such as casting cleaning. Thus, this area was identified for a possible robotic application. Other areas targeted for new technology included the introduction of robotics into the welding shop and the implementation of a computer-aided design (CAD) system.

In early 1980 Malcolm Davis, manager of manufacturing process development, was assigned the task of investigating and implementing robotic technology for possible use in the casting cleaning process. Manufacturing process development is part of the corporate facilities and manufacturing division, which is responsible for the buildings, their contents, and the equipment used in manufacturing. In addition, all new equipment purchases must be approved by this division. Before the robot project, new technology at the foundry had been the responsibility of the group headed by the foundry technical manager.

In September 1980, a development group was physically assigned to the foundry. A robot was delivered to the foundry and the entire project was conducted there. The involvement of the foundry personnel in this project included site selection and preparation (the robot project was carried out 50 feet from the installation of a new cleaning booth) and weekly meetings between the robot development group and the foundry technical group. The superintendent of the foundry joined these meetings once a month.

A Gantt chart prepared on January 19, 1981, is shown in Exhibit 2. One of the first tasks was to provide tools for the robot. In the existing cleaning operation, air tools were the standard type used by humans. It was obvious that the robot was capable of handling tools with much greater horsepower, so the search began for existing tools with higher horsepower that could be used by the robot.

During January and February of 1981, the market and literature were searched for potential tools to be used, but nothing was available. Electric motors were ruled out because they were too heavy and the weight-to-horsepower ratio was too great. Hydraulic motors offered the most promise because the weight-to-horsepower ratio is low and the power source can be remote.

Hydraulic tools that were available on the market could not readily be adapted for use by the robot. The development of these tools by an outside supplier was ruled out because of the cost. Cincinnati Milacron decided it would be more effective to purchase hydraulic motors and then develop the tools themselves around the robot application. An outside engineering firm was hired in March 1981 to do the mechanical drawings, and Milcron did the design work and built the tools in-house.

One of the first tools developed was a chisel, but it did not perform as expected. Effort was then directed toward developing grinding tools, burr cutters, and a cutoff wheel. A total of six tools was developed. It was also necessary to develop a way to change the tools and to then transmit hydraulic power through this tool changer. This was a very extensive endeavor; two iterations of the tool changers were necessary.

Exhibit 3 desribes the robot-aided casting cleaning operation. The robot cleaned its first casting in December 1981. Applications were developed for two types of castings. Castings of each type were cleaned continuously.

The standard time to clean the first casting was 20 minutes for the worker and 16 minutes for the robot. Since this was a smaller casting, the robot spent a considerable amount of time changing tools. The robot, though, could work continuously, while the worker needed to rest. It was estimated that the robot could complete in three days what it would take the worker five days to do. Although the robot's cleaning was more consistent (e.g., grinding lines were identical on all pieces), the quality of the finished casting was not assessed as better than that done by the worker.

The second casting cleaned by the robot was larger than the first. The standard time was 36 minutes for the worker and 22 minutes for the robot. Since the amount of cleaning was greater (as opposed to tool changing), the robot could use the tool more productively over a longer period of time.

The casting cleaning robot is a point-to-point motion robot. It takes from six hours to three days to program the cleaning of each part and each operation requires a separate tape. (In comparison, 12 applications could be stored on a single tape for robot welding operations.) It is estimated that it would take one and a half to two years of programming to have enough parts programmed for the robot to function productively.

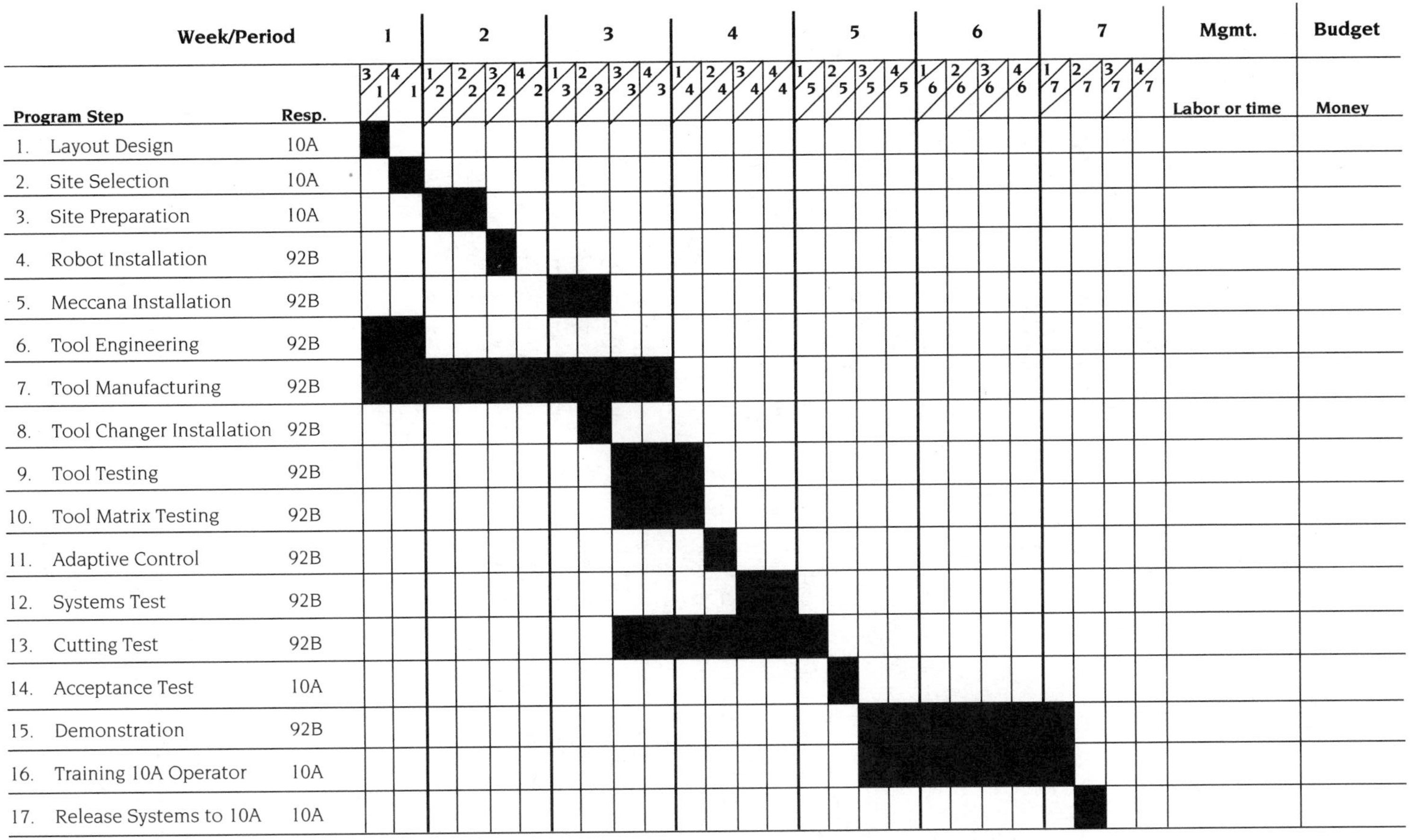

Week/Period	Resp.	1	2	3	4	5	6	7	Mgmt. Labor or time	Budget Money
Program Step										
1. Layout Design	10A									
2. Site Selection	10A									
3. Site Preparation	10A									
4. Robot Installation	92B									
5. Meccana Installation	92B									
6. Tool Engineering	92B									
7. Tool Manufacturing	92B									
8. Tool Changer Installation	92B									
9. Tool Testing	92B									
10. Tool Matrix Testing	92B									
11. Adaptive Control	92B									
12. Systems Test	92B									
13. Cutting Test	92B									
14. Acceptance Test	10A									
15. Demonstration	92B									
16. Training 10A Operator	10A									
17. Release Systems to 10A	10A									

Exhibit 2: Robot-Aided Casting Cleaning—Phase 1 (1/19/81).

641

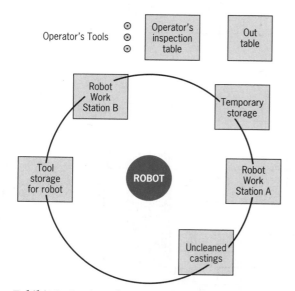

Exhibit 3: Casting Cleaning Robot Operation.

An operator, with the help of a crane, would pick up a raw casting and put it on Work Station A (assume a casting is already at B). The robot would clean as many sides as it could at A and then move to Work Station B and work on the one there. Meanwhile, the operator picks up the casting from A and puts it on the temporary storage table and picks up another raw casting and puts it on A. When the robot is through at B, the operator takes the casting from B to the opera-tor's inspection table, and moves the one from temporary storage to Station B. The operator checks the one on the inspection table to see if anything else needs to be worked on, and if so, does it. When it is completed, the operator moves it to the out table.

The robot is busy all of the time. The worker is idle about 20 percent of the time and is moving castings and working 80 percent of the time. If the robot were adopted, production would be rebalanced to keep the worker busy for greater periods of time.

Current Situation

Malcolm Davis is thus faced with drafting his recommendation. Although some feel that the need for the robot application is not as great now since the cleaning booths have been installed, Malcolm views the booths as a temporary, transitional measure.

The robotic application to casting cleaning is extremely attractive to management because the robot can work in any environment and would qualify as an engineering solution (required by OSHA) to the dust and noise problem. In addition, 12–16 undesirable jobs in casting cleaning could be eliminated.

Discussions with the foundry technical manager revealed that he thinks that future directions will focus on improving the quality of casting in order to reduce the amount of necessary cleaning, as well as examining other methods of metal removing, such as laser cutting and plasma arc cutting.

▶ QUESTIONS

1. Prepare a Gantt chart for the foundry modernization project and the casting cleaning robot project that includes the activities discussed in the case. What interaction was there between the two project groups?

2. A financial feasibility study was not attempted before the casting cleaning project began. Should it have been? What costs and benefits would have been included?

3. Do the cleaning booths reduce the need for the casting cleaning robot? Explain.

4. If you were Malcolm Davis, what recommendations would you make? Why?

5. In June 1982, the project was discontinued. Why do you think it was terminated?

▶ APPENDIX

Glossary*

Blast Cleaning—Removal of sand or oxide scale from castings by the impinging action of sand, metal shot, or grit projected under air, water, or centrifugal pressure.

Captive Foundry—One that produces castings from its own patterns for its own use.

Casting—(verb) Act of pouring molten metal into a mold; (noun) metal object cast to a required shape by pouring or injecting liquid metal into a mold.

Chip—(verb) To remove extraneous metal from a casting by hand or pneumatically operated chisels.

Cleaning—The process of removing all metal that does not belong on the final casting, such as gates, fins, runners, and risers; may also include the removal of adhering sand from the casting.

Core—A preformed sand aggregate inserted into a mold to shape the interior of the casting or that part of the casting which cannot be shaped by the pattern.

Cupola—A vertically cylindrical furnace for melting metal, in direct contact with coke as fuel, by forcing air under pressure through openings near its base.

Fins—Thin projections of excess metal on a casting resulting from imperfect mold or core joints.

Gate—End of the runner in a mold where the rate of flow of molten metal is controlled as it enters the casting or mold cavity.

Gray Iron—Cast iron which contains a relatively large percentage of the carbon present in the form of flake graphite. The metal has a gray fracture.

Holding Furnace—Usually a small furnace for maintaining molten metal at the proper pouring temperature, and which is supplied from a large melting unit.

Hydraulic Motor—An actuator which converts forces from high pressure hydraulic fluid into mechanical shaft rotation.

Jobbing Foundry—One which is equipped to economically produce a single casting or in small quantities from a variety of patterns.

Mold—The form, made of sand, metal, or refractory material, which contains the cavity into which molten metal is poured to produce a casting of desired shape.

Off-Line Programming—A means of programming a robot by developing a set of instructions on an independent computer and then using the software to control the robot at a later time.

Pattern—A form of wood, metal, or other materials, around which molding material is placed to make a mold for casting metals.

Point-to-Point Motion—This is a type of robot motion in which a limited number of points along a path of motion is specified by the controller. The robot moves from point-to-point in a straight line rather than a curved path between points. The latter is often referred to as a continuous path robot and requires larger memory because more points are required.

Respirable Dust—Extremely fine dust; when combined with high levels of quartz silicon, it can be carcinogenic.

Riser—A reservoir of molten metal provided to compensate for the contraction of the metal in a casting as it solidifies.

Robot—A reprogrammable multifunctional manipulator designed to move material, parts, tools, or specialized devices through variable programmed motion for the performance of a variety of tasks.

Runner—The portion of the gate assembly that connects the downgate with the casting ingate or riser.

Snagging—Removal of fins and rough places on a casting by means of grinding.

Sprue—The vertical portion of the gating system where the molten metal first enters the mold.

Teaching—The process of programming a robot to perform a desired sequence of tasks.

---

*Definitions from Charles F. Walton (editor), *Iron Castings Handbook*, Iron Castings Society, Inc., 1981; and J. Gerin Sylvia, *Cast Metals Technology*, Reading, MA: Addison-Wesley Publishing Company, 1972; and *Industrial Robots*, Naperville, IL: Tech Tran Corporation, 1983.

CASE II

BETA COMPANY: THE Z15 ENGINE PROGRAM (A)*
Andrea Malinowksi

Since its founding in 1911, the Beta Company had been the premiere manufacturer of luxury passenger cars in the United States. Beta was known by its competitors and the marketplace as a high-price, high-quality producer. Because of its select market segment and reputation for continually adding unique and innovative features to its cars, Beta sales had traditionally seemed immune to fluctuations in the economy and shifts in the tastes of the general buying public. Beta survived the 1974 oil embargo with few lost sales. By 1976, however, Beta management was concerned that the volatility of oil producing nations and the resulting changing psyche of its consumers would lead to declining sales volumes in the future.

In addition, Beta managers were keenly aware of the increasing threat of imports and the eroding image of U.S. manufacturers as quality producers. Old production methods and management techniques were fading fast in favor of increased automation and more participative management. Beta's parent corporation, United Vehicle Manufacturers (UVM), and the local unions were putting more and more pressure on Beta to shed its image of being an industrial anachronism and begin revamping its organization to produce high-quality products at a lower cost. The future survival of Beta depended on its ability to contend with a marketplace that was quickly becoming more quality and price conscious.

In August 1976, Beta management determined that in order to secure their market position in the future, they needed a vehicle that had the quality of a Beta and the performance and high mileage of imports. This decision led to the beginning of the Z15 engine program.

The Z15 Engine Program

While Beta prided itself on product innovation, it had not had an entirely new engine since the early 60s. All engines had been produced solely at the Clair, Ohio central manufacturing and assembly complex until the early 70s, when a satellite plant was built in Auburn, (about 20 miles from the Clair complex). The Auburn plant supplied machined engine components to Clair through August 1981. Engine assembly continued at Clair only until Auburn was in full production with the Z15 engine for the 1981 model year.

The proposed Z15 engine was a radical departure from traditional automotive engines. It would be lighter, more powerful, and more fuel efficient than engines of comparable size, and this novel design also meant that new production technology would be required at Auburn. The Z15 engine was to be built in a new addition to the Auburn plant which would triple the existing floor space.

As with all major projects in the UVM divisions, final approval for the Z15 engine program and the allocation of corporate funds was the responsibility of the corporate staff. UVM approved the basic Z-15 program proposal in January 1977. The engine was slated to come on stream by August 1980 for the 1981 model year, as shown in the lead time chart in Exhibit 1. With less than two and a half years before pilot engines would be required, UVM released $300 million allocated for the entire project. It was at this time that manufacturing staffs were brought onto the project, including industrial engineering and process engineering. In the Z15 program the process engineering staff, in conjunction with product engineering, had the overall responsibility for the successful implementation of the program. The history of this engine program can be traced by following the work of the process engineering staff from August 1976 through August 1980.

The Beta Company—Process Engineering Staff

In August 1976, the process engineering department at Clair had nearly 100 employees, including 44 engineers. As shown in Exhibit 2, the engineers were di-

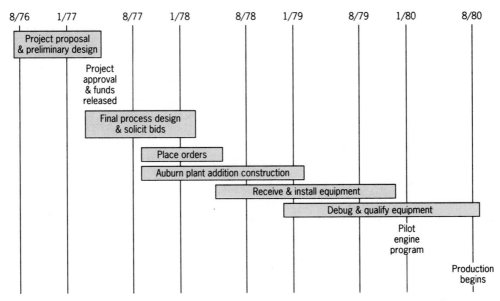

Exhibit 1: Beta Company: Z15 Program Lead Time Chart. (*Source*: Casewriter and company records)

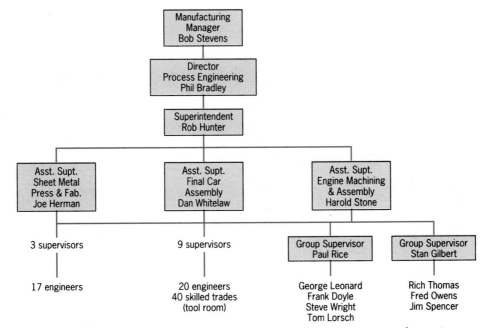

Exhibit 2: Beta Company: Process Engineering Department Organization Chart—August 1976. (*Source*: Casewriter and company records)

vided into three groups: sheet metal press, fabrication, and finishing; final car assembly; engine machining and assembly. At this time the majority of the engineers were in the sheet metal and assembly groups to work on product changes for the 1977 model year. The engine group had dwindled to seven engineers as there had not been any major engine revisions for several years.

It was traditional in process engineering that engineers were rotated about as labor requirements deemed necessary. If there was a major new car assembly program, engineers from other groups which were slow might be put on temporary assignment to the assembly group. New hirings from within or without the company and parent corporation were usually limited to filling openings created by normal attrition. The average age of the engineers in the department was 38, with the range from 22 to 58. The majority of engineers, especially the more recent hires, had engineering degrees. The rest had been promoted to engineers from skilled trade positions in the tool room or tool design. A handful of the engineers had advanced degrees in engineering or management.

The basic responsibility of the process engineer was to carry a part from the finished design stage through to the final product ready for use. For parts already in production, this entailed working with production departments and making equipment or tool-ing improvements. Exhibit 3 shows the engineers' relationship to manufacturing on the organization chart. For new parts, the engineer designed the manufacturing process, procured and installed the equipment, brought the equipment up to running speed producing quality parts, and then looked for any improvements that could be made. There was never a "typical" day for a process engineer. Some days might go entirely as planned while others were determined by the needs of production departments. It was this flexibility to meet the demands of the moment, as well as move to different areas of responsibility with relative ease, that made the process staff well respected within the company.

In 1976 the engineering staff itself was a relatively congenial group. There were weekly departmental meetings for section supervisors who in turn transmitted information to their engineers through weekly group meetings. Most of the engineers knew one another fairly well from working together in various sections. There were card games at lunch and beer drinking together after work. Some of the engineers and their families participated in social activities together. The department layout was conducive to impromptu problem solving sessions and casual conversations, as the engineers were paired in cubicles with partitions that were 3–feet high with another 8 inches of glass on top. (See Exhibit 4 for office layout.)

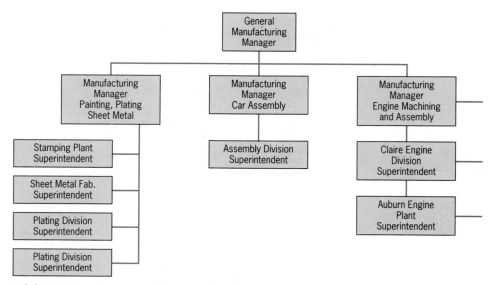

Exhibit 3: Beta Company: Clair Manufacturing Division Organization Chart—August 1976. (*Source*: Casewriter)

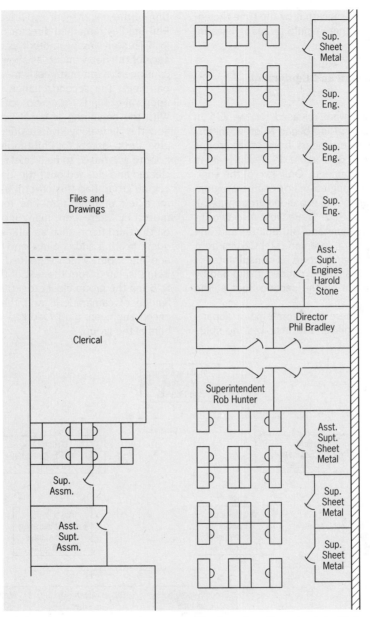

Exhibit 4: Beta Company: Process Engineering Department, Clair Office Layout—January 1977. (*Source*: Casewriter)

The Process Engineering Engine Group

Phil Bradley, director of process engineering, was excited about getting the Z15 program at Beta. The program would bring a boost to Beta as well as the department, with the newly allocated funds providing for much needed additional manpower. Phil had worked closely with product engineering and members of the process engine group on the development of the Z15 proposal submitted to UVM for approval. His life was invested at Beta, and he knew that by the time the engine was in production there would be many lives invested in the Z15.

Phase I: Process Design and Equipment Procurement

Shortly after the funds were released for the Z15 in August 1977, the engine group began to grow, mainly through the transfer of engineers from other groups into the engine group. By August 1977, the engine group had 15 process engineers. Only two of the engineers had ever been through a major engine program before. The average age of the expanded group was 30, with the range from 21 to 52. There were also two industrial engineers (Art Lane and Bill Spatta) and one machining division general foreman (Mel Carter) from Clair who joined the engine group as consultants for the initial project phases. The expanded group had by far outgrown its quarters on the second floor at the Clair complex.

At the same time there were some major departmental changes taking place. The first was the split-

ting of the department activities under two directors. Phil Bradley remained director over the engine group. Rob Hunter was promoted to director over the balance of the department, as shown in Exhibit 5. Hunter continued to run one weekly meeting for the entire department. The second change was the long-awaited approval of funds for new process engineering offices. With the beginning of construction in their old area and the increasing overcrowded conditions, the engine group, except for Phil Bradley, moved to the third floor to what used to be a cafeteria. The area had been cleared and cleaned but little else had been done. The engine group had this cavernous space to themselves for a few months, until the tool design group also moved in. There were many inconveniences to being on the third floor, such as falling plaster, mice, inadequate heating and cooling, and the walk to the copier and file room, which remained on the second floor. Being isolated from the rest of the department served to bring the group closer together. There was a strong feeling of camaraderie and the older, more experienced engineers gladly worked with the newer members of the group.

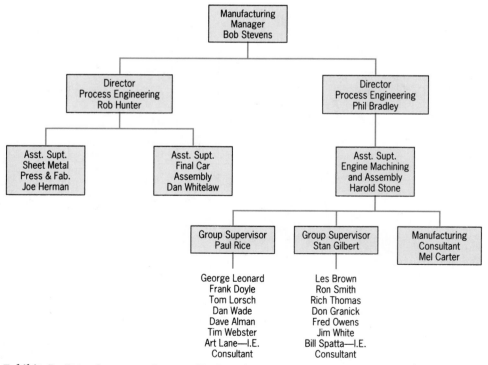

Exhibit 5: Beta Company: Process Engineering Department Organization Chart—August 1977. (*Source*: Casewriter and company records)

By November 1977 the project was well under way. The process engineers in the engine group worked closely with equipment vendors and product engineers to finalize part designs that were functional and that could be manufactured at lower cost. The industrial engineering consultants, Bill Spatta and Art Lane, worked in conjunction with Mel Carter, the process engineers, and some temporarily assigned plant layout engineers to determine what kind of automation would be desirable and the most efficient and effective layout of equipment. In the past, washers and automation had been procured by plant engineering. For the Z15 program, Beta management had shifted this responsibility to the process group.

During this first phase, the engine group had grown accustomed to working 10 to 12 hour days, six and seven days a week. As the amount of overtime increased, the frequency of group and section meetings decreased until there was only the rare project status meeting conducted by Harold Stone. It had also become common for there to be no engine group representative at Hunter's weekly departmental meeting.

The group recognized the limited amount of time to get the enormous job done, and the enthusiasm and energy levels were high enough that the long days didn't seem so long. More than 300 machines had to be purchased, ranging in size from special lathes to 30 station transfer machines. Three to five vendors were selected to bid on every item purchased—from the largest machine to the smallest cutting tool—and each bid had to be evaluated by the engineers before a contract was awarded to a vendor. As the flow of vendors through the office increased, more engineers ate lunch out with salespeople to break up the day. The engineers' time had already been difficult to account for; there were no reprimands for late returns from lunch.

Many of the equipment orders had been placed by February 1978, with deliveries ranging from 9 to 24 months. After the final process and equipment had been determined, the gauging systems were designed and quoted. It was at this time that the quality assurance organization became involved with the Z15. The QA staff had gone through a recent reorganization and increase in manpower, and a group of quality engineers was assigned to the Z15. Their purpose was to ensure that the process was designed to make parts within 80 percent of the tolerance spread, and that gauging would be provided for all pertinent dimensions. The process engineers had never really worked with QA in this way before and there was some frus-

tration on both sides at initial meetings. Their frustration was exacerbated by a new geometric tolerancing code on all drawings and the conversion from English to metric units. Bob Stevens had made it clear, however, that since QA would have the ultimate responsibility for using the gauges in production, it was essential to have their input at the design stage.

Phase II: Receive and Install Equipment

The first machine arrived in August 1978—months before the building was due for completion. The basic structure was complete and floors and foundations were laid as equipment came in. The process engineers spent more and more time at the Auburn plant working with the skilled trades and outside contractors supervising the installation of the equipment. The previous General Manufacturing Manager had been strongly opposed to having permanent offices for engineers at the Auburn plant, but it became clear that some kind of facility was needed for the engineers to store drawings and have a work area with phones. Bradley and Stone had some surplus desks moved into the Auburn warehouse office. The engineers had just completed another move only two months before—this one from the third floor cafeteria to the new process engineering offices at Clair. The new offices had carpeting, indirect lighting, and 5-foot soundproof partitions—all of which served to create a very sedate and professional atmosphere.

Phase III: Debug and Qualify Machines

By January 1979, the Auburn addition had begun to look like an engine plant. With many machines installed, process engineers worked with machine tool servicepeople and Auburn plant skilled trades to cycle the machines and get them running up to speed and producing good parts. Before a machine was accepted for use by production, it had to go through the qualification process: a statistical sampling of 25 consecutive pieces was used to predict the characteristics of the entire population of parts to be produced on that machine. Thus if even two or three pieces from a qualification run were of marginal quality, the entire run could be worthless. The quality engineers, who had become part of the permanent Auburn staff, were responsible for collecting and analyzing the data from the qualification runs. Their job was compounded by the fact that many of the gauges had not yet been received and pieces had to be checked by hand, which was very time consuming.

By this time it was typical for a process engineer to be at the Clair complex only once every week or two. To the dismay of the Auburn warehouse staff, the engineers had moved many of their files and drawings into that office area. To facilitate paperwork processing, Harold Stone stopped at the Auburn plant every night to pick up items to go to the Clair complex. He had also acquired several temporary hourly employees who acted as couriers between Auburn and Clair and made rush pick-ups from local vendors. The engine group had also been expanded through the addition of several more temporary outside contract engineers.

The Auburn plant staff had also expanded during this time. Rob Hunter had been promoted to general plant superintendent, as shown in Exhibit 6, and had started to establish the permanent plant staff through the addition of several assistant superintendents, permanent industrial, plant, and quality engineers, personnel and office administrators, and clerical staff.

The Auburn Plant Social System

In keeping with efforts to shed its old corporate image, the Beta Auburn plant operated under a newly developed social system which encompassed the concepts of quality circles and participative management through the use of business teams. Each team had 10 to 20 hourly employees (quality operators), depending on the labor requirements of the area. For example, the camshaft line had one team of 20 each shift, whereas the crankshaft line had two teams of 15 each on each shift. Foremen and general foremen were replaced by one level of production supervision, team coordinators. Each team also elected a member to act as an assistant team coordinator and these individuals performed some of the standard foreman's functions such as job assignments, and so forth. Through the use of assistant team coordinators, team coordinators were then able to work with two to three teams as both supervisors and facilitators of team functions.

The business teams were fully responsible for the quality of their product and the productivity of their area. Rather than relying on outside support groups for inspection, material handling, cleaning, etc., each team performed these functions internally. The assistant team coordinators (ATCs) led weekly team meetings, which were allotted an hour a week during scheduled working hours, in discussions of product quality problems, team function problems, concerns about their environment, and so forth. The teams developed proposals which the ATC and the team coordinator (TC) would then evaluate and, if warranted,

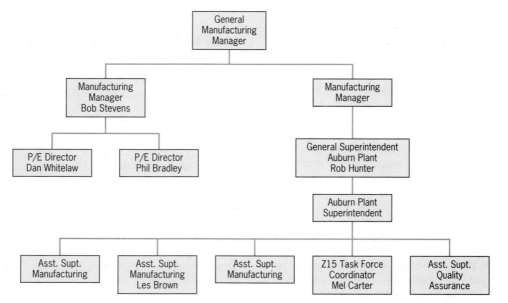

Exhibit 6: Beta Company: Partial Manufacturing Staff Organization Chart—January 1979. (*Source*: Casewriter)

implement. To facilitate this process, team members, ATCs, and TCs were offered the opportunity to attend a four day off-site seminar on problem solving and decision making which had been developed by an outside consultant and taught by trained Auburn employees.

The Auburn salaried staff was not included in the teams, but the distinction between salaried and hourly was erased as neckties were forbidden, and there was a common cafeteria and parking lot. The process engineers, not being part of the permanent plant staff, continued to wear ties and were generally excluded from any meetings concerning the social system.

Almost everyone recognized that the process engineers would be very important to the success of the Auburn Plant business teams. Since a large number of team discussions centered on quality and process improvements, the process engineers were called upon frequently to act as information resources or implementors for business team ideas. Consequently, the process group was required to balance their obligation to the business teams with their normal job responsibilities of installing, debugging, and qualifying new machines. Some of the process engineers were troubled by management expectations of cooperation with the business teams even though the engineers' normal jobs were not reduced in scope.

The development and implementation of the social system was carried on simultaneously with the Z15 program. As the date for pilot engines drew near, the tension at Auburn was further fueled by the new social system as all Auburn employees had to adjust to new operating procedures, new equipment and technology, and a new product.

Phase IV: Pilot Program

By August 1979, the process engineers had been working 70 to 80 hours a week for more than two years and the fatigue had begun to show in heated discussions with production personnel, longer lunches, and more frequent "bull" sessions at bars after work. Two process engineers, Don Granick and Rich Thomas, had left on extended medical leaves. As more machines were qualified and turned over to production, the process engineer had to contend not only with getting the last of the equipment installed and debugged, but also satisfying the needs of production departments when they ran into difficulty with a piece of equipment.

Bob Stevens and Phil Bradley knew that the Z15 program was taking its toll on the engineers and sought to alleviate the situation by bringing in additional temporary supervisors and temporary or outside contract engineers, as shown in the organization chart in Exhibit 7. The addition of new blood seemed to revive the sagging spirits of the veterans. Many of the engineers recognized that old problems took on a new light when looked at with a fresh pair of eyes. Some of the engineers were reluctant to relinquish any of their responsibilities because the temporary engineers were only expected to be in the group for 6 to 9 months. The lines of supervision also seemed to get blurred, with some engineers unclear as to who their supervisor would be in the long run.

In any case, pilot engines were indeed built in November 1979. The Auburn staff seemed to breathe a sign of relief when this hurdle was passed. For the process engineers, however, the pressure only increased. There remained less than eight months until the plant was to begin production of engines for the 1981 model year and much of the equipment was still not running satisfactorily. Some of the pilot engine components had been machined on the outside in job shops because the in-house equipment wasn't ready. To many of the engineers, the August start-up date seemed an impossible goal.

Phase V: Production

Perhaps it was the enormity of the task completed that had the process engineers most suprised and satisfied of all when the Auburn plant began full production in August 1980. Of the more than 300 machines purchased, enough had been installed and debugged to meet initial volume requirements. The many gauges required in the 20 machining and assembly areas were on the floor and ready for use. The hundreds of pieces of automation and material handling equipment were not fully in place and functional, but rapid progress was being made toward that end. The pressure was off Auburn as long as it continued to produce quality engines in the required volume.

Some of the temporary process staff went back to their old jobs and the rest were expected to be gone by the end of the year, as shown in Exhibit 8. Bob Stevens and Phil Bradley realized that the Auburn plant would require a permanent complement of process engineers and, as such, moved the group, including the supervisors, Stone, and Bradley, into the recently expanded Machining Division office, as

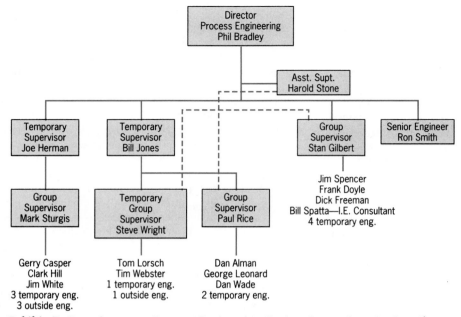

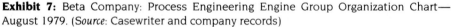

Exhibit 7: Beta Company: Process Engineering Engine Group Organization Chart—August 1979. (*Source*: Casewriter and company records)

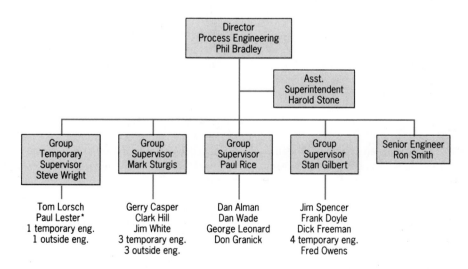

*Paul Lester replaced Tim Webster who had been killed in a car accident.

Exhibit 8: Beta Company: Process Engineering Engine Group Organization Chart—August 1980. (*Source*: Casewriter and company records)

shown in Exhibit 9. It still wasn't clear, however, how many engineers would be permanent at Auburn or where their offices would be. At this time, too, the future of the main complex was uncertain. While Beta sales had been boosted by the introduction of the Z15 engine, UVM sales overall were down drastically, and some major assembly and sheet metal programs at Beta had been cancelled.

Summary

With the pressure at Auburn subsiding, less overtime was required and many of the engineers were back to a 40–hour week, with an occasional Saturday or Sunday. The job ahead of the engine group now was basically to provide service to production departments as they requested help and to look for ways to improve processes. The slower work pace did not seem to enliven the battle-fatigued group, and the completion of the project, coupled with the depressed economic environment, contributed to the uncertain future of the group.

Bob Stevens recognized that the process engine group had been through a difficult period of work on the Z15 engine. He realized that while their jobs were still being done, the attitude of the engineers wasn't what it used to be. Stevens began to wonder what could be done to improve the sagging spirits of his engineers and how to go about doing it. He wasn't sure how he should approach the issue: through group sessions or individual interviews; what questions to ask; what he should expect to find if he talked to the engineers; and how to gather data to confirm his suspicions.

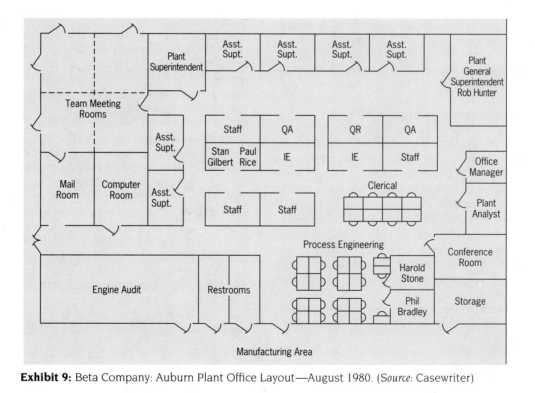

Exhibit 9: Beta Company: Auburn Plant Office Layout—August 1980. (*Source*: Casewriter)

▶ This article has already become a classic on the psychological basis for continuing a project invariably headed for disaster. The authors clearly point out the dangers of certain personality types in project managers matching the needs profile of certain organizations. In these all-too-frequent situations, projects are continued way past the point where commonsense would have called for their termination.

Classic Reading

KNOWING WHEN TO PULL THE PLUG*
Barry M. Staw and Jerry Ross

Last year you authorized the expenditure of $500,000 for what you thought was a promising new project for the company. So far, the results have been disappointing. The people running the project say that with an additional $300,000 they can turn things around. Without extra funding, they cry, there is little hope. Do you spend the extra money and risk further losses, or do you cut off the project and accept the half-million-dollar write-off?

Managers face such quandaries daily. They range from developing and placing employees to choosing plant sites and making important strategic moves. Additional investment could either remedy the situation or lead to greater loss. In many situations, a decision to persevere only escalates the risks, and good management consists of knowing when to pull the plug.

These escalation situations are trouble. Most of us can think of times when we should have bailed out of a course of action. The Lockheed L 1011 fiasco and the Washington Public Supply System debacle (commonly referred to as WHOOPS) are spectacular examples of organizational failure to do so. Decisions to persist with these crippled ventures caused enormous losses.

Of course, all managers will make some mistakes and stick with some decisions longer than they ought to. Recent research has shown, however, that the tendency to pursue a failing course of action is not a random thing. Indeed, at times some managers and even entire organizations, seem almost programmed to follow a dying cause.[1]

What leads executives to act so foolishly? Are they people who should never have been selected for responsible positions? Are these organizations simply inept? Or are they generally competent managers and companies that find themselves drawn into decisional quicksand, with many forces driving them deeper?

Though we think this last description is probably the right one, we don't think the tendency is uncheckable. Managers and organizations that often fall into escalation traps can take steps to avoid them.

Why projects Go Out of Control

As a start to understanding why people get locked into losing courses of action, let's look first at what a purely rational decision-making approach would be. Consider, for example, the decision to pursue or scuttle an R&D or a marketing project. On the basis of future prospects, you'd have made the initial decision to pursue the project, and enough time would have passed to see how things were going. Ideally, you'd then reassess the situation and decide on future action. If you were following a fully rational approach, whatever losses might have occurred before this decision point would be irrelevant for your reassessment. With a cold clear eye, you'd view the prospects for the future as well as your available options. Would the company be better off if it got out, continued with the project, or decided to invest more resources in it? You'd treat any previous expenses or losses as sunk costs, things that had happened in the past, not to be considered when you viewed the future.

In theory, pure rationality is great, but how many managers and organizations actually follow it? Not many. Instead, several factors encourage decision makers to become locked into losing courses of action.

The Project Itself The first set of factors have to do with the project itself. "Is the project not doing well because we omitted an important factor from our calculations, or are we simply experiencing the downside of problems that we knew could occur?" "Are the problems temporary (bad weather or a soon-to-be-settled supplier strike) or more permanent (a steep downturn in demand)?" Expected or short-term problems are likely to encourage you to continue a project. You may even view them as necessary costs or investments for achieving large, long-term gains. If you expect problems to arise, when they do, they may convince you that things are going as planned.

A project's salvage value and closing costs can also impede withdrawal. An executive could simply terminate an ineffective advertising campaign in midstream, but stopping work on a half-completed facility is another story. A project that has very little salvage value and high closing costs—payments to terminated employees, penalties for breached contracts, and losses from the closing of facilities—will be much more difficult to abandon than a project in which expenditures are recoverable and exit is easy. It's understandable why so many financially questionable construction projects are pursued beyond what seems to be a rational point of withdrawal.[2]

Consider the Deep Tunnel project in Chicago, a plan to make a major addition to the city's sewer system that will eventually improve its capacity to handle major storms. Although the project has absorbed millions of dollars, it won't deliver any benefits until the entire new system is completed. Unfortunately, as each year passes, the expected date of completion recedes into the future while the bill for work to be finished grows exponentially. Of course, no one would have advocated the project if the true costs had been known at the outset. Yet, once begun, few have argued to kill the project.

The problem is that the project was structured in ways that ensured commitment. First, the project managers viewed each setback as a temporary situation that was correctable over time with more money. Second, they perceived all moneys spent as investments toward a large payoff they'd reap when the project was complete. Third, expenditures were irretrievable: the laid pipe in the ground has no value unless the entire project is completed, and it would probably cost more to take the pipe out of the ground than it's worth. Thus, like many other large construction and R&D projects, investors in the Deep Tunnel have been trapped in the course of action. Even though what they receive in the end may not measure up to the cost of attaining it, they have to hang on until the end if they hope to recoup any of their investment.

Managers' Motivations Most of the factors concerning projects that discourage hanging on are evident to managers. They may not fully factor closing costs and salvage value into their initial decisions to pursue certain courses of action (since new ventures are supposed to succeed rather than fail), but when deciding whether to continue a project or not, executives are usually aware of these factors. Less obvious to managers, however, are the psychological factors that influence the way information about courses of action are gathered, interpreted, and acted on.

We are all familiar with the idea that people tend to repeat behavior if they are rewarded and to stop it if they are punished. According to the theory of reinforcement, managers will withdraw from a course of action in the face of bad news. This interpretation, however, ignores people's history of rewards. Managers have often been rewarded for ignoring short-run disaster, for sticking it out through tough times. Successful executives—people whose decisions have turned out to be winners even when the outlook had appeared grim—are particularly susceptible. It's tough for managers with good track records to recognize that a certain course isn't a satisfactory risk, that things aren't once again going to turn their way.

Reinforcement theory also tells us that when people receive rewards intermittently (as from slot machines), they can become quite persistent. If a decline in rewards has been slow and irregular, a person can go on and on even after rewards have disappeared. Unfortunately, many business situations that escalate to disaster involve precisely this type of reinforcement pattern. Sales may fall slowly in fits and starts, all the while offering enough hope that things will eventually return to normal. The hope makes it difficult to see that the market may have changed in fundamental ways. Revenues that slowly sour or costs that creep upward are just the kind of pattern that can cause managers to hang on beyond an economically rational point.

Research has also shown other reasons that executives fail to recognize when a project is beyond hope. People have an almost uncanny ability to see only what accords with their beliefs. Much like sports fans who concentrate on their own team's great plays and the other team's fouls, managers tend to see only what confirms their preferences. For example, an executive who is convinced that a project will be profitable will probably slant estimates of sales and costs to support the view. If the facts challenge this opinion, the manager may work hard to find reasons to discredit the source of information or the quality of the data. And if the data are ambiguous, the manager may seize on just those facts that support the opinion. Thus information biasing can be a major roadblock to sensible withdrawal from losing courses of action.

In addition to the effects of rewards and biased information, a third psychological mechanism may be at work. Sometimes even when managers recognize that they have suffered losses, they may choose to invest further resources in a project rather than accept failure. What may be fostering escalation in these cases is a need for self-justification. Managers may interpret bad news about a project as a personal failure. And, like most of us who are protective of our self-esteem, managers may hang on or even invest further resources to "prove" the project a success.

A number of experiments have verified this effect of self-justification. Those who are responsible for previous losses, for example, have generally been found to view projects more positively and to be more likely to commit additional resources to them than are people who have taken over projects in midstream. Managers who are not responsible for previous losses are less likely to "throw good money after bad" since they have less reason to justify previous mistakes.[3]

Reinforcement, information biasing and self-justification—three psychological factors that we're all subject to—can keep us committed to projects or actions we have started. Most managerial decisions, however, involve some additional factors that come into play when other people are around to observe our actions. These are social determinants.

Social Pressures   Managers may persist in a project not only because they don't want to admit error to themselves but also because they don't wish to expose their mistakes to others. No one wants to appear incompetent. Though persistence may be irrational from the organization's point of view, from the point of view of the beleaguered manager seeking to justify past behavior, it can be quite understandable. When a person's fate is tied to demands for performance and when accepting failure means loss of power or loss of a job, hanging on in the face of losses makes sense. Research has shown, for example, that job insecurity and lack of managerial support only heighten the

need for external justification.[4] Thus when a manager becomes closely identified with a project ("that's Jim's baby"), he can be essentially forced to defend the venture despite mounting losses and doubts about its feasibility.

Beyond the personal risks of accepting losses, our ideas of how a leader should act can also foster foolish persistence. Culturally, we associate persistence—"staying the course," "sticking to your guns," and "weathering the storm"— with strong leadership. Persistence that happens to turn out successfully is especially rewarded. For example, when we think about the people who have become heroes in business and politics (Iacocca and Churchill, for examples), we see leaders who have faced difficult and apparently failing situations but who have hung tough until they were successful. If people see persistence as a sign of leadership and withdrawal as a sign of weakness, why would they expect managers to back off from losing courses of action? Recent research demonstrates that even though it may not add to the welfare of the organization, persistence does make a manager look like a leader.[5]

In short, the need to justify one's actions to others and to appear strong as a leader can combine with the three psychological factors to push managers into staying with a decision too long. This combination of forces does not, however, account for all debacles in which organizations suffer enormous losses through excessive commitment. In many of these cases structural factors also play a role.

Organizational Pushes & Pulls   Probably the simplest element impeding withdrawal from losing projects is administrative inertia. Just as individuals do not always act on their beliefs, organizations do not always base their practices on their preferences. All the rules, procedures, and routines of an organization as well as the sheer trouble it takes for managers to give up day-to-day activities in favor of a serious operational disruption can cause administrative inertia. Dropping a line of business may mean changing corporate layoff policies, and moving people to other projects may violate seniority and hiring procedures. Sometimes it's just easier not to rock the boat.

Beyond such simple inertia, the politics of a situation can prevent a bailout. British Columbia's decision to stage the world's fair Expo '86 is one of the most recent public examples of the power of political forces to sustain a costly course of action. Expo '86 was supposed to operate close to the financial break-even point. But as plans for the fair got under way, the expected losses burgeoned. At first, the planners tried to minimize the financial hazards by providing heartening but biased estimates of revenues and costs. When they finally accepted the more dire financial projections, however, and even the director recommended cancellation, the planners still went ahead with the fair. Politically it was too late: the fortunes of too many businesses in the province were tied to Expo, it was popular with the voters, and the future of the premier and his political party were aligned with it. The province created a lottery to cope with the expected $300 million deficit, and the fair opened as scheduled.

Though the Expo example comes from the public sector, political force may also sustain costly business projects. As a venture withers, not only those directly involved with it may work to maintain it, but other interdependent or politically aligned units may support it as well. If the project's advocates sit on governing bodies or budget committees, efforts to stop it will meet further resistance. If a review finally does occur, the estimates of the costs and benefits of containing the venture will very likely be biased.

On occasion, support for a project can go even deeper than administrative inertia and politics. When a project such as a long-standing line of business is closely identified with a company, to consider its discontinuation is to consider killing the very purpose of the company. (Imagine Hershey without chocolate bars or Kimberly-Clark without Kleenex.) A project or a division can become institutionalized in an organization.

Consider the plight of Lockheed with its L 1011 Tri-Star Jet program. Although every outside analysis of the program found the venture unlikely to earn a profit, Lockheed persisted with it for more than a decade and accumulated enormous losses. The problem was not ending the project *per se* but what it symbolized. The L 1011 was Lockheed's major entry in the commerical aviation market (in which it had been a pioneer), and Lockheed shrank from being identified as simply a defense contractor.

Pan American World Airways has recently gone through a similar institutional process. More than most airlines, Pan Am suffered huge losses after deregulation of the industry, it was even in danger of not meeting its debt obligations. Although the prospects for large profits in the airline industry were dim, Pan Am chose to sell off most of its other more profitable assets—first the Pan Am building in New York and then the Intercontinental Hotels Corporation—so as to remain in its core business. Finally, as losses continued, Pan Am sold its valuable Pacific routes to United Air Lines. Following these divestitures, the company was left with only U.S. and international routes in corridors where competition is heavy. Apparently, management didn't seriously consider the possibility of selling or closing the airline and keeping most of the other profitable subsidiaries. Pan Am is, after all, in the airline and not the real estate or hotel business.

Not all the forces we've described are relevant to every case, and not all are of equal influence in the situations where they operate. In many instances, commitment to a course of action builds slowly. Psychological and social forces come into play first, and only later does the structure make its impact. And, in a few cases, because the rational point of withdrawal has long passed, even the economic aspects of a project can cry out for continuation.

Still, some executives do manage to get themselves and entire organizations out of escalating situations. There *are* solutions.

Steps Executives Can Take Themselves

Executives can do many things to prevent becoming overcommitted to a course of action. Some of these solutions they can take care of on their own. Others involve getting the organization to do things differently. Let's look first at the remedies that excutives themselves can apply.

Recognize Overcommitment The most important thing for managers to realize is that they may be biased toward escalation. For all the reasons we have mentioned, executives may delude themselves into thinking that a project will pull through—that success is around the corner. Recognizing overcommitment is, however, easier to preach than to practice. It usually takes enthusiasm, effort, and even passion to get projects off the ground and running in bureaucratic organizations. The organization depends on these responses for vitality. Consequently, the line between an optimistic, can-do attitude and overcommitment is very thin and often difficult to distinguish.

See Escalation for What It Is How, then, can managers know whether they have crossed the threshold between the determination to get things done and overcommitment? Although the distinction is often subtle, they can clarify matters by asking themselves the following questions:

1. Do I have trouble defining what would constitute failure for this project or decision? Is my definition of failure ambiguous, or does it shift as the project evolves?

2. Would failure on this project radically change the way I think of myself as a manager or as a person? Have I bet the ranch on this venture for my career or for my own satisfaction?

3. Do I have trouble hearing other people's concerns about the project, and do I sometimes evaluate others' competence on the basis of their support for the project?

4. Do I generally evaluate how various events and actions will affect the project before I think about how they'll affect other areas of the organization or the company as a whole?

5. Do I sometimes feel that if this project ends, there will be no tomorrow?

If a manager has answered yes to one or more of these questions, the person is probably overcommited to a project.

Back Off   Just knowing that one is under the sway of escalation can help. But knowing is not enough. It is also necessary to take some steps to avoid overcommitment. One way is to schedule regular times to step back and look at a project from an outsider's perspective. A good question to ask oneself at these times is, "If I took over this job for the first time today and found this project going on, would I support it or get rid of it?" Managers could take their cues from bankers. When they take over others' portfolios, bankers usually try to clean up any troubled loans since they want to maximize the future returns associated with their own loan activity. Managers can also encourage their subordinates to reevaluate decisions. Most critical here is establishing a climate in which, regardless of whether the data are supportive or critical of the ongoing project, people convey accurate information. Just stating a "nothing but the truth" policy, however, is usually not enough to change the pattern of information reporting. The messenger with extremely critical but important information needs an explicit reward.

One forum for getting objective and candid feedback is a variant of the currently popular quality circle. Managers could regularly convene key staff members for "decision circles," in which fellow employees would offer honest evaluations of the hurdles a project faces and its prospects. Managers from other departments or sections might also attend or even chair such sessions to ensure an objective look at the problems. Managers might also hold regular "exchanges of perspective" in which colleagues could help each other see the truth about their operations.

Change the Organization   Though it is possible to come up with an array of decision aids to help managers gain an objective perspective about the projects they run, one could argue that the problem of escalation is larger than any one person, that it's organizational in scope. Unfortunately, such a pessimistic view is at least partially correct. Much of what causes escalation is in the nature of organizations, not people.

If organizational action is called for, what can the system do to minimize escalation?

Turn Over Administrators   One way to reduce the commitment to a losing course of action is to replace those associated with the original policy or project. If overcommitment stems from psychological and social forces facing the originators of the action, then their removal eliminates some of the sources of commitment.

Turning over project managers can of course be both disruptive and costly. Moreover, because people who were once associated with the discontinued venture may still be committed to it, management may find it difficult to draw the appropriate line for making a purge. Nonetheless, to make a clean break with the past, many organizations do make occasional personnel sweeps, sometimes more for their symbolic value than because of any real differences in decision making.

Still, we don't recommend turnover as the way to make changes. Like treating the disease by killing the patient, taking committed decision makers off a project may produce nothing but a demoralized staff and disaffected managers hesitant to try again.

Separate Decision Makers   One technique for reducing commitment that is far less drastic than turnover is to separate initial from subsequent decisions concerning a course of action. In some banks, for example, a "workout group" handles problem loans rather than the people who originally funded and serviced the loans. The idea is not only that specialists should be involved in recouping bank funds but also that these officers are able to handle the loans in a more objective way than those who made the first decisions about the accounts.[6] Industrial companies could also make use of such procedures. They could separate funding from new-product development decisions and hiring from promotion decisions. They could keep deliberations on whether to discontinue lines of business apart from day-to-day management decisions.

Reduce the Risk of Failure   Another way to reduce commitment is to lessen the risk of failure. Because project failure can spell the end to an otherwise promising career, an administrator may be forced to defend a losing course of action. In a no-win dilemma, the trapped manager may think, "Things look bleak now, but there's no point in my suggesting that the company withdraw. If the project doesn't succeed, I have no future here anyway."

In some companies, management has reduced the costs of failure by providing rationalizations for losing courses of action and excuses for their managers. People are told that the losses are beyond anyone's control or that the fault lies with more general economic conditions, government regulation, or foreign competition. Although this route takes managers off the hook, it doesn't help them see a losing course for what it is or how they may avoid making the mistakes again.

Most companies do not want to take the pressure off their managers to perform as winners. Yet because a strong fear of failure can cause overcommitment, management is better off setting only a moderate cost for failure, something to avoid but not to fear intensely. A large computer company, for example, puts managers who have made big mistakes in a "penalty box." It makes them ineligible for major assignments for up to a year. After the penalty period, the managers are restored to full status in the organization and are again eligible to run major projects. Organizations trying to cope with escalation situations may find such a compromise between support for failure and demand for competence helpful.

Improve the Information System   Several laboratory experiments have shown that people will withdraw from escalating situations when they see the high costs of persisting.[7] The presentation of such negative data is more difficult in organizations, however. Because no one wants to be the conveyer of bad news, information is filtered as it goes up the hierarchy. Furthermore, because those intimately involved with a project are not likely to distribute unflattering and less-than-optimistic forecasts, information is also biased at the source.

What, then, can organizations do to improve their information reporting? The most common solution is to increase their use of outside experts and consultants. The problem with consultants, however, is that they are no more likely to hear the truth than anyone else in the organization, and they also may not find it easy to tell management what it doesn't want to hear.

A better solution is to try to improve the honesty of reporting throughout the organization. By rewarding process as highly as product, managers can encourage candid reporting. The purpose of rewarding managers for the way a process is carried out is to make them attend as much to the quality of analysis and decision making as to the final results. Instead of acting as champions who inflate the prospects of their own projects and minimize their risks, managers offered process rewards are motivated to recognize problems and deal with them.

At the outset of projects, companies should encourage the creation of fail-safe options, ways to segment projects into small, achievable parts, and analyses of the costs of withdrawal. Later in the life of projects, companies should reward honest recognition of problems and clear examination of the alternatives, including withdrawal.

This kind of reward system is quite different from the usual practice of giving people recognition for success on their projects and punishing them for failure on their undertakings. Yet it is a system that should reduce many of the forces for escalation.

Boosting Experimentation

As we noted earlier in our discussion, an entire organization can be so caught up in supporting a project—especially an institutionalized one—that it ignores the cost of persistence.

Rather than trying to discredit an institutionalized project on economic grounds, a good strategy for withdrawal from it is to reduce its links with the central purposes of the organization. A useful tactic is to label the project peripheral or experimental so that managers can treat it on its own merits rather than as a symbol of the organization's central goal or mission.

Ideally, managers should consider all ventures imperfect and subject to question in an "experimenting organization."[8] Every program should be subject to regular reconsideration (à la zero-based budgeting), and every line of business should be for sale at the right price. In such an experimenting organization, projects wouldn't become institutionalized to the point where mangement couldn't judge them on their own costs and benefits. And because managers in such a system would be judged as much for recognition of problems facing their units and how they cope with them as for success and failure, experimenting organizations should be extremely flexible. When a market or a technology changes, the experimenting organization would not simply try to patch up the old product or plant but would be quick to see when it is best to pull the plug and start anew.

References

1. For more complete reviews and escalation research, see Barry M. Staw and Jerry Ross, "Understanding Escalation Situations: Antecedents, Prototypes, and Solutions" in *Research in Organizational Behavior*. ed. L. L. Cummings and Barry M. Staw (Greenwich, Conn: JAI Press, 1987); and Joel Brockner and Jeffrey Z. Rubin, *Entrapment in Escalating Conflict*. (New York: Springer Verlag, 1985).

2. See Gregory B. Northcraft and Gerrit Wolf, "Dollars, Sense, and Sunk Costs: A Lifecycle Model of Resource Allocation," *Academy of Management Review*, April 1984, p. 22.

3. For experiment results, see Barry M. Staw, "Knee-deep in the Big Muddy: A Study of Escalating Commitment to a Chosen Course of Action," in *Organizational Behavior and Human Performance*, June 1976, p. 27; Alan Tegar. *Too Much Invested to Quit* (New York: Pergamon Press, 1980); and Max H. Bazerman, R. I. Beekum, and F. David Schoorman, "Performance Evaluation in a Dynamic Context: A Laboratory Study of the Impact of Prior Commitment to the Ratee," *Journal of Applied Psychology*, December 1982, p. 873.

4. Frederick V. Fox and Barry M. Staw, "The Trapped Administrator. The Effects of Job Insecurity and Policy Resistance upon Commitment to a Course of Action," *Administrative Science Quarterly*, September 1979, p. 449.

5. Barry M. Staw and Jerry Ross, "Commitment in an Experimenting Society: An Experiment on the Attribution of Leadership from Administrative Scenarios," *Journal of Applied Technology*, June 1980, p. 249.

6. See Roy J. Lewicki, "Bad Loan Psychology, Entrapment and Commitment in Financial Lending," Graduate School of Business Administration Working Paper No. 80–25 (Durham, N.C.: Duke University, 1980).

7. Bruce E. McCain, "Continuing Investment Under Conditions of Failure: A Laboratory Study of the Limits to Escalation," *Journal of Applied Psychology*, May 1986, p. 280; and Edward G. Conlon and Gerrit Wolf, "The Moderating Effects of Strategy, Visibility, and Involvement on Allocation Behavior: An Extension of Staw's Escalation Paradigm," *Organizational Behavior and Human Performance*, October 1980, p. 172.

8. Donald T. Campbell, "Reforms as Experiments," *American Psychologist*, April 1969, p. 409.

Multicultural, Environmental, and Unsolved Issues

We begin this chapter with a disclaimer. As was the case with Chapter 6 on negotiation, it must be noted that this chapter is not a primer on *how to do* multicultural management. That subject is, to quote Chapter 6, "beyond the scope of this book and beyond our expertise." Instead, we raise a number of issues that plague certain projects. For the most part, these projects require input from individuals and groups from different countries. It is not, however, the differences in national boundaries that matter, it is differences in *cultures*. Moreover, it is not merely the differences in culture that matter, it is also differences in the *environments* within which projects are conducted—economic, political, legal, and sociotechnical environments.

These subjects are more carefully defined throughout the chapter, but even at this cursory level it should be obvious that differences in culture and environment are not confined to so-called "international" projects. Different industries have different cultures and environments, as do firms from different regions of a given country, as do different firms from the same geographical area, as do different divisions of a given firm. While the impacts of these dissimilarities is greatest and most visible in the case of international projects, they exist to some extent any time different organizations (including different parts of one organization) are asked to work together on a project.

Inferentially, if a project manager must cope with multiple cultures and different environments, it follows that more than one organization is involved in the project. This fact alone complicates matters. Throughout this book we have noted that the PM must manage and reduce conflict between the parties-at-interest or stakeholders in a project; the project team, client, senior management, and the public. If the parties-at-interest represent different nations, industries, and firms, the conflicts and problems besetting the project are greater by an order of magnitude. In particular, the conceptually simple issue of maintaining communications between the various parties becomes, in reality, almost impossibly complex.

In the first section of this chapter we consider some problems that arise on projects because of cultural differences among the parties-at-interest. Then we examine how various aspects of the environment affect the project. Next, some problems of multiparty, multicultural communications are noted, coupled with a brief discussion of differences in managerial style. The chapter ends with some thoughts on three fundamental problems that must be faced by coming generations of project managers.

Project Management in Practice
A Project Emergency Due to International Politics

In the early 1980s, the SNC Group was involved in a project known as PANAFTEL, a communications project to design and build 62 towers and associated equipment for a microwave system linking five African countries: Senegal, Mali, Burkina Faso, Niger, and Benin. The logistics were the major problem since all the countries had poor material handling, customs, and communications services. The solution involved an extremely detailed logistical plan plus the help of a freight forwarder with direct affiliates in all five of the African countries. Even so, there were some misshipments that caused great confusion and anxiety. In one case, a steel base is even today stranded in a bonded warehouse of a certain harbor because it was cheaper and faster to replace it than to attempt to retrieve it from a country where it had never officially entered.

A serious emergency occurred late in the project involving the site installation of turbo-generators manufactured in Israel and installed by Israeli crews. Before the generators could be installed, the international relations between three of the African countries and Israel had deteriorated to the point where visas for Israeli citizens were not allowed. SNC had to gather enough crews of its own technicians to make the installation at 41 sites, send them to Israel for a three-week crash course, and then bring them to Africa to complete the job.

In this manner, the project was successfully completed and all the generators are effectively supplying energy to the microwave links.

Source: A. Rustin, "The Challenge of Project Management." *Project Management Journal*, Sept. 1985.

▶ 14.1 PROBLEMS OF CULTURAL DIFFERENCES

The term "culture" refers to the entire way of life for a group of people. It encompasses every aspect of living, and has four elements that are common to all cultures: technology, institutions, language, and arts [19].

The *technology* of a culture includes such things as the tools used by people, the material things they produce and use, the way they prepare food, their skills, and their attitudes toward work. It embraces all aspects of their material lives.

The *institutions* of a culture make up the structure of the society. This category contains the organization of the government, the nature of the family, the way in which religion is organized as well as the content of religious doctrine, the division of labor, the kind of economic system adopted, the system of education, and the way in which voluntary associations are formed and maintained.

Language is another ingredient of all cultures. The language of a culture is always unique because it is developed in ways that meet the express needs of the culture of which it is a part. The translation of one culture's language into another's is rarely precise. Words carry connotative meanings as well as denotative meanings. The English word "apple" may denote a fruit, but it also connotes health ("keeps the doctor away"), bribery ("for the teacher"), New York city, a color, a computer, a dance (late 1930s), favoritism ("of my eye"), as well as several other things.

Finally, the *arts* or aesthetic values of a culture are as important to communication as the culture's language. If communication is the glue that binds a culture together, art is the most efficient means of communicating. Aesthetic values dictate what is found beautiful and satisfying. If a society can be said to have "style," it is from the culture's aesthetic values that style has its source.

Culture and the Project

A nation's culture affects projects in many ways. One of the most obvious ways is in how people of different cultures regard time. In the United States and several other Western, industrialized nations, time is highly valued as a resource [17]. We say, "Time is money." It isn't, of course, but the expression is one way of expressing impatience with delay and lateness. Latin Americans, on the other hand, hold quite different views of time. The pace of life differs from one culture to another, just as do the values that people place on family or success. The PM conducting a construction project in South America will learn that to be half-an-hour late to a project meeting is to be "on time." In Japan, lateness causes loss of face. In some cultures, the quality of the work is seen to be considerably more important than on-time delivery. The great value placed on time in the United States and the American's distaste for tardiness leads to a common perception that American managers are "impatient." Arms and Lucas [2] note several other ways American project managers are perceived by workers from other countries, including a deadly, "They just don't understand us."

The fundamental philosophy of staffing projects varies greatly in different cultures. In Latin America, for example, the *compadre* system leads a manager to give preference to relatives and friends when hiring.* North Americans feel that such practices are a major source of inefficiency in Latin American firms. In fact, there appears to be scant evidence that this is so. One private study of several firms in the North American and Latin American chemical industries indicates that the differences in management practices between North American and Latin American chemical firms were, in general, significantly less than the differences between the North American chemical firms and North American clothing manufacturers.

---

* We are quite aware that the *compadre* system is a system of networks of extended family members, and is far more complex than is implied in this simple example.

A view almost uniformly held by non-Americans is that American managers understand everything about technology and nothing about people [2, 17, and elsewhere]. This view apparently originates in the American's desire to "get down to business," while many foreign cultures—certainly Asian, Middle Eastern, Latin American, and southern European—value "getting to know you" as a precursor to the trust required to have satisfying business relationships. In many cultures, the manager is expected to take a personal interest in his/her subordinates' lives, to pay calls on them, to take an interest in the successes of family members, and to hold a caring attitude. This flies in the face of the usual (bad) advice given to an American manager to "Keep your nose out of your employees' personal affairs."

On the other hand, it is clear that American project managers are being urged to value cultural diversity in ways that are often not shared by their foreign cohorts. The following article from the *Wall Street Journal* is printed in its entirety.*

Multiculturism Stalls at the National Divide

Valuing diversity is a uniquely American idea that may not travel well.

Asked by AT&T to study race and gender issues in overseas work places, New York consultants Cornelius Grove and Willa Hallowell found "the values that give impetus to diversity issues here don't necessarily exist abroad," says Mr. Grove.

Based on interviews with AT&T managers and executives, the two report that other societies view ethnic differences as an appropriate basis for assigning workplace roles. In Mexico, for example, an American manager shouldn't expect to find indigenous Indians in management positions, which are controlled by European descendants. In Japan, it took an AT&T manager months to get Japanese managers to talk to key East Indian employees, Ms. Hallowell says.

In the January [1994] issue of the newsletter *Cultural Diversity at Work*, the consultants advise American managers abroad to value equality without judging cultural norms. [20]

Without attesting to the accuracy or fairness of its portrayal of Japanese culture and politics, we would strongly recommend that American project managers read Michael Chrichton's mystery thriller, *Rising Sun* [5]. This book is a rich source of examples of the subtle and not-so-subtle ways in which cultures collide. It is an excellent illustration of the impact that a nation's culture, its technology, language, institutions, and aesthetic values have on human behavior and communications.

Microcultures and the Project

For some years, management theorists have been writing about "corporate culture." We call these "microcultures" to differentiate them from the broader national or regional cultures about which we have been writing. It is just as true, though less ob-

---

*Reprinted by permission of *The Wall Street Journal* © 1994 Dow Jones & Company, Inc. All Rights Reserved Worldwide.

vious, to observe that microcultures vary from industry to industry and from firm to firm just as cultures do from nation to nation. Sales techniques perfectly permissible in one industry, the wholesale automobile industry for instance, would cause outrage and lawsuits in the business-machine industry. Promises have very different meanings in different areas of business. No one takes seriously the "promised" date of completion of a software application project, any more than a finish-date promise made by a home-remodeling contractor, or, for that matter, an author's promise made to a publisher for the delivery of a manuscript on or before the deadline. It is ironic for a society that celebrates the myth of George Washington and the cherry tree to have to depend quite so heavily on *caveat emptor* for the purchase of a used car or insurance policy.

The impact of interindustry, interfirm, and intrafirm microcultural diversity on the project manager is significant. Perhaps more than any other type of manager, the PM is dependent on commitments made by people, both inside and outside the parent organization, who owe little allegiance to the project, have little cause for loyalty to the PM, and over whom the PM has little or no *de jure* authority. In light of this uncertainty, the PM must know whose promises can be relied upon and whose cannot.

Project Management in Practice
Energoproject Holding Integrates Two Diverse Cultures to Achieve Project Success

A major project involving some hundreds of millions of dollars was stymied due to the cultural differences between the owner/client, a state-run Middle East developer, and the contractor, a state-run European international designer and builder of industrial and construction projects. As can be imagined, the difference in the cultures is extreme and includes religions, the role of women in society, the difference in power between managers and workers, and the style of management itself. These differences were exacerbated by the conditions surrounding the project: an isolated desert, poor communication, extremely harsh living/working conditions, and a highly unstable legal/political environment (taxes, regulations, restrictions, even client reorganizations) that was changing daily.

The client and contractor came to realize that the two separate organizational systems created an interface, or boundary, between them that was almost impenetrable. They thus decided to try to integrate the two systems into one unified system. This was done methodically, with a plan being drawn up, environmental impacts recognized, restructuring of the overall organization, designing the integration, and then implementing the design.

As perhaps expected, neither side's personnel were able to give up their perspective to see the larger picture. The project managers kept working on this issue, however, watched for problems, did a lot of management-by-walking-around, and gradually, the integration began to occur, gathering speed

Source: D. Z. Milosevic, "Case Study: Integrating the Owner's and the Contractor's Project Organization." *Project Management Journal*, Dec. 1990.

THE PROJECT STYLE CHARACTERISTICS		ACTIONS
Physical Appearance:	Counterparts working together (teamwork) ◄—— Project-related pictures, charts, and schedules on office walls	Tour the site with counterpart project manager daily Make your office look like a "war room"
Myths and Stories:	We are one team with two sides Both cultures are interesting Both sides' interests should be satisfied We trust young managers Get the job done ◄—— Separate yourself from the position and stick to the problem Both project managers are good, and committed to the project	Whenever possible, let the counterparts have a joint office Organize group visits to local historical sites
Ceremonies:	Gather ideas and information from all over the project organization Frequent meetings at all levels ◄—— Frequent social gatherings and festivities	From time to time, attend lower level joint project meetings Celebrate each key event completion
Management Style:	Plan, organize and control with your counterparts Make decisions ◄—— No finger pointing for wrong decisions, learn the lesson Quickly execute the decision If you need help, don't hesitate to refer to your boss	Ask counterparts for joint report on an issue Recognize high-performance managers monthly

Exhibit 1: Examples of Integrative Actions.

as it went. At project termination, when all costs and engineering changes were hammered out for final payment by tough external bargaining agents (rather than by principled negotiation, typically), no agreement could be reached. Instead, the project managers were brought back and allowed to terminate the project in their own fashion. They simply continued the integration process they had used earlier and quietly phased out the successful project.

▶ 14.2   IMPACT OF INSTITUTIONAL ENVIRONMENTS

In general systems theory, the *environment* of a system is defined as everything outside the system that receives system outputs from it or delivers inputs to it. A culture's institutions are a part of the environment for every project.

Socioeconomic Environment

Of all the nations in which a project manager might find him/herself, the need to interact with governments and representatives of governments is probably lower in the United States than almost anywhere else. This is true regardless of whether the government controls industry or industry controls the government in the country involved. On international projects, therefore, the PM (or the PM's senior management) can expect to deal with bureaucracy at several different levels (i.e., local, regional, and national government functionaries).

Popular movies and television to the contrary, the intentions of foreign governments and their officials are rarely evil. Foreign governments are usually devoted to ensuring that local citizens are well-treated by invading companies, that national treasures are not disturbed, that employment for their nationals is maximized, that some profits are reinvested in the host country, that safety regulations are not violated, and that other unintended exploitations are prevented. At times, rules and regulations may result from ancient traditions—no consumption of alcoholic beverages in Islamic nations, no consumption of pork products in Israel, and avoiding the "A-OK" hand-sign in several South American countries, though the latter is not a rule or regulation.

The job description of any PM should include responsibility for acquiring a working knowledge of the culture of any country in which he/she is to conduct a project. As far as possible, the project should be conducted in such a way that host-country norms are honored. To do so, however, will often raise problems for management of the parent firm. An unwelcome truth is that the cultures of many countries will not offer a female PM the same level of respect shown a male PM. Thus, senior management is faced with the awkward choice of violating its own policy against sex-discrimination or markedly increasing the risk of project failure. The same problem may also exist with the use of a Jewish PM in an Arab country, or an Armenian PM in Turkey.

Legal Environment

As we have noted earlier, the United States is, by far, the most litigious society on this planet. This does not mean that there are fewer disagreements in other societies, but rather that there is less recourse to courts of law—and, therefore, more recourse to negotiation as a means of resolving conflict. Martin examines the nature of the negotiation process in an international setting [14]. He notes the impact that different cultures have on the process of negotiation, with special attention paid to the society's institutional structure and patterns of communication. He concludes that the failure to understand the culture of a nation in which negotiations are taking place puts the ignorant party at a severe disadvantage. The same conclusion is obviously true for microcultures.

Many authors have noted, as we have above, that trust plays an important role in business relationships [8, for example]. The impact of trust on project management, with its dependence on the ability and willingness of others to meet commitments, is clear. The importance of trust is also demonstrated by the critical role played by the *compadre* system in Latin America. Use of a general agreement with the extended family, as trusted suppliers to a project for example, is a substitute for the detailed and highly explicit contracts usually required for dealing with "arms-length" suppliers in the United States.

Finally, it is sometimes forgotten that each nation's laws are a product of its history. Law results from the attempt to reduce conflict by a regularized process. Because the conflicts in a country are, in part, a reflection of its unique culture, it follows that the laws of a nation will also be unique. For instance, the United States has a strong anti-monopoly tradition that is effectuated through its anti-trust law, but this is not the case in several other countries. In some nations, cooperation between local competitors is not discouraged, but collaboration with a foreign competitor is strictly prohibited without express governmental approval. In some nations, certain industries are seen as instruments for implementing governmental economic policy. In others, the very concept of a governmentally determined "industrial policy" is cause for outrage.

But law is constantly changing. In recent years, certain types of collaboration between competitors have grown rapidly, even in the United States [16]. In the United States, SEMATECH is a consortium of semiconductor manufacturers conducting joint research projects in the field, and the Automotive Composites Consortium is a collaborative group formed of Chrysler, Ford, and General Motors to study the use of plastic-processing technologies in automobile manufacture. These are merely two of many collaborative efforts allowed by the National Cooperative Research Act passed in 1984. European nations have also backed research consortia, for example, the ESPRIT program researches information technology. In the period between 1961–1983, Japan had more than 60 research consortia, some with more than 40 members [13].

The move to collaborative projects has also been transnational. Airbus Industrie, the British–French–German–Spanish venture, operating with financial support from its several governments, has achieved outstanding success in commercial aircraft development and production. Other examples are CFM International composed of GE (USA) and Snecma (France), and International Aero Engines composed of Pratt & Whitney (USA), Rolls Royce (UK), Japan Aero Engines, MTU (Germany), and Fiat (Italy).

It seems worth noting that international projects exist in such great numbers because there is some resource required by the project that is not readily available in the host nation. Most commonly, that resource is technological knowledge.* Many firms invited into projects for their proprietary knowledge found, after the project was completed, that their knowledge was no longer proprietary. The world of information technology is replete with cases in which "ownership" of software developed through the joint efforts of two or more firms is strongly disputed. In the United States, such cases are usually settled in the courts. When two or more countries are involved, solution of the problem is not so simple. Patent laws differ from nation to nation, as do national attitudes about the sanctity of patents. Further, what is considered patentable in one nation may not be in another. For example, current research on the identification and replication of gene material is treated quite differently in different nations.

---

* Entry into a heretofore closed foreign market is another common reason for initiating international projects. This was certainly a major factor in the formation of both CFM International and International Aero Engines.

The project manager and senior management must, if proprietary knowledge is valuable, make adequate provision for its protection. How to accomplish that is idiosyncratic to the case at hand. The North American Free Trade Agreement (NAFTA) affords protection of the intellectual property rights of firms to the three signers of the agreement, the United States, Canada, and Mexico. All areas of technology are patentable under NAFTA, and it is the first international agreement to include protection for trade secrets in addition to copyrights and patents [4].

The upshot of all this is that business laws, and laws that affect businesses, vary widely from nation to nation. For the project manager, there is no substitute for qualified legal assistance.

The Business Cycle as an Environment

The project manager must be aware of the general level of business conditions in the nation hosting the project. While it is normal for business cycles in economically developed countries generally to rise and fall together, they rarely match precisely. The depth of the cycle will be greater in one nation than another. The cycle will start or end in one country before it does in another. Therefore, local perceptions about the level of prosperity or recession will differ from region to region. These different perceptions will be reflected in positive or negative attitudes toward investment, and employment. The risks associated with a project will differ from country to country. Even notions about the proper speed for a project to be carried out will be affected.

In times of relatively high unemployment, most nations will erect institutional barriers in order to slow or prevent projects that might negatively affect their balances of trade. These barriers may take the form of mandated delays, failure to approve investments, unwillingness to allow repatriation of earnings, "inability" to locate necessary scarce resources (human and/or capital), severe "foot-dragging" on the part of local officials to grant required "permissions," lack of needed capital equipment, and a great many other forms. Almost all of the above affected a large construction project in a Middle Eastern nation. The creativity of bureaucrats (and we do *not* use that term in a pejorative sense) can be boundless when attempting to impede a project they see as undesirable or untimely.

When questioned about the U.S. trade deficit with Japan, Robert Solow is reported to have responded that a deficit with any one nation was not important. He noted that he consistently ran a "trade deficit" with his barber—and presumably with his plumber and local grocer. While the Noble laureate economist is undoubtedly correct about his barber *et al.*, it should be noted that he runs large positive trade balances with his employer, MIT, and with his consulting clients. Further, while Professor Solow's barber and grocer are unlikely customers for his services, Japan is clearly a potential customer for many goods and services produced in the United States. We would not for a moment argue with the notion of "comparative advantage," but that economic concept assumes reasonable freedom for goods and services to cross national boundaries in both directions. That does not appear to be the case with the importation of foreign goods into Japan. Also [1] presents an interesting discussion of the American-Japanese trade conflict.

Most nations handle such problems in very much the same way that private firms do. They practice commercial reciprocity. It is illegal, in the United States, to restrain trade by specifying reciprocity, but a great many firms manage to buy some required inputs from those customers that are able to supply them. Project managers can earn valuable goodwill by purchasing goods and services from vendors in the host country, and by employing qualified nationals. Indeed, in some cases the hiring of nationals is a condition placed on the project by the host organization. Above all, PMs must be sensitive to economic problems in the host country and be willing to adapt, as far as possible, to local commercial customs.

Technological Environment

Though the state of a nation's technology is not really an "institutional" environment, it is appropriate to mention the issue at this juncture. The ability to complete a project with success is often dependent on the PM's ability to plan the project in such a way as to be compatible with the technology available in the host nation. This point is made in [8] as well as in the following incident.

Operations research pioneer, Russell Ackoff, tells the story of being invited to India as a consultant to the government and being taken on a sight-seeing "inspection" tour in the nearby countryside. He observed several men dipping pails into a water-filled irrigation ditch on one side of the road and carrying the water across the road to a dry ditch on the other side. He then explained to his host, a government official, that if a pipe were installed under the road to connect the two sides, a simple gate could accomplish the water transfer. The gate could be operated by one person, thereby saving labor cost. The official listened politely and then asked, "And how will the men we replace support their families?"

The technology used by any nation is largely a function of the relative cost (supply) of the factors of production—always modified by relevant tradition, policy, and law.

Project Management in Practice
Project Management in Brazil During Unstable Political and Monetary Environments

The government of Rio de Janero in 1983 embarked on a project to build a combined school and carnival stadium to house the crowds that come to see the annual Lent parades and festivities for four days every March, just before Lent. The stadium had to seat 70,000 Samba fans, with the whole facility accommodating 200,000 overall for rock concerts and similar events. The rest of the year the structure would operate as a school for 4000 students. Since the annual cost of facilities for the festival was $10 million a year and the project would only cost $15 million, it would pay for itself very quickly. Groundbreaking took place on October 17 and the

Source: P. C. Dinsmore and J. O. Brizola, "PM Under Rampant Inflation." PM *Network*, Dec, 1993.

The vertical structure after columns were erected.

The completed school in Rio de Janero.

Carnival parade in the new stadium in Rio de Janero.

project had to be done by the following Lent, only four and a half months later.

The challenges of completing such a mammoth task in such a short time were se-verely exacerbated by the project environment of political uncertainty, rampant inflation, governmental bureaucracy, and local contrac-tor politics. However, the extreme public pressure and strong desire by the project participants to complete the project on time led to a successful project completed not only on time but to high-quality standards and within budget. Moreover, the short time span actually contributed to success in some ways, as described in the problems below.

Political Uncertainty

The project began under a new governor of Brazil who wanted to show results in a short time. In general, new governments often make drastic changes in the economy—freezing assets, freezing prices, changing tax rates, changing the banking system, revaluing the currency (or even replacing it)—to correct the mistakes of previous administrations, set the economy straight, and fend off impending problems. Also, the priority of federal programs can often change abruptly because of domestic problems or dwindling funds. The result of such uncertainty is often a "wait and see" attitude in the entire economy, depressing all transactions and projects.

Rampant Inflation

A particularly difficult aspect of economic uncertainty is in judging the "reasonableness" for what things should cost when the inflation spirals upward. Some system is needed to be able to check against price fixing by suppliers and contractors, as well as for simply knowing what items should cost. Thus, sophisticated indexing systems are used to help provide a cost index, but these are imperfect, particularly for individual items that may not have inflated at the same rate as most other

goods. Another complication is knowing when a payment is coming. At the inflation rate of 25 percent per month during this period, even a week's delay in payment by the government can turn a profitable project into a major loss. Thus, another invoice is commonly sent for "escalation" between the time the first invoice was submitted and the time of payment by the customer. This invoice, of course, is also subject to inflation if payment is not forthcoming by the expected time!

Governmental Bureaucracy

Governmental laws on bidding for public projects are extensive and place a heavy bureaucratic burden on all personnel. In addition, bureaucratic delays and forms, licenses, and other such procedural matters can delay and drive up the costs of any project indefinitely. In the case of this project, special simplified bidding and purchasing procedures were established by special government concession, and bureaucratic barriers were circumvented by access to the highest state and local officials for expediting on a case-by-case basis.

Local Contractor Politics

Even local politics with the contractors added problems in that they refused to participate, stating that the project deadline was impossible. Thus, two out-of-state contractors were engaged to conduct the project, after which the local contractors reconsidered and thus obtained contracts for about 30 percent of the project work.

▶ 14.3 MULTICULTURAL COMMUNICATIONS AND MANAGERIAL BEHAVIOR

The importance of language cannot be overstated. Almost every writer on the subject of managing international projects, or of managing any business in another country, advises the manager to learn the language of the host nation. It is usually not necessary (though it is always helpful) for a project manager to be fluent in the language of the host nation. When precise communication is required, a skilled translator can be used. It is, however, usually pleasing to the citizens of the host nation when visiting PMs speak their language, even haltingly.

Language is a complex composite of words, signs, symbols, movements and positions of the body, pictures, sounds, equations, and objects—the things with which we communicate with one another. The ways in which we use the elements of communication, the ways in which we send and receive messages are integral parts of the communication. The media are a part of the message, to paraphrase Marshall McLuhan's famous statement. Even the source and destination of the message may alter its meaning. Identical words may carry quite different meanings depending on the context within which the words are spoken or on who delivers the words to whom. (Consider the words, "I'll give you a ring" spoken by a young man to a young lady at the end of a date.)

Because the communication cannot be separated from the communicator, the managerial and personal behaviors of the project manager are discussed along with the more commonly mentioned aspects of the communication process.

Structure and Style of Communications

Some years ago the American steel industry supported a training program for young engineers educated in India. The program was one of several responses from the United States to the Soviet Union's gift of steel production plants and equipment to India. Based on the (accurate) assumption that American management and production methods in the steel business were significantly better than the USSR's, a project was developed to train the engineers on operations by having them work as first-line supervisors in steel mills in Cleveland and Pittsburgh. At the same time, they attended universities in those cities for academic training in relevant American business practices and techniques. Several problems arose.

All the engineers were reasonably fluent in written and spoken English so they received training in the in-plant communications methods employed by American steel companies. It was several months later before an American academic (who had not been involved in planning the program) pointed out that only 17 percent of the workers in an Indian steel mill could read. This obviated much of the elaborate communication system the engineers were being trained to use, most of which depended heavily on written memoranda and instructions. It is appropriate to wonder why the Indian engineers did not make this fact known to those teaching the communications courses. The reason is, in Asiatic nations, teachers (and senior officials in general) are held in very high regard. It would be impolite, almost unthinkable, to question or correct them.

Cultural differences caused another problem. In the United States, it is common to train supervisors in the steel industry (and also in other industries) by giving them some "hands-on" experience in production methods. The young Indians felt that it was beneath them to pick up and use a shovel while working on the blast furnace floor. To convince the engineers to continue in this aspect of their training, without resentment, required an on-site demonstration by a very senior American executive.

These types of multicultural problems are ubiquitous on international projects. In the United States, delegation is a preferred managerial style. When authority is diffused, information moves to the manager from the delegatees. Workers report to supervisors who, in turn, report to middle and senior managers. In cultures where authority is highly centralized, it becomes the project manager's responsibility to seek out information [17]. At several different points in this book, we have urged the PM never to let the boss be surprised. This is a fundamental tenet of our approach to project management. *The manager of an international project cannot count on being voluntarily informed of problems and potential problems by his/her subordinates.*

The Gogal and Ireland study [8] and the small-sample survey of Graham and Minghe [9] both examine project management as it currently exists in China. They did not examine multicultural projects, but studied projects conducted by Chinese managers and workers in China. They are, nonetheless, instructive. It is clear that management in China is authoritarian, and that the need to negotiate—largely with the state— is just as, if not more, important than it is in the projects of any other culture. The role of negotiation will not decrease for multicultural projects involving China. It will be extended.

Managerial and Personal Behavior

We have already noted the difference in the bottom-up flow of information in American projects and the top-down flow in countries where the management style is authoritarian. There are other cross-cultural differences that create problems for a project manager whose experience is restricted to the United States. In a fascinating paper, Grinbergs and Rubenstein [11] compare the managerial characteristics of Swiss and American managers/engineers of the same general age, education, and salary levels, all of whom were working on software projects.

Several of these comparisons illustrate culturally based differences in managerial and interpersonal style. The study revealed that Swiss managers were "much more formal" with each other than Americans. This demonstrates the interaction of interpersonal style and language. Many languages have both formal and informal modes of addressing other people (e.g., the formal German "Sie" and French "vous" compared to the informal "du" and "tu". If an American in Germany uses "du" to a German counterpart, it will certainly be understood—but it may also carry overtones of rudeness.

Because we have emphasized planning so strongly throughout this book, we find the differences in the Swiss and American approaches to planning of special interest.

> The U.S. respondents did not consider thorough planning and a long-term strategy as absolute prerequisites for beginning a project. . . . Though promptness is highly valued in both countries, long-term strategy is considered much more important in the Swiss company. [11, p. 24]

In addition to these areas, the Swiss and Americans differed in a number of other ways of import to the PM. The Swiss showed a stronger work ethic, were more resistant to change, were more risk averse, more accepting of bureaucracy, and more focused on quality. The Americans were more collegial, more willing to experiment and innovate, had a shorter time horizon, and communicated more openly.

When conducting a project in an Asian nation, an American PM must exercise considerable care when criticizing the work of indigenous subordinates. Loss of face is a serious problem in Oriental cultures. In communist states such as China, the pseudoegalitarianism* may make criticism completely unacceptable [cf. 8 and elsewhere].

In a society with highly structured social classes, it is also difficult to practice participative management. There is, apparently, a built-in assumption that the more educated, higher-class manager's authority will be denigrated by using a participative style. (It is interesting to note that one does not have to leave the United States in order to see this culturally based trait in action. In many U.S. firms, management is quite authoritarian and the social gulf between manager and worker is as wide as in much more class-conscious nations.) The more structured a country's social system, the less direct managerial communication tends to be. In North America, it is common for senior managers to interact with first-line supervisors, and even with blue- and white-collar workers. Communication flows easily across functional lines. In most other areas of the world, the communication will be more indirect, and will tend to follow the lines of authority established on the organizational chart.

Dinsmore and Codas [7] list five factors that they contend require special consideration by the PM heading a multicultural project. We have already noted some of these factors (e.g., the importance of language and culture, the need to deal with the politics and politicians in the host nation, the fact that the PM may have to use indigenous staff members, the possibility of input supply and technology problems, and the need to obey local laws and customs). In addition, they note two other matters that may cause serious problems for the PM. First, there are additional risk factors such as kidnapping, disease, and faulty medical care. Of course, in many countries, project workers will face less risk from crime than in the United States as well as easier access to medical care. Second, Dinsmore and Codas point out that the PM may have to provide for the physical and psychological needs of people who are

---

* We refer to this egalitarianism as "pseudo" because the actual management style is highly authoritarian. Recall George Orwell's *Animal Farm* in which it was noted that all animals were equal, *but some were more equal than others.*

transferred to the host nation and must live in a "strange land with different customs and way of life." [7, p. 458] They refer to this as the "expatriate way of life."

The PM is warned, however, not to go too far in accommodating to foreign cultures. "Going native" is not helpful. An Austrian economist of our acquaintance remarked, "American managers who come over here and wear lederhosen and funny hats are laughable. No one takes them seriously."

Final Comments on Multicultural Projects

The project manager is ill-advised to take on a multicultural project without adequate preparation in the culture and language of the host nation. (The same is true for a multimicrocultural project.) Lack of preparation is apt to cause cultural shock which results in frustration, usually followed by withdrawal. It is a no-win situation. If there are no resources inside the organization to prepare those moving into a different culture, outside consultants with appropriate knowledge and teaching skills are needed. (Note: a current employee of the firm who happens to be of the right nationality is not a suitable resource for the training.) Lessons in the foreign language are mandatory, even if the language training does not extend to technical language.* In most cases, the willingness to speak in the host-nation's tongue on social occasions and for routine business—if not for technical discussions—will be appreciated by the hosts and earn goodwill from the indigenous members of the project team.

Finally, research has shown the importance of the psychosocial aspect of service on project teams. "In practical terms, this finding suggests that it is important for project team members to enjoy working with other team members, and to perceive the project as a valuable way to spend their time." [15, p. 17] This is doubly important for multicultural projects, particularly for expatriate team members. They are away from home and depend, for the most part, on their national cohorts to meet psychosocial needs. Given this cultural isolation, the project becomes a critical source of both psychological and social payoffs, and the PM, with a strong tendency to focus only on task outcomes, must make sure that these other needs are met.

Because all people invariably seem to view the values of other cultures in terms of their own, the process of understanding and working comfortably in another culture requires great effort. But it seems to us that most Americans underestimate their own abilities to manage international projects with skill and sensitivity. Americans seem to feel that being able to speak more than one language, as citizens of many other countries do, implies acceptance and sensitivity to another culture. It takes no more than a quick glance at the Balkans or the Middle East to know that the implication is untrue. If a PM from Toronto can manage a project in Quebec, if a PM from Boston can manage a project in Albuquerque, it is probable

---

* It is interesting to note that English comes closest of any language to being the universal tongue for science, technology, and business. The underlying reason for this is probably the preeminence of American higher education in these fields. This generalization does not, however, apply to China—and possibly not to Paris.

that an American Southern Baptist can function in Israel or a Tex-Mex from Corpus Christi can be effective in Berlin. Multicultural management does take effort, but it is do-able.

▶ 14.4   THREE CRITICAL, UNSOLVED PROBLEMS

At this point in the manuscript of a book, authors are wont to wax philosophical about the future of the subject they have been addressing. We intend to resist the temptation. Instead, we identify three major, unsolved problems. We can suggest no solutions, but it seems apparent to us that they must be solved if project management is going to develop much beyond its current state and move to a higher level of sophistication. One problem concerns the ability of project managers to learn from the experiences of others. The second problem has to do with our ability to manage conflict. The third problem is raised by the consideration of "project management as a career."

On the Need for a Universal Information System

More than 20 years ago, Greiner published his classic article [10] on the fundamental problems that arise as organizations grow, and on the stages of organizational development through which they pass during growth. The fifth and most highly developed stage, he called "growth through collaboration." It is characterized by a managerial focus on problem solving and innovation. The organizational structure is a "matrix of teams," and its managerial style is participative. It is controlled by "mutual goal setting," and the reward system is the "team bonus." We can identify a great many firms that represent, for the most part, the fifth stage of growth: Procter & Gamble, General Electric, Bank One, Microsoft, MCI, 3M, Merck, Merrill Lynch, and Chrysler, among a great many others.

According to Greiner, every stage of growth is followed by a specific type of "crisis" that moves the organization into its next stage of evolution. He was unable to identify the type of crisis that follows growth through collaboration, but we think it is a Crisis of Communication.

In Chapter 11, we discussed the need for postproject control, and in a later chapter the need for a project history. Both were required so that project managers could learn from the successes and failures of their peers, as well as from their own experiences. At this writing, no one has developed an information system that would allow storage and retrieval of the requisite data. Such a system would have to be loaded with all that we learn through experience on our projects. Retrieval is the problem. Information would be stored in the language of the project that generated it, but it would have to be retrieved in the language of the searcher. While "keywords" enable cross-disciplinary communication between a limited few areas of knowledge, we have not yet solved the general problem of n-language information storage and retrieval.

On the Need for Conflict Resolution in Matrix Management

There is little doubt that the use of project organization will continue to grow rapidly in the foreseeable future. There is also little doubt that the lion's share of such projects will be organized internally as matrices. The unfocused nature of functional project organization and the expense of pure project organization make it obvious that when both effectiveness and efficiency are required, the matrix organization will be utilized. Matrix organizations, however, are typified by conflict.

Matrix managers describe themselves as having large responsibilities and no authority. In essence, this complaint has its source in the unwillingness of functional managers to make acceptable (to the project manager) commitments, or to meet their commitments (once made) in a timely manner. One such incident can cause a matrix project to fail. This is the primary source of conflict in matrix projects. It represents a power struggle between the project manager and the rest of the organization. It is inherent in any system that segments the tasks of managers, giving some task responsibilities to one manager and other task responsibilities to others. In a matrix system, the project manager has control over what is done and when, while functional managers control how things are done and who will do them. Once this division of power is made, conflict must result.

The inevitability of conflict as well as the need for resolving it is clearly recognized in the project manager's demands for "support from top management," and for a "clear mission statement, with clear priorities." Almost never are these demands met at a level that would neatly resolve all conflict. Kalu has suggested a framework for managing projects in complex organizations that would develop a distribution of work and responsibility in such a way that conflict would be reduced or avoided [12]. Unfortunately, the data and analytic requirements of Kalu's model are such that only a few very large organizations could experiment with his method.

The level of conflict existing on large numbers of matrix projects is not, in our judgment, insupportable. It is, however, so great that it preoccupies a great many project managers, and diverts their minds and their energies from the work of the project. We need a quantum jump in our knowledge of conflict resolution.

On the Need for New Methods of Rewarding Excellence

In all the history of this and other developed nations, we have never learned how to reward the people who work in our enterprises without promoting them. If an individual excels at a task, we promptly reward that person by taking away that work. This practice gave birth to such interesting axioms as the Peter Principle. The more productive an individual is, the more likely it is that we will reduce the organization's productivity by moving that individual to another job, and we continue in this way until the individual ceases to be productive. Our society needs to develop a reward system that does not require such a sacrifice.

This is a serious problem for all industry, but it has a special application to project management. In Chapter 1, we wrote of the professionalization of project management. We now call into question the degree to which professionalization can progress unless a new method of rewarding excellence is found. Project management is, at best, a middle-management function. It is not, in general, seen as the culmination of a career, but rather as a challenging and interesting stepping stone to senior management. Project-oriented organizations are, however, growing in importance to our economy and the role of the project manager is becoming evermore significant. The job is extraordinarily complex and is demanding beyond belief.

Excellent project managers are rare and their worth exceeds that of rubies. To retain such managerial paragons in positions of managerial value, we must find a way to reward them without removing them from the very work that is so valuable.

Project Management in Practice
Boeing's Key to Future Project Management Success— Multi-Discipline Teams

Although the use of teams to develop airplanes is not a new idea at Boeing—the first Boeing airplane was developed by a team in 1916—the concept of multi-discipline teams to conduct *all* the functional work on new development projects is quite new. Such teams have a cross-functional membership of skilled people who have been organized and empow-

Source: C.G. King, "Multi-Discipline Teams: A Fundamental Element of the Program Management Process," PM *Network*, Aug. 1992.

The Boeing 777.

The Boeing team at work.

ered to develop a specific product(s). This approach facilitates concurrent integration of specifications and design, together with plans for production, deployment, operation, and maintenance.

The Hard Mobile Launcher was one of the early Boeing programs to use multi-discipline teams successfully. More recent uses include the 767 AWACS program, the RAH-66 Comanche helicopter, the 777 commercial jetliner, and the U.S. Air Force's F-22 fighter.

The process is based on the work breakdown structure, with each subelement being handled by a multi-discipline team. The traditional functional organizations coexist with the teams and provide standardized processes, new technologies, and the skilled human resources to staff the teams. As a program moves through its various phases—design, production, delivery—the teams are disbanded and new teams formed to achieve the new subelements that are required. In this manner, the scope of the program is constantly changing in a smooth, fluid evolution.

The benefits of this approach have been well-documented cost and program time reductions, while obtaining enhanced product quality!

▶ SUMMARY

This chapter has provided an overview of the problems and issues facing multicultural project management. It includes the issues of diversity within the project and the effects of several environments within which the project must function.

Specific points made in the chapter were:

- Cultural elements refer to the way of life for any group of people and include technology, institutions, language, and art.
- The project environment includes economic, political, legal, and sociotechnical aspects.

- Examples of problematic cultural issues include the group's perception of time and the manner of staffing projects.
- Language is a particularly critical aspect of culture for the project.
- Three critical, unsolved problems for project management are the need to create an overarching learning information system, the continuing need to identify better methods of conflict resolution, and the most urgent need to find ways of rewarding excellence in projects.

▶ GLOSSARY

Culture—The way of life of any group of people.

Environment—Everything outside the system that delivers inputs or receives outputs from the system.

Microculture—The "corporate culture" within the organization, or even project.

▶ MATERIAL REVIEW QUESTIONS

1. Descibe each of the four elements of culture.
2. Identify some of the important types of project environments.
3. Contrast culture, microculture, and multiculture.

5. In what ways is language crucial in project management?
6. Identify the five multicultural factors requiring special consideration.
7. Describe the three unsolved PM problems.

▶ CLASS DISCUSSION QUESTIONS

1. Contrast cultural differences with environmental differences. Isn't the culture part of the environment?
2. How is communications through art different than through language?
3. What should a firm do when an accepted practice in a foreign country is illegal in its own country?
4. Explain the difference between a trade deficit with your barber and with a foreign nation. What was Solow's point?

5. If employing people to use pails to move water helps the economy, why not use spoons instead and thus hire even more people? How should the official have been answered?
6. In what way is a universal information system an education system?
7. What solution to rewarding excellent work would you suggest?
8. What kinds of ethical dilemmas can working in a foreign culture bring about?

▶ INCIDENTS FOR DISCUSSION

International Microcircuits, Inc.

Diana Bedding, vice-president of sales for International Microcircuits, Inc., was delighted to enter a bid to produce and sell their major industrial product in a small foreign country. However, her top salesperson for that region had just called and informed her of certain "expectations" of doing business in the country:

1. Local materials representing at least 50 percent of the value of the product must be purchased in reciprocity.

2. The local politicians will expect significant donations to their party on a continuing basis.

3. Industrial customers normally receive a 40 percent "rebate" (kickback) when they purchase goods from suppliers such as IM. (IM's profit margin is only 20 percent).

With this new information, Diana was unsure about changing or proceeding with the bid. If it was withdrawn, a lot of effort would be wasted as well as a chance to get a foothold in the international market. But if she proceeded, how could these expectations be met in a legal and ethical way?

Question: Devise a solution that addresses Diana's concerns.

Asian Services, Ltd.

An Australian firm—Asian Services—uses multicultural project teams to provide brokering services for firms wishing to enter into business in certain eastern regions of the former Soviet republic. The diversity of these teams fosters the breadth of knowledge required to identify appropriate contacts and agents who can facilitate the new startup. However, the selection of a project manager continues to be a stumbling block in the process. If a native of the target country is selected, his/her knowledge of procedures and pitfalls is invaluable, but native PMs lack the understanding of how modern businesses operate. On the other hand, a foreign project manager who is up-to-date on contemporary business practice usually trips up on the peculiarities of the local laws, culture, or environment. Clearly, either one can use the other as a critical member of the project team to offer counsel.

Questions: What arrangement of the above choices would you recommend? Why?

▶ PROJECT TEAM CONTINUING ASSIGNMENT

Identify in retrospect, the cultural and environmental issues that affected the project. Classify them in terms of the cultural and environmental subcategories listed in the chapter. Did any of the three unsolved PM problems pose a difficulty for your project?

▶ BIBLIOGRAPHY

1. AHO, C. M. "America and the Pacific Century: Trade Conflict or Cooperation?" IEEE *Engineering Management Review*, Winter 1993.

2. ARMS, P. B., and E. LUCAS. "How Do Foreign Clients Really See American Project Managers?" *Proceedings*, 1978 Annual Seminar/Symposium on Project Management, sponsored by the Project Management Institute, Drexel Hill, PA.

3. BOBROWSKI, P. M., and P. KUMAR. "Learning Project Management Outside the Classroom: The Internship." *Project Management Journal*, March 1992.

4. CHOPRA, K. J. "NAFTA: Implications for Project Management." PM *Network*, November, 1993.

5. CHRICHTON, M. *Rising Sun*. New York: Knopf, 1992.

6. COOKE-DAVIES, T. "Return of the Project Managers." *Management Today*, May 1990.

7. DINSMORE, P. C., and M. M. B. CODAS. "Challenges in Managing International Projects." In P. C.

Dinsmore, ed., *The AMA Handbook of Project Management*. New York: AMACOM, 1993.

8. GOGAL, H. C., and L. R. IRELAND. "Project Management: Meeting China's Challenge." *Project Management Journal*, February 1988.

9. GRAHAM, R. G., and S. MINGHE. "An Empirical Analysis of Project Management in a Selected Area in the People's Republic of China." *Project Management Journal*, June 1988.

10. GREINER, L. E. "Evolution and Revolution as Organizations Grow," *Harvard Business Review*, July-August 1972.

11. GRINBERGS, A., and A. H. RUBENSTEIN. "Software Engineering Management: A Comparison of Methods in Switzerland and the United States." *IEEE Transactions on Engineering Management*, February 1993.

12. KALU, T. C. U. "A Framework for the Management of Projects in Complex Organizations." *IEEE Transactions on Engineering Management*, May 1993.

13. LYNN, L. H., and T. J. McKEOWN. *Organizing Business: Trade Associations in America and Japan*. Washington, D.C.: American Enterprise Institute for Public Policy Research, 1988.

14. MARTIN, M. D. "The Negotiation Differential for International Project Management." In P. C. Dinsmore, ed., *The AMA Handbook of Project Management*. New York: AMACOM, 1993.

15. PINTO, M. B., and J. K. PINTO. "Determinants of Cross-Functional Cooperation in the Project Implementation Process." *Project Management Journal*, June 1991.

16. ROSEGGER, G., and S. J. MANTEL, JR. "Competitors as Consultants: Collaboration and Technological Advance." In J. Allesch, ed., *Consulting In Innovation: Practice, Methods, Perspectives*. Amsterdam: Elsevier, 1990.

17. SMITH, L. A., and J. HAAR. "Managing International Projects." In P. C. Dinsmore, ed., *The AMA Handbook of Project Management*. New York: AMACOM, 1993.

18. STARR, M. K. "The Role of Project Management in a Fast Response Organization." *Journal of Engineering and Technology Management*, Sept. 1990.

19. *The World Book*. Chicago: Field Enterprises, 1962.

20. WYNTER, L. E. "Business and Race." *Wall Street Journal*, January 1, 1994.

CASE

SUPERNET
Samuel J. Mantel, Jr.

Five firms from four countries are playing major roles in a large project devoted to the development and implementation of an extensive communications network. Figure 1 shows the firms together with the roles they play in the project and their countries of origin. The countries of the client and the prime contractor cannot be identified other than to note that both are European.

The client, Custem, contracted with a major supplier of telecommunications electronic components, Primer, for delivery of a large-scale telecommunications network. Primer, in turn, entered into a contract with Clank, a computer manufacturer, for the required computer hardware as well as the operating systems needed to implement and control the network.

Clank, with the approval of the client, entered negotiations with Datum and Exactest. Datum was given responsibility for the development of major elements of the software that could meet the functional requirements of the overall communications system. Exactest was obligated for additional ancillary software for some specific components of the overall system as well as for the development and implementation of a testing strategy for all functional software developed under contracts with Clank, irrespective of what firm wrote the software.

Responsibility for integrating the hardware and software components developed by Clank, Datum, and Exactest also rested with Exactest, well-known for its high-level skill in systems integration. Primer, as

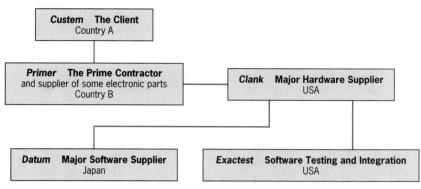

Figure 1: Structure of a multifirm, multicultural project.

prime contractor, was responsible for integrating all project deliverables into the client's environment.

The basic design for software that would meet a large portion of the fundamental specifications for the overall system had been previously developed by another firm, from whom Datum had purchased user rights. Because the client had little experience in the desired technology, Clank served as a consultant in the development of the functional requirements. A senior software engineer in Clank was quite familiar with the original system and the communications industry, in general, and therefore was given technical design responsibility for all deliverables from Clank, Datum, and Exactest. Contractual relationships between the five firms are as indicated in the figure, and the contracts identify the fundamental responsibilities of the various parties.

The history of the project is most easily understood through a sequential list of events that occurred. Editorial comment is not required, but a few "NOTES" have been added for clarification.

- Custem contracts with Primer for delivery of the system; the contract includes delivery dates.
- Primer contracts with Clank for major system hardware and software, including hardware/software integration and delivery dates as specified in the contract with Custem.
- Clank, with Primer assistance, serves as consultant to Custem in the generation of the project's functional requirements.
- Clank begins negotiation with Datum and Exactest. Exactest agrees on its deliverables,

including delivery dates consistent with Clank's commitment to Primer and Custem. Datum agrees on functional specifications for software, but does not agree on delivery dates.

- Primer exerts pressure on Clank to complete the contract with Datum. Clank subsequently completes the contract with Datum, but with delivery dates later than those in the Primer-Clank contract.

  Note: Clank believes that to enter a contract for the system software with any supplier other than Datum would kill the entire project.

- Datum claims there is not sufficient time to update the existing system, develop the new system components, and still make the contracted delivery dates. Further, Datum argues that it is also "too risky" to modify the preexisting software. Thus, Datum suggests to Custem, Primer, and Clank that the previously developed software should not be used at all, and that Datum should write its own, special software for Custem. After extended discussion, Custem, Primer, and Clank agree.

- Datum writes functional specifications. Clank reviews and updates the specifications, and then delivers them to Primer. Primer transmits them to Custem who reviews and documents some needed changes. Datum responds, agreeing with some changes but not with others.

  Note: The "official" design of the program now becomes Datum's write-up of the functional specifications, plus Custem's letter requesting changes, as well as Datum's response accepting some changes and rejecting others.

- Development proceeds, and then, a few months later, Custem discovers the difference between its contracted (with Primer) delivery date and the later date Datum contracted with Clank. Custem meets with Primer, Clank, and Datum and demands that Datum bring its schedule into line with the other firms. (The difference is about six weeks which would alter the contract life by about 10–12 percent.) Datum responds that it cannot be done without some loss of functionality. Custem demands that the delivery date must be met with all of the agreed upon functionality.

- Datum studies the problem for a few weeks and reports back that if a specific set of functions is dropped, four weeks of the six-week delay can be recovered. Custem allows the change. None of the existing contracts are changed, except that Datum now demands a new contract with Clank.

Note: It is apparent to all parties that Custem allowed Datum's request for a slight delay and a reduced level of functionality because Custem's primary objective with this project is "time-to-market." The competition between major communications firms operating in this sector of the world is intense. It is also apparent that Custem is not pleased with the situation.

- Datum misses several crucial, internal milestones, and commits to new dates, but while the software delivered on this new schedule is "on time," it does not meet the promised functional requirements.

- Custem specifies new internal milestones with quality requirements. Datum agrees and Custem states that if the requirements are not met, Datum must open all records and work to Clank, Primer, Custem—a demand that Datum had been strongly refusing, to date.

- Datum fails to meet the internal milestones. Custem insists on reorganizing the project so that Datum workers are directly responsible to Clank's technical control. (Prior to this reorganization, Datum technicians reported only to Datum's senior management who interacted with Clank.) The result is now daily meetings with representatives from all five firms in Datum offices. This "management group" undertakes an organizational redesign in order to institute an appropriate quality level for the software.

▶ QUESTIONS

1. What went wrong?

2. As prime contractor, what should Primer have done?

3. As the client, what steps should Custem have taken to protect itself?

▶ This article describes the opportunities and problems for project management in the future. The importance of international aspects of projects as well as the role of technology is discussed extensively.

READING

THE AGE OF PROJECT MANAGEMENT
David I. Cleland

In the past two decades, the global economy has been transformed. Today, a truly domestic market does not exist. Enterprise managers, the world over, must face competition in a worldwide market place. Not only are their enterprises at stake, their country's competitiveness is at stake as well. Vigorous new companies from countries in the Pacific Rim and elsewhere have challenged many of the traditional industries and their style of management. The creation and application of technology have become key global competitive factors.

Everywhere successful companies are aggressively transferring advanced technology from other countries and integrating it effectively with their other resources. In this way, they are able to build a solid foundation of technology that is relevant to their marketplace and to apply the advances of that technology to the manufacturing of their commercial *products* as well as to the marketing, procurement, and service *processes* required to get products to the customers on a timely basis.

Strategic and project management play key roles in coping with the new global market changes.

The United States clearly has the potential for an ongoing competitive edge in management—but this edge all too often is not used either effectively or efficiently. United States business fears Japan and its competitiveness. But can you think of many truly original products that Japanese companies have taken to the market first—even one product that came from their own basic research laboratories? What they have done so effectively is the management of incremental improvements in both *product* and *process* technology, often utilizing project management techniques in the form of simultaneous (or concurrent) engineering done through product-process design teams.

In the U.S., we seem to know much more about project management than we are able to effectively use! If the Japanese companies are edging ahead of us in the world marketplace because of their use of project management techniques, why can we not do just as well? After all, the major development and continuing refinement of the theory and practice of project management came from the Western nations.

Technological advantage is not enough for survival in the global marketplace. The management of that technology must be better than the competitor's. The prize goes to the company that is better able to practice project management and by so doing integrate product and process development projects into the mainstream of the strategic management of the organization. To do this requires—as it always has—superior knowledge and skills of project and strategic management. But it requires something else of sufficient importance that its absence can make the difference between success and failure. That something else is more a function of the attitudes of the senior managers of the enterprise than anything else:

- The acceptance on the part of the senior managers that project management is not a "special case" of management, and

- Their commitment that it is a key strategy to take the enterprise from its present market share to a superior competitive position in its market future.

Certain developing nations are characterized by a complex of product and process development opportunities, along with construction and other organizational projects which help to position them for their changing environment. Such countries should provide significant opportunities for project management. The need also exists for project management to deal in the best way possible with the management of the "stream of projects" that flows through the established industrial communities of the world.

The flow of projects in Eastern Europe will most probably accelerate in the 1990s. With the erosion of communism in Europe and the movement toward democratic capitalism, the opportunity has arrived to introduce project management into these countries. Their aging plants and equipment require replacement, and project management can facilitate that replacement.

International Projects in Products and Processes

Through the use of project management processes and techniques, product design teams bring about the commercialization of the incremental advancement of technology. Indeed, project management underpins the strategic management of technology, bringing it into an enterprise's *products* and *processes*. Projects are building blocks in the design and execution of strategies and are found at all levels in organizations, cutting across organizational functions and extending to other domestic and international organizations.

For example, the integration of the economic community of Europe in 1992 has already spawned a notable growth in project management. In Europe, state and private corporations are investing massive sums in technologies from telecommunications switches to wonder drugs. European business leaders anticipate that a single European market will emerge in 1992. Europe's governments are funding cooperative research projects that pool the strengths of each country and the cooperating companies. As much as $16 billion is dedicated to develop a wide range of technologies. Mergers are also helping companies to build up technological strength. In all this, project management has become a significant management approach in preparing Europe for the economic and technological impact of the 1992 era [2].

U.S. companies are actively seeking involvement in global projects to bolster U.S. industries. Recently, when IBM and Motorola agreed to participate in a semiconductor research project, IBM also invited other companies to participate, including some from Europe [7].

On the other hand, the acquisition of American technology by foreign companies continues. Just recently Japan's Nikon purchased parts of Perkin-Elmer Corporation's Semiconductor Equipment Group. Perkin-Elmer has long been America's prestigious vendor of equipment to make microchips. Such acquisitions as these are *project*-related, requiring the application of project management processes to acquire the technological capability and integrate it into the mainstream business of the acquirer.

The Wall Street Journal, in an October 26, 1989, feature article described the massive capital expansion plans underway in Japan. Its capital spending is growing at double-digit rates for the second consecutive year in everything from cars to computer chips. This is part of a phased strategy by Japan to expand capacity, modernize factories, and develop new products. Project management plays an important role in these expansions not only in the construction of capital facilities in Japan, but also in other nations where Japanese products will be manufactured and marketed.

The world's total research project budget is approximately $200 billion. Global companies have active strategies to create technology as well as to transfer it from other locales. Wholly new relationships in the form of research consortia, strategic alliances, and other project team-related strategies are being used to discover and create new product and process concepts for opportunities important not only to enterprises, but to nations as well.

Within the global marketplace the time between creation or inception of a new technology in new products and processes is decreasing. Until a few years ago, it took ten or twelve years or more for a scientific discovery to meander from the laboratory to commercial use. Today it may take less than two years.

Because speed has become an important factor in global competitive strategy, project management

concepts and processes applied within the context of simultaneous engineering through product design teams are becoming accepted in competing in the global marketplace. For instance, the Ford Motor Company Tempo-Topaz-Sierra cars, due in the early 1990s, are being developed within a global context. Ford Europe has the lead responsibility; the project manager will manage the design of the new car for both sides of the Atlantic. Dow Chemical is concentrating on new long-range international projects in small groups of technologies—among them, engineering thermoplastics and pharmaceuticals.

"Strategic alliances" is a term used to describe a wide variety of cooperative agreements between companies. These alliances can take the form of cooperative R&D, marketing, production, and product service; all having the purpose of transferring technology and improving the competitive position of the companies entering into the strategic alliance. The conceptualization and implementation of these alliances are done through the use of project management concepts and processes.

International engineering and construction projects are on the move. Petroleum-related projects are again growing. Other projects such as the design, construction, and maintenance of buildings and equipment are growing. The leading A&E firms are extending their services into construction and long-term partnerships with clients where promises are made for ongoing chunks of engineering and construction work. As the developing nations continue to grow and become a force in the global markets, the opportunity for project management in these countries will doubtlessly continue to grow.

Unlimited Domains for Project Management

A brief review of the different domains in which project teams are being used suggests that there are few boundaries for the application of project techniques.

At Xerox, teamwork is critical in making the corporate number-one objective of customer satisfaction happen. This objective comes ahead of return on assets and ahead of market share. Called "Team Xerox" strategy, it is achieved through the policy of "leadership through quality," which makes quality the corporate basic principle and defines it as meeting the customer's requirements all the time. Excellence is measured by the degree of customer satisfaction. Worldwide, there are over 20,000 Team Xerox sales representatives supported by over 36,000 Team Xerox service technicians. Both teams are assisted by highly acclaimed customer training and support programs [5].

A large international company has decentralized its R&D. It concentrates on the development and applications of products rather than research in basic technology areas. The company spends approximately $1.4 billion in customer-funded development projects annually. It has negotiated many strategic alliance-based projects in the high double digits. In recent years the company has moved toward co-location of product development and manufacturing, and "institutionalizing" the idea of product design teams. The organization has traditionally been project-driven and the use of project teams is common.

A large company that dominates the global agricultural equipment market has integrated product and manufacturing into the same organizational units with the result that product and process development are becoming simultaneous. It uses product design teams and product development times have been significantly reduced. The vice-president for technology at this company feels that the "single most significant factor in the improvement of its technology has been the development and use of concurrent engineering project teams." The company is considered one of the leaders in the practice of "concurrent engineering."

In still another large global "systems" company, product design teams are used extensively at the product line levels, and manufacturing is pulled into the development process early. An important responsibility of these product design teams is to perform competitive benchmarking on competitor's products through the use of "reverse engineering" and other techniques to determine the performance parameters of competitive products. Included in the competitive benchmarking is an evaluation of competitive products' cost, delivery time, quality, performance, customer satisfaction, goals, inventory policy, production effectiveness, and staffing.

A competitive evaluation project team in another company is set up to bring a clearer focus to the analysis of competitive products by estimating their costs, target price, and production volume, and assessing the technical aspects and the technological direction of competitive products. The use of "benchmarking" project teams became a necessity in the 1980s, when the company learned that the Japanese could sell products below the company's manufacturing cost. Strategic alliance projects have been quite

successful for the company. In recent years, most of the strategic alliances that have been consummated by this company have been for the development of new technologies. Senior executives have attributed the success of the company's management of technology in part to having a clear sense of strategic direction, to the movement of technical people into key executive positions, to a culture which recognizes that technology is a key component in remaining competitive, and to the willingness of senior people to delegate more responsibility to project teams.

Motorola's secret of competing successfully in the global marketplace includes a strong project-oriented R&D effort, built-in quality, and zealous service. The company has embraced Japanese strategies such as driving relentlessly for market share, sharply upgrading quality, and honing manufacturing processes to reduce costs. Motorola has poured billions into research and development, training, and capital improvements—$1.8 billion, or 19 percent of revenues in 1989. In addition, the company has been forging strategic alliances with chip makers here and abroad. The two most notable have been a 1987 agreement with Toshiba enabling Motorola to re-enter the DRAM business and a recently signed agreement with IBM to jointly develop cutting-edge methods.

At the Japanese Canon company, a matrix management structure evolved out of the reorganization of the company into a product group and systems committee design. Each of three product groups—the Camera group, the Business Machines group, and the Optical Products group— form the vertical axis of the matrix; the Canon systems (along with central staff, i.e., personnel, accounting) represent the horizontal links between each group in R&D, Production, and Marketing. Operations on the line in the factory are carried out under the direction of two bosses, i.e., product and systems managers. The matrix system promotes open information exchanges between line sections and between factories. At the production line level, workers and supervisors are involved in small team activities and projects related to work improvement ideas submitted through the company's suggestion system. The production system within Canon is promoted in part through the use of study teams, committees, conferences and project teams as well as through the support organizations and upper management participation. A key strategy in the company includes the continued attention to the elimination of waste in all facets of the company's operation. A Waste Elimination Promotion team staffed by members from a cross-section of the entire company analyzes waste elimination results and promotes the development or transfer of effective techniques and methods [3].

Merck, the giant drug-making company, has followed a pattern of building project-related strategic alliances in the global marketplace. Other drug companies are also forging cooperative long-term agreements to help them remain competitive [8].

The European Connection

The single European market that is emerging will change the competitive game in the global marketplace. Mergers are building up the ability of the European community to compete. There is no question that Europe's cooperative mega-research projects will have significant influence in changing the structure of global competition.

The historical events in Eastern Europe provide convincing evidence that the Cold War is ending and a new era of social and economic reform is coming about that could launch an unprecedented era of global competition. Free-for-all economic "wars" will replace the threat of "hot wars." Hungary and Poland will likely press for some form of membership in the emerging greater European community. Can Russia be far behind? It may all lead to an economy that will stretch from the Atlantic to Vladivostok.

The opportunities for capitalism to flourish and for emerging technologies to take hold have never been better. The low standard of living in Russia clamors for a new economic system similar to that of the highly developed democratic and capitalistic countries. The drive for economic well-being is mightier than all of the sophisticated weaponry that exists today. Speed will become an increasingly important competitive weapon.

The changing economies will require managers to think and plan for global competition, to think that anything is possible in the changing global social, political, economic, technological, and competitive environments. No possibility can be excluded which will broaden the opportunities for competitive success (and failure).

The vision is emerging of a Europe of shared political values, tied together economically and technologically. The implications of one Europe as a competitive force in the global marketplace is awesome. A larger and more powerful Europe than anyone has heretofore imagined is likely to become a reality—a reality brought about in part by the effective use of project management techniques.

But there are very real pitfalls. In some of the Communist-dominated Eastern European countries the cadre of Communist-appointed managers, or "nomenklatura," have been hated and accused of enjoying many improper privileges and of having been selected for their posts because they paid careful attention to the Communist doctrine and homage to the Communist party bosses.

Whether or not these managers will have the know-how to manage in a market-oriented economy is in serious doubt. Although some may have the needed expertise, many do not. More important, it is doubtful if these managers will be able to function without the respect of the rank-and-file subordinate managers and workers whose cooperation is necessary to make the new competitive economic system work. A massive retraining program will be required, an important part of which is to update the attitudes of these individuals. How to develop in these individuals who have an image of being a "party person," the knowledge, skills, and attitudes to manage an organization undergoing change will be a most demanding task. The individual managers are not totally at fault. Survival as managers in the state-dominated management environment required that they join the party and win its sanction in order to be appointed and perform as a manager.

These Communist-appointed managers have now become the brunt of a lot of hostility, partly because of all the privileges they have had. There is also some desire to take revenge on them for some of the abuses that they have caused in the industrial and management systems. Economic reform in these countries will be difficult, in part because of the need to change the basic management philosophies of the key people.

In addition, they lack the experience in capitalistic-driven management that they will need to run their emerging private businesses. Gordon Feller, head of Integrated Strategies, a California consulting firm, notes that "there are 6000 R&D institutes in the Soviet Union alone. Together, it and Eastern Europe account for one-third of the world's Ph.D. level engineers and scientists [6]." But it takes more than a pool of technical talent to create the new and innovative products and processes needed to compete in the global marketplace. It takes effective management—both in *strategic management* and *project management*.

The Japanese Connection

Japan has used project management to bring about incremental improvements in product and process technology as the center of its competitive capability. Added to these technological improvements is another innovation that will make Japan even more competitive in the future: high levels of research and development expenditures for technological innovation. Japanese companies are moving away from their long dependence on Western technological developments. They are sacrificing short-term profits for long-term technological and competitive advantage and have accelerated their R&D efforts at an extraordinary rate, sensing perhaps that the strategic management of technology will become one of the key competitive factors in global markets in the 1990s.

The move by Japan into R&D is an appropriate and inevitable next stage in the development of the Japanese economy. The growth of the Japanese economy came about not through self-developed technology, but from technology "copied" from abroad. In the period from 1951 through 1984, Japanese companies entered into a total of nearly 42,000 contracts for the importation of technology from abroad. This massive transfer of technology from the United States and Western Europe provided the basis for nearly all of Japan's modern industries. The technology sold to Japanese companies has come back in competitive nightmares. A few strategically driven U.S. companies, such as IBM and Texas Instruments, have used their technology to beat down the barriers of entry into Japan by the building of wholly owned operations there.

Up to the present time then, one of the major keys to Japan's success has been the ability of its government and companies to transfer technology. The typical Japanese company has developed an unusual ability to accept and utilize imported technology. Through "people links" at seminars and symposia, and through literature search, benchmarking, reverse engineering, and continued competitive analysis, the company has assimilated and used technology to global advantage.

The Japanese have proven their ability to conceptualize, design, produce, and market a car in a shorter time than U.S. manufacturers can. Now the Japanese want to cut the time needed to produce a new model still more—from four years to two. Part of the reduced time will come about through more efficient use of concurrent engineering brought to focus through using product design teams.

As a further move to improve competitiveness, the Nissan Motor Company, which has unveiled eleven major model changes since late spring of 1988, is installing flexible assembly systems at its plants in Japan so that different models can be made on the same line at the same time [1]. Some have criticized Japan for its "copying" strategy; yet the imitation of a competitor's products and processes is an accepted strategy in global competition. Economists have stated that imitation of a competitor is part of the basis for economic progress. Let others do the pioneering of the new product, then move in to slightly improve the product. An improvement in the manufacturing and marketing processes can give a real competitive advantage. All too often, U.S. and Western European companies have worried too much about the "NIH" (not-invented-here) syndrome, and have for reasons of company or national pride, failed to monitor and transfer technology from other industrial communities. The United States and Western Europe have had more fundamental breakthroughs in technology and more Nobelists, but less creative adaptations of the technology from other sources. This may very well change. As Japan drives for more R&D, the United States and Western Europe may have to become importers of Japanese technology—a reversal of the competitive game from what has existed from about 1951 to the present.

Several forces have helped Japan in its successful transfer and adoption of technology:

1. A high rate of capital investment;
2. The quality of the Japanese management;
3. The quality and motivation of the Japanese work force;
4. Productive, efficient, quality-driven organizations;
5. A strategic perspective of the corporation; and
6. An ability to analyze and capitalize on knowledge of competitive products and processes.

The Technology Connection

An important conclusion can be drawn from this review of world markets. The strategic management of technology has gained increasing recognition as the competitiveness issue for the 1990s. Effective competition today and in the 1990s will largely depend on the ability of a company to accelerate the life cycle process from the conception to the creation of a technology, and to the use of that technology in the company's products, services and processes. Technology must be exploited and used as a corporate strategic weapon—an asset that can be managed through the vehicle of programs and projects which support corporate strategy.

Projects and programs have been fundamental to the management of technology. In today's acceleration of technology, companies can no longer rely on their internal R&D capabilities alone. One of the principal reasons for this is the shortening of product life cycles, which require faster movement of technology from the labs into the market. This requires improved project management processes, a closer watch over the strategic context of the ongoing new product research, and the process research under way in the organization. "Strategic alliances" in the form of research consortia, acquisitions, mergers, licensing, and joint ventures are being used to pool research and strategies to develop and apply new technologies. The conceptualization and realization of many of these strategic alliances come about through the use of project management processes and techniques.

There is now a proliferation of high-technology projects and advanced manufacturing endeavors. Mastery of the strategic management of technology will be essential to survival in the future as the pace of technology continues to increase, not only in the development and utilization of advanced products, but in the recovery from the use of previous products that have created serious environmental and health hazards for the world.

Most industrial corporations spend 40–70 percent of their pretax income on technology. The role of technology in new business development, the rationale of strategic business planning, plus the ever-present competitive threat will require more integration of technology and business objectives. This integration will only come about by the careful and timely use of project teams to serve as integrative mechanisms.

In the enterprise, project teams provide a useful means of linking research not only with development and technology but with strategic planning as well. Teams of researchers and engineers are used to develop workable prototypes using new technologies. In recent years, IBM has created many special project teams throughout the company to link research and

development in various technological areas. Their main objective is to produce new products.

Projects play a key strategic, technological role in the organization. As building blocks in the design and execution of organizational strategies, projects provide a focus for the resources to react and bring about change in the organization.

Usually projects are created to accommodate the transfer of product and process technology within the company or from outside sources into the company. In general, projects within an enterprise can be classified into:

- Basic research projects directed to extending the boundaries of knowledge in a discipline;

- Product development projects used to design changes in a product;

- Process development projects which bring the state-of-the-art of manufacturing, marketing, sourcing, quality, and other organizational functional processes into being to support the enterprise's products and services; and

- Special projects which are used to further the capability of the organization. These include construction projects to upgrade plants, equipment, and services; training projects to upgrade human skills; projects to reorganize and restructure the organization; projects to provide for the acquisition of new product and process technology; and projects to share resources with other enterprises; "strategic alliances" in the form of joint ventures, cooperative R&D, and other means of sharing. Projects are the leading edge of new technologies and new businesses in the organization. Thus, they play a vital role in the planning for and the execution of organizational resources [4].

Conclusion

The strategic management of technology has taken on new competitive dimensions, for this is a new world. Yet the most dangerous time for an organization is often when the old ways are discarded and attempts are made to change in response to competitive procedures. The changes in the global marketplace are posing extraordinary challenges to the enterprises that seek to survive and grow in the international markets. Survival and growth for today's enterprises depend heavily on products and services. Projects are the basic building blocks in the strategic management of these products and services. If senior managers maintain vigilance over these projects, valuable insights can be gained as to how effectively the organization is preparing for its future.

The opportunities for project management have never been better. Project management has earned an exciting and rightful place in the management discipline and, more importantly, it provides an artful and

systematic strategy to cope with fundamental changes in both contemporary and future organizations. The 1990s promise to be exciting times from any strategic, political, social, economic, and technological perspective. We know a lot about the theory and practice of project management. However, we may not fully appreciate the manifest opportunities that now exist for the application of project management to our changing world.

▶ REFERENCES

1. BORRUS, AMY, and TREECE, JAMES B. "You Know Who Is Flooring It Again." *Business Week*, October 9, 1989.

2. "Can Europe Catch Up in the High-Tech Race?" *Business Week*, October 22, 1989.

3. CANON PRODUCTION SYSTEM. Compiled by the Japan Management Association. Cambridge, MA: Productivity Press, 1987.

4. CLELAND, DAVID I. *Project Management: Strategic Design and Implementation*. Blue Ridge Summit, PA: TAB Professional and Reference Books, 1990.

5. *Fortune*, August 14, 1989.

6. STEWART, THOMAS A. "How to Manage in the New Era." *Fortune*, January 15, 1990.

7. *The Wall Street Journal*. OCTOBER 26, 1989.

8. WEBER, JOSEPH and SMITH, EMILY T. "Merck Wants to Be Alone—But with a Lot of Friends." *Business Week*, October 23, 1989.

Creativity and Idea Generation

The project life cycle can begin with the concept of a new product, a new process, a new service. It can begin with a request for proposal (RFP) to design, construct, or install hardware, software, a telephone system, a building, a road, an aircraft engine. It can even begin with a competitor's new product or the slow realization that the firm is no longer dynamic and is now a follower rather than a leader. The subjects for projects are, like the Queen of the Nile, of infinite variety.

To be successfully carried out, however, they all require creativity. If the purpose of the project is to design a new process for shaping aircraft parts, or a new type of cradle-to-grave mental health insurance, the need for creativity is obvious. But if the project is to construct an office building, and if we have already constructed a dozen or so similar buildings, the need for creativity is not obvious. But those with experience in construction know that buildings are like fingerprints—no two are quite alike. Each one presents unique problems to be solved and requires creative solutions. All projects, therefore, call for creativity, but some call for more than others.

Here we look into the need for creativity. We learn how to foster it and how to discourage it. We even learn that creativity is not an unmixed blessing. We examine processes by which individuals and groups generate ideas, and we develop an understanding of the conditions that favor individual or group approaches to problem solving. We also see that certain organizational structures are useful for fostering idea generation, and conversely, that some organizational arrangements inhibit creativity. Finally, we gaze into our cloudy crystal ball and hazard some opinions on the future of creativity and idea-generation techniques.

Though few project managers may be actively engaged in managing projects at this early point in the project life cycle, they may find the subject of fostering creativity interesting and possibly even useful in their project responsibilities. The subject is particularly important for senior management as well as project managers not only because projects require creativity, but also because solving day-to-day problems requires it.

▶ A.1   CREATIVITY AND THE COMPETITIVE FIRM

Creativity is the attribute of bringing into existence a unique concept or thing that would not have occurred or evolved naturally. The creative person combines, mixes, and expands past experiences so that new, nonobvious concepts, variations, or extensions of knowledge are generated.

In most organizations, creativity is an underutilized resource. M. I. Zeldman summed up [37] an extensive body of writing in his brief warning, "The corporations that will survive and thrive in the future are those that foster creativity today." If we showed that statement to the senior executives of thousands of firms, their reaction would undoubtedly be overwhelming assent. Indeed, it is likely that those senior managers would be annoyed that we dared to bother them with such an obvious statement. But if the Zeldman viewpoint is so widely accepted, so obvious, why is it that in so many firms creativity is stifled and innovation frustrated?

There are, of course, many reasons why managers appear to embrace the idea of creativity while shunning the reality. For example, a key managerial task is to smooth troubled organizational waters. (If this image bothers the reader, it is well to recall the common managerial admonition "Don't make waves.") Change stirs up the organizational waters, but change is the most likely result of creativity. Creativity is like pepper in the soup: A little adds zest, but a lot may well ruin the soup.

Most organizations, even forward-looking, high-technology firms, have a limited tolerance for innovation. Problems of survival arise when the limit is set too low, when the limit on creativity becomes a ban. In addition to the desire to avoid disturbance of organizational balance, creativity may be squelched because it threatens senior managers. The reaction "If we didn't think of it, it can't be a good idea" is so prevalent that it has been immortalized as "the NIH syndrome" (not invented here). The cause of NIH is rarely arrogance, though it usually sounds like arrogance; rather, it is fear. It is hard to admit that an outsider (or young person) can make a creative contribution to "our business." That forces us to admit that we may not know everything about our work. Many people cannot face such a threat to self-esteem.

Another kind of fear reinforces this barrier to creativity. Innovation is risky. Modern managers are taught to be risk avoiders. The brilliant article by Hayes and Abernathy, "Managing Our Way to Economic Decline" [19], makes this point. Risk avoidance is so strong that many firms refuse to undertake risky projects regardless of the magnitude of the potential payoffs; and higher risk is usually associated with higher payoffs, as illustrated in Figure 1.

Risk avoidance—and hence avoidance of creativity—is also manifested in another way, fear of the future. Many firms insist on very short payback periods, not

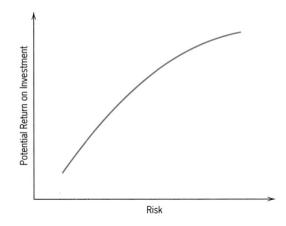

Figure 1: Relationship of risk and ROI.

being willing to fund investments with payback periods of more than two or two-and-a-half years. Some managers attempt to justify such short time horizons by citing the high cost of capital. Such explanations make little sense. A two-year payback period implies a cost of capital of almost 50 percent. Interest rates have been high in past years, but not that high. A more likely explanation of this bias toward the short run is the fact that executives see little personal advantage in long-run projects. Their bonuses and merit rewards are usually tied to current P & L (profit and loss) statements. When rewards are tied to the present, it is not rational to reduce present profits by investing in an uncertain future.

In the face of all this emphasis on short time horizons, not many managers are willing to face up to the obvious implications of short-run policies. Few major industrial projects aimed at increasing productivity, for example, pay back in two or three years. Many require more than five years. It will take about ten years to construct a new integrated steel mill or copper refinery and bring it "on line," assuming no environmental or legal difficulties. Given a 15 percent interest rate, each dollar of revenue received 10 years from now has a present value of about 25 cents. If the cost of capital is 20 percent, the present value of that future dollar (10 years away) is only 16 cents. And it costs hundreds of millions of dollars, spent now and in the near future, to construct a steel mill or copper refinery. Yet the implications of not investing are also very clear. The dilemma needs attention. Several industries have recently lost markets because their plants and equipment are outdated. Over the past three decades, the integrated steel industry, for example, lost a considerable share of its market to foreign mills. The steel industry, however, exercised creativity and began the process of restructuring itself. The large, integrated mills are, for the most part, in economic trouble, but the newer, specialized minimills are thriving.

One response to these pressures and fears is often to purchase the fruits of creativity rather than develop them in-house. Patents can be licensed, and innovative firms can be purchased. Such actions appear to increase the cost of creative ideas, but they also reduce the risk. The firm knows, in general, what it is getting and at what price.

Two other barriers to creativity are common and should be mentioned. Some firms unknowingly institute a climate that mitigates against creativity by firing or transferring people who have failed in a creative activity or project. If failure in risky projects is punished, sensible people will avoid risky projects. Second, some firms inadvertently misuse their best creative talent by promoting them into administrative positions. Scientists often accept these moves because of the higher salary and prestige usually associated with the "promotion." Many firms have recently recognized this error and corrected it by developing *dual-track career ladders* that provide equal rewards for success in research or administration. Eli Lilly and Co. is a notable example.

It requires little imagination to think of other things that could be done to reduce the impact of these barriers to creativity, but unless the barriers are seen as serious, no action is likely to be taken. In the next section, we will look at some ways for firms to enhance rather than discourage creativity.

▶ A.2   CREATIVITY MANAGEMENT

Much has been written about the problems of managing creative people—sometimes inaccurately described as "tweed coat management." Scientists are pictured as undisciplined, absent-minded geniuses with leather patches on the elbows of their threadbare tweed jackets. It is said that they require "total freedom to think," and that they need a manager whose main job seems to be a combination of baby-sitter and clerk/administrator who keeps the lab tidy, files the necessary reports, and sees to it that the scientists eat well-balanced meals.

Fortunately, this Hollywood cartoon of the researcher has little to do with reality. The widespread belief that scientists demand complete freedom in order to think creatively is simply not true. Souder has shown [32] that the creative output of research laboratories is unrelated to the degree of freedom given to the researchers. This apparent contradiction of a commonly held notion makes sense when we reflect on the nature of the individual. Some people, researchers included, think creatively when the area of investigation is constrained. Others are at their best when there are no boundaries to thought. Those who need or desire constraints tend to seek employment in organizations that furnish those constraints. Thinkers who do not function well under constraints choose organizational environments that allow more freedom. Creative thinkers vary widely in personality, style, needs, and even in their approach to problems. A discussion of how to organize creative endeavor is included in Section A.6.

Creativity is more important for some firms than others. Firms make choices about playing the role of leader or follower, at times even deciding to lead in some areas and to follow in others. The would-be leaders must stay abreast of current science. Followers must stay abreast of current technology. (Amid all this discussion of research and science, we should remember that both leaders and followers need creativity to be successful: Leaders need creative effort to extend science and technology; followers need creative effort in applying technology.) Firms seeking the image of high-technology organizations must have a fairly steady stream of new ideas or creative extensions of existing ideas. Ethical drug firms, computer software houses, and electronic component manufacturers are among such firms. Even customers who have no particular need for state-of-the-art technology may still opt to purchase from suppliers who appear to be at the scientific forefront.

The full support of the chief executive officer is mandatory if the organization is to adopt and maintain a creative posture. At the CEO's instigation, the policy-making executives of the firm should develop goals for the various product/service lines in which the firm operates. High-risk, "mold-breaking" creativity is not seen as equally desirable in all areas of operation, no matter how innovative the firm wishes to be. It is well to remember that most firms are not simple, single-purpose entities, but rather are collections of subsidiaries, divisions, departments, and groups that are often like firms themselves.

The strategy of growth and innovation is complex, and even the most innovative firms do not allow all their subunits to be in a wild state of creative flux at the same time. By and large, the strategy of growth and development is carried out through the funding process. In areas where innovation is desired, creative activity is funded. Funds are withdrawn from areas where progress is not needed or has less value.

In addition to the CEO, each unit charged with creativity needs a second person to support innovation, a *promoter*. This person will support implementation of the innovation, and serve as its "champion" [24]. For high-risk areas, special ground rules can be established that permit managers and specialists to work in a supportive environment. Texas Instruments and 3M operate in this way. They allow entrepreneurs to set up "separate" organizations within the firm to exploit the results of their ideas.

Next we explore that aspect of creativity known as *idea generation*. There are many techniques for idea generation, and we will treat them in two categories, individual methods and group methods. Because some of the individual techniques can also be used with groups, but rarely vice versa, we will cover the individual approaches first.

▶ A.3 INDIVIDUAL CREATIVITY

In spite of the fact that people have studied creativity, have taught it, have dedicated institutes to it, and have written about it, not much is known about the fundamental nature of creativity. Creativity is not a technique, nor is it an approach, though some techniques and approaches seem to be associated with creativity. When we ask creative people how they produce their creations, the answers do not fit neatly into recognizable and replicable categories. The techniques to be described in this section do not "produce" creativity, but they do tend to allow people to be creative.

The creative mind seems to associate freely, connecting and disconnecting the familiar and strange in different patterns. Apparent sense, logic, and order may be ignored as the mind "plays" in divergent, rather than the normal convergent, thinking. In this sense, creative thinking is similar to dreaming or fantasizing.

It is useful to understand some characteristics of the human brain. Recent theories about how the brain operates portray it as basically divided into two hemispheres that control different functions. The left hemisphere controls analytic thinking such as verbal, numerical, logical, and judgmental thought. This side is said to be "anchored in time" and seeks control, optimization, and planning. Factual memory is also based here.

The right side is the creative, imaginative side where intuition, imagination, pictorial thinking, and synthesis occur. Symbols and abstract representation are lodged here. This half is said to be "anchored in space" rather than in time. This side is the part of the brain we are trying to stimulate because it appears to be the source of creativity.

According to many articles and books on creativity, such as [21], there are a series of general steps that help the right side of the brain function more actively. First, we begin by considering every object, procedure, system, and process as inadequate to meet our needs. The objects, procedures, systems, and processes should be viewed in terms of the ultimate purposes for which they exist rather than in terms of what they currently "do." A generous amount of time should be allotted to specifying the criteria that the creative idea is to meet. The emphasis should be on listing objectives, not on devising solutions, on determining capabilities, not on improving existing hardware.

Reword and restate the goals. The criteria must be broad, yet specific where specificity is required. Record the criteria and set priorities on them. Are there gaps? Fill them. It does not help to consider solutions until the problem and criteria are fully specified. When the search for solutions begins, it should be pursued as far as possible before any evaluation of potential solutions is permitted. Embrace the long run and the short run with equal fervor. Possibility, not feasibility, is the focus. Practicality is not relevant at this stage of the idea-generation process. The more ideas, the better. Quantity is the watchword; quality will come later. Encourage "idea hopping," the generating of one potential solution by altering a previously suggested idea. Work until you run out of intellectual gas, then start again. Review earlier suggestions to find variations and extensions that add to the possibility list.

Following is a list and brief discussion of some specific techniques to aid in individual free thinking.

1. **Attribute Listing**   Developed by Zwicky and others, this approach assigns attributes to the desired design so that it has new qualities and characteristics. An attribute list can be constructed from words and phrases that describe the desired capabilities, even though the design is unknown. Attribute listing is carried out according to the following ground rules:

    Isolate all of the major characteristics (attributes) of the desired capabilities.

    Consider modifying each characteristic in every way imaginable. Do not limit the proposed changes.

    Once all conceivable modifications have been considered, review them in light of real-world constraints (cost, etc.).

2. **Checklist**   This consists of a set of questions that are "fit" onto the situation to envision new solutions [26]. A typical checklist might be:
   Other applications?
   How can we adapt the product?
   Modify?
   Magnify?
   Reduce?
   Substitute?
   Rearrange?
   Reverse?
   Combine?
   Multipurpose?

3. **Forced Relationships**   Here relevant, and perhaps less relevant, elements are force-fit together to come up with new combinations. The elements can be selected from desirable characteristics for a solution, or from other solutions to similar problems, or even from solutions to problems that are somehow analogous to the present problem. For example, a system that electronically informs drivers on a highway of the road's number/name might be "forced" to include sensors to detect speeders.

4. **Working Backwards**   The idea here is to postulate a "perfect solution" and work backwards from the characteristics of such a solution to the technical capabilities it would have to incorporate.

5. **Black Box**   In this approach, one based on a well-known idea from general systems theory, all the inputs are listed (all elements of the problem or situation) and a separate list is made of all the outputs (the elements of a perfect solution). One then envisions all possible transformation processes that might transform some or all of the inputs into some or all of the outputs. The underlying logic is this: Starting with this (input), what would be required to get that (desired output)?

6. **Directed Dreaming**   This is an attempt to use dreams, or, more appropriately, the subconscious, to engender creative approaches or solutions to problems [13]. This method seems to require a prolonged mental struggle of days or even weeks with the problem. When falling asleep while still pondering the problem (if this is possible), a creative answer may come to the subconscious. It is important to have paper and pencil or tape recorder ready to store the idea until morning.

▶ A.4   GROUP CREATIVITY

The need for creativity is inversely related to the level of our understanding of the problem. The less well understood the problem, the greater the need for creativity. For example, the problem of constructing a warehouse is reasonably well understood, and the degree of creativity required to carry out the construction project is relatively low. The problems involved in developing a long-term habitat for moon dwellers are not well understood, and therefore would require a great deal of creativity.

It has been repeatedly shown [22] that groups are more effective in generating creative solutions to unstructured (poorly understood) problems than individuals. It is also clear that if the problem is structured (well understood), then individuals do a better job of problem solving than groups. (If you doubt this generality, consider the case of using a committee to add a column of numbers—a well-structured problem.) Thus, the fundamental reason for seeking creativity through a group process is that the problem structure is ambiguous.

The discussion on group creativity in the remainder of this section is largely adapted from [5, 8, 33, 35]. (The latter is a particularly valuable reference on techniques to foster group creativity.) It is generally accepted that there are five major advantages associated with using group creativity processes:

1. Groups bring together knowledge and skills not possessed by any individual member of the group.

2. Groups are more effective than individuals in eliminating errors and avoiding mistakes.

3. A group solution is more likely to be accepted by those who must implement it than is the solution of an individual.

4. If the members of a group must act on evidence, it is likely that they will be more productive and effective if they have played a role in developing that evidence.

5. Group members learn from one another, stimulate one another, and add to each other's knowledge and skills—that is, synergism occurs.

The effectiveness of creativity groups can be enhanced if a few simple guidelines [17, 22] are followed. Diversity is a highly desirable quality of such groups. Within the bounds of reason, group members should be as diverse as possible across such dimensions as:

Role	Engineers, managers, technicians, blue- and white-collar production workers, and so on, all represent special viewpoints and may be the source of unique contributions to problem solving.
Specialty	Different areas of study have their individual ways of thinking about and analyzing problems.
Age	Contrary to popular mythology, there appears to be no demonstrable relationship between age and creativity except, possibly, in the field of mathematics. A mix of ages cannot hurt, and probably helps.
Experience	Experience with a problem tends to produce insight, but it also tends to foster overconcern with real or imagined constraints. Inexperienced but intelligent people may develop fresh approaches.
Education	One must never confuse education with wisdom; but, like experience, more is generally better than less.

When a problem arises that requires the use of a creativity group, it should be treated as a project, and the rules of good project management apply. There should be an objective, a leader, a time schedule, a budget, a plan, and an evaluation process. Basic work group tenets should also be observed: hold meetings away from the bustle of business; allow no interruptions; insist that all participants be present; and have a good supply of working materials such as flip charts, blackboards, coffee, paper, pencils, and the rest of the paraphernalia necessary for a successful meeting.

In the initial creativity sessions, the focus should be on the methods of creativity, investigating various methods and technologies used to foster creativity, and forming a good working relationship among the group members. Following these orientation sessions, the groups should be ready to apply its power to the tasks for which it was formed.

Problem recognition and understanding is a critical first step in all problem-solving procedures. A problem not understood cannot be solved. The problem should be stated as precisely and concisely as possible, consistent with its real-world complexity. As noted above, the problem statement should be constructed in terms of the capabilities sought, not in terms of desired hardware. It is difficult but necessary to think of a "land-based people mover," not a "car" or "bus," or of a "container for the foot," not a "shoe."

If the problem is large or complex, it may be advantageous to break it down into subproblems that can be attacked and handled separately. The results may then be combined to secure the overall solution. But it is well to remember that this procedure can result in suboptimization. It should be avoided unless absolutely necessary.

Procedural devices are sometimes helpful in achieving good problem statements. Be concise, but do not arbitrarily limit the length of the statement. It is often useful to require the problem to be restated some minimum number of times, say, four or five. In addition to obtaining a suitable statement of the problem, these reworking techniques also help to familiarize the problem solvers with the various aspects of the problem and its environment. They may even aid in establishing the validity and significance of the problem.

The most commonly used group creativity problem-solving techniques are described below.

Brainstorming   This is probably the best known and most widely used of all the group creativity techniques. It was developed by Alex Osborn [26] in 1953, and has been widely publicized and used since then. The use of brainstorming mushroomed in the middle 1950s, but declined somewhat in the 1960s following some reports alleging the superiority of individual creativity.

A single brainstorming session should probably not last much longer than an hour. All ideas should be recorded. An experienced secretary or recording machine is useful to capture the initial onrush of ideas. Two basic rules should be observed during brainstorming sessions:

1. Criticism, judgment, or analysis of the generated ideas is absolutely prohibited during the session. Critiques can be conducted after the idea-generation sessions have been completed.

2. Quantity is encouraged. Variations, extensions, and combinations of previously generated ideas are often more valuable than the originals. Seemingly wild ideas are welcomed without comment, just as conservative ideas are.

A number of variants of brainstorming have been developed over the years, such as *brainwriting*, where *nominal groups* (see later section and Appendix B) are used. The ideas are written down first, then read aloud and developed.

Synectics This approach, developed by William Gordon [16] in 1944, is most appropriate for very unclear, abstract situations—that is, where the problem has little or no apparent structure. Synectics requires the formation of a tailor-made team that uses analogy and metaphor to approach two tasks: (1) making the strange familiar and (2) making the familiar strange. In the process, participants are urged to leave the mental confines of the everyday world and escape into the bizarre, even the absurd. Some of the types of analogy used are *personal*, where the members see themselves as pieces or parts of the solution; *direct*, where biological and natural analogous elements are employed; *symbolic*, where objective or impersonal images are used to describe the problems; and *fantasy*, where science fiction-type ideas are used as solutions. The synectic approach to creativity requires considerably more training and practice than most other methods. A consultant or facilitator who is expert in leadership of synectic groups is necessary.

Morphology Invented by F. Zwicky in 1947, this method was not publicized until the 1960s. The problem is defined in terms of the various capabilities most likely to be involved in a solution. Highly generalized methods of achieving these capabilities are defined. All possible combinations of these methods are then arrayed in a so-called "morphological box" and examined for technical feasibility. The following five-step process is used.

1. Describe, define, and generalize the problem.
2. Define all factors that influence the solution.
3. Structure these factors into distinctive categories.
4. Analyze the *cells* at the intersection of each category with each other category.
5. Evaluate each of these cells in terms of solution criteria.

As can be imagined, an examination of "all possible combinations" of even a small problem is a serious undertaking. A set of six capabilities, each of which might be achieved by five methods, would require examination of more than 15,000 alternatives.

Bionics Sometimes referred to as *nature analysis*, this is an analogy approach that relies on imitation of nature. The group seeks ways in which animals or plants have solved similar or analogous problems. The use of this technique is limited, but when utilized to handle appropriate problems, it appears to be effective.

Storyboarding The Walt Disney Studios faced a serious creativity problem: how to produce a large number of different short subject cartoon plots. Storyboarding was their answer to the challenge. As usual, a list is made of all problem attributes (all elements in cartoon plot), and of the possible variations each attribute might take (e.g., location: U.S., Egypt, desert isle, etc.). These are printed on cards backed with a self-sticking material such as Velcro®. A wall of a conference room is covered with felt and the attribute cards are arranged and rearranged to form different potential solutions to the problem (plot elements for the cartoon).

This method has much in common with Zwicky's morphological box. Of course, no attempt is made when storyboarding to evaluate all possible combinations. In this manner, a different, feasible combination is being sought, not the best combination.

Delphi This approach has been most widely used for technological forecasting and for the determination of numeric measures of importance (weights), but it also may be used to aid creativity. Delphi focuses the collective knowledge of the group on identifying, forecasting, and solving problems. It adds a formal structure to the group process and avoids the bias usually associated with the presence of strong individual personalities in the group.

The Delphi process begins with group selection. Ground rules and procedures for the particular process must be clearly stated, and sufficient time allowed for the exercise. (The specifics of the Delphi technique are discussed in detail in Appendix B.) While it is a popular tool for technological forecasting and parameter estimation, it is not often used for creativity exercises.

Nominal Group Techniques The nominal group technique is a structured group process that combines both group and individual activities. A coordinator administers the following five-step process:

1. Silent idea generation.
2. Round-robin presentation.
3. Idea clarification.
4. Voting and ranking.
5. Discussion of results.

During silent idea generation, each participant is asked to think of and write down ideas about the specific task. This step is followed by a round-robin presentation wherein participants take turns reading ideas to the group. The coordinator or an assistant records each idea. Any participant may pass on any given round. This process continues until all the ideas of the group have been read and recorded. While this may seem almost identical to brainstorming, the idea flow from nominal groups is not usually as free and uninhibited.

The next step is clarification. The coordinator proceeds through the idea list asking if any clarification is needed. Anyone in the group may clarify any idea, although some courage is usually required to modify someone else's idea.

The participants are then asked to select eight ideas they consider to be the best or most important. These are ranked by the group. The coordinator then tabulates the results, and the group discusses them. A second, abbreviated session may be held to expand on the eight best ideas.

Other Methods In addition to the approaches noted above, there are several less well-known, seldom-used creative problem-solving techniques. Among them are buzz sessions, modified buzz sessions, slipwriting, and reverse brainstorming. All of these methods have one common element: They attempt to utilize the creative potential of groups. (Again, the reader is referred to [35] for an extended discussion of the techniques.)

These techniques work. They increase the output of ideas by individuals and groups. Which techniques work best depends on several factors. Among these are the extent to which people are willing to expose their ideas to their colleagues, penalties for error, schemes for stimulating unusual associations of known ideas, the skill with which the problem is identified and stated, and the stimulation of idea production by each member of the group through the contributions of other group members.

It is now appropriate to mention a matter of crucial importance to the success of any group creativity technique. Research on multidisciplinary projects has shown that problem-oriented individuals are more effective in multidisciplinary problem solving than are discipline-oriented individuals [28]. The distinction is simple. Problem-oriented people give the problem primary consideration. Each views his/her individual area of knowledge only in terms of its potential contribution to solving the problem. Discipline-oriented people view the problem as an opportunity to ply their knowledge or extend it. To the former, knowledge is a means to an end. To the latter, the problem is a vehicle for the demonstration or extension of knowledge. A problem orientation is generally more effective because problem-oriented people welcome any input they see as helpful in problem solving, while discipline-oriented people view as irrelevant (or uninteresting) ideas and discussions not related to their area of expertise. To increase the chance of success, several, if not all, members of the creativity group should be problem-oriented.

Skill in creative problem solving can be acquired and developed. It requires training and the application of effort, but it does not require special mental endowments or "gifts of nature." Almost anyone can be creative by using the principles and methods described in this section and known collectively as *creative problem-solving techniques*.

A.5   EVALUATION OF CREATIVITY METHODS

A 1971 *Industry Week* article [3] indicated that the 13 fastest-growing companies in the United States had programs to encourage employee innovation and creativity. Brainstorming was the most widely known and used method, and there is no reason to believe this has changed. The morphological box was in second place, though it was listed only half as frequently as brainstorming. Use of creativity methods is greatest in the area of product development, with next most frequent uses in value analysis, research, marketing, and planning/organization, in that order. The article noted that half of all the ideas generated and considered for further investigation proved to be viable and were implemented. This is far in excess of the 1 percent usually estimated for the viability of new ideas.

Since the early 1970s, the use of creativity techniques seems to have decreased somewhat. This is felt to result from some disappointment in the use of the techniques, many of which have been oversold by their developers. It is, of course, not possible to measure the contribution of these methods to firm growth and profitability, or even to idea generation itself, because one can argue that the idea "would have occurred anyway." Specific difficulties noted in employing creativity techniques were:

* Insufficient time; overloaded key personnel; inability to find acceptable meeting dates.
* Personal tension; inability to think abstractly; blocks in interpersonal communication; lack of experience; not observing the rules of the method.
* Insufficient knowledge of the problem; lack of top-management support.
* Inability to measure the benefits; patent problems.

The future of specific idea-generation techniques appears mixed. Interested individuals have been quite creative in thinking up new methods for fostering creativity. Among the more interesting recent additions are:

1. **Mechanical Techniques**   These are typically straightforward mechanisms such as Savo Bojicic's "Think Tank," a hollow plastic sphere containing 13,000 words to be used as idea take-offs. As the sphere is turned, the words come into view, stimulating the brain to make various associations.

2. **Electronic Methods**   The techniques of biofeedback and electrical stimulation are included here, and would seem to have much to offer. Considerable experimentation is being conducted on these techniques, and this area will certainly become better developed in the future.

3. **Chemical Techniques**   Several drugs and chemicals appear to produce the kinds of mental states described as desirable in the creativity literature. The primary question is whether or not such chemically induced states are harmless to the individual and can be usefully applied to the task of creative problem solving in an organizational setting. If used at all, these techniques require care and expert control.

4. **Environmental, Psychological**   These approaches involve the use of sound, color, sensory stimulation/deprivation, odor, and so forth, to alter the brain's normal environment to aid creativity. The prime issues here are potential and safety when used in organizational settings.

A final, important point to remember is that individuals in highly stressful situations are rarely creative. A little pressure stimulates, but too much paralyzes creativity because the human body reacts to stress as if preparing to fight or flee. The blood supply to the brain is diminished, and the brain receives less oxygen. The most important factor affecting creativity in the future will be the emphasis and encouragement given it by managers. Supportive organizational leadership is needed. If creativity is sought, failure must be tolerated.

▶ A.6 ORGANIZING TO ALLOW AND ASSIST CREATIVITY

The ways that creative ideas are handled in an organization have a major impact on both the quality and quantity of the flow of ideas. The typical suggestion box is seen as a bottomless repository for good ideas (or for obscene comments on the quality of management).

Over the years, the authors have concluded that several conditions seem to support the development of effective systems for fostering creativity, individual or group, in an organizational environment.

1. Suggestions for system improvement should be submitted directly to a screening committee; that is, they should bypass the usual chain of command.

2. A standard form should be used, insofar as possible, that instructs the submitter on what information is required about the idea. (Note: It is difficult enough to think up a creative idea without having to worry about the best way to present it.)

3. All suggestions should be acknowledged in a timely fashion. Further, the individual submitting the idea should be promptly informed about the progress of the idea through the accept/reject process.

4. All suggestions should be reviewed by a technically competent individual or group.

5. If rewards are given for useful ideas, they should be of appropriate size. No sensible person will spend hours of time working on an idea which, if accepted, will earn a $25 reward.

6. No penalty or negative impact should result from submitting an unsuccessful idea.

7. There must be no penalties attached to successful ideas. No one is likely to submit a labor-saving idea if colleagues may be laid off or fired as a result.

8. Superiors should be encouraged to foster the creativity of subordinates and then rewarded for any creativity that results. This requires a mutually supportive superior/subordinate relationship, not a competitive one.

This prescription for a successful idea-generation system may appear to be ideal, but it is quite realistic. The Lincoln Electric Company is a down-to-earth producer of arc welding machinery and equipment. In that firm, experts consider—and acknowledge—all suggestions. If adopted, the individual who submitted the idea receives one-half of the first year's savings (or added profits). In addition, employees at all levels are guaranteed that no one will be laid off or moved to a lower-paying job as a result of the idea. One result of this policy is that the Lincoln Electric Company has consistently been the productivity leader in its industrial category, electric equipment and parts.

Given policies in basic agreement with the above provisos, an organizational mechanism for fostering and processing suggestions can be developed. The idea should move directly from originator to a screening committee whose membership is broad enough to contain the technical expertise needed to conduct a preliminary evaluation of any suggestions received by the committee. Ideas that seem, to the screening committee, worthy of further investigation are forwarded to an evaluation committee, whose job it is to decide if the idea is worth further development and exploration. (The evaluation and selection of ideas is discussed in Chapter 2.)

BIBLIOGRAPHY

1. ABEND, J. C. "Innovative Management: The Missing Link in Productivity." *Management Review,* July 1979.

2. BARRETT, F. D. "Creativity Techniques: Yesterday, Today and Tomorrow." S.A.M. *Advanced Management Journal,* Winter 1978.

3. BOUCHARD, T. J. "Whatever Happened to Brainstorming?" *Industry Week,* Aug. 2, 1971.

4. CATES, C. "Beyond Muddling: Creativity." *Public Administration Review,* Nov.-Dec. 1979.

5. CLARK, C. H. *Idea Management: How to Motivate Creativity and Innovation.* New York: AMACOM, 1980.

6. CLARK, C. H. *The Creative Organization.* Chicago: University of Chicago Press, 1965.

7. COVINGTON, M. V. *The Productive Thinking Program: A Course in Learning to Think.* Westerville, OH: Merrill Publishing, 1974.

8. CRAWFORD, R. P. *The Techniques of Creative Thinking.* New York: Hawthorn Books, 1966.

9. DACEY, J. S. *Fundamentals of Creative Thinking.* New York: Free Press, 1988.

10. DEAN, B. V. *Evaluating, Selecting and Controlling R & D Projects: Idea Generation and Handling.* New York: AMA Research Study, 1968.

11. DEBONO, E. *Lateral Thinking for Management.* New York: American Management Association, 1971.

12. DEBONO, E. *Serious Creativity: Using the Power of Lateral Thinking to Create New Ideas.* New York: Harper Business, 1992.

13. GARFIELD, P. L. *Creative Dreaming.* New York: Ballantine, 1985.

14. GEE, E. A., and C. TYLER. *Managing Innovation.* New York: Wiley, 1976.

15. GESCHKA, H. "Introduction and Use of Idea-Generating Methods." *Research Management,* May 1978.

16. GORDON, W. J. *Synectics: The Development of Creative Capacity.* New York: Harper Row, 1961.

17. HARRISON, E. F. *The Management Decision-Making Process.* Boston: Houghton Mifflin, 1975.

18. HAYAKAWA, S. I. "What Does It Mean to Be Creative?" *Industry Week,* Sept. 17, 1979.

19. HAYES, R., and W. J. ABERNATHY, "Managing Our Way to Economic Decline." *Harvard Business Review,* July–Aug. 1980.

20. HOWARD, N. "Business Probes the Creative Spark." *Dun's Review,* Jan. 1980.

21. KOBERG, D., and J. BAGNALL. *The Universal Traveler,* 2nd ed. Los Altos, CA: Wm. Kaufmann, 1988.

22. KOLASA, B. J. *Introduction to Behavioral Sciences for Business.* New York: Wiley, 1969.

23. LARSON, R. H. "Developing Creativity in Engineers." *Mechanical Engineering,* Dec. 1978.

24. MEREDITH, J. R. "The Implementation of Computer Based Systems." *Journal of Operations Management,* Oct. 1981.

25. MILLER, B. *Managing Innovation for Growth and Profit.* Homewood, IL: Irwin, 1970.

26. OSBORN, A. *Applied Imagination.* New York: Scribner's, 1953.

27. PARNES, S. *Creative Behavior Guidebook.* New York: Scribner's, 1976.

28. PILL, J. "Technical Management and Control of Large Scale Urban Studies: A Comparative Analysis of Two Cases," Ph.D. dissertation. Cleveland: Case Western Reserve University, 1971.

29. RAWLINSON, J. G. *Creative Thinking and Brainstorming.* New York: Halstead, 1981.

30. RICHARDS, T., and B. FREEDMAN. "A Re-Appraisal of Creativity Techniques in Industrial Training." *European Industrial Training,* Vol. 3, 1979.

31. SOUDER, W. E. "A Review of Creativity and Problem Solving Techniques." *Research Management,* July 1977.

32. SOUDER, W. E. "Autonomy, Gratification, and R & D Outputs: A Small-Sample Field Study." *Management Science,* April 1974.

33. SUMMER, I., and D. E. WHITE. "Creativity Techniques: Toward Improvement of the Decision Process." *Academy of Management Review,* April 1976.

34. VAN GUNDY, A. B. *Managing Group Creativity.* New York: ANACOM, 1984.

35. WARFIELD, J. N., H. GESCHKA, and R. HAMILTON. *Methods of Idea Management*. Columbus, OH: The Battelle Institute and The Academy for Contemporary Problems, 1975.

36. WHITING, C. S. "Operational Techniques of Creative Thinking." *Advanced Management*, Oct. 1955.

37. ZELDMAN, M. E. "How Management Can Develop and Sustain a Creative Environment." S.A.M. *Advanced Management Journal*, Winter 1980.

Technological Forecasting

Forecasting is hard, particularly of the future. **[Anonymous]**

Forecasting is like trying to drive a car blindfolded and following directions given by a person who is looking out the back window. **[Anonymous]**

Technology is the application of science or art. All projects rest on a technological base. They are concerned with using science and art to accomplish some goals. Indeed, most projects rest on a base formed by many technologies. When a project is initiated, decisions must be made about which of the relevant and available technologies to employ. At times, a choice must be made between beginning the project immediately, using currently available technologies, or delaying the project in order to adopt a superior technology that is expected but is not currently available.

In addition to technological choices made for the project itself, it may be necessary to forecast the technologies with which our technological choices and our project results will interact. Our systems must be reasonably compatible with those in the environment that do or will exist across their expected life.

Both reasons for forecasting technology go beyond the obvious need to plan for the technological future. Such planning may or may not be the subject of a special project. For many organizations, technological planning is an ongoing function of management. But whether planning is done as a routine or on a project basis, technological forecasting is required.

We define technological forecasting as the process of predicting the future characteristics and timing of technology. When possible, the prediction will be quantified, made through a specific logic, and will estimate the timing and degree of change in technological parameters, attributes, and capabilities.

As with idea generation, few project managers are engaged with projects at the point in the life cycle at which technological forecasting is normally done. Decisions made at this point, early in the life cycle, influence the subsequent course of the project. Whether implicit or explicit, the decision not to engage in technological forecasting assumes a static technological future. This is a false assumption, but in some cases the assumption is not damaging. We urge project managers, senior managers, and policymakers to make conscious decisions about engaging in technological forecasting, and we urge project managers to study and understand the importance of this process on project management.

We begin by discussing the nature of technological forecasting, its history, and how it has been used. We then survey the major techniques currently in use. Last, we consider how to choose an appropriate forecasting method, the limits of each method, and the general future of technological forecasting. Some of these models require an understanding of basic statistics to employ them, but not to comprehend their use and role.

▶ B.1   CHARACTERISTICS, HISTORY, AND IMPORTANCE OF TECHNOLOGICAL FORECASTING

Note that in the definition, technological forecasting is aimed at predicting future technological capabilities, attributes, and parameters. It is not an attempt to predict how things will be done. Nor is technological forecasting oriented toward profitability. That is, a technological capability or attribute can be forecast to be available at some time in the future, although society may not necessarily want or need the capability.

Consider the process of technological innovation. Many factors influence the progress and direction of technology. For example, science, organizational policy, organization structure, chance, need, and funding all play major roles in determining what technologies are likely to be available to us in the future.

Governmental decisions to support some technologies and not others have a significant impact on technological innovation. For instance, the decision to support the space program had major impacts on miniaturization in the electronics industry, on the use of new materials and styles in the garment industry, and even on the look of television commercials. The federal government's decision not to support the SST affected the technology of air transport in the United States. If technological forecasting predicts that a certain capability is technologically within our reach in the near future, and if the government chooses to support research in this area, it is much more likely that the technology will be developed—for example, new approaches to the generation of electric power. If the government decides to finance implementation of the desired innovation, there will probably be a near-term impact on profits and the speed of diffusion of the new technology.

Another characteristic of technological forecasting is uncertainty about the rate of change of technological capabilities. Many capabilities tend to grow exponentially until they reach some natural limit: for example, aircraft speed, computer memory size and memory access speed, horsepower per liter of internal combustion engines, among many others. This is because new technology builds on older technology, and synergism results from the combination. When one technology impinges on another, the synergy often results in an unexpected and sudden increase in capability. For instance, the development of microcomputers depended on the combined technologies of electronic computer circuitry, miniaturization of electronic circuits, efficient computer programming, and development of information storage devices. Such synergies are difficult to forecast. In the early 1950s, noted science fiction author Isaac Asimov wrote a short story set five hundred years in the future. One artifact featured in this story of the future was a small, hand-held device that could perform complex mathematical calculations when its buttons were properly pushed.

The fact that a new capability is developed does not automatically mean that it will be put to use. The files of the Patent Bureau are jammed with useless inventions. The lack of application potential does not, of course, mean that the capability or scientific finding is worthless. There are many examples of important technological advances that rest on seemingly nonapplicable earlier discoveries. A case in point is Albert Einstein's work on special and general relativity. It depended on earlier work of the mathematician Hendrik Lorentz, work that had no apparent application to physics when it was originally published.

Although varying greatly from industry to industry, the embodiment of a scientific discovery, an *innovation*, has traditionally lagged the discovery itself, the *invention*, by five to seven years [30, 39]. More recently, competitive pressures in worldwide markets have tended to shorten these lags, but they are still significant. Once the innovation is developed, its adoption is also not instantaneous, often taking between 10 and 20 years to reach the point of market saturation. The lag between invention and innovation, and the time required for adoption to be completed are useful for the technological forecaster and the project manager. The fact that invention is a precursor to innovation allows the forecaster to consider the possible nature of innovations before they occur. The time consuming process of adoption gives the project manager some ability to assess the innovation before actually adopting it. (For a detailed discussion and examples of the adoption process, see [30].)

Historically, technological forecasting was based on the guesses of the most recognized and prestigious expert in the area. This is no longer appropriate because technological progress has become dependent on the interaction of several, often diverse, technologies. A single individual rarely has the requisite level of expertise in all relevant areas. Also, the management and funding of the several technologies have a significant impact on the degree and speed of technological change.

The government has played an increasingly important role in technological forecasting. One of the earliest attempts at technological forecasting was the 1937 report *Technological Trends and National Policy, Including the Social Implications of New Inventions* [44], which predicted that plastics, television, synthetic rubber, and a mechanical cotton picker were likely to become widely used and have significant social impacts.

Following World War II, the government established the Scientific Advisory Board to provide guidance for technological development over a 20-year period. This was done, in part, because of the resource bottlenecks and technological barriers encountered during industrial mobilization for the war. Many forecasts were prompted by the development of nuclear power and automation. Then, in the 1960s, a boom occurred in technological forecasting. The number of articles on the subject increased rapidly, as did the membership of societies devoted to forecasting the future. This interest was spurred by several factors:

- The development of space technology.
- Public concern for the environment.
- Public awareness of potential resource limitations.
- Technology as a major factor of international competition.
- Increased availability of computer power.
- Widespread publication of the methods and results of technological forecasting.

In 1972, the government formed a permanent Office of Technology Assessment under the authority of the Technology Assessment Act. The purpose of this office was to equip Congress with the information needed for the support, management, and regulation of applied technologies. All of this governmental attention to technological forecasting resulted in improved forecasting methods, as well as considerable concurrent publicity and general interest in the subject. Business firms saw the obvious value of generating forecasts that helped them identify the probable capabilities of future products. Firms in the so-called high-technology areas led the way in forming in-house capabilities for technological forecasting. Others followed, sometimes setting up their own forecasting groups and sometimes using consultants for *ad hoc* forecasting sessions.

As noted at the beginning of the chapter, the techniques were also used to aid decision making on the choice of production processes as well as products. Forecasting sessions became input for R&D, for marketing life-cycle planning, and for the facility and support functions. High-technology firms saw technological forecasting as a mandatory input to basic corporate planning.

▶ B.2   TECHNOLOGICAL FORECASTING METHODS

The major techniques for technological forecasting may be categorized under two general headings: methods based on numeric data and judgmental methods. In the main, numeric data-based forecasting extrapolates history by generating statistical fits to historical data. A few numeric methods deal with complex interdependencies. Judgmental forecasting may also be based on projections of the past, but information sources in such models rely on the subjective judgments of experts. Again, we emphasize that technological forecasting is most appropriately applied to capabilities, not to the specific characteristics of specific devices.

Numeric Data-Based Technological Forecasting Techniques

Trend Extrapolation   To extrapolate is to infer the future from the past. If there has been a steady stream of technological change and improvement, it is reasonable to assume that the stream will continue to flow. We can distinguish four approaches to the use of trend extrapolation.

1. **Statistical Curve Fitting**   This method is applicable to forecasting functional capabilities. Statistical procedures fit the past data to one or more mathematical functions such as linear, logarithmic, Fourier, or exponential. The best fit is selected by statistical test and then a forecast is extrapolated from this mathematical relationship.

   For example, we can forecast the fastest qualification (pole position) speeds at the Indianapolis 500 Mile Race by plotting pole position speeds against time measured in years (see Figure 1). Beginning with the post-World War I races, the pole position speeds of Indy race cars have exponentially increased. Two technological innovations are quite easily seen in the data. One is the rear-engine car. The first such car appeared in 1961. Qualifying speeds were about 150 mph. In 1964 a rear-engine car won the pole position at slightly less than 159 mph. The growth rate of qualifying speed is significantly higher with the rear-engine technology, so different exponential functions were fitted to front- and rear-engined cars.

   The second easily discernible technological innovation occurred in the early 1970s. It was the use of sophisticated aerodynamic devices (wings at the rear of the car) to create downforce on the cars, allowing them much higher cornering speeds—from 170 mph in 1970, to 179 mph in 1971, to 196 mph in 1973 (with the addition of wings at the front of the car).

2. **Limit Analysis**   Ultimately, all growth is limited, and there is an absolute limit to progress, either recognized or unrecognized. Sooner or later, projections must reflect the fact that improvements may get close to this limit but cannot exceed it. For instance, a trend of increasing energy conversion efficiency cannot eventually exceed 100 percent. As another example, the lowest temperature achieved in the laboratory is presented in Figure 2. The trend of lower and lower temperatures is limited, of course, by absolute zero. (It is interesting to note the rapid improvement in the ability to produce low temperatures that occurred around 1900.)

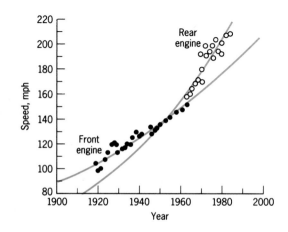

Figure 1: An example of statistical curve fitting.

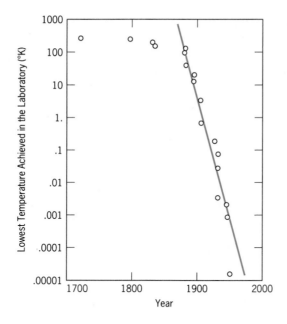

Figure 2: An example of limit analysis.

If the present level of technology being forecast is far from its theoretical extreme, extrapolation may not be unreasonable. If, however, a current technology is approaching its limit, and if this is not recognized, projections of past improvements may seriously overestimate future accomplishments.

3. **Trend Correlation**   At times, one technology is a precursor to another. This is frequently the case when advances made in the precursor technology can be adopted by the follower technology. When such relationships exist, knowledge of changes in the precursor technology can be used to predict the course of the follower technology, as far in the future as the lag time between the two. Further, extrapolation of the precursor allows a forecast of the follower to be extended beyond the lag time. Figure 3 shows an example of a trend correlation, which compares the trends of combat and transport aircraft speeds. Another example of a trend correlation forecast is predicting the size and power of future computers, based on advances in microelectronic technology.

4. **Multivariate Trend Correlation**   Occasionally, a follower technology is dependent on several precursor technologies rather than on a single precursor. In such cases, the follower is usually a composite or aggregate of several precursors. Fixed combinations of the precursors may act to produce change in the follower, but more often the combinations are not fixed and the precursor inputs vary in both combination and strength. For example, improvements in aircraft speed may come from improvements in engines, materials, controls, fuels, aerodynamics, and from various combinations of such factors. An example of a multiple trend correlation forecast using total passenger miles, total plane miles, and average seating capacity is shown in Figure 4.

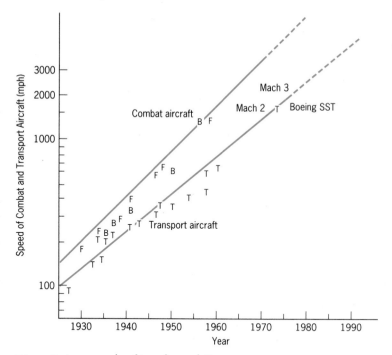

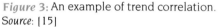

Figure 3: An example of trend correlation.
Source: [15]

Extrapolation of statistically determined trends permits an objective approach to forecasting. It also permits analysis and critique by people other than the forecaster. This approach, however, still has serious limitations and pitfalls. Any errors or incorrect choices made in selecting the proper historical data will be reflected in the forecast. Such errors lower the utility of the forecast, and may completely negate its value. The forecasts given by this methodology are not sensitive to changes in the conditions that have produced the historical data, changes that may significantly alter the trend. Even when it is known that one or more possibly important conditions are going to change, technological advances cannot be predicted from the extrapolation. Statistical trend extrapolation yields a "good" forecast with high frequency, but when the environment changes, it can be quite wrong.

Trend Extrapolation, Qualitative Approaches At times, standard statistical procedures do not result in neatly fitting trends that the forecaster can extrapolate with comfort. In such cases, the forecaster may "adjust" the statistical results by applying judgment, or he or she may ignore the statistics entirely and extrapolate a trend wholly on the basis of judgment. Forecasts generated in this way are less precise than statistically based forecasts, but not necessarily less accurate.

One example of this kind of qualitative trend extrapolation is the prediction of aircraft complexity. The attempts to quantify this trend have not been successful. But the percent of movable or adjustable parts in an aircraft has been extrapolated from the frequency that such elements were introduced in the past, and these fore-

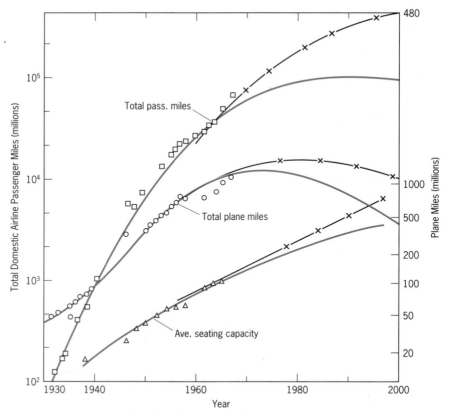

Figure 4: An example of multivariate correlation.
Source: [15]

casts have been reasonably accurate. Specific technical change cannot be predicted this way, but the degree of change can be. This provides useful inputs to planning by indicating the probable trend of past behaviors.

Growth Curves The growth pattern of a technological capability is similar to the growth of biological life. Technologies go through an invention phase, an introduction and innovation phase, a diffusion and growth phase, and a maturity phase. In doing so, their growth is similar to the S-shaped growth of biological life. Technological forecasting helps to estimate the timing of these phases. This growth curve forecasting method is particularly useful in determining the upper limit of performance for a specific technology. An example of growth curve analysis is shown in Figure 5, which depicts the number of telephones per 1000 population as a function of time. The year in which the upper limit of diffusion (one phone per person over 15-years old, or about 700 phones per 1000 population) is reached can be extrapolated from the S-curve, and it occurs between 1990 and 2000.

Several mathematical models can be used to generate growth curves. The choice of model is subjective, depending largely on the analyst's judgment about which of the functional forms most closely approximates the underlying reality of the technical growth under consideration. When using growth curves, the forecaster

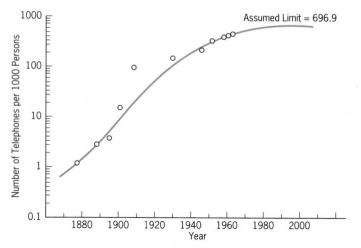

Figure 5: An example of a growth curve.

must be sure that the data are self-consistent—that is, that all data come from the same data set or population.

The forecaster must also remember not to confuse accuracy with precision. It is possible to develop precise capability/time estimates, but their accuracy is illusory. We might read Figure 5 as "697 phones per 1000 population as of 1997," but "about 700 between 1990 and 2000" is a better reflection of the scatter in the data underlying the curve. Finally, the forecaster must remember that growth curves reflect a single technological approach, a given way of achieving a capability. Extrapolation cannot go beyond the saturation level of that specific technological approach. It cannot predict a decline or future rebirth of the growth pattern.

Envelope Curves   A serious constraint on growth curves is overcome by appropriate specification of the capability to be forecast. For example, Figure 6 shows a growth curve for the speed of propeller-driven aircraft. As noted earlier, possible in-

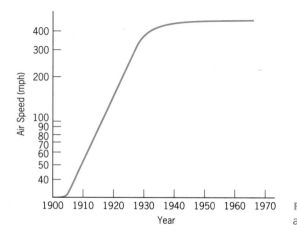

Figure 6: Speed of propeller-driven aircraft. *Source:* [42]

put for Figure 6 must be carefully screened to make sure it includes all available data for propeller-driven aircraft, and *only* data for propeller-driven aircraft.

If we remove the modifier *propeller-driven* from the capability to be forecast, we can add data on jet, ram jet, and rocket planes, as in Figure 7. (We could also have included data on balloons and gliders if we wished.) If we generalize the capability even more to "speed of travel," we get Figure 8, a series of specific growth curves superimposed on one chart and enveloped by a single curve, termed an *envelope curve*. Fundamentally, envelope curves are a combination of growth curve and trend analysis.

Substitution Model   The substitution model is based on three assumptions:

1.   Many technological advances can be considered as competitive substitutions of one method of satisfying a need for another.

2.   Once a substitution progresses, it will proceed to completion.

3.   The rate of substitution of new for old is proportional to the remaining amount of the old left to be substituted.

Experience shows that substitutions tend to proceed exponentially in the early years, and to follow an S-shaped trend curve. When a substitution begins, the new process, products, or service begins to demonstrate its advantages over the past process, products, or service. As the new technology is able to take over some of the market, the pace of substitution increases markedly, and then tapers off as it approaches saturation.

Examples abound. In the area of industrial processes in the steel industry, the replacement of "hot dip" tin-plating by the electrolytic process, the replacement of open hearth furnaces by basic oxygen furnaces, and the replacement of the re-

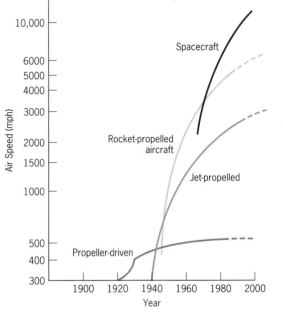

Figure 7: Speed of aircraft. *Source*: [42]

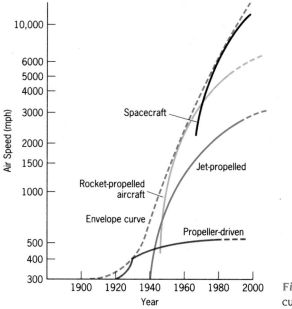

Figure 8: Speed of travel—envelope curve analysis.

versible, single-stand hot rolling mill by the multistand mill are among the many technological substitutions that conform to the S-shaped pattern.

The substitution model can prove useful for several types of investigation—for example, early recognition of technical obsolescence. The major advantage of this model is that it is simple to construct. Like all numeric data-based models, it is fatalistic in that it projects a specific and undeviating future based on past events; it implies that a particular progression of events is inevitable.

Judgment-Based Technological Forecasting Techniques

Monitoring Many forecasting techniques presuppose that the planner knows what to seek. Although the planner may have considerable expertise, occasionally technological surprises occur. Monitoring, or innovation tracking, allows the forecaster to stay abreast of technologies as they develop.

This approach assumes that a new discovery goes through several stages before emerging into public view as an innovation, and that some future technologies are currently in the process of development. The stages to investigate are:

1. Initial idea or suggestion—the concept.
2. Postulation of theory—the research proposal.
3. Verification of theory—the scientific finding.
4. Laboratory demonstration.
5. Field trial.
6. Commercial introduction.
7. Widespread adoption.

If the research is being conducted by a nondefense governmental agency or by a university, the process, with the exception of stage 1 above, is open to view by those who know where to look—learned journals, magazines, trade association letters, and similar sources. Once a sufficient amount of information has been accumulated, the data must be cross-referenced with other information to determine if a new technology or product can be generated by incorporating one or more of these events in order to develop an innovation. In the case of private industry, every attempt is made to keep the process secret as long as possible, and thus emerging technologies are rarely visible before state 5, when the innovation is apparent. Fortunately, a large percentage (49 percent in 1986; see [43]) of basic research is done by universities, so surprises are not common for those who keep up with scientific discovery. Figure 9 shows how innovation can result from a combination of events over time.

Many companies employ internal systems for reviewing the scientific and technical literature, including patents, and have organized means of abstracting and disseminating new items. Government agencies, especially the Department of Defense, use this method to stay aware of changing technologies.

Monitoring techniques may seem unsophisticated, but their potential value is immense. Provided the forecaster collects and screens information properly, this method can provide excellent data to forecast trends. Recently, microcomputer programs have been developed that find and link the related items contained in a large data set—the "hypertext" programs. Such programs are invaluable aids for the process of monitoring innovations.

Network Analysis   Network analysis is a formalization and extension of monitoring. This technique can be used in two distinct ways: (1) as a method of exploring the possible capabilities and systems that might result from extensions of current scientific research and, (2) given a desired capability or end system, as a method for determining what research results are required to achieve the desired capability. The first use is *exploratory* forecasting, and the second is *prescriptive* forecasting. In the

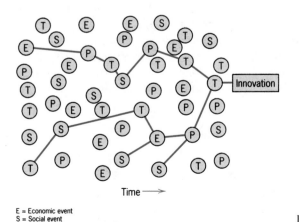

Time ⟶

E = Economic event
S = Social event
P = Political event
T = Technological event

Figure 9: Innovation results for a combination of events over time.

former, possible future technologies are explored; in the latter, desired future capabilities are defined.

The term *network model* results from the fact that networks are commonly used to organize the data. Real examples of the method are quite complex, so consider a hypothetical example.

Assume we have been monitoring the appropriate sources, and we have knowledge of recent research results, r_1, r_2, . . . r_k. We predict that these might be combined as shown in Figure 10, to yield s_1, s_2, . . . s_j scientific capabilities. These capabilities, in turn, could be combined to result in t_1, t_2, . . . t_m technical components. Finally, the technical components can be joined to produce end systems, V_1, V_2, . . . V_n (Figure 11).

Going from research results to end systems is exploratory, but the direction may be reversed. Instead of seeking the system implications of research results, we could begin with one or more related desirable end systems. Going backward through the same chain of logic, we seek the components, and the research results necessary to yield the capabilities. This uses the network to *prescribe* research.

If the various end systems are given weights that reflect their relative importance, it becomes possible to set priorities on the various research results based on the importance of the end system(s) to which the research contributes. One method of finding these priorities is described by Dean (Chapter 11 in [6]) and discussed in detail in Chapter 2 of this book. Dean developed the technique to evaluate research labs after the fact, but if the "evaluation" is *a priori*, it becomes a statement of priorities.

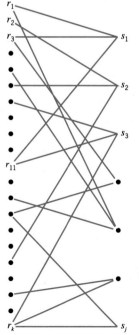

Figure 10: Example of network analysis: interconnection of research results and scientific capabilities.

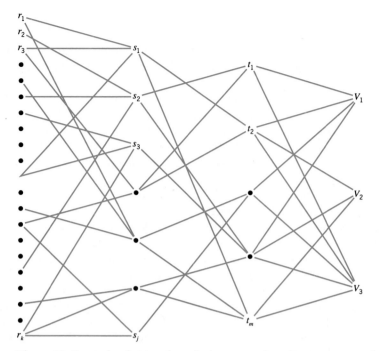

Figure 11: Example of network analysis: connections between research results, scientific capabilities, technical components, and end systems.

It follows that if we know the cost of the research projects, can estimate the relationship between research results and research expenditures, and have a budget constraint, mathematical programming (see Chapter 9) can be used to determine the best order and extent to fund the various research projects.

It is also possible to treat both the prescriptive and exploratory models stochastically—that is, to estimate the probability that the research/capability, capability/component, and component/system connections can be achieved. For the reasons explained in Chapter 2, we do not see this practice as significantly helpful. In any event, no matter how many numbers are applied to the network, the base information is strictly judgmental.

Scenarios   The scenario approach to technological forecasting has gained wide popularity in the past few years. It attempts to describe a future technology or technological event together with its environment. The scenario is a hypothetical view of the future based on past experience and conjecture, usually containing little rigorous analysis. Scenarios may cover any period, but generally extend ten, twenty, or more years into the future. They start with a set of givens. These are then "massaged" and extrapolated to give a picture of future technologies.

Three scenarios are often developed. The first describes the future if current trends continue, and this defines a base for the other two scenarios. The second and third scenarios describe optimistic and pessimistic futures based on assumptions about the environment that differ from the first scenario, giving a best/worst outlook. A diagrammatic model of scenario generation is shown in Figure 12.

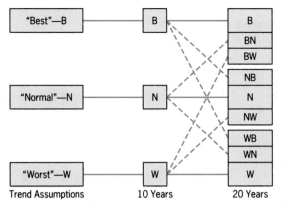

Trend Assumptions	10 Years	20 Years
"Best"—B	B	B
		BN
		BW
		NB
"Normal"—N	N	N
		NW
		WB
		WN
"Worst"—W	W	W

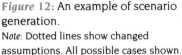

Figure 12: An example of scenario generation.
Note: Dotted lines show changed assumptions. All possible cases shown.

Although the best-known scenarios deal with world events such as famine, war, or environmental destruction (books such as Rachel Carson's *Silent Spring* and George Orwell's *1984* are both elaborate scenarios of the future), scenarios are also useful for forecasting the results of adopting a technological change. When a corporation develops a scenario, it must determine the organizational, economic, social, technological, political, and other variables that may affect their operations. By determining which variables have the greatest impact on the organization and which variables, if any, can be controlled, the organization can get a clearer insight into its potential future and thereby into possible ways of obtaining some control over it.

Morphological Analysis   In the previous appendix we examined the morphological matrix as a technique for fostering creativity. It is also a prescriptive technological forecasting technique because it makes assumptions about what people will want in the future and then investigates the possible ways those wants could be satisfied. Of all the techniques available for forecasting new products or processes, morphology is one of the most systematic. The technique relies on a matrix, usually called a morphological *box*. Figure 13 is an example that uses a morphological box to examine the possible development of clocks. The vertical axis, lettered A, B. C. etc., defines the stages of parameters or the technology under consideration. The horizontal axis, numbered 1, 2, 3, etc., defines alternate methods to achieve the stages or parameters.

The analysis is usually initiated by starting with a well-known or existing solution (A1–B1–C1–D1–E1–F1), and changing one element at a time. Alternate methods (e.g., A2–B2–C1–D1–E1–F1) are analyzed to find potential improvements in current technology. The solutions can be examined for efficiency, and estimates then made of the time when the alternative technologies might be available.

Note that morphological analysis can be used as a creativity technique and a technological forecasting device at the same time. Potential methods to accomplish certain capabilities can be sought and then the times when the required technologies might be available can be estimated. The automobile industry has used morphological studies to meet air pollution and gasoline mileage regulations, deriving possible short-, intermediate-, and long-run solutions to these problems.

Key Parameters	Alternates	1	2	3	4
Energy Source	A	Manual Winding	Vibration	Battery	Solar
Energy Store	B	Weight Store	Spring Store	Bimetallic Coil	No Store
Motor	C	Spring Motor	Electric Motor		
Regulator	D	Balance Wheel	Pendulum	Tuning Fork	Quartz
Gearing	E	Pinion Drive	Chain Drive	Worm Drive	
Indicator Device	F	Dial Hands	Slide Marks	Liquid Quartz	Light Indicators

Figure 13: A morphological matrix for clocks.

Relevance Trees   Most major technological development projects are complex. Their fulfillment is likely to depend on the accomplishment of substantial improvements on existing technologies. These advances are not usually coordinated. Many products result from technological changes that were not originally intended to provide them assistance. The planner must be able to distinguish a large number of potentially supporting technologies and to forecast their futures. Relevance trees, a slight variant of the network analysis discussed earlier, are of great aid in such work.

Relevance trees can be used to study a goal or objective, as in morphological analysis, or to select a specific research project from a more general set of goals, as in network analysis. The methodology of relevance trees requires that the planner determine the most appropriate path of the tree by arranging, in a hierarchical order, the objectives, subobjectives, and tasks in order to ensure that all possible ways of achieving the objectives have been found. The relevance of individual tasks and subobjectives to the overall objective is then evaluated.

An example of a relevance tree is shown in Figure 14. The objective is to develop a means of air pollution control. The subobjectives "Develop Petroleum . . ." and "Develop Alternatives . . ." further define the main objective. Tasks and subtasks are then defined. Once all the "good" alternative ways of achieving the subobjectives have been found, the relevance of individual solutions to the main objective can be evaluated.

Delphi Method   Perhaps the best known of the various judgmental approaches to technological forecasting, the Delphi method uses a panel of individuals who make anonymous, subjective judgments about the probable time when a specific technological capability will be available. The results of these estimates are aggregated by a process administrator and fed back to the group, which then uses the feedback to generate another round of judgments. After several iterations, the process is stopped and areas of agreement or disagreement are noted and documented. Let us now look more closely at some characteristics of this process.

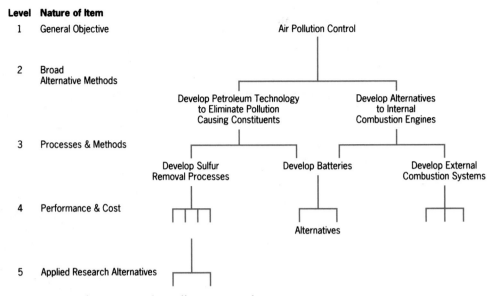

Level	Nature of Item
1	General Objective
2	Broad Alternative Methods
3	Processes & Methods
4	Performance & Cost
5	Applied Research Alternatives

Figure 14: A relevance tree for pollution control.

1. **Opinion Gathering and Distribution**   The key features of the Delphi process are quite simple. Panelists may submit their judgments by mail or may be gathered together in a single room. In either case, the opinions are written and anonymous. If the panelists are in a face-to-face meeting, no discussion of the subjects to be covered is allowed. In this way, loud or aggressive panelists cannot sway the votes of others. The written ballots are collected by the process administrator, who aggregates the responses in a statistical format (i.e., prepares a distribution of the responses). This information is given to all panel members, who can then see how their individual judgments compare with the anonymous views of others on the panel.

2. **Iterative Balloting**   The process is iterative. Additional ballots are passed out to the panel members and they vote again, altering or not altering their previous judgments as they wish. Panelists who found their original vote in the outer reaches of the distribution may, if they feel uncertain about the matter, move their vote toward the majority. There is no pressure on them to do so, however, and those who feel sure about their original vote may choose not to move it at all.

3. **Reasons and Consensus**   This iterative process is sometimes accompanied by anonymous written arguments concerning why some specific judgment is correct or incorrect. The process continues until a consensus is reached (for example, some proportion of respondents—say, 75 percent—cast votes within a predetermined range, such as a 20-year period) or until a predetermined number of iterations has been accomplished, usually four or five. If consensus is reached, a statistical measure of the result, usually the median or mode, is used to represent the actual forecast. If consensus is not reached, the distribution of the final iteration is often displayed with a note that it does not represent a consensus.

4. **Group Composition**   The composition of the group depends on the nature of the capabilities to be forecast. If they are general and abstract, a heterogeneous group is desirable. If highly technical or specific, then specialists in that area and generalists in outside but relevant areas should comprise the group. Attempts should be made to reach a balance between specialists and generalists, and between theoreticians and pragmatists. With a homogeneous group, 10 to 15 persons will probably be adequate. For a heterogeneous group, more may be necessary for representation, but numbers are not the critical factor.

The Delphi method has application beyond its use in technological forecasting. It has been widely used as an aid in policy decision making (e.g., [31]). Its three main characteristics—anonymity, statistical formatting of results, and controlled feedback—make it an acceptable and reliable process for extracting numeric data from subjective opinion. Also, no limits are placed on the factors a Delphi panelist may consider in deciding how to vote. As a result, the process is particularly effective when opinions and judgments must be based on a broad and complex set of underlying factors.

It is most relevant, at this point, to note that the judgmental forecasting methods, like managerial methods in general, are not all equally compatible with different cultures. In nations with a strong tradition of discipline rather than a problem orientation, the Delphi technique is not apt to be workable. Experts in a field are not likely to admit that nonexperts have a right to an opinion, let alone the right to have their opinions considered in a forecast.

Cross-Impact Analysis   This procedure is an extension of the Delphi method. Cross-impact analysis extends the confidence that can be placed on the forecasts of related events. It allows inclusion of an additional set of factors even beyond those usually considered by the respondents in a normal Delphi process.

The purpose of cross-impact analysis is to study the mutual influence of events explicitly and systematically, and to include those influences when forecasting technical capabilities. The set of events being studied for cross-impact potential is subjected to a Delphi analysis where a probability and a date of occurrence is assigned to each event. The events are then entered in a cross-impact matrix, as in Figure 15, where each event's impact is measured against each related event. A revised forecast can be prepared manually or by computer programs that have been developed explicitly for this purpose.

▶ B.3   TECHNOLOGICAL FORECASTING IN USE

In spite of the wealth of models and approaches that are available for technological forecasting, the main elements involved in the determination of future technology are economics, sociopolitics, and existing technology. The forecaster must not ignore any one of these three areas when attempting to forecast technology because they interact in a complex fashion to influence and determine the future. The key to valid technological forecasting is the careful inclusion of realistic and informed judgment into the forecasting methodology.

In terms of choosing a forecasting strategy, one of the crucial factors is the potential economic value of the forecast compared with the cost of making the fore-

If This Event Occurs or Does Not Occur	Initial Forecast		E_1	E_2	E_3	Revised Forecast	
	Date	Probability				Date	Probability
E_1		20					
		40					
		60					
		80					
E_2		20					
		40					
		60					
		80					
E_3		20					
		40					
		60					
		80					

Figure 15: An example of a form for cross-impact analysis.

cast. Some methods are much more expensive than others, and some tend to give better results for certain situations. The ease of entering, storing, fitting curves, and manipulating large amounts of data in microcomputers makes it tempting to "try everything," a strategy that tends to create more confusion than understanding. Technological forecasting can even become a way of procrastinating—the timid manager avoiding the need to act by insisting on more and more forecasts.

The "best" technique depends in part on the environment in which the firm is operating. Many forecasting methods assume a relatively stable environment with constant trends. If such is actually the case, then statistical projection methods may be most appropriate, especially for the short range. Yet a major aspect of technological forecasting rests on the presumption that invention and change will produce technologies that are not simple extensions of the past. If this were not true, much technological forecasting would be unnecessary.

In general, available data should be plotted as a time series to determine underlying patterns that may aid in choosing between alternative forecasting methods. A search for causal relationships is also helpful. Data are generally available for short-range forecasting situations only, which is why extrapolation techniques work best for short-run problems. For long-range forecasts, the judgmental methods are more suitable because, as time periods are extended, the dangers of unjustifiable extrapolation grow rapidly. Among judgmental methods. Delphi is probably the best known and most often used.

Judgmental techniques are also more appropriate when hard data are lacking or when there is insufficient time or funds to collect and analyze hard data. Judgmental techniques are also appropriate when the number of significant problem variables is large and their relationships are complex or not well understood. The various judgmental approaches each have their particular strengths and weaknesses. See Table 1 for a summary of these strengths and weaknesses.

Table 1   Advantages and Disadvantages of Judgmental Technological Forecasting Techniques

Technique	Advantages	Disadvantages
Monitoring	Unsophisticated	Must review a great quantity of material
	First step to any good TF technique	Time-consuming
		Collection/summarization technique
	Low cost	Not a "predictor"
Scenarios	Aids in understanding present	Dependent on select few (the writers)
	Develops a plan of action for future	High cost
		Too general
Morphology	Goal-setting method	Extremely time-consuming
	Exhaustive	Must know all alternatives
	Precise methods	Extremely high cost
	Breaks down whole into component parts	Impossible combinations must be recognized
Relevance trees	Goal-setting method	Unsophisticated
	Structures goal achievement	Too general
		Bad project may not be easily seen
Delphi	First step to other TF techniques	Emphasis on consensus
	Many people can participate	Time-consuming
	Eliminates personality conflict	Does not relate final event to means to achieve final event
Cross-impact	Moderates some problems with Delphi	Very laborious
		Requires Delphi analysis prior to use
	Can be computerized	
	Highlights lack of specific knowledge	Time-consuming
		Must use same people as in Delphi study

Group approaches have special advantages and disadvantages. For one thing, the sharing of information and insights significantly improves the validity of the forecast. Improvement is obtained through combining abilities, illuminating inconsistencies and contradictions, checking errors, and working through fuzzy and indistinct thinking. While it has already been mentioned that groups provide a synergism that builds on the ideas and thoughts of each person, groups also provide synthesis where pieces of previous thoughts and ideas are combined to form a new thought or idea.

Some disadvantages of open discussion (confrontation) groups are:

1. **The Halo (or Horns) Effect**   A person's reputation (or lack of reputation), or the respect (disrespect) in which a person is held can influence the group's thinking.

2. **Bandwagon Effect**   Pressure to agree with the majority.

3. **Personality Tyranny**   A dominant personality forces the group to agree with his or her thinking.

4. **Time Pressure**   Some people may rush their thinking and offer a forecast without sufficient reflection in order not to delay the group.

5. **Limited Communication**   In large groups, not everyone may have an opportunity to provide input. The more aggressive group members or those with the loudest voices may have an exaggerated effect on the group's opinion.

As with methods for fostering creativity, the methods for technological forecasting have an imperfect past and a highly conditional future. But questions about the value of individual methods do not extend to the general subject. Technological forecasting is not a luxury to be enjoyed if it can be afforded; it is a necessity that is recognized and done explicitly or unrecognized and conducted implicitly. Not to forecast is inherently a forecast that the future will be precisely like the past—a forecast certain to be false.

Technological forecasting is a steadily developing art. Several of the methods covered above, both statistical and judgmental, have been computerized, either to make numeric data collection and manipulation more convenient or, through interactive programs, to ease the problems of collecting judgmental data. Current research seems to be focused mainly on developing more sophisticated judgmental methods, and on combining judgmental and statistical methods.

▶ BIBLIOGRAPHY

1. ALLEN, T. J. *Managing the Flow of Technology.* Cambridge. MA: MIT Press, 1977.

2. ARMYTAGE, H., et al. *Hidden Factors in Technology Change.* New York: Pergamon Press, 1976.

3. AYRES, R. U. *Technological Forecasting and Long Range Planning.* New York: McGraw-Hill, 1969.

4. BEDWORTH, D. D. *Industrial Systems: Planning, Analysis, Control.* New York: Ronald Press, 1973.

5. BLOHM, H., and K. STEINBUCK. *Technological Forecasting in Practice.* Lexington, MA: Lexington Books, 1973.

6. BRIGHT, J. R. *A Brief Introduction to Technological Forecasting.* New York: Pergamon Press, 1972.

7. BRIGHT, J. R. *Technological Forecasting for Industry and Government, Methods and Applications.* Englewood Cliffs, NJ: Prentice Hall, 1968.

8. BRIGHT, J. R., and M.E.F. SCHOEMAN. *A Guide to Practical Technological Forecasting.* Englewood Cliffs, NJ: Prentice Hall, 1980.

9. BRODY, H. "Great Expectations: Why Technology Predictions Go Awry." *Technology Review,* July 1991.

10. BROWNLIE, D. T. "The Role of Technology Forecasting and Planning: Formulating Business Strategy." *Industrial Management and Data Systems,* Issue 2, 1992.

11. BURGER, P. C. "A Report on the Development of a Research Agenda for the Product Development and Management Association." *Journal of Product Innovation Management,* Mar. 1989.

12. CETRON, M. J. *Technological Forecasting: A Practical Approach.* Technology Forecasting Institute, 1969.

13. CETRON, M. J., and C. A. RALPH. *Industrial Applications of Technological Forecasting.* New York: Wiley-Interscience, 1971.

14. CHAMBERS, J. C., S. K. MULLICK, and D. D. SMITH. "How to Choose the Right Forecasting Technique." *Harvard Business Review,* July–Aug. 1971.

15. DELANY, C. L. "Technological Forecasting: Aircraft Hazard Detection." *Technological Forecasting and Social Change,* March 1973.

16. FONTELU, E. "Industrial Applications of Cross-Impact Analysis." *Long Range Planning,* Aug. 1976.

17. FUSFELD, A. R. "The Technological Progress Function: A New Technique for Forecasting." *Technological Forecasting and Social Change,* March 1970.

18. GECKELE, G. G. "Evaluating Industrial Technological Forecasting." *Long Range Planning,* Aug. 1976.

19. GARDE, V. D., and R. R. PATEL. "Technological Forecasting for Power Generation—A Study Using the Delphi Technique." *Long Range Planning,* Aug. 1985.

20. GOTTINGER, H. W. "A Strategic Management Decision Support Tool for Technology Management." *International Journal of Technology Management,* Issue 2, 1989.

21. HENRY, B. *Forecasting Technological Innovation.* Norwell, MA: Kluwer Academic, 1991.

22. JANTSCH, E. *Technological Planning and Social Futures.* Cassell, 1972.

23. JONES, H., and B. L. TWISS. *Forecasting Technology for Planning Decisions.* New York: Macmillan, 1978.

24. KLEIN, H. E., and R. E. LINNEMAN. "The Use of Scenarios in Corporate Planning—Eight Case Histories." *Long Range Planning,* Oct. 1981.

25. KLOPFENSTEIN, B. C. "Forecasting Consumer Adoption of Information Technology and Services—Lessons from Home Video Forecasting." *Journal of the ASIS,* Jan. 1989.

26. LANFORD, H. E., and L. V. IMUNDO. "Approaches to Technological Forecasting as a Planning Tool." *Long Range Planning,* Aug. 1974.

27. LEE, J. C., K. W. LU, and S. C. HORNG. "Technological Forecasting with Nonlinear Models." *Journal of Forecasting,* Apr. 1992.

28. LINESTONE, H. H., and M. TRUOTT. *The Delphi Method: Techniques and Applications.* Reading, MA: Addison-Wesley, 1975.

29. MABERT, V. R. "Executive Opinion Short Range Forecasts: A Time Series Analysis Case." *Technological Forecasting and Social Change,* June 1980.

30. MANSFIELD, E. *Industrial Research and Technological Innovation.* New York: Norton, 1968.

31. MANTEL, S. J., JR., *et al.* "A Social Service Measurement Model." *Operations Research,* March–April 1975.

32. MARTINO, J. P. "Looking Ahead with Confidence." *IEEE Spectrum,* March 1985.

33. MARTINO, J. P. *Technological Forecasting for Decision Making,* 2nd ed. Amsterdam: North-Holland, 1983.

34. MARTINO, J. P. "Technological Forecasting—An Overview." *Management Science,* Jan. 1980.

35. MICHMAN, R. D. "Linking Futuristics with Marketing Planning, Forecasting, and Strategy." *Journal of Business and Industrial Marketing,* Spring 1987.

36. MITCHELL, V. W. "Using Delphi to Forecast in New Technology Industries." *Marketing Intelligence and Planning,* Issue 2, 1992.

37. MOGEE, M. E. "Using Patent Data for Technology Analysis and Planning." *Research-Technology Management,* July/August 1991.

38. NAIR, K., and R. SARIN. "Generating Future Scenarios—Their Use in Strategic Planning." *Long Range Planning,* June 1979.

39. ROSEGGER, G. *The Economics of Production and Innovation,* 2nd ed. New York: Pergamon Press, 1986.

40. SCHNAARS, S. P. "Where Forecasters Go Wrong." *Across the Board,* Dec. 1989.

41. TCHIJOV, I., and E. NOROV. "Forecasting Methods for CIM Technologies." *Engineering Costs and Production Economics,* Aug. 1989.

42. Tryckare, *Lore of Flight.* Gothenburg, Sweden: Cagner, 1970.

43. U.S. Bureau of the Census. *Statistical Abstract of the United States: 1987,* 107th ed. Washington, DC: U.S. Government Printing Office, 1986.

44. U.S. Government. *Technological Trends and National Policy, Including the Social Implications of New Inventions.* Washington, DC: U.S. Government Printing Office, 1937.

45. VANSTON, L. K., R. C. LENZ, and R.S. WOLFF. "How Fast Is New Technology Coming?" *Telephony,* Sept. 18, 1989.

46. VAN WYK, R. J. "The Notion of Technological Limits: An Aid to Technological Forecasting." *Futures,* June 1985.

47. WEDLEY, W. C. "New Uses of Delphi in Strategy Formulation." *Long Range Planning,* Dec. 1977.

48. WHEELER, D. R., and C. J. SHELLEY. "Toward More Realistic Forecasts for High-Technology Products." *Journal of Business and Industrial Marketing,* Summer 1987.

49. WILLIS, R. E. "Statistical Consideration in the Fitting of Growth Curves." *Technological Forecasting and Social Change,* Oct. 1979.

50. WILLS, G. "The Preparation and Development of Technological Forecasts." *Long Range Planning,* March 1970.

APPENDIX

C

The Normal Probability Distribution

Cumulative Probabilities of the Normal Probability Distribution (Areas under the Normal Curve from -∞ to Z)

Z	00	.01	.02	.03	.04	.05	.06	.07	.08	.09
.0	.5000	.5040	.5080	.5120	.5160	.5199	.5239	.5279	.5319	.5359
.1	.5398	.5438	.5478	.5517	.5557	.5596	.5636	.5675	.5714	.5753
.2	.5793	.5832	.5871	.5910	.5948	.5987	.6026	.6064	.6103	.6141
.3	.6179	.6217	.6255	.6293	.6331	.6368	.6406	.6443	.6480	.6517
.4	.6554	.6591	.6628	.6664	.6700	.6736	.6772	.6808	.6844	.6879
.5	.6915	.6950	.6985	.7019	.7054	.7088	.7123	.7157	.7190	.7224
.6	.7257	.7291	.7324	.7357	.7389	.7422	.7454	.7486	.7517	.7549
.7	.7580	.7611	.7642	.7673	.7704	.7734	.7764	.7794	.7823	.7852
.8	.7881	.7910	.7939	.7967	.7995	.8023	.8051	.8078	.8106	.8133
.9	.8159	.8186	.8212	.8238	.8264	.8289	.8315	.8340	.8365	.8389
1.0	.8413	.8438	.8461	.8485	.8508	.8531	.8554	.8577	.8599	.8621
1.1	.8643	.8665	.8686	.8708	.8729	.8949	.8770	.8790	.8810	.8810
1.2	.8849	.8869	.8888	.8907	.8925	.8944	.8962	.8980	.8997	.9015
1.3	.9032	.9049	.9066	.9082	.9099	.9115	.9131	.9147	.9162	.9177
1.4	.9192	.9207	.9222	.9236	.9251	.9265	.9279	.9292	.9306	.9319
1.5	.9332	.9345	.9357	.9370	.9382	.9394	.9406	.9418	.9429	.9441
1.6	.9452	.9463	.9474	.9484	.9495	.9505	.9515	.9525	.9535	.9545
1.7	.9554	.9564	.9573	.9582	.9591	.9599	.9608	.9616	.9625	.9633
1.8	.9641	.9649	.9656	.9664	.9671	.9678	.9686	.9693	.9699	.9706
1.9	.9713	.9719	.9726	.9732	.9738	.9744	.9750	.9756	.9761	.9767
2.0	.9772	.9778	.9783	.9788	.9793	.9798	.9803	.9808	.9812	.9817
2.1	.9821	.9826	.9830	.9834	.9838	.9842	.9846	.9850	.9854	.9857
2.2	.9861	.9864	.9868	.9871	.9875	.9878	.9881	.9884	.9887	.9890
2.3	.9893	.9896	.9898	.9901	.9904	.9906	.9909	.9911	.9913	.9916
2.4	.9918	.9920	.9932	.9925	.9927	.9929	.9931	.9932	.9934	.9936
2.5	.9938	.9940	.9941	.9943	.9945	.9946	.9948	.9949	.9951	.9952
2.6	.9953	.9955	.9956	.9957	.9959	.9960	.9961	.9962	.9963	.9964
2.7	.9965	.9966	.9967	.9968	.9969	.9970	.9971	.9972	.9972	.9974
2.8	.9974	.9975	.9976	.9977	.9977	.9978	.9979	.9979	.9980	.9981
2.9	.9981	.9982	.9982	.9983	.9984	.9984	.9985	.9985	.9986	.9986
3.0	.9987	.9987	.9987	.9988	.9988	.9889	.9989	.9989	.9990	.9990
3.1	.9990	.9991	.9991	.9991	.9992	.9992	.9992	.9992	.9993	.9993
3.2	.9993	.9993	.9994	.9994	.9994	.9994	.9994	.9995	.9995	.9995
3.3	.9995	.9995	.9995	.9996	.9996	.9996	.9996	.9996	.9996	.9997
3.4	.9997	.9997	.9997	.9997	.9997	.9997	.9997	.9997	.9997	.9998

Matrix Multiplication

Consider the matrices **A** and **B:**

$$\mathbf{A} = \begin{bmatrix} a_{11}\ a_{12}\ a_{13} \\ a_{21}\ a_{22}\ a_{23} \\ a_{31}\ a_{32}\ a_{33} \end{bmatrix} \qquad \mathbf{B} = \begin{bmatrix} b_{11}\ b_{12}\ b_{13} \\ b_{21}\ b_{22}\ b_{23} \\ b_{31}\ b_{32}\ b_{33} \end{bmatrix}$$

Each element in a matrix is indexed by its position in a row and a column, in that order. So an element, x_{ij}, is in the ith row and the jth column (row first, column second, as in "RC cola").

To find the matrix **C,** which is the product of **A** and **B,** proceed as follows:

$$c_{11} = a_{11}b_{11} + a_{12}b_{21} + a_{13}b_{31}$$
$$c_{12} = a_{11}b_{12} + a_{12}b_{22} + a_{13}b_{32}$$
$$c_{13} = a_{11}b_{13} + a_{12}b_{23} + a_{13}b_{33}$$

Notice that you are multiplying the first, second, and third elements in the first row of **A** by the first, second, and third elements in each of the three columns of **B,** in order.

Now move to the second row of **A** and multiply each of the elements, in order, by each of the elements in each of the three columns of **B.** This will give you c_{21}, c_{22}, c_{23}. Repeat for the third row, and you will have c_{31}, c_{32}, c_{33}.

Example

Given the two by two matrices

$$\mathbf{A} = \begin{bmatrix} 4\ 1 \\ 0\ 5 \end{bmatrix} \qquad \mathbf{B} = \begin{bmatrix} 2\ 5 \\ 1\ 2 \end{bmatrix}$$

find **C = AB.**

$$c_{11} = 4 \times 2 + 1 \times 1 = 9$$
$$c_{12} = 4 \times 5 + 1 \times 2 = 22$$
$$c_{21} = 0 \times 2 + 5 \times 1 = 5$$
$$c_{22} = 0 \times 5 + 5 \times 2 = 10$$

$$\mathbf{C} = \begin{bmatrix} 9 & 22 \\ 5 & 10 \end{bmatrix}$$

Another Example

Given

$$\mathbf{A} = \begin{bmatrix} 4 & 0 & 2 \\ 0 & 1 & 5 \\ 2 & 1 & 1 \end{bmatrix} \qquad \mathbf{B} = \begin{bmatrix} 0 & 1 & 1 \\ 2 & 1 & 2 \\ 1 & 0 & 2 \end{bmatrix}$$

find $\mathbf{C} = \mathbf{AB}$.
Answer:

$$\mathbf{C} = \begin{bmatrix} 2 & 4 & 8 \\ 7 & 1 & 12 \\ 3 & 3 & 6 \end{bmatrix}$$

Caution

The proper order must be maintained in matrix multiplication. With simple numbers, $xy = yx$. This is not usually so in matrix multiplication. Try it!

$$\mathbf{AB} \neq \mathbf{BA}$$

In general, nonsquare matrices cannot be multiplied. However, if the number of columns in $\mathbf{A}$ is equal to the number of rows in $\mathbf{B}$, you can multiply them.

If $\mathbf{A}$ is $m \times k$ and $\mathbf{B}$ is $k \times n$, then $\mathbf{C} = \mathbf{AB}$ will be $m \times n$. For example:

$$\mathbf{A} = \begin{bmatrix} 1 & 1 & 0 & 0 \\ 0 & 1 & 1 & 1 \\ 1 & 0 & 1 & 0 \end{bmatrix}$$

$$\mathbf{B} = \begin{bmatrix} 1 & 0 & 0 \\ 0 & 1 & 1 \\ 1 & 0 & 1 \\ 1 & 1 & 1 \end{bmatrix}$$

$$\mathbf{C} = \begin{bmatrix} 1 & 1 & 1 \\ 2 & 2 & 3 \\ 2 & 0 & 1 \end{bmatrix}$$

For more: see almost any text on "Mathematics for Business," "Finite Mathematics," etc.

▶ **REFERENCES**

J. T. SCHWARTZ. *Introduction to Matrices and Vectors*. New York: McGraw-Hill, 1961. (A slim, easy-to-read volume. Very clearly written.)

KEMENY, SNELL, AND THOMPSON. *Introduction to Finite Mathematics*. Englewood Cliffs, NJ: Prentice Hall, 1957 (and later editions). (A classic text. Clearly written with good material on probability theory, linear programming, and vectors and matrices. Excellent descriptions of "how to do it.")

Probability and Statistics

This appendix is intended to serve as a brief review of the probability and statistics concepts used in this text. Students who require more review than is available in this appendix should consult one of the texts listed in the bibliography.

▶ E.1 PROBABILITY

Uncertainty in organizational decision making is a fact of life. Demand for an organization's ouput is uncertain. The number of employees who will be absent from work on any given day is uncertain. The price of a stock tomorrow is uncertain. Whether or not it will snow tomorrow is uncertain. Each of these *events* is more or less uncertain. We do not know exactly whether or not the event will occur, nor do we know the value that a particular *random variable* (e.g., price of stock, demand for output, number of absent employees) will assume.

In common terminology we reflect our uncertainty with such phrases as "not very likely," "not a chance," "for sure." But, while these descriptive terms communicate one's feeling regarding the chances of a particular event's occurrence, they simply are not precise enough to allow analysis of chances and odds.

Simply put, *probability* is a number on a scale used to measure uncertainty. The range of the probability scale is from 0 to 1, with a 0 probability indicating that an event has no chance of occurring and a probability of 1 indicating that an event is absolutely sure to occur. The more likely an event is to occur, the closer its probability is to 1. This probability definition, which is general, needs to be further augmented to illustrate the various types of probability that decision makers can assess. There are three types of probability that the operations manager should be aware of:

- Subjective probability.
- Logical probability.
- Experimental probability.

Subjective Probability

Subjective probability is based on individual information and belief. Different individuals will assess the chances of a particular event in different ways, and the same individual may assess different probabilities for the same event at different points in time. For example, one need only watch the blackjack players in Las Vegas to see that different people assess probabilities in different ways. Also, daily trading in the stock market is the result of different probability assessments by those trading. The sellers sell because it is their belief that the probability of appreciation is low, and the buyers buy because they believe that the probability of appreciation is high. Clearly, these different probability assessments are about the same events.

Logical Probability

Logical probability is based on physical phenomena and on symmetry of events. For example, the probability of drawing a three of hearts from a standard 52-card playing deck is 1/52. Each card has an equal likelihood of being drawn. In flipping a coin, the chance of "heads" is 0.50. That is, since there are only two possible outcomes from one flip of a coin, each event has one-half the total probability, or 0.50. A final example is the roll of a single die. Since each of the six sides are identical, the chance of any one event occurring (i.e., a 6, a 3, etc.) is 1/6.

Experimental Probability

Experimental probability is based on frequency of occurrence of events in trial situations. For example, in determining the appropriate inventory level to maintain in the raw material inventory, we might measure and record the demand each day from that inventory. If, in 100 days, demand was 20 units on 16 days, the probability of demand equaling 20 units is said to be 0.16 (i.e., 16/100). In general, experimental probability of an event is given by

$$\text{probability of event} = \frac{\text{number of times event occurred}}{\text{total number of trials}}$$

Both logical and experimental probability are referred to as *objective* probability in contrast to the individually assessed subjective probability. Each of these is based on, and directly *computed* from, facts.

▶ E.2   EVENT RELATIONSHIPS AND PROBABILITY LAWS

Events are classified in a number of ways that allow us to state rules for probability computations. Some of these classifications and definitions follow.

1. **Independent events:**   events are independent if the occurrence of one does not affect the probability of occurrence of the others.

2. **Dependent events:** events are termed dependent if the occurrence of one does affect the probability of occurrence of others.

3. **Mutually exclusive events:** two events are termed mutually exclusive if the occurrence of one precludes the occurrence of the other. For example, in the birth of a child, the events "It's a boy!" and "It's a girl!" are mutually exclusive.

4. **Collectively exhaustive events:** a set of events is termed collectively exhaustive if on any one trial at least one of them must occur. For example, in rolling a die, one of the events 1, 2, 3, 4, 5, or 6 must occur; therefore, these six events are collectively exhaustive.

We can also define the union and intersection of two events. Consider two events A and B. The *union of A and B* includes all outcomes in A or B or in both A and B. For example, in a card game you will win if you draw a diamond or a jack. The union of these two events includes all diamonds (including the jack of diamonds) and the remaining three jacks (hearts, clubs, spades). The *or* in the union is the inclusive or. That is, in our example you will win with a jack or a diamond or a jack of diamonds (i.e., both events).

The *intersection* of two events includes all outcomes that are members of *both* events. Thus, in our previous example of jacks and diamonds, the jack of diamonds is the only outcome contained in both events and is therefore the only member of the intersection of the two events.

Let us now consider the relevant probability laws based on our understanding of the above definitions and concepts. For ease of exposition let us define the following notation:

$$P(A) = \text{probability that event } A \text{ will occur}$$
$$P(B) = \text{probability that event } B \text{ will occur}$$

If two events are mutually exclusive, then their joint occurrence is impossible. Hence, $P(A \text{ and } B) = 0$ for mutually exclusive events. If the events are not mutually exclusive, $P(A \text{ and } B)$ can be computed (as we will see in the next section); this probability is termed the *joint* probability of A and B. Also, if A and B are not mutually exclusive, then we can also define the *conditional* probability of A *given that B* has already occurred or the conditional probability of B given that A has already occurred. These probabilities are written as $P(A \mid B)$ and $P(B \mid A)$, respectively.

The Multiplication Rule

The joint probability of two events that are not mutually exclusive is found by using the multiplication rule. If the events are independent events, the joint probability is given by

$$P(A \text{ and } B) = P(A) \times P(B \mid A) \text{ or } P(B) \times P(A \mid B)$$

If the events are independent, then $P(B \mid A)$ and $P(A \mid B)$ are equal to $P(B)$ and $P(A)$, respectively, and therefore the joint probability is given by

$$P(A \text{ and } B) = P(A) \times P(B)$$

From these two relationships, we can find the conditional probability for two dependent events from

$$P(A \mid B) = \frac{P(A \text{ and } B)}{P(B)}$$

and

$$P(B \mid A) = \frac{P(A \text{ and } B)}{P(A)}$$

Also, the $P(A)$ and $P(B)$ can be computed if the events are independent, as

$$P(A) = \frac{P(A \text{ and } B)}{P(B)}$$

and

$$P(B) = \frac{P(A \text{ and } B)}{P(A)}$$

The Addition Rule

The addition rule is used to compute the probability of the union of two events. If two events are mutually exclusive, then $P(A \text{ and } B) = 0$ as we indicated previously. Therefore, the probability of either A or B or both is simply the probability of A or B. This is given by

$$P(A \text{ or } B) = P(A) + P(B)$$

But, if the events are not mutually exclusive, then the probability of A or B is given by

$$P(A \text{ or } B) = P(A) + P(B) - P(A \text{ and } B)$$

We can denote the reasonableness of this expression by looking at the following Venn diagram.

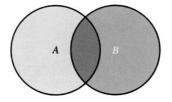

The two circles represent the probabilities of the events A and B, respectively. The shaded area represents the overlap in the events; that is, the intersection of A and B. If we add the area of A and the area of B, we have included the shaded area twice. Therefore, to get the total area of A or B, we must subtract one of the areas of the intersection that we have added.

If two events are collectively exhaustive, then the probability of (A or B) is equal to 1. That is, for two collectively exhaustive events, one or the other or both must occur, and therefore, $P(A \text{ or } B)$ must be 1.

▶ E.3   STATISTICS

Because events are uncertain, we must employ special analyses in organizations to ensure that our decisions recognize the chance nature of outcomes. We employ statistics and statistical analysis to

1. Concisely express the tendency and the relative uncertainty of a particular situation.
2. Develop inferences or understanding about a situation.

"Statistics" is an elusive and often misused term. Batting averages, birth weights, student grade points are all statistics. They are *descriptive* statistics. That is, they are quantitative measures of some entity and, for our purposes, can be considered as data about the entity. The second use of the term "statistics" is in relation to the body of theory and methodology used to analyze available evidence (typically quantitative) and to develop inferences from the evidence.

Two descriptive statistics that are often used in presenting information about a population of items (and consequently in inferring some conclusions about the population) are the *mean* and the *variance*. The mean in a population (denoted as μ) can be computed in two ways, each of which gives identical results.

$$\mu = \sum_{j=1}^{k} X_j P(X_j)$$

where

> k = the number of discrete values that the random variable X_j may assume
> X_j = the value of the random variable
> $P(X_j)$ = is the probability (or relative frequency) of X_j in the population

Also, the mean can be computed as

$$\mu = \sum_{i=1}^{N} X_i / N$$

where

> N = the size of the population (the number of different items in the population)
> X_i = the value of the ith item in the population

The mean is also termed the *expected value* of the population and is written as $E(X)$.

The variance of the items in the population measures the dispersion of the items about their mean. It is computed in one of the following two ways.

$$\sigma^2 = \sum_{j=1}^{k} (X_j - \mu)^2 P(X_j)$$

or

$$\sigma^2 = \sum_{i=1}^{N} \frac{(X_i - \mu)^2}{N}$$

The standard deviation, another measure of dispersion, is simply the square root of the variance or

$$\sigma = \sqrt{\sigma^2}$$

Descriptive Versus Inferential Statistics

Organizations are typically faced with decisions for which a large portion of the relevant information is uncertain. In hiring graduates of your university, the "best" prospective employee is unknown to the organization. Also, in introducing a new product, proposing a tax law change to boost employment, drilling an oil well, and so on, the outcomes are always uncertain.

Statistics can often aid management in reducing this uncertainty. This is accomplished through the use of one or the other, or both, of the purposes of statistics. That is, statistics is divided according to its two major purposes: *describing* the major characteristics of a large mass of data and *inferring* something about a large mass of data from a smaller sample drawn from the mass. One methodology summarizes all the data; the other reasons from a small set of the data to the larger total.

Descriptive statistics uses such measures as the mean, median, mode, range, variance, standard deviation, and such graphical devices as the bar chart and the histogram. When an entire population (a complete set of objects or entities with a common characteristic of interest) of data is summarized by computing such measures as the mean and the variance of a single characteristic, the measure is referred to as a *parameter* of that population. For example, if the population of interest is all female freshmen at your university and all their ages were used to compute an arithmetic average of 19.2 years, this measure is called a parameter of that population.

Inferential statistics also uses means and variance, but in a different manner. The objective of inferential statistics is to infer the value of a population parameter through the study of a small sample (a portion of a population) from that population. For example, a random sample of 30 freshmen females could produce the information that there is 90 percent certainty that the average age of all freshmen women is between 18.9 and 19.3 years. We do not have as much information as if we had used the entire population, but then we did not have to spend the time to find and determine the age of each member of the population either.

Before considering the logic behind inferential statistics, let us define the primary measures of central tendency and dispersion used in both descriptive and inferential statistics.

Measures of Central Tendency

The central tendency of a group of data represents the average, middle, or "normal" value of the data. The most frequently used measures of central tendency are the *mean*, the *median*, and the *mode*.

The mean of a population of values was given earlier as

$$\mu = \sum_{i=1}^{N} \frac{X_i}{N}$$

where

μ = the mean (μ pronounced "mu")

X_i = the value of the *i*th data item

N = the number of data items in the population

The mean of a *sample* of items from a population is given by

$$\bar{X} = \sum_{i=1}^{n} \frac{X_i}{n}$$

where

$\bar{X}$ = the sample mean (pronounced "*X* bar")

X_i = the value of the *i*th data item in the sample

n = the number of data items selected in the sample

The *median* is the middle value of a population of data (or sample) where the data are ordered by value. That is, in the following data set

3, 2, 9, 6, 1, 5, 7, 3, 4

4 is the median since (as you can see when we order the data)

1, 2, 3, 3, 4, 5, 6, 7, 9

50 percent of the data values are above 4 and 50 percent below 4. If there are an even number of data items, then the mean of the middle two is the median. For example, if there had also been an 8 in the above data set, the median would be 4.5[(4 + 5)/2].

The *mode* of a population (or sample) of data items is the value that most frequently occurs. In the above data set, 3 is the mode of the set. A distribution can have more than one mode if there are two or more values that appear with equal frequency.

Measures of Dispersion

Dispersion refers to the scatter around the mean of a distribution of values. Three measures of dispersion are the range, the variance, and the standard deviation.

The *range* is the difference between the highest and the lowest value of the data set, that is, $X_{high} - X_{low}$.

The *variance of a population* of items is given by

$$\sigma^2 = \sum_{i=1}^{N} \frac{(X_i - \mu)^2}{N}$$

where

σ^2 = the population variance (pronounced sigma squared)

The *variance of a sample* of items is given by

$$S^2 = \sum_{i=1}^{n} \frac{(X_i - \bar{X})^2}{n}$$

where

$$S^2 = \text{the sample variance}$$

The *standard deviation* is simply the square root of the variance. That is

$$\sigma = \sqrt{\sum_{i=1}^{N} \frac{(X_i - \mu)^2}{N}}$$

and

$$S = \sqrt{\sum_{i=1}^{n} \frac{(X_i - \overline{X})^2}{n}}$$

σ and S are the population and sample standard deviations, respectively.

Inferential Statistics

A basis of inferential statistics is the *interval estimate*. Whenever we infer from partial data to an entire population, we are doing so with some uncertainty in our inference. Specifying an interval estimate (e.g., the average weight is between 10 and 12 pounds) rather than a *point estimate* (e.g., the average weight is 11.3 pounds) simply helps to relate that uncertainty. The interval estimate is not as *precise* as the point estimate.

Inferential statistics uses probability samples where the chance of selection of each item is known. A random sample is one in which each item in the population has an equal chance of selection.

The procedure used to estimate a population mean from a sample is to

1. Select a sample of size n from the population.
2. Compute $\overline{X}$ the mean and S the standard deviation.
3. Compute the precision of the estimate (i.e., the $\pm$ limits around $\overline{X}$ within which the mean μ is believed to exist).

Steps 1 and 2 are straightforward, relying on the equations we have presented in earlier sections. Step 3 deserves elaboration.

The precision of an estimate for a population parameter depends on two things: the standard deviation of the *sampling distribution*, and the confidence you desire to have in the final estimate. Two statistical laws provide the logic behind Step 3.

First, the law of large numbers states that as the size of a sample increases toward infinity, the difference between the estimate of the mean and the true population mean tends toward zero. For practical purposes, a sample of size 30 is assumed to be "large enough" for the sample estimate to be a good estimate of the population mean.

Second, the central limit theorem states that if all possible samples of size n were taken from a population with any distribution, the distribution of the means of those samples would be normally distributed with a mean equal to the population mean and a standard deviation equal to the standard deviation of the population divided by the square root of the sample size. That is, if we took all of the samples of size 100 from the population shown in Figure 1, the sampling distribution would be as shown in Figure 2. The logic behind Step 3 is that

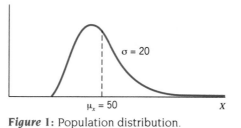
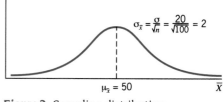

Figure 1: Population distribution.   **Figure 2**: Sampling distribution.

1. Any sample of size n from the population can be considered to be one observation from the sampling distribution with mean $\mu_{\bar{x}} = \mu$ and standard deviation

$$\sigma_{\bar{x}} = \frac{\sigma}{\sqrt{n}}$$

2. From our knowledge of the normal distribution, we know that there is a number (see normal probability table, Appendix C) associated with each probability value of a normal distribution (e.g., the probability that an item will be within ± 2 standard deviations of the mean of a normal distribution is 95.45 percent, $Z = 2$ in this case).

3. The value of the number Z is simply the number of standard deviations away from the mean that a given point lies. That is,

$$Z = \frac{(\bar{X} - \mu)}{\sigma}$$

or in the case of Step 3

$$Z = \frac{(\bar{X} - \mu_{\bar{x}})}{\sigma_{\bar{x}}}$$

4. The precision of a sample estimate is given by $Z\sigma_{\bar{x}}$.

5. The interval estimate is given by the point estimate $\bar{X}$ plus or minus the precision, or $\bar{X} \pm Z\sigma_{\bar{x}}$.

In the previous example shown in Figures 1 and 2 suppose that a sample estimate $\bar{X}$ was 56 and the population standard deviation σ was 20. Also, suppose that the desired confidence was 90 percent. Since the associated Z value for 90 percent is 1.645, the interval estimate for μ is

$$56 \pm 1.645 \left(\frac{20}{\sqrt{100}} \right)$$

or

$$56 \pm 3.29 \quad \text{or} \quad 52.71 \text{ to } 59.29$$

This interval estimate of the population mean is based solely on information derived from a sample and states that the estimator is 90 percent confident that the true mean is between 52.71 and 59.29. There are numerous other sampling methods and other parameters that can be estimated; the student is referred to one of the references in the bibliography for further discussion.

Standard Probability Distributions

The normal distribution, discussed and shown in Figure 2, is probably the most common probability distribution in statistics. Some other common distributions are the Poisson, a discrete distribution, and the negative exponential, a continuous distribution. In project management, the beta distribution plays an important role. A continuous distribution, it is generally skewed, as in Figure 1. Two positive parameters, alpha and beta, determine the distribution's shape. Its mean, μ, and variance, σ^2, are given by:

$$\mu = \frac{\alpha}{\alpha + \beta}$$

$$\sigma^2 = \frac{\alpha\beta}{(\alpha + \beta)^2 (\alpha + \beta + 2)}$$

These are often approximated by

$$\mu = (a + 4m + b)/6$$

and a standard deviation approximated by

$$\sigma = (b - a)/6$$

where:

    a is the optimistic value that might occur once in a hundred times,
    m is the most likely (modal) value, and
    b is the pessimistic value that might occur once in a hundred times.

Recent research [5] has indicated that a much better approximation is given by:

$$\mu = 0.630\, d + 0.185\, (c + e)$$
$$\sigma^2 = 0.630\, (d - \mu)^2 + 0.185\, [(c - \mu)^2 + (e - \mu)^2]$$

where

    c is an optimistic value at one in 20 times,
    d is the median, and
    e is a pessimistic value at one in 20 times.

See Chapter 8 for another method for approximating μ and σ^2

▶ BIBLIOGRAPHY

1. ANDERSON, D., D. SWEENEY, and T. WILLIAMS. *Statistics for Business and Economics.* 4th ed. Minneapolis, Minn.: West, 1990.

2. CONOVER, W. J. *Practical Nonparametric Statistics.* 2nd ed. New York: Wiley, 1980.

3. FREUND, J. E., and R. E. WALPOLE, *Mathematical*

Statistics. 3rd ed. Englewood Cliffs, N.J.: Prentice Hall, 1980.

4. HOAGLIN, D. C., F. MOSTELLER, and J. W. TUKEY. Understanding Robust and Exploratory Data Analysis. New York: Wiley, 1983.

5. KEEFER, D. L., and W. A. VERDINI. "Better Estimation of PERT Activity Time Parameters." Management Science, Sept. 1993.

6. MENDENHALL, W., R. L. SCHAEFFER, and D. WACKERLY. Mathematical Statistics with Applications, 3rd ed. Boston: PWS-Kent, 1986.

7. NETER, J., W. WASSERMAN, and G. A. WHITMORE. Applied Statistics, 3rd. ed. Boston: Allyn and Bacon, 1987.

8. RYAN, T. A., B. L. JOINER, and B. F. RYAN. Minitab Handbook. 2nd ed. Boston: PWS-Kent, 1985.

Sourcenotes

► CHAPTER 1

J. M. Stewart: *Making Project Management Work*
© 1965 by the Foundation for the School of Business at the Indiana University. Reprinted by permission from *Business Horizons* (Fall 1965).

J. R. Meredith, M. M. Hill, and J. M. Comer: *Peerless Laser Processors*
This case research was funded by a grant entitled "Management Issues in High-Technology Manufacturing Industries," from the Cleveland Foundation of Cleveland Ohio, 1985.

► CHAPTER 2

J. R. Meredith and N. C. Suresh: *Justification Techniques for Advanced Manufacturing Technologies*
©1986 Taylor & Francis, Ltd. Reprinted by permission from *International Journal of Production Management* (Vol. 24, No. 5, pp. 1043–1057).

S. J. Mantel, Jr.: *Planning and Budgeting a Social Service System*
Presented at the 7th Annual Meeting of the American Institute for Decision Sciences, Cincinnati, Ohio, Nov. 1975. Printed by permission.

E. Filliben: *Westfield, Inc.: Packaging Alternatives*
Copyright © 1987 by the Darden Graduate Business School Foundation, Charlottesville, VA. Rev. 11/91.

► CHAPTER 3

B. Z. Posner: *What It Takes to Be a Good Project Manager*
©1987 by the Project Management Institute. Reprinted by permission from *Project Management Journal* (March 1987).

J. R. Meredith: *Geartrain International: Medina, Ohio*
This case research was funded by a grant from the Illinois Institute of Technology, Chicago, 1985.

▶ CHAPTER 4

E. W. Larson and D. H. Gobeli: *Matrix Management: Contradictions and Insights*
©1987 by the Regents of the University of California. Reprinted from the *California Management Review*. Vol. 29. No. 4 by permission of the Regents.

J. R. Meredith: *Oilwell Cable Company, Inc.*
This case research was funded by a grant entitled "Management Issues in High-Technology Manufacturing Industries" from the Cleveland Foundation of Cleveland, Ohio, 1985.

▶ CHAPTER 5

H. F. Spirer and A. G. Hulvey: *A Project Management and Control System for Capital Projects*
© 1981 Reprinted with permission from *Proceedings of PMI, Internet 81, 1981*, a publication of the Project Management Institute.

D. P. Slevin and J. K. Pinto: *Balancing Strategy and Tactics in Project Implementation*
Reprinted from *Sloan Management Review*, Fall 1987, pp. 33–41, by permission of the publisher. © 1987 by the Sloan Management Review Association. All rights reserved.

▶ CHAPTER 6

R. J. Burke: *Methods of Resolving Interpersonal Conflict*
©1969 International Personnel Management Association. Reprinted from *Personnel Administration*, July-August 1969, by permission.

J. M. Comer and M. M. Hill: *Cincinnati Milacron, Inc: Robot Welding*
This case research was funded by a grant entitled "Management Issues in High-Technology Manufacturing Industries," from the Cleveland Foundation of Cleveland, Ohio, 1985.

▶ CHAPTER 7

D. H. Hamburger: *Three Perceptions of Project Cost—Cost Is More Than a Four Letter Word*
©1986 by the Project Management Institute. Reprinted by permission from *Project Management Journal*, June 1986, pp. 51–58.

J. R. Meredith: *Automotive Builders, Inc.: The Stanhope Project*
This case research was funded by a grant from the Illinois Institute of Technology, Chicago, 1985.

▶ CHAPTER 8

E. TURBAN and J. R. MEREDITH: *The Sharon Construction Corporation*
From E. TURBAN and J. R. MEREDITH *Fundamentals of Management Science*, 6th ed., Homewood, IL: R. D. Irwin, Inc., ©1994. Reproduced by permission.

D. H. HAMBURGER: *"On-time" Project Completion—Managing the Critical Path*
This article is reprinted from *Project Management Journal*, Sept. 1987, with permission of the Project Management Institute, 130 So. State Road, Upper Darby, PA 19082, a worldwide organization for advancing the state-of-the-art of project management. Phone 215/734-3330. Fax 215/734-3266.

▶ CHAPTER 9

H. F. SPIRER: D. U. *Singer Hospital Products Corp.*
Reproduced with the kind permission of Herbert F. Spirer, Professor of Management and Administrative Sciences, MBA Program at Stamford, University of Connecticut. © 1980 Herbert F. Spirer.

R. V. JOHNSON *Resource Constrained Scheduling Capabilities of Commercial Project Management Software*
This article is reprinted from *Project Management Journal*, Dec. 1992, with permission of the Project Management Institute, 130 So. State Road, Upper Darby, PA 19082, a worldwide organization for advancing the state-of-the-art of project management. Phone 215/734-3330. Fax 215/734-3266.

▶ CHAPTER 10

P. M. BOBROWSKI: *Project Management Control Problems: An Information Systems Focus*
This article is reprinted from *Project Management Journal*, June 1989, with permission of the Project Management Institute, 130 So. State Road, Upper Darby, PA 19082, a worldwide organization for advancing the state-of-the-art of project management. Phone 215/734-3330. Fax 215/734-3266.

B. J. DIXON: *Riverview Children's Hospital*
This case was prepared by B. J. Dixon of the Western Business School. Copyright 1991, the University of Western Ontario.

▶ CHAPTER 11

K. B. CLARK: *Corning Glass Works: The Z-Glass Project*
© 1981 by the President and Fellows of Harvard College. Reprinted by permission of the Harvard Business School.

H. J. THAMHAIN and D. L. WILEMON: *Criteria For Controlling Projects According to Plan*
© 1986 by the Project Management Institute. Reprinted from *Project Management Journal*, June 1986, pp. 75–81, by permission.

▶ CHAPTER 12

R. D. LANDEL: *Delta Electronics, Inc.*
©1985 by the Darden Graduate Business School Foundation, Charlottesville, VA.

A. M. RUSKIN and W. E. ESTES: *The Project Management Audit: Its Role and Conduct*
© 1985 by the Project Management Institute. Reprinted from *Project Management Journal*, August 1985, pp. 64–70, by permission.

▶ CHAPTER 13

B. M. STAW AND J. ROSS: *Knowing When to Pull the Plug*
© 1987 by *Harvard Business Review*, March-April 1987, pp. 68–74.

A. MALINOWSKI: BETA *Company: The Z15 Engine Program* (A)
© 1985 by the Colgate Darden Graduate Business School Foundation, Charlottesville, VA

M. M. HILL and J. M. COMER: *Cincinnati Milacron, Inc: Casting Cleaning*
This case research was funded by a grant entitled "Management Issues in High-Technology Manufacturing Industries" from the Cleveland Foundation of Cleveland Ohio, 1985.

▶ CHAPTER 14

D. I. CLELAND: *The Age of Project Management*
This article is reprinted from *Project Management Journal*, March 1991, with permission of the Project Management Institute, 130 So. State Road, Upper Darby, PA 19082, a worldwide organization for advancing the state-of-the-art of project management. Phone 215/734-3330. Fax 215/734-3266.

S. J. MANTEL, JR: *Supernet* (unpublished).)

Author Index

Subject Index

Photo Credits

Chapter 1: *Pages* 6 *and* 12: Project Management Institute. *Page* 17: Courtesy NASA. **Chapter 2:** *Page* 78: Sygma. **Chapter 3:** *Page* 116: Project Management Institute. *Page* 117: Reuters/Bettmann Archive. **Chapter 5:** *Page* 214: Project Management Institute. **Chapter 7:** *Page* 302: Project Management Institute. **Chapter 8:** *Pages* 334 *and* 335: Project Management Institute. *Page* 359: Courtesy Pittsburgh Convention and Visitor's Bureau. **Chapter 10:** *Page* 443: Project Management Institute. **Chapter 11:** *Page* 529: Courtesy of the Australian Consulate, Barry Le Lievre/Australian Overseas Information Service Photo. **Chapter 14:** *Pages* 671 *and* 672: Project Management Institute. *Pages* 680 *and* 681: Courtesy Boeing Corporation.